Collecting O'BRIEN'S

4th EDITION

TOY CARS & TRUCKS

Identification and Value Guide

HEAVY MACHINERY SERVICE

BUDDY "L"

D1223841

Edited by Karen O'Brien

©2005 KP Books
Published by

kp books
An Imprint of F+W Publications

700 East State Street • Iola, WI 54990-0001
715-445-2214 • 888-457-2873

Our toll-free number to place an order or obtain
a free catalog is (800) 258-0929.

Library of Congress Catalog Number: 2004105227

ISBN: 0-87349-836-4

Designed by Patsy Howell and Brian Brogaard
Edited by Karen O'Brien

Printed in the United States of America

On the Cover
(All toys listed below are courtesy of the Ron O'Brien
Collection. Thanks, Dad!)
Front:
Marx Lumar Van Lines Coast to Coast truck.
1949-52 Tonka Wrecker.
Matchbox Models of Yesteryear 25th Anniversary 1912
    Ford Model T Van, 1978.
Tootsietoy 1960 Chevy El Camino pulling Midget Racer.

Back:
1960 Tonka Suburban Pumper.

Title page:
1956 Buddy "L" Heavy Machinery Service.

Dedication

FOR my dad, Ron O'Brien, whose contagious love of old cars and old toys inspires me still.

And if you've ever discovered a particular toy car or truck and said, "I had one of these when I was a kid," this book is for you, too.

Acknowledgments

FIRST published in 1994, this title's significant growth is due to the diligent efforts of its editors, contributors, and readers. Richard O'Brien established the benchmark for quality with the first two editions, leaving a sizeable legacy to follow, and Elizabeth Stephan accumulated quite a few new photos for the third edition. Their outstanding initial efforts are the foundation upon which this book is based.

The support and dedication of new and continuing contributors made this edition possible. These hobby experts generously shared their knowledge and offered patient encouragement that is evident throughout these pages.

Contributors include Stan Alekna, Tom Billings, Rod Carnahan, Doug Ehrenhaft, Capt. Perry R. Eichor, Brad Fullhart, Jim Geary, Jeff Hubbard, Darryll Jones, Rick Leeman, Dave Leopard, Paul MacLaughlin, Rich Malinowski, John McCurdy, Ron O'Brien, Pim Piët, Larry Planer, Joe Portolano, Randy Prasse, Mark Rich, Dr. Douglas Sadecky, Brian Seligman, David Shrock, Scott Smiles, Bob Smith, Ron Smith, John Taylor, Andrew Tolch, Tom Wetli, and Darin Wood. Several chapters were unaltered from the 3rd edition, and the contributions of those individuals are acknowledged at the beginnings of those sections.

Thanks again to the talented staff of KP Books—Brian Brogaard and Mary Lou Marshall designed the book's

cover, Jamie Griffin designed the front matter, and Patsy Howell created the book's interior design and stuffed many toys into few pages. Sally Olson and Kay Sanders assisted with the interior pages, Sandi Morrison ran the data patterns and worked database miracles, and the members of our scanning department handled hundreds of new images with incredible speed.

Editorial thanks go to Merry Dudley, editor of *Toy Cars & Models* magazine, for data entry and proofreading, and to Tom Bartsch, editor of *Toy Shop* magazine, who also proofread pages. I appreciate your professionalism and encouragement—the next bag of Twizzlers is on me!

Thanks also to the toy collectors, dealers, and toy show organizers who continue to make this hobby a genuine joy in my life. I'm grateful that you always make the time to "talk toys" with me.

And a special thanks to my family and friends for their understanding and support. You're awesome!

— Karen O'Brien
May 2005

Contents

Introduction

WELCOME to the 4th edition of *O'Brien's Collecting Toy Cars & Trucks*.

Summer arrived on June 21, according to the calendar, but the solstice is not the real determiner of summer's arrival for residents of Iola, Wis. Spring in Iola lasts until the second weekend of July when the highly-anticipated annual car show kicks off the summer season. Walking among the variety of show cars, it's easy to see why collecting vehicle toys remains so popular. Many show participants proudly display toy replicas of their vehicles including model kits and die-cast toys of every scale and construction.

"I had one of those when I was a kid," is a popular phrase at the Iola Old Car Show, but I'm never quite sure if the reference is to a real car or a toy.

Old car enthusiasts and toy collectors share a common appreciation for transportation toys and the real cars and trucks that inspired them. Vehicle toys are a special category within the toy collecting community. Not so old as toy ships, but older than toy airplanes, toy cars and trucks chronicle the history of the emerging and departing 20th century rather nicely. As with the design and engineering of their real counterparts, changes in technology and materials used in toy construction and design reflected the socio-economic, artistic, and political conditions of the day.

The broad spectrum of toy cars and trucks within this edition will appeal to collectors of all generations and will likely bring back memories that remind you, "I had one of those when I was a kid."

About the 4th Edition

This new edition features several collector-friendly changes. It is organized alphabetically by toy manufacturer, and the header at the top of each page serves as a quick reference as you thumb through the pages. More than 2,800 photographs assist in the identification of toy cars and trucks from around the world.

The company histories located at the beginning of each manufacturer's section were assembled from a myriad of references including previous editions of this book, collector Web sites, original company catalogs, helpful collectors who submitted useful snippets of information, Mark Rich's excellent book, *Toys A to Z*

"I had one of those when I was a kid."

(Krause Publications, 2001), and several friendly librarians around the country who sorted through their town's records to uncover little-known facts.

More than 1,200 new listings were added to this edition. Researching everything from cast-iron to plastic toys yielded a wide variety of old cars and trucks presented here for the first time. The goal of this ongoing project is to offer an exhaustive compendium, and this edition is a good start in that direction.

A Note on Value

When discussing value, buyers and sellers must remember that a price guide is only a guide and not the sole determiner of a given toy's worth. It is, however, an excellent place to begin the process of acquiring new toys for your collection. As buyers and sellers, *you* determine the value of any given toy. Value is decided ultimately by what a buyer is willing to pay, so do your homework with this value guide and use every available research tool, including fellow collectors, the Internet, and toy shows, to assess the value of the toys you buy and sell.

Become a Contributor

This book is in a constant state of development. New listings, new prices, and more detailed information are added throughout the year. If you have information regarding the toys featured in this book or additional toys that you believe should be included, you are invited to contribute your knowledge. The considerable improvements achieved with this edition would not have been possible without the generous assistance of hobby experts, and the continued support of the collecting community will make future editions even stronger.

We are always seeking photo donations for our archives. Good quality 35mm photos or slides work the best for reproduction in print. Be mindful of the photo's composition—neutral backgrounds (solid colors like white) work better than something with texture.

If you have information or photos to share, please contact me at the following address:

Karen O'Brien
KP Books
700 E. State St.
IOLA, WI 54990
(715) 445-4612
karen.o'brien@fwpubs.com

How To Use This Book

THIS book contains more than 300 toy car and truck manufacturers from different periods of time and different geographic locations. The book is organized alphabetically by those company names. Listings for individual toys include the toy name, a description where possible, the year(s) the toy was produced, the toy number as assigned by the manufacturer, the toy's dimensions, an O'Brien number where applicable, and a value in up to three condition grades.

A note on O'Brien numbers: Richard O'Brien introduced the numbers as a method to catalog various toys. *At no time were these numbers found on the actual toys.* Collectors have found the numbers useful to distinguish toys over the years, and I have included the numbers in parentheses within this edition. The goal of this project was to make the listings as collector-friendly as possible, and the continued inclusion of O'Brien numbers furthers that objective.

A Sample Listing

The following describes how to read a typical listing.

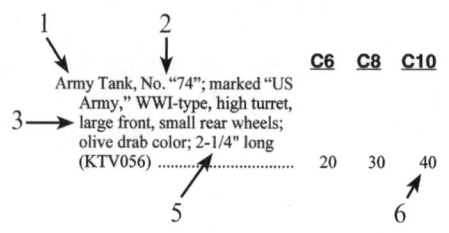

1. Toy name.
2. Toy number.
3. Description.
4. Year of release.
5. Dimensions.
6. Values.

Abbreviations

SEVERAL chapters utilize specialized abbreviations to describe specific characteristics of different toys. Those chapters begin with abbreviation keys before listings are presented.

Other abbreviations include:

n/a Not Applicable. If n/a appears in a price column, then an item has no value in that condition grade. (For example, n/a can apply when an item was released as a part of a set—it will not have a C10 value individually because only the whole set can have a C10 value. But it will have value loose from the set, and those values are typically found in the C6 or C8 column.)

NPF No Price Found. If NPF appears in a price column, then the item's value was not able to be determined. Input from collectors is always welcome to help determine values.

c. Circa; approximately. For example: c.1950.

Condition

DETERMINING the condition of a toy is the single most important factor in assessing its value. The values listed in this guide are for complete toys without missing parts. It should be noted that C10 values for the majority of toys listed here reflect mint toys without their original boxes—boxes add a premium above the C10 price.

To keep up with pricing trends for die-cast toys like Corgi, Hot Wheels, Matchbox, etc., however, C10 value does indicate the presence of original packaging.

Note: Prices in photo captions are listed at C10 condition, whether or not the item pictured is in C10 condition.

Condition code

C6 Good; evident overall wear, well played with but acceptable to many collectors

C8 Very Good; minor overall wear, very clean

C10 Mint; like new

Note: Mint in Box commands a higher price. Condition below C6 brings considerably lower prices.

A.C. GILBERT

Alfred Carlton Gilbert (1884-1961) is best known as the creator of the Erector set. However, Gilbert also produced some very attractive vehicles in the early 1920s.

	C6	C8	C10
Gilmortor Truck, wind-up, early, 10-1/2" long	250	375	500
Racer, wind-up, 9" long	300	500	700
Stutz	500	800	1200
U.S. Mail Truck, copyright 1920, 8" long	375	565	750

A.C. Gilbert Gilmotor windup truck. Photo courtesy Joe and Sharon Freed

A.C. WILLIAMS

A.C. Williams was founded in 1886 when Adam Clark Williams bought the J.W. Williams Company from his father. After a fire in 1893, the firm moved from Chagrin Falls, Ohio, to Ravenna. Toy production began about this time. Small cast-iron toys were Williams' specialty, with banks, cars, and aircraft predominant. A.C. Williams retired in 1919, but the firm continued to make toys until 1938, after which it continued in business in a non-toy capacity. Williams marked few, if any, of its toys. Two clues to an A.C. Williams toy are turned steel hubs and starred axle peens.

	C6	C8	C10
Austin for Car Carrier, cast iron..............	75	128	175
Auto Bank, cast iron, early, 6" long	250	40	550
Bus, cast iron, 5" long	75	125	175
Bus, cast iron, twin coach, 1936, 8-1/4" long	300	425	650
Car Carrier, cast iron, w/three Austins, 1920, 12-1/2" long	350	550	775
Chrysler Roadster, cast iron, 1930s	NPF	NPF	NPF
Coast to Coast Cartage Co. Stake Trailer Truck, cast iron, 10-1/8" long	150	250	375
Coast to Coast Co. Stake Truck, cast iron, two-piece, 7" long	250	400	550
Coupe, cast iron, 1928, 6" long	120	175	250
Coupe, cast iron, 1930s, 7" long	500	800	1100
Coupe, cast iron, 3" long, two-piece body, 1936	75	125	200
Coupe, cast iron, 3-1/2" long	50	75	100
Coupe, cast iron, 4-1/2" long	90	140	200
Coupe, cast iron, w/rumble seat, sidemounts, 1930, 6-3/4" long	150	250	375
Delivery Van, cast iron, 8" long..............	350	525	750

	C6	C8	C10
Doctor's Coupe, cast iron, w/curtains, 5" long...	200	325	450
Double Decker Faegol Bus, cast iron, blue with gold side stripes, 7-3/4" long	500	700	900

A.C. Williams Car Carrier, 3 Austins, 12-1/2".

A.C. Williams vehicles as shown on Kresge's February 15, 1933 sheet.

A.C. Williams Chrysler Roadster, 1930s. Photo courtesy Al Kasishke

A.C. Williams "Coast to Coast Cartage Co." stake trailer truck, 10-1/8". Photo courtesy Bertoia Auctions

	C6	C8	C10
Dump Truck, cast iron, 7" long	100	150	225
Faegol Bus, cast iron, stenciling on roof reads Wisconsin Motor Bus Lines, 7-3/4"	600	800	1400
Fire Pumper, cast iron, interchangeable, 5" long	80	120	175
Ford Model A Sedan, cast iron, nickel-plated cast spoke wheels, 6" long,	600	900	1200
Ford Opera Coupe, cast iron, 5" long	150	225	350
Ford Roadster, cast iron, c.1936	NPF	NPF	NPF
Ford Truck, cast iron, stake truck; rubber tires, available in red, blue, green, and tan; 7-3/4" long			
Grader, cast iron, 6" long	200	300	425
Hook & Ladder, cast iron, 7-1/2" long	125	200	300
Laundry Truck, cast iron, 8" long	375	550	825
Lincoln Touring Car, cast iron, 7" long	175	275	400
Lincoln Touring Car, cast iron, 9-1/4" long	450	675	950
Lincoln Touring Coupe, cast iron, 8-3/4" long	500	850	1250
Machinery Hauler, cast iron, three lowboy trailers, roadscraper, roadroller, tractor, overall length 28-5/8" long	1500	2750	4500
Mack Auto Truck, cast iron, rubber tires; available in red, blue, green, and tan bodies; 6-3/4" long			

	C6	C8	C10
Mack Gas Tank Truck, cast iron, 3-3/4" long	40	70	100
Mack Gas Tank Truck, cast iron, 5-1/8" long	100	150	215
Mack Gas Tank Truck, cast iron, 7-1/4" long	125	200	300
Mack Gasoline-Motor Oil Truck, cast iron, 10-1/4" long	300	600	850
Mack Stake Truck, cast iron, 3-1/2" long	40	70	100
Mack Stake Truck, cast iron, 4-3/4" long	75	110	170
Mack Stake Truck, cast iron, 5-1/8" long	110	160	225
Mack Stake Truck, cast iron, 7" long	350	550	800
Mack Stake Truck, cast iron, 8-1/2" long	175	275	425
Mack Truck, cast iron, 3-1/2" long	40	70	100
Mack Truck, cast iron, 4-3/4" long	50	75	120
Mack Truck, cast iron, 6-3/4" long	90	140	200
Model T Coupe, cast iron, 6" long	125	187	250
Model T Express Truck, cast iron, 7-1/4" long	200	325	475
Motorcycle, cast iron, No. 27, c. 1933, uniformed driver, rubber tires, blue enamel only color available	200	375	550
Moving & Storage Truck, cast iron, 3-1/2" long	100	150	225
Open Bed Truck, cast iron, 8" long	110	175	275
Phaeton, cast iron, driver, lady passenger, open, c.1921, 12" long	NPF	NPF	NPF
Racer, cast iron, 8-3/4" long	100	150	200
Racer, cast iron, boat-tailed, 6-1/2" long	100	180	260

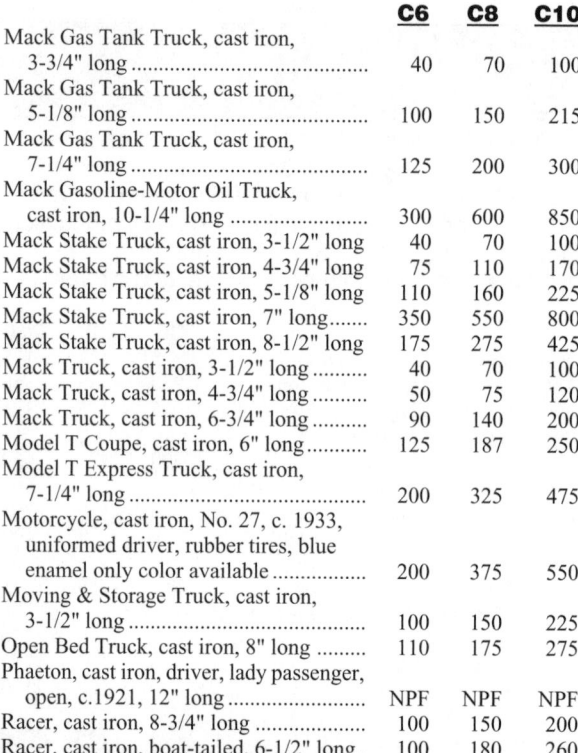

A.C. Williams Coupe, rumble seat, 6-3/4", 1930. Photo courtesy Chic Gast

A.C. Williams Ford Model A Sedan, red with nickel-plated cast spoke wheels, 6". Photo courtesy Al Kasishke

A.C. Williams Lincoln Touring Car, 9-1/4". Photo courtesy Bertoia Auctions

A.C. Williams Ford Roadster, c.1936.

A.C. Williams Machinery Hauler; 3 lowboy trailers, roadscraper, roadroller, tractor, 28-5/8". Photo courtesy Bertoia Auctions

A.C. Williams Mack Gas Tank Truck, 5-1/8", c.1934. Photo courtesy R.W. Cannahan

A.C. Williams Mack Stake Truck, 8-1/2". Photo courtesy Bill Kaufman

A.C. Williams Mack Gas Tank Truck, 7-1/4". Photo courtesy Al Kasishke

A.C. Williams Mack Stake Truck, 4-3/4". Photo courtesy Al Kasishke

A.C. Williams Mack Gas Tank Truck, 10-1/4".

A.C. Williams Coupe, 6", 1928. Photo courtesy Rod Carnahan

A.C. Williams Double Decker Bus, blue with gold side stripes, 7-3/4". Photo courtesy Bertoia Auctions

A.C. Williams Fageol Bus, stenciling on roof reads Wisconsin Motor Bus Lines, 7-3/4". Photo courtesy Bertoia Auctions

A.C. Williams Racer, red, 2 passengers, 7-1/8". Photo courtesy Tim Oei

A.C. Williams Sedan, two-piece, 4-1/2". Photo courtesy Mapes Auctioneers and Appraisers

A.C. Williams Sedan, 1936, 6-3/4".

A.C. Williams Sedan, interchangeable body, 6-3/4", c. 1931.

A.C. Williams Sedan, 6-1/2", c.1930. Photo courtesy Phillips New York

A.C. Williams Tank, 4". Photo courtesy Ed Poole

	C6	C8	C10
Racer, cast iron, driver, tail fin, 8-1/2" long	225	350	525
Racer, cast iron, two passengers, 7-1/8" long	350	550	850
Racer, cast iron, two-man, c.1934, 5-1/2" long	130	200	300
Radiator Car, cast iron, four-casting, nickeled, approx 4" long	75	110	150
Sedan, cast iron, 1936, 6-3/4" long	250	500	700
Sedan, cast iron, 5" long..........................	100	160	220
Sedan, cast iron, approx 3-1/2" long	175	300	450
Sedan, cast iron, c.1920, 4" long.............	60	100	150
Sedan, cast iron, c.1930, cast-iron, streamlined rear fender, 6-1/2" long	200	325	475
Sedan, cast iron, c.1931, interchangeable body, 6-3/4" long	300	450	625
Sedan, cast iron, two-piece, 4-1/2" long ..	100	160	230
Steamroller, cast iron, 1930s, 5-1/2" long	75	110	160
Streamline Sedan, cast iron, 8" long	450	750	1250
Studebaker, cast iron, two-tone sedan, c.1933-34, approx 4" long	100	150	225
Tank, cast iron, 4" long	60	100	140
Taxi, cast iron, 1920s, 5-1/4" long	150	250	350
Touring Car, cast iron, 7" long...............	400	600	850
Touring Car, cast iron, w/two riders, c.1917, 11-3/4" long	550	900	1300

	C6	C8	C10
Touring Car, cast-iron, 9-1/2" long..........	350	450	725
Tractor, cast iron, w/driver, 5" long	100	150	225
Truck with Stake Body Trailer, cast iron, rubber tires; available in red, blue, green, and tan bodies; 7" long			
Truck with Tank Body Trailer, cast iron, rubber tires; available in red, blue, green, and tan bodies; 7" long			
Wrecker, cast iron, 5" long	75	125	175
Wrecker, cast iron, 6-1/2" long	200	350	500
Wrecker, cast iron, 7-3/4" long	350	500	750

A.C. Williams Touring Car, two riders not pictured, 11-3/4", c.1917. Photo courtesy Bob Smith

A.S. TOY COMPANY (NUREMBERG, GERMANY)

The Adolf Schumann Toy Company made toys for approximately twenty years, and like many German toy companies, went out of business in the mid-1930s. Little is known about this small company, and its toys are considered rare. The A.S. trademark is usually on the door of the car.

Contributor: Bob Smith, RATS Toy Shows, 255 Tryon Park, Rochester, NY 14609. (585) 288-7153, bird@oldtoysonline.com. Smith began collecting toys in 1978 after being influenced by some friends who were members of the Genesee Valley Antique Toy Association (GVATA). Starting out with Dinky toys, he soon expanded to Tootsietoys, early hill-climber vehicles, pre war tin cars and early wind-up toys. Smith later joined GVATA and became its president for ten years. He retired from the automobile sales business, and now devotes all of his time to his toy hobby and promotes his toy show. The Rochester Antique Toy Show (RATS) has grown to be one of the largest in the United States.

A.S. Touring Car, tin, 9", c. 1915. Photo courtesy Bob Smith

A.S. Racer w/driver, tin, c. 1908. Photo courtesy Bertoia Auctions

	C6	C8	C10
Racer, w/driver, tin lithographed, c.1908, marked "6", 7" long	700	950	1550
Touring Car, red and black, clockwork motor, glass windshield, c.1915, 9" long	1200	1600	2250

ACME

Acme produced only two toy vehicles, both in clockwork—a 1903 curved-dash Oldsmobile roadster and a delivery truck with a pressed-steel canopied roof. In 1905, Acme's owner, Jacob Lauth, began producing actual automobiles under the name Lauth-Juergens Co.

	C6	C8	C10
Curved Dash Olds, clockwork, c.1903, 11" long	500	750	1000

Acme Curved Dash Olds, c. 1903. Photo courtesy Bob Smith

ACME PLASTIC TOYS, INC.

Collectors may notice a strong similarity between Acme Plastic Toys' vehicles and Thomas Toys, and there is. With an address of 121 East 124th St., New York, New York, Acme handled the marketing of Thomas toys from 1945 to 1950. Toys from this era bear the Acme Plastic Toys mark.

Islyn Thomas, owner of Thomas Toys, bought out Ben Shapiro of Acme in 1950. From that point on, all toys carried the Thomas Toys' mark.

Acme also made other toys—helicopters, planes, baby carriages and strollers, and wagons.

Acme Jeep with original box, yellow jeep with red wheels. Photo courtesy Bob and Alice Wagner

Acme Transporter, green cab, red trailer, two cars, 1950s. Photo courtesy Bob and Alice Wagner

Top to Bottom: Acme Truck and Trailer, green, blue trailer, 9", 1947; Acme Truck Wrecker, red. Photo courtesy Bob and Alice Wagner

	C6	C8	C10
Aerocar PT 560, plastic, marked "Made in U.S.A. Plas-Tex," 7-1/2" long	125	175	200
Airline Limousine, No. 29, 1947, 4-1/2" long	23	25	27
Auto Carrier, No. ?, 9" long	20	25	30
Convertible Coupe, streamlined, No. 77, 4-1/2" long (Acme used the same number for sedan and convertible)	9	11	15
Coupe and House Trailer, No. 30, 1947, 8-1/4" long	20	22	24
Delivery Truck, No. 41, 1947, 4" long.....	16	18	20
Dump Truck, No. 42, 1947, 5" long........	12	14	16
Esso Gas Truck, No. 43, 1947	NPF	NPF	NPF
Jeep, No. 17, movable windshield, 1947, 4-1/2" long	23	25	27
Jeep and Trailer, No. 19, 1947, 8-1/2" long	14	16	18
Limousine and Trailer, No. 55, 6-/4" long	26	31	36
Merry-Go-Round Truck, No. 74, 4-3/4" long	20	25	30

	C6	C8	C10
Motorcycle, plastic, w/rider, No. 72, 4" long..	45	50	55
Motorcycle, plated, No. 125, 4" long.......	NPF	NPF	NPF
Police-Fire Chief Radio Car, No. 67, 4-1/2" long..	23	25	27
Sedan, No. 27, 1947, 4-5/16" long...........	18	20	22
Sedan, streamlined, No. 77, 4-1/2" long ..	11	13	15
Service Motorcycle, w/rider, No. 90, 4-7/16" long..	25	30	35
Texaco Gas Truck, No. 40, 1947, 4" long	21	23	25
Transporter, green cab w/red trailer and two cars, 1950s	20	35	50
Transporter, green cab, red trailer, two cars, 1950s	NPF	NPF	NPF
Truck and Trailer, No. 16, 1947, 9" long.	14	16	18
Truck Wrecker, No. 26, 5" long..............	35	40	45
Truck, streamlined, No. 18, 1947, 5" long	10	12	14
Utility Trailer, streamlined, No. 48, marked "fits items 27-29-40-41," 2-1/2" long	6	8	10

AL OTTO

	C6	C8	C10
Jeep Fire Truck....................................	1000	1700	2500
Jeep Pickup Truck	400	750	1100
Jeepster	1100	1850	2700

	C6	C8	C10
Stock Car Racer, plastic, early, 4-1/2" long	4	10	25
Woody Station Wagon	600	950	150

ALL AMERICAN (LOS ANGELES)

	C6	C8	C10
Hot-Rod, c.1949, 9" long	210	315	420

All-American Hot Rod, red, 1949. Photo courtesy Roger E. Canup

ALL AMERICAN TOY COMPANY (OREGON)

Clay and Beth Steinke founded All American in Salem, Oregon, in 1947. Despite formidable 1950 price of $19.95, All American's most popular toy was its first release, the Timber Toter. Based on the late 1940s Ford trucks, the heavy aluminum cab was originally sand cast before dies were created due to increased demand. The hefty truck was 1:12 scale, measured 36" long, and weighed 10 pounds.

All American continued until 1956, with its location in the Jorgenson Building on Ferry Street. At its peak, it employed forty-two people. In total, it sold 26,000 toys. Collectors should note that toy vehicles made by All American had air-horn steering (a means of steering the truck through the hood using the brass air horn) and Goodyear tires.

Patrick Russell purchased All American Toy Company in 1992. Available now are parts and new limited-edition vehicles. You can reach them at: All American Toy Co., 540 Lancaster SE, Salem, OR 97301; Phone: (503) 399-8609; Web site: www.allamericantoyco.com

	C6	C8	C10
Cargo Liner, model CL-8, 38" long	275	400	600
Cattle Liner, model C-5, 38" long	400	650	925
Dyna-Dump, model D-3, 20" long	250	400	550
Heavy Hauler, model HH-9, 38" long......	300	475	750
Midget Skagit, model MS, battery-powered, 18" long....................	250	450	600
Midget Skagit, model S-I, 16" long	120	240	360
Midget Skagit, model U-1, Midget Skagit	NPF	NPF	NPF
Midget Skagit, model W/T-6	NPF	NPF	NPF
Play-Dozer, model HD-7, 9" long............	300	500	700

	C6	C8	C10
Play-Loader, model HD-6, 11" long	300	500	700
Scoop-A-Veyor, model S-1, sandloader, 6"x10"x16"	NPF	NPF	NPF
Timber Toter, model L-2, w/logs, 38" extended length	260	400	585
Timber Toter Jr., model LJ-4, 20" long ...	100	200	300

1950s Style

	C6	C8	C10
Alis Chalmers K Tractor, new, orange, with or without blade	n/a	n/a	60

The Cargo-Liner, Timber Toter, and Utility truck were other new offerings from All American in 1953. Photo courtesy 1953 All American catalog.

The All American Timer Toter Jr. and an optional trailer. Photo courtesy 1953 All American catalog.

All American Dyna-Dump, white cab with "All American" insignia, red bed. Photo courtesy Roy Bonjour

All American Cattle Liner, 38". Photo courtesy Bob Smith

	C6	C8	C10
Coke Truck, new, red or yellow - 75 produced in each color, air horn steering, Goodyear tires, 24" long	n/a	n/a	500
Heavy Hauler II, new, orange double axle model or yellow triple axle model (add $100); lowboy trailer, 225 produced in each color, 47" long	n/a	n/a	600
Heavy Hauler Limited, new, yellow cab, extended lowboy trailer, 45 produced, 55" long..	n/a	n/a	600
Tilt Bed Trailer, new, yellow, tilting, 16" long 6-1/2" wide	n/a	n/a	170
Timber Toter Jr. II, new, silver gray cab-50 produced, diamond white cab-100 produced; Goodyear tires, air horn steering, with chains, 20" long	n/a	n/a	450
Timber Toter Jr. Trailer, new, red or yellow, Goodyear tires, trailer linkage replicating the 1939 Ford original, with chains, 17" long	n/a	n/a	200
Water Toter, new, yellow and green, air horn steering, Goodyear tires, 100 produced, 22" long..............................	n/a	n/a	600

Kenworth

	C6	C8	C10
18 Wheeler Flatbed w/Sleeper, new, 1:16 scale, sandstone/burgundy - 75 produced, burgundy - 75 produced, 39" long...	n/a	n/a	800
24k Gold Kenworth, new, cab only, black w/24k gold accents, 100 produced, 17" long	n/a	n/a	900
Army Truck, new, tanker truck in olive drab, 100 produced, weighs 10 lbs, 21"	n/a	n/a	795

The All American Model S-1 Scoop-A-Veyor, the Model HD-6 Play-Loader, Model HD-7 Play-dozer as shown in the 1953 All American catalog.

	C6	C8	C10
Cigar Truck, new, Gonzalez-Sanchez Cigar Hauler, 40 produced, 1:16 scale, 10 wheels, white w/ decals, rear door opens, weighs 10 lbs, 22" long	n/a	n/a	595
Dump Truck, new, pearl white w/dark green trim or silver w/metallic green; 100 produced, 1:16 scale, 19" long	n/a	n/a	600
Fire Truck, new, fire tanker truck, customized for each customer with decals and chrome accessories.............	n/a	n/a	735
Meier & Frank Co., new, 10-wheel cargo (box) van, green, air horn steering, 60 produced, weighs 10 pounds, 22" long	n/a	n/a	595
P.I.E. 18 Wheeler, new, 2002, red truck, silver semi trailer, P.I.E. logos, 50 produced, 36" long.......................	n/a	n/a	895
P.I.E. Tanker Truck and Trailer, new, 2002, red truck, silver tanker, additional silver tanker piggy-back, P.I.E. logos, 100 produced, 38" long ...	n/a	n/a	995

ALLIED

Allied, of Corona, New York, only made plastic toys. They specialized in small, inexpensive items, including cars, trucks, boats, pistols, animals, and dollhouse furniture.

	C6	C8	C10
Auto Sales and Station, w/five vehicles ...	65	100	130
Cement Mixer, No. 197, 4" long..............	NPF	NPF	NPF
Construction Set, No. 620, included dump truck, cement truck and emergency truck w/ladder, 15" long box	NPF	NPF	NPF

	C6	C8	C10
Delivery Service Truck	35	52	70
Dump Truck, large, No. 174, 5-1/2" long	NPF	NPF	NPF
Dump Truck, small, No. 191, 4-1/2" long	10	15	20
Emergency Truck, 7" long, No. 129	NPF	NPF	NPF
Furniture Moving Van, large, No. 208, clear trailer ("Viso Box"), 5-1/2" long, price without original ten pieces of furniture	10	15	20
Haulaway Truck and Trailer, w/two small cars and one large car, No. 122, 10" long	15	25	38
Old Fashioned Car, No. 218, 4-1/2" long	NPF	NPF	NPF
Pick-up Truck, 3-1/2" long	8	10	15
Racer, No. 130, 4-5/8" long	15	25	33
Stake Truck, 4-1/2" long	10	15	20
Stake Truck, w/eight assorted farm animals and removable racks, No. 193, 9-1/2" long	NPF	NPF	NPF
Station Wagon, 3-1/2" long	8	10	15

Allied Furniture Moving Van. Photo courtesy Dave Leopard

	C6	C8	C10
Steam Shovel Truck, No. 134, 6" long	NPF	NPF	NPF
Taxi, 3-1/2" long	8	10	15
Tractor, No. 30, 3" long	NPF	NPF	NPF
Van, enclosed, 6" long	10	15	20
Wrecker, 4-3/8" long	15	20	25

ALL-NU

Founded by C. Frank Krupp, All-Nu Products Inc. produced lead figures and vehicles from 1938 until materials restrictions during World War II forced their cessation in 1942. All-Nu continued to produce heavy stock cardboard soldiers and vehicles until 1945. In 1946, All-Nu became Faben Products Inc. and the company lasted until 1950.

The All-Nu Searchlight, Field Kitchen, Tank, and Sound Detector. Photo courtesy Bill Kaufman

	C6	C8	C10
Field Kitchen, lead, marked "Made in USA," approx. 2-1/2" long (ANV001)	NPF	NPF	NPF
Searchlight, lead, marked "Made in USA," approx. 2-3/4" long (ANV002)	NPF	NPF	NPF
Sound Detector, lead, marked "Made in USA," approx., 2-3/4" long (ANV003)	NPF	NPF	NPF
Tank, lead, marked "Made in USA," "USA", 3" long (ANV004)	NPF	NPF	NPF

Cardboard Vehicles	C6	C8	C10
Ambulance, No. Military 154	3	5	7
Army Troop Carrier, No. 155	3	5	7
Cannon, No. 151	3	5	7
Jeep, No. 150	3	5	7
Tank, No. 153	3	5	7
Wheeled AA Gun, No. 152	3	5	7

AMERICAN METAL TOY

This was essentially a toy soldier company, began business in Chicago in 1937, even though President Royce Reyff, along with C. Raymond Pierson incorporated the company in 1939. Because its toys were composed of lead zinc alloy, the lack of metal available during World War II forced the company out of business in 1942.

	C6	C8	C10
Tank, marked "22" on side (AMV004)	50	75	100
Tank, throwing flame, flame not touching hull (AMV002)	45	68	90
Tank, throwing flame, flame touching hull (AMV001)	40	60	80
Tank, throwing flame, marked "25" (AMV003)	60	90	120

AMERICAN NATIONAL

Founded by brothers William, Walter, and Harry Diemer around 1894, American-National of Toledo, Ohio, produced a line of pressed steel trucks as early as 1918 and a wide variety of pedal cars and in the 1920s and 1930s.

	C6	C8	C10
American Railway Express, 27" long	1000	1600	2400
Army Truck, Mack "Giant," 26-1/2" long	800	1400	2000
Chemical Fire Truck, 28" long................	2000	3200	4500
Circus Truck, 27" long	800	1400	2000
Coal Truck..	1500	2500	4200
Duesenberg Bobtail Pedal Car, late 1920s	3000	5500	7000
Dump Truck, 28" long	800	1400	2000
Fire Chief Pedal Truck, 66" long	3000	5000	7900
Fire Pedal Truck, c.late 1920s.................	4000	7500	13,000
Jordan Pedal Car, 40" long......................	1000	1700	2400
Juvenile Auto Dump Truck Pedal Car, 57" long..	2000	3500	5000
Lincoln Dual Cowl Pedal Car	4000	7500	12,000
Moving Van, 28" long..............................	800	1400	2000
Packard, brown, extensive side trim, 28" long..	NPF	NPF	NPF
Packard Convertible, red, 28" long	NPF	NPF	NPF
Packard Coupe Pedal Car, 1928, 56" long	2000	3200	4600
Packard Coupe Pedal Car, steerable front wheels, 54" long...................................	1500	2500	3400

American National American Railway Express, black cab, red and silver tires, green bed, 27" long. Photo courtesy Bertoia Auctions

	C6	C8	C10
Packard Fire Chief Car, 27" long............	3000	5500	10,000
Packard Pedal Car, 1923, 70" long	3000	5500	10,000
Racing Car, 1927	2000	3200	4500
Richfield Gasoline Truck, 27" long	1500	2250	3100
Screenside Truck......................................	1500	2500	3600
Sprinkler Truck	1400	2500	3500
Tanker	1400	2500	3500
Truck, open bed, 29" long........................	700	1150	1700

American National Packard Convertible red, 28" long. Photo courtesy Bertoia Auctions

American National Packard Coupe, 1928 pedal car, red, red centers, white tires, 56" long. Photo courtesy Bertoia Auctions

American National Packard, brown extensive side trim, 28" long. Photo courtesy Bertoia Auctions

American National Packard Coupe, 1923 pedal car, yellow, brown top, 70" long. Photo courtesy Bertoia Auctions

AMERICAN PRECISION CO.

	C6	C8	C10
Allis-Chalmers C Model Tractor, die-cast, 1950	150	225	300

AMF

Rufus L. Patterson founded the American Machine and Foundry Co. in 1900 as a subsidiary of the American Tobacco Co. and became an independent entity following the 1911 collapse of American Tobacco. Under the 1941-62 leadership of Eugene M. Patterson, AMF branched out from its tobacco equipment roots to embrace toys, pedal cars, military equipment, and the bowling equipment for which it is still famous today.

	C6	C8	C10
Pontiac Pedal Car, 1930, 37-1/2" long	1500	2500	3500
Rebel Racer Pedal Car, 1965	200	300	400

AMF Pontiac Pedal Car, 37-1/2", cream, brown, red and yellow Pontiac insignia, 1930. Photo courtesy Bertoia Auctions

ANDY GARD

	C6	C8	C10		C6	C8	C10
Bell Telephone Truck	22	33	45	Pickup Truck, 6" long, soft plastic	7	11	15
Brink's Armored Car, battery-operated	30	45	60	Telephone Truck	30	45	60
Crane, magnetic, battery-operated	62	93	125	Touring Sedan, 19" long	37	56	75
Fire Engine, battery-operated	37	56	75	Telephone Truck	30	45	60
Gee I Jeep, battery-operated	20	30	40	Touring Sedan, 19" long	37	56	75
MG, motor-powered cable steering	100	150	200				

ANIMATE TOY CO.

In 1918, this firm was located at East 17th St., in New York City, and its president was L.T. Savage. By 1931, it had moved to 30 North 15th Street in East Orange, N.J., and employed ten men and forty

Animate Toy Baby Tractor, friction.

Animate Toy Climbing Tractor, 9", driver, red wheels, 1929.

women. In 1934, the president-vice president was George V. Turnbull, and the secretary-treasurer was George H. Webb. Five men and eleven women made up the work force. See also "Woodhaven."

	C6	C8	C10
Baby Haymaker Push Toy Playset, tin, 1916	100	150	200
Baby Tractor, friction, marked "patented June 20, 1916"	85	130	175
Climbing Tractor, wind-up, 9" long, 1929	110	165	225

	C6	C8	C10
Toy Tractor, wind-up, 8-1/2" long	NPF	NPF	NPF
Toy Tractor and Dump Trailer, wind-up, 15-1/2" long	NPF	NPF	NPF
Toy tractor w/Snow Plow, 13" long, wind-up	NPF	NPF	NPF
Toy Tractor w/Sweeper, wind-up, 12-1/2" long	NPF	NPF	NPF
U.S. Baby Tank, wind-up, pat. June 20, 1916 (new in 1918), 2-1/2" long,	37	56	75

ARCADE

In 1869, a foundry in Freeport, Illinois, was organized as a two-man partnership under the name of Novelty Iron and Brass foundry. It was dissolved in 1885 when a new, larger factory was incorporated under the name of Arcade Manufacturing Co. Arcade made industrial castings and household items, but no toys. After a disastrous fire in 1892 and management changes in 1893, toys began to appear in its catalog, and by the early 1900s the line had become so extensive that fifty-page catalog was issued showing a large line of notions and novelties, small stoves, banks, and a few trains, including a unique pile-driver. But it was not until an enterprising young lawyer married the daughter of one of the officers and joined the firm in 1919 that the firm rapidly became one of the major makers of cast-iron toys. Struck by the large numbers of Yellow Cabs in the streets of Chicago, the young man approached the Yellow Cab company with a novel proposition: in return for the sole right to make toy replicas of the cab, the Yellow Cab company would have the exclusive right to use the toy in its advertising. Success was instantaneous.

Arcade went on to duplicate this pattern with miniature Buick, Chevrolet, Ford, Plymouth, and Pontiac automobiles; McCormick-Deering and International Harvester farm equipment; and several makes of trucks and buses.

In the booming 1920s, the company's sales swelled so much that a new and larger plant was built in 1927. Two years later, the stock market crash heralded the Great Depression, and hard times hit the small car business just as it did the large ones.

Cheap competition and dwindling demand for toys costing more than a dime brought the company to the brink of bankruptcy by 1933. But once again the enterprising management gave the firm new life with an exclusive arrangement to provide souvenir replicas of the fairground buses made by G.M.C. for the Chicago Century of Progress. The Depression caused a cheapening of quality, but World War II gave the firm business in military material.

After the war, the company returned to making industrial and household hardware and a few toys, but cheaper toys of die-cast zamac, plastic, rubber, and lithographed tin eclipsed the more expensive cast-iron toys. In 1946, the firm was sold to Rockwell Manufacturing Co. of Pittsburgh. Death and retirement soon finished the change of the old firm, and it followed its guiding directors into oblivion when Rockwell moved to Alabama.

Arcade toys were meant to be played with and are extremely rare in Mint condition. The year listed is the year the toy was introduced.

Contributor: Michael W. Curran, Illinois Antiques, P.O. Box 545, Hampton, IL 61256, 309-496-9426.

	C6	C8	C10
A.C.F. Bus, 1927, 11-1/2" long (AR001)	1700	2700	4100
Allis-Chalmers Tractor and Dump Trailer, No. 2657, 1937, 12-3/4" long w/trailer (AR003)	125	175	275
Allis-Chalmers Tractor and Dump Trailer, No. 2660, 1937, 8-1/4" long (AR003A)	75	125	180
Allis-Chalmers Tractor and Trailer, No. 2650, 1936, 13" long total length (AR002)	200	300	450
Allis-Chalmers Tractor Trailer, No. 2650, 1937, 13" long w/trailer (AR004)	200	310	475
Allis-Chalmers WC Tractor, 1941, 7-3/4" long (AR005)	425	675	1000
Ambulance, blue, No. 188, 1932, 6" long (AR007)	300	500	725
Ambulance, No. 187, 1932, 7-3/4" long (AR006)	350	575	850
Ambulance, white, No. 188, 1932, 6" long (AR007A)	275	425	625

	C6	C8	C10
Ambulance, white-painted version of No. 2620X Chevrolet Panel Delivery Truck, 1936, 4" long (AR008)	350	575	800
American Gasoline Mack Tank Truck, 1925, 13-1/4" long (AR152)	1200	1850	2500
Andy Gump Car, 1920s, 7-1/4" long (AR263)	1250	2250	3500
Anthony Dump Truck, 1927, 8-1/8" long (AR009)	1000	1700	2750
Austin "Roll-A-Plane", 7-1/2" long (AR014)	500	900	1400
Austin Autocrat Road Roller, No. 291, 1928, 7" long (AR010)	300	475	675
Austin Delivery Truck, No. 173, 1932, 3-3/4" long (AR011)	50	75	100
Austin Racer, No. 175X, 1932, 3-3/4" long (AR012)	50	75	100
Austin Roadster, No. 174, 1932, 3-3/4" long (AR013)	125	200	275

Left to right: Arcade A.C.F. Bus, (AR1), 11-1/2", 1927; Arcade Yellow Parlor Coach Bus, 13", 1926. Photo courtesy Bertoia Auctions

	C6	C8	C10
Austin Stake Truck, No. 176X, 1932, 3-3/4" long (AR015)	125	200	300
Austin Wrecker, No. 177X, 1932, 3-3/4" long (AR016)	125	200	300
Avery Tractor, has hood, no stack, 1926, 4-1/2" long (AR018)	110	170	250
Avery Tractor, stack, no hood, 1923, 4-/2" long (AR017)	30	45	60
Borden's Milk Bottle Truck, No. 2640X, 1936, 6-1/4" long (AR019)	1000	1600	2400
Brinks Express Truck, 1932, 11-3/4" long (AR020)	8000	15,000	20,000
Buick Coupe, 1927, 8-1/2" long (AR021)	2500	4400	6250
Buick Sedan, 1927, 8-1/2" long (AR022)	1500	2500	4000
Bullet Racer, No. 139X, 1931, 7-5/8" long (AR191)	900	1300	2300
Bus, Double-Decker, No. 316X, 1929, 8-1/2" long (AR023)	400	600	900
Bus, Double-Decker, No. 317, 1936, stamped "Chicago Motor Coach," 8-1/4" long (AR024)	400	675	950
Cab, brown and white, 1923, 8" long (AR020B)	2200	3700	5500
Cab, brown and white, 1923, 9" long (AR020A)	1800	3000	4500
Cab, green and white, c.1923, 9" long (AR111A)	1200	2000	3200
Car Carrier, cargo has four 25-cent cars or three 50-cent Arcade cars, No. 238, 1931, 24-1/2" long (AR025)	1500	2500	4000
Car Carrier, carries either two No. 114 Ford Sedans and one No. 113X Ford Arcade Coupe or one No. 213 Ford Stake and one each of the others; No. 296, 1932, 24-1/2" long (AR026)	1400	2400	3800
Car Transport, came w/two No. 1501 Sedans, No. 1502 Stake Truck and Wrecker No. 1503; 1937, No. 3107, 18-1/2" long (AR027)	800	1250	1800
Car Transport, holds two sedans, two trucks; No. 2977, 1937, 11-1/4" long (AR028)	425	600	900

	C6	C8	C10
Carry Car Truck and Trailer Set, carries Austin Coupe, Delivery and Stake; No. 2970, 1934, 14-1/4" long (AR029)	650	1000	1650
Caterpillar Tractor, No. 266X, 1931, 3" long (AR033)	25	38	50
Caterpillar Tractor, No. 267X, 1931, 3-7/8" long (AR032)	225	325	500
Caterpillar Tractor, No. 268X, 1931, 5-5/8" long (AR031A)	500	800	1350
Caterpillar Tractor, No. 269X, 1931, 6-7/8" long (AR031)	650	1100	1550
Caterpillar Tractor, No. 270Y (later became No. 2700Y) 1936, 7-3/4" long (AR034)	750	1250	1850
Caterpillar Tractor, No. 271, 1930, 7-1/2" long (AR030)	300	425	650
Century of Progress Bus, does not pivot or detach, 1933, approx. 5-1/2" long (AR038A)	175	275	375
Century of Progress Bus, No. 3200 (became No. 3250 in 1934), 1933, 14-1/2" long (AR035)	250	375	500
Century of Progress Bus, No. 3210, 1933, 12" long (AR036)	200	325	450
Century of Progress Bus, No. 3220, 1933, 10-1/2" long (AR037)	175	275	425
Century of Progress Bus, No. 3230, 1933, 7-5/8" long (AR038)	100	160	225
Century of Progress Yellow Cab, 6-1/2" long (AR038B)	1000	2000	3200
Checker Cab, marked "Checker" on visor, 1932, No. 157, 9-1/4" long (AR040)	15,000	20,000	62,000
Checker Cab, paint variation of No. 1 Yellow Cab, 1923, 9" long (AR039)	2500	4000	6500
Checker Cab, with and without "Checker" on visor, 1932, 9-1/4" long (AR040A)	NPF	NPF	NPF
Chevrolet Coupe, No. 121X, 1929, 8-1/4" long (AR041)	650	1100	1800
Chevrolet Coupe, w/rumble seat, No. 1150X, 1934, 4-3/8" long (AR042)	150	225	325
Chevrolet Panel Delivery Truck, No. 2620X, 1936, 4" long (AR043)	125	175	275

Variations of numerous Arcade ambulances from the 1930s. Photo courtesy Bertoia Auctions

Arcade Austin Autocrat Road Roller, (AR10), 7", 1928. Photo courtesy David W. Mapes Auctions

Arcade Austin "Roll-A-Plane," (AR14), 7-1/2". Photo courtesy Bertoia Auctions

Arcade Brinks Express Truck, (AR20), red, red and white wheels, 1932, 11-3/4". Photo courtesy Bertoia Auctions

	C6	C8	C10
Chevrolet Sedan, double stripe, No. 122X, 1929, 8-1/4" long (AR044A) ...	1250	1750	3000
Chevrolet Sedan, No. 1170X, 1934, 4-1/4" long (AR045)	50	75	100
Chevrolet Sedan, single stripe, No. 122X, 1929, 8-1/4" long (AR044)	900	1500	2200
Chevrolet Stake Truck, 1925, 9" long (AR046)	950	1650	2500
Chevrolet Stake Truck, No. 2610, 1936, 4-1/4" long (AR047)	NPF	NPF	NPF
Chevrolet Superior Roadster, 1925, 7" long (AR048)	1000	1700	2500
Chevrolet Superior Sedan, 1925, 7" long (AR049)	450	700	1050
Chevrolet Superior Touring Car, 1925, 7" long (AR050)	700	1250	2000
Chevrolet Utility Coupe, 1925, 7" long (AR051)	750	1300	1950
Chevrolet Wrecker Truck, No. 2630X, 1936, 4-1/4" long (AR052)	150	225	325
Chief Fire Chief Coupe, No. 1230, 1934, 6-3/4" long (AR053)	1400	2400	3500

	C6	C8	C10
Chief Fire Chief Coupe, No. 1240, 1934, 5" long (AR054)	450	750	1100
Circus Wagon, horse-drawn, driver at top	NPF	NPF	NPF
Coast To Coast GMC Transcontinental Bus, No. 4378X, 1937, 9" long (AR055)	200	325	475
Coast To Coast Greyhound Cruiser Coach bus, No. 4400, 9-1/8" long (AR112A)	225	375	525
Coast To Coast Greyhound Lines Bus, 1937, No. 3850X (AR113A)	250	375	525
Corn Harvester, 1939, No. 4180, 5" long (AR057)	130	200	300
Corn Harvester, 1939, No. 702, 6-1/2" long (AR056)	175	275	400
Corn Planter, 1939, 4-1/2" long (AR058)	60	90	125
Coupe, like above w/o 1922 date on spare, 9" long (AR060)	850	1250	1750
Coupe, marked "1922" on spare tire, 9" long (AR059)	1500	2500	4000

Left to right: Arcade Buick Coupe and Buick Sedan. Photo courtesy Bertoia Auctions

Arcade Cab, (AR111A), green and white, 9", 1920s. Photo courtesy Bertoia Auctions

Page 7 from the No. 51 Arcade catalog.

Arcade Austin Stake Truck, (AR15), 3-3/4", 1932. Photo courtesy Rod Carnahan

Arcade Buick Sedan, (AR22), 8-1/2", 1927. Photo courtesy James S. Maxwell and Virginia Caputo

Arcade Bus, Double-Decker "Chicago Motor Coach," (AR24), 8-1/4", 1936. Photo courtesy Sotheby's New York

Arcade Cabs, Left to right: (AR20A), brown and white, 9", 1923; (AR20B), brown and white, 8" 1923. Photo courtesy Bertoia Auctions

Arcade made several variations of the Century of Progress Bus. Because prices vary with size, make sure you know which one you have. Pictured here is (AR37), No. 3220, 10-1/2" long, 1933. Photo courtesy Mapes Auctioneers and Appraisers

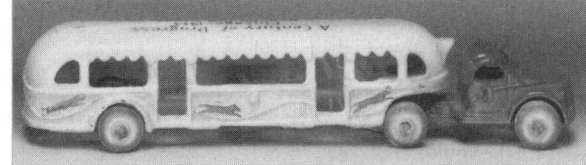

Arcade Century of Progress Bus, (AR38), No. 3230, 7-5/8" long, 1933. Photo courtesy Sotheby's New York

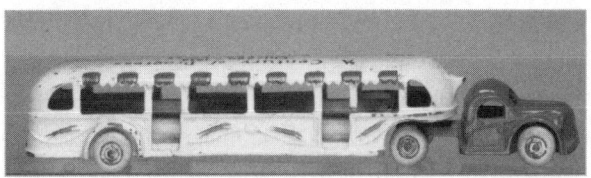

Arcade Century of Progress Bus, (AR36), No. 3210, 12", 1933. Photo courtesy Sotheby's New York

Arcade Checker Cab, (AR39), 9", 1923. Photo courtesy Bertoia Auctions

Arcade issued numerous buses in the 1930s-1940s. Photo courtesy Bertoia Auctions

Arcade Checker Cab, (AR40), 9-1/4", 1932. Photo courtesy Bertoia Auctions

Arcade Chevrolet Coupe, (AR41), 8-1/4", 1929. Photo courtesy James S. Maxwell and Virginia Caputo

	C6	C8	C10
Coupe, no Arcade markings, rumble seat opens, No. 109, 1932, 6" long (AR061)	250	375	550
Deluxe Sedan, same as Yellow Cab No. 1590Y, but w/top lights and w/o sun roof; No. 1590X, 1941, 8-1/2" long (AR062)	475	800	1250
DeSoto Sedan, No. 1460X, 1936, 4" long (AR063)	150	225	325
Double Decker Bus, No. 3180, 1939, 8" long (AR064)	425	625	900
Dump Truck, No. 2320, 1936, 4-1/2" long (AR065)	50	80	120
Dump Truck, No. 3910X, 1941, 7" long (AR066)	275	425	625
Dump Truck, transitional, lighter metal, 1940s, 11-1/4" long (AR066A)	275	425	625
Dump Truck Trailer, No. 234, 1931, 12-/8" long (AR067)	850	1450	2250
Dump Wagon, w/driver, no cab, 1917, 7" long (AR068)	450	650	1000
Express Truck, No. 209X, 1929, 8" long (AR070)	NPF	NPF	NPF
Express Truck, No. 214X, 1929, 5" long (AR071)	NPF	NPF	NPF
Express Truck, No. 270X, 1929, 8" long (AR069)	450	650	1000
Fageol Bus, 12-1/2" long (AR073)	450	700	1000
Fageol Bus, 1925, 12" long (AR072)	375	550	800
Fageol Bus, 8" long (AR074)	325	525	750
Farm Mower, No. 4210X, 1939, 4" long (AR075)	60	90	125
Farm Wagon, horse-drawn, driver, reins, red wagon	NPF	NPF	NPF
Farmall A Tractor, No. 7050, 1941, 7-1/2" long (AR076)	600	1000	1500

	C6	C8	C10
Farmall M Tractor, No. 7070, 1941, 7-1/4" long (AR077)	225	325	500
Farmall Tractor, No. 279, 1929, 6" long (AR078)	500	750	1100
Fire Chief Car, 5-5/8" long, 1941 (AR078A)	150	225	300
Fire Engine, No. 1810, 1936, 6-1/4" long (AR081)	NPF	NPF	NPF
Fire Engine, No. 2340, 1936, 4-1/2" long (AR082)	90	135	180
Fire Engine, No. 6990, 1941, 13-1/2" long (AR083)	700	1150	1650
Fire Engine, pumper, 1923, 7-1/2" long (AR079)	225	375	525
Fire Engine, pumper, No. 1740, 1936, 9" long (AR080)	475	775	1250
Fire Ladder Truck, No. 1820, 1936, 7" long (AR084)	200	300	450
Fire Trailer Truck, ladder truck, No. 1940, 1934, 16-1/4" long (AR085)	450	700	950
Ford Carry Car Truck and Trailer, No. 2400, 1934 (AR086)	NPF	NPF	NPF
Ford Coupe, 1923, 6" long (AR087)	150	250	375
Ford Coupe, 1924, 6-1/2" long (AR088)	275	400	600
Ford Coupe, No. 1190X, 1930s, 4-3/4" long (AR090)	110	175	250
Ford Coupe, rumble seat opens, No. 1610X, 1934, 6-3/4" long (AR089)	150	250	375
Ford Dump Truck, No. 219X, 1929, 7-1/2" long (AR091)	275	400	600
Ford Express Truck, No. 210X, 1929, 8-1/4" long (AR092)	1000	1650	2400
Ford Fordor Sedan, w/removable chauffeur, 1924, 6-1/2" long (AR093)	225	350	525
Ford Sedan, "Center Door," 1923, 6-1/2" long (AR094)	325	400	650

Arcade Chevrolet Sedans, 8-1/4", 1929, L to R: (AR44A), double stripe; (AR44), single stripe. Photo courtesy Bertoia Auctions

Arcade Chevrolets, L to R: (AR45), Sedan, 8-1/4", 1929; (AR42), Coupe w/rumble seat, 4-3/8", 1934. Photo courtesy Chic Gast

Arcade Chevrolet Superior Sedan, (AR49), 1925. Photo courtesy Bertoia Auctions

Arcade Chevrolet Superior Touring Car, (AR50), 7", 1925. Photo courtesy Bertoia Auctions

Arcade Chevrolet Utility Coupe, (AR51), 7", 1925. Photo courtesy Bertoia Auctions

Arcade Circus Wagon, horse-drawn, driver at top. Photo courtesy Liz Isham Cory

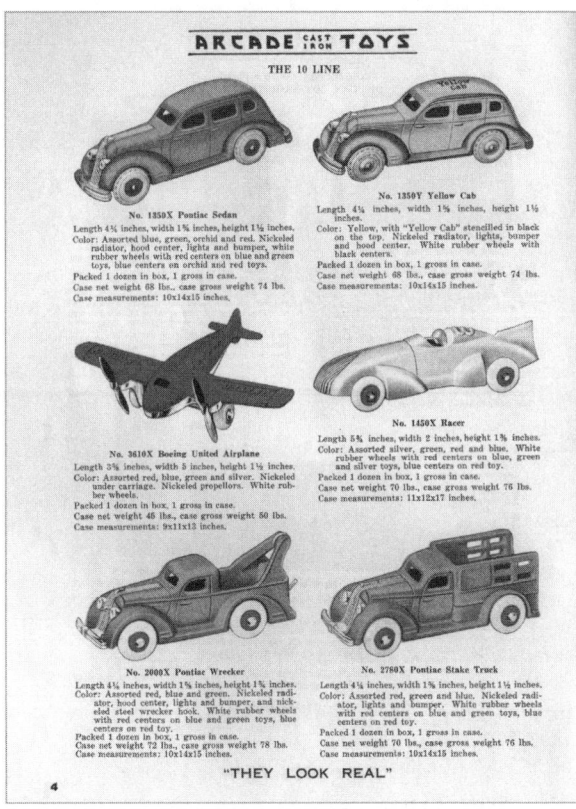

Page 4 from the No. 51 Arcade catalog.

	C6	C8	C10
Ford Sedan, "Century of Progress," 1934, 4-3/4" long (AR097A)	NPF	NPF	NPF
Ford Sedan, "Century of Progress," 1934, 6-7/8" long (AR096)	1000	1750	2750
Ford Sedan, No. 1200, 1930s, 4-3/4" long (AR097)	175	275	400
Ford Sedan, No. 1620X, 1934, 6-7/8" long (AR095)	NPF	NPF	NPF
Ford Sedan with Trailer, No. 1970, 1937, sedan: 12" long, trailer: 5-1/2" long (AR098)	600	1000	1600
Ford Stake Truck, 1925, 8-3/4" long (AR099)	700	1250	1600
Ford Stake Truck, 1927, 9" long (AR100)	1000	1600	2250
Ford Stake Truck, No. 2010X, 1934, 4-3/4" long (AR101)	NPF	NPF	NPF
Ford Touring Car, 1923, 6-1/2" long (AR102)	450	650	900
Ford Touring Car Bank, 1923, 6-1/2" long (AR103)	1100	1800	2700
Ford Tractor and Plow, No. 7220, 1941, tractor: 6-1/2" long, overall length: 8-3/4" (AR104)	425	625	875
Ford Truck, One-Ton Pickup, C-Cab, 1923, 8-1/2" long (AR105)	900	1400	2200
Ford Wrecker, No. 215, 1929, 8-1/4" long to end of hoist (AR106)	500	750	1100
Ford Wrecker, No. 217, 1929 (AR106A)	300	450	650
Ford Wrecker, No. 218, 1930, 4-1/2" long (AR107)	125	175	250
Fordson Tractor, 1923, 5-3/8" long (AR108)	150	225	325
Fordson Tractor, No. 273, 1928, 3-7/8" long (AR110)	50	75	110

A pair of Arcade Coupes, (AR60), 9", 1922. Photo courtesy Bertoia Auctions

Arcade DeSoto Sedan, (AR63), 4", 1936. Photo courtesy Bertoia Auctions

Arcade Double Decker Bus, (AR64), 8", 1939. Photo courtesy Bertoia Auctions

Arcade Dump Truck, (AR66A), 11-1/4", 1940s. Photo courtesy Bertoia Auctions

Arcade Express Truck, (AR69), 8", 1929. Photo courtesy Bertoia Auctions

Arcade Dump Wagon, (AR68), driver, no cab, 1917, 7". Photo courtesy Sotheby's New York

Arcade Fageol Bus, (AR72), 12", 1925. Photo courtesy Virginia Caputo

Arcade Farmall Tractor, 6", 1929. Photo courtesy Perry Eichor

Arcade Farm Wagon, horse-drawn, driver, reins, red wagon. Photo courtesy Liz Isham Cory

	C6	C8	C10
Fordson Tractor, No. 274, 1928, 4-3/4" long (AR109)	100	150	225
Fordson Tractor, No. 275, 1928, 6" long (AR108A)	125	175	275
Fordson Tractor, rubber wheels, No. 2730X, 1934, 3-1/2" long (AR111)	60	110	150
Greyhound Cruiser Coach bus No. 4400, 1941, 9-1/8" long (AR112)	200	300	450
Greyhound Lines Bus, No. 3850 SP, 1937, 7-3/4" long (AR113)	140	225	325
Greyhound Lines Great Lakes Exposition, No. 436, 1936, 6-3/4" long (AR115)	350	475	725
Greyhound Lines Great Lakes Exposition, No. 437, 1936, 11" long (AR114)	450	700	1000

Arcade Fire Engine, Pumper No. 1740, (AR80), with original box, 1936. Photo courtesy Bertoia Auctions

Arcade Fire Engine, (AR83), 13-1/2", 1941. Photo courtesy Bertoia Auctions

Arcade Fire Trailer Truck, (AR85), missing ladders, 16-1/4", 1934. Photo courtesy David Mapes Auctions

	C6	C8	C10
Greyhound Super Coach, No. 4380, 1937, 9" long (AR116)	275	425	575
Ice Truck, No. 1933, c.1941, 6-3/4" long (AR117)	275	375	575
Ice Wagon, horse-drawn	NPF	NPF	NPF
International Delivery Truck, No. 226, 1932, 9-3/4" long (AR118)	500	800	1300
International Delivery Truck, No. 3020, 1936, 9-1/2" long (AR119)	1800	2900	4200
International Dump Truck, No. 236-0, 1931, 10-3/4" long (AR120)	750	1200	1850
International Dump Truck, No. 3030, 1936, 10-1/2" long (AR121)	1000	1600	2350
International Dump Truck, No. 3710, 1937, 9-1/2" long (AR122)	450	700	1000
International Dump Truck, No. 7100, 1941, 11-1/8" long (AR124)	600	900	1250
International Dump Truck, steel chassis and dump box, No. 1670, 1940, 11-5/8" long (AR123)	650	1000	1650
International Harvester Company Public Utility Truck, No. 197, 1932, 11-1/4" long (AR125)	NPF	NPF	NPF
International Pickup Truck, No. 7000, 1941, 9-1/2" long (AR126)	500	750	1100
International Stake Truck, 1935, 12" long (AR127A)	900	1500	2250
International Stake Truck, No. 237-0, 1931, 12" long (AR127)	700	1100	1700

Another view of the Arcade Fire Trailer Truck, 16-1/4", 1934. Photo courtesy Bertoia Auctions

Arcade Ford Coupe, (AR88), 6-1/2", 1924. Photo courtesy Bertoia Auctions

Arcade Ford Dump Truck, (AR91), 7-1/2", 1929. Photo courtesy Bertoia Auctions

Arcade Ford Express Truck, (AR92), 8-1/4", 1929. Photo courtesy Bertoia Auctions

Arcade Ford Fordor Sedan, (AR93), 6-1/2", red, 1924. Photo courtesy Bertoia Auctions

Arcade Ford Sedan "Center Door," (AR94), 6-1/2", 1923. Photo courtesy Bertoia Auctions

Arcade "Century of Progress" Ford Sedans from 1934, L to R: (AR96), 6-7/8"; (AR97A), 4-3/4". Photo courtesy John M. Iannuzzi

Arcade Ford Touring Car, (AR102), 6-1/2", 1923. Photo courtesy Bertoia Auctions

Arcade Ford Touring Car Bank, (AR103), 6-1/2", 1923. Photo courtesy Bertoia Auctions

Arcade Fordson Tractor, (AR108A), 3-7/8", 1928.

Arcade Greyhound Cruiser Coach, (AR112), 9-1/8", 1941. Photo courtesy Sotheby's New York

Arcade Coast to Coast Greyhound Lines Bus, (AR113A), 9", 1937. Photo courtesy Sotheby's New York

Arcade Greyhound Lines Bus, variations on (AR113), 7-3/4", 1937. Photo courtesy Bertoia Auctions

	C6	C8	C10
International Stake Truck, No. 2600, 1937, 9-1/2" long (AR129)	850	1450	2250
International Stake Truck, No. 3090, 1936, 12" long (AR128)	900	1500	2300
International Stake Truck, No. 7090, 1941, 11-1/2" long (AR130)	950	1450	2100
International Wrecker, steel body and crane, No. 1650, 1940, 13" long, (AR131)	500	800	1200
Ladder Truck, No. 1700, 1936, length w/ladders: 12-1/2" long (AR132)	475	725	1000
Ladder Truck, No. 2350, 1936, 4-3/4" long (AR133)	75	110	150
Mack 6 Bus, No. 318, 1929, 13-1/4" long (AR134)	8000	15,000	24,200
Mack Cement Mixer, revolving drum, 1931, 6-11/16" long (AR135)	NPF	NPF	NPF
Mack Chemical Truck, fire engine w/ladders, 1929, 10" long (AR138)	425	625	900

	C6	C8	C10
Mack Chemical Truck, fire engine w/ladders, No. 245R, 1928, 15" long (AR136)	2000	3500	5500
Mack Chemical Truck, fire truck w/ladders, 1929, 15" long (AR137)	800	1300	1900
Mack Dump Truck, 1925, 12" long (AR139)	1000	1700	2750
Mack Dump Truck, No. 248X, 1929, 8-1/2" long (AR140)	600	950	1400
Mack Fire Apparatus Truck, ladder truck, 1929, No. 242, 21" long (AR143)	600	1000	1600
Mack High Dump Truck, No. 244X, "Coal" on side, 1931, 12-3/8" long (AR141)	1000	1500	2200
Mack High Dump Truck, No. 259X, 1931, 8-1/2" long (AR142)	675	1150	1600
Mack Hoist Truck, No. 198, 1932, body: 8" long (AR144)	900	1500	2200
Mack Ice Truck, No. 226, 1931, 8-1/2" long (AR146)	450	675	950
Mack Ice Truck, No. 257, 1930, 10-5/8" long (AR145)	375	550	775
Mack Ice Truck, w/driver, glass "ice" and tongs, No. 257, 1932, 10-3/4" (AR147)	1600	2800	4200
Mack Ladder Truck, c.1928, 17-3/4" long (AR147A)	1100	2000	3100
Mack Side Dump Truck, No. 1960, 1932, 9" long (AR148)	1100	1900	2800
Mack Stake Truck, No. 246X 1929, 12" long (AR149)	1100	1900	2800
Mack Stake Truck, No. 253, 1929, 8-3/4" long (AR150)	950	1500	2250
Mack Tank Truck, "Lubrite" and "Gasoline" on side, 1925, 13-1/4" long (AR153)	1200	2100	3250
Mack Tank Truck, sheet metal tank, marked "Gasoline" and "Mack," No. 241, 1930, 13" long (AR154)	1100	1900	2800

Arcade Greyhound Lines Great Lakes Exposition Bus, 6-3/4", 1936. Photo courtesy John Gibson

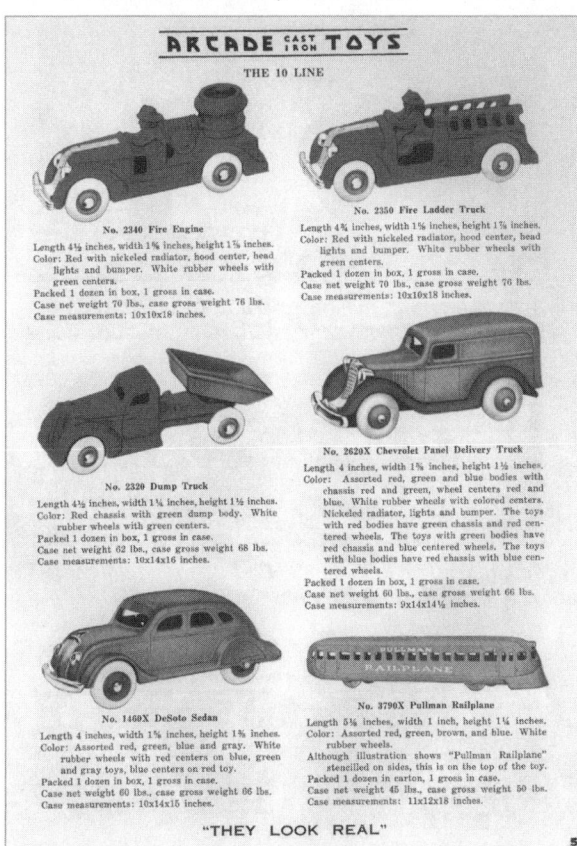

Page 5 from the No. 51 Arcade catalog.

Arcade Ice Wagon, horse-drawn. Photo courtesy Liz Isham Cory

Arcade Ice Truck, (AR117), 6-3/4", 1940s. Photo courtesy Bertoia Auctions

Arcade International Delivery Trucks, L to R: (AR118), 9-3/4", 1932; (AR119) 9-1/2", 1936; (AR118) "Hathaway's Bread Cake" variation, 9-3/4", 1932. Photo courtesy Bertoia Auctions

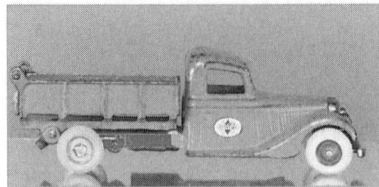

Arcade International Dump Truck, (AR121), 10-1/2", 1936. Photo courtesy Bertoia Auctions

Arcade International Dump Truck, (AR122), 9-1/2", 1937. Photo courtesy Bertoia Auctions

Arcade International Dump Truck, (AR124), red, white bed, 1941, 11-1/8". Photo courtesy Tim Oei

Arcade International Pickup Truck, (AR126), 9-1/2", 1941. Photo courtesy Bertoia Auctions

Arcade International Stake Trucks, L to R: (AR128), 12", 1936; (AR130), 11-1/2", 1941; (AR127A), 12", 1935. Photo courtesy Bertoia Auctions

Arcade International Stake Truck, (AR129), yellow, 9-1/2", 1937. Photo courtesy Bertoia Auctions

Arcade International Delivery Truck, (AR118), green top, light blue and yellow bottom, yellow wheels, 1932, 9-3/4". Photo courtesy Bertoia Auctions

Arcade Ladder Truck, (AR132), 12-1/2" with ladders, 1936. Photo courtesy Bertoia Auctions

Arcade Mack Chemical Truck, (AR136), 15", 1928. Photo courtesy Bertoia Auctions

Arcade Mack 6 Bus, (AR134), 13-1/4", white and red, 1929. Photo courtesy Bertoia Auctions

Arcade Mack Chemical Truck, (AR137), fire ladder truck, 15", 1929. Photo courtesy Bertoia Auctions

	C6	C8	C10
Mack Tank Truck, tank says "Gasoline", 13-1/4" long, 1925, (AR151)	1000	1600	2200
Mack Wrecker, No. 255, 1930, 12-1/2" long (AR155)	1900	3200	4700
McCormick-Deering Farmall Tractor, 1937, 6-1/4" long (AR156)	325	500	750
McCormick-Deering Farmall Tractor, gray, yellow and red wheels, 1937, 6-1/4" long	NPF	NPF	NPF
McCormick-Deering Thresher, 11" long (AR157A)	200	300	450

Arcade Mack Dump Truck, (AR139), 12", 1925.

Arcade Mack High Dump Truck, (AR141), "Coal" on side, 12-3/8", 1931. Photo courtesy Bertoia Auctions

Left to right: Arcade Mack Ice Truck, (AR147), 1932; Arcade Mack Ice Truck, (AR145), 1930. Photo courtesy Bertoia Auctions

Arcade Mack Tank Truck, (AR151), 13-1/4", 1925. Photo courtesy David W. Mapes Auctions

Arcade Mack Ladder Truck, (AR147A), 17-3/4", 1928. Photo courtesy Bertoia Auctions

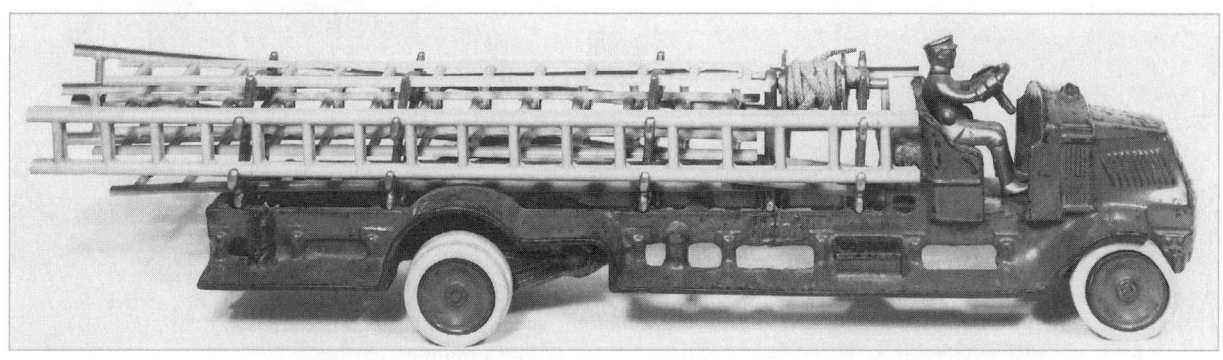

Arcade Mack Fire Apparatus Truck, (AR143), ladder truck, 21", 1929. Photo courtesy Phillips, New York

Arcade Mack Tank Truck, (AR153), "Lubrite" marking, 13-1/4", 1925. Photo courtesy Bertoia Auctions

Arcade Mack Wrecker, (AR155), 1932, 13-3/4". Photo courtesy James S. Maxwell and Virginia Caputo

Arcade McCormick-Deering Thresher, (AR157), 12", 1927. Photo courtesy Liz Isham Cory

Arcade McCormick-Deering 10-20 Tractor, (AR159), 7-1/4", 1925. Photo courtesy Liz Isham Cory

Arcade National Trailways Bus, (AR170), 9-1/4", 1937. Photo courtesy Bob Smith

Arcade Model A Coupe, (AR162), orange, rumble seat, 6-3/4", 1928. Photo courtesy Bertoia Auctions

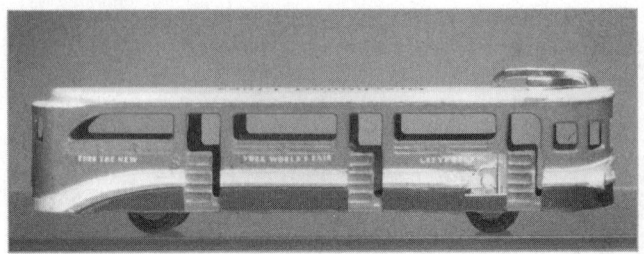

Arcade made several variations of the New York World's Fair Bus. The largest (10-1/2") from 1939, is also the most valuable, (AR171). Photo courtesy Sotheby's New York

Arcade Oliver Tractor, (AR179A), red, driver, white tires with blue centers, 7-1/2", 1937. Photo courtesy Rod Carnahan

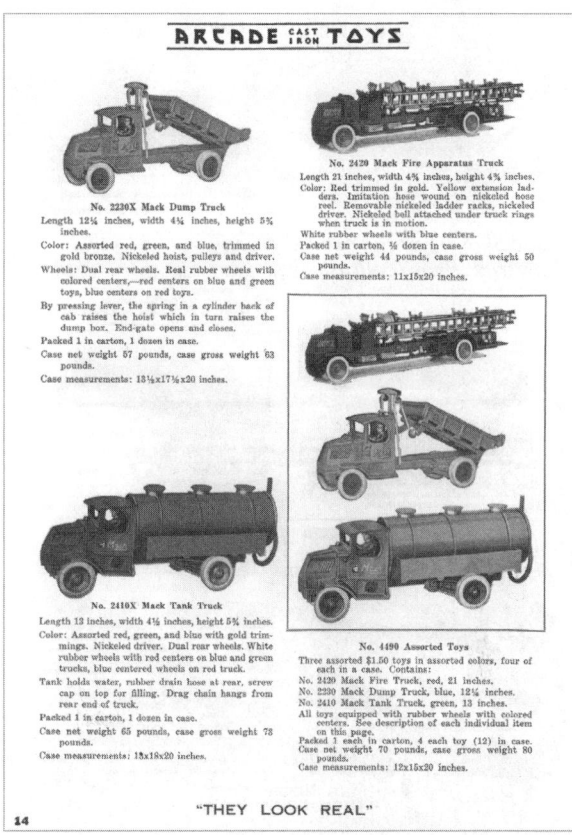

	C6	C8	C10
McCormick-Deering Thresher, 1927, 12" long (AR157)	300	450	650
McCormick-Deering Thresher, 1930, 9-1/2" long (AR158)	200	275	385
McCormick-Deering Tractor, 10-20, 1925, 7-1/4" long (AR159)	400	600	850
Milk Truck, wood box, No. 256, 1931, 13-5/8" long (AR160)	NPF	NPF	NPF
Model A Coupe, No. 113X, 1928, 4-1/8" long (AR163)	125	175	275
Model A Coupe, rumble seat, No. 106, 1928, 6-3/4" long (AR162)	500	850	1300
Model A Coupe, rumble seat, No. 116X, 1928, 5" long (AR161)	200	300	450
Model A Fordor, No. 207, 1928, 6-3/4" long (AR164)	325	475	675
Model A Tudor, No. 108, 1928, 6-3/4" long (AR165)	450	700	1150

Arcade Red Baby Dump Truck, (AR197), 10-3/8", 1923. Photo courtesy Phillips New York

Arcade Red Baby "Weaver" Wrecker, (AR199), red, 12", 1929. Photo courtesy Bertoia Auctions

Arcade Red Coupe, (AR200), 9-3/8", 1931. Photo courtesy Bertoia Auctions

Page 14 from the No. 51 Arcade catalog.

Arcade REO Coupe, yellow, red, black, 1930s. Photo courtesy Harris Auctions

Arcade Service Station, (AR205A). Photo courtesy Bertoia Auctions

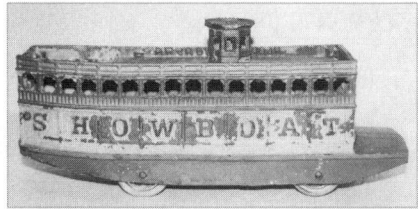

Arcade Showboat was painted green, yellow, red. Photo courtesy Liz Isham Cory

Arcade Stake Trailer, (AR208), 11-5/16", 1931. Photo courtesy Bertoia Auctions

Arcade Stake Trailer, (AR208), 11-5/16", 1931. Photo courtesy Bertoia Auctions

Arcade Army Tank, (AR216), pulls cannon, each 4", 1941. Photo courtesy Ed Poole

Arcade Stake Truck, (AR210A), light blue, 7-1/2", 1929. Photo courtesy Bertoia Auctions

Arcade Trac Tractor, (AR219), 7-1/2", 1941. Photo courtesy Thomas G. Nefos

Arcade Webaco Oil Co. Truck, (AR234A), 13-1/4". Photo courtesy Bob Smith

Arcade White Bus, (AR235), 13-1/4", 1928. Photo courtesy Bertoia Auctions

Arcade White Delivery Truck, (AR236), 8-1/4", 1929. Photo courtesy James S. Maxwell and Virginia Caputo

Arcade Yellow Cab No. 1, (AR248), 9-1/4", 1922. Photo courtesy Bertoia Auctions

	C6	C8	C10
Model T Stake Truck, 1927, 5-3/4" long (AR167)	125	175	275
Model T Stake Truck, 1927, 9" long (AR166)	575	925	1300
Model T Wrecker, 1927, 11" long (AR168)	675	1150	1700
Nash Wrecker, 1936, 4-1/2" long (AR169)	225	400	575
National Trailways Bus, No. 3870, 1937, 9-1/4" long (AR170)	750	1300	1800
New York World's Fair Bus, No. 3750, 1939, 7" long (AR173)	125	200	325
New York World's Fair Bus, No. 3770, 1939, 8-1/2" long (AR172)	300	450	675
New York World's Fair Bus, No. 3780, 1939, 10-1/2" long (AR171)	400	625	925
New York World's Fair Tractor-Train, tractor and one car, No. 7270, 1939; tractor: 3-1/4" long, car: 4-1/4" long (AR174)	200	350	525

	C6	C8	C10
New York World's Fair Tractor-Train, w/three cars, No. 7290, 1939 (AR175)	450	675	900
Oliver Plow, 1923, 6-1/2" long (AR176)	225	375	550
Oliver Plow, No. 4230X, 1941, 6-1/4" long (AR177)	125	200	300
Oliver Superior Spreader, No. 7140, 1941, 9-1/2" long (AR178)	600	950	1400
Oliver Tractor, No. 356, 1937, 7-1/2" long (AR179)	325	500	700
Oliver Tractor, No. 3560, 1941, 7-1/2" long (AR180)	500	800	1200
Oliver Tractor, No. 359, 1937, 5-1/2" long (AR179A)	75	125	185
Panel Delivery Truck, 1925, 8-1/8" long (AR180A)	NPF	NPF	NPF
Pennsylvania Mack Stake Truck, No. 253, 1929, 8-3/4" long (AR151B)	1200	2000	3000
Plymouth Coupe, No. 1340X, 1934, 4-1/2" long (AR181)	400	800	1100

Arcade Yellow Cab, (AR250), 9", 1927. Photo courtesy Sotheby's New York

Arcade Yellow Cab, (AR252), 8", 1927. Photo courtesy Bertoia Auctions

Arcade Yellow Cab Bank, (AR258), 8-1/2", 1927; Green and White Cab, (AR111A), 9", 1923. Photo courtesy Bertoia Auctions

Arcade Yellow Cab Panel Delivery Truck, (AR259), driver, orange and black, 8-1/4". Photo courtesy Bertoia Auctions

Arcade Yellow Coach Double-Decker Bus, (AR260), 14", 1925. Photo courtesy Sotheby's New York

Arcade Yellow Cab, (AR256), 8-1/2", 1941. Photo courtesy Sotheby's New York

Arcade Yellow Cab Bank, (AR257), 8", 1923. Photo courtesy Bertoia Auctions

Arcade Yellow Parlor Coach Bus, (AR262), 9-1/2", 1926. Photo courtesy Sotheby's New York

	C6	C8	C10
Plymouth Sedan, 4-3/4" long, 1934, No. 1330X (AR182)	350	550	775
Plymouth Stake Truck, No. 1840X, 1934, 4-3/4" long (AR183)	NPF	NPF	NPF
Plymouth Wrecker, No. 1830X, 1934, 4-3/4" long (AR184)	125	175	250
Pontiac Fire Pumper, 4-1/2" long (AR184A)	50	75	110
Pontiac Sedan, 1935, 6-1/2" long (AR186)	325	500	700
Pontiac Sedan, No. 1350X, 1934, 4-1/4" long (AR185)	150	225	325
Pontiac Stake Truck, No. 2390X, 1935, 6-1/4" long (AR187)	300	450	650
Pontiac Stake Truck, No. 2780X, 1936, 4-1/4" long (AR188)	NPF	NPF	NPF
Pontiac Wrecker, No. 2000X, 1936, 4-1/4" long (AR189)	125	175	275
Racer, No. 137X, 1932, 5-5/8" long (AR194)	120	175	250
Racer, No. 138X, 1931, 6-3/4" long (AR192)	150	225	300
Racer, No. 1440X, 1937, 8" long (AR195)	NPF	NPF	NPF
Racer, No. 1457, 1937, 5-3/4" long (AR196)	60	90	135
Racer, pre-1923, 7-3/4" long (AR190)	400	600	850
Racer, w/plastic or celluloid windshield, 1932, No. 140X, 10-1/2" long (AR1930)	4000	9000	11,500
Red Baby Dump Truck, No. 2, 1923, 10-3/8" long (AR197)	500	750	1200
Red Baby Truck, No. 1, 1923, 10-3/4" long (AR198)	500	750	1200
Red Baby Weaver Wrecker, 1929, 12" long (AR199)	900	1400	2200

	C6	C8	C10
Red Coupe, No. 1247, 1931, 9-3/8" long (AR200)	900	1700	2600
Red Coupe, No. 1247, 1931, 9-3/8" long (AR201)	900	1700	2400
REO Coupe, yellow, red, black, 1930s	NPF	NPF	NPF
Sand Loading Shovel, No. 298 (later became No. 299), 1932 (AR202)	500	800	1250
Scraper, No. 287, 1929, 8-1/4" long (AR203)	42	63	85
Sedan, No. 1501X, 1937, 4-3/4" long (AR204)	90	135	180
Sedan and Mullins Red Cap Trailer, No. 1497X, 1937; car: 5-5/8" long, trailer: 2-1/2" long (AR205)	400	600	900
Service Station, "Arcade Service" (AR205A)	500	750	1030
Shortline Greyhound Lines Bus, 1937 (AR113B)	1000	1650	2400
Showboat, green, yellow, red	450	750	1100
Side Dump Trailer, fastens to trucks or tractors, 1932, No. 290, 7" long (AR206)	NPF	NPF	NPF
Silver Arrow, 1934, 7-1/4" long (AR207)	275	375	600
Stake Trailer Truck, No. 233, 1931, 11-5/16" long (AR208)	325	550	750
Stake Truck, 1929, 7-1/2" long (AR210A)	325	475	675
Stake Truck, 1932, approx. 6" long (AR209A)	175	300	450
Stake Truck, no Arcade markings, No. 208, 1932, 6" long (AR211)	275	425	600
Stake Truck, No. 1502X, 1937, 4-1/4" long (AR212)	125	175	275
Stake Truck, No. 206, 7-1/4" long (AR208A)	1100	1700	2500

Variation of Arcade Yellow Parlor Coach Bus, (AR261), black roof, yellow, green body, "Pennsylvania Rapid Transit" marking. Photo courtesy Bertoia Auctions

	C6	C8	C10
Stake Truck, No. 208X, 1929, 6" long (AR209)	220	325	475
Stake Truck, No. 213X, 1929, 5" long (AR210)	125	188	250
Steam Shovel, Industrial Derrick, No. 292, 1932, body 6" long (AR213)	750	1125	1600
Tandem Disc Harrow, No. 704, 1939, 6-3/4" long (AR214)	60	90	125
Tank, Army, No. 3960, shoots, 1941, 4" long (AR216)	200	300	450
Tank, Army, No. 400, 1937, 8" long (AR215)	600	950	1500
Texas Centennial Bus, 1936, extremely rare, 10-3/4" long (AR217)	1500	2500	4000
Trac Tractor, No. 7120, 1941, 7-1/2" long (AR219)	1500	2500	3750
Tractor, 1941, No. 7341X, 6-1/4" long, wood wheels (AR224)	400	600	850
Tractor, No. 7200, 1941, 6-1/2" long (AR222)	175	275	400
Tractor, No. 7321X, 1941, 4-1/4" long (AR225)	NPF	NPF	NPF
Tractor, rubber wheels, No. 7240X, 1941, 3-1/8" long (AR227)	100	140	225
Tractor, w/black rubber wheels, No. 4060X, 1941, 6-1/4" long (AR223)	325	500	700
Tractor, wooden wheels, No. 7260X, 1941, 3-1/8" long (AR226)	NPF	NPF	NPF
Tractor and Dump Trailer, No. 7300, 1941, 15-1/2" long (AR228)	600	950	1400
Trac-Tractor, International Harvester, No. 277, 1937, 8-1/4" long (AR218)	800	1200	1700
Trailer, farm, No. 286, 1929, 6-3/8" long (AR229)	150	225	375
Trailer, farm, No. 288, 1929, 4-5/8" long (AR230)	35	52	75
Trailer, farm, No. 289, 1929, 3-3/4" long (AR231)	30	45	70
Transport Trailer Truck, No. 1800, 1934, 7-1/2" long (AR232)	385	550	775
Two-wheeled Jack, No. 216, 1932, 5-1/2" long (AR234)	30	45	60
W&K Truck Trailer, 1923, 8-1/2" long (AR233)	100	150	225
Webaco Fuel Co. Mack Stake Truck, No. 253, 1929, 8-3/4" long (AR151A)	1100	1900	2800
Webaco Oil Co. Truck, 13-1/4" long (AR234A see AR151A)			
White Bus, No. 319, 1928, 13-1/4" long (AR235)	2700	5000	7750
White Delivery Truck, No. 252X, 1929, 8-1/4" long (AR236)	2000	3800	6250
White Delivery Truck, side mounts, No. 252X, 8-1/4" long (AR236A)	1500	2600	4250
White Dump Truck, No. 249, 1929, 11-1/2" long (AR238)	8000	15,000	23,000
White Dump Truck, No. 258X, 1931, 13-1/2" long (AR239)	NPF	NPF	NPF
White Moving Van, No. 251, 1929, 13-1/2" long (AR237)	4000	9000	13,000
White Tank Truck, "Gasoline," No. 254X, 1931, 14-1/8" long (AR240)	1000	1500	2200
Whitehead and Kales Tractor, 1923, 5-3/4" long (AR240A)	160	240	350
Wrecker, no Arcade markings, No. 225, 1932 (AR242)	500	850	1350
Wrecker, No. 1493X, 1937, 6-1/2" long (AR244)	125	200	325

Arcade Andy Gump Car, (AR263), red and green, white tires, 1920s, 7-1/4". Photo courtesy Bertoia Auctions

	C6	C8	C10
Wrecker, No. 1503X, 1937, 4-3/4" long (AR245)	75	125	180
Wrecker, No. 2020X, 1934, 7" long (AR243)	550	900	1400
Wrecker, No. 217, 1928, body: 8" long (AR241)	450	700	1100
Wrecker, No. 3900X, 1941, 8-1/2" long (AR246)	90	135	200
Yellow Baby Dump Truck, 1923, 10-1/2" long (AR246A)	600	1050	1650
Yellow Baby Wrecker, 1929, 12" long (AR247)	650	1100	1750
Yellow Cab, Ford Sedan, 1934, 6-7/8" long (AR254)	1300	2000	3000
Yellow Cab, No. 05, 1927, 8-1/2" long (AR251)	425	650	950
Yellow Cab, No. 1, 1922, 9-1/4" long (AR248)	550	900	1500
Yellow Cab, No. 1, 1927, 9" long (AR250)	600	900	1500
Yellow Cab, No. 1580Y, 1936, 8-1/4" long (AR255)	1700	2800	4250
Yellow Cab, No. 1590Y, 1941, 8-1/2" long (AR256)	175	263	350
Yellow Cab, No. 2, 1923, 8" long (AR249)	500	800	1250
Yellow Cab, No. 2, 1927, 8" long (AR252)	550	850	1300
Yellow Cab, No. 3, 1927, 5-1/4" long (AR253)	500	800	1200
Yellow Cab Bank, 1923, 8" long (AR257)	700	1200	1900
Yellow Cab Bank, 1927, 8-1/2" long, (AR258)	1800	4500	9200
Yellow Cab Panel Delivery Truck, w/driver, 1925, 8-1/4" long (AR259)	1000	1700	2700
Yellow Coach Double-Decker Bus, 1925, 14" long (AR260)	1750	3250	4800
Yellow Parlor Coach Bus, 1926, 13" long (AR261)	700	1250	1900
Yellow Parlor Coach Bus, 1926, 9-1/2" long (AR262)	325	475	675

ARCHER

	C6	C8	C10
Futuristic Auto Carrier, contains four of the 5" futuristic vehicles, No. 349, 14" long (A032A)	NPF	NPF	NPF
Futuristic Convertible, 10" long (A022)	42	63	85
Futuristic Convertible, 5" long (A028)	18	27	36
Futuristic Coupe, 10" long (A024)	42	63	85
Futuristic Coupe, 5" long (A025)	18	27	36
Futuristic Sedan, 5" long (A026)	18	27	36

	C6	C8	C10
Futuristic Truck, 10" long (A023)	55	83	110
Futuristic Truck, 5" long (A027)	18	27	36
Raymobile (A029)	37	56	75
Rocket, red, yellow and black, 13" long (A021)	75	112	150
Scopemobile (A030)	NPF	NPF	NPF
Searchmobile (A031)	NPF	NPF	NPF
Steam Roller, non-space	32	48	65

L to R: Archer Futuristic Coupe; Futuristic Sedan; Futuristic Truck; Gasoline Truck. Photo courtesy Bill Hanlon

Top Left to right: Archer Futuristic Convertible; Futuristic Truck; Futuristic Coupe. Bottom Left to right: Futuristic Convertible, Sedan, Truck. Photo courtesy Bill Hanlon

Archer Raymobile. Photo courtesy Terry Sells

ARGO

	C6	C8	C10
Ambulance, bell rings (AR001)	12	15	20
Armored Car, Army, w/cannon (AR008)	12	15	20
Armored Car, machine gun (AR009)	12	15	20
Chief Car, bell fixed in place (AR010)	12	15	20
Chief Car, bell rings (AR002)	12	15	20
Police Car, gun moves (AR003)	12	15	20
Sedan, windows roll up and down (AR007)	12	15	20
Sedan, windshield wipers work (AR006)	12	15	20
Taxi, meter in roof moves (AR004)	12	15	20
Taxi, meter in windshield moves (AR005)	12	15	20

Argo Ambulance (AR001) and Chief Car (AR002). Photo courtesy Dave Leopard

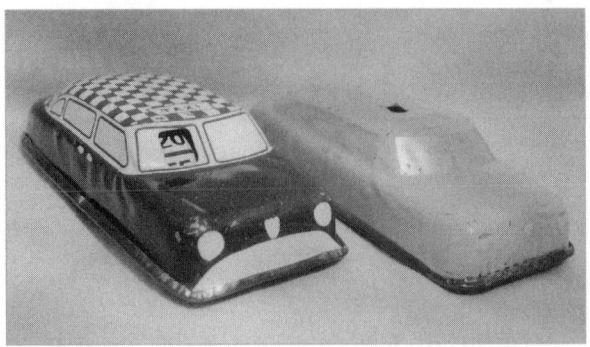

Argo Taxi cabs (AR005) and (AR004). Photo courtesy Dave Leopard

Argo Armored Car (AR008) and Police Car (AR003). Photo courtesy Dave Leopard

ARNOLD

	C6	C8	C10
A560 Motorcycle, wind-up, green, 7-3/4" long	200	325	450
Fire Chief Car, tin lithographed, friction, battery siren, 10" long	150	225	300
Jeep, w/United States Military Police crew, postwar	90	175	300
Jeep, white, w/remote control, postwar, rare	175	275	550
Mac 700 Motorcycle, wind-up, black	325	488	650

	C6	C8	C10
Military Rider, No. A754 , w/rifle motorcycle	388	582	775
Motorcycle, No. A63, wind-up, orange, 8" long	200	325	450
Packard Convertible, 10" long	90	135	180
Police Car, friction, 10" long	250	375	500
Sparkling Fire Truck, U.S. Zone, 4-1/2" wind-up	238	355	475

Arnold jeep, three MP figures, radio. Photo courtesy Jack Matthews

Arnold Mac 700, wind-up, black. Photo courtesy Kent M. Comstock

Arnold jeep, three MP figures, rare white version with green stars. Photo courtesy Jack Matthews

Arnold motorcycles, L to R: orange, 8"; green, 7-3/4". Photo courtesy Kent M. Comstock

AUBURN RUBBER

For more than twenty years, American kids and moms loved rubber toys—children thought they were fun, and moms liked the fact that these toys wouldn't scratch furniture and floors. Unfortunately, the toys disappeared almost as suddenly as they appeared on the market.

The Auburn Rubber Company of Auburn, Indiana, was not the first to introduce rubber toys to the American market, but it was no doubt the largest such company and had the greatest impact on the toy market. Founded in 1910 as the Double Fabric Tire Company, owners William H. Willennar and A.L. Murray produced tire patches and later expanded to automobile tires and tubes. The company was reorganized and renamed the Auburn Rubber Company in the 1920s. Following the 1924 retirement of Willennar, Murray appointed his nephew Dave Sellew vice president. In 1935, Sellew received the titles of president and general manager of the company.

After producing toy soldiers in 1935, Auburn introduced its first vehicle in 1936—a beautiful coffin-nosed Cord Sedan. Today, the Auburn Cord is one of the most prized rubber toys and is seldom seen for sale.

Auburn followed the Cord with a wealth of vehicles, including trucks, farm tractors and implements, motorcycles, racers, fire engines, military vehicles, aircraft, ships, and trains. Production halted in 1942 due to World War II, and peacetime production resumed with a plant acquired in Connellsville, Pennsylvania. Toy production returned to the Auburn, Indiana plant in 1950.

According to catalogs, 1952 was the final year Auburn Rubber exclusively marketed rubber vehicles. By 1955, Auburn's line was mostly vinyl with a few rubber toys left in the line. What appear to be the last rubber toys to be marketed by Auburn were two fire engines shown in the 1956 catalog.

Auburn continued in the toy business in Auburn, Indiana, and later Deming, New Mexico, until going out of business in 1969.

Note: The number in parenthesis coincides with the numbers in Dave Leopard's book *Rubber Toy Vehicles*.

Contributor: Dave Leopard, 2507 Feather Run Trail, West Columbia, SC 29169-4915. Leopard, a retired United States Air Force Colonel is a collector of small, American-made toy cars and trucks. He is considered an expert on the subject of rubber toys and is the author of *Rubber Toy Vehicles 2nd Edition*, a definitive work in this field.

	C6	C8	C10
'35 Ford, two-door slantback sedan, 4" long (AA09)	50	60	75
'35 Ford Coupe, 4" long (AA08)	50	60	75
'36 Cord, four-door, coffin-nose sedan, 6" long (AA01)	70	95	150
'37 International Cabover Stake Truck, "U.S. Army" decal, khaki	30	40	60
'37 International Cabover Stake Truck, "U.S. Army" decal, khaki, minor variations (AT02)	30	40	60
'37 International Cabover Stake Truck, 3-3/4" long (AT05)	20	30	40
'37 International Cabover Stake Truck, 4-1/4" long (AT03)	20	30	40

	C6	C8	C10
'37 International Cabover Stake Truck, 4-1/4" long, minor variations (AT04)	20	30	40
'37 International Cabover Stake Truck, 5-3/8" long (AT01)	22	33	45
'37 International Cabover Stake Truck, ambulance version (AT07)	NPF	NPF	NPF
'37 International Cabover Stake Truck, milk version, 4-1/4" long (AT06)	60	80	100
'37 Olds, four-door sedan, 4-1/2" long (AA02)	35	45	65
'38 GMC Cab/Open Squared-off Trailer, 9" long (AT15)	65	80	105
'38 GMC Carry Car Auto Transport, no top, 11-1/2" long (AT13)	65	75	95

Auburn 1936 Cord, (AA001), four-door sedan, 6". Photo courtesy Max Heiss

Auburn 1937 International Cabover Stake Truck, (AT006), milk version, 4-1/4". Photo courtesy Dave Leopard's book Rubber Toy Vehicles

Left to right: Auburn 1937 International Cabover Stake Truck, (AT001), 5-3/8"; 1937 International Cabover Stake Truck, (AT003), 4-1/4"; 1937 International Cabover Stake Truck, (AT005), 3-3/4". Photo courtesy Dave Leopard's book Rubber Toy Vehicles

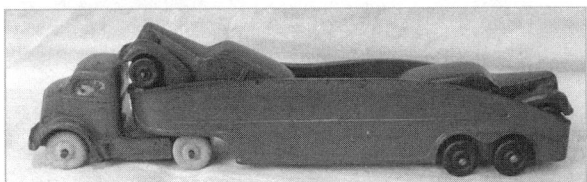

Auburn 1938 GMC Carry Car Auto Transport, (AT014), 11-1/2", rubber on top to carry cars. Photo courtesy Dave Leopard

Auburn 1937 International Cabover Stake Truck, (AT008), ambulance version. Photo courtesy Dave Leopard's book Rubber Toy Vehicles

Auburn 1937 Oldsmobile, four-door sedan, (AA002), 4-1/2". Photo courtesy Dave Leopard's book Rubber Toy Vehicles

Auburn 1938 GMC Cab/Open Squared-Off Trailer, (AT015), 9". Photo courtesy Dave Leopard's book Rubber Toy Vehicles

Auburn 1938 Oldsmobile, four-door sedan, (AA003), 5-3/4". Photo courtesy Dave Leopard's book Rubber Toy Vehicles

Auburn 1939 Plymouth, two-door trunkback sedan, (AA011), 4-1/4". Photo courtesy Dave Leopard's book Rubber Toy Vehicles

Another look at the Auburn 1939 Plymouth, (AA011).

Auburn 1940s Fire Engine, (AE002), hose and ladders, 7-3/4". Photo courtesy Dave Leopard's book Rubber Toy Vehicles

Left to right: Auburn 1946 Lincoln convertible, square headlights, (AA013); 1946 Lincoln convertible, round headlights, (AA014). Photo courtesy Dave Leopard's book Rubber Toy Vehicles

Auburn 1947 Chevy Cab Forward Box Truck, (AT011), 5-3/4". Photo courtesy Dave Leopard's book Rubber Toy Vehicles

Left to right: Auburn 1940 Oldsmobile, (AA005), fender skirts; Auburn 1940 Oldsmobile, (AA004), open fenders. Photo courtesy Dave Leopard's book Rubber Toy Vehicles

Auburn 1940s Fire Engine, (AE004), ladders, no hose, 7-3/4". Photo courtesy Dave Leopard

Auburn 1940s Pumper, (AE003), boiler, 7-1/4". Photo courtesy Dave Leopard

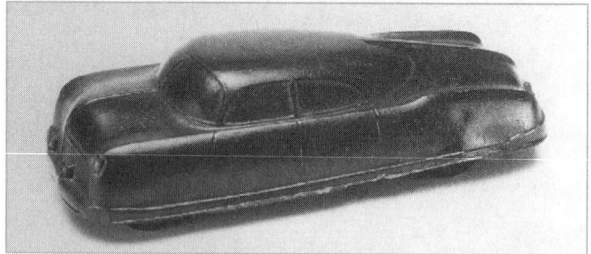

Auburn Late '40s Futuristic Sedan, (AA015), fin down back, 5". Photo courtesy Dave Leopard from his book Rubber Toy Vehicles

Auburn 1948 Buick, (AA06), two-door sedanette, fastback, modified, 7-1/4". Photo courtesy Dave Leopard

Auburn 1950 Cadillac, (AA010), four-door sedan, 7-1/4". Photo courtesy Dave Leopard's book Rubber Toy Vehicles

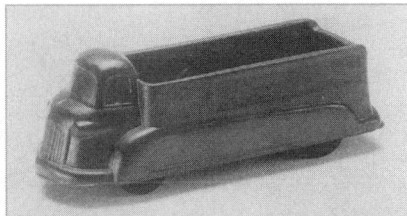

Auburn Cab-forward Box Truck, (AT009), futuristic, 5-1/2". Photo courtesy Dave Leopard's book Rubber Toy Vehicles

Auburn Cabover Box Truck, (AT010), futuristic, 4-1/8". Photo courtesy Dave Leopard's book Rubber Toy Vehicles

Auburn Updated Carry Car Transport, (AT017), 11-3/4". Photo courtesy Dave Leopard's book Rubber Toy Vehicles

Auburn Farm Tractor, Minneapolis-Moline Z, (AF002), 4". Photo courtesy Dave Leopard's book Rubber Toy Vehicles

Auburn Farm Tractor, John Deere A, (AF001), 5". Photo courtesy Dave Leopard's book Rubber Toy Vehicles

	C6	C8	C10
'38 GMC Carry Car Auto Transport, w/rubber on top to carry cars, 11-1/2" long (AT14)	85	120	165
'38 GMC/Cab/Open Squared-off Trailer, no tailgate, 9" long (AT16)	65	85	100
'38 Olds, four-door sedan, 5-3/4" long (AA03)	50	75	100
'39 Buick, Y Job Experimental Roadster, 9-3/4" long (AA07)	NPF	NPF	NPF
'39 Plymouth, two-door trunkback sedan, 4-1/4" long (AA11)	35	40	55
'40 Olds, four-door sedan, fender skirts, 6" long (AA05)	30	40	50

	C6	C8	C10
'40 Olds, four-door sedan, open fenders, 6" long (AA04)	35	45	65
'40s Fire Engine, hose and ladders, 7-3/4" long (AE02)	35	40	55
'40s Fire Engine, ladders, no hose, 7-3/4" long (AE04)	45	55	75
'40s Pumper, boiler, 7-1/4" long (AE03)	35	40	55
'46 Lincoln Convertible, two-door, round headlights, 4-1/2" long (AA13)	20	30	40
'46 Lincoln Convertible, two-door, square headlights, 4-1/2" long (AA12)	20	30	40
'47 Chevy Cab Forward Box Truck, 5-3/4" long (AT10)	25	30	45

Auburn Farm Tractor, Minneapolis-Moline R, early style, (AF003), 7-1/2". Photo courtesy Dave Leopard from his book Rubber Toy Vehicles

Auburn Farm Tractor, Oliver Row Crop 70, (AF005), 8". Photo courtesy Dave Leopard

Auburn Farm Tractor, Graham-Bradley, (AF008), 4-1/4". Photo courtesy Dave Leopard's book Rubber Toy Vehicles

Auburn Blade, (AI014), fits Graham-Bradley tractor, 2-3/4". Photo courtesy Dave Leopard's book Rubber Toy Vehicles

Auburn Farm Tractor, Minneapolis-Moline, later style, (AF004), 7-1/4". Photo courtesy Dave Leopard from his book Rubber Toy Vehicles

Auburn Farm Tractor, McCormick-Deering IH Farmall M, (AF007), 4". Photo courtesy Dave Leopard's book, Rubber Toy Vehicles

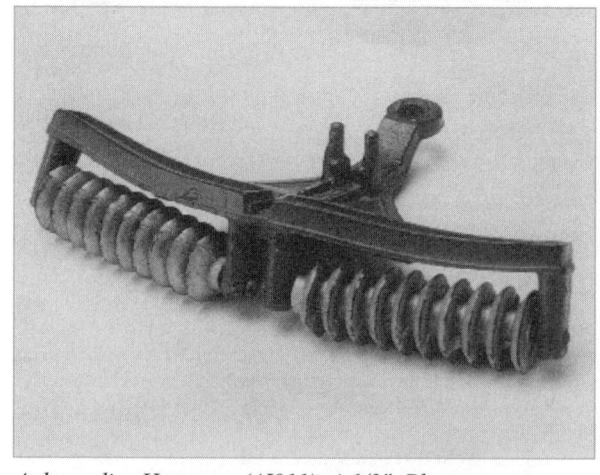

Auburn disc Harrows, (AI011), 4-1/2". Photo courtesy Dave Leopard's book Rubber Toy Vehicles

	C6	C8	C10
'48 Buick, two-door sedanette, fastback, 7-1/4" long (AA06)	50	70	100
'50 Cadillac, four-door sedan, 7-1/4" long (AA10)	50	70	100
'50 Pickup Truck, wheels inside fenders, 4-1/2" long (AT12)	20	30	40
'50s Pickup Truck, wheels outside fenders, 4-1/2" long (AT11)	30	40	50
Ahrens-Fox Fire Engine, 5-1/2" long (AE01)	60	110	150
Army Motor Scout on motorcycle (AC01)	50	70	100
Army Staff Car, '40 Olds w/"U.S. Army" label, sedan, open fenders, 6" long (AA16)	25	38	50

	C6	C8	C10
Blade, 2-3/4", fits Graham-Bradley tractor (AI14)	NPF	NPF	NPF
Cab-Forward Box Truck, smooth sides, futuristic, 5-1/2" long (AT08)	25	30	45
Cabover Box Truck, smooth sides, futuristic, 4-1/8" long (AT09)	20	25	40
Carry Car Transport, updated version of '38 GMC Cab, cab changed, trailer same, 11-3/4" long (AT17)	65	80	100
Cultipacker (Disk Harrows?), David Bradley, 4-3/8" long (AI10)	30	40	60
David Bradley Hay Wagon (AI15)	60	70	110
Disc Harrow, 4-1/2" long (AI12)	30	40	60
Farm Tractor, Graham-Bradley, 4-1/4" long (AF08)	25	38	50

Left to right: Auburn Manure Spreader, David Bradley, (AI004), 4-3/4"; Spreader, (AI005), 4-3/4". Photo courtesy Dave Leopard from his book Rubber Toy Vehicles

Auburn Harrow, (AI009), 4-1/2". Photo courtesy Dave Leopard's book Rubber Toy Vehicles

Auburn Harvester, (AI003), open top, 5-1/2". Photo courtesy Dave Leopard's book Rubber Toy Vehicles

Auburn Open Racer, (AR001), V-6, high fin, 10-1/2".

Auburn Open Racer, (AR002), V-6, low fin, 10-1/2". Photo courtesy Dave Leopard's book Rubber Toy Vehicles

Auburn Open Racer, (AR004), short, boat tail, 6-1/2". Photo courtesy Dave Leopard

Auburn Open Racer, (AR007), short, boat tail, early, 6-1/2". Photo courtesy Dave Leopard's book Rubber Toy Vehicles

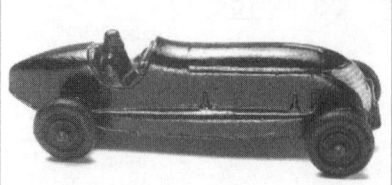

Auburn Open Racer, (AR009), boat tail, no side pipes, 4-3/4". Photo courtesy Dave Leopard's book Rubber Toy Vehicles

Auburn Open Racer, (AR008), no fenders, low fin, long back, 5-1/4". Photo courtesy Dave Leopard's book Rubber Toy Vehicles

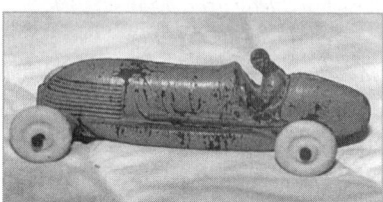

Auburn Open Racer, (AR005), boat tail, 4-3/4". Photo courtesy Dave Leopard's book Rubber Toy Vehicles

Auburn Open Racer, (AR006), small fin, 6-1/4". Photo courtesy Dave Leopard's book Rubber Toy Vehicles

Auburn Plow with riding farmer, (AI012). Photo courtesy Dave Leopard's book Rubber Toy Vehicles

Auburn Trailer, Graham-Bradley, (AI001), two-wheel, 5-3/4". Photo courtesy Dave Leopard's book Rubber Toy Vehicles

Auburn Trailer, Graham-Bradley, (AI002), four-wheel, 4-3/4". Photo courtesy Dave Leopard's book Rubber Toy Vehicles

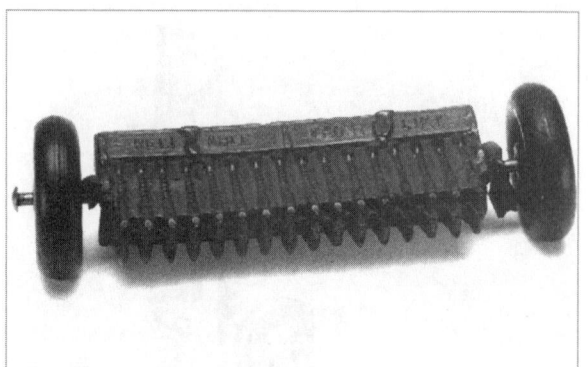

Auburn Reliable Front-Lift Seeder, (AI005), 5". Photo courtesy Dave Leopard's book Rubber Toy Vehicles

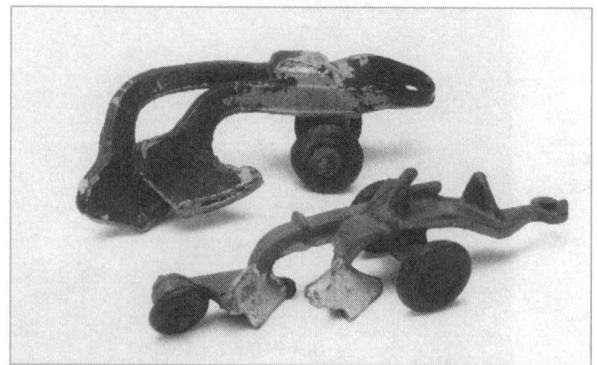

Top to bottom: Auburn Two-Furrow Plow, David Bradley, (AI008), 4-3/4"; Cultipacker, David Bradley, (AI009), 4-3/8". Photo courtesy Dave Leopard's book Rubber Toy Vehicles

*Top row, left to right: Auburn Vinyl Tank; Army Recon Car.
Bottom row, left to right: Jeep with Cannon; Army Truck.*

*Top row (l to r): Auburn Vinyl Howitzer, 155mm, 7" long;
Tank (AM01). Bottom row (l to r): Tank (AM02);
Fieldpiece, 75mm, 7" long. Photo courtesy Ed Poole*

	C6	C8	C10
Farm Tractor, John Deere "A," 5" long (AF01)	30	40	50
Farm Tractor, McCormick-Deering IH Farmall "M," 4" long (AF07)	45	55	75
Farm Tractor, Minneapolis-Moline "R," early style, 7-1/2" long (AF03)	65	80	100
Farm Tractor, Minneapolis-Moline "R," later style, 7-1/4" long (AF04)	60	70	90
Farm Tractor, Minneapolis-Moline "Z," 4" long (AF02)	30	40	50
Farm Tractor, Oliver Row Crop "70," 8" long (AF05)	80	95	120
Ford Stake Truck, 4-3/4" long (AT18)	NPF	NPF	NPF
Futuristic Sedan, fin down back, late 1940s, 5" long (AA14)	20	30	40
Harrow, 4-1/2" long (AI11)	NPF	NPF	NPF
Harvester, open top, 5-1/2" long (AI03)	55	75	110
Manure Spreader, David Bradley, 4-3/4" long (AI04)	20	30	40
Motorcycle Cop, large, 5" high (AC04)	90	120	150
Motorcycle Cop, small, 3-4/5" long (AC03)	50	60	80
Motorcycle Soldiers, w/sidecar (AC02)	50	75	125
Open Racer, boat tail, 4-3/4" long (AR005)	30	45	60
Open Racer, boat tail, no side pipes, 4-3/4" long (AR009)	25	35	50
Open Racer, high fin, 10-1/2" long (AR01)	75	100	150

	C6	C8	C10
Open Racer, midget type, early, 5" long (AR010)	NPF	NPF	NPF
Open Racer, no fenders, low fin, long back, 5-1/4" long (AR008)	20	30	40
Open Racer, short, boat tail 6-1/2" long (AR04)	30	40	55
Open Racer, short, boat tail, early, 6-1/2" long (AR07)	50	60	80
Open Racer, short, tapered tail, large tires, 10-1/2" long (AR03)	45	60	75
Open Racer, small fin, 6-1/4" long (AR06)	25	30	45
Open Racer, V-6, low fin, 10-1/2" long (AR02)	65	75	95
Plow, updated (AI09)	25	30	40
Plow, w/riding farmer (AI13)	NPF	NPF	NPF
Reliable Front-Lift Seeder, 5" long (AI06)	25	30	45
Side-Cutter Sickle Bar Mower, David Bradley, 3-3/4" long (AI07)	25	30	45
Spreader, 4-3/4" long (AI05)	20	30	40
Tank, Marmon-Harrington, 3-1/4" long (AM02)	25	30	40
Tank, Marmon-Harrington, 4-1/2" long (AM01)	30	40	50
Tractor and Cannon, olive green, 11-1/2" long (AM03)	NPF	NPF	NPF
Trailer, four-wheel, Graham-Bradley, 4-3/4" long	30	40	50

Auburn Vinyl Racer, No. 566, red w/yellow wheels, 7".

Auburn Vinyl Fork Lift with driver, 5".

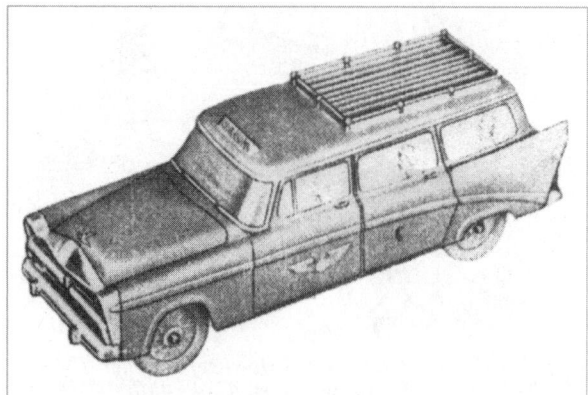

Auburn Vinyl Airport Limousine, 7-1/2".

Auburn Vinyl Police Set with original box. Photo courtesy Kent M. Comstock

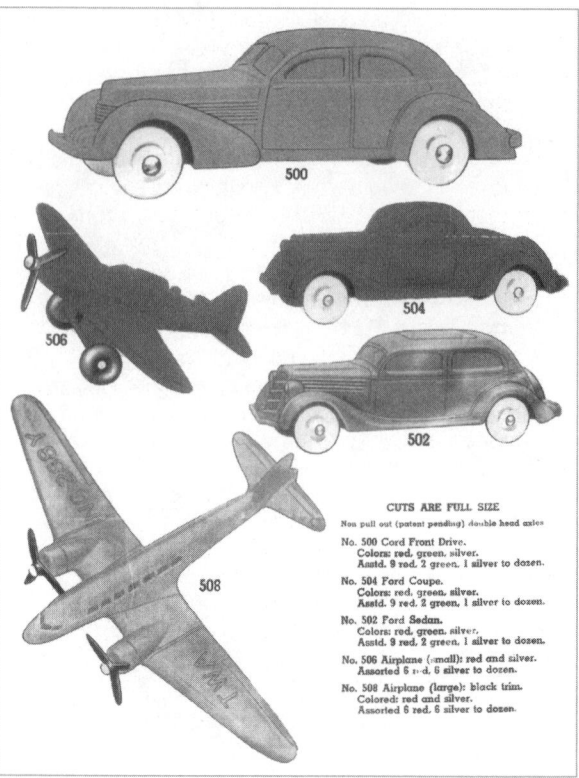

Ad from an Auburn Rubber Co. catalog.

CUTS ARE FULL SIZE

Non pull out (patent pending) double head axles

No. 500 Cord Front Drive.
  Colors: red, green, silver.
  Asstd. 9 red, 2 green, 1 silver to dozen.

No. 504 Ford Coupe.
  Colors: red, green, silver.
  Asstd. 9 red, 2 green, 1 silver to dozen.

No. 502 Ford Sedan.
  Colors: red, green, silver.
  Asstd. 9 red, 2 green, 1 silver to dozen.

No. 506 Airplane (small): red and silver.
  Assorted 6 red, 6 silver to dozen.

No. 508 Airplane (large): black trim.
  Colored: red and silver.
  Assorted 6 red, 6 silver to dozen.

	C6	C8	C10
Trailer, two-wheel, Graham-Bradley, 5-3/4" long (AI01)	45	50	60
Two Furrow Plow, David Bradley, 3-3/4" long (AI08)	20	30	40

Vinyl

	C6	C8	C10
Airport Limousine, No. 504, 7-1/2" long.	10	15	20
Army Recon Car, No. 652	8	12	16
Army Truck, No. 656	8	12	16
Bulldozer, No. 348, 8" long	30	45	60
Cadillac Convertible, 3-1/2" long	6	9	12
Cadillac Convertible, 5" long	12	18	25
Crane Shovel, No. 356	50	75	100
Delivery Truck	10	15	20
Dump Truck, No. 352, 10-1/2" long	35	52	70
Fire Truck, No. 614	10	15	20
Fire Truck Pumper, No. 500, 7-1/2" long	10	15	20
Fork Lift with driver, No. 538, 5" long	35	52	70
Hot Rod, No. 612, 4-1/4" long	10	15	20
Hot Rod Take-A-Part Kit, w/box	50	75	100
Jeep	7	11	15
Jeep, w/Cannon, No. 654	16	24	33

	C6	C8	C10
Krazy Tow Set: Hot Rod and Tow Truck	55	82	110
Motorcycle	32	48	65
Motorcycle Cop, No. 520, 3-7/8" long	25	38	50
Motorcycle Cop, No. 530, 6-1/4" long	35	52	70
Motorcycle Cop, three-wheel, No. 521, 4" long	15	22	30
Police Set, No. 9 w/original box	150	225	300
Racer, 7" long	37	56	75
Racer, No. 556, 10-1/2" long	27	41	55
Ranchero, No. 610, 4-3/4" long	10	15	20
Road Scraper, No. 350, 10-1/2" long	30	45	60
Sedan	20	30	40
Stake Bed Truck, No. 354, 10-5/8" long	10	15	20
Station Wagon, No. 577, 4-5/8" long	12	18	25
Steamroller, No. 362	17	25	35
Streetsweeper, No. 360, 9" long	75	112	150
Take-Apart Hot Rod	32	48	65
Tank, Army No. 650	7	11	15
Telephone Truck, No. 503, 7" long	15	22	30
Tractor, w/plow, 8" overall	16	24	32
Truck, No. 518, 5-1/2" long	14	21	28
Utility Truck, No. 508	12	18	25

AURORA

Founded by Abe Shikes and Joseph Giammarino, the Aurora Plastics Corp. was born in Brooklyn, New York on March 9, 1950. The collaboration in naming their new enterprise is a unique story. Shikes wanted the name to begin with the letter "A" so that the company would appear at the beginning of industry directories. Giammarino recalled Ben Franklin's reflection from the 1787 Constitutional Convention that the sun carved into the back of the president's chair was a rising sun and was determined that their

company would be a rising sun as well. The result was the selection of Aurora, the Roman goddess of the dawn, as the company name and the depiction of a rising sun in the corporate logo.

Plastic beads in a rainbow of colors were the company's mainstay while branching out to produce baby food dishes and other novelties. Joined by John Cuomo in January of 1952, Aurora performed contract services for other firms. An unsuccessful design of plastic clothes hangers contracted for Empire Plastics led to Aurora's entry into the toy market. Without the hook piece, the hanger looked like a bow. The toy bow and arrow set eventually sold more than 7 million copies for Empire and inspired Aurora to market bows of their own.

Inspired by two Hawk model kit planes, Aurora copied their designs and released the Gurmman Panther F9F and the Lockheed F-90 in the fall of 1952. Rather than distribute the kits solely to hobby shops, Aurora innovatively solicited dimestore chain stores with the 69¢ and 89¢ models with great success. By 1953, Aurora created its own line of 1:48 model planes molded in colored plastic.

Expanding production necessitated a new facility and by December, 1953 Aurora moved to West Hempstead, Long Island at 44 Cherry Valley Road. A wide variety of kits followed including ships and planes of different scales and price points.

Aurora entered the model car market unsuccessfully in 1957 with four trucks and returned in 1959 with a line purchased from Advance Molding Corporation and six "Indianapolis 500 Winners" purchased from Best Plastics.

Branching off into other hobby areas, Aurora embraced slot cars in the 1960s and sales eclipsed those of the model kits – but that is another story for another book.

Aurora released two motorized cars in 1961 that ran on two "D" batteries and four smaller-scale "Go Toys" cars that ran on one "C" battery. Although unsuccessful, these cars are collectible today because of their short production run and the remote possibility of finding them unassembled. For the purposes of this book, Aurora's extensive line of model kits will not be listed, but the motorized cars will be included.

The success of the Monsters line of kits immortalized Aurora in the hearts of the 1960s and 1970s generations and despite the company's 1977 exit, those kits pique the imaginations of youngsters to this day through the re-release of popular favorites by Polar Lights.

	C6	C8	C10
T-Jet Mack Stake Truck, HO-scale..........	25	38	50
Vibrator 1962 Ford Sunliner, convertible or hardtop..	40	60	80

AUTOMATIC TOY COMPANY

Around the early 1950s, Automatic Toy Company was located at 77 Alaska St., Staten Island, New York. Its toys are noted for fine tin lithography and precision wind-up motorwork. (Editor's note: I have included non-car and truck toys in this category because no other book lists the offerings of the Automatic Toy Company.

	C6	C8	C10
Auto Speedway, wind-up, one garage, two cars, c.1930	85	128	170
Cop 'N Car, plastic w/motor, siren, 4" long motorcycle, 8-1/2" car, c.1953	NPF	NPF	NPF
Magic Crossroad Track, two wind-up cars, c.1950	85	125	170
Auto Speedway, two garages and three cars...	85	125	170

BANNER

Banner was founded by Emanuel M. Pressner and Bernard Schiller in 1944. A toy importer, Pressner bought an interest in Columbia Protektosite in 1938, the company that cast Beton's plastic toy soldiers. Schiller was eventually edged out.

In 1950, Banner moved from 150 Buckner Blvd., Bronx, New York, to 80 Beckwith Ave., Paterson, New Jersey, where it remained.

Banner manufactured small plastic cars and trucks and specialized in plastic tea sets and metallic plastic forks, knives, and spoons. Banner used "off-falls," blanks formed when holes were cut in steel for car windows and television tubes, to produce their stamped-steel toys.

The company went into Chapter 11 bankruptcy in 1965. They rebounded for a few years, only to be sold in 1967 to Tal-Cap, a toy conglomerate in Minnesota.

Contributor: John Taylor, P.O. Box 63, Nolensville, TN 37135-0063. Taylor has loved antiques his entire life, and is an avid collector of pressed-steel trucks. He became hopelessly hooked on toy trucks in 1994 when he inherited a 1930s Turner ladder truck from his grandmother's estate. Since that time he has amassed an extensive collection of Turner, Steelcraft, Marx, Wyandotte, Metalcraft, Buddy "L," Banner, and Canadian-made pressed-steel trucks. Even though he also rediscovered all of his early 1960s childhood Tonka trucks in his parents' attic, he sold them off because the older stuff was "cooler." When he's not hunting antique trucks, Taylor, a veteran law enforcement agent, is busy hunting criminals. Taylor is married, has one daughter, and lives near Nashville, Tennessee.

Banner Aerial Ladder Truck, metal wheels, 1940s, 20". Photo courtesy John Taylor

Banner American Express Van, 11-1/2". Photo courtesy Ron Fink

Banner American Express Van, tin, 10". Photo courtesy Bob Smith

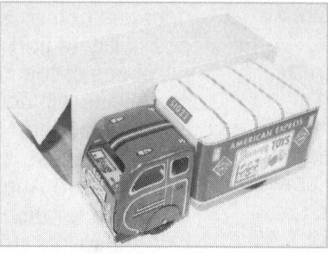

Banner American Express truck, tin, 10". Photo courtesy Bob Smith

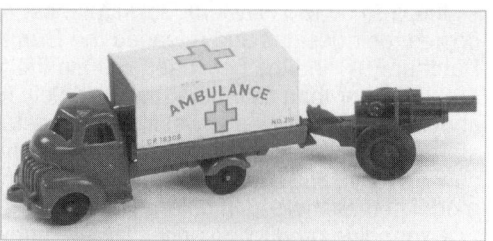

Banner Army Ambulance, tin and plastic, 6".

Left to right: Banner Army Truck, 12"; Banner Army Ambulance. Photo courtesy Roger Johnson and Charles Breslow

Banner Auto Transport, wood wheels, 1940s, 16". Photo courtesy John Taylor

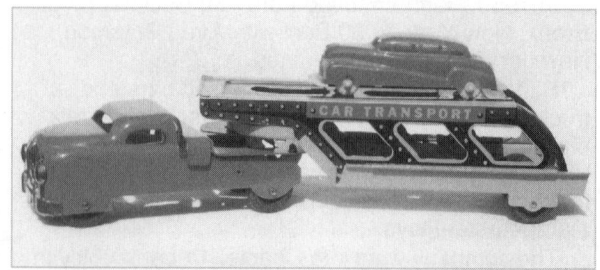

Banner Car Transport, two cars, lithographed trailer, 12". Photo courtesy John Taylor

	C6	C8	C10
Ambulance, Army, tin and plastic, 6" long	12	25	40
American Express Truck, steel cab, 11-1/2" long	150	175	325
American Express Truck, tin, 10" long	75	150	225
American Express Van, tin cab, green body w/white roof, yellow and black trim, 10"	50	125	275
Ariel Ladder Fire Truck, pressed metal wheels, No. 1143, 20" long	50	125	275
Army Truck, 12" long	25	75	125

	C6	C8	C10
Auto Transport, wood wheels, w/4 plastic cars, 1940s, 16" long	150	300	400
Buick Sedan, plastic, 4-1/2" long	5	10	25
Car Transport, lithographed trailer, w/two cars, 16" long	50	100	250
Circus Train, pulled by tractor, c.1949	NPF	NPF	NPF
Clown Van, 4-1/2" long, 1950s	12	25	40
Coronation Milk Van, rare	100	250	400
Cross Country Express, rubber tires, 1950s, 10-1/2" long	50	125	275
Dairy Truck, metal wheels, 13" long	50	125	275

Banner Circus Train, pulled by tractor, late 1940s. Photo courtesy Terry Sells

Banner Clown Van, 1950s, 4-1/2". Photo courtesy Bob and Alice Wagner

Banner Delivery Van, 4-1/4". Photo courtesy Terry Sells

Banner Cross Country Express, late 1940s, early 1950s, 10". Photo courtesy John Taylor

Banner Dump Trucks, plastic, 1950s, 5-1/4". Photo courtesy Bob and Alice Wagner

Banner Fair-Lawn Dairy Truck, 1940s, 11-1/2". Photo courtesy John Taylor

Banner Grocery Service Truck, 13". Photo courtesy John Taylor

Banner Hi-Way Emergency Truck, two spares, jack, late 1940s, 12". Photo courtesy John Taylor

Banner Garbage Truck, Ford, plastic, 1954, 4". Photo courtesy Terry Sells

Banner Grocery Service truck, tin with plastic wheels, 1950s, 11-1/2". Photo courtesy Bob Smith

	C6	C8	C10
Dairy Truck, plastic wheels, 12" long	50	125	275
Delivery Van, plastic, assorted colors, 1949, 4-1/4" long	5	10	25
Dodge, 1950, plastic, 4" long	5	10	25
Dump Truck, metal, 9" long	25	50	75
Dump Truck, plastic, 1950s, 5-1/4" long	10	15	25
Dump Truck, plastic, No. 102, 4-1/2" long	5	10	25
Dump Truck, plastic, w/ or w/out snowplow, bed lifts, tailgate opens, 6" long	NPF	NPF	NPF
Express Truck, plastic, rear door on trailer opens, 1949-50s, 7" long	20	33	45
Fair Lawn Dairy Truck, pressed metal wheels, 1940s, 11-1/2" long	75	175	325
Flying Eagle Express, rare, 12" long	100	250	400
Garbage Truck, Ford, plastic, 1954, 4" long	5	10	25
Gasoline Truck, plastic, "Cross Country Express," assorted colors, 1950s, 5-1/4" long	7	15	25
Gasoline Truck, plastic, assorted color combinations, 1949, 7" long	20	33	45
Grocery Service Truck, plastic wheels, 12" long	50	125	275
Grocery Service Truck, pressed metal wheels, 13" long	50	125	275

	C6	C8	C10
Hi-Way Emergency Tow Truck, w/tools and two spare tires, 1940s, 12" long	150	300	450
Ice Truck, metal wheels, 13" long	50	125	275
Ice Truck, plastic wheels, 12" long	50	125	275
International Harvester Metro 1950 Van, plastic, 4" long	5	10	25
Jewel Tea Van, 9-1/2" long	150	300	450
Kellogg's Express Truck, 4 wheels, 13" long	100	200	325
Kellogg's Express Truck, six wheels, pressed metal wheels, dual metal axles, 1940s, 13" long, very rare	150	300	450
Kroger Van, plastic wheels, 11-1/2" long	75	150	300
Ladder Fire Truck, plastic, ladders molded to sides, raised railing, No. 103, 1950s, 4-3/8" long	NPF	NPF	NPF
LaFrance Fire Truck, plastic, 1950, 4" long	5	10	25
Livestock Truck, plastic, "Cross Country Express," assorted colors, 1950s, 5-1/2" long	5	10	25
Livestock Truck, plastic, 7" long	22	33	45
Lumber Truck, No. 1140, pressed metal wheels, 15" long	75	150	300
Lumber Truck, No. 1140, pressed metal wheels, with original load & chain, 15" long	175	300	500

Banner Kellogg's Express, dual rear axles, 1940s, 13". Photo courtesy John Taylor

Banner Stake Truck, metal wheels, 1940s, 13". Photo courtesy John Taylor

Banner Lumber Truck, metal wheels, 1940s, 15". Photo courtesy John Taylor

Banner Sand and Gravel Truck, steel, 13". Photo courtesy John Taylor

Banner Stake Truck, wood wheels, 1940s, 8". Photo courtesy John Taylor

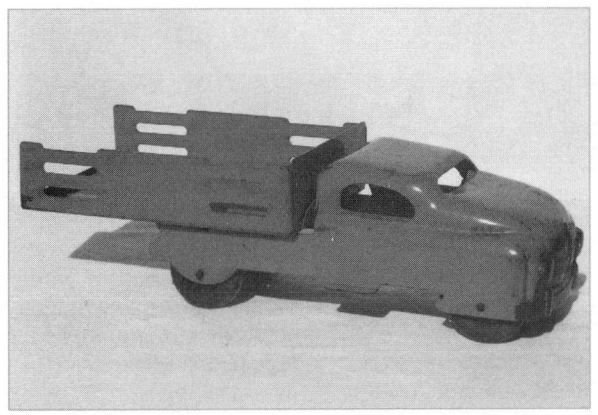

Banner Stake Truck, wood wheels, 1940s, 10". Photo courtesy John Taylor

Banner Toy Truck, #781, 1940s, 11-1/4". Photo courtesy John Taylor

*Banner Trailer Steamshovel w/box, plastic,
6-3/4". Photo courtesy Terry Sells*

*Banner Wonder Bread truck, tin with plastic wheels, 1950s,
11-1/2". Photo courtesy Harvey K. Rainess*

	C6	C8	C10
North American Van Lines Truck and Trailer, 15" long	35	75	225
Nozzle Truck, plastic, wind-up motor w/attached key, 1949, 5-3/8" long	NPF	NPF	NPF
Oil Truck, plastic, No. 101, 4-3/8" long	5	10	25
Pickup Truck, plastic, No. 105, 4-3/8" long	5	10	25
Run Right to Reads Truck, 13" long	50	125	275
Sand & Gravel Dump Truck, 8" long	35	75	100
Sand & Gravel Dump Truck, pressed metal wheels, No. 1142, 13" long	35	75	225
Sand & Gravel Truck, plastic, 7" long	25	38	50
Sand Loader, plastic, conveyor works, rubber wheels, 3" tall	5	10	25
Sanitation Truck, plastic, 1950s, 4-1/2"	7	15	25
Sanitation Truck, plastic, w/ or w/out snowplow, dumper lifts and empties, 6-1/2" long	NPF	NPF	NPF
Sedan, plastic, 1948 to 1950s, 4-1/2" long	5	10	25
Service Station, cardboard w/three plastic trucks, late 1940s-early 1950s	HPF	NPF	NPF
Side Dump Truck, plastic, 1950s, 5-1/4" long	10	20	30
Stake Truck, plastic, 8" long	25	38	50
Stake Truck, plastic, No. 104, 4-1/2" long	5	10	25
Stake Truck, pressed metal wheels, 13" long	25	75	125

	C6	C8	C10
Stake Truck, wood wheels, 1940s, 10" long	25	50	75
Stake Truck, wood wheels, 1940s, 8" long	25	50	75
Station Wagon, plastic, 1948 Oldsmobile, assorted colors, 4-1/4" long	16	24	32
Steam Shovel, plastic, scoop works, assorted colors, 4-1/2" long	5	10	25
Steamroller, plastic, 4" long	5	10	25
Tanker, plastic, 7" long	15	22	30
Town and Country Car, plastic, two-tone in assorted color combinations, wind-up motor w/key attached, 1949 to 1950s, 5" long	20	40	60
Toy Truck, pressed metal wheels, 12" long	75	175	325
Toy Truck Van, 9" long	75	112	150
Tractor, plastic, wheelhorse, 3" long	5	10	25
Trailer Steamshovel, 6-3/4" long	15	25	50
Trailer Truck, plastic, No. 69, cab-over tractor, trailer rear door opens, 1946, 7-1/4" long	NPF	NPF	NPF
U.S. Army Truck, plastic and tin, 6" long	12	25	40
U.S. Mail Truck, 11" long	40	75	175
Whelan's Steel Truck, rare, six wheels	150	300	450
Wonder Bread Truck, steel cab, 10-1/2" long	75	150	300
Wonder Bread Van, tin lithographed, 11-1/2" long	75	150	300

BARCLAY

Barclay, named after Barclay Street in West Hoboken, New Jersey, began in 1924 or late 1923, and was owned by partners Leon Donze (1865-1950) and by Michael Levy (c.1895-1964). In 1929, Levy took over the company and turned it into a major toy manufacturer. Under his guidance, it grew from five employees to a prewar peak of 400 workers and moved several times to increasingly larger quarters.

While known for its toy soldiers, Barclay was the largest producer of lead-alloy vehicles in the 1930s

and early 1940s. The most popular vehicle being the tiny No. 53 racer.

World War II was a difficult time for all toy manufacturers and Barclay was no exception. Forced to lay off all but four of its employees, Barclay moved in the direction of subcontract work. Unfortunately, the firm was never able to regain its prewar success and closed its doors in 1971.

Contributor: Stan Alekna, Toy Soldiers Etcetera, 732 Aspen Ln., Lebanon, PA 17042-9073

	C6	C8	C10
Ambulance, No. 50, red or blue cross, 5" long (BV003)	55	80	110
Ambulance, w/large red cross, No. 194, 3-1/2" long (BV002)	30	45	60
Ambulance, w/small red or blue cross, No. 194, 3-1/2" long (BV001)	35	50	65
Anti-Aircraft Gun Truck, sown in 1931 Barclay catalog, No. 198, 3-1/8" long (BV016)	22	33	45
Anti-Aircraft Gun Truck, w/one man, movable cannon, No. 48, 4" long (BV019)	34	51	65
Anti-Aircraft Gun Truck, w/two men, movable cannon, No. 48, 4" long (BV020)	33	51	65
Armored Army Truck, No. 152, 2-7/8" long (BV006)	14	20	27
Armored Army Truck, No. 152, smaller windows, 2-7/8" long, (BV006A)	15	23	30

	C6	C8	C10
Army Tank Truck, No. 197, c.1935-36, 3-1/8" long (BV007)	18	27	36
Army Tractor, (Minneapolis-Moline "Jeep"), 2-3/4" long (BV009)	20	30	40
Army Truck w/Anti-Aircraft Gun, No. 151, facing forward, 2-1/2" long (BV005)	15	23	29
Army Truck w/Anti-Aricraft Gun, No. 151, facing rear, 2-3/4" long (BV004)	14	21	28
Auburn Speedster, No. 58, c.1931, 3-1/2" long (BV139)	25	37	50
Austin Coupe, No. 43, c.1931, 2" long (BV010)	30	45	60
Beer Truck, No. 376, w/wood barrels, c.1940, 4" long (BV012)	38	57	75
Beer Truck, No. 377, w/barrels (BV013)	40	60	80
Beverage Truck, "Coca Cola" decal, 1960s, 2" long, (BV100A)	18	27	35
Beverage Truck, "Cola" decal, 1960s, 2" long, (BV100B)	15	22	30
Beverage Truck, "Pepsi Cola" decal, 1960s, 2" long (BV100)	18	27	35
Beverage Truck, "Yoo Hoo" decal, 1960s, 2" long, (BV100C)	18	27	35
Beverage Truck, no decal, 1960s, 2" long, (BV100D)	10	15	20
Build and Paint Auto Set, No. 100/4, includes six vehicles, parts, paints, 1930s (BV089)	NPF	NPF	NPF
Build and Paint Auto Set, No. 5004, c.1934 (BV089A)	NPF	NPF	NPF
Build and Paint Set, No. 2004, includes truck, coupe, sedan, parts, paints (BV090)	180	270	360
Build and Paint Set, No. 2004, only inlcudes two vehicles (BV090A)	NPF	NPF	NPF
Bus, futuristic, marked "Made U.S.A.," 3" long (BV014)	34	51	68
Cabover Truck, tailgate, updated, c.1937, 3-1/4" long	20	25	30

Barclay Build and Paint Auto Set, 1930s. Photo courtesy Perry Eichor

Left to right: Barclay Cord Front Drive Coupe (BV031); Parcel Delivery Truck (BV048), 1930s; Golden Arrow Racer (BV043). Photo courtesy Evelyn Besser and Bill Kaufman

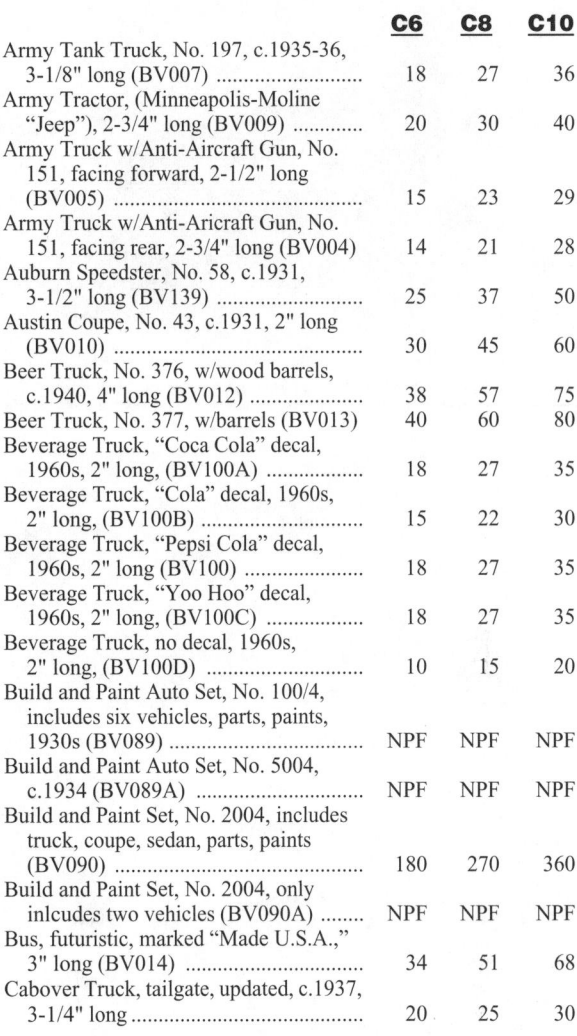

Barclay convertible with vacationers.

Barclay Coupe, 1930s, 3".

Barclay Double Decker Auto Transport (BV035). Photo courtesy Craig Clark

Barclay Fordson Tractor, white rubber tires, red wood wheels, 2-1/8".

This September 1931 Butler Bros. catalog is the earliest catalog appearance known for Barclay vehicles. Note the metal wheels.

Barclay Moving Truck (BV161), decal variants, 1960s, approximately 2". Photo courtesy Stan Alekna

	C6	C8	C10
Cannon Car, battery-powered headlight, shown in 1935 catalog, 3-1/2" long (BV018)	125	175	225
Cannon Car, gunner low, 3-5/16" long (BV015)	15	22	30
Cannon Car, no fitting for bulb, shown in 1935 catalog, 3-1/2" long (BV018A)	22	33	44
Cannon Car, slight casting differences from headlight version, 3-1/4" long (BV017)	25	38	55
Cannon Truck, moveable cannon, olive drab, sloped deck, die-cast, 4" long (BV083)	80	120	150
Cannon Truck, w/movable cannon, only 1 known with original cannon, 4" long (BV021)	NPF	NPF	NPF
Car Carrier, "Trailer" on side of cab, tin trailer w/1 BV170 & 1 BV171 cars, ealry 1930s (BV114)	95	130	165
Car Carrier, cab has 2 side windows, aluminum trailer holds 1 BV108 & 2 BV108A, 1960s, 4-1/2" long, (BV107A)	40	60	80
Car Carrier, Mack cab, tin trailer w/1 BV170 & 1 BV171 cars, 1930s, 4-7/8" long (BV152)	85	120	175
Car Carrier, No. 330, die-cast, cab & trailer w/one BV172 and one BV173 car, 4-1/2" long (BV011)	50	75	100
Car Carrier, No. 44, cab has 2 side windows, aluminum trailer hinged for loading/unloading, 2 BV108 & 2 BV108A cars, 1963, 4-1/2" long (BV107)	65	100	130
Car Carrier, open-cab Mack, long tin trailer w/2 BV010 & 2 BV132 cars, shown in 1935 catalog, 10-1/4" long (BV153)	175	250	325

	C6	C8	C10
Car Carrier, Set No. 330, with one BV172 & one BV173 or with one BV108 & one BV108A, 1960s, 4-1/2" long (BV075)	50	75	100
Chrysler Airflow, c.1936, 2 side windows, 4" long (BV023)	30	45	60
Chrysler Airflow Sedan, large, 1935, No. 1703 (BV127)	25	37	50
Chrysler Imperial Coupe, No. 39, spare tires cast on fenders, metal wheels, c.1931, 2-1/8" long (BV129)	22	33	45
Coast To Coast Bus, die-cast, two-piece, marked "Barclay Toy," No. 405, 2-7/8" long (BV024)	55	85	110
Concrete Truck, Mack cab, marked "Concrete Mixer," mixer rotates, 0 (BV179)	NPF	NPF	NPF
Contractor Set, No. 338, Tractor w/hole hitch for wire, 2 gondola cars, 1930s, approx. 6-1/4" long (BV142)	90	135	175
Convertible, w/vacationers (BV088)	50	75	100
Convertible Sports Car, driver & passenger in white, 1960s, 1-7/8" long, (BV159A)	15	22	30
Convertible Sports Car, driver and passenger in gold, 1960s, 1-7/8" long (BV159)	15	22	30
Cord Front Drive Coupe, No. 40, spare tires cast on fenders, c.1931, 3-5/8" long (BV031)	25	38	50
Coupe, 1 side window; used on BV075, BV107, BV107A, BV157; 1960s, 1-9/16" long, (BV108A)	6	9	12
Coupe, 1930s, marked "Made in U.S.A.," 3" long (BV025)	20	30	40
Coupe, 1934, 4-1/2" long (BV027)	40	60	80
Coupe, 200 series?, spare tire cast on trunk, c.1935, 3-1/8" long (BV145)	40	60	80

Variants of the Barclay Oil Truck (BV100). Left to right: a plain version, Yoo Hoo, Pepsi-Cola Truck, and Coca-Cola. Photo courtesy Stan Alekna

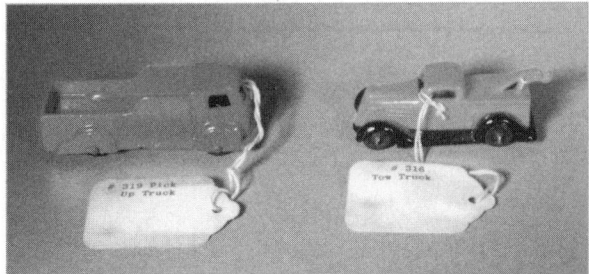

Left to right: Barclay Pickup Truck (BV166); Tow Truck (BV167). Photo courtesy Richard MacNary

Left to right: Barclay Racer, two passenger; Coupe, 1934, 4-1/2"; Wrecker, 1930s, 3-15/16". Photo courtesy Bill Kaufman

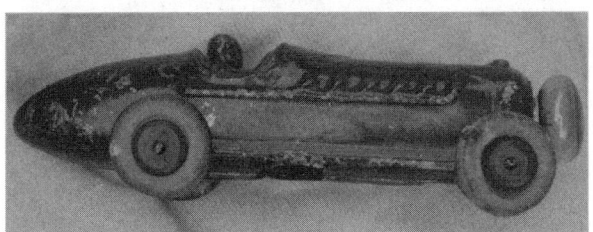

Barclay Racing Car (BV149A), battery-operated flashlight, 4". Photo courtesy Fred Maxwell

Barclay Sedan and Tourist Trailer (BV061), 6-1/2", 1930s.

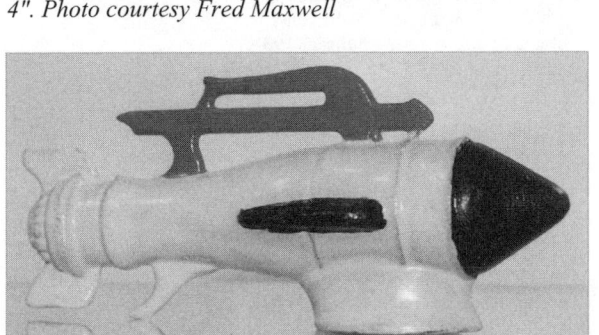

Barclay Rocket Ship No. 610. Photo courtesy Stan Alekna

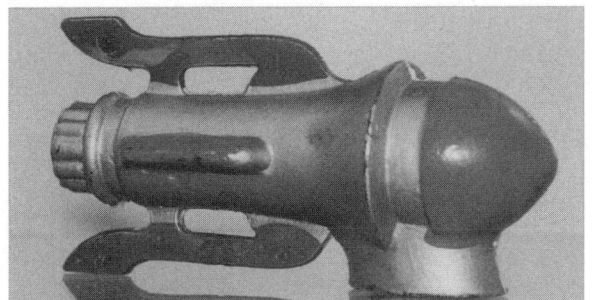

Barclay Rocket Ship No. 611. Photo courtesy Stan Alekna

Left to right: Barclay Streamline Car (BV032), 1930s; Delivery Truck (BV033); Fire Engine (BV41). Photo courtesy Evelyn Besser

	C6	C8	C10
Coupe, c.1935, 2-1/2" long (BV026)	40	70	100
Coupe, die-cast, two-piece, 1930s, "Barclay Toy," 2-7/8" long (BV028) ..	40	50	85
Coupe, luggage trunk on rear, spare tires cast on fenders, 1934, 4-1/2" long (BV030)	45	65	90
Coupe, No. 51, Landau irons at angle, other casting differences from BV132, c. 1931, (BV132A)	22	37	45
Coupe, No. 51, vertical Landau irons, c.1931, 2-3/16" long (BV132)	22	37	45
Coupe, removable spare tire, shown in 1935 catalog, 4-1/2" long (BV146)	30	45	60
Coupe, same as BV030, w/battery-powered light, 1 known, (BV030A)	NPF	NPF	NPF
Coupe, small coupe used for BV011, BV075, BV107, BV107A, 1960s, 1-9/16" long, (BV173)	8	11	16
Coupe, open, w/driver in cap, early 1930s (BV110)	60	90	120
Curtiss Aerocar, coupe (BV145) w/hole pulling trailer, marked "Curtiss Aerocar," (BV169)	NPF	NPF	NPF
Delivery Truck, marked "Bakery Fine Cake Pies," No. 206, c.1934, 3-1/8" long (BV131)	65	90	125
Delivery Truck, No. 309, marked "DELIVERY", 2-15/16" long (BV033)	20	30	40
Delivery Truck, No. 309, marked "Delivery," c.1936, 3-1/2" long (BV136)	22	33	44
DeSoto AirFlow, 1935, 5-3/16" long (BV113)	25	37	50
Double Decker Bus, 4" long (BV034)	60	90	120
Double Transport Set, four cars on upper and lower racks, truck has one side window, 1939-1963, No. 440 (BV157)	50	75	95
Double-Decker Bus, No. 56, c.1931, 3-1/4" long (BV138)	30	45	60
Dump Truck, spring action, ratchet, shown in 1935 catalog, 4" long (BV147)	20	30	40

	C6	C8	C10
Dump Truck, w/movable bed, no decals, 1960s, 2" long (BV094)	9	14	18
Esso Gas Truck, marked "Esso," 1930s, 5" long (BV111)	40	60	80
Express stake Truck, marked "EXPRESS" and "Made in U.S.A.", 1930s, 2-15/16" long (BV037)	30	45	60
Field Kitchen, w/horizontal loop hitch for peg attachment, 2-1/4" long, (BV039A)	20	30	40
Field Kitchen, w/vertical loop hitch for wire attachment, 2-1/4" long (BV039)	20	30	40
Fire Engine, four firemen, black metal wheels, No. 41, 1930s, 2-3/4" long (BV040)	25	37	50
Fire Engine, French-looking (Barclay often copied foreign toys), 4" long (BV041)	NPF	NPF	NPF
Fire Engine, moveable ladder w/climbing fireman in blue, die-cast, only 1 known, No. 390, 1950s (BV038)	NPF	NPF	NPF
Fire Engine, No. 209, Pumper w/bell, c.1934, 3-1/8" long (BV134)	30	45	60
Fire Truck, Hook and Ladder, 2 firemen, water cannon behind driver, 2-3/4" long, (BV177)	40	60	75
Fire Truck, Large Hook and Ladder, small crane behind driver, large hubs, 4-3/4" long, (BV183)	50	75	100
Fire Truck, Large Pumper, small crane attached to boiler, driver only, tires on large hubs, 3-15/16" long, (BV035) ...	NPF	NPF	NPF
Fire Truck, No. 210, Hose truck, c.1934, 3-1/8" long (BV133)	30	45	60
Fire Truck, No. 50 Pumper, steering wheel above hood, 7 hood vents, other mold differences from BV137A, metal wheels, 2-1/4" long (BV137)	30	45	60
Fire Truck, No. 50 Pumper, steering wheel level w/hood, 3 hood vents, metal wheels or wood hubs, c. 1931, 2-1/4" long (BV137A)	30	45	60

Barclay Stake Truck (BV168), 3-1/2". Photo courtesy Craig Clark

Barclay Streamline Sedan (BV125), large.

Barclay was the largest manufacturer of lead-alloy vehicles in the 1930s and 1940s. Photo courtesy Craig Clark

Barclay Army Tank (BV067), two men in turret, white rubber tires, 3-7/8".

Barclay Auto Transport Set (BV011), 4-1/2". Photo courtesy Stan Alekna

Barclay Cannon Car (BV018), 3-1/2". Photo courtesy Brad Fullhart

Barclay Coupe (BV132), vertical Landau irons, 2-3/16". Photo courtesy Doug Ehrenhaft

Barclay Delivery Truck (BV033), 2-15/16". Photo courtesy Doug Ehrenhaft

Barclay Car Carrier (BV114), "Trailer" on side of cab, tin trailer holds BV170 and BV171. Photo courtesy Stan Alekna

Barclay Chrysler Airflow (BV023), 4". Photo courtesy Stan Alekna

Barclay Coupe (BV026), c. 1935, 2-1/2". Photo courtesy Stan Alekna

Barclay Chrysler Imperial Coupe (BV129), c. 1931, metal wheels, 2-1/8". Photo courtesy Doug Ehrenhaft

Barclay Delivery Truck (BV131), marked "Bakery Fine Cake Pies," c. 1934, 3-1/8". Photo courtesy Doug Ehrenhaft

	C6	C8	C10
Fire Truck, Pumper, 2 firemen, marked "Made in U.S.A.," 2-3/4" long, 0 (BV182)	40	60	75
Fire Truck, Pumper, marked "Fire Dept. No. 99," No. 386, 1930s, 5-3/4" long (BV126)	55	81	110
Fire Truck, same as BV035 w/battery-powered headlight, only 1 known, 0 (BV035A)	NPF		
Ford, 1931, 2-1/4" long (BV042)	30	45	60
Fordson Tractor, white rubber tires, red wood wheels, 2-1/8"	NPF	NPF	NPF
Fuel Tractor Trailer, Mack tractor pulling trailer marked "Gasoline,", metal wheels, 4-3/4" long, (BV175)	85	125	175

	C6	C8	C10
Gasoline Tanker, four tank top, 200 Series?, horizontal grille, c. 1935, (BV144B)	30	45	60
Gasoline Tanker, four tank top, 200 series?, vertical grille, c.1935, 3" long (BV144A)	30	45	60
Gasoline Tanker, small, three tank top, c.1931, 2-5/16" long (BV144)	30	45	60
Golden Arrow Racer, marked "Golden Arrow Racer", open cockpit, metal wheels, 4-1/2" long (BV043)	50	75	100
Heavy Truck, "U.S. Army" & insignia decals, standard style cab, c. 1968, 1-11/16" long, (BV104A)	15	22	30

Barclay Fire Truck (BV035), large pumper, 3-15/16". Photo courtesy Brad Fullhart

Barclay Fire Truck (BV035A), battery-powered headlight, only one known, 3-15/16". Photo courtesy Brad Fullhart

Barclay fireman (BV038) at the top of the extended ladder. Photo courtesy Stan Alekna

Barclay Fire Engine (BV038), 5-7/8". Photo courtesy Stan Alekna

Barclay Fire Truck (BV182), Pumper marked "Made in U.S.A.," 2-3/4". Photo courtesy Stan Alekna

Barclay Fire Engine (BV038), with its ladder raised. Photo courtesy Stan Alekna

Barclay Fire Truck (BV133), c. 1934, 3-1/8". Photo courtesy Stan Alekna

Barclay Coupe (BV030A), same as BV030 with battery-powered light, 4-1/2". Photo courtesy Brad Fullhart

Barclay Coupe (BV132A), angled Landau irons, c. 1931, 2-3/16". Photo courtesy Brad Fullhart

Barclay Hook and Ladder Truck (BV122), c. 1935, bell behind driver, 3". Photo courtesy Stan Alekna

Barclay Golden Arrow Racer (BV043), 4-1/2". Photo courtesy Pim Piët

Barclay Race Car (BV050), 3". Photo courtesy Brad Fullhart

Barclay Racer (BV051), closed cockpit, 5-1/2". Photo courtesy Doug Ehrenhaft

Barclay Streamline Racer (BV121), open cockpit, 4 hood vents, 4-3/8". Photo courtesy Brad Fullhart

Barclay Race Car (BV150), manifold pipes on both sides, 4". Photo courtesy Brad Fullhart

Barclay Large Streamline Racer (BV065), No. 363, 6-7/8". Photo courtesy Pim Piët

Barclay Racer (BV053), No. 53, 2". Photo courtesy Doug Ehrenhaft

Barclay Racer (BV054), 4-1/4". Photo courtesy Brad Fullhart

Barclay Silver Arrow Race Car (BV062), 5-1/2". Photo courtesy Brad Fullhart

Barclay Racer (BV055), with tailfin, 3-1/2". Photo courtesy Pim Piët

Barclay Fire Engine (BV134), Pumper with bell, c. 1934, 3-1/8". Photo courtesy Brad Fullhart

Barclay Fire Truck (BV137), Pumper with steering wheel above hood, 2-1/4". Photo courtesy Stan Alekna

Barclay Fire Truck (BV137A), Pumper, steering wheel level with hood, 2-1/4". Photo courtesy Stan Alekna

Barclay Tow Truck (BV141), c. 1935, 3-1/16". Photo courtesy Doug Ehrenhaft

	C6	C8	C10
Heavy Truck, c.1968, approx. 2" long (BV104)	8	13	18
Heavy Truck, white hospital truck, flat front on cab, c. 1968, 1-11/16" long (BV158)	17	25	33
Heavy Truck, white hospital truck, red cross decal on roof, standard style cab, lower & wider canvas over bed vs. BV104, c. 1968, 1-11/16" long, (BV104B)	17	25	33
Hook and Ladder Truck, shown in 1935 catalog, No. 208, bell behind driver, 3" long (BV122)	20	30	40
Howitzer, 4 white or black rubber tires, horizontal loop for peg hitch, 2-7/8" to end of barrel, (BV036A)	20	30	40
Howitzer, 4 white rubber tires, vertical loop for wire attachment, 2-7/8" to end of barrel, (BV036)	20	30	40
Large Streamline Coupe, 1930s (BV143).	40	60	80
Large Streamline Racer, shown in 1935 catalog, No. 363, open cockpit, 3 side vents, wooden hubs, 6-7/8" long (BV065)	45	68	90
Log Truck, w/3 logs, 1960s, 2" long (BV093)	13	20	25
Mack Pickup Truck, 3-1/2" (BV044)	35	50	75
Milk and Cream Truck, white rubber tires, stamped "No. 377," stenciled "Milk & Cream" w/6 silver milk cans, 3-5/8" long (BV045)	45	60	85
Milk Truck, black rubber tires, No. 377, with and without 6 silver milk cans, 3-5/8" long (BV045A)	35	52	65

	C6	C8	C10
Milk Truck, in shape of bottle, silver, No. 567, 5-3/16" long (BV084)	150	225	300
Milk Van Truck, marked "MILK" w/bottle on side, 2-7/8" long (BV085)	30	45	60
Motorcycle, w/flat rider, full-dimensional sidecar, No. 55, metal wheels, 2-3/4" long (BV046)	48	71	95
Moving Truck, "A&P Refrigeration" decal, 1960s, 1-15/16" long, (BV092C)	15	22	30
Moving Truck, "Avis" decal, 1960s, 1-15/16" long, (BV092B)	15	22	30
Moving Truck, "Hertz" decal, 1960s, 1-15/16" long, (BV092A)	13	20	25
Moving Truck, "Sandwiches" decal, 1960s, 1-15/16" long, (BV092E)	12	18	24
Moving Truck, "Stewarts Infared" decal, 1960s, 1-15/16" long, (BV092D)	12	18	24
Moving Truck, "U.S. Army" & insignia decals, c.1968, 1-7/8" long (BV103)	16	24	32
Moving Truck, cargo bed extends over roof of cab, no decals, 1960s, 1-7/8" long (BV161)	10	15	20
Moving Truck, no decal, 1960s, 1-15/16" long (BV092)	9	14	18
Officer's Car, megaphone on roof, olive drab, die-cast, only 2 known, 2-3/4" long (BV008)	NPF	NPF	NPF
Oil Truck, "Milk" decal, 1960s, 1-7/8" long, (BV099C)	19	27	38
Oil Truck, "Shell" decal, 1960s, 1-7/8" long, (BV099A)	17	25	35
Oil Truck, "Sinclair" decal, 1960s, 1-7/8" long (BV099)	17	25	35

Barclay Double-Decker Bus (BV034), 4". Photo courtesy Brad Fullhart

Barclay Fire Engine (BV134), Pumper with bell, c. 1934, 3-1/8". Photo courtesy Brad Fullhart

Barclay Fire Truck (BV137A), Pumper, steering wheel level with hood, 2-1/4". Photo courtesy Stan Alekna

Barclay Motorcycle (BV046), No. 55, with sidecar, 2-3/4". Photo courtesy Brad Fullhart

Barclay Police Car (BV049B), 1939 Packard. Photo courtesy Brad Fullhart

Barclay Stake Truck (BV124), c. 1935, 3-1/8". Photo courtesy Doug Ehrenhaft

Barclay Sedan (BV059), c. 1935, 3-1/8". Photo courtesy Brad Fullhart

Barclay Stake Truck (BV151), rubber tires, 4-3/8". Photo courtesy Brad Fullhart

Barclay Tow Truck (BV141), c. 1935, 3-1/16". Photo courtesy Doug Ehrenhaft

Barclay Tow Car, white rubber tires, red wood wheels, 3".

	C6	C8	C10
Oil Truck, "Sunoco" decal, 1960s, 1-7/8" long, (BV099B)	19	27	38
Oil Truck, "U.S. Army" & insignia decals, c.1968, 1-7/8" long (BV106) ..	15	22	30
Oil Truck, no decal, different fuel tank, 1960s, 1-7/8" long, (BV099E)	10	15	20
Oil Truck, no decals, 1960s, 1-7/8" long, (BV099D)	10	15	20
Oil-Fuel Truck, marked "Oil-Fuel", c.1936, 3-9/16" long (BV047)	20	30	40
Open Bed Truck, "Euclid" decal, c. 1968, 2" long, (BV105A)	10	15	20
Open Bed Truck, "U.S. Army" & insignia decals, c.1968, 2" long (BV105)	16	24	32

	C6	C8	C10
Parcel Delivery, slush mold, No. 45, marked "Parcel Delivery", c.1931, 3-5/8" long (BV048)	100	150	200
Pickup Truck, No. 319 (BV166)	NPF	NPF	NPF
Police Car, 1939 Packard, marked "Radio Police", concave, dished headlights and siren, (BV049B)	30	45	60
Police Car, 1939 Packard, marked "Radio Police", slush mold, No. 317, approx. 3-5/8" long, 1930s (BV049)	34	51	68
Police Car, No. 317, die-cast, 3-5/8" long (BV049A)	25	37	50
Race Car, number decals, gold driver, much wider than BV101, exhaust pipes, 1960s, 1-7/8" long, (BV101A) .	13	20	26

Barclay Sedan (BV061A), with hitch for trailer, 3-1/2". Photo courtesy Brad Fullhart

Barclay Side Dump (BV087), 1-1/2". Photo courtesy Stan Alekna

Barclay Cannon Truck (BV021), with movable cannon, 4". Photo courtesy Stan Alekna

Barclay Wrecker (BV081A), same as BV081 with battery-powered headlight, only one known, 3-15/16". Photo courtesy Brad Fullhart

Barclay Fire Engine (BV040), No. 41, 2-3/4". Photo courtesy Stan Alekna

Barclay Steam Roller (BV064), No. 44. 3-1/4". Photo courtesy Brad Fullhart

Barclay Field Kitchen (BV039A), with loop hitch, 2-1/4". Photo courtesy Brad Fullhart

Barclay Oil Truck: Sinclair decals (BV099); U.S. Army decals (BV106); Shell decals (BV99A); Sunoco decals (BV99B); 1-7/8". Photo courtesy Stan Alekna

Barclay Car Carrier (BV152), Mack cab, tin trailer, two cars, 4-7/8". Photo courtesy Stan Alekna

Barclay Transport (BV075), No. 330, 1960s, 4-1/2". Photo courtesy Stan Alekna

Barclay Tractor Trailer; Hertz decals (BV091C), Allied Van Lines decals (BV091D), no decals with WSW tires, 1960s, 2-7/8". Photo courtesy Stan Alekna

Barclay Fire Truck (BV183), Large hook and ladder, crane behind driver, 4-3/4". Photo courtesy Stan Alekna

Barclay Oil Truck: "Milk" decals (BV099C); No decals (BV099D); No decal different fuel tank (BV099E); 1-7/8". Photo courtesy Stan Alekna

Barclay Car Carrier (BV153), open Mack cab, four cars, 10-1/4". Photo courtesy Stan Alekna

Barclay Tractor Trailer; U.S. Mail decals (BV091), Woolworth decals (BV091A), Railway Express decals (BV091B), 1960s, 2-7/8". Photo courtesy Stan Alekna

Barclay Army Truck (BV103), Moving Truck (BV092), Moving Truck with Hertz decal (BV092A), 1960s, 1-15/16". Photo courtesy Stan Alekna

Barclay Moving Truck; AVIS decal (BV092B), A&P Refrigeration decal (BV092C), Stewarts Infared decal (BV092D), 1960s, 1-15/16". Photo courtesy Stan Alekna

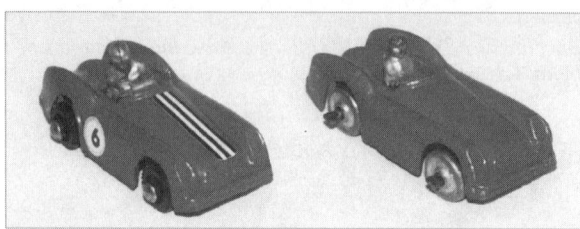

Barclay Racing Car; Gold driver with racing stripes and number decals (BV095), Gold driver wearing cap with no decals (BV-95A), c. 1968, 1-7/8". Photo courtesy Stan Alekna

Barclay Siren Car; Police decals (BV096), Taxi decals (BV163), U.S. Army decals (BV096A), Hippy Car flower decals (BV096B), 1960s, 2-1/8". Photo courtesy Stan Alekna

Barclay Vintage Car: Single high seat and windshield, 1-9/16", (BV098); Single low seat without windshield, 1-5/8", (BV165); Two low seats without windshield, 1-3/4" (BV098A), 1960s. Photo courtesy Stan Alekna

Barclay Vintage Car: Single low seat without windshield, 1-5/8", (BV098B); Bucket seats, rumble seat, no windshield, 1-5/8", (BV098C), 1960s. Photo courtesy Stan Alekna

Barclay Log Truck (BV093), 2". Photo courtesy Stan Alekna

Barclay Dump Truck (BV094), 2". Photo courtesy Stan Alekna

Barclay Racing Car (BV095B), white driver wearing cap with no decals, c. 1968, 1-7/8". Photo courtesy Rick Leeman

Barclay Vintage Car: Same as BV098 with headlamps cast into fenders, 1-9/16", (BV098D); Same as BV165 with headlamps cast into fenders, 1-5/8", (BV165A); 1960s. Photo courtesy Rick Leeman

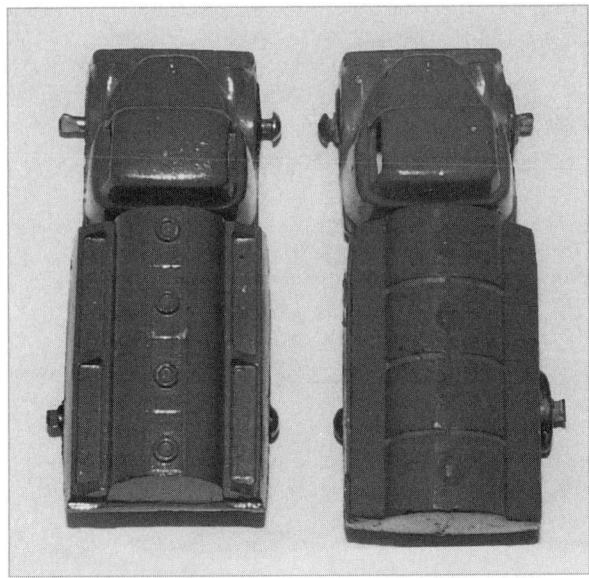

Barclay Beverage Truck: Pepsi Cola decal (BV100); Coca Cola decal (BV100A); Cola decal (BV100B); 1960s, 2". Photo courtesy Stan Alekna

Barclay Beverage Truck: YooHoo decal (BV100C); No decal (BV100D); 1960s, 2". Photo courtesy Stan Alekna

An overhead view of the differences in fuel tanks between BV099D and BV099E. Photo courtesy Stan Alekna

	C6	C8	C10
Race Car, open cockpit, 4 hood vents, wooden hubs, 5-1/2" long (BV062)	45	60	80
Race Car, open cockpit, driver and passenger, 6 manifold pipes on right side only, metal wheels or hubs, 3" long (BV050)	15	22	30
Race Car, open, w/driver's head even with seat, 6 manifold pipes on both sides, 4" long (BV150)	70	105	140
Racer, closed cockpit, 6 manifold pipes, wooden hubs, c.1939, 7" long (BV052)	45	67	90
Racer, closed cockpit, wooden hubs, 5-1/2" long (BV051)	35	52	70
Racer, No. 5, Golden Arrow style racer, shown in 1931 magazine, metal wheels (BV130)	20	30	40
Racer, No. 53, open cockpit, 4 manifold pipes, metal wheels, 2" long (BV053)	45	67	90
Racer, shown in 1936 catalog, No. 306, smooth hoods, open cockpit, white tires, 4-3/8" long (BV120)	55	83	110
Racer, w/driver and passenger, wooden hubs, 4-1/4" long (BV054)	55	83	110
Racer, w/tail fin, marked "Made U.S.A." on right side only, 3-1/2" long (BV055)	25	38	50
Racing Car, c. 1968, no decals, gold driver w/cap, 1-7/8" long, (BV095A) .	15	22	30
Racing Car, c. 1968, no decals, white driver w/cap, 1-7/8" long, (BV095B) .	17	25	35
Racing Car, large, w/driver's head above seat, raised exhaust pipe, shown in 1935 catalog, wooden hubs, 4" long (BV149)	40	60	80
Racing Car, No. 371, large open cockpit, 1930s, 14-1/4" long (BV115)	38	57	75
Racing Car, number decals, gold driver, no fenders, 1960s, 1-7/8" long (BV101)	13	20	26

	C6	C8	C10
Racing Car, racing stripes, no decals, gold driver, c.1968, 1-7/8" long (BV095)	15	22	30
Racing Car, same as BV149 w/battery-powered headlight, shown in 1935 catalog, 4" long (BV149A)	NPF	NPF	NPF
Renault Tank, No. 47, c. 1937, 4" long (BV056)	30	45	60
Roadster, open, w/driver, spare tires cast on fenders, luggage trunk on rear, shown in 1935 catalog, 4-1/2" long (BV154)	60	80	120
Roadster, small roadster used for BV114 & BV152, 1-5/8" long, (BV171)	9	12	18
Rocket Ship, No. 610	NPF	NPF	NPF
Rocket Ship, No. 611	NPF	NPF	NPF
Searchlight Truck, white rubber tires, flat deck, holes along side, c.1940, 4-1/16" long (BV057)	125	175	250
Searchlight Truck, white rubber tires, olive drab, sloped deck, die-cast, 4" long (BV057A)	100	150	200

Barclay Side Dump (BV180), Mack cab, dump bed swivels. Photo courtesy Brad Fullhart

Barclay Race Car: Number decals, gold driver, narrow casting, (BV101); Number decals, gold driver, wide casting, (BV101A); 1-7/8". Photo courtesy Stan Alekna

Barclay Heavy Truck: White Hospital Truck w/Red Cross decal on roof, (BV104); U.S. Army decals, (BV104A); c. 1968, 1-11/16". Photo courtesy Stan Alekna

Barclay Open Bed Truck: U.S. Army decals, (BV105); Euclid decals, (BV105A); c. 1968, 2". Photo courtesy Stan Alekna

Barclay Convertible Sports Car (BV159), 1-7/8"; Volkswagen (BV160), 2-3/16"; Moving Truck (BV161), 1-7/8". Photo courtesy Stan Alekna

Barclay Sedan: U.S. Army decals (BV162); Citroen in metallic colors (BV162A); 2-1/16". Photo courtesy Stan Alekna

Barclay Volkswagen: Stock, in various colors, (BV102); Stock car racer with number decal, (BV102A); Hot Rod with flower decals (BV164); 1960s 1-7/8". Photo courtesy Stan Alekna

Barclay Heavy Truck: White Hospital Truck, flat-front cab, (BV158); White Hospital Truck, standard cab, (BV104B); c. 1968, 1-11-16". Photo courtesy Stan Alekna

Barclay Sedan (BV108), with 2 side windows, 1-9/16". Barclay Coupe (BV108A), with 1 side window, 1-9/16". These cars were issued with auto transports. Photo courtesy Stan Alekna

Barclay Convertible Sports Car, driver and passenger in white, 1960s, 1-7/8". Photo courtesy Rick Leeman

Barclay Car Carrier (BV107A), cab has 2 side windows, aluminum trailer holds BV108 and BV108A, 4-1/2". Photo courtesy Stan Alekna

Barclay Contractor Set (BV142), tractor and 2 gondola cars, 6-1/4". Photo courtesy Brad Fullhart

Barclay Gasoline Tanker (BV144A), vertical grille, c. 1935, 3". Photo courtesy Brad Fullhart

Barclay Gasoline Tanker (BV144B), horizontal grille, c. 1935, 3". Photo courtesy Brad Fullhart

Barclay Coupe (BV145), c. 1935, spare tire cast on trunk, 3-1/8". Photo courtesy Brad Fullhart

Barclay Coupe (BV146), removable rubber spare tire, 4-1/2". Photo courtesy Brad Fullhart

Barclay Sedan (BV140), c. 1934, 3-1/8". Photo courtesy Doug Ehrenhaft

Barclay Dump Truck (BV147), Mack cab, c. 1935, 4". Photo courtesy Stan Alekna

Barclay Racing Car (BV149A), with battery-powered headlight, 4". Photo courtesy Brad Fullhart

Barclay Van (BV176A), marked "Gasoline" on side, 2-7/8". Photo courtesy Brad Fullhart

Barclay Van (BV176B), marked "Gasoline" and "Made in U.S.A." on side, 2-7/8". Photo courtesy Brad Fullhart

Barclay Fire Truck (BV177), Hook and Ladder, 2-3/4". Photo courtesy Stan Alekna

Barclay Sedan (BV178), "Made U.S.A." in fender behind wheel, 3". Photo courtesy Brad Fullhart

Barclay Concrete Truck (BV179), marked "Concrete Mixer," mixer rotates. Photo courtesy Brad Fullhart

	C6	C8	C10
Sedan, "U.S. Army" insignia & decals, 1960s, 2-1/16" long (BV162)	18	24	36
Sedan, 2 side windows; used on BV075, BV107, BV107A, BV157; 1960s, 1-9/16" long (BV108)	2	3	5
Sedan, Citroen in metallic colors, 1960s, 2-1/16" long, (BV162A)	18	24	36
Sedan, die-cast, two-door, marked "Barclay Toy," No. 401, 1930s 2-7/8" long (BV060)	55	80	110
Sedan, four-door, maybe Chrysler, c.1936, approx. 5" long (BV058)	25	37	50
Sedan, marked "Made in U.S.A." on fender behind tire, two-tone paint, rubber wheels, 3" long, (BV178)	NPF	NPF	NPF
Sedan, No. 311, c.1936 (BV135)	24	36	48
Sedan, removable spare tire, two-door, c.1935, 3-1/4" long (BV059)	60	90	120
Sedan, sedan without hitch/hole for trailer, 3-1/2" long, (BV061A)	45	60	90
Sedan, small sedan used for BV011, BV075, BV107, BV107A, 1960s, 1-9/16" long, (BV172)	8	11	16
Sedan, small sedan used for BV114 & BV152, 1-1/2" long, (BV170)	9	12	18
Sedan, w/3 side windows, no spare tire, c.1934, 3-1/8" long (BV140)	20	30	40
Sedan and Tourist Trailer, marked "Made in U.S.A.," 1930s, 6-1/2" long (BV061)	85	125	160
Semi Tractor Trailer, "Allied Van Lines" decal, 1960s, 2-7/8" long, (BV091D)	20	30	40
Semi Tractor Trailer, "Hertz" decal, 1960s, 2-7/8" long, (BV091C)	20	30	40
Semi Tractor Trailer, "Railway Express" decal, 1960s, 2-7/8" long, (BV091B)	20	30	40
Semi Tractor Trailer, "U.S. Mail" decal, 1960s, 2-7/8" long, (BV091)	18	27	35

	C6	C8	C10
Semi Tractor Trailer, "Woolworth" decal, 1960s, 2-7/8" long, (BV091A)	20	30	40
Semi Tractor Trailer, no decal, WSW tires, 1960s, 2-7/8" long, (BV091E)	18	27	35
Side Dump, larger tires in rear, 1960s, 1-5/8" long (BV087)	9	14	18
Side Dump, Mack cab, dump bed swivels, (BV180)	NPF	NPF	NPF
Siren Car, "Chief" and insignia decals, 1960s, 2-1/8" long (BV097)	18	27	35
Siren Car, "Police" decal, 1060s, 2-1/8" long (BV096)	13	20	25
Siren Car, "Taxi" decal, yellow, 1960s, 2-1/8" long (BV163)	15	22	30
Siren Car, "U.S. Army" and insignia decals, 1960s, 2-1/8" long, (BV096A)	15	22	30
Siren Car, Hippy car and flower decals, neon colors, 1960s, 2-1/8" long, (BV096B)	13	20	25
Sport Coupe, removable spare tire, shown in 1935 catalog, 2-7/8" long (BV148)	32	48	65
Stake Truck, marked "Trucking," shown in 1936 catalog, 3-1/2" long (BV168)	NPF	NPF	NPF
Stake Truck, shown in 1935 catalog, 4-3/8" long (BV151)	36	54	72
Stake Truck, shown in 1935 catalog, No. 207, 3-1/8" long (BV124)	38	57	75
Station Wagon, die-cast, two-piece "Barclay Toy," No. 404, 1930s, 2-15/16" long (BV063)	55	80	110
Steam Shovel, Mack cab, shovel moves up and down, (BV181)	NPF	NPF	NPF
Steam-Roller, slush lead w/tin roof, traction type, No. 44, 3-1/4" long (BV064)	30	45	60
Streamline Car, No. 302, 1936, 3-1/4" long (BV032)	45	68	90

	C6	C8	C10
Streamline Coupe, large , No. 361 (BV112)	24	36	48
Streamline Coupe, No. 301, 3-1/4" long (BV123)	38	57	75
Streamline Coupe, shown in 1937 catalog, 5" long (BV155)	NPF	NPF	NPF
Streamline Racer, No. 303, open cockpit, 4 hood vents, 4-3/8" long (BV121)	60	90	120
Streamline Sedan Large, shown in 1935 catalog, No. 362, fenders cover wheels (BV125)	50	75	100
Tank, base on US M2 light tank, 2-1/2" long (BV070)	15	22	30
Tank, die-cast, man in turret, black rubber tires, 2-5/8" long (BV069)	18	27	35
Tank, one man in turret, marked "4562," 3-7/8" long (BV066)	25	37	45
Tank, two men in turret, marked "4562," 3-7/8" long (BV067)	21	31	42
Tank T41, turret swivels, 4-1/4" long (BV068)	25	37	50
Taxi, die-cast, No. 318, 3-1/4" long (BV071A)	30	45	60
Taxi, slush mold, 3-1/4" long (BV071) ...	25	37	45
Tow Car, white rubber tires, red wood wheels, 3" long.............................	NPF	NPF	NPF
Tow Truck, No. 1105 (or 1705), marked "Towing Service," rhinestone headlights, 4-7/8" long (BV117)	82	124	175
Tow Truck, No. 205, shown in 1935 catalog, 3-1/16" long (BV141)	38	57	75
Tow Truck, No. 316 (BV167)	NPF	NPF	NPF
Tow Truck, shown in 1936 catalog, marked "Towing," No. 312, 3-3/8" long (BV119)	50	75	100
Tractor, No. 203, peg hitch, 2-1/8" long (BV109)	17	24	35
Tractor, No. 42, small, shown in 1931 magazine, 2-3/16" long (BV128)	20	30	40
Tractor, No. 7, c.late 1920s-early 1930s (BV116)	22	33	45
Tractor, slush lead, caterpillar type, approx. 2-5/8" long, (BV072)	25	37	50
Truck, white rubber tires, marked "U.S. Motor Unit," wire coupler attaches to rear structure, c.1940, 3" long (BV078)	22	33	44
Truck, white rubber tires, peg hitch, marked "U.S. Motor Unit," c. 1940, (BV078A)	22	33	44
U.S. Army Truck, no hitch, red wood hubs, No. 204, 2-1/2" long (BV076) ...	23	34	46
U.S. Army Truck, white rubber tires, peg hitch, 2-1/2" long, (BV077A)	20	28	35
U.S. Army Truck, white rubber tires, vertical loop for wire hitch, 2-1/2" long (BV077)	20	28	35
Van, marked "Gasoline" and "Made in U.S.A." on side, 2-7/8", (BV176B)	40	60	80
Van, marked "Gasoline" on side, 2-7/8" long, (BV176A)	40	60	80
Van, no lettering on side, 2-7/8" long, (BV176)	40	60	80
Vintage Car, no windshield, 2 low seats, separately cast headlamps, 1960s, 1-3/4" long, (BV098A)	9	14	18

	C6	C8	C10
Vintage Car, no windshield, bucket seats & rumble seat, separately cast headlamps, 1-5/8" long, (BV098C)	9	14	18
Vintage Car, no windshield, single low seat, plastic tires for wheels & steering wheel, headlamps cast into fenders, 1-5/8" long, (BV098B)	9	14	18
Vintage Car, no windshield, single low seat, separately cast headlamps, 1960s, 1-5/8" long (BV165)	9	14	18
Vintage Car, same as BV098, w/small headlamps cast into fenders, 1-9/16" long, (BV098D)	9	14	18
Vintage Car, same as BV165, w/small headlamps cast into fenders, 1960s, 1-5/8" long, (BV165A)	9	14	18
Vintage Car, windshield, single high seat, separately cast headlamps, 1960s, 1-9/16" long, (BV098)	9	14	18
Volkswagen, larger than BV102, 1960s, 2-3/16" long (BV160)	12	18	24
Volkswagen, stock car w/number decal, 1960s, 1-7/8" long, (BV102A)	13	20	26
Volkswagen, various colors including metallic, 1960s, 1-7/8" long (BV102)	13	20	26
Volkwagen, Hotrod w/flower decals, wsw, neon colors, 1960s, approx. 2" long (BV164)	12	18	24
Wheel-A-Rific speedway track, two lead racers, black rubber wheels, sold for $1.00 c.1970, 10" of plastic track (BV079)	50	75	100
White Horse Van, some have sticker reading "Welcome I.C.M.A. compliments THE WHITE MOTOR CO.," approx. 3" long (BV156)	55	83	110
Wrecker, c.1934, 3-15/16 long (BV081)	30	45	60
Wrecker, die-cast, two-piece, marked "Barclay Toy," No. 403, 1930s, 2-7/8" long (BV082)	55	85	110
Wrecker, No. 46, metal wheels, c.1931, 3-1/2" (BV080)	45	68	90
Wrecker, same as BV081, w/battery powered headlight, only 1 known, (BV081A)	NPF	NPF	NPF

Barclay Steam Shovel (BV181), Mack cab, shovel moves up and down. Photo courtesy Brad Fullhart

Barclay Double Transport Set (BV157), four cars on upper and lower racks. Photo courtesy Stan Alekna

Barclay Curtis Aerocar (BV169), Coupe pulling "Curtis Aerocar" trailer. Photo courtesy Brad Fullhart

Barclay Sedan (BV170), used for BV114 and BV152, 1-1/2". Photo courtesy Doug Ehrenhaft

Barclay Roadster (BV171), used for BV114 and BV152, 1-1/2". Photo courtesy Doug Ehrenhaft

Barclay Sedan (BV172), 1960s, used for car carriers, 1-9/16". Photo courtesy Doug Ehrenhaft

Barclay Coupe (BV173), 1960s, used for car carriers, 1-9/16". Photo courtesy Doug Ehrenhaft

Close-up of the BV175 Gasoline trailer. Photo courtesy Brad Fullhart

Barclay Fuel Tractor Trailer (BV175), Mack trailer pulling "Gasoline" trailer, 4-3/4". Photo courtesy Brad Fullhart

BARR RUBBER

Barr Rubber was located in Sandusky, Ohio. The company produced balloons as well as a fine line of rubber 1935 Fords and other toys. The following list with code numbers in parenthesis, was compiled by Dave Leopard. Vehicles are broken down by type.

Contributor: Dave Leopard, 2507 Feather Run Trail, West Columbia, SC 29169-4915.

	C6	C8	C10
'35 Ford, two-door slantback sedan, 4" long (BA002)	35	50	70
'35 Ford Army Truck, 4-3/4" long (BT003)	45	60	90
'35 Ford Coupe, 4" long (BA001)	35	50	70
'35 Ford Panel Truck/Ambulance, 4-1/4" long (BT002)	35	50	70
'35 Ford Stake Body Truck, 4-3/4" long (BT001)	35	50	70

Left to right: Barr Rubber Ford Army Truck; Ford Stake Body Truck, both 4-3/4". Photo courtesy Dave Leopard's book Rubber Toy Vehicles

Barr Rubber Ford Panel Truck/Ambulance, 4-1/4". Photo courtesy Dave Leopard's book Rubber Toy Vehicles

Left to right: Barr Rubber 1935 Ford Slantback Sedan; 1935 Ford Coupe. Photo courtesy Dave Leopard book Rubber Toy Vehicles

BEAUT MFG. CO.

Beut Mfg. Co., North Bergen, New Jersey, was founded in 1946 by Eugene Buhler and Irving Reader (former machinist and salesman, respectively) for Barclay Mfg. Co. The company put out five toys—a taxi cab, a police car, a fire engine, a sedan, and a child's wagon. Beaut was successful at first, selling to Woolworth's and many overseas buyers. Beaut ceased toymaking activities around 1950 because of competition from plastic toys, although they continued until 1982 as a general machine shop.

	C6	C8	C10
Fire Car, No. 4, approx. 3-3/4"	10	15	20
Police Car, approx. 3-3/4"	10	15	20

	C6	C8	C10
Sedan, approx. 3-3/4"	10	15	20
Sedan Delivery, 3-3/4" long	20	30	40
Taxi, No. 1, approx. 3-3/4"	10	15	20
Wagon, No. 50	NPF	NPF	NPF

Beaut Wagon, No. 50.

Left to right: Beaut Police Car; Beaut Taxi. Photo by Bill Kaufman courtesy of George Buhler

BENBROS

	C6	C8	C10
Coronation Coach, similar to Lesney's coach because Benbros made the horses for Lesney's coach	NPF	NPF	NPF
No. 01 Hay Cart, horsedrawn	10	25	40
No. 02 Log Cart, horsedrawn, red wheels	10	25	40
No. 03 A.A. Motorcycle, w/sidecar and police officer	10	25	40
No. 04 Stagecoach, drawn by 4 horses	NPF	NPF	NPF
No. 05 Gypsy Caravan, horsedrawn	10	25	40
No. 06 Milk Cart and Horse, w/milkman	NPF	NPF	NPF
No. 07 Milk Float, w/milkman, pull cart w/3 wheels	NPF	NPF	NPF
No. 08 Foden Timber Tractor	10	25	40
No. 09 Dennis Fire Engine & Ladder	10	25	40
No. 10 Crawler Bulldozer	NPF	NPF	NPF
No. 11 Tractor and Hay Rake	NPF	NPF	NPF
No. 12 Army Scout Car, w/driver, 2-1/4" long	5	15	30
No. 12 Army Scout Car, w/out driver, 2-1/4" long	5	15	30
No. 13 Austin Champ, Jeep w/driver, 2-1/8" long	10	25	40
No. 14 Centurion Tank	10	25	40
No. 15 Vespa Scooter	NPF	NPF	NPF
No. 16 Express Locomotive	10	25	40
No. 16b 1957 Chevrolet Nomad	10	25	40
No. 18 Hudson Tourer, 2-1/4" long	10	25	40
No. 20 Foden 8-wheel flatbed Lorry	NPF	NPF	NPF

	C6	C8	C10
No. 21 Foden 8-wheel open Lorry	NPF	NPF	NPF
No. 22 ERF Petrol Tanker, 6 wheels, 2-1/8" long	10	25	40
No. 23 A.E.C. Box Lorry	10	25	40
No. 24 Field Gun, Howitzer	10	25	40
No. 25 Spyker, silver w/red wheels	NPF	NPF	NPF
No. 26 1904 S.H.P. Vauxhall	NPF	NPF	NPF
No. 27 Rolls Royce	NPF	NPF	NPF
No. 28 Chain Lorry, 8-wheel, flatbed	NPF	NPF	NPF
No. 29 R.A.C. Motorcycle	NPF	NPF	NPF
No. 30 Army Wagon, box van	NPF	NPF	NPF
No. 31 A.E.C. Lorry	5	15	30
No. 32a Foden Compressor Lorry	NPF	NPF	NPF
No. 33 Breakdown Lorry	NPF	NPF	NPF
No. 35 Army Land Rover, 1950s, 1:64-scale	NPF	NPF	NPF
No. 36 Royal Mail Land Rover	NPF	NPF	NPF
No. 37 Police Car	10	25	40
No. 38 Ambulance	NPF	NPF	NPF
No. 39 Bedford CA Milkfloat	10	25	40
No. 40 1956 Ford Convertible	10	25	40
No. 41 Army Hudson Tourer, 2-1/2" long	5	12	22
No. 42 Army Dispatch, motorcycle w/sidecar and rider	10	25	40
No. 44 Bedford Lowside Lorry	NPF	NPF	NPF
No. 46 Bedford Esso Tanker Truck	NPF	NPF	NPF
No. 49 Karrier Coca-Cola Truck	NPF	NPF	NPF

BEST TOY & NOVELTY FACTORY

Best Toy & Novelty was founded by John M. Best Sr. an entrepreneur and printer. Best had lived in Clifton, Kansas, the home of Kansas Toy & Novelty, so he was well-aware of the ups and downs of small toy companies. According to Dee Buchanan, Best's great-granddaughter, Best and his wife Rosanna purchased a company from Kansas Toy & Novelty Company in Vining, Kansas—a suburb of Clifton. The Bests moved the company to the back of their house in Manhattan, Kansas. Although contradictory, evidence from other family members suggests a Best purchase of the assets of a Clifton toy company occurred about 1933.

It started as a family business for his children, relatives, friends, and neighbors, according to Minnie Nelson, Best's daughter. Conrad Morsch was a molder for Best Toy. Items produced included farm implements, tractors, airplanes, buses, and trains, as well as all types of cars. What began as a family hobby grew into a respectable business, supplying toy distributors and dime stores. After several years of operation, it was sold to Ralstoy, a Ralston, Nebraska company, in 1939.

It is not certain precisely when Best started, or what the first number issued in the Best Toy & Novelty series was. Nor do we know if he introduced any new patterns. (See history of "Kansas Toy" in this book).

Donated by Ms. Buchanan was a faded copy of a Best Toy brochure. This appears to be a pre-publication printer's mockup, and undated; but its forty-two illustrations were helpful in identifying many Best Toy and Kansas Toy items in collections. With no paper trail available, this was indeed a find. Many thanks to all who helped and continue to help.

Distinguishing Best Toy vehicles from other slush-mold toys can be very difficult. Molds were passed from one manufacturer to another. Best Toy products can usually be distinguished from other slush-mold toys because they usually have white rubber wheels and are embossed "Made in USA." However, some of the toys used the metal wheels of the Kansas Toy originals, or the later wood hubs with rubber tires. It is also possible that Best Toy modified or rebuilt molds to create variations.

Best molded a great number of designs. To reduce redundancy in this book, we list them here, but will not describe them in detail, if they are adequately covered in Kansas Toy or Ralstoy lists. The following numbered toys and some unnumbered duplicates were found: 6, 10, 14, 17, 20, 25, 26, 27, 31, 32, 34, 35, 36, 37, 39, 40, 41, 42, 43, 45, 46, 47, 49, 51, 54, 55, 57, 58, 59, 60, 67, 70, 71, 72, 74, 76,

ABBREVIATIONS

The following abbreviations are for the details and variations useful in identification.

HG	horizontal grille pattern	**SM**	sidemounted spare
HL	horizontal hood louvers	**SP**	string-pull knob in hand crank area
HO	hood cap, Motometer or ornament	**T**	external trunk
L	lacquer finish	**UV**	unnumbered version
LI	landau irons on convertibles	**VG**	vertical grille pattern
MDW	metal disc wheels	**VL**	vertical hood louvers
MDSW	metal disc solid spokes	**WS, W/S**	windshield
MDWBT	wheels with black painted tires	**WV**	windshield visor
MSW	metal open spoke wheels	**WHRT**	wooden hubs, rubber tires
MWW	metal simulated wire wheels	**WRDW**	white hard rubber disc wheels
OW	open windows	**WRW**	white soft rubber wheels
RM	rearmount spare tire/wheel		(balloon tires)

77, 78, 79, 80, 81, 85, 86, 87, 90, 91, 92, 93, 94, 95, 97, 99, 100, 101, and 102.

Contributors: Perry R. Eichor, 703 North Almond Drive, Simpsonville, SC, 29681. Captain Eichor has been collecting aircraft toys since he was a young officer in the Air Force, his twenty-one years as an Air Force officer only served to deepen his interest in the subject. Today when he is not collecting, researching or writing about aeronautical toys, he works as a criminal justice administrator as well as an appraiser and auctioneer. Original list compiled by Perry Eichor and the late Fred Maxwell.

	C6	C8	C10
Cab Unit, No. "101," International? sleeper cab, slanted grille, HO, two OW, rare; 3-1/4" long (BEV015)	40	60	80
Coupe, No. "92," Dodge?, chopped top, Brewster-like heart shaped grille, HO, long streamlined front fenders; 3-3/4" long (BEV006)	20	35	45
Coupe, No. "93," Cadillac?, streamlined, hood similar to No. 91, grid pattern grille, two OW; 3-5/8" long (BEV007)	20	40	60
Coupe, No. "96," apparently same car as No. 93; it is not known if both were produced; 3-1/2" long (BEV010)	20	45	50
Coupe, No. "98" (BEV012)	15	30	40
Coupe, No. "99," Pontiac?, streamlined, HO, rearmount; 4" long (BEV013)	25	55	85

	C6	C8	C10
Farm Toy Set, all toys from molds belived to have originated at Kansas Toy	NPF	NPF	NPF
Oil Transport, No. "102," streamlined "Gasoline" semi-trailer to No. 101, four tanks, four storage compartments; Total length of cab-trailer - 6-3/4" (BEV016)	50	75	100
Racer, No. "76," square fin on rear	20	30	40
Racer, No. "85," record car w/large square fin, driver, HO, VG, twelve exhaust ports, WHRT, 4" long (BEV001)	30	45	70
Racer, large, No. "97," Bluebird record car, driver, large fin, twelve exhaust ports, hard-rubber wheels, faired; 4-1/2" long (BEV011)	40	75	125
Sedan, No. "100," Pontiac, streamlined, two door, HO, HG, four OW, trunk, 4" long (BEV014)	20	30	40
Sedan, No. "86," Lincoln? two-door fastback, slanted grille w/grid pattern, HL, divided w/s, rear wheel skirts, 4" long (BEV002)	20	30	50
Sedan, No. "87," Brewster? (BEV003)	20	30	45
Sedan, No. "90," two door, airflow, hood reaches front bumper w/no grille, four OW, hard rubber wheels, 3-1/2" long (BEV004)	25	40	70

Best Cab, No. 101, (BEV015), with a Best Oil Transport, No. 102, (BEV016). Photo courtesy Perry Eichor

	C6	C8	C10
Sedan, No. "91," Cadillac? two door airflow, high style vee grille, faired front fenders, 3-1/2" long (BEV005) ..	25	40	70
Sedan, No. "95," two-door, airflow similar to No. 94, w/three headlamps, four OW, trunk, hard-rubber wheels; Chrysler-Briggs show car?; 3-1/2" long (BEV009a)	30	45	75

	C6	C8	C10
Sedan, No. "95," two-door, airflow similar to No. 94, w/three headlamps, four OW, trunk, hard-rubber wheels; w/"Police Dept." shield on doors; centered headlamp may be a siren, one version has "Police" painted on roof; 3-1/2" long (BEV009b)	35	45	60
Sedan, large, No. "94," two door, airflow, similar to No. 90, four OW, taxi lamp on roof; 4-1/2" long (BEV008)	35	45	70

*Best Record
Race Car
No. 76,
Racer No. 85.
Photo courtesy
Perry Eichor*

*Top row from left: Best
Coupe; Best Large
Sedan, two-door
airflow. Bottom row
from left: Best Sedan,
three headlamps, hard
rubber wheels; Best
Sedan, Police Dept.
shield on doors. Photo
courtesy Fred Maxwell*

*Top row, left to
right: Best Sedan,
No. 95; Best Coupe,
No. 93; Best Sedan,
No. 90. Middle row,
left to right: Best
Record Race Car,
No. 85; Best Large
Sedan, No. 94.
Bottom row, left to
right: Best Large
Racer, No. 97; Best
Pontiac Sedan, No.
100. Photo courtesy
Fred Maxwell*

Top row, left to right: Best Coupe; Best Pontiac Sedan, two-door. Middle row, left to right: Best Coupe and Sedan reproduction. Bottom row: Best Sedan reproduction. Photo courtesy Perry Eichor.

Box from a Best Farm Toy Set. All of the toys illustrated are from molds believed to have originated with Kansas Toys. Photo by Perry Eichor courtesy of Fred Maxwell

BICO

	C6	C8	C10
Bico Bus to Joyville, open double-decker, passengers, driver........	2000	3500	5000

BIG BANG

	C6	C8	C10		C6	C8	C10
Army Tank, No. 5T, 8-1/8" long..............	35	50	100	Motor Tank, No. 5T, c.1933, 9-1/2" long	100	200	350

BIG BOY

See Kelmet

BING TOY WORKS

Bing Toy Works was founded by Ignatius and Adolf Bing in 1866 and started producing tin toys in the 1880s. By 1914, it employed more than 5,000 people. Business flourished through the 1920s until the Great Depression. In 1932, after falling to hard times, the company went into receivership. One year later, it ceased production of tin toys entirely. Karl Bub, another German toy manufacturer, took over the company soon after.

Bing trademarks include, "GBN" (Gebrüder Bing Nürnberg) and "BW" (Bing Werkel).

Bing automobiles are difficult to find and are held in high regard by most collectors. The Model T series came in solid black, red, yellow, green, and blue lithograph; the color-lithographed versions are difficult to find.

Contributor: Bob Smith, RATS Toy Shows, 255 Tryon Park, Rochester, NY 14609. (585) 288-7153, bird@oldtoysonline.com.

	C6	C8	C10
Dog Cart, Live Steam, leather seats, 10" long..	3050	6050	9150
Double-Decker Bus, 10" long	700	1250	1950
Fire Ladder Truck, clockwork motor, composition figures, 13" long..............	2050	3550	5250
Fire Pumper, clockwork motor, composition figures, 11" long..............	1850	3250	4650
Garage, tin lithographed, clockwork motor, w/two open cars, c.1925, car length 5-1/2", garage 8" x 6-1/2"	500	800	1050
Garage, Raceabout and Limousine, tin lithographed, clockwork motor; cars 5-1/2" long, garage 8" x 6-1/2", c.1912	500	750	1050
Limousine, blue and black lithographed, clockwork motor, c.1915, 9-1/2" long .	950	1300	1950
Limousine, clockwork motor, maroon and yellow striping, driver, c.1908, 14" long...	1050	2050	4850
Limousine, w/wind-up, driver, 15-1/4" long	750	1150	1850

Bing Garage with two open cars, 1920s. Photo courtesy Bob Smith

Bing Garage, Raceabout and Limousine, autos 5-1/2", garage 8". Photo courtesy Bob Smith

Bing Limousine, circa 1908, maroon with yellow stripes, 14" long. Photo courtesy Bertoia Auctions

Bing Limousine, 9-1/2", issued around 1915. Photo courtesy Bob Smith

Bing Model T Ford Coupe, red, 6-1/2", 1920s. Photo courtesy Bob Smith

A sampling of 1920s Bing Model T Fords—each measures 6-1/2". Photo courtesy Bob Smith

Bing Model T Ford Roadster, 6-1/2", 1920s, red, black, and yellow tin. Photo courtesy Bob Smith

Bing Model T Ford Sedan, blue, 6-1/2", 1920s. Photo courtesy Bob Smith

*A pair of Bing Model T Fords with their original boxes.
Photo courtesy Len Rosenberg*

*Bing Touring Car, Type-I, spoked wheels, male driver,
6", 1920. Photo courtesy Bob Smith*

*Bing Yellow Taxi, 9", c.1924, orange and black. Photo
courtesy Bob Smith*

*Bing Touring Car, Type-II, with female driver, red and
black, 6", 1920s. Photo courtesy Bob Smith*

	C6	C8	C10
Model T Doctor's Coupe, clockwork motor, black, 6-1/2" long	350	475	725
Model T Ford Coupe, clockwork motor, red, black and cream tin lithographed, c.1924, 6-1/2" long	550	800	1350
Model T Ford Roadster, clockwork moto, red, black and yellow tin lithographed, c.1924, 6-1/2" long	650	950	1450
Model T Ford Sedan, clockwork motor, blue, black and cream tin lithographed, c.1924, 6-1/2" long	500	700	1250
Model T Ford Touring Car, clockwork motor, color tin lithographed, c.1924, 6-1/2" long	500	700	1250
Model T Fords, sedan, roadster, touring, and coupe, painted black, c.1923, 6-1/2" long, each	400	500	725
Touring Car, type-I spoked wheels, clockwork motor, red and black, male driver, c.1920, 6" long	300	450	750
Touring Car, type-II, solid wheels, clockwork motor, red and black, female driver, c.1923, 6" long	300	450	750
Touring Car, wind-up, 13" long	650	1150	1800

*Bing Vis a Vis, steam, 10", issued around 1902. Photo
courtesy Bertoia Auctions*

	C6	C8	C10
Two Seater, open, 9-1/2" long	1050	1750	2650
Vis a Vis, steam, driver, c.1902, 10" long	3050	6050	9150
Yellow Taxi, clockwork motor, orange and black lithographed, c.1924, 9" long	850	1550	2350

BONNIE BILT

This Lawrence, Long Island, New York company specialized in plastic toys, producing a variety of construction kits, western play sets, toy soldiers, and did produce a few vehicles as well.

	C6	C8	C10
Armored Car, U.S. Army	11	16	22
Covered Wagon, plastic, horses gallop, 1950s	10	25	50
Tank, plastic	6	9	12
Tank, plastic	6	9	12

BOYCRAFT

Boycraft was the brand name used by Steelcraft for the toys it supplied to Sears-Roebuck in the late 1920s and early 1930s.

	C6	C8	C10
Mack Dump Truck, 22" long	375	563	750
Steam Roller, 16" long	NPF	NPF	NP

Boycraft Mack Dump Truck, 1920s, 22". Photo courtesy Bertoia Auctions

Boycraft Steam Roller, 16". Photo courtesy Joe and Sharon Freed

BRESLIN

Breslin Industries of Toronto made a number of lead-alloy toys, most or all of them copies, particularly of Barclay and Manoil. They can be easily distinguished from the originals because they usually read "Canada" or "Made in Canada."

	C6	C8	C10
Motorized Machine Gunner	30	40	50
Tank	30	40	50
Truck pulling Cannon	30	40	50

Left to right: The Breslin Tank and Motorized Machine Gunner.

Breslin Truck Pulling Cannon.

BRIMTOY (ENGLAND)

Brimtoy (England) made fine toys in tin from 1914-32, when the company merged with Wells to become Wells-Brimtoy Limited.

	C6	C8	C10
Circus Lorry, red plastic cab w/clockwork motor, tin lorry w/circus animal litho, "Brimtoy Circus" on sides, 6" long	10	20	35
Double Decker Bus, tin litho, clockwork motor, "Wells-Brimtoy Distributors Ltd." litho on side, 4-1/4" long	25	50	75
Limousine, 1919, 11" long	300	450	600
Television Lorry, red plastic cab, tin litho lorry says "Television Engineers BBC ITA" on one side and "TV Engineers made in Gt. Britain" on the other, friction drive, 3-1/2" long	15	30	45

Brimtoy Limousine, 1919, black, 11". Photo courtesy Bertoia Auctions

BRINKS

	C6	C8	C10		C6	C8	C10
Armored Car, 9" long	250	375	575	Truck Bank, aluminum, 8" long	40	60	80

BRIO

Basket-maker Ivar Bengtsson founded his workshop in 1884 in a small village outside Osby, Sweden. In 1902, Ivar moved his growing family and growing company to Osby to take advantage of the rail route that made distribution of his products easier. Toys were added to the growing catalog in 1907 with the popular Göinge horse that would stay in production until 1960.

Ivar's three sons, Viktor. Anton, and Emil, joined the company and it was renamed BRIO (Brothers Ivarsson Osby). Under their leadership, the company expanded rapidly. The 1909 catalog contained 999 products and by 1912, it held 2,700 items. As his sons ran the company, Ivar concentrated on new constructions and renovations to BRIO's buildings until his 1948 death.

BRIO developed into an international corporation under the leadership of Anton's son Lennart, who served as chief executive from 1952-70. Today, Lennart's sons, Dag and Bengt Ivarsson, retain the majority ownership of BRIO.

Brio ladder truck, red, yellow and black, red wheels, Brio stenciling on door. Photo courtesy Perry Elchor

Brio Pickup truck. Photo courtesy Perry Eichor

	C6	C8	C10
Ladder Truck, red, yellow and black, red wheels, Brio stenciling on door	NPF	NPF	NPF
Pickup Truck, wooden truck, pre-WWII	50	85	NPF

BRITAINS

William Britain, a gifted toymaker, founded his company in the late 1840s in North East London. Seeking a competitive advantage over the mechanical imports from Germany, William and his sons turned to toy soldiers in the 1890s. Eldest son, William Britain Jr. (1860-1933), invented the hollow casting process for lead soldier manufacture.

Britains toy soldiers were manufactured to the scale of toy trains, resulting in the 54mm standard size by which soldiers are still produced today. Britains made several changes to its products and packaging before the turn of the century, and continued refining their toys with the issue of the large display boxes in 1906.

World War I saw the factory convert from toy production to wartime materials, but the export of toys continued. At that time, Fred Whisstock designed box labels in a single, familiar style. The Home Farm range was introduced following the war, bending to public anti-war sentiment. The expansion of operations through the 1920s positioned the company to survive the Depression years by diversifying the toy lines to include motor vehicles, zoo, circus, and garden themes.

After offering its largest toy line ever in 1940, the factory was once again plunged into wartime production. By 1953, Britains had returned to normal production and faced considerable competition from plastic toys. Britains bought leading plastic toy manufacturer, Herald, in 1959 and had a well-established foothold in the marketplace. Hollow-casting ceased in 1966.

The company thrived over the next four decades with its diverse line of vehicles and plastic farm animals. Die-cast metal soldiers were re-introduced

Britains Farm, Lorry with driver, four-wheel.

in the 1990s to an enthusiastic public. The company was sold to Ertl in 1997 and remains under Ertl leadership today.

(Except where noted, photos by K. Warren Mitchell)

	C6	C8	C10
Armored Car (BR0027d)	NPF	NPF	NPF
Armoured Car (BR1321)	150	325	400
Army Ambulance, wounded man and stretcher, all doors open, 6" long (BR1512)	150	210	275
Army Staff Car, officer and driver, fifth version: black plastic tires; 1958-59 (RB1448d)	125	225	300
Army Staff Car, officer and driver, first version: smooth white tires, black fenders (BR1448)	175	310	385
Army Staff Car, officer and driver, fourth version: lead tires, painted gray, split windshield; 1951-57 (RB1448c)	150	285	350
Army Staff Car, officer and driver, second version: white tires, all khaki body (RB1448a)	165	300	375
Army Staff Car, officer and driver, third version: rectangular windshield, rubber tires; 1948-50 (RB1448b)	145	265	325
Army Tender, covered, caterpillar type (BR1433)	95	150	200

	C6	C8	C10
Army Tender, covered, ten-wheel (BR1432)	125	200	325
Bren Gun Carrier (BR0876)	35	65	85
Covered Lorry, R.A. Gun, drivers (BR10462)	150	350	450
Dispatch Rider (BR0200)	20	30	54
Lorry, Army, Caterpillar type (BR1333)	125	200	300
Lorry, Army, w/driver (BR1335)	115	165	230
Lorry, Army, four-wheeled type (BR1334)	105	130	210
Motorcycle Machine Gun (BR0199)	40	75	110
Police Car, w/two officers (BR1413)	350	600	900
Speed Record Car, The Blubird (BR1400)	135	270	370
Tank, Carden Loyd Type (BR1203)	110	155	230
Triumph Speedtwin Motorcycle, cast w/opaque headlight, 650cc	15	30	50

Farm

	C6	C8	C10
Acrobat Rake (BR0176F)	30	60	94
BP Gas Pump (BR0750)	10	17	22
Cultivator (BR0175F)	8	15	26
Fordson Major Tractor, driver, rubber tires (BR0128F)	60	80	150

Britains Centurion Tank.

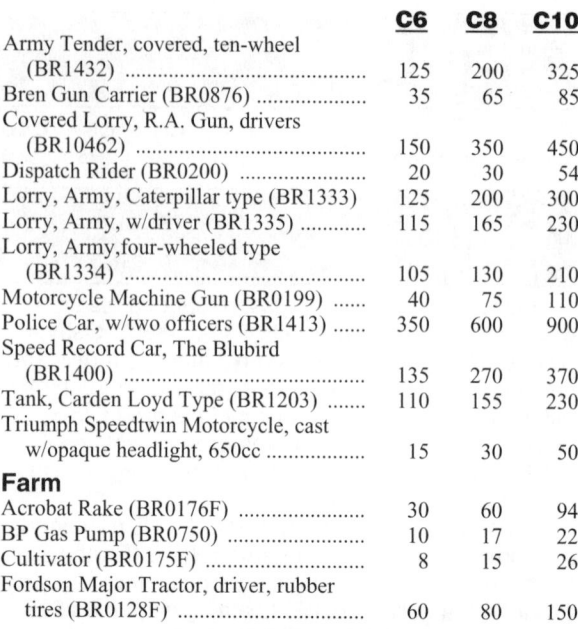

Britains Farm, Tractors, and Implements.

Prewar Britains vehicles include, back row from left: Armored Car; Motorcycle Machine Gun; Dispatch Rider; Armored Car; Tank (Carden Loyd type). Front row from left: Lorry, Army, six-wheeled type; Army Staff Car, officer and driver; Covered Lorry, R.A. Gun, drivers; Army Ambulance, wounded man and stretcher, 6".

Britains Complete Mobile Howitzer Unit.

	C6	C8	C10
Fordson Power Major Tractor, no driver (BR0172F)	50	75	100
Fordson Tractor, metal wheels, driver (BR0127F)	75	125	200
Lorry w/driver, four-wheel (BR0059F) ..	10	17	22
Motorcycle w/sidecar (BR0641)	500	700	1250
Muledozer (BR0174F)	NPF	NPF	NPF
Power Pump (BR07051)	10	17	22
Shell Gas Pump (BR0748)	11	19	25
Shellmax Gas Pump (BR0749)	10	17	22
Three Furrow Plough (BR0173F)	7	11	16
Timber Trailer, w/real log (BR0129F)	25	50	75
Tractors and implements (BR0134F)	200	350	500

Lilliput

	C6	C8	C10
Army Ambulance, measures 3" long (LV/618)	NPF	NPF	NPF
Army Covered Three-ton Truck, removable plastic top (LV/607)	25	38	50
Army Truck, 1-1/2 ton, w/spare wheel (LV/612)	NPF	NPF	NPF
Articulated Lorry (LV/603)	20	30	40
Articulated Truck w/Spare Wheel (LV/614)	NPF	NPF	NPF
Austin Champ, removable hood (LV/609)	NPF	NPF	NPF
Bedford 3-Ton Open Truck, red cab, blue bed (Lv/320)	10	22	40

Postwar Britains vehicles include, back row from left: Bren Gun Carrier; Army Lorry, four-wheeled type towing Mobile Unit; Army Lorry, six-wheeled type; Army Staff Car; Covered Army Tender towing Mobile Searchlight. Front row from left: Army Ambulance; Beetle Lorry towing 4-1/2" Howitzer and Regulation Timber; Dispatch Rider; Austin Champ towing Battalion Anti-Tank Gun.

	C6	C8	C10
Boxed Set, w/accessories and Carter as listed in the 1951 Catalog Supplement, includes: one LV/602, one LV/602; one LV/603; one LV/604; w/driver, one LV/605, w/Milkman, one LV/606 (LV/SA)	65	125	200
Centurion Tank (LV/610)	25	38	50
Covered Army Truck, 1-1/2 Ton, w/spare wheel (LV/613).....................	NPF	NPF	NPF
Farm Lorry, three ton (LV/608)	NPF	NPF	NPF
Farm or Civilian Truck, 1-1/2 ton, w/spare wheel, measures 2-13/16" long (LV/616)	NPF	NPF	NPF
Fordson Tractor with Driver (LV/604) ...	20	30	40
Lilliput Display Box, contains Saloon Car, tractor, tumbrel cart and milk float, farmer, farmer's wife, stable lad, farm girl and dog, horses, cows and calf, sheep and lamb, pig, geese, hurdles and tree, twenty-eight pieces (L7)	75	150	250
Lilliput Railway Personnel and Vehicles, includes: saloon car, lorry, sports car, articulated lorries, Austin "Champ," motorcyclists, station trollies, packing cases, barrels, hampers, porters w/trollies, guards, station master, porters w/luggage, newsvendor, general public asst., forty-three pieces (L11)	NPF	NPF	NPF
Local Authority Ambulance, cream, measures 3" long (LV/617)	8	15	22
Open Army Truck, three ton, w/spare wheel, measures 3-1/4" long (LV/620)	NPF	NPF	NPF
Open Sports Car (LV/601)	20	30	40
Post Office Royal Mail Van, measures 3" long (LV/619)	NPF	NPF	NPF
Saloon Car (LV/602)	20	30	40
Saracen Armoured Personnel Carrier (LV/615)	NPF	NPF	NPF
Sexton Self-Propelled Gun (LV/611)	27	41	55

Postwar

	C6	C8	C10
155mm Gun mounted on Centurion Tank body (BR2175 (also 9748))	200	350	500
Austin Champ (BR2102)	30	50	65
Balloon Barrage Unit, (lorry, winch, balloon) (BR1757)	700	1000	1600
Batallion Anti-Tank Gun (BR2173 (also 9720))	10	14	18
Beetle Lorry and driver (BR1877b)	50	85	125
Bren Gun Carrier, w/full crew (BR1876a)	30	55	75
Centurion Tank (BR2150 (also 9770)) ...	150	275	375

Britains Heavy Duty Lorry, underslung, with driver.

Britains Lorry, Army, four-wheeled type.

	C6	C8	C10
Centurion Tank, painted for Desert Warfare (BR2154)	250	450	600
Complete Mobile Howitzer Unit, 4 pcs., w/limber and caterpillar trailer (BR1727)	300	550	750
Corporation Motor Ambulance, driver, wounded and stretcher (BR1514)	350	600	850
Dispatch Rider, gray, #1791, 2-3/4" long, 1949, 1949, 1791 (BR1791)	30	48	65
Heavy Duty Lorry, underslung, w/driver (BR1643)	600	900	1200
Heavy-Duty Lorry, driver, searchlight, battery and lamp (BR1642)	300	500	700
Howitzer, 4-1/2" long (BR1725)	13	20	30
John Cobb's Railton Wonder Car (BR1656)	200	350	500
John Cobb's Railton Wonder Car, chromium-plated boyd, 10" long (BR1658)	125	200	325

	C6	C8	C10
Light Goods Van, w/driver (BR2024)	250	450	600
Lorry and Trailer, w/hydrogen cylinders (BR1879)	115	165	210
Lorry, ten wheel, w/searchlight on chassis (BR1833)	200	450	675
Lorry, ten wheel, w/two pdr., AA gun on chassis (BR1832)	350	700	1000
Miniature Balloon Barrage Unit, w/lorry, winch and balloon (BR1855)	125	250	350
Mobile Searchlight (BR1718)	30	50	70
Mobile Unit, two-pounder (BR1717)	30	50	70
Motor Ambulance, w/doctor, wounded, nurses, orderlies, eighteen pcs. (BR1897)	175	325	450
Regulation Limber (BR1726)	15	22	27
Underslung Heavy-Duty Lorry (BR1641)	200	350	550

Prewar

	C6	C8	C10
Beetle Lorry and Driver (BR1877)	60	95	135
Bren Gun Carrier, w/full crew (BR1876)	35	65	85

BROOKLIN

The love of cars, both prototype and model, are the reasons John and Jenny Hall created Brooklin Models, Ltd. The firm makes 1:43-scale replicas of white-metal model cars, and many collectors consider Brooklin models to be the standard of the industry—very similar to the "standard of the world" description for Lionel toy trains or Britains toy soldiers. The Brooklin Collection includes some of the greatest and most controversial American motorcars made by U.S. manufacturers in the past six decades.

John Hall began humbly in the basement of his Canadian home in the early 1970s, making windowless resin models by hand, and using wood-burnt Popsicle sticks with the familiar early Brooklin Models logo to keep the resin casting from warping. He named Brooklin Models after Brooklin, a suburb of Ontario, Canada.

While in its infancy, the Brooklin company developed great improvements in technology and process. Therefore, the early Canadian models reflect many changes as Hall experimented with alternative methods of casting materials and color variations in an attempt to perfect his models.

Early in 1974, Hall left his teaching position at Durham College and devoted his full attention to model-making and designing equipment to create finished scale-model cars. Hall continued to dabble in

model-making and scratch-building models for himself and other collectors.

He helped form the Canadian Toy Collector's Society (CTCS) with Ron Faithful and Tony Topley. Through the CTCS, Hall met many collectors from Canada and Buffalo, where he went to his first toy show called "Motoring in Miniatures." At the show, collectors persuaded him to make a Pierce Arrow. Thinking this was a good idea, Hall made two master models out of resin. He then cast eighty-six models at the laborious rate of ten models per week. The hand-painted Pierce Arrow with resin base became car No. 1. The Pierce Arrow was retired in 1993.

In 1975, Hall felt he could raise money at the Canadian Plowing Match held in Toronto, by selling a model of a plow commemorating the event. Two thousand were produced, but only 200 were sold. To say the least, it was not a financial success and the remaining models were melted down. Today, it is a rare and sought-after piece, as many Brooklin collectors have never seen one. (There is one pictured in the hardcover Brooklin Collection Book.)

Initially, Hall did everything to create a Brooklin Model. He carved the master, made the mold, cast the piece, and assembled the models. Two employees helped assemble and paint. As business improved, more people were hired. Today, the business supports twenty-five or more employees, including Jenny Hall, who runs the business office, and John, who oversees the entire operation.

In October of 1979, John and Jenny decided to move back to the United Kingdom and settled in Bath, England. This ceased all future production of Brooklin Models stamped "Made in Canada." The first factory was located in the Huggett Electrical building in Bath. Many of Brooklin's No. 16 Dodger models carry the Huggett logo. American cars are quite popular in Europe, so new markets soon opened up and orders began to pour in.

At the new Brooklin factory in Bath, Brooklin manufacturers more than 50,000 models a year. Since 1988, the models were marketed in a new box, which includes the Statue of Liberty, the New York City skyline and an Edsel with an American flag banner. Gone are the old tan and brown logo boxes. These have been resurrected as of late for promotional issues, lending a nostalgic touch for the collector.

Prices are for items Mint in Box.

Contributor: Vincent Rosa, 28 Arthur Ave., Blue Point, NY 11715, (516) 363-2134. Rosa grew up in Brooklyn, New York, and moved to Long Island, where he attended Adelphi-Suffolk-Dowling College. Rosa holds a master's degree in history from Stony Brook University. His hobbies include collection Lionel trains, toy soldiers of the British Victorian period, and Slingerland Radio-King Drums. Rosa and his wife, Bonnie, operate Model Cars and Trains Unlimited of Blue Point, New York, a firm specializing in the sale of collectible trains, die-cast model cars, and toy soldiers of all types and varieties. In the past, Rosa has contributed to *Greenberg's Guide to Lionel*

H.O. In addition to his books on Brooklin models, Rosa had his short story, "The Man with the Shopping Cart," published in the December 1994 issue of *O-Gauge Railroading*. He has published his own copyrighted work, The Brooklin Collection (1989) and the Official Brooklin Models Collector Guide (1989). Source for Brooklin Models chapter: Rosa, Vincent. 1974-1989 The Brooklin Collection, 1989, 80 pgs. Hardcover with color photos. $49.95 postpaid, comes with free collector's guide. Send to: Model Cars & Trains, Ultd., 28 Arthur Ave., Blue Point, NY 11715, (516) 363-2134.

Canadian Issues	C6	C8	C10
No. 01 1933 Pierce Arrow, blue/gray, (D-1-2-3), approx. thirty made, second issue	n/a	n/a	NPF
No. 01 1933 Pierce Arrow, blue/ gray, (D-5-3), all resin, first issue	n/a	n/a	NPF
No. 01 1933 Pierce Arrow, brown/ cream, (D-1-2-3), approx. thirty made, second issue	n/a	n/a	NPF
No. 01 1933 Pierce Arrow, brown/ cream, (D-5-3), all resin, first issue	n/a	n/a	NPF
No. 01 1933 Pierce Arrow, champagne, (R), maroon interior, third issue	n/a	n/a	350
No. 01 1933 Pierce Arrow, champagne, red interior, third issue	n/a	n/a	350
No. 01 1933 Pierce Arrow, green/gray, (D-1-2-3), approx. thirty made, second issue	n/a	n/a	NPF
No. 01 1933 Pierce Arrow, maroon/gray, (D-1-2-3), approx. thirty made, second issue	n/a	n/a	NPF
No. 01 1933 Pierce Arrow, medium blue, (M), third issue	n/a	n/a	350

BROOKLIN CODES

• **Code I:** All pieces built, assembled, and decaled from the Brooklin factory in England. Also, those pieces produced in the factory, but partially assembled/partially or totally decaled outside, with total knowledge and approval of John Hall. These are considered 100-percent authentic Brooklin. For example, some CTCS, CPCTS, and promotionals such as Mobil and City of Toronto, Bay State Lobster, Model Auto Review, Coca-Cola, et. al.

• **Code II:** Altered or modified Brooklin models outside the factory, done with full approval of the company. At present, there are only a few such models that fall into this category. The first is the series of convertibles produced by the Model Car Shop. Its first car was the Burgundy 1953 Skylark with wire wheels. The only other Code II piece presently is the plated (silver color) Edsel done by Danhausen.

• **Code III:** Altered or modified Brooklin models outside the factory done without the approval of the company. There are many beautiful models in this category that can enhance your collection, but cannot be considered true Brooklin pieces. The excel-

lent convertibles done by Jerry Rettig, the Orange County Fire Dept. Dodge pick-up done by TFC, and the Yellow Corvette with wire wheels done by the Model Car Shop are some examples.

• **Prototypes:** These are pieces that may have been cast differently or paint-tested in color variation and were never intended for sale. These do not fall into any category above. There are many such models and the collector need not feel that his/her collection is incomplete without them. If, however, these pieces were put up for sale by the company or by an individual with permission of the company, then they would be Code 1, such as the turquoise Mercury, and the eleven Tucker samples given to the Tucker Club (so it could choose three promotional colors).

Discontinued Color/Style

Only 1,253 Shelby American G.T. 500 Fast-backs were built in 1968, making it one of the rarest cars in its class. It was the undisputed King of the 1960s muscle cars.

Numbers 1, 16a, 17, 26a, and 31 were discontinued from the Brooklin Collection during 1992.

KEY

Abbreviations can be found in parenthesis in the item's description.

1	Resin baseplate	**12**	Rim limited sides	**CTCS**	Canadian Toy Collectors Society
2	No plastic windows	**13**	No Window; van style	**D**	Discontinued body style
3	Rare (not plentiful, hard to find, in demand)	**14**	Large scale	**L**	Means No. 14 in Tucker Canadian Issue
4	Detailed chassis	**15**	Last 250 made came with certificate		
5	One of a kind	**16**	Gold trim	**M**	Metallic
6	First casting	**App.**	Approximately	**P**	Promotional; Limited run PROTO Prototype
7	No gas cap	**BBC**	British Brooklin Club		
8	With gas cap	**C**	Discontinued color	**R**	Regular Issue
9	Numbered on baseplate	**CPCTS**	Canadian Pacific Coast Toy Show	**SFBBC**	San Francisco Bay Brooklin Club
10	Smooth side	**CTCI**	Classic Thunderbird Collectors International		
11	Small decals				

	C6	C8	C10
No. 01 1933 Pierce Arrow, silver gray, (D-M-1-2-3), third issue	n/a	n/a	350
No. 01 1933 Pierce Arrow, silver gray, (M), third issue	n/a	n/a	350
No. 01 1933 Pierce Arrow, white, (D-1-2-5-3)	n/a	n/a	NPF
No. 02 1949 Tucker, black, (D-2-3-6-L), beige interior	n/a	n/a	200
No. 02 1949 Tucker, black, (D-2-3-6-L), light gray interior	n/a	n/a	200
No. 02 1949 Tucker, dark blue, (D-2-6-2-L), gray interior	n/a	n/a	200
No. 02 1949 Tucker, dark blue, (D-R-M), gray interior	n/a	n/a	200
No. 02 1949 Tucker, maroon, (D-3), fourteen made	n/a	n/a	NPF
No. 02 1949 Tucker, medium blue, (2-6-2-L), gray interior	n/a	n/a	200
No. 02 1949 Tucker, medium blue, (D-M)	n/a	n/a	200
No. 02 1949 Tucker, very dark blue, (D-2-6-2-L), gray interior	n/a	n/a	200
No. 03 1930 Ford Victoria Two-door, beige/olive, (D-4), tan interior, white wheels	n/a	n/a	90

	C6	C8	C10
No. 03 1930 Ford Victoria Two-door, white top beige body, (D-M-2), tan interior, cream wheels	n/a	n/a	275
No. 03 1930 Ford Victoria Two-door, white/medium brown, (D-4), gray interior, white/wheels	n/a	n/a	105
No. 03 1930 Ford Victoria Two-door, white/olive, (D-2), gray interior, white wheels	n/a	n/a	250
No. 03 1930 Ford Victoria Two-door, white/olive, (D-4), tan interior, white wheels	n/a	n/a	250
No. 04 1937 Chevy Coupe, black, (D-4-3), approx. eighteen made	n/a	n/a	NPF
No. 04 1937 Chevy Coupe, buff green, (D-R)	n/a	n/a	325
No. 04 1937 Chevy Coupe, dark green, (D)	n/a	n/a	325
No. 04 1937 Chevy Coupe, dark green, (D-4)	n/a	n/a	325
No. 04 1937 Chevy Coupe, medium green, (D)	n/a	n/a	325
No. 05 1930 Model A Two-door Coupe, black top/brown body, (D), Tudor body, orange wheels	n/a	n/a	525

The most variations and collectible items since 1989 have appeared on the No. 31 Pontiac Van. Since Brooklin models has changed its policy on the number of promotionals produced, a pattern for value has yet to be determined. Values tend to be regional and varied. The average production for promotional tends to be 750 models. The higher the production runs, the lower the after-market prices tend to be.

Lower prices attract more collectors since they have a chance to own at least one or more promotional items.

CHANGES FOR 1992

No. 17A—952 Studebaker convertible replaced No. 17 Studebaker Champion Coupe.
No. 20—1953 Buick Skylark available in red (only as of October 1991
No. 22A—Reworked Edsel; improved casting replaced No. 22A Edsel Citation

No. 31B—1953 Pontiac Sedan Delivery "gulf Oil" replaced by another Gas Co. livery, Mobilgas, and then Sunoco making for an attractive oil company series. Set ongoing, yearly promotionals for the collector and service station enthusiast.

QUICK GENERAL TIPS FOR THE COLLECTOR

Type	Expect To Pay
1st Production (Canada)	$100+
Farley (UK)	$75+
Current Production	$70+
Current Production Specials	$900+
Rare, Limited Edition	
Less than 50 pcs.	$350-$550
Less than 10 units	$1,000+

Prices for rare models and promotionals tend to be higher in England and France. Prices have been rising in the United States where prices for new models vary from $69 to $85.

	C6	C8	C10
No. 05 1930 Model A Two-door Coupe, black top/brown body, (D-4), Tudor body, white wheels	n/a	n/a	500
No. 05 1930 Model A Two-door Coupe, black/black, (D-3), Tudor body, white wheels	n/a	n/a	500
No. 06 1932 Packard, dark beige top maroon body, gray interior	n/a	n/a	NPF
No. 06 1932 Packard, dark gray/maroon .	n/a	n/a	325
No. 06 1932 Packard, light beige/maroon, gray interior	n/a	n/a	NPF
No. 06 1932 Packard, light gray/light gray, blue gray fenders	n/a	n/a	NPF
No. 06 1932 Packard, light gray/metallic gray, maroon fenders, gray interior	n/a	n/a	325
No. 06 1932 Packard, medium gray/medium gray, medium blue fenders	n/a	n/a	NPF
No. 06 1932 Packard, white/maroon, gray interior	n/a	n/a	NPF
No. 07 1934 Chrysler Airflow, cream (off white), (R)	n/a	n/a	190
No. 08 1940 Chrysler Newport Four-door, light green, (M-R), light brown interior	n/a	n/a	175
No. 08 1940 Chrysler Newport Four-door, medium green, (M-R), light brown interior	n/a	n/a	200
No. 08A 1941 Chrysler Newport Pace Car, white, Dearborn Nat. Car Convention, (3), red interior, 200 made	n/a	n/a	475
No. 09 1940 Ford Van, dark blue, (P-12-3), Marque, fifty made	n/a	n/a	600
No. 09 1940 Ford Van, dark blue, (P-12-3, CTCS '79), sixty made	n/a	n/a	800
No. 09 1940 Ford Van, tan, (P-3), Toledo Toy Show, 213 made	n/a	n/a	500

English Issues

	C6	C8	C10
Bk 02 Bx 1948 Tucker, light blue T.A.C.A. second issue, (P), Tucker Club	n/a	n/a	150
BK 15-1 1949 Mercury Pace Car, limited edition	n/a	n/a	99
BK 22-1 1958 Edsel Citation Brooklin No. 22 Video w/Edsel Onvertible, complete set	n/a	n/a	150

The standard version of Brooklin's 1953 Kaiser Manhattan. Photo courtesy Dennis Doty

	C6	C8	C10
BK 25 1948 Tucker, (P), metallic green, Tucker Club	n/a	n/a	350
No. 01 1933 Pierce Arrow, champagne, (M), 100 made	n/a	n/a	350
No. 01 1933 Pierce Arrow, dark blue, (M), gray interior	n/a	n/a	NPF
No. 01 1933 Pierce Arrow, dark silver,(M), gray interior	n/a	n/a	350
No. 01 1933 Pierce Arrow, Light blue, (R-M), gray interior	n/a	n/a	65
No. 01 1933 Pierce Arrow, light silver, (M), gray interior	n/a	n/a	350
No. 01 1933 Pierce Arrow, medium blue, (M), gray interior	n/a	n/a	NPF
No. 01 1933 Pierce Arrow, silver, (M-P), Harrah's, blue interior	n/a	n/a	200
No. 02 1948 Tucker, dark maroon, (D-R-M-8)	n/a	n/a	NPF
No. 02 1948 Tucker, light maroon, (D-R-M-7)	n/a	n/a	195
No. 02 1948 Tucker, light maroon, (D-R-M-8)	n/a	n/a	195
No. 02 1948 Tucker, maroon, (D-2-M) ...	n/a	n/a	195
No. 02A 1948 Tucker, black, (5 Proto) ...	n/a	n/a	NPF
No. 02A 1948 Tucker, champagne, (5 Proto)	n/a	n/a	NPF
No. 02A 1948 Tucker, dark gold, (R-M), tan interior	n/a	n/a	65
No. 02A 1948 Tucker, gold, (P-M), beige interior, Harrah's	n/a	n/a	175
No. 02A 1948 Tucker, gold, (R-M), tan interior	n/a	n/a	65
No. 02A 1948 Tucker, green, (5 Proto) ...	n/a	n/a	NPF
No. 02A 1948 Tucker, Jaguar Coral, (5 Proto)	n/a	n/a	NPF
No. 02A 1948 Tucker, Lazer red, (P-M), Paramount Pictures, semi-limited - 1000 made	n/a	n/a	200

Brooklin 1948 Chevy Police Car, black, white. Photo courtesy Dennis Doty

Brooklin 1952-53 Nash Ambassador LeMans Coupe, yellow, white top. Photo courtesy Dennis Doty

	C6	C8	C10
No. 02A 1948 Tucker, light brown, (P-M), gray interior, Harrah's	n/a	n/a	175
No. 02A 1948 Tucker, maroon, (P-M-3), tan interior, 500 made, Tucker Club	n/a	n/a	200
No. 02A 1948 Tucker, Sierra beige, (5 Proto)	n/a	n/a	NPF
No. 02A 1948 Tucker, Signa Amber, (5 Proto)	n/a	n/a	NPF
No. 02A 1948 Tucker, silver, (P-M), tan interior, Harrah's	n/a	n/a	175
No. 02A 1948 Tucker, stratus silver, (P-M), Paramount Pictures, semi-limited - 1000 made	n/a	n/a	200
No. 02A 1948 Tucker, turquoise, (P-M), Paramount Pictures, semi-limited - 1000 made	n/a	n/a	200
No. 02A 1948 Tucker, white, (5 Proto)	n/a	n/a	NPF
No. 02A 1948 Tucker, Zircon blue, (5 Proto)	n/a	n/a	NPF
No. 03 1930 Ford Victoria Two-door, beige top/medium green body, (D-R-4-15), beige wheels, light brown interior	n/a	n/a	150
No. 03 1930 Ford Victoria Two-door, beige/light green, (D-C-4), beige wheels, light brown interior	n/a	n/a	150
No. 03 1930 Ford Victoria Two-door, beige/light olive, (D-4), beige wheels, light brown interior	n/a	n/a	150
No. 03 1930 Ford Victoria Two-door, beige/tan, (D-4), white wheels, light brown interior	n/a	n/a	175
No. 04 1937 Chevy Coupe, beige, (D-P-3), Webers 87, seventy made	n/a	n/a	NPF
No. 04 1937 Chevy Coupe, blue, (D-P-3-9), Ill. Toy Show '86, 100 made	n/a	n/a	400
No. 04 1937 Chevy Coupe, blue, (P), Brooklin Club England, 275 made	n/a	n/a	NPF

Brooklin 1959 Chevy El Camino, black with red interior. Photo courtesy Dennis Doty

	C6	C8	C10
No. 04 1937 Chevy Coupe, bright green, (P), Ill. Toy Show, 100 made	n/a	n/a	NPF
No. 04 1937 Chevy Coupe, dark green, (D-C-4), beige wheels	n/a	n/a	160
No. 04 1937 Chevy Coupe, dark green, (D-R-4-15), beige wheels	n/a	n/a	160
No. 04 1937 Chevy Coupe, Police, (P), Bay Brooklin Club	n/a	n/a	150
No. 04 1937 Chevy Coupe, red, (D-P), James Leake 87, 150 made, 15th Auc.	n/a	n/a	NPF
No. 04 Model A Ford Two-door Coupe, black top/dark brown body, (D-3), Tudor body	n/a	n/a	150
No. 04 Model A Ford Two-door Coupe, black, (D-P-3), Webers '86, sixty-nine made	n/a	n/a	NPF
No. 04 Model A Ford Two-door Coupe, black/green, (D-R-15)	n/a	n/a	100
No. 04 Model A Ford Two-door Coupe, black/light green, (D-C), New Orleans Fire, 100 made	n/a	n/a	325
No. 04 Model A Ford Two-door Coupe, black/red, (D-P), Philly Fire, 300 made	n/a	n/a	300
No. 06 1932 Packard Standard 8, blue-gray top silver, (3), metallic light blue fenders, red interior	n/a	n/a	200
No. 06 1932 Packard Standard 8, gray light gray, (3), dark gray fenders, red interior	n/a	n/a	200
No. 06 1932 Packard Standard 8, light brown top/cream body, (R), brown fenders, light brown interior	n/a	n/a	125
No. 06 1932 Packard Standard 8, tan/light gray, (3), brown fenders, red interior	n/a	n/a	200
No. 07 1934 Chrysler Airflow, dark blue, (R), black wall tires	n/a	n/a	90+
No. 07 1934 Chrysler Airflow, dark blue, (R), white wall tires	n/a	n/a	90+
No. 07 1934 Chrysler Airflow, light blue, (R), black wall tires	n/a	n/a	65
No. 07 1934 Chrysler Airflow, medium blue, (R), black wall tires	n/a	n/a	90+
No. 07 1934 Chrysler Airflow, medium blue, (R), white wall tires, all variants	n/a	n/a	90+
No. 08 1940 Chrysler Newport, yellow, (R-D-15)	n/a	n/a	125
No. 08A 1941 Chrysler Pace Car, white, (P), Motor Sport, 140 made	n/a	n/a	225
No. 08A 1941 Chrysler Pace Car, white, (P-3), Mtr. Sp. 60th Anv., sixty made	n/a	n/a	350
No. 08A 1941 Chrysler Pace Car, white, (R), Chrysler logo	n/a	n/a	65
No. 09 1940 Ford Van, beige, (P-12-3), Lamberts, 100 made w/certificate	n/a	n/a	650
No. 09 1940 Ford Van, beige, (P-3), Model Auto, fifty made	n/a	n/a	450
No. 09 1940 Ford Van, beige, (P-3), Webers '84, sixty-seven made, rare	n/a	n/a	NPF
No. 09 1940 Ford Van, black, (D-R-12), Ford	n/a	n/a	75
No. 09 1940 Ford Van, black, (P), James Leake '85, 250 made 13th Auc.	n/a	n/a	200
No. 09 1940 Ford Van, black, (R), Ford	n/a	n/a	550
No. 09 1940 Ford Van, blue, (P), Deaf Child Society, 200 made	n/a	n/a	220
No. 09 1940 Ford Van, blue, (P, CPCTS '84), 100 made	n/a	n/a	350

Brooklin 1959 Chevy El Camino, black with red interior.
Photo courtesy Dennis Doty

	C6	C8	C10
No. 09 1940 Ford Van, brown, (P-3), Marque, fifty made	n/a	n/a	350
No. 09 1940 Ford Van, cream, (P), Spanish Armada, 150 made	n/a	n/a	200
No. 09 1940 Ford Van, dark blue, (P-3), BF Goodrich, fifty made	n/a	n/a	400-800
No. 09 1940 Ford Van, dark brown, (P), Hershey	n/a	n/a	375
No. 09 1940 Ford Van, gray, (P), Danhausen, red wheels, 150 made, first issue	n/a	n/a	225
No. 09 1940 Ford Van, green (P-3), Randalls, fifty made	n/a	n/a	390
No. 09 1940 Ford Van, green, (P), Huggett	n/a	n/a	110
No. 09 1940 Ford Van, green, (P-10), Toronto Works, fifty made	n/a	n/a	295-350
No. 09 1940 Ford Van, green, (P-12), Toronto Works, fifty made	n/a	n/a	300
No. 09 1940 Ford Van, light blue, (P, CPCTS '87), 150 made	n/a	n/a	250
No. 09 1940 Ford Van, maroon, (P), Buchi Optik, sixty made	n/a	n/a	400
No. 09 1940 Ford Van, maroon, (P-3), Wessex Model, seventy-five made, rare	n/a	n/a	NPF
No. 09 1940 Ford Van, maroon, (P-3-9), J.U.N.K., fifty made w/certificate	n/a	n/a	800
No. 09 1940 Ford Van, off white, (P), Philly Ambulance, 300 made	n/a	n/a	350
No. 09 1940 Ford Van, orange, (P), James Leake '88, 150 made 16th Auc.	n/a	n/a	225
No. 09 1940 Ford Van, red, (P), Old Toyland, 100 made	n/a	n/a	275
No. 09 1940 Ford Van, red, (P), Springfield Fire, 100 made	n/a	n/a	350
No. 09 1940 Ford Van, red, (P), Weeties	n/a	n/a	150
No. 09 1940 Ford Van, red, (P), Yateley, 150 made	n/a	n/a	225
No. 09 1940 Ford Van, red, (P-12-3, CTCS '80), beige interior, 125 made	n/a	n/a	550
No. 09 1940 Ford Van, red, (P-3), Indian River Fire, fifty made	n/a	n/a	500
No. 09 1940 Ford Van, red, (P-3-10, CTCS '80), light brown interior 125 made	n/a	n/a	550
No. 09 1940 Ford Van, tan, (P), Danhausen, second issue	n/a	n/a	225

	C6	C8	C10
No. 09 1940 Ford Van, white, (P), Harrah's '85, 400 made	n/a	n/a	225
No. 09 1940 Ford Van, white, (P), Nutmeg Ambulance, 300 made	n/a	n/a	200
No. 09 1940 Ford Van, white, (P-3), Maidenhead, 150 made	n/a	n/a	500
No. 09 1940 Ford Van, white, (P-3), Mobil Bk. Tires, twenty-six made	n/a	n/a	NPF
No. 09 1940 Ford Van, yellow, (P), Coke, "Enjoy"	n/a	n/a	325
No. 09 1940 Ford Van, yellow, (P), Coke, marked "Drink"	n/a	n/a	325
No. 09 1940 Ford Van, yellow, (P), Danhausen, 150 made first Issue	n/a	n/a	225
No. 09 1940 Ford Van, yellow, (P), Shell-Model Garage, 140 made	n/a	n/a	175
No. 09 1940 Ford Van, yellow, (P-11), Coke, marked "Drink"	n/a	n/a	325
No. 09 1940 Ford Van, yellow, (P-12-11), Coke, "Drink"	n/a	n/a	325
No. 10 1949 Buick Roadmaster, black, (3), Autosatisfaction, 100 made w/o hood ornnament	n/a	n/a	NPF
No. 10 1949 Buick Roadmaster, black, (3), beige interior, w/hood ornment	n/a	n/a	200
No. 10 1949 Buick Roadmaster, dark gray, (R), beige interior, w/o hood ornment	n/a	n/a	75
No. 10 1949 Buick Roadmaster, light silver gray, (R-C), beige interior, w/o hood ornament	n/a	n/a	65
No. 10 1949 Buick Roadmaster, maroon, (P), beige interior, Mini cars	n/a	n/a	70
No. 10 1949 Buick Roadmaster, medium gray, (R), beige interior, w/o hood ornament	n/a	n/a	75
No. 11 1956 Lincoln Continental Mark II, black, (P), maroon interior, 500 made	n/a	n/a	125
No. 11 1956 Lincoln Continental Mark II, black, (P-9), Accent, first Issue, white interior	n/a	n/a	195
No. 11 1956 Lincoln Continental Mark II, black, (P-9), Accent, gray interior, 400 made	n/a	n/a	150
No. 11 1956 Lincoln Continental Mark II, dark blue, (R-M-C), red interior	n/a	n/a	75
No. 11 1956 Lincoln Continental Mark II, gold, (P-3), Autosatisfaction, fifty made, rare	n/a	n/a	NPF
No. 11 1956 Lincoln Continental Mark II, light blue, (R-M), gray interior	n/a	n/a	65
No. 11 1956 Lincoln Continental Mark II, medium blue, (R-M), gray interior	n/a	n/a	70
No. 11 1956 Lincoln Continental Mark II, white, (5-Proto)	n/a	n/a	NPF
No. 12 1931 Hudson Boattail, beige top black body, (P, CTCS '81), red fenders, 250 made	n/a	n/a	550
No. 12 1931 Hudson Boattail, orange/cream fenders, (R)	n/a	n/a	70
No. 13 1956 Ford T-Bird, beige, (R, CTCI '82), 300 made	n/a	n/a	350
No. 13 1956 Ford T-Bird, dark red, (R)	n/a	n/a	NPF
No. 13 1956 Ford T-Bird, green, (P, CTCI '88), 200 made	n/a	n/a	200
No. 13 1956 Ford T-Bird, red, (R)	n/a	n/a	NPF

	C6	C8	C10
No. 13 1956 Ford T-Bird, tan, (P, CTCI '82)	n/a	n/a	350
No. 13 1956 Ford T-Bird, white, (P), Mini Cars, black interior	n/a	n/a	80
No. 13 1956 Ford T-Bird, white, (P-9), Ill. Toy Show '87, 100 made w/certificate, red interior....................	n/a	n/a	350
No. 14 1940 Cadillac V-16 Convertible, dark bronze-brown, (R-M)...................	n/a	n/a	75
No. 14 1940 Cadillac V-16 Convertible, gold-bronze, (R-M)	n/a	n/a	65
No. 14 1940 Cadillac V-16 Convertible, white top/red body, (P, CTCS '83), 400 made..	n/a	n/a	375
No. 15 1949 Mercury, cream, (C-R), red or gray interior	n/a	n/a	200
No. 15 1949 Mercury, dark blue, (P-M-9), Ill. Toy Show '88, 100 made w/certificate	n/a	n/a	200
No. 15 1949 Mercury, dark green, (R-M)	n/a	n/a	75
No. 15 1949 Mercury, maroon, (P, CTCS)	n/a	n/a	175
No. 15 1949 Mercury, medium green, (R-M)	n/a	n/a	65
No. 15 1949 Mercury, turquoise blue, (Proto), six made	n/a	n/a	NPF
No. 16X 1935 Dodge Pick-up, blue/black, (P), Markham, 500 made...	n/a	n/a	200
No. 16X 1935 Dodge Pick-up, blue/cream, (P-3), B.F. Goodrich, 50 made..	n/a	n/a	700
No. 16X 1935 Dodge Pick-up, Burgundy/cream, (P, CPCTS '86), 150 made..	n/a	n/a	300
No. 16X 1935 Dodge Pick-up, green/beige, (P, CTCS '84), 400 made	n/a	n/a	300
No. 16X 1935 Dodge Pick-up, green/green, (P), A.T.T. w/pole, 400 made...	n/a	n/a	350
No. 16X 1935 Dodge Pick-up, green/green, (P-3), Huggetts, 100 made..	n/a	n/a	300
No. 16X 1935 Dodge Pick-up, olive green, (P), New Eng. Telephone & Pole Truck, 400 made	n/a	n/a	250
No. 16X 1935 Dodge Pick-up, orange body/brown fenders, (P), Avon, seventy-five made	n/a	n/a	400
No. 16X 1935 Dodge Pick-up, orange/brown, (P), J. Leake '86, 150 made w/certificate 14th Auc.	n/a	n/a	300
No. 16X 1935 Dodge Pick-up, red, (P), Yately, 150 made	n/a	n/a	285

Brooklin 1960 Chevy Impala, brown, white striping. Photo courtesy Dennis Doty

	C6	C8	C10
No. 16X 1935 Dodge Pick-up, red/black, (P), Yateley's, 150 made	n/a	n/a	185
No. 16X 1935 Dodge Pick-up, red/brown, barrel seats, (P), McDonald's, Benefit No. 2	n/a	n/a	295
No. 16X 1935 Dodge Pick-up, red/red, (P), Orange City Fire, 400 made.........	n/a	n/a	350
No. 16X 1935 Dodge Pick-up, Yellow, (P), Brasilla Press, 700 made	n/a	n/a	75
No. 16X 1935 Dodge Pick-up, Yellow/blue, (P, CTCS '86), 450 made	n/a	n/a	290
No. 17 1952 Studebaker Starlight, black, (C-R), gray interior	n/a	n/a	110
No. 17 1952 Studebaker Starlight, gray, (R), gray interior	n/a	n/a	65
No. 17 1952 Studebaker Starlight, gray, (R), red interior	n/a	n/a	70
No. 18 1941 Packard Clipper, gold/bronze, (P-M, CTCS '85), 400 made...	n/a	n/a	350
No. 18 1941 Packard Clipper, Khaki/white Stars, (P), Military Staff Car, 160 made	n/a	n/a	400
No. 18 1941 Packard Clipper, maroon, (R)...	n/a	n/a	65
No. 18 1941 Packard Clipper, Yellow, (P), American Taxi, 500 made.............	n/a	n/a	140
No. 19 1936 Dodge Van, beige/ brown, (P), Gems & Cobwebs, 100 made	n/a	n/a	275
No. 19 1936 Dodge Van, beige/brown, (P, CTCS '82), 250 made	n/a	n/a	225
No. 19 1936 Dodge Van, black/ black, (P-R), Sears, semi limited	n/a	n/a	70
No. 19 1936 Dodge Van, blue, (P), Argus De LaMiniature, 100 made	n/a	n/a	295
No. 19 1936 Dodge Van, blue/black, (P), Buchi Optik, 100 made	n/a	n/a	300
No. 19 1936 Dodge Van, brown/ black, (P), Bimbo, 100 made	n/a	n/a	300
No. 19 1936 Dodge Van, brown/black, (P), Hershey	n/a	n/a	300
No. 19 1936 Dodge Van, cream/brown, (P), Camel, seventy-five made.............	n/a	n/a	450
No. 19 1936 Dodge Van, cream/green, (P, St), Martins, approx. 150 made	n/a	n/a	295
No. 19 1936 Dodge Van, cream/orange, (P), Bayview Model, fifty made	n/a	n/a	500
No. 19 1936 Dodge Van, dark blue, (P-3), Maidenhead, 100 made	n/a	n/a	300
No. 19 1936 Dodge Van, dark blue/red, (P), Merley Museum, 100 made	n/a	n/a	300
No. 19 1936 Dodge Van, dark green/light green, Model Auto Review, 100 made	n/a	n/a	295
No. 19 1936 Dodge Van, dark red, (P), Litchfield Fire, 200 made	n/a	n/a	275
No. 19 1936 Dodge Van, gold/black, (P-M-16), Spielgoed Otten, 100 made.	n/a	n/a	250
No. 19 1936 Dodge Van, gold/red, (P-M-16), Collectors Gazette '86, 24k gold, 200 made	n/a	n/a	425
No. 19 1936 Dodge Van, goldish green/black, (P-M), Passport Transport, 150 made	n/a	n/a	275
No. 19 1936 Dodge Van, gray body/black fenders, (3), Burma Shave, approx. fifty made..................................	n/a	n/a	250
No. 19 1936 Dodge Van, gray body/red fenders, (R-C), Burma Shave, black run bds.	n/a	n/a	90

	C6	C8	C10
No. 19 1936 Dodge Van, gray body/red fenders, (R-C), Burma Shave, red run bds.	n/a	n/a	90
No. 19 1936 Dodge Van, gray/ black, (P, CPCTS '85), w/o logo (?)	n/a	n/a	200
No. 19 1936 Dodge Van, green/gray, (P-3), Huggett Elec. '83, 100 made w/certificate	n/a	n/a	325
No. 19 1936 Dodge Van, light blue/dark blue, (P), Mini Wheels of Midland, fifty made	n/a	n/a	395
No. 19 1936 Dodge Van, light blue/dark blue, (R), City Ice	n/a	n/a	65
No. 19 1936 Dodge Van, maroon, (P), Wessex silver Key	n/a	n/a	120
No. 19 1936 Dodge Van, maroon/ black, (P, CPCTS '83), fifty made	n/a	n/a	400
No. 19 1936 Dodge Van, maroon/black, (P-R), Dr. Pepper, semi limited	n/a	n/a	70
No. 19 1936 Dodge Van, orange/brown, (P-3), Avon Club, seventy-five made	n/a	n/a	395
No. 19 1936 Dodge Van, pea green/green, (P-M), Calandre, 100 made	n/a	n/a	300
No. 19 1936 Dodge Van, red, (P), Litchfield Fire, 200 made	n/a	n/a	275
No. 19 1936 Dodge Van, red/black, (P), classic and sport, 200 made	n/a	n/a	200
No. 19 1936 Dodge Van, red/red, (P), Philly Fire, approx. 300 made	n/a	n/a	295
No. 19 1936 Dodge Van, red/red, (P-3), Indian River, fifty made	n/a	n/a	495
No. 19 1936 Dodge Van, silver/black, (P-M, CPCTS '85), w/logo 100 made	n/a	n/a	200
No. 19 1936 Dodge Van, white, (P), Bay St. Lobster, J. Leake redo, fifty made (?)	n/a	n/a	300
No. 19 1936 Dodge Van, white/blue, (P), London Mtr. Fair '85, 100 made	n/a	n/a	300
No. 19 1936 Dodge Van, white/red, (P), Dr. Bernardo's, 100 made	n/a	n/a	300
No. 19 1936 Dodge Van, white/red, (P), ITT Kruse '87, 150 made	n/a	n/a	175
No. 19 1936 Dodge Van, white/red, (P), J. Leake '84, 12th Auction	n/a	n/a	275
No. 19 1936 Dodge Van, Yellow/black, (P), Coca Cola	n/a	n/a	450
No. 19 1936 Dodge Van, Yellow/black, (P-3), Weber's '85, sixty-eight made	n/a	n/a	NPF
No. 19 1936 Dodge Van, Yellow/red, (P), Old Toyland '87, 100 made	n/a	n/a	295
No. 19 1955 Chrysler, black/tan, (P), Mini Cars, 500 made	n/a	n/a	70
No. 19 1955 Chrysler, red, (R), 500 made	n/a	n/a	70
No. 19 1955 Chrysler C-300, (P), Brooklin Club Model, white	n/a	n/a	65
No. 20 1953 Buick Skylark, Aqua, (R-M)	n/a	n/a	NPF
No. 20 1953 Buick Skylark, maroon convertible, Code II, Produced for Model Car Shop - New Model Cars and Trains unlimited blue, PT, NY, very rare, fifty pieces	n/a	n/a	450
No. 20 1953 Buick Skylark, white Convertible, (P), Ketchner Oct. Fest., 100 made	n/a	n/a	350
No. 21 1963 Corvette, blue, (C-R-M)	n/a	n/a	NPF
No. 21 1963 Corvette, red, (P)	n/a	n/a	400
No. 21 1963 Corvette, red, (P), Ill. Toy Show '87, black interior, 100 made	n/a	n/a	375

Brooklin 1952-53 Nash Ambassador LeMans Coupe, yellow, white top. Photo courtesy Dennis Doty

	C6	C8	C10
No. 21 1963 Corvette, red, (P), Ill. Toy Show, 100 made	n/a	n/a	NPF
No. 21 1963 Corvette, red/gray interior, (P), Mini Cars	n/a	n/a	70
No. 21 1963 Corvette, silver, (P-M-3), 350 made	n/a	n/a	300
No. 21 1963 Corvette, white, (R), red interior	n/a	n/a	65
No. 22 1958 Edsel Citation, green, (M-R), w/Cont. Kit	n/a	n/a	65
No. 22 1958 Edsel Citation, lavender-pink, (R-C), gold name	n/a	n/a	NPF
No. 22 1958 Edsel Citation, pink, (R), black name decal	n/a	n/a	75
No. 22 1958 Edsel Citation, pink, (R), gold name decal	n/a	n/a	150
No. 23 1856 Ford Fairlane Victoria, white top/green body, (R)	n/a	n/a	65
No. 23 1856 Ford Fairlane Victoria, white top/green body, (R), marked No. 22 in error	n/a	n/a	90
No. 24 1968 Shelby Mustang, blue, (D-R-M)	n/a	n/a	149
No. 24 1968 Shelby Mustang, green, (D-P-3), Model Expo, 250 made (?); How many are in the hands of collectors is not known	n/a	n/a	NPF
No. 24A 1968 Ford Mustang, red, (R)	n/a	n/a	NPF
No. 25 1958 Pontiac Bonneville Conv., black, (R), gray interior	n/a	n/a	65
No. 25 1958 Pontiac Bonneville Convertible, black, (R-3), burgundy interior, forty made	n/a	n/a	150
No. 26 1956 Chevy Nomad, white top/light blue boyd, (R)	n/a	n/a	65
No. 26 1956 Chevy Nomad, white/Coral, (P, CTCS '87), 375 made	n/a	n/a	275
No. 26X 1956 Chevy Nomad Van, black (P), Das Automobile, 200 made	n/a	n/a	250
No. 26X 1956 Chevy Nomad Van, black, (P), Webers '88, seventy-one made	n/a	n/a	NPF
No. 26X 1956 Chevy Nomad Van, black, (P, CPCTS '88), 150 made	n/a	n/a	195
No. 26X 1956 Chevy Nomad Van, dark blue, (P), cars only, 150 made	n/a	n/a	275
No. 26X 1956 Chevy Nomad Van, maroon, (P), Wessex	n/a	n/a	150
No. 26X 1956 Chevy Nomad Van, red, (P), Fire Chief	n/a	n/a	75
No. 27 1957 Caddy Eldorado Brougham, silver, (R-M)	n/a	n/a	NPF
No. 27-1 1957 Caddy Eldorado Brougham, (P), gold plating, Pacific Coast Toy Show	n/a	n/a	150

	C6	C8	C10
No. 28 1957 Mercury Turnpike Cruiser, bronze/tan, (R-M)	n/a	n/a	65
No. 28 1957 Mercury Turnpike Cruiser, monarch blue, (R-M, CTCS '88), 450 made	n/a	n/a	300
No. 29 1953 Kaiser Manhattan, blue, (R), 500 Produced for Rotterdam Shoppe	n/a	n/a	275
No. 29 1953 Kaiser Manhattan, standard Issue, 1989	n/a	n/a	65
No. 29 1953 Kaiser Manhattan 29X, black, (P)	n/a	n/a	275
No. 29 1953 Kaiser Manhattan 30, standard Issue, 1990	n/a	n/a	65
No. 30-1 1953 Dodge 500 Convertible, convertible, (R), Indianapolis Pace Car	n/a	n/a	95

New Releases

	C6	C8	C10
BRK-101 1952 Muntz Jet Roadster, (R), metallic maroon, open	n/a	n/a	85
BRK-102 1936 Hudson Terraplane 6-62 Custom, (R), green, 4-dr sedan	n/a	n/a	85
BRK-103 1956 Plymouth Plaza, (R), gray, 2-dr sedan	n/a	n/a	85
BRK-103X 1956 Plymouth Plaza, (P), CTCS, "Unionville Fire Chief," red	n/a	n/a	85
BRK-104 1950 Studebaker Commander Landcruiser, (R), maroon, 4-dr sedan	n/a	n/a	85
BRK-105 1947 Cadillac Series 62 Club Coupe, (R), ivory and maroon, available in June 2005	n/a	n/a	85
BRK-105X 1947 Cadillac Series 62 Sedanet, (P), metallic silver/gold, 30th Anniversary edition - only 990 cast	n/a	n/a	85
BRK-106 1938 Lincoln Zephyr, (R), smoke gray, 4-dr sedan	n/a	n/a	85
BRK-107 1954 Studebaker Conestoga Station Wagon, (R), green	n/a	n/a	85
BRK-108 1957 Ford Ranchero, (R), available Fall 2004	n/a	n/a	n/a
BRK-13A 1957 Ford Thunderbird Convertible, (R), light green	n/a	n/a	85
BRK-15A 1950 Mercury Convertible, (R), red	n/a	n/a	85
BRK-15-I 1950 Mercury Convertible, (R), Indianapolis 500 Pace Car, yellow,	n/a	n/a	85
BRK-18A 1947 Packard Super Clipper, (R), blue and silver	n/a	n/a	85
BRK-18B 1947 Packard Custom Super Eight, (R), light blue, 4-dr sedan	n/a	n/a	85
BRK-18C 1947 Packard Super Clipper Club Sedan, (R), gray, available Fall 2005	n/a	n/a	n/a
BRK-19A 1955 Chrysler C-300, (R), white, 2-dr hardtop	n/a	n/a	85

	C6	C8	C10
BRK-19-I 1955 Chrysler C-300, (P), Pan American Road Race, red	n/a	n/a	85
BRK-22A 1958 Edsel Citation, (R), green and white, 2-dr hardtop	n/a	n/a	85
BRK-23AA 1956 Ford Mainline, (R), Michigan State Police, 2-dr sedan	n/a	n/a	85
BRK-27A 1957 Cadillac Eldorado Brougham, (R), blue, 4-dr hardtop	n/a	n/a	85
BRK-28 1957 Mercury Turnpike Cruiser, (D), bronze, 2-dr hardtop	n/a	n/a	85
BRK-29A 1953 Kaiser Manhattan Two-Tone, (R), blue and silver, 4-dr sedan	n/a	n/a	85
BRK-29B 1954 Kaiser Manhattan, (R), metallic green, 4-dr sedan	n/a	n/a	85
BRK-29C 1954 Kaiser Manhattan, (R), white and metallic blue, 4-dr sedan, available February 2005	n/a	n/a	n/a
BRK-30-I 1954 Dodge Convertible, (P), Indianapolis 500 Pace Car, ivory white	n/a	n/a	85
BRK-31-12 1953 Pontiac Delivery, (P), "Vacheauirit," mid-1990s	n/a	n/a	95
BRK-31-8 1953 Pontiac Delivery, (P), "Milano 43," mid-1990s	n/a	n/a	95
BRK-31A 1953 Pontiac Sedan Deliver, (R), Mobil Gas, 1952, 1992	n/a	n/a	NPF
BRK-31A 1953 Pontiac Sedan Deliver, (R), orange Gulf regular issue, 1990	n/a	n/a	NPF
BRK-31A 1953 Pontiac Sedan Deliver, (R), Sunoco, 1953, 1992	n/a	n/a	NPF
BRK-31-I 1953 Pontiac Pickup, (P), Milano 43, black	n/a	n/a	85
BRK-31-J 1953 Pontiac Sedan Delivery, (P), Bender's Wholesale, white	n/a	n/a	85
BRK-31X 1953 Pontiac Sedan Deliver, (P), part of boxed set Brooklin Video No. 1, silver w/tonneau cover, blue	n/a	n/a	NPF
BRK-32 1953 Studebaker Commander, (R), light green, regular Issue, 1990	n/a	n/a	NPF
BRK-32-2 1953 Studebaker Commander Starliner, (P), Pan American Road Race, red	n/a	n/a	85
BRK-32B 1953 Studebaker Commander Starliner, (R), coral and ivory white, 2-dr hardtop	n/a	n/a	85
BRK-33 1938 Phantom Corsair, (R), black body	n/a	n/a	NPF
BRK-33-1 1939 Phantom Corsair, (D), Modelex '91, metallic green	n/a	n/a	85
BRK-33A 1938 Phantom Corsair, (D), tan, original brochure color, mini grid.	n/a	n/a	NPF
BRK-34 1938 Phantom Corsair, (R), maroon, regular issue, dark maroon, 1991	n/a	n/a	NPF

Brooklin 1954 Hudson Italia, silver. Photo courtesy Dennis Doty

Brooklin 1957 Rambler Rebel, silver, brown stripe. Photo courtesy Dennis Doty

	C6	C8	C10
BRK-34A 1954 Nash Lemans Coupe, (P), yellow w/white top	n/a*	n/a	95
BRK-35 1957 Ford Skyliner, (R), tan/gold chrome enhanced	n/a	n/a	75
BRK-35-1 1957 Ford Skyliner, (R), Route 66, yellow, closed	n/a	n/a	85
BRK-35-1 Ford Retractable, (P), Route 66, 1957, mid-1990s	n/a	n/a	95
BRK-35-2 1957 Ford Skyliner, (P), CTCS, metallic green	n/a	n/a	85
BRK-35A 1957 Ford Skyliner Convertible, (R), black, open	n/a	n/a	85
BRK-36 1953 Hudson Hornet, (R), green, tan Interior, 1992	n/a	n/a	NPF
BRK-37 1960 Ford Sunliner, (R), purple metal flake, maroon top, convertible, 1992	n/a	n/a	NPF
BRK-38 1938 Graham Sharknose, (R), khaki tan, 1992	n/a	n/a	NPF
BRK-38 1939 Graham Sharknose Sedan Coupe, (R), silver, 2-dr sedan	n/a	n/a	85
BRK-39 1952 Olds Fiesta, (R), blue and white two-tone - a first for Brooklin models, 1992	n/a	n/a	80
BRK-40 1948 Cadillac, (R), dark Navy blue, red interior, 1992	n/a	n/a	NPF
BRK-40A 1948 Cadillac Series 61 Sedanet Coupe, (R), dark green metallic, 2-dr sedan	n/a	n/a	85
BRK-41 1959 Chrysler Convt., (R), gold, Regular Issue	n/a	n/a	NPF
BRK-41-1 1959 Chrysler 300E Convertible, (P), CTCS, silver and grey	n/a	n/a	85
BRK-41A 1959 Chrysler 300E Convertible, (R), red, open	n/a	n/a	85
BRK-41A Light Milky Gold, (R), mistake a Brooklin factory released	n/a	n/a	NPF
BRK-42 1952 Ford F1, Alka Seltzer	n/a	n/a	185
BRK-42 1952 Ford F1 Ambulance, (R), Jasper County Hospital Services, white w/decals	n/a	n/a	69
BRK-42 1952 Ford F1 Pavel Special Delivery, (P), CTCS, "1992," one of 500	n/a	n/a	185
BRK-42-2 1952 Ford F1, (P), Modelex 91	n/a	n/a	95
BRK-42B 1952 Ford Ranger, (R), Colorado Highway Patrol, white	n/a	n/a	85
BRK-42-X 1952 Ford Panel Truck, (R), Speedy Alka Seltzer, blue	n/a	n/a	85
BRK-43A 1948 Packard Station Wagon, (R), w/o rack	n/a	n/a	69
BRK-43B 1948 Packard Station Sedan, (R), maroon	n/a	n/a	85
BRK-44 1961 Chevrolet Impala, (R), red, 2-dr hardtop	n/a	n/a	85
BRK-44 1961 Chevy Impala, (R), red/white stripe	n/a	n/a	69
BRK-45A 1948 Buick Roadmaster, (R), white/beige interior	n/a	n/a	69
BRK-46 1959 Chevy El Camino, (R), black/red interior	n/a	n/a	69
BRK-46-2 El Camino Pickup, (P), "Modelex," 1994	n/a	n/a	95
BRK-47 1965 Ford T-Bird, (R), red convertible	n/a	n/a	69
BRK-47 1965 Ford Thunderbird Convertible, (R), red, open	n/a	n/a	85
BRK-48 1958 Chevy Impala, (R), Baley blue hardtop	n/a	n/a	69
BRK-49 1954 Hudson Italia, (R), silver	n/a	n/a	69
BRK-50 1948 Chevy Fleetline Aero Sedan, (R), "Country Club Woody"	n/a	n/a	69
BRK-50A 1948 Chevy Police Car, (R), black/white doors, 1996	n/a	n/a	69
BRK-51 1951 Ford Victoria, (R), two-tone green, 2-dr hardtop	n/a	n/a	85
BRK-51X Ford Victoria Hardtop, (P), "Modelex 1995"	n/a	n/a	95
BRK-52 1941 Hupmobile Skylark, (R), maroon	n/a	n/a	69
BRK-53 1955 Cameo Pick-up Truck, (R), red/white	n/a	n/a	69
BRK-53A 1953 Chevroled Cameo Wrecker, (R), Sohio, white, red and blue	n/a	n/a	85
BRK-53X 1955 Chevrolet Cameo, (P), Last Cameo, dark blue, limited edition	n/a	n/a	85
BRK-53X and No. 62 Chevy Cameo and Horse Trailer Set, w/tools, haybales, green/silver trim	n/a	n/a	160
BRK-54 1953 Air Stream-Wonderer, (R), silver	n/a	n/a	69
BRK-54 1953 Streamlined American Caravan, (R), Airstream, aluminum	n/a	n/a	85
BRK-55 1951 Packard Mayfair, (R), maroon/beige top	n/a	n/a	69
BRK-55-1 Packard LaCarrera Panamericana, (P), blue and white, 2-dr hardtop, issued 1997	n/a	n/a	150
BRK-55A 1951 Packard Mayfair, (R), green and yellow, 2-dr hardtop	n/a	n/a	85
BRK-56 1965 Mustang Convertible, (R), yellow, open	n/a	n/a	85
BRK-56X 1964-1/2 Mustang Convertible, (R), Indianapolis 500 Pace Car, white	n/a	n/a	100
BRK-57 1960 Lincoln Continental, (R), convertible, white	n/a	n/a	69
BRK-57X 1960 Lincoln Continental Mk.V Convertible, (P), Anniversary Gold, limited to 100 pieces	n/a	n/a	85
BRK-58 1963-1/2 Ford Falcon Spirit, (R), light green metallic, 1996	n/a	n/a	69
BRK-59 1957 Rambler Rebel, (R), four-door, silver, 1996	n/a	n/a	69
BRK-60 1963 Oldsmobile Starfire, (R), 1996, regal mist metallic, 2-dr hardtop	n/a	n/a	85
BRK-61 1960 Chevy Impala Convertible, (R), bronze color	n/a	n/a	69
BRK-63 1956 Plymouth Fury, (R), ivory white and gold, 2-dr hardtop	n/a	n/a	85
BRK-64 1959 Ford Thunderbird, (R), blue, 2-dr hardtop	n/a	n/a	85
BRK-64A 1959 Ford Thunderbird Convertible, (R), blue, open	n/a	n/a	85
BRK-65 1947 Wesley Slumbercoach, (R), maroon/wood, trailer	n/a	n/a	85
BRK-66 1956 Packard Patrician, (R), metallic gray, 4-dr sedan	n/a	n/a	85
BRK-66X 1956 Packard Patrician, (P), BBC, white and heather, limited edition	n/a	n/a	150
BRK-67 1961 Chrysler Imperial, (R), metallic light green, 2-dr hardtop	n/a	n/a	85

	C6	C8	C10
BRK-67A 1961 Chrysler Imperial Crown Convertible, (R), metalic blue, open, improved detail model available 2002.	n/a	n/a	85
BRK-69 1946 Mercury Sportsman "Woodie" Convertible, (R), maroon/wood, open	n/a	n/a	95
BRK-70 1949 Dodge Wayfarer Coupe, (R), green, 2-dr business coupe	n/a	n/a	85
BRK-71 1955 American Classic Speedboat and Trailer, (R), blue/wood	n/a	n/a	85
BRK-72 1958 Shasta Airflyte Travel Trailer, (R), white and yellow	n/a	n/a	85
BRK-74 1947 Cadillac Series 62 Convertible, (R), metallic blue/green, open	n/a	n/a	85
BRK-75 1960 Edsel Ranger Convertible, (R), cadett blue metallic, open, only 76 of the real cars were built in 1960	n/a	n/a	85
BRK-76 1948 Ford F-1 Pickup, (R), green	n/a	n/a	85
BRK-76X 1948 Ford Fire Truck, (P), SFBBC, "Ford Motor Co.", only 200 cast	n/a	n/a	150
BRK-77 1959 Mercury Commuter Station Wagon, (R), white and red	n/a	n/a	85
BRK-78 1936 Stout Scarab, (R), metallic blue	n/a	n/a	85
BRK-79 1951 Chrysler Imperial Convertible, (R), burgandy, open	n/a	n/a	85
BRK-80 1937 Pierce-Arrow Travelodge, (R), blue	n/a	n/a	85
BRK-81 1936 Pierce-Arrow 1601, (R), blue, 4-dr sedan	n/a	n/a	85
BRK-82 1959 Desoto Adventurer, (R), black, 2-dr hardtop	n/a	n/a	85
BRK-83 1947 Ford V8 Station Wagon, (R), metallic blue/gray, "woodie"	n/a	n/a	85
BRK-84 1934 LaSalle 350 Coupe, (R), metallic gray, 2-dr coupe	n/a	n/a	85
BRK-85 1941 Chrysler New Yorker Convertible, (R), yellow, closed w/black top	n/a	n/a	85
BRK-86 1938 Cadillac 60 Special, (D), silver, 4-dr sedan, 2001	n/a	n/a	85
BRK-87 1949 Desoto Station Wagon, (R), maroon, "woodie"	n/a	n/a	85
BRK-88 1931 Studebaker President Roadster, (R), silver and black, closed w/black top	n/a	n/a	100
BRK-89 1949 Checker Limousine, (R), black, 4-dr	n/a	n/a	85
BRK-89A 1949 Checker Taxi, (R), "New York City," yellow, 4-dr sedan	n/a	n/a	85
BRK-89B 1949 Checker Taxi, (R), "National Cab," ivory white and green, 4-dr sedan	n/a	n/a	85
BRK-90 1935 Plymouth 5-Window Coupe, (R), red	n/a	n/a	85

	C6	C8	C10
BRK-91 1954 Kaiser Darrin Roadster, (R), light green, open	n/a	n/a	85
BRK-91A 1954 Kaiser Darrin Roadster, (R), red, open	n/a	n/a	85
BRK-92 1967 Ford Thunderbird 4-dr Landau, (R), metallic green	n/a	n/a	85
BRK-93 1935 Studebaker Commander Roadster, (R), light yellow, closed	n/a	n/a	85
BRK-93X 1935 Studebaker Commander Roadster, (P), metallic silver, limited edition only 250 cast	n/a	n/a	85
BRK-94 1949 Lincoln Cosmopolitan Convertible, (R), gray, open	n/a	n/a	85
BRK-94X 1949 Lincoln Cosmopolitan Convertible, (R), metallic dark red, open	n/a	n/a	85
BRK-95 1948 Buick Roadmaster Estate Wagon, (R), black	n/a	n/a	85
BRK-96 1931 Marmon Convertible Sedan, (R), maroon and black, closed, 4-dr	n/a	n/a	85
BRK-96A 1931 Marmon Convertible Sedan, (R), metallic light blue w/gray roof, closed, 4-dr	n/a	n/a	85
BRK-97 1955 Dodge Coronet, (R), blue, 4-dr sedan	n/a	n/a	85
BRK-98 1939 LaSalle Touring Sedan, (R), green, 2-dr	n/a	n/a	85
BRK-99 1956 Lincoln Premiere, (R), white and yellow, 2-dr hardtop	n/a	n/a	85
BRK-99A 1956 Lincoln Premiere, (R), white and light yellow, available August 2005	n/a	n/a	n/a
BRK-B Pale Gold, (R), variation of regular issue - color only	n/a	n/a	175

Special Dealer Programme

	C6	C8	C10
1946 Lincoln Continental Special Label, "Dealer Special," black/dark beige interior	n/a	n/a	NPF
BRK 45 D.S. 1948 Buick Roadmaster, D.S., red	n/a	n/a	NPF
No. 63 1956 Plymouth Fury, two-door hardtop, eggshell color, 1997-99	n/a	n/a	75
No. 65 1947 Wesley Slumber Coach, small wooden trailer, 1997-99	n/a	n/a	75
No. 66 1956 Packard Patrician, four-door sedan, metallic gray, 1997-99	n/a	n/a	75
No. 67 1961 Chrysler Imperial Southhamprton, two-door coupe, metallic green, 1997-99	n/a	n/a	75
No. 68 1954 Chevy Bel Air, two-door hard top, coral/ivory, 1997-99	n/a	n/a	75
No. 69 1946 Mercury Sportsman Convertible, maroon, 1997-99	n/a	n/a	75
No. 70 1950 Dodge Wayfarer Coupe, island green/dark red, 1997-99	n/a	n/a	75
No. 73 1949 Oldsmobile 98 Holiday Coupe, praline brown over tawnee buff w/beige interior, 1997-99	n/a	n/a	75

BUCKEYE

The Ohio Art Company was formed in 1908 and is perhaps best known for its early tinplate toys and certainly the enduring Etch-A-Sketch. In the 1950s, Ohio Art created a small line of trucks to compete with the popular Tonka line—Buckeye. Today, Buckeye trucks are considered rare, but are easily mistaken for Tonkas.

Buckeye	C6	C8	C10
Dump Truck, 1950s	65	100	150
Livestock Truck, 1950s	115	172	250
Pickup Truck, 1950s	125	188	285
Red Star Express, red tractor, blue trailer, 1950s	200	325	525

Buckeye Semi Tractor, red. Photo courtesy Calvin L. Chaussee

BUDDY "L"

Buddy "L" toys were first manufactured by the Moline Pressed Steel Company, Moline, Illinois, in 1921, and were named after Buddy Lundahl, the son of the owner, Fred Lundahl. Lundahl started the company eight years earlier, manufacturing auto and truck parts. The toys, originally made as special items for his son, caught the attention of Buddy's playmates. Soon their fathers began asking Lundahl to make duplicate toys for their sons. Lundahl went into the toy business.

Typically twenty-one to twenty-four inches long for trucks and fire engines, the heavy steel construction was strong enough to support a man's weight. These were made until the early 1930s, when the line was modified and lighter weight materials were employed. Before this time, Fred Lundahl had died, having already lost control of the company. The company has changed names several times, being known as the Buddy "L" Corp. and Buddy "L" Toy Co. In recent years, the quotes were dropped from around the L.

Buddy "L," like most toy companies, stopped production of metal toys during World War II. Although the main Buddy "L" plant made nothing bur war-related items, a few wooden toys were produced during the war years.

The early Buddy "L" trains are also popular, and tend to be worth more than the vehicles. Buddy "L" vehicles from the pre-1932 period are almost indestructible; as a consequence, many of the pieces found are either very rusty or have been repainted at some point. The basic metal seems to hold up against time, but repainting and rust drops the price well below "good."

Contributors: John Taylor, P.O. Box 63, Nolensville, TN 37135-0063. Michael W. Curran

1932-on	C6	C8	C10
Aerial Ladder Truck, 25" long	275	375	600
Aerial Ladder Truck, No. 27, red, nickel ladders, brass bell, steel wheels w/spokes embossed, black rubber tires, 1933-34, 40" long	500	850	1400
Aerial Ladder Truck, No. 947, black tires, red rubber wheels, horizontal stripes on radiator, 1940, 30" long	250	375	500
Air Force Truck, No. 5577	100	150	200
Airway Express Van, No. 563	150	225	325
Allied Van Lines Moving Van, No. 366, 31" long	300	450	625
Ambulance Truck	130	195	260
Anti-Aircraft Air Force Blue Truck, GMC	45	65	100
Army Combination Set, No. 5560	200	300	400
Army Electric Searchlight Truck, No. 5545, 1957	125	200	325
Army Half Track, w/cannon	125	200	325
Army Signal Corps Truck, 1941-42, 12" long	140	225	300
Army Supply Corps, cloth top	100	175	250
Army Supply Corps Truck, 12" long	45	70	110
Army Transport, six-spoke wheels, 27" w/towed cannon	150	225	325
Army Transport, w/canvas-top trailer	225	350	475
Army Transport Truck, 19-1/2" long	150	250	350
Army Truck, c.1940, cloth top, 21" long	100	165	250
Army Truck, No. 506, 20-1/2" long	125	170	250
Atlas Van Lines	200	325	500
Automatic Tail-Gate Loader, w/steering handle, 25" long	200	325	475

Buddy "L" Aerial Ladder Truck, 1933-34. Photo courtesy Bertoia Auctions

Buddy "L" Army Supply Corps Truck, 12". Photo courtesy Continental Hobby House

Another view of the Buddy "L" Army Supply Corps Truck, 12". Photo courtesy Calvin L. Chaussee

Buddy "L" produced several Army trucks made of wood. Photo courtesy Richard MacNary

	C6	C8	C10
Baby Ruth/Butterfinger Curtiss Candies Tandem Truck, International-style cab, late 1930s-1940s	750	1500	2000
Baggage Truck, No. 11, 1933, 26-1/2" long	225	350	550
Baggage Truck, No. 203-B, 1930-32, 26" long	3000	5000	8800
Baggage Truck, wood wheels, 1940s, 17" long	95	150	200
Bell Telephone Truck, GMC, three linemen	138	205	275
Brinks Armored Truck	230	345	460
Bus, early 1930s, 23-1/2" long	300	475	750
Camper, 1961	75	125	175
Car Carrier, 1961	125	200	300
Car Lift, 1960s	45	68	100
Cattle Truck	70	105	150
Chain Dump, 1920s	450	679	1000
Chemical Fire Truck, marked "Fire and Chemical," 1949, 22" long	225	425	625
Circus Tractor Trailer, 1960s	200	300	450
City Baggage Dray, No. 439, 1934, 19" long	175	275	400
City Baggage Dray, No. 839, 1939, 20-3/4" long	125	175	275
City Dray, 24" long	1500	2500	4000
Coca-Cola GMC Truck, No. 5646, yellow, decal reads "Drink Coca-Cola the Pause that Refreshes," GMC grille, metal hand truck, 8 green bottles cases, 1957-58, 14" long	150	233	375
Concrete Mixer, 1941, No. 932	100	150	225
Concrete Mixer, No. 5465, 1965	75	100	150

	C6	C8	C10
Concrete Mixer, No. 832, 1950-51 w/motor sound, 10-3/4" long	250	400	575
Concrete Mixer, No. 832, grooved black rubber tires, small nickel hubs, 1949, 9-1/2" long	150	275	400
Concrete Mixer with Truck, No. 54, 1937, 34-1/2" long	100	150	250
Construction Truck, 1960s	50	75	100
Cook Coffee Van, similar to Sunshine Biscuits and Ice Cream vans	200	300	400
Country Squire Station Wagon, 15" long	100	150	250
Curtic Candies Tandem, 1940s, 40" long	750	1500	2000
Curtis Candy Semi, 1950s, 29" long	275	500	650
Curtiss Candy Truck	200	325	450
Dandy Digger, No. 33	75	100	150
Delivery Truck Deluxe Rider, No. 803, 1945-48, 22-3/4" long	225	400	650
Desert Rats Colt Jeep	75	100	150
Double Hydraulic Self-Loader-N-Dump Truck, No. 5892	75	125	225
Dump Truck, No. 434, 1936	212	318	425
Dump Truck, No. 634, 20-1/2" long	125	200	320
Electric Emergency Unit Tow Truck	100	150	250
Emergency Auto Wrecker, No. 3317	75	150	250
Emergency Unit Tow Truck, 1950s	100	150	250
Engine, No. 29, 1933-34, 25-1/2" long	175	300	450
Excavation and Construction Truck and Shovel Set, 1940s, 30" long	300	450	600
Excavator Truck and Shovel, Set No. 948, 1940, 27-1/2" long	275	400	600

Buddy "L" Army Transport Truck, canvas missing, 19-1/2". Photo courtesy Calvin L. Chaussee

Buddy "L" Army Electric Searchlight Truck. Photo courtesy Continental Hobby House

Buddy "L" Automatic Tail-Gate Loader w/steering handle, 25". Photo courtesy Calvin L. Chaussee

Buddy "L" Baby Ruth/Butterfinger Curtiss Candies Tandem Truck, late 1930s, early 1940s. Photo courtesy John Taylor

Buddy "L" Bus, early 1930s, 23-1/2". Photo courtesy Calvin L. Chaussee

Buddy "L" Chemical Fire Truck, 22". Photo courtesy John Taylor

	C6	C8	C10
Express Trailer Truck, No. 35, 1934	475	650	950
Express Truck, screenside, 1932	1200	2000	3000
Farm Machinery Hauler	65	80	130
Farm Supplies Hi-Lift Dump Truck, 1954, 20" long	100	175	275
Farm Supply Truck, No. 634, 1949	170	250	350
Fast Delivery Truck, No. 3313	75	100	150
Fast Freight, 20" long	100	175	225
Fire Hose Truck, 12" long	75	145	185
Fire Ladder Truck, No. 859, 15" long	85	128	170
Fire Ladder Truck, semi, rounded trailer fenders, 1960	100	150	200
Fire Pumper, 1960s	45	60	100
Firestone Service Wrecker	500	800	1100
Freight Hauler, GMC, 1957	200	300	400
Giraffe Truck	75	112	150
Greyhound Bus, 1950s, 7-1/2" long	40	60	80
Greyhound Bus, winds up, 16" long	300	325	500
Grocery Truck	150	225	375

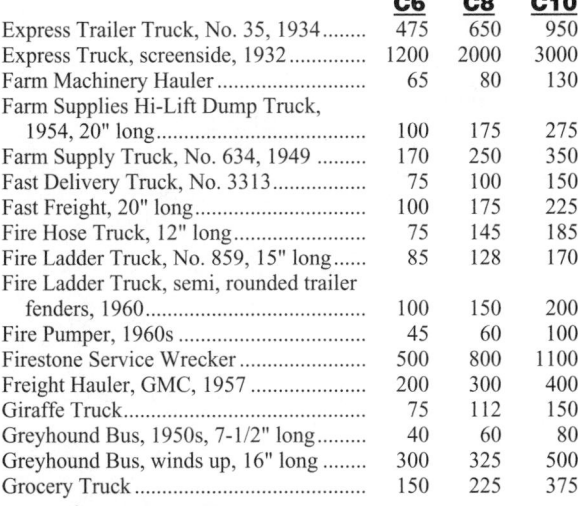

Buddy "L" Concrete Mixer, 1930s. Photo courtesy Calvin L. Chaussee

	C6	C8	C10
Half Track	75	100	150
Heavy Machinery Truck	120	180	250
High Lift Dumper, 1954	150	275	425
Highway Maintenance Dump	50	75	125
Hi-Lift Scoop-A-Dump	65	100	150
Hook and Ladder, 1961	75	125	200
Horse Van, 18" long	75	125	200
Hose Truck, No. 38, 1933, 21-3/4" long	125	225	325
Hot Rod	50	75	100
Hot Rod Station Wagon	60	90	125
Husky Dumper, late 1950s	100	150	225
Hydraulic Aerial Truck, No. 27, 1933-34, 40" long w/ladders down	1200	1300	1500
Hydraulic Dump, 1938, 26" long	900	1400	2400
Hydraulic Dump, 1960s	150	225	400
Hydraulic Dump, No. 5859, 1949	275	400	700
Hydraulic Dump Truck, 1932, 25" long	1100	1700	2800
Hydraulic Dump Truck, No. 10, 1933-34, 23-3/4" long	200	300	450
Hydraulic Highway Maintenance Dumper w/Blade Truck, No. 5552, orange, 1958, 17-3/4" long	125	175	275
Hydraulic Plow Truck	80	120	175
Hy-way Maintenance Mechanical Truck and Concrete Mixer, No. 822, 1949, 36" long	350	525	700
Ice Cream Truck	65	100	140
Ice Truck, No. 12, 1933-34, 26-1/2" long	600	1000	1750
International Delivery Truck, No. 51, 1935, 24-1/2" long	200	300	475
International Ice Truck, 28" long, 1939	500	800	1200
International Wrecker	700	1100	1800
Kennel Truck, w/twelve dogs	75	125	175
Ladder Truck, 1935	375	563	750
Lift Gate Truck	65	100	150
Machinery Hauler	125	200	275
Mack 30-Ton Dump	75	125	190
Mack Quarry Dump	40	60	90
Mack Tandem, 1969	35	60	90

Buddy "L" Fire Ladder truck, semi-rounded trailer fenders, 1960. Photo courtesy Calvin L. Chaussee

Buddy "L" Hi-Lift Scoop-A-Dump. Photo courtesy Thomas G. Nefos

Buddy "L" Hose Truck, 1933, 21-3/4". Photo courtesy Joe and Sharon Freed

Buddy "L" Hydraulic Aerial Truck, 1930s. Photo courtesy Bertoia Auctions

Buddy "L" Hydraulic Dump Truck, 1960s

Buddy "L" Hydraulic Highway Maintenance Truck, 17". Photo courtesy Calvin L. Chaussee

Buddy "L" Ladder Truck, 1935. Photo courtesy Heinz Mueller

Buddy "L" Hy-Way Maintenance Mechanical Truck nd Concrete Mixer, 1949, 36". Photo courtesy Tim Oei

Buddy L Coca-Cola Truck, 1950s, 14", bottles missing. Photo courtesy Calvin L. Chaussee

Buddy "L" Concrete Mixer, 1950-51, 10-3/4". Photo courtesy Bertoia Auctions

	C6	C8	C10
Marshall Field Company, 1966 Step Van	125	200	300
Merry-Go-Round Truck, No. 5429	75	125	175
Milk Delivery Truck, early, 24" long.......	1500	2500	4250
Missile Launcher, GMC..........................	75	125	180
Mister Buddy Ice Cream Van, No. 5353. Made from 1964-67, the 1964-65 model had white plastic bumper and underbody, the 1966-67 was red. The 1967 hubcaps had a "B" in a simple ring. 11-1/2" long.................................	125	200	325
Mobile Repair-It, 1940s, 24" long	200	300	400
Motor Market, 1937, 22" long	175	275	425
Pickup Truck, early 1960s	50	75	125
Railroad Transfer Truck, 1945-48, 23" long...	250	400	550
Railway Express Truck, "Baby Ruth" and "Butterfinger" tandem, 1935.........	1000	1750	2750
Railway Express Truck, 1953, milk ad	125	200	325
Ranchero Stake Truck	100	150	225
Red Baby Pickup, 24" long	500	800	1300
Red Baby Pickup, doors open, 26" long ..	1500	2500	4000
Repair-It, 15" long..................................	125	200	300
Ride-Em Dump, No. 702, 20" long..........	200	300	450
Ride-Em Fire Truck, electric lights, 1920s..	800	1600	2500
Riding Academy, No. 5455 truck, w/three horses	50	75	125
Rival Dog Food Truck, came w/either one or two banks shaped as dog food cans, 1950s, rare..................................	175	325	475

	C6	C8	C10
Robotoy Dump Truck, w/driver, operates on remote control	500	1000	1250
Sand and Gravel Truck, 1950s, 15" long .	75	100	150
Sand and Gravel Truck, No. 3312	100	150	225
Sanitation Truck, late	75	100	150
Scarab, No. 211, no wind-up mechanism	200	350	550
Scarab, No. 711, winds up	200	275	425
Scissors Dump	40	60	100
Scoop Conveyor.......................................	75	100	150
Scoop Dump	100	175	275
Searchlight Truck, GMC, 1950s	75	100	150
Service Truck, 1953	120	180	250
Shell Truck, 13-1/2" long........................	175	275	400
Shell Truck, 1941, 17-1/2" long..............	500	750	1250
Signal Corps Unit, 1957, 24" long	150	250	350
Siren Pull-n-Ride	100	160	240
Stake Truck, GMC, 1960s (?)	100	150	225
Standard Oil Truck, 1933-34, 26" long....	850	1300	2200
Station Wagon, Ford, 1964, 14-1/2" long	60	100	160
Steam Shovel, 1938	100	150	225
Steam Shovel, mechanical, No. 30, 1935, 17-1/2" long, 13-1/2" high..................	150	275	450
Steam Shovel, No. 944, 1940, 17-1/2" long...	200	275	425
Steam Shovel and International Truck, No. 16, 1937, 29-1/2" long, 13-1/2" high	150	275	350
Stepside Pickup Truck, 1950s.................	50	100	150
Store Delivery Truck...............................	75	125	200
Sunshine Biscuits Van	150	250	350

Buddy "L" Delivery Truck, Deluxe Rider, 22-3/4". Photo courtesy Joe and Sharon Freed

Buddy "L" Double Hydraulic Self-Loader-N-Dump Truck. Photo courtesy Thomas G. Nefos

Buddy "L" Scarab No. 711, bumpers missing in photo. Photo courtesy Heinz Mueller, Continental Hobby House

Left to right: Buddy "L" Station Wagon, Ford, 1964; Camper 1961.

Buddy "L" Sunshine Biscuits Van. Photo courtesy Joe and Sharon Freed

Buddy "L" Super Market Delivery Truck, 1950, 13-3/4". Photo courtesy Continental Auctions

Buddy "L" Texaco Tanker, 27". Photo courtesy Calvin L. Chaussee

Buddy "L" Tank Truck, restored, 27". Photo courtesy Calvin L. Chaussee

Buddy "L" Trench Digger, yellow frame, red elevator and conveyor frames, 24". Photo courtesy Bertoia Auctions

Buddy "L" Fire and Chemical Truck, two-tone white and red, No. 646, 1949-51, 25". Photo courtesy John Taylor

Buddy "L" Jr. Milk Delivery Truck. Photo courtesy Bertoia Auctions

Buddy "L" Riding Academy Truck, three horses. Photo courtesy Thomas G. Nefos

Buddy "L" Farm Supplies Hi-Lift Dump Truck, 1954, 20". Note the original retail price!

Buddy "L" Excavator Truck and Shovel Set, 1940. Photo courtesy John Taylor

	C6	C8	C10
Super Market Delivery Truck	80	125	175
Super Motor Market Truck	250	425	650
Supply Truck w/load	100	150	250
Surf Truck, 1953, 12" long	100	150	225
Tank Truck, 1930s, 27" long	500	750	1200
Tank Truck, No. 438, 1935, 19-1/4" long	400	650	1000
Tank Truck, No. 938, 1941, 21-1/2" long	200	300	450
Telephone Truck, GMC	125	175	250
Telephone Truck, w/trailer	75	125	175
Texaco Tanker, 27" long	125	200	325
Texaco Tanker, promo sold at gas stations, 25" long	75	125	200
Towing Service Wrecker, 26" long	175	275	425
Traveling Zoo, post WWII	80	110	150
Trench Digger, yellow frame, red elevator and conveyor frames, 24" long	850	1250	2750
U.S. Mail Truck, "2582," c.1941, 21-3/4" long	325	500	750
U.S. Mail Truck, 1950s, green	NPF	NPF	NPF
U.S. Mail Truck, early 1930s, 22" long	1000	1800	3200
U.S. Mail Truck, No. 5354, 1964	100	150	225
Utility Delivery Truck, No. 946, 25" long, 1941-42	75	125	200
Utility Truck, GMC	75	110	165
Van Freight Carrier, 1940s, 20" long	150	225	300
Volkswagen Bus, 1960s	75	125	200
Water Tower, No. 28, 1936	1250	2250	3500
Wild Animal Circus Truck	100	175	300
Wrecker, 16" long	100	150	250
Wrecker, 1936-37, 27" long	500	900	1500
Wrecker, 1938, 26" long	800	1600	2500
Wrecker, 1940s, 22" long	175	275	375
Wrecker, 1963, w/tools, No. 5427	75	125	225
Wrecker, Emergency Towing Rider, No. 903, 1949, 33" long	75	125	200
Wrecker, No. 13, 1933, 31" long	800	1500	3200
Wrecker, No. 37, 1933, 24" long	125	250	450
Wrecker, No. 437, 1934, 24" long	350	500	850
Wrecker, No. 503, 1940, 1941-42, 19-1/4" long	175	275	375
Wrecker, No. 647, 1949, 26-1/4" long	150	250	375
Wrecker, No. 813, 1938, 32" long	75	125	225
Wrecker, No. 903, 1950, "Buddy L Emergency Towing," 33" long	80	140	225
Wrecker, No. 937, 1939, 25-1/4" long	125	200	325
Wrecker, No. 937, 1941-42 version, 25" long	125	175	300
Wrecker, No. W37, 1939, 25-1/4" long	100	150	250
Wrecking Truck, wood wheels, 1940, scarce variation, 19" long	150	275	325

A page from an L. Gould & Co. catalog

Buddy "L" Wrecker, 1940s. Photo courtesy John Taylor

Buddy "L" Wrecker, 1940s, wood wheels, scarce version, 19-1/2". Photo courtesy John Taylor

Buddy "L" Wrecker, No. 3317, white, red crane, 1954, 15-1/2". Photo courtesy Calvin L. Chaussee

Buddy "L" Wild Animal Circus Truck. Photo courtesy Thomas G. Nefos

Buddy "L" Lumber Truck. Photo courtesy Bertoia Auctions

Buddy "L" made several Repair-It trucks. Photo courtesy Mapes Auctioneers

Buddy "L" Wrigley's Spearmint Railway Express Truck, 1935, with working headlights, 23-1/2". Photo courtesy Rodney A. Heesacker

Buddy "L" Jr. Dump Truck, 22". Photo courtesy Bertoia Auctions

Buddy "L" Sand and Stone truck. Photo courtesy Continental Hobby House

	C6	C8	C10
Wrigley's Spearmint, 1957	150	200	350
Wrigley's Spearmint Railway Express Agency Truck, No. 953, 1940..............	800	1350	2250
Wrigley's Spearmint Railway Express Truck, 1935, headlights light up, 23-1/8" long	750	1250	2250
Wrigley's Spearmint Railway Express Truck, No. 835, 1938, 25" long	750	1250	2000

Buddy L Jr.

	C6	C8	C10
Airmail Truck, 22" long	1500	2500	3750
Baggage Truck, 22" long	1800	3000	4500
Cement Mixer, No. 2006, green w/black steel wheels, 1930-35, 10-1/2" long.....	300	450	600
Dairy Truck, 22" long	1000	1800	2750
Dairy Truck, late	105	158	210
Dairy Truck, No. 2002, 1930-32, 24" long..	350	525	700
Dump Truck, 22" long	800	1200	1850
Dump Truck, early, 24" long	1300	2500	4500
Milk Delivery Truck, No. 2002	2000	3500	5000
Oil Truck, 22" long	1200	2000	2800
Steam Shovel, treads, 24" long	800	1400	2000

Buddy "L" Water Tower Truck, 1930s. Photo courtesy Bertoia Auctions

Buddy "L" Ice Truck, 1933-34, 26-1/2". Photo Tim Oei

Buddy "L" U.S. Mail Truck, 1950s, green. Photo courtesy Calvin L. Chaussee

	C6	C8	C10
Steam Shovel on Treads, No. 2005, 1930-32, 24" long	150	275	400

Construction Equipment

	C6	C8	C10
Aerial Tramway, 1929-30, No. 360	1500	240	3700
Concrete Mixer, 1926-30, No. 280	500	750	1000
Dredge (Clamshell), 1926-30, No. 270....	800	1200	1600
Heavy Shovel (on Treads), 1929-30, No. 220AB, 27-1/2" long....................	2500	4000	7000
Heavy Steam Shovel, 1929-30, No. 220A, 27-1/2" long	400	600	800
Hoisting Tower, 1929-31, No. 350	500	900	1250
Large Derrick, 1922-31, No. 241	275	375	600
Mixer (on Treads), 1929-31, No. 280A ...	1100	1700	2600
Overhead Crane, 1924-27, No. 250	700	1100	1750
Pile Driver, 1926-28, No. 260.................	750	1125	1600
Road Roller, 1929-31, No. 290, only model made these years, 20" long	2100	3700	5280
Sand Loader, 1925-31, No. 230	175	250	350
Sand Screener, 1929-30, No. 300	700	1100	1700
Small Derrick, 1922-31, No. 240.............	300	450	625
Steam Shovel, 1921-31, No. 220	250	375	600
Tractor Dredge (on Treads), 1929-30, No. 270A..	2500	5000	8000
Traveling Crane, 1928-30, No. 250A	NPF	NPF	NPF
Trencher, 1928-31, No. 400	1800	2700	4200

Fire Trucks

	C6	C8	C10
Aerial Ladder, 1926-30, No. 205B	750	1400	2200
Hook & Ladder, 1924-31, No. 205, 26" long..	800	1250	1950
Insurance Patrol, 1926-30, No. 205C.......	1500	2500	3500
Pumper, 1925-30, No. 205A, 23" long	1100	1800	2500

Buddy "L" Mister Buddy Ice Cream Van, 1964-65. Photo courtesy Thomas G. Nefos

Buddy "L" pre-1932 Coach, light green motorbus. Photo courtesy Bertoia Auctions

Buddy "L" Dump Truck (Ratchet), 1921-30. Photo courtesy Joseph and Sharon Freed

Buddy "L" Express Truck, 1921-31. Photo courtesy Bertoia Auctions

Top to bottom: Buddy "L" Hydraulic Dump Truck, 1926-31; Dump Truck (Ratchet), 1921-30. Photo courtesy Tim Oei

Buddy "L" Dump Truck (Ratchet), restored, 1921-30. Photo courtesy Calvin L. Chaussee

Buddy "L" pre-1932 Hook and Ladder. Photo courtesy Calvin L. Chaussee

Another Buddy "L" pre-1932 Hook and Ladder, rubber tires. Photo courtesy Bertoia Auctions

Buddy "L" Pumper, 1925-30. Photo courtesy Bertoia Auctions

Buddy "L" Road Roller, 1929-31, No. 290 20". Photo courtesy Calvin L. Chaussee

Buddy "L" Steam Shovel, 1920s. Photo courtesy Calvin L. Chaussee

	C6	C8	C10
Pumper (Working), 1930-31, No. 205AB, 23" long	1000	1800	3000
Water Tower Truck (Working), 1930-31, No. 205D	2500	4500	7250

Large Trucks

	C6	C8	C10
A Hydraulic Dump Truck, 1926-31, No. 201	600	1100	1700
Auto Wrecker, 1928-31 (Tow Truck), No. 209	1750	2750	4500
Baggage Truck, 1929-31, No. 203B	1400	2300	3500
Coach, 1928-31, light green, No. 208	2000	3300	4800
Coal Truck, 1926-31, No. 202	2500	4000	6500
Dump Truck (Ratchet), 1921-30, No. 201	500	750	1250
Express Truck, 1921-31, No. 200	1000	1600	2500
Hydraulic Dump Truck, 1026-29, No. 201A, black body, red chassis, red disc wheels w/aluminum tires, 25" long	450	950	1400

	C6	C8	C10
Ice Truck, 1926-31, No. 207	600	750	1250
Lumber Truck, 1925-30, No. 203A	1500	2500	4000
Moving Van, 1924-30, No. 204	750	1250	2000
Oil Truck, 1925-30, No. 206A	900	1500	2200
Railway Express, 1926-31, No. 204A	1000	1600	2500
Sand & Gravel Truck, 1926-31, No. 202A	1500	2500	3500
Stake Truck, 1921-24, 1926-28, No. 203	750	1350	1900
Street Sprinkler Truck, 1924-31, No. 206	1250	1750	2750

Model T Series

	C6	C8	C10
Flivver Coupe, 1925-30, No. 210B	400	700	1200
Flivver Roadster, 1925-27, No. 210A	500	750	1250
Flivver Truck, 1925-30, No. 210	900	1400	1900
Ford Dump Cart, 1926-30, No. 211	800	1550	2750
Ford Dump Truck, 1926-30, No. 211A	1100	1700	2650
Ford Express Truck, 1929-30, No. 212	1400	2300	3250
One-Ton Ford Delivery Truck, 1929-30, No. 212A	2000	3500	5000

Pages from a 1930s-era L.Gould & Co. catalog.

Buddy "L" pre-1932 Oil Truck, yellow and black, Hill City inscription. Photo courtesy Calvin L. Chaussee

Buddy "L" Street Sprinkler Truck, 1924-31. Photo courtesy Bertoia Auctions

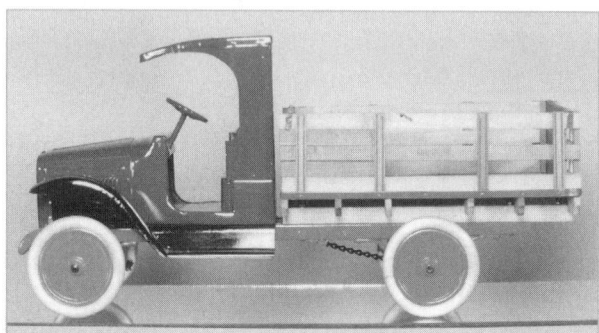

Buddy "L" pre-1932 Stake Truck. Photo courtesy Bertoia Auctions

Buddy "L" Railway Express, 1926-31. Photo courtesy Bertoia Auctions

Buddy "L" Sand and Gravel Truck. Photo courtesy Bertoia Auctions

Buddy "L" Greyhound Bus, wooden. Photo courtesy Bertoia Auctions

Top to bottom: Buddy "L" Coal Truck, 1926-31; Sand and Gravel Truck, 1926-31. Photo courtesy Bertoia Auctions

Buddy "L" Flivver Roadster, 1925-27. Photo courtesy Harry Wolf, Detroit Antique Museum

Buddy "L" Auto Wrecker, 1928-31. Photo courtesy Bertoia Auctions

Wooden

	C6	C8	C10
Aerial Ladder Truck, wooden, 32" long ..	800	1300	1800
Army Combat Car, wooden, w/cannon....	150	225	325
Army Tank, No. 362, wooden, 1943, 13" long..	45	75	125
Army Truck, wooden, canvas top, 13" long..	115	180	275
Army Truck, wooden, canvas top, 16" long..	100	175	275
Big Show Circus Truck, No. 484, wooden, 25-1/2" long.................	750	1000	1500
Buick Convertible, wooden, 18" long......	275	450	750
Coca Cola Truck, wooden, c.WWII, only three known, 19" long.................	1500	2500	4200

	C6	C8	C10
Convertible, No. 499, wooden, blue, 1949, 19" long.....................................	400	700	1000
Fire Chief's Car, No. 483, w/siren, wooden, 1948, 19-1/2" long	475	750	1100
Fire Engine, wooden, 13" long	100	140	220
Fire Ladder Truck, wooden, 1943-45, 37-1/2" long	90	130	190
Fire Station, No, 475, wooden, w/wooden chief car and ladder truck, 1947-49, 20" long..................................	1200	1500	2500
Greyhound Bus, No. 481, wooden, w/bell, 18-1/2" long	450	675	1000
Hook and Ladder Truck, No. 859, wooden, black rubber tires for 1949, 1948-49, 21-1/2" long.........................	250	375	550
Long Distance Moving Van, No. 366, wooden, 1943-47, 31" long.................	225	350	500
Lumber Truck, wooden, 30" long	400	600	900
Milk Farms Truck, wooden.....................	200	300	450
Pepsi-Cola Truck, wooden	800	1000	1600
Popsicle Truck, wooden, 17" long	400	600	900
Pure Ice Truck, No. 357 1943-46, No. 757 in 1947, wooden, w/metal tongs and 3 ice blocks, 16" long	125	175	300
Railway Express Truck, No. 480, wooden, 1947, 16-1/4" long	300	500	750
Station Wagon, No. 371, wooden, 1948-49, 19" long	140	200	325

Buddy "L" Concrete Mixer, 1926-30. Photo courtesy Bertoia Auctions

Buddy "L" Steam Shovel. Photo courtesy Joe and Sharon Freed

Top to bottom: Buddy "L" Baggage Truck, 1929-31; Auto Wrecker, 1928-31. Photo courtesy Bertoia Auctions

Buddy "L" Baggage Truck, No. 203B. Photo courtesy Joe and Sharon Freed

Buddy "L" Army Tank, 1943, wooden, 13". Photo courtesy Jack Matthews

Buddy "L" Coca-Cola Truck, wooden, 19". Photo courtesy Richard MacNary

Buddy "L" Big Show Circus Truck, wood, 1947, 25".

Buddy "L" Fire Station, wooden, with wooden chief car and ladder truck. Photo courtesy Bertoia Auctions

Buddy "L" Long Distance Moving Van, wooden. Photo courtesy Bertoia Auctions

Buddy "L" Fire Chief's Car, 1947, 19-1/2". Photo courtesy William G. Floyd

Buddy "L" Baggage Truck, 1929-31. Photo courtesy James S. Maxwell and Virginia Caputo

Buddy "L" Fire Station, wooden, with wooden chief car and ladder truck. Photo courtesy Bertoia Auctions

Buddy "L" Railway Express Truck No. 480, wooden, 1947; the pressed-steel hand truck came with it. Photo courtesy William G. Floyd

	C6	C8	C10
Taxi, wooden..	450	750	1250
Timber Truck, No. 365, wooden, 1943-47, 25" long	150	225	350
Town and Country Convertible, No. 471, wooden, convertible top folds down, 1947-49, 19" long	300	500	750
Truck, open bed, wooden, 16" long	NPF	NPF	NPF
Victory Jeep and Cannon, wooden	100	150	250
Wrecker, wooden, 18" long.....................	125	175	250

Buddy "L" Station Wagon, wooden, 19". Photo courtesy Joe and Sharon Freed

Buddy "L" Truck w/open bed, wooden, 16".

Buddy "L" Wrecker, wooden, 18". Photo courtesy Perry Eichor

BUFFALO TOY & TOOL WORKS

Buffalo Toys, of Buffalo, New York, began in 1924 and produced a number of lightweight steel toys until World War II. The firm ceased to exist in 1968.

	C6	C8	C10
Blue Bird Racer..	350	475	700
Bumper Car, wind-up, 10" long	55	83	110
Mack Stake Truck, electric lights, circa 1928, 25" long	300	450	700
Niagara Lines, 15-1/2" long, aluminum...	2500	3500	6000
Red Streak Racer, 24" long	350	475	700
Silver Bullet Racer, 26" long	375	525	725
Silver Dash...	175	263	350
Silver Streak	300	450	600
Zepplin, tin, w/4 airplanes, originally retailed for $1.25, 24-1/2" long............	200	575	900

Buffalo Toys Mack Stake Truck, 1920s, 25".

BUILT-RITE

Created by Warren Paper Works, Built-Rite of Lafayette, Indiana, began in 1922 as a cardboard box manufacturer. In 1934, it began to produce cardboard construction toys and stayed in business until the 1970s.

	C6	C8	C10
Airport, No. 18	65	80	95
Armored Car, No. 04................................	15	20	30
Army Battery Set, No. 20.........................	90	125	145
Army Raiders' Victory Unit, No. 50, truck, tank, AA gun, jeep, semitrack truck, twenty soldiers, WWII, No. 50, twenty-eight pieces	75	95	105
Commercial Garage, No. 15	65	80	90
Five Miniature buildings, No. 56, church, school, RR station, firehouse, drugstore, No. 56	35	55	65
Garage and Super Service Station, No. 28	70	85	95

Built-Rite Airport. Photo courtesy Barbara and Jonathan A. Newman

Built-Rite Army Battery Set. Photo courtesy Ed Poole

	C6	C8	C10
House, boxed set w/19" house and garage, twenty-seven pieces of furniture, sedan, baby buggy, shrubbery, etc., No. 415, c.1943, 13" x 20"	65	80	90
Navy Battle Fleet and Coast Artillery Gun, No. 60	35	60	75
Private Garage, brick, No. 7	35	45	55
Service Station, No. 17	65	80	90
Weapons Carrier, No. 83	15	20	30

BURDETTE

	C6	C8	C10
Murray Express Truck, resembles Model T, 26" long	1600	2700	3800

	C6	C8	C10
Murray White Standard Bed Truck	2000	3200	4600

BURNETT

Burnett, Ltd. of Birmingham, England, started producing tinplate toy cars around the turn of the century. Its cars were of excellent quality. Burnett moved the business to London in 1914 and continued to make toys into the 1930s. The company was then purchased by Chad Valley. Burnett toys are quite rare.

Contributor: Bob Smith.

	C6	C8	C10
Cargo Truck, maroon and black, clockwork motor, driver, 8-1/2" long, c.1926	675	875	1400
Limousine, blue/black, clockwork motor, driver, 8" long, c.1925	675	875	1400
Roadster, green/black, clockwork motor, driver, folding windshield, c.1925, 7-1/2" long	675	875	1400
Toyland Bus, 14-1/2" long	675	925	1450

Burnett Cargo Truck, 1920s, maroon and black, 8-1/2" (Coca Cola bottles were not part of the original truck.). Photo courtesy Bob Smith

Burnette Roadster, green and black, c.1925, 7-1/2". Photo courtesy Bob Smith

Burnett Limousine, 1920s, blue and black, 8". Photo courtesy Bob Smith

BW MOLDED PLASTICS

Little is known about BW Molded Plastics, except that in 1954, it was located at 1346 East Walnut Street in Pasadena, California. A variety of plastic toys were made, including musical instruments, tea sets, ships and vehicles.

	C6	C8	C10		C6	C8	C10
Auto Parade Set, pickup truck, convertible, coupe, ladder truck, racer, five piece (BW0873B)	NPF	NPF	NPF	Jeep, 9-1/4" long (BW0886)	NPF	NPF	NPF
				Race Car, 3-1/2" long (BW0000)	13	20	27
Fire Truck, 3-1/2" long (BW0000)	13	20	27	Roly The Steam Roller, "fully mechanized" (BW0879)	NPF	NPF	NPF
Jaguar, 12-1/2" long (BW0888)	NPF	NPF	NPF				

C.A.W. NOVELTY COMPANY

It is remarkable, indeed, that collectors had not found this fine company until 1990. Charles A. Wood not only ran a substantial operation, but he made some of the finest replica toys in the slush-mold industry. Ironically, C.A.W. was in existence longer than most in the slush-mold industry. Founded about 1925, his company was active until lead casting came to a halt due to World War II.

Wood's output showed artistry, ingenuity, and meticulous craftsmanship. All of his toys were smooth, crisp, had detailed moldings, and extra touches such as open windshields and two or three colors on each toy. The early production toys had metal disk wheels with black-painted tires or metal spoked wheels. When you find open, V-shaped, divided windshield, drivers inside cabs, and tri-motored aircraft with the outboard engines mounted on the landing gear struts, you wonder how it was done for the five-cent price. According to Wood, it sometimes took him three or four years to make a mold. The molds are also works of art—machinist's art.

Wood was born about 1891. He lived and worked in Topeka, Kansas and in nearby Clifton, before moving to Clay Center. He was known for his civic pride and good works. After he helped establish the local airport, he built and operated his own aircraft maintenance hanger. A master machinist, he made all his toy molds, production tools, and toy parts—even the plastic wheels.

Over the years, there were rumors of a "small molder in Clay Center." A few years ago, a small monoplane with initials "CAW" marked under its tail was found. Eventually, a collection owned by a relative of Wood as well as a few pieces and some paper memorabilia was discovered in mint condition. Although a complete list has yet to be compiled, some of those "orphans" have been identified. Wood made airplanes, autos, novelties, and trucks. Some of these have been well known to collectors, although unidentified. Clearly, this company and its toys deserve to be more fully known.

The C&H Mfg. Co. was formed in 1940 by Rod Hemphill, the last C.A.W. employee, and Howard Clevenger. According to Mrs. Hemphill, they only used original C.A.W. models. Apparently, this effort at revival managed to reproduce some toys before C&H went under. These are heavier than C.A.W.'s and have black rubber wheels. Their claim to fame is in publication of the accompanying partial flyer that allowed us to solve the paternity of these handsome orphans. However, judging from the catalog numbers and our incomplete list below, there must be several orphans out there. Can any of you collectors help?

The seldom-found C.A.W. trademark, consists of unique, lead-blind hubs fitted over a wire axle. They are sometimes found with ordinary nail axles piercing the hubs.

Contributor: Perry R. Eichor, 703 North Almond Drive, Simpsonville, SC, 29681 and the late Fred Maxwell.

ABBREVIATIONS

The following abbreviations are for the details and variations useful in identification.

HG	horizontal grille pattern	**SM**	sidemounted spare
HL	horizontal hood louvers	**SP**	string-pull knob in handcrank area
HO	hood cap, Motometer or ornament	**T**	external trunk
L	lacquer finish	**UV**	unnumbered version
LI	landau irons on convertibles	**VG**	vertical grille pattern
MDW	metal disc wheels	**VL**	vertical hood louvers
MDSW	metal disc solid spokes	**WS, W/S**	windshield
MDWBT	wheels with black painted tires	**WV**	windshield visor
MSW	metal open spoke wheels	**WHRT**	wooden hubs, rubber tires
MWW	metal simulated wire wheels	**WRDW**	white hard rubber disc wheels
OW	open windows	**WRW**	white soft rubber wheels
RM	rearmount spare tire/wheel		(balloon tires)

C.A.W. Novelty Austin Bantam, part of the three-piece auto set, metal wheels.

C.A.W. Novelty Air Drive Coach, (CWV05), rear propeller drive. Photo courtesy Fred Maxwell

C.A.W. Novelty Dump Truck, (CWV13), hinged dump body.

C.A.W. Novelty Austin Bantam, part of the three-piece auto set, white rubber wheels. Photo courtesy Craig A. Clark

C.A.W. Novelty DeSoto Sedan, airflow, (CWV09), divided windshield. Photo courtesy Gary Franson

C.A.W. Novelty Dump Truck, (CWV13), hinged dump body in "down" position. Photo courtesy Ferd Zegel

	C6	C8	C10
Air Drive Coach, No. 25; blimp-like bus w/fin and rear propeller drive; twelve OW, WRW w/unique fitted hubs which cap hidden axles; there ia also a version w/o propellor; 3-7/8" long (CWV05)	30	50	75
Austin Bantam, two-door sedanette, five OW, HL, plain grille, RM, MDW (easily confused w/other makers' Bantams); 2" long, (CWV12C)	20	30	40
DeSoto Sedan, No. 32, Airflow, divided WS, BOW, HL, VG, HO, WRW; 3-7/8" long (CWV09)	40	85	130
Dump Truck, no number, Ford (?), hinged dump body, divided open WS, two OW, HG, MDW; 3-1/8" long (CWV13)	40	85	140
Fuel Tanker, no number, Ford (?) truck, cab w/driver inside, no WS, HG, three tanks, hose compartment, MSW; 3-3/4" long (CWV04)	40	60	80

	C6	C8	C10
Marvel Racer, No. 31, Streamlined FWD Indy type, driver, torpedo tail w/very small fin, V-grille pattern, eight exhaust ports, aluminum wheels; 3-5/8" long (CWV08)	40	80	120
Marvel Racer, No. 31, Streamlined FWD Indy type, driver, torpedo tail w/very small fin, V-grille pattern, eight exhaust ports, aluminum wheels; also found in a modern bubble-pack, w/lucent hard plastic wheels, "Woodchuck Industries Metal Toys, Clay Center, Ks."; this name may have been a new idea or part of a rare market test; 3-5/8" long (CWV08A)	40	80	120
Midget Coupe Racer, HG, HL, divided open WS, two OW, two colored body, MDW, headlamps and cowl ventilators, 2-1/16" long, (CWV12A)	20	30	40

C.A.W. Novelty Fuel Truck, (CWV04), three tanks.

C.A.W. Novelty Marvel Racer, (CWV08), Indy type, driver, eight exhaust ports. Photo courtesy Gary Franson

C.A.W. Novelty Midget Racer, (CWV12B), part of Auto Set. Photo courtesy Gary Franson

C.A.W. Novelty Midget Coupe Racer (CWV12A), and Fuel Tanker (CWV04). Photo courtesy Craig Clark

C.A.W. Novelty New Design Racer, (CWV10), two oval open windows show driver, rounded tail, 3-3/8". Photo courtesy Gary Franson

C.A.W. Novelty Overland Bus, (CWV03), tour bus, no headlamps, twelve windows. Photo courtesy Gary Franson

C.A.W. Novelty Wonder Special, (CWV07), 3-3/8", three wheels, front wheel skirts. Photo courtesy Gary Franson

C.A.W. Novelty Streamline Coupe, (CWV06), small rear fin, 3". Photo courtesy Perry Eichor

C.A.W. Novelty Sport Roadster, (CWV02), plain grille. Photo courtesy Gary Franson

C.A.W. Novelty Streamline Coupe, (CWV06), small rear fin, white tires, 3". Photo courtesy Craig Clark

	C6	C8	C10
Midget Racer, gilt driver, VL, HG, MDW (easily confused w/Barclay No. 53); 2-1/8" long, (CWV12B)	20	30	40
New Design Racer, No. 38, streamlined coupe, rounded tail, driver visible through two oval OW, HO loop (stringpull?), WRW w/hubs; 3-3/8" long (CWV10)	30	40	50
Overland Bus, no number; Fageol (?) Yellow Line (?) tour bus, HG, no headlamps, twelve windows, shallow observer deck, MDW, left SM; 3-3/4" long (CWV03)	20	40	50
Sport Roadster, no number; later model Buick, no WS, plain grille, VL, RM, right SM, MDW; there is also a version with MSW; 3-1/2" long (CWV02)	30	40	50
Sport Roadster, no number; Open Buick, driver w/gilt or silver cap, no WS, HG, VL, no headlamps, RM, MDW; 3-1/2" long (CWV01)	30	45	60
Streamline Coupe, No. 30; airflow, V-pattern grille, HO, four OW, small rear fin, small winged design on rear-wheel skirts, MDW also WRW; bottom pan goes over rear axle, not under; 3" long (CWV06)	25	50	75
Tank Truck, no number; Ford (?), three fuel tanks, hinged dump body, divided open WS, two OW, HG, MDW; unusual two-piece body connected by rear axle; 3-3/16" long (CWV14)	25	35	45
Tank Truck, no number; Gasoline semi-trailer, two tanks; cab w/divided WS and open windows shows it is part of a set (CWV15)	30	40	60
Three Piece Auto Set, No. 40; includes: (a) Midget coupe racer, CWV12A, HG, HL, divided open WS, two OW,			

	C6	C8	C10
two colored body, MDW, headlamps and cowl ventilators, 2-1/16" long; (b) Midget racer, CWV12B, gilt driver, VL, HG, MDW (easily confused w/Barclay No. 53); 2-1/8" long; (c) Austin Bantam, CWV12C, two-door sedanette, five OW, HL, plain grille, RM, MDW (easily confused w/other makers' Bantams); 2" long; value per each (CWV12)	20	30	40
Transparent Windshield Racer, No. 39; Indy FWD two man racer, v-shaped VG, dual exhausts, boattail, unique hubtires as in No. 25 (also WRW); not complete if divided plastic windshield is missing; 3" long (CWV11)	45	60	75
Wonder Special, No. 33, airflow coupe, three wheeled companion to No. 30 Streamline Coupe; VG, four OW, WRW, front wheel skirts; pan goes over front axle; 3-3/8" long (CWV07)	25	50	75

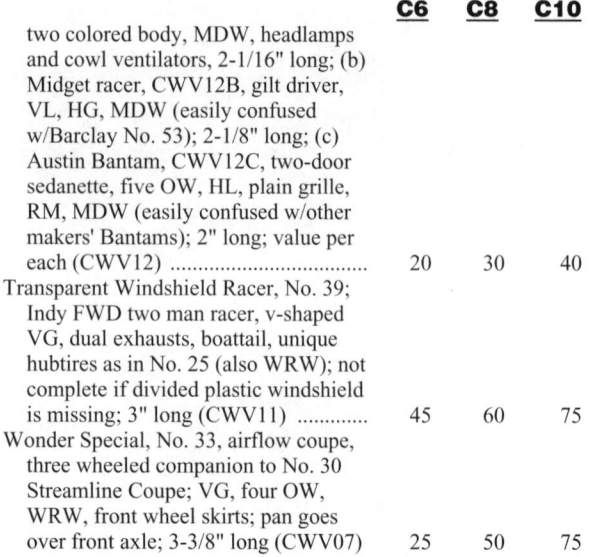

C.A.W. Novelty vehicles, part of a catalog sheet issued by St. Louis-based C&H Mfg. Co., around 1940—after the firm obtained C.A.W.'s molds.

C.A.W. Novelty Tank Truck, (CWV15), semi-trailer, two tanks. Photo courtesy Ferd Zegel

C.A.W. Novelty Tank Truck, (CWV14), three fuel tanks, 3-3/16". Photo courtesy Gary Franson

C.A.W. Novelty Transparent Windshield Racer, (CWV11), Indy type, two-main racer, dual exhausts. Photo courtesy Gary Franson

C.R.

(Charles Rossignol, Paris, 1868-1962)

Rossignol began making toy vehicles in 1895. The company became best known for the toy trains it produced in the nearly 100 years it was in business. In 1920, C.R. came out with a line of toy buses that lasted until the company closed its doors in 1962.

Contributor: Bob Smith, The Village Smith, 62 West Ave., Fairport, NY 14450-2102.

	C6	C8	C10
Dump Truck, clockwork motor, green and yellow, head lamps, dual side mount wheels, c.1935, 16" long	800	1300	2000
Large Bus	1200	2000	2800
Paris Tour Bus, wind-up, tin, green and white, 11-1/2" long, 1930s	250	500	800

	C6	C8	C10
Paris Tour Bus, wind-up, tin, open cab, green and white, 8-1/2" long, 1929	350	600	900
Rolls Royce, tin lithographed, clockwork motor, lights work, 14-1/2" long	1100	1900	2700
Streamline Sedan, wind-up, 14" long	550	700	900

C.R. Streamline Sedan, windup, 1930s, 14". Photo courtesy Bertoia Auctions

C.R. Dump Truck, 1930s, 16", green and yellow. Photo courtesy Bob Smith Collection. Photo by Len Rosenberg

C.R. Rolls-Royce, tin lithographed, 14-1/2". Photo courtesy Bertoia Auctions

CARETTE, GEORGES

Born in France, Carette went to Nuremberg to start his toy factory in 1886. He has since become a legend in the hobby. Next to Märklin, Carette is the most desirable of German toy carmakers. Known for its fine detail and quality of materials, Carette stayed in business until 1917. At the onset of World War I, he fled to France, and his company was taken over by Karl Bub. The Carette limousines were made in three general lengths, 9-inch (twenty-two centimeters), 12-1/2-inch (thirty-two centimeters), and 15-1/2-inch (forty centimeters). The larger size is the most desirable.

Contributor: Bob Smith, RATS Toy Shows, 255 Tryon Park, Rochester, NY 14609. (585) 288-7153, bird@oldtoysonline.com.

	C6	C8	C10
Landauleb Limosine	2600	4100	6800
Limousine, clockwork motor, 16" long	2100	3600	5300
Limousine, doors open, roof rack, c.1911, 12-1/4" long	1700	2800	4400
Limousine, w/chauffeur, c.1910, 12-1/2" long	1300	2300	3400
Limousine Driver, luggage rack, high headlamps, 15" long	2600	4100	6300
Limousine Driver, passenger, clockwork motor, 12-1/2" long	2100	3600	5300

	C6	C8	C10
Open Car, Carette/Bub, clockwork motor, w/tin-plate or cloth dressed driver, red and black, hand brake, forward and reverse gear, c.1911, 6-1/2" long	1000	1600	2300
Open Car, w/driver, 9" long	700	975	1500
Open Phaeton, w/driver, c.1906, 12" long	2100	3600	5600

Carette/Bub Open Car, red and black, 6-7/10".

	C6	C8	C10
Open Toures, wind-up, four-seat, w/two bisque figures, 12-1/2" long	6100	12,100	17,300
Phaeton, four-seat, w/two figures, 9" long	1300	2300	3700
Rear Entrance Tonneau, clockwork motor, w/four figures, 8-1/2" long	1600	2600	4300

Carette Limousine, circa 1911, 9".

Carette Limousine, driver, luggage rack, high headlamps, 15". Photo courtesy Bertoia Auctions

Carette Limousine, 1910, chauffeur, 12-1/2". Photo courtesy Bertoia Auctions

Carette Limousine, chauffeur, passenger, clockwork motor, 12-1/2". Photo courtesy Bertoia Auctions

Carette Open Tourer, four seat, two bisque figures, 12-1/2". Photo courtesy Bertoia Auctions

CASS TOYS

The N.D. Cass Toy Company of Athol, Massachusetts was known simply as "Cass Toys." The company made a variety of wooden toys from its 1896 inception to the 1960s and survived until a spectacular fire destroyed the factory in 1996.

	C6	C8	C10
Delivery Truck Ride 'em, wooden, 30" long	25	38	50
Dump Truck Ride 'em, wooden, 36" long	32	48	65
Station Wagon, wooden, 19" long	60	90	120
Streamlined Truck Ride 'em, 30" long	110	165	220
Tank, wooden, "General Lee," marked "224," 12" long	55	83	110
Truck Ride 'em, wooden, 40" long	150	225	300

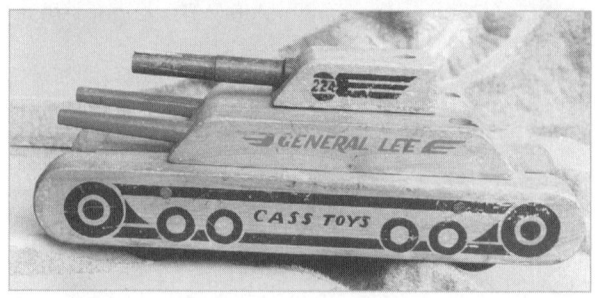

Cass Tank, General Lee, wooden, 12". Photo courtesy Ron Fink

CHAD VALLEY

Chad Valley traces its origins to a printing firm founded in the early 1800s. By 1897, father and son Joseph and Alfred Johnson set up a factory in the village of Harbourne near a stream named, The Chad. Taking their name from that stream, The Chad Valley Works was born. The company gradually moved into game production and released a line of teddy bears in 1915.

Chad Valley Delivery Truck, 10". Photo courtesy Bertoia Auctions

Chad Valley expanded its line and produced a wide variety of toys including vehicles unitl the 1970s. The company was sold to Palitoy in 1978 and the Chad Valley name was sold to Woolworth's in 1988.

	C6	**C8**	**C10**
Aerial Repair Truck, clockwork, 4" long	175	262	350
Bus, Midget series, clockwork motor	20	40	65
Bus, tin wind-up, "Red & White" decals, Burnett-type bus, 12" long, c.1950	125	275	450
Delivery Truck, marked "The Chad Valley Co. Ltd.," 10" long	650	1100	1500
Double Decker Bus, tin, marked "Chad Valley Toys," red or green, 6" long, 1950s	65	100	150
Fordson Major Tractor, 1950s, 6-1/2" long	100	150	200
Open Lorry, No. 225, Midget series, clockwork motor	20	40	65
Race Car, marked "Chad Valley Harborne Made in England" w/a "3" on the side, blue w/gray wheels	NFP	NPF	NPF
Remote Control Car, late 1940s, tin clockwork sedan with remote control steering working through bulb	100	175	250
Sedan, tin wind-up, rear luggage rack, 9-1/4" long	125	188	250
Sunbeam Talbot, Midget series, clockwork motor, bottom reads "A Wee Kin Toy Made in England"	20	40	6

CHAMPION

The Champion Hardware Co., though in business from 1883-1954, produced toys only from 1930-1936, as Depression stopgap. As might be expected from a hardware firm, its toys were cast iron. During its toy years the Geneva, Ohio outfit was headed by C.I. Chamberlin.

	C6	**C8**	**C10**
Airflow, 4-3/4" long	NPF	NPF	NPF
Coupe, Plymouth type, rumble seat opens, 7-1/2" long, auctioned in 1999 .			760
Coupe, Reo type, 7-1/2" long	450	600	900
Delivery Truck, No. 536, 1930s, 8" long	NPF	NPF	NPF

	C6	**C8**	**C10**
Gas and Motor Oil Truck, cast iron, 8" long	275	450	625
Mack Dump Truck, 7" long	150	225	325
Mack Express Truck, 7-1/2" long	100	150	225
Mack Stake Truck, 4-1/2" long, c.1930	75	125	175
Mack Stake Truck, 7-1/2" long	300	525	750
Mack Wrecker, 9" long	350	550	800
Motorcycle, solo policeman, nickel wheels, 5" long (CM02)	125	225	400
Motorcycle, solo policeman, nickel wheels, 7-1/4" long (CM04)	175	300	475

Champion Delivery Truck, 1930s, 8". Photo courtesy Rod Carnahan

Champion Mack Dump Truck, 1930s, 7". Photo courtesy Harry Wolf Detroit Antique Museum

Champion Motorcycle, (CM03), solo policeman, rubber tires, 7-1/4".

Champion Panel Delivery, 7-3/4". Photo courtesy Bertoia Auctions

From left: Champion Motorcycle, (CM02), solo policeman, nickel wheels, 5"; Motorcycle, (CM01), solo policeman, rubber tires. Photo courtesy Kent M. Comstock

From left: Champion Motorcycles, (CM02) and (CM03). Photo courtesy Kent M. Comstock.

Champion Mack Wrecker, 9".

Champion Wrecker, 7-1/2" long. Photo courtesy Bill Kaufman

	C6	C8	C10
Motorcycle, solo policeman, rubber tires, 5" long (CM01)	75	100	175
Motorcycle, solo policeman, rubber tires, 7-1/4" long (CM03)	150	250	425
Motorcycle, w/sidecar, policeman and passenger, rubber tires, 5" long (CM06)	125	200	325
Motorcycle, w/sidecar, policeman and passenger, rubber tires, 6" long (CM07)	200	325	475
Motorcycle, w/sidecar, policeman, rubber tires, 3" long (CM05)	50	80	120
Panel delivery, 7-3/4" long	700	1200	1900

	C6	C8	C10
Race Car, 1935, 7-1/2" long	300	450	650
Race Car, 9" long	150	225	325
Race Car, cast iron, detachable driver, 6" long	150	250	370
Race Car, two riders, 5-1/2" long	160	250	375
Radiator Car, four-casting, nickeled, approx. 4" long	175	250	375
Sedan, 5-1/4" long	100	150	225
Stake Truck, 8" long	275	425	600
Wrecker, 4" long	100	150	225
Wrecker, 9" long	225	350	500
Wrecker, cast iron, 7-1/2" long	225	375	550
Wrecker, C-Cab, 8-1/4" long	900	1500	2250

CHEIN

Chein (pronounced "chain") was founded in 1903 by Julius Chein. The New Jersey company specialized in lithographed metal toys, the majority of them mechanical. In 1918, it was located at 310 Passaic Ave., in Harrison, New Jersey, with 250 employees. World War I forced the ceasation of German toy imports and Chein capitalized by introducing a line of spinning tin tops that became a core offering in their catalogs until the 1970s.

Following Julius' death in 1926, his wife, Elizabeth, took over the company. She was the president and majority stockholder. She soon released the Hercules toy crane and trademarked the "Hercules" name for a series of stamped metal toys. Elizabeth's younger brother, Samuel Hoffman, became president around 1927 and led the company to the 1960s.

In 1934, it had 147 employees. In a 1946-47 directory, it listed 148 male and 132 female employees. Chein made toys until 1979, and is still in business today in Burlington, New Jersey.

Chein Hercules "C" Cab Mack Trucks

Chein introduced the Hercules series vehicles in 1925, and the first model was the Dump Truck. It was made entirely of lightweight stamped-steel (heavy-gauge tin). Chein made at least fourteen different Hercules models, the smallest being seventeen inches long and stretching to thirty inches (with the C-Cab Bull Dog Mack mobile clam truck, including boom). These toys generally retailed between one dollar and $1.25. They were manufactured until the middle 1930s.

Contributor: Bob Smith, RATS Toy Shows, 255 Tryon Park, Rochester, NY 14609. (585) 288-7153

	C6	C8	C10
Airflow, wind-up, w/garage	300	450	600
Army Truck, No. 104, tin, open bed, early, 8-1/2" long	90	135	235
Army Truck, No. 105, tin, olive drab, cannon on back, 1920s, 9-1/2" long	75	125	225
Artillery Truck, No. 225, tin, litho, soldiers, cannon in bed, 1920s, 10" long	150	325	550

	C6	C8	C10
Dan-Dee Dump Truck, tin wind-up, litho, 8" long	200	300	500
Dan-Dee Skid Truck, tin wind-up, litho, open stake truck, 1920s, 9-1/4" long	250	500	750
Dump Truck, No. 212, tin, litho, crank operated, 1920s, 8-3/4" long	200	400	600
Fancy Groceries Truck, tin wind-up litho delivery truck, "Fancy Groceries" on sides, pre-1920, 6" long	175	350	550
Garage, No. 426, tin, litho, produced from the 1920s through 1940s in assorted lithos, 7" long	75	150	225
Greyhound Bus, wind-up, 9" long	120	200	400
Greyhound Lines Push Toy, No. 219, "Greyhound Lines" on litho, 1930s, 9" long	90	175	300
Junior Bus, No. 219, tin, "Junior Bus" on side, 9" long, c.1920s	60	125	185
Junior Oil Tank Truck, No. 22, tin, litho, 1920s, 8-1/2" long	125	250	475
Junior Truck, No. 220, tin, litho, push toy, 1920s, 8-1/4" long	150	275	400
Junior Truck, No. 420, tin wind-up, litho, 1920s, 8-1/4" long	175	275	450
Limosine, tin wind-up, 1930s, 7" long	275	425	600
Locomotive and Tender, No. 80, tin, litho, 1920s, 8-1/2" long	150	250	350
Lumber Truck, No. 224, tin, litho, lumber, 1920s, 8-1/2" long	250	450	650
Mack Army Truck, No. 103, open bed w/canvas cover, 1920s, 8-1/2" long	250	350	500

Chein Greyhound Lines Push Toy, 9". Photo courtesy Bob Smith

Left to right: Chein Army truck 8-1/2"; Chein Moving and Storage Van; Chein Ice Truck, 8-1/2" long. Photo courtesy Bob Smith

Chein Army Truck, open bed, 8-1/2". Photo courtesy Ed Poole

Chein Peanuts Bus. Photo courtesy Continental Hobby House

Chein Racer No. 52, tin windup, 6-1/2". Photo courtesy Bob Smith

Chein Hercules Crane, 23", 1920s. Photo courtesy Bob Smith

Chein Rapid Delivery No. 10, tin windup. Photo courtesy Bob Smith

	C6	C8	C10
Mack Coal Truck, No. 104, tin, litho, 1920s, 8" long	250	450	725
Mack Ice Truck, No. 100, tin, litho, 1920s, 8-1/2" long	250	425	625
Mack Moving and Storage Van, No. 102, 1920s, 7-1/2" long	300	500	700
Mechanical Sedan, No. 44, tin wind-up, litho, 1930s, 7-1/4" long	200	325	450
Peanuts Bus, marked "Happiness Is An Annual Outing"	NPF	NPF	NPF
Playland Whip, No. 340, four bump 'em cars, wind-up	450	650	850

	C6	C8	C10
Racer, "3" on sides, wind-up, 1920s, 6-1/2" long	200	300	400
Racer, No. 223 Junior Racer 5, yellow w/red trim, 1920s, 9" long	325	550	825
Racer, tin wind-up, marked "52," 6-1/2" long	140	190	325
Rapid Delivery Truck, No. 10, tin wind-up, litho "No. 10 Rapid Delivery" on sides, pre-1920, 8" long	325	475	675
Roadster, No. 221, tin lithographed, c.1925, 8-1/2" long	365	525	680
Sedan, No. 137, early version, tin, no floor, 1930s, 5-1/4" long	135	220	310
Sedan, No. 137, later versions, tin wind-up, floor, 1940s-50s, 5-1/4" long	100	150	200

Chein Hercules Mack Motor Express Truck, with original box. Photo courtesy Bob Smith

Chein Hercules Mack Mobil Clam Truck, 30", green, red, black. Photo courtesy Bob Smith

Chein Hercules Fire Pumper, No. 650, 1920s, 18".
Photo courtesy Bob Smith

Back to front: Chein Woodie Sedan, tin windup; Chein Garage.
Photo courtesy Dave Leopard

Chein Hercules Mack Army Truck, canvas cover, 19-3/4".
Photo courtesy Bob Smith

Chein Hercules Mack Coal Truck, 20", black cab, green
bed. Photo courtesy Bob Smith

Chein Hercules Mack Dump Truck, black cab, red dump
body, tailgate opens, 20". Photo courtesy Bob Smith

Chein Hercules Mack Crane Truck, No. 1100, 18". Photo
courtesy Bob Smith

Chein Hercules Dump Truck with original box, No.
250, 20". Photo courtesy Bob Smith

Chein Hercules Mack Ice Truck, 19-1/2", black cab, green
cargo box. Photo courtesy Bob Smith

Chein Hercules Mack Motor Express Truck, 19-1/2", black cab, orange stake bed. Photo courtesy Bob Smith

Chein Hercules Mack Log Truck, black, 18-1/2". Photo courtesy Bob Smith

	C6	C8	C10
Sedan, tin wind-up, six window, 8-1/2" long	300	525	725
Touring Car, tin wind-up, lithographed, 7" long	300	425	550
Woodie Sedan, tin wind-up	NPF	NPF	NPF
Woodie Sedan, tin wind-up, 5-1/4" long..	95	122	145
Woodie Station Wagon, wind-up	150	200	250
Yellow Taxi, "Main 6531" on door, tin wind-up, lithographed, black and orange/yellow, 1920s, 7-3/4" long	235	375	500
Yellow Taxi, "Main 7570" on door, tin wind-up, black and orange/yellow, 1920s, 6" long	175	350	550

Hercules

	C6	C8	C10
Dump Truck, No. 250, open cab, c.1925, 18" long	450	650	1050
Fire Pumper, No. 650, open cab, c.1926, 18" long	700	1250	1800
Ladder Truck, No. 750, open cab, removable ladders, 1920s	700	1250	1900
Mack Army Truck, brown w/canvas cover, 1920s, 19-3/4" long	500	850	1700
Mack Coal Truck, black cab, chassis, green bed, tin coal chute, chute door opens, 1920s, 20" long	600	1000	1800
Mack Crane Truck, No. 1100, crane on back of Mack truck, 18" long, 30" long w/boom	800	1350	2000

	C6	C8	C10
Mack Dump Truck, No. 300, black cab and chassis, red or green dump body, tailgate opens, 1928, 20" long	400	750	1175
Mack Ice Truck, No. 600, black cab, green cargo box, step plate at rear of bed, 1928, 19-1/2" long	600	1000	1800
Mack Log Truck, all black, 1920s, 18-1/2" long	800	1400	2200
Mack Mobile Clam Truck, green, red and black, 30" long inlcuding boom	1800	1400	2100
Mack Motor Express Truck, black cab, orange stake bed, 19-1/2" long	600	1000	1650
Mack Oil Tank Truck, No. 500, black and orange, 1928, 19" long	600	1100	1800
Mack Ready-Mixed Concrete Truck, No. 1150, deluxe model, orange and black lithographed, rotating drum, 1930s, 17" long	800	1400	2200
Mack Wrecking Truck, No. 400, black cab, chassis, tow boom, red bed, 1928, 23-1/2" long (including tow boom)	600	900	1500
Motor Express Semi-Truck, No. 112, driver lithographed in window, c.1934, 15-1/2" long	500	800	1100
Motor Express Truck, No. 700, Mack "C" cab, 1928, 19" long	400	875	1500
Packard Dump Truck	300	550	850
Racer, No. 8, w/driver, spare tire (mounted on rear), red w/yellow trim, "Hercules" across grille, 1920s, 20" long	750	1600	2400
Roadster, color variation of below, in green or yellow w/black fenders	600	1000	1550

Chein Hercules Mack Motor Express Truck, with original box. Photo courtesy Bob Smith

Chein Hercules Mack Mobil Clam Truck, 30", green, red, black. Photo courtesy Bob Smith

	C6	C8	C10
Roadster, red and black, rumble seat, luggage rack, 1920s, 18" long..............	525	900	1400
Royal Blue Line Pullman Bus, No. 550, gray, red, black, 18" long.....................	800	1600	2400

	C6	C8	C10
Sand Crane, No. 200, c.1925, 23" long....	275	400	750
Wrecking Truck, No. 350, open cab, 1920s, 19-1/2" long.............................	550	850	1550

Chein Hercules Mack Ready-Mixed Concrete Truck, orange and black, rotating drum, 17". Photo courtesy Bob Smith

Chein Hercules Mack Oil Tank Truck, 19", black and orange. Photo courtesy Phillips, New York

Chein Hercules Mack Wrecking Truck, 23-1/2", black cab, red bed. Photo courtesy Bob Smith

Chein Hercules Roadster, 18", red and black, rumble seat, luggage rack. Photo courtesy Bob Smith

Chein Hercules Motor Express Semi-Truck, driver printed on glass, 1930s, 15-1/2". Photo courtesy Bob Smith

Left to right: Chein Hercules Roadster, black and red, 18"; Hercules Roadster, yellow with black fenders. Photo courtesy Bob Smith

Chein Hercules No. 8 Racer, red with yellow trim. Photo courtesy Bob Smith

Chein Hercules Royal Blue Line Pullman Bus, gray, red, black, 18". Photo courtesy Bob Smith

C.I.J. (FRANCE)

C.I.J. is an abbreviation for Compagnie Industrielle du Jouet, a French toy manufacturer that was based in Briare. Founded by Fernand Migault and Marcel Gourdet in 1930, C.I.J. specialized in tinplate toys prior to World War II and their large-scale Alfa Romeo P2 Racing Car is highly prized by collectors. Large-scale tin cars were also produced for Renault and Citroën and featured clockwork motors.

Following the war, C.I.J. resumed tin toy manufacture and introduced the first of its soon-to-be successful die-cast series, the 1:43-scale Renault 4CV. The die-cast series focused primarily on French cars done in 1:43 to 1:50 scale. Success through the 1950s was strained at the dawn of the 1960s due to intense competition and the company succumbed in 1965.

	C6	C8	C10
3/12 Mercedes 220, grey or black car, white tires	25	50	100
3/15 Chrysler Widnsor, light grey, dk. blue roof	25	55	125
3/2 Renault Etoile Filante Race Car, blue w/driver	25	50	100
3/21 Renault Shell Tanker, red cab, yellow tank	65	125	200
3/27T Camping Caravan, red w/cream and clear roof	30	65	130
3/3 Facel Vega Facellia, dark grey w/ black roof	25	55	125

	C6	C8	C10
3/46E Pugeuot 403 Ambulance, light grey w/battery-powered roof light	45	90	150
3/48 Renault 4CV, green, assorted colors, 1949-1965	25	55	125
3/49 Renault 4CV Police Car, roof aerial extends, black and white	25	55	125
3/50 Renault 4CV Alpine, white	25	55	125
3/57 Renault Dauphine Police Car, black car w/white fenders and roof, light on roof	25	50	100
3/60S Renault Shell Van, red cab, yellow body	65	125	200
3/62 Renault 1000 KGS Van, "Correspondence SNCF," pale grey w/grey hubs, white tires	60	125	175
3/66 Renault 300 KG Estate truck, w/ metal canopy	25	50	80
3/68 Renault 300 KG Van Postes, dark grey	25	55	125
3/69 Renault 300 KG Estate Gendarmerie, dark blue w/fixed roof antenna	25	55	125
3/92 Renault Estafette van, teal or dark yellow	75	150	250
4/72 Saviem Transformer truck, blue Lorry cabover truck, red plastic electric transformer trailer	200	350	500
P2 Alfa Romeo, clockwork motor, handpainted, hinged filler caps, moveable steering wheel, 20-1/2" long	1200	2200	3100

CITROËN (FRANCE)

Andre Citroën founded his automobile company in 1919 and produced tin toy replicas of them from 1923-36. Most have "Citroën" on the baseplate.

	C6	C8	C10
Fire Truck, clockwork, removable hose reel	650	1100	1600

	C6	C8	C10
Paris Taxi, B2, clockwork, tin, 16" long	550	850	1300
Truck, open bed, wind-up, door opens, 16-1/2" long	550	850	1300

CLARK, DAVID P. & CO.

Founded in 1898 by David P. Clark and located in Dayton, Ohio, D.P. Clark & Co. was the first manufacturer to use the heavy cast-iron flywheel on friction-drive Hill-Climber toys, patented by Israel and Edith Boyer. The cars and trucks were made of heavy sheet metal, wood, and cast iron. Clark also made trains, animals, and other novelty toys with the friction mechanism.

William Schieble, who was a partner in the company, bought Clark's half of the business in 1909. Schieble then changed the firm's name to the Schieble Toy and Novelty Co. Schieble filed for bankruptcy in 1931.

Back on his own, Clark began a new business. Naming his company the Dayton Friction Toy Works, Clark felt free to use the patents from the renamed

This vehicle appears to be a variation of the Clark No. 2 Automobile. Photo courtesy B.R. Blaydes

Schieble Toy Co. Lawsuits followed, and Schieble won. Clark sold the Dayton Toy Works to Nelson Talbot in 1924. He passed away soon after. The company survived for eleven more years.

Contributor: Bob Smith, RATS Toy Shows, 255 Tryon Park, Rochester, NY 14609. (585) 288-7153

	C6	C8	C10
Automobile, No. 10, flywheel drive, w/driver, c.1908, 8-1/4" long	375	550	900
Automobile, No. 2, flywheel drive, four passengers, 10-1/4" long	375	600	975
Battleship, No. 100, flywheel drive, steel, gray, boat rocks when in motion, 4 guns in 2 turrets, c. 1908, 19" long	400	700	1100

The Clark Horseless Carriage was the first toy with flywheel drive. Photo courtesy Bob Smith

Clark No. 2 Automobile, 10-1/4". Photo courtesy Joe and Sharon Freed

Clark Electric Runabout, red, black, gold, early 1900s. Photo courtesy Bob Smith

Clark Team Pumper, bold and red, 11", circa 1908. Photo courtesy Bob Smith

The Clark Horseless Carriage Push Toy could be the first Clark toy. The wood, tin, and cast-iron toy was patented in 1897.

Clark Steam Pumper, early 1900s, 10-1/4". Photo courtesy Bob Smith

Clark Police Patrol, 9-1/2", early 1900s. Photo courtesy Bob Smith

Clark Open Touring Car, 8", circa 1903. Photo courtesy Bob Smith

Clark Runabout, 7-1/4", red, circa 1903. Photo courtesy Bob Smith

Clark Runabout, red, circa 1902, 7-3/4". Photo courtesy Bob Smith

A page from a 1908 toy catalog depicts eight Clark "Hill-Climbing Friction Toys."

Another page from a 1908 toy catalog featuring Clark friction toys.

	C6	C8	C10
Chemical Engine, No. 250, flywheel drive, ladder, chemical reservoir, c. 1908, 10-3/4" long	400	700	1100
Electric Runabout, flywheel drive; two cast iron lady riders, wood, sheet metal and cast iron construction; red, black and gold, c.1902, 7-1/2" long	600	850	1500
Fire Hook and Ladder, No. 4, flywheel drive, 3 ladders, driver, c.1908, 19-1/2" long	500	700	1100
Horseless Carriage, first toy w/flywheel drive; wood, tin and cast iron construction; blue and red, came lady passenger and driver, c.1898, 11-1/2" long	550	700	1075
Horseless Carriage Push Toy, spring suspension, no flywheel mechanism; wood, tin and cast iron construction; green, red and yellow; possibly the first Clark toy. Patented November 2, 1897; 11" long	500	650	1000

	C6	C8	C10
Locomotive, No. 1, flywheel drive, steel, bell, locomotive and tender, c. 1908, 21" long	NPF	NPF	NPF
Open Touring Car, flywheel drive, tin head lamps, red, c.1903, 8" long	325	425	800
Police Patrol, flywheel drive, five riders, red and gold, c.1900, 9-1/2" long	650	900	1500
Runabout, flywheel drive, wood head lamps, red, c.1902, 7-3/4" long	350	500	800
Runabout, flywheel drive, wood, sheet metal and cast iron construction; red, c.1903, 7-1/4" long	350	500	800
Steam Pumper, flywheel drive, gold and red, c.1908, 11" long	350	500	900
Steam Pumper, flywheel drive; wood, sheet metal and cast iron construction; red, silver and gold, c.1903, 10-1/4" long	700	900	1500

CLEVELAND TOY

	C6	C8	C10
Cle-Play Transport, auto transport marked "Cle-Play Transport," two cars, cab-over	NPF	NPF	NPF

	C6	C8	C10
Racer, aluminum, steel wheels, c.1935, 13" long	150	265	375

Cleveland Toy Racer, c.1935, 13". Photo courtesy David W. Mapes Auctions

Cleveland Toy "Cle-Play Transport." Photo courtesy Dave Leopard

COHN (T.COHN)

A popular pre-WWII manufacturer of tin litho noisemakers, sand pails, target games, and party accessories, T. Cohn Inc., located at 200 Fifth Ave., New York, made tin litho play sets, garages, and a few vehicles in the postwar period.

	C6	C8	C10
Fir Chief Pull Car, No. 34, 1940s, metal, 9" long	80	120	160
Superior Sales Service garage, tin, elevator, gas pumps, lift, 1949	125	200	275

T. Cohn Fire Chief pull car No. 34. Photo courtesy Don Hultzman

COMET-AUTHENTICAST

Comet Metal Products Co. Inc was formed by Abraham Slonim in 1919. The company, originally located in Queens, New York, released its first cast-metal soldiers in the 1930s under the

"Brigadiers" brand name. Following World War II, the figures were sculpted by Swedish artist Holger Eriksson and produced by Comet's plant in Ireland, Comet Gaeltacht Industries. Most figures have a

1:108-scale ID models of World War II Japanese tanks by Comet-Authenticast. Back row, left to right: 5051 Amphibian Tankette; 5052 Tankette; 5053 Medium Tank. Front row, left to right: 5054 Medium Tank; 5055 Tankette; 5056 Light Tank; 5057 Heavy Medium Tank. Note: Authenticast GIs are 21mm tall. Photo courtesy Ed Poole

TwoComet-Authenticast 1:108-scale models (Left to right: 5009 Cromwell, 5010 Churchill) and their original boxes. Comet address was given as New York, New York. Authenticast address was given as Richmond Hill, New York. Both have design copyright dates of 1943. Photo courtesy Ed Poole

Quality Casting 1:108-scale German tanks. Back row, left to right: 4051 5cm PAK; 4052 222 Armored Car; 4054 Brumbar; 4055 234/1 Armored Car; 4058 Tiger II (Porsche Turret). Front row, left to right: 4061 7/2 Halftrack with 3.7 FLAK; 4062 2cm Quad FLAF and trailer; 4063 3.7 FLAK on trailer; 4064 88 PAK; 4065 105 Howitzer; 4066 Ferdinand; 4067 Elefant; 4068 250/7 Mortar Halftrack. The Authenticast 20mm GI is shown for comparison. Quality Cast makes many troops closer to the correct scale. Photo courtesy Ed Poole

Using the original molds, Quality Castings reissued vehicles like these Army trucks. Left to right: No. 6033 and No. 6031. Prices are generally in the $8-$10 range. Photo courtesy Ed Poole

Comet-Authenticast 1:108-scale ID World War II German vehicles. Back row, left to right: 5100 PzKwIII; 5101 PzKwI; 5012 Panzerjager; 5103 PzKw IV G; 5104 PzKw IV F. Middle row, left to right: 5105 PzKw II; 5106 PzKw III; 5107 Tiger; 5108 Eight-wheeled Armored Car. Front row, left to right: 5109 Pz35T; 5110 Panther; 5111 Sturmgeschutz; 5112 Halftrack. The Authenticast German soldiers are up to 21mm tall. Photo courtesy Ed Poole

Comet-Authenticast 1:108-scale U.S. ID Models of the Cold War Era. Back row, left to right: 5184 Trailer; 5185 Weapons Carrier; 5186 M-67 Tank; 5187 M48 Tank; 5188 M103 Heavy Tank. Front row: 5189 Atomic Cannon. (Quality Casting). Figures are 15mm tall. Photo courtesy Ed Poole

cross-shaped base, a characteristic that lends to ease of identification.

With the advent of World War II, Comet began a line of identification models for the U.S. government covering planes, ships, tanks, trucks and other military equipment from a variety of nations. Following the war, the company offered the models as toys under the Authenticast brand name.

Comet-Authenticast went out of business in the early 1960s. Its vehicles sell in the $15-30 range, and probably more for something rare, like the Lee Tank. Quality Castings of Alexandria, Virginia, reissued these toys using the original Authenticast molds in the $4-6 price range. Currently, 19th Century Miniatures owns Quality Castings and is reproducing the Quality Castings offerings in the $8 range. Their Web site is: www.oldglory15s.com

Cold War U.S. 1:108-scale ID Models. Back row, left to right: 5192 M3 Medium Tank; 5190 T98 S.P. 105mm Gun; 5191 S.P. 155mm Howizer; 5192 M3 Tank; 5193 Hawk Missile-Transporter (Quality Casting); Launcher and Mobile Radar with crew. Front row, left to right: 5194 Honest John Launcher and crew; 5195 Nike-Ajax Launcher and crew (Quality Casting); 5196 M42 Duster Twin 40mm AA (Quality Casting); 5197 Ontos S.P. Rocket Launcher. Standing figures are 15mm tall. Photo courtesy Ed. Poole

Comet-Authenticast 1:108-scale metal World War II Russian ID Models. Back row, left to right: 5200 KV-1 Heavy Tank; 5201 KV-2 Heavy Tank; 5202 Josef Stalin; 5203 T34 Medium Tank. Middle row: Russian soldiers designed by Holger Eriksson sold by Comet in sets R1 thru 8, the latter two containing tanks; figures are 20mm tall. Front row, left to right: 5204 T70 light tank; 5205 ST2 Armored Carrier; 5206 T34/85 medium tank; 5207 Josef Stalin III. Photo courtesy Ed Poole

Comet-Authenticast 1:108-scale U.S. ID Models. Back row, left to right: 5156 General Pershing; 5166 General Chaffee; 5167 Slugger II; 5168 Slugger; 5169 76mm Sherman. Front row, left to right: 5170 Airborne Tank; 5171 Armored Car (Staghound); 5172 Armored Car (Twin 50); 5173 DUKW; 5174 M32 Tank Recovery. Soldiers were sculpted by Holger Eriksson; the tallest measures 20mm. Photo courtesy Ed Poole

Back row, left to right: 5175 LVTAA Amphibian Tank; 5176 LVT Amphibian; 5176 LTV Utility Tank (Quality Casting); 5178 Medium Tank 105mm (Quality Casting). Front row Left to right: 5180 Walker Bulldog; 5179 General Patton; 5181 6x6 Truck; 5182 Command Car; 5183 Troop Carrier. Note: Comet-Authenticast marching GIs are 20mm tall. Photo courtesy Ed Poole

Back row from left: Quality Castings reproduced original German pieces like those shown here. Back row, left to right: 4017 Wespe; 4018 7.5 PAK; 4023 Opel Blitz; and 4026 88 Flak on boogie wheels. Middle row, left to right: 4027 2 CM FLAF on and off trailer; 4031 3.7 PAK; 4035 7.5 INF gun; 4036 Kubelwagen; and 4037 BMW cycle with MB variant; 4041 Pz38t. Bottom row, left to right: 4042 Wirblewing FLAK; 4044 Hetzer; 4045 Marder III; 4046 250/I Halftrack; 4049 Hummell; RFE Lost Silver DAK (added for scale 22mm tall). Photo courtesy Ed Poole

Comet-Authenticast 1:108-scale U.S. World War II ID Models. Back row, left to right: 5150 75mm Gun on Halftrack; 5151 Heavy Tank M6; 5152 Sherman Tank; 5153 Greyhound Armored Car; 5154 Halftrack. Middle row, left to right: 5155 Hellcat; 5156 Priest; 5157 General Scott; 5158 General Stuart; 5159 Wolverine. Front row, left to right: 5160 Jeep; 5161 Weasel; 5162 Scout Car; 5163 Quack; 5164 King Kong. Authenticast GI with Mine Detector is 20mm tall. Photo courtesy Ed Poole

CONVERSE

Beginning in 1878, Converse transformed Winchendon, Massachusetts, into "Toy Town U.S.A." First incorporated as Mason & Converse, partners Orlando Mason and Morton E. Converse established a modest toy and woodenware business. Five years later, the name was changed to Morton E. Converse & Company. By 1903, the plant was the only factory in the nation solely devoted to toy production and turned out a wide assortment of wooden toys including, hobby horses, trunks, and more than sixty different styles of drums. The plant manufactured some 1,500 drums daily.

When Morton's son Atherton joined the company, the name was changed to Morton E. Converse & Son. The company branched out into tin and steel toy production. Atherton carried on the business after the 1917 death of his father, until his own retirement in 1931. William H. Hezlitt became President and General Manager and the firm merged with the Mason Mfg. Co. to become the Converse-Mason Corporation.

Falling victim to the Depression, the Converse toy factory buildings were sold to the Winchendon Furniture Company in 1934.

Editors Note: My thanks to the Beals Memorial Library of Winchendon, Massachusetts, for sending information on Converse from *Winchendon Years 1764-1964* by Lois Stevenson Greenwood.
—Karen O'Brien

	C6	C8	C10
Auto, pressed steel, painted, clockwork, w/fringe on top, three-seat, 1905, rubber tires	600	900	1200
Fire Engine Ladder Truck, bell, wooden headlight, 1915, 10" long	1250	1875	2500
Fire Engine Ladder Truck, wood headlamps, c.1915, 18" long	1800	3000	4250

	C6	C8	C10
Milk and Dairy Wagon, tin, "145" and "Milk and Dairy Products" on sides, two horses, 12" long	125	250	375
Milk Wagon, tin, "10" and "Milk" on wagon sides, single horse, 11" long	125	250	375
Parcel Post, 1920s, 15" long	1500	2500	3700
Pick-Up Truck, very early, open cab	500	750	1000
Pierce-Arrow Touring Car, open, steers	1200	2200	3000
Roadster, wind-up, open cab, 1908, 15-1/2" long	1200	2200	3000
Touring Auto, open, four-seater	1200	2200	3000
Touring Auto, pressed steel, canvas roof, 1910	1300	2200	3000
Transitional Taxi, clockwork, 10-1/2" long	525	770	1050

Converse Transitional Taxi, clockwork motor, 10-1/2" long. Photo courtesy Sotheby's New York

CONWAY CO.

This small manufacturer was located in Skokie, Illinois, and made a variety of promotional toy delivery trucks in the 1940s and 1950s. The Packard Convertible is their most popular larger-scale toy.

	C6	C8	C10		C6	C8	C10
Kraft Delivery Truck, yellow plastic body, metal frame and wheels, silver trim, "Kraft" advertised on sides, 1950, 4" long	15	30	50	Swift Delivery Truck, red plastic body, metal frame and wheels, "Swift" on sides, friction motor, 4" long	15	30	45
Packard Convertible, plastic body, metal frame, clockwork, electric lights, tires marked "Conway Skokie IL," 1948, 12" long	135	200	325	Wrigley's Delivery Truck, yellow plastic body, metal frame and wheels, "Enjoy Chewing Wrigley's Spearmint" and "Railway Express Agency" on sides, friction motor, 4" long	15	30	45

COR-COR

According to Margaret E. Holland (as reported by Ross Hermann in the July 27, 1992 *Antique News*), the granddaughter of Cor-Cor founder Louis A. Corcoran, this Washington, Indiana firm began on 21st Street in 1925, then expanded to East 3rd and Vantress. After a fire, Cor-Cor built its final plant on Front Street. At this latter location the company changed its name to Corcoran Metal Products. At its height, the firm employed up to 590 people. Corcoran retired in 1941 because of failing health, and died in 1945. His toys are marked "Cor-Cor" on the wheels.

	C6	C8	C10
Airflow, wind-up, electric lights, 18" long	1000	1600	2200
Army Truck	400	650	950
Bus, "Cor-Cor Toys" on side, 23" long	325	495	650
Bus, electric lights	500	750	1000
Chrysler Airflow, wind-up, electric lights, 17" long	600	900	1500
DeSoto Airflow	650	850	1250
Dump Truck, dumps back or side to side, 23" long	225	338	450

Cor-Cor Supplee Ice Cream Truck. Photo courtesy Tim Oei

	C6	C8	C10
Fire Truck, 24" long	200	300	400
Graham Paige Sedan, electric, 20" long	600	1000	1600
Ice Truck	NPF	NPF	NPF
Semi Truck	NPF	NPF	NPF
Supplee Ice Cream Truck	NPF	NPF	NPF
Van, painted metal, c.1928, 23" long	250	380	525

CORGI

Corgi is the registered trademark of Playcraft Toys (a sister corporation to Mettoy before they merged). With a factory based in Swansea, South Wales, its vehicles first appeared in 1956 and featured windows that competitor Dinky did not. The Corgi Model Club was launched that December, and a regular newsletter was published to inform collectors of new releases and company developments. Mettoy became a publicly traded company on June 13, 1964 and was well received by the investing public.

The popularity of its quality die-cast models brought prosperous times through the 1960s and '70s. A declining market led to financial troubles for Corgi in the late 1970s, and by 1983, the company was ready to close, but for a buy-out of the management. The company was reformed and renamed, Corgi Toys Limited in 1984. A new marketing approach was adopted and quality die-cast replicas made their way around the world.

Corgi 69-A Massey-Ferguson 165 Tractor with Shovel, 1967-73. Photo courtesy Dr. Douglas Sadecky

Corgi 102-A Rice Pony Trailer, 1958-65. Photo courtesy Dr. Douglas Sadecky

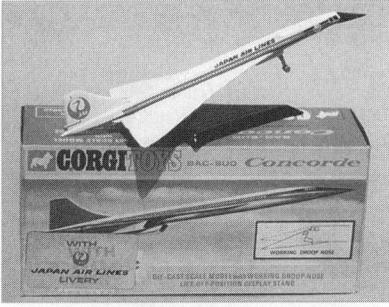

Corgi 653-A Concorde-First Issues, 1969-72. Photo courtesy Dr. Douglas Sadecky

Corgi 1-B Tractor and Beast Carrier, 1966-72. Photo courtesy Dr. Douglas Sadecky

Corgi 54-A Fordson Power Major Halftrack Tractor, 1962-64. Photo courtesy Dr. Douglas Sadecky

Corgi 55-A Fordson Power Major Tractor, 1961-63. Photo courtesy Dr. Douglas Sadecky

In 1990, Mattel purchased Corgi Toys Limited and the Swansea plant was closed in favor of Mattel's Leicester facility. On August 7, 1995, Corgi was once again in private hands under the leadership of Chris Guest. Corgi Classics Limited moved from the Mattel building to another just a mile down the road at the Meridian Business Park.

Following continued product expansion in the 1990s, Corgi was sold to Zindart in 1999. Growth in the new millennium has been evident in the ambitious Unsung Heroes line of military replicas and most recently in the 2004 release of the new Batman series.

AGRICULTURAL

	C6	C8	C10		C6	C8	C10
1-B, Ford Tractor and Beast Carrier, 1966-72, Gift Set included No. 67 Ford 5000 tractor and No. 58 Beast Carrier	60	90	150	4-B, Country Farm Set, 1974-75, No. 50 Massey Ferguson tractor, red No. 62 hay trailer w/load, fences, figures	30	45	75
2-A, Land Rover and Pony Trailer, 1958-62, two versions: green No. 438 Land Rover and a red and black No. 102 Pony trailer (1958-62); tan/cream No. 438 Land Rover and a pony trailer (1963-68); value given is for each individual complete set	50	90	175	5-B, Agricultural Set, 1967-72, No. 69 Massey-Ferguson tractor, No. 62 trailer, No. 438 Land Rover, No. 484 Livestock Truck w/pigs, No. 71 harrow, No. 1490 skip and churns; w/accessories: four calves, farmhand, dog and six sacks	120	180	400
				5-C, Country Farm Set, 1976, same as 4-B but without hay load on trailer	30	45	75

Corgi 201-A Austin Cambridge, 1956-61. Photo courtesy Dr. Douglas Sadecky

Corgi 206-A Hillman Husky, 1956-60. Photo courtesy Dr. Douglas Sadecky

Corgi 202-A Morris Cowley, 1959-60. Photo courtesy Dr. Douglas Sadecky

Corgi 203-A Vauxhall Velox, 1956-60. Photo courtesy Dr. Douglas Sadecky

Corgi 208-M Jaguar 2.4 Litre-Mechanical, 1957-59. Photo courtesy Dr. Douglas Sadecky

Corgi 217-A Fiat 1800, 1960-63. Photo courtesy Dr. Douglas Sadecky

Corgi 216-A Austin A40, 1959-62.
Photo courtesy Dr. Douglas Sadecky

Corgi 220-A Chevrolet Impala,
1960-62. Photo courtesy Dr. Douglas
Sadecky

Corgi 236-A Austin A60 Motor School,
1964-69. Photo courtesy Dr. Douglas
Sadecky

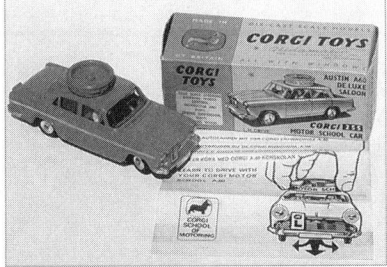

Corgi 255-A Austin A60 Driving
School, 1964-68. Photo courtesy Dr.
Douglas Sadecky

Corgi 207-A Standard Vanguard,
1957-61. Photo courtesy Dr. Douglas
Sadecky

Corgi 259-A2 Citroen LeDandy
Coupe, 1967-69. Photo courtesy Dr.
Douglas Sadecky

	C6	C8	C10
7-A, Massey-Ferguson Tractor and Tipping Trailer, 1959-63, No. 50 tractor and No. 51 trailer, no driver	50	75	125
8-A, Combine, Tractor and Trailer, 1959-62, set of three: No. 1111 combine, No. 50 Massey-Ferguson tractor, and No. 51 trailer.................	110	185	350
9-B, Tractor with Shovel and Trailer, 1968-73, standard colors, No. 69 Massey-Ferguson Tractor and No. 62 Tipping Trailer.....................	65	100	165
13-A, Fordson Tractor and Plow, 1964-66, No. 60 tractor and No. 61 four-furrow plow.....................	55	85	140
15-B, Land Rover & Horse Box, 1968-77, blue/white Land Rover w/horse trailer in two versions: cast wheels (1968-74) and Whizz Wheels (1975-77); accessories include a mare and a foal; value is for each individual complete set	50	75	125
18-A, Fordson Tractor and Plow, 1961-64, No. 55 Fordson Tractor and No. 56 Four Furrow plow.....................	55	85	140
22-A, Agricultural Set, 1962-66, 1962-64 issue: No. 55 Fordson Tractor, No. 51 Tipping Trailer, No. 438 Land Rover, No. 101 Flat Trailer w/No. 1487 Milk Churns; 1965-66 issue: No. 60 Fordson Tractor, No. 62 Tipping Trailer, No. 438 Land Rover, red No. 100 Dropside Trailer w/No. 1487 Milk Churns, a difficult set to find	380	900	1800
29-A, Massey-Ferguson Tractor and Tipping Trailer, 1965, No. 50 Massey-Ferguson tractor w/driver, No. 51 trailer	50	75	125
32-A, Massey-Ferguson Tractor with Shovel & Trailer, 1965-66, No. 54 MF tractor w/driver and shovel, No. 62 trailer..........................	30	75	150
33-A, Tractor and Beast Carrier, 1965-66, No. 55 Fordson tractor, figures and No. 58 beast carrier..........	65	100	165
34-A, David Brown Tractor & Trailer, 1976-79, two-piece set: No. 55 tractor and No. 56 trailer	30	45	75
42-A, Agricultural Set, 1978-80, No. 55 Tractor, No. 56 Tipping Trailer, Silo and mustard yellow conveyor..............	60	90	130
43-A, Silo & Conveyor Belt, 1978-80, w/yellow conveyor and Corgi Harvesting Co. label on silo................	35	50	85
47-A, Ford Tractor and Conveyor, 1966-69, No. 67 tractor, conveyor w/trailer, figures and accessories.........	60	90	175
47-B, Pony Club Set, 1978-80, brown/white No. 421 Land Rover w/Corgi Pony Club labels, horse box, horse and rider	30	45	75
50-A, Massey-Ferguson 65 Tractor, 1959-66, silver metal or plastic steering wheel, seat and grille, red engine hood, red metal or plastic wheels w/black rubber tires	40	60	100
50-B, Massey-Ferguson 50B Tractor, 1973-77, yellow body, black interior and roof, red plastic wheels w/black plastic tires, windows..........................	15	18	75
51-A, Massey-Ferguson Tipping Trailer, 1959-65, two versions: red chassis w/either yellow or gray tipper and tailgate, red metal or plastic wheels, value is for each	10	18	35
53-A, Massey-Ferguson 65 Tractor And Shovel, 1960-66, two versions: red bonnet w/either cream or gray chassis, red metal or orange plastic wheels; value is for each	55	85	140

	C6	C8	C10
54-A, Fordson Power Major Halftrack Tractor, 1962-64, blue body/chassis, silver steering wheel, seat and grille, three versions: orange cast wheels, gray treads, lights in radiator or on sides of radiator. This bizarre little model can be quite difficult to find-especially with original tracks	90	135	225
54-B, Massey-Ferguson Tractor with Shovel, 1974-81, two versions: either yellow and red or red and white body colors; value is for each	20	30	50
55-A, Fordson Power Major Tractor, 1961-63, blue body/chassis w/Fordson Power Major decals, silver steering wheel, seat, exhaust, grille and lights. The 61-A Four Furrow Plough makes a nice companion piece to the model	45	65	110
55-B, David Brown Tractor, 1977-82, white body w/black/white David Brown No. 1412 labels, red chassis and plastic engine	15	25	45
56-A, Four Furrow Plow, 1961-63, red frame, yellow plastic parts	15	20	35
56-B, Tipping Farm Trailer, 1977-80, cast chassis and tailgate, red plastic tipper and wheels, black tires, in two versions	10	15	25
57-A, Massey-Ferguson Tractor with Fork, 1963-67, red cast body and shovel, arms, cream chassis, red plastic wheels, black rubber tires, Massey-Ferguson 65 decals, w/driver	60	90	150
58-A, Beast Carrier Trailer, 1965-71, red chassis, yellow body and tailgate, four plastic calves, red plastic wheels, black rubber tires	24	36	60
60-A, Fordson Power Major Tractor, 1964-66, blue body w/Fordson Power Major decals, driver, blue chassis and			

	C6	C8	C10
steering wheel, silver seat, hitch, exhaust	50	75	125
61-A, Four Furrow Plow, 1964-70, blue frame w/chrome plastic parts	15	20	35
62-A, Tipping Farm Trailer, 1965-72, red working tipper and tailgates, yellow chassis, red plastic wheels, black tires, w/detachable raves	10	15	30
64-A, Jeep FC-150 Pickup with Conveyor Belt, 1965-69, red body, yellow interior, orange grille, two black rubber belts, shaped wheels, black rubber tires; accessories include farmland figure and sacks	45	65	130
66-A, Massey-Ferguson 165 Tractor, 1966-72, gray engine and chassis, red hood and fenders w/black/white Massey Ferguson 165 decals, white grille, red cast wheels; makes engine sound	35	55	90
67-A, Ford 5000 Super Major Tractor, 1967-73, blue body/chassis w/Ford Super Major 5000 decals, gray cast fenders and rear wheels, gray plastic front wheels, black plastic tires, driver	30	45	75
69-A, Massey-Ferguson 165 Tractor with Shovel, 1967-73, gray chassis, red hood, fenders and shovel arms, unpainted shovel and cylinder, red cast wheels, black plastic tires, w/figure. This tractor even featured engine noises!	45	65	120
71-A, Tandem Disc Harrow, 1967-72, yellow main frame, red upper frame, working wheels linkage, unpainted linkage and cast discs, black plastic tires	15	20	45
72-A, Ford Tractor with Trencher, 1970-74, blue body/chassis, gray fenders, cast yellow trencher arm and .			

Corgi 238-A Jaguar Mark X Saloon, 1962-67. Photo courtesy Dr. Douglas Sadecky

Corgi 241-A Ghia L64 Chrysler V8, 1963-69. Photo courtesy Dr. Douglas Sadecky

Corgi 1120-A Midland Red Express Coach, 1961-62. Photo courtesy Dr. Douglas Sadecky

Corgi 35-A London Set, 1964-68. Photo courtesy Dr. Douglas Sadecky

Corgi 445-A Plymouth Sports Suburban, 1963-65. Photo courtesy Dr. Douglas Sadecky

Corgi 104-A Dolphin Cabin Cruiser, 1965-68. Photo courtesy Dr. Douglas Sadecky

Corgi 391-A James Bond Mustang Mach 1, 1972-73. Photo courtesy Dr. Douglas Sadecky

Corgi 497-A2 Man From U.N.C.L.E. THRUSH-Buster, 1968-69. Photo courtesy Dr. Douglas Sadecky

Corgi 802-A Popeye's Paddle Wagon, 1969-72. Photo courtesy Dr. Douglas Sadecky

	C6	C8	C10
controls, chrome trencher, black control lines...	50	75	125
73-A, Massey-Ferguson 165 Tractor with Saw, 1969-73, red hood and fenders, gray engine and seat, cast yellow arm and control, chrome circular saw	55	85	140
74-A, Ford 5000 Tractor with Scoop, 1969-72, blue body/chassis, gray fenders, yellow scoop arm and controls, chrome scoop, black control lines	55	80	130
102-A, Rice Pony Trailer, 1958-65, cast body and chassis w/working tailgate, horse, in six variations, smooth or shaped hubs, cast or wire drawbar. Shown here is the harder-to-find two-tone cream/red variation	20	30	50
112-A, Rice Beaufort Double Horse Box, 1969-72, long, blue body and working gates, white roof, brown plastic interior, two horses, cast wheels, plastic tires	15	30	50
484-A, Dodge Livestock Truck, 1967-72, tan cab and hood, green body, working tailgate and ramp, five pigs	34	51	85

	C6	C8	C10
1104-B, Bedford Articulated Horse Box, 1973-76, cast cab, lower body and three working ramps, yellow interior, plastic upper body, w/horse and Newmarket Racing Stables labels, dark metallic green or light green body w/orange or yellow upper, four horses	32	48	90
1105-B, Berliet Articulated Horse Box, 1976-80, bronze cab and lower semi body, cream chassis, white upper body, black interior, three working ramps, National Racing Stables decals, horse figures, chrome wheels	30	45	75
1111-A, Massey-Ferguson Combine, 1959-63, red body w/yellow metal blades, metal tines, black/white decals, yellow metal wheels	70	105	175
1111-B, Massey-Ferguson Combine, 1968-73, red body, plastic yellow blades, red wheels................................	60	100	160
1112-B, David Brown Combine, 1978-79, No. 55 Tractor, red and yellow combines, white JF labels	30	45	75

AIRCRAFT

	C6	C8	C10
12-C, Glider Set, 1981-83, two versions: white No. 345 Honda, 1981-82; yellow Honda, 1983, value is for individual complete sets.....................................	30	45	75
19-B, Corgi Flying Club Set, 1972-77, blue/orange No. 438 Land Rover w/red dome light, blue trailer w/either orange/yellow or orange/white plastic airplane	24	50	100
49-A, Flying Club Set, 1978-80, green and white No. 419 Jeep w/Corgi Flying Club labels, green trailer, blue/white airplane.............................	36	55	90
648-A, NASA Space Shuttle, 1980, white body, two opening hatches, black plastic interior, jets and base, unpainted retracting gear castings, black plastic wheels, w/satalite	30	45	75
650-A, Concorde-First Issues, 1969-72, BOAC decals	20	40	70
650-B, Concorde-Second Issues, 1976-82, BOAC model on display stand..	15	20	35

	C6	C8	C10
651-A, Concorde-First Issues, 1969-72, Air France decals.................	20	45	85
651-B, Concorde-Second Issue, 1976-82, Air France model on display stand	15	20	35
652-A, Concorde-First Issues, 1969-72, Air Canada decals.................	80	120	200
653-A, Concorde-First Issues, 1969-72, Japan Airlines decals. This rare model was probably an import issue. Ironically, the real Concorde was never part of the Japan Air Lines	280	420	700
806-A, Lunar Bug, 1970-72, white body w/red roof, blue interior and wings, clear and amber windows, red working ramp, Lunar Bug labels...	25	40	95
926-A, Stromberg Jet Ranger Helicopter, 1978-79, black body w/yellow trim and interior, clear windows, black plastic rotors, white/blue labels	45	65	125

AUTOMOBILE

	C6	C8	C10
10-A, Rambler Marlin with Kayak and Trailer, 1968-69, blue No. 263 Marlin w/roof rack, blue/white trailer, w/two kayaks	100	150	250
13-B, Tour de France Set, 1968-72, white and black body, Renault w/Paramount Film roof sign, rear platform w/cameraman and black camera on tripod, plus bicycle and rider	60	90	200
13-C, Tour de France Set, 1981-82, w/white No. 373 Peugeot, red and yellow Raleigh and Total logos, Racing cycles, includes manager figures	25	45	90
20-A, Golden Guinea Set, 1961-63, three vehicle set, gold plated No. 224 Bentley Continental, No. 229 Chevy Corvair and No. 234 Ford Consul	90	150	325
31-A, Buick and Cabin Cruiser, 1965-68, two versions: light blue or dark metallic blue, No. 245 Buick, red boat trailer, dolphin cabin cruiser w/two figures	80	120	280
200-A, Ford Consul, 1956-61, one-piece body in several colors, clear windows, silver grille, lights and bumpers, smooth wheels, rubber tires	45	65	120
200-M, Ford Consul-Mechanical, 1956-59, same as model 200-A but w/friction motor and blue or green body	55	85	160
201-A, Austin Cambridge, 1956-61, available in gray, green/ gray, silver/green, aqua, green/ cream, two-tone green, smooth wheels, shown here with Austin Cambridge-Mechanical	40	60	120
201M, Austin Cambridge-Mechanical, 1956-59, fly-wheel motor, available in orange, cream, light or dark gray, or silver over metallic blue, smooth wheels	50	75	150
202-A, Morris Cowley, 1959-60, long, one-piece body in several colors, clear windows, silver lights, grille and bumper, smooth wheels, rubber tires. The model on the left is the rare blue version, and the car on the right is the 202-M mechanical flywheel version	45	75	140
202-B, Renault 16TS, 1970-72, metallic blue body w/Renault decal on working hatch, clear windows, detailed engine, yellow interior	20	25	50

	C6	C8	C10
202-M, Morris Cowley-Mechanical, 1956-59, same as 202-A but w/friction motor, available in off-white or green body	55	95	170
203-A, Vauxhall Velox, 1956-60, one-piece body in red, cream, yellow or yellow and red body, clear windows, silver lights, grille and bumpers, smooth wheels, rubber tires	50	75	150
203-M, Vauxhall Velox-Mechanical, 1956-59, w/friction motor; orange, red, yellow or cream body	60	90	170
204-A, Rover 90, 1956-60, one-piece body, silver headlights, grille and bumpers, smooth wheels, rubber tires; multiple colors available. The car on the left is the rare two-tone color scheme and the vehicle on the right is the mechanical version in metallic green	50	75	145
204-M, Rover 90-Mechanical, 1956-59, w/friction motor and red, green, gray or metallic green body	60	90	170
205-A, Riley Pathfinder, 1956-61, red or dark blue one-piece body, clear windows, silver lights, grille and bumpers, smooth wheels, rubber tires	45	65	125
205-M, Riley Pathfinder-Mechanical, 1956-59, w/friction motor and either red or blue body	60	95	170
206-A, Hillman Husky, 1956-60, one-piece tan or metallic blue/silver body, clear windows, silver lights, grille and bumpers, smooth wheels. The car on the left is the more rare two-tone version, while the car on the right is the mechanical flywheel version that was only produced for one year in 1959	40	70	125
206-M, Hillman Husky-Mechanical, 1956-59, same as 206-A but w/friction motor, black base and dark blue, gray or cream body	50	100	150
207-A, Standard Vanguard, 1957-61, one-piece red and pale green body, clear windows, silver lights, grille and bumpers, smooth wheels, rubber tires. Pictured with the 207M, the attractive two-tone 207-A version is on the left, and the mechanical version is on the right	50	75	125

Corgi 267-A1 Batmobile, 1966. Photo courtesy Dr. Douglas Sadecky

Corgi 267-C1 Batmobile, 1973. Photo courtesy Dr. Douglas Sadecky

Corgi 270-A James Bond Aston Martin, 1968-77. Photo courtesy Dr. Douglas Sadecky

Corgi 426-A Chipperfield Circus Karrier Booking Office, 1962-64. Photo courtesy Dr. Douglas Sadecky

Corgi 487-A Chipperfield Circus Land Rover Parade Vehicle, 1967-69. Photo courtesy Dr. Douglas Sadecky

Corgi 1121-A Chipperfield Circus Crane Truck, 1960-68. Photo courtesy Dr. Douglas Sadecky

	C6	C8	C10
207-M, Standard Vanguard-Mechanical, 1957-59, w/friction motor and yellow or off-white body w/black or gray base, or cream body w/red roof	55	90	170
208-A, Jaguar 2.4 Litre, 1957-63, one-piece white body w/no interior 1957-59, or yellow body w/red interior 1960-63, clear windows, smooth hubs.	50	80	130
208-M, Jaguar 2.4 Litre-Mechanical, 1957-59, same as 208-A but w/friction motor and metallic blue body	60	90	180
210-A, Citroen DS19, 1957-65, one-piece body in several colors, clear windows, silver lights, grille and bumpers, smooth wheels, rubber tires; colors: red, metallic green w/black roof, yellow w/red roof	56	84	140
211-A, Studebaker Golden Hawk, 1958-60, one-piece body in blue and gold or white and gold, clear windows, silver lights, grille and bumpers, smooth wheels, rubber tires	55	85	140
211-M, Studebaker Golden Hawk-Mechanical, 1958-59, w/friction motor and white body w/gold trim	70	105	175
211S1, Studebaker Golden Hawk, 1960-65, first issue: gold plated body, white flashing, shaped hubs	55	85	140
211S2, Studebaker Golden Hawk, 1960-65, second issue: gold painted body, shaped hubs. The "S" after the catalog number stood for "suspension" which was a new Corgi innovation at the time of the model's release	60	180	180
216-A, Austin A40, 1959-62, one-piece light blue body with dark blue roof or red body w/black roof and clear windows, smooth wheels, rubber tires	35	50	100
216-M, Austin A40-Mechanical, 1959-60, friction motor, red body w/black roof	55	75	170
217-A, Fiat 1800, 1960-63, one-piece body in several colors, clear windows, plastic interior, silver lights, grille and bumpers, red taillights, smooth wheels, rubber tires, colors: blue body w/light or bright yellow interior, light tan, mustard, light blue or two-tone blue body	24	40	80
218-A, Aston Martin DB4, 1960-65, red or yellow body w/working hood, detailed engine, clear windows, plastic interior, silver lights, grille, license plate and bumpers, red taillights, rubber tires, smooth or cast spoked wheels; working scoop on early models	45	65	110
219-A, Plymouth Sports Suburban, 1959-63, dark cream body, tan roof, red interior, die-cast base, red axle, silver bumpers, trim and grille and rubber tires	40	60	100
220-A, Chevrolet Impala, 1960-62, pink body, yellow plastic interior, clear windows, silver headlights, bumpers, grille and trim, suspension, die-cast base w/rubber tires; a second version has a blue body w/red or yellow interior and smooth or shaped hubs	50	75	125
222-A, Renault Floride, 1959-65, one-piece dark red, maroon or lime green body, clear windows, silver bumper, grille, lights and plates, red taillights, smooth or shaped hubs, rubber tires	35	55	95
224-A, Bentley Continental, 1961-66, two-tone green or black and silver bodies, w/red interior, clear windows, chrome grille and bumpers, jewel headlights, red jeweled taillights, suspension, shaped wheels, gray rubber tires	45	65	110
225-A1, Austin Seven Mini, 1961-67, red or yellow body, yellow interior, silver bumpers, grille and headlights, orange taillights	50	75	125
225-A2, second issue, Austin Seven Mini, 1961-67, primrose yellow, red interior, rare	100	200	325
228-A, Volvo P-1800, 1962-65, one-piece body light brown, dark red, pink or dark red body, clear windows, plastic interior, shaped wheels, rubber tires	40	60	100
229-A, Chevrolet Corvair, 1961-66, either blue or pale-blue body w/yellow interior and working rear hood, detailed engine, clear windows, silver bumpers, headlights and trim, red taillights, rear window blind, shaped wheels, rubber tires	36	55	90

	C6	C8	C10
230-A, Mercedes-Benz 220SE Coupe, 1962-64, cream, black or dark red body, red plastic interior, clear windows, working trunk, silver bumpers, grille and plate, spare wheel in boot	40	60	100
231-A, Triumph Herald Coupe, 1961-66, blue or gold top and lower body, white upper body, red interior, clear windows, silver bumpers, grille, headlights, shaped hubs	35	65	110
232-A, Fiat 2100, 1961-64, light two-tone mauve body, yellow interior, purple roof, clear windows w/rear blind, silver grille, license plates and bumpers, red taillights, shaped wheels, rubber tires	22	33	75
233-A, Trojan Heinkel, 1962-72, issued in mauve, red, orange or lilac body, plastic interior, silver bumpers and headlights, red taillights, suspension, smooth, spun, or detailed cast wheels ..	35	55	95
234-A, Ford Consul Classic, 1961-65, cream or gold body and base, yellow interior, pink roof, clear windows, gray steering wheel, silver bumpers, grille, opening hood...........................	35	55	90
235-A, Oldsmobile Super 88, 1962-68, three versions: light blue, light or dark metallic blue body w/white stripes, red interior, single body casting................	40	60	100
236-A, Austin A60 Motor School, 1964-69, light blue body w/silver trim, red interior, single body casting, right-hand drive steering wheel, two figures, steering control on roof; came w/Highway Patrol leaflet	45	65	120
238-A, Jaguar Mark X Saloon, 1962-67, several different color versions w/working front and rear hood castings, clear windshields, plastic interior, gray steering wheel. Shown here in silver and blue versions, pictured at the left are the two suitcases that were included with each car	35	55	110
239-A, Volkswagen 1500 Karmann-Ghia, 1963-68, cream, red or gold body, plastic interior and taillights, front and rear working hoods, clear windshields, silver bumpers; includes spare wheel and plastic suitcase in trunk	35	55	90
240-A, Ghia-Fiat 600 Jolly, 1963-65, light or dark blue body, red and silver canopy, red seats, two figures, windshield, chrome dash, floor, steering wheels................................	45	85	160
241-A, Ghia L64 Chrysler V8, 1963-69, metallic light blue, green, copper or yellow, plastic interior, hood, trunk and two doors working, detailed engine, clear windshield, shaped or detailed cast wheels	25	40	75
245-A, Buick Riviera, 1964-68, metallic gold, dark blue, pale blue or gold body, red interior, gray steering wheel, and tow hook, clear windshield, chrome			

	C6	C8	C10
grille and bumpers, suspension, Tan-o-lite headlights, spoked wheels and rubber tires	30	45	75
246-A1, Chrysler Imperial Convertible, 1965-66, red body w/gray base, working hood, trunk and doors, golf bag in trunk, detailed engine, clear windshield, aqua interior, driver, chrome bumpers...........................	45	65	110
246-A2, Chrysler Imperial Convertible, 1967-68, metallic blue body w/gray base, working hood, trunk and doors, golf bag in trunk, detailed engine, clear windshield, aqua interior, driver, chrome bumpers...........................	50	90	160
247-A, Mercedes-Benz 600 Pullman, 1964-69, metallic maroon body, cream interior and steering wheel, clear windshields, chrome grille, trim and bumpers, working windshield operators; includes instruction sheet	40	60	100
248-A, Chevrolet Impala, 1965-67, tan body, cream interior, gray steering wheel, clear windshields, chrome bumpers, grille, headlights, suspension, red taillights, shaped wheels and rubber tires	50	75	125
251-A, Hillman Imp, 1963-67, metallic copper, blue, dark blue or gold one-piece bodies, w/white/yellow interior, silver bumpers, headlights	30	45	85
252-A, Rover 2000, 1963-66, metallic blue w/red interior or maroon body w/yellow interior, gray steering wheel, clear windshields	30	45	75
253-A, Mercedes-Benz 220SE Coupe, 1967-68, metallic maroon or blue body, cream plastic interior, medium gray base, clear windows, silver bumpers, headlights, grille and license; accessories include plastic luggage and spare wheel in boot. Except for different exterior colors and the inclusion of luggage, this was exactly the same car as the 230-A	40	60	100
255-A, Austin A60 Driving School, 1964-68, medium blue body w/silver trim, left-hand drive steering wheel, steering control on roof; came w/five language leaflet (US version of No. 236).....................	45	65	160
259-A1, Citroen Le Dandy Coupe, 1966, metallic maroon body and base, yellow interior, working trunk and two doors, clear windows, plastic interior, folding seats, chrome grille and bumpers, jewel headlights, red taillights, suspension, spoked wheels, rubber tires	50	75	125
259-A2, Citroen Le Dandy Coupe, 1967-69, metallic dark blue hood, sides and base, plastic aqua interior, white roof and trunk lid, clear windows, folding seats, chrome grille and bumpers, jewel headlights, red taillights, suspension, spoked wheels, rubber tires	70	105	175

	C6	C8	C10
260-A, Renault 16, 1969, metallic maroon body, dark yellow interior, chrome base, grille and bumpers, clear windows, opening bonnet and hatch cover, Renault decal............................	25	35	60
262-A, Lincoln Continental, 1967-69, metallic gold or light blue body, black roof, maroon plastic interior, working hood, trunk and doors, clear windows; accessories include TV w/picture strips for TV	60	90	150
264-A, Oldsmobile Toronado, 1967-68, metallic medium or dark blue body, cream interior, one-piece body, clear windshield, chrome bumpers, grille, headlight covers, shaped or cast spoked wheels	35	55	90
263-A, Rambler Marlin Fastback, 1966-69, red body, black roof and trim, cream interior, clear windshield, folding seats, chrome bumpers, grille and headlights, opening doors	35	55	90
273-A, Rolls-Royce Silver Shadow, 1970, metallic white upper/dusty blue lower body, working hood, trunk and two doors, clear windows, folding seats, chrome bumpers, Golden Jacks wheels	30	50	95
273-B, Honda Ballade Driving School, 1982-83, red body/base, tan interior, clear windows, tow hook, mirrors, bumpers..	10	15	25
274-A, Bentley T Series, 1970-72, red body, cream interior, working hood, trunk and doors, clear windows, folding seats, chrome bumper/grille, jewel headlights, Whizz Wheels	36	55	90
275-A, Rover 2000TC, 1968-70, metallic olive green or maroon one-piece body, light brown interior, chrome bumpers/grille, jewel headlights, red taillights, Golden Jacks wheels	30	45	75
275-B, Austin Mini-Metro, 1981, blue or red body w/plastic interior, working rear hatch and doors, clear windows, folding seats, chrome headlights, orange taillights, black plastic base, grille, bumpers, Whizz Wheels............	18	27	45
276-A, Oldsmobile Toronado, 1968-70, metallic copper, metallic blue or red one-piece body, cream interior, Golden jacks, gray tow hook, clear windows, bumpers, grille, headlights ..	35	55	90

	C6	C8	C10
276-B, Triumph Acclaim HLS, 1981-83, metallic peacock blue body/base, black trim, light brown interior, clear windows, mirrors, bumpers, vents, tow hook	15	18	30
277-B, Triumph Acclaim Driving School, 1982, dark yellow body w/black trim, black roof mounted steering wheel steers front wheels, clear windows, mirrors, bumpers.........	15	25	40
278-B, Triumph Acclaim Driving School, 1982-83, yellow or red body/base, Corgi Motor School labels, black roof mounted steering wheel steers front wheels, clear windows	15	25	50
279-A, Rolls-Royce Corniche, 1979, different color versions w/light brown interior, working hood, trunk and two doors, clear windows, folding seats, chrome bumpers................	10	20	40
280-A1, Rolls-Royce Silver Shadow, 1971-73, metallic silver upper and metallic blue lower body, light brown interior, may or may not include hole in trunk for spare tire, Whizz Wheels ..	25	40	65
280-A2, Rolls-Royce Silver Shadow, 1974-78, metallic blue or gold body, bright blue interior, working hood, trunk and two doors, clear windows, folding seats, spare wheel	25	40	65
281-A, Rover 2000TC, 1971-73, metallic purple body, light orange interior, black grille, one-piece body, amber windows, chrome bumpers and headlights, Whizz Wheels	25	35	60
283-A, OSI DAF City Car, 1971-74, orange/red body, light cream interior, textured black roof, sliding left door, working hood, hatch and two right doors, Whizz Wheels	18	25	45
284-A, Citroen SM, 1971-75, metallic lime gold w/chrome wheels or mauve body w/spoked wheels, pale blue interior and lifting hatch cover, working rear hatch and two doors, chrome inner drs., window frames, bumpers, grille, amber headlights, red taillights, Whizz Wheels	16	24	40
285-A, Mercedes-Benz 240D, 1975-81, silver, blue or copper/beige body, working trunk, two doors, clear windows, plastic interior, two hook, chrome bumpers, grille and headlights, Whizz Wheels......................................	10	15	25

Corgi 9002-A 1927 Bentley, 1964-69. Photo courtesy Dr. Douglas Sadecky

Corgi 9021-A 1910 Daimler 38, 1964-69. Photo courtesy Dr. Douglas Sadecky

Corgi 458-A ERF 64G Earth Dumper, 1958-67. Photo courtesy Dr. Douglas Sadecky

Corgi 237-A Oldsmobile Sheriff's Car, 1962-66. Photo courtesy Dr. Douglas Sadecky

Corgi 412-A Bedford Utilecon Ambulance, 1957-60. Photo courtesy Dr. Douglas Sadecky

Corgi 419-A1 Ford Zephyr Patrol Car, 1960-65. Photo courtesy Dr. Douglas Sadecky

	C6	C8	C10
287-A, Citroen Dyane, 1974-78, metallic yellow or green body, black roof and interior, working rear hatch, clear windows, black base and tow bar, silver bumpers, grille and headlights, red taillights, marching duck and French flag decals, suspension, chrome wheels	15	18	30
289-A, Volkswagen Polo, 1976-79, apple green or bright yellow body, black DBP and posthorn (German Post Office) labels, off white interior, black dash	25	40	65
289-B, Volkswagen Polo Mail Car, 1976-80, bright yellow body, black DBP and Posthorn labels, German issue	25	35	60
291-A, AMC Pacer, 1977-78, metallic red body, white Pacer X decals, working hatch, clear windows, light yellow interior, chrome bumpers and wheels	15	20	50
293-A, Renault 5TS, 1980-81, light blue body, red plastic interior, dark blue roof, dome light, S.O.S. Medicine lettering, working hatch and two doors, French issue	20	35	70
294-A, Renault Alpine 5TS, 1980, dark blue body, off white interior, red and chrome trim, clear windows and headlights, gray base and bumpers, black grille, opening doors and hatchback	15	25	40
302-C, Volkswagen Polo, 1979-81, metallic light brown body, off-white interior, black dash, clear windows, silver bumpers, grille and headlights	15	18	30
325-B, Chevrolet Caprice Classic, 1981-82, working doors and trunk, whitewall tires, two versions: light metallic green body w/green interior or silver on blue body w/brown interior	24	36	60
332-B, Opel Senator Doctor's Car, 1980-81	10	15	25
334-B, Ford Escort 13 GL, 1980, red, blue or yellow body, opening doors	8	15	25
338-B, Rover 3500, 1979, three different body and interior versions, plastic interior, opening hood, hatch and two doors, lifting hatch cover	8	15	25
345-B, Honda Prelude, 1981-82, dark metallic blue body, tan interior, clear windows, folding seats, sunroof, chrome wheels	8	15	20
346-A, Citroen 2CV Charleston, 1981, yellow/black or maroon/black body versions w/opening hood	15	18	30
400-A, Volkswagen 1200 Driving School, 1974-75, metallic red or blue body, yellow interior, gold roof mounted steering wheel that steers, silver headlights, red taillights	25	35	60
401-A, Volkswagen Driving School, 1975-77, metallic blue body, yellow interior, gold roof mounted steering wheel that steers, silver headlights, red taillights	25	40	70
424-A, Ford Zephyr Estate Car, 1960-65, light blue one-piece body, dark blue hood and stripes, red interior, silver bumpers, grille and headlights, red taillights	30	45	75
436-A, Citroen ID-19 Safari, 1963-65, orange body w/red/brown or red/green luggage on roof rack, green/brown interior, working hatch, two passengers, Wildlife Preservation decals	40	70	120
440-A, Ford Cortina Estate Car, 1966-68, 3-1/2" metallic dark blue body and base, brown and cream simulated wood panels, cream interior, chrome bumpers and grille, jewel headlights	35	55	90
443-A, Plymouth Suburban Mail Car, 1963-66, white upper, blue lower body w/red stripes, gray die-cast base without rear axle bulge, silver bumpers and grille, U.S. Mail decals	55	85	140
445-A, Plymouth Sports Suburban, 1963-65, pale blue body w/silver trim, red roof, yellow interior, gray die-cast base without rear axle bulge, shaped wheels	40	60	100
475-A, Citroen Winter Sports Safari, 1964-67, white body in three versions: two w/Corgi Ski Club decals and either w/or without roof ski rack, or one w/1964 Winter Olympics decals	56	84	140
485-A, Austin Mini Countryman, 1965-69, turquoise body, jeweled headlights, opening rear doors, chrome roofrack w/two surfboards, shaped or cast wheels, w/surfer figure	55	80	150

	C6	C8	C10
486-A, Chevrolet Kennel Club Van, 1967-69, white upper, red lower body, working tailgate and rear windows, green interior, four dog figures, kennel club decals; shaped spun or detailed cast wheels, rubber tires	56	90	160
489-A2, Volkswagen Polo German Auto Club Car, 1977-79, yellow body, off-white interior, black dash, silver bumpers, grille and headlights, white roof, yellow dome light........................	25	35	60
489-B, Volkswagen Polo Auto Club Car, 1977-79, yellow body, white roof, yellow dome light, ADAC Strassenwacht labels	15	25	40
491-A, Ford Cortina Estate Car, 1966-69, red body and base or metallic charcoal gray body and base, cream interior, chrome bumpers and grille, jewel headlights	35	55	90
499-A, Citroen Winter Olympics Car, 1967-69, white body, blue roof and hatch, blue interior, red roof rack w/yellow skis, gold sled w/rider, skier, gold Grenoble Olympiade decals on car roof	70	105	200
510-A, Citroen Tour de France Car, 1970-72, red body, yellow interior and rear bed, clear windshield and headlights, driver, black plastic rack w/four bicycle wheels, swiveling team manager figure w/megaphone in back of car, Paramount and Tour de France decals, Whizz Wheels	40	70	120
1003-A, Ford Torino Road Hog, 1981, orange-red body, yellow and gray chassis, gold lamps, chrome radiator shell, windows and bumpers, one-piece body, working horn	15	20	35

Boat

	C6	C8	C10
36-A, Olds Toronado and Speedboat, 1967-70, blue No. 276 Toronado, blue and yellow boat and chrome trailer, w/swordfish decals and three figures ...	60	90	165
37-B, Fiat X 1/9 & Powerboat, 1979-82, green and white automobile, w/white and gold boat, Carlsberg labels.............	30	45	75
38-C, Powerboat Team, 1980-81, white/red No. 319 Jaguar w/red/white boat on silver trailer, Team Corgi Carlsberg, Union Jack and #1 labels on boat........................	25	35	60

	C6	C8	C10
104-A, Dolphin Cabin Cruiser, 1965-68, white hull, blue deck plastic boat w/red/white stripe labels, driver, blue motor w/white cover, gray prop, cast trailer w/smooth wheels, rubber tires...	24	40	80
1119-A, HDL Hovercraft SR-N1, 1960-62, blue superstructure, gray base and deck, clear canopy, red seats, yellow SR-N1 decals	60	90	150

Bus

	C6	C8	C10
11-B, London Set, 1971-75, orange No. 226 Mini, Policeman, No. 418 London Taxi and No. 468 Outspan Routemaster bus, Whizz Wheels	50	75	125
11-C, London Set, 1980-82, No. 425 London Taxi and No. 469 Routemaster B.T.A. bus in two versions: w/mounted Policeman (1980-81); without Policeman, (1982-on); value is for each individual complete set	25	35	60
35-A, London Set, 1964-68, No. 418 taxi and No. 468 bus w/policeman, in two versions: "Corgi Toys" on bus (1964-66); "Outspan Oranges" on bus (1967-68); values for each individual complete set	55	95	170
467-A, Routemaster Bus-Promotionals, 1977, different body and interior versions and promotional labels	15	25	40
468-A, London Transport Routemaster Bus, 1964-75, clear windows w/driver and conductor, released w/numerous advertiser logos, shaped or cast spoked wheels	35	40	70
469-A, London Transport Routemaster Bus, 1975, long, clear windows, interior, some models have driver and conductor, released w/numerous advertiser logos, Whizz Wheels	25	30	50
470-B, Open Top Disneyland Bus, 1977-78, yellow body, red interior and stripe, Disneyland labels, eight-spoked wheels or orange body, white interior and stripe.................	30	50	95
470-C, Green Line Bus, 1983, green body, white interior and stripe, TDK labels, six spoked wheels	10	15	25
471-B, Silver Jubilee London Transport Bus, 1977, silver body w/red interior, no passengers, labels read "Woolworth Welcomes the World" and "The Queen's Silver	15	18	30

Corgi 482-A Chevrolet Impala Fire Chief Car, 1965-69. Photo courtesy Dr. Douglas Sadecky

Corgi 492-A Volkswagen 1200 Police Car, 1966-69. Photo courtesy Dr. Douglas Sadecky

Corgi 506-A Sunbeam Imp Police Car, 1968-72. Photo courtesy Dr. Douglas Sadecky

Corgi 448-A Austin Police Mini Van, 1964-69. Photo courtesy Dr. Douglas Sadecky

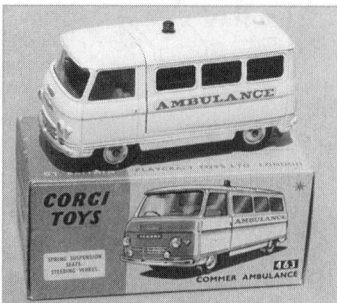

Corgi 463-A Commer 3/4-Ton Ambulance, 1964-66. Photo courtesy Dr. Douglas Sadecky

Corgi 464-A Comer 3/4-Ton Police Van, 1963-68. Photo courtesy Dr. Douglas Sadecky

	C6	C8	C10
701-A, Inter-City Mini Bus, 1973-79, orange body w/brown interior, clear windows, green/yellow/black decals, Whizz Wheels	8	15	25
1004-A, Beep Beep London Bus, 1981, battery-operated working horn, red body, black windows, BTA decals	26	39	65
1120-A, Midland Red Express Coach, 1961-62, red one-piece body, black roof w/shaped or smooth wheels, yellow interior, clear windows, silver grille and headlights. Two box variations shown in this photo	70	105	225
1168-A, National Express Bus, 1983, variety of colors and label variations	8	15	25

Character

	C6	C8	C10
3-B1, Batmobile, Batboat and Trailer, 1967-72, first and second versions: red bat hubs on wheels, 1967-72; red tires and chrome wheels 1972-73	240	360	650
3-B2, Batmobile, Batboat and Trailer, 1973-81, third and fourth versions: 1973; black tires, labels on boat, 1974-76; chrome wheels, boat labels, Whizz Wheels on trailer	120	175	350
7-B, Daktari Set, 1967-75, two versions: No. 438 Land Rover, green w/black stripes, spun or cast spoke wheels, 1968-73; Whizz Wheels, 1974-75, each set	50	75	150
8-B, Lions of Longleat, 1968-74, black/white No. 438 Land Rover pickup w/lion cages and accessories, two versions: cast spoked wheels, 1969-73; Whizz Wheels, 1974, each	60	90	200
14-B, Giant Daktari Set, 1969-73, black and green No. 438 Land Rover, tan No. 503 Giraffe truck, blue and brown No. 484 Dodge Livestock truck, figures	225	350	650
21-C, Superman Set, 1979-81, set of three: No. 265 Supermobile, No. 925 Daily Planet Helicopter and No. 260 Metropolis Police Car	70	120	225
22-B, James Bond Set, 1979-81, set of three: No. 271 Lotus Esprit, No. 649 Space Shuttle and No. 269 Aston Martin	100	200	400
23-B, Spider-Man Set, 1980-81, set of three: No. 266 Spider-Bike, No. 928 Spider-Copter and No. 261Spider-Buggy	80	160	350

	C6	C8	C10
36-B, Tarzan Set, 1976-78, metallic green No. 421 Land Rover w/trailer and Dinghy; cage, five figures and other accessories	100	150	285
40-A, Avengers Set, 1966-69, white Lotus, red or green (rare) Bentley; Jonathan Steed and Emma Peel figures w/three umbrellas	260	390	800
40-B, Batman Set, 1976-81, three vehicle set: No. 267 Batmobile, No. 107 Batboat w/trailer and No. 925 Batcopter, Whizz Wheels on trailer	150	300	800
41-B, Silver Jubilee Landau, 1977-80, Landua w/four horses, two footmen, two riders, Queen and Prince figures, and Corgi dog, in two versions	15	25	50
107-A1, Batboat, 1967-72, black plastic boat, red seats, fin and jet, blue windshield, Batman and Robin figures, gold cast trailer, tinplate fin cover, cast wheels, plastic tires, w/plastic towhook for Batmobile	60	90	175
107-A2, Batboat, 1976-80, black plastic boat w/Batman and Robin figures, small Bat logo labels on fin and on side of boat, chain link labels, Whizz Wheels on trailer	30	45	100
201-B, Saint's Volvo P-1800, 1970-72, one-piece white body w/red Saint decal on hood, gray base, clear windows, black interior w/driver, Whizz Wheels	55	95	200
258-A, Saint's Volvo P-1800, 1965-69, three versions of white one-piece body w/silver trim and different colored Saint decals on hood, driver. Pictured here with the 201-B. Note the wheel and hood logo variation between the two cars	55	85	175
259-B, Penguinmobile, 1979-80, white body, black and white lettering on orange-yellow-blue labels, gold body panels, seats, air scoop, chrome engine, w/penguin figure	20	30	65
261-A, James Bond Aston Martin DB5, 1965-68, metallic gold body, red interior, working roof hatch, clear windows, two figures, left seat ejects, spoked wheels, accessory pack	70	150	300
261-B, Spider-Buggy, 1979-81, red body, blue hood, clear windows, dark blue dash, seat and crane, chrome base			

	C6	C8	C10
w/bumper and steps, silver headlights; includes Spider-Man and Green Goblin figures	50	75	150
262-B, Captain Marvel Porsche, 1979-80, white body, gold parts, red seat, driver, red/yellow/blue Captain Marvel decals, black plastic base, gold wheels	20	30	60
263-B, Captain America Jetmobile, 1979-80, 6" white body, metallic blue chassis, black nose cone, red shield and jet, red-white-blue Captain America decals, light blue seats and driver, chrome wheels, red tires	24	36	60
264-B, Incredible Hulk Mazda Pickup, 1979-80, metallic light brown body, gray or red plastic cage, black interior, Hulk label on hood, chrome wheels; includes green and red Hulk figure	20	30	75
265-A, Supermobile, 1979-81, blue body, red, chrome or gray fists, red interior, clear canopy, Superman figure, chrome arms w/removable "striking fists"	30	45	75
266-A, Chitty Chitty Bang Bang, 1968-72, metallic copper body, dark red interior and spoked wheels, four figures, black chassis w/silver running boards, silver hood, horn, brake, dash, tail and headlights, gold radiator, red and orange wings, handbrake operates side wings	180	270	425
266-B, Spider-Bike, 1979-83, medium blue body, one-piece body, dark blue plastic front body and seat, blue and red Spider-Man figure, amber windshield, black or white wheels	40	60	85
267-A1, Batmobile, 1966, matte black (rare) or gloss black body, gold hubs, bat logos on door and hubs, maroon interior, black body, plastic rockets, yellow headlights and gold rocket control, blue tinted canopy, working front chain cutter, no tow hook, rubber tires. Although it's difficult to tell from this photo, this is the rare first issue matte black finish with no towhook version of the famous Batmobile	200	300	550
267-A2, Batmobile, 1967-72, same as first issue except for gloss black body, gold towhook	200	300	500

	C6	C8	C10
267-C1, Batmobile, 1973, chrome hubs w/red bat logos on door, maroon interior, red plastic tires, gold tow hook, plastic rockets, yellow headlight and gold rocket control, tinted blue canopy w/chrome support, chain cutter. Made for only one year, this version featured red plastic tires and chrome wheels. Also pictured is the back of the rare first-issue window box for this model	140	200	400
267-C2, Batmobile, 1974-79, chrome hubs w/black plastic tires, red bat logos on door, light red interior, gold tow hook, plastic rockets, yellow headlights and gold rocket control, tinted blue canopy w/chrome support	80	120	200
267-D, Batmobile, 1980-81, gloss black body, light red interior, gold towhook, Whizzwheels with 8-spoke chrome hubs	80	110	175
268-A, Green Hornet's Black Beauty, 1967-72, black body, green window/interior, two figures, working chrome grille and panels w/weapons, green headlights, red taillights	175	275	550
268-B, Batbike, 1978-83, black body, one-piece body, black and red plastic parts, gold engine and exhaust pipes, clear windshield, chrome stand, black plastic five-spoked wheels, Batman figure and decals	40	60	125
269-B, James Bond Lotus Esprit, 1977, white body and base, black windshield, grille and hood panel, white plastic roof device that triggers fins and tail, rockets	30	45	95
270-A, James Bond Aston Martin, 1968-77, metallic silver body, red interior, two figures, working roof hatch, ejector seat, bullet shield and guns, chrome bumpers, spoked wheels. Orginally issued in a rare bubble-pack, the subsequent issues were sold in window boxes. On the left, the rare first issue window box; on the right, the more commonly seen version	100	150	325
271-B, James Bond Aston Martin, 1978, metallic silver body and die-cast base, red interior, two figures, clear windows, passenger seat raises to eject	30	45	90

Corgi 1110-A Bedford Mobilgas Tanker, 1959-65. Photo courtesy Dr. Douglas Sadecky

Corgi 1126-A Ecurie Ecosse Transporter, 1961-65. Photo courtesy Dr. Douglas Sadecky

	C6	C8	C10
272-A, James Bond Citroen 2CV6, 1981-86, dark yellow body and hood, red interior, clear windows, chrome headlights, red taillights, black plastic grille. This model was available in a window box, or the more difficult to find photo box shown here	15	35	70
277-A, Monkeemobile, 1968-70, red body/base, white roof, yellow interior, clear windows, four figures, chrome grille, headlights, engine, orange taillights	145	225	450
290-A, Kojak's Buick Regal, 1976-81, metallic bronze brown body, off-white interior, two opening doors, clear windows, chrome bumpers, grille and headlights, red taillights; accessories include Kojak and Crocker figures	25	55	95
292-A, Starsky and Hutch Ford Torino, 1977-81, red one-piece body, white trim, light yellow interior, clear windows, chrome bumpers, grille and headlights, orange taillights; includes Starsky, Hutch and Bandit figures	35	55	100
320-B, Saint's Jaguar XJS, 1978-81, white body, red interior, black trim, Saint figure hood label, opening doors, black grille, bumpers and tow hook, chrome headlights	30	45	85
336-A, James Bond Toyota 2000GT, 1967-69, white body, black interior w/Bond and female driver, working trunk and gun rack, spoked wheels, plastic tires, accessory pack	115	180	375
342-B, Professionals Ford Capri, 1980-82, metallic silver body and base, red interior, black spoiler, grille, bumpers, tow hook and trim, blue windows, chrome wheels; includes figures of Cowley, Bodie and Doyle	30	65	130
348-B, Vegas Ford Thunderbird, 1980-81, orange/red body and base, black interior and grille, opening hood and trunk, amber windshield, white seats, driver, chrome bumper	25	40	85
391-A, James Bond Mustang Mach 1, 1972-73, red and white body w/black hood and opening doors. Because using this model as a Bond vehicle was a last-minute decision, a label was adhered to the right side of the window box. Without this label, no one would know this was a James Bond issue	100	150	300
434-B, Chevrolet Charlie's Angels Van, 1977-80, light rose-mauve body w/Charlie's Angels decals, in two versions: either solid or spoked chrome wheels	15	30	55
435-B, Supervan, 1978-81, silver van w/Superman labels, working rear doors, chrome spoked wheels	15	30	60
436-B, Chevrolet Spider-Van, 1978-80, dark blue body w/Spider-Man decals, in two versions: w/either spoke or solid wheels	26	39	65
497-A1, Man From U.N.C.L.E. THRUSH-Buster, 1966-68, plastic interior, blue windows, two figures, two spotlights, dark metallic blue body, w/3-D Waverly rin	80	130	275
497-A2, Man From U.N.C.L.E. THRUSH-Buster, 1968-69, plastic interior, blue windows, two figures, two spotlights, cream body, w/3-D Waverly ring, RARE	100	350	550
647-A, Buck Rogers Starfighter, 1980, white body w/yellow plastic wings, amber windows, blue jets, color decal, Buck and Wilma figures	32	48	90
649-A, James Bond Space Shuttle, 1979-81, white body w/yellow/black Moonraker labels	30	50	95
801-A1, Noddy's Car, 1969-71, first issue: yellow body, red chassis and fenders, figures of Noddy, Big-Ears, and black, gray, or light tan face Golliwog	200	400	600
801-A2, Noddy's Car, 1972-73, second issue: same as first issue except Master Tubby is substituted for Golliwog	100	200	350
802-A, Popeye's Paddle Wagon, 1969-72, yellow and white body, red chassis, blue rear fenders, bronze and yellow stacks, white plastic deck, blue lifeboat w/Swee' Pea; includes figures of Popeye, Olive Oyl, Bluto and Wimpey. Produced for a short period, the colorful Paddle-Wagon had multiple working features and contained all of the main characters	195	300	525
803-A1, Beatles' Yellow Submarine, 1969, yellow and white hatches, red pinstripes, first issue	200	500	1000
803-A2, Beatles' Yellow Submarine, 1969-70, second issue, yellow and white body, working red hatches w/two Beatles in each	180	270	700
804-A, Noddy's Car, yellow body, red chassis, Noddy alone, closed trunk w/spare wheel	60	90	175
805-A, Hardy Boys' Rolls-Royce, 1970, red body w/yellow hood, roof and window frames, band figures on roof on removable green base	70	105	200
807-A, Dougal's Magic Roundabout Car, 1971-74, yellow body, red interior, clear windows, dog and snail figures, red wheels w/gold trim, Magic Roundabout labels	70	105	175
808-A, Basil Brush's Car, 1971-73, red body, dark yellow chassis, gold lamps and dash, Basil Brush figure, red plastic wheels, plastic tires; w/"Laugh Tapes" and soundbox. Basil Brush could be heard laughing with the aid of laugh tapes and a soundbox that were included with the car	70	105	200
809-A, Dick Dastardly's Racing Car, 1973-76, dark blue body, yellow chassis, chrome engine, red wings, Dick and Muttley figures	40	60	150
811-A, James Bond Moon Buggy, 1972-73, white body w/blue chassis, amber canopy, yellow tanks, red radar dish, arms and jaws, yellow wheels	175	275	525

Corgi 1143-A American LaFrance Ladder Truck, 1968-81. Photo courtesy Dr. Douglas Sadecky

Corgi 470-A Jeep FC-150 Covered Truck, 1965-72. Photo courtesy Dr. Douglas Sadecky

Corgi 478-A Jeep FC-150 Tower Wagon, 1965-69. Photo courtesy Dr. Douglas Sadecky

	C6	C8	C10
851-A, Magic Roundabout Train, 1973, red and blue plastic three-piece train; accessories include figures of Mr. Rusty, Basil, Rosaile, Paul and Dougal	70	195	350
852-A, Magic Roundabout Musical Carousel, 1973, plastic roundabout w/Swiss musical movement, w/Dylan, Rosalie, Paul, Florence and Basil figures, rare	275	425	750
853-A, Magic Roundabout Playground, 1973, contains No. 851 Train, No. 852 Carousel, six figures, seesaw, park bench, shrubs and fowers, rare	295	500	1000
859-A, Mr. McHenry's Trike, 1972-74, red and yellow trike and trailer; accessories include Mr. McHenry and Zebedee figures	70	105	175
925-A, Batcopter, 1976-81, black body w/yellow/red/black decals, red rotors, Batman figure, operable winch	30	50	100
928-A, Spider-Copter, 1979-81, blue body w/Spider-Man labels, red plastic legs, tongue and tail rotor, black windows and main rotor	30	45	85
929-A, Daily Planet Helicopter, 1979-81, red and white body, rocket launcher w/ten spare missiles	24	36	60
930-A, Drax Jet Helicopter, 1979-81, white body, yellow rotors and fins, yellow/black Drax labels	35	75	150
2030-A, Muppet Vehicles, Kermit's Car	15	35	60
2031-A, Muppet Vehicles, Fozzie Bear's Truck	15	30	50
2032-A, Muppet Vehicles, Miss Piggy's Sports Coupe	15	30	50
2033-A, Muppet Vehicles, Animal's Percussionmobile	15	30	50
9004-A, 1927 Bentley "World of Wooster", 1967-69, green body, metallic black chassis, cast spoked wheels, figures of Jeeves & Bertie Wooster	50	100	150

Circus

	C6	C8	C10
12-A, Chipperfield Circus Crane and Cage Wagon, 1961-65, No. 1121 crane truck, No. 1123 cage wagon and accessories	150	225	375
19-A, Chipperfield Circus Land Rover and Elephant Cage, 1962-68, red			

	C6	C8	C10
No. 438 Range Rover w/blue canopy, Chipperfields Circus decal on canopy, burnt orange No. 607 elephant cage on red bed trailer	90	135	275
21-B, Chipperfield Circus Crane and Cage, 1970-72, No. 1144 crane truck, cage w/rhinoceros, red and blue trailer w/three animal cages and animals; very rare gift set	400	700	2000
23-A1, Chipperfield Circus Set, 1st Version, 1963-65, vehicle and accessory set in two versions: w/No. 426 Booking Office	380	600	1300
23-A2, Chipperfield Circus Set, 2nd Version, 1966, vehicle and accessory set w/#503 Giraffe Truck	340	500	1000
30-B, Circus Land Rover and Trailer, 1978-81, yellow/red No. 421 Land Rover w/Pinder-Jean Richard decals; accessories include blue loudspeakers and figures	30	50	90
48-C, Jean Richard Circus Set, 1978-81, yellow and red Land Rover and cage trailer w/Pinder-Jean Richard decals, No. 426 office van and trailer, No. 1163 Human Cannonball truck, ring and cut-out "Big Top" circus tent	90	135	275
426-A, Chipperfield Circus Karrier Booking Office, 1962-64, red body, light blue roof, clear windows, tin lithographed interior, circus decals, smooth or shaped wheels, rubber tires	105	165	325
487-A, Chipperfield Circus Land Rover Parade Vehicle, 1967-69, red body, yellow interior, blue rear and speakers, revolving clown, chimp figures, Chipperfield labels	60	90	175
503-A, Chipperfield Circus Bedford Giraffe Transporter, 1964-71, red "TK" Bedford truck w/blue giraffe box w/Chipperfield decal, two giraffes, shaped, cast spoked or detailed wheels	60	90	175
511-A, Chipperfield Circus Chevrolet Performing Poodles Van, 1970-72, blue upper body and tailgate, red lower body and base, clear windshield, pale blue interior w/poodles in back and ring of poodles and trainer, plastic tires	160	240	550
1121-A, Chipperfield Circus Crane Truck, 1960-68, red body, embossed			

	C6	C8	C10
Chipperfield blue logo, tinplate boom, blue wheels. Pictured here with Chipperfield Circus Cage Wagon 1123-A, that included a set of polar bears or lions and their appropriate label transfers	80	120	225
1123-A, Chipperfield Circus Cage Wagon, 1961-68, red body, yellow chassis, smooth or spun hubs; includes lions, tigers or polar bears	56	84	140
1130-A, Chipperfield Circus Horse Transporter, 1962-72, red Bedford "TK" cab, blue upper/red lower horse trailer, three wheel variations; includes six horses	80	120	235
1139-A, Chipperfield Circus Menagerie Transporter, 1968-72, Scammell Handyman MKIII red/blue cab, blue trailer w/three animal cages, two lions, two tigers and two bears	120	180	375
1144-A, Chipperfield Circus Scammell Crane Truck, 1969-72, red upper cab and rear body, light blue lower cab, crane base and winch crank housing, red interior, tow hook, jewel headlights	175	275	450
1163-A, Circus Human Cannonball Truck, 1978-81, red and blue body; w/Marvo figure	30	45	75

Classics

	C6	C8	C10
9001-A, 1927 Bentley, 1964-69, green body, metallic black chassis, brown interior, black ragtop, spoked wheels, driver	35	50	75
9002-A, 1927 Bentley, 1964-69, red body, metallic black chassis, brown interior, black ragtop, red spoked wheels, driver. The red Bentley is slightly harder to find than the green version	30	60	90
9011-A, Model T Ford, 1964-69, black body & chassis, spoked wheels, two figures	20	40	65
9012-A, Model T Ford, 1964-69, yellow body & spoked wheels, black chassis, two figures	20	40	65
9013-A, Model T Ford, 1964-69, blue body, black chassis, black ragtop, yellow wheels, one figure	20	40	65
9021-A, Daimler 38 1910, 1964-69, orange-red body, gray and yellow			

	C6	C8	C10
chassis, yellow spoked wheels; w/four figures	20	40	65
9031-A, 1910 Renault 12/16, 1965-69, light purple body & spoked wheels, light black chassis	25	50	80
9032-A, 1910 Renault 12/16, 1965-69, pale yellow body & spoked wheels, light black chassis, black ragtop	25	50	80
9041-A, Rolls-Royce Silver Ghost, 1966-69, silver body/hood, charcoal and silver chassis, bronze interior, gold lights, box and tank, clear windows, dash lights, radiator	15	30	60

Construction

	C6	C8	C10
2-B, Unimog Dumper & Priestman Cub Shovel, 1971-73, standard colors, #1145 Mercedes-Benz unimog w/Dumper and 1128 Priestman Cub Shovel	70	135	200
27-A, Priestman Shovel and Carrier, 1963-72, No. 1128 cub shovel and No. 1131 low loader machinery carrier	90	135	225
403-B, Thwaites Tusker Skip Dumper, 1974-79, yellow body, chassis and tipper, driver and seat, hydraulic cylinder, red wheels, black tires two sizes, name labels, Whizz Wheels	10	20	40
409-B1, Unimog Dump Truck, 1971-73, first issue, blue cab, yellow tipper, fenders and bumpers, metallic charcoal gray chassis, red interior, black mirrors, gray tow hook	20	30	50
409-B2, Unimog Dump Truck, 1976-77, second issue, yellow cab, chassis, rear frame and blue tipper, fenders and bumpers, red interior, no mirrors, gray tow hook, hydraulic cylinders	20	30	50
409-C, Allis-Chalmers AFC 60 Fork Lift, 1981, yellow body, white engine hood, w/driver, tan pallets and red containers	15	20	45
458-A, ERF 64G Earth Dumper, 1958-67, red cab, yellow tipper, clear windows, unpainted hydraulic cylinder, spare tire, smooth wheels, rubber tires	30	45	85
459-B, Raygo Rascal Roller, 1973-78, dark yellow body, base and mounting, green interior and engine, orange and silver roller mounting and castings, clear windshield	15	25	45

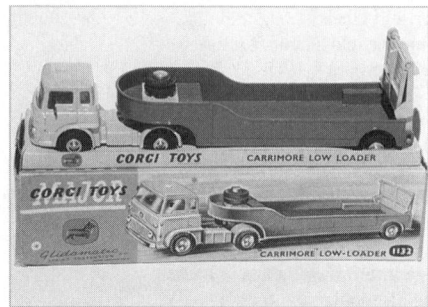

Corgi 1132-A Bedford Carrimore Low Loader, 1963-65. Photo courtesy Dr. Douglas Sadecky

Corgi 1113-A Corporal Missile & Erector Vehicle, 1959-62. Photo courtesy Dr. Douglas Sadecky

	C6	C8	C10
494-A, Bedford TK Tipper Truck, 1968-72, red cab and chassis w/yellow or silver tipper, side mirrors	26	39	65
1007-A, Road Repair Unit, 1982, dark yellow Land Rover w/battery hatch and trailer w/red plastic interior w/sign and open panels, stripe and Roadwork labels	15	25	40
1101-B, Warner & Swasey Crane, 1975-81, yellow cab and body, blue chassis, blue/yellow stripe labels, red interior, black steering wheel, silver knob, gold hook	30	45	75
1102-A, Euclid TC-12 Bulldozer, 1958-62, lime green body w/black or pale gray treads, silver blade surface, gray plastic seat, controls, and stacks; silver grille and lights, painted blue engine sides, black sheet metal base, rubber treads and Euclid decals	80	120	225
1102-B, Berliet Fruehauf Dumper, 1974-76, yellow cab, fenders and dumper; black cab and semi chassis; plastic orange or dark orange dumper body; black interior	30	45	75
1103-A, Euclid Caterpillar Tractor, 1960-63, TC-12 lime green body w/black or pale gray rubber treads, gray plastic seat, driver figure, controls, stacks, silver grille, painted blue engine sides and Euclid decals	50	100	190
1103-B, Caterpillar Tractor, 1960-64, lime green body w/black or gray rubber treads, gray plastic seat, driver figure, controls, stacks	70	105	250
1107-A, Euclid TC-12 Bulldozer, 1963-66, yellow or pale lime-green body, metal control rod, driver, black rubber treads	80	120	200
1110-B, JCB 110B Crawler Loader, 1976-80, white cab, yellow body, working red shovel, red interior w/driver, clear windows, black treads, JCB labels	20	30	50
1113-B, Hyster 800 Stacatruck, 1977, clear windows, black interior w/driver	35	50	85
1121-B, Ford Transit Tipper, 1983, orange cab and chassis, tan tipper, chrome wheels	10	15	25
1128-A, Priestman Cub Power Shovel, 1963-76, orange upper body and panel, yellow lower body, lock rod and chassis, rubber or plastic treads, pulley panel, gray boom, w/figure of driver	40	60	100
1145-A, Mercedes-Benz Unimog & Dumper, 1969-76, yellow cab and tipper, red fenders and tipper chassis, charcoal gray cab chassis, black plastic mirrors or without	25	35	60
1152-B, Scania Dump Truck, 1983, white cab w/green tipper, black/green Barratt labels, black exhaust and hydraulic cylinders, six-spoked Whizz Wheels	7	15	30
1153-A, Priestman Cub Crane, 1972-74, orange body, red chassis and two-piece bucket, unpainted bucket arms, lower boom, knobs, gears and drum castings, clear window, Hi-Grab labels	50	75	125

	C6	C8	C10
1153-B, Scania Dump Truck, 1983, yellow truck and tipper w/black Wimpey labels, in two versions: either clear or green windows; six-spoked Whizz Wheels	7	15	30
1154-A, Mack-Priestman Crane Truck, 1972-76, red truck, yellow crane cab, red interior, black engine, Hi Lift and Long Vehicle or Hi-Grab labels	50	75	125
1154-B, Giant Tower Crane, 1981-82, white body, orange cab and chassis	35	50	85
1155-A, Skyscraper Tower Crane, 1975-79, red body w/yellow chassis and booms, gold hook, gray loads of block, black/ white Skyscraper labels, black tracks	30	45	75
1156-A, Volvo Concrete Mixer, 1977-81, yellow or orange cab, red or white mixer w/yellow and black stripes, rear chassis, chrome chute and unpainted hitch casings	30	45	75

Emergency

	C6	C8	C10
18-B, Emergency Set, 1976-77, three-vehicle set w/figures and accessories, No. 402 Ford Cortina Police car, No. 921 Police Helicopter, No. 481 Range Rover Ambulance	40	60	100
19-C, Emergency Set, 1979-81, No. 339 Land Rover Police Car and No. 921 Police Helicopter w/figures and accessories	30	50	80
33-B, German Life Saving Set, 1980-82, red/white No. 421 Land Rover and lifeboat, white trailer, German labels	30	45	75
35-B, Chopper Squad Rescue Set, 1978-79, blue No. 919 Jeep w/Chopper Squad decal and red/white boat w/Surf Rescue decal, No. 927 Helicopter	40	60	100
44-A, Police Land Rover and Horse Box, 1978-80, white No. 421 Land Rover w/police labels and mounted policeman, No. 112 Horse Box	30	45	75
45-B, Canadian Mounted Police Set, 1978-80, blue No. 421 Land Rover w/Police sign on roof and RCMP decals, No. 102 trailer; includes mounted Policeman	30	50	100
209-A, Riley Pathfinder Police Car, 1958-61, black body w/blue/white Police lettering, unpainted roof sign, gray antenna	50	75	135
213-A, Jaguar 2.4 Litre Fire Chief's Car, 1959-61, red body w/unpainted roof signal/siren, red/white fire and shield decals on doors, in two versions, smooth or spun hubs	60	90	150
223-A, Chevrolet State Patrol Car, 1959-61, black body, State Patrol decals, smooth wheels w/hexagonal panel or raised lines and shaped wheels, yellow plastic interior, gray antenna, clear windows, silver bumpers, grille, headlights and trim, rubber tires	50	75	125
237-A, Oldsmobile Sheriff's Car, 1962-66, black upper body w/white sides, red interior w/red dome light and			

Corgi 416-A RAC Land Rover, 1959-64. Photo courtesy Dr. Douglas Sadecky

Corgi 472-A Public Address Land Rover, 1964-66. Photo courtesy Dr. Douglas Sadecky

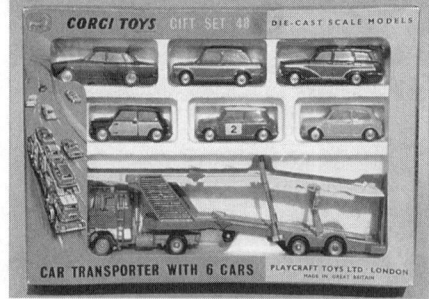

Corgi 48-A Transporter and Six Cars, 1966-69. Photo courtesy Dr. Douglas Sadecky

	C6	C8	C10
County Sheriff decals on doors, single body casting	50	75	125
260-B, Metropolis Police Car, 1979-81, metallic blue body, off white interior, white roof/stripes, two working doors, clear windows, chrome bumpers, grille and headlights, two roof light bars, City of Metropolis labels	20	30	50
284-B, Mercedes-Benz Fire Chief, 1982-83, light red body, black base, tan plastic interior, blue dome light, white Notruf 112 labels, red taillights, no tow hook, German export model	15	25	40
293-A, Renault 5TS, 1977-80, metallic golden orange body, black trim, tan plastic interior, working hatch and two doors, clear windows and headlights ...	15	18	30
295-A, Renault 5TS Fire Chief, 1982, red body, tan interior, amber headlights, gray antenna, black/white Sapeurs Pompiers labels, blue dome light, French export issue	15	25	40
297-A, Ford Escort Police Car, 1982, blue body and base, tan interior, white doors, blue dome lights, red Police labels, black grille and bumpers	8	15	30
326-A, Chevrolet Caprice Police Car, 1980-81, black body w/white roof, doors and trunk, red interior, silver light bar, Police decals	20	30	50
339-B, Rover 3500 Police Car, 1980, white body, light red interior, red stripes, white plastic roof sign, blue dome light, red and blue Police and badge label	8	15	25
373-A, Volkswagen Police Car/Foreign Issues, 1970-76, five different versions, one-piece body, red interior, dome light, silver headlights, red taillights, clear windows, Whizz Wheels	60	90	150
383-A1, Volkswagen 1200, 1970-76, dark yellow body, white roof, red interior and dome light, unpainted base and bumpers, black and white ADAC Strassenwacht labels, Whizz Wheels	60	90	150
383-A2, Volkswagen 1200, 1970-76, seven different color and label versions, plastic interior, one-piece body, silver headlights, red taillights, die-cast base and bumpers	20	45	85

	C6	C8	C10
395-A, Fire Bug, 1972-73, orange body, Whizz Wheels	20	30	50
402-A, Ford Cortina Police Car, 1972-76, white body, red or pink and black stripe labels, red interior, folding seats, blue dome light, clear windows, chrome bumpers, Police labels, opening doors..	15	25	45
405-A, Bedford Fire Tender, 1956-61, divided windshield, red or green body, each w/different decals, smooth or shaped hubs....................................	60	90	175
405-B, Chevrolet Superior Ambulance, 1978-80, white body, orange roof and stripes, two working doors, clear windows, red interior w/patient on stretcher and attendant, Red Cross decals	30	45	75
405M, Bedford Fire Tender-Mechanical, 1956-59, friction motor, red body w/Fire Dept. decals, divided windshield, silver or black ladder, smooth or shaped hubs.........................	70	115	185
406-C, Mercedes-Benz Ambulance, 1980-81, four different foreign versions, white interior, opening rear and two doors, blue windows and dome lights, chrome bumpers, grille and headlights, various labels; accessories include two attendant figures	15	20	35
407-B, Mercedes-Benz Ambulance, 1981, white body and base, red stripes and taillights, Red Cross and black and white ambulance labels, open rear door, white interior, no figures	15	20	35
412-A, Bedford Utilecon Ambulance, 1957-60, divided windshield, cream body w/red/white/blue decals, smooth wheels	50	75	125
412-B, Mercedes-Benz Police Car, 1975-80, white body w/two different hood versions, brown interior, polizei or police lettering, blue dome light......	15	18	30
414-B, Coast Guard Jaguar XJ12C, 1975-77, blue and white body, Coast Guard labels	18	27	45
416-B, Buick Police Car, 1977-78, metallic blue body w/white stripes and Police decals, chrome light bar w/red lights, orange taillights, chrome spoke wheels, w/two policemen.....................	18	27	45

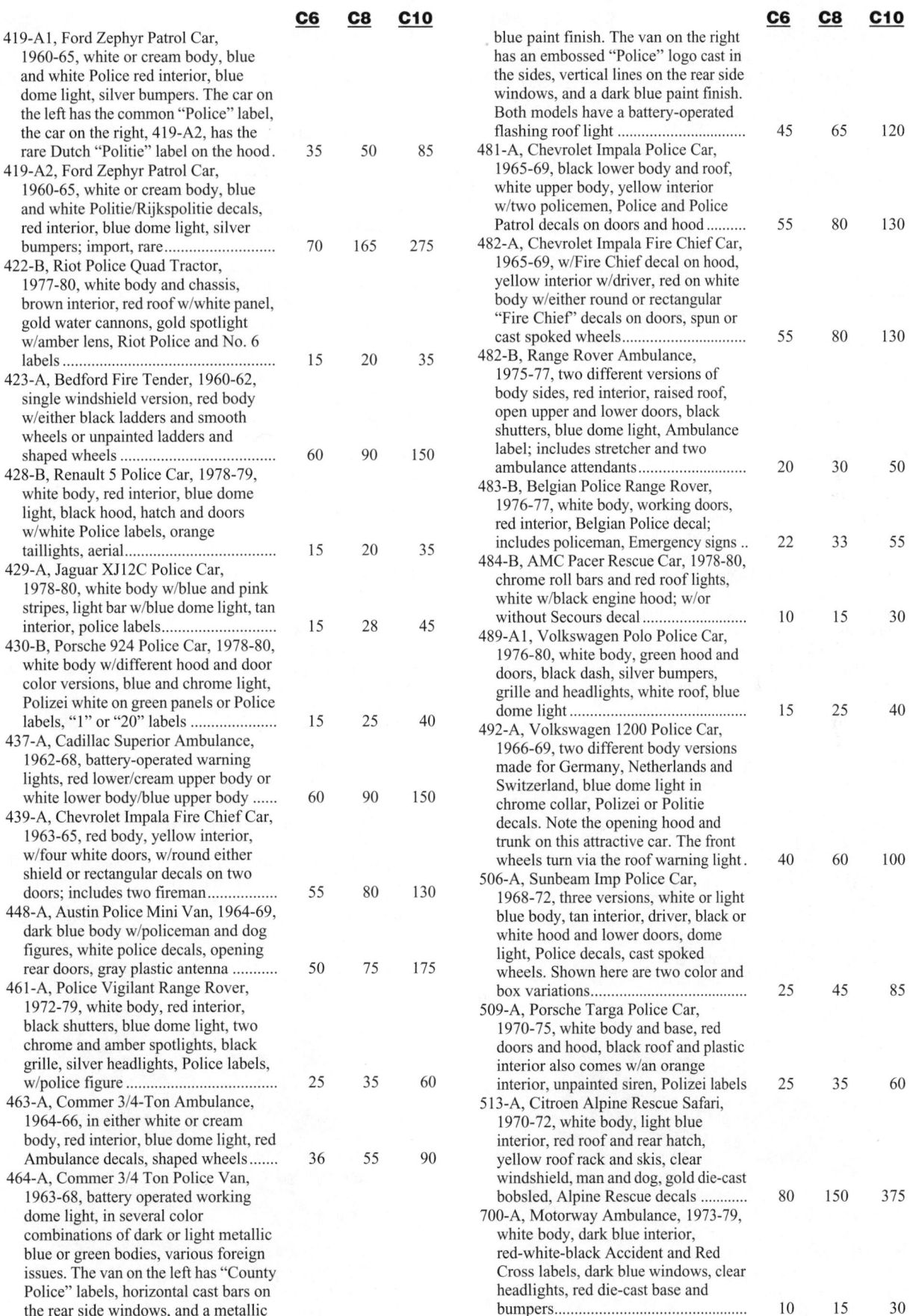

	C6	C8	C10
419-A1, Ford Zephyr Patrol Car, 1960-65, white or cream body, blue and white Police red interior, blue dome light, silver bumpers. The car on the left has the common "Police" label, the car on the right, 419-A2, has the rare Dutch "Politie" label on the hood.	35	50	85
419-A2, Ford Zephyr Patrol Car, 1960-65, white or cream body, blue and white Politie/Rijkspolitie decals, red interior, blue dome light, silver bumpers; import, rare	70	165	275
422-B, Riot Police Quad Tractor, 1977-80, white body and chassis, brown interior, red roof w/white panel, gold water cannons, gold spotlight w/amber lens, Riot Police and No. 6 labels	15	20	35
423-A, Bedford Fire Tender, 1960-62, single windshield version, red body w/either black ladders and smooth wheels or unpainted ladders and shaped wheels	60	90	150
428-B, Renault 5 Police Car, 1978-79, white body, red interior, blue dome light, black hood, hatch and doors w/white Police labels, orange taillights, aerial	15	20	35
429-A, Jaguar XJ12C Police Car, 1978-80, white body w/blue and pink stripes, light bar w/blue dome light, tan interior, police labels	15	28	45
430-B, Porsche 924 Police Car, 1978-80, white body w/different hood and door color versions, blue and chrome light, Polizei white on green panels or Police labels, "1" or "20" labels	15	25	40
437-A, Cadillac Superior Ambulance, 1962-68, battery-operated warning lights, red lower/cream upper body or white lower body/blue upper body	60	90	150
439-A, Chevrolet Impala Fire Chief Car, 1963-65, red body, yellow interior, w/four white doors, w/round either shield or rectangular decals on two doors; includes two fireman	55	80	130
448-A, Austin Police Mini Van, 1964-69, dark blue body w/policeman and dog figures, white police decals, opening rear doors, gray plastic antenna	50	75	175
461-A, Police Vigilant Range Rover, 1972-79, white body, red interior, black shutters, blue dome light, two chrome and amber spotlights, black grille, silver headlights, Police labels, w/police figure	25	35	60
463-A, Commer 3/4-Ton Ambulance, 1964-66, in either white or cream body, red interior, blue dome light, red Ambulance decals, shaped wheels	36	55	90
464-A, Commer 3/4 Ton Police Van, 1963-68, battery operated working dome light, in several color combinations of dark or light metallic blue or green bodies, various foreign issues. The van on the left has "County Police" labels, horizontal cast bars on the rear side windows, and a metallic			

	C6	C8	C10
blue paint finish. The van on the right has an embossed "Police" logo cast in the sides, vertical lines on the rear side windows, and a dark blue paint finish. Both models have a battery-operated flashing roof light	45	65	120
481-A, Chevrolet Impala Police Car, 1965-69, black lower body and roof, white upper body, yellow interior w/two policemen, Police and Police Patrol decals on doors and hood	55	80	130
482-A, Chevrolet Impala Fire Chief, 1965-69, w/Fire Chief decal on hood, yellow interior w/driver, red on white body w/either round or rectangular "Fire Chief" decals on doors, spun or cast spoked wheels	55	80	130
482-B, Range Rover Ambulance, 1975-77, two different versions of body sides, red interior, raised roof, open upper and lower doors, black shutters, blue dome light, Ambulance label; includes stretcher and two ambulance attendants	20	30	50
483-B, Belgian Police Range Rover, 1976-77, white body, working doors, red interior, Belgian Police decal; includes policeman, Emergency signs	22	33	55
484-B, AMC Pacer Rescue Car, 1978-80, chrome roll bars and red roof lights, white w/black engine hood; w/or without Secours decal	10	15	30
489-A1, Volkswagen Polo Police Car, 1976-80, white body, green hood and doors, black dash, silver bumpers, grille and headlights, white roof, blue dome light	15	25	40
492-A, Volkswagen 1200 Police Car, 1966-69, two different body versions made for Germany, Netherlands and Switzerland, blue dome light in chrome collar, Polizei or Politie decals. Note the opening hood and trunk on this attractive car. The front wheels turn via the roof warning light.	40	60	100
506-A, Sunbeam Imp Police Car, 1968-72, three versions, white or light blue body, tan interior, driver, black or white hood and lower doors, dome light, Police decals, cast spoked wheels. Shown here are two color and box variations	25	45	85
509-A, Porsche Targa Police Car, 1970-75, white body and base, red doors and hood, black roof and plastic interior also comes w/an orange interior, unpainted siren, Polizei labels	25	35	60
513-A, Citroen Alpine Rescue Safari, 1970-72, white body, light blue interior, red roof and rear hatch, yellow roof rack and skis, clear windshield, man and dog, gold die-cast bobsled, Alpine Rescue decals	80	150	375
700-A, Motorway Ambulance, 1973-79, white body, dark blue interior, red-white-black Accident and Red Cross labels, dark blue windows, clear headlights, red die-cast base and bumpers	10	15	30

	C6	C8	C10
703-A, Hi-Speed Fire Engine, 1975-78, red body, yellow plastic ladder	16	24	40
921-A, Hughes Police Helicopter, 1975-80, red interior, dark blue rotors, in several international imprints, Netherlands, German, Swiss, in white or yellow	20	30	50
922-A, Sikorsky Skycrane Casualty Helicopter, 1975-78, red and white body, black rotors and wheels, orange pipes, working rear hatch, Red Cross decals	15	20	40
924-A, Bell Rescue Helicopter, 1976-80, two-piece blue body w/working doors, red interior, yellow plastic floats, black rotors, white N428 decals	20	30	50
927-A, Chopper Squad Helicopter, 1978-79, blue and white body, Sure Rescue decals	20	30	50
931-A, Jet Ranger Police Helicopter, 1980, white body w/chrome interior, red floats and rotors, amber windows, Police labels	25	40	65
1001-A, HGB-Angus Firestreak, 1980, chrome plastic spotlight and ladders, black hose reel, red dome light, white water cannon, in two interior versions, electronic siren and lights	35	50	85
1005-A, Police Land Rover, 1981, white body, red and blue police stripes, black lettering, open rear door, opaque black windows, blue dome light, working roof light and siren	15	25	50
1008-A, Chevrolet Caprice Fire Chief Car, 1982, red body, red-white-orange decals, chrome roof bar, opaque black windows, red dome light, chrome bumpers, grille and headlights, orange taillights, Fire Dept. and Fire Chief decals, chrome wheels; includes working siren and dome light	28	42	70
1103-B, Chubb Pathfinder Crash Truck, 1974-80, red body w/either "Airport Fire Brigade" or "New York Airport" decals, upper and lower body, gold water cannon unpainted and sirens, clear windshield, yellow interior, black steering wheel, chrome plastic deck, silver lights; w/working pump and siren....................................	60	90	150
1118-B, Chubb Pathfinder Crash Tender, 1981-83, red body, Emergency Unit decals, working water pump	45	65	110
1126-B, Simon Snorkel Fire Engine, 1977-81, red body w/yellow interior, blue windows and dome lights, chrome deck, black hose reels and hydraulic cylinders.................................	30	45	75
1127-A, Simon Snorkel Fire Engine, 1964-76, red body w/yellow interior, two snorkel arms, rotating base, five firemen in cab and one in basket, three styles of wheels.................................	35	55	100
1143-A, American LaFrance Ladder Truck, 1968-81, first issue: red cab, trailer, ladder rack and wheels; chrome decks and chassis, yellow plastic three-piece operable ladder, rubber tires, six firemen figures, issued 1968-70; second issue: same as first issue except for unpainted wheels, issued 1970-72; third issue: same as earlier issues except for white decks and chassis, silver wheels, plastic tires, issued 1973-81; later issues only had four firemen	60	90	150

Jeep

	C6	C8	C10
10-C, Jeep and Motorcycle Trailer, 1982-83, red working No. 441 Jeep w/two blue/yellow bikes on trailer	15	20	40
14-A, Tower Wagon and Lamp Standard, 1961-65, red No. 409 Jeep Tower wagon w/yellow basket, workman figure and lamp post	40	70	140
29-C, Jeep & Horse Box, 1981-83, metallic painted No. 441 Jeep and No. 112 trailer; accessories include girl on pony, three jumps and three hay bales .	15	30	50
36-C, Off Road Set, 1983, No. 5 label on No. 447 Jeep, blue boat, trailer	15	20	45
409-A, Jeep FC-150 Pickup, 1959-65, blue body, clear windows, sheet metal tow hook, in two wheel versions: smooth or shaped wheels	35	55	90
419-B, Jeep CJ-5, 1977-79, dark metallic green body, removable white top, white plastic wheels, spare tire	8	15	30
441-B, Golden Eagle Jeep, 1979-82, tan and brown or white and gold body, tan plastic top, chrome plastic base, bumpers and steps, chrome wheels......	8	15	25

Corgi 1134-A Bedford Army Fuel Tanker, 1964-65. Photo courtesy Dr. Douglas Sadecky

Corgi 150-A Vanwall Racing Car, 1957-65. Photo courtesy Dr. Douglas Sadecky

Corgi 158-A Lotus-Climax Racing Car, 1969-72. Photo courtesy Dr. Douglas Sadecky

Corgi 227-A Morris Mini-Cooper, 1962-65. Photo courtesy Dr. Douglas Sadecky

	C6	C8	C10
447-B, Renegade Jeep, 1983, dark blue body w/no top, white interior, base and bumper, white plastic wheels and rear mounted spare	8	15	25
448-B, Renegade Jeep with Hood, 1983, yellow body w/removable hood, red interior, base, bumper, white plastic wheels, side mounted spare, No. 8	8	15	25
470-A, Jeep FC-150 Covered Truck, 1965-72, four versions: blue body, rubber tires (1965-67); yellow/brown body; rubber tires w/spun hubs (1965-67); blue or yellow/brown body, plastic tires w/cast spoked hubs. The two major color and wheel variations are pictured here	30	45	75
478-A, Jeep FC-150 Tower Wagon, 1965-69, metallic green body, yellow interior and basket w/workman figure, clear windows, w/either rubber or plastic tires. This was the updated version of the previously released GS14-A which had a red Jeep, smooth wheels and a lamp post	40	60	100

Land Rover

	C6	C8	C10
31-B, Safari Land Rover and Trailer, 1976-80, black and white No. 341 Land Rover in two versions: w/chrome wheels, 1976; w/red wheels, 1977-80; came w/Warden and Lion figures	20	30	60
406-A, Land Rover 109 WB Pickup, 1957-62, yellow, green or metallic blue body, spare wheel on hood, clear windows, sheet metal tow hook, smooth hubs, rubber tires	45	70	100
416-A, RAC Land Rover, 1959-64, light or dark blue body, plastic interior and rear cover, gray antenna, RAC and Radio Rescue decals	60	90	150
417-A, Land Rover Breakdown Truck, 1960-65, red body w/silver boom and yellow canopy, revolving spotlight, Breakdown Service labels	35	55	90
421-B, Land Rover 109WB, 1977-79, working rear doors, tan interior, spare wheel on hood, plastic tow hook	15	18	30
438-A, Land Rover with Canopy, 1963-77, long, one-piece body w/clear windows, plastic interior, spare wheel on hood, issued in numerous colors	35	55	90

	C6	C8	C10
472-A, Public Address Land Rover, 1964-66, green No. 438 Land Rover body, yellow plastic rear body and loudspeakers, red interior, clear windows, silver bumper, grille and headlights; includes figure w/microphone and girl figure w/pamphlets	50	75	145
477-A, Land Rover Breakdown Truck, 1965-77, red body, yellow canopy, chrome revolving spotlight, Breakdown Service labels, shaped hubs or Whizz Wheels	25	35	70

Large Truck

	C6	C8	C10
1-A, Carrimore Car Transporter and Four Cars, 1957-62, three versions: No. 1101 Bedford Carrimore Transporter w/Riley, Jaguar, Austin Healey and Triumph, 1957-60; No. 1101 Bedford Carrimore Transporter w/four American cars, 1959; No. 1101 Bedford Carrimore Transporter w/Triumph, Mini, Citroen and Plymouth, 1961-62; value is for individual complete sets	300	450	800
20-B, Car Transporter & Cars, 1970-73, Scammell tri-deck transporter w/six cars: Ford Capri, the Saint's Volvo, Pontiac Firebird, Lancia Fulvia, MGC GT, Marcos 3 Litre, each w/Whizz Wheels; value is for complete set	200	400	900
28-A, Car Transporter and Four Cars, 1963-66, two versions: No. 1105 Bedford TK Transporter w/Fiat 1800, Renault Floride, Mercedes 230SE and Ford Consul, 1963-65; No. 1105 Bedford TK Transporter w/Chevy Corvair, VW Ghia, Volvo P-1800 and Rover 2000, 1966 only; value is for each individual complete set	200	300	700
41-A, Carrimore Car Transporter and Cars, 1966, Ford "H" series Transporter and six cars; there are several car variations; sold by mail order only	240	360	700
48-A, Transporter and Six Cars, 1966-69, first issue: No. 1138 Ford 'H' Series Transporter w/six cars, No. 252 Rover 2000, blue No. 251 Hillman Imp, No. 440 Ford Cortina Estate, No. 180 Mini w/'wickerwork', metallic maroon No.			

	C6	C8	C10

204 Mini, and No. 321 Mini Rally ('1966 Monte Carlo Rally') racing No. 2; second issue: same as first issue except No. 251 Hillman is metallic gold, No. 204 Mini is blue, No. 321 Mini is substituted for No. 333 SUN/RAC Rally Mini w/autographs on roof. The Car Transporter gift sets were a good way for Corgi to get rid of their excess stock of automobile models **225 365 700**

48-B, Transporter & Six Cars, 1970-73, Scammell transporter w/six cars: No. 180 Mini DeLuxe, No. 204 Mini, No. 339 Mini Rally, No. 201 The Saint's Volvo, No. 340 Sunbeam Imp, No. 378 MGC GT; includes bag of cones and leaflet............................ **250 450 900**

1002-A, BL Roadtrain and Trailers, 1981, white and orange cab, dark blue freighter semi body w/Yorkie Chocolate labels and tanker semi body w/Gulf label; includes playmat **16 24 40**

1100-A, Bedford Carrimore Low Loader, 1958-62, red or yellow "S" cab, metallic blue semi trailer and tailgate; smooth and/or shaped wheels **60 90 150**

1100-B, Mack Trans Continental Semi, 1971-73, orange cab body and semi chassis and fenders, metallic light blue semi body, unpainted trailer rests **35 55 90**

1101-A1, Bedford Car Transporter, 1957, first issue, black die-cast cab base w/blue "S" cab, yellow semi trailer, blue lettering decals, RARE................. **100 200 350**

1101-A2, Bedford Car Transporter, 1957-62, second issue, red cab, pale green upper and blue lower semi-trailer, white decals, working ramps, clear windshield **70 105 175**

1105-A, Bedford Car Transporter, 1962-66, red "TK" cab w/blue lower and light green upper trailer, working ramp, yellow interior, clear windows, white lettering and Corgi dog decals ... **60 90 150**

1106-B, Mack Container Truck, 1972-78, yellow cab, red interior, white engine, red suspension, white ACL labels........ **30 50 80**

1107-B, Berliet Container Truck, 1978, blue cab and semi fenders; white cab

chassis and semi flatbed; each w/United States Lines label **30 45 75**

1108-B, Ford Michelin Container Truck, 1981, blue cab and trailer, white cab chassis and trailer fenders, yellow containers; includes Michelin Man figure...................................... **15 25 50**

1109-B, Ford Covered Semi-Trailer, 1979-80, blue cab and trailer, black cab chassis and trailer fenders, yellow covers...................................... **15 25 50**

1110-A, Bedford Mobilgas Tanker, 1959-65, red "S" cab and tanker w/Mobilgas decals, shaped wheels, rubber tires **100 150 250**

1126-A, Ecurie Ecosse Transporter, 1961-65, in dark blue body w/either blue or yellow lettering, or light blue body w/red or yellow lettering, working tailgate and sliding door, yellow interior, shaped wheels, rubber tires **70 105 225**

1129-A, Bedford Milk Tanker, 1962-65, light blue "S" cab and lower semi, white upper tank, w/blue/white milk decals, shaped wheels, rubber tires...... **100 150 275**

1129-B, Mercedes-Benz Semi-Trailer Van, 1983, black cab and plastic semi trailer, white chassis and airscreen, red doors, red-blue and yellow stripes, white Corgi lettering **15 18 30**

1130-B, Bedford Tanker, 1983, red cab w/black chassis, plastic tank w/chrome catwalk, Corgi Chemco decals **15 20 35**

1131-B, Mercedes-Benz Refrigerator, 1983, yellow cab and tailgate, red semi-trailer, two-piece lowering tailgate and yellow spare wheel base, red interior, clear window.................... **15 18 30**

1132-A, Bedford Carrimore Low Loader, 1963-65, yellow "TK" cab, red trailer with working ramp, clear windows, red interior, suspension, shaped wheels, rubber tires **90 225 350**

1137-A, Ford Express Semi-Trailer, 1965-70, metallic blue cab and trailer, silver roof on trailer, chrome doors marked "Express Service," shaped or detailed cast wheels **60 110 225**

1140-A, Bedford Mobilgas Tanker, 1965-66, red "TK" cab and tanker

Corgi 256-A Volkswagen East African Safari, 1965-69. Photo courtesy Dr. Douglas Sadecky

Corgi 309-A Aston Martin DB4, 1962-65. Photo courtesy Dr. Douglas Sadecky

Corgi 314-A Ferrari Berlinetta 250LM, 1965-72. Photo courtesy Dr. Douglas Sadecky

Corgi 315-A Simca 1000, 1964-66. Photo courtesy Dr. Douglas Sadecky

Corgi 323-A Citroen DS 19 Rally, 1965-66. Photo courtesy Dr. Douglas Sadecky

	C6	C8	C10
w/red, white and blue Mobilgas decals, shaped wheels, rubber tires	100	175	350
1140-B, Ford Transit Wrecker, 1981, white cab and rear body, red roof, silver bed, "24-hour Service" labels	25	35	60
1141-A, Bedford Milk Tanker, 1966-67, light blue "TK" cab and lower semi, white upper tank w/blue/white milk decals	110	165	375
1142-A, Ford Holmes Wrecker, 1967-74, white upper cab, black roof, red rear body and lower cab, mirrors, unpainted or gold booms......................	60	90	200
1144-B, Berliet Holmes Wrecker, 1975-78, red cab and bed, blue rear body, white chassis, black interior, two gold booms and hooks, yellow dome light, driver, amber lenses and red/white/blue stripes	30	45	75
1144-C, Mercedes-Benz Semi-Trailer, 1983, red cab and trailer, black chassis	15	18	30
1146-A, Scammell Carrimore Tri-deck Car Transporter, 1970-73, orange lower cab, chassis and lower deck, white upper cab and middle deck, blue top deck, red interior, black hydraulic cylinders, detachable rear ramp	35	60	130
1147-A, Scammell Ferrymasters Semi-Trailer Truck, 1969-72, white cab, red interior, yellow chassis, black fenders, clear windows, jewel headlights, cast step-hub wheels, plastic tires	60	90	150
1147-B, Scania Container Truck, 1983, yellow truck and box w/red Ryder Truck rental labels, clear windows, black exhaust stack, red rear doors, six-spoke Whizz Wheels......................	7	15	30
1148-B, Scania Container Truck, 1983, blue cab w/blue and white box and rear doors, white deck, Securicor Parcels labels, in red or white rear door colors	7	15	30
1149-A, Scania Container Truck, 1983, white cab and box w/BRS Truck Rental labels, blue windows, red screen, roof and rear doors...................	7	15	30
1150-B, Scania Bulk Carrier, 1983, white cab, blue and white silos, ladders and catwalk, amber windows, blue British Sugar labels, Whizz Wheels	7	15	30
1151-A, Scammell Coop Semi-Trailer Truck, 1970, white cab and trailer fenders, light blue semi-trailer, red interior, gray bumper base, jewel headlights, black hitch lever, spare wheel...	135	210	350

	C6	C8	C10
1151-B, Mack Exxon Tank Truck, 1974-75, white cab and tank, red tank chassis and fenders, red interior, chrome catwalk, Exxon labels	15	35	75
1151-C, Scania Bulk Carrier, 1983, white cab, orange and white silos, clear windows, orange screen, black/orange Spillers Flour labels, Whizz Wheels....	7	15	30
1152-A, Mack Esso Tank Truck, 1971-75, white cab and tank w/Esso labels, red tank chassis and fenders	20	40	80
1157-A, Ford Esso Tank Truck, 1976-81, white cab and tank, red tanker chassis and fenders, chrome wheels, Esso labels...	15	30	60
1158-A, Ford Exxon Tank Truck, 1976-81, white cab and tank, red tanker chassis and fenders, chrome wheels, Exxon labels	15	30	60
1159-A, Ford Car Transporter, 1976-79, metallic lime green or metallic cab and semi, cream cab chassis, deck and ramp	20	30	60
1160-A, Ford Gulf Tank Truck, 1976-78, white cab w/orange chassis, blue tanker body, Gulf labels, chrome wheels	15	25	40
1161-A, Ford Aral Tank Truck, 1977-80, light blue cab and chassis, white tanker body, Aral labels.................................	20	30	50
1164-A, Berliet Dolphinarium Truck, 1980-83, yellow and blue cab and trailer, clear plastic tank; includes two dolphins and a girl trainer	56	84	175
1166-A, Mercedes-Benz Tanker, 1983, tan cab, plastic tank body, black chassis, black and red Guinness labels, w/chrome or black plastic catwalk, clear windows	15	18	30
1167-A, Mercedes-Benz Tanker, 1983, two different versions, white cab and tank, green chassis, chrome or black plastic catwalk, red/white/green 7-Up labels or Corgi Chemo labels..............	15	18	30
1169-A, Ford Guinness Tanker, 1982, orange, tan, black cab, tan tanker body, Guinness labels	20	30	50
1170-A, Ford Car Transporter, 1982, white cab, red chassis and trailer, white labels and ramps.........................	20	30	50

Military

	C6	C8	C10
3-A, RAF Land Rover and Thunderbird Missile, 1958-63, Standard colors, No. 350 Thunderbird Missile on Trolley and 351 RAF Land Rover	100	150	300

	C6	C8	C10
4-A, RAF Land Rover & Bloodhound, 1958-61, set of three standard colored, No, 351 RAF Land Rover, No. 1115 Bloodhound Missile, No. 1116 Ramp and No. 1117 Trolley	150	300	600
6-A, Rocket Age Set, 1959-60, set of eight standard models including: No. 350 Thunderbird Missile on Trolley, No. 351 RAF Land Rover, No. 352 RAF Staff Car, No. 353 Radar Scanner, No. 1106 Decca Radar Van and No. 1108 Bloodhound missile w/ramp	325	650	1400
9-A, Corporal Missile Set, 1959-62, No. 1112 missile and No. 1113 ramp, erector vehicle and No. 1118 army truck	340	510	850
10-B, Centurion Tank and Transporter, 1973-78, No. 901 olive tank and No. 1100 transporter	55	80	130
17-B, Military Set, 1975-80, set of three, No. 904 Tiger tank, No. 920 Bell Helicopter, No. 906 Saladin Armored Car	60	90	150
350-A, Thunderbird Missile and Trolley, 1958-62, ice blue or silver missile, RAF blue trolley, red rubber nose cone, plastic tow bar, steering front and rear axles	55	85	165
351-A, RAF Land Rover, 1958-62, blue body and cover, sheet metal rear cover, RAF rondel label, w/or without suspension, silver bumper	60	90	150
352-A, Standard Vanguard RAF Staff Car, 1958-62, blue body, RAF labels	55	85	140
353-A, Decca Radar Scanner, 1959-60, w/either orange or custard colored scanner frame, silver scanner face, w/gear on base for turning scanner	34	51	85
354-A, Commer Military Ambulance, 1964-66, olive drab body, blue rear windows and dome light, driver, Red Cross decals	50	75	125
355-A, Commer Military Police Van, 1964-65, olive drab body, barred rear windows, white MP decals, driver	55	80	130
356-A, Volkswagen Military Personnel Carrier, 1964-66, olive drab body, white decals, driver	55	95	180
358-A, Oldsmobile 88 Staff Car, 1964-66, olive drab body, four figures, white decals	50	75	125
359-A, Karrier Field Kitchen, 1964-66, olive body, white decals, w/figure	60	90	175

	C6	C8	C10
414-A, Bedford Military Ambulance, 1961-64, clear front and white rear windows, olive body w/Red Cross decals, w/or without suspension	56	84	140
900-A, Tiger Mark I Tank, 1973-78, tan and green camouflage finish, German emblem, swiveling turret and raising barrel castings, black plastic barrel end, antenna; includes twelve shells, fires shells	30	45	75
901-A, Centurion Mark III Tank, 1974-78, tan and brown camouflage or olive drab body, rubber tracks; includes twelve shells	30	45	75
902-A, M60 A1 Medium Tank, 1974-80, green/tan camouflage body, working turret and barrel, green rollers, white decals	30	45	75
903-A, Chieftain Medium Tank, 1974-80, olive drab body, black tracks, Union Jack labels; includes twelve shells	30	45	75
904-A, King Tiger Heavy Tank, 1974-78, tan and rust body, working turret and barrel, tan rollers and treads, German labels	30	45	75
905-A, SU-100 Medium Tank, 1974-77, olive and cream camouflage upper body, gray lower, working hatch and barrel, black treads, red star and #103 labels; twelve shells included, fires shells	30	50	80
906-A, Saladin Armored Car, 1974-77, olive drab body, swiveling turret and raising barrel castings, black plastic barrel end and tires, olive cast wheels, w/twelve shells, fires shells	30	45	75
907-A, Half Track Rocket Launcher & Trailer, 1975-80, two rocket launchers and single trailer castings, gray plastic roll cage, man w/machine gun, front wheels and hubs	20	35	55
907-A, Rocket Launcher and Trailer, 1975-80, steel blue and red launcher, fires rocket	25	35	60
908-A, AMX 30D Recovery Tank, 1976-80, olive body w/black plastic turret and gun, accessories and three figures	35	50	80
909-A, Tractor, Trailer and Field Gun, 1976-80, tan tractor body and chassis, trailer body, base and opening doors, gun chassis and raising barrel castings, brown plastic interior; twelve shells included, fires shells	30	50	80

Corgi 328-A Hillman Imp Rally, 1966. Photo courtesy Dr. Douglas Sadecky

Corgi 333-A BMC Mini-Cooper S "Sun/RAC" Rally Car, 1967. Photo courtesy Dr. Douglas Sadecky

Corgi 459-A ERF 44G Moorhouse Van, 1958-60. Photo courtesy Dr. Douglas Sadecky

Corgi 460-A ERF Neville Cement Tipper, 1959-66. Photo courtesy Dr. Douglas Sadecky

Corgi 483-A Dodge Kew Fargo Tipper, 1967-72. Photo courtesy Dr. Douglas Sadecky

	C6	C8	C10
920-A, Bell Army Helicopter, 1975-80, two-piece olive/tan camouflage body, clear canopy, olive green rotors, U.S. Army decals	24	36	60
923-A, Sikorsky Skycrane Army Helicopter, 1975-78, olive drab and yellow body w/Red Cross and Army labels	15	20	40
1106-A, Decca Airfield Radar Van, 1959-60, cream body w/four or five orange vertical bands, working rotating scanner and aerial	120	180	350
1108-A, Bloodhound Missile and Launching Platform, 1958-61, white and yellow missile, red rubber nose cone; military green ramp	110	165	275
1109-A, Bloodhound Missile on Trolley, 1959-62, white and yellow missile, red rubber nose cone; military green trolley, rubber tires	120	180	300
1112-A, Corporal Missile on Launching Ramp, 1959-62, white missile, red rubber-nose cone	80	120	200
1113-A, Corporal Missile & Erector Vehicle, 1959-62, white missile, red rubber-nose cone, olive green body on erector body	240	360	600
1115-A, Bloodhound Missile, 1959-62, white and yellow missile, red rubber nose cone	70	105	175
1116-A, Bloodhound Launching Ramp, 1959-62, military green ramp	34	51	85
1117-A, Bloodhound Loading Trolley, 1959-62, military green working lift, red rubber nose cone	40	60	100
1118-A, International 6x6 Army Truck, 1959-63, olive drab body w/clear windows, red/blue decals, six cast olive wheels w/rubber tires	70	105	225
1124-A, Corporal Missile Launching Ramp, 1960-61, sold in temporary pack	36	55	90
1133-A, Army Troop Transporter, 1964-65, olive w/white U.S. Army decals	70	105	175
1134-A, Bedford Army Fuel Tanker, 1964-65, olive cab and tanker, w/white "U.S. Army" and "No Smoking" decals	140	210	375
1135-A, Army Heavy Equipment Transporter, 1964-65, olive cab and			

	C6	C8	C10
trailer w/white U.S. Army decals w/red or yellow interior and driver	70	105	325

Miscellaneous

	C6	C8	C10
25-A, Shell or BP Garage Gift Set, 1963-65, gas station/garage w/pumps and other accessories including five different cars; in two versions: Shell or B.P., rare; value is for each set	295	700	1500
490-B, Touring Caravan, 1975-79, white body w/blue trim, white plastic opening roof and door, pale blue interior, red plastic hitch and awning	15	25	40
1401-A, Service Ramp, 1958-60, metallic blue and silver operable ramp	30	45	95

Motorcycle

	C6	C8	C10
25-C, Matra & Motorcycle Trailer, 1980-81, red No. 57 Talbot Matra Rancho w/two yellow and blue bikes on trailer	15	20	35
171-A, Red Wheelie Motorcycle, 1982, red plastic body and fender w/black/white/yellow decals, black handlebars, kickstand and seat, chrome engine, pipes, flywheel-powered rear wheel	10	15	25
172-A, White Wheelie Motorcycle, 1982, white body w/black/white police decals	15	20	35
173-A, Cafe Racer Motorcycle, 1983	15	18	30
681-A, Stunt Motorcycle, 1971-72, made for Corgi Rockets race track, gold cycle, blue rider w/yellow helmet, clear windshield, plastic tires	70	105	175

Racing

	C6	C8	C10
5-A, British Racing Cars, 1959-63, set of three cars, three versions: blue No. 152 Lotus, green No. 151 BRM, green No. 150 Vanwall, all w/smooth wheels, 1959; same cars w/shaped wheels, 1960-61; red Vanwall, green BRM and blue Lotus, 1963, each set	140	210	475
6-B, Volkswagen Racing Tender and Cooper, 1967-69, white No. 490 VW breakdown truck w/racing labels, blue No. 156 Cooper on trailer	50	75	150
12-B, Grand Prix Racing Set, 1968-72, four vehicle set includes: No. 490 Volkswagen Breakdown Truck w/No. 330 Porsche (1969), Porsche No. 371(1970-72), No. 155 Lotus, No. 156 Cooper-Maserati, red trailer	135	210	425

	C6	C8	C10
15-A, Silverstone Racing Layout, 1963-66, seven-vehicle set w/accessories; Vanwall, Lotus XI, Aston Martin, Mercedes 300SL, BRM, Ford Thunderbird, Land Rover Truck; second version has a No. 154 Ferrari substituted for Lotus XI, rare	400	900	1700
16-A, Ecurie Ecosse Racing Set, 1961-66, metallic dark or light blue No. 1126 transporter w/three cars in two versions: BRM, Vanwall and Lotus XI, 1961-64; BRM, Vanwall and Ferrari, 1964-66, value is for individual complete set	140	210	450
17-A, Land Rover and Ferrari Racer, 1963-67, red and tan No. 438 Land Rover and red No. 154 Ferrari F1 on yellow trailer	60	90	150
25-B, Volkswagen Racing Tender and Cooper Maserati, 1970-71, two versions: tan or white No. 490 VW breakdown truck, and No. 159 Cooper-Maserati on trailer; value is for each set	50	75	150
26-B, Matra and Racing Car, 1983, black/yellow No. 457 Talbot Matra Rancho and No. 160 Hesketh yellow car w/Team Corgi trailer and labels	15	35	65
29-B, Ferrari Daytona and Racing Car, 1975-77, blue/yellow No. 323 Ferrari and No. 150 Surtees on yellow trailer	25	40	85
30-A, Grand Prix Set, 1973, sold by mail order only; kit version of No. 151 Yardley, No. 154 JPS, No. 152 Surtees and No. 153 Surtees	60	125	275
32-B, Lotus Racing Set, 1976-79, three versions: "3" on No. 301 Elite and "JPS" on No. 154 Lotus racer; "7" on No. 301 Elite and "JPS" on racer; "7" on No. 301 Elite and "Texaco" on No. 154 Lotus racer; value is for each individual complete set	30	45	95
37-A, Lotus Racing Team Set, 1966-69, 490 VW Breakdown Truck, red trailer w/#318 Lotus Elan Open Top, #319 Lotus Elan Hard Top, #155 Lotus Climax; includes pack of cones, sheet of racing number labels	125	200	375
38-A, Monte Carlo Rally Set, 1965-67, three vehicle set, No. 326 Citroen, No. 318 Mini and No. 322 Land Rover rally cars	295	450	900

	C6	C8	C10
46-A, All Winners Set, 1966-69, first issue: No. 310 Corvette, No. 312 Jaguar XKE, No. 314 Ferrari 250LM, No. 324 Marcos, No. 325 Mustang; second issue: No. 312 Jaguar XKE, No. 314 Ferrari 250LM, No. 264 Toronado, No. 327 MGB, No. 337 Corvette	100	240	450
46-B, Super Karts, 1982, two carts, orange and blue, Whizz Wheels in front, slicks on rear, silver and gold drivers	15	18	30
150-A, Vanwall Racing Car, 1957-65, clear windshield, unpainted dash, silver pipes and decals, smooth wheels, rubber tires, in three versions: green body or red body w/silver or yellow seats	35	65	140
150-B, Surtees TS9 Racing Car, 1972-74, black upper engine, chrome lower engine, pipes and exhaust, driver, Brook Bond Oxo-Rob Walker labels, eight-spoke Whizz Wheels	15	20	40
151-A, Lotus Eleven, 1958-64, red, silver, or light blue/green body, clear windshield and plastic headlights, smooth wheels, rubber tires, racing decals	60	95	160
151-B, McLaren M19A Racing Car, 1972-77, white body, orange stripes, chrome engine, exhaust and suspension, black mirrors, driver, Yardley McLaren #55 labels, Whizz Wheels	15	25	40
152-A, BRM Racing Car, 1958-65, silver seat, dash and pipes, smooth wheels, rubber tires, in three versions: dark green body, 1958-60; light green body w/driver and various number decals 1961-65; light green body, no driver	50	75	150
152-B, Ferrari 312 B2 Racing Car, 1973-75, red body, white fin, gold engine, chrome suspension, mirrors and wheels, Ferrari and #5 labels	16	24	40
153-A, Campbell Bluebird, 1960-65, blue body, red exhaust, clear windshield, driver, in two versions: black plastic wheels, 1960; metal wheels and rubber tires	56	84	175

Corgi 348-A Psychedelic Ford Mustang, 1968. Photo courtesy Dr. Douglas Sadecky

Corgi 24-A Constructor Set, 1963-68. Photo courtesy Dr. Douglas Sadecky

Corgi 453-A Commer Refrigerator Van, 1956-60. Photo courtesy Dr. Douglas Sadecky

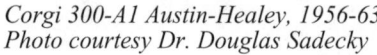

Corgi 300-A1 Austin-Healey, 1956-63. Photo courtesy Dr. Douglas Sadecky

Corgi 310-A Corvette Sting Ray, 1963-68. Photo courtesy Dr. Douglas Sadecky

Corgi 316-A NSU Sport Prinz, 1963-66. Photo courtesy Dr. Douglas Sadecky

	C6	C8	C10
153-B, Surtees TS9B Racing Car, 1972-74, red body w/white stripes and wing, black plastic lower engine, driver, chrome upper engine, pipes, suspension, eight-spoke wheels	15	20	40
154-A, Ferrari Racing Car, 1963-72, red body, chrome plastic engine, roll bar and dash, driver, silver cast base and exhaust, Ferrari and No. 36 decals, shaped or spoked wheels......................	24	36	75
154-B, Lotus Racing Car, 1973-82, black body and base, gold cast engine, roll bar, pipes, dash and mirrors, driver, gold cast wheels, in two versions........	25	35	60
155-A, Lotus-Climax Racing Car, 1964-69, green body and base w/black/white #1 and yellow racing stripe labels, unpainted engine and suspension, w/driver	25	35	65
155-B, Shadow-Ford Racing Car, 1974-76, black body and base w/white/black #17, UOP and American flag labels, cast chrome suspension and pipes, Embassy Racing label..	10	20	50
156-A, Cooper-Maserati Racing Car, 1967-69, blue body w/red/white/blue Maserati and #7 decals, unpainted engine and suspension, chrome plastic steering wheel, roll bar, mirrors and pipes, driver, cast eight-spoke wheels, plastic tires	26	39	65
156-B, Shadow-Ford Racing Car, 1974-77, white body, red stripes, driver, chrome plastic pipes, mirrors and steering wheel, in two versions, Jackie Collins driver figure..................	10	20	45
158-A, Lotus-Climax Racing Car, 1969-72, orange/white body w/black/white stripe and #8 labels, unpainted cast rear wing, cast eight-spoke wheels, w/driver	15	25	50
158-B, Tyrrell-Ford Racing Car, 1974-78, dark blue body w/blue/black/white Elf and #1 labels, chrome suspension, pipes, mirrors, Jackie Stewart driver figure	18	25	50
159-A, Cooper-Maserati Racing Car, 1969-72, yellow/white body w/yellow/black stripe and #3 decals, driver tilts to steer car	18	27	45

	C6	C8	C10
159-B, STP Patrick Eagle Racing Car, 1974-77, red body w/red, white and black STP and #20 labels, chrome lower engine and suspension, black plastic upper engine; includes Patrick Eagle driver figure	20	30	50
160-A, Hesketh-Ford Racing Car, 1975-78, white body w/red/white/blue Hesketh, stripe and #24 labels, chrome suspension, roll bar, mirrors and pipes	15	18	30
161-A, Commuter Dragster, 1971-73, maroon body w/Ford Commuter, Union Jack and #2 decals, cast silver engine, chrome plastic suspension and pipes, clear windshield, driver, spoke wheels	30	45	75
161-B, Tyrrell P34 Racing Car, 1977, dark blue body and wings w/yellow stripes, #4 and white Elf and Union Jack decals, chrome plastic engine, w/driver in red or blue helmet	20	30	55
162-A, Quartermaster Dragster, 1971-73, long, dark metallic green upper body w/green/yellow/black #5 and Quartermaster labels, light green lower body, w/driver.................................	30	45	75
162-B, Tyrrell P34 Racing Car, 1978-79, without yellow labels, First National Bank labels, w/driver in red or orange helmet	20	30	55
163-A, Ford Capri Santa Pod Gloworm, 1971-76, white and blue body w/red, white and blue lettering and flag decals, red chassis, amber windows, gold-based black engine, gold scoop, pipes and front suspension, w/driver, plastic wheels......................................	18	27	45
164-A, Wild Honey Dragster, 1971-73, yellow body w/red/yellow Wild Honey and Jaguar Powered labels, green windows and roof, black grille, driver, Whizz Wheels.....................................	25	40	65
165-A, Adams Drag-Star, 1972-74, orange body, red nose, gold engines, chrome pipes and hood panels, Whizz Wheels	20	30	45
166-A, Mustang Organ Grinder Dragster, 1971-74, yellow body w/green/yellow name, #39 and racing stripe labels, black base, green windshield, red interior, roll bar, w/driver	20	30	50

	C6	C8	C10
167-A, U.S. Racing Buggy, 1972-74, white body w/red/white/blue stars, stripes and USA #7 labels, red base, gold engine, red plastic panels, driver ..	18	25	50
169-A, Silver Streak Jet Dragster, 1973-76, metallic blue body w/Firestone and flag labels on tank, silver engine, orange plastic jet and nose cone....................................	15	25	45
170-A, Radio Luxembourg Dragster, 1972-76, long, blue body w/yellow, white and blue John Wolfe Racing, Radio Luxembourg and #5 labels, silver engine, w/driver	30	45	85
190-A, JPS Lotus Racing Car, 1974-77, black body, scoop and wings w/gold John Player Special, Texaco and #1 labels, gold suspension, pipes and wheels	30	45	75
191-A, McLaren M23 Racing Car, 1974-77, large 1:18-scale red and white body and wings w/red, white and black Texaco-Marlboro #5 labels, chrome pipes, suspension and mirrors, removable wheels	30	60	110
201-C, British Leyland Mini 1000, 1978, red interior, chrome lights, grille and bumper, #8 decal; three variations: silver body w/decals, 1978-82; silver body, no decals; orange body w/extra hood stripes, 1983	16	24	40
227-A, Morris Mini-Cooper, 1962-65, yellow or blue body and base and/or hood, white roof and/or hood, two versions, red plastic interior, jewel headlights, flag, numbers decals. Even though there are various paint and decal versions of this model, any one of them is valuable	80	150	300
256-A, Volkswagen East African Safari, 1965-69, light red body, brown interior, working front and rear hood, clear windows, spare wheel on roof steers front wheels, jewel headlights, w/rhinoceros figure. Although never issued as a gift set, this spectacular little toy could easily have been made into one. A rhinoceros was added as a charging menace to the racing VW......	60	130	285
281-B, Austin Mini-Metro Datapost, 1982-83, white body, blue roof, hood and trim, red plastic interior, hepolite and #77 decals, working hatch and doors, clear windows, folding seats, chrome headlights, orange taillights, Whizz Wheels	15	18	30

	C6	C8	C10
282-A, BMC Mini-Cooper, 1971-74, white body, black working hood, trunk, two doors, red interior, clear windows, orange/black stripes and #177 decals, suspension, Whizz Wheels	30	45	95
291-B, Mercedes-Benz 240D Rally, 1982, cream or tan body, black, red and blue lettering, "dirt," red plastic interior, clear windows, black radiator guard and roof rack, opening doors, racing #5 label.......................	10	15	25
300-C, Ferrari Daytona, 1979, apple green body, black tow hook, red-yellow-silver-black Daytona #5 and other racing labels, amber windows, headlights, black plastic interior, base, four spoke chrome wheels	15	20	35
302-B, Hillman Hunter, 1969-72, blue body, gray interior, black hood, white roof, unpainted spotlights, clear windshield, red radiator screen, black equipment, Golden Jacks wheels; came w/Kangaroo figure.....................	45	70	140
303-A, Mercedes-Benz 300SL Roadster, 1958-66, blue or white body, yellow interior, plastic interior, smooth, shaped or cast wheels, racing stripes and number, driver.............................	45	75	140
303-B, Roger Clark's Capri, 1970-72, white body, black hood, grille and interior, open doors, folding seats, chrome bumpers, clear headlights, red taillights, Racing #73, label sheet, Whizz Wheels	15	25	55
304-A, Mercedes-Benz 300SL Coupe, 1959-65, chrome body, red hardtop, red stripe, clear windows, 1959-60 smooth wheels no suspension, 1961-65 racing stripes.......................	45	65	130
305-B, Mini-Marcos GT850, 1972-73, white body, red-white-blue racing stripe and #7 labels, clear headlights, Whizz Wheels, opening doors and hood	20	30	50
306-B, Fiat X1/9, 1980-81, metallic blue body and base, white Fiat #3, multicolored lettering and stripe labels, black roof, trim, interior, rear panel, grille, bumpers and tow hook, chrome wheels and detailed engine	15	20	35
307-B, Renault 5 Turbo, 1981, bright yellow body, red plastic interior, black roof and hood, working hatch and two			

Corgi 214-M Ford Thunderbird Hardtop-Mechanical, 1959. Photo courtesy Dr. Douglas Sadecky

Corgi 226-A1 Morris Mini-Minor, 1960-71. Photo courtesy Dr. Douglas Sadecky

Corgi 404-A Bedford Dormobile, 1956-62. Photo courtesy Dr. Douglas Sadecky

Corgi 411-A Karrier Lucozade Van, 1958-62. Photo courtesy Dr. Douglas Sadecky

Corgi 413-A Karrier Butcher Shop, 1960-64. Photo courtesy Dr. Douglas Sadecky

	C6	C8	C10
doors, black dash, chrome rear engine, racing #8 Cibie and other sponsor labels	15	18	25
308-B, BMW M1, 1981, yellow body, black plastic base, rear panel and interior, white seats, clear windshield, multicolored stripes, lettering and #25 decal, Goodyear label	15	20	35
309-A, Aston Martin DB4, 1962-65, white top w/aqua green sides, yellow plastic interior, racing Nos. 1, 3 or 7	50	75	125
312-A, Jaguar E Type Competition, 1964-68, gold or chrome plated body, black interior, blue and white stripes and black #2 decals, no top, clear windshield, headlights, w/driver	45	65	130
312-C, Ford Capri S, 1982, white body, red lower body and base, red interior, clear windshield, black bumpers, grille and tow hook, chrome headlights and wheels, red taillights, #6 and other racing labels	15	20	35
314-A, Ferrari Berlinetta 250LM, 1965-72, red body w/yellow stripe, blue windshields, chrome interior, grille and exhaust pipes, detailed engine, #4 Ferrari logo and yellow stripe decals, spoked wheels and spare, rubber tires	30	45	75
315-A, Simca 1000, 1964-66, chrome plated body, No. 8 and red-white-blue stripe decals, one-piece body, clear windshield, red interior	30	45	75
316-B, Ford GT 70, 1972-73, green and black body, white interior, No. 32 label	10	25	45
317-A, Morris Mini-Cooper, 1964-65, red body and base, white roof, yellow interior, chrome spotlight, No. 37 and Monte Carlo Rally decals	60	125	250
318-A, Lotus Elan S2 Roadster, 1965-67, working hood, plastic interior w/folding seats, shaped wheels and rubber tires, issued in metallic blue, Exxon "I've got a Tiger in my tank" label on trunk. The ordinary model is powder blue, but shown here is the rare white version of the car	30	50	110
318-B, Jaguar XJS Motul, 1983, black body w/red/white Motul and No. 4, chrome wheels	8	15	25

	C6	C8	C10
319-B, Lamborghini Miura, 1973-74, silver body, black interior, yellow/purple stripes and No. 7 label, Whizz Wheels	30	45	75
321-A, BMC Mini-Cooper S Rally Car, 1965-66, red body, white roof, five jewel headlights, Monte Carlo Rally decals w/either No. 52 (1965) or No. 2 (1966); rare w/drivers' autographs on roof	100	275	500
321-B, Porsche 924, 1978-81, red or metallic light brown or green body, dark red interior, opening two doors and rear window, chrome headlights, black plastic grille, racing No. 2	10	25	50
322-A1, Rover 2000 Rally, 1965-66, metallic dark red body, white roof, shaped wheels, No. 136 and Monte Carlo Rally decals	50	95	175
322-A2, Rover 2000 Rally, 1965-66, white body, red interior, black bonnet, No. 21 decal, cast spoked wheels	55	135	225
323-A, Citroen DS 19 Rally, 1965-66, light blue body, white roof, yellow interior, four jewel headlights, Monte Carlo Rally and No. 75 decals, w/antenna	70	105	185
323-B, Ferrari Daytona, 1973-78, white body w/red roof and trunk, black interior, two working doors, amber windows and headlights, No. 81 and other labels	15	30	55
324-B, Ferrari Daytona JCB, 1973-74, orange body w/No. 33, Corgi and other labels, chrome spoked wheels	15	25	50
328-A, Hillman Imp Rally, 1966, in various metallic body colors, w/cream interior, Monte Carlo Rally and No. 107 decals	30	65	110
330-A, Porsche Carrera 6, 1967-69, white body, red or blue trim, blue or amber tinted engine covers, black interior, clear windshield and canopy, red jewel taillights, No. 1 or No. 20 decals	30	45	75
333-A, BMC Mini-Cooper S "Sun/RAC" Rally Car, 1967, red body, white roof w/six jewel headlights, RAC Rally and No. 21 decals	90	180	350
337-A, Corvette Sting Ray, 1967-69, yellow body, red interior, suspension, No. 13 decals. This car's decorative appearance definitely places it in the 1960's	30	55	95

	C6	C8	C10
339-A, BMC Mini-Cooper S Rally, 1967-72, red body, white roof, chrome roof rack w/two spare tires, Monte Carlo Rally and No. 177 decals, w/shaped wheels/rubber tires or cast detailed wheels/plastic tires	40	90	180
340-A, Sunbeam Imp Rally, 1967-68, metallic blue body w/white stripes, Monte Carlo Rally and No. 77 decals, cast wheels	20	45	85
340-B, Rover 3500 Triplex, 1981, white sides and hatch, blue roof and hood, red plastic interior and trim, detailed engine, red-white-black No. 1 label	8	15	20
341-B, Chevrolet Caprice Classic, 1981, white upper body, red sides w/red/white/blue stripes and No. 43 decals, tan interior, STP labels	24	36	60
344-A, Ferrari 206 Dino, 1969-73, black interior and fins, in either red body w/No. 30 label and gold hubs or Whizz Wheels, or yellow body w/No. 23 label and gold hubs or Whizz Wheels	24	36	60
348-A, Psychedelic Ford Mustang, 1968, light blue body and base, aqua interior, red-orange-yellow No. 20 and flower decals, cast eight spoke wheels, plastic tire	30	50	100
371-A, Porsche Carrera 6, 1970-73, white upper body, red front hood, doors, upper fins and base, black interior, purple rear window, tinted engine cover, racing No. 60 decals	25	35	60
331-A, Ford Capri 3 Litre GT, 1973-76, white and black body, racing number 5 label	15	20	35
376-A, Corvette Sting Ray, 1970-73, metallic gray body w/black hood, Go-Go-Go labels, Whizz Wheels	40	65	100
380-B, BMW M1 BASF, 1983, red body, white trim w/black/white BASF and No. 80 decals	15	18	30
381-B, Renault 5 Turbo, 1983, white body, red roof, red and blue trim painted on, No. 5 lettering, blue and white label on windshield, facom decal	15	18	25
384-A, Adams Probe 16, 1970-73, one-piece body, blue sliding canopy; metallic burgundy, or metallic lime/gold w/and without racing stripes, Whizz Wheels	15	25	40
384-B, Volkswagen 1200 Rally, 1976-77, light blue body, off-white plastic interior, silver headlights, red taillights, suspension, Whizz Wheels	20	30	50
386-A, Bertone Barchetta Runabout, 1971-73, yellow and black body, black interior, amber windows, die-cast air foil, suspension, red/yellow Runabout decals, Whizz Wheels	15	22	45
394-A, Datsun 240Z, 1973-76, red body w/No. 11 and other labels, two working doors, white interior, orange roll bar and tire rack; one version also has East Africa Rally labels	15	20	35
396-A, Datsun 240Z, 1973-76, white body w/red hood and roof, No. 46 and John Morton labels, Whizz Wheels	15	20	35

	C6	C8	C10
397-A, Porsche-Audi 917, 1973-78, white body, red and black No. 6, L and M, Porsche Audi and stripe labels or orange body, orange, two-tone green, white No. 6, racing driver	15	20	35

Small Truck

	C6	C8	C10
11-A, ERF Dropside Truck and Trailer, 1960-64, No. 456 truck and No. 101 trailer w/No. 1488 cement sack load and No. 1485 plank load	60	90	200
21-A, Milk Truck and Trailer, 1962-66, blue and white ERF No. 456 milk truck w/No. 101 trailer and milk churns	60	130	250
24-A, Constructor Set, 1963-68, one red and one white cab bodies, w/four different interchangeable rear units; van, pickup, milk truck, and ambulance; various accessories include a milkman figure	48	80	160
24-B, Mercedes-Benz and Caravan, 1975-81, truck and trailer in two versions: w/blue No. 285 Mercedes truck and No. 490 Caravan (1975-79); w/brown No. 285 Mercedes and No. 490 Caravan (1980-81); value is for each set	15	30	50
28-B, Mazda Pickup and Dinghy, 1975-78, two versions: red No. 493 Mazda w/"Ford" labels; or w/"Sea Spray" labels, dinghy and trailer	25	35	60
405-C, Ford Transit Milk Float, 1982, white one-piece body, blue hood and roof, tan interior, chrome and red roof lights, open compartment door and milk cases	15	25	40
406-B, Mercedes-Benz Unimog 406, 1970-76, yellow body, red and green front fenders and bumpers, metallic charcoal gray chassis w/olive or tan rear plastic covers, red interior	18	25	45
413-B, Mazda Motorway Maintenance Truck, 1976-78, deep yellow body w/red base, black interior and hydraulic cylinder, yellow basket w/workman figure	18	25	45
415-A, Mazda Camper Pickup, 1976-78, red truck and white camper w/red interior and folding supports	15	25	451
431-A, Volkswagen Pickup, 1964-66, dark yellow or gold body, red interior and rear plastic cover, silver bumpers and headlights, red VW emblem, shaped wheels	45	65	110
440-B, Mazda Custom Pickup, 1979-80, orange body w/red roof, United States flag label	15	18	30
452-A, Commer 5-Ton Dropside Truck, 1956-62, either blue or red cab, both w/cream rear body, sheet metal tow hook, smooth or shaped wheels, rubber tires	40	60	110
453-A, Commer Refrigerator Van, 1956-60, either light or dark blue cab (pictured here), both w/cream bodies and red/white/blue Wall's Ice Cream decals, smooth wheels	80	120	225

	C6	C8	C10
454-A, Commer 5-Ton Platform Truck, 1957-62, either yellow or metallic blue cab w/silver body, smooth or shaped wheels	40	60	120
456-A, ERF 44G Dropside Truck, 1961-64, yellow cab and chassis, metallic blue bed, smooth or shaped wheels	36	55	110
457-A, ERF 44G Platform Truck, 1958-64, light blue cab w/dark blue flatbed body or yellow cab and blue flatbed, smooth hubs	36	55	110
459-A, ERF 44G Moorhouse Van, 1958-60, yellow cab, red body, Moorhouse Lemon Cheese decals, smooth wheels, rubber tires	100	150	295
460-A, ERF Neville Cement Tipper, 1959-66, yellow cab, gray tipper, cement decal, plastic or metal filler caps, w/either smooth or shaped wheels	32	48	85
465-A, Commer 3/4-Ton Pickup, 1963-66, red cab w/orange canopy, yellow interior, Trans-o-Lites	30	45	75
483-A, Dodge Kew Fargo Tipper, 1967-72, white cab and working hood, blue tipper, red interior, clear windows, black hydraulic cylinders, cast spoked wheels, plastic tires	34	51	85
490-A, Volkswagen Breakdown Truck, 1966-72, tan or white body, red interior and equipment boxes, clear windshield, chrome tools, spare wheels, red VW emblem, no lettering	50	75	125
493-A, Mazda B-1600 Pickup Truck, 1975-78, issued in either blue and white or blue and silver bodies w/working tailgate, black interior, chrome wheels	15	20	35
495-A, Mazda 4X4 Open Truck, 1983, blue body, white roof, black windows, no interior, white plastic wheels	15	20	35
702-A, Breakdown Truck, 1975-79, red body, black plastic boom w/gold hook, yellow interior, amber windows, black/yellow decals, Whizz Wheels	15	18	30
1116-B, Shelvoke and Drewry Garbage Truck, 1979, long, orange or red cab, silver body w/City Sanitation decals, black interior, grille and bumpers, clear windows	15	25	40
1117-B, Mercedes-Faun Street Sweeper, 1980, orange body w/light orange or brown figure, red interior, black chassis and unpainted brushing housing and arm castings	15	25	40
1150-A, Unimog with Snowplow (Mercedes-Benz), 1971-76, 6" four different body versions, red interior, cab, rear body, fender-plow mounting, lower and charcoal upper chassis, rear fenders	30	45	75

Sports Car

	C6	C8	C10
311-A, Ford Capri, 1970-72, orange-red or dark red body, gold wheels w/red hubs or Whizz Wheels, two working doors, clear windshield and headlights, black interior, folding seats, black grille, silver bumpers	40	80	145
1-C, Ford Sierra and Caravan Trailer, 1983, blue #299 Sierra, two-tone blue/white #490 Caravan	15	20	35
26-A, Beach Buggy & Sailboat, 1971-76, purple No. 381 buggy, yellow trailer and red/white boat	20	30	55
38-B, Mini Camping Set, 1977-78, cream Mini, w/red/blue tent, grille and two figures	25	40	65
200-B, British Leyland Mini 1000, 1976-78, metallic blue body, working doors, black base, clear windows, white interior, silver lights, grille and bumper, Union Jack decal on roof, Whizz Wheels	18	27	45
203-B, De Tomaso Mangusta, 1970-73, metallic dark green body w/gold stripes and logo on hood, silver lower body, clear front windows, cream interior, amber rear windows and headlights, gray antenna, spare wheel, Whizz Wheels	26	39	65
204-B, Morris Mini-Minor, 1972-73, one-piece body in dark or metallic blue or orange body, plastic interior, silver lights, grille and bumpers, red taillights, Whizz Wheels	30	45	75
214-A, Ford Thunderbird Hardtop, 1959-65, light green body, cream roof, clear windows, silver lights, grille and bumpers, red taillights, rubber tires	50	80	130

Corgi 324-A Marcos Volvo 1800 GT, 1966-69. Photo courtesy Dr. Douglas Sadecky

Corgi 349-A Pop Art Mini-Mostest, 1969. Photo courtesy Dr. Douglas Sadecky

Corgi 101-A Platform Trailer, 1958-64. Photo courtesy Dr. Douglas Sadecky

	C6	C8	C10
214-M, Ford Thunderbird Hardtop-Mechanical, 1959, same as 214-A but w/friction motor and pink body and black roof. This model is fairly hard to find	70	120	215
215-A, Ford Thunderbird Roadster, 1959-65, clear windshield, silver seats, lights, grille and bumpers, red taillights, rubber tires, white body	50	75	125
226-A1, Morris Mini-Minor, 1960-71, light blue or red body w/shaped or smooth wheels, plastic interior, silver bumpers, grille and headlights	40	60	100
226-A2, Morris Mini-Minor, 1960-71, sky blue body w/shaped and/or smooth wheels, plastic interior, silver bumpers, grille and headlights, rare	100	175	350
242-A, Ghia-Fiat 600 Jolly, 1965-66, dark yellow body, red seats, two figures and a dog, clear windshield, silver bumpers and headlights, red taillights, rare	80	175	325
249-A, Morris Mini-Cooper Deluxe, 1965-68, black body/base, red roof, yellow and black wicker work decals on sides and rear, yellow interior, gray steering wheel, jewel headlights	45	65	120
271-A, De Tomaso Mangusta, 1969, white upper/light blue lower body/base, black interior, clear windows, silver engine, black grille, amber headlights, red taillights, gray antenna, spare wheel, gold stripes and black logo decal on hood, suspension, removable gray chassis	32	48	90
286-A, Jaguar XJ12C, 1974-79, five different metallic versions, working hood and two doors, clear windows, tow hook, chrome bumpers, grille and headlights	10	15	35
288-A, Minissima, 1975-79, cream upper body, metallic lime green lower body w/black stripe centered, black interior, clear windows, headlights	15	20	35
298-A, Ferrari 308GTS Magnum, 1982, red body w/solid chrome wheels	24	36	60
299-A, Ford Sierra, 1982, many body color versions w/plastic interior, working hatch and two doors, clear windows, folding seat back, lifting hatch cover	8	15	25
300-A1, Austin-Healey, 1956-63, cream body w/red seats or red body w/cream seats	50	75	125
300-A2, Austin Healey, 1956-63, blue body w/cream seats, shaped hubs, rare	100	215	350
300-B, Corvette Sting Ray, 1970-72, metallic green or metallic red body, yellow interior, black working hood, working headlights, clear windshield, amber roof panel, gold dash, chrome grille and bumpers, decals, gray die-cast base, Golden jacks, cast wheels, plastic tires	40	90	185
301-A, Triumph TR2, 1956-59, cream one-piece body w/red seats, light green body w/white or cream seats, clear windshield, silver grille	70	105	175

	C6	C8	C10
301-B, Iso Grifo 7 Litre, 1970-73, metallic blue body, light blue interior, black hood and stripe, clear windshield, black dash, folding seats, chrome bumpers, Whizz Wheels	15	18	30
302-A, MGA, 1957-65, red or metallic green body, cream seats, black dash, clear windshield, silver bumpers, grille and headlights, smooth or shaped wheels	60	90	150
303-C, Porsche 924, 1980-81, bright orange body, dark red interior, black plastic grille, multicolored stripes, swivel roof spotlight	10	15	25
304-B, Chevrolet Camaro SS, 1972-73, blue or turquoise body w/white stripe, cream interior, working doors, white plastic top, clear windshield, folding seats, silver air intakes, red taillights, black grille and headlights, suspension, Whizz Wheels	30	45	95
305-A, Triumph TR3, 1960-62, metallic olive or cream one-piece body, red seats, clear windshield, silver grille, bumpers and headlights, smooth or shaped hubs	60	90	150
306-A, Morris Marina 1.8 Coupe, 1971-73, metallic dark red or lime green body, cream interior, working hood and two doors, clear windshield, chrome grille and bumpers, Whizz Wheels	15	30	60
307-A, Jaguar E Type, 1962-64, maroon or metallic dark gray body, tan interior, red and clear plastic removable hardtop, clear windshield, folded top, spun hubs	45	65	110
308-A, BMC Mini-Cooper S, 1972-76, bright yellow body, red plastic interior, chrome plastic roof rack w/two spare wheels, clear windshield, one-piece body silver grille, bumpers, headlights, red taillights, suspension, Whizz Wheels	45	65	110
309-B, Volkswagen Polo Turbo, 1982, cream body, red interior w/red and orange trim, working hatch and two door castings, clear windshield, black plastic dash	15	18	30
310-A, Corvette Sting Ray, 1963-68, metallic silver, bronze or red body, two working headlights, clear windshield, yellow interior, silver hood panels, four rotating jewel headlights, suspension, chrome bumpers, w/spoked or shaped wheels, rubber tires. The swivelling jeweled headlights and spoked wheels added real pizzaz to this cool toy	60	90	175
310-B, Porsche 92 Turbo, 1982, black body w/gold trim, yellow interior, four chrome headlights, clear windshield, taillight-license plate decal, opening doors and hatchback	15	20	35
312-B, Marcos Mantis, 1971-73, metallic red body, opening doors, cream interior and headlights, silver gray lower body base, bumpers, hood panel, spoked wheels	20	35	55

	C6	C8	C10
313-A, Ford Cortina GXL, 1970-73, tan or metallic silver blue body, black roof and stripes, red plastic interior, working doors, clear windshield	30	45	75
314-B, Fiat X1/9, 1975-79, metallic light green or silver body w/black roof, trim and interior, two working doors, rear panel, grille, tow hook and bumpers, detailed engine, suspension, chrome wheels	15	20	35
314-C, Jaguar XJS-HE Supercat, 1982-83, black body w/silver stripes and trim, red interior, dark red taillights, light gray antenna, no tow hook, clear windshield	8	15	25
315-C, Lotus Elite, 1976-78, red body, white interior, two working doors, clear windshield, black dash, hood panel, grille, bumpers, base and tow hook	15	18	35
316-A, NSU Sport Prinz, 1963-66, metallic burgundy or maroon body, yellow interior, one-piece body, silver bumpers, headlights and trim, shaped wheels	30	45	75
319-A, Lotus Elan S2 Hardtop, 1967-68, cream interior w/folding seats and tan dash, working hood, separate chrome chassis, issued in blue body w/white top or red body w/white top	30	45	75
319-C, Jaguar XJS, 1978-81, metallic burgundy body, tan interior, clear windows, working doors, spoked chrome wheels	10	15	25
320-A, Ford Mustang Fastback, 1965-66, metallic lilac, metallic dark blue, silver or light green body, spoked or detailed cast wheels	30	45	95
324-A, Marcos Volvo 1800 GT, 1966-69, issued w/either white body w/two green stripes or blue body w/two white stripes, plastic interior w/driver, spoked wheels, rubber tires. The blue version is shown here-the common version is white with racing stripes......	25	40	70
325-A, Ford Mustang Fastback, 1965-69, white body w/double red stripe, blue interior, spun, detailed cast, wire or cast alloy wheels. Shown in the foreground of this photo is an unused number sheet to help jazz up the model	25	45	85
327-A, MGB GT, 1967-69, dark red body, pale blue interior, opening hatch and two doors, jewel headlights, chrome grille and bumpers, orange taillights, spoked wheels, w/suitcase ...	50	75	110
329-A, Ford Mustang Mach 1, 1973-76, green upper body, white lower body and base, cream interior, folding seat backs, chrome headlights and rear bumper	25	35	60
332-A, Lancia Fulvia Zagato, 1967-69, metallic blue body, metallic green or yellow and black body, light blue interior, working hood and doors, folding seats, amber lights, cast wheels	25	35	70
334-A, BMC Mini-Cooper Magnifique, 1966-70, metallic blue or olive green			

	C6	C8	C10
body w/working doors, hood and trunk, clear windows and sunroof, cream interior w/folding seats, jewel headlights, cast detailed wheels, plastic tires......................	34	65	115
335-A, Jaguar E Type 2+2, 1968-69, red or blue body and chassis, working hood, doors and hatch, black interior w/folding seats, copper engine, pipes and suspension, spoked wheels...........	40	60	120
338-A, Chevrolet Camaro SS, 1968-70, metallic gold body w/two working doors, black roof and stripes, red interior, take-off wheels..............	30	45	75
341-A, Mini-Marcos GT850, 1966-70, metallic maroon body, white name and trim decals, cream interior, open hood and doors, clear windows and headlights, Golden Jacks wheels	30	45	75
342-A, Lamborghini Miura P400, 1970-72, w/red or yellow body, working hood, detailed engine, clear windows, jewel headlights, bull figure, Whizz Wheels	40	60	100
343-A, Pontiac Firebird, 1969-72, metallic silver body and base, red interior, black hood, stripes and convertible top, doors open, clear windows, folding seats, Golden Jacks wheels	50	75	125
343-B, Ford Capri 30 S, 1980-81, Silver or yellow body, black markings, opening doors and hatchback..............	15	20	35
345-A, MGC GT, 1969, bright yellow body and base, black interior, hood and hatch, folding seats, luggage, jewel headlights, red taillights	50	75	125
347-A, Chevrolet Astro I, 1969-74, dark metallic green/blue body w/working rear door, cream interior w/two passengers, in two versions: gold wheels w/red plastic hubs or Whizz wheels	18	40	85
349-A, Pop Art Mini-Mostest, 1969, light red body and base, yellow interior, jewel headlights, orange taillights, yellow-blue-purple pop art and "Mostest" decals; very rare. This rare Mini is one of the Holy Grails of any Corgi collection. Very few of these cars were produced in 1969, possibly due to the fact that psychedelia had already passed its prime.....................	1000	1500	2700
370-A, Ford Cobra Mustang, 1982, white, black, red and blue body and chassis, Mustang decal........................	15	18	30
372-A, Lancia Fulvia Zagato, 1970-72, orange body, black working hood and interior, Whizz Wheels	15	25	40
374-A, Jaguar E Type 2+2, 1970-76, in five versions: red or yellow w/nonworking doors; or w/V-12 engine in yellow body or metallic yellow body, Whizz Wheels	35	55	90
375-A, Toyota 2000 GT, 1970-72, metallic dark blue or purple one-piece body, cream interior, red gear shift and antenna, two red and two amber taillights, Whizz Wheels....................	15	30	55

Corgi 441-A Volkswagen Tobler Van, 1963-67. Photo courtesy Dr. Douglas Sadecky

Corgi 471-A1 Karrier Mobile Canteen, 1965-66. Photo courtesy Dr. Douglas Sadecky

Corgi 474-A Ford Thames Wall's Ice Cream Van, 1965-68. Photo courtesy Dr. Douglas Sadecky

	C6	C8	C10
377-A, Marcos 3 Litre, 1970-73, working hood, detailed engine, black interior, Marcos label, Whizz Wheels, issued in orange or metallic blue-green	20	30	55
378-A, MGC GT, 1970-73, red body, black hood and base, black interior, opening hatch and two doors, folding seat backs, luggage, orange taillights, Whizz Wheels	50	75	125
378-B, Ferrari 308GTS, 1982, red or black body w/working rear hood, black interior w/tan seats, movable chrome headlights, detailed engine	15	20	35
380-A, Alfa Romeo P33 Pininfarina, 1970-74, white body, gold or black spoiler, red seats, Whizz Wheels	16	24	45
381-A, GP Beach Buggy, 1970-76, metallic blue or orange-red body, two surfboards, flower label, Whizz Wheels	15	20	35
382-A, Porsche Targa 911S, 1970-75, metallic blue, silver-blue or green body, black roof w/or without stripe, orange interior, opening hood and two doors, chrome engine and bumpers, Whizz Wheels	25	35	60
382-B, Lotus Elite 22, 1970-75, dark blue body w/silver trim, Whizz Wheels	15	18	35
384-C, Renault 11 GTL, 1983, light tan or maroon body and base, red interior, opening doors and rear hatch, lifting hatch cover, folding seats, grille	15	25	40
385-A, Porsche 917, 1970-76, red or metallic blue body, black or gray base, blue or amber tinted windows and headlights, opening rear hood, headlights, Whizz Wheels	15	20	45
387-A, Corvette Sting Ray, 1972, either dark metallic blue or metallic mauve-rose body, chrome dash, Whizz Wheels	40	65	100
388-A, Mercedes-Benz C-111, 1971-74, orange main body w/black lower and base, black interior, vents, front and rear grilles, silver headlights, red taillights, Whizz Wheels	15	20	45
389-A, Reliant Bond Bug 700 E.S., 1971-74, bright orange or lime green body, off white seats, black trim, silver headlights, red taillights, Bug label	15	25	50

	C6	C8	C10
392-A, Bertone Shake Buggy, 1972-74, clear windows, green interior, gold engine, four variations: yellow upper/white lower body or metallic mauve upper/white lower body w/spoked or solid chrome wheels	15	22	45
393-A, Mercedes-Benz 350SL, 1972-79, white body, spoke wheels or metallic dark blue body solid wheels, pale blue interior, folding seats, detailed engine	15	30	60
457-B, Talbot-Matra Rancho, 1981-84, red and black, green and black or white and blue body, working tailgate and hatch, clear windows, plastic interior, black bumpers, grille and tow hook	10	15	25
801-B, Ford Thunderbird 1957, 1982, cream body, dark brown, black or orange plastic hardtop, black interior, open hood and trunk, chrome bumpers	10	20	35
802-B, Mercedes-Benz 300SL, 1982, red body and base, tan interior, open hood and two gullwing doors, black dash, detailed engine, clear windows, chrome bumpers	8	15	25
803-A, Jaguar 1952 XK120 Rally, 1983, cream body w/black top and trim, red interior, Rally des Alps and #414 decals	8	15	25
803-B, Jaguar XK120 Hardtop, 1983, red body, black hardtop, working hood and trunk, detailed engine, cream interior, clear windows, chrome wheels	8	15	25
805-B, Mercedes-Benz 300SC Hardtop, 1983, maroon body, tan top and interior, open hood and trunk, clear windows, folding seat backs, top w/chrome side irons	8	15	25
806-B, Mercedes-Benz 300SC Convertible, 1983, black body, black folded top, white interior, folding seat backs, detailed engine, chrome grille and wheels, lights, bumpers	8	12	25
810-B, Ford Thunderbird 1957, 1983, white body, black interior and plastic top, amber windows, white seats, chrome bumpers, headlights and spare wheel cover	10	20	35
811-B, Mercedes-Benz 300SL, 1983, silver body, tan interior, black dash,			

	C6	C8	C10
clear windows, open hood and two gullwing doors, detailed engine, chrome bumpers............................	8	15	25
1009-A, MG Maestro, 1983, yellow body, black trim, opaque black windows, black plastic grille, bumpers, spoiler, trim and battery hatch, clear headlights, AA Service label	15	20	35

Taxi

	C6	C8	C10
221-A, Chevrolet Impala Taxi, 1960-65, light orange body, base w/hexagonal panel under rear axle and smooth wheels, or two raised lines and shaped wheels, one-piece body, clear windows, plastic interior, silver grille, headlights and bumpers; smooth or shaped spun wheels w/rubber tires	50	75	125
327-B, Chevrolet Caprice Taxi, 1979-81, orange body w/red interior, white roof sign, Taxi and TWA decals..................	20	30	50
373-B, Peugeot 505 STI, 1981-82, red body and base, red interior, blue-red-white Taxi labels, black grille, bumpers, tow hook, chrome headlights and wheels, opening doors..................	8	15	25
411-B, Mercedes-Benz 240D Taxi, 1975-80, orange body, orange interior, black roof sign w/red and white Taxi labels, black on door	15	18	30
418-A1, Austin London Taxi, 1960-65, black body w/yellow plastic interior, w/or without driver, shaped or smooth hubs or rubber tires	36	55	90
418-A2, Austin London Taxi/Reissue, 1971-74, updated version w/Whizz Wheels, black or maroon body	15	20	35
425-A, Austin London Taxi, 1978-83, black body w/two working doors, light brown interior, Whizz Wheels	15	20	35
430-A, Thunderbird Bermuda Taxi, 1962-65, white body w/blue, yellow or green plastic canopy w/red fringe, yellow interior, driver, yellow and black labels	50	75	135
450-B, Peugeot 505 Taxi, 1983, cream body, red interior, red, white and blue taxi decals	8	15	25
451-A, Ford Sierra Taxi, 1983, cream body	8	15	20
480-A, Chevrolet Impala Yellow Cab, 1965-67, red lower body, yellow upper, red interior w/driver, white roof sign, red decals....................................	80	120	200

Trailer

	C6	C8	C10
100-A, Dropside Trailer, 1957-65, cream body, red chassis in five versions: smooth wheels 1957-61; shaped wheels, 1962-1965; white body, cream or blue chassis; or silver gray body, blue chassis, each...............................	10	21	45
101-A, Platform Trailer, 1958-64, in five versions: silver body, blue chassis; silver body, yellow chassis; blue body, red chassis; blue body, yellow chassis	10	20	45
109-A, Pennyburn Workmen's Trailer, 1968-69, blue body w/working lids,			

	C6	C8	C10
red plastic interior, three plastic tools, shaped wheels, plastic tires..................	15	35	50

Vans

	C6	C8	C10
403-A, Bedford Daily Express Van, 1956-59, dark blue body w/white Daily Express decals, divided windshield, smooth wheels, rubber tires	60	90	150
403M, Bedford KLG Van-Mechanical, 1956-59, w/friction motor, red body w/KLG Spark Plugs decals, smooth hubs...	70	125	285
404-A, Bedford Dormobile, 1956-62, two versions and several colors: divided windshield w/cream, green or metallic maroon body; or single windshield w/yellow body/blue roof w/shaped or smooth wheels. Pictured here; the 404-A on the left and the 404M on the right with a mechanical friction motor	50	75	125
404M, Bedford Dormobile-Mechanical, 1956-59, friction motor, dark metallic red or turquoise body, smooth wheels .	60	90	175
407-A, Karrier Mobile Grocery, 1957-61, light green body, grocery store interior, red/white Home Service labels, smooth hubs, rubber tires	70	110	185
408-A, Bedford AA Road Service Van, 1957-62, dark yellow body in two versions: first version with divided windshield, 1957-59 shown; single windshield, 1960-62	50	75	125
411-A, Karrier Lucozade Van, 1958-62, yellow body w/gray rear door, Lucozade decals, rubber tires, w/either smooth or shaped wheels	70	120	225
413-A, Karrier Butcher Shop, 1960-64, white body, blue roof, butcher shop interior, Home Service labels, in two versions: w/or without suspension, smooth hubs. Note the meat hanging in the side windows..................................	65	100	165
420-A, Ford Thames Airborne Caravan, 1962-67, various color versions of body and plastic interior w/table, white blinds, silver bumpers, grille and headlights, two doors........................	35	55	95
421-A, Bedford Evening Standard Van, 1960-62, black body/silver roof or black lower body/silver upper body and roof, Evening Standard decals, smooth wheels	55	80	130
422-A1, Bedford Corgi Toys Van, 1962, yellow upper/blue lower body, Corgi Toy decals, rare....................................	100	225	400
422-A2, Bedford Corgi Toys Van, 1960-62, Corgi Toys decals, w/either yellow body/blue roof or blue body/yellow roof...............................	60	105	200
423-B, Chevrolet Rough Rider Van, 1977-78, yellow body w/working rear doors, cream interior, amber windows, Rough Rider decals..............................	15	18	30
424-B, Security Van, 1976-79, black body, blue mesh windows and dome light, yellow/black Security labels, Whizz Wheels...................................	7	15	25

	C6	C8	C10
428-A, Karrier Ice Cream Van, 1963-66, cream upper, blue lower body and interior, clear windows, sliding side windows, Mister Softee decals, figure inside	90	165	295
431-B, Chevrolet Vantastic Van, 1977-80, off white body w/Vantastic decals	10	15	25
432-A, Chevrolet Vantastic Van, 1977-80, black body w/Vantastic decals	10	15	25
433-A, Volkswagen Delivery Van, 1962-64, white upper and red lower body, plastic red or yellow interior, silver bumpers and headlights, red VW emblem, shaped wheels	55	85	140
434-A, Volkswagen Kombi Bus, 1962-66, off-green upper and olive green lower body, red interior, silver bumpers and headlights, red VW emblem, shaped wheels	50	75	125
435-A, Karrier Dairy Van, 1962-64, light blue body w/Drive Safely on Milk decals, white roof, w/either smooth or shaped wheels	50	75	145
437-B, Chevrolet Coca-Cola Van, 1978-80, red body, white trim, w/Coca Cola logos	15	20	35
441-A, Volkswagen Tobler Van, 1963-67, light blue body, plastic interior, silver bumpers, Trans-o-lite headlights and roof panel, shaped wheels, rubber tires	55	85	140
447-A, Ford Wall's Ice Cream Van, 1965-67, light blue body, dark cream pillars, plastic striped rear canopy, white interior, silver bumpers, grille and headlights. A sidewalk/ street display plus a salesman and small boy dress up this non-musical version of the van	80	160	325
450-A, Austin Mini Van, 1964-67, metallic deep green body w/two working rear doors, clear windows	40	60	100
455-A, Karrier Bantam Two Ton Van, 1957-60, blue body, red chassis and bed, clear windows, smooth wheels, rubber tires	35	55	95
462-A, Commer 3/4-Ton Van, 1970-71, either dark blue body with green roof and Hammonds decals (1971) or white			

	C6	C8	C10
body with light blue roof and CO-OP labels (1970), both w/cast spoked wheels w/plastic tires	45	90	180
466-A1, Commer 3/4-Ton Milk Float, 1964-65, white cab w/light blue body	32	48	80
466-A2, Commer 3/4-Ton Milk Float, 1970, white cab w/light blue body, w/CO-OP decals	40	80	160
471-A1, Karrier Mobile Canteen, 1965-66, blue body, white interior, amber windows, roof knob rotates figure, working side panel counter, Joe's Diner label. In this photo, the model on the left has the common "Joe's Diner" label, while the van on the right (471-A2) features the rare Belgian-issued "patates frites" label	60	90	150
471-A2, Karrier Mobile Canteen, 1965-66, blue body, white interior, amber windows, roof knob rotates figure, working side panel counter, Patates Frites label, Belgium issue	90	150	325
474-A, Ford Thames Wall's Ice Cream Van, 1965-68, light blue body, cream pillar, chimes, chrome bumpers and grille, no figures. This wonderful toy played the Wall's Ice Cream musical tune by turning the hand crank on the rear of the van	55	110	225
479-A, Commer Mobile Camera Van, 1967-72, metallic blue lower body and roof rack, white upper body, two working rear doors, black camera on gold tripod, cameraman	60	105	195
508-A, Commer Holiday Mini Bus, 1968-69, white upper body w/orange lower body, white interior, clear windshield, silver bumpers, grille and headlights, Holiday Camp Special decal, roof rack, two working rear doors. With bathing suits packed in the roof luggage, a trip to the shore was inevitable in this mod van	30	75	130
1006-A, Radio Roadshow Van, 1982, white body, red plastic roof and rear interior, opaque black windows, red-white-black Radio Tele Luxembourg labels, gray plastic loud-speakers and working radio in van	25	35	60

Corgi 420-A Ford Thames Airborne Caravan, 1962-67. Photo courtesy Dr. Douglas Sadecky

Corgi 428-A Karrier Ice Cream Van, 1963-66. Photo courtesy Dr. Douglas Sadecky

Corgi 435-A Karrier Dairy Van, 1962-64. Photo courtesy Dr. Douglas Sadecky

COURTLAND

Walter Rudolph Reach, founder of Courtland toys, was born in Jersey City, New Jersey, in 1905. Educated in local schools, Reach eventually worked his way to Camden, New Jersey, where, in 1937, he opened a successful sign painting business. Beyond the usual commercial trade, he performed extensive contract work for the Campbell's Soup Company. In fact, he painted some of the early Campbell's advertising signs now eagerly sought by advertising collectors. Within a few years, Reach, sensing a rising wave of patriotism within the country, began a second business—The Camden Flag and Banner Company, again taking advantage of his artistic skills. The early war years saw a decline in his work for Campbell, but the flag and banner business flourished.

In the summer of 1943, Reach's friend, Harold Salter, a salesman working for a well-known Philadelphia toy distributor, A. Ponnock & Sons, approached Reach for suggestions on how he might dispose of a railroad boxcar full of "prepared" cardboard. Reach acquired the cardboard at a bargain price; with the thought he'd find some way to capitalize on this potential windfall. He decided on cardboard toys. He quickly fashioned two toys— a two-wheel rabbit cart and a horse cart. Sales success soon followed as a war-weary public, hungry for low-cost toys, snapped up the entire stock. Both sold well.

With the capital from the cardboard toys, Reach founded the Courtland Manufacturing Company, incorporating on May 29, 1944. His friends and business associates formed the company's management team. The first true Courtland toy was produced in 1944—a twelve-inch tractor and trailer truck, made entirely of wood and marked "Courtland" on the sides of the trailer. It achieved widespread sales success when it was introduced to the trade. His wooden Courtland success was short-lived, as his connections with Campbell soon provided him with a ready supply of "rejected" tin from their canning process. (Additionally, over the next several years, Reach purchased "reject" tin-plate from J&L Steel of Bethlehem, Pennsylvania.) A Courtland line of tin toys quickly followed; by the fall of 1945, several toy trucks and play sets fashioned from tin were introduced.

With Reach designing the toys, and his father Erwin as the plant's manager, Courtland was off and running. During 1945, toy production at the Haddon Avenue factory focused on forty-two dedicated employees. Courtland would eventually employ more than 350 persons, father and son, mother and daughter teams were quite common. By late 1945, Courtland began installing mechanical motors in a select number of toys, boosting sales even higher. Courtland prospered with gross sales in 1946 exceeding $600,000. In 1946, Courtland toys could be found in forty-three states and thirteen foreign countries. As evidence of the swift and dynamic growth of the company, the top three domestic orders for tin toys in 1946 came from Sears, Roebuck & Co. of Chicago, for $21,827,26; Loft Candy Company, Long Island, New York, for $14,704.50; and Butler Brothers of Chicago, for $11,711.74.

Reach and his management staff instituted a "child toy testing" program at the plant, whereby a small room in the building was set aside for local children to evaluate the play value of new toy designs by playing with the toys. He observed the children at play to see which toys kept their interest and which toys were played with the least, or not selected for play at all. Reach, over the years, pointed with pride to his "child testing" program, believing that this type of testing was greatly responsible for his overall success.

The 1947 toy sales were five times greater than the same period the preceding year, and factory production was taxed to its production capacity of 20,000 toys a day. During that same year, Courtland's Export Division came into being under the direction of John H. Jackson. The Export Division, located in Basking Ridge, New Jersey, was tasked with the responsibility of coordinating all sales to foreign countries and to administer a newly negotiated contract with General Metal Toys LTD, of Canada. Courtland had, in fact, just completed and shipped the first such order of Walt Reach Courtland Toys with the General Metal Toys, Ltd. markings.

Over the next few years, Courtland introduced several toy innovations, including the streamline design of its trucks and cars and, most notably, the famous "Guaranteed For Life" mechanical motor. This motor, completely enclosed and designed for easy removal from the toy, was offered in both key-wind and friction action, and came with a colorful printed warranty with each toy sold. Hailed by the trade as a decisive marketing tool, the "Motor Guaranteed For Life" warranty provided buyers with the unique opportunity to exchange defective motors for new motors.

Gross sales of more than $1.2 million was reported for the first time in 1948. In 1949, sales rose to a staggering $1.9 million. Also, during 1949, Courtland Manufacturing moved to a newly renovated plant at 6th & Jefferson Street in Camden. During the planning phase for the renovated plant, Reach hired a manufacturing consultant to design the production assembly line so that an entire toy-from start to finish, including piece assembly (hand work), packaging, boxing, sealing, and labeling-could be completed with no toy ever leaving the flow of the production line.

Reach, having borrowed heavily to secure and outfit his new production facility, was hit a severe financial blow. On June 24, 1950, the United States, under a United Nations mandate, entered the Korean Conflict. Essential war materials, which included tin, were diverted to the war effort, effectively denying him the backbone of his toy production. The availability of tin for toy making was reduced to a trickle, with the only source once again being "reject" tinplate. Recalling the early years of the company, this scenario was nothing new to him. What was new this time was that he found himself competing with other toy and novelty manufacturers across America for the meager supply of available tin.

A second, and more devastating blow to Courtland was the discovery, in the fall of 1950, of the introduction of counterfeit toys. These cheap, look-alike knock-offs, with inferior mechanical motors, were flooding the toy market under the Courtland name. The perpetrator, in addition to producing counterfeit Courtland toys, was also printing bogus "Motor Guaranteed For Life" warranty certificates. This caused a two-fold problem. Not only was Courtland faced with the loss of the sale of the toy, but they were also forced to exchange Courtland motors for defective motors, and there were many. To refuse this exchange, at least initially, would have, in all probability, destroyed the highly regarded guarantee. His initial thoughts were that the toys came from an Asian country, such as China or Japan. Subsequent investigating revealed the possibility the toys were coming from Canada, or at least entering the United States from Canada. (The mystery of where the toys originated and by whom has never seen solved).

With the combination of the effects of the war, the decline in sales due to counterfeit toys, and the need to pay the mortgage on the new plant, Reach suddenly found himself with a cash-flow problem. Searching desperately for funds, he turned to the Geo. Borgfeldt Company, a large, national toy distributor, to secure the necessary financial assistance. Besides the debt-service, one of the concessions he made to Borgfeldt was that the sole

distribution of all Courtland toys went to Borgfeldt. Sales continued to sag, and Reach, desperate to hold the company together, approached persons, now known to be less than honorable, for help. Help they did...they helped themselves to his company by taking over the directorship and management positions, firing the original directors, and draining the company of its money by paying themselves high salaries and huge bonuses. Employee rosters were quickly reduced to a minimum.

Within two years, and without Reach, the fledgling toy empire with so much potential, evaporated. Reach, however, was a fighter. Moving to Philadelphia with his family and dreams in 1953, he opened the Courtland Toy Company, attempting to remanufacture several of the original toys and a few new designs under that name; thus, the toys with the Courtland Toy Company, Philadelphia markings. By 1953, though, time has passed for tin-plate as a material for mass toy production. Plastics were in. Even though Reach had used some plastics in his original streamline Courtland designs produced in the 1949-1951 period, he could not retool for plastic-injection molding without considerable expense. Finally, Courtland Toys were truly committed to history and the drive to rival Louis Marx as America's toy king was no more.

Special thanks to Marie Reach, Walt Reach's widow, for the above information. Mrs. Reach, a most gracious lady, opened her home and her memories of Walt and his Courtland toys to us. She, herself employed at the Courtland plant in Camden, provided numerous documents, photographs, artifacts, and anecdotes for our future book on the history of Courtland toys.

Source: *Collector's Guide to American Transportation Toys* by Joe and Sharon Freed.

Contributor: John Taylor, P.O. Box 63, Nolensville, TN 37135-0063.

Friction-Powered

	C6	C8	C10
Dump Truck w/dual rear wheels, 10-1/2" long, 3" wide, 3-3/8" high	250	350	475
FBI Riot Squad Car, No. 7600, 7-1/4" long, 3-1/4" wide, 2-3/4" high	50	100	250
Mechanical Fire Chief Car w/siren, No. 7500, 7-1/4" long, 3-1/4" wide, 3-1/4" high	50	100	250
Mechanical Gasoline Tractor-Trailer, similar to No. 2000; gasoline Truck w/Trailer, marked "Gasoline-Motor Oils", Philadelphia, PA, 13" long, 3" wide, 3-1/4" high	100	150	200
Mechanical Gulf Gasoline Tractor-Trailer, No. 3875, 13" long, 3" wide, 3-1/4" high	200	350	500
Mechanical Military Gun Car, lithographed gunshield, 7-1/2" long, 3-1/4" wide, 2-1/2" high	50	100	200
Mechanical Military Gun Car, painted gun shield, 7-1/2" long, 3-1/4" wide, 2-1/2" high	50	100	200

Left to right: Courtland Gulf Gasoline Tractor-Trailer; unopened wholesale case; battery-operated Traffic Signal; Mechanical Truck Set, box with four trucks; Mechanical Parking Meter and bank, 24-1/2". Photo courtesy Joe and Sharon Freed

	C6	C8	C10
Mechanical State Police Car with siren, No. 7500, 7-1/4" long, 3-1/4" wide, 2-3/4" high	50	100	250
Pop-Up Ladder Fire Truck, No. 5450, 13" long, 3" wide, 3-1/4" high	75	150	300
Space Rocket Patrol Car, No. 4060, 1952, 7-1/4" long, 3-1/4" wide, 2-3/4" high ..	75	150	300
Woody Sedan, No. 4000, blue and tan, 7-1/4" long, 3-1/4" wide, 2-3/4" high. Note: This is one of only four Courtland styled toys stamped "A Walt Reach Toy by Courtland Toy Co. Phila., PA. Made in U.S.A." The only known Courtland-styled toys marked w/the Courtland Toy Company, Philadelphia stamping is this No. 4000 sedan, a non-powered "Fire Chief" car, a private garage similar to No. 9075 and a mechanical parking meter bank..	50	75	150
Woody Sedan, No. 4000, red and tan, 7-1/4" long, 3-1/4" wide, 2-3/4" height	50	75	150

Non-Powered

	C6	C8	C10
Big 4 Truck Parade, No. 1070, 1946, The four 900, 9-1/2" long, 3-1/4" wide, 3" high..................................	NPF	NPF	NPF
Easter Greetings Rabbit Truck, No. 800, 9" long..................................	150	300	450
Fire Patrol No. 2 Truck, No. 900, 1946, 9" long, 3" wide, 2-3/4" high	40	65	125
Ice Cream Truck, No. 900, 1946, ...	40	65	125
Loft Candies Tractor-Trailer, same as No. 2000, marked "Fresh Loft Candy" on sides, rare	NPF	NPF	NPF
Lumber Truck Tractor-Trailer, No. 620, 1946, 13" long, 3" wide, 3-1/4" high ...	75	125	275
Logging Camp Train Set, No. 1050, 1946, 26-3/4" long, 3" wide, 3-1/4" high	NPF	NPF	NPF

	C6	C8	C10
Moving and Storage Truck, No. 900, 1946, 9" long, 3" wide, H 2-3/4" high .	150	225	350
Open Van Tractor-Trailer, No. 600, 1946, 13" long, 3" wide, 3-1/4" high ...	100	150	200
Side Dump Tractor-Trailer, No. 1200, 13" long, 3" wide, 3-1/4" high	30	75	225
Side Dump Tractor-Trailer, No. 610, 1946, 13" long, 13" wide, 3-1/4" high .	100	150	200
Side Dump Tractor-Trailer, No. 700, 1946, 13" long, 3" wide, 3-1/4" high ...	100	150	200
Tractor-Trailer, same tractor as No. 2000 except marked, "Loft-Fresh Candies" on door..................................	150	300	450
Trailer, all-wood open w/high-sides, 12" long..................................	NPF	NPF	NPF
Trailer Truck Parade, No. 1060, 1946, 13" long, 3" wide, 3-1/4" wide	NPF	NPF	NPF
Truck Assortment, No. 900, four trucks w/box	NPF	NPF	NPF

Tin Wind-up

	C6	C8	C10
Assortment, No. 2800, consists of two No. 2000 Gasoline Trucks, two No. 2050 Milk Trucks, two No. 2200 Log Trucks, two No. 2350 Open Van Trucks, two No. 2600 Freight Hauler Trucks and two No. 2700 Side Tipper Trucks; wholesale assortment only, in Mint condition	NPF	NPF	NPF
Assortment, No. 3800, consists of six No. 3100 Dump Trucks; wholesale Assortment Only..................................	NPF	NPF	NPF
Assortment, No. 5800, consists of three No. 2300 Aluminum Open Van Trucks, three No. 2150 Emergency Rescue Squad Trucks, three No. 2375 Sand and Gravel Trucks and three No. 2400 Towing Service Trucks; Wholesale Assortment Only	NPF	NPF	NPF

Left to right: Courtland No. 1300 Fire Patrol No. 2 Truck, 9"; Courtland No. 130 Moving and Storage Truck, 9". Photo courtesy Joe and Sharon Freed

Courtland Dump Truck, friction powered, dual rear wheels, 10-1/2".

Courtland Mechanical Gulf Gasoline Tractor-Trailer, friction powered, 13". Photo courtesy Mapes Auctioneers

Courtland Mechanical Military Gun Car, friction powered, litho gun shield, 7-1/2". Photo courtesy Joe and Sharon Freed

Courtland No. 4000 City Meat Market Delivery Sedan, without motor, 7-1/4". Photo courtesy Joe and Sharon Freed

Courtland No. 4000 Checker Cab Car, green and yellow, 7-1/4". Photo courtesy Joe and Sharon Freed

Courtland No. 5100 Mechanical Black Diamond Coal Truck, 10-1/2". Photo courtesy Joe and Sharon Freed

The Courtland No. 900 Truck Assortment, non-powered, as found in the July 1946 Toys & Novelties. Photo courtesy Richard MacNary

Courtland No. 4000 Fire Chief Car, red and white, 7-1/4". Photo courtesy Joe and Sharon Freed

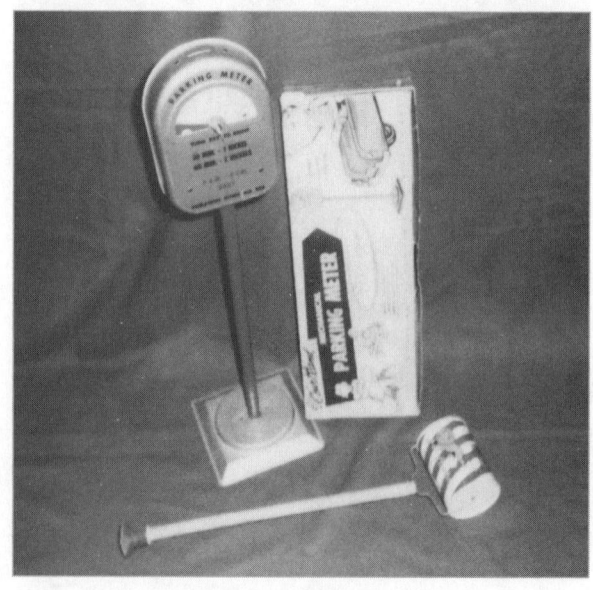

Courtland Mechanical Parking Meter and Bank. Photo courtesy Joe and Sharon Freed

	C6	C8	C10
Bank, No. 7500, base 6" x 6", 24-1/2" high. Note: This is one of only four Courtland toys stamped "A Walt Reach Toy by Courtland Toy Co., Phila. PA. Made in U.S.A." The only known Courtland styled toys marked w/the Courtland Toy Company, Philadelphia stamping is this mechanical parking meter bank, a No. 4000 sedan, a non-power "Fire Chief" car, and a private garage similar to No. 9075	NPF	NPF	NPF
Checker Cab Car, No. 4000, green and white, 7-1/4" long, 3-1/4" wide, 2-3/4" high	75	175	325
Checker Cab Car, No. 4000, green and yellow, 7-1/4" long, 3-1/4" wide, 2-3/4" high	75	175	325
City Meat Market Delivery Sedan, No. 4000, 7-1/4" long, 3-1/4" wide, 2-3/4" high	75	175	325
Country Produce Pickup, No. 4500, 7-1/4" long, 3-1/4" wide, 2-3/4" high	50	100	200
Express Service Pickup, No. 4500 7-1/4" long, 3-1/4" wide, 2-3/4" high ..	75	125	175
Fire Chief Car, No. 4000, red and white, 7-1/4" long, 3-1/4" wide, 2-3/4" high ..	50	100	200

	C6	C8	C10
Fire Chief Car, No. 4000, red, 7-1/4" long, 3-1/4" wide, 2-3/4" high ..	50	100	150
Fire Department with automatic garage door, No. 9050, 7-3/4" x 10-1/8" x 6-3/4"; found to have a non-powered fire chief car w/the Courtland Toy Co., Phila. PA, markings, it is quite possible that some of the 9050 garages were also manufactured in Philadelphia	75	150	300
Mechanical Automatic Ladder Fire Truck, No. 1400, 1947, 9" long, 3" wide, 2-3/4" high	75	150	300
Mechanical Big Four Truck Parade, No. 1070, 1947, 9" long, 3" wide, 2-3/4" high	NPF	NPF	NPF
Mechanical Black Diamond Coal Truck, No. 5100, 10-1/2" long, 3" wide, 3-3/8" high	75	125	275
Mechanical Caterpillar Tractor w/rubber treads, No. 6100, 6" long, 3" wide, 4-1/2" high	85	200	350
Mechanical Chromed Trimmed Tow Truck, No. 8500, tow boom is solid color, 8" long, 3-1/4" wide, 3-1/2" high	65	125	275
Mechanical Chromed Trimmed Tow Truck, No. 8500, tow boom shows			

Courtland Fire Department with automatic garage door, non-powered Fire Chief Car.

Courtland No. 6100 Mechanical Caterpillar Tractor with rubber treads, 6". Photo courtesy Joe and Sharon Freed

Courtland Chrome Trimmed Tow Truck, Walt's Garage, 8". Photo courtesy Joe and Sharon Freed

Courtland No. 5300 Excavating Mechanical Combination Steam Shovel carried by Low-boy tractor-trailer, 15-1/2". Photo courtesy Joe and Sharon Freed

Courtland Pop-Up Ladder Fire Truck, friction powered, red w/yellow ladder. Photo courtesy Joe and Sharon Freed

Courtland Space Rocket Patrol Car, friction powered, red and yellow. Photo courtesy Joe and Sharon Freed

Courtland Woody Sedan, friction powered, red and tan. Photo courtesy Joe and Sharon Freed

Courtland Tractor-Trailer, non-powered, "Loft-Fresh Candies" on door, "Courtland" on trailer. Photo courtesy Joe and Sharon Freed

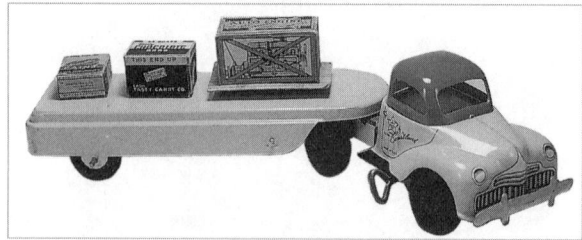

Courtland No. 600 Trucking Terminal Set. Photo courtesy Joe and Sharon Freed

Courtland No. 610 Side Dump Tractor-Trailer, non-powered, 13". Photo courtesy Joe and Sharon Freed

Courtland Tractor-Trailer, non-powered, "Fresh Loft Candy" on trailer sides, extremely rare. Photo courtesy Dutkins of Cherry Hill, N.J.

Courtland No. 620 Log Truck Tractor-Trailer, non-powered, 13". Photo courtesy Joe and Sharon Freed

Courtland all-wood high-side trailer, open, "Courtland" on trailer sides, 13". Photo courtesy Joe and Sharon Freed

Courtland No. 800 Easter Greetings Rabbit Truck, non-powered, 9". Photo courtesy Joe and Sharon Freed

Courtland No. 2100 Mechanical Hook and Ladder Tractor-Trailer, 13". Photo courtesy Joe and Sharon Freed

Courtland No. 1300 Mechanical Ice Cream Truck, 9". Photo courtesy Bob Smith

Courtland No. 2000 Mechanical Gasoline Tractor-Trailer, 13". Photo courtesy Joe and Sharon Freed

Courtland No. 2375 Mechanical Heavy Duty Sand and Gravel Tractor-Trailer, 13". Photo courtesy Joe and Sharon Freed

	C6	C8	C10
detail, 8" long, 3-1/4V wide, 3-1/2" high	65	125	275
Mechanical Combination Steam Shovel, No. 5300, carried by low-boy tractor-trailer, 15-1/2" long, 3-7/8" wide, 10-1/2" high	100	250	400
Mechanical Dump Truck, No. 1600, 7" long, 3" wide, 2-3/4" high	30	55	100
Mechanical Dump Truck, No. 3100, 7" long, 3" wide, 3-1/4" high	30	55	100
Mechanical Emergency Rescue Squad Tractor-Trailer, No. 2150, 13" long, 3" wide, 3-1/4" high	150	200	250
Mechanical ESSO Gasoline Tractor-Trailer, No. 2000, 13" long, 3" wide, 3-1/4" high	200	350	500
Mechanical Express and Hauling Truck, No. 1300, 1947, 9" long, 3" wide, 2-3/4" high	65	125	275
Mechanical Farm Tractor w/o scraper, No. 6050, rear tires are large rubber and front are small rubber tires, 7-1/2" long, 4-3/4" wide, 4-1/2" high	75	100	150
Mechanical Farm Tractor w/o scraper, No. 6075, rear tires are large tin lithographed while the front are small rubber tires, 7-1/2" long, 4-3/4" wide, 4-1/2" high	100	125	175
Mechanical Farm Tractor w/scraper, No. 6000, rear tires are large rubber and front are small rubber tires, 8-3/4" long, 4-3/4" wide, 4-1/2" high	100	150	200
Mechanical Fire Chief Car w/siren, No. 7000, 7-1/4" long, 3-1/4" wide, 2-3/4" high	50	100	250

	C6	C8	C10
Mechanical Fire Patrol No. 2 Truck, No. 1300, 1947, 9" long, 3" wide, 2-3/4" high	65	125	275
Mechanical Freight Haulers Tractor-Trailer, No. 2600, 13" long, 3" high, 3-1/4" wide	30	75	225
Mechanical Gasoline Tractor-Trailer, No. 2000, 13" long, 3" wide, 3-1/4" high	150	250	325
Mechanical Heavy Duty Sand and Gravel Tractor-Trailer, No. 2375, 13" long, 3" wide, 3-1/4" high	30	75	225
Mechanical Hook and Ladder Tractor-Trailer, No. 2100, 13" long, 3" wide, 3-1/4" high	50	100	250
Mechanical Ice Cream Scooter, No. 6500, 6-1/2" long, 3" wide, 4-1/2" high	50	100	250
Mechanical Ice Cream Truck, No. 1300, 9" long, 3" wide, 2-3/4" high	65	125	275
Mechanical Logging Tractor-Trailer, No. 2200, 13" long, 3" wide, 3-1/4" high	30	75	225
Mechanical Milk Tractor-Trailer, No. 2050, "American Dairies", 13" long, 3" wide, 3-1/4" high. Note: 1951 catalog shows Milk Trailer markings that read the same as above except "Approved" is used in the place of the words "Vitamin D." This variation is not known to have been produced.	100	250	400
Mechanical Moving and Storage Truck, No. 1300, 1947, 9" long, 3" wide, 2-3/4" high	50	125	275

Top to bottom: Courtland No. 3100 Mechanical
Dump Truck 7", green, yellow, red; No. 1600
Mechanical Dump Truck, red, 7". Photo courtesy
Joe and Sharon Freed

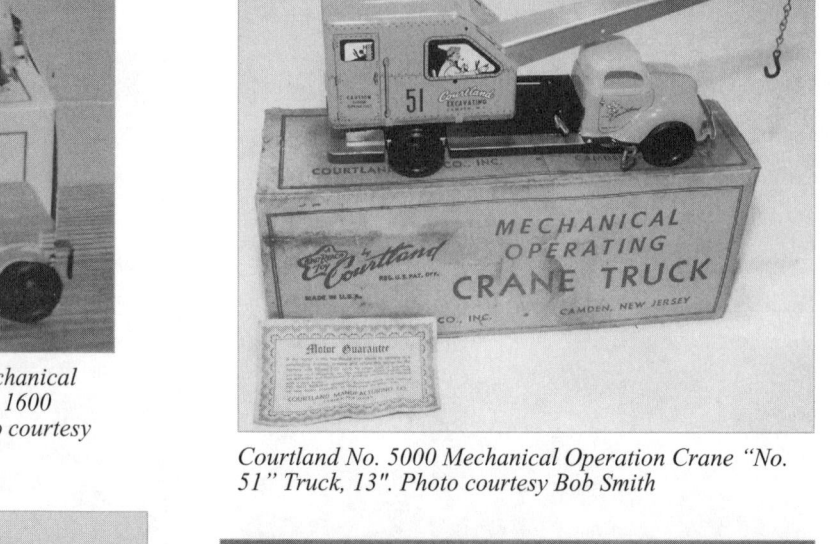

Courtland No. 5000 Mechanical Operation Crane "No.
51" Truck, 13". Photo courtesy Bob Smith

Courtland No. 6050 Mechanical Farm Tractor,
7-1/2". Photo courtesy Continental Hobby House

Courtland No. 2150 Mechanical Emergency Rescue Squad
Tractor-Trailer, 13". Photo courtesy Joe and Sharon Freed

Courtland No. 6075 Mechanical Tractor w/tin wheels.
Photo courtesy Joe and Sharon Freed

Courtland No. 7000 Mechanical Fire Chief Car, with siren,
7-1/4". Photo courtesy Joe and Sharon Freed

	C6	C8	C10
Mechanical Moving and Storage Truck, w/No. 130 lithographed on the sides of the truck bed	50	125	275
Mechanical No. 51 Steam Shovel, No. 5200, 15-1/2" long, 3-3/4" wide, 9-1/2" high	135	185	235
Mechanical Open Van Tractor-Trailer, No. 2300, 13" long, 3" wide, 3-1/4" high	50	125	275
Mechanical Open Van Tractor-Trailer, No. 2350, 13" long, 3" wide, 3-1/4" high	30	75	225
Mechanical Operation, No. 5000, "No. 51" Crane Truck, 13" long, 3-5/8" wide, 5" high	75	150	300
Mechanical Road Roller Truck, No. 1500, 9" long, 3" wide, 3-1/4" high	30	75	225
Mechanical Road Roller Truck, No. 3000 9" long, 3" wide, 3-1/4" high	30	75	225
Mechanical Side Tipper Tractor-Trailer, No. 2700, 13" long, 3" high, 3-1/4" wide	30	75	225

	C6	C8	C10
Mechanical Side Tipper Tractor-Trailer, No. 3900, "Black Diamond Coal Company- 340," 13" long, 3" high, 3-1/4" wide	150	250	325
Mechanical Stake Bed Truck, No. 3200, 7" long, 3" wide, 3-1/4" high	50	100	250
Mechanical State Police Car w/siren, No. 7500, 7-1/4" long, 3-1/4" wide, 2-3/4" high	50	100	250
Mechanical Trailer Tow Truck, No. 2400, 13" long, 3" wide, 3-1/4" high	75	150	300
Mechanical Trailer-Truck, No. 1200, 1947, 13" long, 3" wide, 3-1/4" high	30	75	225
Mechanical Train Set, No. 9000, engine and two gondolas	125	175	250
Mechanical Truck Set, No. 500, w/box, four trucks, assorted, Nos. 2000, 2100, 2200, 2300	200	400	NPF
Modern Bakery Delivery Sedan, No. 4000, 7-1/4" long, 3-1/4" wide, 2-3/4" high	40	100	250

Courtland No. 500 Mechanical Truck Set, box, four trucks. Photo courtesy Joe and Sharon Freed

Courtland No. 2050 Mechanical Milk Tractor-Trailer, American Dairies, 13". Photo courtesy Joe and Sharon Freed

Courtland No. 3900 Mechanical Side Tipper Tractor-Trailer, 13". Photo courtesy Joe and Sharon Freed

Courtland No. 2200 Mechanical Logging Tractor-Trailer, 13". Photo courtesy Joe and Sharon Freed

Courtland No. 1600 Mechanical Dump Truck, 7". Photo courtesy Joe and Sharon Freed

	C6	C8	C10
Modern Decorators Pickup, No. 4500, 7-1/4" long, 3-1/4" wide, 2-3/4" high ..	50	100	200
Private Garage w/automatic door, No. 9075, 7-3/4" x 10-1/8" x 6-3/4". Since the non-powered car which accompanies this garage is found w/Courtland Toy Co., Phila. PA markings, it is quite possible that some of the 9075 garages were also manufactured	75	150	300
Traffic Signal, No. 7800, battery-powered	275	400	550
Trucking Terminal Set, No. 600, two trucks, w/box...................................	NPF	NPF	NPF

Courtland No. 2300 Mechanical Open Van Tractor-Trailer, 13". Photo courtesy Joe and Sharon Freed

Courtland No. 3000 Mechanical Road Roller Truck, 9". Photo courtesy Joe and Sharon Freed

Courtland No. 9000 Mechanical Train Set, 3 piece. Photo courtesy Joe and Sharon Freed

Courtland Modern Bakery Delivery Sedan, 7-1/4". Photo courtesy Continental Hobby House

Courtland No. 8500 Mechanical Chrome Trimmed Tow Truck, tow boom shows detail, 8". Photo courtesy Joe and Sharon Freed

COX (L.M. COX MFG. CO.)

(See also Thimble-Drome)

Founded by Leroy M. Cox in 1946, the L.M. Cox Co. of Santa Ana, California, was the world's largest manufacturer of miniature gas engines in the post-World War II period. Cox began making wooden pop-guns in his home in 1945 and developed a small metal toy race car for his son which led to an expansion of his operation and eventual incorporation. When hobbyists began putting small gas engines in his 12" replica racer, he decided to start selling them with engines.

Cox developed his first 1/20 cid engine and called it the 1-A engine. Sensing a promising future in motorized toys, Cox sunk $75,000 into development, and in 1951, the Space Bug was released as the first Thimble Drome engine. The .049 cid engine was an instant success.

The engine was applied to a variety of cars, planes, and even a hydroplane, and Cox models earned a place in toy history.

	C6	C8	C10
Adam 12, gas powered	90	135	180
Army Command Jeep, gas powered, early 1970s, 12" long	70	112	150
Buck Rogers Invader, gas powered, spaceship flies in the air, 1979	20	40	60
Chaparral Race Car, Jim Hall, gas powered	95	200	400
Corvette, gas powered, 1966, 8" long	90	135	180
Doodle-Bug Racing Car, marked "Thimble Drome Champion" on baseplate, gas powered, box reads "Roy Cox Thimble Drome;"			
Doodle-Bug Ready-to-go Kit; Racing Car;"	125	285	525
Dune Buggy, No. 3700, gas powered, 1960s	85	165	245
Ford GT-40, gas powered	100	185	300
Ford Pinto, gas powered, plastic body, rubber tires, 1972, 12" long	40	90	145
Indy 500 Pace Car, Dan Gurney Indy Eagle racer, gas powered, 1967	95	175	265
Matador, gas powered	40	90	135
Mercedes-Benz Grand Prix Racer, Thimble Drome race car, gas powered, race car	175	325	500
O-Forty-Five Special, Thimble Drome race car, gas powered, teather, No. S-45, 1949	200	410	650
Pinto Funny Car, "Super Funnies" series, plastic body, gas powered, 1972, 12" long	25	60	90
Vega Funny Car, "Super Funnies" series, gas powered, 12" long	25	60	90
Volkswagen, gas powered	35	50	75

CRAFTOYS

Craftoys, a small Omaha, Nebraska, firm, had a brief career casting slush-mold vehicles before World War II when the need for lead brought the pot metal era to a long halt. Craftoys acquired some of their molds when Ralstoy was reorganizing in 1940.

Contributor: Perry R. Eichor, 703 North Almond Drive, Simpsonville, SC 29681 and the late Fred Maxwell.

Collector's Notes

- No. 92 sedan has the same number as a Best Toy Coupe, but they are not the same car.
- No. 100 racer is not the same as the Best Toy No. 100 sedan.
- Second-hand Kansas Toy molds were used for No. 78 mixer, No. 81 racer, No. 102 gasoline semi-tanker, No. 101 fire truck, No. 103 speed car, No. 104 oil truck, and No. 105 station wagon, possibly came from Ralstoy.
- The ancestry of Kansas Toy is evident in the No. 17 tractor and the freight-train set. The designs of the RR coal car, stockcar, and tank car were changed.
- These catalog numbers may or may not be found on the toys. Black rubber wheels are seen to be characteristic of this line, but they are not exclusive with Craftoy.

	C6	C8	C10
Cement Mixer, No. 78, two open windows, marked "Made in USA," 3-3/4" long	20	40	60
Fire Truck, No. 101, Hose Truck or Insurance Patrol, four open windows, 4-1/2" long	40	60	80
Oil Truck, No. 104, 1938 International (?), COE, two open windows, marked "Gas," "Oil" tanker, 3-3/4"	50	80	90

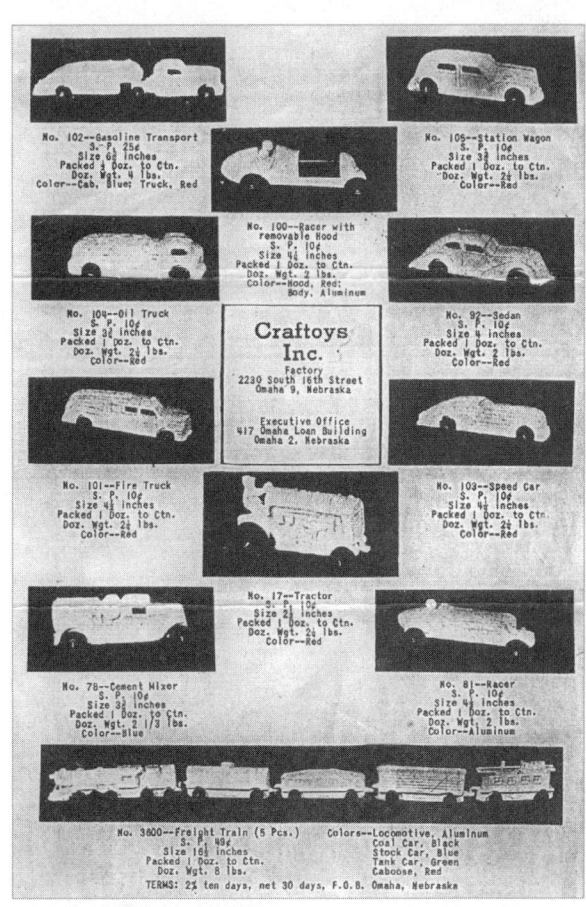

An original Craftoys flyer.

Craftoy Oil Truck, No. 104, tanker, two open windows, 3-3/4". Photo courtesy Fred Maxwell

Top to bottom: Craftoy Racer, No. 100, Indy type, driver, removable tin hood, rounded nose, 4-1/4"; Racer, slanted nose, tin hood, 3-3/4". Photo courtesy Perry Eichor

	C6	C8	C10
Racer, no number, Indy type, driver, removable tin hood, slanted nose, available as a reproduction, 3-3/4" long	50	70	80
Racer, No. 100, Indy type, driver, removable tin hood, rounded nose available as a reproduction, 4-1/4" long	35	50	70
Racer, No. 81, Miller FWD Indy racer, marked "Made in USA", 4-1/2"	30	60	90
Sedan, No. 92, streamlined two-door sedan, four open windows, screen pattern grille, 4" long	20	40	60

Craftoy Speed Car, No. 103, streamlined, closed racer, 4-1/4". Photo courtesy Perry Eichor

Craftoy Tanker, No. 103, semi-trailer, two open windows, 6-3/4". Photo courtesy Ferd Zegel

	C6	C8	C10
Speed Car, No. 103, streamlined closed racer, body trimmed in fantasy streamlines, available as a reproduction, 4-1/4" long,	45	70	95
Station Wagon, No. 105, streamlined, four open windows, 3-3/4" long	30	45	70
Tanker, No. 102, 1938, International K-Line (?), semi-trailer, two open windows, "Gasoline," See Ralstoy, 6-3/4" long	40	60	80
Tractor, No. 17, w/driver, rear wheels larger, visible engine; marked "Fordson" and "Made in USA"; 2-1/2" long	15	30	45

CRAGSTAN

Although best known for their battery-operated robots and vehicles, the Cragstan company of Japan did produce a number of toy cars with friction motors.

	C6	C8	C10
Ambulance, friction	70	105	140
Camper, two-tone green Winnebago camper, 8-1/4" long	25	50	75
Fast Freight Semi-truck, red and white, 9-1/2" long	25	50	75
Fire Chief Car, friction	82	123	165
G Men Car, tin friction, 6-1/2" long	60	90	120
Greyhound Bus, friction, 9" long	35	52	70

Cragstan G Men Car, tin friction, red, 6-1/2". Photo courtesy Ron Fink

D & L PLASTICS

	C6	**C8**	**C10**
Future Car, 1940s	20	30	40

DAISY

The Plymouth Iron Windmill Company of Plymouth, Michigan, (a town that would later become famous for its automobile manufacturers) had a long history of making metal windmills for farmers. With sales on the decline in 1886, General Manager Louis Cass Hough convinced the company to introduce a metal air rifle as a premium for those who purchased windmills.

The air rifle, dubbed "Daisy" after the slang of the day, quickly outpaced demand for windmills, and the company shifted production. By 1890, the twenty-five employees were cranking out some 50,000 Daisy air rifles. In 1895, the company name was changed to the Daisy Manufacturing Company. In the decades that followed, a variety of guns followed as Daisy embraced western and space heroes.

Daisy introduced the line of Daisy-Matic toys in 1963. It consisted of five multi-action battery-powered toys imported from Japan. They were the #60 Tractor and Trailer, #61 Cement Mixer Truck, #62 Dump

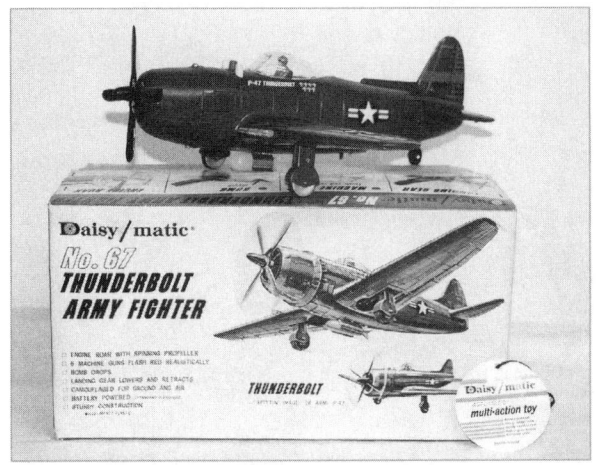

Daisy-Matic No. 67 P-47 Thunderbolt Army Fighter, solid color. Photo courtesy Darryll Jones

Daisy-Matic No. 67 P-47 Thunderbolt Army Fighter, multi-color. Photo courtesy Darryll Jones

Daisy-Matic No. 61 Cement Mixer Truck, International Harvester type. Photo courtesy Darryll Jones

Daisy-Matic No. 61 Cement Mixer Truck, GMC type. Photo courtesy Darryll Jones

Daisy-Matic No. 66 Power Loading Daisy Farms, milk truck. Photo courtesy Darryll Jones

Daisy-Matic No. 62 Dump Truck, International Harvester type. Photo courtesy Darryll Jones

Daisy-Matic No. 62 Dump Truck, GMC type. Photo courtesy Darryll Jones

Daisy-Matic No. 65 Power-Loading Cargo Truck. Photo courtesy Darryll Jones

Truck, #63 Highway Tow Truck, and #64 Tank. Ranging in price from $5-7, the toys enjoyed only a limited run and were discontinued in 1966.

Contributor: Darryll Jones, 4946-W Willis Rd., Georgetown, IN 47122-9164

	C6	C8	C10
Daisy-Matic #60 Farm Tractor & Trailer w/driver, battery-operated, moves forward & reverse, steers, exhaust stack smokes, pulls trailer, 20" long x 5" wide			500
Daisy-Matic #61 Cement Mixer GMC type, battery-operated, moves forward & reverse, mixer turns automatically, headlights work, bed raises & lowers, steers, 12" long x 5" wide			295
Daisy-Matic #61 Cement Mixer I-H type, battery-operated, moves forward & reverse, mixer turns automatically, engine flashes and clicks, bed raises & lowers, steers, 12" long x 5" wide			295
Daisy-Matic #62 Dump Truck GMC type, battery-operated, moves forward & reverse, bed raises & dumps automatically, headlights work, steers, 12" long x 5" wide			295
Daisy-Matic #62 Dump Truck I-H type, battery-operated, moves forward & reverse, bed raises & dumps automatically, engine flashes and clicks, steers, 12" long x 5" wide			295
Daisy-Matic #63 Highway Tow Truck, battery-operated, moves forward & reverse, boom raises & lowers, chain winch feeds/retracts, red roof light flashes, steers, 12" long x 5" wide			250
Daisy-Matic #64 Rapid Fire Tank, battery-operated, plastic, moves forward & reverse, shoots roll caps automatically, muzzle smokes, 10" long x 4-3/4" wide			220
Daisy-Matic #64 Thunder Cap Tank, battery-operated, plastic, moves forward & reverse, shoots roll caps automatically, muzzle smokes, 10" long x 4-3/4" wide			220

Daisy-Matic No. 76 Army Spotlight Truck. Photo courtesy Darryll Jones

Daisy-Matic No. 64 Thundercap Army Tank. Photo courtesy Darryll Jones

Daisy-Matic No. 68 Military Flatbed truck w/Tank. Photo courtesy Darryll Jones

Daisy-Matic No. 60 Farm Tractor 'n Trailer. Photo courtesy Darryll Jones

Daisy-Matic No. 64 Rapid Fire Tank. Photo courtesy Darryll Jones

Daisy-Matic No. 63 Highway Tow Truck. Photo courtesy Darryll Jones

Daisy-Matic No. 74 Super Tank. Photo courtesy Darryll Jones

	C6	C8	C10
Daisy-Matic #65 Power Loading Cargo Truck, battery-operated, moves forward & reverse, steers, tailgate lowers, conveyor runs forward & reverse, 5 Daisy cardboard crates, 10-1/2" long x 4" wide			275
Daisy-Matic #66 Power Loading Daisy Farms Truck, battery-operated, moves forward & reverse, steers, tailgate lowers, conveyor runs forward & reverse, 5 milk containers, 10-1/2" long x 4" wide			320
Daisy-Matic #67 Thunderbolt Army Fighter P-47, battery-operated, one color, engine sound w/spinning propeller, landing gear lowers & retracts, taxi's with steering, machine guns flash w/sound, drops bomb, 13-1/2" long x 14-1/2" wingspan			450
Daisy-Matic #67 Thunderbolt Army Fighter P-47 multi-color, battery-operated, engine sound w/spinning propeller, landing gear			

	C6	C8	C10
lowers & retracts, taxi's with steering, machine guns flash w/sound, drops bomb, 13-1/2" long x 14-1/2" wingspan			450
Daisy-Matic #68 Military Flatbed w/Tank, friction drive truck, #64 Tank unloads from trailer, 21" long, 5" wide			450
Daisy-Matic #74 Super Tank, battery-operated, turret revolves, machine guns flash, shoots shells from cannon, moves forward & spins, shoots roll caps, cannon raises & lowers			400
Daisy-Matic #76 Army Spotlight Truck, battery-operated, moves forward & reverse, spotlight turns 360 degrees automatically, spotlight raises & lowers, 12" long x 5" wide			325
Daisy-Matic #80 Remote Missile Tank, battery-operated, tin litho w/ targets, moves forward & reverse, turret rotates by remote 360 degrees, fires rubber-tipped missile by remote, 10-1/2" long x 5" wide			225

DAYTIME LINES

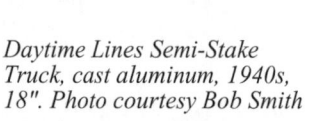

	C6	C8	C10
Semi-Stake Truck, cast aluminum, 1940s, 18" long	300	425	600
Tractor Trailer, 1940s	200	300	400

Daytime Lines Semi-Stake Truck, cast aluminum, 1940s, 18". Photo courtesy Bob Smith

DAYTON FRICTION TOY WORKS

(See David P. Clark history)

	C6	C8	C10
Armored Car, flywheel drive, sheet metal construction, red and gold, c.1909, 11" long	300	500	800
Bus, "The American Deluxe" sticker on side, 1920s, 27" long	500	750	1300
Coal and Ice Truck, tin, friction, c.1920	300	500	800
Coupe, c.1920, 12-1/2" long	450	600	1000
Coupe, pressed steel, 1928, 12" long	225	300	650
Coupe, tin, friction, 17" long	550	700	1100
Dayton Friction, pressed steel, rubber tires, 1920s, 14-1/2" long	300	450	750
Delivery Van, friction	300	450	750
Dump Truck	425	600	950
Fire Ladder Truck, friction, 22" long	300	400	750
Fire Ladder Truck, pressed steel, rubber tires, driver, spoke wheels, two ladders, 18" long	250	400	800

Dayton Friction Car, c.1914. Photo courtesy Tim Oei

	C6	C8	C10
Fire Pumper Truck, flywheel drive, sheet metal construction, white/gold, c.1909, 14-3/4" long	500	650	1000
Friction Car, 1914	NPF	NPF	NPF
Roadster, 14" long	250	350	600
Seven-Passenger Touring Car, flywheel drive, sheet metal contstruction, red and gold, patent date April 2, 1909, 13-1/4" long	200	275	500

	C6	C8	C10
Stake Truck, spoke wheels, driver	350	500	800
Touring Car, unpowered, 13-1/2" long	350	500	800

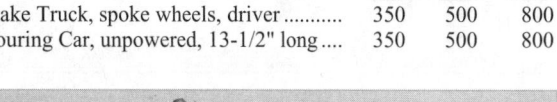

Dayton Seven-Passenger Touring Car, circa 1909, 13-1/4". Photo courtesy Bob Smith

Dayton Armored Car, circa 1909, 11". Photo courtesy Bob Smith

Dayton Fire Pumper Truck, white and gold, circa 1909, 14-3/4". Photo courtesy Bob Smith

Dayton Coupe, tin, friction, 17". Photo courtesy Terry Sells

DELUXE

The Deluxe Game Co. manufactured a variety of service station playsets from the late 1940s to the early 1950s. The company was based in Richmond Hill, Long Island, New York.

	C6	C8	C10
DeLuxe Service Station, 1940s	40	75	100

Deluxe Service Station, with box, 1940s. Photo courtesy Ron Fink

DENT HARDWARE COMPANY

Dent, of Fullerton, Pennsylvania, was in business from 1895-1973. Henry H. Dent, with four partners, was the owner. Dent is known for particularly fine castings in its vehicles. It was also one of the first manufacturers to try (with little success) aluminum toys (in the 1920s). Toys seem to have been phased out during the Depression, sometime near 1937. Dent toys are difficult to identify due to the fact that few, if any, of its toys are marked.

	C6	C8	C10
American Oil Co. Truck, cast-iron, approx. 10-1/2" long	800	1250	1875
American Oil Truck, cast-iron, 15" long	1200	2000	300
Breyer's Ice Cream Truck, cast-iron, removable doors, 1932, 8-1/2" long	700	1150	1700
Bus, cast-iron, 10-1/2" long	500	850	900
Bus, cast-iron, 6-1/4" long	350	500	750
Bus Line, cast-iron, 9" long	450	600	1250
Coast to Coast Bus, cast-iron, 10" long	300	450	650
Coast to Coast Bus, cast-iron, 7-1/2" long	125	175	275

	C6	C8	C10
Coast to Coast Bus, cast-iron, c.1925, 15" long	700	1000	1600
Convertible, cast-iron	400	700	1000
Coupe, cast-iron, 5" long	125	175	250
Dump Truck, cast-iron, C-cab, 15-1/4"	800	1250	2000
Dump Truck, No. 637, cast-iron, no cab all open driver's compartment w/driver, red w/bronze trim, rubber tires, spoke wheels, 8-1/4" long	300	650	1000
Express J&B Stakebed Truck, cast-iron, driver, 1915, 14-1/2"	500	800	1250
Fire Chief, No. 693, cast-iron, sedan in bright red w/bronze trim, bell on hood, driver, 5-1/2" long, c. 1932	250	500	800
Fire Engine, No. 290, cast-iron, bright red w/bronze trim, rubber tires, pumper, c. 1932, 8-1/2" long	250	500	800
Fire Engine, No. 680, cast-iron, bright red, rubber tires, pumper, c. 1932, 6-1/2" long	250	500	800
Fire Ladder Truck, cast-iron, w/driver in front and rear, c. 1915, 8-1/2" long	400	625	925

Dent "American Oil Co.," cast iron, 10-1/2". Photo courtesy Phillips, N.Y.

Another Dent "American Oil" Truck. Photo courtesy Bertoia Auctions

Left to right: Pattern for Dent "Coast to Coast" Bus, circa 1925, 15"; "Public Service" Bus, circa 1926, 13-1/2"; brass pattern for "Public Service" Bus. Photo courtesy Bertoia Auctions

Dent "American Oil" Truck, 15". Photo courtesy Bertoia Auctions

Dent "Breyer's Ice Cream," removable doors, 1932, 8-1/2". Photo courtesy Bertoia Auctions

Dent "New York-Chicago" Bus, 10-1/4". Photo courtesy Bertoia Auctions

	C6	C8	C10
Fire Pumper, cast-iron, normal-sized driver, hose, 11" long	450	800	1250
Fire Pumper, cast-iron, tiny driver, early, 11" long	600	1100	1750
Fire Truck, cast-iron, 7" long	125	200	325
Fire Truck, w/ladder and men, cast-iron, 18" long	800	1250	1900
Fordson Tractor, cast-iron	200	350	525
Freeman's Dairy Truck, cast-iron, sliding doors, milkman, 6"	650	1150	1750
Hose Reeler, cast-iron, w/men, cast iron, large	450	700	1100
Ice Truck, cast-iron, 10" long	400	625	1000
Ice Truck, cast-iron, 6" long	150	225	350
Interburban bus, cast-iron, 10-1/2" long	400	700	1100
Interburban bus, cast-iron, 9" long	225	350	550
La Salle, cast-iron, 4-1/4" long	425	700	975
La Salle Panel Truck, cast-iron	425	700	975
Ladder Truck, cast-iron, 12" long	275	425	625
Ladder Truck, cast-iron, two drivers, 10" long	225	350	550
Mack Cement Truck, cast-iron, extremely rare, 11-1/4" long; auctioned in 1992 in Good-Very Good condition			47,300
Mack Contractor's Truck, No. 688, cast-iron, open cab, three dumping buckets in bed, solid rubber tires, 10-1/2" long	1000	2000	3000
Mack Contractor's Truck, No. 707, cast-iron, two dumping buckets in bed, solid rubber tires, 7-1/2" long	800	1800	2800
Mack Dump Truck, cast-iron, iron wheels, c.1925, 4-1/2" long	50	75	125
Mack Express State Truck, cast-iron	1500	2500	4400
Mack Express Van, No. 685, cast-iron, open cab, solid rubber tires, 6-1/4" long, c. 1932	2000	4500	9900
Mack Tank Truck, cast-iron	1500	2500	3960
Model T Sedan, cast-iron, two door, iron wheels, c.1925	125	175	275
New York-Chicago Bus, cast-iron, 10-1/4" long	350	550	800
Patrol, cast-iron, 6-1/2" long	125	175	275
Phantom, cast-iron, driver	160	250	350
Pioneer Fire Ladder Truck, cast-iron, driver, 13-1/4" long	1200	2000	3250
Police Patrol, cast-iron, 8-3/4" long	700	1125	1650
Public Service Bus, cast-iron, c.1926, 13-1/2" long	1750	3000	4750
REO Speed Wagon, No. 631, cast-iron, no cab all open driver's compartment w/driver, small stake bed, letters "REO" on side, 6-1/4" long, c. 1932	300	650	1000
Road Roller, cast-iron, 4-1/2" long	70	100	160
Road Sweeper, cast-iron	1200	2000	3700
Runabout, cast-iron, driver, tiller, 6" long	200	350	475
Sedan, cast-iron, 1920s, 4-1/2" long	80	140	220
Sedan, cast-iron, 1920s, 7-1/2" long	400	600	850
Sedan, cast-iron, spare tire, has stop and go light, full bumpers on front, 7-1/2" long	800	1250	1800
Stake Truck, cast-iron, driver, four tin milk cans, 15-1/2" long	2000	3600	5500
Steam Roller, No. 717, cast-iron, moving piston rods, 7" long	80	140	200
Steam Roller, No. 718, cast-iron, no moving piston, 5" long	80	140	200
Touring Car, cast-iron, driver and passenger, 12" long	450	700	1100
Touring Car, cast-iron, passengers, driver, 9-1/4" long	500	800	1200

Dent "Police Patrol," 8-3/4". Photo courtesy Phillips, N.Y.

Dent "Public Service" Bus, 1920s, 13-1/2". Photo courtesy Bertoia Auctions

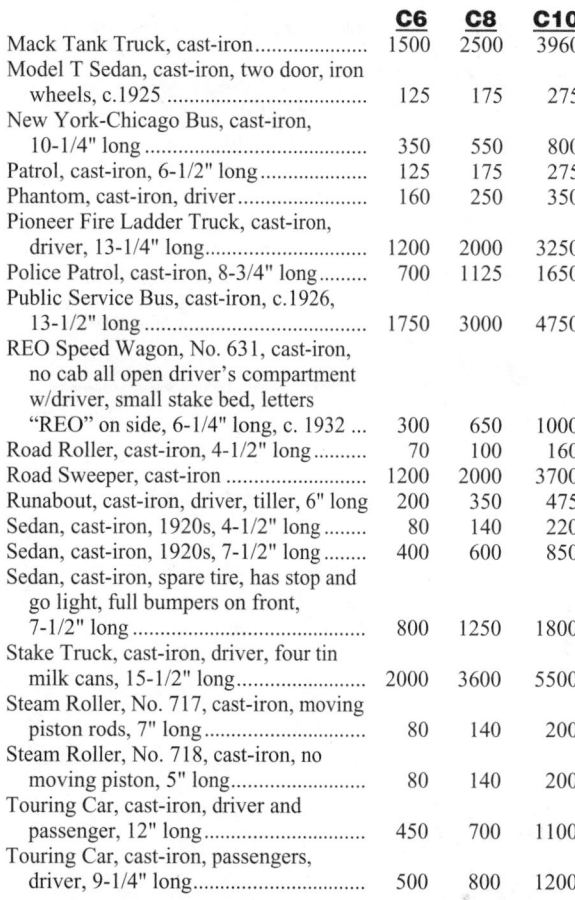

Dent "Pioneer" Fire Ladder Truck, driver, 13-1/4". Photo courtesy Bertoia Auctions

Dent Road Sweeper. Photo courtesy Bertoia Auctions

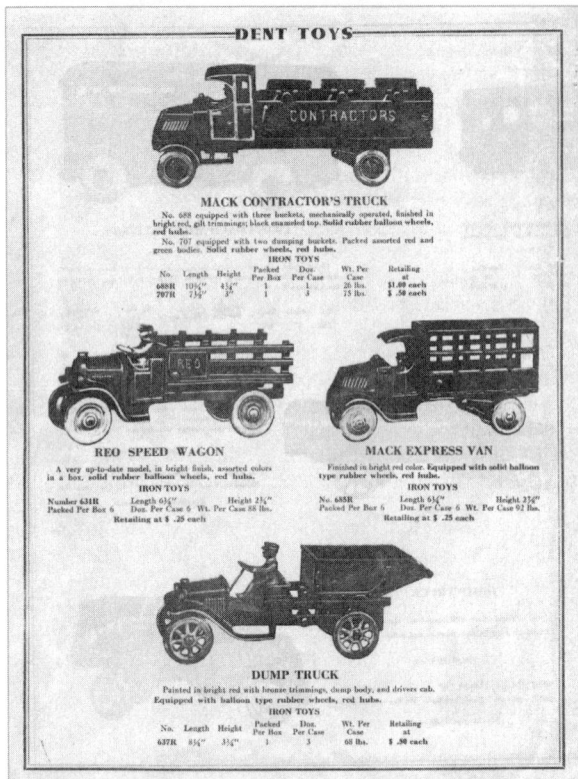

Dent offered a variety of Mack-based trucks in 1932. The catalog shows a Dump Truck, Express Van, Contractors Truck, and REO Speed Wagon.

Dent Road Roller, 4-1/2". Photo courtesy Bertoia Auctions

Dent Junior Supply Co. "New York-Philadelphia," 1920s, 16". Photo courtesy Sotheby's New York

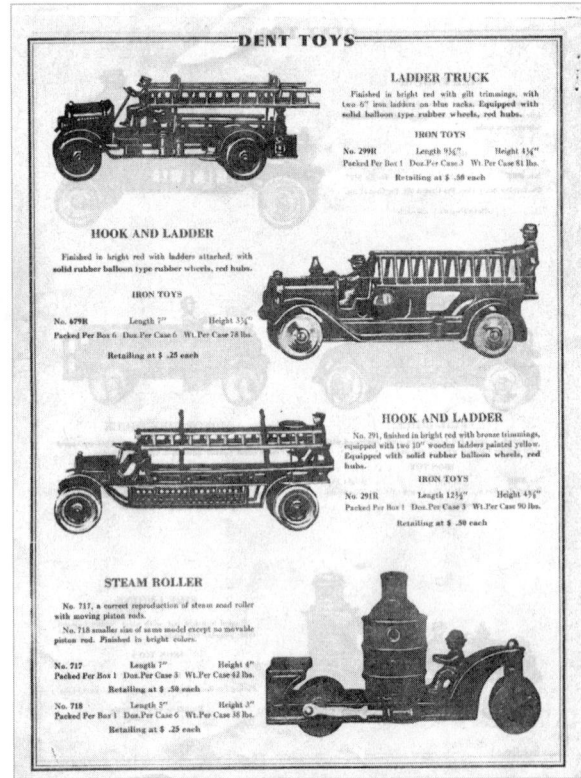

The 1932 Dent catalog shos a Ladder Truck, a pair of Hook and Ladder Trucks, and a Steam Roller.

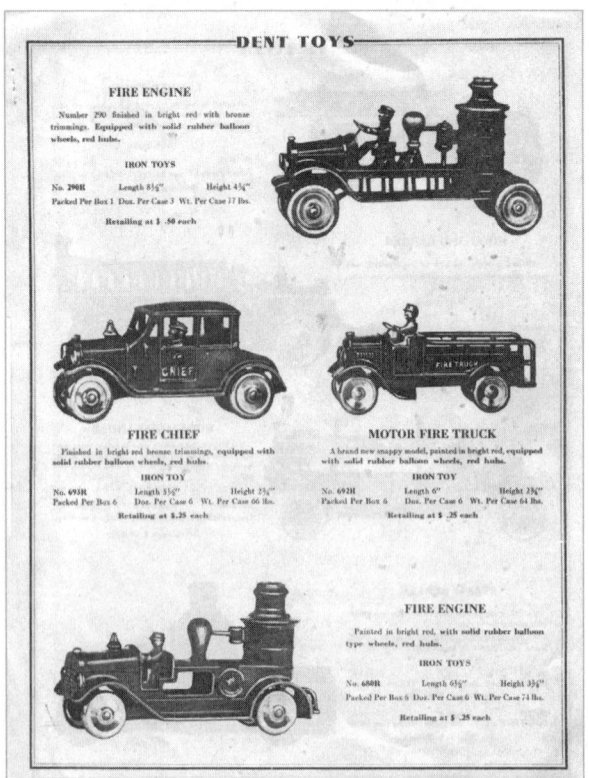

The 1930 Dent catalog also shows a pair of Fire Engines, a Fire Chief Car, and a Motor Fire Truck.

	C6	C8	C10
Truck, cast-iron, marked "Junior Supply Co. New York Philadelphia," c.1923, 16" long	2000	2500	5250
Valley View Dairy, cast-iron, 8" long	500	900	1500
Yellow Cab, cast-iron, approx. 7-3/4" long	800	1250	1800

Dent "Freeman's Dairy" Truck. 6". Photo courtesy Bertoia Auctions

Dent "Valley View Dairy," 8". Photo courtesy Bertoia Auctions

Left to right: Dent Touring Car, driver, passengers, 9-1/4"; Touring Car, driver and passenger, 12". Photo courtesy Bertoia Auctions

Another look at the Dent Junior Supply Co. "New York-Philadelphia" truck. Photo courtesy Sotheby's New York

DINKY

When Dinky Toys were first issued in 1933, they were intended to add a touch of realism to the Hornby train models. The first offering to the public was a set of six small accessories referred to as Model Miniatures and were commonly known as the 22 Series.

The year 1937 saw the introduction of what developed into the finest range of mass-market die-cast military toys ever produced until the birth of Solido. And 1938 saw further consolidation of the vehicle range, which by then contained almost three varieties. During World War II, the Dinky operations were interrupted by the war effort. One of the few new or adapted models during this period was a replica of a petrol tanker painted gray with the word "pool" in white on its sides. The unfortunate part of this period was that many of the toy dies were lost during the equipment shuffling to make room for the wartime production. Christmas 1945 saw production get underway again, and some fifty different toy models went out to the retailers for sale to the public. The hopes for a quick return to the prewar status quo were, however, not to be fulfilled, as metal alloys were put to priority use for much-needed domestic products, and to feed the giant export projects on which the British economy now depended for its survival.

However, by 1952 the postwar boom was gathering momentum as railway accessories and model planes were re-introduced. New products flowed from the design studios to the production lines until finally, in 1954, the production of the first new group of army vehicles arrived on the scene. Also, one of the most significant events of that year for future collectors was the renumbering of all models. The suffix system was no longer manageable, and a lock-number system was allocated to types of vehicles. The larger-scale "Super" Dinky Toys in blue striped boxes with a white background were also introduced in the mid-1950s. It was 1958 before Dinky replied to the challenge of domestic competition from Corgi, which entered the market in 1956, by fitting special features to their models. Pausing for a breath from the introduction of gimmicks to keep abreast of their competition, in 1961, the company produced twenty or so new models and changed over from plain to tread tires on all their vehicles (although military models had them since the mid-1950s).

In June 1969, the company again made a significant change in its vehicle products to attempt to stay with the competition—the introduction of speed wheels, which were eventually to become standard on everything. Six years earlier, after the takeover by Lines Bros., the name of the firm was changed to "Meccano-Triang Ltd." A bad omen, for, in 1971, after a general recession in the toy trade, the company's bank loans were recalled and the whole of the Lines Group went into liquidation. The Meccano assets were transferred to a new company, Maoford, Ltd., which was subsequently named "Meccano (1971) Ltd." New toys were desperately needed. In 1972, the company went into the kit business for the first time.

But by now, the hand of doom was resting on production and even the introduction of space toys would not delay the inevitable, as the Binns Road factory was effectively closed on November 30, 1979. The closure did not save the parent company, which was also having difficulty in the American market. Although Dinky Toy continued to be produced elsewhere for several years, the eventual low labor cost and success of mass-plastic extrusion manufacturing from the Asian export market was the real culprit behind the demise of one of the English-speaking world's finest toy manufacturers, who, in its heyday, produced about three thousand varieties of transportation toys during a marvelous history of almost fifty years in England, France, and India.

Condition

The following is a guide for those with items in less than Mint in Box (C10), Near Mint with Box (C8) and Excellent with Box (C6) condition.

- Near Mint, without box. Some rust, no scratches, all decals in place, deduct thirty percent from C10 value.
- Very Good with box. Some rust, scratched, all decals, no paint missing, deduct forty-five percent from the C10 value.
- Very Good without box. Some rust, scratches, no missing parts or paint, deduct fifty-five percent from the C10 value.
- Good without box. Rust, paint chipped, decals partially missing, no missing parts, deduct sixty per cent from the C10.
- Fair without box. Rusted wheels axle and base, scratches, chipped, missing paint, decals gone missing tires or chains, but not broken, paint still good for the purpose of reconditioning; deduct fifty to sixth percent from the C10 value.
- Items with broken or missing components or with pieces having less than forty percent of the original paint gone have no real value to the collector, unless reconditioned, and then they should only bring lift percent of the C6 value. In addition, it should also be noted that boxes can bring $3 to $50, depending or age and condition

Note: Early military Dinky, except for boxed sets were sold in yellow boxes with black lettering, six or twelve pieces to the box. It should also be noted that prewar items differed from reissue as follows-prewar smooth hubcaps; postwar, rimmed hub caps.

Dinky Chrysler Airflow, No. 30A.

Dinky Panhard Esso Tanker, No. 32C, 1950s.

Dinky B.E.V. Truck, No. 14A/400, 1954-60.

Dinky Search Light Lorry, No. 22S, 1935-41. Photo courtesy W. Kilborn Collection

	C6	C8	C10
No. 003 Chevrolet Impala, 1965-67.........	40	70	100
No. 005 Ford Thunderbird, 1965-67........	40	70	100
No. 006 Rambler, 1965-67.......................	40	70	100
No. 014A B.E.V. Electric Truck, 1948-53	25	50	70
No. 014C Coventry Fork Lift, 1949-53, orange body...................................	35	75	100
No. 022A Maserati Sport 2000, 1958, red body..	55	110	150
No. 022C Motor Truck, 1933-35, blue cab, red or tan body...........................	150	350	650
No. 022C Motor Truck, 1935-40, 1946-50, red, green or blue body........	80	125	200
No. 022F Army Tank, 1933-40, gray or orange body.....................................	75	150	200
No. 022S Search Light Lorry, 1939-40, six to a box, green body.......................	150	250	350
No. 023G Cooper Bristol Racing Car, 1953, green body, Grand Prix racer.....	55	110	150
No. 023H Ferrari Racer, 1953, blue body, Grand Prix racer.................................	35	75	100
No. 023J H.W.M. Racing Car, 1953, green body...................................	55	110	150
No. 023N Maserati Racer, 1953, red body, white stripe.................................	25	70	140
No. 023S Streamlined Racer, 1938-40, 1948-53, land speed record car, red most valuable color.................................	20	40	80
No. 024A New Yorker Convertible, 1956-58, white tires	65	130	175
No. 024B/521 Peugeot, 1956-59, sedan, white tires..............................	55	110	150
No. 024C Citroën DS19, 1956-59, sedan, white tires...	65	132	180

	C6	C8	C10
No. 024C Town Car, 1934-40, blue or green body	85	140	210
No. 024D Plymouth Belvedere, 1957-59.	35	150	300
No. 024E Renault Dauphine, 1957-59	25	75	150
No. 024H Mercedes 190SL, 1958-59, coupe, black tires	50	100	130
No. 024L 2CV Vespa, 1959, blue or orange body, black tires	75	150	200
No. 024M Willy's Jeep, 1946-49, French, open..	100	200	300
No. 024R Peugeot 203 Berline Saloon, 1951-59...	25	100	200
No. 024T Citroen 2CV, 1952-59	25	80	160
No. 024U Simca 9 Arnode, 1953-59, French, sedan, white tires	55	110	150
No. 024X Ford Vedette, 1954-56, French, sedan, gray or navy blue body, white tires	65	130	165
No. 024XT Ford Vedette Taxi, 1956-59..	60	95	150
No. 024Y Studebaker Commander, 1955-59, French, coupe, white tires.....	45	95	125
No. 025B Covered Wagon, 1934-40, 1946-50, blue, gray, green or yellow body	65	115	160
No. 025B Covered Wagon, 1934-40, 1946-50, Carter Paterson logo	150	300	750
No. 025D Citroen 2CV Fire Van, 1959-63	60	130	250
No. 025D Petrol Wagon, 1934-40, 1946-50, gasoline tanker, variety of colors..	150	300	500

Dinky Rolls Royce, No. 30B, 1946-50.

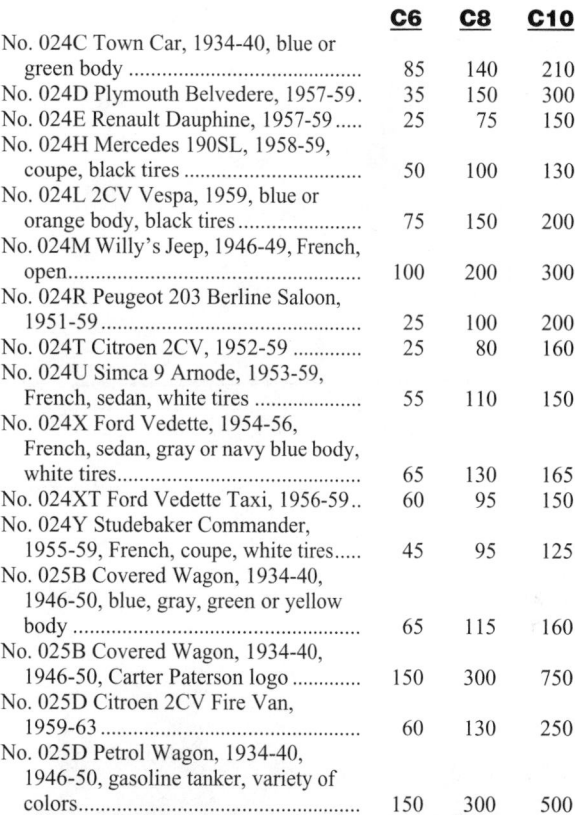

Dinky Range Rover Ambulance, No. 268.

Top to bottom: French Dinky Berliet Army Truck, No. 80D/818, 1958-67; 155mmn Field gun, No. 80E/819, 1973-77. Photo courtesy W. Kilborn Collection

Top row, left to right: French Dinky AMX 13 Char Tank, No. 80C, 1958-67; AMEX Self Propelled Gun, No. 813, 1965. Bottom: Panhard ERB Tank in box, No. 80A, 1957-63. Photo courtesy W. Kilborn Collection

Top to bottom: French Dinky 155mm Field gun No. 80E, 1958-67; Berliet Gazelle Truck, No. 824, 1963. Photo courtesy W. Kilborn Collection

Dinky Medium Tank, with markings, No. 151A. Photo courtesy W. Kilborn Collection

Left to right: Dinky No. 157 Jaguar KX120 Coupe; No. 344 Estate Car. Photo courtesy Phillips, N.Y.

Dinky Medium Tank, without markings, No. 151A, 1930s-1940s. Photo courtesy W. Kilborn Collection

Dinky Transport Wagon, No. 151B, 1937-41. Photo courtesy W. Kilborn Collection

Dinky Light Tank, No. 152A, 1950s, reissued. Photo courtesy W. Kilborn Collection

Dinky Austin Staff Car, No. 152C, 1937-41. Photo courtesy W. Kilborn Collection

Dinky Reconnaissance Car reissue, No. 152B, 1950s. Photo courtesy W. Kilborn Collection

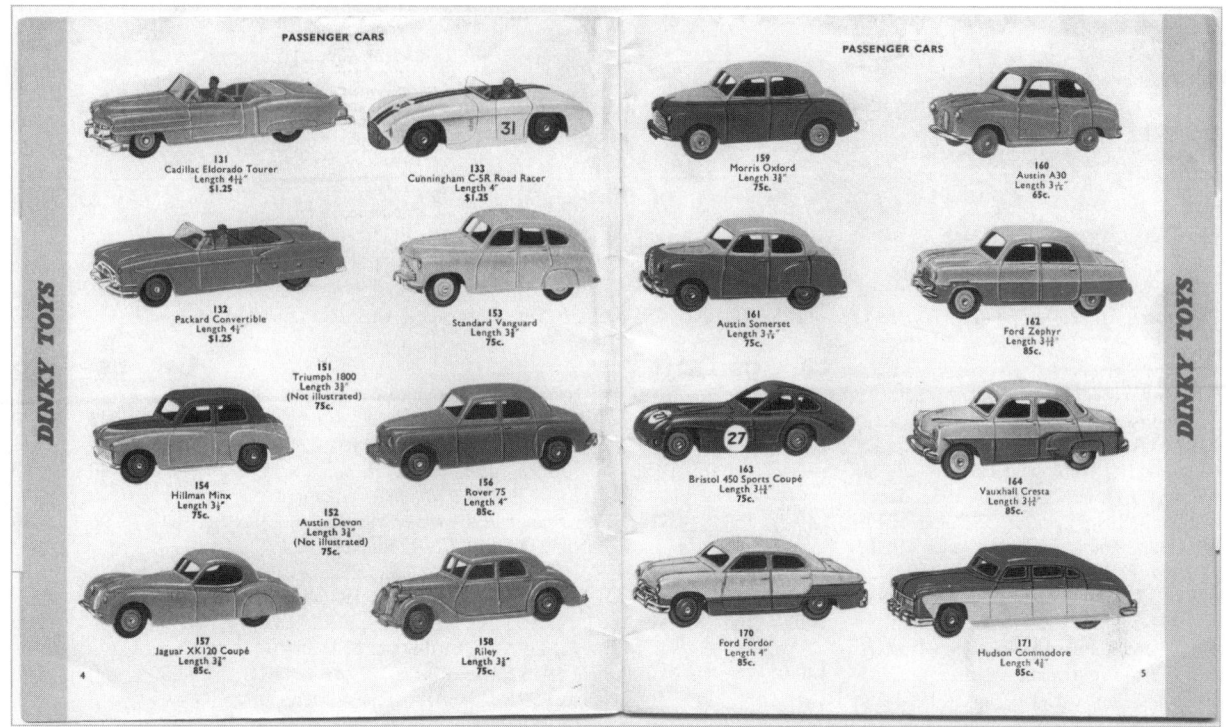

A selection of Dinky passenger cars from a Dinky Toys catalog. (Left Page); Page 5 of a Dinky Toys Catalog shows more Dinky passenger cars. (Right Page)

	C6	C8	C10
No. 025F Market Gardeners Wagon, 1935-40, 1946-49, stake truck	65	115	160
No. 025H Streamlined Fire Engine, 1936-40, 1946-53, red body	75	125	175
No. 025M Bedford Tipper, 1948-53, dump truck, black tires	40	80	100
No. 025R Forward Control Wagon, 1948-53, cab-over truck, open	35	65	90
No. 025V Bedford Refuse Truck, 1948-53, tan body, balck tires	45	85	110
No. 025WM Bedford Military Truck, 1952-53, olive body, black tires	50	125	250
No. 025X Breakdown Truck, 1950-53, wrecker, "Dinky Service" decals	50	100	150
No. 027A Massey-Harris Tractor, 1948-53, red body, driver, yellow wheel hubs, yellow "Massey-Harris" decal	50	75	125
No. 027AC Massey-Harris Tractor and Spreader, 1950, #27A Tractor and #27C Spreader, "Massey-Harris" decals	75	125	175
No. 027AK Massey-Harris Tractor and Hay Rake, 1953, #27A Tractor and #27K Hay Rake, "Massey-Harris" decal	75	125	175
No. 027C Massey-Harris Manure Spreader, 1949-53, red body, yellow "Massey-Harris" decal, 3 silver rotors	50	75	125
No. 027F 1948 Plymouth Estate Wagon, 1950-53, tan and brown body, black tires, black metal base	75	150	200
No. 027F Estate Car, 1950-53	45	75	120
No. 027G Motocart, 1949-53, 3-wheel cart, open, rear body tips	55	110	150

	C6	C8	C10
No. 027H Massey-Harris Disc Harrow, 1951-53, red and yellow body, silver discs	50	75	125
No. 027K Massey-Harris Hay Rake, 1953, red body, yellow wheels	50	75	125
No. 028B Pickfords Delivery Van, 1934-35, Type 1	300	550	1000
No. 028B Pickfords Delivery Van, 1934-35, Type 2	200	375	600
No. 028E Ensign Delivery Van, 1934, orange-red body	300	550	1000
No. 028N Atco Delivery Van, 1935-40, Type 2	200	375	850
No. 028N Atco Delivery Van, 1935-40, Type 3	135	200	350
No. 029D Autobus Parisien, 1948-51, green body	80	135	200
No. 029F/571 Autocar Chausson, 1956-60, French	70	120	200
No. 030A Chrysler Airflow, 1935-40, white tires; 1946-48, black tires	130	250	450
No. 030B Rolls Royce, 1935-40, white tires; 1946-50 black tires	45	95	125
No. 030E Breakdown Lorry, 1935-40, 1946-48, searchlight, tow hook	25	55	95
No. 030F Ambulance, 1935-40, 1946-48, rubber tires, Bentley grille	100	180	275
No. 030G Caravan, 1936-40	50	100	150
No. 030HM Daimler Military Ambulance, 1951-53, same casting as 30H, olive green body	80	125	250
No. 030R Thames Flat Truck, 1951-53, red or green body	45	75	110
No. 030SM Austin Military Truck, 1951-53, same casting as 30S, olive green body	80	125	250

Left to right: No. 174 Dinky Hudson Hornet Sedan; No. 172 Studebaker. Photo courtesy Phillips, N.Y.

	C6	C8	C10
No. 030W Electric Articulated Truck, 1953, semi w/maroon cab	50	85	120
No. 031B Trojan Dunlop Van, 1952-53, red body, "Dunlop" decals	70	110	185
No. 031D Trojan OXO Van, 1953, dark blue body..................	40	160	320
No. 032A Panhard Tractor Trailer SNCF, 1954-59, French	40	120	240
No. 032AB Panhard SNCF Semi Trailer, 1954-59, blue cab	100	165	280
No. 032AJ Panhard Kodak Semi Trailer, 1952-54, yellow cab	140	250	450
No. 032C Panhard Esso Tanker, 1954-59, French	75	120	170
No. 032D Delahaye Fire Truck, 1955-70	120	210	375
No. 033AN Simca Bailly, 1956-59, yellow cab and chassis	55	110	150
No. 033C Simca Glass Truck, 1955-59, red "Saint-Gobain" and "Miroitier" decals	75	120	170
No. 034A Berliet Dumper, 1955-59.........	15	60	120
No. 034B Royal Mail Van, 1938-40, white tires; 1948-52, black tires..........	40	55	90
No. 035A Citroen Wrecker, 1955-59, red body, "Dinky Service" decals	75	120	250
No. 036A Armstrong Siddeley, 1937-40, 1946-48	85	130	225
No. 036A Willeme Log Lorry, 1956-59, orange cab, yellow trailer, black tires, black metal base	75	120	200
No. 036B/896 Willeme Semi Trailer Truck, 1959-71..................	85	130	225
No. 036F British Salmson, 1937-40, 1946-48, four-seat open car	45	90	120
No. 036G Taxi, 1937-40, 1946-49, black tires, many colors..................	45	90	120
No. 037B Police Motorcyclist, 1938-40, blue driver	50	75	125

	C6	C8	C10
No. 037B Police Motorcyclist, 1946-48, blue driver..................	30	45	70
No. 037C Dispatch Rider RCS, 1938-40, green cycle, tan driver..................	25	40	70
No. 037N Field Marshall Tractor, 1953, orange body, silver trim	60	90	150
No. 038A/895 UNIC Bucket Truck, 1957-65	75	120	225
No. 038F Jaguar SS 100, 1946-53, sports car	30	100	200
No. 039A Packard Super 8, 1939-40, 1946-50	25	80	160
No. 039A Unic Auto Transporter, 1957-59, silver semi and cab, black tires	100	200	310
No. 039E Chrysler Royal, 1939-40, 1946-52, sedan, black tires, many body colors..................	150	300	675
No. 040E Vanguard, 1948-53	25	75	150
No. 040F Hillman Minx, 1951-53	20	75	150
No. 040H Austin Taxi, 1951-53, yellow or blue body..................	25	75	150
No. 042A Police Box, 1936-40, 1946-53, blue box..................	40	55	90
No. 042B Police Motorcycle Patrol, 1936-40, motorcycle and sidecar, two figures	50	75	125
No. 042B Police Motorcycle Patrol, 1946-53, motorcycle and sidecar, two figures	30	45	70
No. 044B Motorcycle Patrol & Sidecar, 1935-40, white tires; 1946-48, black wheels	30	50	80
No. 060Y Fuel Tender, 1938-40, red body, 3 wheels, "Shell Aviation Services" decals	100	200	400
No. 061 Ford Perfect, 1958-60, sedan, tan or gray body, gray wheels..................	40	50	80

Left to right: Dinky Transport Lorry with Search Light, No. 161A, 1939-41; Cooker, No. 151C, Water Tanker, No. 151D. Photo courtesy W. Kilborn Collection

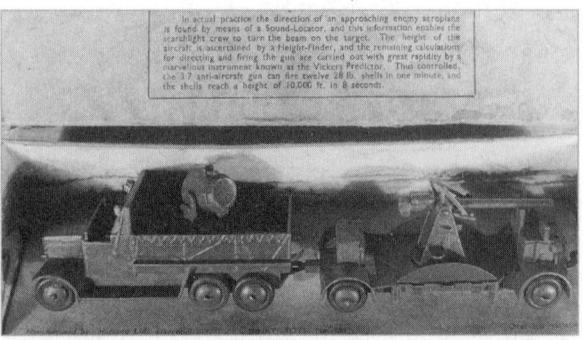

Dinky Mobile Anti-Aircraft Unit set, No. 161, 1939-41. Photo courtesy W. Kilborn Collection

	C6	C8	C10
No. 062 Singer Roadster, 1958-60, orange or tan body, gray wheels	40	50	80
No. 064 Austin Lorry, 1957-62, green body, open truck	40	55	90
No. 066 Bedford Flat Truck, 1957-60, gray body, gray wheels	45	85	110
No. 071 Dublo Volkswagen Van, 1960-64, orange body, black wheels ...	45	90	120
No. 073 Dublo Range Rover and Horse Trailer, 1960-64, green body, gray wheels, tan horse.........	45	95	125
No. 080A Panhard EBR Tank, 1958-63, French	45	55	95
No. 080B Willys Hotchkiss Jeep, 1958-60, French	45	55	95
No. 080BP Willys Hotchkiss Jeep, 1958-63, French	40	80	100
No. 080C AMX13 Char Tank, 1958-67, French, shown with 80A Panhard EBR Tank & 813 AMX Self-Propelled Gun.........	40	80	100
No. 080D Berliet 6x6 Truck, 1958-67, French, shown with 80E Howitzer	45	95	125
No. 080E 155mm Howitzer, 1958-67, French, shown with 824 Berliet Gazelle Truck.........	40	80	125
No. 080F Renault Army Ambulance, 1959-67, French, olive body, black tires.........	25	50	100
No. 100 Lady Penelope's FAB-1, 1966-76, pink limo, Lady Penelope and Parker figures, gold interior	80	135	220

	C6	C8	C10
No. 101 Sunbeam Alpine Sports Car, 1957-60, driver, black tires, plastic windshield.........	90	125	225
No. 101 Thunderbirds 2 & 4, 1974-79, spacecraft w/green body, Thunderbird 4 is a yellow plastic pod that fits into 2, from the television series; #106 has blue body	45	95	125
No. 102 Joe's Car, 1969-75, space car, retractable wings	60	90	140
No. 103 Austin-Healey 100 Sports Car, 1957-60, red or yellow body, driver	85	150	250
No. 103 Spectrum Patrol, 1968-75	80	125	220
No. 104 Spectrum Pursuit Vehicle, 1968-77, light blue body.........	100	200	300
No. 105 Triumph TR2, 1957-60, yellow or gray body, driver	95	125	225
No. 105A Garden Roller, 1948-53, red body	15	25	35
No. 106 "The Prisoner" Mini-Moke, 1968-70, white body, red and white striped canopy, black tires	115	230	340
No. 106 Austin Atlantic Convertible, 1954-58, black or white tires	40	80	100
No. 107 Sunbeam Alpine, 1955-59, racing decals, driver in racing outfit	45	95	125
No. 108 MG Midget, 1955-59, sports car, driver.........	25	100	200
No. 108 Sam's Car, 1969-75.........	65	130	165
No. 109 Austin Healey 100, 1955-59, sports car, driver	25	60	120
No. 110 Aston Martin DB5, 1966-70, red body, opening hood and doors.........	60	120	160

Dinky Lt. Dragon Set, Nos. 162A, 162B, 162C, 1939-41. Photo courtesy W. Kilborn Collection

Dinky Anti-Aircraft Gun on Trailer, No. 161B, 1950s, reissued. Photo courtesy W. Kilborn Collection

Dinky Hudson Hornet Sedan with its original box, No. 174. Photo courtesy Phillips, N.Y.

Dinky Monteverdi 375L, No. 190.

Dinky Plymouth Taxi, No. 278, 1970s.

Dinky Leland Comet Cement Truck, No. 419/533, 1950s.

Dinky Bedford Van, No. 482, 1950s.

Dinky Guy Van Slumberland, No. 514.

Dinky Ford Transit Fire Truck, No. 286, 1969-75.

Dinky B.O.A.C. Coach, No. 283.

Dinky B.O.A.C. Coach, No. 283.

Dinky Foden Flat Truck, No. 503/903.

Dinky Blaw Knox Bulldozer, No. 561.

Left to right: Dinky Austin Paramoke, No. 601, 1966-77; Scout Car, No. 673, 1953-62.

Dinky Honest John Launcher, No. 665, 1964-76. Photo courtesy W. Kilborn Collection

	C6	C8	C10
No. 111 Triumph TR2 Competition, 1956-59, racing decals, driver in racing helmet	80	125	225
No. 112 Purdy's Triumph TR7, 1978-80, yellow body	25	45	80
No. 113 MGB, 1962-68, open, red body	40	80	100
No. 114 Triumph Spitfire, 1963-70	20	75	150
No. 115 Plymouth Fury, 1965-69, sports car, driver and passenger	35	55	80
No. 116 Volvo 1800S, 1966-71	20	60	120
No. 120 Jaguar XKE, 1962-67, coupe, removable black plastic hardtop, black tires	40	85	135
No. 122 Volvo 265 Estate Car, 1977-80, station wagon, many body colors	10	15	25
No. 123 Princess 2200 HL Saloon, 1977-80, sedan, plastic base	15	20	40
No. 124 Rolls Royce Phantom V, 1977-79, limo, blue body, black tires	40	50	82
No. 127 Rolls Royce Silver Cloud, 1964-72, limo, ivory or orange interior	15	30	45
No. 128 Mercedes Benz 600, 1964-79, limo, opening trunk, hood and doors	25	35	55
No. 129 VW Sedan DeLuxe, 1965-76, sedan, blue body, opening hood and doors	45	55	95

	C6	C8	C10
No. 130 Ford Consul, 1963-69, sedan, black tires, many body colors	40	55	90
No. 131 Cadillac Tourer, 1956-62, convertible, driver, yellow or peach body	40	80	100
No. 131 Jaguar Type E 2 + 2, 1968-78, coupe, black cast-metal base	40	80	100
No. 132 Ford 40-RV, 1967-74, GT40 LeMans race car	30	45	70
No. 132 Packard Convertible, 1955-60, green or tan body, driver, black tires	65	130	190
No. 133 Cunningham C-5R Racer, 1955-60, race car, driver in blue helmet	20	50	100
No. 134 Triumph Vitesse, 1963-66, blue or green body	30	42	65
No. 137 Plymouth Fury Convertible, 1963-66	20	60	120
No. 138 Hillman Imp, 1963-73, green or red body, opening trunk and hood	30	42	65
No. 139A Ford Fordor Sedan, 1949-53, black metal base	30	40	60
No. 140 Morris 1100, 1963-69, blue body, black metal base	30	45	75

Dinky Prisoner Mini-Moke, No. 106.

Top to bottom: Dinky Foden ten-ton Truck, No. 622, 1954-64; Medium Artillery Tractor, No. 689, 1957-65.

Dinky Berliet Missile Launch, No. 620, 1973. Photo courtesy W. Kilborn Collection

Top row, left to right: Dinky Army Covered Wagon, No. 623, 1954-63; 5.5 Medium Gun, No. 692, 1955-62. Bottom Left to right: 7.2 Howitzer, No. 693, 1958-67; Three-Ton Army Wagon, No. 621, 1954-63. Photo courtesy W. Kilborn Collection

Top row, left to right: dinky Daimler Ambulance, No. 624, 1944-54; Austin Covered Lorry, No. 625, 1948-54. Bottom: Ford Fordor U.S. Army, No. 675, 1944-54. Photo courtesy W. Kilborn Collection

Top to bottom: Dinky R.A.F. Pressure Fueller, No. 642, 1957-60; Recovery Tractor, No. 661, 1957-65.

	C6	C8	C10
No. 1406 Renault Sinpar, 1968-71, open car, two figures	80	135	220
No. 1406 Sinpar 4x4 Military Police, 1967, French	30	45	75
No. 141 Vauxhall Victor, 1963-67, station wagon, yellow body	40	80	100
No. 1419 Ford Thunderbird, 1969-71	25	70	140
No. 142 Jaguar Mark X, 1962-69, sedan	40	55	85
No. 143 Ford Capri, 1962-67, coupe, blue/turquoise body	45	90	120
No. 144 VW 1500, 1963-66, black metal base	40	55	90
No. 145 Singer Vogue, 1962-67	50	75	100
No. 146 Daimler 2-1/2 litre V8, 1963-67, sedan, black tires	45	55	95
No. 147 Cadillac, 1962-69, sedan, blue or green body	25	60	120
No. 148 Ford Fairlane, 1962-66, sedan, green body	45	85	110
No. 149 Citroen Dyane, 1971-74, four-door sedan, bronze, cream steering wheel, Speedwheels	15	30	45
No. 150 Rolls Royce Silver Wraith, 1959-62, limo, gray body	45	55	95
No. 150 Royal Tank Corp. Personnel Set, 150 a, b, c, d; 1938-41, six pieces	45	90	120

	C6	C8	C10
No. 150A Royal Tank Corp Officer, 1937-41, holding binoculars	10	15	20
No. 150B Royal Tank Corp Private, 1937-41, seated; #150C is standing	15	20	25
No. 150D Royal Tank Corp Driver, 1937-41, seated	10	15	20
No. 150E Royal Tank Corp NCO, 1937-41	10	20	30
No. 151 Royal Tank Corp. Medium Set, 151 a, b, c, d; 1937/41, four pieces	100	200	300
No. 151 Triumph 1800 Saloon, 1954-60, sedan	40	55	90
No. 151 Vauxhall 101, 1966-68	20	50	100
No. 151A Medium Tank, 1937-41	100	200	300
No. 151B Transport Wagon, 1937-41, 1946-48, green body and cover	75	150	200
No. 151B Transport Wagon, reissued 1953-54	40	80	100
No. 151C Cooker Trailer, 1937-41, 1946-48	50	100	125
No. 151D Water Tank Trailer, 1937-41, 1946-48	45	90	120
No. 152 Rolls Royce Phantom V Limousine, 1965-76, limo	32	45	70
No. 152 Royal Tank Corp Light Set, 1937-41, 152 a, b, c; three pieces	125	250	500
No. 152A Light Tank, 1937-41	40	80	100

Dinky Missile Erector Platform, No. 666, 1959-64. Photo courtesy W. Kilborn Collection

Top row: Foden Army Truck, No. 668, 1980. Bottom row, left to right: Landover Bomb Disposal Unit, No. 604. 1977; Convoy Truck, No. 687, 1980. Photo courtesy W. Kilborn Collection

	C6	C8	C10
No. 152A Light Tank, reissued, 1954-55.	30	40	50
No. 152B Reconnaissance Car, 1937-41 .	40	80	100
No. 152B Reconnaissance Car, reissued, 1954-55	40	50	75
No. 152C Austin Staff Car, 1937-41	75	100	125
No. 153 Standard Vanguard, 1954-60	60	85	120
No. 153A U.S. Jeep White Star, 1954-55	40	80	100
No. 155 Ford Anglia, 1961-66	40	50	80
No. 156 Mechanized Army Set, includes 151 a, b, c, d; 152, a, b, c; 161 a, b; 162, a, b, c, 1937/41, twelve pieces	200	1000	1500
No. 156 Rover 75, 1954-60	55	110	150
No. 156 Saab 96, 1966-71, sedan, maroon or blue body	55	90	135
No. 157 BMW 2000 Tilux, 1968-73, sedan, black tires	25	35	50
No. 157 Jaguar XK120, 1954-62, coupe, black metal base, many body colors	65	130	165
No. 158 Rolls Royce Silver Shadow, 1967-73, limo, red or blue body	40	50	80
No. 160 Mercedes Benz 250 SE, 1968-72, sedan, blue body	30	45	70
No. 160 Royal Artillery Personnel Set, 160 a, b, c, d; 1939-40, six pieces	45	90	120
No. 160A Royal Artillery NCO, 1939-41	10	15	20
No. 160B Royal Artillery Gunner, seated, 1939-41	10	15	20
No. 160C Royal Artillery Gunlayer, 1939-41	15	20	25

	C6	C8	C10
No. 160D Royal Artillery Gunlayer, standing, 1939-41	10	15	20
No. 160X Ranco Seated Gunners (3), 1939-41	30	40	60
No. 161 Mobile Anti-Aircraft, 1939-41, Unit 161 a, b, c	600	800	1000
No. 161 Mustang Fastback, 1965-73, black tires	30	40	60
No. 161A AA Gun Trailer, reissued, 1954-55	40	50	70
No. 161A Transport Lorry with Search Light, 1939-41	150	250	500
No. 161B AA Gun Trailer, 1939-41	55	100	180
No. 162 Ford Zephyr Saloon, 1956-60, sedan, black metal base	55	110	150
No. 162 Lt. Dragon Field Gun Set, 1939-40, 1946-49, #162A, #162B, #162C	75	150	300
No. 162 Triumph 1300, 1967-69	40	55	90
No. 162A Lt. Dragon Motorized Tractor, 1939-41	40	80	100
No. 162A Lt. Dragon Motorized Tractor, reissued, 1954-55	35	50	75
No. 162B Ammunition Trailer, 1939-41 .	25	35	50
No. 162B Ammunition Trailer, 1954-55 .	10	15	20
No. 162C 18 PD. Gun, 1939-41	25	35	50
No. 162C 18 PD. Gun, reissued, 1954-55	10	15	20
No. 163 Bristol 450 Sports Coupe, 1956-60, green body	45	95	125

Dinky Bedford Army Truck, No. 640, 1944-54. Photo courtesy W. Kilborn Collection

Left to right: Dinky Tank Transporter, No. 660, 1956-64; Centurion Tank, No. 651, 1954-70. Photo courtesy W. Kilborn Collection

Top to bottom: Dinky One-Ton Cargo Truck, No. 641, 1954-62; Armored Command Vehicle, No. 677, 1952-61. Photo courtesy W. Kilborn Collection

Top row Left to right: Austin Champ "UN white," No. 674, 1954-70; Austin Champ Jeep, No. 674, khaki, 1954-70. Middle: Austin Champ box. Bottom row, left to right: Army Water Tanker, No. 643, 1958-64; Military Ambulance, No. 626, 1956-65. Photo courtesy W. Kilborn Collection

	C6	C8	C10
No. 163 Volkswagen 1600 TL Fastback, 1966-71, red or blue body	30	45	75
No. 164 Ford Zodiac, 1966-71, sedan	30	45	70
No. 164 Vauxhall Crest Saloon, 1957-60, sedan	55	110	150
No. 165 Ford Capri, 1969-74, coupe, Speedwheels	45	55	95
No. 165 Humber Hawk, 1959-63	25	80	160
No. 166 Sunbeam Rapier, 1958-63, sedan, black tires	55	115	155
No. 167 A.C. Aceca, 1958-63, sport coupe	55	90	130
No. 168 Ford Escort, 1968-77, sedan, opening hood and doors	15	25	50
No. 168 Singer Gazelle, 1959-63, sedan, two-tone body colors	55	110	145
No. 169 Ford Corsair 200E, 1967-69, sedan, silver body	30	42	65
No. 169 Studebaker Golden Hawk, 1958-63, sport coupe, green or tan body	55	110	145
No. 170 Lincoln Continental, 1964-70, sedan, blue interior	45	55	95
No. 171 Hudson Commodore, 1954-56, sedan, two-tone body colors	55	110	150
No. 172 Studebaker Land Cruiser, 1954-59, sedan; shown with 174 Hudson Hornet Sedan	65	130	175
No. 173 Nash Rambler, 1958-62	45	90	120
No. 173 Pontiac Parisenne, 1968-73	30	42	65
No. 174 Ford Mercury Cougar, 1969-73	30	45	70
No. 174 Hudson Hornet, 1958-63	55	115	155
No. 175 Hillman Minx, 1958-61	65	130	190
No. 176 Austin A105 Saloon, 1958-63, sedan, first Dinky w/windows	65	130	170
No. 176 NSU R 80, 1969-74, sedan	30	45	75
No. 177 Opel Kapitan, 1961-66	45	95	125
No. 178 Mini Clubman, 1975-80	15	20	40
No. 178 Plymouth Plaza, 1959-63	55	90	130
No. 179 Studebaker President, 1958-63	55	110	150
No. 180 Packard Clipper Sedan, 1958-63	50	90	130
No. 180 Rover 3H, 1979-80	15	20	40
No. 181 Volkswagen, 1956-70, Beetle, black tires	50	100	135

	C6	C8	C10
No. 182 Porsche 356A, 1958-66	55	115	150
No. 184 Volvo, 1961-65	45	95	125
No. 185 Alfa Romeo Coupe, 1961-63, red or yellow body	45	95	125
No. 186 Mercedes-Benz 220SE, 1961-67	40	50	80
No. 187 DeTomaso Mangusta, 1968-77	25	35	50
No. 187 VW Karmann Ghia, 1959-64	45	95	125
No. 188 Jensen FF, 1968-74	30	45	75
No. 189 Lamborghini Marzal, 1968-78	25	35	55
No. 189 Triumph Herald, 1959-64	40	80	105
No. 190 Caravan, 1956-64	30	45	60
No. 190 Monteverdi 375L, 1970-74	30	45	75
No. 191 Dodge Royal Sedan, 1959-64	55	110	145
No. 192 DeSoto Fireflite Sedan, 1958-63	45	90	140
No. 192 Range Rover, 1970-80	15	30	45
No. 193 Rambler Cross Country, 1961-69, station wagon	45	95	125
No. 194 Bentley S2, 1961-67, convertible, driver, black tires	30	60	90
No. 195 Fire Chief's Range Rover, 1971-78, same casting as #192 w/light and fire decals	15	20	35
No. 195 Jaguar 3.4 Saloon, 1960-66	25	80	160
No. 196 Holden Special, 1963-70	40	55	85
No. 197 Morris Mini Traveler, 1961-70	55	110	145
No. 198 Rolls Royce Phantom V, 1962-69	40	80	105
No. 199 Austin Countryman, 1961-70	45	85	110
No. 200 Matra 630, 1971-74, LeMans racing car	15	20	40
No. 201 Plymouth Rally '76, 1979-80	10	20	40
No. 202 Customized Land Rover, 1979-80	5	20	60
No. 202 Fiat Abarth 2000, 1971-74	15	20	35
No. 203 Custom Range Rover, 1979-80, black body	5	20	40
No. 204 Ferrari 312P, 1971-75, red body, number 60 or 24	30	60	90
No. 205 Talbot-Lago, 1962-64, blue body	20	40	60
No. 206 Custom Stingray, 1977-80	5	20	60
No. 208 VW Porsche 914, 1971-79	30	40	60
No. 210 Alfa Romeo 33 LeMans, 1971-73	30	45	70
No. 212 Ford Cortina Rally, 1967-69	40	55	85

	C6	C8	C10
No. 213 Ford Capri Rally, 1971-74	25	35	50
No. 217 Alfa Romeo Scarabo, 1968-74 ...	15	20	40
No. 219 Big Cat Jaguar, 1977-80	5	20	40
No. 220 Ferrari P5, 1970-75	30	40	60
No. 221 Corvette Stingray, 1969-78	30	40	60
No. 222 Hesketh 308E, 1978-80	20	40	75
No. 223 McLaren M8A CanAm, 1970-78	10	20	40
No. 224 Mercedes-Benz C-111, 1970-74	5	20	50
No. 225 Lotus FI Racing Car, 1970-78	25	35	50
No. 226 Ferrari 312, 1972-80..................	15	30	45
No. 227 Beach Buggy, 1974-79	15	20	32
No. 228 Talbot-Lago Race Car, 1954-64 .	55	90	133
No. 231 Maserati, 1954-64, grand prix race car, driver, number 9 on rear	45	95	125
No. 232 Alfa Romeo Race Car, 1954-64, grang prix race car, white driver, number 8	45	95	125
No. 233 Cooper Bristol Race Car, 1954-64, grand prix race car, green body, white driver, number 6	25	70	140
No. 235 H.W.M. Racer, 1954-60, grand prix race car, green body, white driver, number "7" decal	25	70	140
No. 236 Connaught Racer, 1956-59, grand prix race car, green body, driver, number 32	40	85	135
No. 237 Mercedes Racer, 1957-69, grand prix race car, white body, driver, number 30	55	115	155
No. 238 Jaguar Racer, 1957-65	60	120	160
No. 239 Vanwall Racer, 1958-65, grand prix race car, green body, white driver, number 35	20	60	130
No. 240 Cooper Racer, 1963-70, grand prix race car, blue body, white driver, number 20	30	40	60
No. 241 Lotus Racing Car, 1963-71, grand prix race car, blue body, white stripes	20	35	60
No. 242 BRM Racer, 1964-71, grand prix race car, green body, white driver, number 7	25	35	55
No. 242 Ferrari Racer, 1963-71, grand prix race car, red body, white driver, number 36	15	30	60
No. 243 Volvo Police Car, 1978-80	5	30	60

	C6	C8	C10
No. 244 Plymouth Police Car, 1977-80 ...	25	65	135
No. 245 Sports Car Gift Set, 1968-73, #131 Jaguar, #153 Aston-Martin, #188 Jensen FF	85	165	295
No. 250 Police Mini Cooper S, 1968-74, white body	30	45	75
No. 250 Streamline Fire Engine, 1954-62	15	60	120
No. 251 Pontiac Police Car, 1971	30	45	75
No. 252 Bedford Garbage Truck, 1954-64	20	55	100
No. 252 Pontiac RCMP Police Car, 1969-74, dark blue body, ...	40	80	100
No. 253 Daimler Ambulance, 1954-64	15	60	120
No. 254 Austin Taxi, 1954-62	45	85	110
No. 254 Police Range Rover, 1972-80	5	30	60
No. 254 Police Range Rover, 1972-80	15	30	45
No. 255 Ford Zodiac Police Car, 1967-72	40	55	85
No. 255 Mersey Tunnel Police Land Rover, 1955-61, red body, yellow decals	45	55	95
No. 255 Police Mini Clubman, 1977-79 ..	5	30	60
No. 257 Nash Fire Chief's Car, 1961-68 .	55	115	150
No. 258 DeSoto Police Car, 1960-68.......	65	130	165
No. 259 Fire Engine, 1962-69, red body .	45	90	120
No. 260 Royal Mail Van, 1955-61, red body, "Royal Mail" decal	65	115	150
No. 261 Telephone Service Truck, 1956-61	65	130	165
No. 263 Airport Fire Rescue Tender, 1978-80	40	50	80
No. 263 Superior Criterion Ambulance, 1962-68	45	70	110
No. 264 Ford Fairlaine R.C.M.P. Police Car, 1962-68	25	70	125
No. 264 Rover 3500 Police, 1979-80.......	10	30	60
No. 265 Plymouth Taxi, 1960-66	55	115	150
No. 266 ERF Fire Tender, 1976-80	15	50	100

Dinky U.S. Army Jeep (No. 669) with trailer (No. 341), 1954. Photo courtesy W. Kilborn Collection

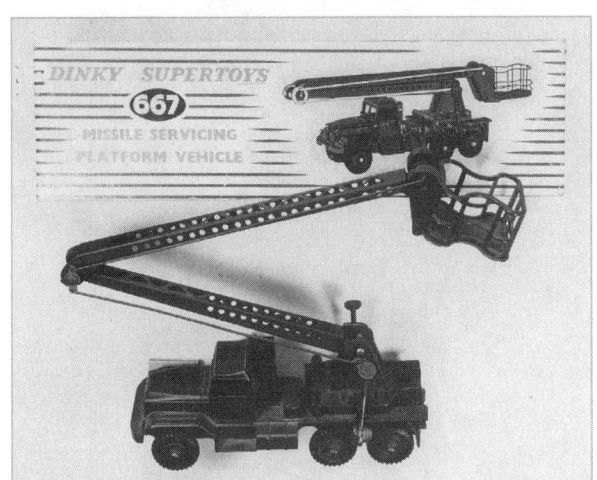

Dinky Missile Service Platform, No. 667, 1960s. Photo courtesy W. Kilborn Collection

Top row, left to right: armored Personnel Car, No. 676, 1955-62; Armored Car, No. 670, 1954-70. Bottom, left to right: Artillery Tractor, No. 688; Gun Trailer, No. 687; Field Gun, No. 686. Photo courtesy W. Kilborn Collection

Top to bottom: French Dinky Panhard EBR Tank, No. 815, 1960s; Berliet Tank Transporter, No. 890, 1960. Photo courtesy W. Kilborn Collection

Left to right: French Dinky UNIMOG Covered Truck, No. 821, 1960; Field Kitchen, No. 823, 1960s. Photo courtesy W. Kilborn Collection

French Dinky AMX Bridge Layer, No. 883, 1964. Photo courtesy W. Kilborn Collection

French Dinky Brockway Bridge Layer, No. 884. Photo courtesy W. Kilborn Collection

Top row, left to right: French Dinky Dodge command Car, No. 810, 1973; Jeep with Anti-Tank Missiles in box, No. 828, 1964. Bottom row, left to right: Jeep with recoil rifle in box, No. 829, 1964; Renault Sinpar, No. 815, 1977. Photo courtesy W. Kilborn Collection

French Dinky M3 Halftrack, No. 822, 1960. Photo courtesy W. Kilborn Collection

French Dinky Berliet Wrecker, No. 826, 1963. Photo courtesy W. Kilborn Collection

French Dinky Panhard FL10 Tank, No. 827, 1963. Photo courtesy W. Kilborn Collection

Top to bottom: French Dinky GMC Wrecker Sahara, No. 808/2, 1970s; GMC Wrecker Khaki, No. 803/3, 1974. Photo courtesy W. Kilborn Collection

Top row, left to right: French Dinky Panhard AML Armored Car, No. 814, 1962-67; Willys Hotchkiss Jeep, No. 80B, 1957-60; Bottom: Willys Hotchkiss Jeep, No. 80BP, 1958-63. Photo courtesy W. Kilborn Collection

	C6	C8	C10
No. 267 "Emergency" paramedic Truck, 1979-80, truck and figure from the "Emergency" television series	10	60	120
No. 267 Superior Cadillac Ambulnce, 1967-71, white and red body, rear door opens, plastic stretcher inside	30	50	80
No. 268 Range Rover Ambulance, 1974-78	5	30	60
No. 268 Renault Dauphine Mini Car, 1962-66, red body	55	115	150
No. 269 Ford Transit Police Van, 1978-80	5	30	60
No. 269 Jaguar Police Car, 1962-66, white body..	65	130	175
No. 270 Ford Panda Police Car, 1969-77, light blue body, Speedwheels	15	35	60
No. 271 Ford Fire Van, 1975-77	15	20	40
No. 271 Touring Secours Motorcycle, 1959, black cycle and sidecar	70	110	200
No. 272 Police Accident Unit, 1975-78 ...	15	30	45
No. 273 Mini Minor Van, 1966-70, R.A.C., blue body, opening rear doors, white roof..	65	115	150
No. 274 Ford Transit Ambulance, 1978-80	5	25	50
No. 274 Mini Minor Van, 1965-73, A.A. decals, yellow body, same casting as #273	65	115	150
No. 274 Mini Minor Van, 1970, Joseph Mason Paints decals, rare....................	150	300	500
No. 275 Brinks Armored Truck, 1964-79	25	40	60
No. 276 Ford Ambulance, 1976-78, white body	15	20	40
No. 277 Police Land Rover, 1979-80	5	30	60
No. 277 Superior Ambulance, 1962-69 ...	40	55	85
No. 278 Plymouth Yellow Cab, 1978-80.	25	35	50
No. 278 Vauxhall Victor Ambulance, 1964-70	15	50	100
No. 279 Diesel Road Roller, 1965-80	30	42	65
No. 279 Plymouth Taxi, 1978-80, yellow cab	12	20	28
No. 280 Midland Bank, 1966-68, silver and cream body, "Midland Bank Limited" decals	60	85	120
No. 280 Observation Coach, 1954-60	55	115	150

	C6	C8	C10
No. 281 Pathe Fiat News Camera Car, 1967-70	65	100	175
No. 282 Land Rover Fire Appliance, 1974-80	45	85	110
No. 283 B.O.A.C. Coach, 1956-63	15	20	40
No. 284 London Austin Taxi, 1972-79	15	30	45
No. 285 Merryweather Fire Engine, 1970-79, red body fire pumper	15	50	100
No. 286 Ford Transit Fire Truck, 1969-75	30	45	70
No. 287 Ford Police Accident Unit, 1967-74	30	40	60
No. 288 Superior Cadillac Ambulance, 1974-79	30	70	100
No. 289 London Bus, 1964-80, doubledecker bus, red body	15	20	40
No. 290 Double Decker Bus, 1954-63	55	115	155
No. 291 Atlantean City Bus, 1974-78......	15	20	40
No. 292 Ribble Regent Bus, 1962-66	30	45	70
No. 295 Atlas Bus, 1973-76......................	40	80	100
No. 297 Silver Jubilee Bus, 1977, Atlantean, celebrating "The Queen's Silver Jubilee," silver body	40	80	100
No. 299 Police Crash Squad Set, 1979, #244 Plymouth Police Car, #732 Bell Police Helicopter, road signs	10	40	80
No. 299 Post Office Set, 1958, #260 Royal Mail Van, #261 Telephone Van, Telephone Box, Telegraph Messenger, Postman..	50	100	175
No. 300 Massey Harris Tractor, 1954-71	45	95	125
No. 301 Field Marshall Tractor, 1954-65, same casting as 027N, orange or red body	60	90	150
No. 301 Field-Marshall Tractor, 1954-65	40	55	85
No. 303 Commando Squad Set, 1978-80, #667, #687, #745	25	60	95
No. 305 David Brown Tractor, 1965-75, driver, working steering......................	30	60	95
No. 308 Leyland Tractor, 1971-78	30	40	60
No. 319 Tipping Trailer, 1961-70............	15	20	35
No. 320 Halesowen Harvest Trailer, 1954-70	15	20	40
No. 321 Massey Harris Manure Spreader, 1954-71	32	45	70
No. 322 Massey-Harris Disc Harrow, 1954-73	15	30	45

	C6	C8	C10
No. 324 Massey-Harris Hay Rake, 1954-1971, same casting as 027K, red body, yellow wheels	25	40	60
No. 340 Land Rover, 1954-71	65	130	175
No. 341 Land Rover Trailer, 1954-71	15	20	35
No. 341 Land Rover Trailer, Army (sold w/No. 669 Super Dinky set), 1954, British, shown with 669 US Army Jeep	15	20	40
No. 342 Austin Mini-Moke, 1967-75	20	30	55
No. 342 Motocart, 1954-60	30	45	75
No. 343 Dodge Farm Truck, 1954-64	65	130	195
No. 344 Estate Car, 1954-61, shown with 157 Jaguar KX120	30	40	60
No. 350 Tiny's Mini-Moke, 1970-76, orange body, giraffe driver	60	85	120
No. 352 Ed Straker's Car, 1971-75	40	55	90
No. 353 Shado 2 Mobile, 1972-80, missile launcher, yellow missiles, "Shado 2" decals	15	60	120
No. 357 Klingon Battle Cruiser, 1976-79, w/white disks	30	55	85
No. 358 U.S.S. Enterprise, 1976-80, off-white, shuttle in shuttle bay, disks for shooting, "NCC-1701" registration	30	65	110
No. 359 Eagle Transporter from Space 1999, 1975-79, white framed spacecraft	35	80	160
No. 360 Eagle Freighter from Space 1999, 1975-79, spacecraft	35	80	160
No. 361 Galactic War Chariot, 1979-80, space vehicle, red driver	5	20	40
No. 371 U.S.S. Enterprise, 1980, small-scale Enterprise, "NCC 1701" decal on white body	5	10	15
No. 372 Klingon Battle Cruiser, 1980, small-scale Battle Cruiser	5	10	15
No. 381 Convoy Farm Truck, 1977-80, Speedwheels	5	15	30
No. 381 Garden Roller, 1954-58	10	20	35
No. 382 Convoy Dump Truck, 1978-80	5	10	20
No. 382 Wheelbarrow, 1954-58	10	20	40
No. 384 Convoy Rescue Truck, 1977-79, red body, Speedwheels	5	20	40
No. 390 Customized Ford Van, 1978-80	5	15	40
No. 400 B.E.V. Truck, 1954-60, blue or gray body	30	45	70
No. 401 Coventry Climax Fork Lift, 1954-64	15	40	80
No. 404 Conveyancer Fork Lift, 1967-79, "CG4" decal or paint on body	15	40	80
No. 405 Universal Jeep, 1954-67	25	60	120

	C6	C8	C10
No. 408 Big Bedford Truck, 1956-63, maroon or blue body, blue a slight premium; #922 from 1954-55	80	120	185
No. 410 Bedford Van, 1972-79, many color and decal variations	15	20	40
No. 411 Bedford Van, 1972-79, panel van	25	60	95
No. 412 Bedford AA Van, 1971-79	5	30	60
No. 417 Ford Motorway Services Van, 1978-80	15	25	40
No. 419/933 Leyland Comet Cement Truck, 1956-59, yellow chassis and cab	85	150	250
No. 421 Electric Articulated Truck, 1954-59, same as #030W, semi w/maroon cab and chassis	50	85	120
No. 422 Thames Flat Truck, 1954-60, same casting as #030R, red or green body	45	75	110
No. 428 Large Trailer, 1956-71, open trailer, gray or red body	10	30	60
No. 430 Johnson 2-Ton Dumper, 1976-80	15	30	60
No. 431 Guy Warrior 4-Ton Truck, 1956-58, blue body, tow hook	150	270	450
No. 437 Muir Hill Two-Wheel Loader, 1962-78, driver, yellow or red body	10	30	60
No. 439 Ford D800 Snow Plow Tipper, 1971-77, dark blue cab, different color tipper	10	40	80
No. 440 Studebaker Mobil Gas Tanker, 1954-61	50	100	175
No. 442 Studebaker Esso Tanker, 1954-58	40	100	200
No. 443 Studebaker National Benzole Tanker, 1957-58	35	75	150
No. 448 Chevrolet El Camino and Trailer, 1963-67, two-tone paint blue and cream, "Acme Trailer Hire" decals	25	75	150
No. 449 Chevrolet El Camino Pickup, 1961-68	35	60	100
No. 449 Ford D800 Johnson Road Sweeper, 1977-79	25	50	75
No. 449 Johnson Road Sweeper D28, 1977-79	10	40	80
No. 451 Trojan Dunlop Van, 1954-57, red body	70	110	185
No. 470 Austin Van, 1954-56, Shell/BP decals	60	110	175

Dinky Road Grader, yellow and red, No. 963.

Dinky Euclid Dump Truck, No. 965.

Dinky Unic Bucket Truck, No. F38A/895.

	C6	C8	C10
No. 471 Austin Van, 1955-63, Nestle's decals	60	110	175
No. 472 Austin Van, 1957-60, Raleigh Cycles decals	60	110	175
No. 481 Bedford 10 Ovaltine Van, 1955-59	25	100	200
No. 482 Bedford Van, 1956-58, "Dinky Toys" decals	60	115	200
No. 485 Santa's Special Model T Ford, 1964-68, Santa and Christmas tree	65	100	150
No. 490 Dairy Van, 1954-56	25	60	125
No. 501 Citroen DS19 Police Car, 1967-70	50	95	175
No. 503/903 Foden Flat Truck, #503 1934-54, #903 1955-60	140	210	450
No. 513 Guy Otter Flat Truck, 1947-54...	80	250	500
No. 514 Guy Van, 1949-54, Slumberland decal 1949-52, Lyons Swiss Rolls decals 1951-54, Weetabix decals 1952-54	135	300	575
No. 522 Citroen DS19, 1959-68, orange or yellow body	25	100	200
No. 523 Simca 1500, 1963-69, sedan	25	75	150
No. 524 Renault Dauphine, 1959-62, sedan	25	75	150
No. 526 Mercedes-Benz 190SL, 1959-63	25	100	200
No. 527 Alfa Romeo 1900, 1959-63, coupe, red or blue body	25	75	150
No. 528 Peugeot 404 Cabriolet Pinninfarina, 1966-71, convertible	25	75	125
No. 530 Citroen DS19, 1964-70, 1963 sedan, maroon or green body	25	75	125
No. 530 Citroen DS23, 1976-78, maroon body	100	200	300
No. 530 VW Karmann-Ghia, 1959-62, coupe	25	75	125
No. 532 Lincoln Premiere, 1959-65, limo, white tires	125	250	425
No. 533 Mercedes-Benz 300 Se, 1963-70, two-door hardtop, black tires	25	75	125
No. 534 BMW 1500, 1963-68, red or green body	25	75	125
No. 535 Citroen 2CV, 1959-63	25	80	160
No. 540 Opel Kadett, 1963-70, two-door sedan	15	35	60
No. 543 Renault Floride, 1960-63, coupe, white tires	35	70	140
No. 545 DeSoto Diplomat, 1960-63, white tires	25	80	160
No. 547 Panhard PL-17, 1960-68	15	35	60

	C6	C8	C10
No. 550 Chrysler Saratoga, 1961-66	70	110	180
No. 551 Ford Police Car, 1960s, green body	50	100	150
No. 555 Comer Fire Engine, 1952-54	25	65	130
No. 561 Blaw Knowx Bulldozer, 1949-54, red body, bulldozer blade, driver	45	75	115
No. 561 Citroen Van, 1959-66, French, sliding door, "Cibie" decal variation brings a premium	50	110	160
No. 561 Renault Mail Car, 1968-72, yellow body	50	85	150
No. 571 Saviem Race Horse Van, 1969-71	125	225	400
No. 583 Pullmore Car Transport, 1953-54	25	70	140
No. 586 Citroen Milk Truck, 1961-65, white body bottle truck	145	275	600
No. 595 Salev Crane, 1959-61, French, driver, black tires	65	100	175
No. 601 Austin Paramoke, 1966-77, British, shown with 673 Scout Car	30	60	120
No. 602 Armoured Command Car, 1980, British	30	50	100
No. 603 Army Personnel Privates, 1955-71, British	25	35	50
No. 604 Landrover Bomb Disposal, 1977, British	20	40	80
No. 609 U.S. 105mm Howitzer, 1977, British, with crew	20	40	80
No. 612 Commando Jeep, 1980, British	10	40	70
No. 615 U.S. Jeep w/105mm Howitzer, 1968-78, #612 Jeep, #609 Howitzer	20	50	100
No. 616 AEC. Arctic Transporter, 1977, British	20	60	120
No. 617 Volkswagen Anti-tank gun, 1977, British	20	50	100
No. 618 AEC. Arctic Trans./ Helicopter, 1976-80, British	35	85	125
No. 619 Bren Gun Set, 1976-78, British	20	55	100
No. 620 Berliet Missile Launcher, 1970-73	55	110	220
No. 621 3-Ton Army Wagon, 1954-63 M/B, British	25	50	100
No. 622 10-Ton Army Truck, 1954-64, British, shown with 689 Artillery Tractor	30	60	120
No. 622 Bren Gun Carrier, 1977, British	20	40	80
No. 623 Army Covered Wagon, 1954-63, British	40	80	140
No. 624 Daimler Ambulance #30H, 1944-54, British, shown with 625 Austin Lorry & 675 Ford Fordor	40	55	85
No. 625 6 Pdr. Anti-tank Gun, 1977, British	15	30	55
No. 625 Austin Covered Lorry/30s, 1948-54, British	30	45	75
No. 626 Military Ambulance, 1956-65, British	40	85	135
No. 640 Bedford Army Truck 25w, 1944-54, British	30	50	95
No. 641 1-Ton Cargo Truck, 1954-62	30	55	85
No. 642 R.A.F. Pressure Fueller, 1957-60, British	40	80	160
No. 643 Army Water Tanker, 1958-64, British	25	50	100
No. 651 Centurion Tank, 1954-70, British	30	50	85

	C6	C8	C10
No. 654 155mm. Mobile Gun, 1980, British	25	55	100
No. 656 Static 88mm. Gun, 1980, British	25	55	100
No. 660 Tank Transporter, 1956-64, British	50	110	200
No. 661 Recovery Tractor, 1957-65, British	35	85	140
No. 662 Static 88mm Gun w/Crew, 1976-77, olive drab	10	40	80
No. 665 Honest John Launcher, 1964-76, British	50	115	200
No. 666 Missile Erector/Platform, 1959-64, British	115	230	450
No. 667 Armoured Patrol Car, 1977, British	15	30	60
No. 667 Missile Service Platform, 1960-64, British	80	115	225
No. 668 Foden Army Truck, 1980, British, shown with 604 Landrover Bomb Disposal & 687 Convoy Army Truck	20	35	60
No. 669 U.S. Army Jeep No. 405 sd/tr, 1944-54, British	20	40	75
No. 670 Armoured Car, 1954-70, British, shown with 676 Personnel Carrier, 687 Gun Trailer, 686 Field Artillery Tractor & 688 Gun Set	25	50	100
No. 673 Daimler Scout Car, 1953-62, British, light armored car	20	40	80
No. 674 Austin Champ Jeep, 1954-70, British	20	40	80
No. 674 Austin Champ UN white, 1958-70, British, rare	100	200	300
No. 675 Ford Fordor U.S. Army No. 139, 1944-54, British	30	75	110
No. 676 Daimler Armored Car, 1972-76	10	35	70
No. 676 Saracen Armoured Personnel Car, 1955-62, British	25	50	100
No. 677 Armoured Commando Vehicle, 1952-61, British	25	55	100
No. 677 Task Force Set, 1972-74, #680 Ferret, #681 DUKW, and #682 Alvis	20	50	100
No. 680 Ferret Armoured Car, 1972-79, British, tan or olive body	10	20	40
No. 681 D.U.K.W. Amphibian, 1972-79, British	10	30	60
No. 682 Stalwart Load Carrier, 1977, British	10	30	60
No. 683 Chieftain Tank, 1972-79, British	20	50	100
No. 686 25-Pounder Field Gun, 1957-70.	20	40	80

	C6	C8	C10
No. 686 Field Artillery Tractor, 1957-70, British	40	80	100
No. 687 Convoy Truck, 1977-80, British	12	20	40
No. 687 Trailer for 25 Pdr., 1957-70, British	10	20	30
No. 688 Gun Set, 1957-70, British	40	50	80
No. 688 Light Artillery Tractor, 1957-61, Morris tractor, spare tire often missing	25	50	80
No. 689 Medium Artillery Tractor, 1957-65, British	25	50	100
No. 690 Scorpion Tank, 1974-80, British	20	40	80
No. 691 Striker Anti-tank Vehicle, 1974-80, British	20	40	80
No. 692 5.5 Medium Gun, 1955-62, British	25	50	100
No. 692 Leopard Tank, 1974-79, British	25	50	100
No. 693 7.2 Howitzer, 1958-67, British	20	40	80
No. 694 Hanomog Tank Destroyer, 1975-80, British	25	65	85
No. 696 Leopard Anti-Aircraft Tank, 1979, British	45	90	120
No. 697 25-Pounder Field Gun Set, 1957-71, #686 Field Gun, #687 Trailer, #688 Tractor	55	110	220
No. 698 Tank Gift Set, 1957-65, #651 Centurion Tank, #660 Transporter	45	70	140
No. 699 Leopard Recovery Tank, 1977, British	25	55	100
No. 800 Renault SINAPAR Radio Tk, French, two figures	15	30	45
No. 801 AMX 13T Tank, 1973-75, reissue of #817	35	70	140
No. 802 (819) 155mm Fieldgun, 1973-77, French	15	20	40
No. 806 Berliet Army Wrecker 6x6, 1973, reissue of #824	45	90	140
No. 807 Renault Ambulance, 1973, French, shown with 825 D.U.K.W. Amphibian	32	45	70
No. 808/2 GMC Wrecker Sahara, 1972-73, French	65	130	170
No. 808/3 GMC Wrecker Khaki, 1974, French	55	115	150
No. 809 GMC Truck 6x6, 1970, French	50	100	250
No. 810 Dodge Command Car, 1972-74, French, shown with 815 Panhard EBR Tank, 828 Jeep/Anti-Tank Missiles & 829 Jeep with Cannon	65	125	185
No. 813 AMX Self Propelled Gun, 1965, French	45	90	180
No. 814 Panhard AML Amoured Car, 1962-67, French	30	60	120
No. 815 Panhard EBR Tank, 1962-67, French	30	70	120
No. 815 Sinpar 4x4 Military Police Vehicle, 1969-70	30	60	120
No. 816 Berliet Gazelle Rkt. Launch, 1969-71, French	55	110	140
No. 816 Hotchkiss Willys Jeep, 1958-59, w/tow hook, French	32	55	110
No. 817 AMX Char 13 Tank, 1959-70, French	25	60	110
No. 820 Renault Army Ambulance, 1959-70, van w/opening rear doors	30	60	90
No. 821 UNIMOG Covered Truck, 1960, French, shown with 823 Field Kitchen	30	60	120
No. 822 M3 Half Track, 1960-71, French	50	100	200

Dinky Commer Fire Engine, No. 955.

	C6	C8	C10
No. 823 Field Kitchen, 1962-67, French .	30	60	120
No. 823 GMC Tank Truck, 1969-70, French, shown with 809 GMC Truck 6x6	125	250	500
No. 824 Berliet Gazelle Truck, 1963-70, French	45	100	150
No. 825 D.U.K.W. Amphibian, 1964-71, French	65	130	165
No. 826 Berliet Wrecker, 1963, French ...	60	120	240
No. 827 Panhard FL10 Tank, 1964-71, French	45	85	110
No. 828 Jeep/anti-tank Missiles, 1964-71, French	35	70	140
No. 829 Jeep with recoil rifle, 1964-71, French	25	50	100
No. 830 Richier Road Roller, 1959-69, French, driver	50	100	150
No. 881 GMC Circus Truck and Trailer, 1969-71, maroon and yellow, 3 animals in cages	50	100	150
No. 882 Peugeot 404 and Circus Caravan, 1969-71, #536 Peugeot and #564 Caravan	25	60	90
No. 883 AMX Bridge Layer, 1964, French	90	180	350
No. 884 Brockway Bridging Truck, 1963, French	85	165	295
No. 890 Berliet Tank Transporter, 1960, French	65	135	250
No. 898 Berliet Transformer Carrier, 1961-65	100	200	450
No. 918 Guy EverReady Truck, 1955-58, blue chassis and cab	80	200	400
No. 920 Guy Heinz Ketchup Truck, 1959-60	250	1000	2000
No. 923 Big Bedford Heinz Truck, 1955-59, baked beans can	100	250	500
No. 923 Big Bedford Heinz Truck, 1955-59, Heinz ketchup bottle	150	500	800
No. 924 Aveling-Barford Centaur Dump Truck, 1972-77	10	30	60
No. 941 Foden Mobilgas Tanker, 1954-57, red tanker, "Mobilgas" decals	145	350	750
No. 942 Foden Regent Tanker, 1955-57, blue tanker, "Regent" decals	135	300	550
No. 943 Leyland Octopus Esso Tanker, 1957-64, red chassis and cab	100	300	600
No. 944 Leland Shell/BP Tanker, 1963-69	125	215	450
No. 948 McLean Tractor Trailer, 1961-67	60	180	360

	C6	C8	C10
No. 953 Continental Touring Coach, 1963-66, blue body	135	200	350
No. 955 Commer Fire Engine, 1955-69...	40	85	135
No. 956 Bedford Fire Escape, 1969-74 ...	60	115	175
No. 958 Guy Warrior Snow Plow, 1961-66	60	150	300
No. 960 Lorry Mounted Concrete Mixer, 1960-68	10	50	100
No. 962 Muir Hill Dumper Truck, 1955-65	25	45	75
No. 963 Road Grader, 1973-75, orange and yellow	20	40	80
No. 965 Euclid Dump Truck, British	45	85	115
No. 967 Muir Hill Loader, British	10	30	60
No. 968 BBC TV Roving Eye Vehicle, British	35	100	200
No. 969 BBC TV Extending Mast Vehicle, British	35	100	200
No. 971 Coles Mobile Crane, 1955-66, yellow body, blue driver, "Coles" decals	40	70	110
No. 972 Coles 20-Ton Crane, 1955-69	10	40	80
No. 973 Eaton Yale Articulated Tractor Shovel, 1971-75	10	40	80
No. 974 A.E.C. Hoynor Transporter, 1969-75, car transporter, blue and yellow, white interior	60	90	130
No. 976 Michigan 180-111 Tractor Dozer, 1967-76	10	40	80
No. 977 Servicing Platform, 1960-64, cream body, black tires, red platform ..	10	40	80
No. 977 Shovel Dozer Frontloader, 1973-77	10	40	80
No. 980 Coles Hydra Crane 150T Truck, 1972-79, yellow or orange cab	10	40	80
No. 981 Horse Box, 1955-61	30	65	120
No. 982 Pullmore Car Transporter, 1954-63, "Dinky Toys Delivery Service" letters	75	125	175
No. 984 Atlas Digger, 1974-79, yellow body, "AB 1702" decals	10	30	60
No. 986 Mighty Antar Transporter w/Propell, 1956-64, red cab, gray semi	125	215	400
No. 991 AEC Shell Chemicals Tanker, 1955-58	35	80	160
No. 994 Loading Ramp, 1955-64	10	20	40
No. F1400 Peugeot 404 Taxi, 1967-71	50	75	100
No. F38A/895 Unic Bucket Truck, 1957-65	75	120	225

DISTLER

Established in 1895 and based in Nürnburg, Germany, the Johann Distler KG Company produced lithographed penny toys, eventually offering more than 500 different novelties. After Johann Distler's death in 1923, his partners assumed leadership and kept the company going. They sold the company in 1936 to Ernst Völk, the Chairman of the Nürnburg Chamber of Commerce.

Following World War II, Distler produced electric toy trains and cars. Although the company enjoyed relative success selling its toys in department (rather than toy) stores through the 1950s, competition from Schuco, Marklin, and Dinky proved too much and Distler ceased production 1962 when the company was sold to a Belgian investor and renamed, Distler Toys S.A. The company closed its doors for good in 1968.

	C6	C8	C10
BMW Wanderer, wind-up, 3 forward gears, 1 reverse gear, working steering	250	375	500

	C6	C8	C10
Coupe, w/driver, clockwork motor	600	1000	1400
Eccentric Saloon Car, wind-up, driver's head springs through roof, 8" long.......	500	800	1100
Electro Magic 7500 Porsche Cabriolet, battery-driven, 1955............................	450	675	900
Jaguar	340	510	680
Limousine, tin lithographed, battery headlights, chauffeur, clockwork motor, 12" long	900	1500	2200

	C6	C8	C10
Packard Convertible, wind-up, 1950s, 9-1/2" long	225	338	450
Studebaker w/ garage, red 1953-54 Studebaker, plastic, station contains batteries and hose connecting to car supplies power	50	100	150
Uncle Wiggly Car	1500	2500	4000

Distler Electro Magic 7500 Posche Cabriolet, battery operated, with original box. Photo courtesy Tim Oei

Distler BMW Wanderer windup. Photo courtesy Tim Oei

DOEPKE "MODEL TOYS"

Charles Wm. Doepke Mfg. Co., Inc., also known as Doepke, was located in Rossmoyne, Ohio. Each of their toys was an authorized replica of the actual vehicle, right down to the decals. The exception was the manufacturer's own "Model Toys" design. Doepke "Model Toys" advertised their toys as outlasting all othersthree to one.

Doepke "Model Toys" were doomed to extinction by lower-priced, lightweight imitators of lesser quality. No company ever matched the heavy-duty construction and realistic operating qualities of the one and only "Model Toys." Of the mass-produced Doepke "Model Toys," several had variations in their basic construction from time to time. Usually these changes were an elimination of the more intricate operating procedures and had little or no effect on the toy's overall appearance.

Doepke accepted orders to make models of actual vehicles for various companies, but the toys with the most allure, playability, feasible mass production design, and greatest entertainment value were mass-produced. The others, those that would not withstand rough handling by young hands or were too expensive, were only manufactured in low numbers, sometimes only one. This is no doubt the explanation for the number gaps between the marketed items.

At the end of World War II, Doepke hit the market with five models, the first in a line of heavy-duty metal operating replicas employing metal tread or authentic miniature tires. The tires were either Goodyear or Firestone, with authentic tread and name and tire sizes. The first five numbers in the toy series were 2000, 2001, 2002, 2006, 2007. Following is a list of the Doepke vehicles.

No. 2000: Wooldridge H.D. Earth hauler, bright yellow, four large tires, 25" long, 10 pounds. Two long doors, the length of the bottom of the dirt-hauling area, could be released to deposit a load.

No. 2001: The Barber-Greene high-capacity bucket loader, 13" high, 10 pounds, dark green, all steel and rolling on steel tread, was designed as a toy to lead earth haulers; hand crank.

No. 2002: Jaeger Concrete Mixer, bright yellow, 15" long, 8 pounds on four wheels, steerable via draw. Though perhaps the best detailed, it did not sell well.

No. 2006: The Adams Diesel Road Grader, dark orange, 26" long, 14 pounds, all six wheels, three axles, and blade adjustable to all angles, exactly like the real thing, steerable via steering wheel.

No. 2007: The Unit Mobile Crane, dark orange, 11-1/2" long, 19-1/2" boom, 8 pounds-8 ounces, with adjustable side jacks, steered via drawbar. It boasted a block and tackle and a removable operating clamshell as a standard accessory.

Doepke catalog illustration of a Model 2010 American LaFrance Pumper. Courtesy Ray Funk, photo by Bill Kaufman

No. 2009: The Euclid Earth-Hauler Truck with uncoupling four-wheel tractor to use to tow other toys. It was 27" long, 11 pounds, Euclid green or light road grader orange, and the trailer dumped in the same way as the Wooldridge.

No. 2010: The American La France Pumper Fire Truck, 18" long, 7 pounds, was bright red with chrome trim, ladder, bell, fire extinguisher, hoses and nozzle, and had a reservoir that held water for hand-operated pressure pump.

No. 2011: The Heiliner Earth Scraper, 29" long, 13 pounds, bright dark red, loaded and dumped and operated on four wheels as the Wooldridge did.

No. 2012: The Caterpillar D6 Tractor and Bulldozer, Caterpillar yellow, 15" long, 7 pounds, with real bulldozer treads for sharp realistic turning and adjustable bulldozer blade, plus heavy draw bar. Diesel motor was cast metal.

No. 2013 eliminated and replaced No. 2001: A Barber-Green mobile high-capacity bucket loader, 22" long, 12" high, and 10 pounds, it had buckets on chains and rubber conveyor belt, and was adjustable and steered by steering wheel.

No. 2014: The American La France Aerial Ladder Truck, 23" long, 42" extended ladder height, 11 pounds, bright red and chrome, with bell, red light, adjustable side jacks, was a single unit truck steered by steering wheel.

	C6	**C8**	**C10**
Coin-operated arcade machine, featured the Doepke unit mobile crane, later version by Williams	150	350	550
Coin-operated arcade machine, featured the Doepke unit mobile crane, original unit by Chicago coin, 1956	150	375	600
Doepke Puzzles	20	90	150

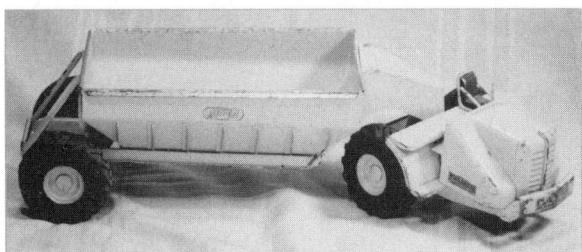

Doepke Wooldridge Earth Hauler, No. 2000, 25". Photo courtesy Calvin L. Chausee

Doepke Unit Mobile Crane, No. 2007, 11-1/2". Photo courtesy Ray Funk

Doepke Barber-Greene high capacity bucket loader, No. 2001, 13". Photo courtesy Calvin L. Chausee

Doepke Jaeger Concrete Mixer, No. 2002, 15". Photo courtesy Calvin L. Chausee

	C6	C8	C10
Doepke Wooden Toys, all Doepke wooden toys are about the same rarity.	25	110	200
Farm Tractor-N-Wagon, No ??, wooden .	75	125	185
No. 2000 Wooldridge H.D. Earth Hauler, 1946-49, all yellow except for driver's seat in black, 25" long	50	200	350
No. 2001 Barber-Greene High Capacity Bucket Loader, fixed chute version, all green 1948-50, orange in 1950,	50	200	350
No. 2001 Barber-Greene High Capacity Bucket Loader, swivel chute version, all green, made 1946-47 only, 13" high	75	330	650
No. 2002 Jaeger Concrete Mixer, 1947-49, all yellow, 15" long	50	225	400
No. 2006 Adams Diesel Road Grader, 1948-56, dark orange 1948, yellow 1949-50, light orange 1951-56, all versions are about the same for rarity, 26" long	50	200	350
No. 2007 Unit Mobile Crane, regular version 1951-56, 11-1/2" long	50	175	300
No. 2007 Unit Mobile Crane, thumbwheeled version 1948-50, 11-1/2" long	50	200	350
No. 2008 American La France Aerial Ladder Truck, 1950, with siren, red	50	200	350
No. 2008 American La France Aerial Ladder Truck, 1951-52, no siren, red	50	175	300
No. 2009 Euclid Earth Hauler Truck (Bottom Dump), 1950-56, forrest green 1950, orange 1951-52, army green/olive drab 1953-56, all color versions of same rarity, 27" long	50	200	350
No. 2010 American-La France Pumper Fire Truck, 1952-56, red, 18" long	75	240	400
No. 2011 Heiliner Earth Scraper, 1951-56, red, Doepke's heaviest toy weighing over 14 pounds, 29" long	75	230	350
No. 2012 Caterpillar D6 Bulldozer, 1952-56, first version 1952 has a spring on the front axle - add 50% to listed prices for this feature, 15" long	75	250	450
No. 2013 Barber-Greene Mobile High-capacity Bucket Loader, 1953-56, dark green, treads, wheels, 22" long	75	240	400
No. 2014 American-La France Aerial Ladder Fire Truck, improved version w/outriggers and a die-cast main ladder that extended to nearly 4 ft. high, red, 23" long	75	250	425

A Doepke American La France Aerial Ladder Truck No. 2008, as shown in a Doepke catalog.

	C6	C8	C10
No. 2015 Clark Airport Tractor and Baggage Trailers, 1954-56, baggage tractor and 2 trailers one w/side panels. Side panels had airline logos, of the 6 different logos planned, only American Airlines and TWA can be found. The others were Braniff, C&S Airlines, Delta, and United. Tractors were red, trailers were yellow or green and side panels could be put on either trailer. First Doepke to have a full color display box, so add 150% to listed value for mint box.	100	275	450
No. 2017 MG, 1954-56, model car kit in gray primer though some were pre-painted red. Came in a large full-color box in 1954-55 and a full-color but smaller box in 1956, add 200% to the listed value for either mint box. 1956 version had plastic wheel hubs instead of metal. 15" long	100	275	450
No. 2018 Jaguar, 1954-56, model car kit, came in large full-color box 1954-55 and a smaller box in 1956. Body only came in pale blue color, any other colors are custom colors by previous owners	100	300	500
No. 2021 Yardbird Handcar, 1954-55, 1st version, yellow base w/red hand cranks, chain cover, and wheels. 34.5" long, 11" wide. Came with enough track to make a circle 12' in diameter,			

Doepke Adams Diesel Road Grader, No. 2006, 26". Photo courtesy Calvin L. Chausee

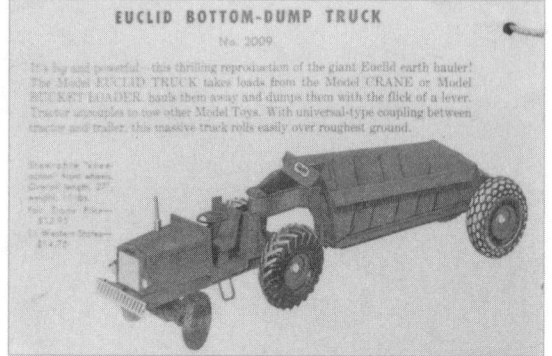

Doepke Euclid Earth Hauler Truck No. 2009, 27", as shown in a Doepke catalog.

Doepke American La France Pumper Fire Truck, No. 2010, 18".

Deopke Heiliner Earth Scraper, No. 2011, 29", as shown in a Doepke catalog.

Doepke American La France Aerial Ladder Fire Truck, 23". Photo courtesy Calvin L. Chausee

Doepke Caterpillar D6 tractor and bulldozer, No. 2012, 15". Photo courtesy Calvin L. Chausee

	C6	C8	C10
weighed 86 lbs., $34.95 on the east coast, $37.95 on the west coast............	125	275	500
No. 2022 Rolybird Pedal Helicopter, 1955-58, blue and yellow w/silver highlights, weighed 35 lbs., 52" long, 37.5" high, 25" wide, sold for $34.95 in the east and $37.95 in the west, rare	150	450	750
No. 2023 Searchlight Truck, 1955-56, American LaFrance searchlight truck was the last regular Doepke steel truck and its rather rare color is all-white	200	525	850
No. 2025 Yardbird Flat Car, 1955-58, flat car goes with the handcar or super yardbird engine made from 1955-58, red and yellow in 1955, red and blue from 1956-58.	75	200	350
No. 2027 Super Yardbird Engine, 1956-58, looks like a streamline engine of the late 1940s to 1960s, this version is powered by a 6-volt car battery and could run on the same 7-inch track the handcar runs on, red and silver, sold new for $225...............	200	425	650
No. 2028 Super Yardbird Engine, 1956-58, gas-powered version, red and silver, sold new for $225.	225	475	750
No. 2029 Yardbird Track Pack, 1955-58, has 8 sections of track..........................	75	150	250
No. 2030 Yardbird Track Pack, 1955-58, has 4 sections of track..........................	50	125	200
No. 2031 Right Switch, 1955-58, right switch for yardbird trains....................	50	150	250
No. 2032 Left Switch, 1955-58, left switch for yardbird trains....................	50	150	250

Doepke Barber-Greene Mobile High-Capacity Bucket Loader, No. 2013, 22" on tracks.

	C6	C8	C10
No. 2033 Yardbird Handcar, 1956-58, 2nd version, blue and red	75	175	300
No. 2034 Crossing Track, 1956-58, crossing track for yardbird trains	75	200	350
No. 2035 Filler Track Set, 1956-58, filler track set for yardbird trains	50	125	200
No. 2036 Flatcar Sides, 1955-58, flatcar sides to make gondola car slats, wood. Red, blue and natural wood color.	75	175	300
No. 2037-2039 Assorted Train Parts, 1955-58, assorted train accessory pieces	50	200	350
No. 2040 Railroad Crossing Sign, 1955-58, railroad crossing sign made out of fibreboard and painted black and white.............................	50	125	200
No. 2042 Road Sign Set, 1955-58, road sign set for yardbird trains made out of fibreboard, contains "Stop," "Yield," and other signs	75	150	250

	C6	C8	C10
No. 2043 Cow Catcher, 1955-58, cow catcher for the super yardbird engines, wood	50	150	250
Popsicle Super Yardbird Trains, 1959, the Popsicle Co. bought the last 250 complete sets of the Super Yardbird trains consisting of an engine, 2 flat cars and sides, the sign sets, station, bench sets, etc. They painted "Popsicle Redball Express" on the sides of the engines and awarded these a part of a sweepstakes contest and as premiums for collected "popsicle points."............	250	575	850

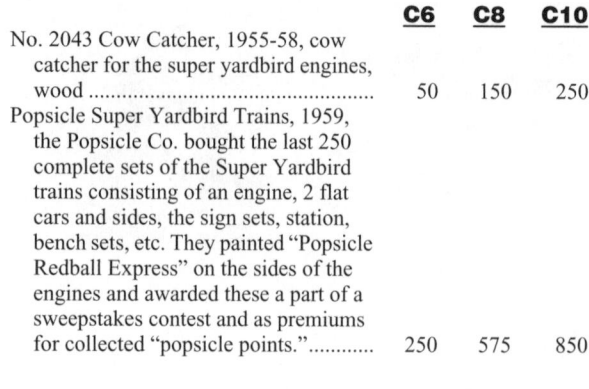

Doepke Searchlight Truck, No. 2023, 1955.

A Doepke "Model Toys" adverstisement.

Doepke Jaguar, No. 2018, 1955. Photo courtesy Calvin L. Chausee

DOLL & CO.

This German toymaker specialized in steam toys in the pre-World War II era.

	C6	C8	C10
Touring Car, open, live steam motor, hand painted tin, four-doors open, 19" long...............................	1500	2700	4000

	C6	C8	C10
Truck, open bed, live steam, chain driven, 19" long	2000	3700	6600

DOOLING BROTHERS

The three brothers began their firm in 1939. There were seven different cars and one variation.

Tether car racing began in the 1930s, when gasoline-powered model airplane engines were bolted to wheeled frames, given a race car covering, and sent racing around oval tracks at speeds in excess of 80mph. The cars were tethered to a central post, hence the name "tether car racing."

The Dooling "61" engine is one of the most famed in all of tether car racing.

C10: New in Box, no Engine
C8: As Run with Engine
C6: Car w/no Engine

Contributor: Rich Malinowski, 10711 S. Cicero Ave., Oak Lawn, IL 60453, Spindizzy2@msn.com

	C6	C8	C10
Arrow, 1948 to late 1950s, 7th car produced, Value in original owner's carrying case: $4000-7000	1000-2000	3500-6500	2500-3500
F Car, 1946, Hornet powered, 6th car produced	1000-1500	2500-4000	2000-3000
Mercury, "18," gasoline powered	1500	2000	2500
Mercury Deluxe Racer, No. "18," gasoline powered, rear drive, made in California in limited numbers between 1939 and 1945, 2nd car produced	900-1800	1500-4500	NPF
Mercury Midget, 1939, first series front drive, 1st car produced	2500-3500	6000-9000	NPF
Mercury Second Series, 1940, gasoline powered, front drive, 4th car produced	1000-2500	2500-6500	NPF
Pee Wee, 1940, gasoline powered, 5th car produced, 12" long	1000-1800	2500-4000	2000-3500
Streamliner, 1939, gasoline powered, 3rd car produced, 16" long	1000-1800	1600-3500	2500-4000

An unrestored Dooling 1939 Mercury Deluxe. Photo courtesy Rich Malinowski

Dooling Brothers' Mercury "18" gasoline-powered racer brought at a 1993 auction. It was made in California in limited numbers between 1939 and 1945. Photo courtesy Jeff Bub Auctions

This restored Dooling Bros. 1946 "F" Car was the sixth car the company released. Photo courtesy Rich Malinowski

The first car Dooling produced was this 1939 Mercury Midget w/first series front frive. Photo courtesy Rich Malinowski

Dooling Bros. second car was this 1939 Mercury Deluxe known as "Rear Drive." This model was restored. Photo courtesy Rich Malinowski

The 1939 Dooling Streamliner was the third car the company produced. Photo courtesy Rich Malinowski

Dooling Bros. fifth car was the 1940 Dooling Pee Wee. Photo courtesy Rich Malinowski

An unrestored Dooling Bros. 1946 "F" Car. Photo courtesy Rich Malinowski

An unrestored example of the Dooling 1940 Mercury Front Wheel Drive car. Photo courtesy Rich Malinowski

Dooling's fourth car was the 1940 Mercury Front Wheel Drive. Collectors know it as the second series front drive car. This example has been restored or "repoped." Photo courtesy Rich Malinowski

The seventh car from Dooling Bros. was this 1948 Dooling Arrow seen here in its original carrying case.

DRUGE

Druge Bros. Mfg. Co. was located at 888 92nd Avenue in Oakland, California. In 1948, its "Hyster" sold for the very high retail price of $9.75.

	C6	C8	C10
Cari-Car Lumber Carrier	100	150	200
Hyster Lumber Carrier, die-cast, yellow, steers w/all four wheels, 11" long, 8" high, 1950s..	120	210	325

Druge Hyster Lumber Carrier. Photo courtesy Tim Oei.

DUNWELL

Dunwell was the trade name given to the toys produced by Metal Products Co. of Clifton, New Jersey. Its trucks appear to have been sold between 1953 and 1958. The line resembles Tonka trucks and examples are rare.

	C6	C8	C10
Auto Transport	65	100	225
Dump Truck	85	125	300
Grain Hauler..	75	125	300
Kroger Semi, refrigerated semi w/"Kroger" decals, 1953-58	250	400	550
Land-o-Lakes Semi, 1956 mail offer, rare	250	400	550
Livestock Truck	75	125	300

	C6	C8	C10
Log Truck, red cab and chassis, round logs..	75	200	350
Red Star Express Lines Truck, rare	300	450	600
Snowcrop Refrigerator Semi....................	200	350	500
Steel Carrier Co. Semi	75	125	300
Wrecker..	100	200	350

Dunwell Log Truck. Photo courtesy Tim Oei

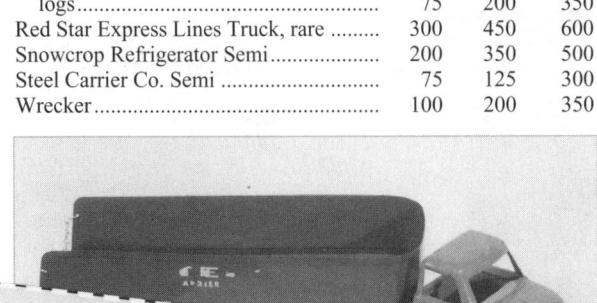

Photo courtesy Tim Oei

Dunwell Livestock Transport. Photo courtesy Tim Oei

oto courtesy Tim Oei

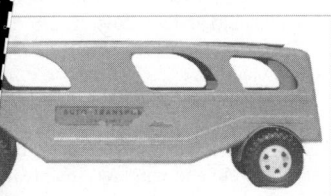

t. Photo courtesy Roy Bonjour

Dunwell Red Star Express Lines Truck. Photo courtesy Bob Smith

MODEL PRODUCTS COMPANY

ducts Co., 93 S. St., Oyster Bay,
ork, may have pioneered the
try that now dominates today's
"Dyna-Mo" brand of HO-scale toys.
pot-metal toys can be identified by
thod of assembling body parts:
tween small posts, and the
earance of the undersides of the

Probably produced in the 1930s, the toys were made by a coarse die-casting process. The earlier vintage cars were made into two to five parts, exclusive of wheels and axles—body, frame, steering wheel, top, and windshield. These parts were then either pinned, clamped, or glued together. Some were packaged as kits, with instructions printed on the box: "Pinch ends of axel [sic] after installing wheels."

The toys were factory painted in as many as four colors per toy.

Contributors: Perry R. Eichor, 703 North Almond Drive, Simpsonville, SC, 29681 and the late Fred Maxwell.

	C6	C8	C10
Convertible, Buick, two-door sedan, top down, one-piece body, solid cast windshield, disk wheels, marked "R-68 HO Buick convertible 55c," late 1930s, 2-3/8" long (D13)	6	9	15
Convertible, Cadillac sedan, two door, late 1930s, 2-3/8" long (D16)	9	6	15

*Top to bottom, left to right:
Dyna-Model Dyna Sedan (D14);
Dyna Limousine (D20); Dyna
Sedan, Buick, 1930s (D12); Dyna
Sedan, Cadillac (D18), late 1930s.
Middle row, left to right: Dyna Taxi,
Buick, late 1930s (D15); Dyna Taxi,
Cadillac, late 1930s (D18); Dyna
Pickup Truck, 2-1/2", late 1930s
(D21); Dyna Pickup Truck, 2-1/2",
late 1930s (D22); Dyna Wrecker,
2-3/4", late 1930s (D23); Dyna
Dump Truck, 2-3/4" (D24). Photo
courtesy Fred Maxwell*

	C6	C8	C10
Delivery Van, Pontiac, open windshield and door windows, late 1930s, 2-3/8" long (D21)	5	8	10
Dump Truck, open windows, hinged body w/realistic load of coal, dual real wheels, three pieces, two colors, 2-3/4" long (D24)	6	9	15
Limousine, Cadillac, open wind-shield and windows incl. rear, late 1930s, 2-1/2" long (D20)	9	6	15
Pickup Truck, GMC (?), one-piece, open windows, one color, 1930s, 2" long (D25)	4	6	8
Pickup Truck, GMC (?), open windows, spoked wheels, two pieces, three colors, late 1930s, 2-1/2" long (D22)	4	6	8
Pickup Truck, Mack (?) marked "US Army" w/Air Corps star decals, late, two piece body, two colors, 1930s, 2" long (D26)	4	6	8
Roadster, Buick (?), open right-hand steering, three colors, 1-7/8" long, four pieces (D04)	4	6	8

	C6	C8	C10
Roadster, Model A Ford (?), top down, open rumble seat, disk wheels, one piece body, unpainted, 2" long (D11)	3	4	6
Roadster, Packard convertible, top down, rumble seat, one-piece body w/glued windshield, spoked wheels, three colors, 1920s, 2" long (D08)	6	9	12
Roadster, Packard convertible, top up, rumble seat, one-piece body w/glued windshield, spoked wheels, three colors, 1920s, 2" long (D09)	6	9	12
Sedan, Buick, open windshield and windows, two colors, 1930s, 2" long (D12)	4	6	8
Sedan, Buick, two door airflow, open windshield and windows, 2-3/8" long (D14)	6	6	12
Sedan, Cadillac sedan, two door, open windshield and windows, late 1930s, 2-3/8" (D17)	9	6	12
Sedan, Pontiac airflow, four door, open windshield and windows incl. rear, 2-3/8" long (D19)	9	6	12

*Top Row, left to right:
Dyna-Model Surey, horseless
carriage (D1); Ford T
Roadster, 1-7/8"; Dyna Touring
Car, 1914 Ford (D7); Dyna
Speedster, antique Mercer
(D3); Touring Car, Stanley
Steamer. Middle Row, left to
right: Touring Car (D5); Model
T Ford (D6); Roadster (D9);
Touring Packard (D10);
Roadster (D8); Bottom row, left
to right: Roadster, top down,
open rumble seat (D11);
Cadillac sedan, late 1930s,
(D17); Buick convertible (D23);
Cadillac convertible (D16).
Photo courtesy Fred Maxwell*

	C6	C8	C10		C6	C8	C10
Speedster, Mercer, right-hand steering, four colors, 2" long, three pieces (D03)	4	6	8	touring with top 60c," 1-5/8" long (D06)	4	6	8
Surrey, horseless carriage, tiller steering, three colors, marked "R-26 HO Surrey, 35c," three piece body kit, 1-3/4" long (D01)	4	6	8	Touring Car, Packard, top down, rumble seat, one-piece body w/glued windshield, spoked wheels, three colors, 1920s, 2" long (D10)	6	9	12
Taxi, Buick sedan, late 1930s, open windshield and windows, two colors, 2-3/8" long (D15)	9	6	15	Touring Car, realistic folded attachable top w/hinge pins, left-hand steering, two colors, 1 7/8" long, five pieces (D05)	5	8	10
Taxi, Cadillac sedan, open windshield and windows including rear, two colors, late 1930s, 2-3/8" long (D18)	9	6	15	Touring Car, Stanley Steamer, open tonneau, right-hand steering, four colors, 2" long, four pieces (D02)	4	6	8
Touring Car, 1914 Ford, cast in one-piece body, top down; glued windshield, three colors, 1-3/4" long (D07)	5	8	10	Truck, Mack (?), tarpaulin covered, two piece body, 2" long (D27)	4	6	8
Touring Car, 1914 Model T Ford, one-piece body, top up, three colors, marked "R-61 HO Model T Ford 1914				Wrecker, GMC (?), open windows, three pieces, four colors, late 1930s, 2-3/4" long (D23)	8	10	14

EBO

	C6	C8	C10
Delivery Truck, early, tin lithographed, clockwork motor, driver, 8" long	400	600	800

ELASTOLIN (HAUSSER)

O&M Hausser (brothers Otto and Max) was founded in 1904 in Ludwigsberg near the German city of Stuttgart in Southern Germany. Hausser, Lineol's larger and fiercest competitor, made a somewhat larger variety of military toys and in the same popular 7-1/2 centimeter scale, but its pieces are generally considered to be a bit less sturdy and well-made (with a few exceptions). Thus, they do not command quite the same prices as do Lineol. Elastolin was Hausser's trade name. (In this section, prices run as part of the picture captions.)

Contributor: Jack Matthews. The author of *Toys Go to War*, Matthews has written for several publications, including Richard O'Brien's *Collecting Toy Soldiers*.

Elastolin Zugwagen, No. 1/734, early, rare, value as shown $3,000. Photo courtesy Jack Matthews

Elastolin Large Prime Mover, No. 731, value as shown $16,000. Photo courtesy Jack Matthews

Elastolin Searchlight Truck, camouflaged, with Luftwaffe crew, early, value as shown, $3,000. Photo courtesy Jack Matthews

Elastolin Prime Mover No. 731, "Chrysler" front, U.S. crew, postwar, value as shown $2,200. Photo courtesy Jack Matthews

Elastolin Prime Mover, No. 730N, camouflaged, value as shown $2,500. Photo courtesy Jack Mathews

Elastolin Six-wheel Prime Mover, No. 730/10, $3,000. Photo courtesy Jack Mathews

Elastolin Panzer Spahwagen, No. 1744, early, rare, value as shown $3,000. Photo courtesy Jack Mathews

Elastolin Prime Mover, No. 730, U.S. crew, postwar, Value as shown $1,500. Photo courtesy Jack Mathews

Elastolin Searchlight Truck, No. 743N with Luftwaffe crew, value as shown, $2,000. Photo courtesy Jack Mathews

Elastolin Early Tank, value as shown, $350. Photo courtesy Jack Mathews

Elastolin Searchlight Truck, No. 743N, value as shown, $2,000. Photo courtesy Jack Mathews

Elastolin postwar Searchlight Truck, No. 744, "Chrysler front" version with U.S. crew, value as shown, $1,200. Photo courtesy Jack Mathews

Elastolin Kubelwagen No. 733/2 (Staff Car), war production, value as shown $900. Photo courtesy Jack Mathews

Elastolin Command Car, No. 733/12, with luggage, very rare, value as shown, $4,000. Photo courtesy Jack Matthews

Elastolin Communications Car, No. 733/10, very rare, value as shown $4,000. Photo courtesy Jack Mathews

Elastolin Zugsmachine, No. 734, rare, value as shown $3,600. Photo courtesy Jack Mathews

Elastolin Searchlight Truck, No. 743, with British crew, value as shown $1,200. Photo courtesy Jack Mathews

Elastolin Searchlight Car, No. 734, with Luftwaffe crew, value as shown $2,400. Photo courtesy Jack Mathews

Elastolin Panzer Spahwagen, No. 744, rare, value as shown $14,000. Photo courtesy Jack Mathews

Elastolin Ambulance, No. 738, camouflaged with rubber tires, value as shown $3,000. Photo courtesy Jack Mathews

Elastolin Flakwagen, No. 739N, camouflaged, with British crew, Value as shown $2,750. Photo courtesy Jack Mathews

Elastolin Kubelauto, No. 1/733, value as shown $650. Photo courtesy Jack Mathews

Elastolin No. 0/730 (very early tank and exceptionally rare), value as shown $2,400. Photo courtesy Jack Mathews

Elastolin Flakwagen, No. 739N, value as shown $2,200. Photo courtesy Jack Mathews

Elastolin Anti-Aircraft Truck, No. 1/740, early, rare, $2,750. Photo courtesy Jack Mathews

Elastolin Anti-Aircraft Truck, No. 0/740, early, rare, value as shown $2,400. Photo courtesy Jack Mathews

Elastolin Kubelauto No. 1/733, with metal wheels, Kreigsproduction, rare, value as shown $700. Photo courtesy Jack Mathews

Elastolin Hauser Tank, early and rare, value as shown, $3,000. Photo courtesy Jack Mathews

Elastolin Heavy Truck towing Kitchen Wagon, No. 794, with crew, very rare, value as shown $4,250. Photo courtesy Jack Mathews

Elastolin Communications Truck, No. 745, light gray, rare, value as shown, $5,000. Photo courtesy Jack Mathews

Elastolin Communications Truck, No. 745, camouflaged, rare, value as shown $5,000. Photo courtesy Jack Mathews

Elastolin Large Prime Mover, No. 731, value as shown $16,000. Photo courtesy Jack Mathews

Elastolin Prime Mover No. 731, "Chrysler" front, U.S. crew, postwar, value as shown $2,200. Photo courtesy Jack Mathews

ELDON

The Eldon Mfg. Co. was based out of Los Angeles, California and located at 1010 E. 62nd St. Eldon was best known for its HO and 1:32-scale slot car sets, but produced a number of vehicle toys as well.

	C6	C8	C10
Aerial Ladder Truck, 21" long	40	60	80
Auto Transport, plastic, includes 4 plastic cars, ramp, 1960s, 20" long	15	30	50
Car Ferry, No. 915, with 18 cars, red plastic, 915	50	100	150

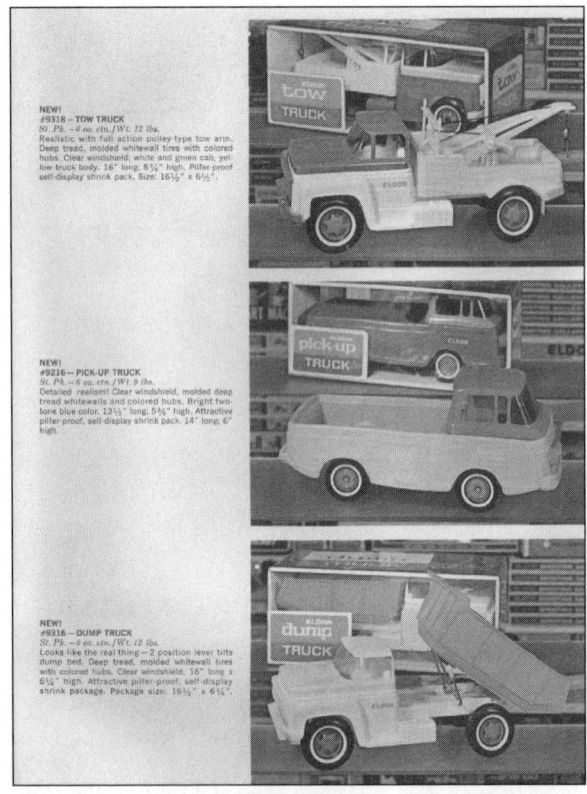

NEW!
#9318 — TOW TRUCK
St. Pk. — 6 cu. cts. /Wt. 12 lbs.
Realistic with full action pulley-type tow arm. Deep tread, molded whitewall tires with colored hubs. Clear windshield; white and green cab; yellow truck body. 16" long; 5½" high. Pilfer-proof self-display shrink pack. Size: 16½" x 6½".

NEW!
#9216 — PICK-UP TRUCK
St. Pk. — 6 cu. cts. /Wt. 9 lbs.
Detailed realism! Clear windshield, molded deep tread whitewalls and colored hubs. Bright two-tone blue color. 13½" long, 5½" high. Attractive pilfer-proof, self-display shrink pack. 14" long; 6" high.

NEW!
#9318 — DUMP TRUCK
St. Pk. — 6 cu. cts. /Wt. 12 lbs.
Looks like the real thing — 2 position lever tilts dump bed. Deep tread, molded whitewall tires with colored hubs. Clear windshield. 16" long x 6½" high. Attractive pilfer-proof, self-display shrink package. Package size: 16½" x 6½".

This page for the 1964 Eldon catalog shows some of the new trucks offered that year.

Dan Gurney racing "Eldon Special" (Lotus 19B) Nassau, Jan. '64

"Tops in realism and excitement!" — that's what world champion race driver Dan Gurney says about Eldon's 1964 road race sets!

Dan Gurney, world champion racing car driver, endorses Eldon Industries Inc's complete line of road race sets and accessories in 1964. His picture and endorsement appears on all packaging of Eldon's road race sets, and in addition, Gurney will be a spokesman for Eldon in their road race TV commercials.

Known in active world-wide racing as a "driver's driver" Dan Gurney has posted many important wins — the French Grand Prix in 1962 — the Daytona Continental, Nassau, the Nurenburgring 1000 Kilometer — as well as many additional wins in American Stock Car racing events.

Dan Gurney's endorsement of Eldon road racing, as part of the promotional program for its model road race sets, will have a more significant meaning for the racing fan than would that of any other racing figure.

ROAD RACE SETS

Race car driver Dan Gurney endorsed all of Eldon's Road Race Sets. This page is from Eldon's Fall 1964 catalog.

	C6	C8	C10
Concrete Truck, 17" long	44	66	85
Corvette, battery-operated, 14" long	44	66	85
Delivery Truck	40	60	80
Dump Truck, 18" long	30	45	75
Ford Lift Gate Truck, 18" long	30	45	75
Hot Rod, 18" long	80	120	160
Hot Rod Kit, batttery operated, snap-together	32	48	65
Mighty Tow Truck	45	68	90
Pink Panther Kit, 1:25-scale plastic model kit, from Bob Reisner's California Show Cars Magazine series, 1970	12	24	40
Road Race Slot Car Set, 1965	35	55	70
Seagrave Fire Pumper, plastic	NPF	NPF	NPF
Stake Truck, No. 989, 18" long	40	60	90
Steam Shovel	20	30	60
Super "100" Slot Car Race Set, plastic, 6 cars - 4 w/engines and 2 interchangable bodies, power pack, track makes over 100 layouts, 1967	65	140	225

	C6	C8	C10
Tank Transport, military	48	72	95
Touch Command Amphibian, battery-operated, plastic, remote, 1960s, 9-1/2" long	12	24	35
Wrecker, plastic, 18" long	40	60	80

Eldon Aerial Ladder Truck, 21". Photo courtesy Terry Sells

ELMAR PRODUCTS COMPANY

Based in New York City and located at 15 W. 24th St., the Elmar Products Co. produced a variety of plastic toys in the 1950s and 1960s.

	C6	C8	C10
Kellogg's Soapbox Derby Car, plastic, cereal premium in the 1950s, spring loaded car w/launcher, rare, 5-1/2" long	25	50	75
Rocket Shooting Tank, plastic, w/3 shells, actually shoots them about 1 foot, converts into a water shooting gun, box has 2 cut-out targets, 3-1/2" long	30	60	110
Soapbox Derby Car, plastic, 5-1/2" long	12	24	40
Tank, plastic, w/3 shells, 4" long	25	50	75

ROCKET SHOOTING TANK
Distributed by Elmar Products Company, 15 West 24th Street, New York City 10, New York. Available in interchangeable colors of red, green, and yellow; 2½" high, 3½" long, 2" wide.
APPROXIMATE RETAIL PRICE . . . . . $ .39

This 1954 ad features Elmar's Rocket Shooting Tank. Note the original retail price. Ad courtesy Islyn Thomas

EMPIRE FORCES

Owned by Gardel Industries at 106 E. 19th St. New York City, Empire Forces released their plaster and composition tanks during World War II c.1943-44.

	C6	C8	C10
E5 Tank, composition (also in plaster)	NPF	NPF	NPF
E6 Tank, composition (also in plaster)	NPF	NPF	NPF

Two Empire tanks, L to R: E5, E6.

ENTEX

Entex, a model kit and toy manufacturer, released numerous highly-detailed plastic kits in the 1970s and 1980s. The images below were scanned directly from company catalogs provided by collector Tom Wetli.

Entex Bugatti Royale, model kit. Catalog courtesy Tom Wetli

Editor's Note: Only a few values have been added, as these listings are brand new, and I've only run across a few at toy shows and in auctions.

	C6	C8	C10
1886 Daimler-Benz, model kit, 1/16-scale, first gas powered car, steerable wheels, ruber tires, molded in color, 1973-74	NPF	NPF	NPF
1896 Peugeot, model kit, 1/43-scale, "Pocket Pak Old Timers," 1973	NPF	NPF	NPF
1901 De Dion Bouton, model kit, 1/16-scale, molded in color, working steering, 1973-74	NPF	NPF	NPF
1905 Rolls-Royce, No. 9017, model kit, 1/16-scale, 150 parts, 1976-78	NPF	NPF	NPF
1906 Rolls-Royce Silver Ghost, model kit, 1/16-scale, 150 parts, molded in color, 1973-74, 1978-80	NPF	NPF	NPF

Entex 1933 Cadillac V-16 Town Car, model kit. Catalog courtesy Tom Wetli

Entex Cobra II, model kit. Catalog courtesy Tom Wetli

Entex Lotus Esprit, model kit. Catalog courtesy Tom Wetli

Entex 1933 Duesenberg Bottail SJ, model kit. Catalog courtesy Tom Wetli

Entex 1967 Corvette, model kit. Catalog courtesy Tom Wetli

Entex 1967 Mustang Convertible, model kit. Catalog courtesy Tom Wetli

Entex 1886 Daimler-Benz, model kit. Catalog courtesy Tom Wetli

Entex 1908 Rolls-Royce "Silver Ghost," model kit. Catalog courtesy Tom Wetli

Entex 1937 Packard 12-cylinder Convertible, model kit. Catalog courtesy Tom Wetli

Entex 1910 Thomas Flyer, model kit. Catalog courtesy Tom Wetli

Entex 1912 Ford Model T, model kit. Catalog courtesy Tom Wetli

	C6	C8	C10
1907 Itala - The First Dune Buggy, model kit, 1/16-scale, won the 1907 race from Peking to Paris, 1972-73, 8-1/2" long..	NPF	NPF	NPF
1908 Rolls-Royce Balloon Car, No. 9001, model kit, 1/16-scale, based on Silver Ghost made for Charles S. Rolls to transport and track his one-man hot-air balloon, 1975-81, 12" long	NPF	NPF	NPF
1910 Thomas Flyer, No. 8490, model kit, 1/16-scale, won the New York to Paris race in 1908, 1974-77, 10" long	NPF	NPF	NPF
1911 Model "T" Ford, model kit, 1/43-scale, "Pocket Pak Old Timers," 1973	NPF	NPF	NPF
1912 Ford Model "T", No. 8469, model kit, 1/16-scale, "The Tin Lizzy," rubber tires, molded in color, 1973-80	NPF	NPF	NPF
1913 Ford Model "T" Van, No. 8497, model kit, 1/16-scale, wood trim, rubber tires, 1974-81, 9-1/2" long	10	20	30
1913 Mercer Raceabout 35J, model kit, 1/43-scale, "Pocket Pak Old Timers," 1973	NPF	NPF	NPF
1914 Dennis Motor Fire Engine, model kit, 1/16-scale, working extension ladder, 500 parts, 1973-76	NPF	NPF	NPF
1915 Ford Model "T" Stake Truck, No. 8498, model kit, 1/16-scale, wood parts, "Columbia Cartage Co." on sides, 1974-81, 12" long	NPF	NPF	NPF
1919 Hispano Suiza, model kit, 1/16-scale, "The Alfonso," 139 parts, molded in color, 1972-74	NPF	NPF	NPF
1928 Lincoln Dietrich, model kit, 1/16-scale, 227 parts, molded in color, 1972-74, 1978-81, 13" long	NPF	NPF	NPF
1928 Mercedes Benz, model kit, 1/43-scale, "Pocket Pak Old Timers," 1973	NPF	NPF	NPF
1928 Mercedes-Benz SS, No. 9031, model kit, 1/16-scale, 1977-81	NPF	NPF	NPF
1929 Mercedes-Benz SSK, No. 9588, model kit, 1/24-scale, 1981, 7-1/2" long	NPF	NPF	NPF
1931 Bugatti Royal Cabriolet, No. 9587, model kit, 1/24-scale, 1981, 9-3/4" long	NPF	NPF	NPF
1931 Ford Model A Delivery Van, No. 9016, model kit, 1/16-scale, bakery decals, 1976-81, 10" long	NPF	NPF	NPF

	C6	C8	C10
1931 Ford Model A Pickup, No. 9015, model kit, 1/16-scale, 1976-81, 10" long	NPF	NPF	NPF
1931 Ford Model A Sedan, No. 9014, model kit, 1/16-scale, 1976-81, 10" long	NPF	NPF	NPF
1933 Cadillac V-16 Town Car, No. 9029, model kit, 1/16-scale, rubber tires, chrome trim, opening doors, hood, trunk, 1977-81	NPF	NPF	NPF
1933 Duesenberg SJ Boattail, No. 9135, model kit, 1/16-scale, "The Weyman Speedster," 1978-81	NPF	NPF	NPF
1935 Morgan, model kit, 1/16-scale, "The Mog," three wheel car, 1973-74	NPF	NPF	NPF
1936 Mercedes 540-K, No. 8499, model kit, 1/16-scale, molded in color, rubber tires, 1974, 13-1/2" long	NPF	NPF	NPF
1936 Mercedes 540-K Sport Roadster, No. 8501, model kit, 1/16-scale, Maharaja version optional, 1976, 13" long	NPF	NPF	NPF
1937 Packard 12-cylinder Convertible Coupe, No. 8499, model kit, 1/16-scale, molded in color, rubber tires, 1974-81, 13-1/2" long	NPF	NPF	NPF
1937 Packard V-12 Formal Sedan, No. 9002, model kit, 1/16-scale, opening hood, 1976-81, 14" long	NPF	NPF	NPF
1937 Rolls-Royce Phantom III, No. 9000, model kit, 1/16-scale, V-12 engine, 1976-81, 13-1/8" long	10	20	30
1939 Jaguar SS100, No. 8500, model kit, 1/16-scale, molded in color, rubber tires, 1974-80	NPF	NPF	NPF
1959-62 Rolls-Royce Silver Cloud II, No. 9111, model kit, 1/25-scale, 1978-81	NPF	NPF	NPF
1967 Corvette, No. 9107, model kit, 1/16-scale, opening doors and hood, rubber tires, 1979, 10" long	NPF	NPF	NPF
1967 Mustang Convertible, No. 9106, model kit, 1/16-scale, opening doors, hood, trunk, 1979-81, 10" long	NPF	NPF	NPF
1969 Corvette, No. 9107, model kit, 1/16-scale, opening doors and hood, 1979-81, 11" long	NPF	NPF	NPF
Alfa Romeo Scarabeo 1600, No. 9132, model kit, 1/16-scale, 1979	NPF	NPF	NPF

Entex MG-TC, model kit. Catalog courtesy Tom Wetli

	C6	C8	C10
Alfa Romeo Scarabeo 1600, No. 9132, model kit, 1/16-scale, opening canopy, 1978, 10" long	NPF	NPF	NPF
BMW 2002 Turbo, No. 9026, model kit, 1/20-scale, opening doors, 1977-78	NPF	NPF	NPF
BMW 3.0 CSI, No. 9030, model kit, 1/12-scale, race car decals, 1977-81	NPF	NPF	NPF
BMW 3.0 CSL, No. 9037, model kit, 1/25-scale, Coupe Sport Long wheelbase, race car, 1977	NPF	NPF	NPF
BMW 3.0 CSL, No. 9134, model kit, 1/16-scale, race car, opening doors, hood, trunk, 1978	NPF	NPF	NPF
BMW 3.5 CSL, No. 9134, model kit, 1/16-scale, racing decals, 1979-80	NPF	NPF	NPF
Bugatti Royale, model kit, 1/16-scale, opening doors and hood, 1972-77	10	20	30
Capri, No. 9036, model kit, 1/25-scale, race car, 1977	NPF	NPF	NPF
Cobra II, No. 9032, model kit, 1/16-scale, racing decals, 1977-79	NPF	NPF	NPF
Datsun 260Z, No. 9008D, model kit, 1/25-scale, 1976	NPF	NPF	NPF
Datsun 280-Z, No. 9046, model kit, 1/16-scale, "The Z," 1977	NPF	NPF	NPF
DeTomaso Pantera, No. 9122, model kit, 1/25-scale, 1978	NPF	NPF	NPF
Europa Lotus, No. 9008L, model kit, 1/25-scale, 1976	NPF	NPF	NPF
Excalibur SSK, No. 9052, model kit, 1/12-scale, removable hood, 1979-81	NPF	NPF	NPF
Fiat X1/9, No. 9028, model kit, 1/20-scale, opening doors, hood, trunk, racing decals, 1977-78	NPF	NPF	NPF
Honda Accord, No. 9043, model kit, 1/20-scale, 1977-78	NPF	NPF	NPF
Honda Civic, No. 9021, model kit, 1/16-scale, CVCC engine, opening doors and hood, 1976	NPF	NPF	NPF
Honda Civic 2-Door, No. 9027, model kit, 1/20-scale, opening doors, hood, trunk, 1977-78	NPF	NPF	NPF

	C6	C8	C10
Jaguar XJ-S, No. 9047, model kit, 1/16-scale, opening doors, hood, trunk, 1977-79	NPF	NPF	NPF
John Player Special, No. 9039, model kit, 1/8-scale, Grand Prix race car, 1977-80, 23" long	NPF	NPF	NPF
Lamborghini Countach, No. 9051, model kit, 1/12-scale, V-12 engine, opening doors, hood, trunk, 1978-79	NPF	NPF	NPF
Lamborghini Countach, No. 9123, model kit, 1/25-scale, 1978-79	NPF	NPF	NPF
Lamborghini Jota, No. 9124, model kit, 1/25-scale, 1978	NPF	NPF	NPF
Lotus Esprit, No. 9121, model kit, 1/25-scale, 1978-79	NPF	NPF	NPF
Lotus Esprit, No. 9133, model kit, 1/16-scale, 1978-79, 10" long	NPF	NPF	NPF
Marlboro McLaren M23-Ford, No. 9191, model kit, 1/8-scale, Grand Prix race car, 1978-80	NPF	NPF	NPF
Mazda Cosmo, No. 9041, model kit, 1/20-scale, 1977-78	NPF	NPF	NPF
Mazda RX3, model kit, 1/20-scale, with Wankel engine, opening hood, trunk, doors, rubber tires, molded in color, (No. 8470 in 1974), 1973-74	NPF	NPF	NPF
Mazda RX4, No. 8492, model kit, 1/20-scale, rotary Wankel engine, 1974	NPF	NPF	NPF
Mazda RX7, No. 9503, model kit, 1/25-scale, 1979	NPF	NPF	NPF
Mercedes 300SL, No. 9113, model kit, 1/25-scale, 1978-81	NPF	NPF	NPF
Mercedes 300SL Gullwing, No. 9019, model kit, 1/16-scale, opening gullwing doors, opening hood and trunk, rubber tires, 1976-80	NPF	NPF	NPF
Mercedes 450SL, No. 9020, model kit, 1/12-scale, opening doors, hood, trunk, 1976-79	NPF	NPF	NPF
Mercer Raceabout, model kit, 1/16-scale, gold plated parts, 1972-77	10	20	30
MG-TC, No. 8223, model kit, 1/16-scale, rubber tires, 1972-81	12	24	40
Mustang II Mach I, No. 9008F, model kit, 1/25-scale, 1976-79	NPF	NPF	NPF
Mustang II Mach I, No. 9024, model kit, 1/16-scale, opening doors and hood, 1976, 11" long	NPF	NPF	NPF
Pantera GTS, No. 9035, model kit, 1/25-scale, race car, 1977	NPF	NPF	NPF
Porsche 911 Carrera, No. 9022, model kit, 1/12-scale, racing type w/opening doors, hood, trunk, 1976-79	NPF	NPF	NPF

Entex 1908 Rolls-Royce Balloon Car, model kit. Catalog courtesy Tom Wetli

Entex 1937 Packard V12 Formal Sedan, model kit. Catalog courtesy Tom Wetli

	C6	C8	C10
Porsche 914, No. 9023, model kit, 1/20-scale, 1976-79, 8" long	NPF	NPF	NPF
Porsche 924, No. 9048, model kit, 1/16-scale, 1979	NPF	NPF	NPF
Porsche 924, No. 9048, model kit, 1/16-scale, opening doors, hood, hatch, headlights, 1978	NPF	NPF	NPF
Porsche 924 Turbo, No. 9151, model kit, 1/16-scale, 1981			
Porsche Carrera 906, No. 9131, model kit, 1/16-scale, gullwing doors, 1979, 10" long	NPF	NPF	NPF
Porsche Carrera 906, No. 9131, model kit, 1/16-scale, race car, gullwing doors, 1978, 10" long	NPF	NPF	NPF

	C6	C8	C10
Porsche Carrera RSR Turbo, No. 9040, model kit, 1/8-scale, RSR 935 Martini Racer, 1977-79, 23" long	NPF	NPF	NPF
Porsche Turbo, No. 9038, model kit, 1/25-scale, RSR 935 Martini Racer, 1977	NPF	NPF	NPF
Rotary Engine Mazda RX2, model kit, 1/20-scale, 130 parts, working doors, hood, trunk, 1972-74	NPF	NPF	NPF
Triumph TR3, No. 9112, model kit, 1/25-scale, 1978-81	NPF	NPF	NPF
Triumph TR7, No. 9044, model kit, 1/20-scale, opening doors, hood, trunk, 1977	NPF	NPF	NPF
VW Bug, No. 9042, model kit, 1/20-scale, opening doors, hood, trunk, 1977-79	NPF	NPF	NPF

ERIE

According to James Apthrope, Erie toys were made by Parker White Metal Company, which apparently began in Erie, Pennsylvania, but moved to Fairview in the early 1960s. However, according to company officials, the firm made toys only prior to World War II. It printed no catalogs.

Contributor: Dave Leopard, 2507 Feather Run Trail, West Columbia, SC 29169-4915.

	C6	C8	C10
Cabover Truck, no tail gate, c.1937, 3-1/4" long (EV15)	25	30	40
Champion Coal Truck, c.1935, 5" long (EV21)	50	60	100
Coupe, futuristic, no chassis, c.1939, 4-1/4" long (EV19)	30	40	60
Ford Ice Truck, "Pure Ice Co.," 1935, 5" long (EV13)	50	60	100
Ford Pickup, painted (EV09)	40	55	80
Ford Pickup Truck, high sides, large rear window, 1935, 5" long (EV11)	40	60	80
Ford Pickup Truck, high sides, small rear window, 1935, 5" long (EV12)	40	60	80
Ford Pickup Truck, low sides, plated, 1935, 5" long (EV10)	45	60	80

	C6	C8	C10
Ford Tow Truck, "Servel Body," 1935, 5" long (EV14)	50	65	90
Lincoln Zephyr Sedan, 1936, 3-1/2" long, plated (EV04)	35	40	65
Lincoln Zephyr Sedan, painted, 1936, 3-1/2" long (EV03)	25	30	50
Lincoln Zephyr Sedan, painted, 1936, 5-1/2" long (EV01)	40	60	80
Lincoln Zephyr Sedan, plated, 1936, 5-1/2" long (EV02)	45	55	85
Packard Roadster, painted, 1936, 3-1/2" long (EV07)	30	35	50
Packard Roadster, painted, 1936, 6" long (EV05)	45	65	95
Packard Roadster, plated, 1936, 3-1/2" long (EV08)	40	50	65
Packard Roadster, plated, 1936, 6" long (EV06)	50	70	100
Sedan, futuristic, fin on trunk, no chassis, c.1939, 4-1/4" long (EV18)	30	40	60
Sedan, sharknose, no chassis, c.1939, 4-1/4" long (EV20)	30	40	60
Tow Truck, no chassis, c.1939, 4-1/4" long (EV17)	30	40	60

Erie Champion Coal Truck, 1935. Photo courtesy John Taylor

Erie Sedan, sharknose, no chassis (cast without fenders and running boards), c.1939, 4-1/4" long. Photo courtesy James Apthrope

ERTL

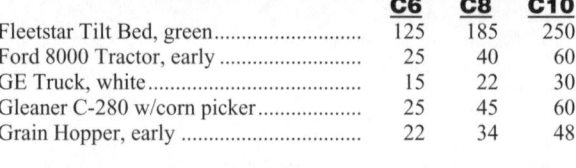

Ertl was begun by Fred Ertl Sr., in 1945, working out of his Dubuque, Iowa, home. As business expanded, the firm moved to Dyersville, Iowa. Ertl learned about using sand molds in his native Germany; very early in the company's history, he began working directly from the original blueprints to make his toy tractors, trucks, and other wheeled toys. Ertl's specialty is farm toys, with rights obtained from such manufacturers as International Harvester and John Deere. Today, Ertl is the largest manufacturer of toy-farm equipment in the world; in addition, it makes a number of other toys, such as cars, trucks, model kits, and airplanes. The company also owns the Britains toy soldier company.

Ertl was purchased by Racing Champions in 1998 and now go by the name Racing Champions-Ertl. The company Web site is www.ertltoys.com.

	C6	C8	C10
Allis-Chalmers B-112 Tractor	70	110	165
Conoco Tanker	75	120	175
Fleetstar Dump Truck, red, ten wheel	125	185	250
Fleetstar Hi-Side Dump Truck, red and white	125	185	250

	C6	C8	C10
Fleetstar Tilt Bed, green	125	185	250
Ford 8000 Tractor, early	25	40	60
GE Truck, white	15	22	30
Gleaner C-280 w/corn picker	25	45	60
Grain Hopper, early	22	34	48

Ertl Cab-Over Dump Truck, white and red. Photo courtesy Bob Smith

Ertl Loadstar Tilt Bed. Photo courtesy Bob Smith

Ertl Loadstar Tow Truck, white and red. Photo courtesy Bob Smith

Ertl Fleetstar Dump Truck, red. Photo courtesy Bob Smith

Ertl Fleetstar Hi-Side Dump Truck, white and red. Photo courtesy Bob Smith

	C6	C8	C10
Greyhound Bus, GM Silversides style, aluminum, Greyhound symbols on sides, 9" long, 1947	75	150	225
IHC Farmal 806, square fender	100	175	230
International Fleetstar Gravity Feed Truck	150	250	350

	C6	C8	C10
International Scout, maroon or blue	85	135	195
John Deere 500 Bulldozer, w/blade	40	70	100
John Deere 6600 Combine	60	100	140
Loadstar Box Van, lavender and white	200	375	575

Ertl Fleetstar Tilt Bed, green. Photo courtesy Bob Smith

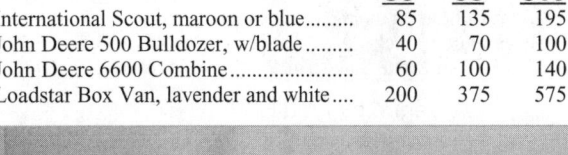

Ertl Van Lines Pup Trailer, white. Photo courtesy Bob Smith

Ertl International Harvester Fleetstar Gravity Feed Truck.

Ertl Loadstar Box Van, lavender and white. Photo courtesy Bob Smith

Ertl International Scout, maroon (top up) and blue (top down). Photo courtesy Bob Smith

Ertl Loadstar Concrete Truck, red and white. Photo courtesy Bob Smith

	C6	C8	C10
Loadstar Concrete Truck, red and white ..	200	350	500
Loadstar Dump Truck	140	250	325
Loadstar Grain/Cattle Stake Truck	140	250	325
Loadstar Tilt Bed, green and gray	125	175	300
Loadstar Tow Truck, white and red	150	275	425
Mary Kay Cosmetics Trailer Truck	65	115	150
Mobile Tanker	40	60	88
Picker	25	40	60
School Bus, GM Silversides style, aluminum, 9" long, c.1950	85	175	285
Texaco Tanker, No. 2	150	250	350
Van Lines Pup Trailer, white	100	150	225
White Cab-Over Dump Truck, white and red	165	265	400

Ertl Grain Hopper, 14-1/2". Photo courtesy Harvey K. Rainess

ERWIN

	C6	C8	C10		C6	C8	C10
Ford, w/windshield wipers	40	60	80	Race Car	55	82	110

F & F CEREAL PREMIUMS

The toy vehicles that were included in Post cereals during the 1950s-1960s were made by the F&F Mold and Die Works of Dayton, Ohio, a company that specialized in manufacturing plastic premiums for the food industry. The Fiedler and Fiedler company was in business from 1945 until 1987, and its entire product-line consisted of plastic premiums.

The small plastic vehicles, about three inches long, were included in Post Grape-Nut Flakes, Corn Flakes, Rice Krispies, etc. over a period of about fifteen years, beginning in 1954. Most of the cereal premiums were cars, but they also made speedboats, which were marked "Century"; several versions of a tractor-trailer truck, which were marked "Ford" on the cab and "Fruehauf" on the trailer; and two versions of a Greyhound bus.

All of the F&F vehicles from 1954 to 1967 are clearly marked with their trademark. Two earlier Fords, a 1950 and a 1951 sedan, have magnets glued underneath the roof, are the same scale and are very similar to other F&F vehicles. Collectors

disagree as to whether these early Fords are in fact F&Fs. Likewise, a series of 1969 Mercurys, identical to earlier F&F vehicles in scale, style, and materials, are marked "JVZ Co." Whether these Fords and Mercurys are properly identified as F&F or not, they are very similar and fit nicely with known F&F vehicles. F & F specialists place great value on certain scarce colors but no attempt is made here to differentiate.

Contributor: Dave Leopard, 2507 Feather Run Trail, West Columbia, SC 29169-4915.

	C6	C8	C10
1950 Ford Sedan, four-door	20	30	50
1951 Ford Sedan, four-door	20	30	50
1954 Ford Crestline Hardtop	10	15	20
1954 Ford Crestline Sedan, four-door	10	15	20
1954 Ford Crestline Sunliner	10	15	20
1954 Ford Customline Ranchwagon	10	15	20
1954 Ford Customline Sedan, two-door ..	10	15	20
1954 Mercury Monterray Convertible	10	15	20
1954 Mercury Monterray Sedan, four-door	10	15	20

A collection of F&F Cereal Premium cars. KP photo courtesy Karen O'Brien

	C6	C8	C10
1954 Mercury Monterray Sedan, two-door	10	15	20
1954 Mercury XM-800 Show Car	10	15	20
1954 Ford Thunderbird Show Car	20	40	60
1955 Ford Country Sedan (wagon)	10	15	20
1955 Ford Customline Sedan, two-door	10	15	20
1955 Ford Fairlane Crown Victoria	10	15	20
1955 Ford Fairlane Sunliner	10	15	20
1955 Ford Thunderbird Convertible	10	15	20
1957 Ford Ambulance	10	15	20
1957 Ford Convertible	10	15	20
1957 Ford Firechief Car	10	15	20
1957 Ford Hardtop Sedan, four-door	10	15	20
1957 Ford Highway Patrol	10	15	20
1959 Ford Thunderbird Convertible	10	15	20
1959 Ford Thunderbird Hardtop	10	15	20
1960 Plymouth Convertible	10	15	20
1960 Plymouth Hardtop Coupe	10	15	20
1960 Plymouth Station Wagon	10	15	20
1961 Ford Thunderbird Convertible	10	15	20

	C6	C8	C10
1961 Ford Thunderbird Hardtop	10	15	20
1961 Ford Thunderbird Roadster, single seat	10	15	20
1966 Ford Mustang Convertible	10	15	20
1966 Ford Mustang Fastback	10	15	20
1966 Ford Mustang Hardtop	10	15	20
1967 Mercury Cougar Hardtop	10	15	20
1969 Mercury Cougar Hardtop	10	15	20
1969 Mercury Cyclone Fastback	10	15	20
1969 Mercury Hardtop, two-Door	10	15	20
1969 Mercury Sedan, four-door	10	15	20
Ford Tractor/Trailer, enclosed	10	15	20
Ford Tractor/Trailer, flatbed	10	15	20
Ford Tractor/Trailer, lowboy	10	15	20
Ford Tractor/Trailer, moving van	10	15	20
Ford Tractor/Trailer Oil Tanker	10	15	20
Greyhound Bus	10	15	20
Greyhound Scenicruiser Double-Decker Bus	10	15	20

FALLOWS TOYS

James Fallows & Sons was originally incorporated as the C.B. Porter Co. In 1894, the name was changed again to Frederick & Henry Fallows Toys. Based in Philadelphia, Penn., the company specialized in tin vehicles, animal-drawn toys, ships, and trains.

	C6	C8	C10
Frederick & Henry, Horseless Carriage, w/driver, cast iron and tin, c.1905, 8" long	900	1350	1800

Fallows Toys Frederick & Henry Horseless Carriage with driver, 8". Photo courtesy Wilkins Collection, Detroit Antique Toy Museum

FIRESTONE

At the San Diego World's Fair of 1935, the Firestone Tire and Rubber Company exhibit included a press that manufactured commemorative Ford Tudors. The rubber replicas were sold to patrons for 10 cents each. The cars were such a hit that Firestone brought the press to the 1936 Great Lakes Exposition in Cleveland, Ohio, and to the Texas Centennial in Dallas, Texas, and manufactured 1936 Ford Tudors. Firestone brought the press to the 1939 Golden Gate Exposition in San Francisco, California, and manufactured 1939 Mercury four-door sedans.

Contributor: Dave Leopard, 2507 Feather Run Trail, West Columbia, SC 29169-4915.

	C6	C8	C10
'35 Ford Sedan, two-door humpback, white rubber tires "Firestone," 4-7/8" long (FA02)	50	60	75
'36 Ford Sedan, two-door humpback, white rubber tires "Firestone," 4-7/8" long (FA03)	70	105	140

	C6	C8	C10
'39 Mercury fastback Sedan, four-door, white rubber tires "Firestone," 4 3/4" long (FA01)	60	75	90

Firestone FA03 (both) with original box. Photo courtesy Ron Smith

FISCHER, HEINRICH & CO.

Fischer's easily recognized mark, a fish swimming through the letter A, is a unique trademark usually found on the rear of the car. The George Brogfeldt store of New Yourk purchased many of the toys produced by Fischer for the American market. Not all of the Fischer toys carried his mark, however. Nifty toys, for example, was one of the trademarks used by the company. The great comic character tin toy, Toonerville Trolley, is one of the best known Fischer toys made under the Nifty trademark.

Contributor: Bob Smith, The Village Smith, 62 West Ave., Fairport, NY 14450-2102

	C6	C8	C10
Automatic Dump Truck, clockwork motor, 10-1/2" long	550	825	1200
Double-Decker Bus, tin clockwork, c.1910, 7-1/2" long	680	1000	1500

Fischer Limousine, 9", green and black, back doors open. Photo courtesy Bob Smith

Fischer Limousine, c.1910. Photo courtesy Bertoia Auctions

Fischer Double-Deck Bus, tin clockwork, 7-1/2". Photo courtesy Harvey K. Rainess

Fischer Limousine, 7-1/2", circa 1918, green and black. Photo courtesy Bob Smith

Fischer Torpedo, 8", red and yellow, tin lithographed. Photo courtesy Bob Smith

Left to right: Fischer Vis-à-Vis, 6-1/2"; Tourer, 8-1/2". Photo by Len Rosenberg courtesy Bob Smith

	C6	C8	C10
Limousine, green and black, clockwork motor head lamps, windshield, c.1918, 7-1/2" long	550	825	1175
Limousine, green and black, clockwork motor, back doors open, c.1915, 9" long	650	975	1275
Limousine, luggage rack, w/driver, 9" long	650	1000	1300
Limousine, maroon, black stripes, w/driver, overhead rack, c.1910, 13" long	1700	2800	4500

	C6	C8	C10
Limousine, w/chauffeur, clockwork motor, 10" long	465	700	930
Torpedo, red and yellow tin lithographed, clockwork motor, c.1912, 8" long	700	1000	1375
Tourer, 8-1/2" long	NPF	NPF	NPF
Tourer, w/chauffeur and two women, 8 1/2" long	500	750	1000
Town Coupe, tin, clockwork motor, approx. 7" long	800	1300	2200
Vis-A-Vis, 6-1/2" long	NPF	NPF	NPF

FISHER-PRICE

Fisher-Price was founded by Herman Fisher and Irving Price on October 1, 1930 in East Aurora, New York. It made (and makes) quality wood toys for small children, colorfully lithographed. Relatively few Fisher-Price toys are cars or trucks. A comprehensive listing of all Fisher-Price toys is available in the annual title, *Toys & Prices*.

	C6	C8	C10
Bouncy Racer, No. 8, 1960, driver bounces	45	90	125
Concrete Mixer, No. 926, 1959	175	310	485
Dinkey Engine, No. 642, 1959	30	60	90
Donald Duck Choo-Choo, No. 450, 1940	350	600	1200
Donald Duck Choo-Choo, No. 465, 1936	750	1150	1600
Elsie's Dairy Truck, No. 745, 1948	400	575	700
Fire Engine, Play Family, No. 720, 1969, w/2 firemen, 12" hose, 9" extension ladder, ringing bell	15	30	45
Fire Truck, No. 630, 1959	30	60	110
Golden Gultch Express, No. 191, 1961	75	150	225
Husky Dump Truck, No. 145, 1963, oversized tires, two passengers bob up and down	50	75	100
Jolly Jalopy, No. 724, 1965, wooden clown car w/oversized plastic tires	11	16	22
Looky Fire Truck, No. 7, 1950, three attached firemen, nickel bell, smiling front grille	85	125	170

	C6	C8	C10
Mickey Mouse Choo-Choo, No. 432, 1938	450	850	1800
Mickey Mouse Choo-Choo, No. 485, 1949, update of the old #432 w/new litho graphics	75	155	255

Fisher-Price Mickey Mouse Choo-Choo, 1938.

Fisher-Price Peter Bunny Truck, No. 472, 1939. Photo courtesy John Murray. Photo by Ross MacKearnin

Fisher-Price Popeye the Sailor, 1936. Photo courtesy John Murray. Photo by Ross MacKearnin

Fisher-Price issued two different Donald Duck Choo-Choo toys. This is the #450 from 1940.

Fisher-Price Elsie's Dairy Cart, No. 745, 1948. Photo courtesy John Murray. Photo by Ross MacKearnin

Fisher-Price Looky Fire Truck, No. 7, 1950. Photo courtesy John Murray. Photo by Ross MacKearnin

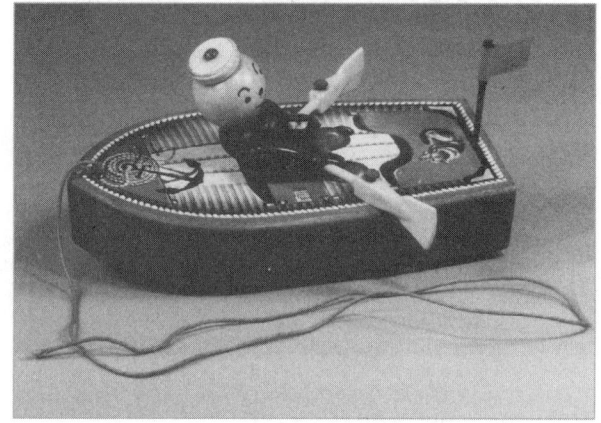

Fisher-Price Racing Rowboat, 1952.

	C6	C8	C10
Mickey Mouse Safety Patrol, No. 733, 1956, Mickey's arms have moveable "Stop" and "Go" signs	262	393	525
Nifty Station Wagon, No. 234, 1960, 3 Little People and dog	225	325	450
Peter Bunny Cart, No. 472, 1939	225	275	375
Popeye the Sailor, No. 703, 1936, movable arms the struck bell	600	1200	2400
Racing Rowboat, No. 730, 1952	105	225	475
Road Roller, No. 152, 1934, circus bear driver, concealed whistle	800	1500	2200
Safety School Bus, No. 983, 1959, 6 Little People, driver, first appearance of "Play Family" figures	200	425	675
Safety School Bus, No. 984, 1961	150	310	475
Smokie Engine, No. 642, 1960	30	60	100
Snorky Fire Engine, No. 168, 1960, 4 firemen, 9-1/2" lift, dog	150	300	425

	C6	C8	C10
Snorky Fire Engine, No. 169, 1961, 4 firemen	175	275	450
Space Blazer, No. 750, 1953	225	550	750
Sports Car, No. 674, 1958, wooden body in red, pink or blue	62	93	125
Stake Truck, No. 649, 1960	50	100	160
Tow Truck, No. 615, 1960, w/crane, tow hook, motor sound, bouncing driver	30	45	60
Tow Truck and Car, Play Family, No. 718, 1969	25	38	50
Tractor, No. 629, 1962, farmer driver w/spinning head	25	38	50
Tractor and Cart, Play Family, No. 716, 1969	10	20	30
Winky Blinky Fire Truck, No. 200, 1954, new litho graphics	65	135	185

FREIDAG

According to a well-illustrated article by Fred MacAdam in the March 1993 *Antique Toy World*, William Freidag formed Freidag Mfg. Co. and Foundry in Freeport, Illinois, in 1920. He pronounced his last name "Firday". Freidag's cast-iron toys are obscure but significant and can easily be confused with those by another maker. Thus, collectors might find it helpful to obtain a copy of the MacAdam article when they're uncertain about any cast-iron toy from 1920-1932.

	C6	C8	C10
Auto, w/chauffeur, 1920s	375	562	750
Bus, 6-3/4" long	225	338	450
Coupe, 1924, 5-3/4" long	290	435	580
Double-Decker Bus, 9-1/4" long	850	1400	2100
Panel Delivery Truck, 7-1/2" long	1200	2200	3200
Pickup Truck, 7-1/2" long	500	750	1000
Racer, w/driver and passenger, 6-1/2" long	400	600	800
Roadster, 1922, 9-1/4" long	500	750	1000
Taxi, 1920s, 7" long	450	675	900
Taxi, w/black driver	600	1000	1400
Truck, flatbed, 10" long	500	750	1000
Yellow Cab, 5" long	550	850	1250

Freidag Double-decker Bus, 9-1/4" long. Photo courtesy Bertoia Auctions. Freidag Roadster, 1922, 9-1/4". Photo courtesy Bertoia Auctions

Freidg Roadster, 1922, 9-1/4". Photo courtesy Bertoia Auctions

Left to right: Freidag Pickup Truck, 7-1/2"; Panel Delivery Truck, 7-1/2". Photo courtesy Bertoia Auctions

FUTURISTIC

Discovered by collector Dave Leopard, these slush-cast lead-alloy vehicles obviously belong together. FU1 appears to be pre-WWII, and the others postwar. The manufacturer is unknown.

	C6	C8	C10
Car pulling house trailer, white tires, 6" long	NPF	NPF	NPF
Coupe, w/fin, black tires, 4-1/4" long	NPF	NPF	NPF
Oil Truck, black tires, reads "Super Oil," 3-3/4" long	NPF	NPF	NPF

Futuristic Coupe with fin, 4-1/4", black tires. Photo courtesy Dave Leopard

Futuristic Oil Truck, 3-3/4". Photo courtesy Dave Leopard

Futuristic Car Pulling House Trailer, 6", white tires. Photo courtesy Dave Leopard

G & K

A German tin toy manufacturer that specialized in tin wind-up toys.

	C6	C8	C10
Delivery Truck, tin wind-up, w/driver, early, 5-1/2" long	475	715	950
Motorcycle, tin wind-up, w/seat-like sidecar, early, 6-1/2" long	800	1300	1800

GAMA

An abbreviation for founder Gerog Adam Mangold, Gama was incorporated in 1882. Gama specialized in tinplate toys with clockwork motors. The high quality of craftsmanship allowed Gama to survive into the 1980s when the company merged with Schuco.

The tinplate Cadillac is the crowning achievement of Gama's tin toy engineering. Produced in response to the successful Japanese tin cars flooding the American market, the Cadillac isn't an accurate reproduction of the real 1954 Cadillac, but an adaptation of the styling of Marusan's 1950 Cadillac with 1954 styling features added.

Responding to the changes in the toy industry, Gama introduced the MiniMod line of die-cast cars in 1959 to compete with the popular Matchbox, Corgi, and Dinky brands. The success of the 1:43-scale

cars propelled the company through the next few decades.

Gama prewar tank, with chain treads (G1), value as shown $500. Photo courtesy Jack Matthews

Gama prewar tank, large (GT2), value as shown $500. Photo courtesy Jack Matthews

Gama pre-war tank, (GT3), large, value as shown, $500. Photo courtesy Jack Matthews

Gama post-war tank, large (GT4), value as shown, $350. Photo courtesy Jack Matthews

Gama postwar tank, large (GT5), value as shown $350. Photo courtesy Jack Matthews

Gama postwar tank, large (GT6), value as shown $350. Photo courtesy Jack Matthews

Gama postwar tank, large (GT7), value as shown $350. Photo courtesy Jack Matthews

Gama postwar tank, large (GT8), value as shown $300. Photo courtesy Jack Matthews

Gama prewar tank, medium size (GT9), value as shown $200. Photo courtesy Jack Matthews

Gama prewar tank, medium size (GT10), value as shown $150. Photo courtesy Jack Matthews

Gama prewar tank, small (GT11), value as shown $200. Photo courtesy Jack Matthews

Two Gama small prewar tanks, left to right: (GT12) value as shown $100, (GT13), value as shown $125. Photo courtesy Jack Matthews

Left to right: Two Gama small prewar tanks (Left to right: GT14 and FT15), value as shown $125, each. Photo courtesy Jack Matthews

Gama Montage tank, small, with original box (GT19), value of tank Mint without box $200. Photo courtesy Joe and Sharon Freed

Left to right: Two Gama small (5"-6") prewar tanks (Left to right: GT16 and GT17), value as shown $125, each. Photo courtesy Jack Matthews

	C6	C8	C10
1948 Buick, tin, clockwork motor, "Made in U.S. Zone, Germany" on bottom, 6-3/4" long	30	60	100
Aerial Ladder w/pump, 3-part ladder extends, 1950s, 23" long	125	210	275
Cadillac, tin, based on 1954 Cadillac, 1950s	350	550	850
Crane w/Clam Bucket, No. 294, tin, battery-operated w/remote, cab-over,			

	C6	C8	C10
moves forward and back, 1950s, 22" long	125	188	295
Dump Truck, tin, battery-operated w/remote, 1950s, 13" long	30	65	100
Stake Truck, tin, red and blue, door decals read "Gama Patent Mechanic," 1950s, 11-1/2" long	40	80	125
Tractor and Trailer, tin, clockwork motor, 17" long	95	145	200

Gama prewar tank, small, with box (GT18), value as shown $175. Photo courtesy Jack Matthews

Gama windup tank, (GT21), WWII type, No. 634, 3-1/4" long. Photo courtesy Harvey K. Rainess

Gama Montage Tank, small, 6-1/4" long, (GT20), value of tank alone, $200. Photo courtesy Jack Matthews

Gama tractor, early, value as shown $250. Photo courtesy Jack Matthews

Gama tractor and wagon, value as shown, $150. Photo courtesy Jack Matthews

GARLAND

Garland made its Red Flyer in Detroit, Mich.

	C6	C8	C10
Red Flyer Hydraulic Dump, Made in Detroit, doors marked "Garland Red Flyer," ride-on	125	188	275

Garland Red Flyer Hydraulic Dump, 25". Photo courtesy Jerry Combs

GARRETT

Garrett Flexible Products of Garrett, Indiana, began in 1978 and was located at 600 E. Quincy St. Its owner was F.H. Thurman, who designed Auburn Rubber's trucks, cars, etc., in the 1950s. He also designed the Garrett line, which was sometimes known as Rubber Toys Unique, with some toys marked "Unique." The company declared bankruptcy in 1985.

	C6	C8	C10
#200 Happy Heidi, rubber, wacky car, grille is mouth, windshield eyes	10	15	25
#220 Aligator Alex, rubber, wacky car, front end is aligator mouth	10	15	25
#225 Lloyd, The Lobster, rubber, wacky car with lobster passenger	10	15	25
#400 Sports Car, rubber, top up	10	15	25
#405 Bobcat Special, rubber, top down, boattail speedster	10	15	25
#415 Racer, rubber, futuristic, round "jet" engine in rear, 7-1/2" long	10	15	25
#420 Utility Truck, rubber, pickup bed, single headlights, 5-1/2" long	10	15	25

Garrett advertisement.

Garrett advertisement.

	C6	C8	C10
#425 Sand Truck, rubber, dump bed, dual stacked headlights	10	15	25
#430 Convertible, rubber, dual headlights, two seater, 7-1/2" long.......	10	15	25
#435 Squad Car, rubber, two sirens on hood, single light on roof	10	15	25

	C6	C8	C10
#500 Mini-Tractor, rubber, no driver.......	10	15	25
#505 Mini-Car, rubber, 4-1/2" long	10	15	25
#510 Mini-Fire Truck, rubber	10	15	25
#520 Mini-Racer, rubber, rear spoiler......	10	15	25
Corvette Sting Ray, 7" long	15	22	30

GARTON

The Garton Toy Company was based in Sheboygan, Wisc., and specialized in pressed-steel pedal cars. The company also produced target games, tricycles, and miniature piano toys.

	C6	C8	C10
Automobile, No. 5707, blue body, white details, 1949, 35" long	NPF	NPF	NPF
Automobile, No. 5728, red body, white details, windshield, 1949, 37" long......	NPF	NPF	NPF
Fire Chief Car, No. 5705, red body, fire bell, 1949, 35" long............................	NPF	NPF	NPF
Fire Chief Car, No. 5735, red body, white details, fire bell, 1949, 37" long...........	NPF	NPF	NPF

	C6	C8	C10
Fire Department Ladder Aerial Car, No. 5754, red body, white details, 2 wooden ladders, 1949, 48" long	700	1100	1700
Ford Pedal Car, 1950s............................	700	1100	1700
Hod Rod Pedal Car	400	650	900
Kiddilac, No. 5733, maroon body, white details, 1950, 45" long	NPF	NPF	NPF
Police Car, No. 5716, white body, red and black details, siren, spot light, radio aerial, 1950, 33" long	NPF	NPF	NPF
Station Wagon, No. 5749, maroon body, ivory details, oak veneer panelling "woodie" style, 1949, 48" long...........	NPF	NPF	NPF
Woody Pedal Car, 1937	1300	2500	3900

GAY PLASTICS

	C6	C8	C10
Back Hoe Truck, blue, cabover, shovel rotates 360 degrees, 1960s, 14" long ...	10	17	25
Fire Truck, red, fire pumper, ladder, 9" long	7	12	18

	C6	C8	C10
Mustang, blue, 4" long............................	4	80	12
Police, three wheeler, 8" long	35	52	70
Truck	5	8	10

GENDRON

Peter Gendron founded Gendron Iron Wheel in 1880 at 210 Summit St. in Toledo, Ohio. Renamed the Gendron Wheel Company, it specialized in vehicles for children and advertised its plant as, "The world's largest factory devoted to the making of children's vehicles."

Their line during the 1920s included velocipedes, wagons, bicycles, tricycles, scooters, and pedal cars. By the 1930s, the company branched out to toy autos and playground equipment. By 1940, the Gendron Wheel Co. abandoned the manufacture of pedal cars and devoted itself solely to hospital equipment.

	C6	C8	C10
Buick Pedal Car, 1920	5000	9500	18,000
Federal Knight Dump Truck	NPF	NPF	11,000

	C6	C8	C10
Gendron/Sampson Army Truck, 27" long..	800	1300	2000
Gendron/Sampson Chemical Fire Truck, 28" long..	1200	2000	2800
Gendron/Sampson Coal Truck, steel, 26" long	1000	1600	2500
Gendron/Sampson Dump Truck, pressed steel, 27" long	850	1350	1900
Gendron/Sampson Screen Side Express Truck, 27" long	650	1100	1500
Gendron/Sampson Stake Truck, 26" long..	1500	2300	3500
Gendron/Sampson Tank Truck, 29" long..	800	1400	2000
Pontiac Pedal Car, 1938	NPF	NPF	NPF
Racer Pedal Car, 38" long.......................	1300	2000	3200
Sportster Pedal Car, 41" long.................	2000	3500	5300
Stearns Pedal Car, c.1920, 41" long.........	1000	1700	2640

GENERAL TOY OF CANADA

	C6	C8	C10
Racer, No. 3, tin wind-up, 4-3/4" long	35	75	112

GIBBS

Founded in 1884 by Lewis E. Gibbs, the Gibbs Mfg. Co. was based in Canton, Ohio. Gibbs made its first toys in 1886. By the 1920s the firm established a line of pull-toys, games, tops, sand toys, and even a few vehicles.

	C6	C8	C10
No. 70 Auto Truck and Trailer, marked "Gibbs No. 701," wooden truck pulls trailer, 1927	150	250	350
No. 72 Tractor and Trailer, farm tractor pulling trailer, wood and metal, 1927, 13-1/2" long	NPF	NPF	NPF
No. 75 Stake Truck, stake truck, wood with metal	NPF	NPF	NPF
No. 77 Rush Delivery Truck, wooden, open sides	NPF	NPF	NPF
No. 78 Lindyplane, monoplane, wood	NPF	NPF	NPF
No. 79 Aeroplane, wood, bi-plane, "G-79" marked on sides, aluminum propeller,	NPF	NPF	NPF
No. 80 Service Station, 1925, wood and metal, 15" long	350	525	700

GIFTCRAFT

(Possibly only a distributor.)

	C6	C8	C10
Fastback Sedan, (possibly only the distributor), Nash, solid rubber, c.1946, 4" long	15	22	30

GILMARK

Based in New York, New York, the Gilmark Merchandising Co. produced cars, trucks, and space vehicles in small scales during the 1950s.

	C6	C8	C10
Esso Gasoline Truck	12	18	25
Jaguar, roadster, 3" long	8	15	25
Rocket Car, driver, 1950s, 4" long	20	30	40
Sedan, w/opening hood, 4" long	8	12	16
Service Truck, plastic, opening tool kit w/3 tools, 1950s, 4" long	15	30	45
Super Highway Fleet, No. 57, plastic, 3 trucks, cabs tilt to display motor, card 12-3/4" long	NPF	NPF	NPF
Tank, plastic, "U.S. Army," 3" long	8	12	25
Tractor/Trailer Hi-Way Transporter	8	12	16
Wrecker, plastic, cab tilts back, hook, 1950s, 4-5/8" long	15	30	45

Gilmark assortment. Front row: 4" Sedan, 3" AA Gun Carriage, Tank, Jeep. Back row: 4" Sedan, 3" Tank, 3-1/2" Truck. Photo courtesy John McCurdy

GIRARD

Girard Model Works was founded by C.G. Wood in 1906, in Girard, Pennsylvania. His son Frank was soon made a partner. In 1918, they began making mechanical toys for an unidentified New York firm. In 1920, they sold them under their name "Wood's Mechanical Toys." The business eventually passed into other hands and had 1,000 employees in 1931.

During the Depression, Girard laid off its salesman, Louis Marx, who stalled Girard customers as he tried to get a plant of his own in business. Since Marx was better known to buyers than the people at Girard, he emerged triumphant, and in 1934, Marx took over the firm. Girard remained in business till 1980.

Girrard Touring Bus, painted tin, circa 1920, 12". Photo courtesy Mapes Auctioneers and Appraisers

Girard Fire Chief Siren Coupe, wind-up, 14". Photo courtesy Bill Kaufman

Girard Wrecker Truck, mechanical boom, 1930s, 10".

Girard Pierce-Arrow Coupe, wind-up, green, orange and cream, 1930s, 14". Photo courtesy Bob Smith

Girard Stake Truck, electric headlights, 10". Photo courtesy Charles L. Jackson

	C6	C8	C10
Army Truck, cloth top, c.1940	150	225	300
Auto Transport, carries two trucks, circa early 1930s	275	413	550
Bus, w/driver, wind-up, 12-1/2" long	188	282	375
Chrysler Speedster, blue body, yellow top, red wheels, wind-up, "Chrysler" in grille, 8-1/2" long.............................	150	275	400
Coupe, 6" long	30	45	60
Coupe, battery-operated, headlights, 14" long...	350	525	700
Fire Chief Car, 15" long	260	300	400
Fire Chief Siren Coupe, wind-up, 14" long	275	450	600
Fire Truck, 1920s, 12" long	50	75	100
Gasoline Tanker, c.1939	85	135	225
Ladder Truck, 1930s, 7" long	175	263	350
Pierce-Arrow Coupe, green, orange and cream, wind-up, c.1932, 14" long........	250	350	500

	C6	C8	C10
Pump Truck, battery-operated, headlights, 10" long	100	150	200
Race Car, No. 2, wind-up, 8" long..........	300	450	600
Race Car, pull rod, 1920s........................	138	205	275
Roadster, electrified, 14-1/2" long	212	318	425
Side Dump, 11-1/2" long	150	225	300
Stake Truck, electric headlights, 10" long	150	225	300
Tank Truck, wood wheels, 11-1/2" long	92	138	185
Touring Bus, painted tin, c.1920, 12" long...	150	225	300
Truck, w/three trailers, 1928	130	195	260
Truck, w/trailer, 1930s, 17" long	100	150	200
Truck and Trailer, marked "Toyland Dairy"	375	565	700
Wrecker Truck, mechanical boom, 1930s, 10" long, scarce	275	450	600

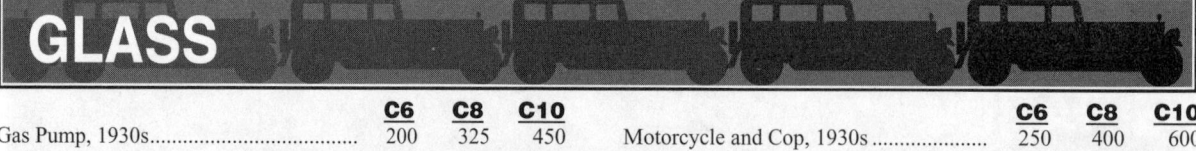

GLASS

	C6	C8	C10		C6	C8	C10
Gas Pump, 1930s....................................	200	325	450	Motorcycle and Cop, 1930s	250	400	600

GLOBE CO.

The Globe Co. was based in Sheboygan, Wisc., and specialized in stamped metal wagons, velocipedes, scooters, and a few vehicles in the 1930s.

	C6	C8	C10
Motorcycle w/Cop, 1930s, 8" long	650	1150	1675
Roadster, separate driver, kids in rumble seat, cast iron, 11-1/2" long	500	750	1000

Globe Co. Roadster, cast-iron, 11-1/2". Photo courtesy Bertoia Auctions

GONG BELL

Located in East Hampton, Conn., the Gong Bell Mfg. Co. was established in 1886. It specialized in toys for young children, and offered a wide variety of bell toys and push toys in wood and cast iron. The firm also manufactured bells. Gong Bell continued wood toy production in World War II and resumed its pull toy lines and toy telephones following the war.

Gong Bell, "Mickey Mouse Bus Lines – Walt Disney Stars." Photo courtesy Wilkinson Collection, Detroit Antique Museum

	C6	C8	C10
Mickey Mouse Bus Lines, No. 125, "Walt Disney Stars" on sides, characters visible in windows, 1960s ..	200	300	400
Milk Truck, w/wooden bottles, 13" long .	225	338	450
Racer, 20" long...	150	225	300

GOODEE

Goodee die-cast vehicles were made by the Excel Products Company of East Brunswick, New Jersey. All of the prototypes for Goodee vehicles appear to be from the years 1953-1955. It would seem that Goodee vehicles were produced in two sizes—three and six inches. Some of the larger models had wind-up motors, which would increase their value.

Contributor: Dave Leopard, 2507 Feather Run Trail, West Columbia, SC 29169-4915.

Large Size

	C6	C8	C10
1953 Ford Police Cruiser	15	25	35
1953 GMC Pickup Truck	15	25	35
1953 GMC Pickup Truck, Military, olive drab, 6"...	15	20	25
1954 DeSoto Station Wagon....................	15	25	35
1955 Ford Fuel Truck	15	25	35
American LaFrance Pumper, red	15	25	35
Military Jeep	15	25	35

Small Size

1953 Cadillac Convertible	10	15	20
1953 Ford Police Cruiser	10	15	20
1953 Lincoln Capri Hardtop	10	15	20

	C6	C8	C10
1953 Studebaker Coupe	15	15	20
1954 DeSoto Station Wagon..................	10	15	20
1955 Ford Fuel Truck	10	15	20
American LaFrance Pumper, red, 3-1/4" long	10	15	20
Land Speed Racer	10	15	20
Land Speed Racer, bubble fenders...........	10	15	20
Military Jeep	10	15	20
Moving Van	10	15	20
Step Van, 3" long	10	15	20

Both large and small versions of the Goodee 1953 GMC Pickup Truck. Photo courtesy Dave Leopard

GREY IRON

Founded as the Brady Machine Shop in Mount Joy, Pennsylvania in 1840, the company was organized as the Grey Iron Casting Company, Ltd. in 1881. As early as 1903 it was manufacturing toy banks and stoves, cap pistols, wheeled toys and trains, as well as a number of non-toy items. The firm's best-known products are toy soldiers.

It is still in business today as the John Wright Company, located in Wrightsville, Penn. They do offer a limited variety of new cast iron toys. The

Grey Iron Midget vehicles, 1-1/2" each. Photo courtesy Stan Alekna

address is P.O. Box 269, Wrightsville, PA, 17368. The company Web site is: www.johnwright.com

	C6	C8	C10
Convertible, Midget, 1-1/2" long	20	30	40
Coupe, Midget, 1-1/2" long	20	30	40
Ford Coupe, w/driver, 5-5/8" long	NPF	NPF	NPF
Ford coupe, w/driver, 8-3/8" long	475	515	950
Racer, Midget, 1-1/2" long......................	20	30	40
Sedan, 1927, 9" long	1000	1500	2000
Sedan, Airflow-type, Midget, 1-1/2" long	20	30	40
Sedan, Older, Midget, 1-1/2" long	20	30	40

Grey Iron Ford Coupe, driver is missing, 8-3/8" long. Photo courtesy Bertoia Auctions

GRIMLAND (MARIETTA, GA.)

This Marietta, Georgia firm released a few trucks as promotional items in the late 1940s.

Contributor: John Taylor, P.O. Box 63, Nolensville, TN 37135-0063.

	C6	C8	C10
Allied Vans, late 1940s, 7-1/2" long	30	70	125
Grey Van Lines, late 1940s, 7-1/2" long	30	70	125
Toys That Last Promo, 7-1/2" long, rare	75	125	200

Grimland "Toys That Last" salesman's promo, 7-1/2". Photo courtesy John Taylor

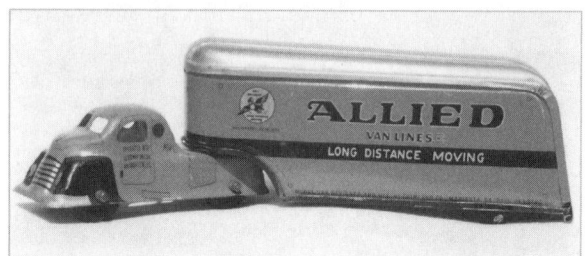

Grimland Allied Van Lines, 7-1/2". Photo courtesy John Taylor

Grimland Grey Van Lines, 7-1/2". Photo courtesy John Taylor

GUNTHERMANN

This Nuremberg, Germany, toy company was founded in 1887. Gunthermann's toy business flourished well into the 1900s despite the fact that S.G. Gunthermann passed away in 1890. His widow married the company manager, Adolf Weigel, and

Weigel's initials were added to the "SG" logo until his death in 1919. The initials were then removed and the logo was changed back to the original "SG." The company was sold to Seimens in 1965.

Contributor: Bob Smith, RATS Toy Shows, 255 Tryon Park, Rochester, NY 14609. (585) 288-7153

Gunthermann Blue Bird Racer, tin lithographed, 20". Photo courtesy Bertoia Auctions

Gunthermann Kaye Don's Sunbeam Silver Bullet Racer, 22". Photo courtesy Bertoia Auctions

Gunthermann Limousine, 1920, green and black, four opening doors, painted driver, 12". Photo courtesy Bob Smith

Gunthermann Vis-à-Vis, driver, wind-up, 10-1/4". Photo courtesy Bertoia Auctions

Another look at the 10-1/4" Gunthermann Vis-à-vis. Photo courtesy Bertoia Auctions

Gunthermann two-way Limousine/Touring Car, brown and yellow, removable top, 1920s. Photo courtesy Bob Smith

	C6	C8	C10
Aerial Ladder Truck, 2 tin firemen, wind-up, extending ladder, red, 1950s, 14" long	175	285	550
Auto Candy Container, driver in open, closed cab	625	975	1600
Blue Bird Racer, tin lithographed, clockwork motor, 20" long	1075	1775	2550
Car, two-seat, open, driver w/top hat, c.1899, 7" long	925	1675	2700
Clown Car, clockwork motor, 6" long	975	1775	2500
Double-Decker Bus, electric headlights, early 1930s, 12" long	550	725	1150
Fire Ladder Truck, four firemen, overhead ladder, 16" long	1875	3075	4600
Fire Pumper, handpainted tin, clockwork motor, two firemen, c.1898, 8-1/4" long	1575	2775	4100
Fire Pumper, three firemen (composition), 8-1/4" long	1675	2875	4200
Fire Pumper, wind-up, early 7-3/4"	875	1375	2200
Georgian Window Limousine, driver, clockwork motor, c.1908	1175	1775	2700
Gordon Bennett coupe, 5-3/4" long	1275	2275	3200
Hansom-type Auto	825	1375	1950
Horseless Carriage, clockwork motor, driver, 7" long	1175	1775	2700

	C6	C8	C10
Kaye Don's Sunbeam Silver Bullet Racer, 22" long	875	1475	2200
Limousine, green/black, clockwork motor, fur opening doors, painted driver, c.1920, 12" long	1225	1875	2800
Limousine/Touring Car, two-way, brown and yellow, clockwork motor, adjustable steering and headlamps, a removable top converts car to touring model. 10-1/4" long	925	1525	2300
Motorcycle and Rider, 7" long	1575	2875	3900
Motorcycle and Rider, 8-1/4" long	1075	1775	2600
Open Phaeton, driver, wind-up, 7" long	725	1175	1800
Paris-Berlin Race Car	1175	1775	2700
Taxi, convertible back, driver, clockwork motor, c.1912, 10-1/2" long	1175	2175	3100
Tour Bus, tin, wind-up, tin hubcaps, two-tone color, see-through portion of roof - plastic, baseplate has litho map from Rome to Amsterdam, rubber tires, 1950s, 11" long	200	325	600
Trolley Bus, w/passenger, aluminum, trolley wires on roof, 8-1/2" long, 1940s	275	425	700
Vis-à-Vis, driver, wind-up, 10-1/4" long	1325	2575	3300
Vis-à-Vis, driver, wind-up, 5" long	875	1475	2200

GYRO

Richard B. Munday became head of Dayton Friction Works in 1926, where he patented a horizontal flywheel and called his toys "Gyro" after the gyroscope. Gyro shut its doors in 1935.

	C6	C8	C10
Airplane, pressed steel, friction motor, wheels, single prop, 13-1/2"	NPF	NPF	NPF
Bus, pressed steel, friction motor, 26"	NPF	NPF	NPF
Coal and Ice Dump Truck, pressed steel, friction motor, 14-1/2"	250	275	500
Coupe (Large), pressed steel, friction motor, 18-1/2"	NPF	NPF	NPF
Coupe (Small), pressed steel, friction motor, 13-1/2"	NPF	NPF	NPF
Delivery Truck, pressed steel, friction motor, panel delivery, 14-1/2"	NPF	NPF	NPF
Dump Truck (Large), pressed steel, friction motor, 20-1/4"	NPF	NPF	NPF
Dump Truck (Small), pressed steel, friction motor, 14-1/2"	NPF	NPF	NPF
Fire Engine, pressed steel, friction motor, pumper, 14"..	NPF	NPF	NPF
Hook & Ladder, pressed steel, friction motor, 18"	NPF	NPF	NPF
Locomotive & Tender, pressed steel, friction motor, 17"	NPF	NPF	NPF
Roadster, pressed steel, friction motor, 13-1/2"	NPF	NPF	NPF
Sport Roadster, pressed steel, friction motor, 18-1/2"	NPF	NPF	NPF
Trolley Car, pressed steel, friction motor, 21"...	NPF	NPF	NPF

Gyro toys, as seen in a 1929 Butler Bros. catalog.

HAFNER

Chicago's Hafner began in 1900 as the Toy Auto Company, though it may not have produced its first model until the following year. By 1904, the firm's name became W.F. Hafner and eventually became the American Flyer company. Mr. Hafner set off on his own when he started the Hafner Manufacturing Company in 1914; his son joined him in 1918. Hafner manufactured wind-up trains until it was purchased in 1950 by Wyandotte.

	C6	C8	C10
Auto Express Co. Truck, clockwork, steel, 8-1/2" long.................................	450	675	900

	C6	C8	C10
Runabout, w/upholstered driver's seat, steel clockwork, 7" long	450	675	900
Touring Car, pressed steel, clockwork, 10" long..	750	1125	1500
Transitional Phaeton, two figures, 9-1/2" long	1500	2500	3500

Left to right: Hafner Auto Express Co. Truck, 8-1/2"; Hafner Runabout, 7". Photo courtesy Sotheby's N.Y.

Hafner Transitional Phaeton, pressed steel, 9-1/2". Photo courtesy Bertoia Auctions

Hafner Touring Car, pressed steel, 10". Photo courtesy Bertoia Auctions

Hafner Touring Car without top. Photo courtesy Bertoia Auctions

HALSAM

Halsam is best known for its American Logs (similar to Lincoln Logs, but preferred by some collectors), which went into production in 1934. It was also well-known for its blocks, and, as can be seen by the accompanying illustrations, its trucks came with loads of them.

	C6	C8	C10
Truck With Blocks, No. 449, cab-over, contains ten 1-5/16" blocks, 1934, 11" long	NPF	NPF	NPF
Truck With Blocks, No. 450, cab-over, contains ten 1-5/16" blocks, 1934, 15-1/2" long	NPF	NPF	NPF
Truck With Blocks, No. 451, cab-over, contains twenty-four 1-3/4" blocks in two layers, 1934, 17" long	NPF	NPF	NPF

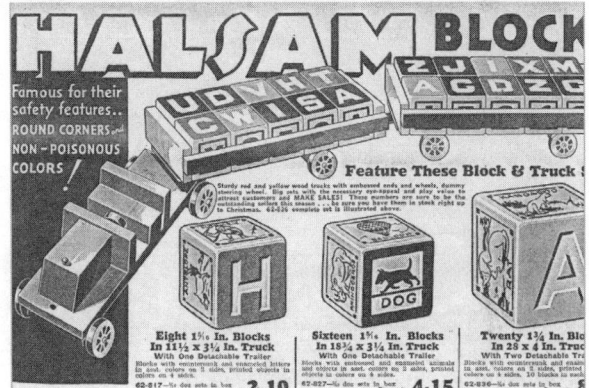

A Halsam trailer truck as shown in the September 1934 Butler Bros. catalog.

Halsam No. 451 wood truck, possibly the wrong blocks, 16-1/2" long. Photo courtesy John McCurdy

Halsam No. 450 wood truck, holds single row of blocks. Photo courtesy John McCurdy

HANDI-CRAFT CO.

	C6	C8	C10
Auto Casting Set, price w/box, No. 891, 1940s	72	105	145

HAPPY SAM

	C6	C8	C10
Driving Wood Truck, c.1920s, 8" long....	80	120	160

HARRIS

The Harris Toy Company of Toledo, Ohio, began production of cast iron toys in the late 1880s. They produced animal-drawn vehicles, trains, as well as vehicles. The firm, which also jobbed for Dent, Hubley, and Wilkins, stopped making toys in 1913.

	C6	C8	C10
Tiller Auto, cast-iron, w/driver	450	675	900

HENRY, M.A. (NEW YORK)

The M.A. Henry company was based in New York.

	C6	C8	C10
Tank/Jeep, composition, 8" long..............	NPF	NPF	NPF

M.A. Henry Tank/Jeep, composition, 8" long.
Photo courtesy Harold Haseley

HESS PROMOTIONAL TOYS

One can trace the roots of the Amerada Hess Corp. (formally Hess Oil & Chemical) back many years before a promotional toy was even considered. Hess entered retail gasoline marketing around 1958 with a minority purchase of the Meadville Corp. Meadville operated clean, oversized service stations under the brands of Save Way and Safeway in some large Northeast cities. The Hess branch was introduced in 1959; by 1962 the company operated about twenty-eight stations under its own brand name. By 1965, several other fuel companies were bought, and some of their stations were renamed as "Heass."

It wasn't until 1964 that the first toy tanker truck was sold at Hess stations. Almost every year since then (around Thanksgiving Day) a high quality plastic toy vehicle bearing the Hess name has been offered. These highly detailed toys are said to be exact replicas of actual vehicles in the Hess fleet; although from 1987 to present, the toys design was changed to reflect non-fleet vehicles. The toys are produced in limited quantities and over the past few years, customers have been restricted to two toys, because of great demand. Each vehicle is packaged in a colorful box and batteries are included in the purchase price. It's important to note that to maintain the value, keep all the packaging that comes with the tox (box, inserts, battery card, etc.).

The 1964 toy truck commonly referred to as the "B Mack" was manufactured by Marx in Hong Kong and sold at the stations for $1.39. The cab of the truck was green with yellow fenders and red chassis. The tank trailer featured a green and white body with the Hess anme applied to both sides of the tank and cab. The truck had operating head and tail lights, powered by a battery located under the tank. It came with a small red funnel that enabled the tank to be filled with liquid and a drain hose to empty it. This unique toy truck can be hard to find in original condition today.

Not commonly known by collectors, this same truck design was offered under the private labeling of several other fuel companies: Billups Petroleum, Aetna (which was the North Carolina-based Taylor Oil Co., operating under the Travelers Brand), Wilso (also on the Delhi-Taylor supply system), Service of North Carolina and Gant. Each of these marketers sold the B Mack toy truck in 1964. By 1965, the Billups brand name had been eliminated in the Eastern part of the United States and their stations were sold to Hess. Hess continued the toy promotion the following year (1965) with the reissue of the B Mack.

A few Hess Promotional Toy history highlights:

The first non-land vehicle, the Hess Voyager, was released in 1966. The second, the Hess Helicoptor, was released in 2001.

In 1967, Hess offered a newly-designed semi-tanker truck often referred to as the "red velvet bottom." This term describes the box, not the truck.

The merger of Hess Oil and Chemical with Amerada Petroleum Corp. took place in 1969, producing the present-day name, Amerada Hess. To commemorate this occasion, the 1968-69 toy truck was re-labeled with the new corporate name and given to Hess employees.

The first pumper truck was offered in 1970 for $1.69.

Amerada Hess opted not to offer a toy promotion at their stations in 1973.

The first semi-box truck with opening side and rear doors made its appearance in 1975.

Amerada Hess, in maintaining high standards of service, provided training to its service-station personnel on location by means of a modified GMC motor home. In 1980, a toy replica of the Hess Training Van was chosen as the holiday promotion.

A reissue of the 1933 Chevy appeared in 1983, with a new feature—a savings bank.

In 1987, the new white and green color scheme was introduced.

Hess promotional toys are still being released. For more information, go to the company Web site: www.hesstoytrucks.com

	C6	C8	C10
1964 B Model Mack Tanker Truck, made in Hong Kong	n/a	n/a	1900
1965 B Model Mack Tanker Truck, made in Hong Kong	n/a	n/a	1900
1966 Hess Voyager Tanker Ship, Made in U.S.A.	n/a	n/a	2300
1966, B Mack Tanker Truck, silver, "W" tooled into grill	n/a	n/a	2500
1967 Tank Truck, split window, w/faux red velvet base on box, Made in U.S.A.	n/a	n/a	2400
1968 Tank Truck, split window, without red velvet box, made in Hong Kong	n/a	n/a	675
1969 Tank Truck, split window without red velvet box, made in Hong Kong	n/a	n/a	675
1969 Tank Truck, split window, Amerada Hess, Hong Kong, never sold to the general public	n/a	n/a	2500
1970 Pumper Fire Truck, red, made in Hong Kong, by Marx	n/a	n/a	695

	C6	C8	C10
1971 Pumper Fire Truck, red, made in Hong Kong, by Marx, marked "Season's Greetings"	n/a	n/a	3000
1972 Tanker Truck, split window	n/a	n/a	395
1974 Tanker Truck, split window	n/a	n/a	350
1975 Tractor Trailer, box-type w/three oil drums, no labels on drums, one-piece cab, made in both Hong Kong and the United States	n/a	n/a	395
1976 Tractor Trailer, two-piece cab, three oil drums, marked "Hess," made in Hong Kong	n/a	n/a	395
1977 Tanker Tractor Trailer, made in Hong Kong, rear label is 1-1/2" x 1"	n/a	n/a	175
1978 Tanker Tractor Trailer, made in Hong Kong	n/a	n/a	185
1980 GMC Training Van, made in Hong Kong	n/a	n/a	395
1982, 1933 Chevy Tanker Delivery Truck, marked "first Hess truck," made in Hong Kong	n/a	n/a	95

Hess Promotional Tanker Tractor Trailer, similar to the 1977 truck except it was issued as a bank, 1984. Photo courtesy John and Suzanne Adivari

Hess Promotional box-type Tractor Trailer, three "Hess" oil drums, 1987. Photo courtesy Thomas G. Nefos

Hess Promotional B Model Mack Tanker Truck, 1964. Photo courtesy Thomas G. Nefos

Hess Promotional Hess Voyage Tanker Ship, 1966. Photo courtesy John and Suzanne Adivari

Hess Promotional split-window Tank Truck with red velvet on box, 1967. Photo courtesy John and Suzanne Adivari

Hess Promotional Tank Truck, similar to 1967 except no red velvet box, 1968-69. Photo courtesy John and Suzanne Adivari

Hess Promotional 1967 "Red Velvet" Truck. Photo courtesy Thomas G. Nefos

Hess Promotional Red Pumper Fire Truck, 1970. Photo courtesy Thomas G. Nefos

Hess Promotional Race Car Transporter, 1988. Photo courtesy John and Suzanne Adivari

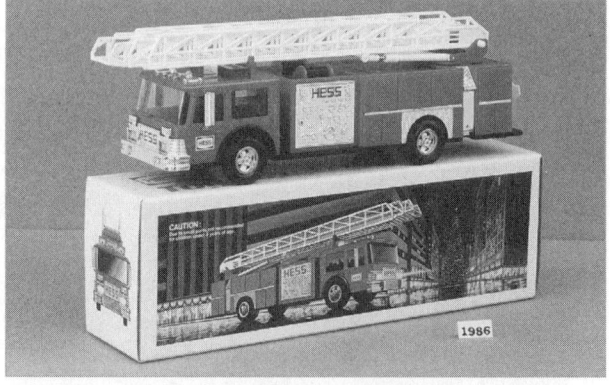

Hess Promotional Red Aerial Ladder Fire Truck, 1986. Photo courtesy John and Suzanne Adivari

Hess Promotional Red Pumper Fire Truck, "Seasons Greetings," 1971. Photo courtesy John and Suzanne Adivari

Hess Promotional box-type Tractor Trailer with three oil drums, 1975, no labels on drums. Photo courtesy John and Suzanne Adivari

Hess Promotional 1975 Box Truck. Photo courtesy Thomas G. Nefos

Hess Promotional box-type Tractor Trailer, three "Hess" drums, 1976. Photo courtesy Thomas G. Nefos

Hess Promotional Tanker Tractor Trailer, 1977. Photo courtesy John and Suzanne Adivari

Hess Promotional 1977-78 Tanker Truck. Photo courtesy Thomas G. Nefos

Hess Promotional Eighteen-wheeler Box Truck with race car, 1992. Photo courtesy John and Suzanne Adivari

Hess Promotional Semi-Tanker Truck, air horn sounds, 1990. Photo courtesy John and Suzanne Adivari

Hess Promotional GMC Training Van, 1980. Photo from John and Suzanne Adivari

Hess Promotional 1933 Chevy Tanker Delivery Truck, 1982. Photo courtesy John and Suzanne Adivari

*Hess Promotional Trucks from 1988, 1991, and 1992.
Photo courtesy Thomas G. Nefos*

Hess Promotional Aerial Ladder Fire Truck, 1989.

	C6	C8	C10
1983, 1933 Chevy Tanker Delivery Truck, marked "first Hess truck," made in Hong Kong	n/a	n/a	495
1984 Tanker Tractor Trailer, bank	n/a	n/a	495
1985, 1933 Chevy Tanker Delivery Truck, bank	n/a	n/a	125
1986 Aerial Ladder Fire Truck, bank, red, made in Hong Kong	n/a	n/a	100
1987 Tractor/Trailer, box-type, w/three drums labeled "Hess," made in Hong Kong and China	n/a	n/a	85
1988 Race Car Transporter, w/friction-powered car, made in Hong Kong	n/a	n/a	470
1989 Aerial Ladder FireTruck, white, dual siren sounds, bank made in China	n/a	n/a	85
1990 Semi-tanker Truck, white, w/back-up/air horn sounds, made in China	n/a	n/a	55
1991 Race Car Transporter, w/friction-powered car, made in China	n/a	n/a	50
1992 Eighteen Wheeler Box Truck, track w/race car, made in China	n/a	n/a	45
1993 Patrol Car, white and green w/sirens and lights, larger scale than previously-issued toys	n/a	n/a	50
1993 Semi-tanker Truck, white w/back-up/air horn sounds, not sold to			

	C6	C8	C10
general public, given as gift to bulk diesel fuel dealers	n/a	n/a	1000
1994 Rescue Truck, white and green w/red ladder, larger scale than previously-issued toys	n/a	n/a	45
1995 Flat-bed Semi, white and green w/helicopter cargo, both w/working lights	n/a	n/a	45
1996 Emergency Truck, white and green, extending ladder, siren, lights, 12" long	n/a	n/a	40
1997 Toy Truck and Racers, white and green semi-truck w/2 race cars, battery-operated lights, 15" long	n/a	n/a	35
1998 Recreation Van with Dune Buggy and Motorcycle, white and green RV, dune buggy, motorcycle, battery-operated lights	n/a	n/a	35
1999 Toy Truck and Space Shuttle w/Satellite, white and green, battery-operated lights and sounds, working Shuttle bay doors	n/a	n/a	35
2000 Fire Truck w/Ladder Trailer, white and green, red ladder, battery-operated lights and siren sounds	n/a	n/a	25
2001 Helicopter w/Motorcycle and Cruiser, white and green, battery-operated lights and sounds, Cruiser looks like SUV, friction motors on Motorcycle and Cruiser	n/a	n/a	25

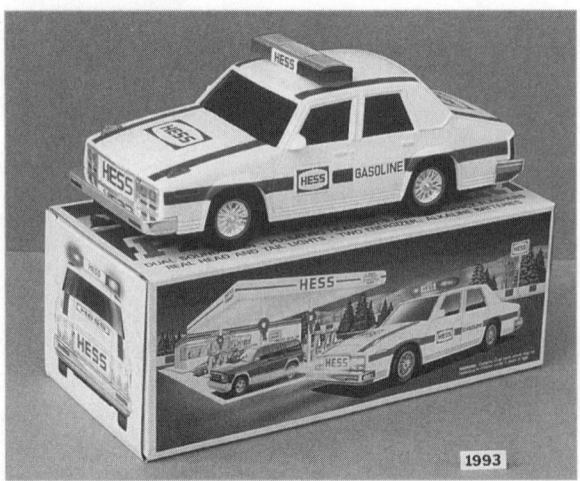

*Hess Promotional Patrol Car, white and green, 1993.
Photo courtesy John and Suzanne Adivari*

*Hess Promotional Hess Premium Diesel truck, same as
1990 tanker except not sold to general public; given as gift
to bulk diesel fuel dealers, 1993. Photo courtesy John and
Suzanne Adivari*

	C6	C8	C10
2002 Toy Truck and Airplane, white and green, bi-plane, ramp, battery-operated lights	n/a	n/a	25
2003 Toy Truck and Race Cars, white and green semi w/2 Indy cars	n/a	n/a	25
2004 Sport Utility Vehicle and Motorcycles, 40th Anniversary release, white and green, working lights, motorcycles have friction motors	n/a	n/a	20
2005 ?, toy not released at time of printing	n/a	n/a	n/a

Hess Promotional Toy Truck and Helicopter, white and green, 1995.

HESS TOY COMPANY

(Nuremburg, Germany 1825-1934)

Founded in 1825 by Matthieu Hess, this is one of the oldest toy makers in Germany. Matthieu passed away in 1886, leaving the business to his son, Johann Leonard, beginning the "J.L.H." trademark. Most Hess-mobile cars used a unique friction mechanism which had a power-lock on top of the cowl and a hand crank in the front. When cranking the handle, a momentum would build up. You would then lift the power-lock, releasing the dreveshaft to turn the rear wheels.

Contributor: Bob Smith, RATS Toy Shows, 255 Tryon Park, Rochester, NY 14609. (585) 288-7153, bird@oldtoysonline.com

	C6	C8	C10
Hessmobile Open Phaeton, driver, 8-1/2" long, c.1918	875	1375	2050
Hessmobile Racer, w/driver, hand crank, 8" long	475	775	1100
Limousine, clockwork, green/red, 9" long	675	875	1250
Limousine, friction drive, blue/black, c.1920, 9" long	775	1125	1450
Limousine, friction drive, green/black, c.1920, 7-1/2" long	650	750	1050
Open Two-Seat Car, 10-1/2" long	825	1475	2150
Open Two-Seat Car, tin lithographed, approx. 8" long	825	1400	1950
Racer, tin lithographed, two seat, open, clockwork motor, 8-3/4" long	825	1400	1950
Racer, w/driver, 5"	575	875	1350
Speedster, w/driver, crank friction drive, 8" long	425	675	950

Hess Toy Company cars. Top: Limousine, 9" long. Bottom: Limousine, 7-1/2" long. Photo courtesy Bob Smith

HILLER

	C6	C8	C10
Comet Race Car, fuel-powered, marked "3," c.1940-42	800	1300	1800
Comet Race Car, non-powered, marked "4," c.1942, 18" long	550	825	1200

Hiller Comet Race Car, fuel-powered, 1940s, 3". Photo courtesy William G. Floyd

HOGE MFG. CO.

Hampden Hoge (pronounced, "Hoagie") founded the Hoge Mfg. Co. in 1909. By 1919, Hoge had left his Manhattan, New York, company, which continued to produce office supplies exclusively until 1931, when its toy division was formed. The Mattatuck Mfg. Co. was contracted to produce the Hoge-designed toys, which included stamped-steel locomotives, and a few vehicles. The toy line ceased in 1939 and in 1958, Mattatuck purchased and dissolved Hoge.

	C6	C8	C10
Fire Chief Car, No. 266, battery-operated, lights, siren gets louder as car increases speed, rubber tires, 14-1/4" long	250	450	650
Fire Chief Car, No. 267, same as No. 266 w/bell on rear of car that works from interior switch that also controls headlights, battery operated, 14-1/4" long	275	475	675
Police Chief Car, No. 265, battery-operated lights, siren sounds when car is pushed or pulled, two-tone green, rubber tires, 14-1/4" long	250	450	650

Hoge Fire Chief Car. Photo courtesy Bob Smith

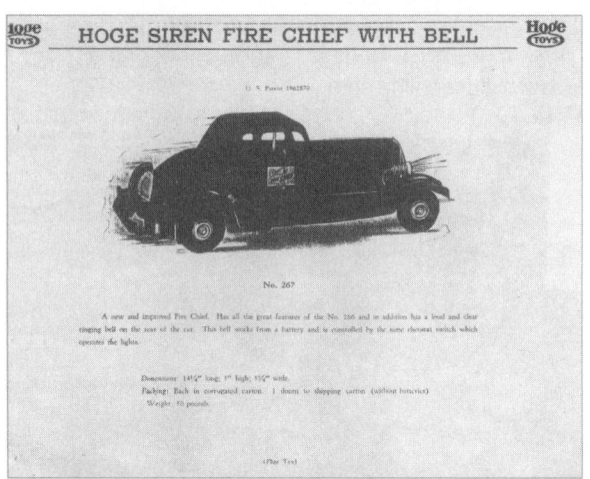

The Hoge Siren Fire Chief car, as shown in a Hoge No. 35 catalog.

Hoge Fire and Police Chief cars, as shown in a Hoge catalog.

HOLGATE

Holgate was founded by Cornelius Holgate in Philadelphia. About 1930 it began turning out educational wooden toys and numerous vechiles in its Kent, Penn. plant. It merged with Playskool in 1958; now owned by Hasbro.

	C6	C8	C10
Army Tank, wooden, ten wheels, 12" long	65	82	130
Army Transport Truck, wooden, 6 wheels, 10 wooden peg passengers, 1940s, 9-1/4" long	30	55	85
Bus, "Holgate Jack Rabbit Bus Line" on sides, wooden, driver and 12 passengers removable, pull toy, 11" long, 1930s	35	65	100
Convertible and Trailer, wooden, car has 2 people, trailer has 4 people, pull toy, 16" long overall	30	60	90
Fairyland City Train Set, wooden, engine plus 5 cars with fairy tale themes, 1940s	45	90	135
Hook & Ladder Truck, wooden, 4 firemen, 2 ladders	30	55	85
Neighborhood Trolley, wooden, pull toy, Trolley from Mr. Roger's Neighborhood, stamped "Fred Rogers" on bottom, 1960s	30	55	85
Roadster, wooden, pull toy, headlights, spare tire, holes for two wooden passengers, 7-1/2" long	30	55	85

HOLMES COAL CO.

Delivery Truck, pressed steel, marked	C6	C8	C10
"Holmes Coal Co.," 17-1/2" long	4100	600	800

This "Holmes Coal Co." truck may be a promotional item produced by Marx. Photo courtesy Sotheby's New York

HOT WHEELS

It all started in 1968 when Mattel issued the original sixteen metallic colored toy cars. Customized versions of cars commonly found on America's highways, the Hot Wheels cars were a direct attempt to compete with the successful Matchbox line. Detroit auto makers reveled in muscle car mania through the 1960s, and Hot Wheels became the first toy line devoted to minature die-cast muscle cars.

An instant hit with boys, girls, and adults, Mattel expanded the color palette so that each car was offered in at least nine colors (a few were offered in as many as 20 unique colors). The 1968 catalog promised just two colors for each car. Originally manufactured in Hong Kong and the U.S., today, Hot Wheels cars are assembled in China and Malaysia as reflected on their bases.

More than 35 years later, Hot Wheels cars are still being offered in staggering varieties and have developed a loyal following of dedicated collectors. Collector clubs can be found across the globe and there are several popular Internet destinations including www.hotwheelscollectors.com, the home of the Hot Wheels Redlines Collectors Club.

Listed are issued from 1968 to 1977 (the red-line era). These are the most sought after by toy collectors, especially if they are still in their original blister package (C10). Most are found, however, in used condition. The (C8) designation is used here to reflect near mint status of a loose car.

Redlines

	C6	C8	C10
'31 Doozie, 1977, orange, tan top, brown fenders, Model No. 9649	n/a	15	55
'56 Hi Tail Hauler, 1977, orange, redline, Model No. 9647	n/a	15	60
'57 Chevy, 1977, red, yellow & white tampo, "57 Chevy", Model No. 9638 .	n/a	20	85
Alive '55, 1973, assorted, Model No. 6968..	n/a	125	600
Alive '55, 1974, blue, Model No. 6968 ..	n/a	90	350
Alive '55, 1974, green, Model No. 6968 .	n/a	50	110
Alive '55, 1977, chrome, redline, Model No. 9210..	n/a	15	55
Ambulance, 1970, met. blue, white back with red cross & blue light on top, Model No. 6451	n/a	30	130

	C6	C8	C10
American Hauler, 1976, blue cab, white plastic box, American-flag-style tampo, "American Hauler", Model No. 9118	n/a	30	70
American Tipper, 1976, red metal cab, white plastic tipper bed, American flag tampo, "American Tipper", Model No. 9089	n/a	25	65
American Victory, 1975, light blue, American flag tampo, "9" on sides, silver interior, exposed silver engine, Model No. 7662	n/a	20	45
AMX/2, 1971, dark met. red, rear engine covers lift up, metal chassis, Model No. 6460	n/a	40	130

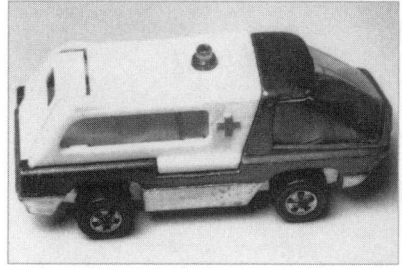
Hot Wheels Ambulance.

Hot Wheels Carabo.

Hot Wheels Classic '32 Ford Vicky.

Hot Wheels Classic '36 Ford Coupe.

Hot Wheels Classic Nomad.

Hot Wheels Custom Charger.

	C6	C8	C10
Backwoods Bomb, 1975, blue body with green & yellow tampo on sides, plastic camper shell on bed, "Keep On Camping," silver base, Model No. 7670	n/a	40	100
Baja Bruiser, 1974, yellow, blue in tampo, Model No. 8258	n/a	300	1200
Baja Bruiser, 1974, yellow, magenta in tampo, Model No. 8258	n/a	300	1200
Baja Bruiser, 1974, orange, stars & stripes side tampo, "Firestone," "Cragar," and "Ford", Model No. 8258	n/a	30	90
Baja Bruiser, 1976, light green, Model No. 8258	n/a	400	1300
Baja Bruiser, 1977, blue, redline or blackwall, Model No. 8258	n/a	25	85
Beatnik Bandit, 1968, met. blue, tan interior, clear bubble, exposed engine, Model No. 6217	n/a	15	75
Boss Hoss, 1970, chrome, black stripes on top, Club Kit, black number "9" in white circle on side, Model No. 6499	n/a	50	160
Boss Hoss, 1971, met. green, black "8" in white circle on side, exposed engine, Model No. 6406	n/a	125	250
Brabham-Repco F1, 1969, met. green, long tailpipes on silver engine, black "1" in white circle on side, blue-tinted windows, Model No. 6264	n/a	20	65
Breakaway Bucket, 1974, dark blue, orange tampo w/ yellow designs, Model No. 8262	n/a	40	120
Bugeye, 1971, magenta, white interior, Model No. 6178	n/a	30	n/a
Bugeye, 1971, red, black interior, hood lifts to expose engine, Model No. 6178	n/a	30	140

	C6	C8	C10
Buzz Off, 1973, assorted, Model No. 6976	n/a	110	500
Buzz Off, 1974, blue, Model No. 6976	n/a	30	90
Buzz Off, 1977, gold plated, redline or blackwall, Model No. 6976	n/a	15	30
Bye-Focal, 1971, met. green, opening hood, bifocals & "Bye Focal" on side, Model No. 6187	n/a	125	400
Carabo, 1974, yellow, Model No. 7617	n/a	500	1400
Carabo, 1974, light green with blue and red stripes, opening gull-wing style doors, Model No. 7617	n/a	35	100
Carabo, 1974, green, with blue & orange tampo, opening doors, Model No. 6420	n/a	35	80
Cement Mixer, 1970, "Heavyweights" series, met. green, orange plastic cement mixer, Hot Wheels logo, Model No. 6452	n/a	30	100
Chaparral 2G, 1969, white, back opens to expose metal engine, Model No. 6256	n/a	20	140
Chevy Monza, 1977, chrome, yellow & black tampo, Model No. 9202	n/a	n/a	50
Chevy Monza 2+2, 1975, orange enamel finish, "Monza" rally stripes on hood and roof, Model No. 7671	n/a	40	110
Chevy Monza 2+2, 1975, light green enamel with "Monza" rally stripes on hood and roof, black plastic interior, Model No. 7671	n/a	200	800
Chief's Special Cruiser, 1976, red, redline, Model No. 7665	n/a	25	65
Classic '31 Ford Woody, 1969, met. red, metal engine, Model No. 6251	n/a	30	90
Classic '32 Ford Vicky, 1969, met. gold, metal engine, black roof, Model No. 6250	n/a	30	95
Classic '36 Ford Coupe, 1969, blue, Model No. 6253	n/a	20	60

Hot Wheels Classic '36 Ford Coupe in original package.

Hot Wheels Chaparral 2G.

Hot Wheels Boss Hoss.

Hot Wheels Custom Fleetside.

Hot Wheels Custom Mustang.

Hot Wheels Demon, 1970.

	C6	**C8**	**C10**
Classic '36 Ford Coupe, 1969, red, opening back reveals rumble seat, black roof, Model No. 6253	n/a	35	100
Classic '57 T-Bird, 1969, met. orange, hood opens to reveal engine, Model No. 6252	n/a	30	140
Classic Cord, 1971, met. green, opening hood, detachable plastic soft-top roof (often missing), Model No. 6472	n/a	35	100
Classic Nomad, 1970, met. aqua, opening hood, metal engine, Model No. 6404	n/a	55	150
Classic Nomad, 1970-71, blue, opening hood, metal engine, Model No. 6404	n/a	55	150
Cockney Cab, 1971, blue, British flag tampo on rear, "Cockney Cab", Model No. 6466	n/a	50	210
Cool One, 1976, Magenta body, "Cool One" letting on front, lightning tampo on body. Available as blackwalls variation, Model No. 9120	n/a	30	60
Corvette Stingray, 1977, red body, red, white, yellow & blue tampo, Model No. 9241	n/a	n/a	40
Custom AMX, 1969, met. green, hood lifts to expose engine, Model No. 6267	n/a	100	225
Custom Barracuda, 1968, met. green, hood opens to reveal metal engine, Model No. 6211	n/a	80	400
Custom Camaro, 1968, met. orange, black roof, opening hood, Model No. 6208	n/a	100	750
Custom Camaro, 1968, white enamel— an almost mythical car, and apparently none "in-pack", Model No. 6208	n/a	n/a	n/a
Custom Charger, 1969, Assorted body colors, white plastic interior, opening hood, Model No. 6268	n/a	100	250

	C6	**C8**	**C10**
Custom Continental Mark III, 1969, met. pink, opening hood, metal engine, Model No. 6266	n/a	20	400
Custom Corvette, 1968, met. orange, opening hood, assorted interior color, Model No. 6215	n/a	90	400
Custom Cougar, 1968, met. green, opening hood, black interior, Model No. 6205	n/a	80	400
Custom El Dorado, 1968, met. green, black interior, black top, opening hood, Model No. 6218	n/a	40	180
Custom Firebird, 1968, met. orange, metal engine, opening hood, Model No. 6212	n/a	50	280
Custom Fleetside, 1968, met. purple, black roof, opening bed cover, Model No. 6213	n/a	60	250
Custom Mustang, 1968, assorted w/open hood scoops or louvered windows, Model No. 6206	n/a	400	1400
Custom Mustang, 1968, assorted, Model No. 6206	n/a	80	450
Custom Police Cruiser, 1969, Black and white paint scheme on a Plymouth with "Police" and star tampos, red dome light. A nice companion car to the the 6469 Fire Chief Cruiser, Model No. 6269	n/a	65	205
Custom T-Bird, 1968, met. brown, opening hood, metal engine, Model No. 6207	n/a	50	225
Custom VW Bug, 1968, met. aqua, oversized engine, sunroof, Model No. 6220	n/a	30	125
Demon, 1970, blue, exposed engine, called "Prowler" in 1973, Model No. 6401	n/a	25	100

Hot Wheels Deora.

Hot Wheels Double Header.

Hot Wheels Hiway Robber.

Hot Wheels Jack Rabbit Special.

Hot Wheels King Kuda.

Hot Wheels Mantis.

	C6	C8	C10
Deora, 1968, assorted, Model No. 6210 .	n/a	60	375
Double Header, 1973, green, blue-tinted windshield, Model No. 5880	n/a	120	450
Double Vision, 1973, orange, white interior, blue-tinted windows, Model No. 6975	n/a	110	400
Double Vision, 1973, met. green, flip-up plastic canopy over the seats, rear engine, Model No. 6975	n/a	110	400
Dump Truck, 1970-72, metal cab & chassis, unpainted base, plastic dump truck bed, "Heavyweights" series, Model No. 6453	n/a	25	50
Dune Daddy, 1973, green, blue-tinted windshield, white interior, Model No. 6967	n/a	110	400
Dune Daddy, 1975, orange body with sixties-style flowers on hood, Model No. 6967	n/a	225	600
Dune Daddy, 1975, light green with sixties-style daisy tampos on hood, Model No. 6967	n/a	25	75
El Rey Special, 1974, green, yellow & red "Dunlop," number "1" tampos, silver metal base, Model No. 8273	n/a	40	120
El Rey Special, 1974, dark blue, Model No. 8273	n/a	225	900
El Rey Special, 1974, light blue with orange tampos, unpainted metal base, Model No. 8273	n/a	310	1250
El Rey Special, 1974, light green, Model No. 8273	n/a	75	175
Emergency Squad, 1975, red body, yellow & white side tampos, silver plastic base, very much in the mold of the paramedic vehicle used on the TV show, "Emergency!", Model No. 7650	n/a	25	75

	C6	C8	C10
Evil Weevil, 1971, met. blue, black "8" inside white circle, sunroof, blue-tinted windows, Model No. 6471	n/a	75	175
Ferrari 312P, 1970, gold chrome, back opens to expose metal engine, black "60" in white circles, Model No. 6417	n/a	30	60
Ferrari 312P, 1973, red, back opens to expose metal engine, black "60" in white circles, Model No. 6973	n/a	300	600
Ferrari 512S, 1972, blue, opening rear hood & cockpit, Model No. 6022	n/a	75	250
Ferrari 512-S, 1972, met. magenta, opening rear hood & cockpit, Model No. 6021	n/a	75	250
Fire Chief Cruiser, 1970, red Plymouth Fury, matches Custom Police Cruiser, #6269, Model No. 6469	n/a	15	85
Fire Engine, 1970, met. red cab, black ladder, rear is red plastic, white hoses, Model No. 6454	n/a	25	140
Fire-Eater, 1977, blue-tinted window, blue plastic hoses, Model No. 9640	n/a	n/a	40
Ford J-Car, 1968, met. aqua, back opens to reveal metal engine, Model No. 6214	n/a	20	70
Ford MK IV, 1969, red, back opens to reveal metal engine, Model No. 6257.	n/a	15	75
Fuel Tanker, 1971, white cab & chassis, plastic fuel tanker section, removable fuel hoses, "Heavyweights" series, Model No. 6018	n/a	75	200
Funny Money, 1972, gray armored car body on funny car chassis, orange plastic bumper (usually missing), "Funny Money" labels, Model No. 6005	n/a	70	335

Left to right: Hot Wheels Mongoose and Snake Funny Cars.

Hot Wheels Mongoose Dragster.

Hot Wheels Mongoose Funny Car.

Hot Wheels Mongoose and Snake Dragsters.

Hot Wheels Noodle Head.

Hot Wheels Olds 442.

	C6	C8	C10
Funny Money, 1974, plum w/floral tampo, Model No. 7621	n/a	n/a	85
Funny Money, 1977, gray, "Brink's" in white on side, Model No. 7621	n/a	60	150
Funny Money, 1977, gray body, white "Brink's" on sides, body lifts open, Model No. 7621	n/a	n/a	50
Grass Hopper, 1971, met. red, shown without white plastic canopy, Model No. 6461	n/a	45	125
Grass Hopper, 1974, light green, engine, orange & blue side tampo, blue-tinted windshield, Model No. 7622	n/a	40	100
Grass Hopper, 1975, light green, no engine, Model No. 7622	n/a	90	350
Gremlin Grinder, 1975, green, blue-tinted windows, yellow, orange & black tampo, exposed engine, Model No. 7652	n/a	35	85
Gremlin Grinder, 1976, chrome, orange, black & green tampo, exposed engine, Model No. 9201	n/a	20	40
Gun Bucket, 1976, olive-green body, white "Army" star & number tampos on hood, black plastic anti-aircraft gun & treads, Model No. 9090	n/a	25	60
Gun Slinger, 1975, olive, Model No. 7664	n/a	25	50
Hairy Hauler, 1971, assorted, with lifting front canopy, Model No. 6458	n/a	20	65
Heavy Chevy, 1970, met. Blue, exposed engine, black "8" in white circle on side, Model No. 6189	n/a	75	200
Heavy Chevy, 1970, assorted, Model No. 6408	n/a	65	200
Heavy Chevy, 1974, yellow, exposed engine, orange & red side tampo, "7", Model No. 7619	n/a	90	200
Heavy Chevy, 1974, light green, Model No. 7619	n/a	200	750
Heavy Chevy, 1977, chrome, redline or blackwall, Model No. 9212	n/a	40	120
Hiway Robber, 1973, red, black interior, exposed engine, Model No. 6979	n/a	75	400
Hood, The, 1971, met. light green, exposed engine, black interior, Model No. 6175	n/a	25	150
Hot Heap, 1968, met. yellow, white interior, exposed engine, Model No. 6219	n/a	20	100
Ice T, 1971, yellow, with "Ice T" on plastic roof, Model No. 6184	n/a	40	200
Ice T, 1973, Body in assorted colors, black plastic interior, plastic roof (mostly in white), silver base. Blackwall wheels variations also produced at the same time, Model No. 6980	n/a	200	650
Ice T, 1974, yellow with hood tampo, Model No. 6980	n/a	200	525
Ice T, 1974, light green, Model No. 6980	n/a	25	75
Indy Eagle, 1969, assorted colors with tinted plastic windshield and silver rear engine and tailpipes, Model No. 6263	n/a	15	40
Indy Eagle, 1969, gold, Model No. 6263	n/a	75	240
Jack Rabbit Special, 1970, white, blue stripe, clear windshield, Model No. 6421	n/a	15	75
Jack-in-the-Box Promotion, 1970, white, Jack Rabbit w/decals, Model No. 6421	n/a	300	n/a
Jet Threat, 1971, met. yellow, blue-tinted windshield, Model No. 6179	n/a	45	185
Jet Threat, 1973, light blue, blue-tinted windshield	n/a	45	160
Jet Threat II, 1976, plum w/yellow flames, blue-tinted windshield, exposed engine, Model No. 8235	n/a	n/a	55
Khaki Kooler, 1976, khaki body, "Military Police", black interior, smoke-colored windshield, Model No. 9183	n/a	n/a	45
King Kuda, 1970, chrome, Club Kit, Model No. 6411	n/a	75	300
King 'Kuda, 1970, met. green, exposed engine, blue-tinted windshield, Model No. 6411	n/a	25	180
Large Charge, 1975, green, red & yellow tampos, blue-tinted windows, Model No. 8272	n/a	25	80
Light My Firebird, 1970, Convertible in assorted finishes, with decal number on doors and exposed silver engine in front. Brown plastic interior, Model No. 6412	n/a	35	75
Lola GT 70, 1969, dark green, opening rear, clear windows, Model No. 6254	n/a	20	60
Lotus Turbine, 1969, met. brown, blue-tinted windshield, Model No. 6262	n/a	20	75
Lowdown, 1976, light blue, Model No. 9185	n/a	30	75
Mantis, 1970, assorted, Model No. 6423	n/a	20	60
Maserati Mistral, 1969, assorted, Model No. 6277	n/a	50	125
Maxi Taxi, 1976, Oldsmobile 442 body, yellow w/checkboard & "Maxi Taxi" tampo, black plastic interior, Model No. 9184	n/a	25	60
McClaren M6A, 1969, orange, blue-tinted windshield, Model No. 6255	n/a	20	65

Hot Wheels Olds 442.

Hot Wheels Paddy Wagon.

Hot Wheels Pit Crew Car.

	C6	C8	C10
Mercedes 280SL, 1969, red, opening hood, metal engine, blue-tinted windows, Model No. 6275	n/a	25	85
Mercedes 280SL, 1973, assorted, Model No. 6962	n/a	100	450
Mercedes C-111, 1972, assorted, Model No. 6169	n/a	80	250
Mercedes C-111, 1973, assorted, Model No. 6978	n/a	300	1200
Mercedes C-111, 1974, red, with stars and stripes tampo, Model No. 6978	n/a	55	100
Mercedes-Benz 280SL, 1969, met. blue, blue-tinted windows, opening hood, metal engine, Model No. 6275	n/a	25	70
Mighty Maverick, 1970, assorted, Model No. 6414	n/a	45	130
Mighty Maverick, 1975, blue, orange, yellow & white tampo, blue-tinted windows, Model No. 7653	n/a	50	100
Mighty Maverick, 1976, chrome, yellow & blue tampo, blue-tinted windows, "Super Chromes" series, Model No. 9209	n/a	25	50
Mod-Quad, 1970, met. red, black interior, four metal engines, top opens, Model No. 6456	n/a	20	170
Mongoose, 1973, red/blue, Model No. 6970	n/a	400	1400
Mongoose Funny Car, 1970, red, opening body, white, blue & yellow tampo, Model No. 6410	n/a	50	210
Mongoose II, 1971, met. blue, opening body, Model No. 5954	n/a	75	350
Mongoose Rail Dragster, 1971, blue, two pack, Model No. 5952	n/a	75	n/a
Monte Carlo Stocker, 1975, yellow, blue-tinted windows, black interior, Model No. 7660	n/a	45	120
Motocross I, 1975, red plastic seat and tank, unpainted gray die-cast body, Model No. 7668	n/a	100	200
Moving Van, 1970, met. blue, white trailer, "Heavyweights" series, Model No. 6455	n/a	50	150
Mustang Stocker, 1975, yellow w/red in tampo, Model No. 9203	n/a	300	900
Mustang Stocker, 1975, yellow with magenta and orange tampo with "Ford" and "450 HP", Model No. 7664	n/a	80	135
Mustang Stocker, 1975, white, Model No. 7664	n/a	400	1200
Mustang Stocker, 1976, chrome, Model No. 9203	n/a	40	90

	C6	C8	C10
Mustang Stocker, 1977, chrome, redline or blackwall, Model No. 9203	n/a	40	90
Mutt Mobile, 1971, met. red, dogs in back, Model No. 6185	n/a	80	300
Neet Streeter, 1976, blue, red & white roof stripes, Model No. 9244	n/a	30	75
Nitty Gritty Kitty, 1970, gold chrome, metal engine, blue-tinted windows, Model No. 6405	n/a	25	200
Noodle Head, 1971, assorted, Model No. 6000	n/a	55	165
Odd Job, 1973, red, white topper, exposed engine, Model No. 6981	n/a	100	600
Odd Rod, 1977, yellow plastic bucket around seats, clear plastic hood with flame graphics, Model No. 9642	n/a	30	100
Odd Rod, 1977, plum, blackwall or redline, Model No. 9642	n/a	200	400
Olds 442, 1971, assorted, Model No. 6467	n/a	400	800
Open Fire, 1972, met. red, modified AMC Gremilin, oversized engine & six wheels, Model No. 5881	n/a	100	450
Paddy Wagon, 1970, blue, with plastic covering over bed, Model No. 6402	n/a	20	75
Paddy Wagon, 1973, blue, Model No. 6966	n/a	30	120
Paramedic, 1975, white with yellow and red stripes and "Paramedic" lettering, Model No. 7661	n/a	30	65
Peepin' Bomb, red, exposed engine, blue-tinted windshield	n/a	45	150
Peepin' Bomb, 1970, met. yellow, clear windshield, exposed engine, Model No. 6419	n/a	20	70
Pit Crew Car, 1971, white, Model No. 6183	n/a	30	350
Poison Pinto, 1976, light green body, skull & crossbones, "Poison Pinto" tampo, late-era redlines, Model No. 9240	n/a	25	65
Police Cruiser, 1973, white Olds 442, "Police" labels on doors, opening hood & red dome light on roof, Model No. 6963	n/a	200	110
Police Cruiser, 1974, white, Model No. 6963	n/a	45	125
Police Cruiser, 1977, white Olds 442 with black doors, yellow police tampos on doors, non-opening hood, blue light, Model No. 6963	n/a	30	65
Porsche 911, 1975, yellow, with blue and red stripes on hood and roof, Model No. 7648	n/a	40	75

	C6	C8	C10
Porsche 911, 1975, orange, Model No. 6972	n/a	25	65
Porsche 911, 1976, chrome, red & green tampo, black interior, Model No. 9206	n/a	20	40
Porsche 917, 1970, silver, clear windshield, opening back, Model No. 6416	n/a	25	140
Porsche 917, 1973, red, opening back, blue-tinted windshield, Model No. 6972	n/a	300	700
Porsche 917, 1974, red, Model No. 6972	n/a	175	500
Porsche 917, 1974, orange, Model No. 6972	n/a	40	75
Power Pad, 1970, met. red, clear windshield, black interior, exposed engine, shown w/o camper, Model No. 6459	n/a	30	125
Prowler, 1973, assorted, Model No. 6965	n/a	200	1000
Prowler, 1974, orange with demon flame tampo on roof (which makes sense, considering this car was known as "The Demon" in its previous incarnation in 1970. Unpainted metal base, Model No. 6965	n/a	35	75
Prowler, 1974, light green, Model No. 6965	n/a	500	1000
Prowler, 1976, chrome, yellow & red flames, devil tampo, exposed engine, Model No. 9207	n/a	n/a	85
Python, 1968, met. red, black top, exposed engine, Model No. 6216	n/a	20	75
Racer Rig, 1971, red/white, "Heavyweights" series, Model No. 6194	n/a	100	375
Ramblin' Wrecker, 1975, white, "Larry's 24 Hour Towing", blue lift, Model No. 7659	n/a	n/a	80
Ranger Rig, 1975, medium green w/yellow lettering & design, Model No. 7666	n/a	20	75
Rash 1, 1974, green, blue-tinted windshield, yellow & white tampo, exposed engine, Model No. 7616	n/a	50	140
Rash I, 1974, blue, Model No. 7616	n/a	300	800
Rear Engine Mongoose, 1972, red, Model No. 5699	n/a	200	600
Rear Engine Snake, 1972, yellow, blue w/red stars tampo, Model No. 5856	n/a	200	600
Red Baron, 1970, red, cross on helmet, Model No. 6400	n/a	15	80

	C6	C8	C10
Red Baron, 1973, red, note no Iron Cross on the helmet, Model No. 6964	n/a	30	200
Road King Truck, 1974, yellow cab and trailer with metal chassis, tilting dumper section, availabe in set only, Model No. 7615	n/a	600	1200
Rock Buster, 1976, yellow, Model No. 9088	n/a	20	35
Rock Buster, 1976, chrome dune buggy with black plastic rollcage and interior, racing graphics on hood and sides, Model No. 9507	n/a	15	30
Rocket-Bye-Baby, 1971, met. yellow, metal rocket on top, Model No. 6186	n/a	60	280
Rodger Dodger, 1974, magenta Dodge Charger, flame tampos on hood & roof, exposed silver engine, red plastic exhaust pipes, Model No. 8259	n/a	40	125
Rodger Dodger, 1974, blue, Model No. 8259	n/a	200	550
Rodger Dodger, 1977, gold plated, blackwall or redline, Model No. 8259	n/a	30	80
Rolls-Royce Silver Shadow, 1969, silver, opening hood shows detailed engine, Model No. 6276	n/a	30	90
Sand Crab, 1970, red, black interior, clear windshield, Model No. 6403	n/a	20	75
Sand Drifter, 1975, green, Model No. 7651	n/a	150	375
Sand Drifter, 1975, yellow, flame tampo on hood, black plastic interior & covering over bed, Model No. 7651	n/a	45	85
Sand Witch, 1973, green, blue-tinted windshield, opening rear hood, Model No. 6974	n/a	125	450
S'Cool Bus, 1971, yellow, lift-up funny car body, silver chassis, Model No. 6468	n/a	175	750
Scooper, 1971, met. green, yellow scoop & rear, Model No. 6193	n/a	100	220
Seasider, 1970, met. light green, exposed engine, plastic boat, Model No. 6413	n/a	60	200
Second Wind, 1977, white w/yellow & red striping, number "5" on hood, Model No. 9644	n/a	35	90
Shelby Turbine, 1969, met. purple, Model No. 6265	n/a	20	85
Short Order, 1971, blue, extending plastic tailgate, exposed engine, Model No. 6176	n/a	50	230

Hot Wheels Racer Rig.

Hot Wheels Sand Crab.

Hot Wheels S'Cool Bus.

Hot Wheels Seasider.

Hot Wheels Sky Show Fleetside.

Hot Wheels Snake Dragster.

	C6	C8	C10
Show Hoss II, 1977, yellow funny car Mustang II body lifts up over silver base, black plastic rollcage, redline or blackwalls versions available, Model No. 9646	n/a	300	600
Show-Off, 1973, orange, exposed engine, blue-tinted windows, Model No. 6982	n/a	140	550
Sidekick, 1972, met. green, exposed engine, Model No. 6022	n/a	80	300
Silhouette, 1968, Body in assorted colors, plastic dome canopy over seats, exposed front engine, Model No. 6209	n/a	20	90
Sir Sidney Roadster, 1974, yellow, red flames, exposed engine, brown top, Model No. 8261	n/a	50	90
Sir Sidney Roadster, 1974, light green, Model No. 8261	n/a	325	650
Sir Sidney Roadster, 1974, Orange body with brown plastic roof and exposed silver engine. Red flame tampos, silver metal base, Model No. 8261	n/a	375	700
Six Shooter, 1971, met. blue, exposed engines, blue-tinted windshield, Model No. 6003	n/a	75	225
Sky Show Fleetside (Aero Launcher), 1970, met. blue, orange plastic ramp, Model No. 6436	n/a	400	850
Snake, 1973, white/yellow, Model No. 6969	n/a	600	1500
Snake Funny Car, 1970, yellow, body opens, metal engine, Model No. 6409	n/a	60	300
Snake II, 1971, white, Model No. 5953	n/a	60	275
Snake Rail Dragster, 1971, white, exposed engine, part of a two-pack with blue Mongoose Rail, Model No. 5951	n/a	75	1250
Snorkel, 1971, assorted, Model No. 6020	n/a	90	200
Special Delivery, 1971, blue, exposed engines, U.S. Mail tampo, Model No. 6006	n/a	45	250
Splittin' Image, 1969, met. orange, clear windows, exposed engine, Model No. 6261	n/a	15	75
Spoiler Sport, 1977, light green van, tropical island scene on side panels, Model No. 9641	n/a	25	50
Steam Roller, 1974, white body, stars & stripes tampo, three stars reversed out of red stripe on hood; the more common model, Model No. 8260	n/a	25	70
Steam Roller, 1974, white body with red white and blue graphics, seven stars on front, Model No. 8260	n/a	100	300
Street Rodder, 1976, black, flames, exposed engine, clear windshield, Model No. 9242	n/a	40	85

	C6	C8	C10
Street Snorter, 1973, light green, blue-tinted windows, Model No. 6971	n/a	100	500
Street Snorter, 1973, assorted, Model No. 6971	n/a	110	400
Strip Teaser, 1971, blue, opeing back, exposed engine, Model No. 6188	n/a	65	200
Strip Teaser, 1973, blue, exposed engine, driver area opens to reveal black interior	n/a	n/a	140
Sugar Caddy, 1971, assorted, Model No. 6418	n/a	45	120
Super Van, 1975, Toys-R-Us, Model No. 7649	n/a	100	350
Super Van, 1975, blue body, yellow flames, Model No. 7649	n/a	110	270
Superfine Turbine, 1973, red, exposed engine, black interior, Model No. 6004	n/a	40	850
Sweet 16, 1973, red, exposed engine, trunk opens to expose spare, Model No. 6007	n/a	125	650
Swingin' Wing, 1970, met. red, blue-tinted windows, Model No. 6422	n/a	25	85
T-4-2, 1971, met. yellow, black top, exposed metal engines, blue-tinted windows, Model No. 6177	n/a	50	175
Team Trailer, 1971, white/red, detailed plastic interior & opening door on trailer, Model No. 6019	n/a	95	250
TNT-Bird, 1970, met. green, white stripe, blue-tinted windshield, exposed engine, Model No. 6407	n/a	60	125
Top Eliminator, 1974, blue lift-up funny car body on silver chassis, green, light tan, and orange "Hot Wheels" tampo w/stripes on sides, Model No. 7630	n/a	50	165
Torero, 1969, gold chrome, opening hood, clear windows, white interior, Model No. 6260	n/a	15	75
Torino Stocker, 1975, red, blue-tinted windshield, black interior, Model No. 7647	n/a	35	95
Tough Customer, 1975, olive, with rotating turret and white numbering tampos, Model No. 7655	n/a	30	60
Tow Truck, 1970, assorted, Model No. 6450	n/a	30	80
Tri-Baby, 1970, blue, interesting engine casting under opening rear hood, Model No. 6424	n/a	20	85
T-Totaller, 1977, black, Red Line, six-pack only, Model No. 9648	n/a	500	1000
Turbofire, 1969, met. yellow, opening rear, clear windshield, Model No. 6259	n/a	15	75

Hot Wheels Sweet 16.

Hot Wheels Tow Truck.

Hot Wheels VW Beach Bomb.

	C6	C8	C10
Twin Mill, 1969, met. aqua, clear windows, two exposed engines, Model No. 6258	n/a	15	85
Twin Mill, 1973, met. red, blue-tinted windshield, two exposed engines.........	n/a	n/a	145
Twin Mill II, 1976, orange, two engines, blue-tinted windows, blue, white & red tampo, Model No. 8240	n/a	10	45
Vega Bomb, 1975, green, Model No. 7658	n/a	250	800
Vega Bomb, 1975, orange, this model is right on the cusp of the Redlines era— blackwall versions (like this one as #7654) were becoming a more common sight, Model No. 7658	n/a	40	120
Volkswagen, 1974, orange w/stripes on roof, Model No. 7620	n/a	100	400
Volkswagen, 1974, orange enamel, bug graphic on roof, Model No. 7620	n/a	30	125
Volkswagen Beach Bomb, 1969, surf boards on side raised panels, Model No. 6274	n/a	115	400

	C6	C8	C10
Volkswagen Beach Bomb, 1969, surf boards in rear window, Model No. 6274	n/a	7000	n/a
Warpath, 1975, white, stars & stripes tampo, opening plastic engine covers, Model No. 7654	n/a	60	115
Waste Wagon, 1971, met. yellow, orange receptacle, "Heavyweights" series, Model No. 6192	n/a	90	250
What-4, 1971, met. green, blue-tinted windshield, Model No. 6001	n/a	50	225
Whip Creamer, 1970, met. yellow, clear slide-back plastic canopy, Model No. 6457	n/a	25	120
Winnipeg, 1974, yellow body, orange spoiler, blue & orange tampo, Model No. 7618	n/a	n/a	210
Xploder, 1973, red, black interior, blue-tinted windows, Model No. 6977	n/a	100	500
Z Whiz, 1977, gray body, orange & yellow tampo, Model No. 9639	n/a	35	70
Z Whiz, 1977, white, redline, Model No. 9639	n/a	1500	n/a

HUBLEY

The Hubley Manufacturing Company was founded in 1892 by John Hubley. It made iron toys from the start at its plant in Lancaster, Pennsylvania. In the beginning, all toys were cast iron, and some early toys included coal ranges, circus wagons, and mechanical banks. Hubley's cast-iron toys were popular almost from the start, and have long been collector's items because they were well made and attractive.

By 1940, however, the cast-iron toy, due to the increased cost of freight and foreign competition, was slowly becoming a thing of the past. At this time,

when Hubley was the largest producer of cast-iron toys and cap pistols in the world, it began to introduce die-cast zinc alloy toys. During World War II, Hubley was ninety-eight-percent engaged in war production.

After the war, Hubley manufactured die-cast toys and plastic toys exclusively. In 1952, Hubley manufactured 9,763,610 toys and 11,184,878 cap pistols, about ten times the amount of toys and pistols it produced in 1930, but with a line of toys eighty-percent smaller than in 1930. It is the combination of the relative scarcity (and multiplicity)

Left to right: Hubley Ladder Truck, 13"; Ahrens Fox Hose Reel, 11-1/4". Photo courtesy Bertoia Auctions

Hubley Auto Carrier, 1950s, with two Cadillacs.

Hubley Auto Transport, all metal with four different color plastic Packards, 18" without ramp. Photo courtesy Harvey Rainess.

Hubley Avery Tractor, 4-3/4". Photo courtesy Ron Carnahan

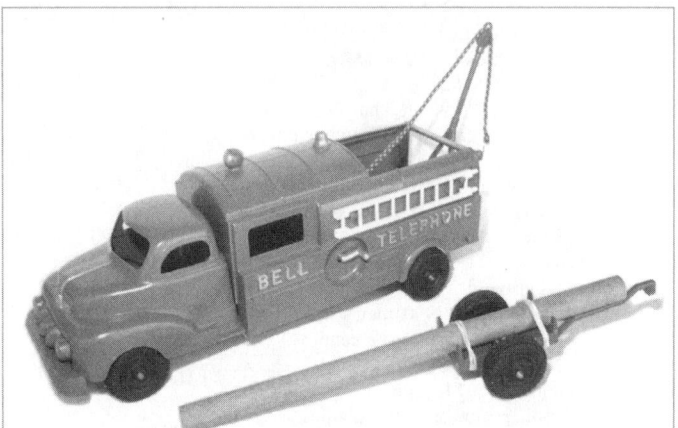

Hubley Bell Telephone, postwar truck, 24". Photo courtesy Thomas G. Nefos

Hubley Bell Telephone, 5-1/4".

Hubley Bell Telephone trucks. Top row, left to right: 3" long; 3-3/4" long; 5-1/4" long; 7" long. Bottom row, left to right: 8-1/4" long; 9-1/4" long. Photo courtesy Bertoia Auctions

Hubley Borden's Milk Cream truck, deluxe version, 7-1/2" long. Photo courtesy Phillips New York

Hubley Borden's Milk Cream truck. Left to right: 6" long; 3-5/8" long. Photo courtesy Bertoia Auctions

of the older toys, plus the preference by collectors for cast-iron over die-cast zinc alloy and plastic toys that makes the prewar toys the most attractive to collectors. Hubley was acquired by Gabriel Industries in late 1965, and released holster sets, cap pistols, vehicles, hobby kits, and a number of other toys.

Contributor: Kent M. Comstock contributed the original list of motorcycles.

	C6	C8	C10
Ahrens Fox Hose Reel, 11-1/4" long	2000	4500	8000
Air Compress Truck, 7" long	37	56	75
Airflow type, marked "Hubley, U.S.A." c.1937, approx. 3-1/2" long	20	30	40
Allis Chalmers Model WC Tractor, w/driver, 7" long	100	160	225
American LaFrance Ladder and Hose Truck, 15" long	100	175	275
Army Ambulance, No. 476, late	60	90	120
Army Motor Truck, No. 807, w/driver, 15" long	1100	1800	2400
Auto, 6-1/2" long	80	120	160
Auto, Chevy (?), 1922, 9" long	400	650	1000
Auto, die-cast, black plastic wheels, 1950s	12	18	25
Auto, No. 358, c.1928, 7-1/2" long	150	225	300
Auto Carrier, w/three cars and one pickup truck, c.1939, 10" long			
Auto Carrier, w/two Packards, 1950s	80	120	160
Auto Express, cast iron, 9" long	900	1450	2000
Auto Transport, all-metal, w/four different-color plastic Cadillacs, 18" long without ramp	175	263	350
Auto Transport, plastic, marked "Hubley Transport," 13" long	125	188	250
Avery tractor, marked "No. 2," very early, 4-3/4" long	120	180	240
Bell Telephone, post-WWII, 24" long	60	90	120
Bell Telephone Truck, 3" long	200	300	400
Bell Telephone Truck, 3-3/4" long	150	235	310
Bell Telephone Truck, 5-1/4" long	200	320	450
Bell Telephone Truck, accessories, 1950s	85	128	170
Bell Telephone Truck, marked "Bell Telephone", w/tools, 12" long	179	263	350
Bell Telephone Truck, w/derrick and windlass, auger, trailer w/10" pole, three digging tools, and two loose ladders, 1931, 9-1/4" long	550	950	1300
Bell Telephone Truck, w/tools, 8-1/4" long	400	600	800

	C6	C8	C10
Bell Telephone Truck, w/two ladders, tools, 7" long	600	1000	1400
Borden's Milk Truck, 3-5/8" long	250	375	500
Borden's Milk Truck, marked "Borden's Milk Cream," deluxe versions, rubber tires, clicker, 7-1/2" long	1250	1875	2500
Borden's Milk Truck, marked "Borden's Milk Cream," standard versions, 6" long	1000	1500	2000
Bulldozer, 12" long	150	225	300
Bulldozer, 9" long	92	93	125
Bulldozer, die-cast, front scoop, rubber treads, c.1950, 10-1/4" long	78	118	155
Bus, 1930s, 8" long	60	90	120
Bus, c.1938, rubber wheels, 5-1/2" long	50	75	100
Bus, cast iron, marked "Coast to Coast," 1927, 13" long	450	675	900
Bus, die-cast, 9" long	20	30	40
Bus, futuristic type, c.1935, 3-1/2" long	60	90	120
Bus, futuristic, No. 617, 7-3/4" long	150	225	300
Cab, black and white 1920s	1200	2000	3000
Cadillac, die-cast, 1941, 7" long	40	60	80
Car and Trailer, No. 2278 car and No. 2279 house trailer, c.1939	150	225	300
Caterpillar Tractor, 9" long	62	93	125
Caterpillar Tractor, driver in cab, 3-1/4" long	100	150	200
Cattle Truck, plastic, 12" long	30	45	60
Cement Mixer, 18" long	400	600	800
Cement Mixer, marked "Jaeger"	475	712	950
Cement Mixer, Wonder, 1930s, 3-1/2" long	125	188	250
Cement Mixer Truck, 8" long	2000	3800	6500
Champion Stake Truck, white rubber tires, 1930s, 8-1/2" long	140	210	280
Chemical Truck, w/ladders, 13" long	200	300	400
Chevrolet 1932 Coupe Kit, w/box	12	18	25
Chevrolet 1932 Paheton Kit, 1960s, w/box	27	41	55
Chevrolet 1932 Roadster Kit, 1960s, w/box	20	30	40
Chrysler Airflow, electrified, white rubber tires on wood hubs, 8" long	600	900	1200
Chrysler Airflow, racing car, c.1938	100	150	200
Chrysler Airflow, take-apart body, 4-1/2" long	125	188	250
Chrysler Airflow, take-apart body, 6-3/4" long	312	468	625
Coal Truck, cast iron, w/driver, 16-3/4" long	1200	1800	2500
Coal Truck, marked "Coal," c.1922, 9-1/2" long	438	657	875

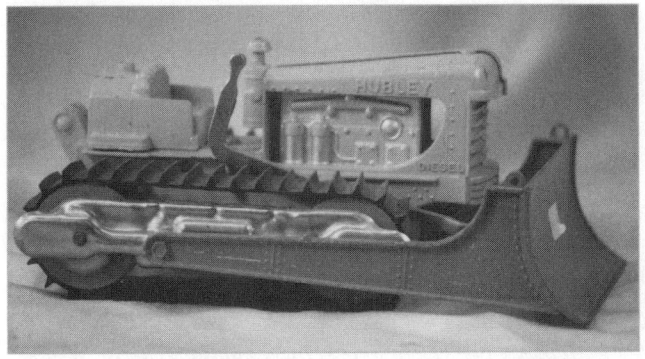

Hubley Bulldozer, 12". Photo courtesy Calvin L. Chaussee

Hubley Caterpillar Tractor, 3-1/4".

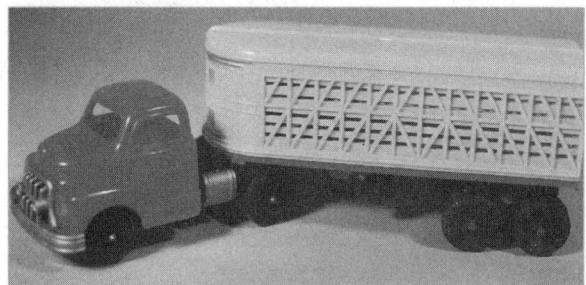

Hubley Cattle Truck, plastic, 12".

Hubley Coast to Coast Bus, cast-iron, 1927, 13". Photo courtesy Bertoia Auctions

Hubley Cement Mixer Truck, 8". Photo courtesy Bertoia Auctions

Hubley Chrysler Airflow, 4-1/2".

Hubley Corvette, 13-1/2".

Hubley Coal Truck, 1920s, 9-1/2". Photo courtesy Christie's East

Hubley made several versions of the Chrysler Airflow, the most valuable of which is an eight-inch car with white rubber tires on wood hubs.

Hubley, futuristic type, 3-1/2", 1930s. Photo courtesy Mapes Auctioneers and Appraisers

Hubley Compressor Truck, Ingersoll Rand, 8-1/4". Photo courtesy Bertoia Auctions

L to R: Hubley Delivery Van, "Merchants Delivery," 6-1/2" long; Arcade Ambulance, 1930s, 6" long. Photo courtesy Chic Gast

Hubley Delivery Van, 4-1/2", 1932.

	C6	C8	C10
Compressor Truck, Ingersoll Rand, 8-1/4" long	2500	4500	7000
Convertible, die-cast and iron, 7" long	100	150	200
Convertible, hard top, 1950s	50	75	100
Corvette, No. 509, red common color, yellow rare, 1955-56, 13" long	160	235	325
Coupe, 1920s, 4-1/2" long	100	150	200
Coupe, 1930s, 3-1/2" long	40	60	80
Coupe, 1933 Ford	90	135	180
Coupe, c.1939, 6-1/2" long	110	165	220
Coupe Roadster, rumble seat, rubber tires, 11" long	125	187	250
Crane, wooden wheels, 1940s	65	100	135
De Soto Air flow, 4" long	100	150	200

	C6	C8	C10
Delivery Truck, marked "Merchants Delivery," 1920s, 6" long	400	600	800
Delivery Van, 1932, 4-1/2" long	700	1300	1800
Diesel Low Boy, w/grader	115	172	230
Diesel Road Roller, 10" long	50	75	100
Duesenberg Town Car, built-it, model, w/box, 9" long	26	39	52
Dump Truck, 1930s, 3-1/2" long	40	60	80
Dump Truck, 1952	112	168	225
Dump Truck, 5-1/2" long	50	75	100
Dump Truck, c.1938, 7-1/2" long	1000	1600	2400
Dump Truck, Mack, six tires, 1930s, 10-3/4" long	1000	1800	2800
Dump Truck, No. 902, late	55	83	110

Hubley Kiddietoy Dump Truck, 8". Photo courtesy John Taylor

Hubley Hook and Ladder fire truck, plastic, rubber wheels. Photo courtesy John Taylor

Hubley Kiddie Toy Motor Express, tailgate opens, plastic, 6-1/2". Photo courtesy Harvey Rainess

Hubley Kiddie Toy Stake Truck. Photo courtesy Bob and Alice Wagner

Hubley Merchants Delivery, 1920s, 6". Photo courtesy Bertoia Auctions

Hubley Fire Ladder Truck, early, 7-1/2". Photo courtesy Rod Carnahan

Hubley Flatbed Truck, all metal, No. 506. Photo courtesy Harvey Rainess

Hubley Huber Road Rollers, left to right: 5-3/8" long; 4-1/2" long; 3-1/2" long. Photo courtesy Bertoia Auctions

Hubley Jaguar, 7-1/2". Photo courtesy Bob Smith

Hubley Dump Truck, Mack, 1930s, 10-3/4" long. Photo courtesy James S. Maxwell and Virginia Caputo

Hubley Fire Pumper.

Hubley Tractor, Ford Powermaster, No. 961.

Hubley Huber Road Roller, 8". Photo courtesy Mapes Auctioneers and Appraisers

Hubley Crane, 1940s, wooden wheels. Photo courtesy Harvey Rainess

Hubley Lincoln Zephyrs. Left to right: 6" long; 5-1/4" long. Photo courtesy Bertoia Auctions

Hubley Life Saver Truck, 1930s, holds pack of Life Savers, 4-1/4". Photo courtesy Bertoia Auctions

	C6	C8	C10
Dump Truck, plastic and metal, 8" long ..	25	38	50
Fire Chief's Car, plastic, red and black, rubber wheels, 1949, approx. 5" long ..	NPF	NPF	NPF
Fire Engine, die-cast, white rubber tires w/wooden rims, c.1941	40	60	80
Fire Engine, No. 526, c.1936, 10-1/2" long	175	263	350
Fire Engine Pumper, 1930s, 5" long	65	98	130
Fire Engine Pumper, Ahrens-Fox, 10" long...	250	375	500
Fire Engine Pumper, Ahrens-Fox, 7" long	400	600	800
Fire Engine Pumper, cast iron, black rubber tires, driver, boiler-trailer, c.1920, 12-1/2" long	350	525	700
Fire Engine Pumper, early, No. 504........	350	525	700
Fire Engine Pumper, No. 2254, 1930s	170	255	340
Fire Engine Pumper, No. 554, two firemen, early, 14" long	1700	3200	6820
Fire Engine Pumper, postwar?, 7" long ...	55	82	110
Fire Engine Pumper, terraplane front, 1930s, 6-1/4" long	185	275	370
Fire Engine Pumper, w/searchlight, 7" long...	55	83	110
Fire Engine Pumper, w/two firemen, 8-1/2" long..	275	362	550
Fire Ladder Truck, 19-1/2" long	850	1400	1900
Fire Ladder Truck, driver, early 1930s, 14" long...	500	800	1200

	C6	C8	C10
Fire Ladder Truck, early, 7-1/2" long	130	195	260
Fire Ladder Truck, early, 8-1/2" long	250	375	500
Fire Truck, 5" long.................................	100	150	200
Fire Truck, w/searchlight, white rubber tires w/wooden rims.............................	55	82	110
Fish Hatchery Truck, w/net, fish, 1950s ..	65	98	130
Flatbed Truck, all metal, No. 506	118	177	235
Ford Coupe, 1936....................................	40	50	80
Ford Model A Coupe Kit, 1960s, w/box..	25	38	50
Ford Model A Phaeton Kit, 1960s, w/box	25	38	50
Ford Model A Pickup Kit, 1960s, w/box .	25	38	50
Ford Model A Roaster Kit, 1960s, w/box	32	48	65
Ford Model A Station Wagon Kit, 1960s, w/box	25	38	50
Ford Model A Town Car Kit, 1960s, w/box	25	38	50
Ford Model A Victoria Kit, 1960s, w/box	25	38	50
Ford Powermaster Tractor, No. 961	NPF	NPF	NPF
Ford Tractor and Disk	85	128	170
Fordson Front-End Loader, cast iron, early 1930s, 9" long..............................	1000	1800	2700
Fuel Truck, cast iron, 5-1/2" long	100	150	200
Grader	56	84	112
Graham, 4" long	85	125	170
Hook and Ladder, No. 463......................	28	42	56
Hook and Ladder, No. 468......................	130	195	260
Hook and Ladder, No. 473......................	82	123	165

Hubley Kiddie Toy Taxi. Photo courtesy Bob and Alice Wagner

Hubley Mack Gasoline Truck, 8-3/4". Photo courtesy Bertoia Auctions

	C6	C8	C10
Hook and Ladder Truck, cast iron, 19-1/2" long	200	300	400
Huber Road Roller, 13" long..............	2500	3850	5000
Huber Road Roller, 14" long..............	1600	2500	3800
Huber Road Roller, 15" long..............	3000	4500	6000
Huber Road Roller, 3-1/2" long	75	112	150
Huber Road Roller, 4-1/2" long	110	165	220
Huber Road Roller, 5-3/8" long	125	188	250
Huber Road Roller, 8" long....................	455	682	960
Huber Road Roller, wind-up, 1932, 7-1/2" long....................	3500	6500	9500
Indianapolis 500 Racer Kit, metal, 9" long....................	150	225	300
Jaguar XK-120, No. 455, red (rare) in 1955 only, yellow common issue, two-tone color as well, die-cast, 7-1/2" long	62	93	145
Jeep, metal, 6-3/4" long..........................	20	27	35
Jeep and Speedboat, late	25	38	50
Kiddie Toy, aluminum, "457," 7" long	50	75	100
Kiddie Toy, plastic, black rubber tires, marked "3," 6-5/8" long	150	200	250
Kiddie Toy Auto Transport, w/Cadillacs .	80	120	160
Kiddie Toy Buick Convertible, No. 465, 7" long....................	65	98	130
Kiddie Toy Convertible, 1930s	100	150	200
Kiddie Toy Dump Truck, No. 322, plastic, green w/red dump bed, cab tilts forward, 1950s, 6-1/4" long	NPF	NPF	NPF
Kiddie Toy Dump Truck, No. 475, plastic cab w/metal dump, 8" long	50	75	150
Kiddie Toy Dump Truck, No. 476	70	105	140

	C6	C8	C10
Kiddie Toy Dump Truck, No. 510	125	188	250
Kiddie Toy Fire Ladder Truck, No. 520, 19" long....................	250	375	500
Kiddie Toy Fire Truck, plastic, w/rubber wheels	17	26	35
Kiddie Toy Hook and Ladder, No. 454, 7" long....................	65	98	130
Kiddie Toy Ladder Truck, No. 324, plastic, removable white ladders, cab tilts forward, 1950s, 6-3/4" long	65	100	140
Kiddie Toy Log Truck, No. 356, 12" long	72	105	145
Kiddie Toy MGTD Roadster, No. 432, 6" long....................	110	165	220
Kiddie Toy Midget Racers, No. 20, set of 3 metal body racers w/rubber tires; green, yellow, red	200	400	600
Kiddie Toy Motor Express, No. 330, plastic, green and red, tailgate opens, 1950s, 6-7/8" long....................	25	45	60
Kiddie Toy Pickup Truck, 1930s	100	150	200
Kiddie Toy Pumper, plastic, red w/painted chrome trim, rubber wheels, 1950s, 6" long	67	10	135
Kiddie Toy Racer, die-cast rubber tires, No. 457, 6-1/2" long	46	69	92
Kiddie Toy Road Roller, green plastic w/red wood wheels, No. 315, 1952, 6" long	50	75	100
Kiddie Toy Sedan, four-door, 1930s........	115	172	230
Kiddie Toy Sedan, two-door, 1930s	100	150	200
Kiddie Toy Stake Truck, Ford 1946, No. 461	45	90	170

Hubley Mack Gasoline Truck, 10-3/4". Photo courtesy Bertoia Auctions

Hubley Milk Cream Truck, 1930s, cast-iron, white rubber tires, 3-1/2". Photo courtesy Mapes Auctioneers and Appraisers

Hubley toys as shown in Woolworth's 1954 Christmas catalog/comic book.

Hubley Mr. Magoo Car, battery-operated, 1961.

Hubley Nu-Car Transport, w/four cars, 17". Photo courtesy Christie's East

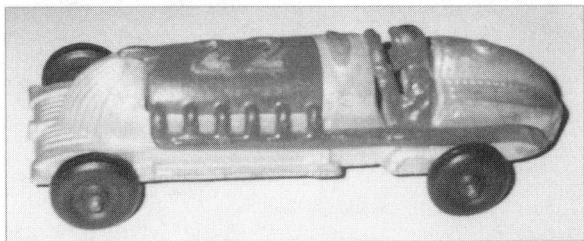

Hubley Racer, No. 22, aluminum and cast-iron, circa 1940, 7-3/8". Photo courtesy Rod Carnahan

Hubley Racer, No. 5, nickeled iron and aluminum, hood opens, 9-1/2". Photo courtesy Christie's East

Hubley Nite Coach, metal wheels, went on Nu-Car carrier, 1930s, 3-1/2". Photo courtesy Chic Gast

Hubley made several versions of the Packard in the 1920s-1930s.

Hubley Packard, fifteen parts, 1929, 11". Photo courtesy Bertoia Auctions

Hubley Panama Digger, Mack, 13". Photo courtesy Joe and Sharon Freed

Hubley Racers. Left to right: 9-1/2" long; with exhaust stacks, 11" long; with early wheels, 9-3/8" long; streamlined, 7-1/4" long. Photo courtesy Bertoia Auctions

Hubley Racer, 5". Photo courtesy Bill Kaufman

Hubley Racer, 1930s, 7-1/2".

Hubley automobiles as shown in an ad from the September 1934 Butler Bros. catalog.

Hubley Railway Express Truck, rubber tires, 5".

	C6	C8	C10
Kiddie Toy Stake Truck, marked "Patrol," c.1937	27	41	55
Kiddie Toy Taxi, No. 5, marked "Taxi"	7	12	25
Kiddie Toy Tow Truck, "No. 2" on roof, No. 452, 1950s, 6-3/8" long	37	56	75
Kiddie Toy Tractor, die-cast, 1960s, 5-1/2" long	12	18	25
Kiddie Toy Tractor, No. 472	42	63	85
Kiddie Toy Wrecker, 8" long	67	105	135
Ladder Truck, 1929, 13" long	500	750	1000
Ladder Truck, 1930s, 10" long	110	165	225
Ladder Truck, 7" long	175	263	350
Ladder Truck, c.1940, 13-1/2"	375	562	750
Ladder Truck, circa late 1930s, 5" long	45	67	90
Ladder Truck, terraplane front, 1930s, 6" long	70	105	140
Ladder Truck, w/eagles, early, 16" long	700	1150	1600

	C6	C8	C10
Ladder Truck, w/three ladders, w/two aces, 7-1/4" long	225	338	450
LaSalle, die-cast, 1940s	90	135	180
Life Saver Truck, hole in rear is large enough to hold pack of Life Savers, 4-1/4" long	700	1150	1600
Life Saver Truck, small hole in rear, can't hold Life Savers	NPF	NPF	NPF
Limousine, six-door, 1920s, 7" long	165	250	330
Lincoln Zephyr, 6" long	120	180	240
Lincoln Zephyr, 7-1/4" long	233	350	465
Lincoln Zephyr, die-cast, 5-1/4" long	25	38	50
Lincoln Zephyr and House Trailer, cast iron, 14" long overall	400	600	800
Log Truck, 13" long	100	150	200
Log Truck, 16" long	70	105	140
Log Truck, No. 469	45	100	200
Log Truck, plastic, No. 356, 12" long	75	112	150
Log Truck, w/five chained logs, black rubber tires, die-cast, approx. 19" long	138	205	275
Low Boy Hauler, w/road grader, 21" long	115	172	230
Low Boy Truck, trailer, tractor	200	300	400

Hubley Road Roller, 4-5/8". Photo courtesy Bertoia Auctions

Hubley Huber Road Roller, 8". Photo courtesy Bertoia Auctions

Hubley "Sport Car" MG, die-cast, 9". Photo courtesy Bob Smith

Hubley Stake Bed Truck, 7". Photo courtesy Mapes Auctioneers and Appraisers

Hubley Stake Truck, white cab, blue bed.

Hubley "10 Ton" Stake Truck, 7". Photo courtesy Bob Smith

Hubley "10 Ton" Stake Truck, 8-1/4". Photo courtesy Bertoia Auctions

Hubley Stake Truck, No. 452, postwar.

Hubley Steam Shovel, "General," 9" long. Photo courtesy Bertoia Auctions

	C6	C8	C10
Mack Dump Truck, 8-1/2" long	600	950	1400
Mack Dump Truck, w/driver, 11-1/2" long	900	1400	2200
Mack Gasoline Truck, 10 3/4" long	800	1350	1800
Mack Gasoline Truck, 8-3/4" long	700	1100	1500
Mack Gasoline Truck, c.1925, 13-1/4" long	550	900	1300
Mack Truck Steam Shovel-Digger, nickel wheels and scoop, c.1920, 7" long	450	675	920
MG, No. 432, issed in sets, red, yellow, or green, produced from 1955-58 and 1962, 1957-58 models have black seats, 5-3/4" long	48	75	115
MG, No. 485, silver chassis, issued in red 1954-56, yellow and green 1957-58, 9" long	60	90	150
Mighty Metal Power Shovel	100	150	200
Milk Truck, cast iron, white rubber tires, "Milk Cream," 1930s, 3-1/2" long	262	393	525
Model T Coupe, 4" long	100	150	200
Monarch Tractor, 5-1/2" long	600	900	1200
Motor Express Tractor and Trailer, black rubber tires, 500 series, approx. 19" long	130	195	260
Motor Express Truck and Trailer, No. 2287, 8" long	175	263	350
Motor Express Truck and Trailer, No. 352, plastic, 12" long	75	112	150
Motor Express Truck and Trailer, plastic, 12" long	70	105	140
Motorized Steam Pumper, 4" long	50	75	100
Mr. Magoo Car, battery-operated, includes cloth roof top, five actions, 1961, 9" long	145	215	290
Nite Coach, metal wheels, went on "Nu-Car" carrier, 1930s, 3-1/2" long	30	45	60

	C6	C8	C10
Nu-Car Transport, five cars, 17" long w/trailer	500	900	1250
Oliver Orchard Tractor, 5-1/2" long	88	132	175
Packard, "Phaeton" Kit, w/box, 1930	25	38	50
Packard, fifteen parts, straight eight, 1929, 11" long	6000	12,000	16,000
Packard Dietrick Convertible Model Kit, w/box	25	38	50
Packard Roadster Kit, w/box	25	38	50
Packard Sedan, 1939-1940s, 5-1/2" long	25	40	75
Panama Digger, 9-1/2" long	800	1200	1650
Panama Digger, hard to find, approx. 3-1/2" long	300	450	600
Panama Digger, Mack, 13" long	1100	1650	2200
Patrol Car, w/driver and policeman, 15-1/2" long	700	1200	1600
Patrol Car, w/driver and three firemen, 8-1/4" long	312	468	625
Pickup, cast iron, 3-1/2" long	22	33	45
Pickup, Dump, die-cast, Ford, No. 470, 1958, 9-1/2" long	20	30	40
Pipe Truck, No. 803, 9-1/2" long	35	52	70
Power Shovel, 14" long	60	90	120
Racer, "1," cast iron, white rubber wheels	150	200	250
Racer, "12," cast iron, white rubber tires, red grille, 5-1/2" long	100	125	150
Racer, "22," aluminum and cast iron, 7-3/8" long	100	150	200
Racer, "5," cast iron, white rubber tires w/wooden hubs, tail fin, marked "1791," 5-1/16" long	200	250	300
Racer, "6," nickel-plated cast iron, white rubber tires w/wooden hubs, one piece driver, exhaust and grille, marked "2137," 4-3/4" long	200	250	300

Hubley Elgin Street Sweeper, cast-iron, 1931, 8". Photo courtesy Chic Gast

Hubley Tanker, plastic, 12-1/2". Photo courtesy Terry Sells

Hubley Woody Station Wagon, takeapart, 5". Photo courtesy Bertoia Auctions

Hubley Wrecker, No. 20, circa 1940, 6". Photo courtesy Mapes Auctioneers and Appraisers

Hubley Yellow Cab, 1920s, 7-3/4". Photo courtesy Sotheby's, New York

Hubley Yellow Cab, spare on rear, shown with an Arcade street sign, 1920s, 7-3/4". Photo courtesy Chic Gast

Hubley Yellow Cab, rear luggage rack folds down, 8". Photo courtesy Chic Gast

Hubley Motorcycle, removable rider, 4-1/4". Photo courtesy Kent M. Comstock

Hubley Motorcycle solo, Cop, rubber or nickel wheels, 4". Photo courtesy Mapes Auctioneers and Appraisers

Hubley Motorcycle w/removable civilian rider, 9". Photo courtesy Kent M. Comstock

Hubley Motorcycle, Harley-Davidson with sidecar, two policemen, rubber or nickel wheels, 5-1/4". Photo courtesy Kent M. Comstock

Hubley Motorcycle, plastic, Kiddie Toy, 5". Photo courtesy Terry Sells

Hubley Motorcycle with civilian driver, rubber or nickel wheels, 6-1/4". Photo courtesy Kent M. Comstock

Hubley Motorcycle Hillclimber, rubber or nickel wheels, 6-1/2". Photo courtesy Kent M. Comstock

Hubley Motorcycle Package Truck, Harley-Davidson Parcel Post, 9-1/2". Photo courtesy Sotheby's New York

Hubley Motorcycle Package Truck, Indian, Air Mail, 9-1/2". Photo courtesy Bertoia Auctions

	C6	C8	C10
Racer, "7," cast iron, marked "1791" on driver, 5-1/4" long	150	200	250
Racer, "7," cast iron, white rubber tires w/wooden hubs, large scalloped tail, one-piece casting, marked "2309," 5-3/4"	150	200	250
Racer, 1930s, tail fin, exhaust stacks, driver, 8-1/2" long	650	1000	1500
Racer, aluminum and cast iron, No. 22, 1940, 7-3/8" long	105	158	210
Racer, aluminum, white rubber tires, tail fin, 3-3/4" long	50	75	100
Racer, animated exhaust stacks, driver, 11" long	1200	2000	3000
Racer, animated exhaust stacks, driver, 8" long	550	875	1250
Racer, cast iron, exhaust stacks, tail fins, white rubber tires w/wooden hubs, driver part of casting, marked "2229" on car, 5-3/8" long	75	100	125
Racer, cast iron, exhaust stacks, white rubber tires, wooden hubs, tail fins, marked "1791" on driver and "2233" on cast iron, 6" long	150	200	250
Racer, cast iron, flat slanted grille, tail fin 4-1/4" long	50	100	150
Racer, cast iron, white rubber tires w/wooden hubs, electric light, marked "2125B on casting" and 1878B18" on driver, 6-1/2" long	350	450	550
Racer, Closed Cabin, 1930s, 8" long	250	375	500
Racer, die-cast, 12" long	65	93	130

	C6	C8	C10
Racer, die-cast, black rubber tires, 4" long	25	38	50
Racer, driver, 1930s, 6-1/2" long	200	300	400
Racer, driver, 1930s, 7" long	215	322	430
Racer, driver, electric headlights, 7" long	NPF	NPF	NPF
Racer, driver, rubber tires, 8" long	125	188	250
Racer, driver, tail fin, 1930s, 6" long	210	325	450
Racer, marked "1790," approx. 5" long	160	240	320
Racer, marked "No. 1," 8" long	250	375	500
Racer, No. 2241, 1930s, 7-1/2" long	45	68	90
Racer, No. 2330, aluminum	500	800	1200
Racer, No. 5, die-cast, large wheels	75	11	2150
Racer, No. 5, early wheels, 9-3/8" long	1100	1800	2600
Racer, No. 5, hood raises to show engine, painted and nickeled iron and aluminum, 9-1/2" long	1300	2000	3000
Racer, No. 629, 1936, 6-3/4" long	300	475	650
Racer, No. 677, 8-1/2" long	700	1200	1600
Racer, No. 7, early 1930s, 5-1/4" long	188	282	375
Racer, No. 8, streamlined, 7-1/4" long	225	338	450
Racer, plastic, 6-1/2" long	44	66	88
Racer, w/two passengers, 1930s, 5-1/2" long	125	188	250
Railway Express Truck, rubber tires, 5" long	200	300	400
Renault Dauphine, plastic	45	68	90
Road Grader, 12" long	70	105	140
Road Grader, 1950s, 15" long	40	60	80
Road Grader, die-cast, 10" long	27	41	55
Road Roller, Hercules, 4-5/8" long	80	120	160
Road Roller, plastic, wood wheels	25	38	50
Road Roller, w/driver, late 1920s, 8" long	300	450	600

Hubley Motorcycle Racer, nickel wheels, 5-3/4". Photo courtesy Kent M. Comstock

Hubley Motorcycle Trike "Crash Car," HM39. Photo courtesy Bertoia Auctions

Hubley Motorcycle Trike, "Flowers," rubber (left) or nickel (right) wheels, blue, 4-1/2". Photo courtesy Kent M. Comstock

Hubley Motorcycle Trike Indian Traffic Car, removable rider, red and blue, 12". Photo courtesy Bertoia Auctions

Hubley Motorcycle Trike Indian Crash Car, 11-1/2". Photo courtesy Bertoia Auctions

Hubley Motorcycle Trike Indian Traffic car, HM16, 9" long. Photo courtesy Sotheby's New York

Hubley Motorcycle Trike, "Say It With Flowers", cast-iron, 10-1/2". Photo courtesy Bertoia Auctions

Hubley Motorcycle Trike Indian Crash Car, removable driver, HM27, 11-1/2" long. Photo courtesy Kent M. Comstock

	C6	C8	C10
Road Scraper, No. 481	37	52	75
Roaster, driver, early 1920s, 7-1/4" long	900	1600	2200
School Bus, die-cast, 1960s, 9" long	35	52	70
Sedan, cast iron, 1920, 7" long	100	150	200
Sedan, cast iron, 1928, 7" long	150	225	300
Sedan, cast iron, four-door, 1930s, 6" long	110	165	220
Sedan, die-cast, 7" long	62	93	125
Sedan, early, 4-1/8" long	67	100	135
Sedan, looks like Ford, rubber wheels, two-door, 3-1/2", c.1938	60	90	120
Sedan, plastic, painted silver trim, rubber wheels/tires, assorted colors, 4" long	10	20	30
Sedan, sidemount tire, 1930s, 5" long	165	198	230
Service Car, 4-1/4" long	60	90	120
Service Car, cast iron, including wheels, 1930s, 5" long	200	300	400
Shovel Truck, c.1938, 8-1/2" long	550	900	1250
Shovel Truck, No. 726, c.1930, 10" long	NPF	NPF	NPF
Speedster, No. 6, early, 7" long	225	350	435
Sport Car, No. 485	70	105	140
Stake Bed Truck, 5" long	95	142	190
Stake Bed Truck, 7" long	225	338	450
Stake Bed Truck, cast iron, 3-1/2" long	50	75	100
Stake Dump, die-cast	30	45	60
Stake Truck, cast iron, marked "10 ton," 7" long	300	425	600
Stake Truck, late 1930s	160	240	325
Stake Truck, marked "10 ton," 8-1/4" long	350	525	700
Stake Truck, No. 460	44	66	88

	C6	C8	C10
Stake Truck, No. 614, 1930s	75	112	150
Stake Truck, w/trailer, No. 927, 21" long, two pieces	40	60	80
Stake truck, white cab w/blue bed, 12" long	NPF	NPF	NPF
Stake Truck, white cab, blue bed	NPF	NPF	NPF
Stake-type Truck, No. 452, black rubber tires, post WWII	40	60	80
Station Wagon, No. 476, 1940s-50s, 8-1/2" long	35	52	70
Steam Roller, 5" long	150	225	300
Steam Shovel, marked "General," 10-1/2" long	440	660	880
Steam Shovel, marked "General," 15" long	450	700	1000
Steam Shovel, marked "General," 6" long	175	263	350
Steam Shovel, marked "General," 7" long	375	562	750
Steam Shovel, marked "General," 8-1/4" long	300	450	600
Steam Shovel, marked "General," 9" long	400	625	850
Steam Shovel, No. 325, 4-1/2" long	115	173	230
Stock Truck, plastic, 12" long	112	168	225
Street Sweeper, cast iron, marked "Elgin, The," 1931, 8" long	3500	5000	7500
Studebaker Car Carrier, 10" long	200	300	400
Studebaker Roadster, frame and body separate	300	450	600
Studebaker Stake Truck	20	30	40
Studebaker Touring Car, cast iron	325	518	650
Studebaker Town Car, cast iron, 5" long	250	375	500
Take-Apart Coupe, 6" long	225	338	450

Hubley Motorcycle policeman, Harley-Davidson, nickel wheels, 5-1/2". Photo courtesy Kent M. Comstock

Hubley Motorcycle policeman, 1950s, die-cast with plastic driver, 8-1/2". Photo courtesy Kent M. Comstock

Hubley Motorcycle policeman, Harley-Davidson, swivel head, rubber or nickel wheels, 7-1/4". Photo courtesy Mapes Auctioneers and Appraisers

Hubley Motorcycle policeman, battery-operated head-light, 6". Photo courtesy Max Heiss

Hubley Motorcycle Trike Indian Crash Car, 9-3/8". Photo courtesy Bertoia Auctions

Hubley Motorcycle Trike Crash Car, 6-1/2". Photo courtesy Bertoia Auctions

Hubley Motorcycle with removable cop; red, green, or yellow; 9-1/4". Photo courtesy Kent M. Comstock

Left to right: Hubley Motorcycle trike Popeye Spinach Cycle, HM37, 5-3/8"; Hubley Popeye Patrol, HM38, 8-3/8". Photo courtesy Bertoia Auctions

Hubley Motorcycle with removable civilian driver, Harley-Davidson, 9". Photo courtesy Kent M. Comstock

Hubley Motorcycle with removable cop, Harley-Davidson, olive green, blue or orange, HM23, 9". Photo courtesy Bertoia Auctions

	C6	C8	C10
Take-Apart Roadster, 1930	120	180	240
Take-Apart Sedan, early 1930s, 6" long	150	230	325
Take-Apart Stake Truck, 4-3/4" long	200	300	400
Take-Apart Station Wagon, 1920s	250	400	550
Take-Apart Two Truck, early	238	355	475
Tank Truck	100	150	200
Tanker, plastic, marked "Hubley Tanker," 12-1/2" long	NPF	NPF	NPF
Taxi, die-cast, black rubber tires	20	30	40
Telephone Truck, plastic	25	38	50
Thunderbird, #486, 1955 Ford Thunderbird, issued in red (common) and yellow (rare) w/black plastic top, 1955-56, 8-7/8" long	120	180	255
Thunderbird, No. 475, 1955 Ford Thunderbird, issued in red or yellow w/out top, 1957, 8-7/8" long	120	180	255

	C6	C8	C10
Touring Auto, 1920s, 7" long	165	248	330
Touring Auto, 1921, 11-1/2" long	NPF	NPF	NPF
Touring Auto, cast iron, chauffeur and rider, 1915, 9-1/2" long	750	1125	1500
Tow Truck, cast iron, 8-3/4" long	140	210	280
Tow Truck, Ford, die-cast, 9" long	62	93	125
Tractor, 1930s, 5" long	250	450	600
Tractor, 960 H	68	102	1035
Tractor, die-cast, w/scoop, 13" long	58	87	115
Tractor, Ford 4000, 10-1/2" long	40	60	80
Tractor, Ford 6000	80	120	160
Tractor, Ford No. 961, w/plow, 15" long	100	150	200
Tractor, No. 472	40	60	80
Tractor, No. 490	50	75	100
Tractor, scale model, 7" long	88	132	175
Tractor, steam boiler in front, early 1920s, 4-3/4" long	125	187	250

	C6	C8	C10
Tractor Loader, No. 501, 1950s, 11" long	78	118	155
Tractor Shovel, driver, 9-1/2" long	750	1300	1750
Tractor Trailer, 1950s	75	112	150
Tractor Trailer and Road Scraper, No. 506, die-cast, 19" long	150	225	300
Trailer Truck, c.1936-38	100	150	200
Transitional Fire Patrol, cast iron, driver, firemen, 1920, 12" long	1000	1500	2000
Truck, w/eight wooden barrels, marked "5 Ton Truck," c.1920, 17" long	750	1200	1700
VW, metal w/sunroof, marked "Beetle Bug," 1969	50	75	100
Water Tower, early, two drivers, 14" long	850	1400	2000
Woody Station Wagon, takeapart, 5" long	NPF	NPF	NPF
Wrecker, 3-1/2" long	42	63	85
Wrecker, 4-3/4" long	75	112	150
Wrecker, Ford, No. 474, 10" long	82	123	165
Wrecker, rubber wheels, 1930, 4-1/2" long	110	165	220
Wrecker, Service Car, chrome wheels	45	68	90
Wrecker, white wheels on large hubs, c.1940, 6" long	100	150	200
Wrecking Truck, cast iron, rubber tires, 1930, 7-1/2" long	150	225	300
Yellow Cab, 1920s, 7-3/4" long	550	850	1200
Yellow Cab, rear luggage racks folds down, 8" long	300	450	600

	C6	C8	C10
Yellow Cab, spare tire, 1920s, 8-1/4" long	600	950	1400

Motorcycles

	C6	C8	C10
Motorcycle, Harley Davidson w/sidecar, two policemen, rubber or nickel wheels, 5-1/4" long (HM35)	250	350	500
Motorcycle, Harley Davidson, sidecar, civilian driver, woman passenger, 9" long (HM33)	800	1400	2200
Motorcycle, Harley-Davidson w/policeman, swivel head, 6-1/2" long, early, "Harley" on both sides (HM32)	600	850	1100
Motorcycle, Popeye Patrol, 8-3/8" long (HM38)	2000	3500	5500
Motorcycle, removable rider, 4-1/4" long (HM34)	50	75	125
Motorcycle, rubber or nickel wheels, marked "Cop," 4" long (HM01)	50	75	100
Motorcycle, tandem, marked "PDH" rubber or nickel wheels, 4-1/8" long (HM04)	100	150	250
Motorcycle, w/cast-in policeman, black rubber tires, 4-1/2" long (HM34A)	50	75	100
Motorcycle Civilian Driver, rubber or nickel wheels, 6-1/4" long (HM13)	250	400	600

Hubley Motorcycle with sidecar, Cop rider and passenger (passenger missing), 4". Photo courtesy Max Heiss

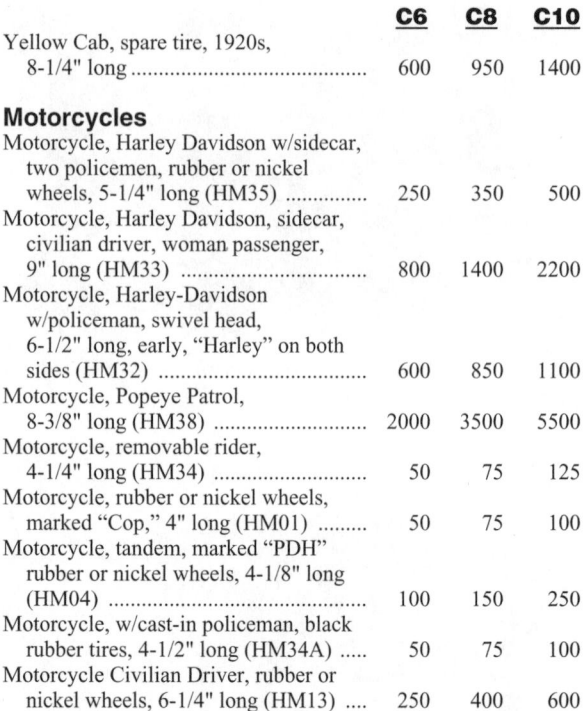

Hubley Motorcycle with sidecar, two removable cops, red, battery-operated headlight, HM19, 8-1/2". Photo courtesy Sotheby's New York

Hubley Motorcycle with sidecar, Indian, two cops, red, 9". Photo courtesy Kent M. Comstock

Hubley Motorcycle with sidecar, Harley-Davidson, two removable cops, olive green, HM20, 9". Photo courtesy Kent M. Comstock

Hubley Motorcycle with sidecar, Indian Armored Car, two removable cops, red, 8-1/2". Photo courtesy Bertoia Auctions

Hubley Motorcycle, Harley Davidson w/Policeman, 6-1/2" long. Photo courtesy Wilkinson Collection, Detroit Antique Museum

	C6	C8	C10
Motorcycle Hillclimber, rubber or nickel wheels, marked "HD-45," 6-1/2" long (HM11)	400	600	800
Motorcycle Package Truck, "Harley Davidson Parcel Post," w/detachable blue rider 9-1/2" long (HM25)	1300	2000	2900
Motorcycle Package Truck, "Indian Air Mail," w/detachable blue rider, 9-1/2" long (HM26)	1100	2000	2700
Motorcycle Policeman, battery-operated headlight, 6" long (HM17)	300	450	600
Motorcycle Policeman, Kiddie Toy, No. 310, plastic, w/removable plastic cop, assorted colors, 1950-1965, 5" long (HM40)	15	30	60
Motorcycle Policeman, marked "Harley Jr.," nickel wheels, 5-1/2" long (HM09A)	150	300	450
Motorcycle Policeman, marked "Harley Jr.," nickel wheels, 5-1/2" long (HM09A)	300	450	600
Motorcycle Policeman, nickel wheels, marked "Harley Davidson," 5-1/2" long (HM09)	275	363	550
Motorcycle Policeman, No. 479, die-cast w/plastic driver, spoked wheels, "PD," 1950-51, 8-1/2" long (HM15)	400	500	750
Motorcycle Policeman, swivel head, rubber or nickel wheels, marked "Harley Davidson," 7-1/4" long (HM10)	500	750	1200
Motorcycle Policeman, w/detachable cop, battery-operated headlight, red, 8-1/2" long (HM18)	600	750	1000
Motorcycle Racer, marked "Speed," 4-1/4" long (HM03)	165	248	330

	C6	C8	C10
Motorcycle Racer, nickel wheels, 5-3/4" long (HM12)	375	550	800
Motorcycle Trike, "Crash Car," 6-1/2" long (HM39)	225	338	450
Motorcycle Trike, cast iron, "Say It with Flowers," 10-1/2" long (HM31)	8000	13,000	18,000
Motorcycle Trike, Indian "Crash Car," 9-3/8" long (HM36)	1400	2200	4500
Motorcycle Trike, Indian "Crash Car," removable rider, axes and hose red 11-1/2" long (HM27)	1500	2000	3000
Motorcycle Trike, Indian "Traffic Car", rubber tires, 9" long (HM16)	700	1000	1600
Motorcycle Trike, Indian "Traffic Car," removable rider, red and blue, 12" long (HM28)	1500	2000	3000
Motorcycle Trike, marked "Flowers," 5-1/4" long (HM08A)	900	1500	3100
Motorcycle Trike, nickel wheels, blue, marked "Flowers," 3-3/8" long (HM07)	500	800	1200
Motorcycle Trike, Popeye Spinach Cycle, separate rider, 5-3/8" long (HM37)	650	1100	1750
Motorcycle Trike, rubber or nickel wheels, blue, marked "Flowers," 4-1/2" long (HM08)	500	800	1200
Motorcycle Trike, rubber or nickel wheels, marked "Crash Car," 4-3/4" long (HM05)	50	75	125
Motorcycle Trike, traffic car nickel wheels, 3-5/8" long (HM06)	75	125	200
Motorcycle w/removable civilian rider, "Harley Davidson," olive green, blue, or orange, 9" long (HM22)	1250	2000	3000

Hubley Motorcycle, Harley-Davidson with Policeman, HM32, 6-1/2". Photo courtesy Wilkinson Collection, Detroit Antique Museum

Hubley Motorcycle, Indian w/removable cop, HM24, 9-1/4". Photo courtesy Kent M. Comstock

	C6	C8	C10
Motorcycle w/removable cop, "Harley Davidson," olive green, blue, or orange, 9" long (HM23)	700	1500	1880
Motorcycle w/removable cop, "Indian," nickel four-cylinder motor, red, green, or yellow, 9-1/4" long (HM24)	800	1300	1800
Motorcycle w/sidecar, "Harley Davidson," two removable cops, olive green, 9" long (HM20)	600	1000	1400
Motorcycle w/sidecar, "Indian Armored Car," two removable cops, red, 8-1/2" long (HM29)	1200	2000	2750

	C6	C8	C10
Motorcycle w/sidecar, "Indian," two removable cops, red, 9" long (HM21)	600	900	1200
Motorcycle w/sidecar, civilian driver and passenger, 6-1/2" long (HM14)	300	500	750
Motorcycle w/sidecar, Cop rider and passenger, 4" long (HM02)	110	165	220
Motorcycle w/sidecar, two removable cops, battery-operated headlight, red, 8-1/2" long (HM19)	800	1900	2650

IDEAL

Rose and Morris Michtom founded the Brooklyn, N.Y. based Ideal Novelty & Toy Co. in 1903. Their early success with the original line of teddy bears led to an expanded line of dolls, stuffed toys, and other playthings. In the postwar era, Ideal changed its name to the Ideal Toy Corp., adopted the new plastics technologies, and released a large variety of vehicle toys in addition to metal toy lines.

	C6	C8	C10
Ambulance, plastic, white w/1 red cross on roof, plastic wheels, 4-1/2" long	10	17	25
Ambulance, plastic, white w/red crosses, rubber tires, No. AM-40 in 1950, No. 3004 1951-53, 6-1/4" long	NPF	NPF	NPF
American LaFrance Aerial Ladder Truck	95	143	190
American LaFrance Fix-It Tow Truck, w/1952 Pontiac car and tools	150	225	300
Army Ambulance, 5" long	20	30	40
Army Jeep, "Mighty Mo," siren, plastic, 1953, 13" long	25	38	50
Army Van, 4" long	20	30	40
Atomic Rocket Launching Truck, 12" long	32	48	65
Auto Laundry	55	83	110
Barracuda Coupe, 1964, plastic, 4" long	15	23	30
Beverage Truck, No. 3025, plastic, 1951-54, 4-1/2" long	NPF	NPF	NPF
Beverage Truck, No. BT-10, plastic, 1947-49, 4-1/8" long	NPF	NPF	NPF
Blazer Fire Chief and Barking Dog, No. 4197, plastic, large driver and dog figures, dog barks as truck is pushed, 1954-55, 6-3/4" long	NPF	NPF	NPF
Bulldozer, plastic	50	75	100

	C6	C8	C10
Bungalow Bar Truck, No. BBT-40 in 1950, No. 3044 in 1951-52; plastic ice cream wagon, white w/red trim, "Ice Cream" on back, opening side doors, 5-3/4" long	NPF	NPF	NPF
Bus, plastic, 6" long, 1950s	25	50	75
Cadillac, four-door, 1948, plastic, 4" long	25	38	50
Car Carrier, No. 3055, plastic, w/three 3" cars, ramp lowers, 1952-55, 9-1/4" long	NPF	NPF	NPF
Car Trailer, plastic, c.1945, 3" long	20	30	40
Carousel Truck, No. MGR-75, plastic, carousel on rear of truck turns as truck moves, 1949-50, 6-1/2" x 3" x 3"	50	75	135
Cattle Truck, 13" long	25	38	50
Cement Mixer, No. CM-50, plastic, drum rotates, lever raises drum, 1947-50, 6-1/4" long	NPF	NPF	NPF
Coal Truck, No. DT-50, plastic, 1947-48, 5-1/2" long	21	31	42
Comic Cop Car, plastic; six 3" cops, 3 sitting, 3 standing in red or blue; black or yellow car w/seats that rock as car is pushed, No. 4193, 1953-54, 6-1/4" long	NPF	NPF	NPF

Left to right: Ideal Army Ambulance, 5"; Van, 6". Photo courtesy Bob and Alice Wagner

Ideal Talking FBI Car, No. 3072, talks. Photo courtesy Tim Oei

Ideal Dump Truck, 5-3/4". Photo courtesy Dave Leopard

Ideal Cattle Truck, 13". Photo courtesy Terry Sells

	C6	C8	C10
Corvette, plastic, assembly of 61 parts with screws, opening trunk and hood, clear plastic con-vertible top, white, plastic tires, No. 3083, 1954-55, 16" long..	75	125	175
Coupe, No. SC-10, 1 side window, 1947-49, 4-3/8" long	NPF	NPF	NPF
Dairy Farm Van, No. MT-40 in 1950, No. 3067 in 1951-52; plastic milk truck, back doors open, side doors slide open, white w/"Ideal Dairy Farm" decals, 4-3/4" long	25	40	75
Danger Patrol Truck, No. 3300, plastic, battery-powered light, tools, green w/tin litho interior, 1950s....................	90	135	180
Delivery Truck, No. TD-40 in 1949-50, No. 3052 in 1951-52; plastic, sliding side doors, opening rear doors, 5" long...	NPF	NPF	NPF
Dick Tracy Copmobile, plastic, siren, microphone, battery-operated, steering, "Dick Tracy" decals, 1968	40	80	125

	C6	C8	C10
Diner, plastic, two 2-7/16" cars, figure, No. 4254, 1951-53, 7" long, 5-1/2" wide	NPF	NPF	NPF
Dragnet Talking Police Car	60	90	120
Dream Racer, plastic, black w/gold paint and chrome, plastic wheels, No. 3043, 1954-55, 13-1/2" long........................	NPF	NPF	NPF
Dump Truck, No. 3075, plastic, lever raises dump bed, assorted colors, 5-3/4" long	NPF	NPF	NPF
Dump Truck, No. DT-50 in 1949, No. 4870 in 1950-51; plastic, dump bed raises, 5-3/4" long	21	32	42
Emergency Truck, No. 3301, plastic, blue, battery-powered light, friction motor, siren, tin litho interior, tools, 1954, 12-3/4" long	NPF	NPF	NPF
Emergency Van, 6" long.........................	10	35	45
Farm Implements, No. STR-60, plastic, seeder 5-1/4" long, mower 5-1/2" long, assorted colors, 1940s........................	NPF	NPF	NPF
FBI Car, No. 3072, talks	NPF	NPF	NPF

Another view of the Ideal Talking FBI Car.

Ideal Fix-It Luxury Coupe on left, plain color version on right; plastic, 1954-58, 9" long. Photo courtesy John McCurdy

Ideal Two-Car Garage, plastic. Photo courtesy Dave Leopard

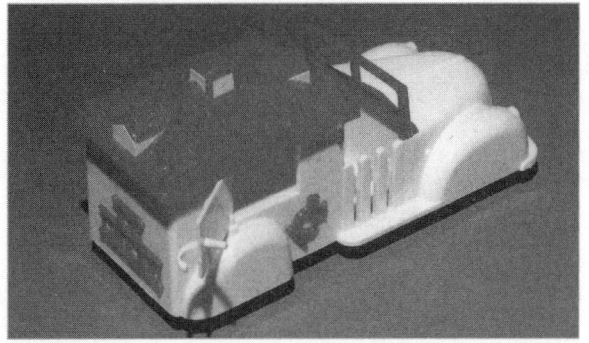

Ideal Ice Cream Truck, 5-1/2", 1948-1954. Photo courtesy Bob and Alice Wagner

Ideal Jeep, with original box, 1940s. Photo courtesy Terry Sells

Left to right: Ideal Pickup Truck, streamlined with canopy and gas tank filler, 4-1/2"; Pickup Truck, streamlined, 4-1/2". Photo courtesy Bob and Alice Wagner

Ideal Rolls-Royce, plastic, 8". Photo courtesy Ron Fink

Ideal Sanitation Truck, plastic, 5-1/2". Photo courtesy Terry Sells

Ideal Robert the Robot Mechanical Bulldozer, battery-operated. Photo courtesy Don Hultzman

Ideal Rocket Cycle, 6-1/2". Photo courtesy Terry Sells

Ideal Scooter, plastic, 4". Photo courtesy Terry Sells

Ideal Sedan, 9-1/4". Photo courtesy Terry Sells

Ideal Shell Truck, 12-1/2". Photo courtesy Terry Sells

	C6	C8	C10
Ferrari, plastic, assembly of 35 parts using screws, opning hood, assorted colors, rubber tires, No. 3084, 1954-55, 7-1/2" long	NPF	NPF	NPF
Fire Engine, No. 3037, plastic, red w/white extension ladder, 1953, 8" long	NPF	NPF	NPF
Fire Pumper	34	51	68
Fix-It Cadillac, 12" long	75	112	150
Fix-It Convertible, No. 3058, w/spare parts, hood and trunk open, rubber tires, plastic wheels, cardboard license plates, 1952-55, 13" long, 1955, 3058 .	65	135	200
Fix-It Fire Chief Fire Truck	72	108	145
Fix-It Luxury Coupe, No. 3061, plastic, opening hood, trunk, and doors; tools; moving windshield wipers, assorted colors, 1953-54, 10" long	NPF	NPF	NPF
Fix-It Pontiac Starfire, plastic, assembly of 130+ parts using screws, body molded in clear plastic, working lights, opening hood and trunk, vinyl tires, 1957, 20" long	NPF	NPF	NPF
Fix-It Tow Truck	90	135	180
Fix-It Tow Truck and Car w/Dented Fender, No. 3001, metal and plastic, replacement parts for salmon sedan, tools, 1955-57, 20-1/2" long	NPF	NPF	NPF
Fix-It Truck, No. FT-100 in 1950, No. 3059 in 1951-54; plastic, w/tools, 8-1/2" long	62	93	145
Ford Truck	40	60	80
Ford Wagon	40	60	80
Gambles Semi Truck, plastic, 12" long	36	54	72
Garage with 2 Cars, 6" plastic garage has opening overhead door, 2 5-1/4" cars and/or trucks of assorted colors, No. GAR-90 in 1950, No. 3030 in 1951	NPF	NPF	NPF

	C6	C8	C10
Gas Station, plastic, station has 2 opening overhead doors, comes with three 2-7/16" cars and one 2-5/16" tow truck. No. GS-100 in 1950, No. 3032 1951-53, station measures 8-1/4" long	NPF	NPF	NPF
Grocer Truck, No. PA-10 in 1950, No. 3065 in 1951-52; plastic, "Grocer" decals, 5" long	NPF	NPF	NPF
Hi-Speed Car Wash, plastic, lever moves cars along belt and water washes the Jeep and Sedan included, No. 3031, 1952-55, 1950s	32	48	65
Ice Cream Truck, 1948-54, 5-1/2" long	30	60	100
Ideal Car Trailer, plastic, four cars, 27" long	40	60	80
Jaguar, plastic, assembly of 35 parts using screws, opening hood, rubber tires on plastic wheels, No. 3082, 1954-55, 8-1/2" long	NPF	NPF	NPF
Jeep, c.1945	20	30	40
Jet Racer	50	75	100
Ladder Truck, No. 3054, plastic w/aluminum ladder, bumper, metal windshield and rack, ladder extends to 44", searchlight, toolbox, 1955-57, 36-1/2" long	50	98	135
MC Sports Car, plastic, opening hood, gearshift works, 3 gears, rubber tires, plastic wheels, assorted colors, No. 4054, 1953-55, 9" long	50	125	200
Mercedes-Benz, plastic, assembly of 35 pieces with screws, opening hood, lift-off roof, assorted colors, rubber tires, No. 3079, 1954-55, 9" long	35	65	110
Milk Delivery Truck, No. MD-10, plastic, white, "Milk Farms" decals, 1951-52, 4-1/2" long	NPF	NPF	NPF

Ideal Steam Shovel, plastic, 7-1/2". Photo courtesy Dave Leopard

Ideal Turbo-Jet Car, No. 4867. Photo courtesy Tim Oei

	C6	C8	C10
Motorcycle w/Sidecar, plastic, removable cop, assorted colors, rubber tires on plastic spoke wheels, No. MC-120, 1950s, 3-3/4" long	NPF	NPF	NPF
Motorific, 1951 GMC Wrecker	20	30	40
Moving Van, No. VA-10 in 1950, No. 3078 in 1951; plastic, 4-3/8" long	NPF	NPF	NPF
Mower and Tractor, No. MTR-100, plastic, sold together, steering wheel turns tractor wheels, blades slice as mower is pulled, 1948-49, 9" long	NPF	NPF	NPF
Nellybelle Jeep	14	21	28
Oil Tanker Truck, No. OT-10, plastic, 1947-49, 4-1/8" long	NPF	NPF	NPF
Old Smokey Comical Fire Engine, No. 4198, plastic, driver, funny motion as truck is pulled, 1954-55, 12" long	NPF	NPF	NPF
Oldsmobile, 1954, 19" long	150	225	300
Painter's Truck, No. 3073, plastic, opening cab doors, extension ladder, step ladder, 2 paint brushes, 5 water color containers, 1952-54, 11-1/2" long	NPF	NPF	NPF
Panel Truck, No. 1-1729	20	30	40
Panel Truck, No. PT-40 in 1949-50; No. 3085 in 1951-52; plastic, rear doors open, assorted color combinations, rubber tires, 6-1/4" long	27	40	75
Patton Tank, 6" long	12	18	25
Pegaso, plastic, assembly of 35 parts using screws, opening hood, assorted colors, rubber tires, No. 3064, 1954-55, 8"	NPF	NPF	NPF
Pickup Truck, American, 1948, 4" plastic	20	30	40
Pickup Truck, Ford, 1940, 4" plastic	14	21	27
Pickup Truck, No. TR-2, plastic, 1945-47, 4-1/2" long	NPF	NPF	NPF
Pickup Truck, streamlined, 1950s, No. 1-788, 4-1/2" long	7	11	14
Pickup Truck, streamlined, w/canopy and gas tank filler, 1950s, 4-1/2" long	4	10	20
Police Car, plastic, rubber tires, metal wheels, friction motor, siren, assorted colors, No. MPC-60F in 1950, No. 3332 1951-53, 6-1/4"	15	25	40
Porsche, plastic, assembly of 35 parts using screws, opening hood, rubber			

	C6	C8	C10
tires, assorted colors, No. 3707, 1955, 8-1/4" long	NPF	NPF	NPF
Race Car, 10" wind-up	50	75	100
Race Car, plastic, "4" cast into hood, assorted colors, rubber wheels, 1949, 6-1/4" long	NPF	NPF	NPF
Race Car, plastic, assorted colors, No. RC-10, 1948-49, 4-1/2" long	NPF	NPF	NPF
Race Car, plastic, wind-up motor, white rubber tires, assorted 2-tone colors, white plastic driver, No. RCM-120, 1948-50, 8-1/4"	50	90	135
Road Building Set, No. RB-200 in 1950, No. 4870 in 1951; plastic, 8 vehicles, square cab cement mixer & square cab steam shovel only available in this set, box measures 15" long	NPF	NPF	NPF
Road Roller, No. RR-25 in 1949-50, No. 4870 in 1951; plastic, driver, 4-1/2" long	NPF	NPF	NPF
Robert the Robot, battery-operated	150	225	300
Rocket Car, w/wind-up launcher, 11" long	NPF	NPF	NPF
Rocket Cycle, 6-1/2" long	100	150	200
Rocket Launcher Truck, 12" long	55	83	110
Rolls Royce, 12" long	11	16	22
Rolls Royce, plastic, assembly of 35 parts with screws, opening hood, assorted colors, rubber tires, N. 3068, 1954-55, 8-1/2" long	30	55	85
Sanitation Truck, No. STR-100, plastic, opening rear door, sliding doors on sides, 1948, 6" long	20	35	50
Scooter, plastic, 4" long	NPF	NPF	NPF
Sedan, plastic, 1950-51, 9-1/4" long	20	35	50
Sedan, plastic, 5" long	14	21	28
Sedan and House Trailer, sold as set, No. AHT-70. Same as AUMT-120, but sedan has no wind up motor, 1948-50	NPF	NPF	NPF
Sedan and House Trailer, sold as set, No. AUMT-120. Sedan has wind-up motor w/attached key, rubber tires, 5-1/4" long. Trailer has sliding side door, plastic wheels, 7" long. Set produced 1948-49	NPF	NPF	NPF
Sedan w/Teardrop Trailer, No. AT-1, plastic, 1947, 8-3/8" long. Trailer			

Back row, left to right: Ideal Van, sliding front door, 4-1/2"; Dairy Farm Van. Front row: Van, 6". Photo courtesy Bob and Alice Wagner

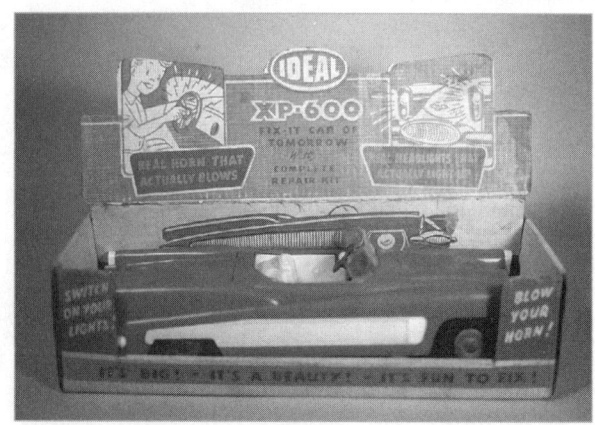

Ideal XP-600 Fix-It Car of Tomorrow, 16". Photo courtesy Terry Sells

	C6	C8	C10		C6	C8	C10
(No. TR-1) was available separately from 1946-49.	26	39	52	Tow Truck, plastic and metal, 17" long	100	150	200
Seeder and Tractor, plastic, sold together, steering wheel turns, hopper doors open as seeder is pulled, 9" long	NPF	NPF	NPF	Tractor, 1948, plastic, 4" long	20	30	40
Semi Truck, 12" long	26	39	52	Tractor and Hay Rake, No. HTR-100, plastic, sold together, steering wheel turns, rake moves as it is pulled, 1947-49, 9" long	NPF	NPF	NPF
Service Truck, 8" long	22	33	45				
Service Van, 5" long	20	30	40				
Shell Truck, 12-1/2" long	25	38	50	Tractor and Plough Wagon, No. PWT-80 in 1950, No. 4790 in 1951-52; plastic, tractor plough moves up and down, wagon dumps, 12-1/2" long	NPF	NPF	NPF
Signal Corps Truck, 5" long	20	30	40				
Speed King Dream Racer, plastic, 13" long	50	75	100				
Speedy Pete Pull Toy Racer, plastic w/paper litho on cardboard cylinder; plastic driver, end pieces, wheels; No. 4501; 1955, 16" long	45	90	125	Trailer, No. 1-409	7	11	15
				Trailer, No. TR-1, teardrop, plastic, 1946-49, 3-1/8" long	NPF	NPF	NPF
Steam Shovel, 7-1/2" long	22	33	45	Trailer, Square, No. TR-5, open box trailer, plastic, 1947-49, 3-1/4" long	NPF	NPF	NPF
Steam Shovel, No. SS-75, plastic, scoop works, cab rotates on flatbed truck, 1948-51, 9" long	NPF	NPF	NPF	Trailways Bus, No. 3093, plastic, 2-tone colors, opening door, sign w/city names moves, 1952-53, 10" long	NPF	NPF	NPF
Steering Farm Tractor	7	11	15				
Steve Canyon Glider Bomb Truck, 17" long	60	90	120	Turbo-Jet Car, No. 4867, w/10" tin-litho Automatic Launching Platform, car is 12" long	60	95	155
Talbot, plastic, assembly of 35 parts using screws, opening hood, ruber tires, assorted colors, No. 3703, 1955, 8" long	NPF	NPF	NPF	U.S. Army Military Police Car, olive drab plastic, "Military Police" on doors, friction motor, 6" long	30	65	95
				Van, 6" long	10	35	45
Taxi, yellow plastic w/red paint, No. TA-10 in 1950, No. 3024 in 1951, 4-3/4" long	10	20	30	Van, sliding front door, 4-1/2" long	10	25	60
				Work Truck	35	52	70
Television Repair Truck, No. 3019, light blue plastic w/clear topper, yellow accessories, 1954	55	110	175	XP-600 Fix-It Car of Tomorrow, No. 3062, four removable tires, opening hood and trunk, 1953-55, 16" long, 1955, 3062	75	150	250
Thunderbird, plastic, assembly of 35 parts using screws, opening hood, ruber tires, assorted colors, No. 3702, 1955, 8-1/2" long	NPF	NPF	NPF	XP-600 Fix-It Car of Tomorrow, plastic, convertible, less detailed version of No. 3062, opening hood and trunk, tools, No. 3009, 1956-57, 16" long	NPF	NPF	NPF

INGAP

Located in Padova, Padua, Italy, INGAP is an anachronym for Industria Nazionale Giocattoli Automatica. The Italian toymaker is known for its pre-WWII tin litho toys, and plastic 1:87-scale cars during the postwar period.

	C6	C8	C10
Mouse Car, wind-up, Italian, 6" long	1650	2475	3300

Ingap Mouse Car. Photo courtesy Christie's East

IRWIN TOY CORPORATION

Irwin was founded in 1922 by Irwin Cohn. Located at first in New York City, it began as a maker of celluloid baby rattles and pinwheels, soon becoming the largest manufacturer of pinwheels in the United States. In the late 1940s, it produced the first polyethylene toy—a seven-inch car. Irwin, which eventually moved to Leominster and Fitchburg in Massachusetts (with an additional plant in Nashua, New Hampshire), sold out to Miner Industries in 1973.

Irwin State Police Car, 6-1/2", plastic friction. Photo courtesy Ron Fink

Irwin Sedan Delivery, Pickup Truck in red, and Pickup Truck in black. Each is based off of the 1952 Chevrolet line and each is 6" long. Photo courtesy John McCurdy

	C6	C8	C10
Army Bus	27	41	55
Army Cadillac Staff Car, plastic windshield..	15	22	30
Army Dump Truck, plastic	12	18	25
Barney Rubble Car.................................	12	18	25
Big Mike Tow Truck, battery-operated ...	55	82	110
Buick Convertible, plastic wheels, assorted colors, 1948, 5" long.............	10	20	30
Bus, plastic, clear plastic top shows interior, 1940s, 5-1/2" long	NPF	NPF	NPF
Chevrolet Panel Delivery, 6" long	10	15	20
Chevrolet Pickup Truck, 1952, 5-1/3" long	10	15	20
Dream Car Convertible, metal, 16" long..	200	300	400
Dump Truck, 1950s, 8-1/2" long	15	22	30
Ford Sunliner, plastic friction, 9" long.....	50	15	100
GI Joe Motorcycle and Sidecar	100	150	200
Horse Van, 16" long...............................	25	38	50
Human Cannonball Truck, w/net and two figures, 1960s, 19" long	41	62	83
Ice Cream Truck, plastic	55	82	110
Jaguar Roadster, 6" long	35	52	70
Log Truck...	20	30	40

	C6	C8	C10
Packard Sedan, friction, 1952, 9" long	25	30	35
Panel Truck, plastic, assorted colors including blue and black, 1950s, 6" long...	20	35	50
Pickup Truck, metal, 6" long	24	36	48
Pickup Truck, plastic, assorted colors including blue and black, 1950s, 5-1/2" long	20	35	50
Plumbing and Heating Truck, w/tools, etc., 1960s	62	93	125
Police Car, plastic, 12" long....................	25	38	50
Pontiac Hardtop Coupe, friction, 1952, 6" long	15	20	25
Racer	17	26	35
Sedan, plastic, painted details, 1945 to late 1940s, 5-3/8" long.........................	NPF	NPF	NPF
Sedan Delivery, Chevrolet, c.1952, 6" long...	10	20	30
Skipper convertible, 1962	150	225	300
State Police Car, plastic friction, 6-1/2" long	15	22	30
Station Wagon, plastic, box reads "Mechanical Station Wagon Spring Wound," wind-up motor w/attached key, blue w/woodie details painted on, roof rack has 2 suitcases, rubber wheels, No. 104, 1940s, 12" long	NPF	NPF	NPF

Irwin Chevrolet Pickup Truck, 1952. Photo courtesy Dave Leopard

Irwin Pickup Truck, 6", metal. Photo courtesy Ron Fink

Irwin Pontiac Hardtop Coupe, 6", friction. Photo courtesy Dave Leopard

Irwin Police Car, 12", plastic friction. Photo courtesy Ron Fink

	C6	C8	C10
Steeraway Wonder Car, battery operated, driver, 1955 to late 1950s, 16" long.....	85	150	225
Taxi Cab, trunk opens, 12" long	125	188	250
Telephone Repair Truck...........................	100	150	200

	C6	C8	C10
Tow Truck, 8"	27	41	55
Wonder Car, No. 1431, battery-operated; red, white, blue w/chrome accents; magic wand steering, 1952	45	75	100

IVES

Bridgeport, Conn. was the home of the Ives Corp. Originally founded in 1868 by Edward R. Ives as the E.R. Ives Co., the company made baskets from its Plymouth, Conn. factory. Ives moved the company to Bridgeport in 1870. He joined with his brother-in-law, Cornelius Blakeslee in 1872 and changed the name to Ives and Blakeslee & Co.

Collectors simply know it as "Ives" and the name is synonymous with high-quality cast-iron toys. Many of its cast-iron offerings are animal-drawn units. Its popular trains sustained company growth through the 1920s, but the company fell victim to the Great Depression and filed for bankruptcy in 1929. The Lionel Co. bought the company and produced "Lionel-Ives" trains through 1931.

	C6	C8	C10
Fire Patrol, cast-iron, 20-1/2" long...........	500	700	900
Hook and Ladder Wagon, cast-iron, 26-1/2" long	600	800	1200
Horse Drawn Ladder Truck, cast-iron, 21" long...............................	900	1200	1500
Horseless Carriage Runabout, 6-1/2" long, 6" high to the top of jockey cap on driver.............................	2500	3750	5000
Steamer, cast iron, two drivers, 19-1/2" long	500	750	1000

Ives Fire Patrol, cast-iron, 10-1/2".

Ives Hook & Ladder Wagon, cast-iron, 26-1/2".

Ives Horse Drawn Ladder Truck, cast-iron, 21".

J & S PRODUCTS

Based in Los Angeles, Calif., J&S is noted only for the 1950s production of its Hudson. The 9" die-cast toy featured a solid body (including the windows) and black rubber tires.

	C6	C8	C10
Hudson, die-cast, w/suspension	68	102	135

JANE FRANCIS TOYS

Jane Francis Toys operated in Wilkinsburg, Pennsylvania, from 1942-1946 and in Somerset, Pennsylvania, from 1947-1949. Starting as a stuffed-toy maker, the company introduced a line of die-cast cars in 1945. The last Jane Francis toys were manufactured in 1949.

	C6	C8	C10
Gulf Service Station, complete	235	475	950
Gulf Service Station, No. 749, cardboard station, 2 trucks, rubber tires in rack, hoist, gas pumps, 1946........................	300	525	750
Gulf Truck, tin cover, No. 447, 5" long (JF05)	30	45	75

Jane Francis Gulf Service Station, 1940s. Photo courtesy Barbara Francis Vanyo

Jane Francis Gulf Truck, tin cover, 5". Photo courtesy Dave Leopard

Jane Francis Pickup Truck, 5". Photo courtesy Dave Leopard

	C6	C8	C10
Pickup Truck, 5" long, No. 447 (JF03) ...	20	25	30
Pickup Truck, 6-1/2" long (JF01)	30	40	50
Pickup Truck, No. 347, 5" long (JF02) ...	20	25	30
Sedan, fastback, futuristic, 6-1/2" long (JF06)	25	30	40
Sedan, fastback, futuristic, w/wind-up motor, 6-1/2" long (JF07)	30	40	50
Tow Truck, No. 447, 5" long (JF04)	30	40	65

Jane Francis Tow Truck, 5". Photo courtesy Dave Leopard

JAPANESE BATTERY-OPERATED VEHICLES

"Made in Japan" are the words toy collectors look for in their pursuit of high-quality mechanical tin toys. Before World War II, these words were synonymous with cheap, poor-quality, drab-looking toys made from recycled materials and ideas. Most of the toys were people-animal oriented, with less emphasis on vehicle, nautical, or aircraft-type toys. They were powered wither by a spring or a flywheel and didn't last too long or do too much, as far as play-value goes. These cheap toys kept Japan a third-rate toy-manufacturing nation until after World War II, when Japan's surrender resulted in economic chaos for this industrial nation.

In its quest for economic recovery and to compete in a toy market already dominated by Germany and America, the Japanese knew they had to come up with a new, different, and exciting type of toy that would make them more desirable than their competitors. The Japanese toy designers concentrated their technology on a different type of toy operation. Not satisfied with the limited edition and short duration of spring-driven or flywheel-propelled toys, the toy engineers developed a small electric motor, powered by flashlight batteries. This mini-motor took up less room than other mechanisms, had a longer-running duration, and enabled the toy to perform more functions. This development opened up an entirely new dimension in toy design and introduced the concept of the battery-operated toy.

The toy designers integrated this new concept into hundreds of automation-like toys, capable of as many as eight different types of actions, all in one cycle. These unique toys were an instant hit with the foreign market, especially in the United States. These clever, unusual, and high-quality toys made Japan the dominant toy producer and exporter for the next twenty-thirty years.

Again, Japan flooded the market with these ingenious, well-made toys while quality control remained a high priority. These merits were not only apparent in their figural toys, but also in their vehicle line. Here, the Japanese toy makers concentrated on very fine detail and quality, especially in their scale-model passenger cars, with the ultimate goal of making them look like the real thing. They succeeded. Their workmanship carried over into their other vehicle lines, such as motorcycles, emergency and construction vehicles, as well as their novelty (silly) and comic character cars, trucks, and space toys.

No other nation was able to equal or surpass the impetus and determination of the Japanese toy makers, until Japan relinquished its domination by realigning its economy in the electronic-automotive field.

Now that they are approaching middle age, it is no wonder that these fine toys remain in great demand today and are often very pricey!

	C6	C8	C10
007 Aston Martin, 1966, Gilbert Co., 11-1/2" long, eight actions (includes ejectable passenger)	250	375	500
007 Secret Agent's Car (Impala), 1960s, Spesco Co., (Joy Toy), 15" long, five actions	200	300	400
American Circus Television Truck, 1950s, Exelo Co., 9-1/4" long, six actions, RAE (includes detachable metal antenna)	600	900	1200
Anti-Aircraft Jeep, 1950s, "K" Co., 9-1/2" long, five actions	100	150	200
Anti-Aircraft Jeep, 1950s, T-N Co. 11" long, six actions (includes detachable tin radar antenna)	150	225	300
Antique Gooney Car, 1960s, Alps Co., 9" long, four actions	70	105	140
Armored Attack Set, 1960s, Marx Co., jeep 6-1/4" long and tank 5-1/4" long, plus fifteen 2" plastic figures	200	300	400
Army Radio Jeep—J1490, 1950s Linemar Co., 7-1/4" long, four actions	90	135	180
Automatic Toll Gate, 1955, Sears, 16"x17" base, six actions (includes 8" tin Valiant)	150	225	300
Auto-top Ferrari Convertible, 1960s, Bandai Co., three actions, 11" long	450	675	900
Batmobile, 1972 National Periodical Publications, ASC Co., 12" long, three actions	200	300	400
Big Ring Circus Truck, 1950s, M-T Co., 13" long, three actions	150	225	300
Big Shot Cadillac, 1950s, T-N Co., 10" long, four actions, rare	200	300	400
Big Wheel Coca Cola Truck, 1970s, Taiyo Co., three actions	80	120	160
Big Wheel Family Camper, 1970s, 10" long, three actions	80	120	160
Big Wheel Ice Cream Truck, 1970s 10" long, three actions	70	105	140
Bulldozer, 1950s, M-T Co., 11" long, six actions	90	135	180
Bulldozer, 1950s, T-N Co., 7-1/2" long, five actions	80	120	160
B-Z Porter Baggage Truck, 1950s, M-T Co., 7-1/2" long, 6-1/2" high, minor toy, includes three pcs. of luggage (tin)	150	205	300
Cadillac Car, 1949, Ashai Toy Co., 10" long, three actions	150	225	300
Caterpillar Tank M-1, 1950s, M-T Co., five actions, 8-1/2" long, 11" long w/barrel extended	150	220	300
Chaparral 2F Car, 1960s, Alps Co., 11" long, five actions	90	135	180
Chemical Fire Engine, 1950s, HTC Co., 10" long, four actions	110	165	220
Circus Fire Engine, 1960s, M-T Co., 11" long, four actions	140	210	280
Climbing Donald Duck On His Friction Fire Engine, 1950s Linemar Co., four actions, 12" long	400	600	800
Clown Circus Car, 1960s, M-T Co., 8-1/2" long, 9" high, five actions	130	195	260
Coin Taxi, 1960s, Daiya Co., 6-1/2" long, minor toy	50	75	100
Comic Hungry Bug, VW auto, 1970s, Tora (S-T) Co., 7-3/4" long, five actions	40	60	80

Condition of a Toy and its Relation To Price

The value of a battery-operated toy depends not only on its desirability, rarity, and complexity, but very much on its condition. A toy in Mint condition is generally worth twice as much as a toy in Good condition. A toy in Very Good condition will be equally priced between Good and Mint.

C10, Mint: It means just that—the condition in which the toy was originally issued regardless of age. It will also be in perfect mechanical condition, complete with all accessory parts, when applicable, and will look brand new. The cloth or fur (plush) covering on some battery toys may reveal some discoloration or yellowing due to age, but this should not affect its value as a Mint toy, as long as it is clean. All toys in this category must be in perfect working condition. The original box in Mint condition will significantly enhance the value of any Mint toy.

C8, Excellent: Indicates the condition of a battery toy that has seen some use and is starting to show its age. It will still be in perfect working order and have all its accessory parts, where applicable. It will have some age-soiling, but will have no rust or corrosion. Overall, it will have an appearance of freshness and still be highly desirable to the fussy collector.

C6, Good: Applies to a battery toy that has seen considerable use, wear and tear, some age soiling, but still in perfect working condition with no missing parts or accessories. The "wet" toys may show some slight surface rust that can be easily removed. A toy in Good condition is still a welcome addition to any toy collection, but will be targeted for upgrading by a piece in better condition.

Any battery toy below the condition of Good will reflect a drastic reduction value. Toys in good shape, but missing accessory parts, will not lose as much value as those that are severely rusted, corroded, painted over, have parts broken off, and are totally inoperable. These toys in Poor condition are usually collected for their scrap value by the toy repairer, and seldom are they worth more than $10.

The key to grading is to use common sense and avoid wishful thinking. Since grading the condition of a toy may be difficult at times, consulting with an expert in the field, if possible, could clear up any lingering doubts.

Source: *Collecting Battery Toys 2nd Edition* by Don Hultzman.

Guidelines for the Care and Repair of your Battery-Operated Toy

Your prized battery toy needs special care. When it stops working, you now have a frustrating disaster on your hands. To avoid this, the following suggestions should be of some help.

Bettery toys, like other mechanical toys, should be operated periodically to keep them loosened up. Using a lightweight spray lubrication now and then will help considerably, if the mechanism is accessible. Do not over-lubricate, as the excess may stain any cloth or fur covering on some battery toys.

A good quality car wax or polish will keep the lithographed and bare metal parts looking like new—especially on the "wet" toys. Always test an obscure lithographed area to make sure the polish doesn't soften or dissolve the paint. Care should be exercised when polishing metal parts adjoining any cloth or plush covering, as the substance may stain the coverings. Light surface rust usually disappears with a careful polishing. Nothing can be done for deep rust or corrosion without ruining the value of the toy. Repainting will only further reduce the value and is not recommended.

Should your battery toy fail to operate, the following steps might be helpful.
1. Make sure it is not gunked-up, and that no moving parts are binding.
2. Make sure the battery contacts are not dirty or corroded—if so, clean them with crocus cloth. Always use fresh batteries.
3. Lighly tap the toy with your finger or lightly nudge one of the moving parts while the switch is on.

If none of these steps work, your toy needs major surgery. This means the toy must be completely torn down, repaired, and reassembled. Most battery toys are repairable as long as they have not been destructively tampered with and no parts are missing or corroded beyond repair. This job is best left to an expert in toy repair and should never be attempted by one who doesn't know what he is doing. Expert repairs will not affect the value of a battery toy, so long as the repair is undetectable and the toys look and function exactly as it did before the repair. Such repairs are acceptable in toy collecting circles. Expert repairs are also expensive but well worth the investment, if it means the difference between a Mint and Good toy, since an inoperable toy is practically worthless, regardless of condition.

	C6	C8	C10
Comic Musical Car, 1960s, T-N Co., four actions, 6" long, 8-1/2" tall	70	105	140
Comic Road Roller, 1960s, Bandai Co., four actions, 9" long	70	105	140
Corvair Bertone, 1970s, Bandai Co., four actions, 12" long	50	75	100
Corvette Sting Ray Sport Coupe, 1968, Eldon Co., 13-1/2" long, minor toy	100	150	200
Cragstan Beep Beep Greyhound Bus, 1950s, Cragston Co., 20" long, three actions	120	330	240
Cragstan Firebird III, 1956, Alps Co., 11-3/4" long, three actions	300	450	600
Crane Tractor, 1950s, SKK Co., 7-1/2" long, 11-1/2" high extended	70	105	140
Crazy Car, 1950s, Marusan Co., five actions, 9" long	70	105	140
Desert Patrol Jeep, 1960s, M-T Co., 11" long, four actions, includes turret gunner	100	150	200
Dick Tracy Police Car, 1949, TN Co., 9" long, four actions	100	150	200
Disney Fire Engine, 1950s, Linemar Co., 11" long, four actions	440	660	880
Disneyland Fire Engine, 1950s, Linemar Co., 18" long, five actions	300	450	600
Dreamboat Hot-Rod-See Hot Rod, "Dump Truck No. 7343," 1960s, T-N Co., 10-1/4" long, seven actions	150	225	300
Electric School Bus, 1950s, M-T Co., 9-1/2" long, minor toy	80	120	160
Electro Special Racer, 1950s, Yonezawa Co., 10" long, three actions	100	150	200
Electro Toy Racer, 1950s, Yonezawa Co., three actions, 10" long	1000	1500	2000
Electronic Fire House, 1940s, Banner Co., 7" square, minor toy (includes plastic fire engine)	80	120	160
Expert Motor Cyclist, 1950s, MT Co., 12" long, five actions	450	675	900
F.D. Fire Engine, 1960s, Y-M Co., 10" long, 12" high when ladder is extended, four actions	100	150	200
Farm Truck, 1950s, T-N Co., five actions, 9" long	100	150	200
Farm Truck, 1960s, Alps Co., 11" long, three actions	120	180	240
Ferris Wheel Truck, 1950s, T-N Co., 11" long, four actions	400	600	900
Fire Chief Mystery Action Car, 1960s, T-N Co., 9-3/4" long, four actions	120	180	240
Fire Chief No. 8 Car, 1960s, Y Co., 11-1/4" long, three actions	90	135	180
Fire Command Car, 1950s, T-N Co., five actions	170	255	340
Fire Engine, 1950s, Marusan Co., four actions, 9" long	150	225	300
Fire Engine, 1950s, S-H Co., three actions, 8" long	100	150	200
Fire Engine, 1950s, T-N Co. (Electro Toy), three actions, 9" long-ladder extends 13"	150	225	300
Fire Engine, 1950s, Y Co., 12" long, ladder extends 16", six actions	100	150	200
Firebird Racer, 1950s, Tomiyama Co., four actions, 14-1/4" long	300	450	600
Ford Model T, 1950s, Nihonkogei Co., 10-1/4" long, four actions (includes detachable tin roof)	60	90	120

Japanese battery-operated Anti-Zircraft Jeep, T-N, 1950s, 11". Photo courtesy Don Hultzman

Japanese battery-operated Antique Gooney Car, Alps, 1960s, 9". Photo courtesy Don Hultzman

Japanese battery-operated Batmobile, ASC, 1972, 12". Photo courtesy Don Hultzman

Japanese battery-operated Big Wheel Coca-Cola Truck, Taiyo, 1970s. Photo courtesy Don Hultzman

Japanese battery-operated Bulldozer, Shaking Old-Timer Car, Tractor. Photo courtesy Don Hultzman

	C6	C8	C10
Ford Mustang 2x2, 1960s, Wenmac-AMF Co., four actions, 16" long	70	105	140
Fork Lift Truck, 1960s, M-T Co., 10-1/4" high, minor toy	100	150	200
Go Kart, 1950s, Rosko Co., 10" long, three actions, includes detachable head	100	150	200
Go Kart, 1960s, M-T Co., 6-1/2" long, minor toy (includes control wire w/steering key)	100	150	200
Go-Stop Benz Racer, 1950s, Marusan Co., three actions, 11" long	150	220	300
Grand-Pa Car, 1950s, Y Co., 9" long, four actions	60	90	120
Greyhound Bus, 1950s, KKK. Co., minor toy, 7-1/4" long	100	150	200
Greyhound bus with Headlights, 1950s, Linemar Co., 10-1/4" long, three actions	120	180	240
Greyhound Bus-Scenicruiser, 1950s, I.Y. Metal Toy Co., 16" long, three actions	100	150	200
Handy-Hank Mystery Tractor, 1950s, T-N Co., 9" long, four actions	90	135	180
Happy Clown Car, 1960s, Y Co., 6-1/2" long, three actions	80	120	160
Happy Tractor, 1960s, Daiya Co., 8" long, four actions	40	60	80
Highway Drive, 1950s, T-N Co., 15-1/2" long, three actions (includes tin magnetic car)	60	90	120
Highway Patrol Jeep, 1950s, Daiya Co., 10" long, four actions	70	105	140

	C6	C8	C10
Highway Patrol Police Special, 1960s, Y Co., five actions, 11-1/2" long	100	150	200
Highway Skill Driving, 1960s, K Co., 13" long, three actions	70	105	140
Hot Rod Car, 1950s, T-N Co., 10" long, minor toy	200	300	400
Hot Rod Custom 'T' Ford, 1960s, Alps Co., four actions, 10-1/2" long	100	150	200
Hot Rod Limousine, 1960s, Alps Co., four actions, 10-1/2" long	200	300	400
Ice Cream Truck, 1960s, Bandai Co., 10-1/2" long, five actions	150	225	300
James Bond-007 Car-M101, 1960s, Daiya Co., 11' long, seven actions, includes ejectable driver, See M101 Aston Martin	NPF	NPF	NPF
James Bond's Aston-Martin, See 007 Aston Martin	NPF	NPF	NPF
Jeep No. 10560, 1950s, Cragstan, 5-1/2" long, a minor action toy	70	105	140
Jeep-USA, 1950s, TKK Co., 12-1/2" long, a minor toy	60	90	120
John's Farm Truck, 1950s, T-N Co., 9" long, seven actions	140	210	280
K-55 Electric Tractor, M-T Co., three actions, 7" long	70	105	140
King Size Fire Engine, 1960s, Bandai Co., three actions, 12-1/2" long	150	225	300
Kissing Couple, 1950s, Ichida Co., 10-3/4" long, five actions	150	225	300
Ladder Fire Engine, 1950s, Linemar Co., five actions, 13" long	170	255	340

Japanese battery-operated Caterpillar Tank M-1, 1950s, M-T, 11". Photo courtesy Don Hultzman

Japanese battery-operated Crazy Car, Marusan, 1950s, 9". Photo courtesy Don Hultzman

Japanese battery-operated Farm Truck, Alps Co., 1960s, 11". Photo courtesy Don Hultzman

Japanese battery-operated Fire Chief Mystery Action Car, T-N, 1960s, 9-3/4". Photo courtesy Don Hultzman

Japanese battery-operated Farm Truck, T-N, 1950s, 9". Photo courtesy Don Hultzman

Japanese battery-operated Fire Command Car, T-N, 1950s. Photo courtesy Don Hultzman

Japanese battery-operated Go-Kart, M-T Co., 1960s, 6-1/2". Photo courtesy Don Hultzman

Japanese battery-operated Fork Lift Truck, 1960s, M-T Co., 10-1/4". Photo courtesy Don Hultzman

	C6	C8	C10
Love-Beetle-Volks, 1960s, K.O. Co., 10" long, three actions	60	90	120
M-101 Aston Martin Secret Ejector Car, 1960s, Daiya Co., 11" long, six actions (includes ejectable passenger)	200	300	400
Magic Action Bulldozer, 1950s, T-N Co., 9-1/2" long, three actions	100	150	200
Marvelous Car, T-Bird, 1956, T-N Co., three actions, 11" long	250	375	500
Marvelous Fire Engine, 1960s, "Y" Co., 11" long, four actions	100	150	200
Melody Camping Car, 1970s, "Y" Co., 10" long, three actions	100	150	200
Merry-Go-Round Truck, 1950s, M.T. Co., 11" long, four actions	400	600	800
Mickey Mouse and Donald Duck Fire Engine, 1960s, M-T Co., 16" long, three actions	200	300	400
Mickey Mouse Sand Buggy, 1960s M-T Co., 11" long, four actions	150	225	300
Military Air Defense Truck, 1950s, Linemar Co., four actions, 15-1/4" long	100	150	200
Military Command Car, 1950s T-N Co., five actions, 11" long	150	225	300

	C6	C8	C10
Million Bus, 1950s, KKK Co., three actions, 12" long, rare	1250	1875	2500
Mobile Satellite Tracking Station, 1960s, Y Co., six actions, 9" long, (includes detachable antenna) rare	400	600	800
Monkee-Mobile, 1967, ASC Co., (Aoshin Co.) Minor Toy, 12" long	250	375	500
Motorcycle Cop, 1950s, Daiya Co., 10-1/2" long, 8-1/4" high, five actions	200	300	400
Musical Cadillac Car, 1950s, Irco Co., 9" long, minor toy	300	450	600
Musical Comic Jumping Jeep, 1970s, M-T Co., 12" long, six actions	90	135	180
Musical Ice Cream Truck, 1960s, Bandai Co., 10-1/2" long, five actions	100	150	200
Mystery Fire Chief Car No. 81, 1950s, Sanshin Co., 9-1/4" long, three actions	120	180	240
Mystery Police Car, 1960s, T-N Co., 9-3/4" long, 6" wide, 4" high, three actions	100	150	200
Newbuggy Crazy Car, 1970s, M-T Co., 10" long, minor toy	50	75	100
News Service Car, 1960s, TPS Co., 10" long, four actions	150	225	300

Japanese battery-operated Greyhound Bus. Photo courtesy Don Hultzman

Japanese battery-operated Highway Patrol Police Special, Y Co., 1960s, 11-1/2".

Japanese battery-operated John's Farm Truck, T-N, 1950s, 9". Photo courtesy Don Hultzman

Japanese battery-operated M-101 Aston Martin Secret Ejector Car, Daiya, 1960s, 11". Photo courtesy Don Hultzman

Japanese battery-operated Old Timer Car, Cragstan, 1950s, 9". Photo courtesy Mapes Auctioneers and Appraisers

Japanese battery-operated Military Command Car, T-N Co., 1950s, 11". Photo courtesy Don Hultzman

Japanese battery operated Marvelous Fire Engine, Y Co., 1960s, 11". Photo courtesy Don Hultzman

Japanese battery-operated Kingsize Fire Engine, Bandai, 1950s. Photo courtesy Don Hultzman

Japanese battery-operated Old Fashioned Fire Engine, M-T, 1950s, 12-1/2". Photo courtesy Don Hultzman

Japanese battery-operated Kissing Couple, Ichida, 1950s, 10-3/4". Photo courtesy Don Hultzman

Japanese battery-operated Monkee-Mobile, ASC Co., 1967, 12". Photo courtesy Don Hultzman

Japanese battery-operated Musical Ice Cream Truck, Bandai, 1960s, 10-1/2". Photo courtesy Don Hultzman

Japanese battery-operated Turn-O-Matic Gun Jeep, T-N, 1960s, 10". Photo courtesy Don Hultzman

Japanese battery-operated Fire Command Car, T-N, 1950s. Photo courtesy Don Hultzman

Japanese battery-operated Strange Explorer, DSK, 1960s, 7-1/2".

Japanese battery-operated Mobile Satellite Tracking Station, Y Co., 1960s, 9". Photo courtesy Don Hultzman

Japanese battery-operated Santa Claus on Scooter, M-T, 1960s, 10". Photo courtesy Don Hultzman

	C6	C8	C10
Nutty Mads Car (Drincar), 1960s, Marx Co., 9-1/4" long, three actions	200	300	400
Ol' MacDonald's Farm Truck, 1960s, Frankonia, four actions (includes plastic pig, cow and chicken)	110	165	220
Old Fashioned Car, 1950s, S-H Co., 10" long, four actions	50	75	100
Old Fashioned Fire Engine, 1950s, M-T Co., four actions, 12-1/2" high	110	165	220
Old Ford Touring Car, 1950s, Z Co., 10" long, four actions	50	75	100
Old Time Automobile, 1950s, "Y" Co., 8-3/4" long, three actions (includes detachable tin lithographed driver and steering wheel)	100	150	200
Old Timer, Car, 1950s, Cragstan Co., 9" long-three actions	100	150	200
Oldtimer Automoball, 1950s, M-T Co., 10" long, three actions, includes celluloid ball	90	135	180
Oldtimer Sunday Driver, 1960s, Daiya Co., 9" long, four actions	70	105	140
P.D. No. 5-Police Patrol Car (Buick), 1960s, Askakusa Toy Co., 11-1/2" long, three actions	90	135	180
Passenger Bus, 1950s, "Y" Co., 16" long, four actions	300	450	600
Patrol Auto-Tricycle, 1960s, T-N Co., 19" long, 7-1/2" high, four actions	160	240	320
Pick-Up Truck, T-N Co., 10" long, four actions	90	135	180
Piston Action Bulldozer, 1960s, Linemar Co., 7-1/2" long, two cycles	100	150	200
Police Auto Cycle, 1960s, (motorcycle and plastic driver), Bandai Co., five actions, remote control	150	225	300
Police Motorcycle, 1950s, M-T Co., 11-3/4" long, seven actions	160	240	320
Police No. 5 Police Car, 1950s, T-N Co., four actions, 9-1/2" long	100	150	200
Police Patrol Jeep, 1960s, T-N Co., four actions, lights, bump and go, noise, smoke, 9-1/4" long	100	150	200
Pom Pom Tank, 1950s, S&E Co., 12" long, five actions	100	150	200

	C6	C8	C10
Popcorn Vendor Truck, 1960s, T-N Co., 9" long, three actions	130	195	260
Porsche With Visible Engine, 1964, Bandai Co., 10" long, three actions	90	135	180
Power Shovel, 1950s, Alps Co., 15" long, extended, six actions	150	225	300
Racecar No. 25, 1950s, Alps Co., three actions, 9" long, rare	800	1200	1600
Radar Jeep, 1950s, T-N Co., 11" long, four actions	100	150	200
RCA-NBC Mobile Color TV Truck, 1950s, Yonezawa Co., 9" long, four actions	350	525	700
Reversible Diesel Electric Tractor, 1950s, Marx Co., minor toy	90	135	180
Road Construction Roller, 1950s, Daiya Co., 8-1/2" long, four actions	90	135	180
Road Grader, 1960s, T-N Co., 12" long, three actions	80	120	160
Road Roller, 1950s, M-T Co., 9" long, four actions	110	165	220

Japanese battery-operated Mystery Police Car, T-N, 1960s, 9-3/4". Photo courtesy Don Hultzman

Japanese Road Roller, M-T, 1950s, 9". Photo courtesy Don Hultzman

Japanese battery-operated Ol' MacDonald's Farm Truck, 1960s. Photo courtesy Mapes Auctioneers and Appraisers

	C6	C8	C10
Robotank TR-2, 1960s, T-N Co., four actions, 5" high	200	300	400
Romance Car M-841, 1950s, "M" Co., 8" long, three actions	110	165	220
Santa Claus on Hand Car	100	150	200
Santa Claus on Scooter, 1960s, M-T Co., 10" high, four actions	100	150	200
School Bus, 1950s, Cragstan, 20-1/2" long, minor toy	60	90	120
Searchlight Jeep, 1950s, T-N Co., 16" long overall, (7-1/2" Jeep and 8-1/2" artillery) four actions	100	150	200
Secret Service Action Car (Green Hornet motif), 1960s, ASC Co., 11" long, four actions, rare	300	450	600
Shaking Classic Car, 1960s, T-N Co., 7" long, four actions	60	90	120
Shaking Old-Timer Car, No. 2511-1, 1960s, T-N Co., 9" long, four actions, includes plastic driver	60	90	120
Sheriff Car, 1950s, T-N Co., four actions, 10" long	90	135	180
Sight Seeing Bus, 1950s, Yonezawza Co., minor toy, 9" long	150	225	300
Sight Seeing Bus, 1960s, Bandai Co., 14-1/2" long, four actions	150	225	300
Siren Fire Car, 1950s, M-T Co., 9" long, four actions	130	195	260
Siren Patrol Car, 1960s, M-T Co., four actions, 12-1/2" long	80	120	160
Siren Patrol Motorcycle, 1960s, M-T Co., three actions, 12" long	200	300	400

	C6	C8	C10
Smokey the Bear Jeep, 1950s, M-T Co., 10" long, four actions	300	450	600
Smoking Bulldozer, 1960s, WKC Co., 9" long, four actions	100	150	200
Smoking Volkswagen, 1960s, Aoshin Co., 10-1/2" long, four actions	60	90	120
Smoky Bill on Old Fashioned Car, 1960s, T-N Co., 9" long, four actions	110	165	220
Smoky Joe-Fancy Mobile, 1960s, T-N Co., four actions, smokes, lights, bump and go, noise, 9" long	90	135	180
Sports Car Race Set, 1960s, TPS Co., Minor Toy, 8"x14" base, includes four plastic race cars	100	150	200
Steam Roller, 1950s, "Y" Co., 8" long, four actions (includes tin trailer)	110	165	220
Steam Roller (Road Roller), 1950s, T-N Co., (Rosko), 12" long w/trailer, four actions	150	225	300
Steerable Tank, 1950s, Linemar Co., 9" long, five actions	60	90	120
Strange Explorer, 1960s, DSK Co., 7-1/2" long, four actions	70	105	140
Sunbeam Jeep No. 1, 1940s, 10" long, unmarked, three actions	100	150	200
Sunbeam Side Car (Motorcycle), 1950s, Marusan Co., 9-1/2" long, three actions	800	1200	1600
Sunday Driver, 1950s, M-T Co., 10" long, four actions (includes detachable driver)	70	105	140

Japanese battery-operated Police Auto Cycle, Bandai, 1960s. Photo courtesy Don Hultzman

Japanese battery-operated Police Motorcycle, M-T, 1950s, 11-3/4". Photo courtesy Don Hultzman

*Japanese battery-operated Police Car, T-N, 1950s, 9-1/2".
Photo courtesy Don Hultzman*

*Japanese battery-operated Power Shovel, Alps Co., 1950s,
15". Photo courtesy Don Hultzman*

	C6	C8	C10
Superman Truck, 1950s, Linemar Co., 10-1/4" long, three actions, rare	800	1200	1600
Surrey Jeep, 1960s, T-N Co., 11" long, three actions	90	135	180
Swinger, The (Mustang Mach I), 1960s, T.P.S. Co., 10-1/2" long, three actions	50	75	100
Talking Police Car-Mystery Action, 1960s, Y Co., 14" long, three actions ..	70	105	140
Tank, Daisymatic No. 64	100	150	200
Tank, Daisymatic No. 80	100	150	200
Tank M-103, 1950s, M-T Co., 7" long, three actions	90	135	180
Tank M-107-US Army, 1950s, Y Co., 6" long, four actions, includes four missiles	110	165	220
Tank M-35, 1950s, HTC Co., 8" long, three actions	110	165	220
Tank M-4 Combat Tank, 1960s, Taiyo Co., 11-1/2" long, 13" w/gun barrel extended, five actions	80	120	160
Tank M-41, 1970s, J Co., 8-1/4" long, four actions	110	165	220
Tank M-48-T, 1960s, T-N Co., 8-1/4" long, four actions	100	150	200
Tank M-56, 1940s, M-T Co., 7-1/2" long, wheel drive	100	150	200
Tank M-71, 1950s, M-T Co., 5-3/4" long, five actions	100	150	200
Tank M-81, 1960s, M-T Co., 8-1/2" long, seven actions	100	150	200
Tank M-X, 1950s, T-N Co., 8-1/2" long, five actions	70	105	140

	C6	C8	C10
Tank Robot, 1960s, S-H Co., five actions, 10" tall	250	375	500
Tank T-5, 1950s, T-N Co., 8-1/2" long, three actions, includes detachable radar antenna	120	160	240
Tank X-3 (Explorer Defense), 1950s, Cragstan Co., 7-3/4" long, five actions, includes six cartridge shells	130	195	260
Tank X-75, 1950s, M-T Co., 9" long, three actions, includes tin gun and darts	110	165	220
Taxi (yellow cab), 1950s, Linemar Co., 7-1/2" long, five actions	70	105	140
Taxi Cab, 1950s, "Y" Co., 8-1/2" long, five actions	70	105	140
Taxi Cab, 1960s, "Y" Co., four actions, 9" long	80	120	160
Teddy-Go-Kart, 1960s, Alps Co., 10-1/2" long, four actions	90	135	180
Tiny Jeep, 1950s, WACO Co., 4-1/4" long, minor action	30	45	60
Tiny Tank, 1950s WACO Co., 4-1/4" long, minor action	30	45	60
Tom and Jerry Highway Patrol, 1960s, M-T Co., 8" long, three actions	120	180	240
Tom and Jerry Jumping Jeep, 1960s, M-T Co., 9" long, three actions	150	225	300
Tractor, 1950s, Showa Co., 7-1/2" long, four actions, includes lithographed tin figure (driver)	110	165	220
Tractor, 1960s, Y Co., 6" long, three actions	100	150	200

*Japanese battery-operated Sunday Driver, M-T,
1950s, 10". Photo courtesy Don Hultzman*

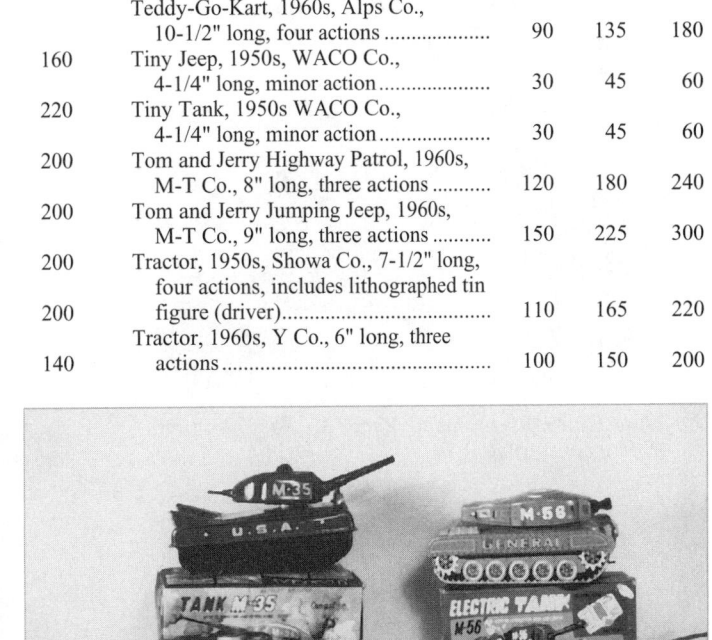

Japanese battery-operated Tank M-81, M-T, 1960s, 8-1/2".

	C6	C8	C10
Tractor On Platform, 1950s, T-N Co., tractor 9" long, trailer 7" long, minor toy	100	150	200
Turn-O-Matic Gun Jeep, 1960s, T-N Co., 10" long, five actions	100	150	200
Twin Racing Cars, 1950s, Alps Co., three actions, 7" long; 10" long w/coupling rod)	200	300	400
Visible Ford Mustang, 1960s, Bandai Co., 10" long, four actions	90	135	180

	C6	C8	C10
Volkswagen Convertible, 1950s, T-N Co., three actions, 9-3/4" long	250	375	500
Volkswagen No. 7653, 1960s, Bandai Co., 10" long, three actions	80	120	160
Volkswagen With Visible Engine, 1960s, K.O. Co., 7" long, three actions	110	165	220
Volkswagen With Visible Engine No. 4049, 1960s, Bandai Co., 8" long, three actions	110	165	220
Volkswagen-Eletrik, 1950s, Mignon Co., 8-1/2" long, three actions	100	150	200

JAPANESE (ETC.) TIN CARS

Tin toy cars have been manufactured since the first horseless carriages roamed the streets of the United States and Europe. They ranged in size and price from the tiny one-inch penny toy to the twenty-eight-inch Eldorado, which sold for $10. Although there are German, Spanish, and French toy cars listed here, our concentration will be the 1950s—the Golden Era of Japanese tin toy cars. These examples enjoy much popularity today, and prices have been raised by the limitlessness of some people's insanity. Keep one thing foremost in your mind when trying to sell a toy at the mint price—the person who paid that price already has one. (All photos by Ron Smith except where noted.)

Contributor: Ron Smith, 33005 Arlesford, Solon, OH, 44139, 440-248-7066, fax 440-519-0906. Smith has always loved toy cars and planes, he can still show you his first Dinky Toy his aunt bought him at Fred Harvey's Toy Store in Cleveland's Terminal Tower Building. Smith has collected die-cast cars, trucks, and planes, cast-iron toys and plastic promotional cars, but for the past fifteen years he has specialized in tin-plate cars and planes. Smith lives in Ohio with his wife Joan and their two cats, T-2 and Bogart.

Source: *The Big Book of Tin Toy Cars* by Ron Smith and William C. Gallagher.

	C6	C8	C10
Agajanian Racer No. 98, friction, Y Co., 18" long, 1950s (J286)	600	1200	2400
Aston-Martin DB5 (James Bond), friction, Gilbert, 11-1/2" long, 1960s (J001)	90	175	400

Japanese Tin 1950s Agajanian Racer No. 98, Y, friction, 18". Photo courtesy Ron Smith

Japanese Tin Atom Car, Yonezawa, friction, 17". Photo courtesy Ron Smith

Japanese Tin 1960s Aston-Martin DB6, Asahi, friction, 11". Photo courtesy Ron Smith

Japanese Tin 1960s Aston-Martin DB5 (James Bond), Gilbert, friction, 11-1/2". Photo courtesy Ron Smith

Japanese Tin 1960s BMW 1500, Ichiko, friction, 8". Photo courtesy Ron Smith

Japanese Tin 1958 Buick Century, Bandai, friction, 8". Photo courtesy Ron Smith

Japanese Tin 1958 Buick Century, Yonezawa, friction, 12". Photo courtesy Ron Smith

Japanese Tin 1959 Buick Convertible, Ichiko, battery-operated/friction, 12". Photo courtesy Ron Smith

Japanese Tin 1950s Buick Futuristic Le Sabre, Yonezawa, friction, 7-1/2". Photo courtesy Ron Smith

	C6	C8	C10
Aston-Martin DB6, friction, Asahi Toy Co., 11" long, 1960s (J002)	200	400	600
Atom Car, friction, Yonezawa, 17" long, 1950s (J284)	300	600	1200
Atom Jet Car, friction, Y Co., 30" long (J283)	500	1000	2000
Austin Healey 100 Six Convertible, friction, Bandai, 8" long, 1959 (J002B)	60	90	160
Austin Healey 100 Six Coupe, friction, Bandai, 8" long, 1959 (J002A)	60	90	160
BMW 1500, friction, Ichiko, 8" long, 1960s (J002C)	90	150	250
BMW 600 Isetta, friction, Bandai, 9" long, 1950 (J016)	200	400	600
BMW Isetta (three wheels), friction, Bandai, 6-1/2" long, 1950 (J017)	75	125	200
Buick, friction, Marusan, 7" long, 1953 (J003)	75	125	250
Buick, friction, T.N., 11" long, 1959 (J008)	90	150	300
Buick, B/O-friction, Ichiko, 12" long, 1959 (J009)	100	250	300
Buick, friction, Ichiko, 17-1/2" long, 1960 (J010)	150	250	600
Buick, friction, T.N., 11" long, 1961 (J011)	50	100	200
Buick Century, friction, Bandai, 8" long, 1958 (J007)	80	100	150
Buick Century, friction, Yonezawa, 12" long, 1958 (J006)	400	650	1500
Buick Emergency Car, friction, T.N., 14" long, 1961 (J012)	50	75	100
Buick Futuristic Le Sabre, friction, Yonezawa, 7-1/2" long, 1950s (J276)	200	300	500
Buick Le Sabre, friction, Ashai Toy Co., 19" long, 1966 (J014)	100	200	400
Buick Roadmaster, friction, Yoshiya, 11" long, 1955 (J005)	125	250	500

	C6	C8	C10
Buick Sportswagon, friction, Asakusa, 15" long, 1968 (J015)	100	150	200
Buick Station Wagon, battery, unknown, 8" long, 1954 (J004)	75	150	200
Buick Wildcat, friction, Ichiko, 15" long, 1963 (J013)	250	500	900
Cadillac, friction, Marusan, 11" long, 1950 (J018)	300	500	1000
Cadillac, battery, Marusan, 11" long, 1950 (J019)	400	800	1800
Cadillac, battery, T.N., 13" long, 1952 (J021)	100	250	450
Cadillac, friction, Alps, 11-1/2" long, 1952 (J020)	250	400	800
Cadillac, battery, Joustra, 12" long, 1954 (J023)	150	300	550
Cadillac, friction, Gama, 12" long, 1954 (J022)	200	300	500
Cadillac, friction, Yonezawa, 18" long, 1960 (J027)	150	200	350
Cadillac, friction, Bandai, 17" long, 1960s (J026)	125	175	375
Cadillac, friction, Yonezawa, 22" long, 1962 (J030)	100	250	400
Cadillac, friction, Bandai, 17" long, 1963 (J031)	125	200	350
Cadillac, friction, Ichiko, 22" long, 1965 (J033)	200	400	600
Cadillac, friction, Ashahi Toy Co., 17" long, 1965 (J032)	200	400	600
Cadillac, friction, unknown, 10-3/4" long, 1967 (J035)	65	120	185
Cadillac, friction, K.O., 10-1/2" long, 1967 (J034)	100	150	300
Cadillac 60, friction, unknown, 9" long, 1961 (J028)	70	80	100
Cadillac Convertible, friction, Bandai, 12" long, 1959 (J025)	60	110	220

Japanese Tin 1959 Buick Hardtop, T.N., friction, 11". Photo courtesy Ron Smith

Japanese Tin 1955 Buick Roadmaster, Yoshiya, friction, 11". Photo courtesy Ron Smith

Japanese Tin 1963 Buick Wildcat, Ichiko, friction, 15". Photo courtesy Ron Smith

Japanese Tin 1950 Cadillac, Marusan, friction, 11". Photo courtesy Ron Smith

Japanese Tin 1952 Cadillac, Alps, friction, 11-1/2". Photo courtesy Ron Smith

Japanese Tin 1952 Cadillac, T.N., battery, 13". Photo courtesy Ron Smith

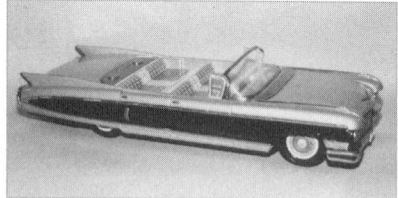

Japanese Tin 1961 Cadillac, battery, Joustra, 12". Photo courtesy Ron Smith

Japanese Tin 1959 Cadillac, Bandai, friction, 12". Photo courtesy Ron Smith

Japanese Tin 1967 Cadillac, friction, K.O., 10-1/2". Photo courtesy Ron Smith

Japanese Tin 1959 Cadillac Convertible, Bandai, friction, 12". Photo courtesy Ron Smith

Japanese Tin 1959 Cadillac Convertible, Bandai, friction, 12". Photo courtesy Ron Smith

Japanese Tin 1961 Cadillac Fleetwood, SSS, friction, 17-1/2". Photo courtesy Ron Smith

Japanese Tin 1959 Cadillac Sedan, Bandai, friction, 12". Photo courtesy Ron Smith

Japanese Tin 1950 Champion Racer No. 42, German, friction, 18". Photo courtesy Ron Smith

Japanese Tin 1950 Champion Racer No. 15, German, friction, 18". Photo courtesy Ron Smith

Japanese Tin 1950s Champion's Racer No. 98, Y, friction, 18". Photo courtesy Ron Smith

Japanese Tin 1954 Chevrolet, Marusan, friction, 11". Photo courtesy Ron Smith

	C6	C8	C10
Cadillac El Dorado, friction, Ichiko, 28" long, 1967 (J036)	200	300	500
Cadillac Fleetwood, friction, SSS, 17-1/2" long, 1961 (J029)	100	200	350
Cadillac Sedan, friction, Bandai, 12" long, 1959 (J024)	75	100	150
Champion Racer No. 15, friction, German, 18" long, 1950 (J289)	600	900	1800
Champion Racer No. 42, friction, Gem, 18" long, 1950 (J288)	600	900	1800
Champion's Racer No. 98, friction, Y Co., 18" long, 1950s (J287)	600	900	1850
Chevrolet, friction, Marusan, 11" long, 1954 (J049)	250	500	1100
Chevrolet, battery, Marusan, 10-3/4" long, 1955 (J050)	300	800	1500
Chevrolet, friction, Marusan, 11-1/2" long, 1960 (J060)	200	400	800
Chevrolet, friction, unknown, 11" long, 1962 (J065)	125	250	375
Chevrolet Camaro, friction, T.N., 14" long, 1967 (J046)	125	175	350
Chevrolet Camaro, friction, Modern Toys, 11" long, 1967 (J047)	25	50	75
Chevrolet Camaro, friction, Taiyo, 9-1/2" long, 1967 (J045)	10	20	30
Chevrolet Camaro Rusher, battery, Taiyo, 9-1/2" long, 1971 (J048)	10	20	30
Chevrolet Convertible, friction, Bandai, 9-1/2" long, 1956 (J053)	80	100	150
Chevrolet Convertible, friction, Bandai, 8" long, 1958 (J056)	60	90	125
Chevrolet Corvair, friction, Bandai, 8" long, 1960s (J043)	30	50	75
Chevrolet Corvair, friction, Ichiko, 9" long, 1963 (J044)	50	65	95
Chevrolet Corvette, friction, Bandai, 7" long, 1953 (J037)	125	225	400
Chevrolet Corvette, friction, Yonezawa, 9-1/2" long, 1958 (J038)	200	300	600
Chevrolet Corvette, friction, Bandai, 8" long, 1962 (J039)	30	50	75
Chevrolet Corvette, battery, Ichida, 12" long, 1964 (J041)	150	225	400
Chevrolet Corvette, friction, Bandai, 8" long, 1965 (J040)	40	60	80
Chevrolet Corvette, battery, Taiyo, 9-1/2" long, 1968 (J042)	20	40	80
Chevrolet Hardtop, friction, Japan, 9" long, 1960 (J060A)	90	150	300
Chevrolet Impala, friction, unknown, 18" long, 1963 (J066)	200	300	500

	C6	C8	C10
Chevrolet Impala Convertible, friction, Bandai, 11" long, 1961 (J063)	100	150	300
Chevrolet Impala Sedan, friction, Bandai, 11" long, 1961 (J062)	100	150	300
Chevrolet Pickup, friction, Bandai, 9-1/2" long, 1956 (J052)	60	90	120
Chevrolet Pickup Truck, friction, Bandai, 8" long, 1958 (J055)	50	65	90
Chevrolet Red Cross Ambulance, friction, Bandai, 8" long, 1958 (J054)	20	30	50
Chevrolet Secret Agent, battery, unknown, 14" long, 1962 (J064)	50	75	150
Chevrolet Sedan, friction, Bandai, 8" long, 1958 (J058)	75	100	150
Chevrolet Sedan/Convertible/ Wagon, friction, SY, 11-1/2" long, 1959 (J059)	200	400	800
Chevrolet Station Wagon, friction, Bandai, 9-1/2" long, 1956 (J051)	60	90	120
Chevrolet Station Wagon, friction, Bandai, 8" long, 1958 (J057)	50	65	125
Chrysler, friction, Guntherman, 11" long, 1950 (J070)	100	300	600
Chrysler, friction, Yonezawa, 8" long, 1955 (J071)	100	200	300
Chrysler, battery, unknown, 13" long, 1958 (J073)	300	400	800
Chrysler Imperial, friction, Asahi Toy Co., 16" long, 1962 (J077)	600	1200	2200
Chrysler Imperial Convertible, friction, Bandai, 8" long, 1959 (J074)	50	100	175
Chrysler Imperial Sedan, friction, Bandai, 8" long, 1959 (J075)	75	90	150
Chrysler New Yorker, friction, Alps, 14" long, 1957 (J072)	600	1200	1800
Chrysler Valiant, friction, Bandai, 8" long, 1960 (J076)	20	40	50
Citroen DS 19 Convertible, friction, Bandai, 12" long, 1960 (J067)	175	300	500
Citroen DS 19 Sedan, friction, Bandai, 12" long, 1960 (J068)	200	400	600
Citroen DS19 Sedan, Convertible, Wagon, friction, Bandai, 8" long, 1960 (J66A)	75	125	200
Citroen ID 19 Station Wagon, friction, Bandai, 12" long, 1960 (J069)	100	150	300
Coke Truck, battery, Japan, 12" long, 1960s (J17B)	125	225	400
Corvair Bertone, battery, Bandai, 12" long, 1963 (J277)	75	200	400

Japanese Tin 1955 Chevrolet, battery, Marusan, 10-3/4". Photo courtesy Ron Smith

Japanese Tin 1960 Chevrolet, Marusan, friction, 11-1/2". Photo courtesy Ron Smith

Japanese Tin 1962 Chevrolet, friction, 11". Photo courtesy Ron Smith

Japanese Tin 1967 Chevrolet Camaro, T.N., friction, 14". Photo courtesy Ron Smith

Japanese Tin 1971 Chevrolet Camaro Rusher, Taiyo, battery, 9-1/2". Photo courtesy Ron Smith

Japanese Tin 1960s Chevrolet Corvair, Bandai, friction, 8". Photo courtesy Ron Smith

Japanese Tin 1953 Chevrolet Corvette, Bandai, friction, 7". Photo courtesy Ron Smith

Japanese Tin 1958 Chevrolet Corvette, Yonezawa, friction, 9-1/2". Photo courtesy Ron Smith

Japanese Tin 1964 Chevrolet Corvette, Ichida, battery, 12". Photo courtesy Ron Smith

Japanese Tin 1960 Chevrolet Hardtop, friction, 9". Photo courtesy Ron Smith

Japanese Tin 1961 Chevrolet Impala Convertible, Bandai, friction, 11". Photo courtesy Ron Smith

Japanese Tin 1961 Chevrolet Impala Sedan, Bandai, friction, 11". Photo courtesy Ron Smith

Japanese Tin 1963 Chevrolet Impala, Bandai, friction, 18". Photo courtesy Ron Smith

Japanese Tin 1962 Chevrolet Secret Agent, battery, 14". Photo courtesy Ron Smith

Japanese Tin 1959 Chevrolet Sedan/ Convertible/Wagon, SY, friction, 11-1/2". Photo courtesy Ron Smith

Japanese Tin 1955 Chrysler, friction, Yonezawa, 8". Photo courtesy Ron Smith

Japanese Tin 1959 Chrysler Imperial Convertible, Bandai, friction, 8". Photo courtesy Ron Smith

Japanese Tin 1958 Chrysler, battery, 13". Photo courtesy Ron Smith

	C6	C8	C10		C6	C8	C10
Daihatsu Auto Tricycle, friction, Nomura, 11" long, 1950s (J275)	100	150	300	Edsel Station Wagon, friction, T.N., 11" long, 1958 (J089)	150	200	300
Daihatsu Midget, friction, Kokyu Shokai, 5" long, 1950 (J269)	75	100	200	Edsel Wagon, friction, Haji, 10-1/2" long, 1958 (J087)	200	300	400
Daihatsu Midget, friction, Yonezawa, 7" long, 1950s (J270)	75	100	200	Electrospecial No. 21, battery, Y Co., 10" long (J290)	300	600	1200
Datsun Bluebird 1200, friction, Bandai, 8" long, 1960s (J079)	90	125	250	Ferrari, battery, Bandai, 11" long, 1958 (J148)	90	150	300
DeSoto, friction, Masudaya, 8" long, 1930s (J081)	300	400	800	Ferrari 250 G. Convertible, friction, A.T.C., 9-1/2" long, 1957 (J147)	200	300	600
DeSoto Hardtop, friction, Japan, 7", 1950s (J081A)	50	75	150	Ferrari Berlinetta, friction, Bandai, 9-1/2" long, 1960s (J092A)	50	75	125
Divco Dugans Bakery Truck, friction, unknown, Japan, 7-1/2" long, 1950s (J080)	300	400	600	Ferrari Berlinetta 250 Le Mans, friction, Asahi, 11" long, 1960s	115	265	375
DKW 1000 Convertible, friction, Bandai, 8" long, 1960 (J078)	90	200	300	Ferrari Super America Convertible, friction, Bandai, 12" long, 1960s (J150)	100	200	300
Dodge Hardtop, X, Buddy L, 13" long, 1969 (J085A)	50	70	90	Ferrari Super America Coupe, friction, Bandai, 12" long, 1960 (J149)	100	200	300
Dodge Pickup, friction, unknown, 18-1/2" long, 1959 (J084)	400	600	1200	Ferrari, No. 3, friction, Bandai, 8" long, 1960s (J147B)	85	150	190
Dodge Sedan, friction, T.N., 11" long, 1958 (J082)	300	400	800	Fiat 600 Sedan, friction, Bandai, 8" long, 1960s (J151)	50	65	95
Dodge Truck, friction, unknown, 24" long, 1959 (J083)	350	500	1000	Ford, wind-up, Italy, 10" long, 1946 (J092B)	100	200	400
Dodge Yellow Cab and Checker cab, friction, T.N., 12" long, 1968 (J085)	90	125	200	Ford, friction, Bandai, 7" long, 1956	60	125	175
Dream Car, friction, Y Co., 17" long (J278A)	400	600	1200	Ford, friction, Haji, 11" long, 1960 (J119)	85	150	225
Dream Car Buick Phantom, friction, Tipp & Co., 12" long, 1950s (J278)	300	400	800	Ford Ambulance, friction, Bandai, 12" long, 1955 (J098)	150	200	250
Dream Car Firebird III, friction, Alps, 11" long, 1960s (J279)	100	200	300	Ford Convertible, friction, Bandai, 12" long, 1955 (J100)	200	400	600
Edsel, friction, Yonezawa, 10-1/2" long, 1958 (J092)	300	400	600	Ford Convertible, friction, Haji, 11-1/2" long, 1956 (J102)	400	600	800
Edsel Ambulance, friction, Haji, 11" long, 1958 (J088)	200	250	300	Ford Convertible, friction, Rico, 17" long, 1964 (J124)	300	500	800
Edsel Convertible/Sedan, friction, Haji, 10-1/2" long, 1958 (J086)	300	500	900	Ford Country Sedan, friction, Bandai, 10-1/2" long, 1961 (J120)	100	160	225
Edsel Hardtop, friction, Asahi, 10-3/4" long, 1958 (J090)	100	200	350	Ford Country Sedan, friction, Asahi, 12" long, 1962 (J121)	200	350	700
Edsel Hardtop, friction, Toy Nomura, 8-1/2" long, 1958 (J091)	100	150	250	Ford Country Squire Station Wagon, friction, Bandai, 8" long, 1958 (J112)	40	60	100

Japanese Tin 1959 Ford Retractable, T.N., friction, 11". Photo courtesy Ron Smith

Japanese Tin 1949 Ford Sedan, Guntherman, wind-up, 11". Photo courtesy Ron Smith

Japanese Tin 1950s Ford Sedan, Ichiko, friction, 10". Photo courtesy Ron Smith

Japanese Tin 1957 Chrysler New Yorker, Alps, friction, 14". Photo courtesy Ron Smith

Japanese Tin 1960s Ferrari Berlinetta 250 Le Mans, Asahi. Photo courtesy Ron Smith

Japanese Tin 1960 Citroen DS 19 Sedan, Bandai, friction, 12". Photo courtesy Ron Smith

Japanese Tin Coke Truck, battery, 12". Photo courtesy Ron Smith

Japanese Tin 1950s DeSoto, Hardtop, friction, 7". Photo courtesy Ron Smith

Japanese Tin 1958 Dodge Sedan, T.N., friction, 11". Photo courtesy Ron Smith

Japanese Tin 1959 Dodge Pick Up, friction, 18-1/2". Photo courtesy Ron Smith

Japanese Tin Dream Car, Y, friction, 17". Photo courtesy Ron Smith

Japanese Tin 1958 Edsel Convertible/ Sedan, top up, Haji, friction, 10-1/2". Photo courtesy Ron Smith

Japanese Tin 1958 Edsel Convertible/ Sedan, top down, Haji, friction, 10-1/2". Photo courtesy Ron Smith

Japanese Tin 1958 Edsel Hardtop, friction, Toy Nomura, 8-1/2". Photo courtesy Ron Smith

Japanese Tin 1958 Edsel Station Wagon, T.N., friction, 11". Photo courtesy Ron Smith

Japanese Tin 1958 Edsel Wagon, Haji, friction, 10-1/2". Photo courtesy Ron Smith

Japanese Tin 1960s Ferrari Berlinetta, Bandai, friction, 9-1/2". Photo courtesy Ron Smith

Japanese Tin 1962 Chrysler Imperial, Asahi, friction, 16". Photo courtesy Ron Smith

Japanese Tin 1960s No. 3 Ferrari, Bandai, friction, 8". Photo courtesy Ron Smith

Japanese Tin 1946 Ford, Italian, wind-up, 10". Photo courtesy Ron Smith

Japanese Tin 1960 Ford, Haji, friction, 11". Photo courtesy Ron Smith

	C6	C8	C10
Ford Fairlane Hardtop/Convertible, friction, Sankei Gangu, 9" long, 1958 (J114)	90	115	125
Ford Fairlane Hardtop/Convertible, friction, Bandai, 8" long, 1958 (J113)	40	60	125
Ford Fairlane Skyliner, friction, Sankei Gangu, 9" long, 1959 (J115)	90	115	125
Ford Falcon, friction, Bandai, 8" long, 1960s (J118)	20	30	60
Ford Ford Fairlane Sedan, friction, Ichiko, 10" long, 1950s (J105)	100	200	300
Ford Galaxie Hardtop, friction, MT, 11" long, 1965 (J125)	125	150	300
Ford Good Humor Ice Cream Truck, friction, KTS, Japan, 10-3/4" long, 1950 (J095)	150	500	750
Ford GT, battery, Bandai, 10" long, 1960s (J146)	65	85	125
Ford Gyron, battery, Ichida, 11" long, 1960 (J280)	135	315	450
Ford Hardtop, friction, Yonezawa, 12" long, 1956 (J101)	300	500	800
Ford Hardtop, friction, T.N., 12" long, 1957 (J106)	100	200	300
Ford Hardtop, battery, Japan, 12" long, 1958 (J114A)	150	200	400
Ford Hardtop, friction, Rico, 17" long, 1964 (J123)	300	500	800
Ford Hardtop, friction, Ichiko, 13" long, 1964 (J122)	200	300	500
Ford Hardtop and Police and Fire Chief and Yellow Cab, friction, Marusan, 11" long, 1954 (J095A)	125	175	350
Ford Mustang, battery, Bandai, 13" long, 1967 (J144)	45	65	100
Ford Mustang (FBI), friction, Bandai, 11" long, 1965 (J141)	75	100	300
Ford Mustang Convertible, battery, Yonezawa, 13-1/2" long, 1965 (J142)	90	125	250
Ford Mustang Fastback, friction, Bandai, 11" long, 1965 (J139)	45	65	90

	C6	C8	C10
Ford Mustang Fastback, friction, T.N., 17" long, 1966 (J143)	120	200	300
Ford Mustang Hardtop/ Convertible, Fric/Bat., Bandai, 11" long, 1965 (J140)	75	125	150
Ford Panel Delivery, reads "Standard Coffee," friction, 10" long, 1960 (J119A)	800	1500	2500
Ford Panel Truck, friction, reads "Standard Coffee," Bandai, 12" long (J108A)	1000	2000	3000+
Ford Panel Truck, friction, reads "Standard Coffee," Bandai, 12" long, 1955 (J99A)	600	800	1500
Ford Panel Truck, friction, reads "Flowers," Bandai, 12" long, 1955 (J099)	200	400	600
Ford Pickup, friction, Bandai, 12" long, 1955 (J096)	150	250	300
Ford Retractable, friction, T.N., 11" long, 1959 (J117)	80	100	150
Ford Retractable Top, friction, K. Japan, 10" long, 1958 (J110)	70	90	150
Ford Retractable Top, battery, T.N., 11" long, 1958 (J111)	100	125	175
Ford Sedan, wind-up, Guntherman, 11" long, 1949 (J093)	150	300	400
Ford Sedan, wind-up, Guntherman, 11" long, 1951 (J094)	150	300	400
Ford Sedan, friction, Marusan, 13" long, 1956 (J103)	500	800	2000+
Ford Sedan/Con./Wagon/Pickup, friction, Joustra, 12" long, 1957 (J107)	150	200	275
Ford Sedan/Convertible/ Wagon/Pickup, friction, Bandai, 12" long, 1957 (J108)	200	250	300
Ford Station Wagon, friction, Bandai, 12" long, 1955 (J097)	150	250	300
Ford Station Wagon, friction, Nomura, 7-1/2" long, 1957 (J109)	60	80	100
Ford Station Wagon, friction, T.N., 12" long, 1959 (J116)	100	150	200

Japanese Tin 1950s Pontiac Convertible, KS, friction, 14". Photo courtesy Ron Smith

Japanese Tin 1950s Pontiac Coupe, KS, friction, 14". Photo courtesy Ron Smith

Japanese Tin 1954 Pontiac Hardtop/Convertible, Minister-Indai, friction, 11". Photo courtesy Ron Smith

Japanese Tin 1955 Ford Ambulance, Bandai, friction, 12". Photo courtesy Ron Smith

Japanese Tin 1955 Ford Convertible, Bandai, friction, 12". Photo courtesy Ron Smith

Japanese Tin 1956 Ford Convertible, Haji, friction, 11-1/2". Photo courtesy Ron Smith

Japanese Tin 1961 Ford Country Sedan, Bandai, friction, 10-1/2". Photo courtesy Ron Smith

Japanese Tin 1962 Ford Country Sedan, Asahi, friction, 12". Photo courtesy Ron Smith

Japanese Tin 1965 Ford Galaxie Hardtop, MT, friction, 11". Photo courtesy Ron Smith

Japanese Tin 1954 Ford Hardtop, Marusan, friction, 11". Photo courtesy Ron Smith

Japanese Tin 1957 Ford Hardtop, T.N., friction, 12". Photo courtesy Ron Smith

Japanese Tin 1958 Ford Hardtop, battery, 12". Photo courtesy Ron Smith

Japanese Tin 1964 Ford Hardtop, Ichiko, friction, 13". Photo courtesy Ron Smith

Japanese Tin 1965 Ford Mustang Fastback, Bandai, friction, 11". Photo courtesy Ron Smith

Japanese Tin 1966 Ford Mustang F.B., T.N., friction, 17". Photo courtesy Ron Smith

Japanese Tin 1965 Ford Mustang Hardtop/Convertible, Bandai, friction/battery, 11". Photo courtesy Ron Smith

Japanese Tin 1955 Ford Panel Truck "Flowers," Bandai, friction, 12". Photo courtesy Ron Smith

Japanese Tin 1955 Ford Pick Up, friction, Bandai, 12". Photo courtesy Ron Smith

Japanese Tin 1956 Ford Sedan, Marusan, friction, 13". Photo courtesy Ron Smith

Japanese Tin 1957 Ford Sedan/Con./Wagon/Pickup, Joustra, friction, 12". Photo courtesy Ron Smith

Japanese Tin 1955 Ford Station Wagon, Bandai, friction, 12". Photo courtesy Ron Smith

Japanese Tin 1956 Ford Wagon, Nomura, friction, 10-1/2". Photo courtesy Ron Smith

Japanese Tin 1959 Ford Station Wagon, T.N., friction, 12". Photo courtesy Ron Smith

Japanese Tin 1960s Ford Taunus 17M Convertible/Hardtop, Bandai, friction, 8". Photo courtesy Ron Smith

Japanese Tin 1956 Ford Thunderbird, T.N., friction, 11". Photo courtesy Ron Smith

Japanese Tin 1956 Ford Thunderbird, T.N., battery, 11". Photo courtesy Ron Smith

Japanese Tin 1963 Ford Thunderbird Retractable, Yonezawa, battery, 11". Photo courtesy Ron Smith

Japanese Tin 1964 Ford Thunderbird Hardtop, Asahi, friction, 12". Photo courtesy Ron Smith

Japanese Tin 1964 Ford Thunderbird, Ichiko, friction, 16". Photo courtesy Ron Smith

Japanese Tin 1965 Ford Thunderbird Hardtop, Bandai, friction, 10-3/4". Photo courtesy Ron Smith

Japanese Tin 1968 Ford Torino, friction, S.T., 16". Photo courtesy Ron Smith

Japanese Tin Jaguar XKE Convertible, friction, T.T., 10-1/2". Photo courtesy Ron Smith

Japanese Tin 1950s Lancia, friction, Bandai, 8". Photo courtesy Ron Smith

Japanese Tin 1956 Lincoln, friction, Ichiko, 16-1/2". Photo courtesy Ron Smith

Japanese Tin 1964 Lincoln, friction, 10-1/2". Photo courtesy Ron Smith

Japanese Tin 1956 Lincoln Continental Mark II, Linemar, friction, 12". Photo courtesy Ron Smith

	C6	C8	C10
Ford Taunus 17M Convertible, friction, Bandai, 8" long, 1960s (J145)	20	40	80
Ford Thunderbird, battery, T.N., 11" long, 1956 (J129)	200	300	400
Ford Thunderbird, friction, T.N., 11" long, 1956 (J127)	200	300	400
Ford Thunderbird, friction, Bandai, 8" long, 1959 (J130)	50	60	80
Ford Thunderbird, friction, Ichiko, 16" long, 1964 (J137)	125	225	425
Ford Thunderbird Convertible, friction, Bandai, 7" long, 1955 (J126A)	50	100	150
Ford Thunderbird Convertible, friction, Bandai, 8" long, 1959 (J131)	50	60	80
Ford Thunderbird Convertible, friction, Asahi, 12-1/2" long, 1964 (J135)	150	200	400
Ford Thunderbird Hardtop, friction, Asahi, 12" long, 1964 (J136)	150	200	400
Ford Thunderbird Hardtop, friction, Bandai, 10-3/4" long, 1965 (J138)	60	90	160
Ford Thunderbird Hardtop Clear Top, friction, T.N., 11" long, 1956 (J128)	200	300	400
Ford Thunderbird Retractable, battery, Yonezawa, 11" long, 1961 (J132)	90	120	175
Ford Thunderbird Retractable, battery, Yonezawa, 11" long, 1962 (J133)	105	120	175
Ford Thunderbird Retractable, battery, Yonezawa, 11" long, 1963 (J134)	80	150	200
Ford Torino, friction, S.T., 16" long, 1968 (J126)	200	350	800
Ford Wagon, friction, Nomura, 10-1/2" long, 1956 (J104)	125	225	300
GM's Gas Turbine Powered Firebird II, friction, Asahi, 8-1/2" long, 1956 (J281)	125	200	350
International Cement Mixer, friction, SSS, 19" long, 1950s (J152)	275	300	800
International Grain Hauler, friction, SSS, 23" long, 1950 (J153)	275	300	800
Jaguar 3.4 Convertible, friction, Bandai, 8" long, 1960s (J160)	50	60	120
Jaguar 3.4 Sedan, friction, Bandai, 8" long, 1960s (J159)	50	60	120
Jaguar XK140, friction, Bandai, 9-1/2" long, 1960s (J157)	40	60	90
Jaguar XK150 Hardtop Convertible, friction, Bandai, 9-1/2" long, 1960 (J154)	75	125	200
Jaguar XKE, battery, Bandai, 10" long, 1960s (J158)	90	125	200
Jaguar XKE Convertible, friction, T.T., 10-1/2" long, 1960s (J155)	75	150	250
Jaguar XKE Coupe, friction, Lendolet Auto, 10-1/2" long, 1960s (J156)	50	75	120
Jaguar XKE120, friction, Alps, 6-1/2" long, 1965 (J161)	90	150	350

	C6	C8	C10
Lancia Coupe and Convertible, friction, Bandai, 8" long, 1950s (J161B)	50	90	150
Land Rover 88 Station Wagon, friction, Bandai, 8" long, 1960s (J171)	30	40	60
Lincoln, friction, unknown, 12" long, 1954 (J162)	175	275	400
Lincoln, friction, Ichiko, 16-1/2" long, 1956 (J165)	150	250	375
Lincoln, friction, unknown, 10-1/2" long, 1964 (J169)	90	175	275
Lincoln Continental Mark II, friction, Linemar, 12" long, 1956 (J164)	600	1200	2500
Lincoln Continental Mark III Convertible, friction, Bandai, 12" long, 1959 (J166)	90	125	200
Lincoln Continental Mark III Sedan, friction, Bandai, 12" long, 1959 (J167)	90	125	175
Lincoln Hardtop/Convertible, friction, Yonezawa, 11" long, 1960 (J168)	100	150	300
Lincoln Sedan, friction, Yonezawa, 12" long, 1955 (J163)	250	600	1200
Lotus Elite, friction, Bandai, 8-1/2" long, 1950s (J170)	25	35	45
Lotus Ford Racer, battery, Junior, 16" long, 1960s (J170A)	200	400	600
Mazda Auto Tricycle, friction, Bandai, 8" long, 1950s (J274)	75	125	250
Mazda Auto Tricycle K 360, friction, Bandai, 6" long, 1950s (J268)	75	100	200
Mercedes Benz, friction, Ichiko, 12-1/2" long, 1960s (J175)	115	155	200
Mercedes Benz, battery, SSS, 12" long, 1962 (J190)	200	250	350
Mercedes Benz, friction, Ichiko, 24" long, 1970 (J191)	125	150	200
Mercedes Benz 219 Convertible, friction, Bandai, 8" long, 1960s (J177)	50	80	120
Mercedes Benz 219 Sedan, friction, Bandai, 8" long, 1960s (J176)	50	70	110
Mercedes Benz 230 SL, battery, Yanoman, 14-1/2" long, 1960 (J180)	125	155	185
Mercedes Benz 230 SL, battery, Alps, 10" long, 1960s (J179)	65	75	95
Mercedes Benz 230 SL, battery, Modern Toys, 15" long, 1960s (J178)	175	210	250
Mercedes Benz 250 S, friction, Daiya, 14" long, 1960 (J182)	110	155	175
Mercedes Benz 250 SE, battery, Ichiko, 13" long, 1960s (J181)	110	140	185
Mercedes Benz 300 SL, battery, T.N., 11" long, 1950s (J183)	125	150	200
Mercedes Benz 300 SL, battery, KS, 7" long, 1950s (J184)	45	65	85
Mercedes Benz 300 SL, battery, Dist. Cragstan, 9" long, 1950s (J185)	65	95	125

Japanese Tin 1959 Lincoln Continental Mark III Convertible, Bandai, friction, 12". Photo courtesy Ron Smith

Japanese Tin 1959 Lincoln Continental Mark III Sedan, Bandai, friction, 12". Photo courtesy Ron Smith

Japanese Tin 1960 Lincoln Hardtop/ Convertible, Yonezawa, friction, 11". Photo courtesy Ron Smith

Japanese Tin 1955 Lincoln Sedan, Yonezawa, friction, 12". Photo courtesy Ron Smith

Japanese Tin 1960s Lotus Ford Racer, Junior, battery, 16". Photo courtesy Strine

Japanese Tin 1950s Mazda Auto Tricycle, Bandai, friction, 8". Photo courtesy Ron Smith

Japanese Tin 1950s Mercedes Benz 300 SL, T.N., battery, 11". Photo courtesy Ron Smith

Japanese Tin 1960s Mercedes Benz 219 Sedan, Bandai, friction, 8". Photo courtesy Ron Smith

Japanese Tin 1960s Mercedes Benz 219 Convertible, Bandai, friction, 8". Photo courtesy Ron Smith

Japanese Tin 1967 Mercury Cougar Hardtop, Asakusa Toys, friction, 15". Photo courtesy Ron Smith

Japanese Tin 1956 Mercury Hardtop, Alps, friction, 9-1/2". Photo courtesy Ron Smith

Japanese Tin 1958 Mercury Hardtop, Yonezawa, friction, 11-1/2". Photo courtesy Ron Smith

Japanese Tin 1960s Messerchmitt Three-wheel Sedan, Bandai, friction, 8". Photo courtesy Ron Smith

Japanese Tin 1955 MG, friction, SSS, 6". Photo courtesy Ron Smith

Japanese Tin Midget Special No. 6, Y, friction, 7". Photo courtesy Ron Smith

Japanese Tin 1952 Oldsmobile, Y, friction, 11". Photo courtesy Ron Smith

Japanese Tin 1961 Oldsmobile Convertible/Wagon, Yonezawa, friction, 12". Photo courtesy Ron Smith

Japanese Tin 1956 Oldsmobile Sedan, Ichiko/Kanto, friction, 10-1/2". Photo courtesy Ron Smith

	C6	C8	C10
Mercedes Benz 300 SL, friction, Marusan, 8-1/2" long, 1957 (J187)	150	250	325
Mercedes Benz 300 SL Coupe and Convertible, friction, Bandai, 8" long, 1950s (J186)	65	95	150
Mercedes Benz 600, friction, unknown, 10" long, 1960s (J188)	95	125	175
Mercedes Benz Racer, friction, Line Mar, 9-1/2" long, 1950s (J173)	95	150	185
Mercedes Benz Racer W196, battery, Marusan, 10" long, 1950s (J174)	150	200	250
Mercedes Benz Taxi, battery, Bandai, 10" long, 1960s (J189)	75	100	125
Mercedes Limousine, friction, Tipp & Co., 14" long, 1950s (J172)	500	800	1000
Mercury Cougar Hardtop, friction, Asakusa Toys, 15" long, 1967 (J197)	200	400	800
Mercury Cougar Hardtop, battery, Taiyo, 10" long, 1967 (J196)	25	45	65
Mercury Hardtop, battery, Rock Valley Toys, 9-1/2" long, 1954 (J192)	100	125	200
Mercury Hardtop, friction, Alps, 9-1/2" long, 1956 (J193)	600	800	1500
Mercury Hardtop, friction, Yonezawa, 11-1/2" long, 1958 (J195)	250	325	500
Mercury Station Wagon, friction, Bandai, 8" long, 1958 (J194)	60	80	100
Messerschmitt Four-wheel Convertible, friction, Bandai, 8" long, 1960s (J204)	200	500	600
Messerschmitt Three-wheel Sedan/Convertible, friction, Bandai, 8" long, 1960s (J205)	200	250	350
MG, friction, SSS, 6" long, 1955 (J200B)	50	70	100
MG Magnette Mark III Convertible, friction, Bandai, 8" long, 1960s (J203)	95	125	150
MG Magnette Mark III Sedan, friction, Bandai, 8" long, 1960s (J202)	95	125	150
MG TD, friction, SSS, 6-1/2" long, 1954 (J199)	35	65	85
MG TF, friction, unknown, 8-1/2" long, 1952 (J198)	50	75	95
MG TF, friction, Bandai, 8" long, 1955 (J200)	95	125	150
MGA, friction, A.T.C., 10" long, 1957 (J201)	175	300	600
Midget Special No. 6, friction, Y Co., 7" long (J291)	200	350	700
Mitsubishi Auto Tricycle, friction, Bandai, 11" long, 1950s (J272)	100	150	300
Mitsubishi Auto Tricycle Leo, friction, Bandai, 5" long, 1950s (J271)	75	100	200
Nash, battery, MSK, 8" long, 1950s (J206)	40	70	90
Nash Ambassador, friction, Sankei Gangu, 8" long, 1956 (J207)	100	125	150
Oldsmobile, friction, Y Co., 11" long, 1952 (J207A)	150	350	500
Oldsmobile Convertible/Wagon, friction, Yonezawa, 12" long, 1961 (J214)	75	125	200
Oldsmobile Sedan, friction, Ichiko/Kanto, 10-1/2" long, 1956 (J208)	200	400	700
Oldsmobile Sedan, friction, Y Co., 16" long, 1958 (J212)	300	400	700
Oldsmobile Sedan, friction, A.T.C., 12" long, 1958 (J210)	200	300	600
Oldsmobile Sedan, friction, Ichiko, 12-1/2" long, 1959 (J213)	75	125	175
Oldsmobile Super 88 Sedan, friction, Masudaya, 16" long, 1956 (J209)	200	300	500
Oldsmobile Super 88 Sedan, friction, A.T.C., 13" long, 1958 (J211)	250	325	425
Oldsmobile Toronado, battery, Bandai, 11" long, 1966 (J215)	65	110	150
Oldsmobile Toronado, friction, Ichiko, 17-1/2" long, 1968 (J216)	300	400	500
Opel Sedan, friction/battery, Yonezawa, 11-1/2" long, 1950s (J217)	70	90	125
Orient Auto Tricycle, friction, Yonezawa, 9" long, 1950s (J273)	75	100	200

Japanese Tin 1956 Pontiac Hardtop, friction, T.N., 8". Photo courtesy Ron Smith

Japanese Tin 1967 Pontiac Firebird, Akasura, friction, 15-1/2". Photo courtesy Ron Smith

Japanese Tin 1967 Pontiac Firebird, Bandai, friction, 10". Photo courtesy Ron Smith

Japanese Tin 1958 Oldsmobile Sedan, friction, A.T.C., 12". Photo courtesy Ron Smith

Japanese Tin 1959 Oldsmobile Sedan, Ichiko, friction, 12-1/2". Photo courtesy Ron Smith

Japanese Tin 1956 Oldsmobile Super 88 Sedan, Masudaya, friction, 16". Photo courtesy Ron Smith

Japanese Tin 1966 Oldsmobile Toronado, Bandai, battery, 11". Photo courtesy Ron Smith

Japanese Tin 1968 Oldsmobile Toronado, Ichiko, friction, 17-1/2". Photo courtesy Ron Smith

Japanese Tin 1953 Packard Convertible/Sedan, Alps, friction, 16". Photo courtesy Ron Smith

Japanese Tin 1957 Packard Hawk Convertible, Schuco, battery, 10-3/4". Photo courtesy Ron Smith

Japanese Tin 1957 Plymouth Fury Hardtop, Y, friction, 11-1/2". Photo courtesy Ron Smith

Japanese Tin 1958 Plymouth Fury, Bandai, friction, 8". Photo courtesy Ron Smith

Japanese Tin 1956 Plymouth Hardtop, friction, 8-1/2". Photo courtesy Ron Smith

Japanese Tin 1956 Plymouth Hardtop, Alps, battery, 12". Photo courtesy Ron Smith

Japanese Tin 1959 Plymouth Hardtop, A.T.C., friction, 10-1/2". Photo courtesy Ron Smith

Japanese Tin 1961 Plymouth Sedan, Ichiko, friction, 12". Photo courtesy Ron Smith

Japanese Tin 1961 Plymouth Station Wagon, Ichiko, friction, 12". Photo courtesy Ron Smith

Japanese Tin 1961 Plymouth T.V. Car, Ichiko, battery, 12". Photo courtesy Ron Smith

Japanese Tin 1960 Renault, Bandai, friction, 7-1/2". Photo courtesy Ron Smith

Japanese Tin Rolls 1960 Royce Silver Coupe Convertible, Bandai, friction, 12". Photo courtesy Ron Smith

Japanese Tin 1960s Rolls Royce Silver Coupe Sedan, Bandai, friction, 12". Photo courtesy Ron Smith

	C6	C8	C10
Packard Convertible/Sedan, friction, Alps, 16" long, 1953 (J222)	500	800	1600
Packard Hawk Convertible, battery, Schuco, 10-3/4" long, 1957 (J223)	300	400	800
Plymouth Convertible, friction, A.T.C., 10-1/2" long, 1959 (J229)	330	770	1100
Plymouth Fury Convertible, Sedan, Wagon, friction, Bandai, 8" long, 1958 (J227)	75	90	165
Plymouth Fury Hardtop, friction, Y Co., 11-1/2" long, 1957 (J226)	300	400	600
Plymouth Futy Hardtop, friction, Kusama, 10" long, 1964 (J233)	60	80	100
Plymouth Hardtop, battery, Alps, 12" long, 1956 (J225)	300	400	800
Plymouth Hardtop, friction, unknown, 8-1/2" long, 1956 (J224)	100	200	300
Plymouth Hardtop, friction, A.T.C., 10-1/2" long, 1959 (J228)	200	400	600
Plymouth Sedan, friction, Ichiko, 12" long, 1961 (J230)	150	300	550
Plymouth Station Wagon, friction, Ichiko, 12" long, 1961 (J231)	150	250	500
Plymouth T.V. Car, battery, Ichiko, 12" long, 1961 (J232)	100	150	300
Pontiac Convertible, friction, KS, 14" long, 1950s (J218B)	150	300	450
Pontiac Coupe, friction, KS, 14" long, 1950s (J218C)	150	300	450
Pontiac Dream Car, friction, Mitsubishi, 10" long, 1950s (J282)	100	300	600
Pontiac Firebird, friction, Bandai, 10" long, 1967 (J220)	30	55	100
Pontiac Firebird, friction, Akasura, 15-1/2" long, 1967 (J219)	200	400	900
Pontiac Firebird (w/wipers), battery, Bandai, 9-1/2" long, 1967 (J221)	40	55	75

	C6	C8	C10
Pontiac Hardtop, friction, TN, 8" long, 1956 (J218D)	150	300	500
Pontiac Hardtop/Convertible, friction, Minister-India, 11" long, new issue, made from old Asahi molds, 1954 (J218A)	10	20	30
Pontiac Star Chief, friction, Asahi, 11" long, 1954 (J218)	250	350	500
Porsche, W/W, Geshia (Ger.), 9" long, 1960s (J233D)	200	400	600
Porsche, wind-up, JNF (Ger.), 9" long, 1960s (J233C)	200	400	600
Porsche, friction, T.T., 9-1/2" long, 1960s (J233B)	75	125	200
Porsche 911, battery, Bandai, 10" long, 1960 (J234)	65	95	125
Porsche 911, friction, T.T., 9-1/2" long, 1960s (J234B)	75	125	200
Porsche Speedster, battery, Distler, 10-1/2" long, 1950s (J235)	200	300	600
Rambler Rebel Station Wagon, friction, Bandai, 12" long, 1960s (J240)	60	90	150
Record Racer NSU, friction, Bandai, 18" long, 1950s (J285)	100	150	250
Renault, friction, Bandai, 7-1/2" long, 1960 (J241)	60	90	120
Rolls Royce, friction, HTC, 6" long, 1960s (J235B)	75	100	150
Rolls Royce (w/Electric Lights), battery, Bandai, 12" long, 1960s (J238)	100	200	400
Rolls Royce Sedan, friction, TN, 10" long, 1960s (J235C)	300	500	800
Rolls Royce Silver Coupe Convertible, friction, Bandai, 12" long, 1960 (J236)	100	150	300
Rolls Royce Silver Coupe Sedan, friction, Bandai, 12" long, 1960s (J237)	100	150	250

Japanese Tin 1960 VW Karmann-Ghia, Bandai, friction, 7". Photo courtesy Ron Smith

Japanese Tin 1960s Volvo, K.S., friction, 7". Photo courtesy Ron Smith

Japanese Tin 1954 Studebaker, Yoshiya, friction, 9". Photo courtesy Ron Smith

Japanese Tin 1950s Volkswagen Convertible, T.N., friction, 9-1/2". Photo courtesy Ron Smith

Japanese Tin 1950s Volvo, wind-up, 11". Photo courtesy Ron Smith

Japanese Tin 1960s Volkswagen, Bandai, battery, 11". Photo courtesy Ron Smith

Japanese Tin 1960s Volkswagen Convertible, Bandai, battery, 11". Photo courtesy Ron Smith

Japanese Tin 1960s Volkswagen with/ without sun roof, Bandai, friction, 15". Photo courtesy Ron Smith

Japanese Tin 1960s Porsche, Geshia German, 9". Photo courtesy Ron Smith

Japanese Tin 1950s Porsche Speedster, battery, Distler, 10-1/2". Photo courtesy Ron Smith

Japanese Tin 1960s Rambler Rebel Station Wagon, Bandai, friction, 12". Photo courtesy Ron Smith

Japanese Tin 1960s Rolls Royce, HTC, friction, 6". Photo courtesy Ron Smith

Japanese Tin 1958 Chevrolet Station Wagon, Bandai, friction, 8". Photo courtesy Ron Smith

Japanese Tin 1960s Studebaker Avanti, Bandai, friction, 8". Photo courtesy Ron Smith

Japanese Tin 1960s Porsche 911, T.T., friction, 9-1/2". Photo courtesy Ron Smith

Japanese Tin 1960s Porsche, T.T., friction, 9-1/2". Photo courtesy Ron Smith

Japanese Tin 1960s Rolls Royce Sedan, TN, friction, 10". Photo courtesy Ron Smith

	C6	C8	C10
Saab 93 B, friction, Bandai, 7" long, 1960s (J244)	40	60	80
Studebaker, friction, Yoshiya, 9" long, 1954 (J243)	150	200	375
Studebaker Avanti, friction, Bandai, 8" long, 1960s (J242)	90	150	225
Subaru 360, friction, Bandai, 7" long, 1960s (J245)	75	100	125
Toyopet Crown, Friciton, Bandai, 9" long, 1960s (J248)	100	200	300
Toyota, friction, Ichiko, 16" long, 1960s (J249)	150	275	325
Toyota 2000 GT, friction, A.T.C., 15" long, 1967 (J250)	150	275	325
Triumph TR-3 Convertible, friction, Bandai, 8" long, 1960s (J246)	50	75	150
Triumph TR-3 Coupe, friction, Bandai, 8" long, 1960s (J247)	50	75	150
Vespa, friction, Bandai, 9" long, 1960s (J251)	50	75	125
Volkswagen, wind-up, German, 6" long, 1950s (J262A)	75	150	300
Volkswagen, battery, Bandai, 10-1/2" long, 1960s (J263)	25	50	75
Volkswagen, battery, Bandai, 11" long, 1960s (J264)	25	50	75
Volkswagen, friction, Bandai, 8" long, 1960s (J262)	25	40	80
Volkswagen Bus, battery, Tipp & Co., 9" long, 1950s (J257)	300	400	600
Volkswagen Bus, Bat/Fric, Bandai, 9-1/2" long, 1960s (J256)	75	125	175
Volkswagen Bus, friction, A.T.C., 12" long, 1960s (J253)	125	175	350

	C6	C8	C10
Volkswagen Bus, friction, Bandai, 8" long, 1960s (J255)	50	60	75
Volkswagen Convertible, friction, T.N., 9-1/2" long, 1950s (J258)	100	150	250
Volkswagen Convertible, battery, Taiyo, 10-1/2" long, 1960s (J261)	25	40	70
Volkswagen Convertible, battery, Bandai, 11" long, 1960s (J260)	110	145	200
Volkswagen Convertible, battery, Bandai, 7-1/2" long, 1960s (J259)	50	70	90
Volkswagen Pickup Truck, friction, Bandai, 8" long, 1960s (J254)	50	60	75
Volkswagen with/without Sun Roof, friction, with Bandai, 15" long, 1960s (J265)	60	90	125
Volvo, wind-up, Sweden, 11" long, 1950s (J265A)	600	1000	2000
Volvo 444 and 445, friction, KS, 7" long, 1960s (J265B)	100	200	350
Volvo P-1800 Coupe, friction, SSS, 11" long, 1960s (J265E)	600	1200	1800
Volvo P-1800 Coupe, friction, Ichiko, 9" long, 1960s (J265C)	200	300	600
Volvo P-1800 Wagon, friction, Ichiko, 9" long, 1960s (J265D)	200	300	600
VW Karmann-Ghia Coupe/Convertible, friction, Bandai, 7" long, 1960 (J252)	100	150	300
Willys Jeep FC - 150 Pickup, friction, T.N. Toy Nomura, 11" long, 1960s (J266)	50	75	95
Zuendapp Janus, friction, Bandai, 8" long, 1950s (J267)	125	150	300

JEP (J DE P)

J de P was founded in 1899 as the *Societe Industrielle de Ferblanterie*. The name was changed to *Jouets de Paris* (J de P) in 1928, as the company introduced a new line of toy cars. Four years later, the name was again changed to *Jouets en Paris* (JEP). This name stayed until 1965, when the company went out of business.

Contributor: Bob Smith, RATS Toy Shows, 255 Tryon Park, Rochester, NY 14609. (585) 288-7153, bird@oldtoysonline.com.

	C6	C8	C10
Autobus, six-wheel, green/cream, clockwork motor, front/rear wheel steering, marked "Madeline-Bastille," c.1928, 10-1/4" long	1400	1800	2300
Bugatti Racer, tin lithographed, clockwork motor, "2," 8-1/2" long	700	900	1150

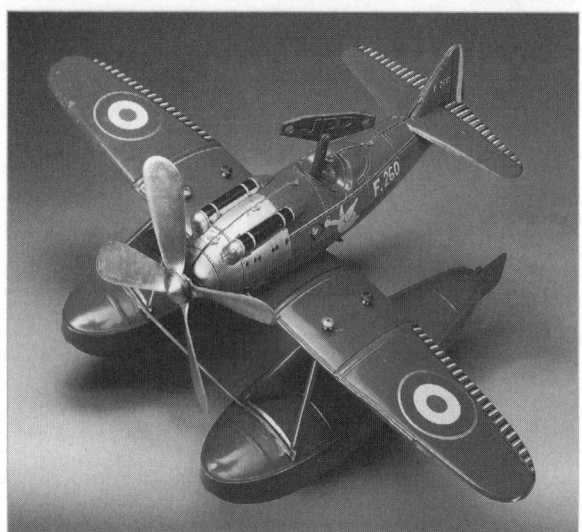

JEP Seaplane, tin wind-up, 13-1/2". Photo courtesy Christie's East.

JEP Bugatti Racer, tin lithographed, clockwork motor, "2" on side, 8-1/2". Photo courtesy Auction Team Breker

JEP Rolls Royce Open Phaeton, steel, electric headlights, clockwork motor, 19-1/2". Photo courtesy Bertoia Auctions

	C6	C8	C10
Bus, wind-up, 10-1/2" long	700	950	1300
Delage Limousine, green and black, clockwork motor, horn, battery-operated spot light, full steering, c.1929, 13-1/2" long	1500	2650	3800
Hispano Suiza, clockwork motor, lights work, 20" long	2200	4200	6800
Peugeot Coupe, clockwork, pre-WWII	500	700	800
Plymouth, wind-up, door opens, 13" long	600	800	1000
Rolls Royce Open Phaeton, clockwork motor, steel, electric headlights, 19-1/2" long	2200	3700	5200
Seaplane, tin wind-up, 13-1/2" long	NPF	NPF	NPF

JEP Hispano Suiza, steel, electric headlights, clockwork motor, 20". Photo courtesy Auction Team Breker

JEP Delage Limousine, green and black, late 1920s, 13-1/2".

JOHNNY LIGHTNING/TOPPER

The Deluxe Reading Company changed its name to "Topper Toys" in the early 1960s. The company introduced its famous line of Johnny Lightning cars in 1969 with 11 models that looked like customized versions of real cars. The line was so popular that 31 new models were introduced in 1970 and 5 more debuted in 1971.

	C6	C8	C10
'32 Roadster, 1969	25	60	125
A.J. Foyt Indy Special, black wall tires, 1970	40	60	250
Al Unser Indy Special, black wall tires, 1970	100	200	500
Baja, 1970	45	125	200
Big Rig, came w/add on extras called Customs; prices reflect fully accessorized cars, 1971	65	150	275
Bubble, Jet Powered, 1970	45	75	150
Bug Bomb, black wall tires, 1970	40	90	225
Condor, black wall tires, 1970	150	250	1200
Custom Camaro, prototype, only six known to exist, 1968-69	n/a	6000	n/a
Custom Charger, prototype, only six known to exist, 1968-69	n/a	6000	n/a
Custom Continental, prototype, only six known to exist, 1968-69	n/a	4000	n/a
Custom Dragster, mirror finish, 1969	150	250	1000
Custom Dragster, w/plastic canopy, 1969	60	150	200
Custom Dragster, without canopy, 1969	35	75	135
Custom El Camino, mirror finish, 1969	200	350	1125

	C6	C8	C10
Custom El Camino, w/opening doors, 1969	150	275	500
Custom El Camino, w/sealed doors, 1969	110	300	500
Custom Eldorado, w/opening doors, 1969	150	275	350
Custom Eldorado, w/sealed doors, 1969	150	300	1000
Custom Ferrari, w/opening doors, 1969	150	275	500
Custom Ferrari, w/opening doors, mirror finish, 1969	300	450	1000
Custom Ferrari, w/sealed doors, 1969	40	80	130
Custom GTO, mirror finish, 1969	200	475	1100
Custom GTO, w/opening doors, 1969	200	450	1500
Custom GTO, w/sealed doors, 1969	200	450	1700
Custom Mako Shark, w/opening doors, 1969	125	350	500
Custom Mako Shark, w/opening doors, mirror finish, 1969	200	500	1800
Custom Mako Shark, w/sealed doors, 1969	40	75	225
Custom Mustang, prototype, only six known to exist, 1968-69	n/a	6000	n/a
Custom Spoiler, black wall tires, 1970	35	65	150
Custom T-Bird, mirror finish, 1969	200	400	5000
Custom T-Bird, w/opening doors, 1969	100	250	475
Custom T-Bird, w/sealed doors, 1969	150	300	800
Custom Toronado, mirror finish, 1969	450	650	2000
Custom Toronado, w/opening doors, 1969	225	400	1000
Custom Toronado, w/sealed doors, 1969	300	500	1500
Custom Turbine, mirror finish, 1969	150	225	500
Custom Turbine, red, black, white painted interior, 1969	50	150	200

	C6	C8	C10
Custom Turbine, w/unpainted interior, 1969	30	60	125
Custom XKE, w/opening doors, 1969	150	275	475
Custom XKE, w/opening doors, mirror finish, 1969	300	450	800
Custom XKE, w/sealed doors, 1969	35	80	110
Double Trouble, black wall tires, 1970	75	180	1500
Flame Out, black wall tires, 1970	60	125	350
Flying Needle, Jet Powered, 1970	45	100	225
Frantic Ferrari, unpainted base, silver exposed engine, 1970	35	50	90
Glasser, Jet Powered, 1970	40	75	150
Hairy Hauler, came w/add on extras called Customs; prices reflect fully accessorized cars, 1971	65	150	275
Jumpin' Jag, black wall tires, 1970	35	80	175
Leapin' Limo, black wall tires, 1970	50	125	400
Mad Maverick, black wall tires, 1970	75	150	450
Monster, Jet Powered, 1970	40	75	150
Movin' Van, black wall tires, 1970	35	65	90
Nucleon, black wall tires, 1970	40	100	225
Parnelli Jones Indy Special, black wall tires, 1970	45	90	250

	C6	C8	C10
Pipe Dream, came w/add on extras called Customs; prices reflect fully accessorized cars, 1971	65	150	275
Sand Stormer, black roof, black wall tires, 1970	50	100	200
Sand Stormer, black wall tires, 1970	20	40	90
Screamer, Jet Powered, 1970	45	90	200
Sling Shot, black wall tires, 1970	50	95	250
Smuggler, black wall tires, 1970	35	75	150
Stiletto, black wall tires, 1970	60	110	300
TNT, black wall tires, 1970	40	75	175
Triple Threat, black wall tires, 1970	40	90	200
Twin Blaster, came w/add on extras called Customs; prices reflect fully accessorized cars, 1971	65	150	275
Vicious Vette, black wall tires, 1970	35	80	225
Vulture w/wing, black wall tires, 1970	75	130	500
Wasp, black wall tires, 1970	75	125	400
Wedge, Jet Powered, 1970	45	80	200
Whistler, black wall tires, 1970	75	125	300
Wild Winner, came w/add on extras called Customs; prices reflect fully accessorized cars, 1971	60	125	250

JONES & BIXLER

In 1899, Charles A. Jones and Louis S. Bixler founded the Jones & Bixler Co. Located in Freemansburg, Penn., the company began its cast-iron vehicle toys in 1903 and the company continued until 1914.

	C6	C8	C10
Auto, cast iron, driver, rider	1200	2000	3200
Express J & B Truck, 15-1/2" long	900	1350	1800
Peerless Racer, cast iron, 5" long	500	800	1100
Red Devil Touring Car, cast iron, driver, 8-1/2" long	550	850	1200

Jones & Bixler Express J&B Truck, 15-1/2". Photo courtesy Sotheby's New York

JUDY COMPANY, THE

The Judy Company of Minneapolis made educational toys, including a farm set called "Happy's Farm Family" (patented in 1945) which included a solid rubber car, pickup truck, and tractor, along with human and animal figures.

Contributor: Dave Leopard, 2507 Feather Run Trail, West Columbia, SC 29169-4915.

Judy vehicles, L to R: Sedan (JA01), Pickup Truck (JT01). Photo courtesy Dave Leopard from his book, Rubber Toy Vehicles

Judy vehicles at top of box, L to R: (JF01), (JT01), (JA01). Photo courtesy Dave Leopard from his book, Rubber Toy Vehicles

	C6	C8	C10
Farm Tractor, two-dimensional (part of set), solid rubber, 3-1/2" long (JF01) ..	15	20	25
Pickup Truck, two-dimensional (part of set), solid rubber, 5-1/4" long (JT01) ..	15	20	25

	C6	C8	C10
Sedan, two-dimensional, (part of set), solid rubber, 5-1/4" long (JA01)	15	20	25
Cadillac and Trailer, w/furniture, bushes, plastic, 1950, car is 9" long..................	10	20	30

KAHN

	C6	C8	C10
Cadillac and Trailer, w/furniture, bushes, plastic, 1950, car is 9" long..................	10	20	30

Kahn Sedan, plastic, without the house trailer sold with it, 9" long. Photo courtesy John McCurdy

KANSAS TOY & NOVELTY COMPANY

Arthur Haynes, an auto mechanic, began molding toys in his Clifton, Kansas, shed for local stores in 1923. With clever hands and an artist's eye, he charmed his friends and local townspeople with his bright-colored toys. He made his patterns from advertising pictures, from local vehicles and probably from other makes of toys, such as Tootsietoy. He made his own production tools. His range was diverse, for he made miniatures of aircraft, autos, trains, farm equipment, zeppelin, and a few animals, novelties, and charms.

Haynes believed that he invented the hollow-casting of metal toys, so he must have started with solid toys. One day, he dropped his full mold, spilling its hot metal. To his delight he had a perfect, hollow toy vehicle, with promise of savings of metal and shipping costs.

This was a town enterprise from the beginning. Jess Foster, news editor, helped with alloy mixtures; Mr. Hadsell, Union Pacific agent, suggested they send samples to Woolworth's in New York. Clayton D. Young, a traveling salesman, saw the toys, joined the company, and built a profitable business with the chain stores, including Kress, Kresge, and Sears-Roebuck; he later became a partner. At its peak of international sales in the late 1920s, the firm employed as many as sixty-five in two shifts during the Christmas-order season.

They were young people who had grown up together, this familiarity lead to an informal and relaxed workplace. This informality was reflected in the local name for the plant, "The Hoopie Factory." Two or three of their early toys, No. 26 and No. 33, were stripdowns—hoopies, probably raced locally. Whether "Whoopee," tractor toy No. 48, was a local spelling of this or whether it celebrated a fat, cheering order, is not known.

Teamwork was a must, for a molder, according to Ernest Istas, could produce 2,000 toys a day. Helen Istas was the secretary; Bill Haynes was another molder, showing the family nature of the work force, with its clippers (trimmers), painters, clampers (axles), and boxers. Butch Morgison, one of our sources, was each of these during his long career with the company. It was discovered that Clayton Stevenson (see Lincoln White Metal Works and Midwest Toy), a basement toymaker and then employee of a foundry, furnished some molds and patterns. He must have created those realistic designs from three-piece molds with their intricate frontends (see No. 8, No. 58, No. 60, No. 80, No. 88, No. 91). These features must have slowed production and added to costs, but made for collector value and rarity.

During its good years, Kansas Toy & Novelty created more designs and produced more toys than

Kansas Toy, L to R, Top: KTV14, KTV35, KTTV69. Middle: Best "85," KTV52, KTTV71. Bottom: Craftoy?, KTV24, Best "97." Photo courtesy Fred Maxwell

Kansas Toy, L to R, Top: KTV24, KTV26, KTV37. 2nd Row: KTV27, KTV29. 3rd Row: KTV 38, KTV40, KTV43. 4th Row: KTV45, KTV52, KTV53. Bottom: KTV62 (small version?), KTTV67. Photo courtesy Fred Maxwell

any producer of white-metal toys except Barclay. Young withdrew his share and retired around 1930. With the loss of these assets and the onset of the Depression, the company went downhill. George Hoeffer reorganized the company and moved the factory down the road, but this effort lasted only a few months. An era was coming to an end. This later history is scanty, but there is evidence that Haynes kept trying until toy No. 100 in 1935.

High-numbered toys are rare. Changes of wheel types suggest that Haynes was having problems. Perhaps he had always overreached, for looking back at the diversity of his toys and novelties, it is remarkable from a few mechanics in a small Midwest town.

Contributor: Perry R. Eichor, 703 North Almond Drive, Simpsonville, SC, 29681 and the late Fred Maxwell.

	C6	C8	C10
Army Tank, No. "74"; marked "US Army," WWI-type, high turret, large front, small rear wheels; olive drab color; 2-1/4" long (KTV056)	20	30	40
Box Car, No. "38"; marked "KT & N RR," Union Pacific shield (possibly an early promotional), four MDW, 3-1/4" long (KTV029)	15	20	30
Caboose, No. "40"; marked "KT & N RR," stack, brakeman's cab, MDW, 2-3/4" long (KTV031)	15	25	35
Canoe, No. "50"; two paddling Indians "Rain-in-the-Face," and "Chief Big Foot," 4 wheels, 3-1/2" long (KTV073)	NPF	NPF	NPF
Coupe, no number; crude, slant roof, no head lamps, shallow rear body, no fenders, lacquer; possibly first "hoopie"			

Kansas Toy Molds

Because KT&N founded a molding dynasty, with its molds still in use today after passing through several companies, extra details and comments have been included to eliminate collector and dealer confusion. Many Kansas Toy & Novelty toys were not numbered, some of them were twins of the numbered versions; and not all numbered toys were Kansas Toy & Novelty.

- Some toys were made in two or three versions/variations.
- Some toys were made in two or three sizes (5 cents, 10 cents, and 15 cents)
- Most wheels were metal (disk or simulated spoked or wire. Tractor/farm wheels were large disk or open spoke with wide rims; a unique track laying version with rubber tracks used metal or wood wheels.) Rubber tires on wood hubs (popularized by Tootsietoy Grahams in 1932) were tried on No. 75 and later; followed by soft rubber (balloon) wheels and hard-rubber white discs with painted black tires.
- Many had string-pull loops or knobs on the lower grille.
- All colors were used, including gold, silver, and pink.
- A few were found with bi-colored bodies (may have been salesman samples). Many early toys were finished in Egyptian lacquer, so this the bright metal gleamed through. A mint example with this unique finish has a modern, glittery look.
- "Made in USA" embossing is a clue to Best Toy and later, as this copyright addition came from laws of the mid-1930s. Black rubber tires were used later by Ralstoy and others.
- For Kansas Toy & Novelty airplanes, cannon, and novelties, see "Aircraft" and "Miscellaneous" sections in *O'Brien's Collecting Toys*. For additional pictures and different views see "Best Toy & Novelty" in this book.
- The "dynasty" mentioned above included Best Toy, Ralstoy, Craftoy, and Eccles Bros., in that order. The Ralstoy of today, with its line of die-cast trucks, is the same company on a different track.
- The following sequential listing has been carefully researched, but additions are still trickling in. The first toy is controversial. One source said it was a solid casting; probably true, but did it ever reach the market? Some said it was the large Indy racer; others said it was the midget racer without a driver.

Note: There are so few original Kansas Toy & Novelty toys with higher numbers in today's market, compared to later reproductions, that it is not known which went into production. They are shown earlier in this book as Best Toys to save duplication.

ABBREVIATIONS

HG	horizontal grille pattern	**SM**	sidemounted spare
HL	horizontal hood louvers	**SP**	string-pull knob in hand crank area
HO	hood cap, Motometer or ornament	**T**	external trunk
L	lacquer finish	**UV**	unnumbered version
LI	landau irons on convertibles	**VG**	vertical grille pattern
MDW	metal disc wheels	**VL**	vertical hood louvers
MDSW	metal disc solid spokes	**WS, W/S**	windshield
MDWBT	wheels with black painted tires	**WV**	windshield visor
MSW	metal open spoke wheels	**WHRT**	wooden hubs, rubber tires
MWW	metal simulated wire wheels	**WRDW**	white hard rubber disc wheels
OW	open windows	**WRW**	white soft rubber wheels
RM	rearmount spare tire/wheel		(balloon tires)

	C6	C8	C10
or stripdown made; 3-1/8" long (KTV004)	40	75	100
Coupe, No. "35"; convertible, LI, VL, HG, HO, RM, MWW; 2-1/4" long; also an UV (KTV026)	30	55	75
Coupe, No. "66"; stream-lined three-wheeler, six OW, MWW; 3-1/2" long (KTV051)	60	80	100
Coupe, No. "8"; Cadillac Convertible (?), three-piece mold casting different from the three No. 8 versions, basic body suggests same pattern-maker, if not Kansas Toy & Novelty, then it is Midwest Toy; rectangular VG, HO, no headlamps, VL, MWW, SM, WV, two OW, body trim, kickplates, door handles, LI, T, MDWBT, rare, 3-1/4" long (KTV006)	40	60	80
Coupe, No. "8"; Convertible, LI, VL, HG, WV, SP, RM, MWW, no HO, no headlamps, enamel finish. 3-1/8" long; there is also UV w/"Chrysler," headlamps and HO, or w/MDSW (KTV007)	20	30	50
Coupe, No. "8"; trunk Convertible, T, HO, VG, SM, MDW; 3-1/8"-long; Note: No. 8 is the lowest numbered vehicle found. Its realistic, high quality signals the ending of a novice			

Kansas Toy, L to R, Top: KTV33A, Ralstoy (?), KTV38. Middle: KTV23, KTV21, KTV34. Bottom: KTV46, KTV18, KTV47. Photo courtesy Perry Eichor

	C6	C8	C10
toymaker's experimental phase (KTV008)	40	60	80
Dirt scraper, No. "65"; 1-7/8" blade, adjustable, on same frame as number 62; 3-5/8" long; Note: This is part of a unique towed farm set w/several hinged or moving parts, each a different color and large 1-1/4" spoked tractor wheels (KTV050)	40	60	80
Dirt Tumble, No. "64"; adjustable dumping scoop, 1-1/2" wide on same frame as No. 62, six pieces, four colors; 4" long; Note: This is part of a unique towed farm set w/several hinged or moving parts, each a different color and large 1-1/4" spoked tractor wheels (KTV049)	50	75	100
Disk Harrow, No. "62"; eight disks on same 1-5/8" wide frame as No. 61; thirteen pieces, including disks and wheels, four colors, 4" long. Note: This is part of a unique towed farm set w/several hinged or moving parts, each a different color and large 1-1/4" spoked tractor wheels. Has been seen w/tin snap-on seats. (KTV047)	40	60	80
Dump Truck, No. "42"; Ford (?), driver, no cab, diamond emblem on hinged dump body, VL, HG, SP, MWW; 3-1/2" long (KTV033)	40	60	80
Farm Tractor, no number; "Fordson" on radiator and crankcase, VG and towhook, w/small plain MDW, three-piece molded grille; 2-5/8" long (KTV018)	25	35	45
Farm Tractor, No. "17"; "Fordson", driver, HG, crank, no tow hook, large 1-1/4" and 3/4" MDW w/four holes in disks; also found w/same size six spoke wheels; 2-7/8" long; see No. 57 (KTV017)	25	35	45
Farm Tractor, No. "48"; "Caterpillar," "Whoopee," driver, VL, HG, HO, SP, tow loop, w/larger-3/4" track-laying wheels, metal or wood, for rubber track (KTV036A)	25	40	55

Kansas Toy, Top: KTV41. Bottom: L to R: KTV53 (repro), trailer for KTV41. Photo courtesy Fred Maxwell

Kansas Toy towed implements, Top: KTV46, KTV49. Bottom: KTV47, KTV50. Photo courtesy Fred Maxwell

Kansas Toy Roadster, KTV64, open sport Duesenberg No. 77. Photo courtesy Craig A. Clark

Kansas Toy, Top: Roadsters KTV39 and KTV40. Bottom: Coupe KTV26 and Sedanette KTV43. Photo courtesy Fred Maxwell

Kansas Toy autos with hard rubber wheels, Top: KTTV59, KTV45. Middle: KTTV63. Bottom: KTTV67, KTTV72. Photo courtesy Fred Maxwell

Kansas Toy vehicles with wood hubs, Top: KTTV64, KTTV65. Bottom: KTTV66, KT&N #85. Photo courtesy Fred Maxwell

Kansas Toy Overland Bus, KTV12. Photo courtesy Bob Ackerly

Kansas Toy, L to R: Tour Bus KTV37 and Fire Engine KTV53. Photo courtesy Fred Maxwell

Kansas Toy Fordson Tractor, KTV17. Photo courtesy Fred Maxwell

Noted for its outstanding cast-iron vehicles, A.C. Williams released this 6-1/2-inch long Sedan around 1930 in assorted colors, $475. *Photo courtesy Al Kasishke*

American National was a Toledo, Ohio, firm that produced pressed-steel toys and pedal cars before World War II. This American Railway Express is 27 inches long, $2,400. *Photo courtesy Bertoia Auctions*

The Acme Plastics Co. produced plastic toys until the company was purchased by Thomas Toys in 1950. This is the No. 27 Sedan from 1947, $22. *KP Photo courtesy Karen O'Brien*

Located in Freeport, Ill., the Arcade Mfg. Co. was famous for its cast-iron toys. In 1941, Arcade released the No. 7100 International Dump Truck, $1,250. *Photo courtesy Tim Oei*

The All-American Toy Co. of Salem, Ore., made pressed-steel trucks from 1948-55. This is its C-5 Cattle Liner, $925. *Photo courtesy Bob Smith*

In return for the exclusive rights to manufacture cast-iron replicas of real Yellow Cabs, Arcade granted the firm permission to use the toys in its advertising. This version was released in 1932 and once brought $62,000 at auction. *Photo courtesy Bertoia Auctions*

Specializing in inexpensive dime-store toys, the Allied Molding Co. used plastic exclusively. The Furniture Moving Van features a clear "Viso Box" trailer, $20. *Photo courtesy Dave Leopard*

Dependable Mack trucks were a favorite of pre-World War II toymakers. On the left is Arcade's Mack Ice Truck, No. 257, from 1932. On the right is an earlier version of the No. 257 that was released in 1930. *Photo courtesy Bertoia Auctions*

Cartoonist Sidney Smith was hired by *Chicago Tribune* editor Capt. Joseph Patterson to write and draw the unheroic adventures of an ordinary family, The Gumps, in 1917. The strip's success led to toys based on its characters. The family's chinless patriarch was immortalized in cast iron when Arcade released the Andy Gump Car in the 1920s, $3,500. *Photo courtesy Bertoia Auctions*

This Arnold Mac 700 Motorcycle is propelled by a wind-up motor, $650. *Photo courtesy Kent M. Comstock*

The Auburn Rubber Co. was the world's largest producer of rubber toys. This 1936 Cord was the first automobile model the Auburn, Ind.-based firm released, $150. *Photo courtesy Max Heiss*

The Banner Plastics Co. also worked in pressed steel, releasing this Sand and Gravel truck in the late 1940s, $225.
Photo courtesy John Taylor

Banner moved from the Bronx to Paterson, N. J., in 1950. It was just about the same time that the Cross Country Express was released, $275. *Photo courtesy John Taylor*

Besides its toy soldiers, Barclay was a leading producer of lead-alloy dime-store vehicles in the pre-WWII period. This Stake Truck (BV168) was released in 1936.

The Bing Toy Works was one of Germany's finest tin toy manufacturers. Here is the Bing Yellow Taxi, circa 1924, $2,200. *Photo courtesy Bob Smith*

Bing's Model T Coupe and Roadster were released around 1924 and are each 6-1/2-inches long, $1,200 and $1,300, respectively. *Photo courtesy Len Rosenberg*

Breslin was a Canadian firm that produced copies of Barclay and Manoil lead-alloy toys. Shown here are the Tank and Motorized Machine Gunner, $50 each. *Photo courtesy Hank Anton*

Swedish toymaker Ivar Bengtsson established his workshop in 1884, and his sons later renamed the company Brio. Fine wooden toys are a Brio hallmark, as evidenced by this striking Ladder Truck. *Photo courtesy Perry Eichor*

High-quality 1:43-scale white-metal models are the stock-in-trade of Brooklin Models, which was named for a suburb of Ontario, Canada. This is the Brooklin 1950 Mercury Convertible Indianapolis 500 Pace Car, $85. *Photo courtesy Dennis Doty*

Another favorite from Brooklin is this 1936 Stout Scarab, $85. *KP Photo courtesy Karen O'Brien*

Buddy "L" toys were first manufactured by the Moline Pressed Steel Co. in 1921. The No. 201 "Ratchet" Dump Truck was produced from 1921-30, $1,250. *Photo courtesy Joe and Sharon Freed*

Buddy "L" trucks manufactured before World War II are listed under the "Large Trucks" heading in that chapter. On top is the Buddy "L" Baggage Truck No. 203B that was manufactured from 1929-31, $3,500. The bottom truck is the Buddy "L" Auto Wrecker No. 209 released from 1928-31, $4,500. *Photo courtesy Bertoia Auctions*

English tinplate car manufacturer Burnett produced its toys from the turn of the 20th century into the Depression-era, when it was purchased by Chad Valley. The Burnett Roadster appeared circa 1925 and features a clockwork motor, $1,200. *Photo courtesy Bob Smith*

The Charles A. Wood Novelty Co. was one of the longest-lived of the slush-mold toy companies. Founded around 1925, the firm fell victim to the materials shortages of World War II. The C.A.W. Fuel Tanker has three tanks and painted tires, $45. *Photo courtesy Bob Ackerly*

The most desirable of the pre-WWII German tinplate toy car manufacturers, Carrette toys feature exceptional detail. This Limousine features a clockwork motor and is 12-1/2″ long, $5,000. *Photo courtesy Bertoia Auctions*

The Champion Hardware Co. only produced its cast-iron toys during the Depression years. At left is the Policeman on motorcycle #2, $400; at right is #3, $425. *Photo courtesy Kent M. Comstock*

The J. Chein (pronounced "chain") Co. was the master of tin-litho toys. The Hercules line of trucks was introduced in 1926. This is the Chein Hercules Mack Motor Express Truck, $1,450. *Photo courtesy Bob Smith*

The David P. Clark & Co. was founded in 1898 and famous for its flywheel friction motor that propelled its toy vehicles as found in this Electric Runabout, circa 1902, $1,300. *Photo courtesy Bob Smith*

Another example of the fine craftsmanship of the David P. Clark & Co. is this Fire Engine Steam Pumper, circa 1908, $700. *Photo courtesy Bob Smith*

Corgi released its first die-cast vehicles in 1956. This 1974 release is a Citroen SM, #284. The 1:43-scale car features Whizzwheels—a compromise in realism made in 1970 to offset the speedy trends established by Mattel's Hot Wheels cars, $40. *KP photo courtesy Karen O'Brien*

In 1958, Studebaker produced only 858 Golden Hawk automobiles. Corgi's 1:43-scale Studebaker Golden Hawk, #211S, was produced from 1960-63, $180. *Photo courtesy Dr. Douglas Sadecky*

The Courtland Mfg. Co. released its first toy, a 12″ wooden tractor/trailer, in 1944 and soon followed with a line of pressed-steel trucks. This is the Courtland Mechanical Black Diamond Coal Truck, $300. *Photo courtesy Joe and Sharon Freed*

Like so many other toy companies of the post-WWII era, Courtland included a space toy in its lineup to appeal to the widest audience. The Courtland Space Rocket Patrol Car, #4060, has a friction motor and was released in 1952, $250. *Photo courtesy Joe and Sharon Freed*

Craftoy was a pre-WWII producer of slush-mold metal dime-store vehicles. This is its Speed Car No. 103, $85.
Photo courtesy Perry Eichor

Japanese tin toy manufacturer Cragstan produced numerous highly-detailed toys in the post-WWII period. This friction-powered Yellow Cab is a fine indication of Cragstan's talents with tin lithography, $85.

David P. Clark founded the Dayton Friction Toy Works after William Scheible purchased Clark's half of the David P. Clark Co. This is his 13-1/4-inch long Seven Passenger Touring Car, circa 1909, $300.
Photo courtesy Bob Smith

Although few Dent toys feature company markings, their finely-detailed castings separate Dent toys from other cast-iron toymakers. Left to right: Touring Car, 9-1/4″ long, $1,200; Touring Car, 12″ long, $1,100. *Photo courtesy Bertoia Auctions*

Dinky die-cast vehicles were first released in 1933 to complement model train layouts. Their popularity soared when the military vehicles were issued in 1937. This assortment of Dinky vehicles includes, Leyland Cement Wagon, $250; Mighty Antar w/Propeller, $400; Guy Slumberland Van, 1949-52, $575.

German manufacturer Distler specialized in toy trains and vehicles in the post-WWII period. Here is the rare yellow U.S. version of the Distler BMW Wanderer windup, $500. *Photo courtesy Tim Oei*

Heavy-gauge pressed-steel construction toys were a specialty of the Dopke Model Toy Co. Their Wookdridge Earth Hauler, #2000, was released from 1946-49, $350.

Based in Oakland, Calif., the Drudge Bros. Mfg. Co. released its Hyster Lumber Carrier in 1948, $325. *Photo courtesy Tim Oei*

Dunwell released its pressed-steel trucks from 1953-58, making examples difficult to find today. Here is the Dunwell Red Star Express Lines Truck, $675. *Photo courtesy Tim Oei*

Erie enjoyed only a brief production period for its vehicle toys including this Champion Coal Truck, circa 1935, $105. *Photo courtesy John Taylor*

The Ertl Co. has released a seemingly limitless variety of toys in its 60-year history. Ertl's affordable pressed-steel trucks like this Van Lines box truck have held their value nicely, $225. *Photo courtesy Bob Smith*

The Heinrich Fischer & Co. was well-known for its high-quality tin vehicles and its "Nifty" line of tin toys. The Fischer Torpedo is 8-inches long, and has a clockwork motor, $1,375. *Photo courtesy Bob Smith*

The Freidag Mfg. Co. was located in Freeport, Ill., and produced cast-iron vehicles before falling victim to the Depression. Left to right: Pickup Truck 7-1/2″ long, $1,000; Panel Delivery Truck 7-1/2″ long, $3,200. *Photo courtesy Bertoia Auctions*

The manufacturer of this "Futuristic" Coupe with fin (FU2) has the black rubber tires that would identify it as a post-WWII creation, although its manufacturer is unknown. Anyone? *Photo courtesy Dave Leopard*

Founded in 1882, Gama was known for the intricate mechanical clockwork motors in its tin toys. This is the prewar Gama No. 70 Tank (GT18), $175. *Photo courtesy Jack Matthews*

The Girard Model Works specialized in mechanical wind-up toys. Louis Marx was once the sales manager for the firm. This is the rare Girard Wrecker Truck, $600. *Photo courtesy John Taylor*

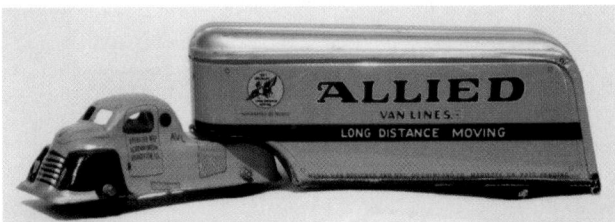

Grimland was based in Marietta, Ga. Its Allied Van Lines truck measured 7-1/2″ long, $115. *Photo courtesy John Taylor*

The Gunthermann Vis-à-Vis features a wind-up motor and driver. It measured 10-1/4″ long, $3,100. *Photo courtesy Bertoia Auctions*

Hoge Mfg. Co. toys were only produced from 1931-39, making them rare finds today. This is the 15-inch long Hoge Fire Chief Car, $650. *Photo courtesy Bob Smith*

Goodee vehicles were produced in just two sizes—3 and 6 inches in length. Here is the Goodee 1953 GMC Pickup, large and small versions; $15 each. *Photo courtesy Dave Leopard*

Gunthermann toys are identified by their "SG" logo that was derived from the founder's initials. This TwoWay Limousine/Touring Car was released in the 1920s and is 10-1/4″ long, $2,100. *Photo courtesy Bob Smith*

The Amerada Hess Corp. released its first promotional toy in 1964 and continues to produce them annually. Here is the Hess Promotional Toy 1991 Race Car Transporter, $50. *Photo courtesy John and Suzanne Adivari*

In 1968, Mattel changed the face of die-cast toys forever. It released 16 1:64-scale "hot rod" cars, some of which were based on real cars of the day. Others were pure fantasy. This Hot Wheels Redlines Custom Firebird was based on the Pontiac Firebird, $250. *KP photo courtesy Tom Michael*

An instant hit with kids and collectors, Hot Wheels cars featured a unique wheel/axle design that allowed the cars to travel faster than any other die-cast car on the market at the time. This Hot Wheels Redlines Mantis was released in 1970, $60. *KP photo courtesy Tom Michael*

Called "Redlines" because of the distinctive redwall present on the tires, these early Hot Wheels cars are the favorite of collectors. The Hot Wheels Redlines Bugeye debuted in 1971, $75. *KP photo courtesy Tom Michael*

Hot Wheels Redlines were popular with girls, too. I still have the Paddy Wagon that I played with as a kid, but mine isn't in as nice condition as this example, $75. *KP photo courtesy Tom Michael*

The Hubley Mfg. Co. embraced the use of plastics in its post-WWII toys. This Hubley Auto Transport with a pair of Cadillacs displays the same attention to detail that characterized the firm's prewar toys, $160. *Photo courtesy Terry Sells*

The Hubley Mfg. Co. was established in 1892 and was known for its fine cast-iron toys, including this 7-inch long "10 Ton" Stake Truck, $600. *Photo courtesy Bob Smith*

This Hubley Packard from 1929 was cast in 15 different parts and measures 11″ long. This rarity achieved $16,000 at auction and is one of the "Holy Grails" of Hubley collecting.
Photo courtesy Bertoia Auctions

Detailed casting techniques led to outstanding motorcycle replicas including this 9-inch long Hubley Motorcycle (HM21) with two removable Policemen, $1,200. *Photo courtesy Kent M. Comstock*

Ideal's toy production soared in the post-WWII era, as the company embraced plastics and released a wide variety of games and toys. Here is the Ideal Turbo-Jet Car No. 4867, $155. *Photo courtesy Tim Oei*

The Irwin Toy Corp. was another manufacturer that produced plastic vehicles. Its State Police Car featured a friction motor and was 6-1/2″ long, $30. *Photo courtesy Ron Fink*

Based in Wilkinsburg, Pa., the Jane Francis Co. specialized in stuffed toys and released a line of die-cast vehicles in 1945. Here is the Jane Francis Gulf Truck (JF05), $75. *Photo courtesy Dave Leopard*

The wild success of 1966's *Batman* television series sent toy manufactures worldwide scrambling to produce related toys. Appearing in the Japanese Battery-Operated Vehicles chapter is this colorful Batmobile, $400. *Photo courtesy Heinz Mueller*

Bandai cars are distinguishable by a "B" on the baseplate. In the Japanese Tin Cars chapter is this friction-motored Renault (J241) from Bandai. Released in 1960, this car is 7-1/2″ long, $120. *Photo courtesy Ron Smith*

Incorporated in 1899, JEP (J de P) produced elegant tin cars with clockwork motors. This is the 13-1/2-inch long JEP Delage Limousine circa 1929, $3,600. *Photo courtesy Bob Smith*

Topper Toys proved that Mattel wasn't the only company that could release a successful 1:64-scale die-cast line in 1969, when the Johnny Lightning series debuted. This Johnny Lightning Sand Stormer was issued in 1970.

Known to collectors as Johnny Lightning/Topper cars, its short-lived production period make them rare and highly desirable today. An icon of the line is the futuristic Johnny Lightning Nucleon from 1970, $225.

The humble beginnings of the Kansas Toy & Novelty Co. in the garage shop of founder Arthur Haynes gave the slush-mold toys their charm. Here is the Kansas Toy Sedanette No. 58, (KTV43), $45. *Photo courtesy Ferd Zegel*

Based in Nuremburg, Germany, Karl Bub produced some of the finest tin automobiles prior to World War II. This 14-inch long Karl Bub Limousine is circa 1925, $7,500. *Photo courtesy Bob Smith*

Kelmet based many of its trucks off of the design of 1920s-era White trucks. Made of heavy steel, they were the toy equivalent of their workhorse inspirations. This is the Kelmet No. 501 Big Boy White Dump Truck, $2,700. *Photo courtesy Joe and Sharon Freed*

Kenton is known for its quality cast-iron vehicle toys and its famous line of Gene Autry cap pistols. Left to right: 1926 Coupe, 10″ long, $9,000; 1923 Sedan, 10″ long, $6,000; 1926 Sedan, 10-1/4″ long, $15,000. *Photo courtesy Bertoia Auctions*

You never know what you'll see at your local toy show. Connie Foundos walked into the Portage, Ind., show last spring with this nice Keystone Water Tower Pump truck, $1,500.
Photo courtesy Karen O'Brien

In 1928, Kilgore began making cast-iron toys in its Westerville, Ohio, plant, and later introduced plastic toys to its line. This is the Kilgore Motorcycle (KM7), $750. *Photo courtesy Kent M. Comstock*

Kingsbury was one of only a few manufacturers to place motors in its pressed-steel toys. Here is the rare Kingsbury Fire Chief Car, $2,000. *Photo courtesy Bob Smith*

Made in Lansing, Iowa, Slik-Toys were made of aluminum or plastic. Left to right: Pickup No. 9703, $30; Tank Truck No. 9705, $30; Sedan No. 9702, $30. *Photo courtesy Dave Leopard*

Lapin specialized in plastic toys and was among the first to use plastic before World War II. This assortment of Chevrolet Stake Trucks was available from 1939-54, $25 each.
Photo courtesy Bob and Alice Wagner

Ernst Paul Lehmann began production of his mechanical tin vehicles in 1881. Top row left to right: Gnom Series BV-Aral Tanker, 4-1/2″, $600; Gnom Series Opel Dump Truck, 4-1/2″, $550. Bottom row left to right: Gnom Series Racing Car, 4-1/2″, $650; Gnom Series Sedan, $500. *Photo courtesy Bob Smith*

A postwar producer of pressed-steel trucks, Lincoln Toys was based in Walkerville, Ontario, Canada. This is the 14-inch long Lincoln Toys Sand Truck Dump, $225. *Photo courtesy Bob Smith*

Using three-piece molds to create greater detail in its slush-mold dime-store toys, Lincoln Metal Works of Lincoln, Neb., produced some of the finest castings in the industry. This Bluebird Speed Car, (LWV3), is 4″ long, $110. *Photo courtesy John Taylor*

Founded in 1906, Lineol was known for its authentically detailed tin military vehicles. The Lineol No. 1218 Bridge Truck is a rare treat, $6,500. *Photo courtesy Jack Matthews*

My fondness for Canadian-owned Londontoys began at the Iola Car Show when I found this Fire Engine, $25. *KP photo courtesy Karen O'Brien*

A good relationship with a favorite toy dealer can lead to some terrific additions to your collection. Such was the case at the Toledo Toy Show last year when I ran into that same dealer from the Iola show. This gorgeous Londontoy Bus appeared from under his table and went home with me, $55. *KP photo courtesy Karen O'Brien*

The storied history of Louis Marx and the toy empire he created and maintained through the 20th century is the stuff of legend. This is the Marx Merchants Transfer truck from 1929, $700. *Photo courtesy Bob Smith*

Louis Marx incorporated his company in 1921 and based his early designs on those of the Strauss Co. The endless variety of Marx toys included military toys like this battery-operated Marx Combat Tank, "U.S. Tank Division," $45. *Photo courtesy Heinz Mueller*

Early Marx toys were less detailed than their European counterparts, but priced for mass consumption. Featuring battery-powered headlights, the Marx Electric Motor Driven Coupe, circa 1933, was 15″ long, $850. *Photo courtesy Bob Smith*

While perusing a toy show for his favorite pressed-steel Tonka trucks, my dad couldn't resist this strikingly colorful Marx Lumar Van Lines truck, $325. *KP photo courtesy Ron O'Brien*

The Lesney Co. debuted its Matchbox cars in 1953 with the Coronation coach. The miniature replicas of real vehicles quickly caught on. This is the Matchbox Regular Wheels Iron Fairy Crane from 1969-70, $18. *KP Photo courtesy George Cuhaj*

The term "Regular Wheels" describes Matchbox cars produced before the 1970 change to "Superfast" wheels in response to the Hot Wheels phenomenon. This Matchbox Regular Wheels Road Roller was released in 1962, $60.

Introduced in 1956, the Matchbox Model of Yesteryear line celebrated the vehicles of the past. I found this Y-12 1909 Thomas Flyabout that was first issued in 1967 at the 2004 National Farm Toy Show, $20. *KP photo courtesy Karen O'Brien*

Frank Hornby founded Meccano in 1901. Famous for its construction sets, the company branched out in 1932 to include mechanical car constructor sets, which were only in production until 1940. This Meccano No. 2 Car was the largest of the three cars offered. *Photo courtesy Christie's East*

This rare Metalcraft Waldorf Lager Truck, circa 1935, is 13-inches long and has all of its barrels. It was produced in St. Louis, Mo., during the Depression. *Photo courtesy Andrew Tolch*

The distinctive designs of Midgetoy cars and trucks hint at a deco style that sets them apart from other die-cast toymakers. This is the 6-inch long Midgetoy Tanker Truck from 1963, $30. *Photo courtesy Thomas G. Nefos*

Slush-mold toymaker C.E. Stevenson also created the Mid-West Metal Novelty Mfg. Co. of Clifton, Kan. This Mid-West Buick Sedan makes its debut in this edition, $60. *KP photo courtesy Karen O'Brien*

Nosco is best known for producing the plastic prizes found in boxes of Cracker Jack. If this remarkable Hot Rod is any indication, it's a shame Nosco didn't release more vehicles, $160.
Photo courtesy Terry Sells

Another Northern Illinois toy dynasty, Nylint began producing toys in 1946. This is the No. 4500 Ranch Truck from 1961, $200.
Photo courtesy Thomas G. Nefos

Ford trucks were a favorite subject for Nylint. Its No. 8200 Bronco was 12-1/2″ long, $100. *KP photo courtesy Ron O'Brien*

Enamel paint and decals only appearing on one side are two characteristics of Oh Boy! trucks. This is an Oh Boy! American Express Truck No. 205, $2,200. *Photo courtesy Bob Smith*

The Orobr Toy Works released this 8-3/4-inch long clockwork-motored Touring Car around 1918, $950. *Photo courtesy Bob Smith*

Promotional models are called "promos" by collectors, and the same rules governing the valuation of the real cars upon which they are based apply—popular cars in rare (or very cool colors) command the highest prices. This promo is the Silver Anniversary edition 1978 Corvette, $85. *KP photo courtesy Ron O'Brien*

Red is a popular color on real Corvettes, too. I borrowed this 1979 promo from my dad's collection for this photo, $65.
KP photo courtesy Ron O'Brien

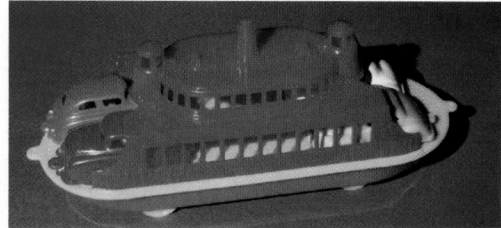

Pyro is best known for its outstanding model kits, but it did get around to releasing some very nice plastic vehicles in the 1950s. This Pyro Ferry and Cars is 7″ long, $60.
Photo courtesy Bob and Alice Wagner

Ranlite was a durable plastic similar to Bakelite that was used in automobile manufacture for control knobs and radios in the 1930s. The body of this Ranlite Singer Saloon shown with its w/box and catalog is molded in Ranlite. *Photo courtesy Gates Willard*

After successful turns producing plastic airplanes and dollhouse furniture, the Renwal Mfg. Co. turned to toy vehicles in the late 1940s. This Renwal No. 60 car is another find from the Iola Old Car Show, $55. *KP photo courtesy Karen O'Brien*

Distinctive among pre-WWII slush-mold toy makers, Savoye models are distinguished by their oversized, bright red, wooden wheel hubs. Here is the Savoye Tractor (SA18). *Photo courtesy Bill Conover*

Schuco toys are a marvel of German engineering ingenuity and display a sophistication of movement that few toys of today could match. Here is the Schuco Old Timer 1913 Mercer windup, $150.
Photo courtesy Al Kasishke

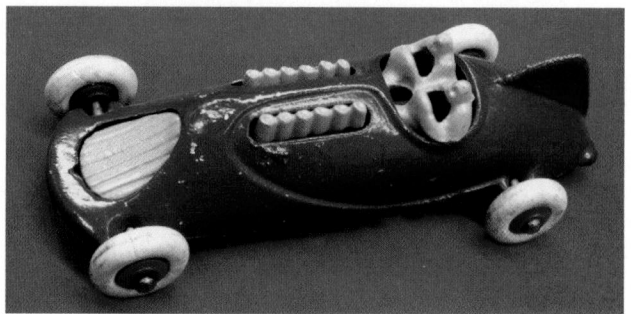

Sharon toys are made of aluminum and are unfortunately without any maker's marks. This is the Sharon Racer No. 11R, $225.
Photo courtesy Perry Eichor

Smith-Miller produced quality pressed-steel toys following World War II. I found this Stake Truck at the Portage, Ind. toy show last spring, $500. *Karen O'Brien photo courtesy "Toy" George Hollis*

The cab-over design of Smith-Miller trucks was based on GMC trucks of the era. The Smith-Miller Tanker has two hoses, $750.
KP photo courtesy Larry Planer

This Smith-Miller Dump has a working hand crank that operates the dump bed. Thanks to Larry Planer for lending me his Smitty trucks for these photos, $500. *KP photo courtesy Larry Planer*

Built tough, Smith-Miller trucks are one of the few manufacturers whose toys are highly desirable in every condition grade. This Smith-Miller Materials Truck is missing the sides of the bed, $550. *KP photo courtesy Larry Planer*

We know that Steer O Toys was based in Chicago, Ill., but little else. Anyone? This is the Steer O Toys Convertible, $600. *Photo courtesy Tim Oei*

Ferdinand Strauss became the founder of the mechanical toy industry in America and launched the career of Louis Marx. This is the tin wind-up Strauss Interstate Bus, $850. *Photo courtesy Bob Smith*

Structo is one of the few pressed-steel manufacturers to produce toys in both the pre-and post-WWII periods. A fine example of prewar engineering is this Structo Dump Truck #811, circa 1930s, $750. *Photo courtesy John Taylor*

This Structo Weekender was too ugly not to put in this very colorful section of the book, $180. *KP photo courtesy Ron O'Brien*

Sun Rubber of Barberton, Ohio specialized in a line of rubber vehicles and had some fun with Disney characters, as evidenced by this Donald Duck Roadster No. 12018, $150. *Photo courtesy Dave Leopard*

Former Ideal employee, Islyn Thomas, founded his company in 1944 and specialized in plastic toys. The toys are identified by the "Thomas Toy" enclosed in a circle molded inside the roof. This is the Thomas Toys No. 1-183 Sedan, $25. *KP photo courtesy Karen O'Brien*

The whitewall tires are a giveaway that this Tonka Suburban Pumper is from the early 1960s and its two-piece grill is indicative of trucks made before 1962, $350. *KP photo courtesy Ron O'Brien*

I found this 1963-64 Tonka Wrecker on the table of Ty Travers at the November Kalamazoo Toy Show and had to have it, $150. *KP photo courtesy Karen O'Brien*

The first sci-fi hero, Buck Rogers came to life as a short story by Philip Francis Nowlan in the August 1928 edition of *Amazing Stories* magazine. The character's success launched numerous toys, including the Buck Rogers No. 1033 Attack Ship from Tootsietoy, $225.

A division of the National Sewing Machine Co., short-lived Vindex produced high-quality toys from 1928-32. Left to right: Packard Club Sedan, 1929; Oldsmobile Sedan, 1929. *Photo courtesy Bertoia Auctions*

F&F Mold and Die Works manufactured cereal premiums for Post cereals in the 1950s and 1960s. Here is an assortment of F&F Cereal Premium cars, $20 each. *KP photo courtesy Karen O'Brien*

All-Metal Products made stamped metal parts for the auto industry until the fall of 1921, when it used some of the scrap to make children's playthings, Wyandotte Toys was born. This is the Wyandotte Sedan with Trailer, circa 1938, $225. *Photo courtesy Brian Seligman*

Lithography became a Wyandotte specialty in the 1950s, as did combining plastic and metal materials. This Emergency Auto Service truck has a plastic cab and metal bed with litho graphics, $145. *Photo courtesy Brian Seligman*

Art-deco influences are a hallmark of early Wyandotte toys, as evidenced by the gorgeous fenders on this Wyandotte Boat-Tail Racer, circa 1934, $195. *Photo courtesy Brian Seligman*

Kansas Toy Farm vehicles, Top: Two examples of a KTV17. Middle: KTV23, KTV21. Bottom: KTV23, KTV17. Photo courtesy Fred Maxwell

Kansas Toy Commercial vehicles, Top: KTV20, KTV33. Middle: KTV34, KTV36. Bottom: KTV38, KTV41 (with later wheels). Photo courtesy Fred Maxwell

	C6	C8	C10
Farm Tractor, No. "57"; Fordson, driver, SP, MDW rear, MSW front; 1-3/4" long; smaller version of No. 17 there is also an UV (KTV042)	25	35	45
Fire Engine, No. "70"; Seagrave (?) pumper, driver, VL, HG, MDW; 2-1/4" long (KTV053)	30	50	75
Indy Racer, No. "10"; driver, boattail, exhaust right, VL, HG, HO, SP, M.S.W. or MWW; 3-1/8" long; There is also UV (KTV014)	25	35	50
Large coupe, no number; Chrysler Convertible, MWW and and golf doors; 5" long; larger version of No. 8 (KTV009)	20	30	40
Large Coupe, no number; crude, high-bodied "Ford," HO, HG, no headlamps, SP, VL, five windows, door handles, wheel type unknown because only a reproduction has been found, 3-1/4" long (KTV000)	20	30	40
Large Farm Tractor, no number; Deere Model D, two color, steering shaft, fly wheel, belt drive wheel, rear fenders, large 2" and 1" twelve-spoke wheels; 4-7/8" long (KTV019)	35	50	75
Large Indy Racer, no number; driver, boattail, HO, MDW, lacquer, 6" long (KTV003)	50	80	120

	C6	C8	C10
Locomotive-tender, No. "36"; marked "KT & N RR," six MSW, four MDW, 0-6-4; 4-3/8" long (KTV027)	20	30	40
Midget Racer, no number; no driver, torpedo tail, HO, SP, VL, HG; 5/8" MDW w/simulated lug nuts; lacquer finish (KTV001)	20	30	40
Midget Racer, no number; no driver, torpedo tail, HO, SP, VL., HG, 3" long w/driver, plain MDW, lacquer; easily confused w/another maker's copy; see No. 31 and No. 67 (KTV002)	70	105	140
Midget racer, No. "31"; driver, torpedo tail, VL, HG, HO, MWW, lacquer; 2-1/8" long; there is also UV; see No. 67 (KTV024)	20	30	40
Midget Racer, No. "67"; Driver, torpedo-tail, VL, HG, HO, MDW; 1-1/2"; smaller version of No. 31; there is also an UV (KTV052)	25	50	70
Overland Bus, no number; "Fageol", nine male passengers, driver and "baggage" cast on windows; HG, RM, MDW 3-1/2" long; There is also an UV w/various family passengers on windows (KTV013)	35	50	70

Kansas Toy Canoe, KTV73. Photo courtesy Ferd Zegel

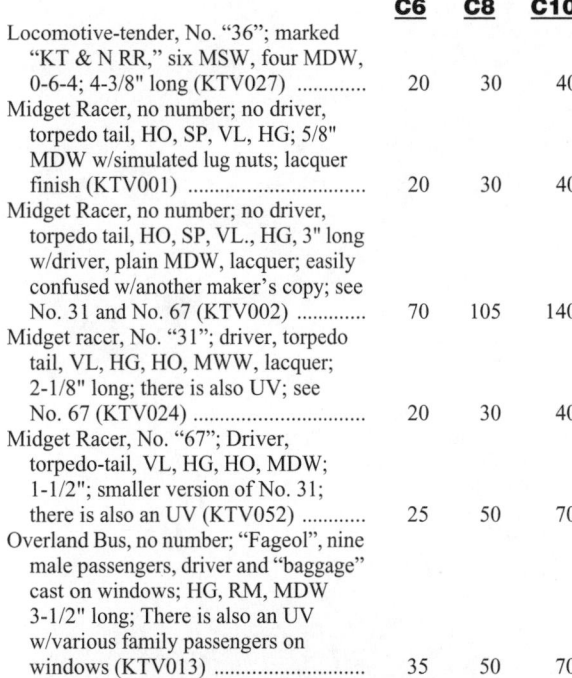

Kansas Toy Army Tank, No.74, high turret, large front, 2-1/4". Photo courtesy Perry Eichor

Top row, left to right: Kansas Toy Coupe, no number; Sedan, no number. Middle row: a pair of 3-1/8" Coupes (No. 8). Bottom row, left to right: a pair of 2-1/4" Coupes (No. 35); Sedanette, No. 58, 2-1/4". Photo courtesy Fred Maxwell

Top row, left to right: Kansas Toy Coupe, No. 8, 3-1/8"; Roadster, No. 15, 3-1/8". Bottom row, left to right: Sedan, No. 60, 3-1/2"; Coupe, No. 80, 3-1/2". Photo courtesy Perry Eichor

Kansas Toy Coupe, No. 66, three-wheeler, 3-1/2". Photo courtesy Ferd Zegel

Left to right: Kansas Toy Coupe, No. 8, 3-1/8"; Coupe, No. 8, 3-1/4". Photo courtesy Fred Maxwell

Kansas Toy Coupe, No. 35, 2-1/4". Photo courtesy Bob Ackerly

Back row: Kansas Toy Dump Truck, No. 42, driver, no cab, 3-1/2". Front row: two Ralstoy versions of the Kansas Toy truck. Photo courtesy Perry Eichor

Left to right: Kansas Toy Dump Truck, No. 42, 3-1/2" and a later version of the Dump Truck. Photo courtesy Fred Maxwell

Left to right: Kansas Toy Farm Tractor, No. 17, 2-7/8"; Disc Harrow, No. 62, 4"; Planter, No. 61, 4". Photo courtesy Chic Gast

*Top to bottom: Kansas Toy Large Coupe, no number, 5";
Coupe, No. 35, 2-1/4". Photo courtesy Ferd Zegel*

*Kansas Toy Large Indy Racer, no number, driver, boat-tail,
6".*

*A pair of Kansas Toy Deere Model D tractors, 4-7/8".
Photo courtesy Ferd Zegel*

*Top row, left to right: Kansas Toy Midget Racer, no
number, no driver, 3"; Midget Racer, no number, with
driver, 3". Bottom row, left to right: Indy Racer, No. 10,
driver, 3-1/8"; Midget Racer, No. 24, driver, 2-1/28";
Midget Racer, No. 67, driver, 1-1/2". Photo courtesy Fred
Maxwell*

	C6	C8	C10
Overland Bus, No. "9"; "Fageol," solid windows; 3-1/2" long (KTV012)	25	40	60
Pickup Truck, No. "51"; Ford w/cab; VL, HG, tow loop, MDW, lacquer; 2-3/4" long; there is also an UV (KTV038)	20	30	40
Planter, No. "61"; marked "KTN No. 61," V-blade plough w/seed hopper, four-piece including wheels, three colors; 4" long; Note: This is part of a unique towed farm set w/several hinged or moving parts, each a different color and large 1-1/4" spoked tractor wheels. Has been seen w/tin snap-on seats. (KTV046)	40	60	80
Plough, No."63"; single blade on same shaft as number 61, 4" long; Note: This is part of a unique towed farm set w/several hinged or moving parts, each a different color and large 1-1/4" spoked tractor wheels (KTV048)	40	60	80
Pullmar Car, No. "37"; marked "KT & N RR," four MDW; 3-1/2" long (KTV028)	15	25	35
Racer, no number; miniature solid-cast version of No. 10, moving wheels, charm loop on nose; 1" long (KTV057)	15	25	35
Racer, No. "26"; "Bearcat" stripdown, long hood, motometer, three intakes, driver, open frame, left four cylinder exhaust, 4" long; see No. 33 (KTV022)	85	125	150

	C6	C8	C10
Racer, No. "33"; "Bearcat" stripdown, 3" long; smaller version of No. 26 (KTV025)	85	125	150
Racer, No. "46"; 1929 Golden Arrow record car, driver, large tail fin, MWW; 2-7/8" long (KTV035)	25	45	60
Roadster, "54", Buick, driver w/cap, rumble seat, no trunk, plain hood and grille, no headlamps, SM, MWW; 2-1/4" long; there is also an UV; see No. 77 (KTV040)	60	75	100
Roadster, no number; solid WS, plain grille, HO, VL, SP, RM, MDSW, HG, two golf club doors; 3-1/8" long (KTV015A)	25	40	60
Roadster, no number; solid WS, plain grille, HO, VL, SP, RM, MDSW, HG, w/open rumble seat; might not be Kansas Toy & Novelty (KTV016)	NPF	NPF	NPF
Roadster, No. "14"; open "Chrysler," solid W.S., plain grille, HO, VL, SP, RM, MDSW; 3-1/8" long (KTV015)	20	30	45
Roadster, No. "54"; Buick, driver w/cap, rumble seat, T, plain hood and grille, no headlamps, SM, MWW; 2-3/8" long; there is also an UV; see No. 77 (KTV039)	30	50	70
Sedan, no number; "Chevrolet," six windows, LI, WV, VL, SP, RM, MWW, HG, HO, MSW; 3-1/4" long (KTV011)	20	30	40
Sedan, no number; "Chevrolet," six windows, LI, WV, VL, SP, RM, MWW; 2-7/8" long (KTV010)	20	30	40

Overland Bus, No. 9, 3-1/2". Photo courtesy Fred Maxwell

Kansas Toy Racer, No. 46, Golden Arrow Record Car. Photo courtesy Fred Maxwell

Kansas Toy Roadster, no number, open rumble seat. Photo courtesy Bob Straub

Kansas Toy Sedanette, No. 58, Austin Bantam, unique fighting cock on door panels, 2-1/4". Photo courtesy Ferd Zegel

Top row, left to right: Kansas Toy Separator-Thresher, No. 27, 3"; Steam Tractor, No. 21, Case, 3". Bottom row: Steam Tractor, No. 71, crew of two, 2-1/2". Photo courtesy Fred Maxwell

From left: Racer, No. 26, 4"; Racer, No. 33, 3". Photo courtesy Perry Eichor

This is a catalog photo of the Kansas Toy No. 92 Toy Racer. Photo from M.C.P. catalog.

Kansas Toy Roadster, No. 54, rumble seat, plain hood and grille, no headlamps, 2-3/8". Photo courtesy Fred Maxwell

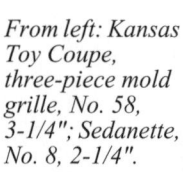

From left: Kansas Toy Coupe, three-piece mold grille, No. 58, 3-1/4"; Sedanette, No. 8, 2-1/4".

Kansas Toy Steam Road Roller, No. 43, driver, boiler, wooden rollers, 3-1/4". Photo courtesy R.F. Sapita

Kansas Toy Tour Bus, No. 59, 1928 Pickwick double-deck night coach, 3-3/8". Photo courtesy Fred Maxwell

Left to right: Kansas Toy Dump Truck, No. 42; Truck-Semi, No. 55, stake trailer, 4". Photo courtesy Ferd Zegel

	C6	C8	C10
Sedan, no number; crude limousine or stretch taxi, six windows, louvered rear quarters, HO, VL, HG, T, SP, large MDW, lacquer; 3-3/8" long (KTV005)	20	30	40
Sedan, No. "60", 1930 Reo Royale (?) or Chrysler two-door. brougham, plain hood, vee-VG, square rear deck, MDW, MDWSM; 3-1/2" long; there is also an UV w/MWW and MWWSM, three-piece molded grille (KTV045) ..	45	60	75
Sedanette, No. "58"; Austin Bantam, unique fighting cock on door panels, four OW, H.L., VG, RM, MWW, three-piece molded grille; 2-1/4" long (KTV043)	25	40	70
Separator-Thresher, No. "27"; tow hook, auto-type MSW (not tractor rims), lacquer or enamel; 3" long; there is also UV; see No. 72 (KTV023)	25	40	50
Separator-Thresher, No. "72"; tow hook for No. 71 (KTV055)	25	40	50
Steam Road Roller, No. "43"; driver, SP, boiler, wooden rollers; 3-1/4" long (KTV034)	30	45	60
Steam Tractor, No. "25"; "Case," crew of two, tow loop, large front, small rear M.S.W. and flywheel; 3" long; see number 71; also an UV w/no name (KTV021)	25	40	60
Steam Tractor, No. "71"; crew of two, tow-loop; 2-1/2" long; small version of No. 25 (KTV054)	30	40	60
Stock Car, No. "41"; marked "KT & N RR," MDW (KTV032)	15	25	35
Tank Car, No. "39"; marked "KT & N RR," ladder, filler, MDW; 3-1/8" long (KTV030)	15	25	35

	C6	C8	C10
Tour Bus, No. "49"; 1928 Pickwick COE "Nite Coach," HG, SP, MDW duals; 2-3/8" long; there is also an UV; see No. 59 (KTV037)	20	30	40
Tour Bus, No. "59"; 1928 Pickwick COE double-deck night-coach, screen grille; 3-3/8" long; larger version of No. 49; also an UV w/dual wheels (KTV044)	75	100	125
Truck, No. "20"; Ford (?), solid W.S., two OW, three tanks, VL, HG, rear faucet, M.W.W; there are versions w/ and w/o driver. 3-1/8"; there is also an UV version (KTV020)	40	60	80
Truck-Semi, No. "55"; Ford, stake trailer, VL, HG, MDW; 4" long (KTV041) ...	40	60	80
Warehouse Tractor, No. "48"; "Caterpillar," "Whoopee," driver, VL, HG, HO, SP, tow loop, MWW; 3" long; there is also an UV (KTV036)	25	38	50

Transitional

	C6	C8	C10
Army Tank, No. "74"; marked "US Army," two gun turret, olive dab color; 2-1/4" long; a different tank than No. 74 listed earlier (KTV061)	40	50	60
Concrete Mixer, No. "78", truck w/water tank and mixing barrel, VG, HL, WHRT; Found both w/ and w/o a bottom pan; sometimes called a fuel tanker; 3-3/4" long (KTV065)	40	60	80
Coupe, No. "75"; Graham-like (Tootsietoy), VG, SM, T, WHRT, 1933 issue, 4-1/4" long (KTV062)	20	30	40
Coupe, No. "80"; convertible, top up, LI, two OW, VG, T, HRDW w/MDW, SM (a different sidemounts castings); 3-1/2" long (KTV068)	30	45	70
Coupe, No. "80"; convertible, top up, LI, two OW, VG, T, MWW w/MWW, SM, three-piece molded grille; 3-1/2" long (KTV067)	30	45	70

Kansas Toy Truck, No. 20, three tanks, 3-1/8". Photo courtesy Fred Maxwell

Kansas Toy Warehouse Tractor, No. 48, KTV36, Caterpillar, driver, 3". Photo courtesy Fred Maxwell

Kansas Toy Racer, No. 81, 1933 issue, 4-3/8". Photo courtesy Bob Ackerly

A pair of Kansas Toy Pierce-Arrow Silver Arrow Sedans (No. 82), 4". Photo courtesy Ferd Zegel

Back row, left to right: Kansas Toy Sedan, No. 79, two-door, 4-1/4"; Racer, No. 76., Auburn Speedster, 4-1/4". Middle row, left to right: Coupe, No. 80, 3-1/2"; Sedan, No. 60,1930s REO or Chrysler, 3-1/2". Bottom row: Sedanette, No. 58, three-piece molded grille, 2-1/4". Photo courtesy Perry Eichor

Kansas Toy Sedan, No. 84, 3-5/8", possibly a DeSoto Airflow, 1934 issue. Photo courtesy Bob Ackerly

	C6	C8	C10
Indy Racer, No. "83"; FWD, driver, VG, H.L., right exhaust, WHRT, 4-5/8" long (KTV071)	40	70	80
Racer, No. "76"; Auburn speedster, low driver, headrest fairing, SP, HG, slanted louvers, large oval fin, kickplates, HWRW or WHRT; 4-1/4" long (KTV063)	30	45	60
Racer, No. "81"; 4-3/8". Miller FWD, driver, eight cylinder right exhaust, HG, WHRT, 1933 issue (KTV069)	NPF	NPF	NPF
Roadster, No. "77"; open sport Duesenberg, W.S down, driver, VG, slanted louvers, SM, T, WHR; 4" long (KTV064)	25	40	60
Sedan, No. "79," two-door, Graham-like, four OW, VG, HL, RM, WHRT w/five removable tires; found both w/ and w/o bottom pan; 4-1/4" long (KTV066)	20	30	40
Sedan, No. "82"; Pierce-Arrow Silver Arrow fastback, six OW, HRDW, three-piece molded grille; 4" long (KTV070)	40	75	100
Sedan, No. "84", DeSoto (?) Airflow, four OW, HO, HG, HL, HRDW, 1934 issue; 3-5/8" long (KTV072)	40	75	100

KARL BUB

Bub had one of the longest reigns in the toy business. The company produced high-quality toys from 1851-1966 and was based in Nuremberg, Germany. Bub took over the Carette Toy Co., in 1917, after Georges Carette fled to France at the onset of World War I. He also took over the Bing Toy Works in 1932. Bub used much of the technology practiced by Carette. His toys were of the better-quality toys to come out of Germany in the early 1900s. Bub produced many of the fine toys sold by F.A.O. Schwarz Co., of New York.

Contributor: Bob Smith, RATS Toy Shows, 255 Tryon Park, Rochester, NY 14609. (585) 288-7153, bird@oldtoysonline.com.

	C6	C8	C10
Coupe, rumble seat, clockwork motor	NPF	NPF	NPF
Limousine, clockwork, 14" long	2100	4100	7700
Limousine, green and black, doors open, front crack clockwork motor, 9-3/4" long	800	1250	1800
Limousine, red and black, clock-work motor, opening doors, hand brake, c.1915, 14" long	1300	2100	2900
Limousine, wind-up, 8" long	500	700	1000
Limousine, wind-up, driver, 11" long	800	1500	2200

Karl Bub Limousine, green and black, 9-3/4". Photo courtesy Bob Smith

Karl Bub Limousine, red and black, circa 1915, 14". Photo courtesy Bob Smith

Karl Bub Limousine, 9-3/4". Photo courtesy Bob Smith

Karl Bub Limousine, clockwork, 1920s, 14". Photo courtesy Sotheby's, New York

Karl Bub Mercedes Limousine, circa 1928, 13-1/2". Photo courtesy Bob Smith

Karl Bub Roadster, driver, circa 1908, 9". Photo courtesy Bertoia Auctions

Karl Bub Sedan, 1919, high headlamps, wind-up, 14". Photo courtesy Bertoia Auctions

	C6	C8	C10
Mercedes Limousine, green and black, doors open, windshield folds, head lamps, tool box's clockwork motor, head lamps, steering, c.1928, 13-1/2" long	1150	1850	2600

	C6	C8	C10
Roadster, driver, c.1908, 9" long	900	1600	2500
Sedan, wind-up, high headlamps, 1919, 14" long	900	1700	2700
Toures, wind-up, two seat, 9-1/2" long	1000	1800	2600

KELMET (Also known as Trumodel and Big Boy)

Kelmet was founded in Chicago in 1925 by several wholesale toy representatives. It was their wish to compete with the large toy-steel vehicles of the period. Some work was sub-contracted through A.C. Gilbert. White trucks were a Kelmet staple after the company acquired the rights in 1924 and were sold under the trade name "Big Boy." In 1926, the company acquired the construction toy lines of the Noble Mfg. Co. and their "Trumodel" steel toys.

Identification is simple; the toys were big (about two feet) and heavy (about ten pounds). Beyond that simplicity, the "White" and "Big Boy" diamond-shaped decals plus the white balloon rubber tires are a good indication. Note: Some early models had black rubber tires on spoked or solid stamped wheels.

Kelmet Army Truck, 1929, 25". Photo courtesy Joe and Sharon Freed

	C6	C8	C10
Aerial Ladder Truck, No. 510, "Big Boy," open cab, pressed steel, red, 2 fire extinguishers, bell, 2 wooden ladders, 1926, 30" long	800	1250	1700
Army Truck, No. 513, dump truck w/canvas canopy stamped "Army Truck," 1928-29, 25" long	800	1250	2000
Chemical Truck	900	1400	2000
Coal Pocket Loader, No. 508, "Big Boy," coal elevator w/2 chutes, red and black, 1926, 23" high	1200	2000	3000
Sand Loader	1000	1700	2400
Scissor Dump Truck, 25" long	600	950	1400

Kelmet White Dump Truck, No. 501, 25". Photo courtesy Joe and Sharon Freed

	C6	C8	C10
Steam Excavator, No. 506, "Big Boy," w/same cab and chassis as No. 502, large boom, clamshell bucket, black and red, 1926, 25" long	NPF	NPF	NPF
Steam Shovel, No. 502, "Big Boy," black vertical boiler, 4 wheels, rotating cab, black and red, 1925, 20" long	325	488	650
Trumodel Derrick, w/power hoist and tip bucket, 54" long	1000	1700	2500
White Crane Truck, No. 507, "Big Boy," open cab truck, chassis has clamshell digger attached, black and red, 1926, 26" long	2500	4000	6000
White Dump Truck, No. 501, "Big Boy," diamond-shaped decals on bed sides reads "White," 1925-26, 25" long	1200	2000	2700

Kelmet Aerial Ladder Truck, 30". Photo courtesy Bill Bertoia Auctions

	C6	C8	C10
White Fire Engine, No. 504, "Big Boy," w/ladder, spoked or stamped wheels, bell on 1927 model, 1925-27, 27" long	1200	2000	3000
White Tank Truck, No. 505, "Big Boy," 3 caps on top of tank, white rubber tires, 1926-27, 25" long	1500	2700	4700

KENTON

Kenton Lock Manufacturing Co., was incorporated in May 1890, in Kenton, Ohio. In November of 1894, it became the Kenton Hardware Manufacturing Co. Around this period, it began producing cast-iron toys with a still bank to commemorate the 1893 World's Columbian Exhibition in Chicago. It was a detailed replica of the Administration Building known as the "Columbia Bank."

In 1903, Kenton brought out its first toy vehicle line, named the "Red Devils," since most cars in those days were painted red. The company was reorganized as the Kenton Hardware Company in 1912. In 1930, L.S. Bixler, of Jones & Bixler, was its president. The last catalog was produced in 1952 and from there, the company embarked on a downward slide to it's demise in November of 1956.

	C6	C8	C10
Ambulance, cast iron, 7" long	700	1200	1800
Army Motor Truck 807, cast iron, 14" long	600	950	1450
Auto, cast iron, 6" long	900	1600	2400
Auto, clockwork, tiller, driver w/top hat, very early, approx. 4" long	250	400	650
Auto Dray Truck, black driver, passenger, 9" long	9000	1700	2600
Auto Express 548, w/driver, 9-1/4" long	1500	2500	3800
Auto Hansom, 7-3/4" long	475	550	800
Boat-tail Cut-Down Speedster, 1910, 7" long	120	180	260
Buckeye Ditcher, 11-3/4" long	1400	2500	4250
Buckeye Ditcher, 9" long	500	750	1200
Bus, 12-3/4" long	600	900	1500
Bus, 1920s, 10-3/4" long	375	525	750
Bus, cast iron, 8" long	325	500	700
Bus, double- decker, 1920, 7-1/4" long	1000	1500	2200
Bus, double-decker, 12" long	500	800	1300

	C6	C8	C10
Bus, double-decker, 13-1/2" long	1500	2600	4500
Bus, double-decker, 1920s, 6" long	375	575	900
Bus, double-decker, 9-1/2" long	500	750	1100
Bus, double-decker, c.1902s, 8-1/8" long	1000	1600	2500
Bus, twin coach, 8-1/2" long	950	1500	2350
Bus, w/Mama Katzenjammer, Uncle Heine, Alphonse, Gloomy Gus, Happy Hooligan, marked "Seeing New York 899," 10-1/2" long	2000	3900	6350
Cattle Truck, cast iron, c.1938, 8" long	150	225	325
Cement Mixer Truck, 1932, 8-1/2" long	1400	2500	4000
Circus Truck, 10" long	1300	2000	2700
City Service Truck, C-cab, 10-1/4" long	1500	2800	3700
Coal Dump Truck, 8-1/2" long	140	210	280
Coal Dump Truck, w/driver, c.1932, 10-1/2" long	800	1350	2000
Coast-to-Coast Bus	350	525	700
Contractors Dump Truck, 3-bucket, 9-3/4" long	500	800	1150
Contractors Dump Wagon, cast iron, 8-1/2" long	500	750	1000
Coupe, 5" long	230	345	460
Coupe, 6-1/2" long	450	638	850

Kenton Ambulance, 7". Photo courtesy Sotheby's

Kenton Army Motor Truck, 14". Photo courtesy Sotheby's

Kenton Auto Hansom, 7-3/4". Photo courtesy Bertoia Auctions

Kenton Buckeye Ditcher, 9". Photo courtesy Sotheby's

Kenton Bus, double-decker, 13-1/2". Photo courtesy Sotheby's

Kenton Seeing New York 899 Bus, 10-1/2". Photo courtesy Bertoia Auctions

Kenton Bus, 12-3/4". Photo courtesy Bertoia Auctions

Kenton Bus, double-decker, 12". Photo courtesy Bertoia Auctions

Kenton Bus, double-decker, 8-1/8". Photo courtesy Sotheby's

Kenton Bus, double-decker, 9-1/2". Photo courtesy Sotheby's

Kenton Bus, double-decker, 1920s, 6". Photo courtesy Bertoia Auctions

Kenton Bus, double-decker w/passengers, 9-1/2". Photo courtesy Phillips New York

Kenton Coal Dump Truck, with driver, 1930s, 10-1/2". Photo courtesy Bertoia Auctions

	C6	C8	C10
Coupe, 8" long	700	1100	1600
Coupe, separate driver, 10" long, 1926	1500	4500	9000
Dump Truck, 6" long	337	505	675
Dump Truck, hinged self-locking gate, 8-1/2" long	500	800	1100
Emergency Truck, black rubber tires, takes batteries for headlights and spotlight, 1930s	180	270	360
Fire Apparatus Truck	400	600	800
Fire Pump Truck, early w/driver, approx. 10" long	185	278	350
Fire Pumper, 1911, 11-1/2" long	NPF	NPF	NPF
Fire Pumper, 1920s, 14-1/2" long	800	1200	1600
Fire Pumper, early, 5-3/4" long	120	180	240
Fire Pumper, w/gong, c.1920, 18" long	350	525	700
Fire Truck, w/pumper, 15" long	1200	2000	2800
Franklin, air-cooled, 8-1/2" long	1300	1950	2600
Hose Reel Fire Truck, 8-3/4" long	325	488	650
Hose Truck, open cab, green, driver, rider, hose, ladders, 1920s, approx. 6-3/4" long	350	525	700
Hudson, postwar electric lights	50	75	100
Ice Truck, tongs and glass ice, 7-1/2" long	1000	2000	3000
Ice Truck, tractor trailer 1930s, 10-1/2" long	1000	1700	2400
Ice Truck, w/driver, 7-7/8" long	425	638	850
Jaeger Cement Mixer, 7" long	550	825	1250
Jaeger Cement Mixer, 7-3/8" long	650	950	1500
Jaeger Cement Mixer, 8" long	1000	1500	2000
Jaeger Cement Mixer, iron wheels, 6-1/2" long	262	393	525
Jeager Mixer Cement Truck, cast iron, 9" long	1000	2000	3000
Ladder Truck, 11-1/2" long	280	420	560
Ladder Truck, 17-1/4" long	750	1200	1700

	C6	C8	C10
Ladder Truck, 20" long	1100	1800	2500
Ladder Truck, 22" long	1500	2400	3500
Ladder Truck, cast iron, approx. 7-1/2" long	300	450	600
Ladder Truck, driver, early 1930s, 9" long	90	135	180
Ladder Truck, pressed steel ladders, 16" long	500	850	1100
Limousine, driver, c.1915, 7-3/4" long	500	700	1000
Lumber Truck, cast-iron, white rubber tires, red cab and chassis, green open stake bed, wood planks, 1930s, 12" long	300	600	950
Merchant Delivery Truck	450	675	900
Oil Gas Truck, 10-1/2" long	800	1400	2100
Overland Circus, w/hippo, 7-1/4" long	700	1150	1600
Overland Circus, w/lion, 9" long	800	1300	1800
Overland Circus Cage Truck, w/driver, 7-1/2" long	900	1500	2000
Overland Circus Calliope Truck, rare, 10" long	NPF	NPF	NPF
Patrol Wagon, w/driver and three fireman, 1920s-1930s, 9" long	650	1100	1600
Phaeton touring Car, 12" long	350	562	700
Pickwick Nite Coach, cast iron, 14" long	1900	2750	3800
Pickwick Nite Coach, cast iron, 6" long	350	700	1050
Pickwick Nite Coach, cast iron, 7-1/2" long	600	1100	1500
Pickwick Nite Coach, cast iron, 9-1/2" long	1400	2500	3700
Pickwick Nite Coach, cast iron, streamlined back or square back, 11" long	575	1150	1500
Pontiac, 4-1/2" long	262	393	525
Pontiac and Trailer, 10" long	350	525	725
Racer, 7-1/2" long	142	213	285
Racer, cast iron, early, 9" long	600	1000	1400
Red Devil Auto, w/driver, 1906, 6" long	225	338	450
Red Sedan, 1929, 8" long	NPF	NPF	NPF

Kenton Coal Dump Truck, with driver, 1930s, 10-1/2". Photo courtesy Bertoia Auctions

Kenton Contractors Dump Truck, 3-bucket, 9-3/4". Photo courtesy Sotheby's

Kenton Fire Pumper Truck, early, with driver, approximately 10". Photo courtesy Rod Carnahan

Kenton Fire Pumper, circa 1920,18". Photo courtesy Mapes Auctioneers and Appraisers

Kenton Franklin, air-cooled, 8-1/2". Photo courtesy Sotheby's

Kenton Ice Truck, driver, 7-7/8". Photo courtesy Bertoia Auctions

Kenton Ice Truck, tractor trailer, 1930s, 10-1/2". Photo courtesy Bertoia Auctions

Kenton Jaeger Cement Mixer Truck, 8". Photo courtesy Hake's

Kenton Jaeger Cement Mixer, 6-1/2" iron wheels. Photo courtesy Sotheby's

Kenton Jaeger Cement Mixer Truck, rubber wheels. Photo courtesy Sotheby's

Kenton Speed Stake Truck, circa 1927, 5-1/2". Photo courtesy Bertoia Auctions

Kenton Runabout Auto, driver, circa 1908, 6-1/2". Photo courtesy Christie's East

Kenton Road Roller, Gallon Master, 7". Photo courtesy Bertoia Auctions

	C6	C8	C10
Road Grader, 1950, 7-1/4" long	135	205	275
Road Grader, 5-1/2" long	125	188	250
Road Grader, cast iron, rubber tires, nickel-plated moveable blade, 7-1/2" long	155	230	310
Road Roller, "Galion Master," 5-1/2" long	115	172	230
Road Roller, "Galion Master," 7" long	150	225	300
Roadster, w/driver, c.1908, 6" long	300	450	600
Runabout Auto, 1900, 5" long	170	225	340
Runabout Auto, cast iron, driver, c.1908, 6-1/2" long	700	1050	1400
Sand and Gravel Truck, 1940s	165	248	330
Sedan, 4" long	110	165	225

	C6	C8	C10
Sedan, 8-1/2" long..................................	2000	3000	5000
Sedan, rubber tires, take apart body, late 1930s, 7" long	1400	2100	2800
Sedan, separate drive, 1923, 10" long......	1500	3000	6000
Sedan, separate driver, 1923, 10" long	1500	3000	6000
Sedan, separate driver, 1926, 10-1/4" long	4500	9500	15.000
Speed Stake Truck, 9-1/8" long	450	850	1250
Speed Stake Truck, c.1927, 5-1/2" long ..	50	75	100
Sprinkler Truck, early, 8" long	300	450	600
Stake Truck, 6" long	337	405	675
Steam Roller, marked "Galion Master," 6-1/2" long	225	338	450
Steam Shovel, Marion, 7-1/4" long	600	900	1200
Tank, cast iron, 2-1/2" long	80	120	160

Kenton Limousine, driver, circa 1915, 7-3/4". Photo courtesy Sotheby's

Kenton Overland Circus Cage Truck with hippo, 7-1/4". Photo courtesy Bertoia Auctions

Kenton Pickwick Nite Coach, 11". Photo courtesy Phillips New York

Kenton Patrol Wagon, driver, three firemen, 9". Photo courtesy Bertoia Auctions

Kenton Speed Stake Truck, 9-1/8". Photo courtesy Bertoia Auctions

Kenton Contractors Dump Truck, 3-bucket, 9-3/4". Photo courtesy Bertoia Auctions

	C6	**C8**	**C10**
Touring Car, open, driver and passenger, 1923, 9" long	650	975	1300
Touring Car, open, driver and passenger, detachable steering wheel, 1924, 7-3/4" long	NPF	NPF	NPF
Touring Car, w/driver, 6" long	225	338	450
Tow Auto, 1920s, 9-1/2" long	1600	2400	3200
Yellow Cab, 1950s, 6-3/8" long	300	450	600

Left to right: Kenton Sedan, 1923, separate driver, 10"; Coupe, 926, separate driver, 10"; Sedan, 1926, separate driver, 10-1/4". Photo courtesy Bertoia Auctions

Kenton Touring Car, open, driver and passenger, 1923, 9". Photo courtesy Bertoia Auctions

Left to right: Kenton Pickwick Nite Coaches, 7-1/2" and

KEYSTONE

Keystone of Boston had an odd assortment of products—movie projectors, steel trucks, wooden boats, and pressed-wood forts and garages. Founded in 1922 or 1923 by Chester Rimmer and Arthur Jackson, it was first located in a small shop in Maiden, Mass., under the name "Jacrim," using parts of partners' last names. In the 1920s, Keystone's steel toy trucks were released in conjunction with the Packard Motor Company and based on Packard designs. By the 1930s, Keystone's large trucks were a solid competitor for Buddy "L" and featured nickel hubcaps, and some steerable "Ride On" designs.

Rimmer retired in 1958 and sold out to various companies. Keystone's Boston address was 288 A Street.

	C6	**C8**	**C10**
Aerial Ladder, No. 79, Packard, extension ladder, 2 side ladders, "Keystone Aerial Ladder" decals, 1928, 27-1/2" long	600	1000	1650
Ambulance, No. 73, Packard, canvas side curtains, military, 27" long	775	1400	2000
American Railway Express, No. 43, Packard, w/3 or 4 screen panel body, black cab, red chassis, green panel, 1925, 26" long	1000	1700	2600

	C6	**C8**	**C10**
Bus, plastic, side door opens, destination sign, 1950s, 7-1/4" long	25	50	80
Bus Terminal, pressed board terminal w/2 plastic busses, 1950s	100	200	350
Chemical Pump Engine, No. 57, open cab, water tank, hose reel, bell, 4 ladders, 1926, 27-1/2" long	700	1200	1600

Keystone American Railway Express, 26". Photo courtesy Joe and Sharon Freed

Keystone Dump Truck. Photo courtesy Calvin L. Chausee

Keystone Dump Truck, No. 41. Photo courtesy Bertoia Auctions

Keystone Fire Truck, No. 49, 27-1/2". Photo courtesy Joe and Sharon Freed

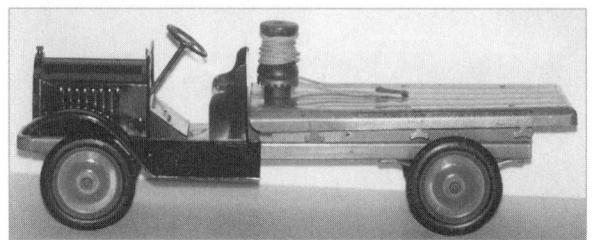

Keystone made several Koaster Trucks, the version with skids, a hoist cable, and windlass is considerably more valuable than the truck without those features. Photo courtesy Joe and Sharon Freed

Keystone Moving Van, 26". Photo courtesy Mapes Auctioneers and Appraisers

Keystone Plastic Bus, 7-1/4". Photo courtesy Joe and Sharon Freed

Keystone Police Van, 1920s.

Keystone Plastic Sedans, circa 1950, 4-1/2". Photo courtesy Terry Sells

Keystone Ride 'em Water Tower with Real Pump, 1945, 29". Photo courtesy Joe and Sharon Freed

Keystone Ride 'em Dump Truck, circa 1945, 29". Photo courtesy Joe and Sharon Freed

Keystone Dump Truck, 26-1/2". Photo courtesy PB Eighty Four

Keystone vehicles, as shown in a 1928 Butler Bros. catalog.

One of several versions of Keystone's Steam Shovel—the 26" version shown here is more valuable than the 34-1/2". Photo courtesy Calvin L. Chaussee

	C6	C8	C10
Chemical Pump Engine, Ride 'Em, No. 57, w/seat and steering handle, 1932, 27-1/2" long	500	1000	1500
Circus Truck, Ride 'Em, No. 82, Packard, open cab, hinged sides have "World's Greatest Circus" artwork, three removable cages, 1932, 26" long	1500	3000	6500
Coast to Coast Bus, Ride 'Em, No. 84, Packard, light green and black, wind-up, 31" long	1100	1900	2700
Dugan Brothers Truck, Ride 'Em, Packard, looks like Keystone Moving Van, has Dugan Bros. Bakery decals, rare, 1932, 27" long	2400	4400	6400

Keystone Dugan Brothers Ridem Truck, 27". Photo courtesy Joe and Sharon Freed

Keystone Dump Truck, 26-1/2". Photo courtesy PB Eighty Four

Keystone U.S. Army Truck, 26". Photo courtesy Calvin L. Chaussee

Keystone Tank, wooden, metal firing mechanism, 6". Photo courtesy Ed Poole

	C6	C8	C10
Dump Truck, "Keystone" embossed on door, electric lights, 1937, 23" long.....	300	500	700
Dump Truck, cab over, 25' long	230	345	475
Dump Truck, No. 41, Packard, crank raises dump bed, opening tailgate, black body, red chassis, 1925, 26-1/2" long	450	750	1100
Dump Truck, Ride 'Em, c.1945, 29" long	200	300	425
Express Truck, wind-up, 20" long	100	175	250
Fire Truck, No. 49, Packard, open cab, 4 ladders, red, 1925, 27-1/2" long........	275	425	675
Fire Truck, No. 52, Packard, open cab, 2 ladders, "Fire Department" decals, "Ride 'em" version in 1932, 1926, 27-1/2" long	600	1100	1500
Hydraulic Dump Truck, No. 62, Packard, hydraulic piston lifts truck bed, black cab, red chassis, 1927, 26" long...........	550	950	1450
Koaster Truck, No. 54, Packard, w/2 skids, hoist cable, windlass, 1926, 26" long when skids retracted	800	1350	1900
Koaster Truck, No. 55, Packard, without skids and windlass, 1927, 26" long......	450	675	1150
Ladder Truck, 24" long	250	400	750
Mack Fire Truck, Ride 'Em, cab over engine	235	375	600
Milk Truck, Ride 'Em, No. 87, Packard, white, 1932, 27" long..........................	1400	2300	3300
Moving Van, No. 58, Packard, opening rear doors, "Keystone Moving Van Long Distance Moving" decals, 1926, 26" long..	750	1300	1850
Plastic Sedan, hood lifts, gas tank fills and drains out oil pan, 1948 to early 1950s, 4-3/4" long..............................	25	40	75
Police Patrol, No. 51, "Ride 'em" version in 1932, black, screen sided body, rear step-up platform w/brass railing, 1926, 27-1/2" long	700	1200	1975
Police Van, 1920s	NPF	NPF	NPF
Pure Milk Divco, motor drive, No. D-402	150	225	300
Service Center w/vehicles	70	105	140

	C6	C8	C10
Sprinkler Truck, No. 53, Packard, sprinkler detaches, black cab, tank 12" long, 1925, 26" long.....................	800	1300	2000
Steam Roller, No. 60, red and black, air pressure whistle, brass bell, 1929, 20" long...	600	850	1250
Steam Roller, Ride 'Em, No. 60, air whistle, bell, black and red, 1930, 20" long...	232	348	465
Steam Shovel, No. 46, 26" long when arm is extended	425	638	450
Steam Shovel, No. 47, 34-1/2" long when arm is extended, 1925, 21" long	250	375	500
Steam Shovel, Ride 'Em, No. 47, extension arm, boiler, 1928, 21" long..	200	300	400
Tank, wooden w/metal firing mechanism, 6" long...	NPF	NPF	NPF
Traffic Outfit, plastic, gas pump, battery-operated traffic light, 2 parking meters, sedan (4-3/4" long) w/opening hood and fillable gas tank, No. 737, 1949, box measures 12-3/4" x 12-1/4" x 1-1/2"	NPF	NPF	NPF
Truck Loader, No. 44, digger w/loader, 1926, 17-3/4" high	500	800	1100
U.S. Army Truck, No. 48, Packard, canvas cover over truck bed, 1927, 26" long..	432	648	865
U.S. Mail Truck, No. 45, black cab w/"Packard" decal on grille, green screen-sided body w/"U.S. Mail" decals on sides, 1925, 26" long...........	750	1450	2000
Water Pump Tower, No. 56, Packard, open cab, bell, 2 ladders, tower raises, water tank pumps water through tower nozzle, red, 1925, 29" long	700	1250	1650
Water Pump Tower, Ride 'Em, No. 56, decal reads: "Water Tower with Real Pump," 1938, 29" long	200	300	400
Water Tower, No. 59, same design as No. 56 w/out working water pump and tank, 1929, 29" long.............................	1300	2100	3000
Wrecking Car, No. 78, Packard, open cab, crane, 1928, 27" long	775	1400	1950

KILGORE

The Kilgore Mfg. Co. Inc., of Westerville, Ohio, began toy making in 1925. Kilgore introduced its low-priced cast-iron toys in 1928, and cap pistols quickly became the most popular line. It also did well with a number of attractive trucks, fire engines, and cars, as well as scattered aircraft and ships. Some

subsidiary manufacturing was done in Lancaster, Penn., and Canada. In 1937, Kilgore began making plastic cars, trucks, planes, and buses, and later added plastic cap pistols, placing it among the first companies to produce plastic toys.

Kilgore remained in business until 1978.

	C6	C8	C10
Arctic Ice Cream Truck, 8" long	600	1000	1400
Arctic Ice Cream Truck, 9" long	500	750	1000
Arctic Ice Cream Truck, w/three interchangeable bodies, 6-3/8" long	550	1000	1400
Auto, LF 1300A, w/driver	180	270	360
Aviation Semi Tanker Ford, 1931, 12-1/4" long	2000	4000	5200
Bus, double decker, c.1930, 6" long	450	675	900
Bus, plastic, stamped "Bus" on sides, advertised in 1937, 4-3/8" long	20	25	30
Convertible with Rumble Seat, w/driver, early 1930s, 7" long	160	240	320
Coupe, cast iron, 1930s, 5" long	70	105	140
Coupe, cast iron, 4" long	60	90	120
Coupe, streamlined, plastic, assorted colors, 1938, 4" long	22	33	45
Dump Truck, 1930s, 7" long	180	270	360
Dump Truck, cast iron, 5-window cab, vertical hood louvers, c.1934, 8-1/2" long	800	1500	2180
Dump Truck, cast iron, c.1934, 5-3/4" long	160	240	320
Express Truck, plastic, assorted colors, stamped "Express" on sides, advertised in 1937, 4" long	22	33	45
Fire Chief Sedan, plastic, advertised in 1937, 4" long	22	33	45
Fire Ladder Truck, 7-1/2" long	200	300	400
Fire Pumper, cast iron, 4" long	80	120	160
Fire Pumper, cast iron, 5" long	88	132	175
Ford Deluxe Sedan, 1934, 7" long	NPF	NPF	NPF
Ford Wrecker, 1931, 10-3/4" long	1200	2100	3100
Livestock Truck, 1930s, 7" long	700	1050	1400
Livestock Truck, 6-1/4" long	165	248	330
Livestock Truck, 8" long	600	900	1200
Low Boy Machinery Hauler, 1931, 12-1/4" long	900	1500	2300
Model T Coupe, 5" long	200	300	400
Open Town Car, plastic, 4" long	15	20	25
Packard Luxury Sedan, take-apart body, 8-1/4" long	800	1200	1600
Pierce-Arrow Roadster, take-apart body, 6-1/8" long	250	375	500
Police Car, plastic, 1937, 4" long	22	33	45

Kilgore Arctic Ice Cream Truck, 6-3/8" with three interchangeable bodies. Photo courtesy Bertoia Auctions

One of several versions of Kilgore's Arctic Ice Cream Truck–this is the 9" version.

Kilgore Motorcycle with delivery box, nickel wheels, 5-7/8". Photo courtesy Kent M. Comstock

Left to right: Kilgore Motorcycle Trike Special Delivery, white rubber tires, 4-1/4"; Kilgore Motorcycle with sidecar, nickel wheels. Photo courtesy Kent M. Comstock

Kilgore Tank, 2-1/2". Photo courtesy Ed Poole

Kilgore Aviation Semi Tanker Ford, 12-1/4". Photo courtesy Bertoia Auctions

Kilgore Bus, double decker, circa 1930, 6". Photo courtesy Christie's East

Kilgore Coupe, streamlined, plastic, 4". Photo courtesy Dave Leopard

Kilgore Dump Truck, circa 1934, 5-3/4". Photo courtesy James S. Maxwell and Viginia Caputo

Kilgore Express Truck, plastic, 4". Photo courtesy Dave Leopard

Kilgore Stutz Roadster, thirteen parts.

Kilgore Livestock truck, 8". Photo courtesy Rod Carnahan

Kilgore Fire Chief Sedan, plastic, 4". Photo courtesy Dave Leopard

Kilgore Taxi, plastic, 4". Photo courtesy Dave Leopard

Kilgore Stake Truck, take-apart, 5". Photo courtesy Bertoia Auctions

	C6	C8	C10
Pontiac, cast iron, 1930, 10" long (See Stutz)...	NPF	NPF	NPF
Race Car, Rocket, 1930s, 4-1/4" long......	112	168	225
Race Car, Rocket, 1930s, 6-1/2" long......	225	338	450
Roadster, 4" long..................................	68	102	135
Roadster, driver, rumble seat, 6" long......	230	345	460
Roadster, driver, rumble seat, 8" long......	375	563	750
Sedan, 3-1/4" long..................................	70	105	140
Sedan, 5" long	175	263	350
Sedan, plastic, assorted colors, 1938, 4-1/2" long..	NPF	NPF	NPF
Stake Truck, 3-1/2" long.........................	62	93	125
Stake Truck, take-apart, 5" long...............	112	168	225
Stutz Roadster, thirteen parts	1100	1500	2500
Tank, cast iron, 2-1/2" long.....................	30	45	60
Taxi, plastic, advertised in 1937, assorted colors, 4-1/4" long	22	33	45
Toy Town Delivery Truck, 6-1/8" long ...	200	300	400
Tractor, w/scoop......................................	100	150	200

Motorcycles

	C6	C8	C10
Motorcycle, solo, removable rider, rubber tires, 6-1/2" long (KM006)	400	600	1000
Motorcycle, solo, rubber tires, 5-3/4" long (KM005)	150	225	350
Motorcycle, w/delivery box, nickel wheels, 5-7/8" long (KM007)	250	500	750

Kilgore Toy Town Delivery Truck, 6-1/8". Photo courtesy Bertoia Auctions

	C6	C8	C10
Motorcycle, w/sidecar nickel wheels, 4-1/4" long (KM003)	125	200	300
Motorcycle, w/sidecar nickel wheels, 5" long (KM004)	175	250	400
Motorcycle solo, police, white rubber tires, single headlight, 4" long (KM001)	75	100	150
Motorcycle trike, Special Delivery, white rubber tires, disc wheels in back-spoke wheel in front, 4-1/4" long (KM002) ..	150	225	350

KINGSBURY

Kingsbury had its origins in 1886 in Keene, New Hampshire. Its owner was Harry T. Kingsbury, who bought the Wilkins Toy Co., apparently not phasing out that firm's name until 1919. Steel and spring motors characterize Kingsbury's toys, with cars, fire engines, farm equipment and racing cars its primary output. Kingsbury is still in business, but gave up toy production in 1942.

One version of Kingsbury's Airflow. Photo courtesy Mapes Auctioneers & Appraisers

Kingsbury Auto Delivery Truck, No. 749, circa 1908. Photo courtesy Phillips

Kingsbury Cannon Truck, wind-up, circa 1939, 15". Photo courtesy Orville C. Britor

Kingsbury Coupe, circa 1930, rumble seat, electric lights, 12-1/2". Photo courtesy Christie's East

Kingsbury Fire Chief Coupe, wind-up, 12-1/4". Photo courtesy Bob Smith

Kingsbury Fire Pumper, cast-iron.

Kingsbury Greyhound Bus, wind-up, 18". Photo courtesy Bob Smith

Kingsbury Fire Pumper, 1930s, 20". Photo courtesy Calvin L. Chaussee

Kingsbury Lincoln Zephyr and Travel Trailer, 22-1/2", circa 1936.

Kingsbury Golden Arrow Racer, pressed steel, wind-up, 20". Photo courtesy Kevin Sharp. Detroit Antique Toy Museum

	C6	C8	C10
Aerial Ladder Truck, pressed steel, wind-up, ladder rises automatically to height of 38" when the truck runs into any obstruction, fireman on ladder climbs up and down by turning crank at base of ladder, early version new in 1905; c.1941, 24" long	250	375	625
Aerial Ladder Truck, wind-up, 1920s, 33" long	1200	2000	3000
Aerial Ladder Truck, wind-up, 1920s, 9" long	250	375	550
Airflow, clockwork motor, battery-operated lights and sound, rubber tires, c. 1935, 14" long	275	400	750
Airflow, pressed steel, rubber tires, no motor, c.1935, 14" long	275	375	600
Army Truck, c.1941	125	175	250
Auto, steel, wind-up, very early, 9-3/4" long	325	525	750

	C6	C8	C10
Auto Delivery Truck, No. 749, c.1908	700	1200	1800
Bluebird Racer	750	1200	2000
Brougham Sedan, pressed steel, wind-up, 13" long	550	900	1500
Cannon Truck, clockwork, very early, 11" long	150	250	350
Cannon Truck, wind-up, c.1939, 15" long	150	250	350
Caterpillar, wind-up, 8-1/2" long	150	250	350
Cattle, 1930s, 19" long	100	185	275
Chemical Fire Truck, clockwork motor, c.1929, 14" long	950	1750	2750
Chemical Ladder Truck, 35" long	1100	2000	3000
Combination Chemical Truck, 26" long	1250	2250	3500
Contractors Tractor	150	225	300
Coupe, electric lights, No. 444, 13-1/2" long	500	800	1200
Coupe, No. 244	800	1300	2000
Coupe, No. 344, 13-1/2" long	500	900	1100
Coupe, No. 74200	550	900	1300

	C6	C8	C10
Coupe, rumble seat, electric light, c.1930, 12-1/2" long	325	488	650
Coupe, wind-up, 11" long	800	1400	1900
Coupe, wind-up, has music box, electric lights, 14" long	500	825	1250
Delivery Stake Truck, w/driver, 1923, 9" long	225	325	450
DeSoto, pressed steel wind-up, c.1938, 14-1/2" long	275	375	600
Divco Borden's Van, No. 254, white step van, "Borden's" decals, 1937, 9" long.	350	525	750
Divco Grocery Van	300	450	650
Divco U.S. Air Mail Truck	300	450	675
Dray Stake Truck, early 1930s	150	225	325
Dump Truck, 11-1/2" long	450	700	1100
Dump Truck, clockwork, early 1930s, 16" long	350	525	750
Dump Truck, tin, driver, 10" long	200	300	450
Express Truck, late	200	275	375
Fire Chief Coupe, 1930s, 14" long	325	550	850
Fire Chief Coupe, No. 341, wind-up, rubber tires, bell, 1927, 13" long	750	1250	2000
Fire Pumper, 1920s, 23" long	1000	1700	2700

	C6	C8	C10
Fire Pumper, 1930s, 20" long	300	450	650
Fire Pumper, 9-1/2" long	200	300	400
Fire Pumper, very early, clockwork, iron and steel, 11" long	300	450	675
Fire Truck, 18" long	220	330	440
Fire Truck, mechanical ladder, cast-iron driver, 1915, 9-1/2" long	235	355	470
Ford Sedan and House Trailer, pressed steel, 1937, 23" long	350	535	700
Golden Arrow Racer, No. 337, pressed steel, wind-up, 1927, 21" long	465	700	930
Greyhound Bus, GM Silversides style, pressed steel, white rubber tires, 1940s, 18" long	135	275	425
Greyhound Bus, GM/Yellow Coach, pressed steel, white rubber tires, wind-up motor, 1930s, 18" long	350	500	850
Huckster Truck, 9-1/2" long	800	1200	2090
Ladder Truck, 10-1/2" long	100	150	200
Ladder Truck, 33" long	1000	2300	3600
Ladder Truck, early, 19" long	1700	3000	4700
Ladder Truck, pressed steel, wind-up, No. 225, 1930s, 15" long	275	375	475

Kingsbury Sand Loader, 12". Photo courtesy Calvin L. Chaussee

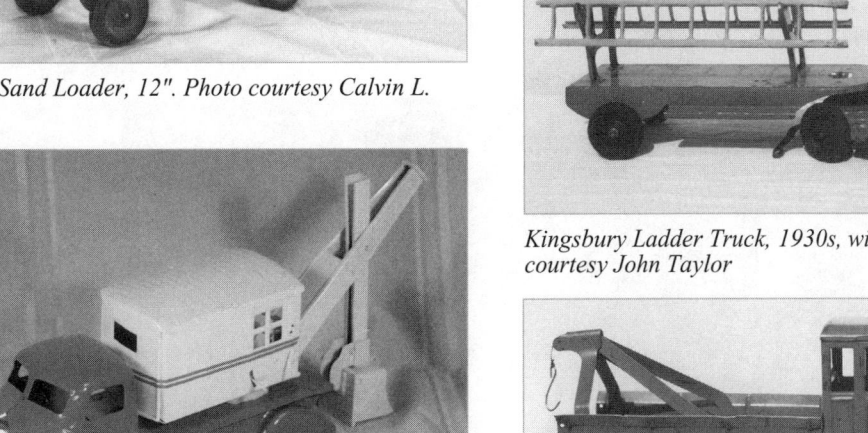

Kingsbury Truck with Crane, 1930s. Photo courtesy Calvin L. Chaussee

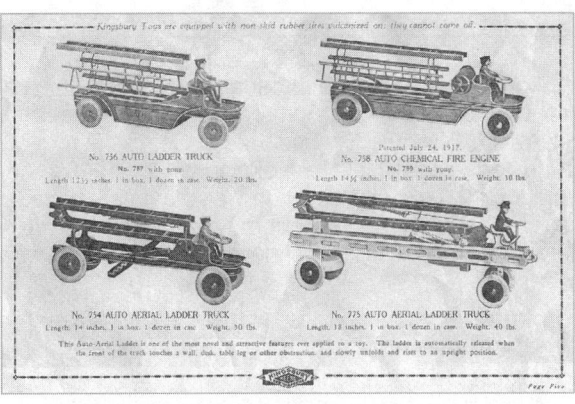

An illustration from a Kingsbury catalog c.1922.

Kingsbury Ladder Truck, 1930s, windup, 15". Photo courtesy John Taylor

Kingsbury Wrecker, late 1920s, windup, 14". Photo courtesy John Taylor

	C6	C8	C10
Ladder Truck, steel, driver, 22" long	150	250	350
Ladder Wagon Fire Truck, tin, rubber tires, 23-1/2" long	100	175	275
Lincoln Zephyr and Travel Trailer, c.1936, 22-1/2" long	325	500	700
Little Jim Delivery Truck, 13" long	300	450	550
Little Jim Tow Truck, 11" long................	300	450	650
Little Jim Tractor	250	375	500
Little Jim Truck.......................................	700	1100	1600
Mail Truck, w/driver, early, 7" long	500	800	1100
Panama Dump Truck, clockwork, 1923, 14" long...	750	1000	1400
Phaeton Auto, rubber slip tires, 1900, 9-1/2" long	750	1125	1500
Pure Milk Truck	132	198	265
Rack Truck, pressed steel, wind-up, 16" long...	350	525	700
Roadster, 11" long..................................	350	525	700
Roadster, No. 242, electric headlights, spring motor, luggage rack, 13" long...	550	950	1250
Roadster, No. 433, same as No. 242	NPF	NPF	NPF

	C6	C8	C10
Sand Loader, 12" long	125	188	250
Sedan, No. 300..	1300	2000	2900
Semi-Truck, cab over	155	250	325
Stake Truck, clockwork, c.1926, 25" long...	300	450	600
Studebaker Cannon Truck........................	150	225	400
Sunbeam Racer, sheetmetal, red w/rubber tires on steel wheels, clockwork motor, 19" long...	500	750	1050
Tractor, mechanical, w/driver, 8" long	160	240	320
Tractor and Cart, tin, w/iron driver, white rubber wheels, 1930s	150	250	450
Transit Truck, 1930s, 19" long	150	250	400
Truck with C Cab, tin, 10" long..............	175	262	350
Truck with Carne, 1930s, 20" long	175	300	500
Windup Car, curved dash, driver, 9" long	225	337	450
Wrecker, pressed steel, wind-up, 13" long...	250	375	500
Wrecker, pressed steel, wind-up, 1927, 14" long...	550	750	950
Yellow Cab, 1934	350	525	700

KINGSTON PRODUCERS

The Kingston Products Co. was founded in Kokomo, Ind. It was the manufacturer of "Kokomo Toys"—its toy division. Some Kokomo Toys are stamped, "Kokomo Stamped Metal Company." Kingston released its electric racers in the 1920s and into the 1930s, but production was ultimately halted by the Depression. The company survived past World War II and became known for its roller skates.

	C6	C8	C10
Duesenberg, w/transformer and steel track, 12" long..................................	1500	2700	3700
Dump Truck	150	225	300
Electric Truck......................................	150	225	300
Electricar, the Red Arrow, 1930s, 15" long..	150	225	300
Electricar Set, racer and truck	500	750	1000
Ice Truck	150	225	300
Wrecker..	150	225	300

KNAPP

Knapp Electric Inc. was located in Indianapolis, Ind., and was founded in 1894. It offered several electric-powered toys before World War II. It was among the first companies to use batteries to power its toys.

	C6	C8	C10
Electric Automobile, battery-activated, pressed steel, c.1903, 11" long	1500	2400	4000

Knapp "Electric Automobile," c. 1903. Photo courtesy Sotheby's New York

LAKETOY

	C6	C8	C10
John Wanamaker Delivery Van, wooden, 10-1/2" long	180	270	350

LANSING SLIK-TOYS

Lansing Slik-Toys were produced by the Lansing Co. Inc., and made in Lansing, Iowa. They sometimes bear the name "Kipp," in addition to the "Lansing" and "Slik-Toy" trademarks. Most Slik-Toys are made of aluminum in a single casting, but some were made of hard plastic. It seems that all Slik-Toys have a four-digit number beginning with "9." If a toy bears such a number, even if it has no other markings, it is almost surely a Slik-Toy.

Contributor: Dave Leopard, 2507 Feather Run Trail, West Columbia, SC 29169-4915.

Left to right: Lansing Silk-Toys Pickup Truck, 4"; Tank Truck, 4", plastic; Sedan 1949 Buick, plastic. Photo courtesy Dave Leopard

A Lansing Slik Toys ad as seen in the July, 1946 issue of Toys & Novelties.

	C6	C8	C10
Bulldozer	65	98	130
Combine	150	225	300
Corn Picker, goes w/Oliver 77 Tractor	225	338	450
Fire Truck, No. 9606, 6" long	25	35	45
Fire Truck, No. 9700, 3-1/2" long	25	35	45
Fire Truck, No. 9706, plastic, 4" long	20	25	30
Grader, 17" long	70	132	175
Grader, 9-1/2" long	40	75	100
Metro Van, No. 9618, 5" long	30	40	50
Oliver 77 Tractor, approx. 7-3/4" long	142	217	285
Open Stake Truck, No. 9602, 7" long	30	40	60
Pickup Truck, No. 9601, 7" long	30	40	60
Pickup Truck, No. 9605, 6" long	30	40	60
Pickup Truck, No. 9703, plastic, 4" long	20	25	30
Roadster, No. 9701, aluminum, 3-1/2" long	25	35	45
Sand and Gravel Dump, 12" long	70	105	140
Sedan, No. 9600, fastback, 7" long	25	35	50
Sedan, No. 9600, fastback, taxi version, 7" long	40	50	65
Sedan, No. 9604, four-door, 6" long	20	30	40
Sedan, No. 9702, Buick, plastic, c.1949	15	20	30
Stake Truck, No. 9616, 6" long	25	30	40
Stakebody Truck, No. 9500, 11" long	50	65	85
Station Wagon, No. 9704, plastic, 4" long	20	25	30
Tank Truck, No. 9603, 7" long	25	35	50
Tank Truck, No. 9607, 6" long	20	30	40
Tank Truck, No. 9705, plastic, 4" long	20	25	30
Tractor/Trailer Rig, No. 9610, milk tanker, 8" long	30	45	60
Tractor/Trailer Rig, No. 9611, grain trailer, 8" long	30	40	55
Tractor/Trailer Rig, No. 9612, (log trailer) 18" long	25	40	55
TractorTtrailer Rig, No. 9613, (flatbed trailer), 8" long	25	35	45
Wrecker, No. 9617, 5" long	20	25	35
Wrecker, No. 9707, plastic, 4" long	20	25	30

LAPIN

Lapin Products, Inc., was among the first to manufacture plastic toys and toy parts prior to World War II. It released several toy vehicles in the 1950s and 1960s.

Contributor: Dave Leopard, 2507 Feather Run Trail, West Columbia, SC 29169-4915.

	C6	C8	C10
1939 City Bus, rare, 4" long	20	30	40
1939 Four-door Sedan, 4" long	17	26	35
1939 Hudson Coupe, 4" long	17	26	35
1949 Cadillac Convertible, 6" long	15	20	30
1949 Cadillac Convertible, 9" long	20	30	40
1949 Cadillac Sedan, 6" long	15	20	30
1949 Cadillac Sedan, 9" long	20	30	40
1949 Chevrolet Stake Truck, No. 285, assorted colors, 1950s, 5" long	12	18	25

Several Lapin 1939 Coupes. Photo courtesy Bob and Alice Wagner

An assortment of Lapin Chevrolet Stake Trucks. Photo courtesy Bob and Alice Wagner

An assortment of Lapin 6" Cadillacs. Photo courtesy Bob and Alice Wagner

Lapin 1939 Four-door Sedans. Photo courtesy Bob and Alice Wagner

Lapin 1939 Hudson Coupe. Photo courtesy Dave Leopard

LEE STOKES INDUSTRIES

Lee Stokes started his firm in 1945 in New Oxford, Pennsylvania. Except for the first three, he created all his own models. Thirty-one different types were sold; six in O-gauge, the rest in HO, to take advantage of the postwar interest in HO-gauge trains and accessories. The cars were made of a very tough compound of plaster and urea formaldehyde, so that they stand up. The firm, with eitht employees, sold internationally, as well as in the United States. It moved to Bel Air, Maryland, in 1950 and closed in 1955. Stokes died in 1991. Prices average $30; up to $50 for the Rolls-Royce.

Contributor: Dave Leopard, 2507 Feather Run Trail, West Columbia, SC 29169-4915.

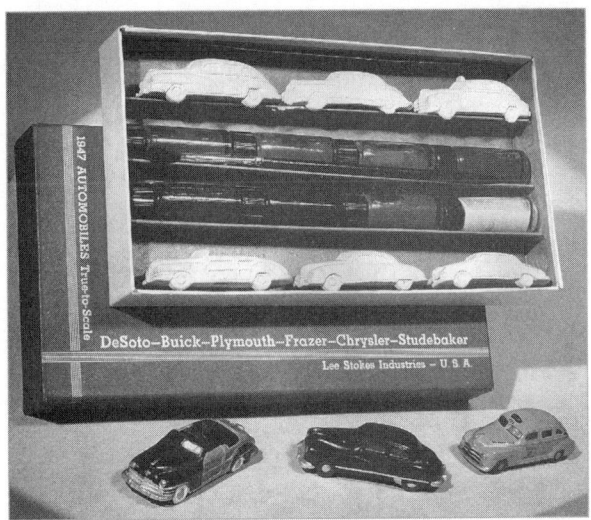

	C6	C8	C10
1949 Chevrolet Coupe, 2-1/2" long (LV02)	10	15	20
1949 Ford Tudor, HO-scale	10	20	30
Ambulance, HO-scale	10	20	30
Dump Truck, HO-scale	10	20	30
MG, HO-scale	10	20	30
Rolls-Royce, HO-scale	20	40	60
Taxi, HO-scale	10	20	30
Tractor/Trailer, modern decal, c.1948 Reo, 5-1/2" long (LV01)	20	25	30
Woody Station Wagon, HO-scale	10	20	30

A 1948 Lee Stokes kit that included DeSoto, Buick, Plymouth, Frazer, Chrysler and Studebaker models. Photo courtesy Lee Stokes Industries; B. Richmond, photographer

LEHIGH BITSI-TOYS

These heavy die-cast toys with black rubber tires were produced around 1950 and were known as "Bitsi-Toys."

Contributor: Dave Leopard, 2507 Feather Run Trail, West Columbia, SC 29169-4915.

	C6	C8	C10
Chevrolet Coupe, (1949 model), 2-1/2" long (LV002)	10	20	25
Tractor Trailer, "Modern" decal, (1948 model), 5-1/2" long (LV001)	20	25	30

LEHMANN, ERNST PAUL

Ernst Paul Lehmann began manufacturing toys in 1881, using the EPL trademark. Its founder passed away in 1934, but the company continued in business under the management of his cousin, Johannes Richter. At the end of World War II, Richter moved to West Germany. He opened a new factory in Nuremberg in 1951. The Lehmann Company is still in business making toys.

Lehmann Toys have become a common word among early tin-toy collectors. These wonderful mechanical machines are more sought-after than any other wind-up toy, though they usually command a high price. The company used many different color variations from year to year on some of its toys, giving the collector a wide variety to choose from. While some Lehmanns are very rare, it is not too difficult to build a collection of them. Most Lehmanns carry a model number for easy reference. A box adds twenty to forty percent to the value.

Contributor: Bob Smith, RATS Toy Shows, 255 Tryon Park, Rochester, NY 14609. (585) 288-7153, bird@oldtoysonline.com.

Lehmann Aha Delivery Van, 1920s tin wind-up, 5-1/2". Photo courtesy Bertoia Auctions

Lehmann Autobus tin wind-up. Photo courtesy Bertoia Auctions

Lehmann Echo Motorcycle, 1907, 9". Photo courtesy Kent M. Comstock

Lehmann Galop Racer, tin wind-up with garage. Photo courtesy Bertoia Auctions

Top row, left to right: Gnom Series BV-Aral Tanker, 4-1/2"; Gnom Series Opel Dump Truck, 4-1/2". Bottom row, left to right: Gnom Series Racing Car, 4-1/2"; Gnom Series Sedan. Photo courtesy Bob Smith

Lehmann Lu Lu Delivery Truck tin wind-up, 7-1/4". Photo courtesy Bertoia Auctions

Lehmann EHE & Co., open bed, tin wind-up.

Lehmann Gnom No. 808 Autohutt with two No. 807 tin-lithographed sedans. Photo courtesy Bob Smith

Lehmann Ito Sedan, 1920s, 6-1/2". Photo courtesy Christie's East

Lehmann Am Pol, 5-3/4". Photo courtesy Bertoia Auctions

Lehmann Uhu Amphibious Car. Photo courtesy
Sotheby's

Lehmann Mixtum Comic Car, 4". Photo
courtesy Bertoia Auctions

Lehmann Motor Car Kutsche, 1897, 5-1/2" long.

*Lehmann
Mensa
Delivery Van,
circa 1912,
5-1/4". Photo
courtesy Bob
Smith*

*Lehmann
Motor Coach,
1920s, 5-1/2".
Photo courtesy
Sotheby's*

*Lehmann Terra
tin wind-up.
Photo courtesy
Bertoia Auctions*

*Lehmann Uhu
Amphibious
Car. Photo
courtesy
Sotheby's*

*Lehmann Tut Tut, man in
car with horn, 6-3/4". Photo
courtesy Christie's East*

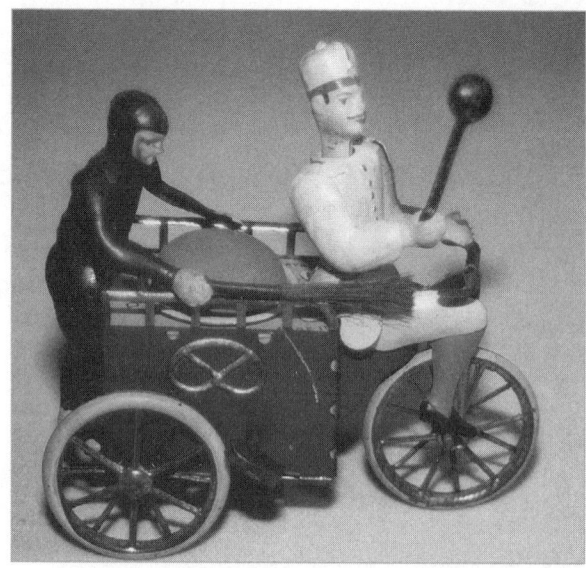

*Lehmann Baker and Chimney Sweep, tin wind-up, 5-1/4".
Photo courtesy Kent M. Comstock*

	C6	C8	C10
Aha Delivery Van, tin wind-up, 1920s, 5-1/2" long	500	850	1400
Auto Post, tin wind-up, 5" long	650	1100	1700
Autobus, tin wind-up	800	1400	2000
Autohutte Garage, No. 771, 6" long	200	300	600
Baker and Chimney Sweep, tin wind-up, c.1900-1935, 5-1/4" long	2000	3800	6200
Berolina Car, tin wind-up	1500	2500	3700
Deutsche Reichspost, wind-up, postal truck w/driver, 1927	800	1400	2400
Echo Motorcycle, tin wind-up, No. 725, 1907, 9" long	1000	1700	3000
EHE & Co. Truck, tin wind-up, open bed	320	550	1000
Galop Racer, No. 1, tin wind-up w/garage	800	1200	1800
Gnom No. 808 Autohutt Garage, w/two no. 807 Sedans, tin lithographed, c.1935	500	750	1400
Gnom Series No. 807 Sedan, various colors, tin lithographed, c.1935, 4-1/2" long	200	350	700
Gnom Series No. 808 Racing Car, various colors colors, tin lithographed, c.1935, 4-1/2" long	250	400	850
Gnom Series No. 813 Opel Dump Truck, red/green, tin lithographed, c.1935, 4-1/2" long	200	350	750
Gnom Series No. 835 BV-Aral Tanker, blue/gray, tin lithographed, c.1938, 4-1/2" long	250	400	800
IHI Meat Van, lithographed tin, clockwork, cloth sides, 6-5/8" long	1200	1800	2400
Ito Sedan, tin wind-up, 1920s, 6-1/2" long	500	850	1400
Lana Auto, tin wind-up	1200	2000	3000
Lehmann Am Pol, 5-3/4"	NPF	NPF	NPF
Lehmann's Autobus 590, tin wind-up, brown	1000	1800	2500
Lehmann's Autobus 590, tin wind-up, red	800	1400	2000
Li La Car, tin wind-up, early, 5-1/2" long	1000	1700	2500
Lo Lo Car, tin wind-up, w/driver, early	500	750	1100
Lu Lu Delivery Truck, tin wind-up, 7-1/4" long	1500	2700	4000

	C6	C8	C10
Mensa Delivery Van, No. 688, red/blue, clockwork motor, three wheel, steering, c.1912, 5-1/4" long	1200	1900	3000
Mixtum Comic Car, 4" long	1200	2200	3200
Motor Car Kutsche, tin wind-up, 1897, 5-1/2" long	400	550	800
Motor Coach, tin wind-up, 1920s 5-1/2" long	325	475	600
Naughty Boy, tin wind-up	650	1200	1500
New Century Cycle, tin wind-up, 1907, 5" long	400	650	1000
Oho, tin wind-up, c.1903	325	575	850
Onkel, tin wind-up	375	575	900
Panne Touring Car, tin wind-up, 6-1/2" long	550	850	1200

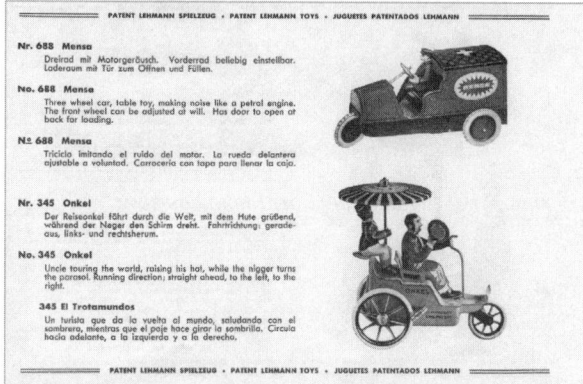

The Mensa Delivery Van and the Onkel, as they appeared in a reprint of an 1881 Lehmann catalog.

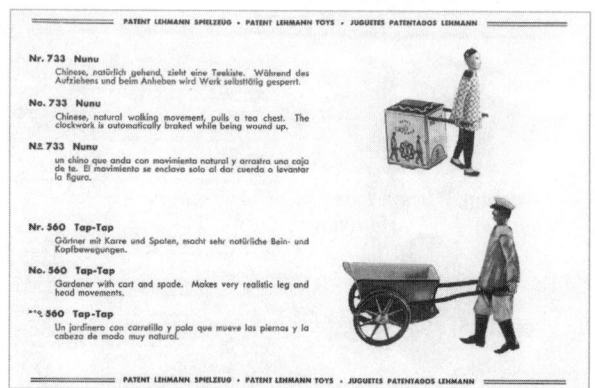

Reprint page from an 1881 Lehmann catalog.

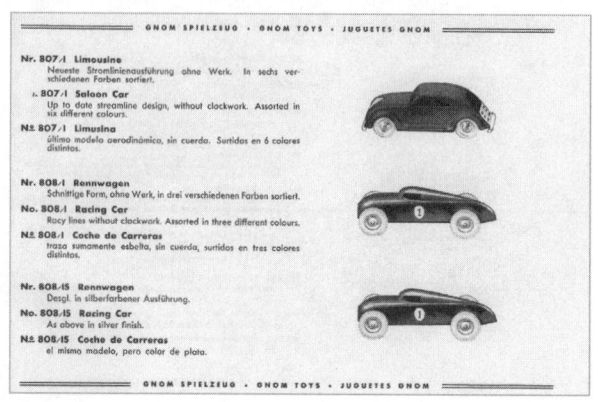

Another reprint page from an 1881 Lehmann catalog.

	C6	C8	C10
Peter Clown Car	1000	1600	2200
Royal Mail Van, lithographed tin, clockwork, w/driver, 6-3/4" long	1200	1800	2200
Sedan, tin wind-up, 5-1/2" long	275	400	550
Terra, tin wind-up	650	1100	1650

	C6	C8	C10
Tut-Tut, tin wind-up, man in car w/horn, 6-3/4" long	650	1100	1700
Uhu Amphibious Car, tin wind-up	800	1850	2400
Velleda, lithographed tin, clockwork, open sedan w/chauffer	900	1500	2000

LIDO

Lido was founded in October 1947 by brothers Seymour and Effram Arenstein, with the purchase of Elite Toy Co. from David Krotman. Krotman made plastic bubble pipes, scissors, and a horn. Located in Bronx, New York, the firm was near the Lido Country Club, hence the name. For $6,800, the Arensteins bought the molds and the name. Lido's toys were small and always plastic. Eventually, the Arensteins were known as the "Louis Marxes of low-end" toys.

At its peak, Lido employed close to 1,000 people. In the years after the 1950s, they employed several thousand indirectly in Hong Kong, Japan, and Taiwan. They sold out, due to disagreements, to Bala Corporation of Philadelphia, which liquidated a year later. What was left was eventually bought by Gabriel Industries. From 1973-1990, Seymour Arentstein owned Joy Toy.

	C6	C8	C10
Auto, w/trailer hitch, 9-1/2" long	15	22	30
Bus, plastic in red, blue, yellow, or green; 1940s, 5-1/2" long	10	20	30
Bus, plastic, 3" long	4	6	10
Convertible, plastic, assorted colors, rubber wheels, 1949 to early 1950s, 6" long	10	17	25
Fire Truck, plastic ladder truck, rubber wheels, 1949, 6" long	10	20	33
Fire Truck, plastic, red, 3" long	4	6	8

	C6	C8	C10
Gasoline Tanker, plastic, assorted colors, rubber wheels, 1949, 6" long	10	20	35
Jeep and Trailer, plastic, 3" long	5	8	10
Moving Van, plastic, assorted colors, rubber wheels, 1949, 6" long	10	20	35
Pickup Truck, plastic, assorted colors, rubber wheels, 1949, 6" long	10	20	30
Racer, plastic, 3" long	4	6	8
Service Truck, plastic, 3-1/2" long	8	12	17
Touring Car, plastic, 6" long	7	14	20

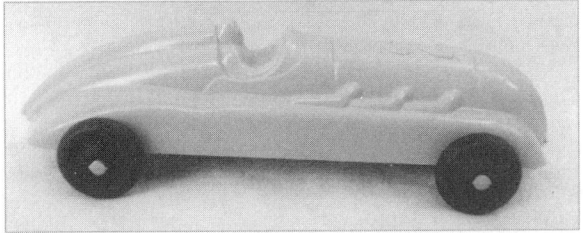

Lido Racer, 3". Photo courtesy Dave Leopard

Lido Auto, trailer, hitch, plastic, 9-1/2". Photo courtesy Ron Fink

Lido assortment. Front row: Touring Car, Racer, Oil Truck, Jeep; 3" long. Middle row: Touring Car, Fire Truck, Bus; 3" long. Back row: Touring Car, 6" long. Photo courtesy John McCurdy

Lido Convertible, 1950s. Photo courtesy Dave Leopard

LIMOUSINE

	C6	C8	C10
Limousine, tin wind-up, license plate reads "N.Y. 1918," lithographed, approx. 6" long	140	210	280

LINCOLN TOYS

Lincoln Toys was founded in 1946 as Lincoln Specialities by the father and son team of Haven and Frederick Kimmerly as a division of their company, Windsor Steel. Located in Walkerville, Ontario, Canada, Lincoln Toys specialized in pressed-steel trucks. By 1953, the company offered a variety of 24 different vehicles including dump trucks, construction equipment, A Massey-Harris 44 tractor, and a rare airplane. The company was in business until 1958.

Contributor: John Taylor, P.O. Box 63, Nolensville, TN 37135-0063.

Lincoln Toys Sand Truck Dump, 14". Photo courtesy Bob Smith

	C6	C8	C10
Allied Van Lines Truck, 23" long	175	325	475
Auto Transport, 2 steel cars, 25" long	175	350	700
Auto Transport, Double Decker w/4 plastic cars	150	275	425
Borden's Milk Truck, 18-1/2" long	150	300	450
Cement Truck, 13" long	100	250	400
Coca Cola Truck, w/12 wood cases, 16" long	300	600	900
Crane Truck	100	200	350
Department of Highways Dump Truck, 19" long	100	200	350
Dump Truck, "Phil Wood," 7" long	75	150	300
Dunlop Wrecker, 13" long	100	250	400
Dunlop Wrecker, 7" long	75	200	350
Dunlop Wrecker, rare, 9" long	75	200	350
Dunlop Wreckers, 11" long	100	250	400
Express Truck, 11" long	75	150	300
Express Truck, Trans Canada	125	275	425
Fire Truck, 2 ladders, 8" long	75	150	300
Heinz Pickle Truck	300	450	600
Hi Dump Truck, 20" long	50	125	275
Highway Express, 17" long	125	275	425
Ice Truck, "Ice Delivery," 13-1/2" long	100	250	400
Jeep, Lincoln's first and only wooden toy was a small Jeep	NPF	NPF	NPF
Ladder Truck, steel, 1950s, available in both 15" and 17" version	100	200	350

	C6	C8	C10
Lincoln Transport, early 1950s, 24" long	175	275	350
Lincoln Van Lines	100	250	400
Lowney's Chocolate Bars Truck, 24" long	200	450	600
Phil Wood Dump Truck, 12" long	50	100	250
Phil Wood Dump Truck, 16" long	50	100	250
Phil Wood Dump Truck, 7" long	75	150	300
Planter's Peanuts, rare, 14" long	NPF	NPF	NPF
Red Cross Ambulance, rare, 14" long	NPF	250	NPF
Sand Dump Truck, 14" long	75	200	350
Sanitation Truck, 13-1/2" long	150	300	450
Sedan, steel, 7-1/4" long	50	100	200
Shovel, 16" long	125	175	275
Simpson's Dept. Store Truck, 14" long	NPF	450	NPF
Telephone Service Truck	125	350	800
Tow Truck, different variations of Dunlop Wrecker, 13" long	100	250	400
Tow Truck, round fenders, 14" long	100	250	400
Tow Truck, w/two spares, 16" long	150	300	450

LINCOLN WHITE METAL WORKS

This Lincoln, Nebraska, firm is now recognized as the maker of many high-quality prewar slush mold "orphan toys." This long obscurity is all the more surprising because Clayton E. Stevenson, founder, was a many-talented personage in the Dime Store Toy industry—an artist, skilled craftsman, and salesman with worldwide contacts. He had made toys at home since the early 1920s (see Mid-West Metal Novelty Co.); as a salesman for Western Diecasting Co., he furnished some molds to Kansas Toy and may have furnished some to Tip Top Toy and others. His specialty were toys made from a the three-piece mold. The third piece was used to cast those uniquely realistic front-ends (grille, headlamps, fenders). These molds, and the more-complex molds for those beautiful tri-motored aircraft (Lincoln's Fokker and C.A.W.'s Fords), were surprising in this competitive industry, because it slowed production and added to costs. For us collectors it created rarity.

Stevenson had a remarkably long toy making career, about fifteen years, through the Great Depression. What we know came from a story in the Nov. 20, 1931, *Nebraska State Journal*, an article in the January 1984 *Antique Toy World*, and from biographical information, photos, and toys saved by his daughter, Marian Horn. Stevenson, an auto mechanic, was born in 1896 and raised in Axtell, Kansas. He, and his wife, Ester, moved to Lincoln in 1931, and started marketing toys in his name at 1250 Dakota Street. For a new business, he had a rapid rise. In his first season he made 800,000 toys in three months. He was manager, purchaser, worker, and salesman. As his business grew (30,000 toys a day and twenty-seven to thirty laborers at one time), he

moved to a larger facility at 2204 Y Street. In 1935, he was listed at 3433 J Street. The toys were sold to Woolworth, Kress, Kresge, and Schwartz Paper Co., stores, as well as all over the country, especially California and New York, and even abroad.

The factory was sold in 1940, after nine years of production, due to shortages of lead and rubber and the rising costs of labor—all due to expansion of war production. (We were not told who bought what, although a few clues point to nearby Ralstoy. Although 1940 is the date given by a family member, the business was not listed in Lincoln directories after 1937.)

A variety of toys were made—tiny airplanes, midget racers, larger speed cars, brilliant sedans, small coupes, tri-motor plane models, and miniature sawmills. They range in size from three inches to seven inches long. Stevenson, who made the molds, used pictures of planes and cars shown in magazines. For his midget racer, he used a picture of a Miller special. His sedan was a replica of the front-drive Cord. His coupe was a Nash model. His tri-motor plane was taken from a photo of a Ford product. Early toys used metal wheels and tin propellers and had neat patterned bottom pans. Later toys had rubber wheels. This list below is incomplete. Collectors with more information are welcome to send the info to the contributor listed below, or directly to the editor at the address listed in the Introduction of this book.

Note: Abbreviations in this chapter are the same as used in the Kansas Toy Co. chapter.

Contributors: Perry R. Eichor, 703 North Almond Drive, Simpsonville, SC, 29681 and the late Fred Maxwell.

	C6	C8	C10
Brougham, Graham (?), vertical V-grille, SM, fiour OW, T, made from three-piece mold, 3-1/2" long (LWV021)	50	75	110
Bus, Overland, HO, HG, VL, ten OW, 3-1/2" long (LWV027)	30	45	70
Coupe, Graham (?), slanted vee-grille, divided WS, two OW, SM, T, from three-piece mold, 3-3/8" long (LWV015)	30	40	50
Coupe, Graham (?), VG, SM, two OW, LI, T, made from three-piece mold, 3-1/2" long (LWV018)	30	40	60
Coupe, Oldsmobile, streamlined, slanted vee-grille, HO, HL, divided W.S., two OW, RM, patterned pan, 4" long (LWV016)	30	40	60
Coupe, slanted hood, rear-mount hub for rubber tire, slanted grill (see Tootsie Graham); 4-1/2" long (LWV019)	40	60	80
Coupe, streamline, Pontiac, HO, VG, HL, two OW, H trim on front fenders, embossed folded "trunk rack", patterned pan, 3-3/8" long (LWV014)	40	60	80

	C6	C8	C10
Coupe, streamlined Lincoln (?), slanted vee-grille, divided WS, two OW, patterned pan, 3-1/2" long (LWV017)	35	50	70
Coupe, vertical hood, wrap-around (?), rear window, T (LWV020)	40	60	80
Fire Engine, steam pumper, two man crew, hose real compartment, HO, HG, 3-1/4" long (LWV012)	40	80	110
Fire Engine Pumper, w/fireman on rear step, Graham-like grille, fenders faired bumper to bumper, patterned pan, marked "Made in USA," "Patrol No. 79," 3-3/4" long (LWV009)	75	100	125
Indy Racer, large (LWV030)	NPF	NPF	NPF
Indy Racer, large driver, slanted V-grille, horizontal cooling fins, torpedo tail (LWV028)	50	75	100
Indy Racer, large, driver, unusual grille design (LWV029)	50	75	100
Indy Racer, Miller FWD Special, driver, rounded grille, horizontal cooling fins alongside hood, torpedo tail, 5-1/8" long (LWV001)	60	80	100

Lincoln White Metal Overland Bus, 3-1/2". Photo courtesy Bob Ackerly

Left to right: Lincoln White Metal Sedan, Pierce-Arrow Silver Arrow; Coupe, possibly a Graham, 3-3/8"; Sedan, Chrysler Airflow, 3-3/4". Photo courtesy Perry Eichor

Top to bottom: Lincoln White Metal Coupe, stream-lined Pontiac, 3-3/8"; Coupe, three-piece mold, 3-1/2"; Brougham, vertical vee-grille, three-piece mold, 3-1/2". Photo courtesy Fred Maxwell

Lincoln White Metal Coupe, slanted hood, 4-1/2". Photo courtesy Ferd Zegel

Lincoln White Metal Fire Engine, steam pumper, two-man crew, 3-1/4". Photo courtesy Fred Maxwell

Left to right: Lincoln White Metal Indy Racer, 5-1/8"; Indy Racer, large, driver, torpedo tail. Photo courtesy Perry Eichor

Lincoln White Metal Fire Engine with fireman on rear step, Graham-like grille, 3-3/4". Photo courtesy Perry Eichor

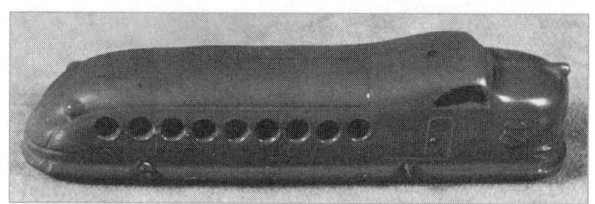

Railcar, hidden rubber wheels, 4-1/2". Photo courtesy Perry Eichor

	C6	C8	C10
Indy Racer, small, two-man, FWD, rounded hood, four cylinder, exhaust left side (LWV025)	40	60	80
Limousine, Graham (?) VG, MDW SM, four OW, LI, T, made from three-piece mold, 3-1/4" long (LWV023)	40	60	80
Limousine, Nash (?), VG, VL, MWW SM, four OW, T, made from three-piece mold, 2-1/2" long (LWV024)	40	60	80
Racer, Indy Miller type, similar to above, 4-1/4" long (LWV034)	40	60	90
Racer, Indy Miller type, smaller version of Indy Racer Miller FWD Special, 4" long (LWV033)	30	45	60
Railcar, Streamline, marked "UNION PACIFIC" and shield symbol, two OW in cab, eighteen OW in passenger section, hidden rubber wheels, patterned pan, marked "Made In USA," 4-1/2" long (LWV011)	80	140	200
Sedan, Chrysler airflow, two-door, HO, divided open WS, HL, plain pan, 3-3/4" long (LWV006)	40	70	100

	C6	C8	C10
Sedan, DeSoto (?), two-door, HO, HL, four OW, very streamlined airflow rear (LWV035)	40	60	80
Sedan, Ford V-8 (LWV032)	NPF	NPF	NPF
Sedan, Lincoln Auto Co. (?) (LWV031)	NPF	NPF	NPF
Sedan, Pierce-Arrow Silver Arrow, vertical vee-grille, head-lamps and front fenders faired, six OW, divided WS, plain pan, 3-1/2" long (LWV005)	40	70	100
Sedan, Pontiac, two-door, HO, grid pattern grille, HL, four OW, trunk, 3-7/8" long (LWV007)	30	40	60
Speed Car, Bluebird record car, driver, V-8 engine w/intake ports, triangular fin w/wing design embossed, 4" long (LWV003)	55	85	110
Speed Car, Bluebird record car, driver, V-8 engine w/intake ports, triangular fin w/wing design embossed, 6" long (LWV002)	60	80	125
Speed Car, Bluebird, w/crossed flag on fin, V12, horizontal trim, patterned pan, 4-1/8" long (LWV013)	75	125	200

Lincoln White Metal Tanker Truck, six tanks, eight compartments, 3-3/4". Photo courtesy Fred Maxwell

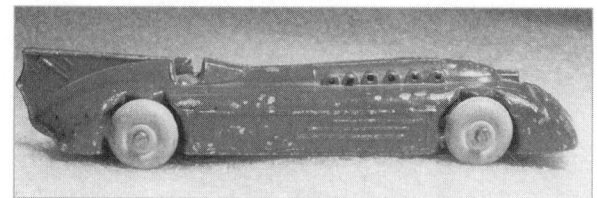

Lincoln White Metal Speed Car, Bluebird, V12, 4-1/8". Photo courtesy Perry Eichor

Left to right: Lincoln White Metal Sedan, Pierce-Arrow Silver Arrow, 3-1/2"; Lincoln White Metal Sedan, Chrysler Airflow, 3-3/4". Photo courtesy Perry Eichor

Lincoln White Metal Sedan, possibly Lincoln Auto Co. Photo courtesy Fred Maxwell

Lincoln White Metal Racer, Indy-type, LWV34. Photo courtesy Ferd Zegel

Top to Bottom: Lincoln White Metal Limousine, possibly a Nash, 2-1/2"; Limousine, possibly a Graham, 3-1/4"; Lincoln White Metal Coupe, possibly a Graham, 3-3/8". Photo courtesy Fred Maxwell

Left to right: Lincoln White Metal Fire Engine; Sedan, Ford V-8; Fire Engine variation. Photo courtesy Fred Maxwell

Lincoln White Metal Sedan, possibly a two-door DeSoto. Photo courtesy Bob Ackerly

Lincoln White Metal Speed Car, Bluebird record car, triangular fin with wing design, 6". Photo courtesy Chic Gast

Top to bottom: Lincoln White Metal Speed Car, Bluebird record car, driver, V-8 engine with intake ports, 6"; Lincoln White Metal Speed Car, Bluebird, smaller version of above, 4". Photo courtesy Perry Eichor

Left to right: Lincoln White Metal Sedan, Pierce-Arrow Silver Arrow, 3-1/2"; Coupe, slanted vee-grille; Coupe, Oldsmobile, streamlined vee-grille, 4". Photo courtesy Fred Maxwell

Lincoln White Metal Speed Car, Bluebird, 4". Photo courtesy John Taylor

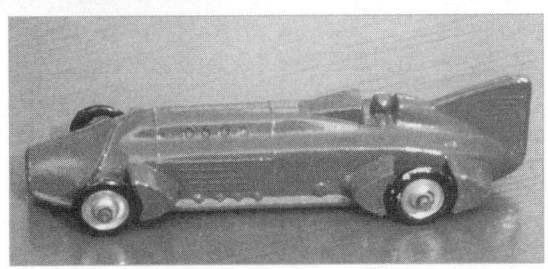

Lincoln White Metal Wrecker, high style with chopped top, Graham-like grille. Photo courtesy Perry Eichor

Lincoln White Metal Stake Truck, open stakes, 3-1/2". Photo courtesy Bob Ackerly

	C6	C8	C10
Speed Car, V-12 version of Bluebird w/triangular fin, possibly Lincoln Metal Works, 4-5/8" long (LWV004?)	60	90	120
Stake Truck, slanted HG, divided WS, two OW, open stakes, rounded pan, 3-1/2" long (LWV022)	20	30	40
Tanker Truck, COE, two OW, six tranks, eight compartments, patterned pan,			

	C6	C8	C10
marked "Made in USA", 3-3/4" long (LWV010)	60	80	100
Tractor, small Fordson (LWV026)	15	25	40
Wrecker, high style w/chopped top, Graham-like grille, two OW, fenders faired bumper to bumper, solid crane w/grid pattern and hook, patterned pan, marked "Made in USA," 3-1/2" long (LWV008)	40	60	90

LINDSTROM

The Lindstrom Tool & Toy Company made wind-up toys of light pressed steel, as well as tin. Located in Bridgeport, Connecticut, Lindstrom began making toy cars about 1913. It seems to have ceased production in the 1940s.

	C6	C8	C10
Bumper Car, tin wind-up, 6-1/2" long	60	90	120
Ladder Truck, Mack type	138	247	275
Long Distance Moving Van, trailer only	75	112	150
Lumber Truck, steerable front wheels, tin, w/driver, No. 160, 10" long	125	187	250
Parcel Post Truck, tin wind-up, No. 2......	200	300	400

	C6	C8	C10
Racing Car, tin wind-up, 1930s, 6" long..	90	135	185
Skeeter Bug, tin wind-up, bumper car, 1930s, 7" long	120	180	240
Steam Roller, mechanical, No. 181, 12" long...	50	75	100
U.S. Mail Truck, No. 1, early, 7" long.....	500	800	1200

LINEOL

Germany's Lineol was founded by Oscar Weiderholz in 1906, in the Berlin suburb of Brandenburg. Its military tinplate line was considered superior to all others (although in sales, Elastolin dominated the field). Authentic in detail, most were painted in camouflage colors. With a few exceptions, all Lineol military tinplate toys were made in scale for its 7-1/2 centimeters (2-15/16 inches) composition toy soldiers.

Lineol Armored Car, No. 1215, rare, value as shown $3,500. Jack Matthews Collection

Lineol Ambulance, No. 1041, value as shown $4,000. Jack Matthews Collection

Lineol Command Staff Car, No. 1211 (solid olive drab), value as shown $1,300. Jack Matthews Collection

Lineol Panzer Tank, No. 1280, value as shown $2,000. Jack Matthews Collection

Lineol Command Staff Car, No. 1211 (camouflage), value as shown $1,500. Jack Matthews Collection

Lineol Communications Car, No. 1205/5, very rare, value as shown $6,000. Jack Matthews Collection

Lineol Six-wheeled Prime Mover, No. 1225/6, gray, lade vehicle made, value as shown $3,000. Jack Matthews Collection

Lineol Six-wheeled Prime Mover with camouflage top, No. 1225/6, camouflage top, last vehicle made, $3,000. Jack Matthews Collection

Lineol Searchlight Truck, No. 1010, value as shown $4,500. Jack Matthews Collection

Lineol Staff Car, No. 1206/5, with luggage rack, value as shown $6,000. Jack Matthews Collection

Note: All vehicles in this chapter have their prices listed at the end of the photo caption.

Contributor: Jack Matthews.

Lineol Bridge Truck, No. 1218, value as shown $6,500. Jack Matthews Collection

Lineol early tank, value as shown $450. Jack Matthews Collection

Lineol Troop Lorry, No. 1011, early, value as shown $3,500. Jack Matthews Collection

Lineol truck, No. 1210, value as shown $1,500. Photo courtesy Jack Matthews Collection

Lineol gun truck w/German crew, No. 1009, early, value as shown $4,500. Photo courtesy Jack Matthews Collection

LIONEL (TRAINS)

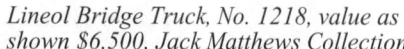

	C6	C8	C10
Electric Racing Automobile Set	1600	2500	3750
Log Truck (Beck), steers via horn on top of cap, large, late 1940s	60	90	120

Lionel Electric Racing Automobile set. Photo courtesy Sotheby's New York

LLEDO

Lledo was founded in 1983 by Jack Odell, a former executive at Lesney Products & Co. Odell's goal was to produce quality die-cast at an affordable price. Lledo, Odell spelled backwards, is the only major die-cast manufacturer to produce models in the United Kingdom (Enfield, Essex). In 1996, the

An assortment of Liedo vehicles. Photo courtesy Iain C. Baillie

company was purchased by HCG Group Limited (the Hobbies Collectables and Gifts Group).

The first six models, part of the Day Gone line, were launched in April 1983 and consisted of five horse-drawn vehicles. Also issued was a 1920 Model "T" Ford Van which could very well be the most popular toy vehicle ever produced. The scale of the early models was erratic, especially for buses and trucks. Most models were motor vehicles from the 1920s-1940s era with a few exceptions. In 1996, the Vanguard line was launched. Based on vehicles from the 1950s and 1960s, they are generally 1:45-scale for cars and 1:64-scale for trucks.

From the beginning, Lledo exploited the collectibles market and over the years many millions of models have been produced. Its product proved very popular in the promotional market and steps were taken to distinguish general release lines from promotional lines.

A systematic numbering system was developed. Day Gone models are marked with a "DG" followed by a casting number. Promotional models, marked with at "LP" followed by a casting number, each have a different face plate and weren't intended for general release. The Vanguard series are identified by "VA" followed by the casting number, while the promotional models done from this line are marked with a "PM". There are about eighty-eight different DG/LP castings and twenty-six PM castings. The Marathon series is made up of six different truck or bus castings done in a larger scale.

The casting number in each series is followed by a three-digit livery number while the annual catalogs published by RDP Publications, the main source of information for Lledo models, applies a final letter to define variants-which can be extremely important in identifying the more expensive models. Specific lines were included a gray series of 144 sets of seventeen of the DG castings issued in 1986 for promotional use in the United States; a United States-dedicated series (the so-called 500 series) which consisted of eight DG castings without logos; eight castings were released under the name Edocar in the Netherlands in 1986; and the "Fantastic Set of Wheels" series,

distributed by Hartoy, Inc., was developed in 1985 for the U.S. market in 1985.

Logos on the models available to the general public are tampo printed while the logos on the promotional models were label printed for small runs and tampo printed for larger runs.

While the models are popular in Great Britain, there has been considerable expansion of their distribution in the United States, and an American collector's club has been formed.

Lledo models have virtually no value if they are not Mint in box (C10). Many of the models can be secured for relatively low prices ($10-$15) but it seems unlikely there will be any significant increase in price for the average model. A complete set of the castings (amounting to more than 150) can be secured for a relatively modest investment, although individual liveries cost considerably more. Promotional releases tend to bring higher prices because of the scarcity as compared to general release liveries. However, the collector should be aware that limited edition models with certificates of authenticity are rapidly increasing in value.

With nearly 140 castings and possibly some 7,000 in total different liveries, detailed pricing becomes more impossible these figures will give some guide to a collector.

Editor's Note: More information on Lledo can be found in the newsletter of The Lledo Enthusiast & Variations Club. As reported by Model Auto Review in their June 2005 online newsletter, the Lledo newsletter's founder, Bill Alexander, has announced in the Vol. 6 No. 3 issue that the Vol 6. No. 6 issue which will ship in September 2005 will be the last. He cites the recent decision of parent company Corgi to drop the Lledo line. Alexander may be reached at 33 North Town Moor, Maidenhead, Berks, SL6 7JR, England. The Lledo Collector's Club may be reached online at www.lledo.com or by mail at Lledo Collectibles, P.O. Box 4000, Southampton, SO14 0ZR, England.

Contributor: Iain C. Baillie, Town Mill, 191 High Street, Old Amersham, Bucks HP7 OEQ, England.

LONDONTOY

Londontoy die-cast vehicles were produced in London, Ontario, from 1945-1950. They were also molded in the United States by the Leslie Henry Company, by special arrangement with Londontoy. The American versions are characterized by the absence of the "Made in Canada" marking, and the larger American versions sometimes had a three-dimensional baseplate, which stimulated the vehicle drivetrain. The larger versions were sometimes equipped with a heavy flywheel friction-motor or a windup mechanism. Oil tankers and beverage trucks sometimes bore advertising for actual brandnames. Either motors or advertising would add to the values below.

Contributor: Dave Leopard, 2507 Feather Run Trail, West Columbia, SC 29169-4915

Four-inch Size

	C6	C8	C10
1941 Chevrolet Master Deluxe Coupe, No. 14, die-cast	15	20	30
1941 Ford Open Cab Fire Truck, No. 16, die-cast, red	15	20	30
1941 Ford Pickup Truck, No. 12, die-cast	15	20	30
Beverage Truck, No. 15, die-cast, assorted colors	15	20	30
City Bus, No. 17, die-cast, assorted colors	15	20	30
Oil Tanker, No. 13, die-cast	15	20	30

Larger Than Six Inches

Car Transporter	NPF	NPF	NPF
Dump Truck	NPF	NPF	NPF
Lumber Truck	NPF	NPF	NPF
Moving Van, tin body	NPF	NPF	NPF
Stake Body Truck	NPF	NPF	NPF

Londontoy Bus, 4". KP photo courtesy Karen O'Brien

Left to right: Londontoy Pickup Trucks, 1941, 4"; Londontoy Ford Pickup, 1941, 6". Photo courtesy Dave Leopard

Left to right: Londontoy Chevrolet Master Deluxe Coupes, 1941, 4"; Chevrolet Master Deluxe Coupe, 1941, 6". Photo courtesy Dave Leopard

Left to right: Londontoy 1941 Ford Open Cab Firetruck, 4"; Firetruck 6". Photo courtesy Dave Leopard

Left to right: Londontoy Oil Tanker, 4"; Londontoy Oil Tanker, 6". Photo courtesy Dave Leopard

Londontoy Beverage Truck, 4". KP photo courtesy Karen O'Brien

Six-inch Size

	C6	C8	C10
1941 Chevrolet Master Deluxe Coupe, die-cast	25	30	45
1941 Ford Pickup Truck, die-cast	25	30	45
Beverage Truck, No. 55, die-cast	25	30	40
Candian Greyhound Bus, No. 33, die-cast, blue and silver, "Canadian Greyhound" on sides, 5" long	50	100	150
City Bus, No. 57, die-cast, assorted colors	25	50	75

Londontoy Fire Engine, 4". KP photo courtesy Karen O'Brien

	C6	C8	C10
Fire Chief Car, No. 54, die-cast, wind-up motor	25	35	50
Fire Truck, die-cast	25	30	45
Oil Tanker, die-cast	25	30	45
Panel Delivery, die-cast	NPF	NPF	NPF
Six-window Sedan, die-cast	30	50	70
Thunderbolt Racer, die-cast	NPF	NPF	NPF
Tractor and Van Trailer, die-cast	60	80	100

LUPOR METAL PRODUCTS

Joe Portellano founded Lupor Metal Products.

Lupor made metal toys in the post-WWII period in the Bronx, NY. President Louis Portollano machined original tooling for the toys. His son, Joe, was the Vice President. The toys ranged in retail price from 29 cents to $2.99. Like so many American toymakers of the period, competition from Asian imports (that were produced for a fraction of the cost) forced Lupor to cease production.

	C6	C8	C10
Ambulance, friction, 7" long	50	78	105
Army Ambulance, friction, 7" long	50	75	0
Bus, tin, friction motor, "Lupor Bus Line," 1930s, 4-1/4" long	15	30	50
City Cab, No. 39, tin, wind-up, yellow and red, 7" long	15	30	60
FBI Car, tin litho, yellow, friction motor, 4-3/8" long	15	30	60

	C6	C8	C10
Fire Chief Car, No. 57, tin, wind-up, 7" long	45	70	95
Gasoline Tanker, tin litho, yellow, "Gasoline," 4" long	10	20	30
Lupor Citrus Fruit Trailer Truck, tin, "Lupor Citrus Fruit Transport," 9" long	40	60	85
Police Car, friction, 1949 Ford, 7" long	44	66	88
Race Master, tin wind-up, 11" long	100	150	200
Racer, no wind-up, 12" long	30	45	60
Racer, tin wind-up, No. 8, 1930s	138	205	275
Seafood Transport Trailer Truck	40	60	85
Sedan, friction, 7" long	38	57	75
Sportster, plastic, friction motor, assorted colors, rubber wheels, 1954, 5-1/4" long	NPF	NPF	NPF
Trailer Truck	25	38	50

M & L TOY CO. INC.

M&L was incorporated Oct. 21, 1947. It was located on Paterson Plank Road in Union City, New Jersey, and got its name from the two brothers (or father and son) who owned it. Morris and Louis (last name unknown). The company may have begun in 1946, and lasted until at least 1948. It made vehicles, trains, jeweled swords, water guns, mechanical toys, and plastic horns. Most—or all—of its vehicles seem to have been sold unpainted and with plastic wheels. The alloy used in the vehicles was more than ninety-nine-percent zinc, with a smidgen of aluminum added. Most of its toys were copies. There were

M&L Fire Pumper. Photo courtesy Craig A. Clark

Top to bottom: Compare this M&L Cabin Racer to this Barclay prototype. Photo courtesy Perry Eichor

M&L Coupe, 1930s. Photo courtesy Bill Conover

M&L Sedan, streamlined. Photo courtesy Bill Conover

about thirty employees. By 1948, it was at 123-33rd Street in Union City. Many, and perhaps all of their vehicles, were copies of discontinued Barclays.

	C6	C8	C10
Cabin Racer (2)	12	18	25
Coupe, spare tire post, 1930s (5)	12	18	25
Fire Ladder Truck (4)	12	18	25
Fire Pumper (3)	12	18	25
Racer, 2-3/4" long (1)	20	35	50
Sedan, streamlined (6)	12	18	25

MANOIL

Manoil was owned by two brothers, Jack and Maurice Manoil. Its sole sculptor was Walter Baetz, the man responsible for Manoil's seven early vehicles, which were Manoil's first toys, debuting in 1934. The firm originally located in Manhattan, then Brooklyn, and finally in Waverly, New York, closed down in about 1955. Manoil is best known for its toy soldiers and military toys, but did release a number of vehicles including some made of plastic following World War II.

	C6	C8	C10
No. 070 Soup Kitchen, large number	9	13	18
No. 071 Shell Carrier With Soldier On Shell Box, has loop	11	16	23
No. 071A Armored Car w/Siren, siren cast separately	25	38	50
No. 071A Armored Car w/Siren, siren cast w/vehicle	32	48	65
No. 071A Shell Carrier w/Soldier On Shell Box, no loop	10	15	20
No. 072 Water Wagon, larger number	10	15	20
No. 072A Water Wagon, small number	10	15	20
No. 072B Water Wagon, No. number	10	15	20
No. 073 Tractor, loop front	10	15	20
No. 073A Tractor, plain front	11	16	23
No. 074 Armored Car w/Anti-Tank Gun	22	33	45
No. 075 Armored Car w/Anti-Aircraft Gun	27	41	55
No. 095 Tank	8	12	17
No. 096 Large Shell on Truck	9	13	18
No. 097 Pontoon on Wheels	22	33	45
No. 098 Torpedo on Wheels	10	15	20
No. 103 Gasoline Truck	10	15	20
No. 104 Chemical Truck	11	16	22
No. 105 Five Barrel Gun on Wheels	12	18	25
No. 700 Sedan, futuristic	40	60	80
No. 701 Sedan, futuristic	45	68	90
No. 702 Coupe, futuristic	45	68	90

	C6	C8	C10
No. 703 Wrecker, futuristic	80	120	160
No. 704 Roadster, futuristic, Pat. No. 95701	45	68	90
No. 705 Sedan, futuristic, Pat. No. 95792	45	68	90

Manoil Aerial Ladder, No. 711. Figures were not included with engine. Photo courtesy Old Toy Soldier magazine

Top row, left to right: Manoil Sedan, futuristic, No. 705;
Roadster, No. 708; Roadster, vertical radiator, No. 708.
Bottom row, left to right: Sedan, No. 707; Oil Tanker, 710;
Fire Engine, 4", No. 709. Photo courtesy Marjorie and Peter
Ruben

Manoil Aerial Ladder with original box. Photo courtesy
Old Toy Soldier magazine

Manoil P-7 Roadster, plastic, early 1950s. KP photo
courtesy Karen O'Brien

Manoil P-8 Sedan, plastic, early 1950s. KP photo courtesy
Karen O'Brien

	C6	C8	C10
No. 706 Rocket, futuristic bus-like vehicle, Pat. No. 95793	60	90	120
No. 70A Soup Kitchen, small number	9	13	18

Plastic Vehicles

	C6	C8	C10
No. P-10 Tow Truck, assorted colors, rubber tires, 1949, 3-3/8" long	12	18	25
No. P-11 Towing Truck	12	18	25
No. P-12 Tractor, w/tow hitch, 2" long	12	18	25
No. P-13 Dump Cart	12	18	25
No. P-7 Roadster/Convertible, assorted colors, rubber tires, 1949, 3-1/4" long	12	18	25
No. P-8 Sedan, assorted colors, rubber tires, 1949, 3" long	12	18	25
No. P-9 Pick-Up, assorted colors, rubber tires, 1949, 3" long	12	18	25
Road Grader w/Trailer, assorted colors, rubber tires, 1949, 5" long	12	18	25

Postwar Vehicles

	C6	C8	C10
Four Speedsters Boxed Set, includes roadster and sedan	250	375	500
No. 707 Sedan, 4-1/2" long	22	33	44
No. 708 Roadster, horizontal radiator	27	41	55
No. 708A Roaster, vertical radiator	50	75	100
No. 709 Fire Engine, 4" long	18	28	38
No. 710 Oil Tanker	13	19	26
No. 711 Aerial Ladder	200	300	400
No. 712 Pumper	200	300	400

Manoil Pumper, No. 712, with original box. Figures were
not included with the engine. Photo courtesy Old Toy
Soldier magazine

	C6	C8	C10
No. 713 Bus	12	18	24
No. 714 Towing Truck	10	15	20
No. 715 Commercial Truck	10	15	20
No. 716 Sedan	10	15	20
No. 717 Hard Top Convertible	12	18	24
No. 718 Convertible	10	15	20
No. 719 Sport Car	10	15	20
No. 720 Rance Wagon	10	15	20

MÄRKLIN VEHICLES

Well-known today as a toy train manufacturer, the German Märklin Company enjoyed a fine reputation for quality toys long before 1933-1934, when a series of constructional motor vehicles was introduced. Märklin had been making multipurpose construction sets similar in concept to Erector in the United States and Meccano in England, and released specialized sets that would appeal to the young automotive engineer.

PREWAR NUMBERINGS

* Means not reissued postwar

1101C	Chassis		*** 1108G**	Armored Car body, camouflaged (more than one pattern)
1103St	Streamline Coupe body; early version is two-tone blue; later version is all green with brown roof		**1109M**	Clockwork motor
			* 1110B	Electric Lighting Set
* 1104	Pullman Limousine body; early version is beige and green; later version is ivory with gray roof		*** 99R**	Driver (lightweight composition material)
			* 1133R	Mercedes Racing Car. red, complete with chassis and motor; smaller scale
1105L	Lorry (Pick-up) body; red/green		**1133AL**	Mercedes Racing Car, aluminum. Complete with chassis and motor, smaller scale
* 1106T	Tanker Body; red/blue			
1107R	Racing (Sports Car) body, red/white			

A clever merchandising scheme was developed. You could buy a boxed set of parts to build a complete chassis, but a motor would have to be purchased separately. The body of your choice was still another kit to buy, and up to six types were available by the late 1930s. If you wished to have other types of vehicles, alternative body kits were available. Complete sets with body, motor, and chassis were also sold, and some sets included more than one body. Märklins were costly, and, in the 1930s, many could afford to buy only one piece at a time. The quality of finish is superb, and some pieces are decorated with hand striping.

The group of constructional vehicles could be referred to as The 1100 series. However, there was no 1102. The 1100 Series was revived after the war, but 1104P, 1106T, 1108G, 1110B, 1133R, and 99R were not made again. Märklin phased out the remaining constructional vehicles in the mid-1950s. Why is no value guide currently possible for Märklin toys? Very few are changing hands at toy shows and auctions, and not enough data exists to develop a reliable and useful listing of values.

Since 1990, Märklin has issued seven limited-edition constructional vehicles that look as though they could be members of the original 1100 series, but there are many detail differences. The Tanker, Racing Car, and Lorry are very similar to the originals, but the three vans and the Fire Engine are probably based upon 1930s prototypes that never reached production. Perhaps one of these could have been the missing link, Number 1102! All of the "new" Märklins have electric headlights, and they were completely assembled at the factory.

Construction Sets

	C6	C8	C10
1101C Chassis	NPF	NPF	NPF
1103St Streamline Coupe Body, Early is 2-tone blue, later is all green w/brown roof	NPF	NPF	NPF
1104 Pullman Limousine Body, early is beige and green, later is ivory w/gray roof	NPF	NPF	NPF
1105L Lorry (Pick-up) Body, red/green	NPF	NPF	NPF
1106T Tanker Body, red/blue	NPF	NPF	NPF
1107R Racing (Sports Car) body, red/white	NPF	NPF	NPF

Märklin Limited Edition Trucks. Left to Right: Postal Van, 1990; Fire Engine, 1991; and Lorry (1992); all have working electric headlights. Photo courtesy Gates Williard. Photo by E.W. Williard

Limited editions, left to right: Märklin Reichspost Van, 1994; Racing Car, 1995. Photo courtesy Gates Willard. Photo by E.W. Willard

Left to right: Märklin Standard Tanker, 1993; Geld Transporter, 1993. Photo courtesy Gates Willard. Photo by E.W. Willard

Märklin Lighting Set with instructions and original battery. Photo courtesy Gates Willard. Photo by E.W. Willard

Märklin No. 1106T Tanker with original box; two tinplate cars were included. Photo courtesy Gates Willard. Photo by E.W. Willard

Märklin No. 1103St Streamlined Coupe. Photo courtesy Gates Willard. Photo by E.W. Willard

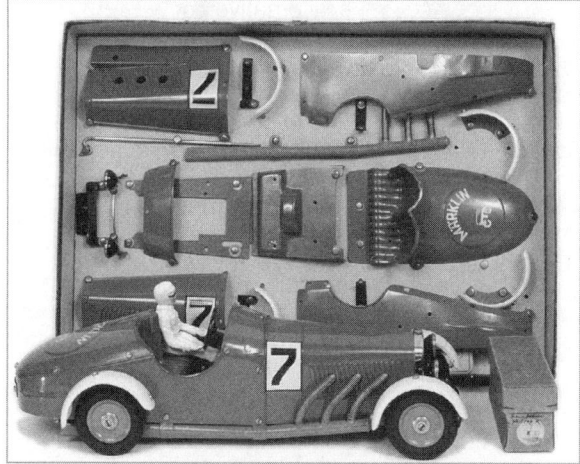

Märklin No. 1107R racing car with original composition 99R driver; behind it is the unassembled car in its box. Photo courtesy Gates Willard. Photo by E.W. Willard

Märklin No. 1104 Pullman Limousine. Photo courtesy Gates Willard. Photo by E.W. Willard

Märklin No. 1108G Armored Car, camouflage-type paint. Photo courtesy Gates Willard. Photo by E.W. Willard

Märklin No. 1105L Lorry. Photo courtesy Gates Willard. Photo by E.W. Willard

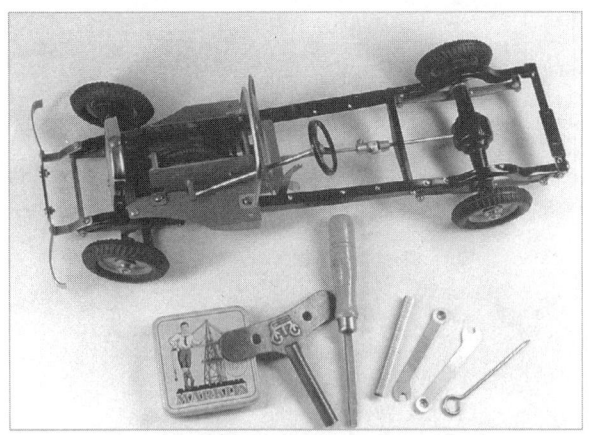

Märklin Assembled Chassis with parts box, cast-iron key and tools; No. 1109M clockwork motor is installed. Photo courtesy Gates Willard. Photo by E.W. Willard

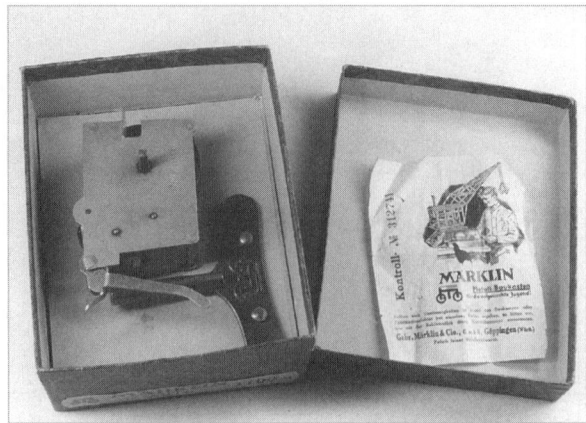

Märklin boxed No. 1110B Lighting Set with instructions and original battery. Photo courtesy Gates Willard. Photo by E.W. Willard

Märklin Kubelwagen, die-cast, 3-1/2". Photo courtesy Terry Sells

Märklin Mercedes Racing Car, composition driver, cast-iron key, windup, 12". Photo courtesy Gates Willard. Photo by E.W. Willard

Märklin Road Working Machine, 3-5/8". Photo courtesy Virginia Caputo

Märklin Troop Carrier, die-cast metal, ten wheels, 5". Photo courtesy Terry Sells

Märklin Water Truck, faucet works, 15". Photo courtesy Bertoia Auctions

Märklin Troop Carrier, die-cast metal, 4-1/2". Photo courtesy Terry Sells

	C6	C8	C10
1108G Armored Car Body, camouflaged (more than one pattern)	NPF	NPF	NPF
1109M Clockwork motor	NPF	NPF	NPF
1110B Electric Lighting Set	NPF	NPF	NPF
1133AL Mercedes Racing Car, aluminum, complete w/chassis and motor, smaller scale	NPF	NPF	NPF
1133R Mercedes Racing Car, red, complete w/chassis and motor, smaller scale	NPF	NPF	NPF
99R Driver, made of lightweight composition material	NPF	NPF	NPF

Die-Cast

	C6	C8	C10
308 El Racer, 12" long	250	375	500
Armored Car, camouflaged, 14-1/2" long	1000	1700	2400
Kubelwagen, 3-1/2" long	325	490	650
Mercedes Racing Car, wind-up, 12" long	425	638	850
Road Working Machine, 3-5/8" long	100	150	200

	C6	C8	C10
Sedan Bus, No. 32, two-toned, 1938, 5-1/5" long	100	175	285
Troop Carrier, 4-1/2" long	325	490	650
Troop Carrier, ten wheels, 5" long	450	675	900
Water Truck, early, faucet works, 15" long	1300	2500	3600

Limited Editions

	C6	C8	C10
Fire Engine, red, No. 1990, 1990	NPF	NPF	NPF
Geld Transporter (Armored Truck), blue/black, No. 1993, 1993	NPF	NPF	NPF
Lorry, red/green, No. 1992, 1992	NPF	NPF	NPF
Racing Car, red/white, No. 1995, 1995	NPF	NPF	NPF
Reichspost (Postal Van), dark red/black, No. 1994, 1994	NPF	NPF	NPF
Reichspost (Postal Van), yellow/black, No. 1990, 1990	NPF	NPF	NPF
Standard Tanker, red/blue, No. 1993, 1993	NPF	NPF	NPF

MARX

By the 1950s, Louis Marx was the largest manufacturer of toys in the world; six large factories in the United States and ownership of interest in factories in seven other countries. Marx, born in Brooklyn in 1896, was working for the so-called toy king, Ferdinand Strauss, when he was in his teens. By 20, his energy and enterprise had made him a director of that company. A falling out with Strauss persuaded him to go into business for himself. In 1921, he and his brother began making their own toys, including some adaptations of items by the now-defunct Strauss. Marx's watchword seems to have been quality at the lowest possible price, and he was such a favorite with toy buyers that he had virtually no need for salesmen or advertising.

Marx made virtually every type of toy, with the exception of dolls. In April 1972, he sold his company to the Quaker Oats Company, which in 1976 sold it to Europe's largest toy manufacturer, Dunbee-Combex-Marx. The company went into bankruptcy in 1980. Marx died in 1982, at the age of 85. In 1982, American Plastics bought much of the Marx assets; in 1990, it began producing toys from the original molds. Marx eventually ended up in the hands of Jay Horowitz, the current president. Horowitz produces Marx action figures based on the original molds and has licensed Jim and Debby Flynn to produce new tin lithographed trains.

The company is available online at www.marxtoys.com or may be reached at: Marx Toys & Entertainment Corp., 101 S. 15th St., Sebring, Ohio 44672, (620) 224-2945.

The Official Marx Toy Museum is dedicated to preserving the history and legacy of Marx toys and the people who made them. It is available online at www.marxtoymuseum.com, or may be reached at The Official Marx Toy Museum, 915 Second St., Moundsville, WV 26041, (304) 845-6022.

Contributor: Scott Smiles, 157 Yacht Club Way #112, Hypoluxo, FL 33462

	C6	C8	C10
1st Batt. F.D. Chief's Car, tin wind-up, w/siren, battery-operated headlights, 16" long	225	325	425
A&P Box Truck	50	100	250
A&P Trailer Truck, 28" long	50	100	250
Acme Markets Trailer Truck, blue and white cab	75	150	300
Aerial Ladder Truck, late	135	202	270
Aerial Water Tower Truck, wind-up, 15" long	275	363	550
Aero Oil Company Truck, friction, c.1930, 5-1/2" long	225	375	500
Air Force Truck, "Air Defense Group" ride 'em toy, No. 3290, 32" long	125	188	250
Air Force Truck, canvas top, 20" long	105	158	210
Airflow, 4" long	40	50	100
Airport Transport, 6-1/2" long	30	40	65
All State Wrecker, 19" long	100	200	350
Allied Van Lines, tin friction, Linemar, 1950s	100	150	200

	C6	C8	C10
Allstate Super Service Station, w/plastic gas pumps	25	45	85
Allstate Super Trailer	150	300	450
Ambulance, No. 8500, 1930s, approx. 14" long	150	275	475
Ambulance, No. 8600, 1930s, approx. 14" long	240	360	550

Marx Allstate Super Service Station. Photo courtesy Ron Fink

Marx A & P Truck.

Marx Acme Markets Trailer Truck. Photo courtesy John Taylor

Marx Aero Oil Company Truck, friction, 5-1/2". Photo courtesy Bob Smith

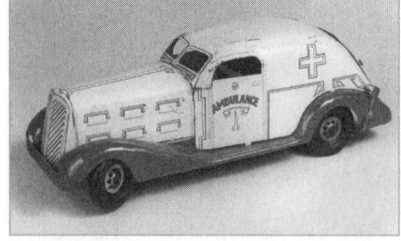

Marx Ambulance, with siren, 1930s, tin windup 14-1/2". Photo courtesy Mapes Auctioneers and Appraisers

Marx Anti-Aircraft Unit Civilian Defense Truck, plastic, 12". Photo courtesy Terry Sells

Marx Armored Bank, 6". Photo courtesy Richard MacNary

Marx Amos & Andy Fresh-Air Taxi, 1930s 8". Photo courtesy Bob Smith

Marx Army Command Car, friction, tin and plastic, siren, 19-1/2". Photo courtesy Terry Sells

Marx Army Truck, cloth cover. Photo courtesy Phillips

Marx Army Truck, marked "USA 4153147," 13-3/4". Photo courtesy Bill Kaufman

Marx Auto Transport, friction powered, with three racers. Photo courtesy Continental Hobby House

Marx made several versions of the Auto Transport. The 31" version from 1958 with two Corvettes and two Thunderbirds is the most valuable. Photo courtesy Calvin L. Chaussee

Marx Arrow Special Delivery, 1940s, 13". Photo courtesy John Taylor

Marx Automatic Fire House, 1950s, Fire Chief Car, Volunteer Fire Dept. Garage. Photo courtesy Don Hultzman

Marx Beat It the Komical Kop, tin, wind-up, 7". Photo courtesy Ed Hyers Antiques

Marx Dippy Dumper, Brutus celluloid figure, 1930s, 9". Photo courtesy Don Hultzman

Marx Brake Kar with screeching noise. Photo courtesy Continental Hobby House

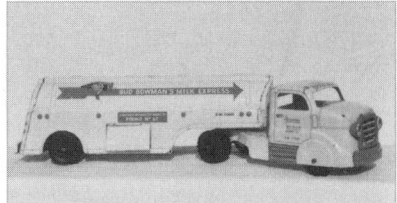

Marx Bud Bowman's Milk Express Truck. Photo courtesy John Taylor

Marx Caterpillar Climbing Tractor, tin, wind-up, 10". Photo courtesy Continental Hobby House

Marx Bus, circa 1940, 4-1/2". Photo courtesy Richard MacNary

Marx Cadillac, Untouchables-type, 5-1/4". Photo courtesy Gary Linden

	C6	C8	C10
Ambulance w/Siren, tin wind-up, 1930s, 14-1/2" long	250	375	550
Ambulance, Army, tin wind-up, marked "M.D. War Dept.," 1930s, 13-1/2" long	300	450	800
American LaFrance Hose Truck, late, 21" long	175	263	350
American Railroad Express Agency, Inc., open cab, early 1930s, 7" long	150	250	450
American Railway Express Agency Van, wind-up, Bulldog Mack	250	400	575
American Railway Express Agency Van, wind-up, closed driver's window, 9" long	300	450	625
American Tractor, tin wind-up, w/implements, 1920s, 10" long	132	198	265

	C6	C8	C10
American Truck Co. Moving Truck, friction, No. 65	65	98	130
Amos & Andy Fresh-Air Taxi, tin wind-up, 1930s, 8" long	450	750	1150
Anti-Aircraft, friction, plastic and tin, Unit No. 1 Fire Control Truck	90	135	180
Anti-Aircraft Unit Civilian Defense Truck, No. 12, friction, plastic, 12" long	110	165	220
Armored Bank Truck, c.1940, 6" long	75	112	150
Armored Trucking Co., tin wind-up	150	275	400
Army Command Car, friction, tin and plastic, siren and flashing signal light, 19-1/2" long	NPF	NPF	NPF
Army Corps of Engineers, canvas top, 20" long	125	188	250
Army Jeep w/Searchlight Trailer, steel	100	150	250
Army Scout Stake Truck, c.1940	60	90	120
Army Staff Car, plastic friction, 9" long	9	14	18
Army Staff Car, tin wind-up, 1930s	150	225	325
Army Staff Car, tin wind-up, w/flasher and siren, 1940s, No. W-601158, 11" long	200	300	425
Army Tractor, wind-up, 1930s	135	203	270
Army Troop Carrier, plastic, w/searchlight	62	93	125
Army Truck, c.1952, marked "USA 41573147," 13-3/4" long	100	150	200
Army Truck, plastic cab	85	128	170
Army Truck, tin lithographed, c.early 1930s, 8" long	108	162	215
Army Truck, tin wind-up, cloth cover, 1930s, 10" long	350	525	700
Army Truck, w/cannon, 1950s	65	98	130
Army Truck, w/canopy, mark "U.S. Army 5th Div.," late 1950s	80	120	160
Army Truck, w/covered trailer and cannon trailer, c.1940	200	300	400
Arrow Racer, tin wind-up, No. 2, 1930s, 4" long	70	110	155
Arrow Special Delivery Truck, 1940s, 13" long	40	75	175

Marx Carousel Truck, 1967, 8". Photo courtesy Scott Smiles

	C6	C8	C10
Arrow Special Delivery Truck, wind-up, 1940s, 13" long	50	125	225
Auto Hauler, friction, w/three 1965 Mustangs, 18" long	175	263	350
Auto Hauler, w/four plastic cars	135	102	270
Auto Hauler, w/two Airflows, 1930s	150	210	300
Auto Hauler, wind-up, two cars, c.1950, 10" long	125	200	275
Auto Transport, four steel cars, c.1939	275	400	500
Auto Transport, friction powered, with three friction racers, detachable ramp	50	100	150
Auto Transport, includes two Corvettes, two T-Birds, everything tin, c.1958, 31" long	275	363	550
Auto Transport, w/three cars, 1950s, 21" long	225	338	450
Auto Transport, w/two tin lithographed cars, 1950s, 34" long	150	225	300
Auto Transport, wind-up, Mack C-Cab, w/three cars, 1920s, 12" long	250	375	575
Auto Transwalk, truck w/three cars, No. T-50447B, 1930s	185	278	350
Auto-Laundry Car Wash	125	188	250
Automatic Fire House Fire Chief Car, tin wind-up, 1940s, 7-1/2"-long car, w/9"-long Volunteer Fire Dept. Garage	125	175	250
Automatic Garage, comes w/one friction car	35	52	70
Automatic Reversing Road Roller, tin wind-up, 1925, 9" long	200	300	400
Baby Wrecker Truck, battery-operated	50	75	100
Baggage Express Truck, 1940s, 11" long	75	200	350
Bakery Truck, reads "Rolls Pies & Cakes," 11" long	75	150	325
Beat It the Komikal Kop, tin wind-up, 1930s; 7" long	300	400	525
Big Boss Car Carrier, 42" long	80	120	160
Big Bruiser Tow Truck, 1960s	50	75	100
Big Job Dump Truck, plastic, 28" long	50	75	100
Big Lizzie Car, tin wind-up, early 1930s, 7-1/4" long	130	225	300
Big Load Van Company Truck, wind-up, Bulldog Mack, 1930s, 13" long	235	352	470
Big Parade, tin wind-up, moving vehicles, soldiers, etc., 1928; 24" long	525	875	1150
Big Shot Cannon Truck, plastic, fires cap-loaded missiles, 22" long	52	76	105
Big Silver Mack Dump Truck, tin wind-up	250	375	500
Block Truck, 1940s, 11" long	75	200	350
Blondie's Jalopy, tin wind-up, 1941; 16" long	1250	2000	3000
Blue Bird Gas Station	150	225	300
Bluestreak Racer, No. 3, tin, wind-up, 1930s, 4" long	55	83	110
Bottom Dump, late	40	60	80
Bouncing Benny Pull Car, tin litho car, oversized rubber tires, 1939, 7" long	150	225	300
Brake Kar, w/screeching noise	105	157	210
Brutus Dippy Dumper	450	675	900
Bud Bowman's Milk Express Truck	75	225	375
Builders Dump Truck, 1930s	75	200	350
Builders Stake Truck, 11" long	75	200	350
Bulldozer Climbing Tractor, tin wind-up, caterpillar type, 1950s, 10-1/2" long	175	275	400
Bumper Auto, tin wind-up, streamlined, large bumpers, c.1939	120	180	240

Marx Charlie McCarthy in his Benzine Buggy tin windup. Photo courtesy Bob Smith

	C6	C8	C10
Bus, c.1940, 4-1/2" long	90	135	180
Bus, Coast to Coast Greyhound, tin, one deck, wind-up motor, 1920s, 9" long	100	200	300
Bus, Coast to Coast Greyhound, tin, two decks, wind-up motor, 1920s, 9" long	125	250	400
Bus, Continental Flyer, tin, wind-up motor, front axle, two rear axles, green and yellow, 1930s, 12" long	125	250	450
Bus, Greyhound, pressed steel, friction motor, 1930s, 6-1/2" long	20	40	65
Bus, plastic, assorted colors, 1950s, 4-1/2" long	15	30	45
Bus, Royal Bus Line, tin, wind-up motor, red and yellow, black rubber tires, 1930, 10" long	75	145	210
Bus Terminal, Greyhound terminal, tin, 1938, 16" long	65	165	300
Bus Terminal, tin playset, clock, gas pumps, 1937, 12" long	65	140	225
Busy Bridge, tin wind-up, 1937, 24" long	300	400	550
Busy Parking Station, wind-up, 1930s, 17" long, w/2" tin race car	150	225	300
Cadillac, Untouchables type, 5-1/4" long	35	52	70
Cadillac Coupe, wind-up, 1931, 12" long	432	648	865
Cadillac Roadster, tin wind-up, trunk w/tools on luggage carrier, 1930s; 13" long	250	400	550
Canadian Tire Trailer Truck, 25" long	75	125	275
Cannon Truck, 1930s, 10" long	75	150	300
Car Carrier, wind-up, carries Airflow	58	85	115
Car Wash and Garage, tin lithographed	125	188	250
Cargo Truck, postwar, 16" long	80	120	160
Carousel Truck, marked "1967," 8" long	50	75	100
Carpenter Stakebed Truck, w/dolly, approx. 14" long	50	125	275
Caterpillar Climbing Tractor, tin wind-up, 10" long	10	140	190
Cement Truck, plastic, assorted colors, 1950s, 5" long	10	18	25
Charlie McCarthy and Mortimer Snerd Private Car, tin wind-up; 1939; 16" long	1000	1700	2400

Marx City Sanitation Dept., "Help Keep Your City Clean," 12-3/4". Photo courtesy Calvin L. Chaussee

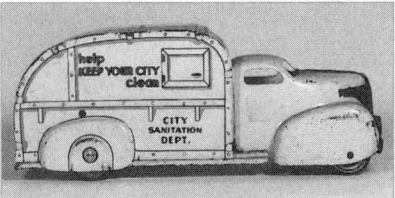

A side view of the Marx City Sanitation Dept. truck. Photo courtesy Bill Kaufman

Marx Cloverdale Farms Milk Truck, 11-1/2". Photo courtesy John Taylor

Marx Coca-Cola Truck, 1950s, shelf sidecases. Photo courtesy Don Hultzman

Marx Coast to Coast Delivery Truck, 1930s, 6". Photo courtesy Richard MacNary

Marx Coca-Cola Truck, plastic, 10-1/2". Photo courtesy Terry Sells

Marx Coo Coo Car, 1920s, 7-1/2". Photo courtesy Don Hultzman

Marx Curtiss Candy Truck, plastic. Photo courtesy Gary Linden

Marx Deluxe Coupe, electric headlights, 15". Photo courtesy Bob Smith

Marx Cunningham Drug Stores Truck, plastic, 1950s. Photo courtesy John Taylor

Marx Deluxe Delivery Truck, 13". Photo courtesy John Taylor

Marx Deluxe Delivery Truck. Photo courtesy Thomas G. Nefos

Marx Deluxe Tractor, tin wind-up, c.1932. Photo courtesy Orville C. Britton

Marx Deluxe Trailer Truck, plastic cab, metal trailer, 1950s. Photo courtesy John Taylor

Marx Doughboy Tank, World War II pot helmet, circa 1950. Photo courtesy Harvey K. Rainess

	C6	C8	C10
Charlie McCarthy in His Benzine Buggy, tin wind-up; 1938; 7-1/2" long	400	525	700
Chief-Fire Dept. No. 1, friction drive, c.1948	90	135	180
Circus Truck, plastic, w/6 animals: tiger, alligator, leopard, polar bear and cub, buffalo; blue and red, cage sides open, 11" long.....................	110	165	225
Cities Service Towing Service, 20-1/2" long	75	125	275
City Freight Trailer Truck, 1950s, 19" long, rare	125	250	400
City Hospital Ambulance, tin wind-up, 10" long............................	475	713	950
City Sanitation Dept., "Help Keep Your City Clean" on sides, pressed steel, c.1940, 12-3/4" long	50	100	275
Climbing Tractor, tin wind-up, sparkling, 1960s, 8-1/2" long................	90	135	180
Climbing, Fighting Tank, tin and plastic, 5-1/2" long	22	33	45
Climbing, Fighting Tank, tin wind-up	175	263	350
Cloverdale Farms Milk Truck, 11-1/2" long	75	150	300
Coal Dump Truck, No. 964, 21" long	140	210	280
Coal Truck, electric motor and lights, early	200	300	500
Coal Truck, No. 964J	122	188	245
Coast to Coast Delivery Truck, 1930s, 6" long..	75	100	150
Coast to Coast Transfer Semi Truck, 1950s, 24" long...........................	100	150	200
Coca-Cola Truck, No. 1005, red cab and chassis, yellow stakes, late 1940s, 17" long..	200	275	425
Coca-Cola Truck, plastic, 6 removable cases, yellow w/Coke decals, 1949-51, 10-1/2" long	145	235	325
Coca-Cola Truck, shelf sidecases, 1950s .	75	150	300
Coca-Cola Truck, Sprite decal, stamped steel, late 1940s to early 1950s, 20" long..	160	250	450
Coke Coal City Coal Co. Truck, tin wind-up	255	383	510
Comicar the Snappy Flivver	275	363	550
Construction Tractor Hauler, reverses, w/driver, 14" long	175	263	350
Contractors and Builders Dump Truck, 1939, 11" long................................	75	200	350
Convertible Roadster, nickel-plated tin, 1930s, 11" long	200	300	400
Coo Coo Car, tin wind-up, 1931; 7-1/2" long	225	425	575
Corvette Coupe, plastic, friction, 8" long..	42	63	85
Coupe, steel wind-up, electric headlights, 14" long..	390	585	780
Crane Truck, approx. 20" long................	188	292	375
Crazy Dora Nodder-Head, tin wind-up	100	150	200
Crescent Ice Truck, 11" long..................	50	100	250
Cunningham Drug Stores Stake Truck, 1930s, 11" long...........................	75	200	350
Cunningham Drug Stores Truck, plastic, 1950s, scarce	30	45	75
Curtiss Candy Truck, plastic, dump truck, red w/black rubber wheels, marked "Curtiss Candy Company" on door, originally came w/10 packs of candy, 1950, 9" long.................................	40	80	125

	C6	C8	C10
Dairy Truck and Trailer, w/bottles, 1930s	125	263	350
Dan Dipsey Car, plastic nodder, wind-up, 1950s, 5-3/4" long......................	175	275	375
Daredevil Motor Drome, wind-up car, 1930s, 5-1/2" high, 9" diameter	100	150	200
Day and Nite Service Service Center.......	75	112	150
DC Semi Tractor Trailer, late	100	150	200
De Luxe Tractor, six wheels, four w/treads, tin wind-up, c.1932	250	375	500
Delivery Truck, w/friction motor, 1950s .	175	250	325
Delivery Van, 1940s, 3-3/4" long	35	75	200
Delivery Van, plastic, stamped "Delivery" on sides, assorted colors, 1950s, 10" long	50	90	120
Deluxe Auto Transport, pressed steel and plastic w/two plastic sedans, 1950s, 24" long.....................................	75	200	300
Deluxe Auto Transport, w/o cars, approx. 22" long.....................................	50	125	200
Deluxe Coupe, wind-up, electric lights, 15" long.....................................	450	650	950
Deluxe Delivery Co. Box Truck, 1940s, 11" long.....................................	150	300	450
Deluxe Delivery Co. Box Truck, early Type 1 chassis w/Kingsbury wind-up..	300	450	600
Deluxe Delivery Ride 'Em Truck, pressed steel, "Deluxe Delivery" decals, red cab and seat, gray sides, 1930s, 26" long.....................................	150	325	550
Deluxe Delivery Super Series Truck, wind-up, 1940s, 13" long...................	150	225	275
Deluxe Delivery Truck, tin, 1950s 11" long.....................................	40	75	225
Deluxe Mechanical Coupe, 1930s, 8" long.....................................	155	235	310
Deluxe Trailer Truck, plastic cab, metal trailer, 1950s	35	75	225
Dept. of Police Car, friction, 1930s, 8" long.....................................	125	228	450
Dick Tracy Police Station, w/7" long automatic siren car, 1950s	150	300	450
Dick Tracy Riot Car, friction motor, c.1946, 7-1/2" long	30	75	225
Dick Tracy Squad Car, friction, No. 1, 6-3/4" long	30	75	225
Dick Tracy Squad Car, No. 1, 11" long ...	100	200	400
Dipsy Doodle Bug Dodgem Car, Dan or Dora, tin wind-up, 6" high	67	105	135
Disney Parade Roadster, w/four characters	250	350	450
Donald Duck Dipsy Car, tin wind-up w/plastic Mickey or Donald, 1953, 5-3/4" long.................................	250	400	550
Donald Duck on Tractor, friction, plastic, 1950s, 3-1/2" long........................	100	150	200
Dora Dipsy Car, plastic nodder, wind-up, 1950s, 5-3/4" long........................	150	200	275
Dottie the Driver, wind-up, 1950s, 6-1/2" long.................................	80	120	160
Doughboy Tank, tin wind-up, no extending side turrets; 1937, 10" long .	125	200	250
Doughboy Tank, tin wind-up, soldier w/gun pops out, two extending side turrets, w/top turret, 1932, 10" long.....	175	225	275
Doughboy Tank, WWII pot helmet, tin wind-up, c.1951; 10" long	125	200	250
Driver Training Car, tin wind-up, 1950s, 6" long.................................	105	160	250

Marx Doughboy Tank, no extending side turrets.

Marx Disney Parade Roadster. Photo courtesy Don Hultzman

One of Marx's numerous Dump Trucks. Photo courtesy Perry Eichor

Marx Dump Truck, circa 1940, 4-1/2". Photo courtesy Bob Smith

Marx Easter Dump Truck with yellow cab and rare pink dump bed, late 1930s, 6". Photo courtesy John Taylor

Marx Easter Dump Truck with blue cab and yellow dumb bed, coal shute, 1940, 7". Photo courtesy John Taylor

Marx E-12 Tank, sponsons swing down for flint replacements; very similar to the Sparkling Climbing Fighting Tank. Photo courtesy Bill Holt

Marx East-West Fast Freight Trailer Truck. Photo courtesy John Taylor

Marx Electric Combat Tank, battery-operated. Photo courtesy Continental Hobby House

Marx Electric Motor Driven Coupe, electric lights, circa 1933, 15". Photo courtesy Bob Smith

Marx Fire Chief Car, right-hand drive (made in England), 7-1/2". Photo courtesy Richard MacNary

Marx Fire Dept. Chief Car, tin, 1950s, 11". Photo courtesy Bill Kaufman

Marx Gold Star Transfer Company Trailer Truck. Photo courtesy John Taylor

Marx Funny Flivver, 1920s, 8". Photo courtesy Bertoia Auctions

Marx Giant King Racer, 1930s. Photo courtesy 1929 Butler Bros. Catalog

Marx G-Man Pursuit Car, 1930s.

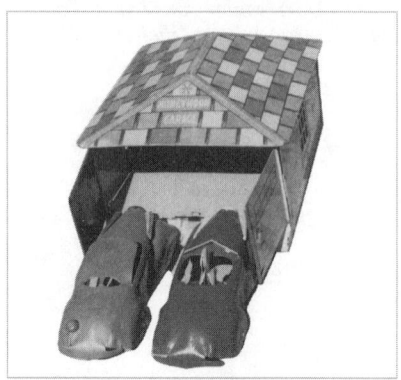

Marx Honeymoon Garage with the two original cars. Photo courtesy James Apthorpe

Marx Gravel Mixer, 1940s, 9-1/2". Photo courtesy John Taylor

Marx Home Dairy Truck, 10-1/2", bottles missing. Photo courtesy John Taylor

Marx Highboy Climbing Tractor, sparkles, 1950s, 10". Photo courtesy Don Hultzman

Marx Hook and Ladder Fire Truck. Photo courtesy Continental Hobby House

	C6	C8	C10
Drive-UR-Self Car, tin wind-up, 1950s, 11" long......	225	338	450
Dump Truck, 14" long	37	56	75
Dump Truck, 1937-41, 6" long	75	100	250
Dump Truck, 1955 Chevy.......................	62	93	125
Dump Truck, c.1940, 4-1/2" long	50	95	250
Dump Truck, c.1941, 7-1/2" long	60	90	120
Dump Truck, hard plastic........................	42	63	85
Dump Truck, late, 9-1/2" long	50	75	100
Dump Truck, No. 1018, 1950s, 18" long .	192	290	385
Dump Truck, No. 1084	30	45	60
Dump Truck, No. 2083, late, 20" long.....	50	75	100
Dump Truck, No. 695B, 17" long	75	112	150
Dump Truck, steel wind-up, c.1940, 4-1/2" long	75	175	325
Dump Truck, tin wind-up, 13" long	200	300	400
Dump Truck, two-color, No. T751, 1930s	82	124	165
Dump Truck, w/treads, 1920s	137	205	375
Dump Truck, wind-up, 6" long	85	160	220
E-12 Tank, sponsons swing down............	88	132	175
Earth Hauler, c.1964	110	165	220
Easter Dump Truck, 1930s, 6" long, scarce	100	250	400
Easter Stake Truck, 1938, 10-1/2" long ...	200	350	500
Easter Stake Truck, w/coal chute, c.1940, 7" long..	75	200	350
East-West Fast Fright Trailer Truck	75	175	325
Electric Combat Tank, battery-operated ..	80	120	160
Electric Lighted Car, Silver finish, Pontiac, 10" long..................................	60	90	120
Electric Motor Driven Coupe, electric lights, c.1933, 15" long............................	350	550	850
Electric Speedway Cars, track, transformer..	300	450	600
Electrically Lighted Truck and Trailer Set, No. T-5715, 1930s, 15" long	150	220	300
Elmer's Racing Fuel trailer Truck, tin, 1950s..	112	168	225

	C6	C8	C10
Falcon, w/plastic bubble top, black rubber tires	125	188	250
Fanny Farmer Candy Truck, plastic.........	50	75	125
Farm Tractor, battery-operated	40	60	80
Fighting Tank, wind-up, plastic top, No. 462, 6" long..	37	56	75
Fire Chief Car, 1920s	175	263	350
Fire Chief Car, 1948 Hudson, 12" long ...	162	245	350
Fire Chief Car, friction...........................	68	102	135
Fire Chief Car, right-hand drive (made in England), 7-1/2" long	100	150	200
Fire Department Car	100	150	200
Fire Dept. Chief Car, tin wind-up, 1950s, 11" long..	40	60	80
Fire Engine Pumper, friction, late 1920s .	275	363	550
Fire Ladder Truck, 14" long	60	90	120
Fire Ladder Truck, c.1940, 6" long..........	50	75	100
Fire Ladder Truck, plastic, all red, friction motor, 1950s, 5-1/2" long	NPF	NPF	NPF
Fire Truck, 25" long	225	338	450
Fire Truck, plastic, w/siren, 1950s	70	105	140
Firestone Truck, 14-1/2" long	125	275	425
First National Stores Tractor Trailer, late 1950s-early 1960s, 25" long	150	275	325
Fix-All Convertible and Wrecker Set	125	188	250
Fix-All Farm Tractor, plastic, 40+ pieces, tools, driver, assorted colors, rubber tires, 1953, 9" long..............................	100	165	225
Fix-All Hard-Top Convertible, plastic, 30 pieces w/tools & equipment, assorted colors, 1953, 10" long..........................	75	125	175
Fix-All Jeep, plastic, 30+ pieces, folding windshield, tools, assorted two-tone colors, plastic wheels, 1953, 7" long ...	NPF	NPF	NPF
Fix-All Mercury Station Wagon, plastic, 64 pieces w/tools & equipment, assorted colors, wood paneling decals, plastic wheels, 1953, 14" long	115	172	250

	C6	C8	C10
Fix-All Motorcycle, plastic, 12" long	00	0	0
Fix-All Sports Car, plastic, 50+ pieces, tools, assorted colors, 1953, 12-1/2" long	NPF	NPF	NPF
Fix-All Wrecker, plastic, 30+ pieces, tools, opening hood, 1953, 10-1/4" long	100	150	210
Fix-It Motorcycle, plastic, 12" long	88	132	175
Fix-It Tow Truck, w/accessories..............	100	150	200
Flatbed Truck, plastic, assorted colors, metal wheels, playset type, 1950s, 3-3/8" long	18	25	38
Ford Convertible, 1951, 11" long	55	83	110
Funny Flivver, tin wind-up, 8" long, c.1926..	225	275	350
Gang Buster Car, No. 7200, 1930s, approx. 14" long...................................	550	825	1100
Garage, tin, marked "Volunteer Fire Department" and "Chief FD," w/1950s car..	130	195	260
Gas Island, 1930s	100	200	300

	C6	C8	C10
Gasoline Trailer Truck, wind-up..............	188	282	375
General Alarm Fire House	350	525	700
Giant King Racer, tin wind-up, marked "711," 1930s	110	165	220
Giant Reversing Tractor Truck, tin wind-up, w/tools, marked "Hauling," 14" long...	100	150	200
Glendale Coal Company Dumper	50	100	250
Glendale Wrecker	50	100	250
G-Man Pursuit Car, No. 7000, 1935s, 14-1/2" long	375	550	700
Gold Star Transfer Company Trailer Truck	75	175	325
Gravel Mixer, 1940s, 9-1/2" long	150	225	325
Gravel Truck, 13" long	88	132	175
Gravel Truck, 9" long	55	83	100
Grocery Truck, 1950s, 14-1/2" long	62	93	125
Guided Missile Truck, No. 4488..............	220	330	440
Gulf Service Station	300	450	600
Gyro Rocket Car	85	128	170
Handyman Repair Truck, 16-1/2" long....	50	100	250

Marx Hydraulic Dump. Photo courtesy Continental Hobby House

Marx Ice Truck, 1941. Photo courtesy Terry Sells

Marx Jet Speed Racer, battery-operated, with box. Photo courtesy Continental Hobby House

Marx International Agent Car, tin windup.

Marx Joy-Rider, 1929, College Boy driver, 8". Photo courtesy Bertoia Auctions

Marx Lonesome Pine Trailer and Convertible Sedan, 1930s, 19". Photo courtesy Bob Smith

Marx Lifesavers Truck, plastic, 9-1/2". Photo courtesy Terry Sells

Marx Magnetic Crane Truck, 1940s, 8-1/2". Photo courtesy Bob Smith

Marx Mechanical Coupe, 1933, 8". Photo courtesy Bob Smith

Marx Mickey Mouse Dipsy Car, 1950s, 5-1/4". Photo courtesy Don Hultzman

Marx Midget Climbing Fighting Tank, third version, 1951. Photo courtesy Harvey K. Rainess

Marx Midget Climbing Fighting Tank, 1930s, 5-1/2". Photo courtesy K. Warren Mitchell

	C6	C8	C10
Happitime Service Station	238	357	475
Hauler and Closed Van Trailer, plastic	62	93	125
Hauler and Open Van Trailer, plastic	90	135	180
Hauling tractor, wind-up, six-wheel, 14" long	150	220	300
Heavy Duty Express Truck, cloth cover	95	142	190
Heavy Duty Hydraulic Dump	72	108	145
Heavy Duty Power Shovel	112	168	225
Highboy Climbing Tractor, tin wind-up, 10-1/2" long	75	112	150
Highboy Tractor, tin wind-up, sparkles, 10" long	100	150	200
High-Lift Loader, c.1964	112	168	225
Highway Patrol Car (TV series), plastic and metal, friction, 9" long	88	132	175
Hi-Mac Dump Truck and Driver	125	188	250
Hi-Way Express Truck, 16" long, late 1940s	75	200	350
Hi-Way Express Van Lines Truck	100	150	200
Home Dairy Truck, metal, 11" long	40	75	225
Home Dairy Truck, plastic cab, 1950s, 10-1/2" long	25	50	100
Honeymoon Garage, tin lithographed, 1935, 7-1/4" long with two 6" cars (blue and green)	100	150	200
Hook and Ladder Fire Truck	NPF	NPF	NPF
Hot Rod, marked "777 Super"	160	240	320
Hot Rod, open cab, driver, plastic, 7-1/2" long	45	68	90
Hot Rod Coupe, plastic, 5" long	42	63	85
Hot Rolls, Cakes & Pies Delivery Van, w/bell, 11-1/2" long	75	125	275
Howard Johnson's Truck, plastic, 10" long	25	50	75
Hydraulic Dump	75	100	150
Ice Cream Truck, plastic, all red, friction motor, 1950s, 5-3/4" long	NPF	NPF	NPF
Ice Truck, c.1941, 11" long	50	100	250
Ice Truck, w/tongs and ice	100	175	400
Intercity Delivery, cabover, 18" long	50	75	225
International Agent Car, lithographed tin, friction, 1950s	60	100	195
International Agent Car, tin wind-up	30	55	125
International Task Force Truck, w/soldiers	55	82	110
Invasion Force Truck	45	68	90
Jalopy Pickup Truck, tin wind-up, 7" long	80	120	160
Jeep, 11" long	100	150	200
Jeep and Trailer	108	162	225

	C6	C8	C10
Jet Speed Racer, battery-operated, with box	NPF	NPF	NPF
Joy-Rider, tin wind-up, college boy driver, 1929, 8" long	250	375	500
Jumpin' Jeep, tin wind-up, 1947, 6" long	125	175	225
Kentucky Derby Stables Trailer Truck, rare, 1950s, 15" long	250	400	550
King Racer, tin wind-up, 1930s, 8-1/2" long	500	800	1100
Landau, 6" long	38	58	75
Lazy-Day Dairy Farm Pick-up Truck, w/trailer, 22" long	115	172	230
Lazy-Day Farms Stake Truck, late, 18" long	50	75	225
Liberty Bus Co., 1930s	150	225	300
Lifesavers Truck, plastic, 9-1/2" long	75	100	150
Light Duty Climbing Tractor, tin wind-up, 1930s	162	243	325
Limping Lizzie Car, tin wind-up	200	300	400
Livestock Truck	75	112	150
Loader Dump, 17" long	100	150	200
Loblaws Trailer Truck, late	200	350	500
Lone Eagle Oil Company Tank Truck, Bulldog Mack, wind-up, 12" long	700	1100	1600
Lonesome Pine Trailer and Convertible Sedan, 1930s, 19" long	360	540	720
Lowboy, 1953, 34" long	112	168	225
M.D. War Dept. Ambulance, 1930s	650	975	1300
Machinery Moving Truck, No. 1016	75	150	300
Mack Dump Truck, tin wind-up, City Coal Co., 1930s 13" long	350	525	700
Mack Tank Truck	250	375	500
Magic Barn, w/tractor	95	143	190
Magic Garage and Car, wind-up, garage, 1950s, 10" long, car: 7" long	50	100	250
Magnetic Crane, 17" long	100	150	275
Magnetic Crane Truck, 1940s, 8-1/2" long	425	640	850
Main Street, tin wind-up, 1927, 24" long	300	400	500
Maintenance Truck, two ladders at each side of truck, c.1929, 6" long	30	45	60
Mammoth Truck Train, truck w/five trailers, No. T-50-12345, 1930s	175	262	350
Marbrook Farms Sparkling Tractor and Trailer Set, tin wind-up, 21" long	75	112	150
Marco Oil Tanker, c.1940	150	225	300
Marcrest Dairy Truck, 14" long	50	125	275
Marcrest Livestock Semi, 20" long	50	100	200

Marx Midget Special Race Car, No. 7, 1930s, 5". Photo courtesy Scott Smiles

Marx Midtown Service Center. Photo courtesy Ron Fink

Marx Midget Racer No. 7, premier windup. Photo courtesy Richard MacNary

Marx Midget Special Racer, No. 2, driver in old headgear and goggles, 5". Photo courtesy Richard MacNary

Marx Motorcycle Policeman w/sidecar, litho "Police" and "3," 8". Photo courtesy Phillips NY

Marx Moving Van, circa 1940, 4-1/2". Photo courtesy Richard MacNary

Marx Mystic Motorcycle, 1936, 4-1/4". Mike Adams photo courtesy Scott Smiles

Left to right: Marx Old Jalopy tin windup; Linemar Old Jalopy, smaller. Photo courtesy Ed Hyers Antique Toys

Marx New Flivver, 1920s, 7", tin windup. Photo courtesy Bob Smith

Marx Old-Fashioned Antique Automobile. Photo courtesy Gary Linden

Marx Newberry's Semi Truck. Photo courtesy John Taylor

Marx P.D. Motorcycle Cop, windup, siren, late 1930s, 8". Photo courtesy Kent M. Comstock

Marx P.D. Police Motorcycle w/Sidecar, 1930s, 3-1/2". Photo courtesy Gary Linden

Marx Pepsi-Cola Truck, 10-1/2". Photo courtesy Terry Sells

Marx Pepsi-Cola Truck, plastic, 7".
Photo courtesy Terry Sells

Marx Pet Shop Delivery, 1950s, 10".

Marx Pickup Truck, electric
headlights, 11", with original box.
Photo courtesy Richard MacNary

	C6	C8	C10
Marshall's Delivery Van, late, plastic	30	45	75
Marshall's Drug Stores Stake Truck, 13" long	40	75	225
Marx-A-Power Giant Bulldozer, battery-operated	68	102	135
Mayflower Van, 13" long	115	173	230
Meadow Brook Dairy, stake truck w/trailer	100	225	375
Meat Delivery Truck, plastic, 9-3/4" long	90	135	180
Mechanical Coupe, tin wind-up, c.1933, 8" long	275	400	575
Mechanical Gasoline Truck, wind-up1936, 9-3/4" long	125	275	425
Mechanical Roadster, tin wind-up, 1950s, 11" long	100	150	200
Mechanical Sparkling Tank, late	35	52	70
Mechanical Speed Racer, tin wind-up, 1950, 6-1/4" long	125	175	225
Mechanical Station Wagon, tin wind-up	125	188	250
Mechanical Taxi Cab, tin wind-up, 1950s, 11' long	80	120	160
Mechanical Tractor, plastic and tin wind-up, 6" long	62	93	125

	C6	C8	C10
Mechanical Tractor, tin wind-up, 6" long, 1930s	110	165	220
Mechanical Tractor with Earth Grader, tin wind-up, 21-1/2" long	105	158	210
Mechanical Trailer Truck, wind-up	300	450	600
Merchants Transfer Truck, tin wind-up, 1929, 10" long	275	450	700
Mickey Mouse Dipsy Car, tin car, plastic Mickey, 1953, 5-3/4" long	200	300	400
Mickey Mouse Motorcycle, Linemar, tin friction, 1950s, 3-1/2" long	300	475	700
Midget Climbing Fighting Tank, third version, 1950s	50	100	125
Midget Climbing Fighting Tank, tin wind-up, c.1935, approx. 5-1/2" long	75	115	150
Midget Climbing Tractor, tin wind-up, c.1950, 5-1/2" long	75	100	125
Midget Racer, plastic wind-up, 1950s, 6" long	50	75	100
Midget Racer, premier wind-up, No. 7	100	150	200
Midget Special Race Car, driver in old headgear and goggles, No. 7 racer, tin wind-up, 1930s, 5" long	100	150	200

Marx Police Car, based on 1954
Chevrolet. Photo courtesy Gary Linden

Marx Racer, No. 3, 1930s, 5". Photo
courtesy Richard MacNary

Marx Racer, No. 7, tin windup, 5".
Photo courtesy Richard MacNary

Marx Racer, 1930s, tin windup, 5".
Photo courtesy Richard MacNary

Marx Racer, No. 8, nickel-plated. Photo
courtesy Perry Eichor

Marx Racer, No. 4, 1942, sedan-like.
Photo courtesy Richard MacNary

Marx Radar Jeep's Four-Wheel Trailer, plastic radar screen turns as wheels rotate. Photo courtesy Richard Jansen

Marx Radar Jeep, operating machine gun, two figures, "U.S. Armed Forces Mobile Radar" on hood. Photo courtesy Richard Jansen

Marx Road Grader, 17".

Marx RCA Panel Truck, 1950s, with original box, 8". Photo courtesy John Taylor

Marx Rookie Cop on Motorcycle, c.1950, 8". Photo courtesy Kent M. Comstock

Marx Roy Rogers Horse Trailer. Photo courtesy Harvey K. Rainess

Marx Rex Race Car, 1920s, tin windup. Photo courtesy Thomas G. Nefos

Marx Royal Van Co., 9".

Marx Searchlight Truck, 1941, 9". Photo courtesy John Taylor

Marx Salerno Cookies-Crackers, Dodge cab, 1950s, 11". Photo courtesy John Taylor

Marx Sand & Gravel Truck, w/scoop, 16". Photo courtesy Calvin L. Chaussee

Marx Sand Mechanical Dump Truck, c.1939, 9". Photo courtesy Charles D. Richards

Marx Siren Sparkling Fire Engine, 9", friction, 1930s. Photo courtesy John Taylor

Marx Siren Fire Chief Car, c.1930, 15". Photo courtesy Bob Smith

Marx Siren Police Patrol Car, 1933, 15". Photo courtesy Bob Smith

Marx Sparkling Climbing Fighting Tank, cannon recoils, 10". Photo courtesy Bill Holt

Marx Sparkling Climbing Fighting Tank with its original box. Photo courtesy Charles D. Richards

Marx Sparkling Climbing Bulldozer Tractor, 8-1/2", tin windup. Photo courtesy Continental Hobby House

	C6	C8	C10
Midget Special Race Car, tin wind-up, driver in old headgear and goggles, No. 2, 1950, 5" long	100	150	200
Midtown Service Center	200	300	400
Mighty Marx Jeep	10	15	20
Military Power-Mite Bulldozer	45	68	90
Military Power-Mite Dump Truck	45	68	90
Military Truck, mark "U.S. Mobile Guided Missile Squadron"	180	270	360
Milk Truck, step-down, tailgate, 1940s, 11" long	75	150	300
Milk Truck, Studebaker-type	150	300	450
Milton Berle Car, tin wind-up, 1950s, 5-3/4" long	200	325	450
Mobile Crane, c.1940	80	120	160
Model T Ford, plastic	40	60	80
Mortimer Snerd's Tricky Auto, tin wind-up, 1939, 7-1/2" long	450	650	875
Moto-Fix Truck	80	120	160
Motor Market, 14" long	50	125	275
Motor Market Truck, 1940s, 10" long	75	175	325
Motorcycle Policeman w/Sidecar, tin wind-up, marked "Police" and "3," license plate reads "102D," c.1940, approx. 8" long	200	325	450
Motorcycle Trooper, tin wind-up, 1935	175	275	400
Moving Van, c.1940, 4-1/2" long	100	150	200
Mystery Car, tin wind-up, press down to operate	145	318	290
Mystery Police Cycle, 1930s, 4-1/2" long	175	275	400

	C6	C8	C10
Mystery Taxi, press down to operate, 1930s	100	150	275
Mystic Motorcycle, tin wind-up, first version, 1936, 4-1/4" long	100	125	150
Mystic Motorcycle, tin wind-up, second version, 1940, 4-1/4" long	150	175	200
Navy Jeep, No. 1078	65	97	130
Navy Jeep, w/searchlight trailer	100	150	200
Nevins Cut Rate Stores Stake Truck, 1940s	125	275	425
New Flivver, tin wind-up, 1920s, 7" long	250	350	500
New Rocket Racer, 1930s, 16" long	200	300	450
Newberry's Box Van, 1950s, 12" long	75	175	325
Newberry's Semi Truck	75	200	350
North American Van Lines, wind-up, 14" long	75	150	300
Nutty Mads Car (Drincar), battery-operated, three action, 1960s, 9-1/4" long	125	210	300
Oklahoma Tire & Supply Trailer Truck, rare	75	200	350
Old Jalopy, tin wind-up, w/college boys, 1950s, 5-3/4" long	150	225	300
Old Jalopy, tin wind-up; 1950s; 4-3/4" long	125	200	250
Old-Fashioned Antique Automobile, plastic	20	30	35
P.D. Motorcycle Cop, wind-up, siren, 8" long, late 1930	200	275	375
P.D. Motorcyclist, tin wind-up, approx. 4" long	150	225	325
P.D. Police Motorcycle w/Sidecar, tin wind-up, 1930s, 3-1/2" long	200	325	450

Marx Sparkling Climbing Tractor, 1940s.

Marx Speed Boy, motorcycle, 9-1/2". Photo courtesy Kent M. Comstock

Marx Speed Cop, two 4" tin windup cars, track, 1930s.

Marx Stake Truck, 4-1/2". Photo courtesy Richard MacNary

Marx Sunny Side Service Station, 1930s, complete. Photo courtesy Don Hultzman

Marx Super Roadster, plastic. Photo courtesy Continental Hobby House

Marx Tank, plastic, turret and machine gun rotate, 6" long. Photo courtesy John McCurdy

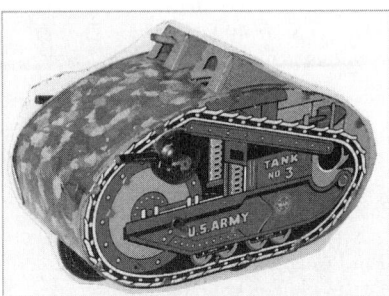

Marx Tank No. 3, no top turret, two guns on roof. Photo courtesy Harvey K. Rainess

Marx Tip Over Motorcycle, 1930s, 8". Photo courtesy Bob Smith

Marx Toyland Farm Products Truck, 1931, 10-1/2". Photo courtesy Bob Smith

Marx Toy Town Express Van Lines Deluxe Service Truck. Photo form Ron Chonjnacki

Marx Tri-City Express Truck. Photo courtesy John Taylor

Marx made several Tricky Taxis.

Marx Tricky Taxi variation.

Marx Tricky Taxi w/box, tin, wind-up, 4-1/2". Photo courtesy William G. Floyd

Marx Turnover Tank No. 3. Photo courtesy Max Heiss

Marx "Untouchables" Rolls-Royce, 5-1/4". Photo courtesy Gary Linden

Marx U.S. Army Searchlight Trailer.
Photo courtesy Calvin L. Chaussee

Marx U.S. Army Truck, plastic, 6-1/2".
Photo courtesy Ron Fink

Marx U.S. Army Troop Transport,
plastic, 6". Photo courtesy Ron Fink

	C6	C8	C10
Paddy Wagon, 5" long	150	225	300
Panel Truck, plastic, 8-1/4" long.............	NPF		
Panel Wagon	40	60	80
Parcel Post U.S. Mail, tin wind-up, early, 8-1/2" long	225	338	450
Pepsi-Cola Truck, 1945, 8" long.............	95	150	250
Pepsi-Cola Truck, 1950s, 11" long	50	125	200
Pepsi-Cola Truck, plastic, 10-1/2" long ...	175	250	375
Pepsi-Cola Truck, plastic, 1950s, 7" long	100	150	200
Pepsi-Cola Truck, plastic, 7" long	145	215	290
Pet Shop Delivery, plastic, w/6 dogs, red and blue, 1950s, 11" long	55	82	110
Peter Rabbit Eccentric Car, tin wind-up ..	145	225	325
Pickup Truck, 1968, 6" long	12	18	25
Pickup Truck, marked "Package Service," electric headlights, c.1941, 11" long...	75	200	350
Pickup Truck, marked "Package Service," w/box and load, electric headlights, c.1941, 11" long	175	350	600
Pickup Truck, plastic, assorted colors, 1950s, 5" long	10	18	25
Pinched, tin wind-up, c.1927, 10" long....	400	650	900
Polar Ice Truck, steel, came with 2 glass ice blocks and ice tongs, red cab, yellow stake body, 1940s, 13" long	50	125	275
Police Car, 1954, Chevy	NPF	NPF	NPF
Police Car, plastic, wind-up motor w/attached key, green and white w/police decals, late 1940s, 10" long...	NPF	NPF	NPF
Police Patrol motorcycle w/Sidecar, tin wind-up, 1935	150	225	300
Police Siren Motorcycle, tin wind-up, 1930s, 8" long	175	275	350
Police Squad Sidecar, wind-up, yellow, 8" long...	200	325	400
Pontiac, friction, 1954, 10" long	30	45	60
Popeye Dippy Dumper Truck	450	675	900
Popeye Transit Co. Trailer Truck	550	825	1200
Power Caterpillar Climbing Tractor, tin wind-up	125	188	250
Power Grader, No. 1759, black or white wheels, 17-1/2" long	35	52	70
Power House Dump Truck, late, 25" long	50	125	275
Power Shovel, c.1964..............................	90	135	180
Power Snap Caterpillar Climbing Tractor, tin wind-up, 1950s, 8" long....	80	120	160
Powerhouse Dump Truck..........................	250	375	500
Precinct Police Patrol Armored Truck, tin wind-up, circa early 1930s, 10-1/2" long	2000	3000	4000

	C6	C8	C10
Pumper Fire Truck, pressed steel, tin litho, plastic, white w/red trim, "V.F.D." decals, actually pumps water through hose, open cab w/plastic windshield, hydrant, 1950s, 22" long ..	125	235	350
Pure Milk Dairy Truck, w/glass bottles, pressed steel, tin wheels, c.1940	125	225	350
Racer, No. 2, tin wind-up, 1930s, 5" long	75	125	150
Racer, No. 3, plastic wind-up...................	162	243	325
Racer, No. 3, tin wind-up, 1930s, 5" long	75	112	150
Racer, No. 8, nickel-plated	100	150	200
Racer, tin wind-up, No. 2, 1930s 13" long	100	150	200
Racer, tin wind-up, No. 4, 1930s, 5" long	75	125	150
Racer, tin wind-up, No. 5, 1930s, 5" long	75	125	150
Racer, tin wind-up, No. 7, 1930s, 5" long	75	125	150
Racer, tin wind-up, sedan-like, No. 4, 1942	88	132	175
Racing Car, marked "21," early, 7" long .	175	263	350
Racing Car, tin wind-up, w/two-man team, marked "12," c.1940	150	200	250
Racing Car, wind-up, lithographed, plastic driver, marked "27," c.1950	150	225	300
Racing Car, wind-up, lithographed, w/plastic driver, marked "12," 1950s ..	300	450	600
Racing Car, wind-up, marked "61," this is the earliest Marx racer to appear with a number, 1930s, 6" long	90	135	180
Radar Jeep, w/plastic seats, console interior, operating machine gun (2-1/2" long), and 1-1/2" diameter radar screen; two figures	75	250	500
Radar Jeep w/2-wheel trailer, plastic, jeep and trailer wheels match; add.......	30	45	85
Radar Jeep w/4-wheel electric searchlight trailer, plastic, military, wheels match; add...	40	65	125
Radar Jeep w/4-wheel trailer, plastic rotating (turn w/wheels) radar acreen (8-3/4" long) and one or two figures (wheels match); add	50	100	300
Rapid Express Truck, wind-up, 9" long...	50	125	275
RCA Panel Truck, plastic, opening rear door, extension ladder, order book, 1950s, 8-1/2" long..............................	50	100	250
REA Express Truck, No. 1021	100	200	350
Reads Drugstore Stake Truck, c.1940, 14" long..	50	125	275
Reads Drugstore Stake Truck, plastic cab, 14-1/2" long..................................	75	125	175
Reversible Coupe, tin wind-up, marked "The Marvel Car," c.1936, 16" long....	275	425	550
Reversing Road Roller, tin wind-up	125	188	250

	C6	C8	C10
Reversing Tank, tin wind-up, 1930s	65	98	130
Rex Mars Planet Patrol, tin wind-up, 1950s, 10" long	225	325	425
Rex Race Car, tin wind-up, open cockpit racer, dark red body, black fenders, yellow tires, driver, "50-50" on license, 1923, 8-1/4" long	145	244	375
Ridem Fire Truck, 30" long	155	243	325
Road Grader, heavy-duty, 17" long	35	56	75
Road Roller, has driver, tin wind-up, c.1930, 8-1/2" long	125	188	250
Roadside Rest, four pumps, car, garage, 1930	450	700	1000
Rocker Dump, No. 1752, 17-1/2" long	110	165	220
Rocket Racer, tin wind-up, red w/yellow, green, blue and black, driver, "Rocket Racer" on sides, 16" long, 1935	350	425	675
Rookie Cop, w/siren, 1930s, 8-1/2" long, tin wind-up	232	348	465
Rookie Cop on Motorcycle, No. 216, wind-up, yellow, c.1950, 8" long	200	300	375
Roy Rogers Horse Trailer	100	200	350
Roy Rogers Horse Trailer, w/Jeep and figures	125	250	425
Royal Bus Line, tin wind-up, 10" long	100	150	200
Royal Coupe, 1920s, 9" long	375	563	750
Royal Oil Company Truck, Mack, 9" long	400	600	800
Royal Van Co., tin wind-up, reads "We Haul Anywhere," 9" long	350	525	700
Sabre Car	87	132	175
Safe Driving School - see Driver Training Car			
Salerno Cookies - Crackers Dodge Cab, 1950s, 11"	75	150	300
Salerno Cookies and Crackers Truck	75	150	300
Sand & Gravel Truck, w/scoop, 16" long .	30	75	175
Sand and Gravel Dump Truck, 21" long	115	172	230
Sand and Gravel Dump Truck, late 1940s, 13" long	30	75	175
Sand and Gravel DumpTruck, 10" long, 1940s	30	75	175
Sand and Gravel Truck, tin wind-up, "reads Builders Supply Co.," 1920	100	150	200
Sand Loader	60	90	120
Sand Mechanical Dump Truck, Sand and Gravel, c.1939, 9" long	55	95	140
Sanitation Truck, plastic, assorted colors, 1950s, 5" long	10	18	25
Scenic Bus, plastic, 10" long	40	60	80
School Bus, 12" long	35	52	70
Scoop Dump, postwar, 20" long	138	206	275
Searchlight Truck, c.1941, 9" long	75	175	325
Secret Agent Car	110	165	220
Sedan, c.1937, 4" long	50	95	140
Sedan, c.1940, 4-1/2" long	50	95	140
Sedan, plastic, single post, assorted colors, early 1950s, 6-1/2" long	NPF	NPF	NPF
Service Station, 1929	262	393	525
Service Station, plastic, with Take-A-Part-Car 4" sedan, opening bay doors, gas pumps, 1953, 8-1/4" long	NPF	NPF	NPF
Sheriff Sam and His Whoopee Car, tin wind-up, 1950s, 6" long	180	270	360
Shop-Rite Tractor/Trailer, late	50	75	125
Side Dump Truck, four-color, No. T-475, c.1940	60	90	120

	C6	C8	C10
Signal Corps Truck, plastic	50	75	95
Silver Streak Racer, plastic wind-up, 6" long..	70	105	140
Sinclair Trailer Truck, 1950s, 18-1/2" long	75	200	350
Sinclair Truck, steel, 1930s, 17" long	200	325	475
Single Track Speedway, wind-up car, eight track sections, 1938, 4" long.......	60	90	120
Siren Fire Chief, reads "F.D. 1st Batt.," c.1930, 15" long	375	550	750
Siren Police Car, 1933, 15" long.............	250	350	475
Siren Police Patrol, 1930s, 15" long	375	550	750
Siren Sparkling Fire Engine, friction, 1930s, 9" long	50	125	275
Snappy Gus Car	500	750	1050
Sparkling Climbing Fighting Tank, tin wind-up, cannon recoils	138	206	275
Sparkling Climbing Tank, 1939...............	140	210	280
Sparkling Climbing Tractor, tin wind-up, 8-1/2" long	62	93	125
Sparkling Climbing Tractor, tin wind-up, 1940s	150	225	300
Sparkling Climbing Tractor and Trailer, tin wind-up, 16" long	55	82	110
Sparkling Doughboy Tank	175	263	350
Sparkling Heavy Duty Bulldog Tractor w/Road Scraper, tin wind-up, 11" long	125	188	250
Sparkling Hot Rod Racer, plastic wind-up, 1950s, 8" long......................	37	56	75
Sparkling Jet Futuristic Car, friction motor, 10" long	87	132	175
Sparkling Soldier Motorcycle, tin wind-up, c.1940	250	375	500
Sparkling Super Power Tank, tin wind-up, 9-1/2" long	110	165	220
Sparkling Tank, tin wind-up, 4" long	55	82	110
Sparkling Tank, tin wind-up, prewar, 9" long..	120	180	240
Sparkling Tractor, tin wind-up, tractor w/plow blade, 1939.............................	140	210	280
Sparkling Turn Over Tank, tin wind-up ..	40	60	80
Sparks Racer, tin wind-up, yellow body w/red trim, driver, "Sparks" on sides, 1928, 15" long....................................	150	300	475
Speed Boy 4 Motorcycle, wind-up, 9-1/2" long	250	375	550
Speed Boy Delivery Motorcycle, tin wind-up, 1930s, 9-3/4" long	250	375	525
Speed Boy Delivery Motorcycle, tin wind-up, battery lights, 1930s, 9-3/4" long	300	425	550
Speed Cop, includes two tin wind-up cars and track, 1930s, cars: 4" long...........	175	275	795
Speedway Bus, plastic wind-up, 4" long .	25	38	50
Speedway Coupe, plastic wind-up, 4" long..	250	375	500
Speedway Jeep	25	38	50
Sports Coupe, 1930s, 15" long................	200	300	400
Stake, wind-up, 4-1/2" long	75	175	325
Stake Truck, c.1939, 20" long.................	100	150	200
Stake Truck, c.1940, 14" long.................	50	75	125
Stake Truck, c.1940, 4-1/2" long	50	95	250
Stake Truck, c.1941, 6" long..................	75	100	250
Stake Truck, No. 1008	60	90	120
Stake Truck, three-color, No. E-271, c.1940	100	150	200
Stake Truck, two-color, 1930s, 12" long .	65	98	130
Station Wagon, plastic, assorted colors, early 1950s, 5" long	NPF	NPF	NPF

Marx U.S. Army Truck, with horns, cloth top, 18-1/2". Photo courtesy Joe and Sharon Freed

Marx U.S. Army Truck, 4-1/2". Photo courtesy Richard MacNary

Marx U.S. Army Truck, plastic, 6-1/2". Photo courtesy Ron Fink

Marx U.S. Mail Truck, 9-1/2". Photo courtesy Phillips

Marx Utility Service Truck, with trailer, linemen, 1950s. Photo courtesy John Taylor

Marx U.S.A. Mobile Artillery Truck. Photo courtesy Bill Holt

Marx Walgreen's Ice Trailer Truck, 21". Photo courtesy John Taylor

Marx Whoopee Car, laughing cows on wheels, driver looks like cowboy. Photo courtesy Bertoia Auctions

Marx Whoopee Car, Yale-Princeton pennants, with original box. Photo courtesy Bertoia Auctions

Marx Woolworth's Trailer Truck, 1960s. Photo courtesy John Taylor

Left to right: Marx Wrecker, 4-1/2"; Sedan, 4-1/2". Photo courtesy Richard MacNary

Marx Willys Steel Jeep, hood opens, windshield folds down, 12". Photo courtesy Richard Jensen

Marx Willys Jeep, steel, c.1940, 12". Photo courtesy Calvin L. Chaussee

Marx "Yellow Cab,"—Marx's first plastic car. The original has "Made in U.S.A." on the underside of the roof. The 1990s reissue bears a Marx emblem. Photo courtesy Bob and Alice Wagner

	C6	C8	C10
Station Wagon with Trailer, plastic, friction motor, assorted colors, rubber wheels, 1947, 6" long	NPF	NPF	NPF
Streamline Convertible, friction	138	207	275
Streamline Speedway, tin figure-eight track, two wind-up cars, 1938, 31" long	140	210	280
Streamlined Coupe, steel, hardtop, no windshield supports, c.1937, 6" long	180	270	360
Streamlined Coupe, tin wind-up	110	165	220
Studebaker Dump, 1950s	110	165	220
Studebaker Shovel Truck	125	188	250
Studebaker Stake Truck, 1950s	100	150	200
Stutz Electric Car, tin wind-up, w/driver, 1930, 36" long	225	338	450
Stutz Roadster, tin wind-up, 1928, 15" long,	350	500	650
Sunnyside Service Station, 1930s, complete	400	600	800
Sunshine Fruit Growers Semi, wind-up, 14" long	100	225	375
Super Hi-Way Service Wrecker	42	63	85
Super Hot Rod 777, tin friction, 1950s, 11" long	150	225	325
Super Roadster, plastic	NPF	NPF	NPF
Super Service Center	175	263	350
Super Streamline Racer, tin wind-up, 1950s, 17" long	120	180	240
Superman Tank, battery-operated, three actions, 1950s, Linemar Co., 10-1/4" long	500	750	1000
Superman Tank, Linemar, wind-up, 1940, 4" long	500	800	1100
Take-A-Part Fire Engine, plastic, all red, 1950s, 4-1/2" long	40	75	115
Take-A-Part Jaguar, 1950s	115	172	230
Take-A-Part Wrecker, plastic, all silver, 1950s, 4-7/8" long	40	75	115
Tank, late, machine gun on top of turret	55	82	110
Tank, plastic and metal wind-up, 392-U.S. Tank Division	22	33	45
Tank, plastic, turret rotates on hull, machine gun rotates on turret rear, 6" long	24	50	80
Tank, tin wind-up, No. 3, two machine guns or cannon on top of roof (no turret), "U.S. Army" and "Tank No. 3"	80	120	160
Tank, tin, sparkles, friction, 1940, 3-1/2" long	20	30	40
Tank, wind-up, marked "U.S. Tank Co. No. 4," 1931, 5-1/4" long	60	90	120
Tank, wind-up, No. 4, marked "U.S. Army"	100	150	200
Tank 392-U.S. Tank Division, battery-operated, three actions, 1950s 9-1/2" long	60	90	120
Tank Truck, c.1940, scarce, 5" long	75	200	350
Tank Truck, Oil & Gas, 1937-41, 6" long	75	100	250
Taxi, plastic, wind-up motor w/attached key, yellow, rubber wheels, late 1940s, 5" long	NPF	NPF	NPF
Taxi Cab, plastic, wind-up motor w/attached key, green and white w/taxi decals, late 1940s, 10" long	NPF	NPF	NPF
Taxi Hauler, two taxis, c.1940	75	150	300
Telephone Repair Unit, thirty pieces	275	415	550
Telephone Truck, plastic, 11" long	50	75	125
Thimble-Drome Racer No. 1, plastic wind-up, 6" long	35	52	70

	C6	C8	C10
Thrifty Stores State Truck, c.1940	160	240	320
Tip Over Motorcycle, tin wind-up, c.1933, 8" long	225	375	500
Tow Truck, c.1941, 11" long	100	175	250
Toy Town Express Van Lines Deluxe Service Truck	50	100	250
Toyland Dairy Truck, tin wind-up, 1940s, 10" long	125	175	225
Toyland Farm Products Truck, tin wind-up, w/twelve wooden bottles, 10-1/2" long, c.1931	500	675	1000
Track and Trailer Set, no ballon tires	125	188	250
Track and Trailer Set, wind-up, 1930s, similar to climbing tractor set, but w/rounded and radiator front and copper finish metal. Tin plow attaches to front, silver metal trailer attaches to rear; has tin, copper finish and "ballon" tires	160	240	320
Tractor, plastic	20	30	40
Tractor, tin wind-up, 1920s	60	90	120
Tractor, tin wind-up, early 1940s	50	75	100
Tractor and Trailer, tin wind-up, 16-1/2" long	95	138	190
Tractor Service, tractor, cardboard garage box, three pieces of farm equipment, 1940s	225	338	450
Tractor with Scoop Loader, pressed steel, yellow and red, 13" long	80	165	250
Traffic Light, plastic, battery-operated, yellow, 1950, 8" tall	NPF	NPF	NPF
Tri-City Express Truck, 13" long	50	100	250
Tri-City Freight Truck, rare, 19" long	200	350	500
Tricky Motorcycle, non-fail action w/wind-up, 1930s, 4-1/4" long	90	135	180
Tricky Taxi, friction, 1935, 4-1/2" long	75	125	150
Tricky Taxi, tin wind-up, 1935, 4-1/2" long	100	150	175
Tricky Tommy Big Brain Tractor, battery-operated	62	93	125
Truck w/Trailer, c.1940, 19" overall	88	132	175
Trucking Terminal	90	135	180
Turn Over Tank, tin wind-up, No. 8	70	105	140
U.S. Air Force Radio Jeep, w/driver and rider	138	207	275
U.S. Air Force Searchlight Truck	88	132	175
U.S. Air Force Truck, cloth top	92	138	185
U.S. Army Searchlight Trailer, battery-operated light, olive drab	30	45	60
U.S. Army Troop Transport, plastic, 6" long	15	22	30
U.S. Army Truck, 4-1/2" long, c.1940	100	150	200
U.S. Army Truck, cloth top, late	72	108	145
U.S. Army Truck, late, canvas cover, plastic cab	60	90	120
U.S. Army Truck, Mack, wind-up, cloth cover, 1920s, 10" long	90	135	180
U.S. Army Truck, plastic, 6-1/2" long	15	25	40
U.S. Army Truck, w/horns, cloth top, 18-1/2" long	80	120	160
U.S. Mail Truck, 12-1/2" long	45	68	90
U.S. Mail Truck, 12-1/2" long	30	75	225
U.S. Mail Truck, late, 24" long	200	300	400
U.S. Mail Truck, tin wind-up, 9-1/2" long	250	350	475
U.S. Navy Jeep, w/searchlight, 23" long	138	205	275
U.S.A. Mobile Artillery Truck	55	80	115
Uncle Wiggily Crazy Car, He Goes A Ridin', tin wind-up, 1935, 7-1/2" long	450	700	925
United Van Lines Semi, wind-up, 14" long	75	200	350

	C6	C8	C10
Univeral Gas Service Station, 1940s, 6-1/2" high, base 12" long	138	208	275
Universal Bus Terminal, 12" long	95	142	190
Untouchables Rolls Royce, tin friction, 5-1/4" long	42	63	85
Untouchables Touring Car, tin friction	35	52	70
UPS Truck, plastic, 10" long	75	125	175
Utility Service Truck, w/trailer	175	325	475
Wacky Taxi, tin wind-up	75	112	150
Walgreen Ice Cream Trailer Truck, 21" long, scarce	175	350	425`
Walgreen's Ice Cream Trailer Truck, 21" long, rare	200	350	500
Walt Disney Television Car, 1950s, 7-1/2" long	225	325	500
War Tank, tin wind-up, 5-1/4" long	68	102	135
Wars Service Station	138	205	275
Western Auto Truck, 25" long	60	90	120
Whoopee Car, tin wind-up, laughing cows on wheels, driver looks like cowboy, 1932	275	425	550
Whoopee Car, tin wind-up, marked "Yale-Princeton" pennants on wheels	225	325	425
Whoopee Car with Flappers, tin wind-up, 7-1/2" long	100	150	200
Willys Jeep, steel, hood opens, windshield folds down, c.1940, 12" long	60	90	120
Willys Jeep and Trailer, 22" long	75	125	275
Willys Jeepster, plastic wind-up	25	50	75
Willys Steel Jeep, hood opens, windshield folds down; w/metal, rubber, or plastic wheels, 1946-67, 11" long	65	125	210
Willys Steel Jeep, same as other w/electric lights, 11" long	75	135	250
Willys Steel Jeep, same as other, with mechanical or electric horn, 11" long	65	135	225
Willys Steel Jeep, same as other, with removable cloth top, 11" long	85	175	325
Willys Tow Jeep, c.1940	100	200	350
Woodie Sedan, tin lithographed wind-up, 11" long	100	150	200
Woodie Sedan, tin lithographed wind-up, 6-3/4" long	48	72	95
Woolworth's Trailer Truck, 1960s	200	375	450
Wreckage Service Truck, tin, battery lights	75	112	150
Wrecker, 10" long, 1920s	100	150	200
Wrecker, 6-1/2" long, c.1940	75	125	275
Wrecker, c.1940, 5" long	100	250	400
Wrecker, No. T-16, 1930s	150	225	300
Wrecker, plastic, assorted colors, 1950s, 5" long	10	18	25
Wrecker, plastic, assorted colors, metal wheels, playset type, 1950s, 3-5/8" long	15	26	38
Wrecker, Studebaker, 7" long	75	175	325
Wrecker, w/tool box, 1940s, 11" long	175	325	475
Wrecker, wind-up, 1940, 5" long	125	275	425
Yellow Cab, first Marx plastic car, 4" long. Original has "MADE IN U.S.A." under roof. (1990s reissue has Marx emblem)	27	41	55
Yellow Cab, tin wind-up, marked "LMN 52," 1940s, 6-1/2" long	162	245	325

Linemar

	C6	C8	C10
Air Defense Pom-Pom Gun, battery-operated, five action, 14" long	120	180	240
Army Pickup Truck, tin friction, 6-1/2" long	35	52	70
Army Searchlight Truck	100	150	200
Army Stake Truck, tin, friction, 7" long	35	52	70
Coca-Cola Truck, friction, tin, 3" long	50	75	100
Donald Duck Convertible, tin friction, 1950s, 5" long	250	350	500
Donald Duck Dipsy Car, wind-up, 1953, 5-3/4" long	300	450	600
Donald Duck Disney Flivver, 1950s, 5-1/2" long	250	375	550
Donald Duck Dump Truck, 1950s, 5" long	250	375	550
Donald Duck Fire Chief Crazy Car, tin wind-up, rubber hat	750	1300	1700
Donald Duck In His Convertible, friction, 1950s, 6" long	225	350	525
Ferris Wheel Truck, battery-operated, four actions, 11" long	140	210	280
Friction Car, 8-1/2" long	30	45	60
Futuristic Roadster 1955, friction toy, 1955, 12" long	75	165	245
Mercedes Racer, 9" long	138	208	275
Military Police Car, battery-operated, six actions, 1950s, 8-1/2" long	90	135	180
NAR Television Truck, battery-operated, four actions, included six film strip inserts, 1950s, 12" long	250	375	500
NBC Television Truck, battery-operated, five actions, 1950s, 9" long	200	325	450
Nutty Mad Car, friction, c.1965, 4" long	70	105	150
Old Jalopy, tin wind-up, small, 1950s	48	72	95
Police Car, 1954 Chevy, 7-1/2" friction	60	90	120
Searchlight Truck, Studebaker	90	135	180
Stake Truck, friction, 15-1/2" long	108	162	215
Steerlab Tank, battery-operated, five actions, 1950s, 9" long	50	75	100
Taxy Yellow Cab, battery-operated, five actions, 7-1/2" long	60	90	120
Television Truck, three actions, battery-operated, 1950s, 11" long	200	300	400

Marx Linemar Air Defense Pom-Pom Gun, battery-operated, 14". Photo courtesy Don Hultzman

Marx Linemar Army Pickup Truck, tin friction, 6-1/2". Photo courtesy Ron Fink

Marx Linemar Army Stake Truck, tin, friction, 7". Photo courtesy Ron Fink

Marx Linemar Coca-Cola Truck, tin, friction, 3". Photo courtesy James S. Maxwell and Virginia Caputo

Marx Linemar Donald Duck Dipsy Car, 1950, 5-1/4", tin windup. Photo courtesy Don Hultzman

Marx Linemar Futuristic Roadster, 1955, 12". Photo courtesy Carl Thatcher

Marx Linemar Nutty Mad Car, battery-operated, 1965, 4". Photo courtesy Don Hultzman

Marx Lumar Contractors Dump Truck, 17". Photo courtesy Continental Hobby House

Marx Lumar Inter-City Delivery Service, 1950s, 16-1/2". Photo courtesy John Taylor

Lumar

	C6	C8	C10
Aerial Ladder Truck	118	177	235
Allied Van Lines	50	100	175
Army Truck	80	120	160
Army Truck and Electric Searchlight Trailer	100	150	200
Auto Transport, 28" long	145	218	290
Carry All Low Boy	32	48	65
Construction Co. Dump Truck, friction motor, 1950s, 12" long	75	150	300
Contractors Crane	65	98	130
Contractor's Dump, No. 1084, 21" long	75	150	250
Contractors Dump Truck, No. 962, 1940s, approx. 17" long	75	150	250
Contractor's Dump Truck, LM 2314, 1950s, 18" long	50	100	250
Contractors Steam Shovel	70	105	140
Dairy Truck	75	100	175
Dump, 22" long	85	128	170
Dump Truck	100	150	200
Emergency Searchlight Unit, tin lithographed, 19" long	75	150	300
Emergency Searchlight Unit Truck, 18" long	75	150	300
Handyman's Repair Truck, 16-1/2" long	50	100	175
Hi-Lift Loader	90	135	275
Hook and Ladder, 33" long	212	318	425

	C6	C8	C10
Hydraulic Dump	75	112	150
Intercity Delivery Service, 16-1/2" long	100	175	225
Inter-city Delivery Service Truck, 16-1/2" long	50	125	200
Jeep and Trailer	50	100	250
Police Car, battery-operated, 1954 Chevy	75	100	125
Power Grader	52	78	105
Rocker Dump, 18" long	60	90	120
Rocket Truck	77	108	155
Scoop-A-Dump	140	210	280
Shop-Rite Trailer Truck, 1970s, 24" long	27	41	55
Stake Truck, 14" long	60	90	120
Steam Shovel	75	112	150
Telephone Service Truck	120	180	240
U.S. Army Truck, cloth top, 18-1/2" long	75	112	150

Marx Lumar Wrecker Service, 1950s, 22". Photo courtesy John Taylor

Marx Lumar Emergency Searchlight Unit, 1950s, 19". Photo courtesy John Taylor

Marx Lumar Utility Truck, with tools. Photo courtesy Continental Hobby House

Marx Lumar Van Lines, straight body. Photo courtesy Bob Smith

	C6	C8	C10		C6	C8	C10
Utility Truck, w/tools	125	225	375	Willys Jeep	35	75	150
Van Lines, straight body	50	100	250	Wrecker Service Truck, rare, 1950s,			
Van Lines Trailer Truck, red and yellow				22" long	100	200	350
w/blue roof, 1950s, 17" long	50	125	275				

MASON & PARKER

After 1907, the Mason & Parker Mfg. Co. specialized in wood toys at their Winchendon, Mass. plant. Founded by H.N. Parker and Orlando Mason in 1899 to produce pressed-steel toys, the company is best known for its wood toys, blackboards, and other products in the pre-WWII period.

	C6	C8	C10
Baby Auto, 1907, 7" long	450	700	1000
Truck, w/cloth top, wooden, c.WWII	20	30	40
Truck, w/log load, wooden, c.WWII	20	30	40

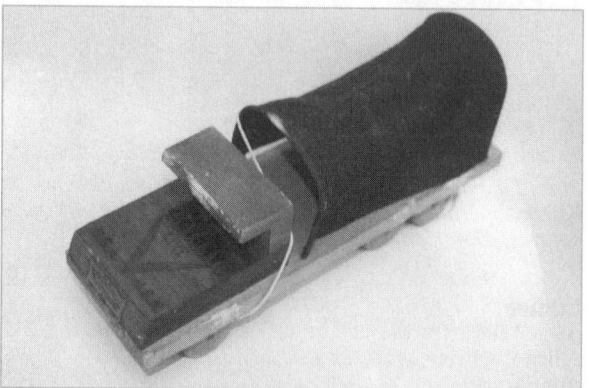

Mason & Parker Truck with log load, wooden. Photo courtesy Jack Matthews

Mason & Parker Truck with cloth top, wooden. Photo courtesy Jack Matthews

MATCHBOX

Matchbox Toys grew out of a company begun in 1947 by two Navy friends, Leslie Smith and Rodney Smith (no relation). Manufacturing toys was not even planned at this point. On June 19, 1947, the two partners combined portions of their first names, and the name "Lesney" was born. In 1948, Lesney Products produced their first toy, a 4 1/2-inch Aveling Barford Road Roller. Encouraged by the brisk sales, three other toys were produced that year—a 4 1/2" Caterpillar Bulldozer, a 3 1/8" Caterpillar Tractor, and a 3 3/4" Cement Mixer. These rare early Lesney toys are quite valuable. It was decided to package the toys in a matchbox-type box, and thereafter the toys would be known as "Matchbox."

These small vehicles quickly became very popular, and all other toy lines were discontinued. These first small vehicles had metal wheels, but these were quickly changed to plastic. These early wheels are now known to collectors as "regular" wheels, not to be confused with the "Superfast" wheels that were introduced in 1969-70. To compete with the success of Mattel's Hot Wheels, Matchbox cars were outfitted for speed with thin axles and slick new wheels, hence the name "Superfast."

It is not uncommon to find slight color and style variations for the same vehicle. These variations were often due to paint or part shortages, and these variations are now highly sought-after by collectors.

Matchbox toys were first marketed in the United States in 1958; by the early 1960s, they became a household standard. The year 1956 saw the introduction of the "Models of Yesteryear" line. The King-Size line was first developed and marketed in 1957 and was known as Major Packs through 1966. It was just called King-Size from 1965-70. Matchbox marked its 40th anniversary of in 1993 and for its 50th anniversary in 2003, released the "Matchbox Across America" series to celebrate each of the 50 states.

Contributor: The following list is derived from the *Standard Catalog of Die-Cast Vehicles, Revised Edition.*

	C6	C8	C10
Major Packs (1957-1966)			
M1-1, Caterpillar Earth Mover, 1957, Yellow tractor, driver, and scraper, unpainted metal wheels, black plastic tires, 4-1/2"	30	65	125
M1-2, B.P. Autotanker, 1961, Green lower body, yellow & white upper body, BP decals, green windshield, black plastic wheels, silver-painted headlights, no interior, 4"	25	50	90

	C6	C8	C10
M2-1, Bedford Articulated Walls' Ice Cream Lorry, 1957, Light-blue cab, silver-painted grille, headlights and bumper, cream trailer with Wall's decals, metal or gray plastic wheels, no interior, 3-7/8"	60	110	160
M2-2, Davies Tyres Truck, 1961, Orange cab, trailer base, & doors, silver-gray trailer body with Davies Tyres decals, silver grille, headlights, & bumper, gray or black plastic wheels, 4-3/8"	60	110	160
M2-3, Articulated Truck Box, 1961, Silver-gray cab, dark-red trailer, LEP decals, three different color variation of trailer base & doors, 4-3/8"	60	110	160
M3-1, 10-Wheel Transporter with Centurion Tank, 1959, Olive cab, trailer, & tank, black plastic wheels on truck, metal, gray or black plastic wheels on tank, 6-1/8". Also known as Thornycroft Antar with Sankey 50-ton Tank Transporter and Centurion Mark III Tank	60	110	160
M4-1, Ruston-Bucyrus Model 22 RB Excavator, 1959, Dark red body, yellow base, shovel, & arms, gray or green treads, red or yellow decals	45	100	150
M4-2, GMC Tractor with Hopper Train, 1964, Maroon cab, blue windows, silver headlights & bumper, silver-gray trailers, Fruehauf labels, red plastic wheel with gray or black plastic tires, 11-1/4". This model was incorporated into the King-Size line as K4-1	45	110	150
M5-1, Massey-Ferguson Combine Harvester, 1960, Red body, yellow combines, tan driver, white decals, unpainted metal wheels or various orange/ yellow plastic wheel combinations with black plastic tires, 4-3/8"	40	85	135
M6-1, 18-Wheel Pickford Scammell Tractor & Transporter, 1960, Dark-blue tractor and trailer wheel supports, dark-red trailer, white Pickfords decals, black plastic wheels	80	165	235
M6-2, Racing Car Transporter, 1965, Green body, white interior, clear windows, yellow/white/black decals, red plastic wheels, black plastic tires, 5". Incorporated into the King-Size line as K-5 in two years later	25	45	80
M7-1, Ford Thames Cattle Truck, 1960, Red cab, trailer base, & rear fenders, tan			

Matchbox Mercedes-Benz Ambulance, No. 3, 1968.

	C6	C8	C10
or dark-red trailer body & doors, gray or black plastic wheels	60	110	160
M8-1, Mobilgas Petrol Tanker, 1960, Red cab & trailer, silver grille, headlights, & bumper, Mobilgas decals, gray or black plastic wheels	75	160	225
M8-2, Car Transporter, 1964, Turquoise cab, orange trailer, white decals & interior, orange plastic wheels with gray plastic tires, tinted windshield, 8-1/2"	25	50	100
M9-1, Inter-State Double Freighter, 1962, Dark-blue cab, silver grille & headlights, gold airhorns, dark-blue or unpainted trailer connector, two different shades of gray trailers & doors possible, yellow or orange Cooper-Jarrett decals, black plastic wheels, 11-3/8"	60	120	180
M10-1, Whitlock "Dinkum" Rear Dumper, 1962, Yellow cab, body, & dumper, black & white decals, unpainted metal or red plastic wheels with black plastic tires, 4-1/4"	30	60	100

King Size (1965-1970)

	C6	C8	C10
K1-1, Hydraulic Shovel, 1960, Yellow body and front loader, no plastic windows, no interior, gray plastic wheels	30	65	95
K1-2, Foden Tipper Truck, 1964, Red cab and chassis, orange dumper bed with "Hoveringham" decals or labels on sides, red plastic wheels with removable black plastic tires, blue plastic windows, no interior, axle suspension system to roll over bumps, silver metal horns on cab, 4-1/2"	25	45	70
K1-3, O & K Excavator, 1970, Red body with silver excavator arm, red hubs with eight black plastic removable tires, "MH6", "O&K" and white stripe labels on sides, 4-15/16"	15	25	35
K2-1, Dumper Truck, 1960, Blocky red body and chassis with open cab, gray or black plastic tires on green metal hubs, "Muir-Hill" decals	25	45	75
K2-2, KW-Dart Dump Truck, 1964, Yellow articulated body with silver trim on engine and hood. Red hubs with removable black plastic tires, "KW-Dart" decals with arrow graphic, no window plastic, 5-5/8"	30	65	95
K2-3, Scammell Heavy Wreck Truck, 1969, White or gold body with red plastic hubs and black removable wheels, silver metal hooks, red towing arm, silver horns on cab roof, "Esso" labels on doors, 4-3/4"	22	45	70
K3-1, Caterpillar Bulldozer, 1960, Yellow body with green rubber treads and unpainted metal or yellow or red plastic roller wheels, cast tow hook, red-painted engine	25	50	80
K3-2, Hatra Tractor Shovel, 1965, Orange-red body with articulating center and lifting loader. Blue-tinted plastic windows, "Hatra" decals on sides of cab, red hubs with black plastic removable tires, 6"	36	65	110

	C6	C8	C10
K3-3, Massey-Ferguson Tractor and Trailer, 1970, Red cab and hood with gray engine and base, yellow hubs with removable black plastic tires, white grille, green plastic windows. Trailer with yellow chassis, red dumper bed, yellow hubs with black removable tires. Set measures 8"..................................	17	28	60
K4-1, International Tractor, 1960, Red body with "McCormick International" and "B-250" decals, green, red or orange hubs with black plastic removable tires, 2-7/8". Early versions with green metal hubs have approx. 80 MIP value..................................	25	40	65
K4-2, GMC Tractor with Hopper Train, 1967, Red tractor with two silver hopper trailers, red plastic hubs with black plastic removable wheels, opening chutes, "Fruehauf" decals on each trailer, set measures, 11-1/4".........	55	90	145
K4-3, Leyland Tipper, 1969, Red cab and chassis, silver dumper bed, red hubs with black plastic removable tires, (duals in rear), "Wates" and "LE Transport" labels most common. Amber plastic windows, yellow plastic interior, 4-1/2". Some hard-to-find models with green cabs exist, but have approx. 300 MIP values. Other models include orange cabs with green dumper beds	12	20	45
K5-1, Tipper Truck, 1961, Yellow body, silver-painted grille, silver metal or red plastic hubs with black tires, "Foden" decal on sides of hood, 4-1/4". First-version siver-hub models about 80 MIP..	25	50	80
K5-2, Racing Car Transporter, 1967, Medium-green body, cream plastic interior, clear plastic windows and skylights, red plastic hubs with black removable tires, decals on sides show racing car graphic with "Racing Transporter," "BP," and "LeMans, Sebring, Silverstone, Nurburgring." Silver metal base. Opening tailgate reveals tilting ramp and space for two racing cars, 5". This model entered the King-Size line, after being number M-6 in the Major Packs series	25	50	80
K5-2, Racing Car Transporter, View of vehicle showing the ramp and car storage are a K6-1, Allis-Chalmers Earth Scraper, 1961, Orange scraper with silver metal or red plastic hubs and black plastic tires. Adjustable scaper bed with springs (sometimes missing) "Allis-Chalmers" decals, 5-7/8"	42	75	130
K6-2, Mercedes-Benz "Binz" Ambulance, 1967, White body with blue plastic windows and dome light, black base, red cross decal on hood and shield decals on opening doors, opening rear hatch with white plastic patient and red plastic blanket, silver hubs with black plastic tires, silver metal grille and bumpers, "True Guide" steering, 4-1/8"...	12	25	62

Matchbox Merryweather Marquis Fire Engine, No. 9, 1959. Photo courtesy Gary Linden

	C6	C8	C10
K7-1, Curtiss-Wright Rear Dumper, 1961, Yellow articulated body with silver metal hubs and black plastic tires, tilting dumper bed, "Curtiss-Wright" decals, red-painted engine block, 5-3/4"	40	85	135
K7-2, SD Refuse Truck, 1967, Red cab & chassis, silver rear refuse unit, "Cleansing Service" decals or labels, red plastic wheels with black plastic tires, cream-colored plastic interior, clear plastic windows, 4-5/8"	15	25	45
K8-1, Prime Mover and Transporter with Caterpillar Tractor, 1962, Orange body & trailer, yellow "Laing" decals, metal towhook, unpainted metal or red plastic wheels with black plastic tires, yellow tractor with green treads and no blade, set measures 12-1/2"	125	180	275
K8-2, Car Transporter, 1967, Green or yellow cab, orange or yellow trailer, orange or red plastic wheels with black plastic tires, "Car Auction Collection" and "Farnborough Meashan" decals on trailer, 8-1/2"	25	45	70
K8-3, Caterpillar Traxcavator, 1970, Various versions of shades of yellow cab, orange shovel & arms, figure, yellow or black wheels with green or black treads, "available mid-1970" in catalog, 4-1/4"	15	25	35
K9-1, Diesel Road Roller, 1962, Green body, red metal rollers, gray or red driver, red "Aveling Barford" decals on sides with white reversed type, 3-3/4"...	35	65	95
K9-2, Claas Combine Harvester, 1967, Green or red body, red or yellow reels, "Claas" decals or labels, yellow plastic wheels with black plastic tires, 5-1/2" ...	20	40	60
K10-1, Aveling-Barford Tractor Shovel, 1963, Light-blue body & shovel, red seat, with or without air filter, unpainted metal or red plastic wheels with black plastic tires, 4-1/8"	30	60	90
K10-2, Pipe Truck, 1967, Yellow cab & trailer chassis, black house-shaped			

	C6	C8	C10

decal on cab doors, gray plastic pipes, red plastic wheels with black plastic tires, later issues had Superfast wheels and pink cab and chassis, 8" 20 40 85

K11-1, Fordson Tractor and Trailer, 1963, Blue tractor body & trailer chassis, light-gray trailer bed, orange metal or plastic wheels with black plastic tires, 6-1/4"... 25 45 70

K11-2, DAF Car Transporter, 1969, Metallic blue cab with gold trailer or yellow cab with orange & yellow trailer, DAF labels, red plastic wheels with black plastic tires or Superfast Wheels, 9".. 20 50 85

K12-1, Heavy Breakdown Wreck Truck, 1963, Green body, yellow boom, with or without roof lights, unpainted metal or red plastic wheels with black plastic tires, 4-3/4"... 25 50 75

K12-2, Scammell Crane Truck, 1970, Yellow cab & crane, red plastic wheels with black plastic tires or orange body & crane with Superfast wheels, 6" 20 35 50

K13-1, Ready-Mix Concrete Truck, 1963, Orange body & mixer with unpainted metal or red plastic wheels with black plastic tires, green plastic windows, no interior, "Readymix" or "RMC" decals on mixer barrel, 4-1/2".......................... 25 50 80

K14-1, Taylor Jumbo Crane, 1964, Yellow body & crane, green windows, red or yellow weight box, red plastic wheels with black plastic tires, 5-1/4" ... 25 50 75

K15-1, Merryweather Fire Engine, 1964, Red body, gray extending ladder, red plastic wheels with black plastic tires or Superfast wheels, 6-1/8"......................... 25 45 65

K16-1, Dodge Tractor with Twin Tippers, 1966, Green cab & trailer chassis, yellow dumps, Dodge Trucks decals, red plastic wheels with black plastic tires; later issues had yellow cab with blue dump & Superfast wheels, 11-7/8" 70 135 200

K17-1, Low Loader with Bulldozer, 1967, Green Ford cab & trailer, red plastic wheels with black plastic tires, red Case bulldozer body, yellow roof & blade, green treads, "Laing" or "Taylor Woodrow" decals or labels, later issues had Superfast wheels and lime-green cab and trailer, 9-1/2" 65 100 150

K18-1, Articulated Horse Box, 1967, Red Dodge cab with tan trailer, clear windows on trailer, gray ramp, four white horses, red plastic wheels with black plastic tires, later issues had Superfast wheels , 6-5/8" 35 55 90

K19-1, Scammell Tipper Truck, 1967, Red cab & yellow dump, red plastic wheels with black plastic tires or Superfast wheels, 4-3/4"........................ 20 35 50

K20-1, Tractor Transporter, 1968, Red Ford cab & trailer, red plastic wheels with black plastic tires, green plastic windows, 3 blue tractors with yellow wheels, later issues had Superfast wheels, 9"... 65 100 150

K21-1, Mercury Cougar, 1968, Gold body, red or white interior, unpainted

metal wheels with black plastic tires, 4-1/8". Shown in blue in 1968 catalog, announcing model would be available mid-year... 25 50 75

K22-1, Dodge Charger, 1969, Dark-blue body, light-blue interior, unpainted metal wheels with black plastic tires with "True Guide" steering, 4-1/2". Shown in 1969 catalog, announcing available mid-year...................................... 25 50 75

K23-1, Mercury Police Car, 1969, White body, red interior, blue dome lights, police labels, unpainted metal wheels with black plastic tires with "True Guide" steering or Superfast wheels, 4-3/8". Introduced in 1969 catalog as being available mid-year....................... 20 35 50

K24-1, Lamborghini Miura, 1969, Red body, white interior, unpainted metal wheels with black plastic tires and "True Guide" steering, many color & wheel variations exist, 4"...................... 20 35 55

Regular Wheels (1953-1969)

1-1RW, Road Roller, 1953, One of the first Matchbox offerings, this model had a "steamroller"-style large-roofed cab that matched the large toy produced by Lesney. Green paint on body can vary in shade, red metal wheels and rollers.. 40 75 125

1-2RW, Diesel Road Roller, 1955, Second in the series, but first with a smaller cab, roller attachment a little more snug than the first version, red metal wheels and roller, driver available in light and dark tan variations, gold-painted upright tow hook, 2-1/4"... 30 45 85

1-3RW, Road Roller, 1958, Third in the series, this casting kept the driver, but changed the tow hook at rear of the tractor. It still featured red metal wheels and rollers, 2-1/4" 45 70 90

1-4RW, Diesel Road Roller, 1962, Green with orange/red plastic wheels, open window on cab behind driver, tow hook

Matchbox Land Rover, No. 12, 1953. Photo courtesy Gary Linden

Matchbox Bedford Lomas Ambulance, No. 14, 1962. Photo courtesy Gary Linden

Matchbox Dennis Refuse Truck, No. 15, 1963.

	C6	C8	C10
on back. 2-5/8", "Aveling Barford Road Roller" on base near rear wheels	12	35	60
1-5RW, Mercedes-Benz Truck, 1968, Light pea-green, with orange or yellow plastic canopy, truck could be hitched to a matching trailer, released the same year, 3"	5	12	20
2-1RW, Dumper, 1953, This first version featured a gold-painted front grille on a green body with red dump bed, 1-1/2"	22	40	90
2-2RW, Dumper, 1957, Second casting is larger than first, with less painted detail. First issue with metal wheels, second with gray plastic wheels. Green body, red dumper bed, 2". Pictured here 2-3RW Muir-Hill Dumper	20	55	80
2-3RW, Dumper, 1961, Short, blocky cab with "Laing" or "Muir-Hill" decal on right-hand door. Red cab with pea-green dumper bed, black plastic wheels, 2-1/8". Although the cab is different, this model is very similar to the K-2 dumper released one year earlier. "Muir-Hill" decal versions can have about 100 MIP value	7	12	30
2-4RW, Mercedes-Benz Trailer, 1968, Pea-green trailer released same year as Mercedes-Benz Truck, 1-5RW. Also came with orange or yellow canopy, 3-1/2"	5	10	20
3-1RW, Cement Mixer, 1953, Another early Matchbox, this model mirrors one of Lesney's first larger die-cast toys. Variations seem to exist in castings, earlier models measure slightly larger at 1-3/4" length than the later ones, coming in at 1-1/2" length. Orange metal or gray plastic wheels	25	55	90
3-2RW, Bedford Tipper Truck, 1961, Available in red and maroon dumper variations, as well as gray and black plastic wheels, 2-1/2". Gray plastic wheeled version harder to find, about 120 MIP	10	20	45

3-3RW, Mercedes-Benz "Binz" Ambulance, 1968, White or cream body with Red Cross label or decal and plastic patient on stretcher. This was a smaller version of the K-6 ambulance released one year earlier, 2-7/8".

	C6	C8	C10
Unpainted base with textured surface along sides and near back tailgate	9	20	35
3-3RW, Mercedes-Benz "Binz" Ambulance, 1968, Variation photo showing cream paint and decal version of Mercedes ambulance	6	12	20
4-1RW, Tractor, 1954, Red Massey-Harris tractor body and fenders; a small version of larger Lesney Massey-Harris toy tractor	35	65	95
4-2RW, Massey-Harris Tractor, 1957, Red with no fenders. An update on the previous model, this tractor was re-released painted green in 1994 as an anniversary issue. Metal wheel and gray plastic wheel variations, some casting variations with 1-1/2" and 1-3/4" lengths	40	75	135
4-3RW, Triumph Motorcycle w/Sidecar, 1960, Light metallic blue with 24-spoke silver wheels and black tires, 2-1/8"	17	30	85
4-4RW, Dodge Stake Truck, 1967, Yellow cab and body with green plastic stakes. A popular model, Matchbox made many toy trucks with this Dodge cab style, 2-7/8". Models with blue-green stakes, a very slight color difference, can have about 150 MIP value	6	9	19
5-1RW, Double Decker Bus, 1954, First of Matchbox's London Buses, this one featured decals that read "Buy Matchbox Series" on the side, 2"	15	45	80
5-2RW, Double Decker Bus, 1958, Second London Bus, casting slightly larger, at 2-1/4" length. "No. 5" cast into front of bus, no interior. Available with metal and gray plastic wheels, with a variety of decals	40	80	120
5-3RW, Routemaster London Bus, 1961, Red, with gray or black plastic wheels, "Visco-Static" decal most common. No interior in bus, major change from last model: a wider front grille, with cast headlights on front fenders	20	45	80
5-4RW, Routemaster London Bus, 1965, Red body, white plastic interior-first Matchbox model bus to feature one. Like 5-3RW, the "Visco-Static" decals and labels are the most common, 2-3/4"	6	12	30

	C6	C8	C10
6-1RW, Quarry Truck, 1954, Orange body with gray dumper bed. No interior. Most commonly seen with metal wheels, crimped or rounded axles, 2-1/4"	20	40	75
6-2RW, Quarry Truck, 1959, Yellow body, black plastic wheels most common, red, white and black decal on cab doors, cab extends the full width of the front of truck, appears first in 1959 catalog with black plastic wheels	12	30	65
6-3RW, Euclid 10-Wheel Quarry Truck, 1964, Yellow body, no decals, exposed engine shows on casting, partial cab does not extend across body of truck, 2-5/8"	7	15	30
6-4RW, Ford Pickup, 1969, Red, with white plastic camper top and white or silver plastic front grille. Featured "Autosteer," a Matchbox innovation making its appearance in the 1969 catalog, that "turns the front wheels in either direction by simple pressure." 2-3/4"	10	20	30
7-1RW, Horse-Drawn Milk Float, 1954, Orange wagon body, white painted driver, brown horse. Available with metal spoked or gray solid plastic wheels, 2-1/4". Quite a detailed little model	45	60	120
7-2RW, Ford Anglia, 1961, Light blue body, no interior, gray, silver or black plastic wheels, silver painted grille, bumper and headlights, 2-5/8", black painted baseplate, tow hook. Gray plastic wheel versions, about 90 MIP; silver plastic wheel versions, about 55 MIP	15	22	45
7-2RW, Ford Anglia, 1961, A view of a gray-plastic-wheel version of the Ford Anglia, a harder-to-find variation	20	40	90
7-3RW, Ford Refuse Truck, 1967, Red body, gray and silver dumper section, tilts together when dumped, no interior, black plastic wheels, green window plastic, 3"	7	12	20
8-1RW, Caterpillar Tractor, 1955, Yellow or orange with cast driver, silver painted grille. Unpainted roller wheels for treads, 1-1/2". Fully exposed engine under hood. Note: Orange variation harder to find, MIP value can reach over 200; yellow versions with painted drivers also about 200 MIP	20	40	85
8-2RW, Caterpillar Tractor, 1959, Yellow, different casting with engine partially covered by hood, and cast "roller wheels" between two actual turning metal wheels. Driver cast with toy, 1-3/4", green or gray rubber treads	25	65	90
8-3RW, Caterpillar Crawler Tractor, 1961, Yellow body with cast driver, metal or plastic tread wheels, very similar to previous casting, models with silver plastic roller wheels about 90 MIP	20	40	65
8-4RW, Caterpillar Crawler Tractor, 1965, Yellow, cast without driver, black plastic roller wheels, 2", gray or black rubber treads	12	22	30

	C6	C8	C10
8-5RW, Ford Mustang Fastback, 1966, White, with red interior and tow hook. Black plastic tires on silver wheels. Unique steering lever on driver's side allows front wheels to turn left or right, 2-7/8", orange versions are quite rare, about 300 MIP	12	20	45
9-1RW, Fire Escape, 1955, Red with cast driver, metal wheels, gold-painted trim, 2-1/4", no front bumper in casting	20	45	80
9-2RW, Fire Escape, 1957, Red, cast with driver, metal wheels most common, versions with gray plastic wheels about 400 MIP, front bumper included in casting, 2-1/4"	20	45	80
9-3RW, Merryweather Marquis Fire Engine, 1959, Red body with cab, gold ladder, black plastic wheels (first versions had gray plastic wheels), ladder colors can vary, 2-5/8", simply called "Fire Truck" in 1966 catalog	20	55	70
9-4RW, Boat and Trailer, 1967, Plastic blue and white boat with blue die-cast trailer, black plastic wheels. First time a stand-alone trailer makes appearance in regular wheels line	7	15	30
10-1RW, Mechanical Horse and Trailer, 1955, Red, three-wheeled cab and gray stake-style trailer, metal wheels, 3"	55	70	95
10-2RW, Mechanical Horse and Trailer, 1957, Second casting of Scammell Scarab, red three-wheeled cab and light-tan stake-style trailer with fenders. Grille can be painted or unpainted, metal wheels, 3". Appears first in 1957 catalog/flyer	40	60	95
10-3RW, Sugar Container Truck, 1962, Blue Foden truck body with "Tate & Lyle" decal, with silver, gray, or black plastic wheels (shown). Popular Foden cab design, 2-5/8". Gray-wheeled models tend to have higher MIP values, up to 200	15	30	65
10-4RW, Pipe Truck, 1967, Red Leyland die-cast body, silver grille and baseplate, gray plastic pipes. "Ergomatic Cab" written on baseplate, 3". The Ergomatic cab was a new feature on large British trucks, including Leyland and AEC, beginning in the mid-sixties, so this model reflected the latest advance at time of release	12	25	50
11-1RW, Road Tanker, 1955, Yellow or red ERF truck body, metal wheels, "Esso" decal on rear of tank, 2", painted side gas tanks, crimped axles	40	75	100
11-2RW, Road Tanker, 1959, Red ERF truck body, metal wheels, gray or black plastic wheels, variations include silver painted side gas tanks and grilles, slightly larger casting, 2-1/2"	35	60	100
11-3RW, Jumbo Crane, 1965, Yellow, red plastic hook, large black plastic wheels in front near cab, small in back-1966 catalog illustration looks more like King Size version, K-14, with what appears to be a die-cast hook. Some with red counterweights, 3". Shown here with 42-3RW Iron Fairy Crane	8	15	30

	C6	C8	C10
11-4RW, Scaffold Truck, mid-1969, Mercedes-Benz truck, silver body with yellow plastic scaffold sections in stake-style bed. "Builders Supply Company" decal on side, 2-5/8", released late in 1969, just before transition to Superfast	8	12	20
12-1RW, Land Rover, 1957, Dark green body with tan driver, metal wheels. No real windshield, just a low flat piece of the casting appearing where the base of a windshield would be. Slight casting variations, some 1-5/8" length, later editions, 1-3/4" length. Silver-painted grille	8	40	80
12-2RW, Land Rover, 1960, Dark green, black or gray plastic wheels (black more common). Open cab, model shown has bent windshield. "Land-Rover Series II" on black baseplate	5	40	75
12-3RW, Safari Land Rover, 1965, Dark green body, dark brown plastic luggage on top, white interior, white tow hook, black plastic baseplate. First issue of the Safari Land Rover, says "Land Rover Safari" on base, 2-3/4"	8	15	25
12-3RW, Safari Land Rover, 1967, Medium-blue body, light reddish-brown plastic luggage, white plastic interior and tow hook, black plastic baseplate with "Land Rover Safari." Second issue of same casting in blue	8	15	25
13-1RW, Wreck Truck, 1955, Tan Bedford truck with red tow hook and scaffold, metal wheels, silver-painted grille and bumper, 2-1/4"	35	50	75
13-2RW, Wreck Truck, 1958, Tan Bedford body, red boom section, metal or gray plastic wheels, no interior, slightly smaller than previous casting at 2"	40	60	90
13-3RW, Wreck Truck, 1961, Red body with metal or plastic tow hook, and gray or black plastic wheels, decal on side of truck says "A.A. & R.A.C. Matchbox Garages Breakdown Service," silver trim on front grille	18	45	115

Matchbox MG Midget Sports Car, No. 19, 1955. Photo courtesy Gary Linden

	C6	C8	C10
13-4RW, Wreck Truck, 1966, Dodge Wreck Truck with yellow cab, green tow bed, red plastic hook, clear red plastic cab light, BP decals or labels, 3", black plastic wheels. Variations with colors reversed, (green cab and yellow body) are extremely rare. "Dodge Wreck Truck" on green base near rear wheels	7	12	30
14-1RW, Ambulance, 1956, Cream painted body, metal wheels, Red Cross decal, word "Ambulance" cast in raised letters along side of vehicle, 2" .	20	45	85
14-2RW, Ambulance, 1958, Daimler with cream or off-white body with metal or gray plastic wheels, Red Cross decal, slightly larger casting at 2-1/4", word "Ambulance" cast in raised letters	18	60	90
14-3RW, Lomas Ambulance, 1962, White body with black plastic wheels and "LCC Ambulance" decals, 2-5/8", referred to simply as "Ambulance" in catalog. "LCC" is an abbreviation for the "London County Council," responsible for designing and building ambulances in the 1950s and 1960s to its own specifications, later adapted by Daimler and other companies	10	20	45
14-4RW, Iso Grifo, 1968, Dark blue, almost purple body, light blue plastic interior and tow hook, opening doors, 3", in 1968 catalog, "available in early 1968," steering wheel on right-hand side, black tires on silver wheels, textured baseplate	9	17	25
15-1RW, Prime Mover Truck, 1956, Orange body, silver grille and trim, metal wheels. Harder to find editions: yellow body with metal wheels and orange with gray plastic wheels	22	45	70
15-2RW, Atlantic Prime Mover, 1959, Orange body, black plastic wheels, spare tire in bed of truck, no interior	25	45	80
15-3RW, Dennis Refuse Truck, 1963, Blue body, gray dumper section, red and white decals or labels say "Cleansing Service," and have cross-in-shield design at center. Black plastic knobby wheels, no interior, 2-1/2"	7	14	30
15-4RW, Volkswagen 1500 Saloon, 1968, White Volkswagen Beetle body with "137" decals or labels, black plastic tires on silver wheels, 2-7/8"	7	12	25
16-1RW, Transporter Trailer, 1956, Tan, flat bodied trailer with ramp and non-skid surface for vehicles, one axle and metal wheels in front near towbar, two axles with metal wheels on back near ramp, 3", ramp fold up onto trailer body	17	30	60
16-2RW, Atlantic Transporter, 1960, Orange trailer body, black plastic wheels, 4 axles; two at front near drawbar, two at back near ramp, non-skid tire tracks on trailer, pictured here with 15-2RW Atlantic Prime Mover	17	40	75
16-3RW, "Mountaineer" Dump Truck w/Snowplough, 1964, Gray cab and body with orange dumper section,			

	C6	C8	C10

snowplow on front with orange and white striped decal, black plastic wheels, 3", gray plastic wheel version about twice MIP value .... **18　30　50**

16-4RW, Case Bulldozer, 1969, Red body with yellow blade and cab, "Available mid-1969" in 1969 1st issue catalog, 2-1/2"...................................... **9　18　32**

17-1RW, Removals Van, 1956, Green, blue or dark red body, metal wheels, "Matchbox Removals Service" decal, green more common color .... **15　60　100**

17-2RW, Removals Van, 1958, Green body, with "Matchbox Removals Service" decal on sides, metal or gray plastic wheels .... **35　75　120**

17-3RW, Metropolitan Taxi, 1960, Dark red with gray or silver plastic wheels, gray more common, silver can have 130+ MIP value, gray-wheel values shown .... **25　40　75**

17-4RW, 8-Wheel Tipper, 1963, Red Foden body, orange dumper section, black plastic wheels, no interior, 3", "Hoveringham" decal on tipper. A "little brother" to the 8-Wheel Tipper K-1 in the King Size line .... **9　18　37**

17-5RW, Horse Box, 1969, Red AEC (Associated Equipment Company) Ergomatic cab and truck body, green plastic box with gray door, two white plastic horses, black plastic wheels, 2-7/8", "Available mid-1969" in 1969 catalog, 1st edition .... **8　12　25**

18-1RW, Bulldozer, 1956, Yellow body, tow hook, red blade, metal roller wheels, driver in hat cast as part of toy . **18　35　85**

18-2RW, Bulldozer, 1958, Yellow body, tow hook, yellow blade, driver cast into body, metal roller wheels. Engine partially covered on side .... **25　78　110**

18-3RW, Caterpillar Bulldozer, 1961, Yellow body, tow hook, yellow blade, driver cast into body, metal or black plastic rollers. Driver shown here is painted, but normally they were the same color as casting .... **18　40　80**

18-4RW, Caterpillar Crawler Bulldozer, 1964, Yellow body, curving tow hook, no driver, black plastic roller wheels. Casting essentially the same as 18-3, but with flatter blade and no driver .... **7　18　40**

18-5RW, Field Car, 1969, Yellow body, white plastic interior, generally red wheels with black plastic tires. Many collectors consider this vehicle to be an International Scout model, and in fact the side view bears close resemblance. However, the front grille also looks a bit like a French SINPAR Renault military vehicle (although they were produced in the 1970s). "Available mid-1969" in catalog. Auto-Steer model. 2-5/8" .... **7　11　18**

19-1RW, Sports Car, 1956, White or cream body with metal wheels, painted driver, silver grille .... **45　70　150**

19-2RW, MG "A" Sports Car, 1958, White body, metal or gray plastic wheels, painted driver, can have rounded or crimped axles, silver-painted grille and headlights, 2-1/4" .... **58　85　150**

19-3RW, Aston Martin Racer, 1961, Green body, white or gray driver, 24-spoke wheels with black plastic tires. Variable number decals on body .. **45　80　165**

19-4RW, Lotus Racing Car, 1966, Green or orange body, white plastic driver, yellow wheels with black plastic tires, No. "3" decal or label, 2-3/4". Green pictured in 1966 catalog, but orange variation included in G-4 Racetrack Set that same year. Driver missing in this photo .... **11　22　50**

20-1RW, Heavy Lorry, 1956, Dark red ERF truck body, metal or gray plastic wheels, no interior, dropside stake bed appearance with fuel tanks along sides. Can have silver-painted grille, some casting variations, 2-1/4" and 2-5/8" ..... **18　40　100**

20-2RW, Transport Truck, 1959, ERF dropside truck with dark blue body, gray or black plastic wheels, "Ever Ready For Life" decal along stake sides, model also called "Heavy Lorry" in 1959 catalog .... **18　45　90**

20-3RW, Taxi Cab, 1965, Chevrolet Impala Taxi Cab with yellow body, red or white plastic interior, (red is harder to find) black plastic wheels, 3" .... **11　18　30**

21-1RW, Bedford Coach, 1956, Light pea-green body with red and yellow "London to Glasgow" decals above windows, metal wheels......................... **22　40　68**

21-2RW, Bedford Coach, 1958, Light pea-green body with red and yellow "London to Glasgow" decal above windows, metal or gray plastic wheels, "Bedford Duple Luxury Coach" on black base, 2-1/2", silver painted grille and front bumper, no interior .... **25　60　95**

21-3RW, Milk Delivery Truck, 1961, Commer truck with light green body, white or cream plastic cargo and gray or black plastic wheels, 2-1/4", cow or milk bottle decal on cab doors. Both variations shown here .... **15　35　65**

21-4RW, Foden Concrete Truck, 1969, Yellow Foden cab and plastic mixer with orange body, dark green plastic windows, eight black plastic wheels, 3". Worm-gear under second set of wheels turns mixer as truck rolls forward .... **5　9　22**

22-1RW, Vauxhall Cresta, 1956, Red body with white roof, no interior, metal wheels, silver painted grille and bumpers, tow hook .... **22　40　62**

22-2RW, Vauxhall Cresta, 1958, Different casting than previous version. Longer, more "Chevy-like" body with low tailfins and wraparound front and rear windshields. Many paint variations exist, some pushing MIP price well into the hundreds of dollars. Can have gray or black plastic wheels or metal wheels **30　72　150**

22-3RW, Pontiac Grand Prix, 1964, Red body, black plastic wheels, gray plastic interior & tow hook, 3", opening doors, "Pontiac G.P. Sports Coupe" on black painted baseplate .... **12　22　45**

	C6	C8	C10
23-1RW, Caravan, 1956, Pale blue body, metal wheels, 2-1/2"	17	30	75
23-2RW, Trailer, 1958, Pale blue-green or lime-green body, metal or gray plastic wheels	22	40	75
23-3RW, Bluebird Dauphine Trailer, 1960, Metallic tan or green body, opening door, no interior or plastic windows, black or gray plastic wheels. Variations with green bodies are hard to find, and can be quite valuable. More common tan variation prices given below	25	40	85
23-4RW, Trailer Caravan, 1966, Yellow or pink body, black plastic wheels, white plastic interior, 3", pink more common beginning in 1968 and after. Yellow version about 45 MIP value	9	17	30
24-1RW, Hydraulic Excavator, 1956, Yellow or orange body with metal wheels; larger two at rear and smaller at front, figure cast as part of body, front dumping bucket	18	40	75
24-2RW, Hydraulic Excavator, 1959, Yellow body, black or gray plastic wheels, larger at rear or cab, smaller in front near dumper bucket. Figure cast in piece, 2-5/8"	17	28	45
24-3RW, Rolls-Royce Silver Shadow, 1967, Deep red sedan body, white plastic interior, opening trunk, silver wheels with black plastic tires, clear plastic windshield and windows, unpainted silver metal grille, headlights and front bumper, 3". Black baseplate with "A" near front axle	7	11	25
25-1RW, Bedford Dunlop Van, 1956, Dark blue Bedford panel van, with yellow "Dunlop" decals on sides, no interior or plastic windows	18	40	80
25-2RW, Volkswagen Sedan, 1960, Volkswagen 1200 Sedan, blue-silver body, gray plastic wheels, opening rear engine hood, green or clear plastic windows, black base	45	65	100
25-3RW, Petrol Tanker, 1964, Yellow Bedford cab, green body, white tanker with "BP" decal. Cab tilts to reveal white plastic interior. Black plastic wheels, 3". Called "B.P. Tanker" in 1966 catalog. Blue versions with "Aral" decals on tanker section harder to find, about 200 MIP	8	14	25
25-4RW, Ford Cortina, 1968, Light brown body, cream-colored plastic interior and tow hook, black plastic wheels, "Auto-Steer," textured pattern on unpainted baseplate near front and rear axles, opening doors, 2-5/8". Interesting to note that its first catalog appearance in 1968 showed a blue car with the subhead "Available in mid-1968." The blue color wouldn't be used until the 1970 Superfast version was released. Yellow roof rack included in 1969 G-4 Race'n Rally Gift Set	6	9	17
26-1RW, Ready Mixed Concrete Lorry, 1957, Orange ERF cab and body with silver-painted grille and side gas tanks, metal or gray plastic wheels, 1-3/4", metal mixer section, four wheels	18	45	88

	C6	C8	C10
26-2RW, Ready-Mix Concrete Truck, 1961, Orange die-cast Foden cab and body with plastic orange mixer section. Gray or black plastic wheels, 2-1/2". Six wheels, says "Foden Cement Mixer" on base	9	19	40
26-3RW, GMC Tipper Truck, 1968, Red cab with green plastic windows, silver-gray tipper bed, green chassis, black plastic wheels with duals at rear, 2-5/8", 1968 catalog shows subhead "Available early 1968" and model with yellow tipper bed	6	10	18
27-1RW, Bedford Low Loader, 1956, Green Bedford cab with silver trim, tan trailer, metal wheels, 3", no windows or interior	28	48	90
27-2RW, Bedford Low Loader, 1958, Green Bedford cab with silver trim, tan trailer, metal or gray plastic knobby wheels, slightly larger casting at 3-3/4" length. No windows or interior	30	75	140
27-3RW, Cadillac Sixty Special, 1960, Silver-gray or silver-purple Cadillac body with cream or pink colored roof, plastic windows, no interior and gray or black plastic wheels, red base, tow hook, red-painted taillights and silver-painted trim	28	45	90
27-4RW, Mercedes 230SL, 1966, White Mercedes convertible with red plastic interior, opening doors, black plastic wheels, tow hook, 2-3/4", "Available early 1966" in catalog	7	13	25
28-1RW, Bedford Compressor Lorry, 1956, Orange or yellow Bedford cab and chassis with Caterpillar-type compressor engine on back, painted-silver grille and trim, 1-3/4", metal wheels. Pictured here with 28-2RW Thames Compressor Truck	20	30	50
28-2RW, Ford Thames Compressor Lorry, 1959, Yellow Ford Thames truck cab and chassis with black plastic wheels, no interior or window plastic, silver headlights and grille	25	40	60
28-3RW, Mark Ten Jaguar, 1964, Light metallic brown body with opening hood, black plastic wheels, black-painted base. Engine can be painted the same as body color or left unpainted, 2-3/4". White plastic interior, clear window plastic, tow hook	12	20	30
28-4RW, Mack Dump Truck, 1969, Orange Mack truck body with orange dumper bed, black plastic tires on orange or yellow wheels, 2-5/8", green window plastic, unpainted base	7	18	25
29-1RW, Bedford Milk Delivery Van, 1956, Tan body with white plastic milk bottles and boxes, silver trim, metal or gray plastic wheels, no interior or window plastic, 2-1/4"	18	30	80
29-2RW, Austin A55 Cambridge, 1961, Medium green body with light green roof, gray or black plastic wheels, green window plastic, no interior, black-painted base with tow hook, 2-1/2"	17	30	72
29-3RW, Fire Pumper, 1966, Red LaFrance fire engine body, white			

	C6	C8	C10
plastic ladders along sides, unpainted base and trim, green window plastic, no interior, blue dome light, black plastic wheels, 3". With or without "Denver" decal	6	11	22
30-1RW, Ford Prefect, 1956, Light sage-green or light brown body with metal or gray plastic wheels, (light blue harder to find, 200 or more MIP). No window plastic or interior, silver-painted grille, headlights and bumpers, red-painted taillights. Tow hook, black-painted base, 2-3/8"	15	40	80
30-2RW, Magirus-Deutz Crane Truck, 1961, Silver cab and truck body with orange boom section and gray or black plastic wheels. Hook can be metal or plastic. Black-painted baseplate under front cab section, 2-3/8"	17	30	72
30-3RW, 8-Wheel Crane, 1965, Medium-dark green body with 8 black plastic wheels, orange crane section, yellow plastic hook, 3"	5	11	20
31-1RW, American Ford Station Wagon, 1957, Yellow body with metal or gray plastic wheels, silver painted bumpers and headlights, no interior or window plastic, 2-5/8". Appears brown in 1957 leaflet catalog	15	40	78
31-2RW, Ford Fairlane Station Wagon, 1960, Mint green with pink-white roof, gray or black plastic wheels, silver-painted trim, tow hook. Yellow-painted versions are harder to find, and can bring higher MIP values (up to 300). Two box variations shown.	22	55	78
31-3RW, Lincoln Continental, 1964, Dark blue or mint-green body, white plastic interior, clear window glass, opening trunk, 3" Metallic tan versions rare, over 1000 MIP at auction	6	10	22
32-1RW, Jaguar XK140 Coupe, 1957, Cream body with metal or gray plastic wheels, 2-3/8", called "Fixed Head Coupe" in 1957 catalog/flyer. Silver-painted grille, red-painted taillights	30	45	70
32-2RW, E-Type Jaguar, 1962, Metallic red body, spoked wheels with gray or black tires, green or clear window plastic, 2-5/8", white plastic interior	20	40	80

Matchbox B.P. Tanker, No. 25, 1960.

	C6	C8	C10
32-2RW, Leyland Petrol Tanker, 1968, Medium-green Ergomatic cab and chassis, eight black plastic wheels, white tanker section, "BP" decals or labels, silver or white plastic grille and bumper, 3". A blue and white version with "Aral" labels is harder to find, and can have 120 or more MIP value. "Available early 1968" in catalog	4	7	15
33-1RW, Ford Zodiac, 1957, A variety of body colors exist for this model: blue, dark green, blue-green, silver, tan & orange and turquoise. Dark green and tan and orange models more common, with around 80-90 MIP values. 2-5/8"	20	40	80
33-2RW, Ford Zephyr 6, 1962, Blue-green body, white plastic interior, gray or black plastic wheels, silver front grille and headlights, slight tailfins, black painted base, 2-1/2". Some models with black wheels have a lighter blue-green color than earlier versions	8	15	30
33-3RW, Lamborghini Miura, 1969, Yellow or gold body with red or cream plastic interior, 2-3/4", silver wheels with black plastic tires, opening doors. Gold cars with cream interiors (as shown in 1969 catalog) have high MIP values, around 200	4	12	25
34-1RW, Volkswagen Microvan, 1957, Blue panel van body, no interior, "Matchbox International Express" yellow type decal on sides, with silver-painted bumper and headlights, 2-1/4". Mostly found with metal or gray plastic wheels, decal on side with "Matchbox International Express" in yellow lettering	30	50	95
34-2RW, Volkswagen Camping Car, 1962, Light sea-green body, gray or black plastic wheels, opening side doors, top window plastic, camper section interior, 2-5/8"	20	40	90
34-3RW, Volkswagen Camper, 1967, Silver body with opening camper section doors, orange plastic interior, yellow window plastic, raised roof with windows and top window plastic, black plastic wheels, 2-5/8"	10	18	45
34-3RW, Volkswagen Camper, 1967, Another view of the Volkswagen Camper	10	18	45
34-4RW, Volkswagen Camper, 1969, Silver body, opening doors to camper section, slightly raised roof with window plastic on top but no windows, orange plastic interior, black plastic wheels. Interestingly, the size of this vehicle remained the same since the 1962 release at 2-5/8". Makes first appearance in 1969 catalog	11	17	35
35-1RW, Marshall Horse Box, 1957, Red ERF cab with silver-painted grille and headlights, brown horse box with opening side door, metal and gray plastic wheels most common, 2-1/8". Silver plastic wheel version, about 180 MIP; black plastic wheel version, about 135 MIP	15	30	80

	C6	C8	C10

35-2RW, Snow-Trac Tractor, 1964, Red body with unpainted base, six black tread roller wheels, green window plastic, 2-1/4". White or gray treads, some versions have "Snow-Trac" cast in side of tractor, (as seen in 1968 and 1969 catalogs) others have decal, and some variations have neither, (as seen in the 1966 catalog). Gray-tread models may have slightly higher MIP values, although decal models (based on the tenuous nature of decals) may start to become more desirable 9 17 40

36-1RW, Austin A 50, 1957, Blue-green body, no interior, metal or gray plastic wheels, silver-painted grille, headlights and bumper, tow bar, 2-3/8" 20 35 75

36-3RW, Opel Diplomat, 1966, Gold body, black-painted metal base, white plastic interior and tow hook, opening hood, silver or gray plastic motor, 2-3/4". Pictured in elusive sea-green in 1966 catalog with caption "Available mid 1966." These (possibly) first versions are rarely seen 4 10 20

37-1RW, Coca-Cola Lorry, 1956, Yellow-orange truck with Coca-Cola decals on sides and back of truck, metal or gray plastic wheels, 2-1/4", no step on the running board on cab, silver-painted trim on running boards, grille. Some versions have "uneven" loads of cast Coca-Cola cases (as seen in 1957 flyer) in the bed of the truck. These typically run about 150 MIP. "Even" load versions in gray plastic wheels comparable MIP price. Even-load metal wheel version prices shown below 30 55 95

37-2RW, Coca-Cola Lorry, 1960, Yellow body, black baseplate, "even" cast crate load on bed, Coca-Cola decals on sides and back, 2-1/4", gray or black plastic wheels. Gray plastic wheel versions tend toward higher MIP values, about 110 .... 25 40 80

37-3RW, Cattle Truck, 1966, Yellow Dodge cab and chassis, gray plastic cattle box, originally included two white plastic steers, 2-1/2". Introduced in 1966 catalog as a new model, but hadn't yet replaced the #37 Coca-Cola truck in the line-up 4 7 15

38-1RW, Refuse Wagon, 1957, Silver-gray or dark-gray cab and almost tanker-truck shaped rounded-top bed and "Cleansing Department" decals. Metal or gray plastic wheels. 1957 flyer shows model painted green and without the decals. Casting variations must account for size difference: 2-1/8" and 2-1/2" lengths 18 45 85

38-2RW, Vauxhall Victor Estate Car, 1963, Yellow station wagon with opening rear hatch, gray, silver or black plastic tires, red or green plastic interiors, clear plastic windows. 2-1/2". 18 32 60

38-3RW, Honda Motorcycle with Trailer, 1967, Blue-silver Honda motorcycle with kickstand and orange or yellow trailer. Trailer may or may not included labels or decals. 3". As with many motorcycle-related toys, these fairly common models are increasing in value.. 12 25 40

39-1RW, "Zodiac" Convertible, 1957, Pink body, turquoise interior, driver, tow hook. Metal, gray or silver plastic wheels. Casting variations: Model can measure 2-5/8" or 2-1/2". Silver-painted grille, gray-painted headlights, red-painted taillights, light green baseplate.. 27 68 95

39-2RW, Pontiac Convertible, 1962, Purple Pontiac convertible body with gray or silver plastic wheels; yellow body with gray, silver or black plastic wheels. Yellow with black plastic wheels is most common, around 55 MIP. Purple version with silver plastic wheels is hard to find (pictured above and in color section). 2-3/4". Yellow with gray or silver wheels prices shown below.. 28 55 95

39-3RW, Ford Tractor, 1967, Blue Ford tractor body with yellow die-cast hood, yellow wheels with black plastic tires, 2-1/8", tow hook. Versions of this tractor exist in all-blue, being part of the King Size K-20 set 7 16 25

40-1RW, Bedford 7-Ton Tipper, 1957, Red Bedford cab and chassis, tan dumper bed, metal or gray plastic wheels, silver painted trim. Casting variations: Size varies between 2-1/8" and 2-1/4". Shown in all-green color in 1957 flyer 15 40 80

40-2RW, Long Distance Bus, 1961, Blue-silver coach body with tailfins at rear, 3", green window plastic, silver-painted grille. With gray, silver or black plastic wheels. (Gray or silver-wheel versions about 55 MIP value.) Black-wheel version values given below 7 15 28

40-3RW, Hay Trailer, 1967, Blue die-cast trailer body with yellow die-cast stake-ends, often missing. Yellow plastic wheels with black plastic tires, 3-3/8"... 3 8 12

41-1RW, "D" Type Jaguar, 1957, Green D-type body, metal driver in later catalogs, but not in 1957 flyer, "41" decal, metal or gray plastic tires, 2-1/4". Photo shows 41-1RW and second release with a larger casting, 41-2R 20 45 70

41-2RW, Jaguar Racing Car ("D"-Type), 1961, Second issue of car featured a green body and tan driver, but came in a variety of wheel types, from more common gray and silver plastic wheels to rare spoked versions and black plastic wheels 25 40 80

41-3RW, Ford G.T., 1966, Generally white Ford G.T. bodies with yellow plastic wheels and black plastic tires. Clear window plastic, blue rally stripe on hood with "6" or "9" reversed in white. Visible rear engine, 2-5/8". "Available early 1966" in 1966 catalog. Black base, red plastic interior. Versions with differently-colored wheels or bodies are hard to find 5 12 20

	C6	C8	C10
42-1RW, Bedford "Evening News" Van, 1957, Mustard-yellow Bedford panel van body with die-cast billboard on roof and red decal "First With The News" in white type. "Evening News" on panel side of van and "Football Results" in red type decals on each door. Metal, gray or black plastic wheels, (gray and black shown). 2-1/4"	17	40	95
42-2RW, Studebaker Station Wagon, 1965, Blue body with blue or light blue sliding roof, white plastic interior and tow hook, clear window plastic, white plastic dog and hunter figure included with original (often missing), 3"	15	30	65
42-3RW, Iron Fairy Crane, 1969-70, Red body, yellow crane arm, yellow plastic hook and seat, black plastic wheels, 3". Introduced in 1970 catalog, as a "non-Superfast" toy	4	11	18
43-1RW, Hillman "Minx", 1958, Blue body, light gray roof, no window plastic or interior, silver-painted grille, metal or gray plastic wheels, 2-1/2", first appears in 1958 catalog	12	40	75
43-2RW, Aveling-Barford Tractor Shovel, 1962, Yellow tractor body with cast yellow or red driver and yellow or red bucket, black wheels, 2-5/8". All yellow versions can have 140 MIP value. Model prices for yellow with red bucket and yellow with red driver shown	15	30	55
43-3RW, Pony Trailer, 1968, Yellow body with clear window plastic on sides and top, gray/brown plastic door, black plastic wheels, 2 white plastic horses, 2-5/8"	6	11	25
44-1RW, Rolls Royce Silver Cloud, 1958, Blue metallic Rolls Royce body, metal, gray or silver plastic wheels, crimped axles, no interior, no window plastic, silver-painted grille and bumpers, 2-5/8"	18	35	80

Matchbox Bedford Dunlop Van, No. 25, 1956. Photo courtesy Gary Linden

	C6	C8	C10
44-2RW, Rolls Royce, 1962, Metallic tan or metallic silver/gray body, opening trunk, black plastic wheels, white plastic interior, clear window plastic, black base, silver-painted grille, 2-7/8"	12	20	40
44-3RW, Refrigerator Truck, 1967, Red GMC cab and chassis, green refrigerator box, green window plastic, black plastic wheels, opening rear door on box, 3"	4	7	13
45-1RW, Vauxhall "Victor", 1958, Yellow body, silver-painted headlights and grille, can have no windows, clear or green plastic windows. No interior. Metal, gray, silver or black plastic wheels, 2-3/8"	18	40	85
45-2RW, Ford Corsair, 1965, Cream-yellow body, red plastic interior and tow hook, gray or black plastic wheels, silver-painted grille and headlights, green plastic roof rack and boat (not shown), 2-5/8". Gray-wheeled versions may have higher MIP values	6	12	30
46-1RW, Morris Minor 1000, 1958, Dark blue or dark green body, metal or gray plastic wheels, black base, no interior, no plastic windows, 2". Dark blue with gray plastic wheels harder to find, with higher MIP values	45	65	100
46-2RW, Pickford's Removal Van, 1960, Dark blue or green body, silver-painted grille, no interior, no plastic windows, gray, silver or black plastic wheels, 2-5/8". Decals can have 2 or 3 lines. Many variations of this model exist, although versions with 2-line decals seem hard to find, bumping up the MIP price from what is shown here	30	80	150
46-3RW, Mercedes 300SE, 1968, Medium blue or green body, white plastic interior, opening doors and trunk, black plastic wheels, unpainted base extends to bumpers and front grille, 2-7/8"	9	18	25
47-1RW, Trojan "Brooke Bond" Van, 1958, Red body, metal or gray plastic wheels, decals on van box read "Brooke Bond Tea," tea leaf decal on each door, silver-painted headlights, 2-1/4"	18	45	95
47-2RW, Commer Ice Cream Van, 1963, Blue, cream or metallic blue body with white plastic interior, clear plastic windows and black plastic wheels, 2-1/4". Color and decal variations change MIP values considerably. Metallic blue versions with square roof decals are more rare than cream-colored models with plain (non-striped) side decals (see color section)	20	45	75
47-3RW, DAF Tipper Container Truck, 1969, Green or silver-gray cab and chassis, yellow tipper bed with removable gray top. Red plastic grille and baseplate under cab, black plastic wheels, 3". Makes first appearance in 1969 catalog. Green version higher MIP value, about 40	3	8	18
48-1RW, "Meteor" Sports Boat on Trailer, 1958, Blue and yellow plastic boat with slight rise for windshield, black die-cast			

	C6	C8	C10
trailer, metal or gray plastic wheels, 2-3/4"	25	40	70

48-2RW, Sports-Boat and Trailer, 1961, Plastic red and white boat with gold or silver outboard motor, blue die-cast trailer, gray or black plastic wheels, 3-1/2". Boat can come with red deck and white hull or white deck and red hull 12 25 60

48-3RW, Dumper Truck, 1967, Red Dodge cab, chassis and dumper bed, silver plastic baseplate, bumper and front grille, black plastic wheels, 3" 3 8 18

49-1RW, Army Half-Track, 1958, Dark olive-green with star-in-circle U.S. insignia on hood, no interior, metal, gray or black plastic wheels and rollers, gray treads (often missing as they are here) 2-1/2". Known as Army Half-Track and Military Personnel Carrier, this toy stayed in the 1-75 lineup for many years 18 30 55

49-2RW, Mercedes Unimog, 1967, Two color variations, one tan and blue and the other blue and red, green plastic windows, yellow plastic wheels with black plastic tires, silver-painted grille, tow hook cast, 2-1/2" 8 12 25

50-1RW, Commer Pickup, 1958, Tan or red and gray body, with metal, gray or black plastic wheels, 2-1/2", silver-painted grille and headlights 25 45 60

50-1RW, Commer Pickup, 1958, A view of the red and gray variation of the Commer Pickup with black plastic wheels 40 75 150

50-2RW, John Deere-Lanz Tractor, 1964, Green body, yellow plastic wheels, gray or black plastic tires, cast tow hook, 2-1/8". After John Deere acquired the German manufacturer Lanz in the 1950s, a variety of toy manufacturers, including Matchbox, produced models of this tractor. Photo shows black-tire version tractor with 51-2RW Tipping Trailer. Note: Gray-tire versions have slightly higher MIP value, about 55 ...... 14 20 35

50-3RW, Kennel Truck, 1969, Dark green die-cast body, white or silver plastic grille, green window plastic, truck bed partitioned into four sections, to hold one plastic dog each (included), clear plastic canopy over truck bed, "Auto-Steer" front wheels, black plastic wheels, 2-3/4" 9 20 35

51-1RW, Albion "Portland Cement" Lorry, 1958, Yellow Albion truck cab and chassis, two decal variations: "Portland Cement" and "Blue Circle Portland Cement." Metal, gray, silver or black plastic wheels, silver-painted trim, tan-painted cement bag load on flatbed, no interior, no window plastic, 2-1/2". Silver plastic wheel versions have about 150 MIP values 18 40 80

51-2RW, Tipping Trailer, 1964, Green body, yellow wheels, tilting bed, black or gray plastic tires, three yellow barrels, 2-5/8" 8 12 25

51-3RW, 8-Wheel Tipper, 1969, Orange or yellow Ergomatic AEC cab and chassis with silver-gray tipper bed, 8 black plastic wheels, green plastic windows, no interior, "Douglas" or "Pointer" labels on the sides of tipper bed, 3". Orange models with "Douglas" appear to have higher MIP values, about 40 ...... 9 16 28

52-1RW, Maserati 4CLT Racecar, 1958, Yellow or red body with spoked wheels and black tires or solid black plastic wheels. Open cockpit with driver, mostly seen with "52" decal, 2-3/8", silver-painted grille 20 35 70

52-2RW, BRM Racing Car, 1965, Blue or red body, white plastic driver, yellow wheels, black plastic tires, 2-3/4". Generally carries no. "5" decals on hood and sides 7 12 25

53-1RW, Aston Martin, 1958, Light green, metal or gray plastic wheels, no interior, no plastic windows, 2-1/2", silver-painted grille 18 35 70

53-2RW, Mercedes-Benz 220SE, 1963, Red or maroon body, opening doors, white plastic interior, clear plastic windows, 2-3/4", silver, gray or black plastic wheels 10 30 55

53-3RW, Ford Zodiac Mk. IV, 1968, Blue-silver body, opening hood, white plastic interior, clear plastic windows, black plastic wheels, 2-3/4" 3 6 12

54-1RW, Army Saracen Carrier, 1958, Olive-green "turtle-shaped" body, six black plastic wheels, rotating turret on top, 2-1/4". One of Matchbox's first military vehicle releases. Like rescue and construction vehicles, military toys tend to be in rough shape, so finding mint or MIP examples can be a little tough 8 18 40

54-2RW, S&S Cadillac Ambulance, 1965, White Cadillac ambulance body with red cross decal or label, blue plastic windows, detailed white plastic interior, black plastic wheels, silver-painted grille, red plastic dome lights, 2-7/8" 9 18 40

55-1RW, D.U.K.W. Amphibian, 1958, Olive-green body, metal, gray or black plastic wheels, 2-3/4", another in the early military grouping of Matchbox vehicles 15 35 60

55-2RW, Ford Fairlane Police Car, 1963, Dark or light blue Ford Fairlane with white plastic interior, clear plastic windows, red dome light, silver-painted grille, black plastic wheels. Dark blue version is harder to find; about 300 MIP. Light blue values shown 22 40 85

55-3RW, Ford Galaxie Police Car, 1966, White body, white plastic interior with molded figure, black plastic wheels, red, white and blue stars-in-shield decals, unpainted base, red dome light.. 17 25 40

55-4RW, Mercury Police Car, 1969, White Mercury sedan with white plastic interior, featuring two officers, silver hubs with black plastic tires, blue dome light, clear plastic windows, unpainted

	C6	C8	C10
base, "Auto-Steer" front wheels, 3-1/16". A new model, this police car was released at the same time as a Mercury station wagon, #73. Both share auto-steer feature and a baseplate, reading "55 or 73"...............	16	28	60
56-1RW, Trolley Bus, 1958, Red double-decker body with sloped front, no interior; six metal, gray, or black plastic wheels, "Drink Peardrax" decals on sides, flat trolley poles on roof, "OXO" decal on front, 2-5/8". Note that MIP metal wheel versions have sold for 250. Common prices for gray and black wheel versions shown...........................	20	45	70
56-2RW, Fiat 1500, 1965, Pea-green Fiat 1500 sedan with dark or light brown plastic luggage on roof, red plastic interior, silver-painted grille and headlight details, black plastic wheels, 2-5/8", black plastic base. Red versions of this car were included with the G-1 Service Station Gift Set, and are tough to find, usually over 100 mint value. Standard green values shown................	4	9	15
57-1RW, Wolseley 1500, 1958, Pale green body, no plastic windows, no interior, silver-painted grille, bumpers and headlights, red-painted taillights, black-painted base, 2-1/8"	20	35	70
57-2RW, Chevrolet Impala, 1961, Medium-blue body with light-blue top, cast tow hook, clear plastic windows, no interior, silver, gray or black plastic wheels.....................................	25	50	110
57-3RW, Land Rover Fire Truck, 1966, Red Land Rover body with "Kent Fire Brigade" and fire dept. insignia decals on sides, blue plastic windows and dome light, white plastic ladder (removable) on top, black plastic wheels, 2-1/2"	6	11	25
58-1RW, British European Airways Coach, 1958, Rounded metal blue bus body, no plastic windows, no interior, gray plastic wheels, "British European Airways" decals, 2-1/2"......................	30	50	85
58-2RW, Drott Excavator, 1962, Red or orange body, silver-painted motors on some red variations, orange motor on some orange models, 2-5/8"	15	35	60
58-3RW, DAF Girder Truck, 1968, Cream-colored cab and chassis, red plastic grille, green plastic windows, no interior, "Available mid-1968" in 1968 catalog, black plastic wheels, 12 red plastic girders, 3"	10	20	32
59-1RW, Ford "Singer" Van, 1958, Light green Ford Thames van with "Singer" decals on panel sides and "S" logo decals on doors. No plastic windows, no interior, silver-painted grille, gray plastic wheels, 2-1/8". Dark green models seem hard to find, about 250 MIP	35	55	100
59-2RW, Ford Fairlane Fire Chief Car, Red Ford Fairlane casting (same as 55-2RW Ford Fairlane police car) black plastic wheels, white plastic interior, clear plastic windows...........................	25	45	80

Matchbox Bedford Compressor Truck, No. 28, 1956. Photo courtesy Gary Linden

	C6	C8	C10
59-3RW, Ford Galaxie Fire Chief Car, 1966, Red Ford Galaxie body, white plastic interior with figure cast as part of interior (like police car version) unpainted base and metal grille and headlight section, fire chief decals or labels on side doors and hood, clear plastic windows, white plastic tow hook, blue plastic dome light, 2-7/8"	9	12	30
60-1RW, Morris J2 Pick-Up Truck, 1958, Blue pick-up body, gray, silver or black plastic tires, "Builders Supply Company" decals on sides, silver-painted grille, no plastic windows, no interior, 2-1/4"	18	30	60
60-2RW, Site Hut Truck, 1967, Blue Leyland Ergomatic cab and flatbed chassis, silver plastic grille and headlights, blue plastic windows, no interior, black plastic wheels, plastic yellow hut on back with green roof, 2-1/2"......................................	3	6	12
61-1RW, Ferret Scout Car, 1959, Olive-green, open-cockpit armored car body, tan-colored driver, four black plastic wheels, (one spare on side), 2-1/4"......................................	9	12	30
61-2, Alvis Stalwart, 1967, White body with green plastic windows and green or yellow wheels with black plastic tires. Plastic canopy over bed (not shown), no interior, 2-5/8". Yellow wheels are less common and have approx. 75 MIP values.........................	9	17	30
62-1RW, General Service Lorry, 1959, Olive green body with six black plastic wheels, no plastic windows, no interior	20	32	60
62-2RW, TV Service Van, 1963, Cream colored body with "Rentaset" or "Radio Rentals" decals on sides, red plastic accessories: antenna, 3 TV sets and ladder. No interior, 2-1/2"..................	20	50	110

	C6	C8	C10
62-3RW, Mercury Cougar, 1969, Lime-green Mercury Cougar body with unpainted base, silver wheels with removable black plastic tires (like other Mercury models in the line), opening doors, red plastic interior, "auto-steer" front wheels, tow hook, 3"	10	18	24
63-2RW, Fire Fighting Crash Tender, 1964, Block-shaped red body with white plastic ladder (missing in this photo) and white plastic lettering on sides. No plastic windows, no interior, black plastic wheels, 2-3/8"	12	30	50
63-3RW, Dodge Crane Truck, 1969, Yellow Dodge cab and chassis, red or yellow plastic hook, black grille and headlights, green plastic windows, no interior, six black plastic wheels, swivelling crane section, 3"	6	10	18
63-3RW, Service Ambulance, 1959, Olive green truck-ambulance chassis, black plastic wheels, no interior, no plastic windows, red cross decals on sides	8	22	50
64-1RW, Scammell Breakdown Lorry, 1959, Olive green body, box cab, green, silver or gray hook, six black plastic wheels	25	45	70
64-2RW, M.G. 1100, 1966, Green car body, white plastic interior with driver in front and dog peeking out of rear window, clear plastic windows, black plastic wheels, unpainted base, white plastic tow hook, 2-5/8"	3	7	12
65-RW, Jaguar 3.4 Litre, 1959, Blue body, no interior, no plastic windows, gray plastic wheels, silver-painted grille. Shown here with 65-2RW Jaguar 3.8 Litre Sedan	18	35	65
65-2RW, Jaguar 3.8 Litre Sedan, 1962, Red body, opening hood, silver-painted grille and headlights, gray, silver or black plastic wheels, green plastic windows, no interior, 2-5/8"	11	20	50
65-3RW, Combine Harvester, 1967, Red Claas combine with yellow plastic grain reel and yellow wheels with removable black plastic tires, 3". A popular casting for Matchbox, matching the King-Size model (K-9) version	3	7	12
66-1RW, Citroen DS19, 1959, Yellow body, silver-painted grille, no window plastic, no interior, gray plastic wheels	15	32	55
66-2RW, Harley-Davidson Motorcycle with Sidecar, 1962, Gold metallic body with spoked wheels, 2-5/8". This piece has escalated in value due to Matchbox and Harley-Davidson collector cross-over	65	95	160
66-3RW, Greyhound Bus, 1967, Silver-gray body, "Greyhound" decals or labels, yellow plastic windows, white plastic interior, black plastic wheels, 3"	8	12	25
67-1RW, Saladin Armoured Car, 1959, Olive-green body, rotating turret (gun barrel in photo is broken, a common occurrence with these models) six black plastic wheels, 2-1/4"	11	18	30
67-2RW, Volkswagen 1600 TL, 1967, Red body, white interior, unpainted base running up into headlights, clear window plastic, opening doors, 2-11/16". One version with snap-on plastic roof rack was included with Race 'n Rally G-4 gift set, harder to find	11	17	25
68-1RW, Austin Mark II Radio Truck, 1959, Olive-green body, no window plastic, no interior, black plastic wheels	18	35	65
68-2RW, Mercedes Coach, 1966, White and blue-green or white and orange body, clear window plastic, white plastic interior, black plastic wheels, 2-7/8". Blue-green version harder-to-find with approx. 130 MIP values. More common orange-version values shown	7	11	15
69-1RW, Commer 30 CWT Nestlé's Van, 1959, Dark red or red van with Nestlé's decals on panel sides, sliding doors, no window plastic, no interior, silver-painted grille, gray plastic wheels	22	40	90
69-2RW, Hatra Tractor Shovel, 1965, Yellow or orange body with black plastic removable tires. Hubs can be yellow or red, 3-1/8". Models with red hubs seem to have higher MIP values, about 90-125	11	17	30
70-1RW, Ford Thames Estate Car, 1959, Pale blue and yellow van-shaped body with clear or green plastic windows, no interior, silver-painted grille. Gray, silver or black plastic wheels	25	40	70
70-2RW, Grit Spreader, 1966, Red Ford cab and chassis, yellow hopper section, green plastic windows, no interior, black plastic wheels, silver metal grille, gray or black plastic "pulls" that open bottom chute, 2-5/8"	7	9	20
71-1RW, Service Water Truck, 1959, Olive-green truck chassis with water tank on back, black plastic wheels, spare black plastic tire behind cab, no plastic windows, no interior	28	40	75
71-2RW, Jeep Pick-Up Truck, 1964, Red body, opening doors, black partial base, black plastic wheels, clear plastic windows, silver-painted grille, 2-5/8". Early models came with green plastic interior (shown in 1964 catalog) and are hard to find, about 175 MIP. White plastic interior more common; prices shown	12	22	40
71-3RW, Ford Heavy Wreck Truck, 1969, Red cab, green plastic windows and dome light, red plastic hook, black plastic wheels, "Esso" label, white grille extending from white base with "1968" date, 3". A nice, hefty model	12	20	40
72-1RW, Fordson Major Tractor, 1959, Blue tractor with gray or black plastic tires, and orange hubs in rear and in variations, on front. Silver-painted grille, 2". Gray-tire version and black-tire version with box variations shown	18	30	75
72-1RW, Fordson Major Tractor, 1959, Another variation of the Fordson tractor with orange hubs and black tires, front and rear. This is the version of the tractor that appeared in its last catalog appearance in 1966	18	30	75

	C6	C8	C10
72-2RW, Standard Jeep, 1967, Yellow body with upright windshield, black base, red plastic interior and tow hook, black plastic removable tires over yellow hubs, spare tire on back, 2-3/8" .	12	20	40
73-1RW, RAF Refueller Truck, 1960, Blue body with RAF decal on top of truck behind cab, no plastic windows, no interior, gray plastic wheels	20	45	75
73-2RW, Ferrari Racing Car, 1962, Red racing car body with "73" and Ferrari decals on sides, spoked wheels, white or gray plastic driver, 2-5/8"	20	35	80
73-3RW, Mercury Commuter, 1969, Lime green body with clear plastic windows, white plastic interior (including two dogs peeking out of the back), black plastic removable tires with silver hubs, "Auto-Steer" front steering, 3-1/16"	9	12	25
74-1, Mobile Refreshment Bar, 1960, Silver trailer body with opening sides and plastic interior, "Refreshments" decals below side openings, silver or gray plastic wheels, medium-blue baseplate models about 190 MIP, 2-5/8". Common prices with lighter blue bases shown below........................	28	45	95
74-2RW, Daimler Bus, 1966, Cream, green or red bodies with white plastic interior, black plastic wheels, "Esso Extra Petrol" decals or labels, 3". First appears in 1966 catalog as new model, "Available mid 1966" with no series number	7	14	25
75-1RW, Ford Thunderbird, 1960, Pink and cream 1959 Ford Thunderbird body, green plastic windows, no interior, silver, gray or black plastic wheels..	20	50	90
75-2RW, Ferrari Berlinetta, 1965, Dark or light green body with white plastic interior and tow hook, clear plastic windows, spoked wheels or silver hubs, (with black plastic removable tires), 2-7/8". Red-colored versions of this model are very rare, about 750 MIP. Common prices shown below	11	18	40

Superfast (1970-1982)

	C6	C8	C10
1-1SF, Mercedes Truck, 1970, Gold-colored body, orange plastic tarp cover, green window plastic, narrow transitional Superfast wheels, silver plastic grille and half-baseplate, tow hook cast with body, 3"	4	8	18
1-2SF, Mod Rod, 1972, Yellow body, amber window plastic, exposed silver-plastic engine in back, red or black Superfast wheels, "wildcat" label on hood, 2-7/8"	6	12	25
1-3SF, Dodge Challenger, 1976, Red or blue body, white or red plastic interior, black wheels, plastic air scoops on hood, blue-tinted windshield plastic, white plastic roof, 2-7/8"	5	12	18
2-1SF, Mercedes Trailer, 1970, Gold-colored body with orange plastic canopy, thin transitional wheels, 3-1/2"	5	9	20
2-2SF, Hot Rod Jeep, 1972, Pink body, exposed silver plastic engine with black			

	C6	C8	C10
plastic exhaust pipes, white plastic seats, lime-green base and bumpers, 2-5/16"	4	7	12
2-3SF, Hovercraft, 1976, Metallic-green hovercraft body with light brown plastic base and thin "hidden wheels" beneath, 3-1/6"	1	3	6
3-1SF, Mercedes-Benz "Binz" Ambulance, 1970, White body with opening hatch and patient on stretcher, red cross labels, blue window plastic, white plastic interior, thin transitional wheels, (later issued with thicker wheels as part of TP-10 Two-Pack), 2-7/8"	7	11	25
3-1SF, Mercedes-Benz "Binz" Ambulance, View of wider-wheel version without opening rear hatch, included as part of TP-10			
3-2SF, Monterverdi Hai, 1974, Orange body with number "3" label on hood, blue window plastic, thick black wheels, opening doors, 3"	5	7	17
3-3SF, Porsche Turbo, 1979, Charcoal-gray, red or white exterior with rally number "14," plastic interior can be yellow, tan or brown, plastic tow hook, opening doors	1	2	5
4-1SF, Stake Truck, 1970, Yellow, or orange-yellow cab and chassis with green window plastic, no interior, green plastic stake-side cargo area, silver metal base, grille and headlights, 2-7/8"	3	8	15
4-2SF, Gruesome Twosome, 1972, Gold with cream interiors and pink or purple window plastic. Two exposed engines, unpainted base, 2-7/8"	2	4	11
4-3SF, Pontiac Firebird, 1976, Blue body with silver plastic interior, amber window plastic, unpainted base and bumpers, 2-7/8"	1	3	5
4-4SF, '57 Chevy, 1981, Red or light purple with unpainted or black base, opening hood with silver plastic engine underneath	1	3	5
5-1SF, Lotus Europa, 1970, Pink or blue body, white plastic interior, opening doors, 2-7/8", thin or thick Superfast wheels. Blue model shown in 1970 catalog, but pink was advertised afterward until model removed from lineup..	4	9	20
5-2SF, Seafire, 1976, White body with "Seafire" label on front, blue base, blue or orange driver, exposed silver plastic engine with red plastic exhaust pipes. This casting has been used many times by Matchbox, returning in 5-Packs in the 1990s	1	3	5
6-1SF, Ford Pick-Up Truck, 1970, Red body, white plastic camper top, silver or white plastic grille, 2-3/4", black or charcoal base	8	15	25
6-2SF, Mercedes Tourer, 1973, Orange or yellow 350SL body with black plastic top, amber windows, light yellow or cream plastic interior, 3", unpainted base. Later models in light or dark red with white plastic roof, or red or metallic blue with no roof.....................	3	7	14

	C6	C8	C10

7-1SF, Ford Refuse Truck, 1970, Red-orange cab with gray plastic and silver metal garbage dumper bed, 3". The same model as the old regular-wheels version, just with thin or thick Superfast wheels .... | 4 | 8 | 12

7-2SF, Hairy Hustler, 1973, Bronze body, with amber windows, number "5" racing labels on front and side, or white body with checkered labels on hood and roof, and red stripes on fenders, black metal base.............................. | 2 | 4 | 7

7-3SF, Volkswagen Golf, 1977, Lime green, dark green, yellow or red body, amber window plastic, black plastic, detachable surf boards on roof rack, yellow plastic interior, black or charcoal base, tow hook .... | 4 | 7 | 12

8-1SF, Ford Mustang Fastback, 1970, White, red or orange-red body, white or red plastic interior (red is harder-to-find), tow hook, 2-7/8". Red models with red plastic interiors are the most rare, selling for around 400 MIB . | 65 | 80 | 120

8-2SF, Wildcat Dragster, 1971, Orange or pink body with silver engine protruding from hood, and "Wild Cat" labels on sides, tow hook, 2-7/8". This is the same casting used on the Mustang Fastback model 8-1SF .... | 3 | 5 | 11

8-3SF, De Tomasa Pantera, 1975, White body with "8" labels, blue base, red plastic interior, or blue body, tempo "17", black base, 3" .... | 2 | 4 | 10

9-1SF, Boat and Trailer, 1970, Blue die-cast boat trailer with thin Superfast wheels and plastic blue and white boat, 3-1/2"... | 4 | 9 | 20

9-2SF, AMX Javelin, 1972, Lime-green or blue body (blue included with Twin-Pack #3, Javelin and Pony Trailer), black or silver plastic air scoop, light yellow or white plastic interior, opening doors, tow hook, 3-1/16" .... | 3 | 6 | 10

9-3SF, Ford Escort RS 2000, 1979, White body with Ford and Shell rally labels, clear window plastic, black base, tan plastic interior .... | 3 | 5 | 8

10-1SF, Pipe Truck, 1970, Red or orange cab and chassis, gray or yellow plastic pipes, thin or wide Superfast wheels, silver grille, green window plastic, 3". Red models about 35 MIB, orange model values shown below .... | 7 | 14 | 23

10-2SF, Piston Popper, 1973, Blue or yellow Mustang Mach I body with

	C6	C8	C10

silver Rola-Matic engine with red plastic pistons that move as car is rolled along. Yellow plastic interior, unpainted base, 2-7/8" .... | n/a | 5 | 10

10-3SF, Plymouth Gran Fury Police Car, 1979, Black and white with "Metro Police" on doors and hood, blue police lights on roof, amber or blue window plastic, unpainted or silver base. Introduced in 1979/80 catalog, it hadn't yet replaced Piston Popper in the lineup | 1 | 4 | 7

11-3SF, Scaffold Truck, 1970, Silver Mercedes-Benz truck with red plastic base and grille, yellow plastic scaffold sections in back, "Builders Supply Company" labels on sides of truck, green window plastic, no interior, 2-5/8"... | 4 | 6 | 13

11-2SF, Flying Bug, 1973, Red metallic Volkswagen Beetle with Iron Cross label on hood, oversized face with silver helmet peeking up from car, opaque windows, tailwing and yellow plastic jet engine section on back. Silver or unpainted base, 2-7/8" .... | 4 | 9 | 16

11-3SF, Car Transporter, 1978, Orange body with black base and light tan/cream car carrying section with red, yellow and blue plastic cars. Dark blue window plastic, no interior .... | 3 | 5 | 9

11-4SF, Cobra Mustang, 1982, Orange body with opening hood, chrome interior, yellow windows, "The Boss" in white lettering on sides, number "5" on roof. Another in the many variations of the old "Boss Mustang" casting........ | 1 | 3 | 6

12-1SF, Safari Land Rover, 1970, Gold body with white plastic interior, red-brown plastic luggage, tow hook, thin Superfast wheels, 2-3/4". Blue versions of this model exist as Superfasts, but are extremely rare, so prices shown are for gold models only . | 8 | 14 | 25

12-2SF, Setra Coach, 1971, Metallic yellow and white or burgundy and white with clear or green window plastic, white plastic interior, unpainted base, 3" .... | 3 | 6 | 14

12-3SF, Big Bull, 1975, Orange bulldozer body and rollers, green base and blade, silver plastic engine and trim, 2-1/2"..... | 1 | 3 | 5

66-2SF, Citroen CX Station Wagon, 1980, Blue body with cream or light yellow plastic interior, clear or blue window plastic, unpainted or silver base .... | 2 | 5 | 10

13-1SF, Wreck Truck, 1970, Yellow Dodge cab and tow boom with green

Matchbox Jaguar, E Type, No. 32.

Matchbox Volkswagen Camper, No. 34, 1961.

Matchbox Coca-Cola Truck, No. 37, 1956. Photo courtesy Gary Linden

	C6	C8	C10

bed. "BP" labels on sides, thin Superfast wheels, red window plastic and dome light, no interior, red plastic tow hook, 3". This is another transitional model that is becoming hard to find 17 30 48

13-2SF, Baja Buggy, 1972, Lime green body, orange plastic interior, no window plastic, thick Superfast wheels, flower label on hood, silver plastic engine with orange plastic exhaust pipes, 2-5/8" 2 4 9

13-3SF, Snorkel Fire Engine, 1977, Red body with blue or amber window plastic, yellow or white snorkel section, unpainted metal base. Models with amber-colored window plastic tend to have higher MIP prices, about 15. This fire engine first appeared in the 1977 catalog with a white snorkel as a new model to watch for, not yet replacing Baha Buggy in the lineup...................... 1 4 7

14-1SF, Iso Grifo, 1970, Dark or medium blue with thin Superfast wheels, light blue or white plastic interior, unpainted base, 3" 6 12 25

14-2SF, Mini-Ha-Ha, 1976, Red body with blue opaque window plastic, silver plastic rotary engine protruding through hood, large rear wheels, head with pilot's helmet showing through roof, circular British RAF side labels on doors.. 3 8 17

15-1SF, Volkswagen 1500, 1970, White, cream or red body with white plastic interior, tow hook, unpainted base, "137" labels on doors, 2-7/8" 7 12 20

15-2SF, Fork Lift Truck, 1973, Red body with larger wheels at front, gray or yellow plastic lifting forks on yellow metal or unpainted track, "Lansing Bagnall" or "Hi-Lift" side labels, unpainted, black or green base, 2-3/4" .. 3 6 9

15-3SF, Hi Ho Silver, 1981, Silver Volkswagen Beetle (same casting as "Volks Dragon") with "Hi Ho Silver" and "31" tempo. Black base, clear window plastic, red plastic interior, 2-5/8". Having "31" on the roof is an interesting choice of graphic, considering it was the same vehicle casting as the 31-2SF 4 7 12

16-1SF, Case Bulldozer, 1970, Red with yellow engine, cab and blade and green or black rubber tracks, 2-1/2". This model was released at the same time as the Superfast line-notice that the box has "speed lines" just like the other models 5 8 15

16-2SF, Badger, 1974, Block, metallic bronze-red body with surface detail tools, ladders, etc., and plastic "Rola-Matic" radar. Green window plastic, no interior, six thick wheels, 2-3/4". Later editions in olive green were included as part of TP-14 Two-Pack 4 7 12

16-3SF, Pontiac Firebird, 1981, Metallic light or dark tan, Firebird tempo on hood, light tan plastic interior .... n/a 2 5

17-1SF, Horse Box, 1971, Red or orange AEC Ergomatic cab with green or gray plastic horse box, gray or mustard door, and two white plastic horses, 2-7/8"...... 3 7 12

17-2SF, The Londoner, 1973, Red body with "Berger Paints" or "Swinging London Carnaby Street" side labels (most common). White plastic interior, no window plastic, 3". There are many color and label variations of this model, some limited runs that command MIP values over 200. However, prices shown are for the common red-colored "Berger" and "Swinging London" versions 1 3 8

18-1SF, Field Car, 1970, Yellow body with tan plastic roof, white plastic interior, no window plastic, unpainted base, spare tire, tow hook, thin or thick wheels, 2-7/8". Other variations as part of Two-Packs in the 1970s, included orange with checked hood label and black plastic roof, olive green with light-tan plastic roof and hood label, red with light-tan plastic roof and "44" hood label-almost all with black plastic interiors. White editions are harder to find, about 250-300 in MIP condition. Prices shown reflect the more common models listed... 7 12 25

18-2SF, Hondarora, 1975, Red or orange body with silver or black forks and black seat are the most common, some with gas-tank labels, some without. Olive-drab military models were part of the TP-11 set with the olive-drab field car. 2-1/2".. n/a 2 5

19-1SF, Lotus Racing Car, 1970, Dark metallic purple, white plastic driver, wide Superfast wheels, "3" decal on sides, 2-3/4"....................................... 9 20 48

19-2SF, Road Dragster, 1971, Red or metallic pink body with unpainted base, exposed silver plastic engine, white plastic interior, wide wheels, clear window plastic, "8" labels on hood and roof, 3". Some models have "Wynns" or scorpion labels and are pink or orange-red and harder to find, about 80 MIP 2 5 10

19-3SF, Cement Truck, 1977, Red cab and chassis, unpainted metal base, green window plastic, no interior, yellow plastic mixer, with or without black or red stripes, 3" 1 3 6

Matchbox Opel Diplomat, No. 36, 1966.

Matchbox Army Saracen Personnel Carrier, No. 54, 1959. Photo courtesy Gary Linden

Matchbox Ford Police Car, No. 55, 1963. Photo courtesy Gary Linden

Matchbox Fiat 1500, No. 56, 1965. Photo courtesy Gary Linden

Matchbox Ford Zodiac MKIV, No. 53, 1968.

Matchbox DAF Girder Truck, No. 58, 1968.

Matchbox Ford Singer Van, No. 59, 1959. Photo courtesy Gary Linden

Matchbox Scammel Army Wreck Truck, No. 64, 1959. Photo courtesy Gary Linden

Matchbox Army Austin MKII Radio Truck, No. 68, 1959. Photo courtesy Gary Linden

Matchbox Commer 30 CWT Van, Nestle's, No. 69, 1959. Photo courtesy Gary Linden

Matchbox RAF 10-Ton Pressure Refueler Tanker, No. 73, 1959. Photo courtesy Gary Linden

Matchbox 1911 Renault Two-seater, Y-2, 1963.

Matchbox Dodge Dragster, No. 70, 1971.

	C6	C8	C10
20-1SF, Lamborghini Marzal, 1970, Pink or dark red with amber window plastic, white plastic interior and thin wheels; or pink or orange-pink with thick wheels, 2-3/4"	4	9	18
20-2SF, Police Patrol, 1975, White Range Rover with orange stripe "Police" label, frosted window plastic and blue or orange revolving police light (part of the Rola-Matics series). 2-7/8". Other models include orange Site Engineer from Gift Pack #13, olive-drab military ambulance model, and orange Paris-Dakar model, each with approx. 25-35 MIP value. Common white model values given below	1	4	8
20-2SF, Police Patrol: Site Engineer, 1977, Orange body with rotating orange dome light, "Site Engineer" labels on doors, plain metal base. Part of #13 Construction Gift Pack	5	8	14
20-2SF, Police Patrol: Paris-Dakar Rallye, 1983, Gold body with black and white checkered label and "Securitie-Rallye Paris Dakar 83" on sides, black base, red rotating dome light	5	9	13
20-2SF, Police Patrol: County Sheriff, 1982, White body with blue doors and roof, star design on hood and doors, "County Sheriff" in blue type on sides, blue rotating dome light	3	5	8
20-2SF, Police Patrol: British Police, 1983, White body with yellow and black/white checkered "Police" labels on sides. Blue rotating dome light, black base	4	8	12
21-1SF, Foden Concrete Truck, 1971, Yellow cab, orange truck bed with yellow plastic mixer, eight thin wheels, 3"	8	12	25
21-2SF, Rod Roller, 1973, Yellow body with red plastic seat, star and flames label on hood, (later editions without black plastic roller wheels, some with red or metallic red hubs on rear, black plastic steering lever, 2-1/2". Prices for metallic red hub versions about 45 MIP	3	8	17
21-3SF, Renault 5TL, 1979, Yellow, blue, white or silver-gray body, clear or amber window plastic, tan or red plastic interior, tow hook, 2-1/2". Some yellow models have "Le Car" tempo	2	6	10
22-1SF, Pontiac Grand Prix, 1970, Purple body, thin wheels, silver grille and black base, 3"	12	22	55
22-2SF, Freeman Inter-City Commuter, 1971, Purple-red body with white plastic interior, clear window plastic, unpainted base, some with side labels, 3"	2	4	8
22-3SF, Blaze Buster, 1976, Red body with yellow or black plastic ladder, silver plastic interior, amber window plastic, black or silver base, 3-1/16". Black-ladder versions about 25 MIP value	2	4	7
22-4SF, 4 x 4 Big Foot, 1982, Silver body, white plastic camper top, blue window plastic, black base, "Big Foot" and "26" tempos on sides and hood	2	5	12

	C6	C8	C10
23-1SF, Volkswagen Camper, 1970, Blue or orange body with plastic orange lift-up top reveals white plastic interior, amber or clear window plastic. Some models with sailboat labels on sides, 2-5/8". Military olive-drab versions without lift-up camper top were included as ambulances with TP-12 Two-Pack	9	22	45
23-2SF, Atlas Tipper, 1976, Blue body with orange or silver tipper section, wide wheels, amber or clear window plastic, silver or gray plastic interior, 2-3/4". Later versions available with red body	1	3	7
23-3SF, Ford Mustang GT-350, 1981, White body, blue Shelby stripes, exposed engine in front, "GT 350" on sides	3	6	14
24-1SF, Rolls-Royce Silver Shadow, 1970, Metallic-red body, white plastic interior, clear window plastic, opening trunk, silver metal grille and headlights, black or silver base, 3"	5	9	20
24-2SF, Team Matchbox, 1973, Metallic green, red or orange body, "8" or "44" label (included with TP-9, Field Car and Racing Car Two-Pack), white plastic driver, 2-7/8". Metallic green version, about 35 MIP, orange version about 85 MIP. Values for red shown	1	4	9
24-3SF, Diesel Shunter, 1979, Dark green and red or yellow and red body, no window plastic, labels read "Rail Freight" or "D1496-RF"	n/a	2	5
25-1SF, Ford Cortina GT, 1970, Metallic tan or blue body, white plastic interior, opening doors, tow hook, 2-5/8". Metallic tan versions, the first of the transitional Superfast models, are harder-to-find and have approx. 70-80 MIP values	8	12	25
25-2SF, Mod Tractor, 1973, Metallic purple body, black base, some with "V" cast on fenders, some without, silver plastic exposed engine, yellow plastic seat, 2-1/4". Harder to find editions have headlights cast in rear fender, about 60 MIP	1	3	7
25-3SF, Flat Car and Container, 1979, Black or charcoal flat car with tan or red plastic container with "NYK Worldwide Service" labels	1	3	5
26-1SF, GMC Tipper Truck, 1970, Red tipping cab, green engine and base, silver dump bed, green window plastic, no interior, 2-5/8"	5	9	20
26-2SF, Big Banger, 1973, Red with dark-blue window plastic, no interior, large silver plastic engine and exhaust pipes, "Big Banger" side labels, 3". Later versions were brown with "Brown Sugar" side labels or white with "Cosmic Blues" tempo	4	9	18
26-3SF, Site Dumper, 1977, Yellow body with yellow or red dumper bed, or orange body with silver-gray dumper bed, no window plastic, black or brown base, black plastic interior	2	4	7
27-1SF, Mercedes 230SL, 1970, Yellow convertible body with black plastic			

	C6	C8	C10

interior, or white body with red plastic interior, clear window plastic, silver base, thin wheels, 2-3/4" 8 12 25

27-2SF, Lamborghini Countach, 1973, Pale-orange body with "3" label on hood, or red-orange with "8" tempo and stripes, silver or gray plastic interior, amber or blue window plastic, opening rear hood, 3".. 3 7 16

28-1SF, Mack Dump Truck, 1970, Light-green body and dumper bed, silver base, wide wheels, no interior, amber window plastic, 2-5/8". Olive-drab versions were released with Case bulldozer in TP-16 Two-Pack 6 10 22

28-2SF, Stoat, 1973, Metallic bronze-tan body with rotating (Rola-Matic) soldier holding binoculars. Black base, wide wheels, 2-5/8". Olive-green versions with all-black wheels were included in TP-13 Two-Pack along with an olive version of 73-2SF Weasel armored vehicle 2 6 12

28-3SF, Lincoln Continental Mk V, 1979, Red body, white plastic roof, light-yellow or gray interior, silver base. First introduced in the 1979/80 catalog, this model had not yet replaced the Stoat in the lineup, but was due to be "available in your shops later this year" 3 6 12

29-1SF, Fire Pumper, 1970, Red body, blue window plastic and dome light, white plastic ladders and reels, silver base, thin wheels, 3" 12 32 70

29-2SF, Racing Mini, 1971, Orange-red body with yellow "29" labels, clear window plastic, white plastic interior, unpainted silver-gray base and grille, 2-1/4". Also included with TP-6 Two-Pack 5 8 16

29-3SF, Shovel-Nose Tractor, 1977, Yellow body with silver or black plastic engine and interior, shovel can be red or black plastic, 2-7/8". Lime green models with yellow plastic shovels are harder to find, about 65 MIP value. Models with yellow body, black plastic and stripes (as shown) were included in the G-5 Giftset in the 1979/80 catalog. Orange models with red plastic shovels, also about 65 MIP value 5 8 16

30-1SF, 8-Wheel Crane, 1970, Red with gold crane section, red plastic hook, no window plastic, yellow plastic hook, 3" 10 20 45

30-2SF, Beach Buggy, 1971, Pink body with yellow "spatter paint," white or yellow plastic interior and side tanks, no window plastic, 2-9/16". White interior versions have approx. 20 MIP value.. 4 7 12

30-3SF, Swamp Rat, 1977, Squared-boat body with olive-green deck, tan plastic hull, rotating striped army gunner (Rola-Matic), "Swamp Rat" labels, 3-1/16".. 3 7 9

31-1SF, Lincoln Continental, 1970, Lime-green body with thin wheels, opening trunk, clear window plastic, white plastic interior, 3"........................ 12 21 38

31-2SF, Volksdragon, 1972, Red Volkswagen Beetle body with clear window plastic, white or yellow plastic interior, silver plastic engine, "eyes" label, unpainted base, 2-5/8"................. 6 10 16

31-3SF, Caravan, 1978, White body with amber or blue window plastic, some with orange stripe with white reversed bird graphic label, unpainted base, light-yellow plastic interior, 2-3/4" 1 3 6

32-1SF, Leyland Petrol Tanker, 1970, Green cab and chassis, white tank, "BP" labels, thin wheels, blue or amber window plastic, no interior, chrome plastic base, 3" 6 10 22

32-2SF, Maserati Bora, 1973, Magenta body with yellow plastic interior, clear window plastic, opening doors, "8" stripe label on hood, lime green, dark green or unpainted base, 3".................... 3 7 13

32-3SF, Field Gun, 1978, Olive-green with black plastic barrel that fired shells attached to sprue on tan plastic base with soldiers, 3". An interesting piece, in that it included a diarama with the toy. Field Gun was removable from base 3 6 11

33-1SF, Lamborghini Miura, 1970, Gold body, opening doors, white plastic interior, thin wheels, unpainted base, 2-3/4".. 7 12 22

33-2SF, Datsun 126X, 1973, Yellow body with silver plastic interior, orange base, opening rear hood, amber window plastic, 3". Some versions have black and red flame tempo detail on hood and roof.. 1 4 8

33-3SF, Police Motorcycle, 1978, White motorcycle with blue plastic policeman rider, silver plastic engine, "Police" on saddlebags, silver or black wire spoked wheels, 2-7/8". Models included with the K-71 Porsche Polizei set had green plastic riders and detailing 1 4 7

34-1SF, Formula 1 Racing Car, 1970, Magenta or yellow body, white plastic driver, silver plastic engine, wide wheels, "16" striped label on hood, clear windshield plastic, 2-7/8" 5 8 14

34-2SF, Vantastic, 1976, Modified orange Ford Mustang body, white plastic interior, blue window plastic, early models with large silver plastic engine, later models with closed hood, white base, 2-7/8" 2 6 12

35-1SF, Merryweather Marquis Fire Engine, 1970, Red body, blue window plastic, gray plastic reels and instrument panel, white plastic ladder, blue dome lights, "London Fire Service" labels, narrow or wide tires, 3". This model was also included with TP-2 Two-Pack (900 Range). A modified casting was later used for 63-5SF Snorkel Fire Engine 4 7 12

35-2SF, Fandango, 1975, White body with red plastic interior, "35" label with stripe on hood, rotating (Rola-Matic) fan behind driver, clear window plastic, 3". Also red body with red or white

Matchbox Lambretta Motorcycle with sidecar, No. 36, 1960. Photo courtesy Gary Linden

Matchbox Darrier Refuse Collector, No. 38. Photo courtesy Gary Linden

Matchbox Morris Minor 1000, 1957, No. 46. Photo courtesy Gary Linden

	C6	C8	C10
plastic interiors, a later release. Versions with white body and red interior and a number "6" label are harder to find, and about 40 MIP	1	3	10
36-1SF, Opel Diplomat, 1970, Metallic green-gold color, opening hood, thin wheels, 2-3/4"	6	11	20
36-2SF, Hot Rod Draguar, 1971, Metallic pink or purple body with white or light yellow plastic interior, clear bubble window plastic, large silver engine, wide wheels, 2-7/8"	5	8	18
36-3SF, Formula 5000, 1977, Orange with blue label number "3" and blue plastic driver, or red with "Texaco" and "Champion" labels and yellow plastic driver, 2-7/8"	1	4	8
37-1SF, Cattle Truck, 1970, Yellow Dodge cab and chassis, green plastic windows, no interior, gray-brown plastic stake-side bed with two white plastic cows, 2-1/2"	6	11	20
37-2SF, Scoopa Coopa, 1973, Blue or pink body with yellow plastic interior, amber plastic windshield, unpainted base, 2-7/8". Pink models have a daisy-shaped sticker on the roof section, and were shown first in the 1976 catalog	1	3	8
37-3SF, Skip Truck, 1977, Red cab and chassis, clear or amber plastic windows, yellow bucket, white plastic interior, 2-3/4"	2	4	6
38-1SF, Honda Motorcycle with Trailer, 1970, Yellow motorcycle trailer with thin wheels and "Honda" labels. Green or pink motorcycle, silver spokes, 3"	7	11	19
38-2SF, Stingeroo, 1973, Purple chopper-style bike with cream-colored plastic horse head on seat, two wide wheels in rear, one solid wheel in front, purple plastic forks, silver plastic engine, 3-1/8"	6	10	22
38-3SF, Armored Jeep, 1977, Dark olive-drab with white star emblem on hood, black base and grille, black plastic gun on back (swivels), all-black wide wheels	4	7	10
39-1SF, Ford Tractor, 1970, Blue body with yellow hood and wheels or all-blue body (included with K-20 Tractor Transporter), 2-1/8". This was another			

	C6	C8	C10
regular-wheels holdover into the Superfast era	7	16	25
39-2SF, Clipper, 1973, Metallic magenta body with light metallic green base, yellow plastic interior, flip-up cockpit, and "clicking" exhaust pipes that moved up and down as the car rolled along. One of the first in the Rola-Matics series, 3"	1	4	9
39-4SF, Rolls-Royce Mark II, 1979, Silver body with red plastic interior or metallic red body with yellow plastic interior. Clear window plastic, opening doors, unpainted base, silver grille and headlights. Introduced in the 1979/80 catalog, but had not replaced Clipper in the 1-75 lineup	2	5	9
40-1SF, Hay Trailer, 1970, Blue with yellow wheels and stakeside attachments, 3-3/8". Another holdover from the regular wheels series, this model was replaced in 1972 with the Superfast Guildsman	3	8	12
40-2SF, Guildsman, 1972, Pink with white plastic interior and light-green window plastic, star and flames label on hood; or, red body with white plastic interior with amber window plastic and "40" label on hood (first appears in 1976 catalog), 3"	4	8	16
40-3SF, Horse Box, 1978, Orange cab and chassis, no interior, green window plastic, cream-colored plastic box with light-brown door, two white plastic horses, 2-7/8". This model was reissued in the 1990s with green and blue color variations	2	6	10
41-1SF, Ford GT, 1970, White or red with red plastic interior, blue stripe and number "6" label on hood, thin or wide wheels	8	15	28
41-2SF, Siva Spyder, 1973, Red body with cream-colored plastic interior, black segment wraps behind cabin, wide wheels, clear window plastic, 3". Blue versions with stars and stripes label motif available in 1976 catalog	3	7	12
41-3SF, Ambulance, 1979, White body, blue window plastic and dome lights, opening rear doors, unpainted base, white plastic interior, "Emergency Medical Service" or "Ambulance" with red cross labels, 2-1/2"	3	6	12

	C6	C8	C10
42-1SF, Iron Fairy Crane, 1971, Red with open cab (no window plastic) yellow plastic interior, yellow crane section with yellow plastic hook, wide wheels, 3". Continued as a regular wheels model, but only for the 1970 catalog, then converted to Superfast..................	15	25	45
42-2SF, Tyre Fryer, 1973, Light or dark-blue body, open cockpit, yellow plastic seat, large silver plastic engine behind driver, large Superfast wheels in rear, wide wheels in front, 3".................	2	6	12
42-3SF, Mercedes Container Truck, 1978, Red cab and chassis, blue window plastic, no interior, unpainted or black base, plastic container with "SeaLand," "NYK" or "Matchbox" labels, 3"..........	1	3	6
42-4SF, '57 T-Bird, 1981, Red body, white interior, clear windshield, silver metal base..	1	3	6
42-4SF, '57 T-Bird, 1982, Later version with black body, red interior, yellow windshield, plain base...........................	1	3	7
43-1SF, Pony Trailer, 1970, Yellow body with green base, clear window plastic, two white plastic horses, narrow wheels, brown plastic door, 2-5/8". Orange version with horse label included with TP-3 Two-Pack	5	8	15
43-2SF, Dragon Wheels, 1973, Green Volkswagen Beetle funny-car body hinged to silver plastic and metal base, "Dragon Wheels" labels on sides, 2-7/8"..	4	7	14
43-3SF, Steam Loco, 1979, Red and black body, red base, "4345" labels on sides, 2-11/16"...	1	3	6
44-1SF, Refrigerator Truck, 1970, Yellow GMC cab and chassis with red refrigeration box, green window plastic, 3". The first release in 1970 was painted like the regular wheels version with red cab and chassis and green refrigeration box. These are hard to find and command approx. 145 MIP values	6	11	18
44-2SF, Boss Mustang, 1973, Yellow body with opening black hood, silver plastic interior, amber plastic window, unpainted base, 3"..................................	3	6	12
44-3SF, Passenger Coach, 1979, Red body, cream-colored plastic top, green window plastic, black base, "431 & 432" or "GWR" labels, 2-7/8"...............	1	3	6
45-1SF, Ford Group Six, 1970, Metallic green body with white plastic interior, silver plastic engine, clear window plastic and number "7" label; or red body with amber-colored windows and number "45" labels, (a later version, first appearing in 1973), 3"	4	10	22
45-2SF, B.M.W. 3.0 CSL, 1975, Orange body with opening doors, yellow plastic interior, amber or blue plastic windows, silver base, "BMW" label on hood, 2-7/8"..	3	7	15
46-1SF, Mercedes 300SE, 1970, Gold or blue body, white plastic interior, opening trunk, (some early models with opening doors, too) thin wheels, unpainted base, grille and headlights,			

	C6	C8	C10
2-7/8". Blue models are hard to find and may command MIP values of 100 or more. Olive-drab staff car versions as part of TP-14 Two-Pack set, about 15 in NM condition.................................	4	8	16
46-2SF, Stretcha Fetcha, 1973, White with blue windows, white plastic interior, red base, "Ambulance" red cross labels, wide wheels, opening rear hatch, 2-3/4"	2	4	8
46-3SF, Ford Tractor & Harrow, 1979, Blue Ford tractor with cab, no window plastic, gray engine block and base, black wheels with or without orange-yellow painted hubs, yellow plastic disk or harrow included (not shown). Also included with hay trailer in TP-11 Two-Pack	1	6	14
46-4SF, Hot Chocolate, 1982, Metallic brown and black funny car body with white stripe. This car was an update on the "Dragon Wheels" funny car	2	5	8
47-1SF, DAF Tipper Container Truck, 1970, Silver-green cab and chassis, plastic tipping box with removable top, red plastic grille and partial base, green plastic windows, no interior, 3". A Superfast update of the regular wheels model..	6	10	22
47-2SF, Beach Hopper, 1973, Blue with pink "spatter" paint, brown plastic interior, tan plastic driver that "hops" as car moves along (a Rola-Matic model), wide wheels, sun label on hood, 2-5/8".	2	5	9
47-3SF, Pannier Locomotive, 1979, Green body, "GWR" labels, metallic brown base. This model had not yet replaced the Beach Hopper in the 1-75 catalog lineup, but was introduced as being available later in the year	2	5	8
47-4SF, Jaguar SS, 1982, Red body, silver grille, headlights and windshield, light-brown plastic interior, wide wheels	1	4	7
48-1SF, Dumper Truck, 1970, Blue Dodge cab and chassis, yellow dumper bed, green plastic windows, no interior, silver plastic grille, bumper and partial base, 3". A Superfast version of the 48-3RW regular wheels model	10	18	32
48-2SF, Pi-Eyed Piper, 1973, Blue body, oversized plastic engine on hood, number "8" label on roof, silver exhaust pipes along sides, no interior, blue plastic windows, 2-1/2"	5	8	20
48-3SF, Sambron Jack Lift, 1978, Yellow body with yellow plastic lifting forks, no window plastic, 3-1/16"....................	2	4	7
49-1SF, Unimog, 1970, Blue or metallic blue-green with red base, green plastic windows, wide wheels, 2-1/2". Another update of a regular wheels model, in the 1-75 lineup until 1973. An olive-drab version with a plastic container for artillery shells in the bed was part of the TP-13 Two-Pack in 1979.....................	7	12	25
49-2SF, Chop Suey, 1973, Magenta seat, red plastic fork, yellow plastic bull's head on handlebars, silver plastic engine, black roller-style wheels, 2-7/8"	5	9	17
49-3SF, Crane Truck, 1977, Yellow body with swiveling crane section,			

	C6	C8	C10
extendable crane arm, red plastic hook, six wide wheels, 3"	3	6	12
50-1SF, Kennel Truck, 1970, Dark-green Ford truck body, with four white plastic dogs and clear plastic canopy over bed. Green plastic window, no interior, thin wheels, 2-3/4"	8	17	40
50-2SF, Articulated Truck, 1973, Short yellow cab with green plastic windows and blue trailer with yellow plastic chassis, wide wheels, 3". Some have arrow labels, some do not. Notice the difference in the wheels on the trailer. ..	1	4	7
51-1SF, 8-Wheel Tipper, 1971, Yellow AEC cab and chassis, silver tipper bed, green plastic windows, no interior, "Pointer" labels, silver grille and headlights and partial base, 3"	8	18	40
51-2SF, Citroen SM, 1973, Dark red metallic body, opening doors, unpainted base, white plastic interior and tow hook, clear plastic windows, 2-7/8". In 1976, the paint scheme changed to blue with a red stripe and number "8" on roof............................	4	7	12
51-3SF, Combine Harvester, 1979, Red with yellow reel and auger, black Superfast wheels, Superfast wheels with yellow hubs or regular wheels, 2-7/8"....................................	1	3	7
52-1SF, Dodge Charger Mk III, 1970, Metallic red or metallic lime-green body with black plastic interior, lift-up canopy, wide wheels, 3". Early red models also featured "hood scoop" labels	4	7	18
52-2SF, Police Launch, 1977, White body with blue plastic base and two blue plastic officers, labels on sides read "Police," silver metal horns on cabin roof, dark-blue plastic windows, thin wheels, 3-1/16"	1	4	7
53-1SF, Ford Zodiac Mk IV, 1970, Metallic green body, opening hood, silver engine with spare tire, white plastic interior, clear plastic windows, 2-3/4"....................................	7	10	22
53-2SF, Tanzara, 1973, Orange body, amber plastic windows, opening rear hood shows silver plastic engine, wide wheels, silver plastic interior, unpainted base, 3". Models in 1976 had a bicentennial color scheme; white with red and blue stripes and number "53" on hood..............................	2	4	7
53-3SF, CJ6 Jeep, 1978, Red body, tan plastic roof, yellow plastic interior, unpainted metal base	3	7	12
54-1SF, Cadillac Ambulance, 1970, White body, blue plastic interior, white plastic interior, red cross labels, white or silver-painted grille, narrow wheels, 2-7/8". Shown here with its regular wheels predecessor	12	22	40
54-2SF, Ford Capri, 1971, Red with black hood or all pink with white plastic interior, unpainted base, opening hood, wide wheels, 2-7/8". All-red models were included with boat and trailer in TP-5 Two-Pack starting in 1977	2	5	11

	C6	C8	C10
54-3SF, Personnel Carrier, 1978, Olive-green with tan plastic troops and gun, black base, wide wheels, 3"..........	3	7	12
55-1SF, Police Car, 1970, White Mercury sedan, clear windows, white plastic interior with molded figures, police label on hood, shield labels on doors, blue or red dome light, thin wheels, 3-1/16".................	8	17	30
55-2SF, Mercury Police Car, 1971, White station wagon body with blue or red dome lights, thin or wide wheels, unpainted base and grille, clear plastic windows, 3-1/16". Early versions had shield labels on doors and "Police" label on hood. Versions from 1973 to 1975 had only arrow-shaped red "Police" label. This car was a minor casting variation of the Mercury Commuter 73-1SF	7	15	27
55-3SF, Hellraiser, 1976, White body with red plastic interior, silver plastic rear engine, clear windshield, wide wheels, stars and stripes label on hood. Or, blue body and white plastic interior, stars and stripes label, 3".................................	2	5	12
55-4SF, Ford Cortina 1600 GL, 1979, Metallic gold with clear plastic windows, opening doors, unpainted base, red plastic interior. Introduced in 1979/80 catalog, but not yet part of the 1-75 lineup	2	6	12
56-1SF, BMC 1800 Pininfarina, 1970, Metallic gold or orange body, thin or wide wheels, opening doors, clear plastic windows, unpainted base, white plastic interior, 2-3/4". Later models modified the casting of the rear wheel wells to accommodate the wider Superfast wheels that became standard by 1973. This was a new model in the 1-75 lineup, not an adapted regular wheels casting like many others in 1970. Orange body versions about 16 MIP	4	7	12
56-2SF, Hi-Tailer, 1975, White body with yellow or blue plastic driver, silver plastic rear engine, red, white and blue striped label with "5, Team Matchbox and MB," 3"	2	4	9
56-3SF, Mercedes 450 SEL, 1979, Blue body, opening doors, light-yellow plastic windows, clear plastic windows, unpainted base. Introduced in 1979/80 catalog, had not yet replaced Hi-Tailer in the 1-75 lineup..............................	1	3	6
57-1SF, Eccles Caravan, 1970, Cream or light-yellow trailer body with four thin wheels, stripe and flower label on sides, red or orange plastic roof, green or light-yellow plastic interior, 3-1/16". Like many models, the Eccles Caravan continued on in a Two-Pack set, the TP-4 Holiday Set	4	7	16
57-2SF, Wild Life Truck, 1973, Yellow body, red plastic windows, "Ranger" label on hood with elephant illustration, silver plastic grille, wide wheels, red plastic lion circles in truck bed as it is pushed along (Rola-Matic), no interior, clear plastic canopy over truck bed.......	4	7	14

	C6	C8	C10

58-1SF, DAF Girder Truck, 1970, Off-white or lime-green cab and chassis, red plastic girders, red plastic grille and partial base, green window plastic, no interior, 3". Off-white versions aren't real common and have approx. 65 MIP value .... 6　11　20

58-2SF, Woosh-N-Push, 1973, Yellow body with open cockpit, red plastic interior, silver plastic exhaust, number "2" label on back of roof; or metallic red body, cream plastic interior, number "8" label with stars and stripes on roof (1976 version), 3" .... 2　4　8

58-3SF, Faun Dumper, 1977, Yellow body and dumper bed, black base, red plastic windows, 2-3/4" .... 1　3　5

59-1SF, Ford Galaxie Fire Chief Car, 1970, Red body, white plastic interior and tow hook, clear plastic windows, thin wheels, shield labels on doors, blue dome light, 2-7/8". Oddly, this model dropped from the lineup for one year and returned, briefly, for 1972 .... 12　22　45

59-1SF, Mercury Fire Chief Car, 1971, Red sedan body with white plastic interior (early versions with two figures), unpainted base, blue dome light, thin or wide wheels, shield and fire chief labels or fire helmet labels, also included in TP-10 Two-Pack with a dual dome light arrangement.............. 4　8　16

59-3SF, Planet Scout, 1976, Metallic green with lime-green or red with yellow body, silver plastic interior, yellow plastic windows, wide wheels, 2-3/4".. 2　4　8

60-1SF, Truck with Site Office, 1970, Blue Leyland truck with Ergomatic cab, yellow plastic hut with green plastic roof, thin wheels, green plastic windows, silver plastic grille and partial base, 2-1/2" .... 6　10　22

60-2SF, Lotus Super Seven, 1972, Orange or yellow body with unpainted base, black plastic interior, clear plastic windshield, ghost and flame label on hood, or checker pattern with "60" along length of car, 2-7/8" .... 5　9　16

60-3SF, Holden Pick-Up, 1978, Red with yellow plastic motorcycles in bed and

yellow plastic interior, unpainted base, checkered label with "500" on hood, 3-1/16" .... 4　7　14

60-4SF, Piston Popper, 1982, Yellow body with "Piston Popper" on hood and number "60" on sides. Unpainted metal base, red Rola-Matic pistons like the earlier version

61-1SF, Alvis Stalwart, 1970, White body, with yellow plastic canopy (not shown) green plastic wheels with removable black tires, "BP Exploration" labels on sides, 2-5/8". Olive-green versions were included with TP-16 Two-Pack in 1979 ... 9　17　30

61-2SF, Blue Shark, 1972, Blue body with unpainted base, white plastic driver, silver plastic rear engine, black plastic exhaust pipes, clear plastic windshield, "86" or Scorpion label (harder to find, about 50 MIP), 3" .... 3　8　15

61-3SF, Wreck Truck, 1979, Red truck body, black base, red plastic windows and dome lights, no interior, white towing arms with red plastic hooks....... 3　6　10

62-1SF, Mercury Cougar, 1970, Lime-green body with red plastic interior and tow hook, opening doors, 3".................. 9　16　25

62-2SF, Rat Rod Dragster, 1971, Light-green body, clear plastic windows, red plastic interior, exposed engine through hood, "Rat Rod" labels on sides, 3". A reworking of the Mercury Cougar casting .... 5　8　18

62-2SF, Renault 17TL, 1974, Red body with opening doors, white plastic interior, blue plastic windows, some with stripe and number "6" label, some without, 3". A version with "Fire" labels was included in the G-12 Rescue Gift Set in the 1977 catalog .... 2　5　12

62-3SF, Chevy Corvette, 1982, Black body with yellow and orange stripes running from hood to trunk, white plastic interior, plain base with side-pipes... 2　5　8

62-1SF, Dodge Crane Truck, 1970, Yellow body with rotating crane section, yellow plastic hook, black base, green plastic windows, no interior, 3" ... 6　11　20

63-2SF, Freeway Gas Tanker, 1974, Short red cab with black base and wide

Matchbox Trojan Brooke Bond Van, No. 47, 1957. Photo courtesy Gary Linden

Matchbox Army Half Track MKIII, No. 49, 1958. Photo courtesy Gary Linden

Matchbox Y-12 1909 Thomas Flyabout, 1967. KP photo courtesy Karen O'Brien

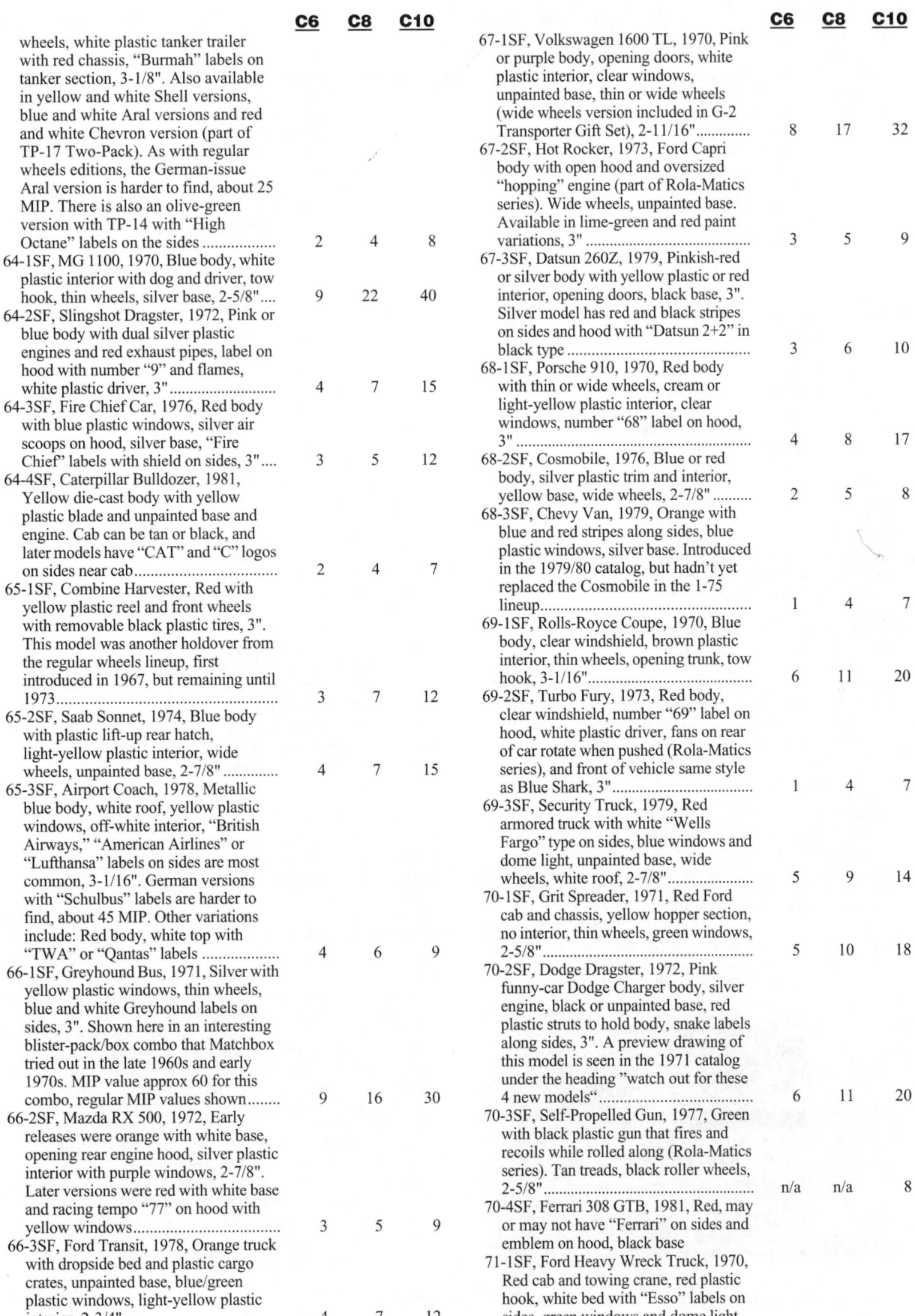

	C6	C8	C10

wheels, white plastic tanker trailer with red chassis, "Burmah" labels on tanker section, 3-1/8". Also available in yellow and white Shell versions, blue and white Aral versions and red and white Chevron version (part of TP-17 Two-Pack). As with regular wheels editions, the German-issue Aral version is harder to find, about 25 MIP. There is also an olive-green version with TP-14 with "High Octane" labels on the sides 2 4 8

64-1SF, MG 1100, 1970, Blue body, white plastic interior with dog and driver, tow hook, thin wheels, silver base, 2-5/8".... 9 22 40

64-2SF, Slingshot Dragster, 1972, Pink or blue body with dual silver plastic engines and red exhaust pipes, label on hood with number "9" and flames, white plastic driver, 3" 4 7 15

64-3SF, Fire Chief Car, 1976, Red body with blue plastic windows, silver air scoops on hood, silver base, "Fire Chief" labels with shield on sides, 3".... 3 5 12

64-4SF, Caterpillar Bulldozer, 1981, Yellow die-cast body with yellow plastic blade and unpainted base and engine. Cab can be tan or black, and later models have "CAT" and "C" logos on sides near cab 2 4 7

65-1SF, Combine Harvester, Red with yellow plastic reel and front wheels with removable black plastic tires, 3". This model was another holdover from the regular wheels lineup, first introduced in 1967, but remaining until 1973 .... 3 7 12

65-2SF, Saab Sonnet, 1974, Blue body with plastic lift-up rear hatch, light-yellow plastic interior, wide wheels, unpainted base, 2-7/8" 4 7 15

65-3SF, Airport Coach, 1978, Metallic blue body, white roof, yellow plastic windows, off-white interior, "British Airways," "American Airlines" or "Lufthansa" labels on sides are most common, 3-1/16". German versions with "Schulbus" labels are harder to find, about 45 MIP. Other variations include: Red body, white top with "TWA" or "Qantas" labels 4 6 9

66-1SF, Greyhound Bus, 1971, Silver with yellow plastic windows, thin wheels, blue and white Greyhound labels on sides, 3". Shown here in an interesting blister-pack/box combo that Matchbox tried out in the late 1960s and early 1970s. MIP value approx 60 for this combo, regular MIP values shown 9 16 30

66-2SF, Mazda RX 500, 1972, Early releases were orange with white base, opening rear engine hood, silver plastic interior with purple windows, 2-7/8". Later versions were red with white base and racing tempo "77" on hood with yellow windows.................................... 3 5 9

66-3SF, Ford Transit, 1978, Orange truck with dropside bed and plastic cargo crates, unpainted base, blue/green plastic windows, light-yellow plastic interior, 2-3/4" 4 7 12

67-1SF, Volkswagen 1600 TL, 1970, Pink or purple body, opening doors, white plastic interior, clear windows, unpainted base, thin or wide wheels (wide wheels version included in G-2 Transporter Gift Set), 2-11/16".............. 8 17 32

67-2SF, Hot Rocker, 1973, Ford Capri body with open hood and oversized "hopping" engine (part of Rola-Matics series). Wide wheels, unpainted base. Available in lime-green and red paint variations, 3" 3 5 9

67-3SF, Datsun 260Z, 1979, Pinkish-red or silver body with yellow plastic or red interior, opening doors, black base, 3". Silver model has red and black stripes on sides and hood with "Datsun 2+2" in black type 3 6 10

68-1SF, Porsche 910, 1970, Red body with thin or wide wheels, cream or light-yellow plastic interior, clear windows, number "68" label on hood, 3" 4 8 17

68-2SF, Cosmobile, 1976, Blue or red body, silver plastic trim and interior, yellow base, wide wheels, 2-7/8" 2 5 8

68-3SF, Chevy Van, 1979, Orange with blue and red stripes along sides, blue plastic windows, silver base. Introduced in the 1979/80 catalog, but hadn't yet replaced the Cosmobile in the 1-75 lineup... 1 4 7

69-1SF, Rolls-Royce Coupe, 1970, Blue body, clear windshield, brown plastic interior, thin wheels, opening trunk, tow hook, 3-1/16".................................... 6 11 20

69-2SF, Turbo Fury, 1973, Red body, clear windshield, number "69" label on hood, white plastic driver, fans on rear of car rotate when pushed (Rola-Matics series), and front of vehicle same style as Blue Shark, 3" 1 4 7

69-3SF, Security Truck, 1979, Red armored truck with white "Wells Fargo" type on sides, blue windows and dome light, unpainted base, wide wheels, white roof, 2-7/8" 5 9 14

70-1SF, Grit Spreader, 1971, Red Ford cab and chassis, yellow hopper section, no interior, thin wheels, green windows, 2-5/8" 5 10 18

70-2SF, Dodge Dragster, 1972, Pink funny-car Dodge Charger body, silver engine, black or unpainted base, red plastic struts to hold body, snake labels along sides, 3". A preview drawing of this model is seen in the 1971 catalog under the heading "watch out for these 4 new models"....................................... 6 11 20

70-3SF, Self-Propelled Gun, 1977, Green with black plastic gun that fires and recoils while rolled along (Rola-Matics series). Tan treads, black roller wheels, 2-5/8" .... n/a n/a 8

70-4SF, Ferrari 308 GTB, 1981, Red, may or may not have "Ferrari" on sides and emblem on hood, black base

71-1SF, Ford Heavy Wreck Truck, 1970, Red cab and towing crane, red plastic hook, white bed with "Esso" labels on sides, green windows and dome light,

	C6	C8	C10
white grille, 3". Olive-green versions with all-black wheels were included in 1978's TP-16 Two-Pack	11	17	32
71-2SF, Jumbo Jet, 1973, Motorcycle with blue seat and handlebars, black roller-style wheels, silver plastic engine, red elephant head on handlebars, 2-3/4"	6	9	18
71-3SF, Cattle Truck, 1978, Red or metallic gold with plastic yellow or cream stake bed, black plastic cattle, blue or green windows, 2-7/8". Also included in the 1979 TP-19 Two-Pack in red with a matching trailer and plastic cattle	2	5	8
72-1SF, Standard Jeep, 1970, Yellow body with red plastic seats, black bumpers, spare tire on back, 2-3/8". An update of the 72-2RW Standard Jeep, but in this case the spare couldn't actually be used	8	12	30
72-2SF, SRN Hovercraft, 1972, White top with black plastic base and "SRN6" with British flag labels on sides, red plastic propeller, thin wheels in underside of hull, blue plastic windows, 3-1/16"	1	2	5
72-3SF, Bomag Road Roller, 1979, Yellow body with red plastic interior and engine, black plastic roller, silver or yellow hubs. Introduced in 1979/80 catalog, but hadn't yet replaced the SRN Hovercraft in the 1-75 lineup	1	4	7
72-4SF, Maxi Taxi, 1982, Yellow Ford Capri body with Rola-Matic engine that hops when car is moved, an update of the Hot Rocker model. Checkered taxi tampos and rates on sides, "Maxi Taxi" on roof, black base	1	4	7
73-1SF, Mercury Commuter, 1970, Metallic lime-green body with thin wheels, clear windows, white plastic interior with dogs looking out the back, unpainted base, 3-1/16". By 1972, this car had changed to red with a bull's head label on the hood and luggage rack grooves on the roof, with approx. 16 MIP value. Prices for green model shown	6	14	25
73-2SF, Weasel, 1973, Medium metallic-green armored vehicle with black turret that turns as the car is rolled			

Different versions of Matchbox boxes. Photo courtesy Gary Linden

	C6	C8	C10
(Rola-Matics series), wide wheels, all-black or with silver hubs, 2-7/8". Olive-green versions were issued as part of TP-13 Two-Pack	2	5	8
74-1SF, Daimler Bus, 1970, Red or pink body, white plastic interior, thin or wide wheels, "Esso Extra Petrol" and Esso logo labels on sides, 3"	5	11	20
74-2SF, Toe Joe, 1974, Metallic lime-green body with green plastic towing arms and red plastic hooks, yellow windows, unpainted base, 3". Versions with yellow bodies and red towing arms with black plastic hooks were included with the Racing Mini in TP-6 Two-Pack	3	6	12
74-3SF, Mercury Cougar Villager, 1979, Lime-green or blue body, pale yellow interior, unpainted base, opening tailgate, 3-1/16"	2	5	11
75-1SF, Ferrari Berlinetta, 1970, Red with white plastic interior, thin wheels, unpainted base, 2-7/8". Some early models were produced in green, echoing the regular wheels editions, but they are rare and can have 350 MIP values	12	22	40
75-2SF, Alfa Carabo, 1971, Pink with yellow or white base, models in 1976 had yellow stripes running across top of car. White plastic interior, clear windows, 3"	2	5	11
75-3SF, Seasprite Helicopter, 1977, White body, red base, blue windows, regular wheels landing gear, black plastic rotor, "Rescue" labels on tail section, 2-7/8" ..	4	6	9

Models of Yesteryear

	C6	C8	C10
Y-01 1911 Ford Model T, 1964	n/a	n/a	45
Y-01 1925 Allchin Traction Engine, 1956, first Model of Yesteryear released	n/a	n/a	150
Y-01 1936 Jaguar SS 100, 1977	n/a	n/a	17
Y-02 1911 'B' Type London Bus, 1955 ..	n/a	n/a	90
Y-02 1911 Renault 2-Seater, 1963...........	n/a	n/a	36
Y-02 1914 Prince Henry Vauxhall, 1970	n/a	n/a	21
Y-03 1907 London 'E' Class Tramcar, 1955	n/a	n/a	125
Y-03 1910 Benz Limousine, 1965	n/a	n/a	50
Y-03 1934 Riley MPH, 1972	n/a	n/a	20
Y-04 1909 Opel Coupe, 1966	n/a	n/a	30
Y-04 1930 Duesenberg Model J, 1976	n/a	n/a	10
Y-04 Sentinel Steam Wagon, 1956..........	n/a	n/a	120
Y-04 Shand Mason Fire Engine, 1960, horse drawn..	n/a	n/a	150
Y-05 1907 Peugeot, 1968	n/a	n/a	33
Y-05 1927 Talbot Van, 1978	n/a	n/a	10
Y-05 1929 LeMans Bentley, 1956...........	n/a	n/a	75
Y-05 1929 Supercharged 4-1/2 Litre Bentley, 1960	n/a	n/a	30
Y-06 1913 Cadillac, 1967	n/a	n/a	33
Y-06 1916 A.E.C. "Y" type Lorry Truck, 1955	n/a	n/a	72
Y-06 1926 Type 35 Bugatti, 1961	n/a	n/a	89
Y-06 Rolls-Royce Fire Engine, 1978.......	n/a	n/a	14
Y-07 1912 Rolls-Royce, 1967	n/a	n/a	48
Y-07 1913 Mercer Raceabout Sportcar, 1961	n/a	n/a	16
Y-07 1914 4-Ton Leyland, 1955	n/a	n/a	125
Y-08 1914 Stutz Roadster, 1968	n/a	n/a	36

	C6	C8	C10
Y-08 1914 Sunbeam Motorcycle with Sidecar, 1962	n/a	n/a	113
Y-08 1926 Morris Cowley Bullnose, 1955	n/a	n/a	66
Y-08 1945 MGTC Sports Car, 1978	n/a	n/a	11
Y-09 1912 Simplex, 1967	n/a	n/a	54
Y-09 1924 Fowler Big Lion Showman Engine, 1967	n/a	n/a	54
Y-10 1906 Rolls-Royce Silver Cloud, 1968	n/a	n/a	20
Y-10 1908 Grand Prix Mercedes Racing Car, 1957	n/a	n/a	30
Y-10 1928 Mercedes-Benz, 36/220, 1963	n/a	n/a	54
Y-11 1912 Packard Landaulet, 1963	n/a	n/a	42
Y-11 1920 Aveling & Porter Steam Roller, 1957	n/a	n/a	93
Y-11 1938 Lagonda Drophead Coupe, 1972	n/a	n/a	19
Y-12 1899 Horse-Bus (London), 1957	n/a	n/a	110
Y-12 1909 Thomas Flyabout, 1967	n/a	n/a	50
Y-12 1912 Model T Ford, 1979	n/a	n/a	15
Y-13 1911 Daimler, 1965	n/a	n/a	60
Y-13 1918 Crossley Truck, 1972	n/a	n/a	22
Y-14 1911 Maxwell Roadster, 1965	n/a	n/a	27
Y-14 1931 Stutz Bearcat, 1972	n/a	n/a	18

Matchbox Y-1 4 Stutz Bearcat, 1972. Photo courtesy Gary Linden

	C6	C8	C10
Y-15 1907 Rolls-Royce Silver Ghost, 1960	n/a	n/a	48
Y-15 1930 Packard Victoria, 1969	n/a	n/a	16
Y-16 1904 Spyker Veteran Automobile, 1961	n/a	n/a	48
Y-16 1928 Mercedes SS, 1971	n/a	n/a	19
Y-17 1938 Hispano Suiza, 1972	n/a	n/a	19
Y-18 1937 Cord 812, 1979	n/a	n/a	20
Y-19 1935 Auburn 851, 1980	n/a	n/a	21
Y-20 1938 Mercedes 540K, 1981	n/a	n/a	17
Y-21 1929 Woody Wagon, 1981	n/a	n/a	11
Y-22 Model A Van	n/a	n/a	15

MECCANO

The Meccano Company closed its doors at the Liverpool, England, factory on Nov. 30, 1979. It was a sad ending to a great company founded by Frank Hornby early in the twentieth century. His construction sets had become very popular by the time the first specialized Meccano car constructor sets appeared for Christmas in 1932. The largest of the three cars to be made, it was later dubbed the No. 2 Motor Car Constructor Outfit. In 1933, the smaller No. 1 outfit became available at a much lower price. At about the same time, an accessory electric lighting set was made available for the No. 2 car only. The two-seater sports car probably appeared in 1934. It is in scale with the No. 1 constructor and has the same wheels and was sold fully assembled. The two car constructor sets were marketed in the United States, but the two-seater sports car was imported in very small numbers, if at all. In any case, it is rare in the United States and scarce in England. Meccano cars went out of production in 1940. A wooden garage was made, but few were sold. A beautiful miniature Kaye Oil can, made of copper and brass, is a much-sought-after accessory.

Meccano Two-Seater Sports Car (non-constructional). Photo courtesy Gates Willard. Photo by E.W. Willard

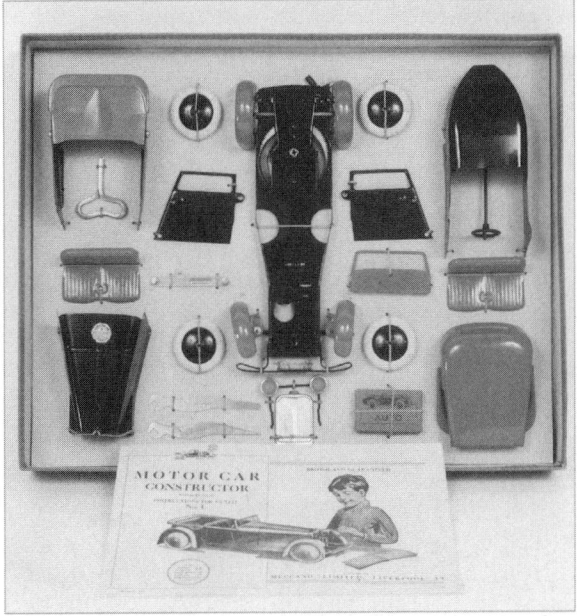

Later (1939-40) No. 1 Car Constructor in its original box. Photo courtesy Gates Willard. Photo by E.W. Willard

Left to right: Late French No. 1 Car; Late English No. 1 Car. Photo courtesy Gates Willard. Photo by E.W. Willard

Left to right: No. 1 Constructor Car; Two-Seater Sports Car (non-constructional). Photo courtesy Gates Willard. Photo by E.W. Willard

Left to right: Early (1933) No. 1 Car; 1933-40 No. 1 Car. Photo courtesy Gates Willard. Photo by E.W. Willard

A factory-assembled No. 1 Constructional Car with original box. Photo courtesy Gates Willard. Photo by E.W. Willard

Left to right: Late French No. 1 Car; Late English No. 1 Car. Photo courtesy Gates Willard. Photo by E.W. Willard

Left to right: Early two-seater Sports Car with box; later two-seater Sports Car with box (picture box was discontinued). Photo courtesy Gates Willard. Photo by E.W. Willard

Five different ways to assemble the English No. 1 Car—an original box is also pictured. Photo courtesy Gates Willard. Photo by E.W. Willard

A size comparison of the No. 1 and No. 2 Constructor Cars. Photo courtesy Gates Willard. Photo by E.W. Willard

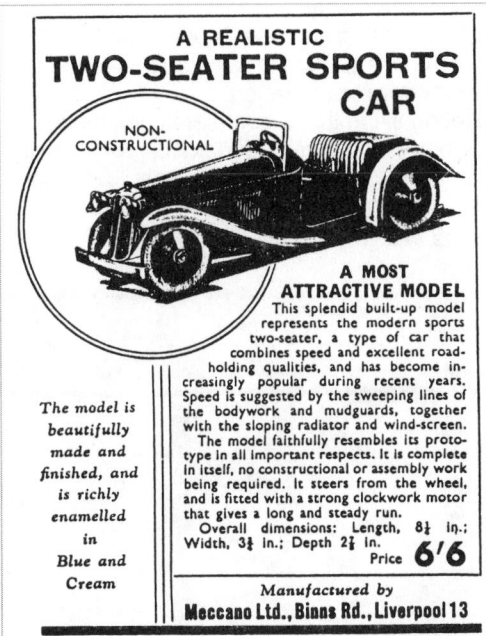

A December, 1936 ad in Meccano Magazine *for the Meccano two-seater sports car. Photo courtesy Gates Willard*

A late 1930s French Meccano Constructional Car with original box, alternative parts and instruction sheet. Photo courtesy Gates Willard. Photo by E.W. Willard

IDENTIFICATION

The following should help you identify approximately when an English Meccano car was made (note that over the years, parts can get substituted and moved around).

English No. 1 Meccano Car Constructor

Early (1933 to 1934)—Removable rubber tires on stamped steel wheels; yellow opaque headlight lenses, large oval decal (hood).

Later (1934 to 1940)—Solid-rubber wheels with metal disks; translucent gray headlight lenses, metal disks; translucent gray headlight lenses, small round decal (hood).

Colors:

Fenders: yellow/Body: green
Fenders: cream/Body: blue
Fenders: red/Body: cream
Fenders: red/Body: black
Fenders: blue/Body: red

English No. 2 Meccano Car Constructor

Early (1932 to 1933)—Soft alloy wheels; Dunlop tires; rubber spare tire; no holes in seat or dashboard; tall handbrake lever; opaque yellow headlight lenses; splitpin steering mechanism assembly; large oval decal (rear body sections); smaller box; colors-All had cream fenders; body was painted red, blue, or green. (Note: This set was auctioned in 1995 in excellent condition for $990.)

Later (1933 to 1940)—Hard die-cast wheels (subject to metal fatigue); Dunlop (more common) or Firestone tires; soft alloy cast metal tire cover; holes in seat and dashboard for figure and switch for lighting set; short handbrake lever; gray translucent headlight lenses; simplified steering assembly; round decal (rear body sections); larger box.

Colors

Fenders: yellow/Body: green
Fenders: cream/Body: blue
Fenders: red/Body: cream
Fenders: red/Body: black
Fenders: blue/Body: red

Two-Seater Sports Car

Early—Opaque yellow headlight lenses; colors-same as No. 1 and No. 2 constructor cars (two-tone) except yellow-green and red-black combination were not made; picture on box lid shows a red car with cream fenders; but the reverse of this combination was actually used; all had hand-painted black running boards.

Later—Translucent gray headlamp lenses; colors-the lasts cars were painted single colors-all blue with slightly darker blue wheel discs and all red with maroon wheel discs; hand painting of running boards black was phased out, cost savings passed on to the buyer, prices were slightly reduced; no picture label on box lid.

The French Meccano Factory also manufactured both car construction sets, and these are identified by decals stating that they were made in France. Earlier models appear to be the same as their English counterparts, but the tires of the French No. 1 car can be marked Hutchinson, instead of Dunlop. Later French No. 1 cars continued to have removable tires on stamped steel wheels, while the English No. 1 cars changed to solid-rubber wheels with metal disks on the outside only. The last French No. 1 cars retained the original chassis and wheels, but all of the sheet metal and radiators were revised to create a more modern appearance.

Recognizing that a complete construction set in a large box could be a bit formidable for a novice collector, Meccano produced some lower-priced, factory-assembled cars in both sizes, and the box was big enough only for one assembled car, with no

No. 2 Car assembled and placed on a store display stand with an original box in the background. Photo courtesy Gates Willard. Photo by E.W. Willard

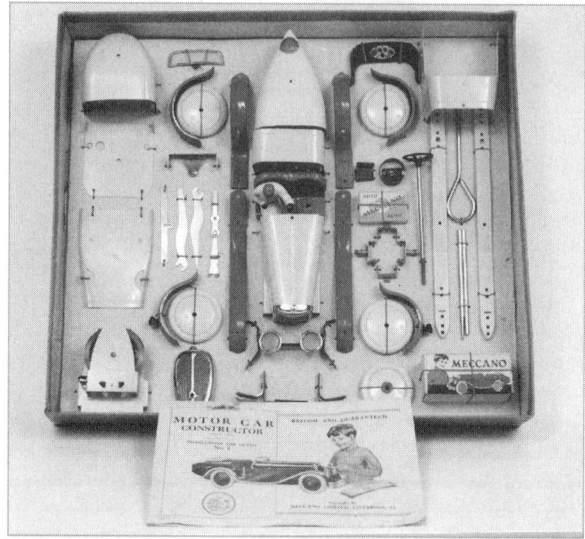

No. 2 Car Constructor shown as purchased at the store. Photo courtesy Gates Willard. Photo by E.W. Willard

Left to right: Early (1932) No. 2 Constructor Car; Late (1933-40) No. 2 Constructor Car. Photo courtesy Gates Willard. Photo by E.W. Willard

Left to right: Firestone and Dunlop (more common) tires for No. 2 Car. Photo courtesy Gates Willard. Photo by E.W. Willard

Left to right: Miniature K oil can compared to a real one; Electric Lighting Set with instructions; No. 2 Car to give concept of scale. Photo courtesy Gates Willard. Photo by E.W. Willard

Left to right: Meccano 1932 No. 2 Constructor Car; 1933-40 No. 2 Constructor Car. Photo courtesy Gates Willard. Photo by E.W. Willard

extra alternative pieces. Individually boxed assembled cars are identical to those sold in the larger sets. They were not very popular, and individually boxed cars are rare today. Why is no value guide possible for Meccano toys? Very few are currently changing hands, and not enough data exists to develop a reliable and useful listing of values. If you are a collector specializing in these vehicles, contact the editor to help out for the next edition of this book.

METAL CAST

Metal Cast Products, formed by the reorganization (circa 1925) of the toy soldier and novelty company S. Sachs, made hand-operated slush-casting molds for small businesses and hobbyists—what some have called the home-casting industry. Since identical molds were sold to many customers, actual makers cannot be identified unless the maker engraved their names on their products. One who did was Fred Green Toys, whose name is found prominently on its toys. Metal Cast offered full-support services to its customers, including marketing, printing, publishing, and parts. A variety of wheels may be found on its vehicles, including Tootsietoy-like metal disk wheels, metal spoke wheels, wood wheels with rubber tires, and white or black rubber wheels.

There aren't many of these home-cast vehicles on the market today, not many were made. Perhaps it was the lack of identity, but demand today seems weak. However, collectors of the unusual should find many enjoyable collectibles; most of those I have seen were well designed and professionally finished.

Contributors: Perry R. Eichor, 703 North Almond Drive, Simpsonville, SC, 29681 and the late Fred Maxwell.

	C6	C8	C10
Cadillac Sedan, No. 40, second version, two-door, 5-3/4" long	20	30	40
Cadillac Sedan, No. 40, two-door, 5-1/4" long	20	30	40
Coupe, No. 63, convertible, two open windows, sidemounts, trunk	20	30	40
Dump Truck, No. 42	20	30	40
Dump Truck, No. 43, COE unique chassis w/activating mechanism, 5-1/4" long	20	30	40
Fire Engine, no number, similar to No. 65 w/o water cannon, 3-7/8" long	6	10	14
Fire Engine, No. 61, hook and ladder truck, crew of two, 4-1/2" long	25	50	60

Metal Cast Cadillac Sedan, No. 40, second version, 5-3/4". Photo from Metal Cast catalog

Top row, left to right: Metal Cast Greyhound Bus; Racer, Bluebird type, Nol. 62, 4-1/2". Middle row, left to right: Limousine, No. 40; Sport Coupe, No. 60. Bottom row: Truck, No. 20, stake-body, 1920s. Photo courtesy Perry Eichor

Metal Cast Racer, No. 92, Indy type with bulging radiator, no driver, torpedo tail. Photo courtesy Bob Ackerly

Top to bottom: Van Truck, No. 01-02, 6", $40; Tank Truck, No. 01-03; Cadillac Sedan, No. 04, 5-3/4". Photo courtesy Perry Eichor

Metal Cast Dump Truck, No. 42. Photo from Metal Cast catalog

Metal Cast Streamline Sedan, six open windows, No. 60, 4". Photo from Metal Cast catalog

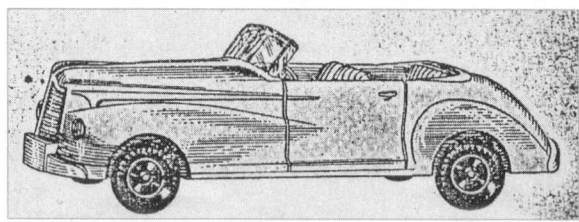

Metal Cast Packard Convertible, second version, No. 41, 5-3/4". Photo from Metal Cast catalog

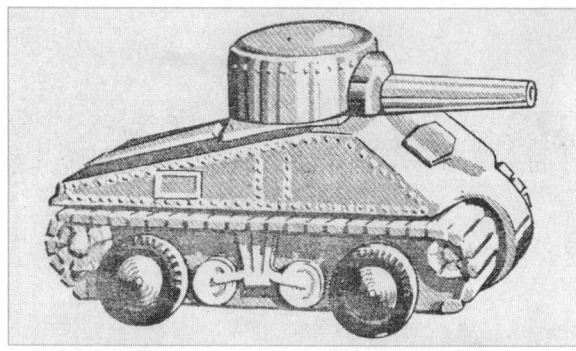

Metal Cast War Tank, No. 39. Photo from Metal Cast catalog

Metal Cast Fire Engine, hook and ladder truck, No. 61, 4-1/2". Photo from Metal Cast catalog

A page from a 1949 Metal Cast catalog.

	C6	C8	C10
Fire Engine, No. 65, steam pumper w/water cannon, driver, 4" long	NPF	NPF	NPF
Greyhound Bus, no number	30	50	70
Limousine, no number	20	30	40
Open Rack Truck, No. 01-04, COE cab, stake semi-trailer, 6" long	15	25	35
Packard Convertible, No. 41, 2-door, top down, 5-1/4" long	20	30	40
Packard Convertible, No. 41, second version, 5-3/4" Long	20	30	40
Packard Convertible, No. 45, 6" long	20	30	40
Racer, No. 62, Bluebird type, blunt-nosed, V-8, record car, driver, 4-1/2" long	40	60	80
Racer, No. 92, large Indy-type w/bulging radiator, no driver, torpedo tail	40	60	80
Sedan, No. 44, postwar, 6" long	20	30	40
Sport Coupe, No. 60, vee grille, Graham (?), from three-piece mold; very similar to Kansas Toy's No. 75	20	30	40
Streamline Sedan, No. 60, DeSoto (?) Airflow, six open windows, smooth grille, rubber tires, 4" long	20	30	40
Tank Truck, No. 01-03, same COE cab, semi-fuel tanker, marked "FRED GREEN TOYS," "Made in U.S.A.," 6" long	20	30	40
Truck, No. 64, Dodge (?), stake-body, 1920s, two open windows, 4-1/4" long	NPF	NPF	NPF
Van Truck, No. 01-02, COE, cab, semi-trailer moving van; trailer also found in a Fred Green version, 6" long	20	30	40
War Tank, No. 39, early heavy Sherman Tank, 4" long	35	50	65
War Tank, No. 55, early WWI type w/side turrets	20	30	40

METAL MASTERS

Located in Philadelphia, Penn., Metal Masters Co. specialized in metal children's toys including telephones and managed to release a number of vehicles.

Contributor: Dave Leopard, 2507 Feather Run Trail, West Columbia, SC 29169-4915.

	C6	C8	C10
Bus, c.1938, 7-1/4" long (MM002)	25	35	50
Fire Truck, removable ladders, c.1940, 10" long (MM012)	50	65	85
Fire Truck, variation of pickup, c.1938, 7" long (MM004)	35	55	75
Fire Truck, wind-up motors, w/ladders, c.1940, 10" long (MM013)	60	90	120
Jeep, c.1947, 5-1/2" long (MM006)	20	30	55
Pickup Truck, c.1938, 7" long (MM003)	25	38	50
Roadster, c.1938, 7" long (MM001)	25	38	50
Station Wagon, ambulance version, c.1940, 8-1/2" long (MM009)	45	55	75
Station Wagon, c.1940, 8-1/2" long (MM007)	40	50	85
Station Wagon, wind-up motor, c.1940, 8-1/2" long (MM008)	45	55	85
Tow Truck, marked "ABC Towing Service," c.1940, 10" long (MM010) .	50	75	100
Tow Truck, variation of pickup, c.1938, 7" long (MM005)	35	45	55
Tow Truck, wind-up motor, c.1940, 10" long (MM011)	55	80	110
Tractor, w/driver, 5" long (MM014)	55	82	110

METALCRAFT

The Metalcraft Corp. of St. Louis, Mo., got its biggest boost in the toy industry by capitalizing on Charles A. Lindbergh's 1927 flight in the Spirit of St. Louis. Metalcraft produced numerous Spirit of St. Louis airplane models and later added zeppelins and trains.

In January 1931, metalcraft rolled out the first of their pressed steel trucks and steam shovels. The majority of the trucks exhibited advertising on the sides. Metalcraft was the leader in advertising toys of national giants like Coca-Cola, Heinz, and Shell Oil. The tireless ad agents garnered contracts from small regional bakeries, grocers, and candy makers, as far away as upstate New York.

Al Korte was the main designer of all the trucks. The battery-operated (electric headlight) grille was patented in 1933 and the art deco streamlined design, noted here as long nose trucks, began shortly thereafter. Metalcraft was still in city directories as late as 1938, but Al Korte had already left the company. As a cost-cutting measure, the very last trucks came with solid rubber wheels and dummy headlights. The original factory where the trucks were produced still stands today in North St. Louis.

Metalcraft Clover Farm Stores. Photo courtesy Bob Smith

Metalcraft Coca-Cola Truck, late 1920s to early 1930s, ten bottles in rack, 11 ". Photo courtesy Detroit Antique Museum. Photo by Harry Wolf

Metalcraft Machinery Hauling. Photo courtesy Calvin L Chaussee

Metalcraft Steam Shovel. Photo courtesy Calvin L Chaussee

Metalcraft Heinz Truck, 12". Photo courtesy Calvin L. Chaussee

Metalcraft White House Truck. According to Andrew Tolch, "There are less than 5 known to exist. It was for a Department store and sold at the store or redeemed if you spent a certain high-dollar amount that day in the store. It is the only Metalcraft to feature this customized odd brown color, almost brown with a green tint. It is circa 1931-32." Photo courtesy Andrew Tolch

Metalcraft boxes, with the exceptions of Heinz, Shell, and Coca-Cola, are extremely hard to find. The Coca-Cola truck box has been reproduced, so be careful. A C10 price does not include an original box. Original boxes can add 25 to 30% to the price of a C9 or C10 truck.

Contributor: Andrew Tolch can be reached through his Web site: www.Andystoys.com, or at 8225 Mackenzie Rd., St. Louis, MO 63123. He is the organizer of the St. Louis Toy Show, one of the Midwest's finest vintage toy shows.

	C6	C8	C10
Acme Stores Truck, long nose	800	1500	NPF
Bunte Candies Truck, 12" long	250	400	650
Buster Brown Shoes Truck	600	NPF	NPF
Clover Farm Stores Truck, long nose	350	600	900
Coca-Cola Truck, pressed steel, rubber tires, w/ten bottles in rack, reads "Every Bottle Sterilized," 11" long	400	650	975
Coca-Cola Truck, ten bottles, long nose, stamped metal, 12" long	500	850	1350
Coca-Cola Truck, w/ten bottles, steel wheels, 1930s, 10-1/2" long	350	525	700
CW Coffee Delivery Van, 11" long	175	325	500
CW Coffee Dump Truck, 10-3/4" long	225	400	550

	C6	C8	C10
CW Coffee Steam Shovel	50	100	150
CW Coffee Wrecker	225	400	550
Deckers Iowana Truck	600	1200	1900
Delivery Truck Van, steel, no advertising, green or orange, 11" long.	300	425	600
Esso Stake Truck, w/barrels, 12" long	500	900	1300
First Prize Meats Truck, long nose	500	950	NPF
Forbes Coffee Machinery Hauling, red and green w/steel wheels	500	975	1400
Forbes Coffee Stake Truck	350	600	800
Goodrich Silvertown Tires Wrecker, battery-operated lights, long nose	225	450	775
Goodrich Silvertown Tires Wrecker, w/three spare tires	150	350	425
Hardy's Salt	250	400	600
Hardy's Salt Steam Shovel	70	120	165
Heinz 57 Stake Truck, green and white w/steel wheels	800	1900	NPF
Heinz Truck, marked "Baked Beans, Bottled Vinegar" and "Rice Flakes," c.1932, 12" long	150	300	425
Kroger Food Express Truck, 11" long	300	450	675
Krug Bakery Truck, battery-operated lights	450	675	950
Leslie Vacuum Packed Coffee Delivery Van, green	500	700	1000

Metalcraft CW Coffee Dump Truck, 10-3/4".

Metalcraft Decker's Iowana, sweet heart grille. Photo courtesy Bob Smith

Metalcraft Meadow Gold Butter Truck, battery lights, 13". Photo courtesy Bob Smith

Left to right: Metalcraft Coca-Cola Truck, 11"; Heinz Truck with original box. Photo courtesy Bertoia Auctions

Metalcraft Waldorf Lager Truck. According to Andrew Tolch, "It is somewhat scarce and very rare to find with the original 8 wooden kegs. Goodrich rubber tires, c.1935, 13" long." Photo courtesy Andrew Tolch

Metalcraft Express Truck. According to Andrew Tolch, "It is the only version along with some late-model Machinery Haulers to feature the optional dimmer switch along with the headlight switch. Not all Express trucks have this, though. It seems that this truck was sold primarily in the Northern United States and Canada. Goodrich rubber tires, c.1932-34, 12-1/2" long." Photo courtesy Andrew Tolch

Metalcraft Sand-Gravel Dump. Photo courtesy Bob Smith

Metalcraft Plee-zing Quality Products Delivery Van, 11". Metalcraft tried to beat the Depression by tying its toys to participating advertisers. Its pressed-steel toys were inexpensive, but by 1937 the company was defunct. Photo courtesy Mapes Auctioneers and Appraisers

Metalcraft Shell Motor Oil, with eight oil drums. Photo courtesy Bob Smith

Metalcraft Pure Oil Co. tanker, electric lights, sweetheart grille, 14-3/4". Photo courtesy Bob Smith

	C6	C8	C10
Leslies Coffee Dump Truck	475	675	950
Lily of the Valley Coffee Delivery Van	500	800	1150
Machinery Hauling Truck, red	475	675	950
Meadow Gold Butter Truck, battery-operated lights, long nose	425	800	1250
Metalcraft Express Logo Stake Truck	250	475	750
National Candy Company St. Louis Truck, long nose	500	900	1500
Old Judge Coffee Truck, long nose	550	1200	NPF
Old Sol Cleaning Truck, rubber tires, battery-operated headlights	450	800	1200
Plee-zine Dump Truck	225	400	575
Plee-zing Quality Products Delivery Van, green, 11" long	225	375	550
Plee-zing Steam Shovel	70	125	165
Plee-zing Wrecker Truck	225	375	550
Pure Oil Co. Tanker, electric lights, 14-3/4"	375	675	1100
Rain Proof Polish Truck, rubber tires, battery-operated headlights	475	750	NPF
Rite-Way Grocer Delivery Van	400	675	1000
Rite-Way Grocer Stake Truck	375	650	975
Rold Gold Pretzels Delivery Van, steel wheels	400	675	975
Sand-Gravel Dump Truck	125	225	350
Shell Motor Oil Truck, includes eight oil drums	150	375	675
Smile Soda Stake Truck, rubber tires, battery-operated headlights	400	650	1000

	C6	C8	C10
Sohio Oil Stake Truck, long nose	500	950	1350
Speck Baking Stake Truck, rubber tires, battery-operated headlights	450	850	1275
St. Louis Logo Truck, green, 11" long	175	325	400
St. Louis Logo Truck, red, 11" long	275	475	600
Standard Oil Stake Truck, battery-operated headlights	400	675	1200
Steam Shovel, #4	40	90	130
Sunshine Biscuits Delivery Van, yellow w/running baker-man logos	375	650	1100
Sunshine Biscuits Stake Truck	175	275	475
Tag Soap Delivery Truck, no "Werks" in the title	300	550	775
Tag Soap Steam Shovel, no "Werks" in the title, red	70	125	175
Tow Truck, Towing and Repairing St. Louis, orange bed	250	425	550
Tow Truck, Towing--Repairs, yellow bed	275	450	575
Towing & Repairs Truck, orange bed	125	275	400
Toy Town Grocery Truck	225	375	500
Waldorf Lager Truck, long nose, sweet heart grill	450	800	1300
Weatherbird Shoes Truck	600	NPF	NPF
Webbs Coffee Truck, long nose, battery-operated headlights	600	1200	1600
Werks Tag Soap Delivery Van	150	300	475
Werks Tag Soap Dump Truck, red and black	225	400	600
Werks Tag Soap Steam Shovel	50	115	150
Weston's English Biscuits Truck	225	350	550
White House Delivery Van, steel wheels	500	950	NPF
White King Express Truck, 12" long	175	300	500

METALGRAF COMPANY

Metalgraf Company manufactured toys from 1920 until 1939. It is still in business today, but has not produced toys for many years. A Metalgraf car is seldom found offered for sale. They are considered rare and are especially hard to find in the United States.

Contributor: Bob Smith, RATS Toy Shows, 255 Tryon Park, Rochester, NY 14609. (585) 288-7153, bird@oldtoysonline.com.

	C6	C8	C10
Touring Car, gray/black lithographed, clockwork motor, steering, 10" long, c.1922	1400	2000	3200

Metalgraf Touring Car, 1920s, 10". Photo courtesy Bob Smith

METTOY

Before it became famous as the parent company of Corgi Toys in 1956, Mettoy Playcraft Ltd. produced toy vehicles. Founded in 1943, the firm was located in Swansea, South Wales.

	C6	C8	C10
Bus, streamlined, wind-up, 7-1/4" long	95	140	190
Citroen Sedan, 11" long	188	282	375
Clown on Motorcycle, 7-1/4" long	550	800	1210
Computacar, program cards direct car, 1960s	20	40	65
Coupe	400	600	800

	C6	C8	C10
Dan Dare Spaceship Eagle, No. 8230, tin, sparks, litho reads "Earth-Mars-Venus Express" and "SS Eagle," 1950s	100	200	300
Motorcycle, c.1940	425	638	850
Motorcycle, No. 49, tin wind-up, 8" long	262	393	525
Racer, No. "7," 5" long	750	1400	1800
Racer, No. "7," tin, clockwork motor, blue, 15-1/2" long	85	175	265
Rolls Royce, 14" long	500	800	1200
Sedan, 14" long, c.1930	300	450	600
Steam Roller, clockwork	100	150	200
Tractor, tin wind-up, 8" long	55	83	110

MIDGETOY

During postwar slack times at A&E Tool & Gage Co. of Rockford, Illinois, a die-cast toy company was born that would eventually rank second only to Tootsietoy in the industry. A&E, named for owners Alvin and Earl Herdklotz, had been making precision gages since 1943. Reluctant to let workers go when business slowed after the war, the Herdklotz brothers turned to toy making. The company had already made tooling work for regional toy companies, including Nylint, Structo, and Lansing Slik-Toys.

Their first toy was the Chevy truck of 1946. Interchangeable bodies snapped onto the chassis to make a stake, oil, or dump truck. That toy, and many which followed, reflected an appealing and distinctive sense of design at work, essentially a 1930s deco sensibility that was especially apparent in the King-Size and Jumbo series of vehicles.

Two futuristic designs appeared next—the Spaceship and the Rear Engine Auto. The spaceship was modeled after a comic strip Buck Rogers spaceship but never marketed as such, for licensing reasons. The Rear-Engine Auto, with its swept-back, two-door body and swept-up tail lights, was an original design. After this flirtation with the future, Midgetoy settled on the course it would take the next three decades, producing solidly built toys based on existing vehicle models.

Leaving toys in production for many years was standard practice for the company. The popular train sets, for instance, were issued continuously from their introduction in the late 1950s until the company closed its doors in the early 1980s. They remain common in collecting circles today, even in Mint in Package (C10) form.

In 1981, the Herdklotz brothers sold the company to a group of investors. The new owners unfortunately let the business languish, and introduced few new toy designs. The new Midgetoy company also packaged toys produced by other companies. After one investor suffered a fatal heart attack, the Herdklotz brothers bought back the company in 1985 to shut it down.

The Herdklotz brothers retained ownership of the company's old inventory during the change of ownership. They started releasing these essentially factory-fresh toys in the 1990s, with the result that collectors have a plentiful supply of later, plastic-wheeled versions of Midgetoy's line in excellent condition. These later versions of the toys frequently had masking and decals, unlike earlier versions. Some collectors show preference for these over older examples.

The axle arrangement used in the toys was patented by Midgetoy in 1957. The hidden wheels gave the toys their distinctive look until the 1970s, when the company introduced a line of small, exposed-axle vehicle toys akin to Tootsietoy's Jam-Pac vehicles. The move was made necessary by the rising cost of zinc. Midgetoy did continue producing some larger vehicles until the end, however.

In the listings below, dates in parentheses refer to the year of first release of the model. Early versions of the smaller vehicles possessed black rubber tires, here designated **brt**, as opposed to the later black plastic tires, or **bpt**. The later versions are usually worth sixty to seventy percent of the earlier versions.

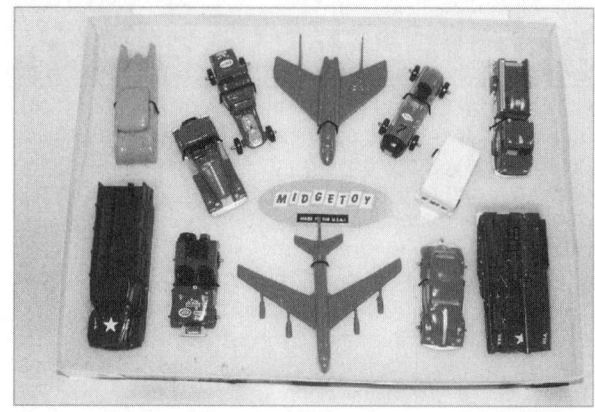

Part of a Midgetoy salesman's sample box. Photo courtesy Thomas G. Nefos

Larger toy vehicles apparently had black rubber tires from beginning to end, although the early tires have a fatter and rounder appearance, and the later ones have a central ridge. Masking and decals, however, are sure signs of later production or pieces made for upscale stores.

Al Herdklotz passed away December 28, 2002. He was 87 years old.

The given dates refer to the year of the model's introduction.

Contributor: John W. Vayo, P.O. Box 201, Ringwood, IL 60072-0201. John recently self-published a book, *Midgetoy: An All American Toy Story*, detailing the history and toys of Midgetoy.

Airplanes	C6	C8	C10
Army 707 Jet Cargo Plane, four engines on the wings	7	10	15
Army B-57 Bomber Jet Plane, two jet engines on the wing	7	10	15
Army F-86 Sabre Jet Plane, wing tanks on the end of each wing	7	10	15
Modified Jet Trainor Plane	7	10	15
Navy Cougar Jet Plane, high tail section	7	10	15
Navy Cutlass Jet Plane, two rudders on the wing	7	10	15

Ford Tractor-Trailer Series, 8" Vehicles

	C6	C8	C10
Auto Transporter with loading ramp, w/2 cars, 1962	12	25	35
Hook and Ladder Aerial Fire Truck, 1963	12	20	30
Oil Tanker, 1962	15	22	30
Oil Tanker, marked "Midgetoy Oil Co."	15	22	30
Shipping Van, 1962	15	25	35
Shipping Van, marked "Allied Van Lines"	20	30	40
Shipping Van, marked "Midgetoy Van Lines, Inc."	20	30	40
Shipping Van, marked "North American Van Lines"	20	30	40

Jumbo Series, 6" Vehicles

	C6	C8	C10
American La France Pumper, brt	11	18	27
Ford Oil Tanker, 1957, brt	10	17	25
Ford Oil Tanker, marked "Midgetoy Oil Co."	10	17	25
Four-door Convertible, brt	10	17	25
Mobile Artillery, 1957, brt	10	17	25
Scenicruiser Bus, late 1950s, 3 axles w/brt	12	20	30
Scenicruiser Bus, marked "Midgetoy Bus Line"	10	17	25
Utility Truck, brt	10	17	25

Junior Series, 2-1/2" to 3-1/2" vehicles

	C6	C8	C10
American La France Pumper, closed cab, early 1950s	6	10	15
American La France Pumper, open cab, late 1950s	6	9	15
Army Amphibious Vehicle, brt, 1949	8	14	22
Army Howitzer, bpt	2	5	7
Army Howitzer, brt, 1949	4	7	10
Army Jeep, brt, 1950	5	8	15
Cadillac Convertible, brt, 1949	6	11	17
Chevy Dump Truck, 1946	10	17	n/a
Chevy Oil Truck, 1946	10	17	n/a
Chevy Stake Truck, 1946, set w/1 cab and 3 car bodies on tray	20	30	40
Corvette Convertible, brt, late '50s	7	12	18
Ford Hot Rod, 2-3/8 inches, brt	8	12	20
Ford V-8 Hot Rod, bpt	8	10	15
Ford V-8 Hot Rod, brt, 1948, 3" long	10	15	25
Ford Wrecker, brt, 2-3/4" w/boom, late 1950s	10	16	25
MG Sports Roadster, brt, 1958	6	9	13

Midgetoy Stake Truck. Photo courtesy Mark Rich

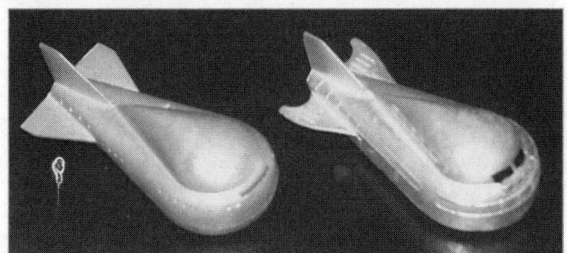

Left to right: Midgetoy Spaceship without open windows; Midgetoy Spaceship with open windows. Photo courtesy Mark Rich

Midgetoy Scenicruiser Bus. Photo courtesy Thomas G. Nefos

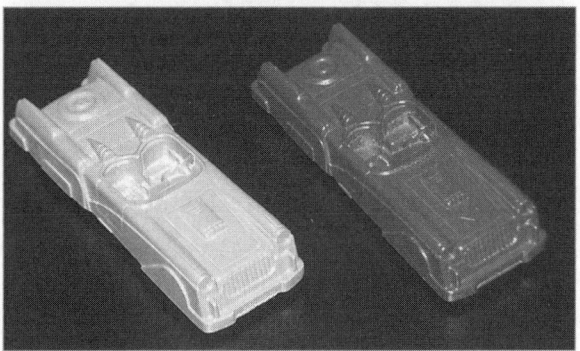

Two examples of Midgetoy convertibles. Photo courtesy Mark Rich

	C6	C8	C10
Oldsmobile Convertible, brt, rare, 1950s .	10	20	50
Oldsmobile Sedan, brt, rare, 1950s	10	20	50
Open Cockpit Curtis Craft Racer, 1950 ...	8	14	22
Rear-Engine Auto, no rear window, brt, 1948	12	22	30
Rear-Engine Auto, rear window outlined, bpt	7	12	18
Scenicruiser Bus, brt, 1955	6	10	15
Spaceship, no open window, three brt	30	45	60
Spaceship, no open window, two brt	25	40	50
Spaceship, open window, two bpt............	8	14	22
Spaceship, open window, two brt	20	32	45
Sunbeam Racer, bpt	5	8	12
Sunbeam Racer, bpt, heavily decaled	7	12	18
Sunbeam Racer, brt, 1950	8	14	22
Volkswagen Beetle, bpt, 1960	6	10	15

King-Size Series, 4" Vehicles

	C6	C8	C10
American La France Pumper, brt, early 1950s	8	16	25
Army Half-Track, late '50s, brt	7	13	20
Army Personnel Carrier, laten '50s, brt ...	7	13	20
Army Tank, brt..	7	13	20
Cadillac Four-door Sedan, late '50s, brt ..	7	13	20
Cadillac Four-door Sedan, military..........	7	12	18
Cadillac Two-door Coupe, early '50s, brt	12	18	28
Chrysler-style Convertible Roadster, brt .	8	14	22
Ford Pickup Truck, early 1950s, brt	8	14	22
Oil Tanker Truck, late '50s, brt...............	9	15	24
Oil Tanker Truck, military, brt.................	7	13	20
Van, no side windows, late '50s	10	15	22
Van, open side windows, late 1950s, brt..	7	12	18
Van Ambulance, late 1950s, brt..............	10	16	22
Van Ambulance, Red Cross, late '50s, brt	10	18	25

Midget Series, 2-1/2" to 3" Vehicles

	C6	C8	C10
Cadillac Ambulance, 1971	5	8	12
Corvette '68 L88 Stingray, 1971..............	2	5	8
Ford Mark IV, 1971	2	4	5
Ford Mustang, 1971	1	2	3
Ford Pickup Truck, 1971	2	5	10
Ford Torino, 1971	1	2	3
Ford Torino Fire Chief Car, 1971	2	4	6
Ford Torino Police Car, 1971	2	5	8

Midgetoy Oil Tank Truck, 1957, 6". Photo courtesy Thomas G. Nefos

	C6	C8	C10
Ford Wrecker, 1971	3	5	7
Jaguar XKE, 1971....................................	3	6	10

Miscellaneous

	C6	C8	C10
Boat Trailer, various designs	3	5	8
Camping Trailer	6	10	15
Fire Axe, metal, found in sets	n/a	n/a	1
Gas Pumps, metal...................................	8	15	20
Gas Pumps, plastic	n/a	1	2
Race Car Trailer for Pee Wee Car, w/car	3	5	8
Railroad Signals, four different metal signals	n/a	n/a	1
Rifle, metal, found in sets	n/a	n/a	1
Sledge, metal, found in sets	n/a	n/a	1
Utility Trailer, 1-1/2" long	2	4	5
Utility Trailer, 2" long	3	5	8
Utility Trailer, military, 1-1/2" long	2	4	5

Pee-Wee/Mini Series, Under 2" Mini Vehicles

	C6	C8	C10
American La France Fire Truck, 1969.....	1	2	5
Chevy-style Dragster, 1969	1	2	3
Corvette Convertible Dragster, 1969	1	2	5
Drag Racer, 1969	1	2	3
Ford Dragster, 1969	1	2	3
Ford GT, 1969.......................................	1	2	3
Jeep, 1969	n/a	1	3
MG Roadster, 1969	1	2	3
Open Cockpit Racer, 1969	n/a	3	5
Porsche Convertible Dragster, 1969	1	2	5

Sets

	C6	C8	C10
Dixie Chargers, three car set, 1981	7	10	18
Train, diesel, five-piece set	10	15	28

Midgetoy American La France Fire Truck, 1957, 6". Photo courtesy Thomas G. Nefos

Midgetoy Shipping Van, "Midgetoy Van Lines, Inc." Photo courtesy Mark Rich

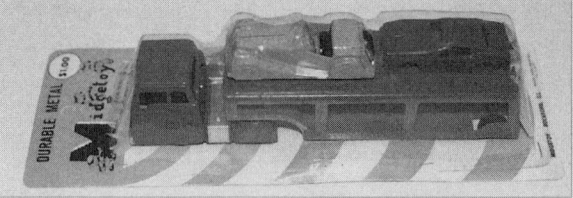

Midgetoy Auto Transporter with MG and Mustang, 1960s. Photo courtesy Thomas G. Nefos

Midgetoy Truck Set, Chevrolet chassis with three iner-changeable bodies, 1946. Photo courtesy Thomas G. Nefos

Midgetoy Oil Tank Truck, 1957, 6". Photo courtesy Thomas G. Nefos

	C6	C8	C10
Train, diesel, Mint on blister pack	n/a	20	35
Train, freight, five-piece set	10	15	28
Train, freight, Mint on blister pack	n/a	20	35
Train, passenger, five-piece set	10	15	28
Train, passenger, marked "Amtrak Super Liner," Mint on blister pack	n/a	20	35
Train, passenger, Mint on blister pack	n/a	20	35
Train, western, four-piece set	10	15	28
Train, western, package marked "Train That Won the West," Mint in blister pack	n/a	20	35

MID-WEST METAL NOVELTY MFG. CO.

In the late 1920s, the American auto industry, led by Ford, was not only booming but dominating global production, and vehicle toys were keeping up with their prototypes. There were three companies that developed a thriving slushmold toy business— C.A.W. Novelty Co., Mid-West Metal Novelty Co., and Kansas Toy and Novelty Co. These were in small Northern Kansas towns, Clay Center and Clifton, only a few miles apart. These toy makers had other things in common—they loved racers, they all used metal-disk wheels and black-painted tires, they tended to follow the lead of Tootsietoy, and the companies left almost no paper trail.

This lack of documentation accounts for the difficulty toy historians have had identifying some excellent models and toys. The above clues suggest that Mid-West was C.E. Stevenson's business title. Stevenson, an active businessman, was at the center of all this. In 1923, he started casting toys at home. In 1925, he joined Western Diecasting of Clay Center, probably as an outside salesman. Shortly after Kansas Toy started, he contracted to furnish molds to them. He may also have sold master patterns and those prepainted wheels to C.A.W. and Kansas Toy, for all these were probably made in the foundry of Western Diecasting. The sole surviving newsclip on Mid-West in a 1929 *Toys and Novelties* magazine shows a deluxe (five-window) coupe, a fairly exact copy of the Tootsietoy Buick, but with Kansas Toy black-painted tires.

But what else did Mid-West make? Over the years a group of vehicle toys with a similar look have been found-Tootsietoy copies or look-a-likes; Tootsietoy wheels, including those distinctive lug boltheads; metal-disk wheels with a suggested rim between wheel and tire; most important, several versions of Buick coupe seen in the 1929 *Toys and Novelties*. The most likely maker was Stevenson, before he moved on to a larger city in 1931 and started Lincoln (Nebraska) White Metal Works, with which he thrived for years, despite the Depression.

Contributors: Perry R. Eichor, 703 North Almond Drive, Simpsonville, SC, 29681, and the late Fred Maxwell.

	C6	C8	C10
Buick Coupe, no lamps, disk wheels, five grooved solid windows, HG, HO, VL, SM, three variations, four open windows; five smooth windows; MDW w/"lug bolts," 3" long (MW03)	25	40	55
Buick Sedan, disk wheels, six open windows, HO, VL, OW, WV, 0 (MW15)	25	40	55
Bus, overland/safety, no lamps, no doors, no spares, HG, HO, ten open windows, disk wheels (same bus later reissued by by Lincoln White Metal Works), 3-1/2" long (MW12)	40	50	60
Bus, Yellow Coach, school-bus body, no doors, thirteen solid grooved windows, HG, RM, painted disk wheels, 3-3/4" long (MW10)	30	40	60
Large Coupe, no lamps, large die-cast (?), five grooved solid windows, disk wheels w/lug bolts, HG, HO, VL, 3-1/2" long (MW01)	40	60	80
Large Racer, driver crouched and hunched over steering wheel, boattail, medium-sized disk wheels w/lug bolts, HG, HO, VL, 3-5/8" long (MW05)	40	60	80

	C6	C8	C10
Large Truck, AC Mack, Buick or Packard, long hood, top up, HG, HO, VL, door handles and hinges, RM, rear bumper, 3-5/8" long; variation—two colors, three solid windows, painted disk wheels (MW07)	40	60	80
Large Truck, AC Mack, gas tank ahead of windshield, V6, screen louvers, full-sized solid stake body w/open rear (for pouring), 3-1/4" long; Uunique slushmold design w/solid, curved pan (MW06)	40	60	80

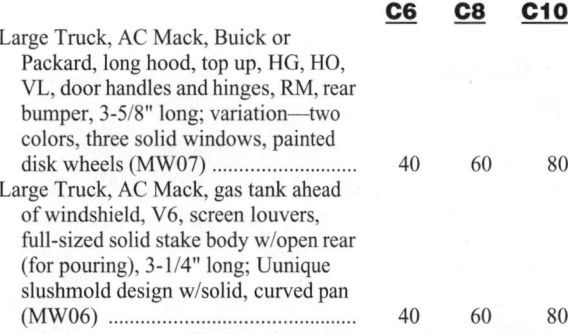

From left: Mid-West Yellow Taxicab, grooved solid windows, 2-3/4"; Large Coupe, disc wheels, 3-/2". Photo courtesy Fred Maxwell

ABBREVIATIONS

The following abbreviations are for the details and variations useful in identification.

HG	horizontal grille pattern	**SM**	sidemounted spare
HL	horizontal hood louvers	**SP**	string-pull knob in hand crank area
HO	hood cap, Motometer or ornament	**T**	external trunk
L	lacquer finish	**UV**	unnumbered version
LI	landau irons on convertibles	**VG**	vertical grille pattern
MDW	metal disc wheels	**VL**	vertical hood louvers
MDSW	metal disc solid spokes	**WS, W/S**	windshield
MDWBT	wheels with black painted tires	**WV**	windshield visor
MSW	metal open spoke wheels	**WHRT**	wooden hubs, rubber tires
MWW	metal simulated wire wheels	**WRDW**	white hard rubber disc wheels
OW	open windows	**WRW**	white soft rubber wheels
RM	rearmount spare tire/wheel		(balloon tires)

	C6	C8	C10
Midget Racer, driver crouched and hunched over steering wheel, torpedo tail, small disk wheels w/lug bolts, HG, HO, VL, 2-3/4"; variation: narrower body and large wheels (the postwar Barclay?); M & L reproduction is more often found (MW04)	40	50	60
Sedan, Ford A, two-door, finely detailed screen grille, headlamps and fenders (made w/a three-piece mold, a Stevenson specialty); VL, WSV, four open windows, door handles and hinges, painted disk wheels, 2-3/4" long (MW13)	40	60	80

An advertisement for Mid-West Metal Novelty Manufacturing Co.

Left to right: Mid-West Touring Car, top up, no seats, 3-1/8"; Touring Car, driver and lady, top down, 3-1/8". Photo courtesy Fred Maxwell

Top to bottom: Mid-West Large Roadster, 3-5/8"; Another version of the Large Roadster; Town Car, 3-5/8". Photo courtesy Fred Maxwell

Top: Two versions of the Mid-West Midget Racer, 2-3/4"; Bottom row: Large Racer, 3-5/8". Photo courtesy Fred Maxwell

Two versions of the Mid-West Yellow Taxicab. Photo from Fred Maxwell

Mid-West Buick Sedan, 3". KP photo courtesy Karen O'Brien

Two versions of the 3" Mid-West Buick Coupe. Photo courtesy Fred Maxwell

Mid-West Sedan, two-door Ford A, 2-3/4". Photo courtesy Fred Maxwell

	C6	C8	C10
Touring Car, Ford T, driver and lady passenger w/muff, top down, no lamps, plain grille, HO, VL, door handles, disk wheels, 3-1/8" long (MW08)	50	80	120
Touring Car, top up, no seats, HG, HO, VL, RM, side lamps, door handles, disk wheels, 3-1/8" long (MW09)	30	40	50
Town Car, w/chauffeur, long hood, HG, HO, VL, LI, three colors, five solid windows, grooved, door handles and hinges, disk wheels, 3-5/8" long (MW11)	50	75	100
Yellow Taxicab, no lamps, door handles, seven "grooved" solid windows, MDW w/rims but no bolts, HG, HO, VL, 2-3/4" long; other versions have driver and passenger embossed on front windows, other windows open (MW02)	40	60	80

	C6	C8	C10
Sedan (?), Buick, finely detailed screen grille, headlamps and fenders, "B" cast on grille, HO, VL, side lamps, WSV, six open windows, door-hinges, RM, painted wheels, 3-1/16" long; a similar car has been attributed to Barclay Mfg. (MW14)	40	60	80

MILITARY VEHICLES

Identification Models and Miscellaneous items

1:36-scale Metal Identification Models; World War II U.S. Top row, left to right: "Heavy Tank M-6"; "Med. Tank, M4-2" (Turret Revolves); "Med. Tank M-4"; "Med. Tank M-3". Front row, left to right: "Light Tank M-3"; "Light Tank M-3" (turrent revolves); "3" Gun Car. M-5"; "105 MM Howitzer Motor T32 My M7 Priest M-7". Note: Britians Ltd. GI included for scale. Photo courtesy Ed Poole

1:36-scale metal Identification Models; World War II U.S. Top row, left to right: "Half TRK Car M2"; "Half TRK pers. car - M3"; "75 MM Gun Car. M-3 Half Track Car M2" (decal not original but AAF Acceptance tag dated "Jul 3 1946" is); "Scout Car M-3 A-1". Front row, left to right: "Armoured Car T-17"; "Duck" (1/48th scale); "37MM Gun Car. M6". Note: Britians Ltd. GI included for scale. Photo courtesy Ed Poole

1:36-scale metal Identification Model, World War II German. Top row, left to right: "Ger. Light med. tank L.T. 3.5"; "Praga" Ger. Tank 7 ton T.N.H.P. Ex. (Czech); "Ger. Light Med. Tank C.K.V. D.8.H." Front row, left to right: "German Light Amphibian Tank C.K.D.F4.H.E."; "Ger. Light Arm. car Horch 1936 SD:K 223"; "Ger. Heavy 8 wheeled armor, car." Note: Jones 54mm soldier included for scale. Photo courtesy Ed Poole

Prime Mover (after Barclay) and Howitzer (after Tootsietoy) from Junior Caster Model No. E45; homecast. Photo courtesy Ron Eccles. Photo by Ed Poole

1:36-scale metal Identification Models; WWII Japanese (Decals not original). Top row, left to right: "Japanese Medium Tank - Cometal"; "Japanese Cruiser Tank – Cometal"; "Japanese Heavy Medium Tank - Cometal." Front row, left to right: "Japanese Amphibian Tank"; "Japanese 1938 Tankette"; "Japanese L.M. Tank M2595 Comet"; "Japan. Tankette M2592 – 1932 Comet." Note: Britains Ltd. 54mm Soldier added for scale. Photo courtesy Ed Poole

Some contemporary Russian die-casts. Top row, left to right: 76mm Gun; T34-85 Tank; 100mm Gun in 1:43-scale by UEHA (?). Front row, left to right: T34 Tank; Two YA3-469 Cars in 1:43 scale by Schelano B CCCP. Dinky soldiers added for scale is 30mm tall. Photo courtesy Ed Poole

Dale 1:36-scale Identification model bought in an Army "PX" post World War II; mailing label already attached to box. Photo courtesy Ed Poole

1:36-scale metal Identification models; World War II British. Top row, left to right: Churchill Tank, "Infantry Tank MKIV Comet NY"; armoured car, "Humber MKII Comet NY"; Convenanter Tank, "Cruiser MKV"; Bren Gun, "UK Cruiser MKVI Crusader Comet NY," "Universal Carrier." Front row, left to right: Bren Gun Carrier, "Universal Carrier"; Valentine Tank, "MKIII UK Cruiser Comet NY"; Matilda II Tank, "UK Infantry Tank MKIIA Comet NY"; armoured car, "MKI Daimler Comet NY"; "Carden Loyd Carrier." Note: Britains 54mm "Tommy" for scale. Photo courtesy Ed Poole

1:108-scale metal Identification Models; WWII British. Numbering is that of the manufacturer Comet/Authenticast but a Denzil Skinner model is substituted for No. 5012. Front row, left to right: No. 5000 Convenanter IV; No. 5001 Churchill MKV; No. 5002 Universal Carrier; No. 5003 Humber Armoured Car; No. 5004 Carden Loyd Carrier. Middle row, left to right: No. 5005 Valentine; No. 5006 Matilda; No. 5007 Crusader; No. 5009 Cromwell. Front row, left to right: No. 5008 Daimler Armoured Car, No. 5010 Churchill MKVII; No. 5011 Sherman VC 5012 Centurion. Note: Authenticast GI by Holger Eriksson is 23mm tall. Photo courtesy Ed Poole

Miscellaneous small metal AFVs. Top row, left to right: Crescent (England) Russian Tank; British Cruiser Tank and Humber Armoured Car; Daimler Ambulance and tank by unknown makers. Front row, left to right: Series by Unknown Maker-Patton Tank, Sherman Tank, Armored car, Tank and Amphibian. U.S. Markings but imprinted "JAPAN". Note: Comet GI is 20mm tall. Photo courtesy Ed Poole

Miscellaneous small die-cast military vehicles. Top row, left to right: Mattel "Hot Wheels Gun Bucket"; Corgi Junior (England) Daimler Scout Car; Lesney "Matchbox Rola-matics" No. 73 Weasel; Sherman Tank (made in Hong Kong, pencil sharpener). Front row, left to right: Efsi (Holland) T-Ford 1919 Ambulance; Budgie Toy (England) Tank Transporter; 25pdr Gun Howitzer (maker unknown). Note: Comet GI 20mm tall. Photo courtesy Ed Poole

Homecastings from Ever-Ready Mould No. ML21 (American Craft Manufacturing Company, Chicago), "Big Bertha in Action," Gun barrel 11.5cm long; Photo by Ed Poole

Miscellaneous Small metal AFVs. Top row, left to right: HR Products WWI Rhomboidal tanks; Renault FT tank; Quality Castings Desert War 2018 Stuart "Honey"; 2019 MKVI light tank; 2020 Cruiser MK IV. Front row, left to right: Denzil Skinner (England) – British tank Series BZ Centurion, B25 Vickers MKVI and MKII Medium; British Armoured Car Series Bill Daimler; B23 Rolls Royce and Armoured Truck (number unknown). Note Comet GI is 20mm tall. Photo courtesy Ed Poole

Some Military Vehicles by Miscellaneous British manufacturers Top row, left to right: Lone Star Bren Gun Carrier towing Gun; Skybirds Artillery Tractor towing Howitzer; TriAng Mini-Toys Jeep, Lledo Days Gone Ambulance. Front Row, left to right: Charbens Armoured Car; Crescent Armoured Car towing Limber and Gun Corgi Major; International 6x6 Truck; Corgi Toys Hong Kong King Tiger Tank; Lone Star Jeep. Note: Skybird soldier shown for scale is 30mm tall. Photo courtesy Ed Poole

Die-cast Military Vehicles from Various Countries. Top row, left to right: "Henschel Bau J 1926 Made in W. Germany" (maker unknown); Mercedes Benz 1937 Cabriolet Feuhrerwagen by RIO (Italy); Fiat Antocarro Militaire 1914 by RIO; Military truck; Rader Truck by TEKNO (Denmark); Ambulance by TEKNO. Front row, left to right: Liasson Car by Brumm (Italy); "Dodge 6X6 Made in France" (marked FJ within a geared wheel); three tanks by Play Art (Hong Kong)-Tiger I, Panther and Sherman; Two jeeps-front by Play Art and behind by Fun Ho! (New Zealand); Zylmex "King Tiger" (Hong Kong). Note: Starlux soldiers shown are 30mm tall. Photo courtesy Ed Poole

1:36-Scale metal Identification Models. WWII German (Jones 54mm Soldier included for scale.) L to R, Back row: "Ger. Light Tank P.Z.K.W.1 Maybach 1936." "Ger. Light Tank (P)Z.K.1 Command Tank," "Ger. Light Tank PZ:KW:2," Ger. Light Med. Tank PZ.KW3. Type 'C'." Photo courtesy Ed Poole

1:24-scale metal Identification Models; World War II. Top row, left to right: Amphibian Tractor, 105mm S.P. (illegible) M7; Half-trak car; M2. Front row, left to right: Jeep (some of these movable wheel versions are also marked "Dale"); "4X4 Ton Truck- Jeep" (fixed wheel version); "Cletrac" (bulldozer). Note: Manoil 3-1/4" GI for scale. Photo courtesy Ed Poole

Miniature metal military vehicles as Souvenirs (Heyde 50mm soldier included for sacle). L to R – Back row: Renault Tank Inkwells, "G.B.W. 1919..Carton Steel Company" (turret hinges back to uncover inkpot); "G.B.W. 1919. Renault Constructeur" (turret Cupola unstoppers; piece repainted and gun replaced); "Depose S.R. Tour Eiffel" (turret hinges to left – like Mignot but lacks recessed wheels). Front row: Ashtray Decorations Fourth tank from left bears soldered plaque, "State Capitol Columbus Ohio." Photo courtesy Ed Poole

Five and Dime Corps HG troops with Tri-ang Jeep (England), 16cm long. Photo courtesy Ed Poole

1:36-scale metal Identification Models; WWII Japanese (Decals not original). Top row, left to right: "Japanese Medium Tank - Cometal"; "Japanese Cruiser Tank – Cometal"; "Japanese Heavy Medium Tank - Cometal." Front row, left to right: "Japanese Amphibian Tank"; "Japanese 1938 Tankette"; "Japanese L.M. Tank M2595 Comet"; "Japan. Tankette M2592 – 1932 Comet." Note: Britains Ltd. 54mm Soldier added for scale. Photo courtesy Ed Poole

Three Battle of Britain 50th Anniversary Commemorative sets; vehicles each about 8cm in length. Photo courtesy Ed Poole

Arnold (Germany) Jeep with Five and Dime Corps troops and mascot; Jeep 17cm long. Photo courtesy Ed Poole

MINIATURE VEHICLE CASTINGS

Though these appear to be toys from the 1930s, they were first produced in 1985. The models were carved and cast by owner Robert E. Wagner. Made of die-cast lead from silicone molds, they were sold for $21 each; at least 3,500 have been sold. Some are beginning to appear at toy shops and on dealer lists. The average length is about 4-1/2 inches, and the New Jersey firm's name is visible (sometimes dimly) on a piece of tin soldered to the bottom. The toys today seem to sell at slightly more than double their original price.

Following is a list of Miniature Vehicle Castings:
- 1937 Ford Two-door Sedan
- 1938 Ford Standard Sedan Delivery
- 1934 Olds Two-door Humpback
- 1936 Olds Four-door Humpback
- 1937 Hudson Terraplane Two-door
- 1938 Dodge Step Van
- 1937 Plymouth Five-window Coupe
- 1937 Dodge Two-door Humpback
- 1938 Plymouth Two-door Sedan
- 1941 Ford COE Truck (flatbed or dump)
- 1936 Hudson Two-door Sedan
- 1937 Studebaker Three-window Coupe
- 1936 Plymouth Four-door Sedan
- 1936 Plymouth Four-door Taxi
- 1935 Pontiac Three-window Coupe
- 1940 Dodge Two-door Sedan
- 1939 Dodge Two-door Sedan
- 1941 Divco Milk Truck (Sunrise Dairy)

Left to right: 1937 Hudson Terraplane; 1935 Hudson. Photo courtesy Bob and Alice Wagner

Left to right: Miniature Vehicle Castings 1934 Olds; 1936 Olds. Photo courtesy Bob and Alice Wagner

From left: Miniature Vehicle Castings 1938 Plymouth two-door Sedan; 1937 Plymouth Coupe, five windows; 1937 Dodge two-door Humpback. Photo courtesy Bob and Alice Wagner

Miniature Vehicle Castings 1938 Dodge Step Van. Photo courtesy Bob and Alice Wagner

Left to right: Miniature Vehicle Castings 1941 Ford C.O.E. Truck; 1937 Studebaker three-window Coupe; 1936 Plymouth Taxi. Photo courtesy Bob and Alice Wagner

MINIC

(Minic history by Gates Willard).

Established by George Lines in the 1870s, the original Lines company of England made wooden rocking horses. Lines' brother, Joseph joined the firm and ultimately bought out his share. After World War I, three of Joseph Lines' sons formed a company called Lines Bros., Ltd. and its logo was a triangle, and its products came to be known as Tri-ang Toys. By the mid 1930s, the company was making prams, cycles, pedal cars, stamped steel trucks, wooden toys, doll houses, and many other kinds of playthings.

In 1935, the Tri-ang Minic Miniature Clockwork Vehicles were introduced. Only fourteen models were available that first year. Three to seven inches in length, they were robustly made of heavier gauge steel than that used by competing German manufacturers. They had brightly plated radiators and wheels. The trucks and some of the cars even had plated fenders. Painting was done by a dipping and baking process which caused runs, as well as thick and thin areas, but the finishes were durable. Subtle shades of red, blue, green, beige, orange, and yellow, plus black and chrome were tastefully combined to make some unusually attractive color schemes. The road vehicles had white rubber tires and each Minic came boxed with a stamped steel key and a little color folding catalogue inside the box.

The first Minics must have been successful, because in 1936 many new types were added and a few even had electric lights. A miniature Shell gasoline can appeared on the left running board of most cars and trucks. By early September 1939, England was at war and the Shell can had been deleted. The white tires were replaced with black, and the plated trunk rack on the ordinary cars was replaced by a decal number plate and a plain rear bumper. Since 1935, many new models were added and none discontinued. The factory claimed that more than seventy types were available. However, by 1940, some vehicles were painted in army camouflage, while others, such as the electric lighted types, were phased out. The non-military vehicles had some parts chemically blackened instead of plated. Steering wheels were later attached with miniature split pins instead of being pressed onto a brass column.

After the war ended, Minics were rushed back into production. The British economy required exports, and large quantities of Minics were sent to the United States, which was starved for metal toys. Minics seem to have been available in many areas of the country, whereas there had been very few outlets before the war. The first postwar Minics often had leftover prewar parts and boxes. Stronger colors were used (mostly bright red, dark blue, and shades of green) and the quality of finish was below the prewar standard. Tooling was wearing out and the stampings often lacked definition. In time, quite a few new types and variations were produced before the company ceased operations in the 1970s.

In addition to the vehicles, various garages, service stations, and even a fire station were made prewar and postwar. The numbering system used below was instituted about 1938 or 1939. In general, the lower the number, the cheaper the item. However, new toys announced 1939 or 1940 were tacked on to the end of the existing list (65M-79M). Some of this last group were never put into production before toy manufacturing ended during World War II.

Why is there no value guide for prewar Minic toys? Very few are currently changing hands and not enough data exists to develop a reliable and useful listing of values.

Mint in Box versions of postwar Minic vehicles average between $95 and $225.

01M Ford Saloon Sedan, 1936
01MCF Ford Saloon, camouflaged, fewer than 100 known, 1939-1940 (none produced postwar)
02M Ford Light Van, 1936
03M Ford Royal Mail Van, 1936
04M Sports Saloon, two-window sedan; headlights, radiator and bumper stamped from one piece, 1935; it is a possibility that a small number were made following WWII w/a new tooling for radiator and matte-black baseplate
05M Limousine, three-window sedan; headlights, radiator and bumper stamped from one piece, 1935; a small number were made following WWII w/a new tooling for radiator and matte-black baseplate

06M Cabriolet, coupe, headlights, radiator and bumper stamped from one piece, 1935; a small number were made following WWII w/a new tooling for radiator and matte-black baseplate
07M Town Coupe (Town Car), headlights, radiator and bumper stamped from one piece, 1935; a small number were made following WWII w/a new tooling for radiator and matte-black baseplate
08M Open Touring Car, headlights, radiator and bumper stamped from one piece, 1935; a small number were made following WWII w/a new tooling for radiator and matte-black baseplate
09M Streamline Saloon Airflow Sedan, 1935
10M Delivery Lorry (Pickup Truck), headlights, radiator and bumper stamped from one piece, 1935

Left to right: 2M Minic Ford Light Van, 1936; 3M Ford Royal Main Van; 1M Ford Saloon (Sedan); 1 MCF Ford Saloon, camouflaged. Photo courtesy Gates Willard. Photo by E.W. Willard

Left to right: 15M Minic Petrol Tank Lorry (Oil Tanker), 1936; 78M Pool Tanker, 1940; 31M Mechanical Horse and Fuel Oil Tanker, 1936; 79M Mechancial Horse and Pool Tanker, 1940. Photo courtesy Gates Willard. Photo by E.W. Willard

Minic Service Station with pumps, oil bin and electric lamps advertising Shel and Pratts. Photo courtesy Gates Willard. Photo by E.W. Willard

Left to right: Minic Fire Station; small 00 Service Station. Photo courtesy Gates Willard. Photo by E.W. Willard

11M Tractor, headlights riveted to bar held in place by radiator, 1935

11MCF Tractor, camouflaged, 1940 (none produced postwar); fewer than fifty known to exist

12M Learner's Car, 1936, 1, 5

13M Racing Car, headlights, radiator and bumper stamped from one piece, 1936, fewer than 100 known to exist

14M Streamline Sports, 1935

15M Petrol Tank Lorry Oil Tanker, 1936, fewer than 100 known to exist

15MCF Petrol Tank Lorry, headlights, radiator and bumper stamped in one piece, camouflaged, 1940 (none produced postwar); fewer than 100 known to exist

16M Caravan, non-electric, house trailer, 1937

17M Vauxhall Tourer, headlights riveted to bar held in place by radiator, 1937

18M Vauxhall Town Coupe, headlights riveted to bar held in place by radiator, 1937

19M Vauxhall Cabriolet, headlights riveted to bar held in place by radiator, 1937

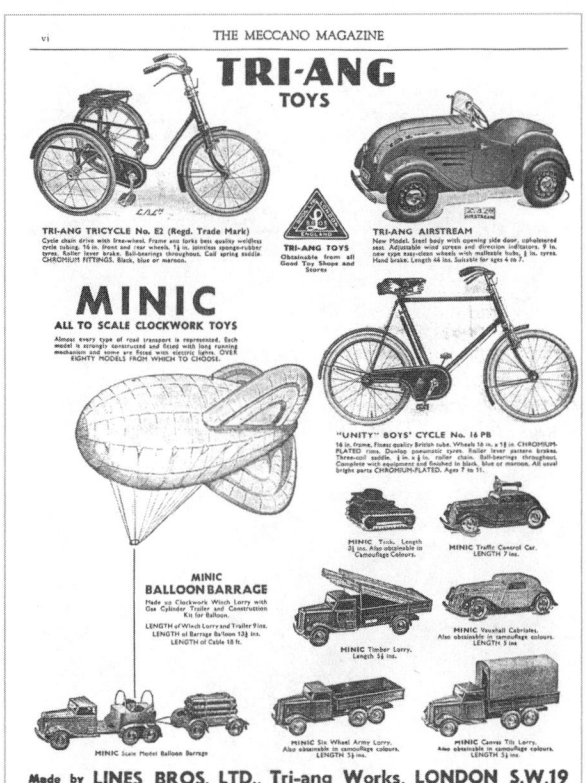

An ad from a 1940 Meccano Magazine *featuring The Balloon Barrage. At the time this toy debuted, England had been at war for a year. Photo courtesy Gates Willard*

This was the first Minic advertisement as shown in Meccano Magazine. *Courtesy Gates Willard*

Left to right: 7M Minic Town Coupe, 1935; 6M Cabriolet, 1935; 8M Open Touring Car, 1935. Photo courtesy Gates Willard. Photo by E.W. Willard

Left to right: 24MCF Minic Luton Van, camouflaged, 1940; 24M Luton Transport Van, 1936. Photo courtesy Gates Willard. Photo by E.W. Willard

Left to right: 4M Minic Sports Saloon, 1935; 5M Limousine, 1935. Photo courtesy Gates Willard. Photo by E.W. Willard

Four Minic Tourers. Left to right: 35M Rolls; 36M Daimler; 37M Bentley, non-electric (electric versions were never made); 55ME electric-lighted Bentley Tourer. Note the battery box in back in place of the rear seat. Photo courtesy Gates Willard. Photo by E.W. Willard

Minic Mechanical Horse and Pantechnicon. Left to right: typical 1935-1936 version; rare Brockhouse promotional. Photo courtesy Gates Willard. Photo by E.W. Willard

Left to right: 18M Minic Vauxhall Town Coupe, plain bumper and number plate, 1937; 8M Open Touring Car, with luggage rack and Shell can, 1935. Photo courtesy Gates Willard. Photo by E.W.Willard

Left to right: 21M Minic Transport Van, 1935; 22M Carter Paterson Van, 1936; 21M Transport Van, 1935; 21MCF Transport Van, camouflaged, 1940. Photo courtesy Gates Willard. Photo by E.W. Willard

Top to bottom: Minic Delivery Lorry with cases, 1936; Mechanical Horse and Trailer with cases; Delivery Lorry (Pickup Truck), 1935; Tip Lorry (Dump Truck), 1936. Photo courtesy Gates Willard. Photo by E.W. Willard

Left to right: 33M Minic Steam Roller; 11MCF Camouflaged Tractor; 26M Tractor and 11M Trailer with cases. Photo courtesy Gates Willard. Photo by E.W. Willard

Left to right: 37M Minic Bentley Tourer, non-electric, 1938; 55ME Bentley Tourer, electric. Photo courtesy Gates Willard. Photo by E.W. Willard

Left to right: Minic 12M Learner's Car, 1936; 13M Racing Car, 1936. Photo courtesy Gates Willard. Photo by E.W. Willard

The Minic Rolls Royce Sedanca with electric headlamps as sold by Bloomingdale's department store in New York City for $1.98. Also shown are the key and catalog that were included with every Minic, plus instruction/information sheets. Photo courtesy Gates Willard. Photo by E.W. Willard

Minic Sunshine Saloons. Left to right: 47M Rolls, non-electric; 45M Daimler, non-electric; 46M Bentley, non-electric. Photo courtesy Gates Willard. Photo by E.W. Willard

Two 38M Minic Caravan Sets. Left to right: 5M Limousine and 16M non-electric Caravan, 1937; 34M Tourer with Passengers, 1937, 34ME Caravan with electric light. Photo courtesy Gates Willard. Photo by E.W. Willard

Minic electric-lighted Sunshine Saloons. Left to right: Rolls; Daimler; Bentley. Photo courtesy Gates Willard. Photo by E.W. Willard

Left to right: Minic 32M Dust Cart, 1936; 54M Traction Engine and Trailer set, 1939. Photo courtesy Gates Willard. Photo by E.W. Willard

Left to right: 50ME Minic Rolls Sedanca; 51 ME Daimler Sedanca; 42M Rolls Sedance; 43M Daimler Sedanca. The two Minic Sedancas on the left have electric lights; the battery is inside the opening trunk. A turn screw operated the lamps. The two cars on the right are non-electric and there is no separate trunk lid. All postwar Rolls, Bentleys an. Photo courtesy Gates Willard. Photo by E.W. Willard

Left to right: 48M Minic Breakdown Lorry; 48CF Camouflaged Breakdown Lorry; 49ME Searchlight Lorry; 49MECF Camouflaged Searchlight Lorry. Also shown is an original Everready battery. Photo courtesy Gates Willard. Photo by E.W. Willard

19MCF Vauxhall Cabriolet, camouflaged, headlights riveted to bar held in place by radiator, 1940 (none produced postwar); fewer than 100 known to exist

20M Light Tank, painted either dark glossy green or gray, 1935 (none produced postwar)

20MCF Light Tank, camouflaged, 1940 (none produced postwar); fewer than fifty known to exist

21M Transport Van, headlights, radiator and bumper stamped in one piece, decals not used during first year produced, 1935

21MCF Transport Van, camouflaged, headlights, radiator and bumper stamped in one piece, 1940 (none made after WWII); fewer than 100 known to exist

22M Carter Paterson Van, headlights, radiator and bumper stamped in one piece, 1936

23M Tip Lorry Dump Truck, headlights, radiator and bumper stampd in one piece, 1936

24M Luton Transport Van Moving Van, headlights, radiator and bumper stamped in one piece, 1936

24MCF Luton Van, camouflaged, 1940 (none produced postwar)

25M Delivery Lorry w/cases, headlights, radiator and bumper stamped in one piece, 1936

26M Tractor and trailer with cases, 1936

27M, 28M - Numbers not used

29M Traffic Control Car (Police Car), headlights rivited to bar held inplace by radiator, 1938

30M Mechanical Horse and Pantechnicon, headlights, radiator and bumper stamped in one piece, decals not used during first year of production, 1935; a special non-numbered issue Brockhouse promotional was made c.1937; reportedly fewer than 100 made

31M Mechanical Horse and Fuel Oil Tanker, headlights rivited to bar held inplace by radiator, 1936

32M Dust Cart (Garbage Truck), headlights rivited to bar held inplace by radiator, 1936

33M Steam Roller, 1935

34M Tourer with Passengers, headlights, radiator and bumper stamped in one piece, 1937 (none produced postwar); fewer than 100 known to exist

35M Rolls Tourer, Non-electric, headlights rivited to bar held inplace by radiator, no front bumper, 1937 (none produced postwar)

36M Daimler Tourer, Non-electric, headlights rivited to bar held inplace by radiator, 1937 (none produced postwar)

37M Bentley Tourer, Non-electric, headlights rivited to bar held inplace by radiator, 1938 (none produced postwar)

38M Caravan Set (Limousine and Non-electric caravan), 1937; fewer than fifty known to exist

39M Taxi, 1938, rare if found in colors other than dark blue

40M Mechanical Horse and Trailer with cases, headlights, radiator and bumper stamped in one piece, 1936; fewer than 100 known to exist

41ME Caravan with electric light, 1937 (none produced postwar); fewer than 100 known to exist

42M Rolls Sedanca, Non-electric, headlights rivited to bar held inplace by radiator, no front bumper, 1937; fewer than 100 known to exist

43M Daimler Sedanca, Non-electric, headlights rivited to bar held inplace by radiator, 1937; fewer than 100 known to exist

44M Traction Engine, 1938; fewer than 100 known to exist

45M Bentley Sunshine Saloon, (Sunroof Sedan), Non-electric, headlights rivited to bar held inplace by radiator, 1938; fewer than fifty known to exist

46M Daimler Sunshine Saloon, non-electric, headlights rivited to bar held inplace by radiator, 1938; fewer than fifty known to exist

47M Rolls Sunshine Saloon, Non-electric, headlights rivited to bar held inplace by radiator, 1938; fewer than fifty known to exist

48M Breakdown Lorry (Wrecker Truck), headlights, radiator and bumper stamped in one piece, 1936

Minic toys, as pictured in the September 1937 issue of Meccano Magazine. *Courtesy Gates Willard*

The Minic line was becoming more sophisticated when this ad appeared in Meccano Magazine. *Courtesy Gates Willard*

Left to right: 50ME Rolls Sedanca; 51ME Daimler Sedanca; 42M Rolls Sedanca; 43M Daimler Sedanca. Four Minic Sedancas, the Rolls and Daimler on the left have electric lights, but the Rolls and Daimler on the right are non-electric. Bentley Sedancas were never made. Photo courtesy Gates Willard. Photo by E.W. Willard

Left to right: 56ME Minic Rolls Sunshine Saloon, electric, 1938; 51ME Daimler Sedanca, electric, 1937; 55ME Bentley Tourer, electric, 1938; 47M Rolls Sunshine Saloon, non-electric, 1938; 43M Daimler Sedanca, non-electric, 1937; 37M Bentley Tourer, non-electric, 1938. Photo courtesy Gates Willard. Photo by E.W. Willard

Left to right: 61M Minic Double-Deck Bus; 53M Single-Deck Bus. These buses were produced in red, beige or two-tone green. All four were separately numbered in trade catalog. Photo courtesy Gates Willard. Photo by E.W. Willard

Left to right: 62ME Minic Fire Engine, with electric headlamps and attachments (hoses are in an opening compartment), 1936; 39M Taxi, 1938; 29M Traffic Control Car (Police Car), 1938. Photo courtesy Gates Willard. Photo by E.W. Willard

Left to right: 71M Minic Mechanical Horse and Milk Trailer, 1939; 72M Mechanical Horse and Lorry with barrels, 1939. Photo courtesy Gates Willard. Photo by E.W. Willard

Left to right: 67M Minic Farm Lorry; 68M Timber Lorry; 72M Mechanical Horse and Lorry with barrels. Photo courtesy Gates Willard. Photo by E.W. Willard

Left to right: 17M Minic Vauxhall Tourer, 1937l; 18M Vauxhall Town Coupe; 19M Vauxhall Cabriolet; 19MCF Vauxhall Cabriolet, camouflaged, 1940. Photo courtesy Gates Willard. Photo by E.W. Willard

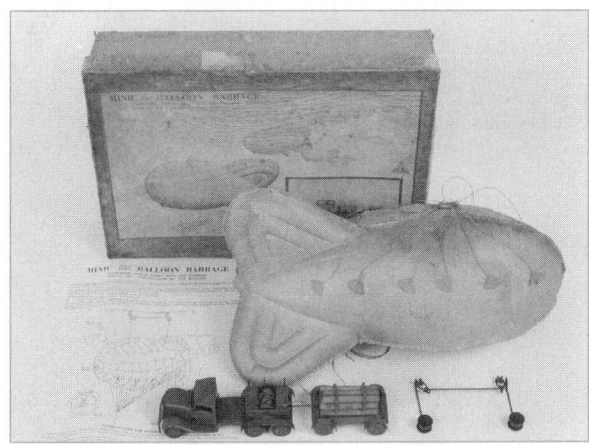

76M Minic Balloon Barrage Wagon and Trailer. Photo courtesy Gates Willard. Photo by E.W. Willard

Left to right: 69M Minic Canvas Tilt Lorry; 69MCF Camouflaged Canvas Tilt Lorry; 66M Six-wheel Army Lorry; 66MCF Camouflaged Six-wheel Army Lorry. Photo courtesy Gates Willard. Photo by E.W. Willard

48MCF Breakdown Lorry, camouflaged, headlights, radiator and bumper stamped in one piece, 1940 (none produced postwar); fewer than fifty known to exist

49ME Searchlight Lorry, headlights, radiator and bumper stamped in one piece, 1936 (none produced postwar)

49MECF Searchlight Lorry, camouflaged, headlights, radiator and bumper stamped in one piece, 1940 (none produced postwar); fewer than fifty known to exist

50ME Rolls Sedanca, electric, no front bumper, electric headlights, 1936 (none produced postwar); fewer than fifty known to exist

51ME Daimler Sedanca, electric, electric headlights, 1937 (none produced postwar); fewer than fifty known to exist

52M Single Deck Bus, red, 1936

53M Single Deck Bus, green, 1936

54M Traction Engine and Trailer, 1939; fewer than fifty known to exist

55ME Bentley Tourer, electric (production probably delayed), electric headlights, 1938 (none produced postwar); fewer than fifty known to exist

56ME Rolls Sunshine Saloon, electric, electric headlights, 1938 (none produced postwar); fewer than fifty known to exist

57ME Bentley Sunshine Saloon electric, electric headlights, 1938 (none produced postwar); fewer than fifty known to exist

58ME Daimler Sunshine Saloon electric, electric headlights, 1938 (none produced postwar); fewer than fifty known to exist

59ME Caravan Set, tourer with passengers and caravan with electric light, 1937 (none produced postwar); fewer than fifty known to exist

60M Double Deck Bus, red, 1935

61M Double Deck Bus, green, 1935 (none produced postwar); fewer than fifty known to exist

62ME Fire Engine, electric headlights, 1936

63M No. 1 Presentation Set, 1937 (none produced postwar); fewer than fifty known to exist

64M No. 2 Presentation Set, 1937 (none produced postwar); fewer than fifty known to exist

65M Construction Set, 1936 (none produced postwar); fewer than fifty known to exist

66M Six Wheel Army Lorry, ten wheel, painted dark glossy green, headlights, radiator and bumper stamped in one piece, 1939 (none produced postwar); fewer than 100 known to exist

66MCF Six Wheel Army Lorry, camouflaged, headlights, radiator and bumper stamped in one piece, 1939-1940; fewer than 100 known to exist

Left to right: Minic 15MCF Camouflaged Petrol Tank Lorry, 1940; 20M Light Tank, 1935; 20MCF Camouflaged Light Tank, 1940. Photo courtesy Gates Willard. Photo by E.W. Willard

67M Farm Lorry, headlights, radiator and bumper stamped in one piece, 1939-1940; fewer than fifty known to exist

68M Timber Lorry, headlights, radiator and bumper stamped in one piece, 1939; fewer than fifty known to exist

69M Canvas Tilt Lorry (Enclosed Army Truck), ten wheel, painted dark glossy green, headlights, radiator and bumper stamped in one piece, 1939-1940; fewer than fifty known to exist

69MCF Canvas Tilt Lorry, camouflaged, ten wheel, headlights, radiator and bumper stamped in one piece, 1940-1940

70M Coal Lorry not made, cataloged but never made, 1939 ·

71M Mechanical Horse and Milk Trailer, number on box is "70M," headlights, radiator and bumper stamped in one piece, 1939; fewer than fifty known to exist

72M Mechanical Horse and Lorry with Barrels, number on box is "71M," headlights, radiator and bumper stamped in one piece, 1939; fewer than fifty known to exist

73M Cable Lorry, prewar, not made, cataloged as prewar, but not made until postwar, 1939

74M Log Lorry, number on box is "75M," headlights, radiator and bumper stamped in one piece, 1939; fewer than fifty known to exist

75M Ambulance, prewar, not made, cataloged as prewar, but not made until postwar, 1939

76M Balloon Barrage Wagon and Trailer, production delayed until 1940 made in camouflage only; should have been numbered 76MCF; 1939-1940; fewer than fifty known to exist

77M Double Deck Trolley Bus, cataloged but never made, 1939

78M Pool Tanker, headlights, radiator and bumper stamped in one piece, 1939-1940; fewer than fifty known to exist

79M Mechanical Horse and Pool Tanker, headlights, radiator and bumper stamped in one piece, 1939-1940; fewer than fifty known to exist

MINNITOYS BY OTACO LIMITED

Based in Ontario Canada, Minitoys produced a number of pressed steel trucks with advertising themes.

Contributor: John Taylor, P.O. Box 63, Nolensville, TN 37135-0063

	C6	C8	C10
Auto Wrecker, #216,	350	500	800
B/A Gasoline Trailer Truck, 29" long	300	450	725
Beaver Lumber Truck, 1950s, 29" long	300	450	725
Country Good Soups Trailer Truck, 1950s, 29" long	275	425	700

Minnitoys Heinz Ketchup Trailer Truck, 1950s, 29". Photo courtesy John Taylor

Minnitoys Heinz Pickles Trailer Truck, Canada, 1950s, 29". Photo courtesy John Taylor

	C6	C8	C10
Daily Star Weekly Truck, 29" long.........	400	800	1275
Fina Trailer Truck, 29" long	400	600	1000
Heinz Ketchup Trailer Truck, 1950s,			
29" long...	250	400	650
Heinz Soups, 29" long.............................	NPF	NPF	1500
Heinz Tomato Juice	250	400	650
Heinz Tomato Juice Trailer Truck	275	425	675
Hienz Pickles Trailer Truck, 1950s,			
29" long...	225	375	600
Hochelaga Superflame	600	NPF	NPF
Imperial Esso, 29" long	350	500	800
Irving Gasoline Tanker Truck, 1950s,			
16" long...	400	600	1000
Minni Construction Dump Truck,			
hydraulic, 1950s, 16" long	200	350	550
Minnitoy Wrecker, 1950s, 18" long.........	350	500	800
North Star Oil Ltd, 29" long....................	350	500	800
Shell Tanker Truck, 1950s, 29" long	225	375	600
Sunoco Trailer Truck, 29" long................	500	NPF	NPF

	C6	C8	C10
Super Test Trailer Truck, 29" long	350	500	800
Texaco Gasoline Tanker Truck, 1950s,			
29" long...	225	375	600
Tippet-Richardson Moving & Storage,			
29" long...	400	600	1000
White Rose Tanker Trailer, 1950s,			
29" long...	350	500	800

Minnitoys Good Soups Tractor Trailer, French inscription.
Photo courtesy John Taylor

MISCELLANEOUS

	C6	C8	C10
Bus, "Twin Coach Buffalo, Niagara			
Lines," 15-1/2" long, aluminum	2500	3500	6000
Roberts Refuse Dump Truck, 1950s	68	102	135
Roberts U-Ride-It Fire Rescue Van,			
21" long...	175	263	350
Robot Bus, see Woodhaven."Rocket"			
Pedal Car...	450	675	900

	C6	C8	C10
Roi-Tan Cigars, promotional car			
w/pic of Sophie Tucker......................	130	195	260
Scientific Forklift	100	135	67
Tractor, looks like Arcade, but has			
nickeled driver, 3" long	NPF	NPF	NPF

MITTEN

Although the Mitten Toy Mfg. Co. was best known for its puppets and toy animals, it did release at least one toy vehicle from its Broadway, N.Y. location.

	C6	C8	C10
Dunlop Stake Truck, 16" long	100	150	200

MODERN TOYS (MT)

The Chicago-based Modern Toy Co. released several vehicle toys in the boomer era.

	C6	C8	C10
Convertible, 9" long	125	188	250
Mobilgas Tanker	80	120	160
Stunt Car, No. 27, battery-op	35	52	70
Tin Lizzie, wind-up.................................	NPF	NPF	NPF

Modern Toys Tin Lizzie.
Photo courtesy Tim Oei

MOHAWK TOY

The Mohawk Metal Toy Company was founded by Samuel Hoffman (brother-in-law of Julius Chein, who left Chein to start Mohawk and return at the request of his sister, Elizabeth, who assumed the Chein presidency after the 1926 death of her husband) and was only in business from 1919 to 1921. During its

short history, Mohawk produced a number of tin vehicles in addition to metal novelties.

	C6	C8	C10
Blue Bird Taxi, wind-up, 6" long..............	188	282	375
Dump Truck, tin, 7" long, 1920	NPF	NPF	NPF
Main Street Trolley Car, tin, 6-1/2" long .	NPF	NPF	NPF

	C6	C8	C10
Metropolitan Groceries, tin wind-up, 6" long..	170	255	340
Racer, No. 13, wind-up, driver, front window, 6-3/4" long	125	250	375
Yellow Taxi	275	363	550

MOKO

Moses Kohnstam not only manufactured toys, he also ran a large wholesale house and had his toys made to order by toy companies such as Guntermann, Distler, and Fischer. He became a distributor for Gama, Tippco, Levy, Carette, and other companies. Most special-order toys carried the "MOKO" logo. Kohnstam died in 1912, leaving the business to his sons, Willi and Emil. His other son, Julius, had opened a branch office in England before 1900. The company closed in 1933, as many other Jewish businesses in Germany prior to World War II. Emil fled to England, while Willi stayed in Germany. Willi died one year later. Emil joined his brother Julius to help run the English firm. Julius died in 1935. The MOKO Company survived, however, and is still in business today.

Contributor: Bob Smith, RATS Toy Shows, 255 Tryon Park, Rochester, NY 14609. (585) 288-7153, bird@oldtoysonline.com

	C6	C8	C10
Flying Police Squad, clockwork motor battery searchlight, 10" long	1200	2100	2900
Kohnstam Sedan, four-cylinder, green/black, c.1928, 8" long	600	850	1350
Limousine, six-cylinder, green/black, 9-1/2" long, clockwork motor runs car in forward and reverse while pistons on top of engine move up and down; doors and hood open; c.1927, 9-1/2" long	900	1200	2000
Motorcycle w/rider, spring action, 7-1/2" long	1300	2200	3000
Motorcycle w/rider, tin clockwork, 8-1/2" long	1600	2800	4200

Moko Six-Cylinder Limousine, green and black, late 1920s, 9-1/2".

Moko Motorcycle and Rider, tin clockwork, 8-1/2". Photo courtesy Bertoia Auctions

Moko Motorcycle and Rider, spring action, 7-1/2". Photo courtesy Bertoia Auctions

MORMAC

	C6	C8	C10
Convertible, plastic, 9-3/4" long	30	45	60

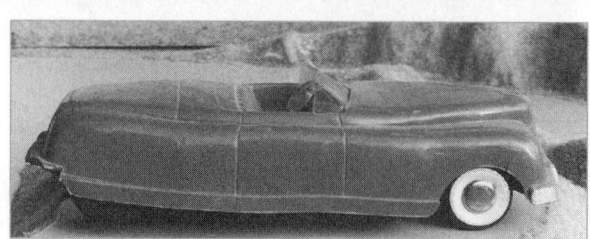

Mormac Convertible, plastic, 9-3/4". Photo courtesy Ron Fink

MOXIE

The Main-based soft drink company that advertised "Beverage Moxie Nerve Food" or Moxie for short, began in 1884 and enjoyed national popularity until it was surpassed by Coca-Cola in the 1920s. Known for its aggressive advertising campaigns, Moxie appeared in signage across the country. One of the company's more unusual advertising gags was the Moxiemobile or Moxie Horse Car. A life-sized horse was fabricated within a real car bearing Moxie logos (if you know the make and model of that car, be sure to drop me a line and let me know) and the driver sat mounted on the horse. The steering column ran up through the horse so the "horse rider" could drive the car.

The tin toy replica of that Moxie Horse Car is represented in the listing below.

	C6	C8	C10
Horse Car, based on the actual Moxie soft drink promotional vehicle, tin lithographed, 8" long	275	500	750

MPC (MULTIPLE PRODUCTS CORP.)

Known for its dime-store plastic figures, MPC also released vehicles.

	C6	C8	C10
Dump Truck, 7-1/4" long	11	16	22
Firewagon, three figures, ten accessories	12	18	25
Halftrack, plastic, 1960s	12	18	25

MPC Halftrack, plastic, 1960s.
Photo courtesy John McCurdy

MURRAY

Known for its pedal cars and as the parent company of the Steelcraft pressed-steel toys, the Murray-Ohio Mfg. Co. was an active manufacturer of wheeled toys. The firm survived the Depression because of its Steelcraft line and began wheeled toy production following World War II, making tricycles, wagons, and pedal cars. It ceased operations in 1973.

	C6	C8	C10
Buick Pedal Car, 1949	1500	2700	4600
Camaro Pedal Car, 1968	88	132	175
Champion Pedal Car	500	850	1150
Clipper Pedal Car	550	900	1200
Comet Pedal Car, 1956	800	1400	2000
Country Squire Station Wagon Pedal Car, 1955	325	488	650

	C6	C8	C10
Earth Mover Pedal Car, 1959	550	850	1200
Fire Chief Pedal Car	500	800	1100
Fire Truck Pedal Car	200	300	400
Golden Wildcat Pedal Car, 1961	425	635	850
Pace Car Pedal Car, 1959	500	800	1100
Pontiac Station Wagon Pedal Car, 1948	950	1500	2200
Racer Pedal Car, No. 8, 1960	215	322	430
Radio Sports Car, 1959	480	720	960
Speedway Pace Car, 1959	500	800	1100
Suburban Pedal Car, 1950	550	850	1200
Super Wildcat Pedal Car, 1961	350	525	700
Tee Bird Pedal Car, 1961	140	210	280
Tractor Pedal Car, c.1950	400	600	800

NEFF-MOON

Neff-Moon, of Sandusky, Ohio, was owned by William Moon and Charles Neff. Production of its pressed steel toys began in 1923. Its toys featured bodies that could be used interchangeably on a single chassis. The firm, which was located above a grocery, was apparently an early victim of the Depression.

	C6	C8	C10
10 Toys in 1 Set, No. 14	500	750	1040
Coupe	NPF	NPF	NPF
Dump truck	NPF	NPF	NPF

Neff-Moon Coupe. Photo courtesy Don Hultzman

Neff-Moon Emergency Truck. Photo courtesy Don Hultzman

Neff-Moon Sedan, 12". Photo courtesy Don Hultzman

Neff-Moon Dump Truck. Photo courtesy Don Hultzman

	C6	C8	C10
Emergency Truck	NPF	NPF	NPF
Groceries Van	175	262	350
Sedan	NPF	NPF	NPF
Sedan, 12" long	500	800	1100
Sedan Delivery Truck	350	525	700
Taxi, 12" long	350	525	700
Tow Truck, c.1925, 16" long	200	300	400
Truck, interchangable	NPF	NPF	NPF

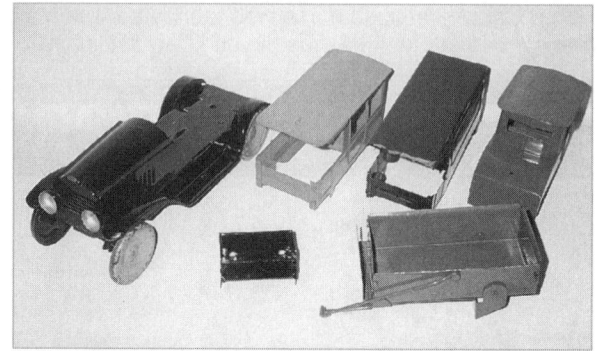

Neff-Moon Convertible Auto Sets and Interchangeable Toys. Photo courtesy Don Hultzman'

NIFTY

The Nifty trademark was owned by the George Borgfelt Corp. of New York City. Nifty was among the first companies to acquire rights to produce toys attached to specific cartoon characters.

	C6	C8	C10
Bus, double decker, tin wind-up, 9" long	800	1400	2200
Felix the Cat Car, "Speedy Felix"	1000	1700	2750
Skidoodle, tin wind-up	1800	2900	4000
Truck, automatic tilter, w/driver, 9-1/2" long	600	950	1350

Nifty Speedy Felix the Cat car.

Nifty Skiddodle. Photo courtesy PB Eighty-four

Felix the Cat "Speedy Felix" in car. Photo courtesy Christie's East

NOMA

Famous for its inventive electric Christmas lights, the Noma Electric Corp. altered production during World War II to products made of non-essential materials. The result included several toys.

	C6	C8	C10
Car and Trailer, 1940s	65	98	130
Low Boy, wooden	100	150	200
Steam Shovel, wooden	90	135	180
Tank, wooden, WWII	30	45	60
Truck, wooden, 1940s	45	68	90

Noma Tank, wooden with a 4" wood peg sticking out at the top for reasons unknown. Photo courtesy Jack Matthews

NORTH & JUDD

North & Judd, located in New Britain, Connecticut, made cast-iron toys for S.H. Kress during the year of 1930. Its original designs appear to have been marked with the company's name, but, for the most part, its toys are unmarked. The company currently makes quality hardware.

	C6	C8	C10
Austin Convertible, open top, marked "North & Judd"	NPF	NPF	NPF
Austin Sedan, two-door, marked "North & Judd"	NPF	NPF	NPF
Bus, looks like Dent, 4-2/3" long	NPF	NPF	NPF
Ford Model A Coupe, looks like Arcade,has driver in window, trunk at rear, left cab 1-1/2" long	NPF	NPF	NPF
Ford Model T Stake Truck, like Arcade's, but marked "Anchor Truck Co." (an anchor is North & Judd's trademark), 8-3/4" long	1500	2500	4200

	C6	C8	C10
Motorcycle Cop, Hubley's "Cop," separate nickeled driver is held by mushrooms at front of handle-bars and on driver's feet	NPF	NPF	NPF
Semi-Trailer Stake Truck, marked "North & Judd"	NPF	NPF	NPF

North & Judd Semi-Trailer Stake Truck. Photo courtesy Terry Sells

NOSCO PLASTICS

Nosco Plastics was a division of the National Organ Supply Company of Erie, Penn. Founded in 1920 by Harry H. Kugel, National Organ Supply produced replacement parts for commercial pipe organs. The forward-thinking Kugel realized that the electric organ would one day be a reality and sought to diversify the company's offerings. In 1934, the patent for the first electric organ was granted to Laurens Hammond. National Organ Supply created its Nosco Plastics Division the following year and produced custom injection-molded plastic parts.

Nosco Hot See Hot Rod, friction, 10-1/4". Photo courtesy Terry Sells

Nosco Doodle-Bug, 9-1/2". Photo courtesy Terry Sells

Nosco Cop-Cycle, friction, 5-1/2". Photo courtesy Terry Sells

Nosco Vizy Vee Stockar Racer, 9-1/4". Photo courtesy Terry Sells

Following World War II, Nosco Plastics ventured into the toy business with two vehicles, the wind-up bus and station wagon. The toys were a hit and the line expanded in 1949 to include more wind-up toys, several planes, and even a few trains. Given the high quality of Nosco's offerings, it's a shame that they didn't produce a greater variety of toys, but the majority of their business was to supply large

The Vizy Vee and the Hot 'See Hot Rod were among the vehicles pictured in this Nosco advertisement.

quantities of the plastic figures and novelties found as prizes in Cracker Jack boxes.

Some of its toys appear in a 1952-53 *Toy Year Book*. In 1954 its address in Erie was 17th and Cascade Street. The toy division was sold to Saunders Tool & Die Co. of Aurora, Ill., in 1955 and the Nosco name never appeared on another toy.

	C6	C8	C10
Ace Indianapolis Mechanical Racer, No. 6390, plastic, wind-up w/attached key, "5" on hood, 1949, 8" long	60	100	160
Auto-Mite "Woodie" Station Wagon, plastic w/plastic gears and keys, 1949, 3-1/2" long			
Auto-Mite Coupe, plastic, wind-up motor w/attached key, plastic wheels, assorted colors, 1949, 3-5/8" long	20	40	65
Auto-Mite Sedan, plastic, 2-door sedan, wind-up motor w/attached key, assorted colors, No. 6360, 1949, 3-1/2" long	20	40	65
Auto-Mite Wrecker, plastic w/plastic gears and keys, No. 6360, 1949, 3-1/2" long	NPF	NPF	NPF
Bus, marked "Nosco Lines," assorted colors, wind-up motor w/attached key, 1948, 4" long	20	40	65
Cop-Cycle, friction, with sidecar, driver and passenger, No. 6357, 1949, 5-1/2" long	125	275	400
Doodle-Bug, No. 6381, plastic, wind-up w/attached key, rubber tires, 1949, 9-1/2" long	100	200	300
Fire Truck, No. 6386, plastic, friction motor w/siren, 6 firemen, tools, 1949, 7-1/2" long	NPF	NPF	NPF
Hot'See Hot Rod, friction, see through working 4-cylinder motor, No. 6490, 1951, 10-1/4" long	80	120	160
Pokey Joe Fire-Pumper, No. 6430, plastic, 10-1/2" long	NPF	NPF	NPF
Roaring Roadster, blue, red and yellow plastic, friction motor, #66 on trunk, rubber tires, yellow driver, 1950s, 8" long	75	135	185
Station Wagon, assorted colors, wind-up motor w/attached key, assorted colors, No. 6335SW, 1948, 4" long	20	40	65
Vizy Vee Stockar Racer, No. 6565, friction motor, visible V-8, assorted colors, 1952, 9-1/4" long	70	110	180

NYLINT

The Nylint Tool and Manufacturing Company was formed in 1937 by Bernard C. Klint and David Nyberg (thus its name) in Rockford, Illinois. Toy production began in the spring of 1946. Since 1951, the firm has concentrated on the production of heavy-duty scale reproductions, in steel, of earth-moving equipment and over-the-road trucks. Jeff L. Hubbard provided part of the following list.

Exclusives

	C6	C8	C10
Admiral TV Van, No. 5802, Ford Econoline with decals on both sides and all doors; special premium available through Admiral TV delaers, very rare, 1966	75	325	650
Big Dig Shovel, No. SR1100, Sears exclusive; orange and black, all steel except for rubber tracks; later versions (non-exclusives) available in orange yellow and black while track wheels were yellow plastic, 1964-65	50	140	275
Chase and Sanborne Stake Truck, No. 4501, same as No. 4500 but with coffee boxes (add 75 percent premium if present), 1964	75	175	350

Nylint Ranch Truck, Chase & Sanborn version, 14". Photo courtesy Bob Smith

	C6	C8	C10
Culligan Water Van, No. 5803, dark blue Ford Econoline with white top and Culligan decals on sides and doors; very rare, 1966	75	275	550
Gambles Stores Pickup, No. 8001, white Ford Econoline with green top, 1966...	75	175	350
Hertz Rental Truck, No. 8401, same as No. 8400 but exclusive to Sears; yellow cab, black base, silver cargo box, Hertz decals; rare, 1967	85	250	500
JC Penney Wrecker, No. 6001, light blue Ford Econoline Wrecker with white boom; available only form the JC Penney's wishbook, 1966	75	250	500
Lawn and Garden Set, No. SR1200/ 5439, Sears exclusive, 1964-65	50	175	350
Michigan Shovel (crane), No. 2201, redesigned version (made to look like Tonka mobile crane); clamshell bucket; this toy continued with number changes until the mid-1980s, 1966-73 .	50	150	300
Mobile Home Trailer, No. 6602, dark blue cab with white top, no extras, large "N" logo on cab doors, 1966	75	325	650
Mobile Home Trailer, No. 6603, American Transit Mobile Home Movers and other variations, 1964-66 .	100	350	700
Mobile Home Trailer, No. 6601, aqua blue or turquoise with white or light tan top, 27 pieces of furniture, one-piece grille/ bumper on front, round "6601" decal on cab doors, 1965	75	300	600
Philco Radio Camper, No. 5302	75	325	650
Telescopic Crane, No. 2500, green with white boom for 1959 NY Toy Fair (won award for toy of the year); rare, 1957-60	150	225	450
Trailblazer Camper, No. 5301, green and white Econoline camper, 1969-72	35	65	125

Nylint Elevating Scraper.

	C6	C8	C10
Truck and Haul-It Trailer, No. 9401, rare; knock-off of U-Haul Trailer with similar decals, 1969	50	175	350
Twin Hopper Dump Truck, No. 1420, Sears exclusive; yellow semi tractor pulling two hopper dump trailers, black dump doors and operating levers, 1967..	125	225	450
U-Haul Van, No. 5801, orange Ford Econoline, white U-Haul decals, 1966-67	50	200	400
U-Haul Van Set, No. SR1000/ 5465, Sears exclusive; orange and white Ford Pickup, U-Haul Van (closed type), and trailer with race car, 1962 ...	75	200	400
Western Auto Econoline Pickup, No. 5201, rare, 1964	75	225	450

Regular Issue

	C6	C8	C10
Aerial Ladder Fire Truck, No. 1210, red with white ladders and black handwheels; Nylint's first large fire truck, 1968-74......................................	75	140	275
Aerial Ladder Fire Truck, No. 1211, second version of No. 1210 (less steel), 1975-	50	100	200
Airport Courtesy Van, No. 6900, Ford Econoline Van, yellow with Holiday Inn decals on sides and doors; rare, 1964, 12" long.................................	75	350	700
Amazing Car, No. 600, wind-up; green or blue; box commands a premium (contains operating instructions), 1946-49	75	150	300
Amazing Car, No. 600, wind-up; red; box commands a premium (contains operating instructions), 1946-49	50	125	250
Ambulance, No. 6700, white Ford Econoline Van with red crosses on sides and doors; included stretcher, interior seats, red flasher light, 1964-67, 12" long	50	150	300
American Oil Emergency Truck, No. 6000, red Ford Econoline Wrecker, white boom, with or without American Oil decals, 1963-69, 11-1/4" long........	50	150	300
Army Ambulance, No. 7300, olive drab Ford Econoline Van, stretcher, red cross decals on sides and doors, red flasher light on top, 1965, 12" long	50	175	350
Backhoe, No. 1310, yellow backhoe on rubber crawler tracks with black base, 1968-73	75	140	275
Beach Buggy, No. 2310, 1969-72............	25	40	75
Big Dig, No. 1100, regular version..........	50	115	225
Big Dig, No. 1101, re-design of No. SR1100 to look like Tonka's Mighty Cranes; orange, yellow and black with yellow plastic track wheels, 1967-70...	50	100	200
Big Haul Dump, No. 9200, yellow and black, reminiscent of Tonka's Mighty Dump Truck, 1966-68	45	125	250
Big Haul Dump, No. 9201, same as No. 9200 but larger wheels, 1969-72...	45	125	250
Bobcat Loader, No. 2070, yellow and black trim, 1970-................................	35	65	125
Boysen Paints Stake Truck, No. 4502, same as No. 4500, 1964....................	75	200	400
Bronco Bobcat, No. 2410, dark red Bronco with white top and larger wheels, 1969-72.................................	35	85	175

	C6	C8	C10
Bronco Petmobile, No. 1710, dark blue Ford Bronco, white plastic cage for dogs, 1968-70s	40	115	225
Bronco Police Car, No. 1610, white Ford Bronco with lights and black trim, 1968	35	75	150
Bulldozer, No. 4200, orange with towbar instead of winch (1967-70); yellow with towbar (1971-72), 1967-72	50	125	250
Bulldozer, No. 4200, all yellow with rear chain winch (1961-65); yellow with orange winch (1967-70); black plastic motor, 1961-70	50	150	300
Camper Pickup, No. 4400, red Ford pickup truck with two-piece front grille/bumper, white topper camper, two green air mattresses, 1961-63, 13-1/2" long	50	125	250
Car Carrier, No. 8900, yellow car carrier; three cars (1967-68); two cars (1969-77); several color variations for cars, 1967-77	50	150	300
Construction Four-Wheel Platform Dump, No. 4600, 15-3/4" long	100	150	225
Construction Set, No. 5700, orange No. 5000 Dump and Cement Mixer with yellow drum, Econoline Pickup Truck and Open Stake Trailer; rare, 1962-64.	100	300	600
Countdown Rocket Launcher, No. 3500, three rockets (Atlas, Jupiter, Thor) in various colors; gray gantry crane, dark blue base with yellow, black, or red countdown dial; last Nylint toy from the 1950s and second plastic toy, 1959-61, 21" long	50	125	250
Custom Camper Econoline Pickup Truck, No. 5300, aqua green truck and plastic camper with opening windows and rear door, slide-out steps under rear door, 1962-66, 12-1/2" long	50	125	250
Custom Camper on Pickup Truck with Boat, No. 5400, with red and green sailboat on trailer, 1962-65, 23-1/2" long	75	175	350
Deliverall, No. 1000, wind-up; three-wheeled scooter with large cargo box; white, yellow, red, blue and black; rare, 1946-51, 10" long	100	300	600
Dump Truck, No. 5100, red truck, yellow dump box, two-piece grille/bumper (1962-64); red/yellow truck, one-piece grille/bumper (1965); light green truck, white dump box, one-piece grille/bumper (1966), 1962-66, 13-1/2"	50	140	275

Nylint Ford Cab-over Tow Truck, 17". Photo courtesy Bob Smith

	C6	C8	C10
Dump Truck with Cement Mixer, No. 5000, yellow truck with round decal on doors and two-piece front grille/bumper (1962-64); yellow/green truck with special decal on mixer (1965); yellow body, green dump box, large N logo decal on doors (1966); cement mixer is always yellow, 1962-66, 20-1/2" long	75	200	400
Econoline Pickup Truck, No. 5200, dual headlights (1962); teardrop headlights (1963-72); red/white truck (1962-65); yellow with black roof (1966-72), 1962-72, 11-1/4" long	50	125	250
Electronic Cannon Truck, No. 2400, with yellow radar antenna and four rockets, 1957-59, 22-1/2" long	75	150	300
Electronic Cannon Truck, No. 2400, no radar antenna; four red/black-tipped rockets; Nylint's second battery-operated toy, 1956	75	150	300
Elevating Scraper, No. 2010, two-wheel tractor with large earthmover with rubber belt, pan scraper trailer (looked like a Caterpillar earthmover), 1969-73	75	200	400
Elgin Street Sweeper, No. 2300, battery-operated version, closed cab; yellow cab roof, red/yellow body (1956); red cab roof, yellow body (1957), 1956-57	50	175	350
Elgin Street Sweeper, No. 1100, wind-up; yellow with red and black highlights, white plastic driver; bottom and side brooms rotate, 1950-52, 8-1/4" long	50	175	350
Farm Set, No. 9900, one of four farm sets made by Nylint; included light blue and white Ford Bronco, Ford			

Nylint Tournarocker, 1950s, open tractor, driver, 18". Photo courtesy Thomas G. Nefos

Nylint Vacationer Bronco and Travel Trailer, 1960s, 20". Photo courtesy John Taylor

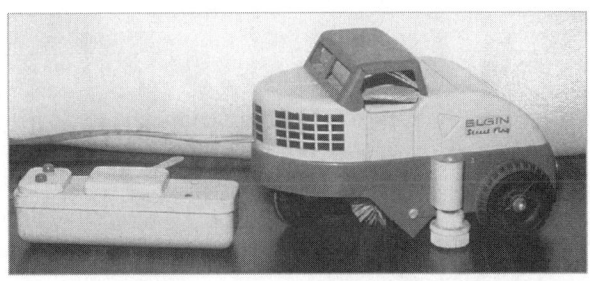

Nylint Elgin Street Sweeper, 1950s, battery-operated, closed cab. Photo courtesy Frank McCormick

	C6	C8	C10
Econoline Pickup, Stake Truck and trailer, 1968-71	75	175	350
Farm Set, No. 5600, with light blue/ white No. 4500 Stake Truck, light blue/white No. 5200 Econoline Pickup Truck and other assorted pieces, 1962-64	75	175	350
Ford Bronco, No. 8200, listed in the 1965 catalog as a Roustabout but was changed to a Bornco right after the catalog was printed, 1965-69, 12-1/2" long	50	140	275
Ford Econoline Van, No. 5800, purple with white decals; dark pink or maroon (1964 only), 1963-64, 12" long	50	175	350
Ford Pickup & U-Haul Box Trailer, No. 4100, orange pickup, white cab roof, orange trailer with white/cream top and opening rear door; trucks made before 1965 have two-piece front grille (trucks from 1965-66 with one-piece front grille/bumper and I-beam suspension), 1961-66	75	175	350
Ford Platform Tilt Truck, No. 3900, metallic blue, white cab roof with tilt cab, narrow side panels on rear bed, 1960, 15-3/4" long	75	175	350

Nylint Payloader, No. 1600, 1950s. Photo courtesy Continental Hobby House

Nylint Speed Swing, No. 2000, 1955-58, 19". Photo courtesy Thomas G. Nefos

	C6	C8	C10
Ford Rapid Delivery Truck, No. 3600, dark blue cabover Ford truck with white stake racks and working lift gate, tilt cab with motor; first Nylint toy of 1960s, 1960-62, 18-1/4" long	75	175	300
Ford Sales & Service, No. 3800, aqua green with utility rack and ladder, 1960-61, 13-5/8" long	50	175	350
Ford Speedway Truck with Racer, No. 4000, dark tan pickup with white top and trailer and race car, 1960-63, 24-3/4" long	75	140	275
Ford U-Haul Rental Fleet, No. 4300, includes orange Ford pickup, orange U-Haul van and orange U-Haul open trailer; pickup has two-piece front grille bumper (1961-64), one-piece bumper and I-beam suspension (1965), 1960s	75	225	450
Fun on Farm Econoline Truck Set, No. 7100, 29 piecesFord Econoline Pickup with farm family, farming items, plus small cans of paint to customize your farm family, 1964-65, 11-1/4" long	50	175	350
Grader-Loader, No. 3000, first version with remote bucket release (1959 only); yellow, black bucket; first Nylint construction toy to have plastic tractor wheels (to keep shipping weight low), 1959-62, 23-3/4" long	75	150	300
Guided Missile Carrier, No. 2800, first version (1958), non-firing missiles, 1958-59, 15-1/2" long	75	125	250
Guided Missile Carrier, No. 2800, later version (through 1960), firing cone of missiles, side-mounted forklift with red/ yellow pallet, white missile with red fins and red nose cone, 1958-59	75	125	250
Happy Acres Truck with Horses, No. 4700, same as No. 4500 but red truck with white stakes, large picture decal on doors, 1961-63, 14" long	75	150	300
Happy Ranchers Set, No. 7200, Stake Truck with Open Stake Trailer, both light blue and white, 1964	75	175	350
Highway Emergency Unit Truck, No. 3400, large cabover Ford wrecker, white with red cab roof, red dolly and wrecker boom; later versions without boom hoist (only hook hoist); with whitewall tires and tilt cab with motor (1963 only), 1959-63, 18-5/8" long (3400)	50	150	300

Nylint Michigan Shovel, No. 2200, 1955-65, 31-1/2".

	C6	C8	C10
Hopper Dump, No. 1410, regular single-trailer version; yellow with black dump doors, 1968-69	75	150	300
Horse Van Semi Truck, No. 6300, brownish-gold truck, white doors, decals, four horses and ponies; two-piece grille/bumper on front (1963-64); one-piece grille/bumper (1965-67); light blue and white truck (1967 only), 1963-67, 23-1/2"	50	175	350
Hot Rod, No. 1910, 1969-72	25	40	75
Hydraulic Big Haul Dump Truck, No. 9801, orange and black, new tires, 1969-73	35	140	275
Hydraulic Big Haul Dump Truck, No. 9800, orange and black, 1967-68	35	140	275
Hydraulic Dump, No. 4600, same as No. 2700 but orange with yellow/black decals, front grille guard in yellow/black, hollow plastic wheels, 1961-66	50	125	250
Hydraulic Dump Truck, No. 6100, beige truck with red dump box; two-piece grille/bumper (1963-64); one-piece grille bumper (1965-70), 1963-70	75	150	300
Jalopy, No. 6800, Ford hot rod in red with white top or light blue with white top (1964); also No. 6801 with seats, available in same colors as 1964 version (1965-68); No. 6802 purple and white (1969-71); No. 6803 neon green top and purple body (1972-78), 1964-78, 9-5/8" long	25	150	300
Jumbo Street Roller, No. 2050, roller in front, wheels in back; large red roller in front and red operator's cab (1971); yellow and black (1972-77), 1971-77 ..	50	100	200
Jungle Wagon, No. 9000, two-tone green Ford Econoline with cages to transport wild animals, 1966-72	45	140	275
Junior Jack Hammer, No. 2900, with air compressor package that connected to toy with 4' rubber hose; Nylint's first plastic toy; red/black jack-hammer, yellow/red/black compressor box, 1958-59, 19-1/2" long	50	125	250
Kennel Truck, No. 6200, pink Ford Econoline, plastic dog cage in back, 12 dogs (12 different breeds); paper band around cage featuring the dog breeds on it (1964 only), 1963-69, 11-1/2" long	175	265	525

Nylint Traveloader, 1950s, 30". Photo courtesy Thomas G. Nefos

	C6	C8	C10
Lawn and Garden Set, No. 1200, new number; same as No. 7000, 1965	50	125	250
Lawn and Garden Set, No. 7000, dark green Econoline Pickup with white roof; included lawn mower and other garden equipment, 1964	50	150	300
Lift Truck (fork lift), No. 700, red and yellow; box commands a premium (contains operating instructions), 1946-49	75	125	250
Lift Truck (fork lift), No. 700, green and yellow; box commands a premium (contains operating instructions), 1946-49	75	140	275
Michigan Shovel (crane), No. 2200, 10 wheels, clamshell bucket, single headlights, grille plate, steering (1955-56); six wheels, single or dual headlights, embossed front grille or grille plate (1956-60); no steering, grille sticker (1961-63); magnet added to bucket but only drop-down outriggers (1964-65); only Nylint toy to have real rubber tires through its first 10 years, 1955-65, 31-1/2" long ...	50	150	300
Missile Launcher, No. 2600, orange, white radar antenna, white missiles with black tips, 1959	100	175	350
Missile Launcher, No. 2600, blue-gray, white radar antenna, white missiles with black tips, 1957-60, 31-1/2" long	50	125	250
Mobile Home Semi Truck, No. 6600, aqua blue cab with white or light tan roof, nine pieces of furniture, two-piece grille/ bumper on front, round "6600" decal on cab doors, 1964, 30" long......................................	75	300	600

Nylint Guided Missile Carrier, No. 2800, 1958. Photo courtesy Calvin L. Chausee

Nylint Pepsi Truck, No. 5500, 16-1/2". Photo courtesy Bob Smith

Nylint Electronic Cannon, No. 2400, 1956. Photo courtesy Calvin L. Chaussee

Nylint Ford U-Haul Rental Fleet, No. 4300, three pieces. Photo courtesy Thomas G. Nefos

	C6	C8	C10
Payloader, No. 1600, dark green, 1958	50	175	350
Payloader, No. 1600, light green and yellow, 1956-58	50	175	350
Payloader, No. 6500, red and yellow, 1963-66	50	100	200
Payloader, No. 1600, red and yellow, 1951-55, 18" long	50	175	350
Payloader, No. 1600, yellow, 1958	50	175	350
Payloader, No. 1600, tan, 1951	50	175	350
Payloader Tractor-Shovel, No. 3100, first version yellow with levers in cab (1959 only); red/yellow with levers in cab (1959-60); without levers (1961-62); less than 1,300 made, replica of Hough machine; all toys had steel track base and rubber tracks, 1959-62, 17-5/8" long	75	175	350
Pepsi Delivery Truck, No. 5500, red, white and blue Ford C-600 truck with decals, six cases of Pepsi and hand truck, 1962-67, 16-1/2"	50	225	450
Platform Dump Truck, No. 3900, yellow, white cab roof, narrow side panels on rear bed; last truck to feature tilt cab, 1961	75	175	350
Pony Farm Van Set, No. 8000, white Ford Econoline Pick,up, green cab top, large green/white Pony Farm decal on sides, four ponies, 11-1/4" long	75	175	350
Power & Light Lineman Truck, No. 3200, yellow cab and flasher light, orange trailer, black rear hoist with tools, rope, yellow spool of wire, two stained poles; orange with yellow cab and flasher light, orange trailer, yellow wire spool, 1959-61, 35-3/4" long	75	175	350
Power & Light Posthole Digger Truck, No. 3300, orange, yellow cab roof, orange trailer, yellow posthole assembly and tool box cover, plastic tools, four wooden phone poles, 1959-61, 35-3/4" long	75	175	350

	C6	C8	C10
Power Pony, No. 900, light tan, black, yellow; three-wheeled pony performed tricks; rare, 1949	100	250	500
Pumpmobile, No. 1200, wind-up; Howdy Doody cowboy-like figure (unlicensed), yellow, red and blue, 1950-52, 8-5/8" long...........................	100	300	600
Race Team, No. 5900, Ford Econoline with race car (white and other colors) and red trailer, 1963-66......................	50	175	350
Race Team, No. 7800, white Econoline Pickup, red trailer, white race car, 1965-69	50	150	300
Race Team, No. 9600, Ford Econoline Pikup and trailer with race car, red and white, 1967-69	40	140	275
Ranch Truck, No. 4500, light blue Ford stake truck, two-piece front grille/bumper, white stake racks, round decals on doors, 1961-64, 14" long	50	100	200
Road Grader, No. 1400, first version; small wheels and steel grille plate; orange, 1951, 19-1/4" long	75	125	250
Road Grader, No. 1400, second version; larger 3-3/4" wheels and grille plate; orange, 1952-53	50	175	350
Road Grader, No. 7900, yellow and black, 1965-68, 15" long.....................	25	100	200
Road Grader, No. 1400, third version; embossed grille, large 3-3/4" wheels; orange (1954-55), yellow (1956-58), 1954-58	50	175	350
Road Grader, No. 7910, yellow with larger wheels, 1969............................	40	65	125
Safari Hunt Set, No. 8800, Ford Bronco with white top, cage trailer with wild animals; cage has door, trailer has slide-out ramp and winch for loading, 1966-71	75	200	400
Scootscycle/Servicecycle, No. 800, wind-up; red, blue, yellow or black; rare, 1946-51, 7-1/4" long...................	75	225	450
Speed Swing Loader, No. 2000, orange or yellow; by Pettibone-Mulliken Co. orange and black (1955), yellow and black (1956-58), 1955-58, 19" long.....	50	125	250
Sportsman Set, No. 9700, truck with boat and trailer; white and other colors, 1967-69	50	140	275
Sportster, No. 9500, pink Ford Bronco, 1967-69	45	140	275
Stake Pickup Truck, No. 9100, light blue and white Ford Econoline stake truck, 1966-69	35	125	250
Street Sprinkler Truck, No. 3700, white tank truck, operating nozzles on front bumper, tilt cab, 1960-61, 18" long	75	175	350
Suburban Fire Department Set, No. 7408, red Ford Econoline Pumper Fire Truck, Fire Rescue Econoline Van, Fire Chief's Bronco; Rescue Van and Fire Chief's Bronco available only in this set, 1966-70..................................	75	225	450
Suburban Fire Pumper, No. 8100, Ford Econoline Pumper fire Truck with water cannon; a garden hose could be connected to the cannon to shoot water; hard to find in good condition since the pressure from the garden hose usually blew up the truck, 1965-70, 12-1/2" long.......................	50	150	300

	C6	C8	C10
Telescopic Crane, No. 2500, red with yellow boom, four-wheel steering, extendable boom, 1957-60	100	150	300
Texaco Service Van, No. 8300, red Ford Econoline Van, white decals, red flasher light, 1965, 12" long	50	200	400
Tin Lizzy Hot Rod Pickup, No. 9300, red and other colors, 1967-72	35	100	200
Tournadozer, No. 2100, orange with black seat and motor; first version with larger 4-7/16" wheels (1956), 1956-59, 20" long	75	150	300
Tournahauler, No. 1700, third version; dark green embossed grille, 1954-55	50	125	250
Tournahauler, No. 1700, second version dark green with grille plate, 1953-54	50	125	250
Tournahauler, No. 1700, first version; yellow, 1953	100	200	400
Tournahauler, No. 1700, fourth version; light green, 1956	50	125	250
Tournahopper, No. 1500, second version; embossed front, 3-3/4" wheels; yellow (1954-55), orange (1956). After 1953, these are replicas of Letourneau-Westinghouse machines, 1954-56	75	175	350
Tournahopper, No. 1500, first version; grille plate on front of closed tractor; yellow with black decals; replica of a R.G. Letourneau machine, 1952-53, 22-1/2" long	75	175	350
Tournaractor, No. 1900, yellow and black with 4-7/16" wheels; by J.D. Adams, 1954-55, 14-3/4" long	50	175	350
Tournarocker, No. 1300, second version; closed cab, no driver, grille plate on front, larger 3-3/4" wheels; all yellow; also by R.G. Letourneau, 1953-54, 18" long	75	125	250
Tournarocker, No. 1300, first version; open tractor w/driver; orange (1951) or mustard yellow (1952); scale model of			

	C6	C8	C10
a machine by R. G. Letourneau, 1951-52, 18" long	50	150	300
Tournarocker, No. 1300, third version; embossed grille details, larger 3-3/4" wheels; all yellow (1955), orange and yellow (1956-57); also by R.G. Letourneau, 1955-57	75	125	250
Traveloader, No. 1800, first version with smaller blades on front feeder belt (1953); second version with larger blades (1954-55); both versions orange with black decals, black belts on front feeder, black rear conveyor belt, 1953-55, 30" long	75	125	250
Truck and Horse Trailer, No. 8700, Ford Bronco, two-axle horse trailer with yellow top, 1966-70	50	145	285
Truck and U-Haul Trailer, No. 9400, Ford Econoline Pickup and open trailer, orange and white, 1967-68	50	140	275
Twister Exploration Car, No. 1810, yellow and black; Nylint's version of Tonka's Crater Crawler, 1969-73	25	100	200
U-Haul Cube Van, No. 8400, five-ton cube van, 1966-67, 22" long	75	175	350
U-Haul Truck, No. 8411, Chevy, 1975	100	125	175
U-Haul Truck & Trailer, No. 8410, 1974, 22" long	100	150	200
U-Haul Van, No. 4900, open trailer, orange and cream, U-Haul decals, 1961, 9" long	50	100	200
U-Haul Van, No. 4800, closed trailer, orange and cream, U-Haul decals, 1961, 8" long	50	100	200
Uranium Hauler, No. 2700, olive drab hydraulic bumper, yellow/ black front guard, 1958-59, 22-1/2" long	50	125	250
Vacationer Set, No. 8600, blue and white Ford Bronco and camper trailer, 1966-70	50	150	300

Nylint U-Haul Truck, Chevy, 1975. Photo courtesy Thomas G. Nefos

Nylint American Oil Emergency Truck, No. 6000, 11-1/4". Photo courtesy Bob Smith

OH BOY

(Kiddie Metal Toys, Plainfield, N.J.)

President Louis Portolano was also a tool and die maker for Kiddies Metal Toys. Established in the early part of the twentieth century, Kiddie Metal Toys produced toy vehicles under the logo O Boy! In the early 1920s, the company hired Louis Emmets, a skilled lithographer previously employed by J. Chein & Co. Emmets worked with George Borgfeldt to produce the type of toys the public wanted. Very successful early on, Kiddie Metal Toys' volume was close to $1,000,000 in the early 1920s.

Oh Boy Hook & Ladder Truck, No. 130, red, 1920s, 21". Photo courtesy Bob Smith

Oh Boy American Express Truck, No. 205. Photo courtesy Bob Smith

Oh Boy Dump Truck, No. 100, 1920s, 19". Photo courtesy Bob Smith

In 1925, Kiddie Metal Toys began a line of large light pressed-steel vehicles. These trucks ranged in length from nineteen to twenty-seven inches. The gauge of metal used on the Oh Boy! trucks was the same gauge metal that Chein used on its Hercules Trucks. Other similarities in these trucks, include body style and wheel types. Some collectors believe that Louis Emmets brought this strong influence with him from J. Chein & Co. The Oh Boy! toys, however, were finished with enamel paint, while Chein used lithography on the Hercules vehicles. Another peculiarity of the Oh Boy! toys was the installing of decals on only one side.

Kiddie Metal Toys made a wide variety of toys such as tea sets, sand pails and roulette games. Kiddies Metal Toys, Inc. closed its door in 1931, after going through tough times from the Depression.

Contributor: Bob Smith, RATS Toy Shows, 255 Tryon Park, Rochester, NY 14609. (585) 288-7153, bird@oldtoysonline.com.

	C6	C8	C10
No. 100 Dump Truck, black/gray, w/or without decals, c.1926, 19" long	450	800	1200
No. 100 Dump Truck, black/red or all black, w/or without decals, c.1926, 19" long	400	700	1075
No. 105 Bus, blue, c.1926, 19-1/2" long	550	1250	1850
No. 110 Racer, red, c.1926, 19" long	800	1700	2600
No. 115 Ice Truck, green, c.1926, 19-1/2" long	500	850	1200
No. 120 Delivery Truck, closed cab, stake sides, black/red, c.1927, 19" long	500	1000	1450
No. 120 Delivery Truck, pen cab, stake sides, black/red, c.1927, 19" long	400	900	1400

	C6	C8	C10
No. 125 Wrecker Truck, black/red, c.1926, 19" long	500	1150	1750
No. 130 Hook & Ladder Truck, red, c.1926, 21" long	650	950	1450
No. 135 Fire Engine, red w/copper plated boiler and hand rails, c.1926, 19" long	700	1200	1850
No. 135 Fire Engine, red w/orange boiler and hand rails, c.1926, 19" long	600	950	1550

Oh Boy toys, as shown on a page from a late 1920s Butler Bros. catalog. Manufacturer's numbers are in parentheses.

Oh Boy American Express Truck, No. 205. Photo courtesy Bob Smith

Oh Boy Fire Engine, No. 135, orange boiler, hand rails. Photo courtesy Bob Smith

Oh Boy Dump Truck, same as No. 100 Dump Truck except black and red. Photo courtesy Bob Smith

Oh Boy Fire Patrol Truck, No. 140, red, 1920s, 23". Photo courtesy Bob Smith

Oh Boy Wrecker Truck, No. 125, black, red, 1920s, 19". Photo courtesy Bob Smith

Oh Boy Racer, No. 110, red, 1920s, 19". Photo courtesy Bob Smith

	C6	C8	C10
No. 140 Fire Patrol Truck, red, c.1926, 23" long	450	950	1550
No. 200 Auto Steam Shovel, four-wheel chassis w/vertical boiler, red/black, c.1927, 23" long	700	1400	2200
No. 200 Auto Steam Shovel, red/black, mounted on open cab truck chassis, c.1927, 27" long	650	1350	2100

	C6	C8	C10
No. 205 American Express Truck, green, c.1927, 22" long	800	1700	2400
No. 209 Mail Truck, olive green, c.1927, 22" long	800	1700	2400
No. 210 Moving Van, black/red, c.1927, 22" long	800	1700	2400

OHIO ART

Ohio Art was started in October 1908, by a dentist, H.S. Winzeler. Originally, its intent was to make metal picture frames (thus, its name). But in 1917, the firm bought C.E. Carter (Erie Toy Plant) and began producing metal toys, including a climbing monkey on a string for Ferdinand Strauss. Winzeler later sold the plant to Louis Marx, but continued making tin toys, while Marx, according to Ohio Art history, used the former Carter plant as the foundation of his own company. Ohio Art is still making toys in Bryan, Ohio.

Ohio Art 1953 Buick LeSabre Showcar, 8" long. Photo courtesy John McCurdy

	C6	C8	C10
1953 Buick LeSabre Showcar, plastic, never had a windshield, 8" long	12	24	35
Tank Bank, No. 15, 1941	78	117	155
Traffic Control, tin wind-up cars, 1950s, 3-1/2" long, base 19"x13"	40	60	80

OHLSSON & RICE

Irv Ohlsson grew up building model planes and soon started constructing engines to make them fly. He subcontracted machinist Harry Rice to produce tooling for his engines, and by 1941, the duo were in business. Initial success was interrupted by World War II, but resumed once materials again became available. The O&R engines were dependable, easy to maintain, and operate.

By 1947, the O&R product line also included model airplane propellers and several gas-powered cars. Rapid expansion of the product line ultimately led to the demise of this Los Angeles, Calif.-based company.

	C6	C8	C10
Midget Racer, aluminum body, rubber tires, 1940s	260	375	575
No. 76 Racer, gas-powered	500	750	1075
Pusher Racer, 11" long	270	455	540

OROBR

Orobr Toy Works was founded by three partners, Neil, Muller, and Blechschmidt. The company produced numerous lower-end toy vehicles, many of which were made for the American market. Even though a large amount of toy vehicles are found with the Orobr mark, there is not much information in print about the company. Orobr made some toys that do carry a fair value, and they make a nice accent to any collection.

Contributor: Bob Smith, RATS Toy Shows, 255 Tryon Park, Rochester, NY 14609. (585) 288-7153, bird@oldtoysonline.com.

	C6	C8	C10
Bus	550	850	1250
Double-Decker Bus, wind-up, 9-1/2" long	450	750	1150
Double-Decker Bus, wind-up, c.1915, 6" long	350	550	650
Express Wagon, wind-up, 1920s, 6" long	350	600	750
Limousine, open front cab, luggage rack on top, clockwork motor, c.1910, 5-1/2" long	400	650	850

	C6	C8	C10
No. 24 Orobr Mercedes Pullman Limousine., six window, lithographed in three-tone green/red/white, electric lights, clockwork motor, four opening doors, driver, c.1920, 9-1/2" long	1150	1750	2450
No. 25 Touring Car, red/gray, clockwork motor, fold down rear seats, c.1918, 8-3/4" long	550	750	100
No. 26 Model T Ford Sedan, black, 6" long, clockwork motor, 1920s; add $200 for different color	275	375	575
No. 27 Model T Ford Sedan, black, 7-3/4" long, clockwork motor, full interior, 1920s	275	375	575
No. 28 Model T Ford Touring Car, black/gray, clockwork motor, 7-3/4" long	600	800	1050
Steam Roller, tin wind-up, 6" long	250	350	500
Taxi, tin, 6" long	400	550	800

Top row: Orobr Model T Ford Sedan, 6". Front row, left to right: Model T Ford Sedan, 7-3/4"; Model T Ford Touring Car, 7-3/4". Photo courtesy Bob Smith

Orobr Six-Window Mercedes Pullman Limousine, green, red and white, electric lights, opening doors, driver, circa 1920, 9-1/2". Photo courtesy Bob Smith

PAGCO

In the 1950s and 1960s, the Pagliuso Engineering Co. manufactured toy race cars with spring-driven and gas-powered engines. The company used the Pagco name and was based in Glendale, Calif.

	C6	C8	C10
Racer, w/motor, 11" long	80	125	160

PARKER BROS.

Game manufacturer Parker Bros. was founded in 1883 by George Parker. Prior to World War I, the firm released its Toy Town Garage complete with tin penny cars.

	C6	C8	C10
Toy Town Garage, three lithographed tin penny cars w/paper lithographed garage, c.1910	600	900	1200

PAYA (SPAIN)

Based in Spain, Rapheal Paya made his first tin toy in 1902. In 1906, his sons Pascuale, Emilio, and Vincente built the Paya factory—the first toy factory in Spain. With a reputation for high quality and brilliant lithography, Paya toys expanded operations through the Depression years. The company shut down toy operations during the war, and resumed when materials once again becme available.

Be aware when evaluating Paya toys that modern reproductions from the original tooling exist.

	C6	C8	C10
Bugatti Racer, tin, open cockpit w/driver, 19" long	275	500	750
Chrysler Airflow Sedan, tin lithographed, clockwork motor, 13" long	325	468	625
Coupe, handpainted and stenciled, clockwork motor, doors open, 13" long	600	1350	2100

	C6	C8	C10
Limousine, handpainted and stenciled, lights work, clockwork motor, 19" long	650	1200	1650
Motorcycle and Rider, tin wind-up, 10-1/2" long	325	468	625
Sedan, steel, doors open, battery lights, 19" long	500	850	1200

Paya Motorcycle and Rider, tin windup, 10-1/2" long. Courtesy Bertoia Auctions

PAYTON

New York-based Payton Products specialized in dime-store plastic figures and toy vehicles in the 1950s and 1960s.

	C6	C8	C10
Bulldozer, soft plastic	12	18	25
Cement Mixer	12	18	25
Tiger Tank, No. 411	20	30	40
Tow Truck	12	18	25

A Payton flyer advertising some of its vehicles.

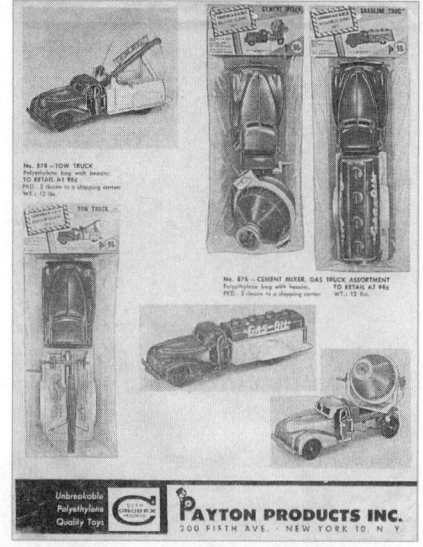

PERFECT RUBBER CO.

The Perfect Rubber Co. was based in Mansfield, Ohio. It is best known for its realistic replicas of the 1935 and 1936 Pontiac slantback sedan.

	C6	C8	C10
1935 Slantback Sedan, "suicide" door handle placement, 3-3/4" long	35	52	70
1936 Slantback Sedan, no "suicide" door handles - this is the only difference between the two years, 3-3/4" long	35	52	70

The Perfect Rubber Co. 1935 Slantback Sedan, 3-3/4" (Pontiac Premium). Courtesy Dave Leopard from his book, Rubber Toy Vehicles.

PETER-MAR

Ralph Lohr was the owner of Peter Products Manufacturing in Muscatine, Iowa. He was an entrepreneur, artist, and musician. Lohr operated a music store in the early 1920s. In 1941, he started manufacturing wooden kitchen items, such as clothes racks, stools, ladders, and ironing boards. Lumber was limited to government contracts during World War II, and Lohr was faced with closing the business. It

Another original Peter-Mar promotional flyer. Courtesy of Mary Gaeta

An original Peter-Mar promotional flyer. Courtesy of Mary Gaeta

was at this time that he discovered scrap lumber could be purchased from government contractors, and he started to design toys. The first of these were military vehicles. Farm toys were also very popular, so he began making tractors, hay racks, trailers, and wagons. Other toys were Noah's Ark, Humpty Dumpty, Lucky Dog, Village Smitty, Old Woman in a Shoe, Trolley Cars, Carousel, and Ferris Wheel.

The company was named after Lohr's son Peter, and Mary, the daughter of his partner, Clifford Hakes.

After more than sixty years, these toys are still popular and sought-after. When these toys are found in antique stores, the prices for a Noah's ark in Mint condition are $300. The Village Smitty, a

pound-a-peg-type toy, has been sold for as much as $65. These toys are well constructed and durable.

Contributor: Mary Gaeta is a lifetime resident of Muscatine, Iowa. She graduated from Saint Mathias School and Muscatine Community College. She has abeen active in family business, has enjoyed a life-long interest in antiques, and has managed an antique consignment business for many years.

	C6	C8	C10
Hay Wagon	42	63	85
Jeep, wood	NPF	NPF	NPF
Milk Wagon	42	63	85
Tractor, wood	90	135	180
Trailer, wood	67	100	135

PINARD

Based in France, Eugine Pinard made tin toys prior to World War I.

	C6	C8	C10
Cannon Truck, searchlight on grill, WWI, 13" long	475	713	950

Pinard Cannon Truck, c.WWI, searchlight on grill, 13". Courtesy Bertoia Auctions

PLASTICRAFT

Plasticraft was one of the first producers of plastic toys following World War II. Located on Kearny, New Jersey, and noted for their soft-plastic, oversized soldiers, the company produced several vehicle toys as well.

	C6	C8	C10
1902 Spyder, plastic, 1960s, 5"	3	7	10
1908 Oldsmobile, plastic, 1960s, 5"	3	7	10
Easter Bunny Truck, plastic, bunny moves as truck is pushed, 1950s, 4" long	5	10	15

Plasticraft L to R: Stanley Steamer, 1908 Oldsmobile, and 1902 Spyder; 1960s, 5" long. Photo courtesy John McCurdy

	C6	C8	C10
Jeep, articulating driver, plastic, 4" long .	5	8	10
Stanley Steamer, plastic, 1960s, 5"	3	7	10
Toy Trucks Set, plastic, 2 trucks- tanker and dump, No. 159, originally retailed for 59¢, 1950s	4	8	12
Truck, plastic..	6	9	12

PLASTICVILLE U.S.A.

Bachmann Bros. of Philadelphia, Pennsylvania capitalized on the booming post-WWII plastics market and offered a line of affordable plastic accessories for Christmas tree floor displays in 1946. The fences were soon adopted by model railroaders and by 1950, Bachmann expanded the line to include bushes, trees, a wishing well, a foot bridge and a trellis. Scale buildings and vehicles soon followed. White plastic wheels/tires are characteristic of Plasticville U.S.A. vehicles.

	C6	C8	C10
HO gauge			
Gas Station, No. 2608-100, red and white, came with yellow sedan	5	10	15
O/S gauge			
Ambulance, gray, blue, orange, tan. Tan is rare. 1950s	4	8	12
Bus, gray, blue, orange, tan. Tan is rare. 1950s...	4	8	12
Fire Ladder Truck, red, white ladder, 1950s, 5" long	7	14	20
Fire Pumper Truck, red, white hose, 1950s, 5" long	7	14	20
Gas Station, red and white, 2 pump sets, one yellow sedan.................................	5	10	15
Jet Bomber, gray, 1950s......................	10	17	25
Jet Fighter, gray, 1950s.......................	10	17	25
Pickup Truck, 3" long	7	14	20

	C6	C8	C10
Sedan, red, yellow, light green, dark green, orange, light blue, dark blue, turquoise, black, 1950s	7	14	20
Vehicle Assortment 1802.........................	NPF	NPF	NPF
Vehicle Assortment 45987, 1 car, 1 bus, 1 ambulance, 1 fire pumper.......	NPF	NPF	NPF
Vehicle Assortment V-10, 4 cars, 1 bus, 1 fire ladder truck, 1 fire pumper truck, 1 ambulance, 2 jet planes, assorted colors, 1950s	NPF	NPF	NPF
Vehicle Assortment V-6, 2 cars, 1 ladder truck, 1 bus, 1 fire pumper truck, 1 ambulance, assorted colors, 1950s....	NPF	NPF	NPF
Willys Jeep, 3" long	7	14	20

Plasticville O-gauge assortment. Front row: 3" Willys Jeep, 3" Chevy Sedan. Middle row: 3" Sedan, 5" Fire Engine, 3" Sedan, 3" Pickup Truck. Back row: 5" Pumper Engine, 5" Ladder Engine. Photo courtesy John McCurdy

PLAYBOY

The Playboy line of trucks was released by the Murray-Ohio Mfg. Co. of Cleveland, Ohio prior to World War II.

	C6	C8	C10
Delivery Truck, "Playboy Trucking Co.," 21" long..	225	338	450

	C6	C8	C10
Dump Truck, 22" long	150	225	30
Intercity Bus, cream color, 23-1/2" long..	300	450	600
Tow Truck, marked "Playboy Trucking Co.," white, 22" long	250	400	650

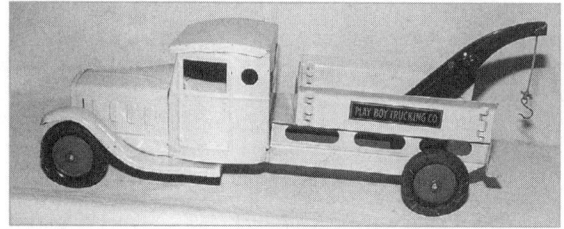

Playboy Tow Truck, "Playboy Trucking Co.," white, 1930s, 22". Photo courtesy Bob Smith

Playboy Delivery Truck, "Playboy Trucking Co." Photo courtesy Calvin L. Chaussee

PLAYWOOD PLASTICS

This World War II-era company was a subsidiary of Transogram. Playwood's products were made of wood composition, and its factory was located at 133 Floyd St., Brooklyn, New York.

	C6	C8	C10
Dispatch Rider on Cycle, No. 407 (?)	7	11	15
Dispatch Rider on Cycle, round base, head higher, No. 407a (?)	7	11	15
Motorcyclist, leather-type helmet (probably post-WWII), Nos. 438 or 436	NPF	NPF	NPF

PRECISION PLASTICS

Philadelphia-based Precision Plastics was incorporated in 1941 and released its Woodie Station Wagon in 1947. It used the division name U.S. Plastics for its toys.

	C6	C8	C10
Convertible, plastic, wind-up motor w/attached key, assorted two-tone color combinations, rubber wheels, No. R-252, 1948, 7" long	NPF	NPF	NPF
Motorcycle Racer, plastic, wind-up motor w/attached key, white and red, No. MB-80, 1948, 5" long	NPF	NPF	NPF
Sedan, plastic, wind-up motor w/attached key, plastic or rubber wheels, assorted colors, No. P-250, 1948, 5"	NPF	NPF	NPF
Station Wagon, plastic, box reads "Road King Station Wagon," plastic, no motor, assorted two-tone color combinations, plastic wheels, No. SW-69, 1947, 7"	30	55	80
Station Wagon, plastic, wind-up motor w/attached key, assorted two-tone color combinations, rubber wheels, 1948 to early 1950s, 7" long	55	82	125

PREMIER TOY CO.

Based in Brooklyn, New York, this plastic toy manufacturer specialized in novelties and toy vehicles in the 1950s and 1960s.

	C6	C8	C10
Coupe, plastic, assorted colors, plastic wheels, early 1950s, 4-3/4" long	NPF	NPF	NPF
Heavy Tank, No. 144	30	45	60
No. 52 Station Wagon, plastic, plastic wheels, assorted colors, early 1950s, 4-3/4" long	15	22	30
Sedan, plastic, assorted colors, plastic wheels, early 1950s, 4-5/8" long	NPF	NPF	NPF

Premier Station Wagon No. 52, plastic, 4-3/4". Photo courtesy Ron Fink

PRESSMAN TOY CO.

Primarily known for its games, Pressman also produced a variety of toys including its remarkable ambulance.

Founded in 1922 by World War I veteran Jack Pressman, the company prospered through the 1920s and acquired the license for Chinese Checkers in 1928. The game was a runaway success and Pressman branched out to Table Tennis, building sets, and sewing kits. In the 1930s, Pressman acquired licenses for Dick Tracy and Little Orphan Annie toys, and was among the first to produce toys based on Walt Disney's first feature-length animated film, *Snow White and the Seven Dwarfs* in 1937.

Jack Pressman married Lynn Rambach in 1942, moved the factory from Brooklyn, New York, to Paterson, New Jersey, and opened new offices in Manhattan. Lynn was named Vice President and the company was named Pressman Toy Corporation. Lynn's business savvy led to the production of the Doctor Bag in 1956. Its popularity led to a Nurse Bag and similar items for Barbie and Ken.

Jack Pressman died in 1959, leaving Lynn as president. At the time, she was one of only three women in executive positions within the toy industry. Madame Alexander and Ruth Handler (creator of Barbie) were the other two. Returning to the licensing success of the 1930s, Lynn was among the first to produce toys based on television shows.

James Pressman was appointed president in 1977.

	C6	C8	C10
Ambulance, plastic, 30 parts, rubber wheels, white, bell rings when			

	C6	C8	C10
ambulance is pushed, rubber wheels, 14" long	45	70	125

PROCESSED PLASTIC

Based in Aurora, Ill., Processed Plastic was known for its plastic dime-store toys and vehicles.

	C6	C8	C10
1963 Corvette, plastic, yellow, No. 9110, 1960s, 9" long	10	20	30
Army Tank, plastic	37	56	75
Army Wrecker, plastic, 9" long	35	52	70
Bulldozer, plastic, yellow, red, and blue; scoop lifts/dumps, 1950s, 6-3/4" long	25	38	50
Clamshell Truck, plastic, red "B-Line Construction Co." decal, clamshell crane, 9-3/8" long	10	20	30
Dump Truck, plastic, lever lifts dump bed, stamped "City Sand and Gravel Co." on sides, No. 100, 1948, 8-1/2" long	25	38	50
Dump Truck, plastic, red cab and yellow dump bed, bed lifts manually, 1950s, 7-3/4" long	10	20	30
Dump Truck, plastic, spring-activated dump, red cab and yellow dump bed, No. 200, 1949, 10" long	25	45	70

	C6	C8	C10
Fire Ladder Truck, plastic, red, 2 metal ladders, rubber wheels, 1950s, 6" long	25	38	50
Hot Rod, plastic, driver, open engine, rubber wheels, 1950s, 5" long	NPF	NPF	NPF
Jeep w/Machine gun, plastic, machine gun rotates, 1960s	5	10	15
Locomotive, plastic, red "Toyland Express" engine, yellow waving bear conductor, 1960s, 10" long	5	10	18
MGA, plastic, 1960s, 4" long	20	35	50
Mobile Crane, plastic, cab rotates on flatbed truck, shovel lifts, rubber wheels, 1952, 10" long	25	38	50
Race Car, plastic, "7," assorted colors, driver, No. 549, 1950s, 8" long	NPF	NPF	NPF
Tow Truck, plastic, metal tow arm, crank winch, rubber wheels, No. 300, 1951, 9-1/4" long	25	38	60

PRODUCT MINIATURES

	C6	C8	C10
International Pickup Truck, plastic, yellow w/IH decals, metal grille and bumper, rubber tires, red plastic wheels, metal hub caps, 1948, 9-1/2" long	50	100	185

	C6	C8	C10
International Stake Body Truck, plastic, blue w/removable stakes, metal grille and bumper, 1940s, 11" long	50	125	210
Sedan, plastic, friction motor, early 1950s GM-style	25	50	75
Tru Toy Delivery Van, plastic, yellow, Divco-style, 1940s	25	50	75

PROMOTIONALS

Promotionals are scale models of the full-size cars (usually) offered by car salesmen to the children of potential buyers. Almost always produced in 1:25-scale plastic or pot metal, most potmetal promos were discontinued by the early 1950s. The most dominant manufacturers were—Aluminum Model Toys (AMT), Banthrico (BAN), JoHan Models (JH), Master Caster (MC), Model Products Corp. (MPC), National Products (NP), Product Miniatures (PM), and Scale Model Products (SMP).

They are still being made today, but in reduced numbers. In recent years, as few as three or four different models were produced, whereas in the mid 1960s, as many as fifty different models were produced. The most popular full-size cars are usually the popular promo.

When using this guide, remember that sometimes even Mint in box items may not get you the C10 price. The plastic of the 1950s and early 1960s had a tendency to warp and each car had a specific place where warp occurred. In addition, the plating on the grille or bumpers might be flaking or dull. Something as small as a missing hood ornament or a cracked vent window post can reduce your C10 to a C6.

Contributor: Paul McLaughlin, Promos columnist for *Toy Cars & Models* magazine.

	C6	C8	C10
Aero Willys Four-door Sedan, BIR, 1953	80	160	325
Aerocar Convertible, GLA, 1953	40	80	150
AMC Hornet, JH, 1974	NPF	NPF	NPF
AMC Hornet, JH, Two-door sedan, 1973	NPF	NPF	NPF
AMC Pacer, MPC, 1975	NPF	NPF	NPF
AMC Ramber American Two-door Hardtop, JH, 1965	NPF	NPF	NPF
AMX Two-door Hardtop, JH, 1969	20	30	60
AMX Two-door Hardtop, JH, 1970	20	30	60
Barracuda Two-door Fastback, AMT, 1965	15	45	95
Barracuda Two-door Fastback, AMT, 1966	15	35	75

	C6	C8	C10
Barracuda Two-door Hardtop, AMT, 1967	15	35	75
Barracuda Two-door Hardtop, MPC, 1968	40	75	140
Barracuda Two-door Hardtop, MPC, 1969	30	45	100
Barracuda Two-door Hardtop, MPC, 1970	65	135	260
Barracuda Two-door Hardtop, MPC, 1971	80	160	325
Buick Century Convertible, AMT, 1956	30	60	110
Buick Convertible, AMT, 1955	20	40	75
Buick Electra 225 Convertible, AMT, 1962	30	50	100
Buick Electra 225 Convertible, AMT, 1963	30	70	120
Buick Electra 225 Two-door Hardtop, AMT, 1962	20	50	100
Buick Electra 225 Two-door Hardtop, AMT, 1963	2	50	100
Buick Four-door Hardtop, BAN, 1956	30	50	95
Buick Four-door Sedan, AMT, 1954	20	40	85
Buick Four-door Sedan, AMT, 1955	20	40	65
Buick Four-door Sedan, BAN, 1952	30	60	110
Buick Four-door Sedan, NP, 1947	40	80	150
Buick Four-door Sedan, NP, 1948	30	65	130
Buick Four-door Sedan, NP, 1949	50	100	150
Buick Invicta Convertible, AMT, 1959	20	40	85
Buick Invicta Convertible, AMT, 1960	30	60	110
Buick Invicta Convertible, AMT, 1961	30	60	110
Buick Invicta Two-door Hardtop, AMT, 1959	20	40	75
Buick Invicta Two-door Hardtop, AMT, 1960	30	60	110
Buick Invicta Two-door Hardtop, AMT, 1961	20	40	90
Buick Regal, PD, Two-door hardtop, 1988	10	20	30
Buick Riviera Two-door Hardtop, AMT, 1963	30	70	130
Buick Riviera Two-door Hardtop, AMT, 1964	20	50	95
Buick Riviera Two-door Hardtop, AMT, 1965	45	80	160
Buick Riviera Two-door Hardtop, AMT, 1966	20	30	70
Buick Riviera Two-door Hardtop, AMT, 1967	20	30	60
Buick Riviera Two-door Hardtop, AMT, 1968	30	50	105
Buick Riviera Two-door Hardtop, AMT, 1969	20	40	75
Buick Roadmaster Convertible, AMT, 1957	30	60	110
Buick Roadmaster Convertible, AMT, 1958	20	60	100
Buick Roadmaster Four-door Hardtop, AMT, 1956	20	40	80
Buick Roadmaster Two-door Hardtop, AMT, 1957	30	60	110
Buick Roadmaster Two-door Hardtop, AMT, 1958	20	40	90
Buick Sedan, BAN, 1953	30	50	110
Buick Sedan, NP, 1950	30	55	110
Buick Skylark Convertible, AMT, 1954	40	80	140
Buick Skylark Two-door Hardtop, AMT, 1966	36	81	160
Buick Special Station Wagon, AMT, 1961	20	40	60

	C6	C8	C10
Buick Special Station Wagon, AMT, 1962	10	25	50
Buick Two-door Hardtop, BAN, 1954	20	40	90
Buick Two-door Hardtop, BAN, 1955	20	40	75
Buick Wildcat Convertible, AMT, 1964	55	110	160
Buick Wildcat Convertible, AMT, 1965	54	108	215
Buick Wildcat Two-door Hardtop, AMT, 1964	60	110	225
Buick Wildcat Two-door Hardtop, AMT, 1965	54	117	235
Buick Wildcat Two-door Hardtop, AMT, 1966	20	40	80
Buick Wildcat Two-door Hardtop, AMT, 1969	10	30	60
Buick Wildcat Two-door Hardtop, AMT, 1970	10	20	40
Cadillac 62, Two-door Hardtop, AMT, 1956	20	40	80
Cadillac Convertible, JH, 1963	10	30	60
Cadillac Convertible, JH, 1964	20	40	80
Cadillac Convertible, JH, 1965	20	40	80
Cadillac Convertible, JH, 1966	20	40	80
Cadillac Convertible, JH, 1967	20	30	60
Cadillac Convertible, JH, 1968	10	20	40
Cadillac Coupe deVille, JH, Two-door hardtop, 1967	20	30	60
Cadillac Coupe deVille, JH, Two-door hardtop, 1968	10	20	40
Cadillac Coupe deVille, JH, Two-door hardtop, 1969	10	30	40
Cadillac Coupe deVille, JH, Two-door hardtop, 1977	10	20	30
Cadillac Coupe deVille, JH, Two-door hardtop, 1978	10	20	30
Cadillac Coupe deVille, JH, Two-door hardtop, 1979	10	20	30
Cadillac Eldorado, JH, Two-door hardtop, 1973	15	30	45
Cadillac Eldorado, JH, Two-door hardtop, 1974	15	30	45
Cadillac Eldorado, JH, Two-door hardtop, 1975	15	30	45
Cadillac Eldorado, JH, Two-door hardtop, 1976	15	30	45
Cadillac Eldorado Two-door Hardtop, BAN, 1956	30	65	130
Cadillac Eldorado Two-door Hardtop, JH, 1967	20	40	80
Cadillac Eldorado Two-door Hardtop, JH, 1968	10	20	40
Cadillac Eldorado Two-door Hardtop, JH, 1969	10	30	40

Promotionals, Chevrolet El Camino Pickup, 1960, AMT. Photo courtesy Ron Smith

	C6	C8	C10
Cadillac Eldorado Two-door Hardtop, JH, 1970	20	30	60
Cadillac Eldorado Two-door Hardtop, JH, 1971	10	30	60
Cadillac Eldorado Two-door Hardtop, JH, 1972	10	20	40
Cadillac Fleetwood Four-door Hardtop, JH, 1959	20	40	80
Cadillac Fleetwood Four-door Hardtop, JH, 1960	20	40	80
Cadillac Fleetwood Four-door Hardtop, JH, 1961	20	40	80
Cadillac Fleetwood Four-door Hardtop, JH, 1962	20	40	85
Cadillac Fleetwood, Four-door Hardtop, JH, 1958	10	30	60
Cadillac Four-door Sedan, BAN, 1952	30	60	120
Cadillac Four-door Sedan, BAN, 1954	30	60	120
Cadillac Four-door Sedan, BAN, 1955	40	60	120
Cadillac Two-door Hardtop, AMT, 1955	20	50	95
Cadillac Two-door Hardtop, JH, 1963	10	30	60
Cadillac Two-door Hardtop, JH, 1964	20	40	80
Cadillac Two-door Hardtop, JH, 1965	20	40	80
Cadillac Two-door Hardtop, JH, 1966	20	40	80
Cadillac Two-door Hardtop, JH, 1970	10	20	40
Camaro Convertible, AMT, 1967	40	80	140
Camaro Convertible, AMT, 1969	40	90	180
Camaro Convertible, MPC, 1968	50	90	185
Camaro Convertible Indy 500 Pace Car, AMT, 1967	125	250	500
Camaro Convertible Indy 500 Pace Car, AMT, 1969	80	150	310
Camaro IROC-Z, AMT, 1989	10	20	30
Camaro IROC-Z, AMT, 1990	10	20	30
Camaro IROC-Z, MPC, 1987	10	20	30
Camaro IROC-Z, MPC, 1988	10	20	30
Camaro Two-door Hardtop, AMT, 1967	40	80	160
Camaro Two-door Hardtop, AMT, 1969	40	80	150
Camaro Two-door Hardtop, AMT, 1970	30	60	120
Camaro Two-door Hardtop, MPC, 1971	20	40	80
Camaro Two-door Hardtop, MPC, 1972	20	40	80
Camaro Z-28, AMT, 1992	10	25	40
Camaro Z-28, AMT, coupe, 1993	10	25	40
Camaro Z-28, MPC, 1982	10	25	40
Camaro Z-28, MPC, 1983	10	25	40
Camaro Z-28, MPC, 1984	10	25	40
Camaro Z-28, MPC, 1985	10	25	40
Camaro Z-28, MPC, 1986	10	25	40
Camaro Z-28 Indy 500 Pace Car, AMT, decals to apply, 1993	10	25	40
Chevrolet Silverado C-1500 Pickup, AMT, 1989	10	20	30
Chevelle Convertible, AMT, 1969	40	80	100
Chevelle Malibu SS Two-door Hardtop, AMT, 1965	20	40	80

	C6	C8	C10
Chevelle Malibu Station Wagon, AMT, 1965	30	50	95
Chevelle SS Convertible, AMT, 1970	30	60	120
Chevelle SS Two-door Hardtop, AMT, 1970	30	60	120
Chevelle SS Two-door Hardtop, MPC, 1972	20	40	80
Chevelle Station Wagon, AMT, 1964	20	40	80
Chevelle Two-door Hardtop, AMT, 1964	30	50	120
Chevelle Two-door Hardtop, AMT, 1969	30	60	125
Chevelle Two-door Hardtop, MPC, 1971	20	40	80
Chevrolet 150 Four-door Sedan, PMC, 1953	30	60	120
Chevrolet 150 Four-door Sedan, PMC, 1954	40	80	180
Chevrolet 150 Two-door Sedan, PMC, 1953	30	70	130
Chevrolet 150 Two-door Sedan, PMC, 1954	40	80	160
Chevrolet 210 Four-door Sedan, PMC, 1953	30	70	120
Chevrolet 210 Four-door Sedan, PMC, 1954	30	60	120
Chevrolet 210 Two-door Sedan, PMC, 1953	30	60	120
Chevrolet 210 Two-door Sedan, PMC, 1954	40	80	160
Chevrolet Apache Pickup, AMT, 1961	40	80	150
Chevrolet Apache Pickup, SMP, 1959	25	55	90
Chevrolet Bel Air Convertible, PMC, 1954	50	100	200
Chevrolet Bel Air Four-door Sedan, PMC, 1953	30	60	120
Chevrolet Bel Air Four-door Sedan, PMC, 1954	40	60	125
Chevrolet Bel Air Two-door Hardtop, BAN, 1950	30	60	120
Chevrolet Bel Air Two-door Hardtop, PMC, 1951	30	60	130
Chevrolet Bel Air Two-door Hardtop, PMC, 1952	30	60	120
Chevrolet Bel Air Two-door Hardtop, PMC, 1953	30	60	140
Chevrolet Bel Air Two-door Hardtop, PMC, 1954	40	80	160
Chevrolet Bel Air Two-door Sedan, PMC, 1953	30	70	125
Chevrolet Bel Air Two-door Sedan, PMC, 1954	27	63	125
Chevrolet Bel-Air Convertible, SMP, 1957	40	60	120
Chevrolet Beretta, AMT, 1990	8	16	25
Chevrolet Beretta, AMT, 1990	8	16	25
Chevrolet Beretta GT, AMT, 1989	8	16	25
Chevrolet Beretta GT, MPC, 1988	8	16	25
Chevrolet Camaro, MPC, 1968	NPF	NPF	NPF
Chevrolet Camaro, MPC, Two-door hardtop, 1973	50	100	150
Chevrolet Cameo Pickup, PMC, 1956	40	80	135
Chevrolet Caprice, MPC, Two-door hardtop, 1974	20	40	60
Chevrolet Caprice, MPC, Two-door hardtop, 1975	20	40	60
Chevrolet Caprice, MPC, Two-door hardtop, 1976	20	40	60
Chevrolet Caprice Two-door Hardtop, MPC, 1973	25	50	75
Chevrolet Cavalier, MPC, 1983	10	20	30
Chevrolet Cavalier, MPC, Two-door, 1982	10	20	30

Promotionals, Chevrolet Impala Two-door hardtop, 1963, AMT. Photo courtesy Ron Smith

	C6	C8	C10
Chevrolet Chevette, MPC, 1977	10	20	30
Chevrolet Chevette, MPC, 1978	10	20	30
Chevrolet Chevette, MPC, 1979	10	20	30
Chevrolet Convertible, BAN, 1949.........	40	80	160
Chevrolet Convertible, BAN, 1950.........	40	80	150
Chevrolet Convertible, PMC, 1951.........	60	120	240
Chevrolet Convertible, PMC, 1952.........	60	110	240
Chevrolet Convertible, PMC, 1953.........	40	80	160
Chevrolet El Camino Pickup, AMT, 1960	20	60	120
Chevrolet El Camino Pickup, AMT, 1964	30	60	120
Chevrolet El Camino Pickup, AMT, 1965	36	63	125
Chevrolet El Camino Pickup, MPC, 1979	20	40	60
Chevrolet El Camino Pickup, MPC, 1980	20	40	60
Chevrolet El Camino Pickup, MPC, 1980	20	40	60
Chevrolet El Camino Pickup, MPC, 1981	20	40	60
Chevrolet El Camino Pickup, MPC, 1982	20	40	60
Chevrolet Fleetline Four-door, BAN, 1949	40	80	150
Chevrolet Fleetline Four-door, BAN, 1950	30	60	120
Chevrolet Fleetline Four-door, PMC, 1951	40	80	160
Chevrolet Fleetline Two-door, BAN, 1949	40	80	150
Chevrolet Fleetline Two-door, BAN, 1950	40	70	140
Chevrolet Fleetline Two-door, NP, 1947.	40	80	160
Chevrolet Fleetline Two-door, NP, 1948.	40	80	160
Chevrolet Fleetline Two-door, PMC, 1951	40	80	150
Chevrolet Fleetline Two-door, PMC, 1952	30	60	150
Chevrolet Fleetside Pickup, AMT, 1965 .	40	80	160
Chevrolet Fleetside Pickup, AMT, 1966 .	50	140	180
Chevrolet Fleetside Pickup, AMT, 1967 .	30	60	115
Chevrolet Fleetside Pickup, AMT, 1969 .	30	60	120
Chevrolet Fleetside Pickup, AMT, 1970 .	30	60	120
Chevrolet Fleetside Pickup, MPC, 1968 ..	30	55	115
Chevrolet Fleetside Pickup, MPC, 1971 ..	30	60	110
Chevrolet Fleetside Pickup, MPC, 1972 ..	30	50	100
Chevrolet Four-door Hardtop, PMC, 1956	30	60	120
Chevrolet Four-door Hardtop, PMC, 1957	30	60	120
Chevrolet Four-door Hardtop, SMP, 1957	NPF	NPF	NPF
Chevrolet Four-door Sedan, PMC, 1955 .	30	60	115
Chevrolet Four-door Sedan, PMC, 1956 .	30	60	120
Chevrolet II Two-door Hardtop, AMT, 1965	25	50	100
Chevrolet Impala Convertible, AMT, 1961	50	100	200
Chevrolet Impala Convertible, AMT, 1962	50	100	200
Chevrolet Impala Convertible, AMT, 1963	80	160	300
Chevrolet Impala Convertible, AMT, 1964	40	70	140
Chevrolet Impala Convertible, AMT, 1965	30	70	140
Chevrolet Impala Convertible, AMT, 1966	30	60	120
Chevrolet Impala Convertible, AMT, 1967	40	60	115
Chevrolet Impala Convertible, AMT, 1969	20	40	80
Chevrolet Impala Convertible, AMT, 1970	20	40	80
Chevrolet Impala Convertible, MPC, 1968	40	80	160
Chevrolet Impala Convertible, MPC, 1971	20	40	80
Chevrolet Impala Convertible, SMP, 1958	30	60	115
Chevrolet Impala Convertible, SMP, 1959	30	60	125
Chevrolet Impala Convertible, SMP, 1960	30	60	110
Chevrolet Impala Four-door Hardtop, AMT, 1961	60	120	200
Chevrolet Impala Four-door Hardtop, PMC, 1958	20	40	60
Chevrolet Impala Four-door Hardtop, PMC, 1959	NPF	NPF	NPF
Chevrolet Impala Four-door Hardtop, SMP, 1959	25	55	90
Chevrolet Impala Four-door Hardtop, SMP, 1960	20	50	90
Chevrolet Impala SS Budget Rent-A-Car, AMT, 1966....................	40	80	175
Chevrolet Impala Two-Door Hardtop, AMT, 1961	35	70	110
Chevrolet Impala Two-door Hardtop, AMT, 1962	80	10	300
Chevrolet Impala Two-door Hardtop, AMT, 1963	60	110	220
Chevrolet Impala Two-door Hardtop, AMT, 1964	40	80	150
Chevrolet Impala Two-door Hardtop, AMT, 1965	30	60	115
Chevrolet Impala Two-door Hardtop, AMT, 1966	30	60	120
Chevrolet Impala Two-door Hardtop, AMT, 1967	25	60	115
Chevrolet Impala Two-door Hardtop, AMT, 1969	20	40	80
Chevrolet Impala Two-door Hardtop, AMT, 1970	20	40	70

Promotionals, Lincoln Continental MK III Four-door hardtop, 1958, AMT. Photo courtesy Ron Smith

Promotionals, Ford Edsel convertible, 1958, AMT. Photo courtesy Ron Smith

	C6	C8	C10
Chevrolet Impala Two-door Hardtop, MPC, 1968	30	60	120
Chevrolet Impala Two-door Hardtop, MPC, 1971	20	40	80
Chevrolet Impala Two-door Hardtop, MPC, 1972	15	30	60
Chevrolet Impala Two-door Hardtop, SMP, 1958	27	54	110
Chevrolet Impala Two-door Hardtop, SMP, 1959	20	40	80
Chevrolet Impala Two-door Hardtop, SMP, 1960	20	30	60
Chevrolet Monte Carlo, AMT, 1970	20	40	75
Chevrolet Monte Carlo, AMT, 1971	25	50	100
Chevrolet Monte Carlo, MPC, 1972	20	40	85
Chevrolet Monte Carlo, MPC, 1978	10	20	30
Chevrolet Monte Carlo, MPC, 1979	10	20	30
Chevrolet Monte Carlo, MPC, 1980	10	20	30
Chevrolet Monza, MPC, 1978	10	20	30
Chevrolet Monza, MPC, 1979	10	20	30
Chevrolet Monza 2+2, MPC, 1976	10	20	30
Chevrolet Monza 2+2, MPC, 1977	10	20	30
Chevrolet Monza 2+2, MPC, 1980	10	20	30
Chevrolet Monza 2+2, MPC, Two-door, 1975	10	20	30
Chevrolet Nova Convertible, AMT, 1962	30	60	120
Chevrolet Nova Convertible, AMT, 1963	40	80	170
Chevrolet Nova Station Wagon, AMT, 1963	15	30	60
Chevrolet Nova Two-door Hardtop, AMT, 1962	40	80	160
Chevrolet Nova Two-door Hardtop, AMT, 1963	25	50	100
Chevrolet Pickup, AMT, 1958	20	40	80
Chevrolet Pickup, AMT, 1962	60	120	250
Chevrolet Pickup, AMT, 1963	60	120	250
Chevrolet Pickup, PMC, 1957	30	60	120
Chevrolet Pickup, PMC, 1959	40	80	170
Chevrolet Pickup, SMP, 1960	50	40	185
Chevrolet Silverado C-1500 Pickup, AMT, 1990	7	14	25
Chevrolet Silverado C-1500 Pickup, AMT, 1990	7	14	25
Chevrolet Silverado C-1500 Pickup, AMT, 1992	7	14	25
Chevrolet Silverado C-1500 Pickup, AMT, 1993	7	14	25
Chevrolet Silverado C-1500 Pickup, MPC, 1988	7	14	25
Chevrolet Station Wagon, PMC, 1956	20	40	80
Chevrolet Station Wagon, PMC, 1958	20	50	75
Chevrolet Station Wagon, SMP, 1957	NPF	NPF	NPF
Chevrolet Station Wagon, SMP, 1957	30	60	120
Chevrolet Station Wagon, SMP, 1959	20	40	80
Chevrolet Station Wagon, SMP, 1960	20	40	70
Chevrolet Styline Four-door Sedan, BAN, 1949	40	70	130
Chevrolet Styline Four-door Sedan, BAN, 1950	30	60	120
Chevrolet Styline Four-door Sedan, PMC, 1951	30	60	120
Chevrolet Styline Four-door Sedan, PMC, 1952	30	60	120
Chevrolet Styline Two-door Sedan, BAN, 1949	30	60	120
Chevrolet Styline Two-door Sedan, BAN, 1950	30	60	120
Chevrolet Styline Two-door Sedan, PMC, 1951	30	60	130

	C6	C8	C10
Chevrolet Styline Two-door Sedan, PMC, 1952	40	70	150
Chevrolet Suburban Indianapolis 500 Official Truck, BCG, 1993	10	20	30
Chevrolet Two-door Coupe, BAN, 1949	60	120	240
Chevrolet Two-door Coupe, BAN, 1950	30	60	115
Chevrolet Two-door Coupe, PMC, 1951	30	60	130
Chevrolet Two-door Coupe, PMC, 1952	40	80	150
Chevrolet Two-door Hardtop, BAN, 1955	40	80	145
Chevrolet Two-door Hardtop, BAN, 1956	40	70	140
Chevrolet Two-door Hardtop, PMC, 1955	30	60	120
Chevrolet Two-door Hardtop, PMC, 1956	30	60	120
Chevrolet Two-door Hardtop, SMP, 1957	30	60	120
Chevrolet Vega, MPC, 1974	20	40	60
Chevrolet Vega, MPC, 1976	20	40	60
Chevrolet Vega, MPC, 1977	20	40	60
Chevrolet Vega, MPC, coupe, 1972	20	40	60
Chevrolet Vega, MPC, hatchback, Two-door coupe, 1971	20	40	60
Chevrolet Vega, MPC, Two-door, 1973	20	40	60
Chevrolet Vega, MPC, Two-door, 1975	20	40	60
Chrysler 300 Convertible, JH, 1962	15	30	60
Chrysler 300 Convertible, JH, 1963	35	70	140
Chrysler 300 Convertible, JH, 1964	30	70	140
Chrysler 300 Convertible, JH, 1965	30	60	120
Chrysler 300 Convertible, JH, 1966	15	30	60
Chrysler 300 Convertible, JH, 1967	10	20	45
Chrysler 300 Convertible, JH, 1968	10	20	45
Chrysler 300 Convertible Indy 500 Pace Car, JH, 1963	60	130	270
Chrysler 300 Two-door Hardtop, JH, 1962	15	30	60
Chrysler 300 Two-door Hardtop, JH, 1963	30	6	120
Chrysler 300 Two-door Hardtop, JH, 1964	20	40	80
Chrysler 300 Two-door Hardtop, JH, 1965	40	80	170
Chrysler 300 Two-door Hardtop, JH, 1966	40	60	150
Chrysler 300 Two-door Hardtop, JH, 1967	10	20	35
Chrysler 300 Two-door Hardtop, JH, 1968	10	20	45
Chrysler Four-door Hardtop, JH, 1957	15	40	60
Chrysler Four-door Sedan, BAN, 1949	NPF	NPF	NPF
Chrysler Four-door Sedan, BAN, 1950	30	60	120
Chrysler Four-door Sedan, BAN, 1954	30	60	95
Chrysler Four-door Sedan, NP, 1948	20	40	90
Chrysler New Yorker Four-door Hardtop, JH, 1958	15	35	65
Chrysler New Yorker Four-door Hardtop, JH, 1959	10	20	45
Chrysler New Yorker Two-door Hardtop, JH, 1960	10	20	45
Chrysler New Yorker Two-door Hardtop, JH, 1961	10	20	60
Chrysler Turbine Two-door Hardtop, JH, 1964	10	30	65
Chrysler Two-door Hardtop, BAN, 1953	3	50	100
Corvair 700 Four-door Sedan, AMT, 1961	20	40	80
Corvair Corsa Convertible, AMT, 1965	30	63	120
Corvair Corsa Convertible, AMT, 1966	20	30	60
Corvair Corsa Two-door Hardtop, AMT, 1965	40	80	150

	C6	C8	C10
Corvair Corsa Two-door Hardtop, AMT, 1966	30	60	130
Corvair Four-door Sedan, SMP, 1960	20	40	80
Corvair Monza Convertible, AMT, 1963	30	60	115
Corvair Monza Convertible, AMT, 1964	40	90	170
Corvair Monza Coupe, AMT, 1961	25	50	100
Corvair Monza Two-door Hardtop, AMT, 1962	50	100	200
Corvair Monza Two-door Hardtop, AMT, 1963	30	65	120
Corvair Monza Two-door Hardtop, AMT, 1964	40	90	170
Corvair Monza Two-door Hardtop, AMT, 1967	30	60	120
Corvette Convertible, AMT, 1958	80	180	360
Corvette Convertible, AMT, 1959	80	180	325
Corvette Convertible, AMT, 1960	90	180	390
Corvette Convertible, AMT, 1962	150	275	560
Corvette Convertible, AMT, 1989	15	30	50
Corvette Convertible, AMT, 1990	20	40	60
Corvette Convertible, AMT, 1992	20	40	60
Corvette Convertible, AMT, 1993	20	40	60
Corvette Convertible, AMT, license plate variations, 1990	15	30	50
Corvette Convertible, BAN, original, 1954	20	50	95
Corvette Convertible, MPC, 1987	15	30	50
Corvette Convertible, MPC, 1988	20	40	60
Corvette Convertible, PMC, 1954	90	200	410
Corvette Convertible, PMC, all white, 1953	NPF	NPF	NPF
Corvette Convertible, SMP, 1961	150	275	560
Corvette Coupe, AMT, license plate variations, 1990	20	40	60
Corvette Coupe, MPC, 1984	20	40	60
Corvette Coupe, MPC, 1985	20	40	60
Corvette Coupe, MPC, 1986	20	40	60
Corvette Sting Ray Convertible, AMT, 1963	95	140	450
Corvette Sting Ray Convertible, AMT, 1964	120	250	500
Corvette Sting Ray Convertible, AMT, 1965	120	250	500
Corvette Sting Ray Convertible, AMT, 1966	200	450	900
Corvette Sting Ray Convertible, AMT, 1967	200	400	800
Corvette Sting Ray Convertible, AMT, 1969	90	180	360
Corvette Sting Ray Convertible, AMT, 1970	80	160	320
Corvette Sting Ray Convertible, MPC, 1968	100	200	400
Corvette Sting Ray Coupe, AMT, 1963	150	300	600
Corvette Sting Ray Coupe, AMT, 1964	120	250	500
Corvette Sting Ray Coupe, AMT, 1965	150	300	600
Corvette Sting Ray Coupe, AMT, 1966	200	400	800
Corvette Sting Ray Coupe, AMT, 1967	225	450	900
Corvette Sting Ray Coupe, AMT, 1969	140	280	560
Corvette Sting Ray Coupe, AMT, 1970	80	160	320
Corvette Sting Ray Coupe, MPC, 1968	120	140	380
Corvette Sting Ray Coupe, MPC, 1971	90	180	360
Corvette Sting Ray Coupe, MPC, 1972	90	180	360
Corvette Sting Ray Coupe, MPC, 1973	75	150	225
Corvette Sting Ray Coupe, MPC, 1974	100	220	325
Corvette Sting Ray Coupe, MPC, 1975	75	150	225
Corvette Sting Ray Coupe, MPC, 1976	75	150	225
Corvette Sting Ray Coupe, MPC, 1977	25	50	85
Corvette Sting Ray Coupe, MPC, 1979	15	30	65
Corvette Sting Ray Coupe, MPC, 1980	10	20	30
Corvette Sting Ray Coupe, MPC, 1981	15	30	45
Corvette Sting Ray Coupe, MPC, 1982	15	30	45
Corvette Sting Ray Coupe, MPC, 25th anniversary model, 1978	25	50	85
Corvette Sting Ray Coupe, MPC, no side trim, 1978	50	100	150
Corvette ZR-1 Coupe, AMT, 1989	10	20	30
Corvette ZR-1 Coupe, AMT, 1990	10	20	30
Corvette ZR-1 Coupe, AMT, 1992	10	20	30
Corvette ZR-1 Coupe, AMT, 1993	10	20	30
DeSoto Adventurer Two-door Hardtop, JH, 1960	20	30	50
DeSoto Fireflite Four-door Hardtop, JH, 1956	20	40	60
DeSoto Fireflite Four-door Hardtop, JH, 1958	20	30	60
DeSoto Fireflite Four-door Hardtop, JH, 1959	10	25	55
DeSoto Four-door Sedan, BAN, 1949	NPF	NPF	NPF
DeSoto Four-door Sedan, JH, 1955	20	40	75
DeSoto Four-door Sedan, NP, 1948	20	40	80
DeSoto Sportsman Four-door Hardtop, JH, 1957	20	40	80
Diamond T Dump Truck, PMC, 1956	20	40	90
Diamond T Semi-Truck, PMC, 1956	20	40	90
Divco Milk Truck, AMT, 1951	70	120	250
Dodge Challenger, MPC, 1970	60	120	230
Dodge Challenger, MPC, 1971	50	100	200
Dodge Challenger, MPC, 1972	30	60	120
Dodge Challenger, MPC, 1973	30	60	100
Dodge Charger, MPC, 1973	30	60	100
Dodge Charger, MPC, 1974	30	60	100
Dodge Charger R/T Two-door Hardtop, MPC, 1969	60	100	200
Dodge Charger R/T Two-door Hardtop, MPC, 1970	50	100	210
Dodge Charger Two-door Hardtop, MPC, 1966	40	80	150
Dodge Charger Two-door Hardtop, MPC, 1967	50	100	200
Dodge Charger Two-door Hardtop, MPC, 1968	65	130	260
Dodge Charger Two-door Hardtop, MPC, 1971	70	140	265
Dodge Charger Two-door Hardtop, MPC, 1972	30	60	120
Dodge Cornet Four-door Sedan, BAN, 1953	NPF	NPF	NPF
Dodge Coronet 500 Convertible, MPC, 1965	40	90	180
Dodge Coronet 500 Two-door Hardtop, MPC, 1965	50	100	200
Dodge Coronet Convertible, MPC, 1969	50	10	200
Dodge Coronet Two-door Hardtop, MPC, 1968	60	120	240
Dodge Coronet Two-door Hardtop, MPC, 1969	50	100	200
Dodge Custom 880 Convertible, MPC, 1965	40	80	160
Dodge Custom Royal Four-door Hardtop, AMT, 1956	30	60	110
Dodge Custom Royal Two-door Hardtop, AMT, 1955	20	30	70
Dodge Custom Royal Two-door Hardtop, JH, 1958	20	30	65
Dodge Custom Royal Two-door Hardtop, JH, 1959	10	25	50
Dodge Dart, MPC, 1975	25	50	75
Dodge Dart, MPC, 1976	25	50	75
Dodge Dart Convertible, JH, 1962	20	30	60

	C6	C8	C10
Dodge Dart Police Car, JH, 1962	60	120	240
Dodge Dart Two-door Hardtop, JH, 1962	10	30	60
Dodge Four-door Sedan, BAN, 1949	NPF	NPF	NPF
Dodge Four-door Sedan, BAN, 1950	20	40	95
Dodge Four-door Sedan, BAN, 1951	20	40	90
Dodge Four-door Sedan, BAN, 1952	20	50	95
Dodge Four-door Sedan, BAN, 1954	20	40	80
Dodge Four-door Sedan, NP, 1948	20	60	95
Dodge Intrepid, BCG, Four-door sedan, 1993	7	14	25
Dodge Monaco, MPC, 1977	15	30	45
Dodge Monaco, MPC, 1978	15	30	45
Dodge Monaco 500 Two-door Hardtop, MPC, 1966	40	80	150
Dodge Monaco Two-door Hardtop, MPC, 1965	30	60	120
Dodge Phoenix Two-door Hardtop, JH, 1960	20	40	70
Dodge Phoenix Two-door Hardtop, JH, 1961	20	30	65
Dodge Pickup, NP, 1950	30	60	120
Dodge Polara 500 Convertible, MPC, 1966	40	80	160
Dodge Polara Convertible, JH, 1963	20	40	80
Dodge Polara Convertible, JH, 1964	30	40	90
Dodge Polara Two-door Hardtop, JH, 1963	30	40	85
Dodge Polara Two-door Hardtop, JH, 1964	30	40	85
Dodge Police Car, JH, 1961	20	40	85
Dodge Stake Truck, NP, 1950	30	60	120
Dodge Stealth, AMT, 1993	10	20	30
Dodge Stealth Coupe, AMT, 1992	10	20	30
Dodge Stealth R/T Turbo Coupe, AMT, comes with Indy 500 decals, 1991	10	20	30
Dodge Viper Roadster, AMT, 1993	10	20	30
Dodge Viper Roadster, AMT, Indy 500 Pace Car, 1992	10	20	30
Edsel Convertible, AMT, 1958	50	100	190
Edsel Corsair Convertible, AMT, 1959	40	80	160
Edsel Corsair Two-door Hardtop, AMT, 1959	40	80	160
Edsel Ranger Convertible, AMT, 1960	40	80	160
Edsel Ranger Two-door Hardtop, AMT, 1960	40	80	160
Edsel Two-door Hardtop, AMT, 1958	40	60	90
Euclid Dump Truck, BAN, 1958	20	30	60
Euclid Dump Truck, BAN, 1965	10	20	60
Euclid Quarry Dump Truck, PM, 1950	20	40	80
Ford Convertible, AMT, 1954	20	50	100
Ford Crestline Convertible, AMT, 1953	NPF	NPF	NPF
Ford Custom 300 Two-door Sedan, AMT, 1957	70	140	300
Ford Custom Four-door Sedan, AMT, 1950	20	40	80

Promotionals, Chrysler Imperial Two-door hardtop, 1958, AMT. Photo courtesy Ron Smith

	C6	C8	C10
Ford Custom Four-door Sedan, AMT, 1952	20	40	75
Ford F-100 Pickup, AMT, 1961	40	60	130
Ford F-100 Pickup, AMT, 1962	30	60	110
Ford F-100 Pickup, AMT, 1963	30	60	110
Ford F-150 Pickup, AMT, 1992	10	20	30
Ford F-150 Pickup, AMT, 1993	10	20	30
Ford Fairlane 500 Convertible, AMT, 1958	30	60	110
Ford Fairlane 500 Two-door Hardtop, AMT, 1958	20	30	75
Ford Fairlane 500 Two-door Hardtop, AMT, 1964	20	40	80
Ford Fairlane 500 Two-door Hardtop, AMT, 1965	20	30	60
Ford Fairlane 500 Two-door Sedan, AMT, 1962	20	40	60
Ford Fairlane Cobra Two-door Hardtop, AMT, 1970	10	30	60
Ford Fairlane Convertible, AMT, 1957	30	50	100
Ford Fairlane Four-door Sedan, HUB, 1960	20	30	60
Ford Fairlane Four-door Sedan, HUB, 1961	20	30	60
Ford Fairlane Two-door Hardtop, AMT, 1957	20	40	80
Ford Fairlane Two-door Hardtop, AMT, 1963	20	40	65
Ford Fairlane Two-door Hardtop, AMT, 1966	20	60	110
Ford Falcon Convertible, AMT, 1963	30	60	115
Ford Falcon Convertible, AMT, 1965	20	40	80
Ford Falcon Futura Two-door, AMT, 1966	20	40	80
Ford Falcon Futura Two-door Sedan, AMT, 1962	10	20	30
Ford Falcon Ranchero Pickup, SMP, 1961	10	30	60
Ford Falcon Sprint Convertible, AMT, 1964	20	40	80
Ford Falcon Sprint Two-door Hardtop, AMT, 1964	20	40	80
Ford Falcon Two-door Hardtop, AMT, 1965	20	40	80
Ford Falcon Two-door Hardtop, AMT, 1969	10	20	40
Ford Falcon Two-door Sedan, AMT, 1960	10	30	60
Ford Falcon Two-door Sedan, AMT, 1961	10	20	30
Ford Four-door Sedan, AMT, 1948	30	60	120
Ford Four-door Sedan, AMT, 1949	NPF	NPF	NPF
Ford Four-door Sedan, AMT, 1951	20	40	85
Ford Four-door Sedan, AMT, 1953	20	35	75
Ford Four-door Sedan, AMT, 1954	20	40	80
Ford Four-door Sedan, AMT, 1956	30	50	100
Ford Four-door Sedan, BAN, 1950	30	60	120
Ford Four-door Sedan, BAN, 1953	20	35	75
Ford Galaxie 500 Convertible, AMT, 1959	30	50	95
Ford Galaxie 500 Convertible, AMT, 1962	30	50	100
Ford Galaxie 500 Convertible, AMT, 1963	20	40	80
Ford Galaxie 500 Convertible, AMT, 1966	20	30	60
Ford Galaxie 500 Four-door Hardtop, AMT, 1960	20	40	80
Ford Galaxie 500 Two-door Hardtop, AMT, 1959	30	50	95

	C6	C8	C10
Ford Galaxie 500 Two-door Hardtop, AMT, 1961	20	40	80
Ford Galaxie 500 Two-door Hardtop, AMT, 1962	15	30	65
Ford Galaxie 500 Two-door Hardtop, AMT, 1963	20	40	80
Ford Galaxie 500 Two-door Hardtop, AMT, 1966	20	30	60
Ford Galaxie 500XL Convertible, AMT, 1964	20	40	85
Ford Galaxie 500XL Convertible, AMT, 1965	20	30	60
Ford Galaxie 500XL Two-door Hardtop, AMT, 1964	20	40	85
Ford Galaxie 500XL Two-door Hardtop, AMT, 1965	20	30	60
Ford Galaxie 500XL Two-door Hardtop, AMT, 1967	20	30	60
Ford Galaxie 500XL Two-door Hardtop, AMT, 1968	20	30	60
Ford Galaxie 500XL Two-door Hardtop, AMT, 1969	20	30	60
Ford Grand Torino Two-door Hardtop, JH, 1972	10	20	40
Ford LTD Four-door Hardtop, AMT, 1970	20	30	60
Ford Maverick Two-door Sedan, JH, 1969	10	15	25
Ford Pace Car Convertible, AMT, 1953	70	150	300
Ford Panel Truck, NP, 1951	20	40	90
Ford Pickup, AMT, 1960	30	60	120
Ford Pickup, BAN, 1953	40	80	160
Ford Pickup, NP, 1950	40	80	150
Ford Pickup, NP, 1951	20	50	100
Ford Ranchero Pickup, PMC, 1959	20	40	60
Ford Ranger Pickup, AMT, 1993	10	20	30
Ford Stake Truck, NP, 1951	20	40	80
Ford Starliner Hardtop, AMT, 1961	25	60	120
Ford Starliner Hardtop, AMT, Two-door, 1960	20	50	100
Ford Station Wagon, AMT, 1959	20	40	80
Ford Station Wagon, HUB, 1960	20	40	80
Ford Station Wagon, HUB, 1961	20	40	80
Ford Station Wagon, HUB, 1962	20	40	80
Ford Station Wagon, PMC, 1955	30	50	100
Ford Station Wagon, PMC, 1956	30	50	100
Ford Station Wagon, PMC, 1957	20	40	80
Ford Station Wagon, PMC, 1958	20	40	100
Ford Sunliner Convertible, AMT, 1955	40	80	150
Ford Sunliner Convertible, AMT, 1956	20	40	85
Ford Sunliner Convertible, AMT, 1960	20	50	110
Ford Sunliner Convertible, AMT, 1961	20	50	110
Ford Taurus SHO, AMT, Four-door sedan, 1989	10	20	30
Ford Taurus SHO, AMT, Four-door sedan, 1990	10	20	30
Ford Torino Two-door Hardtop, AMT, 1969	30	60	115
Ford Two-door Sedan, MC, 1948	30	60	120
Ford Two-door Sedan, MC, 1950	30	60	120
Ford Victoria Four-door Sedan, AMT, 1956	20	40	85
Ford Victoria Four-door Sedan, BAN, 1955	30	60	120
Ford Victoria Two-door Hardtop, BAN, 1955	20	50	100
Geo Storm, AMT, 1990	7	14	20
Geo Storm, AMT, 1992	7	14	20
Geo Storm, AMT, 1993	7	14	20
GMC Dump Truck, NP, 1950	30	60	100

	C6	C8	C10
GMC Pickup, NP, 1950	30	60	100
Henry J Two-door Sedan, AMT, 1951	40	80	150
Hornet Two-door Sedan, JH, 1970	10	20	40
Hudson Four-door Sedan, MC, 1948	50	100	200
Hudson Four-door Sedan, MC, 1950	40	80	150
Hudson Four-door Sedan, MC, 1951	40	80	160
Hudson Hornet Four-door Sedan, MC, 1954	NPF	NPF	NPF
Imperial Convertible, AMT, 1961	40	60	120
Imperial Convertible, AMT, 1962	20	50	100
Imperial Convertible, AMT, 1963	20	50	100
Imperial Convertible, AMT, 1964	45	90	180
Imperial Convertible, AMT, 1965	50	100	200
Imperial Convertible, AMT, 1966	60	110	230
Imperial Convertible, SMP, 1959	20	45	90
Imperial Convertible, SMP, 1960	10	30	60
Imperial Crown Convertible, SMP, 1958	20	45	90
Imperial Crown Two-door Hardtop, AMT, 1964	45	90	180
Imperial Crown Two-door Hardtop, SMP, 1958	20	45	90
Imperial Two-door Hardtop, AMT, 1961	40	60	120
Imperial Two-door Hardtop, AMT, 1962	20	50	100
Imperial Two-door Hardtop, AMT, 1963	50	100	175
Imperial Two-door Hardtop, AMT, 1965	20	40	80
Imperial Two-door Hardtop, AMT, 1966	60	110	230
Imperial Two-door Hardtop, AMT, 1967	40	80	140
Imperial Two-door Hardtop, JH, 1968	10	20	50
Imperial Two-door Hardtop, SMP, 1959	20	45	90
Imperial Two-door Hardtop, SMP, 1960	10	30	60
International Dump Truck, PMC, 1951	30	60	120
International Dump Truck, PMC, 1953	25	50	100
International Dump Truck, PMC, 1958	10	20	50
International Pickup, PMC, 1947	50	100	190
International Pickup, PMC, 1950	40	70	140
International Pickup, PMC, 1951	40	80	150
International Pickup, PMC, 1956	20	40	85
International Pickup, PMC, 1957	20	45	90
International Pickup, PMC, 1958	NPF	NPF	NPF
International Scout Convertible, ESK, 1965	20	30	60
International Semi, PMC, 1953	30	60	120
International Semi Mayflower, PMC, 1953	20	40	90
International Semi-Truck, PMC, 1951	30	60	110
International Semi-Truck, PMC, 1958	NPF	NPF	NPF
International Stake Truck, PMC, 1951	30	60	120
International Stake Truck, PMC, 1953	30	60	120
International Stake Truck, PMC, 1958	10	20	50
International Telephone Truck, NP, 1947	30	60	130
International Tilt Cab Semi, PMC, 1955	25	50	100
Javelin Two-door Hardtop, JH, 1968	10	30	60
Javelin Two-door Hardtop, JH, 1969	10	30	60
Javelin Two-door Hardtop, JH, 1970	20	30	65
Javelin/AMX Two-door Hardtop, JH, 1971	10	30	50
Javelin/AMX Two-door Hardtop, JH, 1972	10	30	50
Jeep Station Wagon, AUT, 1950	40	90	180
Kaiser Four-door Sedan, BAN, 1953	80	150	310
Lincoln Continental Four-door Convertible, AMT, 1961	20	40	80
Lincoln Continental Four-door Convertible, AMT, 1962	30	60	120
Lincoln Continental Four-door Convertible, AMT, 1963	20	30	60
Lincoln Continental Four-door Convertible, AMT, 1964	20	40	85
Lincoln Continental Four-door Convertible, AMT, 1965	10	20	40

	C6	C8	C10
Lincoln Continental Four-door Sedan, AMT, 1961	20	40	80
Lincoln Continental Four-door Sedan, AMT, 1962	30	60	120
Lincoln Continental Four-door Sedan, AMT, 1963	20	40	60
Lincoln Continental Four-door Sedan, AMT, 1964	40	80	170
Lincoln Continental Four-door Sedan, AMT, 1965	30	60	90
Lincoln Continental Four-door Sedan, AMT, 1966	20	40	80
Lincoln Continental Four-door Sedan, AMT, 1967	20	40	85
Lincoln Continental Four-door Sedan, AMT, 1968	10	20	40
Lincoln Continental Mark II Two-door Hardtop, AMT, 1956	40	80	150
Lincoln Continental Mark II Two-door Hardtop, AMT, 1957	40	80	150
Lincoln Continental MK III Four-door Hardtop, AMT, 1958	10	30	60
Lincoln Continental MK IV Convertible, AMT, 1959	20	40	60
Lincoln Continental MK IV Two-door Hardtop, AMT, 1959	20	40	60
Lincoln Continental MK V Convertible, AMT, 1960	10	30	50
Lincoln Continental MK V Two-door Hardtop, AMT, 1960	10	20	50
Lincoln Cosmopolitan Four-door Sedan, NP, 1950	100	250	425
Lincoln Four-door Sedan, BAN, 1951	30	60	100
Lincoln Four-door Sedan, BAN, 1953	30	60	100
Lincoln Two-door Hardtop, BAN, 1954	30	60	100
Mack Tanker Truck, NP, 1950	30	60	120
Mercedes 300 SL Convertible, HUB, 1958	25	40	80
Mercedes 300 SL Coupe, HUB, 1958	25	40	80
Mercury Comet, JH, 1972	30	60	90
Mercury Comet Convertible, AMT, 1963	10	30	60
Mercury Comet Cyclone GT, AMT, 1966	65	110	180
Mercury Comet Cyclone GT Pace Car, AMT, red, 1966	100	200	300
Mercury Comet Cyclone GT Pace Car, AMT, white, 1966	80	165	250
Mercury Comet Four-door Sedan, AMT, 1960	20	40	60
Mercury Comet Two-door Hardtop, AMT, 1964	60	120	240
Mercury Comet Two-door Sedan, AMT, 1961	10	20	30
Mercury Comet Two-door Sedan, AMT, 1962	10	25	50
Mercury Comet Two-door Sedan, JH, 1971	10	20	30
Mercury Cougar Two-door Hardtop, AMT, 1968	10	20	60
Mercury Four-door Sedan, BAN, 1951	30	60	120
Mercury Four-door Sedan, NP, 1949	NPF	NPF	NPF
Mercury Meteor Custom Two-door Sedan, AMT, 1962	30	60	120
Mercury Meteor Two-door Hardtop, AMT, 1963	30	60	120
Mercury Monterey Convertible, AMT, 1961	20	35	70
Mercury Monterey Convertible, AMT, 1962	30	60	120
Mercury Monterey Convertible, AMT, 1963	20	40	80

Promotionals, International Pickup, 1956, Product Miniatures. Photo courtesy Ron Smith

	C6	C8	C10
Mercury Monterey Four-door Sedan, BAN, 1953	20	40	95
Mercury Monterey Two-door Hardtop, AMT, 1961	10	20	40
Mercury Monterey Two-door Hardtop, AMT, 1962	30	60	120
Mercury Monterey Two-door Hardtop, AMT, 1963	20	40	80
Mercury Monterey Two-door Hardtop, BAN, 1954	20	40	95
Mercury Monterey Two-door Hardtop, BAN, 1955	30	60	120
Mercury Park Lane Breezeway Two-door Hardtop, AMT, 1964	40	80	160
Mercury Park Lane Convertible, AMT, 1959	20	35	70
Mercury Park Lane Convertible, AMT, 1960	20	35	70
Mercury Park Lane Convertible, AMT, 1964	20	40	80
Mercury Park Lane Two-door Hardtop, AMT, 1959	20	40	75
Mercury Park Lane Two-door Hardtop, AMT, 1960	20	35	70
Mercury Park Lane Two-door Hardtop, AMT, 1965	10	20	40
Mercury Park Lane Two-door Hardtop, AMT, 1966	10	25	50
Metro Panel Truck (double), PMC, 1952	20	40	80
Metro Panel Truck (single), PMC, 1952	20	40	80
Metropolitan Convertible, HUB, 1958	60	120	240
Metropolitan Two-door Hardtop, HUB, 1958	60	120	240
Mustang, UMC, 1981	NPF	NPF	NPF
Mustang 2 + 2 Two-door Hardtop, AMT, 1966	40	80	175
Mustang 2 + 2 Two-door Hardtop, AMT, 1967	60	120	220
Mustang Convertible, AMT, 1965	30	50	100
Mustang Convertible, AMT, 1966	20	40	80
Mustang Convertible Indy 500 Pace Car, AMT, 1964	50	100	200
Mustang II, MPC, 1974	NPF	NPF	NPF
Mustang II, MPC, 1975	NPF	NPF	NPF
Mustang Mach I Two-door Fastback, AMT, 1969	60	120	245
Mustang Mach I Two-door Fastback, AMT, 1971	40	80	150
Mustang Mach I Two-door Hardtop, AMT, 1972	30	60	120
Mustang Two-door Convertible, AMT, 1964	30	60	120
Mustang Two-door Fastback, AMT, 1965	30	50	100
Mustang Two-door Hardtop, AMT, 1964	25	50	90

	C6	C8	C10
Mustang Two-door Hardtop, AMT, 1965	20	40	90
Mustang Two-door Hardtop, AMT, 1966	30	60	115
Nash 600 Four-door Sedan, NP, metal, 1949	NPF	NPF	NPF
Nash Four-door Sedan, NP, 1950	20	40	60
Nash Four-door Sedan, PMC, 1953	20	40	95
Nash Four-door Sedan, PMC, 1954	30	50	100
Nash Golden Airflight Four-door, PMC, 1952	3	50	100
Oldsmobile 442 Two-door Hardtop, JH, 1969	20	40	80
Oldsmobile 442 Two-door Hardtop, JH, 1970	20	40	60
Oldsmobile 442 Two-door Hardtop, JH, 1971	20	40	60
Oldsmobile 88 Convertible, AMT, 1965	30	60	110
Oldsmobile 88 Four-door Hardtop, JH, 1961	20	30	60
Oldsmobile 88 Four-door Hardtop, JH, 1962	20	40	80
Oldsmobile 88 Two-door Hardtop, AMT, 1965	20	50	100
Oldsmobile 98 Four-door Hardtop, JH, 1957	20	40	75
Oldsmobile 98 Four-door Hardtop, JH, 1959	20	40	75
Oldsmobile 98 Two-door Hardtop, JH, 1960	20	30	60
Oldsmobile Cutlass, JH, 1973	25	50	75
Oldsmobile Cutlass, JH, 1974	25	50	75
Oldsmobile Cutlass, JH, 1975	25	50	75
Oldsmobile F-85 442 Two-door Hardtop, JH, 1968	20	40	60
Oldsmobile F-85 Convertible, JH, 1964	30	60	120
Oldsmobile F-85 Cutlass Convertible, JH, 1962	20	40	60
Oldsmobile F-85 Cutlass Two-door Sedan, JH, 1962	20	40	60
Oldsmobile F-85 Station Wagon, JH, 1961	10	20	30
Oldsmobile F-85 Two-door Hardtop, JH, 1964	30	60	120
Oldsmobile Four-door Hardtop, JH, 1956	25	40	85
Oldsmobile Four-door Hardtop, JH, 1958	20	40	65
Oldsmobile Four-door Sedan, BAN, 1953	25	40	85
Oldsmobile Four-door Sedan, CRU, 1949	NPF	NPF	NPF
Oldsmobile Starfire Convertible, JH, 1962	20	40	80
Oldsmobile Starfire Convertible, JH, 1963	10	30	50
Oldsmobile Starfire Two-door Hardtop, JH, 1963	10	30	60
Oldsmobile Tornado, AMT, 1968	30	60	90
Oldsmobile Toronado Two-door Hardtop, JH, 1966	10	30	50
Oldsmobile Toronado Two-door Hardtop, JH, 1969	10	30	50
Oldsmobile Toronado Two-door Hardtop, JH, 1970	10	20	40
Oldsmobile Toronado Two-door Hardtop, JH, 1971	20	40	60
Oldsmobile Toronado Two-door Hardtop, JH, 1972	10	20	30
Oldsmobile Two-door Hardtop, BAN, 1954	25	40	85
Oldsmobile Two-door Hardtop, BAN, 1955	25	40	85
Opel GT 1900 Coupe, AMT, 1969	20	50	100

	C6	C8	C10
Opel Sedan, PMC, 1959	10	20	30
Packard Convertible, MC, 1948	30	60	120
Packard Four-door Sedan, BAN, 1953	35	60	120
Packard Four-door Sedan, BAN, 1954	35	60	120
Packard Henesey Ambulance, AMT, 1951	60	120	250
Pinto Runabout Two-door Sedan, AMT, 1972	10	15	25
Pinto Two-door Sedan, AMT, 1971	10	15	25
Plymouth Belvedere Four-door, JH, 1956	20	40	80
Plymouth Belvedere Two-door Hardtop, JH, 1957	20	40	80
Plymouth Belvedere Two-door Hardtop, JH, 1958	10	30	60
Plymouth Cuda Two-door Hardtop, MPC, 1972	50	90	175
Plymouth Duster, MPC, 1972	30	60	120
Plymouth Duster, MPC, 1973	NPF	NPF	NPF
Plymouth Duster, MPC, 1974	NPF	NPF	NPF
Plymouth Duster Two-door Hardtop, MPC, 1971	20	50	100
Plymouth Four-door Hardtop, PMC, 1954	30	40	80
Plymouth Four-door Sedan, AMT, 1949	NPF	NPF	NPF
Plymouth Four-door Sedan, AMT, 1950	20	40	85
Plymouth Four-door Sedan, BAN, 1953	30	60	120
Plymouth Four-door Sedan, JH, 1955	20	40	80
Plymouth Four-door Sedan, PMC, 1953	20	40	80
Plymouth Four-door Taxi, PMC, 1953	20	40	85
Plymouth Fury Convertible, JH, 1962	30	50	100
Plymouth Fury Convertible, JH, 1963	20	40	85
Plymouth Fury Convertible, JH, 1964	20	40	80
Plymouth Fury Convertible, JH, 1967	20	30	60
Plymouth Fury Drivers Ed., JH, 1965	80	120	180
Plymouth Fury III Convertible, JH, 1965	30	70	130
Plymouth Fury III Convertible, JH, 1966	20	40	80
Plymouth Fury III Convertible, JH, 1968	20	30	60
Plymouth Fury III Convertible Indy 500 Pace Car, JH, 1965	60	120	265
Plymouth Fury III Driver's Training, JH, 1965	25	50	110
Plymouth Fury III Driver's Training, JH, 1966	35	70	125
Plymouth Fury III Two-door Hardtop, JH, 1965	30	60	120
Plymouth Fury III Two-door Hardtop, JH, 1966	20	40	80
Plymouth Fury III Two-door Hardtop, JH, 1968	10	30	50
Plymouth Fury Police Car, JH, 1962	40	80	150
Plymouth Fury Taxi, JH, 1959	30	50	110
Plymouth Fury Taxi, JH, 1960	30	65	130
Plymouth Fury Taxi, JH, 1962	50	100	200
Plymouth Fury Two-door Hardtop, JH, 1958	30	60	115
Plymouth Fury Two-door Hardtop, JH, 1959	20	40	80

Promotionals, 1978 Corvette Silver Anniversary edition. Photo courtesy Ron O'Brien

	C6	C8	C10
Plymouth Fury Two-door Hardtop, JH, 1960	20	40	60
Plymouth Fury Two-door Hardtop, JH, 1961	20	40	90
Plymouth Fury Two-door Hardtop, JH, 1962	30	50	100
Plymouth Fury Two-door Hardtop, JH, 1963	20	40	85
Plymouth Fury Two-door Hardtop, JH, 1964	30	60	120
Plymouth Fury Two-door Hardtop, JH, 1967	10	30	50
Plymouth GTX Two-door Hardtop, JH, 1969	20	40	80
Plymouth GTX Two-door Hardtop, JH, 1970	20	50	100
Plymouth Police Car, JH, 1961	25	50	100
Plymouth Roadrunner, MPC, 1973	65	130	200
Plymouth Roadrunner, MPC, 1974	NPF	NPF	NPF
Plymouth Roadrunner, MPC, 1975	NPF	NPF	NPF
Plymouth Roadrunner Two-door Hardtop, MPC, 1971	30	65	130
Plymouth Roadrunner Two-door Hardtop, MPC, 1972	30	60	120
Plymouth Sedan, BAN, 1955	20	40	80
Plymouth Sedan, NP, 1948	30	60	120
Plymouth Station Wagon, JH, 1960	10	30	60
Plymouth Station Wagon, PMC, 1954	30	70	140
Plymouth Taxi, JH, 1957	40	65	130
Plymouth Taxi, JH, 1958	40	60	120
Plymouth Taxi, JH, 1961	30	65	135
Plymouth Two-door Sedan, BAN, 1956	20	40	80
Plymouth Volare, MPC, 1978	10	20	30
Plymouth Volare, MPC, Two-door hardtop, 1977	10	20	30
Pontiac Bonneville Convertible, AMT, 1958	30	60	120
Pontiac Bonneville Convertible, AMT, 1959	20	40	80
Pontiac Bonneville Convertible, AMT, 1960	20	40	80
Pontiac Bonneville Convertible, AMT, 1961	30	60	120
Pontiac Bonneville Convertible, AMT, 1962	60	120	240
Pontiac Bonneville Convertible, AMT, 1963	40	80	130
Pontiac Bonneville Convertible, AMT, 1964	40	80	140
Pontiac Bonneville Convertible, AMT, 1965	40	65	130
Pontiac Bonneville Convertible, MPC, 1966	40	65	130
Pontiac Bonneville Convertible, MPC, 1967	30	60	115
Pontiac Bonneville Convertible, MPC, 1968	30	50	110
Pontiac Bonneville Convertible, MPC, 1969	20	40	80
Pontiac Bonneville Convertible, MPC, 1970	30	60	95
Pontiac Bonneville Two-door Hardtop, AMT, 1958	20	40	80
Pontiac Bonneville Two-door Hardtop, AMT, 1959	20	40	80
Pontiac Bonneville Two-door Hardtop, AMT, 1960	20	40	80
Pontiac Bonneville Two-door Hardtop, AMT, 1961	30	60	120
Pontiac Bonneville Two-door Hardtop, AMT, 1962	40	80	160
Pontiac Bonneville Two-door Hardtop, AMT, 1963	30	50	90
Pontiac Bonneville Two-door Hardtop, AMT, 1964	30	60	120
Pontiac Bonneville Two-door Hardtop, AMT, 1965	40	90	140
Pontiac Bonneville Two-door Hardtop, MPC, 1966	40	75	150
Pontiac Bonneville Two-door Hardtop, MPC, 1967	30	60	115
Pontiac Bonneville Two-door Hardtop, MPC, 1968	20	40	75
Pontiac Bonneville Two-door Hardtop, MPC, 1969	20	40	80
Pontiac Bonneville Two-door Hardtop, MPC, 1970	10	25	50
Pontiac Firebird, MPC, 1975	NPF	NPF	NPF
Pontiac Firebird, MPC, 1976	NPF	NPF	NPF
Pontiac Firebird, MPC, 1977	NPF	NPF	NPF
Pontiac Firebird, MPC, 1978	NPF	NPF	NPF
Pontiac Firebird, MPC, 1979	NPF	NPF	NPF
Pontiac Firebird, MPC, 1980	NPF	NPF	NPF
Pontiac Firebird, MPC, 1980	NPF	NPF	NPF
Pontiac Firebird 400, MPC, 1973	NPF	NPF	NPF
Pontiac Firebird 400, MPC, 1974	NPF	NPF	NPF
Pontiac Firebird 400 Two-door Hardtop, MPC, 1971	20	30	70
Pontiac Firebird 400 Two-door Hardtop, MPC, 1972	20	30	70
Pontiac Firebird Convertible, MPC, 1967	50	100	180
Pontiac Firebird Convertible, MPC, 1968	60	110	225
Pontiac Firebird Convertible, MPC, 1969	30	70	120
Pontiac Firebird Trans Am, AMT, 1993	15	30	45
Pontiac Firebird Two-door Hardtop, MPC, 1967	50	10	180
Pontiac Firebird Two-door Hardtop, MPC, 1968	40	80	160
Pontiac Firebird Two-door Hardtop, MPC, 1969	27	63	115
Pontiac Firebird Two-door Hardtop, MPC, 1970	20	40	80
Pontiac Four-door Hardtop, JH, 1956	20	40	60
Pontiac Four-door Sedan, AMT, 1951	20	40	60
Pontiac Four-door Sedan, AMT, 1952	20	40	60
Pontiac Four-door Sedan, BAN, 1949	NPF	NPF	NPF
Pontiac Four-door Sedan, JH, 1955	20	40	60
Pontiac Four-door Sedan, NP, 1947	40	60	120
Pontiac Four-door Sedan, NP, 1948	40	60	120
Pontiac Grand Prix Two-door Hardtop, AMT, 1964	40	80	140
Pontiac Grand Prix Two-door Hardtop, AMT, 1965	40	80	150
Pontiac Grand Prix Two-door Hardtop, MPC, 1969	20	40	80
Pontiac Grand Prix Two-door Hardtop, MPC, 1970	20	40	80
Pontiac Grand Prix Two-door Hardtop, MPC, 1971	20	40	80
Pontiac Grand Prix Two-door Hardtop, MPC, 1972	20	40	80
Pontiac GTO Two-door Hardtop, MPC, 1970	30	25	100
Pontiac GTO Two-door Hardtop, MPC, 1971	20	40	85
Pontiac GTO Two-door Hardtop, MPC, 1972	20	40	80
Pontiac Sedan, BAN, 1953	30	60	90
Pontiac Sedan, BAN, 1955	20	40	60
Pontiac Star Chief Convertible, AMT, 1957	40	80	160

	C6	C8	C10
Pontiac Star Chief Four-door Hardtop, AMT, 1957	30	60	120
Pontiac Tempest Four-door Sedan, AMT, 1961	20	30	60
Pontiac Tempest GTO Convertible, AMT, 1965	65	140	300
Pontiac Tempest GTO Convertible, MPC, 1966	70	140	300
Pontiac Tempest GTO Convertible, MPC, 1967	70	140	300
Pontiac Tempest GTO Convertible, MPC, 1968	40	80	160
Pontiac Tempest GTO Convertible, MPC, 1969	40	80	160
Pontiac Tempest GTO Two-door Hardtop, AMT, 1964	65	120	250
Pontiac Tempest GTO Two-door Hardtop, AMT, 1965	65	140	300
Pontiac Tempest GTO Two-door Hardtop, MPC, 1966	70	140	300
Pontiac Tempest GTO Two-door Hardtop, MPC, 1967	70	140	300
Pontiac Tempest GTO Two-door Hardtop, MPC, 1968	40	80	160
Pontiac Tempest GTO Two-door Hardtop, MPC, 1969	40	80	100
Pontiac Tempest LeMans Convertible, AMT, 1962	20	30	60
Pontiac Tempest LeMans Convertible, AMT, 1963	30	60	120
Pontiac Tempest LeMans Convertible, AMT, 1964	30	60	120
Pontiac Tempest LeMans Two-door Hardtop, AMT, 1964	30	60	120
Pontiac Tempest LeMans Two-door Sedan, AMT, 1962	20	30	60
Pontiac Tempest LeMans Two-door Sedan, AMT, 1963	30	60	120
Pontiac Two-door Sedan, AMT, 1953	20	40	60
Pontiac Two-door Sedan, AMT, 1954	20	40	60
Pontiac Two-door Sedan, JH, 1955	20	40	60
Rambler Ambassador Convertible, JH, 1967	10	20	30
Rambler Ambassador Convertible, JH, 1968	10	20	30
Rambler Ambassador Two-door Hardtop, JH, 1966	10	20	30
Rambler Ambassador Two-door Hardtop, JH, 1967	10	20	30
Rambler Ambassador Two-door Hardtop, JH, 1968	10	20	30
Rambler Ambassador Two-door Hardtop, JH, 1969	10	20	30
Rambler American Convertible, JH, 1962	10	20	40
Rambler American Convertible, JH, 1963	10	30	40
Rambler American Convertible, JH, 1964	10	20	30
Rambler American Convertible, JH, 1965	10	20	40
Rambler American Convertible, JH, 1966	10	20	40
Rambler American Two-door Hardtop, JH, 1964	10	20	50
Rambler American Two-door Hardtop, JH, 1966	10	20	40
Rambler American Two-door Sedan, JH, 1961	10	30	40
Rambler American Two-door Sedan, JH, 1962	10	20	40
Rambler C.C. Station Wagon, JH, 1966	10	20	30
Rambler Classic Four-door Sedan, JH, 1962	10	20	40
Rambler Classic Four-door Sedan, JH, 1963	10	30	50

	C6	C8	C10
Rambler Classic Four-door Sedan, JH, 1964	10	20	40
Rambler Classic Four-door Sedan, JH, 1965	10	20	40
Rambler Classic Station Wagon, JH, 1962	10	20	40
Rambler Classic Station Wagon, JH, 1963	10	30	50
Rambler Classic Station Wagon, JH, 1964	10	20	40
Rambler Convertible, NP, 1951	30	60	120
Rambler Cross Country Station Wagon, JH, 1960	25	55	90
Rambler Cross Country Station Wagon, JH, 1961	10	30	65
Rambler Dauphine Four-door, HUB, 1958	10	20	45
Rambler Marlin Two-door Fastback, JH, 1965	20	40	80
Rambler Marlin Two-door Fastback, JH, 1966	20	40	80
Rambler Sedan, BAN, 1953	20	50	100
Rambler Station Wagon, JH, 1959	10	30	65
Rambler Two-door Hardtop, BAN, 1952	30	60	120
Rambler Two-door Hardtop, BAN, 1954	30	60	120
Rambler Unit Frame Construction Demo, JH, 1961	50	100	150
Rolls Royce Silver Ghost Four-door Sedan, HUB, 1958	30	60	120
Studebaker Golden Hawk Two-door, AMT, 1956	30	60	90
Studebaker Lark Convertible, JH, 1962	10	25	50
Studebaker Lark Two-door Hardtop, JH, 1959	10	25	50
Studebaker Lark Two-door Hardtop, JH, 1960	10	25	50
Studebaker Lark Two-door Hardtop, JH, 1961	10	25	50
Studebaker Lark Two-door Hardtop, JH, 1962	10	25	50
Studebaker Stake Truck, NP, 1950	90	180	350
Studebaker Starliner Coupe, AMT, 1953	20	40	80
Studebaker Starliner Coupe, AMT, 1954	20	40	80
Studebaker Starliner Coupe, BAN, 1953	20	40	80
Studebaker Two-door Sedan, AMT, 1950	30	60	110
Studebaker Two-door Sedan, AMT, 1951	30	60	110
Studebaker Two-door Sedan, AMT, 1952	20	40	80
Studebaker Two-door Sedan, NP, 1947	40	80	150
Studebaker Two-door Sedan, NP, 1948	30	60	120
Studebaker Two-door-Hardtop, AMT, 1955	20	40	80
Thunderbird Convertible, AMT, 1955	50	75	150
Thunderbird Convertible, AMT, 1956	40	60	80
Thunderbird Convertible, AMT, 1957	30	40	60
Thunderbird Convertible, AMT, 1959	20	40	75
Thunderbird Convertible, AMT, 1960	20	50	100
Thunderbird Convertible, AMT, 1961	30	60	120
Thunderbird Convertible, AMT, 1962	50	110	195
Thunderbird Convertible, AMT, 1963	50	90	180
Thunderbird Convertible, AMT, 1964	30	60	120
Thunderbird Convertible, AMT, 1965	20	40	75
Thunderbird Convertible, AMT, 1966	20	40	75
Thunderbird Two-door Hardtop, AMT, 1958	20	40	75
Thunderbird Two-door Hardtop, AMT, 1959	20	40	75
Thunderbird Two-door Hardtop, AMT, 1960	20	40	75
Thunderbird Two-door Hardtop, AMT, 1961	30	60	120

Promotionals, 1979 Corvette. Photo courtesy Ron O'Brien

	C6	C8	C10
Thunderbird Two-door Hardtop, AMT, 1962	30	60	120
Thunderbird Two-door Hardtop, AMT, 1963	20	40	80
Thunderbird Two-door Hardtop, AMT, 1964	20	40	80
Thunderbird Two-door Hardtop, AMT, 1965	20	40	75
Thunderbird Two-door Hardtop, AMT, 1966	20	40	60
Thunderbird Two-door Hardtop, AMT, 1967	10	25	50
Thunderbird Two-door Hardtop, AMT, 1968	10	25	50
Thunderbird Two-door Hardtop, AMT, 1969	10	25	50
Thunderbird Two-door Hardtop, AMT, 1970	10	25	50

	C6	C8	C10
Thunderbird Two-door Hardtop, AMT, 1971	10	25	50
Torino Cobra Two-door Hardtop, AMT, 1971	10	20	60
Triumph TR-3A Convertible, HUB, 1958	20	40	90
Triumph TR-3A Hardtop, HUB, 1958	20	40	90
Valiant Four-door Sedan, AMT, 1960	10	20	40
Valiant Four-door Sedan, AMT, 1961	10	20	40
Valiant Hatchback Two-door, MPC, 1972	10	20	30
Valiant Signet 200 Two-door Hardtop, AMT, 1964	10	60	80
Valiant Signet 800 Two-door Hardtop, AMT, 1962	30	60	120
Valiant Signet 800 Two-door Hardtop, AMT, 1963	10	60	80
Valiant Two-door Hardtop, AMT, 1961	10	20	40
Valiant Two-door Hardtop, AMT, 1965	20	30	60
Valiant Two-door Hardtop, AMT, 1966	80	160	320
Volkswagen Karmann Ghia, PM, 1959	10	20	40
Volkswagen Sedan, PM, 1959	10	20	30
White C.O.E Truck, NP, 1950	50	100	200
Willys 3/4-ton Army Truck, BAN, 1969	20	40	80
Willys Jeep FC Pickup, AUT, 1961	30	50	100
Willys Jeep FC Stake Truck w/plow, AUT, 1961	30	50	100
Willys Jeep Jolly, AUT, 1961	20	50	100
Willys Jeep Stake Truck, AUT, 1961	30	50	100
Willys Jeepster, MPC, 1968	10	20	40
Willys-Jeep Army Stake Truck, BAN, 1967	10	25	50

PYRO

Pyro is probably best known for its plastic model kits produced in the 1950s and 1960s, but it did produce a nice line of toy vehicles in the 1950s. The originals of these were military vehicles made around the time of the Korean War. Available in two sizes, they came in three different colors—khaki, olive drab, and gray (for Navy and Marine) plastic. Each model was heat-stamped with stars and other identifying marks. Lionel used the large Pyro military vehicles as loads for its Navy and Marine trains. The loads were all gray and had no figures glued in place. After the Korean War came the inevitable decline in sales of war toys, and the vehicles were issued in civilian roles (i.e. Horse Transport) and specialty roles (i.e., Coca-Cola Truck). Pyro also produced a wide range of toys and trinkets for Planters Peanuts.

Specialty advertising issued included at least one political truck—an "Elect Marvin Griffin for Governor-Get On The Griffin Bandwagon" truck. Griffin was governor of Georgia from 1954 to 1958. Military sets continued in production into the mid to late 1950s. A 1956 Pyro advertisement in *Toys & Novelties* magazine declared: "Military Toys Are Hot Again!" The ad pictured boxed military sets C-242, C-243, and C-244. Toys gradually faded behind Pyro's growing line of model kits. The company went out of business in 1969. It was located in Pyro Park, Union City, New Jersey. At its height, it had 400 employees.

Contributor: Terry Sells.

Pyro toys, as advertised in a December 1951 Woolworth's catalog.

Pyro Coca-Cola Truck, 5-1/2". Photo courtesy Terry Sells

Pyro Elect Marvin Griffin Governor, Get On The Griffin Bandwagon Truck, 5-1/2". Photo courtesy Terry Sells

Pyro City Builders Truck, 5-1/2". Photo courtesy Terry Sells

Pyro Mr. Peanut's Peanut Wagon, 5-1/2". Photo courtesy Terry Sells

Pyro Planters Peanuts Stake Truck, semi, 5-1/2". Photo courtesy Terry Sells

Pyro Design-A-Car set, builds fourteen models, with box. Photo courtesy Terry Sells

Pyro Ice & Coal Truck, 5-1/2". Photo courtesy Terry Sells

Pyro Planters Peanuts semi with trailer, 5-1/2". Photo courtesy Terry Sells

Pyro Ranch Horse Transport, 5-1/2". Photo courtesy Terry Sells

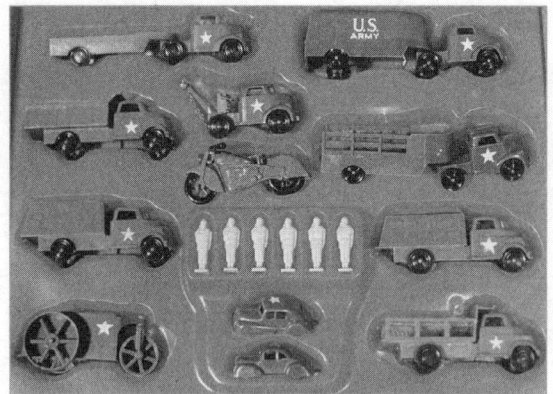

Contents of Pyro's twenty-one-piece U.S. Army Set. Photo courtesy Terry Sells

Cover for Pyro's twenty-one-piece U.S. Army Set. Photo courtesy Harvey K. Rainess

	C6	C8	C10
Army Tank P-1020, plastic	30	45	60
Balloon Racer, plastic, 3-1/2" long	12	18	25
Bulldozer, plastic, front loader	35	70	100
Canteen Truck, plastic	30	45	60
City Bottling Truck, plastic, 4" long	11	16	22
City Builders Truck, plastic, 5-1/2" long	NPF	NPF	NPF
Coca-Cola Truck, plastic, 5-1/2" long	75	112	150
Design-A-Car Set, plastic, builds fourteen models, w/box	35	52	70
Express Truck, plastic, 1950s	15	22	30
F7U Cutlass, plastic, 6" long	15	22	30
Ford, plastic, No. C-295, 1932	5	8	10
Ice & Coal Truck, plastic, 5-1/2" long	NPF	NPF	NPF
Lumber Loader, plastic	20	35	50
Lunch Wagon Truck, plastic, 5-1/2" long	18	27	37
Mobile Anti-Aircraft Truck, plastic, P-1015	48	72	95
Mobile Radar Truck, plastic, P-957	48	72	95
Mobile Searchlight Truck, plastic, P-958	48	72	95
Mobile Sound Truck, plastic, P-956	48	72	95
Motorcycle, plastic	32	48	65
Motorcycle w/Sidecar, plastic, w/molded baby in sidecar, assorted colors, 1950s, 3-3/8" long	NPF	NPF	NPF
Mr. Peanut's Peanut Wagon, plastic, 5-1/2" long	NPF	NPF	NPF

	C6	C8	C10
Planters Peanuts Semi w/Trailer, plastic, 5-1/2" long	NPF	NPF	NPF
Planters Peanuts Stake Truck, plastic, semi, 5-1/2" long	NPF	NPF	NPF
Pyro Ranch Horse Transport, plastic, 5-1/2" long	NPF	NPF	NPF
Race Car, plastic, "2" on hood, driver, assorted colors, 1950s, 3-3/4" long	10	18	30
Race Car, plastic, "7" on hood, driver, assorted colors, 1950s, 3-3/4" long	10	18	30
Race Car, plastic, 4" long	20	30	40
Range Patrol Truck, plastic, 5" long	15	22	30
Road Roller, plastic	12	18	25
Soap Box Supersonic Racer, plastic, driver, "7" assorted colors, 1950s, 4-3/4" long	75	112	150
Soldier Transport, plastic, P-955	20	30	40
Steam Roller, plastic	12	18	25
Truck, plastic, marked "Elect Marvin Griffin Governor" or "Get On The Griffin Bandwagon," 5-1/2" long	NPF	NPF	NPF
Twin 40-mm Mobile Gun, plastic, P-1087	48	72	95
U.S Army Ambulance, plastic	12	18	24
U.S Army Mobile Units Set, plastic	NPF	NPF	NPF
U.S Army Set, plastic, 21 pieces	17	26	35
U.S Army Stake Trailer Truck, plastic, 5-1/2" long	10	15	20
U.S Army Truck, plastic	9	13	19
U.S Navy Truck, plastic	10	15	20
U.S.M.C. Truck, plastic	10	15	20

RAINBOW

The Rainbow Rubber Company was based in Butler, Pa., during the mid-1930s.

Contributor: Dave Leopard, 2507 Feather Run Trail, West Columbia, SC 29169-4915

	C6	C8	C10
'35 Oldsmobile Coupe, 3-3/4" long (RA001)	50	60	80
'35 Oldsmobile Sedan, four-door, 3-1/4" long (RA002)	50	60	80
'35 Oldsmobile Sedan, four-door, 5" long (RA003)	65	95	125

Rainbow 1935 Studebaker Stake Side Pickup, 5-1/4". Photo courtesy Dave Leopard's book Rubber Toy Vehicles

	C6	C8	C10
'35 Studebaker (?) Stake Side Pickup, 5-1/4" long (RT001)	50	60	80
Racer, open, tapered tail, 4" long (RR001)	35	40	55
Racer, open, tapered tail, 5" long (RR002)	NPF	NPF	NPF

Rainbow Open Racer, tapered tail, 4". Photo courtesy Dave Leopard's book Rubber Toy Vehicles

Left to right: Rainbow 1935 Oldsmobile Sedan, 5"; Rainbow 1935 Oldsmobile Sedan, 3-1/4". Photo courtesy Dave Leopard's book Rubber Toy Vehicles

Two different looks at the Rainbow 1935 Oldsmobile Coupe, 3-3/4". Photo courtesy Dave Leopard's book Rubber Toy Vehicles

RALSTOY

Ralston Toy & Novelty Co. was founded in July 1939 to manufacture slush mold toys and novelties. It was formed by Dr. Felix Despecher, former mayor of Ralston, Neb., A.M. Erickson, and Henry C. Nestor to acquire the assets of Best Toy Co. of Manhattan, Kan., and the surviving molds of Kansas Toys Co. of Clifton, Kan. These assets included the temporary services of John M. Best, his molder Conrad Morsch, and about 140 molds from these pioneering slush mold toy-vehicle companies. The new enterprise was located in a building formerly occupied by the American Legion at 7632 Burlington St. This continued a low-cost toy line familiar to collectors since Kansas Toy was founded in 1923.

With the death of its founder, the young company was forced into reorganization. Lawyer Paul Massey, reorganized the company, but had to give up production of pot metal toy vehicles soon thereafter due to the need of lead for World War II. To survive, Massey turned to the production of wooden toys. One of Ralstoy's well known toys was a model of the Army Jeep, of which about two million copies were sold through the dimestores, mainly Woolworth and Kresge. Other wooden toys included an Army tank, a Navy PT boat, and a (rumored) DUKW amphibious landing craft. These toys were completely made in Ralston, except for Jeep wheels, which were made in Omaha by blind workers (when war-time labor became short, handicapped workers were hired).

After the war the company turned to die-casting toys and novelties. As the business expanded it moved to 5707 S. 77th St., where it is today

ABBREVIATIONS

The following abbreviations are for the details and variations useful in identification.

HG	horizontal grille pattern	**SM**	sidemounted spare
HL	horizontal hood louvers	**SP**	string-pull knob in hand crank area
HO	hood cap, Motometer or ornament	**T**	external trunk
L	lacquer finish	**UV**	unnumbered version
LI	landau irons on convertibles	**VG**	vertical grille pattern
MDW	metal disc wheels	**VL**	vertical hood louvers
MDSW	metal disc solid spokes	**WS, W/S**	windshield
MDWBT	wheels with black painted tires	**WV**	windshield visor
MSW	metal open spoke wheels	**WHRT**	wooden hubs, rubber tires
MWW	metal simulated wire wheels	**WRDW**	white hard rubber disc wheels
OW	open windows	**WRW**	white soft rubber wheels
RM	rearmount spare tire/wheel		(balloon tires)

Ralstoy Army Tank, No. 107, two-gun turret, 3-1/8". Photo courtesy Fred Maxwell

Ralstoy Army Tank, wooden. Photo courtesy Ed Poole

Ralstoy Large Sedan, No. 2R, black rubber wheels, 5-5/8". Photo courtesy Fred Maxwell

Ralstoy vehicles, Top: RAV5 Transporter w/Tank #74, Cannon #34, and Aircraft #32 (?). Middle: RAV6 Anti-Aircraft Unit, RAV8 Railway (?) Cannon. Bottom: RAV7 Tank #107, Cannon. Photo courtesy Ed Poole

Back row: Ralstoy Tanker Truck, No. 102, 6-3/4". Middle row, two variations on No. 48 Tractor—one without the rubber tracks and one with. Photo courtesy Perry Eichor

producing a well-known line of promotional trucks under Art Massey.

The history of those numbered molds is confusing. Although market values will depend on other factors than the actual makers, the following information should be of assistance to collectors. Ralstoy did label a few of its toys. They liked bottom pans, introduced by Best to increase rigidity of these fragile toys; this provided a surface to emboss "Ralstoy" and "Made in USA." Military olive-drab colors reflected the growing war consciousness. Wheels are not a good

clue, even when the latest fad, black rubber wheels, were used.

Ralstoy probably reproduced many pieces from its acquired molds, but there is no practical way to know who made them when they are not labeled. (See Best Toy Co. and Kansas Toy Co. in this book.)

The toys described below are mostly new issues.

Contributors: Perry R. Eichor, 703 North Almond Drive, Simpsonville, SC, 29681 and the late Fred Maxwell.

	C6	C8	C10
Army Jeep Wooden, WWII issue, marked "Ralstoy 78 HR1," white star on hood, white grille and headlamps, no steering wheel, rearmount spare; crude, assembled w/nails; 5-1/8" long; also available in metal version, details not available; (RAV010)	20	30	40
Army Tank, No. "107," reads "US Army," wood grooved-3/4" tracklaying wheels, two-gun turret, larger version of No. 74; 3-1/8" long; two other versions: also version w/black rubber wheels, and one unnumbered version (RAV007)	20	30	40
Army tank, No. "74," marked "US Army," two gun turret; entirely different tank than Kansas Toy No. 74; 2-1/4" long (RAV003)	20	30	40
Army Tank Wooden, marked "USA W356" and "Rakstoy" on bottom, WWII issue (RAV011)	30	50	60

	C6	C8	C10
Dump Truck, No. "42," International (?) COE, two OW, hinged tin dump body, different casting than Kansas Toy Dump Truck No. 42; 3-3/8" long (RAV00I1)	20	30	40
Fire-rescue Truck, die-cast, streamlined, w/cast on roof, six open windows, tandem rear axles w/wheel skirts, possibly an early postwar issue, 6" long (RAV013)	30	45	70
Ford Tractor, 1948, w/trailer, 9" overall	30	45	60
Indy Racer, slanted grille, removable tin hood, torpedo tail. 3-3/4" long; earlier attributed to Craftoy, it is now known to be a different casting since it is also found w/large white rubber wheels it is more likely Ralstoy (RAV014)	30	50	70
Large Gun Truck, "US Army Anti-aircraft Unit," three axle carrier, AA gun, searchlight and crew of three; 5-5/8" long (RAV006)	28	42	56
Large Transporter, "Ralstoy" International (?) sleeper cab w/two			

	C6	C8	C10
OW, vertical grille, steel semi-trailer w/No. 74 tank, No. 34 muzzle-loading cannon and No. 32 aircraft, olive drab color; Not known if Ralstoy issued them as a set; 9" long overall (RAV005)	20	45	60
Mayflower Moving Van, 8-1/2" long	20	25	50
Phillips 66 Tanker	37	56	75
Sedan, large, No. "2R," die-cast, Cadillac (?), marked "Ralstoy" and "Made in USA," four open vent windows, divided open windshield, three open rear windows, burnished white metal, long fenders, rear-wheel skirts, bumper guards, black rubber wheels, possibly an early postwar issue, 5-5/8" long (RAV012)	10	20	30

	C6	C8	C10
Tanker Truck, No. 102, "Ralstoy" International (?) sleeper cab w/two OW, vertical grille; trailer marked "Gasoline" and "No. 102," four tanks and four storage compartments; Ralstoy cab found in commercial finish or military olive drab Trailer was Best Toy; entire length: 6-3/4", sleeper cab length: 3-3/8", semi-trailer length: 4" (RAV004)	25	45	70
Tractor, No. "48," Caterpillar tractor, marked "Whoopee," driver in different color, grooved wood-3/4" wheels w/rubber tracks on Kansas Toy body; 3" long (RAV002)	20	30	60

RANGER STEEL CO.

Ranger Steel Products Co. was located in Roslyn Heights, New York.

	C6	C8	C10
Auto Laundry, tin litho station is 14" long, 3 tin 2-1/4"-long cars, crank			

	C6	C8	C10
moves cars through on rubber conveyor, 1950s	40	80	125
No. 450 Cross Country Turnpike, two wind-up racers, etc.	85	128	170

RANLITE

Whatever happened to Automobiles (Geographical) Limited of Halifax, Yorkshire, England? Except for the Ranlite Toys made from 1931 to 1932, there is no information about the company and what else it may have manufactured. The only advertising known is in the December 1931 issue of the *Meccano Magazine*. It is possible that the company was yet another Depression casualty. Ranlite's toys were quite expensive for their time, and it is unlikely that they were a marketing success. Cartainly, very few have survived.

Complex in design these were quite different from other toys made in the 1930s. Bodies and wheels were molded in "Ranlite", which was similar to Bakelite, a hard and brittle plastic commonly used to make control knobs and radio cases. The chassis and fenders of the two cars were stamped out of heavy-gauge steel. The large clockwork motor

powered the rear axle. The front wheels were steerable. At extra cost, a remote-cable control kit was available so that the vehicle could be wound up

Ranlite Golden Arrow Racing Car with original box, key and advertising brochure. Photo courtesy Gates Willard. Photo by E.W. Willard.

Ranlite Austin with original box, sunroof is in open position. Photo courtesy Gates Willard. Photo by E.W. Willard

Ranlite Singer with original box and closed sunroof. Photo courtesy Gates Willard. Photo by E.W. Willard

Ranlite, left to right: Singer, Austin, with Hammond Petrol Pump in between. Courtesy Gates Willard. Photo courtesy E.W. Willard

and steered around obstacles. Wheels could be removed and reinstalled with the small hub-nut wrench provided. The hollow Dunlop "Simi Pneumatic" tires were removable. The boxes were made of heavy cardboard, but the maroon paper covering tends to fade badly.

Two popular English saloons (sedans) were realistically modeled. Body and chassis of the Singer and the Austin are identical, but the radiator and hood are unique to each. The Austin has more wire spokes per wheel than the Singer. Both cars have a sliding sunroof. Upper and lower body sections were cast separately, which allowed for variations in color schemes. The Austin has a rear-mounted spare wheel and luggage rack, but no bumpers. The Austin name appears on a diagonal bar across the radiator, and the hood has vertical louvers. The Singer has a small letter "s" at the top front of the radiator, and the bonnet louvers are horizontal. The Singer has double-bar, spring-steel bumpers on the front and rear, resulting in a total length of 10-3/4-inches,

whereas the bumperless Austin is ten inches long. Of the two cars, the Singer is scarcer. The fold-away key wind is permanently attached underneath so the body is not spoiled by having a visible key hole. No headlamps were fitted. The die-cast key wind, differential gears, and front axle are subject to metal fatigue, which has often destroyed them.

The Golden Arrow racing car is 16-1/2-inches long and it is a beautifully proportioned model of the famous Seagrave Record Car. Except for the tires, it does not share parts with the two passenger cars. The key is separate and not attached to the motor. It has steerable front wheels and a remote-control cable was also available at extra cost.

The petrol (gasoline) pump is made of Bakelite. It has a flexible hose made of a tightly coiled spring and is a gold model of a contemporary English Hammond pump. There is no value guide to (or for) Ranlite toys, since few are currently changing hands and not enough data exists to develop a reliable and useful listing of values.

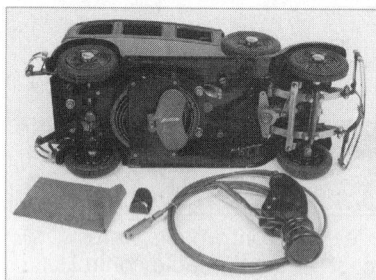

The underside of a Ranlite Singer with a hub nut wrench and envelope. Photo courtesy Gates Willard. Photo by E.W. Willard

Left to right: Rear view looks at the Ranlite Singer and Austin. Photo courtesy Gates Willard. Photo by E.W. Willard

A reprint of a Ranlite catalog page. Photo courtesy Gates Willard

REALISTIC

Realistic toys were made by Freeport Toys Mfg. Co., in Freeport, Illinois, during the late 1940s and early 1950s. It used some original Arcade molds to produce cast-aluminum vehicles. Realistic seemed to specialize in buses and produced varieties of both

Greyhound and Trailways buses. Its bus models were often sold as souvenirs at bus terminals.

Contributor: Dave Leopard, 2507 Feather Run Trail, West Columbia, SC 29169-4915.

	C6	C8	C10
1939 Yellow Cab, 8-1/4" long (RV001) .	60	75	100
Flex Clipper Bus, aluminum, No. 201 (RV005)	60	75	100
Greyhound Bus, aluminum, No. 101, silver sides, 8-3/4" long (RV002)	75	110	150
Hook and Ladder Truck, No. 501, 8-1/2" long (RV007)	55	75	110
Racer, No. 401, 5-1/2" long (RV006)	60	75	100
Trailways Bus, aluminum, 8-3/4" long (RV004)	125	200	325
Trailways Bus, aluminum, Clipper, No. 301, various decals as Realistic produced these for sale at bus terminals, 9-1/4" long (RV003)	125	200	325

A realistic ad in the August 1947 Toys & Novelties magazine.

REHRBERGER

	C6	C8	C10
David Moving Van, c.1924, 7-1/4" long..	2000	3500	5000

Rehrberger "David" Moving Van, c.1924, 7-1/4". Photo courtesy Bertoia Auctions

RELIABLE

Reliable was based in Toronto, Canada. The company is perhaps best known as a doll manufacturer, but it did release plastic vehicles in the postwar period.

	C6	C8	C10
Bus, plastic, red, 1950s, 6-1/4" long	30	60	95
Cement Mixer, plastic, drum spins when truck is pushed, assorted colors, 1950s, 4-1/2" long..............................	20	35	50
Convertible, plastic, driver, No. 581-1, 1950s...	8	17	30
Curbside Delivery Van, plastic, 10-3/4" long	60	93	125
Delivery Truck, plastic, 1950s, 4-1/2" long	25	38	50
Lowboy w/crane, plastic, 6-1/2" long	NPF	NPF	NPF
Pickup Truck, plastic, 1950s, 4-1/2" long	20	38	55

	C6	C8	C10
Rolls-Royce, plastic, red, No. 974-1, 1950s...	8	17	25
Sedan, plastic, assorted colors, plastic wheels, 1950s, 4-1/2" long	20	35	50
Stake Truck, plastic, wind-up w/detachable key, driver, opening doors, rubber tires, 1950s, 6" long.......	20	35	50
Super Deluxe Mechanical Sedan, plastic, wind-up w/detachable key, assorted colors, trim painted in silver, rubber tires, metal wheels, late 1940s, 6" long..	50	75	100
Tanker Truck, plastic, red, 1950s, 4" long..	15	25	40
Tow Truck, plastic, 10-1/2" long	25	46	62
Tractor-Trailer, plastic, 6-1/4" long........	NPF	NPF	NPF

Reliable Bus, plastic, 6-1/4". Photo courtesy Terry Sells

Reliable Lowboy with crane, plastic, 6-1/2". Photo courtesy Terry Sells

Reliable Super Deluxe Mechanical Sedan, plastic windup, 6". Photo courtesy Terry Sells

Reliable Tractor-Trailer, plastic, 6-1/4". Photo courtesy Terry Sells

RELIANCE MOLDED PLASTICS, INC.

Reliance was located at 335 Barton St., Pawtucket, R.I.

	C6	C8	C10
Indian Scout Motorcycle, plastic, movable handlebars, revolving wheels, No. 249, c.1948, 5" long	NPF	NPF	NPF

Reliance Indian Scout.

REMCO

Remco Industries Inc., was located on Cape May St. in Harrison, N.J. One of the biggest toy manufacturers of the post-WWII period, Remco made a large variety of toys including, dolls, space toys, and vehicles among others. Battery-operated plastic toys were a specialty.

	C6	C8	C10
Barney's Auto Factory, builds convertible or sedan, w/box, 1961	145	240	320
Bulldog Tank	55	100	145
Dune Buggy Wheelies Camper, No. 7146, battery-operated, 1971	25	50	75
Electronic Mobile Loudspeaker and Signal System, 1955, 24" long	50	75	100
Flintstones Motorized Sports Car & Trailer, battery-operated, 1961	75	150	250
Flying Dutchman Antique Car, battery-operated	40	72	95
Mighty Matilda, battery-operated battleship, 1963, 35" long	100	200	350
Mighty Mike Motorized Trucks, battery-operated, chassis w/interchangable snap-on truck beds	10	20	30
Movieland Drive-In Theatre, battery-operated, includes six small cars, ad cards, filmstrips, 1959, 14" long	125	200	300
Mr Kelly's Car Wash, 1960s	60	98	130
Old-Timer Convertible, 22" long	50	75	110
Pickup Truck, plastic, resembles the Swiss-made AEBI Farmwagon, 7" long	8	14	20

	C6	C8	C10
Road Devils Injector & Racer Set, wind up crank on Injector and release car when tachometer hits a certain level, 1972	12	24	40
Shark Racer, No. 610, battery-operated, plastic, 1961, 20" long	65	100	135
Supercar, Mike Mercury, battery-operated, based on the puppet tv show	12	24	40
Tiger Joe Tank, 1959	110	165	220
Tricky School Bus, 1968	30	52	75
Tricky Tommy Turtle, battery-operated, 1967	25	50	75
Tru-Smoke Diesel Dump Truck, 1969	20	30	40
U-Drive Auto, w/driver	36	54	72

Remco Pickup Truck, 7" long. Photo courtesy John McCurdy

RENWAL

Accounts vary as to whether Renwal Manufacturing Company was founded in 1939 by Irving Rosenblum or Irving Lawner. What is indisputable is that Lawner spelled backward is Renwal. The firm seems to have begun as a manufacturer of a glass knife. A plastic knife replaced it and presumably led to the manufacture of plastic toys, which went on sale at least as early as August 1945. Its initial line consisted of WWII-era air-planes

and dollhouse furniture. Vehicles were probably introduced in late 1946 or 1947 (the earliest known Renwal catalog is from 1948). The firm's early ads proclaimed it was, "Famous for toys and houseware products."

In 1945, Renwal's showroom and factory were at 902 Broadway, New York City. An additional showroom at 200 Fifth Avenue seems to have been given up by 1946. In 1950, Renwal moved to Toyland

Park, Mineola, New York. It seems to have remained there until the end (1970s). When it went out of business, its tooling was sold to Chein, which in turn sold it to Revell. (Years in parenthesis indicate the earliest known year of production.)

	C6	C8	C10
No. 0023 Motorcycle and Side Car w/Passenger, Handlebars steer, 1949, 5-1/4" long	40	75	100
No. 0039 Convertible Sedan w/Driver, doors open, top slides back, trunk opens, 1948, 6-1/2" long	30	45	70
No. 0046 Coal Truck w/Driver, doors open, body raises, 1948, 7-1/2" long	50	75	100
No. 0048 Transport Truck w/Driver, doors open, body swings, 1948, 10-3/4" long	65	100	125
No. 0049 Gasoline Truck w/Driver, doors open, tank holds water, 1948, 7-3/4" long	50	75	100
No. 0049 Gasoline Truck w/Driver, doors open, tank holds water, top reads "Super-X," working faucet inside rear door, 1950, 7-3/4" long	50	75	100
No. 0050 Dump Truck w/Driver, doors open, body raises, "Sand-Gravel," 1948, 7-1/2" long	55	90	125
No. 0056 Cement Mixer Truck, mixer revolves, rear cap comes off, tank raises, 1948, 7-1/4" long	75	112	150
No. 0057 Fire Truck w/Three Fireman, 1948, 7" long, 8" high when ladder extended	48	72	95
No. 0058 Racing Car, marked "Speed King," 1948, 6-3/8" long	30	50	75
No. 0059 Sedan, 1948, 4-1/4" long	15	30	45
No. 0060 Coupe, 1948, 4-1/4" long	15	30	45
No. 0061 Racer, 1948, no driver, assorted colors, 4-3/4" long	15	30	45
No. 0062 Truck (pick-up), 1948, 4-1/4" long	5	8	10
No. 0079 Auto Carrier Truck w/Driver, four autos, cab turns, doors open, elevator raises cars for upper level, 1949, 13" long	50	100	175
No. 0088 Racer, (1950), 4-3/8" long	20	30	45
No. 0090 Two-door Sedan w/Driver, doors and trunk open, 1949, 6-1/2" long	45	60	95
No. 0091 Taxicab w/Driver, cab doors and trunk open, 1949, 6-1/2" long	42	63	85
No. 0092 Plastic Garage, 1949, 6-1/2" long	50	75	100
No. 0093 Panel Truck, "Delivery," 1949, 4-1/4" long	15	25	40
No. 0094 Gasoline Truck, "Gasoline," 1949, 4-1/4" long	15	25	40
No. 0099 Stake Wagon, gates removable, tongue hinged, 1950, 8-3/8" long	NPF	NPF	NPF
No. 0101 Stake Truck w/Driver, doors open, gates removable, 1950, 7-3/4" long	50	100	150
No. 0102 Coupe, 1950, 4-1/4" long	8	10	15
No. 0103 Sedan, 1950, 4-1/4" long	8	10	15
No. 0104 Convertible, 1950, 4-1/4" long	10	15	20
No. 0105 Fire Engine, w/ladder, 1950, 4-1/4" long	10	12	20
No. 0106 Friction Motor Convertible w/Driver, 1950, 9-1/2" long	50	75	150

	C6	C8	C10
No. 0107 Speed King Friction Motor Racer w/Driver, 1950, 10-1/4" long	NPF	NPF	NPF
No. 0110 Auto Jack, raises cars 1-1/2", 1950, base 3-3/4" long	5	8	10
No. 0113 Friction Motor Fire Truck w/Driver and two Firemen, w/water tank, pump, unwinding hose, nozzle w/water release, siren, gear-controlled ladder, 1950, 11-1/2" long, 16" high when ladder extended	NPF	NPF	NPF
No. 0123 School Bus, plastic, assorted colors, 4-7/16" long	7	15	25
No. 0124 City Bus, plastic, assorted colors, 4-7/16" long	14	21	30
No. 0126 Hook and Ladder Truck w/Drivers, cab turns, doors open, rear wheels turn, 1950, 15-3/4" long, 16" high when ladder extended	60	80	100
No. 0131 Cement Mixer, crank turns mixer, mixer revolves, tilts; can be filled and emptied, doors open, 1951-53, 9-7/8" long	50	70	90
No. 0132 Gasoline Truck, "Gas Oil," rear and cab doors open, tank can be filled and emptied through plastic hose, which folds up inside rear doors (1951), 12" long	NPF	NPF	NPF
No. 0133 Heavy Duty Tow Truck w/Driver, adjustable crane, windlass clicks, doors open, 1951, 11" long	50	70	90
No. 0134 Heavy Duty Dump Truck w/Driver, crank operates hoist, cab doors and tailgate open, 1951, 10-7/8" long	50	70	90
No. 0135 Heavy Duty Coal Truck w/Driver, crank operates hoist, load divider, unloading chute, cab doors open, 1951, 10-3/4" long	50	70	90
No. 0143 Sedan, 3-1/8" long	9	14	18
No. 0144 Coupe, 3-1/16" long, new in 1950	7	11	20
No. 0145 Fire Truck, 3-1/4" long, new in 1950	7	15	20
No. 0146 Hook and Ladder, 3-1/4" long	7	10	20
No. 0147 Convertible, 3-1/8" long	6	12	16
No. 0148 Gasoline Truck, 3-1/8" long	6	9	14
No. 0149 Pickup Truck, 3-3/16" long	7	10	20
No. 0150 Racer, 3-1/4" long	17	26	37
No. 0151 Fire Chief Coupe, 1950, 4-1/4" long	NPF	NPF	NPF
No. 0152 Police Coupe, 1950, 4-1/4" long	12	18	24
No. 0153 Taxi, 1950, 4-1/4" long	10	15	21
No. 0167 Fire Truck Builder Kit, w/ladder, hose reel, crank, firemen, driver, 1953, truck 7" long	NPF	NPF	NPF
No. 0168 Auto-Boat, auto on one side, boat on other, 1954, 6-1/2" long	20	30	50
No. 0173 Speedway Racer w/Driver, 1953, 9-1/2" long	85	128	170
No. 0174 Cadillac Convertible with Driver, top goes up and down, 1953, 5-1/2" long	20	30	50
No. 0175 Motorcycle w/Sidecar Construction Kit, 1953, motorcycle 5-1/4" long	NPF	NPF	NPF
No. 0176 Two-door Sedan Construction Kit w/Driver, w/spare wheel, doors and trunk open, 1953, 6-1/2" long	NPF	NPF	NPF

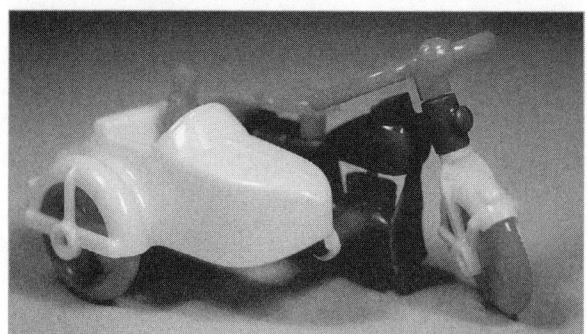

Renwal Motorcycle and Side Car with Passenger, No. 23, handlebars steer, 1949, 5-1/4". Photo courtesy Terry Sells

Another version of the No. 39 Convertible Sedan with top up and opened trunk. Photo courtesy Bob and Alice Wagner

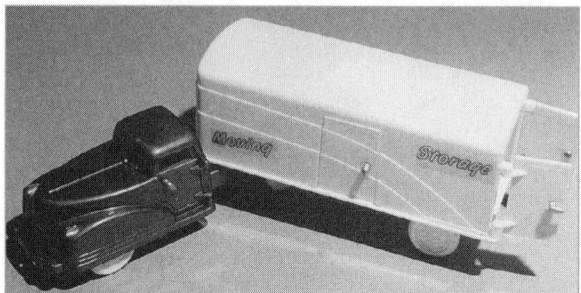

Renwal Transport Truck, No. 48, doors open, body swings, 1948, 10-3/4". Photo courtesy Bob and Alice Wagner

Renwal Fire Truck with Three Fireman, No. 57, 1948, 7"— 8" when ladder is extended. Photo courtesy Bob and Alice Wagner

Renwal Convertible Sedan with Driver, No. 39, doors open, top slides back, trunk opens, 1948, 6-1/2". Photo courtesy Terry Sells

Renwal Heavy Duty Coal Truck with Driver, No. 46, crank operates hoist, 1951, 10-3/4". Photo courtesy Terry Sells

Renwal Gasoline Truck with Driver, No. 49, doors open, tank holds water, 1948, 7-3/4". Photo courtesy Bob and Alice Wagner

Back row: Renwal Racing Car, No. 58, 6-3/8". Front row, left to right: Racer, No. 150, 3-1/4"; Racer, No. 88, 4-3/8". Photo courtesy Terry Sells

Renwal Cement Mixer Truck, No. 56, 1948, 7-1/4". Photo courtesy Terry Sells

	C6	C8	C10
No. 0177 Taxicab Construction Kit w/Driver, w/spare, doors and trunk open, 1953, cab 6-1/2" long	35	52	70
No. 0178 Fire Truck, w/two firemen, 1953, 15" long, ladder extends to 16"	NPF	NPF	NPF
No. 0179 Fire Truck, two firemen, 1953, 7-1/2" long, 8" high w/ladder extended	30	45	60
No. 0186 Tractor w/Driver, 1953, 5-1/4" long	NPF	NPF	NPF
No. 0188 Motorcycle Cop, plastic, assorted colors, 1953, 9" long	50	75	100
No. 0189 Motorcycle Cop, plastic, assorted colors, 1953, 3-3/4" long	NPF	NPF	NPF
No. 0191 Trailer Truck, w/two Boats, 1953, 13-1/4" long	NPF	NPF	NPF
No. 0192 Trailer Truck, w/eight Logs, 1953, 13-1/4" long	NPF	NPF	NPF
No. 0195 Two-Car Garage, w/two cars, doors open, 1954, 4-1/8" x 3-5/8" x 2-1/4"	12	18	25
No. 0196 Pick-up Truck, 1953, 11" long	NPF	NPF	NPF
No. 0201 Old Fashioned Car w/Driver, open top, 1954, 8-1/2" long	NPF	NPF	NPF
No. 0206 Convertible, no motor, 1952, 9-1/2" long	NPF	NPF	NPF
No. 0207 Racer, no motor, 1952, 10-1/4" long	NPF	NPF	NPF
No. 0210 Take-Apart Hot Rod, 10-1/2" long, 1954	90	135	180
No. 0213 Fire Engine, w/water tank, pump, unwinding hose, nozzle w/water release, siren, gear-controlled ladder, no motor, 1952, 11-1/2" long, 16" high when ladder extended	NPF	NPF	NPF
No. 0216 Champion Racer, friction motor, dome over driver, siren, 1954, 10-3/8" long	NPF	NPF	NPF
No. 0218 Toytown Service Garage Set, w/five 3-1/4" cars, 1955, 7" x 5" x 2-7/8"	NPF	NPF	NPF
No. 0220 Take-Apart Racer, 1954, 10-1/2" long	NPF	NPF	NPF

	C6	C8	C10
No. 0221 Coal Truck Kit, 1954, truck 7-1/2" long	NPF	NPF	NPF
No. 0222 Dump Truck Kit, 1954, truck 7-1/2" long	NPF	NPF	NPF
No. 0223 Transport Kit, 1954, truck 10-3/4" long	NPF	NPF	NPF
No. 0224 Gasoline Truck Kit, 1954, truck 7-3/4" long	NPF	NPF	NPF
No. 0226 Cement Mixer Kit, 1954, truck 7-1/4" long	NPF	NPF	NPF
No. 0235 Motorized Fuel Truck, friction, driver, doors open, body raises, rear door opens to slide out chute, 1954, 7-1/2" long	NPF	NPF	NPF
No. 0236 Motorized Sand Truck, friction, doors open, body raises, rear gate opens, 1954, 7-1/2" long	NPF	NPF	NPF
No. 0237 Motorized Tank Truck, friction, doors open, tank cap opens for filling, rear door opens to faucet, 1954, 7-3/4" long	NPF	NPF	NPF
No. 0238 Motorized Ready-Mix Concrete Truck w/Driver, friction motor, doors open, mixer revolves as truck moves, raises, rear cap comes off, 1954, 7-1/8" long	NPF	NPF	NPF
No. 0239 Motorized Moving Van w/Driver, friction motor, cab, trailer doors open, 1954, 10-5/8" long	NPF	NPF	NPF
No. 0243 Racer w/Driver, 1954, 9-1/2" long	NPF	NPF	NPF
No. 0248 Motorized Fire Truck w/Siren, friction motor, driver, two firemen, 1955, 15" long, ladder extends to 16"	NPF	NPF	NPF
No. 0259 Engine Running Racer, transparent engine block shows action, 1955, 10-1/2" long	NPF	NPF	NPF
No. 0260 TV MobileTruck, camera, spotlight, microphone, cable "Renwal-TV" on side, 1956	75	112	150
No. 0270 Steam Shovel Construction Kit, 1953, truck 8-1/8" long	NPF	NPF	NPF

Renwal Gasoline Truck, No. 132, 1951, rear and cab doors open, 12". Photo courtesy Terry Sells

Renwal Cadillac Convertible with Driver, No. 174, top goes up and down, 1953, 5-1/2". Photo courtesy Terry Sells

Renwal Motorcycle Cop, No. 188, 1953, 9". Photo courtesy Gary Linden

Renwal Coupe, No. 60, 1948, 4-1/4". KP Photo courtesy Karen O'Brien

Renwal Motorcycle Cop, No. 189, 1953, 3-3/4". Photo courtesy Terry Sells

Renwal Auto Carrier Truck, No. 79, four autos, cab turns, doors open, 1949, 13". Photo courtesy Bob and Alice Wagner

Renwal Two-Car Garage with two Cars, No. 195, 1954. Photo courtesy Dave Leopard

Renwal, top to bottom: No. 62 Pickup, No. 61 Racer, No. 60 Coupe, No. 59 Sedan. Amended from ad brochure c.1948. Courtesy Islyn Thomas

Renwal Two-door Sedan with Driver, No. 90, doors and trunk open, 1949, 6-1/2". Photo courtesy Bob and Alice Wagner

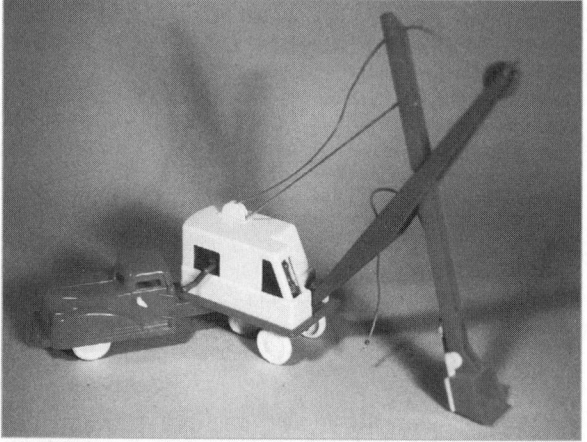

Renwal Steam Shovel Truck with Truck Driver and Steam Shovel Operator, No. 86, doors open, cab swings, shovel can be raised, 1949, 19". Photo courtesy Terry Sells

Renwal Plastic Garage, No. 92, 1949, 6-1/2". Photo courtesy Dave Leopard

Renwal Taxicab with Driver, No. 91, 1949, doors and trunk open, 6-1/2". Photo courtesy Bob and Alice Wagner

Renwal Hook & Ladder Truck with Drivers, No. 126, cab turns, doors open, rear wheels turn, 1950, 15-3/4" and 16" when ladder is extended. Photo courtesy Terry Sells

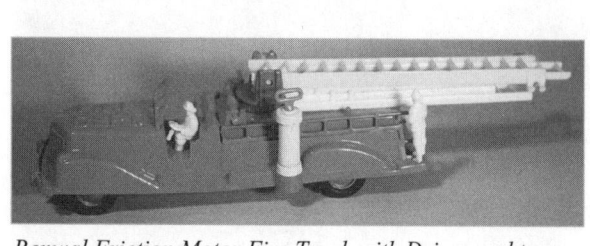

Renwal Friction Motor Fire Truck with Driver and two Firemen, No. 113, 1950, 11-1/2" and 16" with extended ladder. Photo courtesy Terry Sells

Renwal Friction Motor Convertible with Driver, No. 106, 1950, 9-1/2". Photo courtesy Bob and Alice Wagner

	C6	C8	C10
No. 0271 Hook and Ladder Construction Kit, w/two drivers, firemen, 1953, truck 15-3/4" long	NPF	NPF	NPF
No. 0284 U.S Army Tank	3	5	7
No. 0301 Customized Service Truck, 1:32-scale, 1964	NPF	NPF	NPF
No. 0313 Motorized Pumper Fire Truck, w/driver and two firemen, w/siren and extension ladder friction, throws water through plastic hose, 1955, 11-1/2" long	NPF	NPF	NPF
No. 0329 Gasoline Truck, soft plastic, 6" long	8	12	16
No. 0501 Car and Whistle Set, plastic, #45 Whistle, #59 Sedan, #60 Coupe, #61 Racer w/o driver, #62 Truck, 1948	NPF	NPF	NPF
No. 0621 Truck, same as No. 62, 1951, 4-1/4" long	NPF	NPF	NPF
No. 0813 Visible Auto Chassis, early 1960s, over three feet long	NPF	NPF	NPF
No. 086 Steam Shovel Truck w/Truck Driver and Steam Shovel Operator, doors open, cab swings, shovel can be raised, lowered, extended via handle on side of cab, 1949, 19" long	45	68	90
No. 2039 Convertible w/Driver, w/simulated chrome trim, 1952, 6-1/2" long	32	48	65
No. 2057 Fire Truck, w/simulated chrome trim, 1952	48	72	95
No. 2061 Racer, w/simulated chrome trim, w/driver, 1949-56, 4-3/4" long	NPF	NPF	NPF
No. 2088 Racer, but w/chrome trim, 1952	NPF	NPF	NPF
No. 2090 Sedan w/Driver, w/simulated chrome trim, 1952, 6-1/2" long	NPF	NPF	NPF
No. 2091 Taxicab, w/simulated chrome trim, 1952	60	90	120
No. 2093 Delivery Truck, w/chrome trim, 1952	10	15	20
No. 2094 Gasoline Truck, w/chrome trim, 1952	10	15	20
No. 2102 Coupe, w/chrome trim, 1952	10	15	20
No. 2103 Sedan, w/chrome trim, 1952	10	15	20
No. 2104 Convertible, w/chrome trim, 1952	10	15	20
No. 2621 Truck, w/chrome trim, 1952	10	15	20
No. 8001 Ferrari Racer, metal, motorized, 1955, 9-1/4" long	100	150	200
No. 8002 Maserati Racer, metal, motorized, 1955, 9-1/4" long	NPF	NPF	NPF

	C6	C8	C10
No. 8003 Pontiac Convertible, metal, motorized, 1955, 8-1/4" long	60	90	120
No. 8004 Plymouth Convertible, metal, motorized, 1955, 7-7/8" long	NPF	NPF	NPF
No. 8005 Chevrolet Sedan, metal motorized, 1955, 7-7/8" long	NPF	NPF	NPF
No. 8006 Ford Sedan, metal, motorized, 1955, 7-7/8" long	NPF	NPF	NPF
No. 8007 Sedan, metal, 1955, 6" long	NPF	NPF	NPF
No. 8008 Gasoline Truck, metal, 1955, 6" long	27	41	55
No. 8009 Racer, metal, 1955, 7" long	NPF	NPF	NPF
No. 8010 Delivery Truck, metal, 1955, 6" long	40	50	70
No. 8011 Pickup Truck, metal, 1955, 6" long	30	45	60
No. 8012 Hot Rod, metal, 1955, 6-1/2" long	NPF	NPF	NPF
No. 8013 Jeep, metal, 1955, 5-5/8" long	NPF	NPF	NPF
No. 8014 Fire Truck, metal, 1955, 6" long	NPF	NPF	NPF
No. 8015 Convertible, metal, 1955, 6" long	35	52	70
No. 8028 Citroen, metal, 1955, 6" long	NPF	NPF	NPF
No. 8029 Porsche, metal, 1955, 5-3/4" long	NPF	NPF	NPF
No. 8030 Pegasa, metal, 1955, 6" long	NPF	NPF	NPF
No. 8031 Lancia, metal, 1955, 6" long	NPF	NPF	NPF
No. 8032 Rolls Royce, metal, 1955, 6-1/8" long	NPF	NPF	NPF
No. 8033 Jaguar, metal, 1955, 6-1/8" long	NPF	NPF	NPF
No. 8034 MG, metal, I 955, 6" long	NPF	NPF	NPF
No. 8035 Mercedes-Benz, metal, 1955, 5-7/8" long	NPF	NPF	NPF
No. 8036 Kaiser-Darrin, metal, 1955, 6-1/8" long	NPF	NPF	NPF
No. 8037 Austin-Healey, metal 1955, 6" long	NPF	NPF	NPF
No. 8853, 3-1/2" metal replicas of Renwal's plastic convertible, sedan, coupe, pick-up truck, gasoline truck, fire truck, hook and ladder, racer; 1955	NPF	NPF	NPF
No. 8854, 4-1/4" to 4-1/2" metal replicas of Renwal's plastic convertible, coupe gasoline truck, city bus; 1955	NPF	NPF	NPF
Nos. 0186 and 0187 Tractor and Trailer, 1953	NPF	NPF	NPF

Renwal Gasoline Truck with Driver, No. 49, like other truck but with Super-X inscription, 1950. Photo courtesy Bob and Alice Wagner

Renwal Dump Truck with Driver, Sand-Gravel, No. 50, doors open, body raises, 1948, 7-1/2". Photo courtesy Terry Sells

Renwal Gasoline Truck, No. 8008, die-cast metal, 1955, 6". Photo courtesy Terry Sells

REPUBLIC TOOL PRODUCTS CO.

Based in Dayton, Ohio, the Republic Tool Products Co. was in business from 1922-32. Charles Black received a patent for a unique cover to protect the friction mechanism between the rear wheels from dirt and moisture, and is stamped with the patent date, No. 1, 1921. Black had been employed at the Dayton Toy Works until 1922, when he left the company to form a partnership with Elijah Miller, another ex-Dayton employee. The company ceased making Republic Toys in 1932. Although Republic Toys were produced for a mere ten years, they have become an important part of American toy manufacturing history.

Contributor: Bob Smith, RATS Toy Shows, 255 Tryon Park, Rochester, NY 14609. (585) 288-7153, bird@oldtoysonline.com.

	C6	C8	C10
Bus, 1920s, 28" long	500	675	1050
Cargo Truck, friction drive, green, c.1922, 13" long..................................	325	475	750
Chemical Truck.......................................	225	350	500
Coupe	325	475	750
Dayton Racer, operates on large spring-wind motor cranked from front of car gray/blue/red, 1910 or 1922, 11" long......................................	350	525	800
Ladder Truck, 17" long...........................	300	425	625
Ladder Truck, friction, 24" long	300	450	650
Limousine, friction drive, blue, c.1922, 11" long...	300	450	675
Momentum Dump Truck, w/driver, pat. 11/1/21, 20" long	350	525	750
Roadster, friction drive, red, 11" long, c.1922...	275	425	650
Taxi Cab w/Driver, sheet-metal, friction, c.1926...	325	475	700

Republic Cargo Truck, friction drive, green, 1920s, 13". Photo courtesy Bob Smith

Republic Limousine, friction drive, 11". Photo courtesy Bob Smith

Republic Roadster, friction drive, 1920s, 11". Photo courtesy Bob Smith

Republic/Dayton Racer, spring-wind, c.1910 or 1922, 11". Photo courtesy Bob Smith

REUHL PRODUCTS, INC.

Reuhl Prod. Inc., toys were named after their founder, Andy Reul (the "H" was added to the name to help in the pronunciation). Although Reul was working in his newly founded business before World War II, he didn't really get established until 1945. In the beginning, Reuhl made his models out of wood, Bakelite, Fiberglas, and plastic. His work with plastic was outstanding. When he started getting large orders for scale models from Caterpillar Heavy Equipment Corp. and Massey-Harris Farm Equipment, Reul switched to die-cast metal.

His castings were far superior to anything previously produced by other manufacturers. His attention to detail brought these 1:24-scale construction models to be miniature duplicates of the real thing. Most Massey-Harris models were done in

1:20-scale and had the same fine detail. Reuhl Products were too expensive for most retail stores. Because only a few retail outlets were able to sell the products successfully, they became almost exclusively sold at the Caterpillar and Massey-Harris dealer showrooms. Reuhl Products went out of business in 1958 after losing its two major customers—Caterpillar and Massey-Harris. Although some of today's products have great detail, Reuhl Products were the finest-made farm and construction models in the industry, and they are highly sought after on today's market.

Note: A clean, original box for any Reuhl model can double its value.

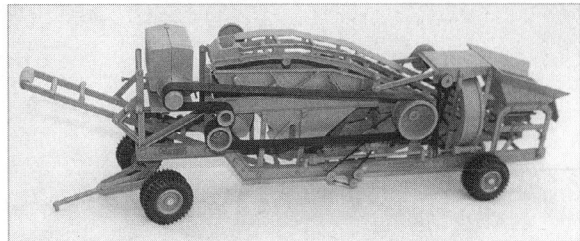

Reuhl Cedar Rapids Pitmaster Gravel Crusher. Photo courtesy Bob Smith

	C6	C8	C10
American Portable Material Elevator	NPF	NPF	NPF
Caterpillar 1948 D7 Dozer, plastic kit, 1:24-scale, Reuhl/Curver, could also be purchased assembled	200	375	675
Caterpillar D7 Dozer, die-cast, 1:24-scale	275	475	750
Caterpillar DW-10 Wheel Tractor, die-cast, 1:24-scale	325	475	750
Caterpillar No. 12 Grader, die-cast, 1:24 scale	600	900	1350
Caterpillar No. 70 Four-wheel Scraper, die-cast, 1:24 scale	400	600	950
Caterpillar Ripper, die-cast w/plastic wheels, 1:24-scale	185	400	625
Caterpillar Scraper 1948 No. 70, plastic kit, 1:24-scale, could also be purchased assembled	250	450	750
Catterpillar DW-10 Tractor with No. 10 Scraper, die-cast, 1:24-scale	700	1100	1800
Catterpillar No. 10 Two-wheel Scraper, die-cast, 1:24-scale	325	500	850
Cedar Rapids Pitmaster Gravel Crusher, 221 parts	800	1450	2100

	C6	C8	C10
I.H. Farmall Cub Tractor, plastic kit, 1:16-scale, could also be purchased assembled	175	350	575
Lorain Shovel	700	1250	1900
Massey-Harris 3 Buttom Row, die-cast, 1:20-scale, made to fit 44 tractor	175	300	525
Massey-Harris 44 Tractor, diecast, 1:20 scale, die-cast or plastic rims	325	475	775
Massey-Harris Disc Harrow, die-cast, 1:20-scale, made to fit 44 tractor	175	310	525

Reuhl Cedar Rapids Pitmaster Gravel Crusher. Photo courtesy Bob Smith

Reuhl Massey-Harris 44 Tractor. Photo courtesy Bob Smith

Reuhl Lorain Shovel. Photo courtesy Bob Smith

Reuhl Massey-Harris 3 Bottom Plow. Photo courtesy Bob Smith

Reuhl Massey-Harris Disc Harrow. Photo courtesy Bob Smith

Reuhl Caterpillar D7 Dozer. Photo courtesy Bob Smith

Reuhl Massey-Harris Loader. Photo courtesy Bob Smith

Reuhl Massey Harris Self-propelled Combine. Photo courtesy Bob Smith

A Reuhl flyer from 1950. Courtesy Ray Funk

	C6	C8	C10
Massey-Harris Loader, die-cast, 1:20-scale, made to fit 44 tractor	175	325	550
Massey-Harris Pull-type Combine, die-cast, 1:20-scale, made to fit 44 tractor	354	572	1162
Massey-Harris Roadmaster Wagon, die-cast, 1:24-scale, made to fit 44 tractor	125	225	400
Massey-Harris Self-propelled Combine, die-cast, 1:20-scale, made to fit 44 tractor	354	572	1162
Model Race Car Type I, molded Fiberglas, 17" long	275	425	700

	C6	C8	C10
Model Race Car Type II, molded Fiberglas	375	550	850

REVELL

Revell seems to have begun in 1951 and soon produced more cars a year than Ford, General Motors, and Chrysler put together. Located in Venice, California, the firm was founded by Lewis H. Glaser.

Revell Maxwell Auto. This seems to have been Revell's first toy. Photo courtesy Charles D. Richards

Revell Antique Autos, as shown in the Toy Yearbook from 1953-54.

	C6	C8	C10
Backfiring Hot Rod	42	63	85
Caterpillar Grader, plastic, steering wheel controls front wheels, blade adjusts, yellow, 1952, 12" long	40	68	90
Caterpillar Tractor and Wagon, plastic, wagon dumps, yellow, 1952, 12" long	60	90	120
Gardening Service Truck, plastic, ladder, wheelbarrow, lawnmower, flower pots, watering can, 1953, 10-1/2" long	65	110	140

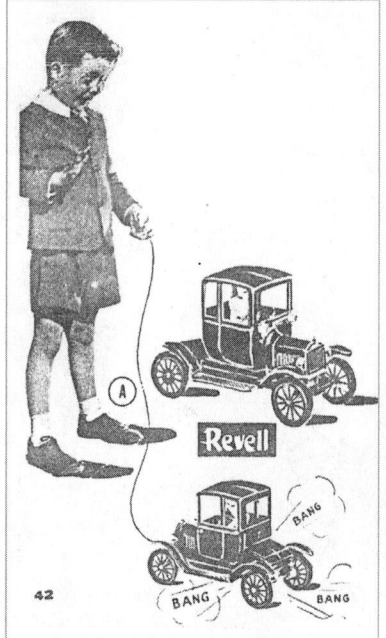

An ad from the 1952-53 Toy Yearbook. "Revell Back-Firing Ford: Constructed of durable plastic, this is an authentic replica of the famous 1917 Model T Closed Coupe. It runs along freely as a pull toy and when the trigger is squeezed, the engine backfires with a loud BANG! The clever metal backfiring mechanism takes any standard roll of caps. $3."

	C6	C8	C10
Jr. Mechanic Gift Set, plastic, contains Plumbing Service Truck, Gardening Service Truck, Television Service Truck. 1953, box measures 15-1/4" long	NPF	NPF	NPF
Maxwell Auto, 1950-51	37	56	75

	C6	C8	C10
Plumbing Service Truck, plastic, w/tools, 1953, 10-1/2" long	67	100	135
Police Motorcycle, w/sirens	17	26	35
Prestige Auto Carrier, two cars	135	202	270
Television Service Truck, plastic, tv, ladder, tools, 1953, 10-1/2" long	65	110	140

RICH TOYS

The Rich Illinois Mfg. Co. used its trademark name Rich Toys on its line of wooden playthings in the 1920s and 1930s. The company eventually moved to Iowa and later to Mississippi. It produced only a small number of vehicle toys as the product line focused on doll houses, wooden horses, and children's furniture.

	C6	C8	C10
Borden's Farm Products Wagon, tin and wood, single horse, "Borden's Farm Products" and "Milk & Cream" on sides, w/milk bottles, 20" long	175	325	500
Borden's Milk Wagon, tin and wood, single horse, "Borden's" on wagon sides, 19" long	175	325	500
National Biscuit Company Truck, w/two trailers, wood, w/wooden Nabisco boxes	800	1400	2200
Texaco Gas Station, 16" x 22"	205	308	410

RICHARD APPEL (NEW YORK)

	C6	C8	C10
Victory Tank, wooden, WWII	22	33	45

Richard Appel Victory Tank.
Photo courtesy Jack Matthews

RICHARD TOYS

	C6	C8	C10
Heavy Transport Rid 'em, steel 32" long.	225	338	450

RICHMOND

	C6	C8	C10
Dump Truck, steel, 12" long	50	75	150
Tow Truck, 13" long, scarce	50	125	275

Richmond Dump Truck, 12". Photo courtesy John Taylor

Richmond Tow Truck, 13". Photo courtesy John Taylor

RICO TOY CO.

Located in Alicante, Spain, the Rico Toy Co. produced tin mechanical and battery-operated toys. The company dates back to the 1930s, (its offerings were often compared to the Paya Co) and lasted at least to the 1960s.

	C6	C8	C10
BMW, 1930s, 13" long	800	1400	2200

	C6	C8	C10
Bonnet Bus, tin wind-up, 6-1/4" long	262	393	525
Silver Bullet Racer, driver, wind-up, 11" long	300	450	600
Streamline Car, c.1935 tin wind-up, 7-3/4" long	262	393	525
Tom and Jerry Car, battery-operated, three actions, 1960s, 13" long	262	393	525

ROSS TOOL AND MANUFACTURING CO.

Another postwar plastic toy manufacturer was the Ross Tool and Mfg. Co.

	C6	C8	C10
Convertible, plastic, w/woman and dog, 1949, 3" long (RO008)	6	8	10
Hose Truck, plastic, 3" long (RO009)	6	8	10
Hot Rod, plastic, 5" long (RO007)	15	20	30
Ladder Truck, plastic, attached driver and ladder, 1950s, 4-3/4" long (RO001)	12	15	20
Mack Dump Truck, plastic, 1950s, 4-1/4" long (RO002)	20	25	35

	C6	C8	C10
Mack Gasoline Truck, plastic, 1950s, 4-5/8" long (RO004)	20	25	35
Mack Moving Van, plastic, 1950s, 4-5/8" long (RO003)	20	25	35
Racer, plastic, "2" on back, 1949, 4" long (RO005)	15	20	25
Racer, several varieties, plastic, 1949, approx 3" long (RO006)	6	8	10

Ross Convertible, woman and dog, 3". Photo courtesy Dave Leopard

Ross Hot Rod, plastic, 5". Photo courtesy Dave Leopard

Ross Ladder Truck, plastic, 4-7/5". Photo courtesy Dave Leopard

Ross Racer, plastic, 4". Photo courtesy Dave Leopard

Ross Hose Truck, plastic, 3". Photo courtesy Dave Leopard

RSA

A trademark of the Rico Co., a pre- and post-war toy manufacturer based in Spain.

	C6	C8	C10
Motorcycle, driver, 6-1/2" long	225	338	450
Motorcycle, driver, rider, tin wind-up, 9" long	700	1100	1500
Motorcycle, sidecar, driver, rider, tin wind-up, 10" long	1200	2000	3400

Left to right: RSA Motorcycle, sidecar, 10" and Motorcycle, driver, 9". Photo courtesy Bertoia Auctions

RUBBER VEHICLES UNKNOWN MFGS.

The following list, with its number codes, was compiled by Dave Leopard. Vehicles are broken down by types. The gaps in the numbering indicate vehicles that have been identified since the list was made up.

Contributor: Dave Leopard, 2507 Feather Run Trail, West Columbia, SC 29169-4915.

	C6	C8	C10
'34 Dodge Rack Truck, 4-7/8" long (UT004)	NPF	NPF	NPF
'35 Chrysler Four-door Airflow Sedan, rear spare, ad on roof, 4-3/4" long (UA007)	NPF	NPF	NPF
'35 Chrysler Two-door Airflow Sedan, 5-1/8" long (UA008)	75	95	125
'35 DeSoto Four-door Airflow Sedan, 5" long (UA006)	75	95	125
'35 LaFayette (?) Sedan, fastback, solid, w/tires, 4" long (UA012)	30	40	50
'35 Plymouth Four-door Sedan, 4-7/8" long (UA008A)	NPF	NPF	NPF
'36 Plymouth Four-door Trunkback Sedan, 4-7/8" long (UA009)	75	112	150
'37 Plymouth Four-door Trunkback Sedan, 4-7/8" long (UA010)	75	112	150
'46 Nash Two-door Fastback Sedan, hollow, molded tires, 4" long (UA011)	12	18	25
Open Racer, left side header pipes, solid rubber, 3-1/2" long (UR001)	NPF	NPF	NPF
Open Racer, solid, rubber tires on wood hubs, 6" long (UR003)	NPF	NPF	NPF
Open Racer, V-8, solid, large tires on wood hubs, 4" long (UR002)	NPF	NPF	NPF

Rubber Vehicles, 1935 DeSoto Four-door Airflow Sedan, 5". Photo courtesy Dave Leopard's book Rubber Toy Vehicles

Rubber Vehicles, 1935 Sedan, possibly a LaFayette, 4". Photo courtesy Dave Leopard's book Rubber Toy Vehicles

Rubber Vehicles, 1935 Plymouth Four-door Sedan, 4-7/8". Photo courtesy Dave Leopard's book Rubber Toy Vehicles

Rubber Vehicles, 1946 Nash, Two-door Fastback Sedan, 4". Photo courtesy Dave Leopard

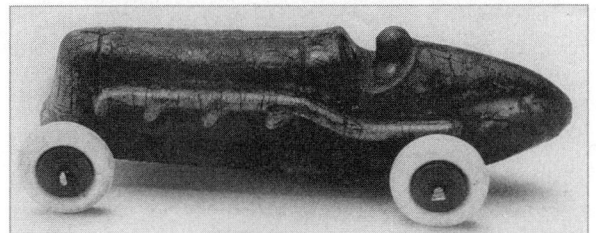

Rubber Vehicles, Open Racer, V-8, large tires on wood hubs, 4". Photo courtesy Dave Leopard's book Rubber Toy Vehicles

Rubber Vehicles, Open Racer, (UR01). Photo courtesy Dave Leopard

Rubber Vehicles, 1935 Chrysler Four-door Airflow Sedan, rear spare, ad on roof, spare, 4-3/4". Photo courtesy Dave Leopard's book Rubber Toy Vehicles

Rubber Vehicles, 1935 Chrysler Two-door Airflow Sedan, 5-1/8". Photo courtesy Dave Leopard's book Rubber Toy Vehicles

Rubber Vehicles, 1937 Plymouth Four-door Truckback Sedan, (UA10). Photo courtesy Dave Leopard's book Rubber Toy Vehicles

Rubber Vehicles, Open Racer, rubber tires on wood hubs, 6". Photo courtesy Dave Leopard's book Rubber Toy Vehicles

SAUNDERS TOOL & DIE CO.

The Saunders Tool & Die Co. was located in Aurora, Illinois. Charles Coddington, the Research Assistant at the Aurora Public Library kindly supplied the following: "The company was listed in City Directories for 1943-56. The business address was 500 Rathbone Ave. in Aurora at the south end of town. The officers were Paul B. Saunders, President; Stanley G. Cherwin, Vice President; and Mrs. Ann J. Drucks, Secretary."

Saunders Convertible, plastic windup, 10-3/4". Photo courtesy Ron Fink

A look at the Saunders Fire Chief with its original box. Photo courtesy Continental Hobby House

Left to right: Saunders Hot Rod, friction, 7"; Stock Car Racer with removable hood, friction, 8". Photo courtesy Bob and Alice Wagner

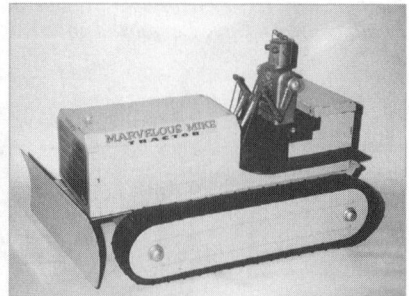

Saunders Marvelous Mike, 1950s, battery-operated, 17". Photo courtesy Don Hultzman

	C6	C8	C10
Bump and Dump Truck, 10-3/4" long	40	60	80
Convertible, plastic, wind-up w/attached key, rubber tires, 10-1/4" long	40	72	95
Fire Chief Car, plastic, No. 250, siren, wind-up, 10" long	42	63	85
Fire Truck, wind-up, plastic, 12" long	45	68	90
Frazer Convertible, plastic wind-up	75	112	150
Hot Rod, plastic, driver, friction, No. 400, 1950, 7" long........................	34	51	68
Jaguar, plastic, fricion motor, driver, opening hood, rubber tires, No. 700, 1952, 8-3/4" long	40	100	150
Ladder Truck...	55	80	110
Marvelous Mike, battery-operated, four actions, 1950s, 17" long........................	118	177	235
Military Police Car, friction, 9" long	NPF	NPF	NPF
Nu-Style Sportster Convertible	50	75	100
Packard Convertible, 1947, 10-1/2" long.	62	93	125
Police Car..	27	41	55
Police Rescue Car	48	72	95
Race Car..	16	24	32
Race Car, wind-up, 8" long.....................	42	63	85
Sand Dump Truck	55	82	110

Saunders Fire Chief, car windup, 10". Photo courtesy Dave Leopard

	C6	C8	C10
Searchlight Truck.....................................	85	128	170
Sedan, wind-up	42	63	85
Semi Trailer, 1960s, 16" long	88	132	175
Semi Van..	32	48	65
Stock Car Racer, w/removable hood, friction, 8" long......................................	60	125	175
Super Battle Tank, 8" long.......................	27	41	55
Super Motor Bus......................................	55	82	110
Super Searchlight Fire Truck, battery, bulb, on/off switch, 12" long	NPF	NPF	NPF

SAVOYE PEWTER TOY COMPANY

Savoye was incorporated August 1930. In 1931, Savoye Pewter Toy Co., manufacturer of pewter toys (pewter was often the word used for lead alloy or pot metal) was listed in directory at 69 Paterson Plank Road in North Bergen, N. J., with six male and three female employees. The names of the owners may have been Selma and Joseph Wigh. In 1934, at the same address, the workforce was seven males and two females. Slush-mold toys were probably its only product. Savoye was in the 1936 phone book yet not in the February 1937 directory. Collectors identify vehicle toys as Savoye

if they have a somewhat coarse appearance, heavy slush-mold body, and white rubber tires on oversized red wooden hubs that are smooth on the outside surface (no axle showing); but whether this is simply lore is not known at present. The son of one of the owners of Tommy Toy Co. thinks some Savoye-looking vehicles were made by Tommy Toy. If so, it's possible Savoye sold its molds to nearby Tommy Toy.

Contributor: Perry R. Eichor, 703 North Almond Drive, Simpsonville, SC, 29681 and the late Fred Maxwell.

	C6	C8	C10
Ambulance, same as the Tommy Toy ambulance (SA025)	16	24	32
Bus, cross-country bus, partial upper deck, twelve OW, rear-mount spare; 3-3/8" long (SA8)	20	30	40
Bus, heavy 5th Ave. sight-seeing bus, open overhanging upper deck, twelve OW, gilt or silver trim; 4-3/4" long (SA7)	62	93	125
Bus, tour bus, two OW, reads "Motor Coach," dual-axle semi-trailer, twelve OW, gilt trim, also came w/single axle; 7-1/2" long (SA009)	NPF	NPF	NPF

	C6	C8	C10
Coal Truck, dump body on chassis, driver and steering wheel, open windshield, 4-3/8" long (SA27)	NPF	NPF	NPF
Coupe, slanted louvers, fantasy grille and large black rubber wheels (possibly not original), 3-3/8" long (SA004)	14	21	28
Coupe, two OW, silver VG (Graham like), VL, 3-3/8" long (SA003)	20	30	40
Dump Truck, 4-3/8" long (SA10A)	NPF	NPF	NPF
Fire Engine, Steam pumper, driver and fireman w/high style gilt helmets, large ten-spoke metal wheels, possibly an early Savoye, 3-3/4" long (SA17 ?)	NPF	NPF	NPF

Left to right: Savoye Ambulance; Van, Police Patrol, 4"; Van, Police Patrol, 4", with Barclay wheels. Photo courtesy Ferd Zegel

Bus marked "Motor Coach," 7-1/2". Photo courtesy Ferd Zegel

Left to right: Savoye Bus, heavy 5th Ave. sightseeing bus, 4-3/4"; Tractor, Caterpillar (?), 4-3/4"; Oil car from Savoye's Tank Car Set. Photo courtesy Craig A. Clark

Savoye Cross-country Bus, partial upper deck, with window variation. Photo courtesy Al Lane

Savoye Convertible, open. Photo courtesy Al Lane

Savoye Tow Truck. Photo courtesy Craig A. Clark

Left to right: Savoye Dump Truck, 4-3/8"; Coal Truck, with open windshield, driver and steering wheel, 4-3/8". Photo courtesy Ferd Zegel

Left to right: Savoye Fire Truck, driver and steersman, 4-1/4"; Fire Truck, driver and fireman, two detachable ladders, 3-3/4".

Savoye Moving Van, six wheels, 3-7/8" (this model was repainted).

Savoye Gun Truck, Army, driver and gunner, 3-1/4". Photo courtesy Bill Conover

Savoye Fire Engine, steam pumper, driver and fireman, 3-3/4". Photo courtesy Fred Maxwell

Savoye Pickup Truck.

	C6	C8	C10
Fire Truck, driver and fireman w/high style gilt helmets, two detachable ladders on high rack, oversized wheel wells, oversized tires, 3-3/4" long (SA16)	NPF	NPF	NPF
Fire Truck, driver and steersman w/high style gilt helmets, bell on hood, two ladders (glued on), oversized wheel wells, oversized tires, 4-1/4" long (SA15)	NPF	NPF	NPF
Gun Truck, Army, driver and gunner (smooth gear under gun barrel distinguishes it from similar gun trucks); 3-1/4" long (SA21)	NPF	NPF	NPF
Moving Van, six wheels, 3-7/8" long (SA023)	105	158	210
Open Convertible, w/driver in Cap (SA026)	10	15	20
Pickup Truck (SA022)	20	30	40
Racer, w/driver and co-pilot, 4-1/4" long (SA24A)	NPF	NPF	NPF
Racer, w/driver, 4-1/4" long (SA024)	NPF	NPF	NPF
Roadster, 3-1/2" long (SA002)	NPF	NPF	NPF
Roadster, driver, open rumble seat, silver VG, (reminiscent of Tootsietoy Graham), VL, 3-1/2" long (SA001)	NPF	NPF	NPF
Tank Car Set, marked "Oil," "Cap 80000," not known whether Savoye sold these as a set; 10-1/4" long overall, 3-1/4"-long cab, 3-1/2"-long tank car (SA20)	40	60	80

	C6	C8	C10
Tow Truck, coupe cab, chain and hook on crane, 4" long (SA013)	NPF	NPF	NPF
Tow Truck, w/oversized crane, wire hook, 5-3/4" long (SA014)	NPF	NPF	NPF
Tractor, Caterpillar (?) tractor w/stack, 2-3/4" long (SA18)	10	15	20
Tractor, Caterpillar (?), w/large ten-spoke metal wheels, possibly an early Savoye (?), 3" long; same casting as Tommy Toy but longer wheelbase than Barclay No. 7 (SA019)	NPF	NPF	NPF

Savoye, Top row: SA10, SA15. Middle row: SA7, SA6. Bottom row: SA14, SA12. Photo courtesy Fred Maxwell

Savoye Truck with stake body, 5-3/4". Photo courtesy Perry Eichor

Savoye Tractor, SA19 (?). Photo courtesy Fred Maxwell

Savoye Van, milk grade, sidemounts, 3-1/4". Photo courtesy Al Lane

Top row, left to right: Savoye Roadster, 3-1/2"; Savoye Roadster, 3-1/2". Middle row, left to right: Bus, 4-3/4"; Coupe, two open windows, 3-3/8". Bottom row: Savoye bus, Mack Cab, "Motor Coach," 7-1/2". Photo courtesy Fred Maxwell

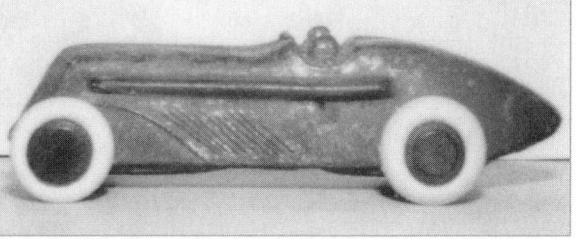

Savoye Racer, driver and co-pilot, 4-1/4".

Left to right: A Barclay tractor compared to Savoye Tractor, 2-3/4". Photo courtesy Bill Conover

	C6	C8	C10
Truck, heavy "Beer Truck," six wood barrels set in cast depressions, 4-3/8" long (SA010)	40	60	80
Truck, stake body, 4-1/2" long (SA011)	12	18	24
Truck, stake body, hinged tailgate w/chains, 5-3/4" long (SA012)	NPF	NPF	NPF

	C6	C8	C10
Van, marked "Police Patrol," policeman on rear step, six OW, gilt trim, SM; 4" long (SA6)	24	36	48
Van, reads "Milk Grade A," two OW, SM; 3-1/4" long (SA005)	20	30	40
Van, reads "Police Patrol," policeman on rear step, six OW, gilt trim, solid windows; 4" long (SA006A)	24	36	48

SCHIEBLE TOY & NOVELTY CO.

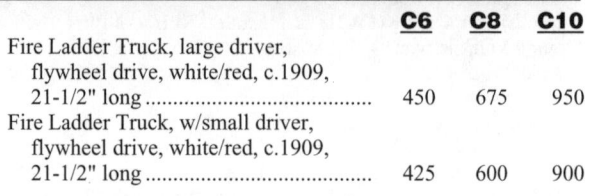

William E. Schieble was a partner in D.P. Clark & Co. for nearly ten years. In 1909, after some disagreements with Clark, he broke up the partnership and became the sole owner. At this time, Schieble changed the name of the company to Schieble Toy & Novelty. Things went well during the 1920s, but, as did many manufacturing companies, Schieble declared bankruptcy, in 1931.

Contributor: Bob Smith, RATS Toy Shows, 255 Tryon Park, Rochester, NY 14609. (585) 288-7153, bird@oldtoysonline.com.

	C6	C8	C10
Armored Car	350	525	750
Bus, No.110, Parlor Coach, 1920s, 20" long	425	650	900
Cannon Truck	450	675	950
Coupe, 18" long	400	575	925
Delivery Truck	450	650	925
Fire Engine Pumper, flywheel drive, red/gold, c.1917, 11-3/4" long	350	550	875
Fire Engine Pumper, light works, 1920s, 20" long	425	625	875
Fire Ladder Truck, 1920s, 20" long	375	550	800

	C6	C8	C10
Fire Ladder Truck, large driver, flywheel drive, white/red, c.1909, 21-1/2" long	450	675	950
Fire Ladder Truck, w/small driver, flywheel drive, white/red, c.1909, 21-1/2" long	425	600	900

Schieble Racer, team, c.1910, 12". Photo courtesy Wilkinson Collection, Detroit Auto Museum

Schieble Fire Truck, flywheel drive, circa 1917, 11-1/2". Photo courtesy Bob Smith

Left to right Schieble Fire Ladder Truck with flywheel drive and large driver, 21-1/2"; Fire Ladder Truck with flywheel drive, small driver, 21-1/2". Photo courtesy Bob Smith

Schieble Fire Engine Pumper, flywheel drive, c.1917, 11-3/4". Photo courtesy Bob Smith

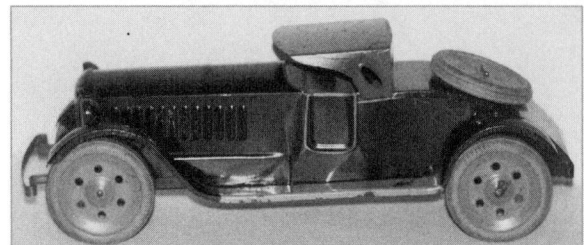

Schieble Roadster, spare tire on back, 18-1/2". Photo courtesy Joe and Sharon Freed

Schieble Mack Semi Dump Truck, 1920s, 22". Photo courtesy Bob Smith

	C6	C8	C10
Fire Truck, flywheel drive, red/gold, c.1917, 11-1/2" long	350	525	800
Mack Semi Dump Truck, (Chein lookalike) c.1925, 22" long	475	775	1050
Packard Express Truck	450	675	950
Pickup Truck	400	625	950
Racer, team, steel wind-up, c.1910, 12" long	500	750	1050

	C6	C8	C10
Roadster, 13" long	275	450	800
Roadster, spare tire on back, 18-1/4" long	450	675	1000
Sedan, 17" long	550	850	1000
Tank, WWI type	350	525	700
Touring Car, c.1909, 14" long	375	575	875
Wrecker	550	925	1450

SCHOENHUT

Although best known for its wooden Humpty Dumpty Circus (1903) and Teddy Roosevelt's Adventures in Africa (1909) figures, the A. Schoenhut company enjoyed a long toymaking history (1972-1935) and released a few vehicles.

	C6	C8	C10
Every Boy Auto Build 5 in 1 Toy, wood set to build, boxed	45	67	90
Stutz Racer, 10" long	150	250	350

SCHUCO

Schuco was founded in 1912 by Heinrich Muller and Herr Schreyer. They later called Schreyer and Co., and adopted the name "Schuco" as its trademark. Schuco toys, noted for their ingenious mechanisms, were produced in the 1930s into the 1950s, and marked either "Germany" or "U.S. Zone Germany." Toy with other markings are reissues.

	C6	C8	C10
Akustico 2002, BMW-based design, 2 clockwork motors, 1936-59, 5-1/2" long	87	130	175
Alarm Car, Opel Admiral, Opel-based body, flashing roof light, green or white body, 1967-69, 8-1/2" long	75	150	225
Anno 2000, 1940s, 5-1/2" long	80	120	160
Beach Buggy 355120, plastic body, clockwork motor, 4-speeds, removable wheels, 1:16-scale, 1975, 9" long	15	32	48
BMW 327, 1:18-scale tinplate, coupe or cabriolet, assorted two-tone colors, clockwork steering, new release, 1990s, 9-1/2" long	25	50	85
Buick, No. 5311, 9" long	200	300	400
Cadillac DeVille Convertible 5505, plastic, 1960s, 11" long	80	120	160
Combinato 4003, two clockwork motors, column gearshift, speedometer, working horn, 1953, 7-1/2" long	150	300	450
Command Car, "The Car of the Future," front license plate reads "A.D.2000," 1937-51, 5-1/2" long	100	210	350

	C6	C8	C10
Command Car Garage, designed to be used with the Command Car, telephone, 1950	50	100	150
Control Car, Opel Admiral, Opel-based body, flashing roof light, white or red body, no flashing light, 1967-69, 8-1/2" long	75	150	225
Dalli 1011, tin car and plastic driver, clockwork motor, reaches end of table raises hands and car turns, 1960s, 6-1/2" long	112	168	225
Electro Ingenico 5300, Buick-inspired design, remote control, clockwork motor, 1952, 8-1/2" long	175	365	575
Elektro Ingenico 5311, Buick-inspired design, remote control, battery-powered, 1952, 8-1/2" long	250	382	510
Examico 11, updated version of the Examico 4001, similar features, hood "Schuco" badge, 1957-68, 7-1/2" long	150	300	450
Examico 4001, five-speed BMW, clockwork motor, working clutch, handbrake, 1936-59, 6" long	165	248	330
Fernlenk, Auto No. 3000	92	138	185
Fex 1111, streamlined sedan, clockwork motor, rolls over, 1951-65, 6" long	90	135	180
Fx-Atmos, almost 2" long, late 1950s-early 1960s	NPF	NPF	NPF
Gas Station 3054, 1950s, 8" long	60	90	120

Schuco Examico, 1950s, 6".

Schuco Mercer Auto, 1950s, 7-1/2".

Schuco Micro Racer, 1950s, 4".
Photo courtesy Don Hultzman

	C6	C8	C10
Girato Mercedes 250SE, plastic body, tin baseplate, clockwork motor, 1967, 9" long..................................	100	200	300
Grand Prix Racer 1070, based on Ferrari Formula One racer, clockwork motor, 1955-66, 6" long..............	80	120	160
Jaguar 1250, 1940s, 5-1/2" long..............	160	240	320
Lasto 3042, 1950s, 4-1/2" long truck.......	60	90	120
Limousine 1010, two-tone paint versions most desirable, 1939-65, 5-3/4" long...	100	220	350
Magico Alfa Romeo 2010, based on Alfa Romeo Giulietta, clockwork motor, antenna stop/starts car, remote steering, 1964, 9-1/2" long..................	200	400	600
Magico Auto 2008, responds to blowing, rubber roof antenna, 1951-65, 5-1/2" long	300	450	600
Magico Car and Garage, 1950s, 6" long ..	120	180	240
Matra-Ford Formula One, plastic body, clockwork motor, 9-1/2" long.............	30	60	90
Mercedes 170V Limo, available as sedan, police car, cabriolet, panel van, tanker truck, or pickup truck; clockwork motor, new release, 1990s, 9-1/2" long	25	50	85
Mercedes 190SL 2095, clockwork motor, remote steering, 1956-69, 8" long........	145	220	315
Mercedes 190SL Elektro Phanomenal 5503, battery-operated via the electric Gasoline Pump 5506, column gearshift, remote steering, 1955, 8-1/2" long	150	300	450
Mercedes TYP SSK 1928, 1950s, 4" long	100	150	200
Mercedes-Benz 0303 Bus, die-cast, opening doors, 1975, 7" long	30	60	95
Mercer Auto 1225, 1950s, 7-1/2" long	75	112	150
Micro Racer 101, die-cast, Porsche style, 1950s, 3-1/2" long...............................	90	135	180
Micro Racer 102, die-cast, Indy style, 1950s, 3-1/2" long...............................	90	135	180
Micro Racer 104, die-cast, Indy style, 1950s, 3-1/2" long...............................	90	135	180
Micro Racer '57 Ford Custom 1045, die-cast, 1950s, 4" long......................	80	120	160
Micro Racer Alpha Romeo 1048, die-cast, 1950s, 4" long......................	90	135	180
Micro Racer Ferrari F1 1040, die-cast, 1950s, 4" long......................................	75	105	145
Micro Racer Ford Custom Hot Rod 1036, die-cast, 1950s, 4-1/2" long	100	150	200
Micro Racer Go Kart 1035, die-cast, 1950s, 4" long......................................	100	150	200
Micro Racer Hotrod 1036, die-cast, 1950s, 4" long......................................	90	135	180
Micro Racer Mercedes Benz 190SL 1044, die-cast, 1950s, 4" long.............	110	165	220
Micro Racer Mercedes Benz 220S 1038, die-cast, 1950s, 4" long........................	100	150	200
Micro Racer Mercedes F1 1043, die-cast, 1950s, 4" long	75	112	150
Micro Racer Mercer 35J 1036/1, die-cast, 1950s, 4" long........................	100	150	200
Micro Racer Porsche Coupe 1047, die-cast, 1950s, 4" long........................	110	165	220
Micro Racer Rally 1034, eight three lane tracks, 1950s, 10' 6" long....................	60	90	120
Micro Racer Stake Truck 1049, die-cast, 1950s, 4" long	90	135	180
Micro Racer USA Midget Racer 1041, die-cast, 1950s, 4" long......................	72	112	150
Micro Racer USA Midget Racer 1042, die-cast, 1950s, 4" long......................	100	150	200
Micro Racer Volkswagen 1046, die-cast, 1950s, 4" long	90	135	180
Micro Racer Volkswagen Polizei 1039, die-cast, 1950s, 4" long......................	100	150	200
Mirakocar 1001, non-fall action, 1951, 4-1/2" long..	72	108	145
Monkey Car, orange-black, smiling monkey, 1930s, 6" long	1400	2100	2800
Motodrill Clown 1007, composition head, 1950s, 5" long motorcycle	1000	1500	2000
Mystery Car 1010, non-fall action, 1950s, 5-1/2" long.............................	90	135	180
Patent 1001, sedan, clockwork motor, steep raked grille, assorted colors, when car reaches end of table it does a 90-degree turn and keeps moving, 1936-52, 4-1/2" long............................	45	90	130
Patent 1250, sedan, clockwork motor, assorted colors, 1938-52, 5-1/2" long ..	60	125	210
Porsche 911 Monte Carlo Rallye Car, plastic body, battery operated, removable wheels, 1:16-scale, 1972	40	80	125
Porsche Carrera RS 356 180, plastic body, clockwork motor, 1:16-scale, 1973	30	60	90
Radio 4012, musical car, 2 clockwork motors, plastic windshield, 1952-64, 6" long..	238	355	475
Radio 5000, rare, 2 clockwork motors, one for movement and the other for music, 1938, 5-1/2" long....................	350	700	1000
Razzia 5509, based on the Mercedes 190SL, battery and clockwork powered, two passengers, available as police or fire chief's car, 1958, 8-1/2" long	200	400	600
Rollyvox 1080, based on the Mercedes 190SL, rocket-shaped hood ornament, plastic windshield, flywheel driven, working steering wheel, 1957-69, 8-1/2" long	125	250	400
Sonny Mouse 2005, BMW-based, Akustico body, clockwork motor, "Mouse" figure drives, 1956-60, 5-1/2" long...	150	300	500
Sonny Peter 2006, BMW-based, Akustico body, clockwork motor, "Peter" figure drives, 1956-60, 5-1/2" long...	150	300	500
Station Car 3118, 1950s, 4-1/2" long.......	60	90	120
Studio Racer 1050, based on 1936 Mercedes Silver Arrow Grand Prix racer, clockwork motor, includes tools, one of the most popular and enduring of all Schuco toys, 1936-on, 5-1/2" long...	125	188	250
Synchromatic 5700, resembles Packard Hawk, "Packard" across hood deck, rechargable battery-powered, instrument panel light, 1958-69, 11" long..	500	750	1000
Tacho Examico 4002, same body as Radio Auto 4012, clockwork motor, column gearshift mimics motion of real car, working steering wheel, 1951-56, 6" long	175	365	575
Telesteering 3000 Limo, 1950s, 4" long..	72	105	145

	C6	C8	C10
Telesteering Car 3000, sedan, 4-speed gear, clockwork motor, 12 wooden posts, wooden ball, 2 flags, steering wheel w/connecting wire, 1938-60, 4" long	75	150	225
Texi 5735, same body as Alfa Romeo 2010, clockwork motor, blonde female driver, 1960, 9-1/2" long	225	475	750
Varianto 3010, two tin car playset, 1950s, cars are 4-1/2" long	100	150	200
Varianto 3010 Super, service station w/two cars, 1950s, 4-1/2"-long cars	170	225	340
Varianto 3041 Limo, clockwork motor, "Schuco" stamped in trunk, 1950s, 4" long	50	90	125
Varianto 3064, all plastic, 1950s, 8" long	30	45	60
Varianto Box 3010/30, tin garage and 3041 Limo, 1950s, 4-1/2" long	50	100	150
Varianto Bus 3044, clockwork motor, plastic windows, 1950s, 4-1/4" long	70	105	140
Varianto Electro 3112u, long truck, 1950s, 4-1/2" long	60	90	120
Varianto Electro Lastwagen 3112, long truck, Elecktro rechargable, 1950s, 4" long	60	90	120
Varianto Elektro 3118 Station Car, station wagon design, rechargable battery power, 1957, 4-1/2" long	65	140	210
Varianto Elektro Express 3114, futuristic van, rechargable battery power, 1955, 4-1/2" long	65	140	210

Schuco Studio Racer, 1950s, 5-1/2". Photo courtesy Don Hultzman

	C6	C8	C10
Varianto Elektro Tankwagen 3116, rechargable battery operated, tinplate, "Aral" or "Shell" decals on sides, 4-1/2" long	65	140	210
Varianto Lasto 3042, long truck, clockwork motor, "Schuco 3042" stamped into doors, plastic pickup bed, 1950s, 4-1/4" long	80	120	160
Varianto Sani Ambulance, clockwork motor, same workings as Varianto Bus, 4-1/4" long	50	100	150
Varianto Service Station 3055, recharges Varianto vehicles, tin litho, 6" long	45	90	140
Varianto Traffic Lights 3051, four-way intersection, 1953, 11" x 11"	64	140	210
Varianto Van 3116, clockwork motor, same workings as Varianto Bus, 4-1/4" long	50	100	150

SEIBERLING RUBBER

The Sieberling Lates Products Co. was based in Barberton, Ohio. The firm began making rubber toys in 1931 and released its two vehicles in 1934. They were small and large examples of a 1935 Ford.

Contributor: Dave Leopard, 2507 Feather Run Trail, West Columbia, SC 29169

	C6	C8	C10
'35 Ford Two-door Slantback Sedan, 4" long (GA02)	30	40	50
'35 Ford Two-door Slantback Sedan, 5" long (GA01)	40	50	65

Seiberling, 1935 Ford Two-door Slantback Sedan, 4". Photo courtesy Dave Leopard from his book, Rubber Toy Vehicles

Seiberling, 1935 Ford Two-door Slantback Sedan, 5". Photo courtesy Dave Leopard from his book, Rubber Toy Vehicles

Seiberling, Left to right: 1935 Ford Two-door Slantback Sedan 5" and 4" long. Photo courtesy Dave Leopard from his book, Rubber Toy Vehicles

SHARRON

Sharron toys are die-cast aluminum, with two-piece construction similar to cast-iron vehicles from the 1930s. Sharron toys were made for a brief time at the Eastern Mennonite College in Harrisonburg, Va., during the Depression era. The molds were designed by a craftsman from Hubley, and the toys were made at the school from melted-down scrap aluminum. The toys are not marked in any way, but the originals bore a small paper tag that read, "Indestructible Aluminum Toys."

Sharron No. 13SD Mack Side Dump Truck. Photo courtesy Perry Eichor

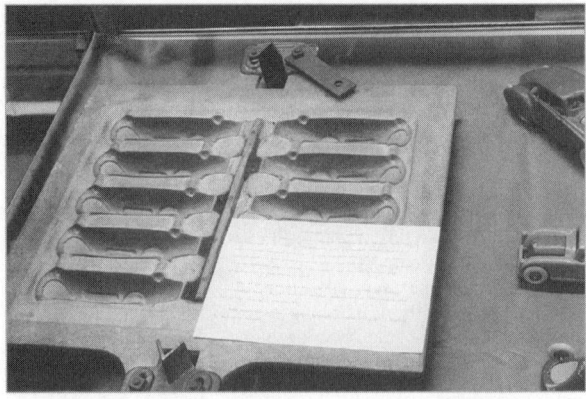

Sharron match plate. Photo courtesy Perry Eichor

Sharron 1934 Rohr, 5". Photo courtesy Perry Eichor

Sharron's No. 10S Pierce Arrow with its original tag. Photo courtesy Perry Eichor

Another look at Sharron's No. 10S Pierce Arrow-Sedan (back) and the No. 20S Pierce Arrow-type Sedan. Photo courtesy Perry Eichor

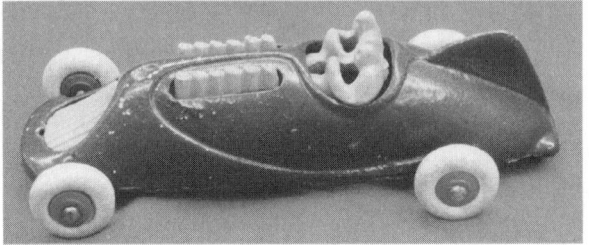

Sharron No. 11 R Twelve-cylinder, two-man Racer. Photo courtesy Perry Eichor

Clockwise from top: Sharron No. 11R Twelve-cylinder Racer; No. 20S Pierce Arrow-type Sedan; two versions of No. 10S Pierce Arrow-type Sedan; No. 13SD Makc Side Dump Truck; Another version of No. 11R Racer; Another version of No. 20S Pierce Arrow-type Sedan. Photo courtesy Perry Eichor

Manufacture of the toys was part of the work-study program at the school, and it apparently landed some large orders with chain stores.

As of the late 1990s, Julian Thomas owned the plates, which produced eight of the smaller cars in one pouring.

	C6	C8	C10
Dump truck, aluminum, Mack, side-dump, No. 13SD, 4" long	100	175	250
Open Racer, aluminum, 6" long (SV03) .	80	100	130
Pierce Arrow-type Sedan, aluminum, No. 10S	50	100	150

	C6	C8	C10
Pierce Arrow-type Sedan, aluminum, No. 20S, 6-1/2" long..........................	75	135	200
Pierce-Arrow Silver Arrow, aluminum, 1933, 6" long (SV01)	125	175	225
Racer, aluminum, two-man, twelve cylinder, No. 11R, 5-3/4" long	75	145	225
Racer, aluminum, unnumbered, spring loaded, 12" long.................................	NPF	NPF	NPF
Rohr, aluminum, 1934, 5" long (SV02)	100	150	200
Trolley Car, aluminum (SV04)	NPF	NPF	NPF

SHERWOOD TOY CO.

	C6	C8	C10
Roy Rogers Nellybelle Pedal Car, 1954 ..	800	1400	2000

SHROCK BROTHERS

The Shrock Bros., Tom and Dave, are the owners of an autobody shop that gave birth to a line of toys devoted to Studebaker. After restoring several real Studebakers, one that was used in the film, *The Color Purple*, they released their first pewter replica of a 1940 Studebaker President Boat-tail Speedster in 1:43 scale.

Shrock Bros. used 1:43 scale from 1985 to 1993. In 1988, they released the first line of 1:55-scale Studebakers that included 1941-64 Pickups, and 1959-60 Larks in five body styles. In 1994, the 1:72-scale line debuted, and it remains the preferred scale.

For more information, you may contact Shrock Bros. online at: www.shrockbrothers.com, or via the mail at: Shrock Body Shop, 3999 Tyrone Pike, Coalport, PA 16627

1:43

	C6	C8	C10
1931-32 Indy Racer, 1991......................	n/a	n/a	175
1936 COE Cab and Chassis, March 1985, six produced in pot metal....................	n/a	n/a	NPF
1936 COE Circus Tractor and Trailer, 1990, 11 in plastic	n/a	n/a	NPF
1936 COE Streamline Tractor and Trailer, 1989, 15 in plastic	n/a	n/a	NPF

Shrock Bros. 1933-32 Indy Racer, 1:43-scale, 1991. Photo courtesy Jim Geary

	C6	C8	C10
1936 COE Tandem Stake Truck, 1991	n/a	n/a	NPF
1936 Tractor, November 1985-86, with 5th wheel but no trailer, 14 produced in plastic	n/a	n/a	NPF
1936-38 COE Cab and Chassis, 1985......	n/a	n/a	NPF
1936-38 COE Dump, 1990	n/a	n/a	175
1940 President Boat-tail Speedster, 1986 Type 1	n/a	n/a	NPF
1940 President Boat-tail Speedster, Re-issued..	n/a	n/a	175
1949-53 2R 1-ton Wrecker, 1993 with modified Studebaker bed	n/a	n/a	NPF
1949-53 2R Milk Truck, 1994	n/a	n/a	NPF
1949-53 2R PA Fire Warden Truck, 1994	n/a	n/a	NPF
1949-53 2R16 Dump Truck, 1993	n/a	n/a	NPF
1949-53 2R16 Stake Truck, 1993	n/a	n/a	NPF
1949-53 2R16 Tractor and Flatbed Trailer, 1993, with front wind deflector	n/a	n/a	NPF
1949-53 2R16 Tractor and Lowboy Trailer, 1993	n/a	n/a	NPF
1949-53 2R5 & 2R10 Pickup, 1993.........	n/a	n/a	175
1949-53 Brush Fire Truck, 1994.............	n/a	n/a	300
1950 Champion Convertible, 1995	n/a	n/a	NPF
1950 Champion Starlight Coupe, 1995.....	n/a	n/a	NPF
1951 Commander Convertible, 1994.......	n/a	n/a	NPF
1951 Commander Starlight Coupe, 1994	n/a	n/a	NPF
1955 Commander Regal Starlight, 1995..	n/a	n/a	NPF
1955 E13 Dump Truck, 1991...................	n/a	n/a	NPF
1955 E13 Stake Truck, 1991	n/a	n/a	NPF
1955 E28 Dump Truck, 1991...................	n/a	n/a	NPF
1955 E28 Stake Truck, 1991	n/a	n/a	NPF
1955 E38 Dump Truck, 1991...................	n/a	n/a	NPF
1955 E38 Stake Truck, 1991	n/a	n/a	NPF
1955 President Speedster, 1995	n/a	n/a	NPF
1955 President Starlight Coupe, 1995	n/a	n/a	NPF
1955 President Starliner HT, 1995...........	n/a	n/a	NPF
1955-59 E12 Pickup, 1990......................	n/a	n/a	175
1955-59 E12 Pickup, 1990 w/two-tone paint scheme	n/a	n/a	200
1955-59 E5 Pickup, 1990........................	n/a	n/a	175
1955-59 E5 Pickup, 1990 w/two-tone paint scheme	n/a	n/a	200
1955-59 E7 Pickup, 1990.......................	n/a	n/a	175

Shrock. Bros. 1935 Commander 4-door Landcruiser, 1:72-scale, 1994. Photo courtesy Jim Geary

Shrock Bros. 1935 President 4-door Convertible, 1:72-scale, 1994. Photo courtesy Jim Geary

Shrock Bros. 1936 COE Excavator, 1:72-scale, 1999. Photo courtesy Jim Geary

Shrock Bros. 1936 COE Cab and Chassis, 1:43-scale, 1985. Photo courtesy Jim Geary

Shrock Bros. 1938 K 20 Human Canon Truck, 1:72-scale, 2003. Photo courtesy Jim Geary

Shrock Bros. 1938 4-door Convertible, 1:72-scale, 1995. Photo courtesy Jim Geary

Shrock Bros. 1939 Club Sedan, 1:72-scale, 1996. Photo courtesy Jim Geary

Shrock Bros. 1939 Coupe Express, 1:72-scale, 1996. Photo courtesy Jim Geary

Shrock Bros. 1940 President Boat-tail Speedster, 1:72-scale, 1996. Photo courtesy Jim Geary

Shrock Bros. 1941 Champion 4-door Sedan, 1:72-scale, 1997. Photo courtesy Jim Geary

Shrock Bros. 1947-49 Champion Business Coupe, 1:72-scale, 1998. Photo courtesy Jim Geary

Shrock Bros. 1947-49 Commander, 1:72-scale, 1998. Photo courtesy Jim Geary

Shrock Bros. 1949-53 2 R 5 Pickup, 1:72-scale, 1999. Photo courtesy Jim Geary

Shrock Bros. 1950 Champion Convertible, 1:72-scale, 1998. Photo courtesy Jim Geary

Shrock Bros. 1951 Auto Cannon, 1:72-scale, 2002. Photo courtesy Jim Geary

	C6	C8	C10
1955-59 E7 Pickup, 1990 w/two-tone paint scheme	n/a	n/a	200
1956 2E13 Dump Truck, 1991	n/a	n/a	NPF
1956 2E13 Stake Bed, 1991	n/a	n/a	NPF
1956 2E13 Wrecker, 1993, with custom Studebaker bed	n/a	n/a	NPF
1956 2E28 Dump Truck, 1991	n/a	n/a	NPF
1956 2E28 Stake Truck, 1991	n/a	n/a	NPF
1956 2E28 with Box Van, 1992	n/a	n/a	NPF
1956 2E38 Dump Truck, 1991	n/a	n/a	NPF
1956 2E38 Stake Truck, 1991	n/a	n/a	NPF
1956 2E38 Tractor and Fruehauf Trailer, 1991	n/a	n/a	NPF
1957 3E13 Wrecker, 1993	n/a	n/a	NPF
1957 E28 Dump, 1991	n/a	n/a	NPF
1957-58 3E13 Dump Truck, 1992	n/a	n/a	NPF
1957-58 3E13 Stake Truck, 1992	n/a	n/a	NPF
1957-58 3E13 Wrecker, 1994, with custom wrecker body	n/a	n/a	NPF
1957-58 3E28 Dump Truck, 1992	n/a	n/a	NPF
1957-58 3E28 Stake Truck, 1992	n/a	n/a	NPF
1957-58 3E38 Dump Truck, 1992	n/a	n/a	NPF
1957-58 3E38 Long Wheel Base Stake Truck, 1994	n/a	n/a	NPF
1957-58 3E38 Stake Truck, 1992	n/a	n/a	NPF
1957-58 3E38 Tractor and Lowboy Trailer, 1992	n/a	n/a	NPF
1957-59 E12 4x4 Pickup, 1989	n/a	n/a	200
1957-59 E7 4x4 Pickup, 1989	n/a	n/a	200
1958 E38 Semi Lowboy, 1991	n/a	n/a	NPF
1958 Packard 3E12D 4x4 Pickup, 1993	n/a	n/a	275
1959 4E13 Dump Truck, 1993	n/a	n/a	NPF
1959 4E13 Stake Truck, 1993	n/a	n/a	NPF
1959 4E28 Dump Truck, 1993	n/a	n/a	NPF
1959 4E28 Stake Truck, 1993	n/a	n/a	NPF
1959 4E38 Dump Truck, 1993	n/a	n/a	NPF
1959 4E38 Stake Truck, 1993	n/a	n/a	NPF
1959 4E38 Tractor and Lowboy Trailer, 1993	n/a	n/a	NPF
1962-63 96BBC 7E 45 Diesel Wrecker, 1995	n/a	n/a	NPF
1962-63 96BBC 7E 45 Dump Truck, 1994	n/a	n/a	NPF
1962-63 96BBC 7E 45 PA Snow Plow Truck, 1994	n/a	n/a	NPF
1962-63 96BBC 7E 45 Tractor and Lowboy Trailer, 1994	n/a	n/a	NPF
1962-63 96BBC 8E 45 Diesel Wrecker, 1995	n/a	n/a	NPF
1962-63 96BBC 8E 45 Dump Truck, 1994	n/a	n/a	NPF
1962-63 96BBC 8E 45 PA Snow Plow Truck, 1994	n/a	n/a	NPF

	C6	C8	C10
1962-63 96BBC 8E 45 Tractor and Lowboy Trailer, 1994	n/a	n/a	NPF
1963 8E45 Diesel Wrecker, 1995	n/a	n/a	NPF
1963 Diesel 96 BBC/Lowboy, 1992	n/a	n/a	NPF
1963 Diesel Dump, 1993	n/a	n/a	NPF
1963 Diesel Dump with Plow Mount, 1993	n/a	n/a	NPF
2000 E2K Pickup, 2000	n/a	n/a	250

1:55

	C6	C8	C10
1941-48 Flat Bed Trailer, 1992	n/a	n/a	NPF
1941-48 Fruehauf Van Trailer, 1992	n/a	n/a	NPF
1941-48 M 16 Tractor, 1992	n/a	n/a	NPF
1941-48 M5 Pickup, 1993	n/a	n/a	NPF
1946 M 16 Tandem Axel Grain Truck, 1992	n/a	n/a	NPF
1949-53 2R16 Tractor, 1999	n/a	n/a	NPF
1949-53 2R5 Pickup, 1989	n/a	n/a	NPF
1957-59 3E7 Pickup, 1992	n/a	n/a	NPF
1959-60 Lark 2-door HT, 1995	n/a	n/a	NPF
1959-60 Lark 2-door Sedan, 1995	n/a	n/a	NPF
1959-60 Lark 2-door Station Wagon, 1995	n/a	n/a	NPF
1959-60 Lark 4-door Sedan, 1995	n/a	n/a	NPF
1960 Lark 4-door Station Wagon, 1995	n/a	n/a	NPF
1960 Lark Convertible, 1995	n/a	n/a	NPF
1960-62 Champ Stepside Pickup, 1992	n/a	n/a	NPF
1961-64 Champ Fleetside Pickup, 1993	n/a	n/a	NPF

1:72

	C6	C8	C10
1935 Big Chief Dump, 1994	n/a	n/a	70
1935 Big Chief Tractor & Car Carrier Set, 1994	n/a	n/a	425
1935 Big Chief w/Flatbed Trailer, 1994	n/a	n/a	100
1935 Commander 4-door Landcruiser, 1994	n/a	n/a	70
1935 Commander Convertible, 1994	n/a	n/a	70
1935 Commander Coupe, 1994	n/a	n/a	70
1935 President 4-door Convertible, 1994, w/ dual side mounts	n/a	n/a	70
1935 President 4-door Landcruiser, 1994	n/a	n/a	70
1935 President Convertible, 1994	n/a	n/a	70
1935 President Coupe, 1994	n/a	n/a	70
1936 COE Excavator, 1999	n/a	n/a	100
1936 Streamlined COE Tractor & Aero Car Trailer, 1996	n/a	n/a	150
1936 Streamlined COE Tractor & Jungle Cat Trailer, 2001	n/a	n/a	150
1936-38 COE Car Carrier Set, 1995	n/a	n/a	425
1936-38 COE Tractor & Flatbed Trailer, 1995	n/a	n/a	100
1936-38 COE Tractor or Dump, 1995	n/a	n/a	70
1938 4-door Convertible, 1995	n/a	n/a	70
1938 4-door Sedan, 1995	n/a	n/a	70
1938 Business Coupe, 1995	n/a	n/a	70
1938 Club Sedan, 1995	n/a	n/a	70
1938 Coupe Express, 1995	n/a	n/a	70
1938 K 10 Brush Fire Truck, 2003	n/a	n/a	70
1938 K 20 Human Canon Truck, 2003	n/a	n/a	200
1938 President Stock Car, 2003	n/a	n/a	70
1938-40 K 10 Pickup, 2001	n/a	n/a	60
1938-40 K 20 Tractor & Dump, 2001	n/a	n/a	70
1938-40 K 30 Excavator, 2001	n/a	n/a	100
1939 4-door Convertible, 1996	n/a	n/a	70
1939 4-door Sedan, 1996	n/a	n/a	70
1939 Business Coupe, 1996	n/a	n/a	70
1939 Club Sedan, 1996	n/a	n/a	70
1939 Coupe Express, 1996	n/a	n/a	70
1940 Champion 2-door Sedan, 1997	n/a	n/a	70
1940 Champion 4-door Sedan, 1997	n/a	n/a	70
1940 Champion Business Coupe, 1997	n/a	n/a	70

Shrock Bros. 1951 Commander 2-door Sedan, 1:72-scale, 1998. Photo courtesy Jim Geary

Shrock Bros. 1951 Commander Convertible, 1:72-scale, 1998. Photo courtesy Jim Geary

Shrock Bros. 1952 Commander Convertible, 1:72-scale, 1998. Photo courtesy Jim Geary

Shrock Bros. 1952 Commander Starliner HT, 1:72-scale, 1998. Photo courtesy Jim Geary

Shrock Bros. 1952 Commander 2-door Sedan, 1:72-scale, 1998. Photo courtesy Jim Geary

Shrock Bros. 1953 Commander Convertible, 1:72-scale, 1999. Photo courtesy Jim Geary

Shrock Bros. 1953 Commander Starlight Coupe, 1:72-scale, 1999. Photo courtesy Jim Geary

Shrock Bros. 1954 Commander Starlight Coupe, 1:72-scale, 2001. Photo courtesy Jim Geary

Shrock Bros. 1955 E7 1/2-ton Pickup, 1:72-scale, 1999. Photo courtesy Jim Geary

Shrock Bros. 1955 E13 Stake Truck, 1:43-scale, 1991. Photo courtesy Jim Geary

Shrock Bros. 1955 President Speedster, 1:43-scale, 1995. Photo courtesy Jim Geary

Shrock Bros. 1956 2E28 with Box Van, 1:43-scale, 1992. Photo courtesy Jim Geary

Shrock Bros. 1956 Power Hawk, 1:72-scale, 2002. Photo courtesy Jim Geary

Shrock Bros. 1958 Packard Hawk, 1:72-scale, 2003. Photo courtesy Jim Geary

Shrock Bros. 1959-60 Lark 4-door Sedan, 1:55-scale, 1995. Photo courtesy Jim Geary

Shrock Bros. 1960 Lark 4-door Station Wagon, 1:55-scale, 1995. Photo courtesy Jim Geary

	C6	C8	C10		C6	C8	C10
1940 Champion Coupe Delivery, 1997....	n/a	n/a	70	1953 Commander Starliner HT, 1999......	n/a	n/a	70
1940 President 4-door Sedan, 1996	n/a	n/a	70	1953 Roadster, 1999	n/a	n/a	70
1940 President Boat-tail Speedster,				1953 Starlight Express, 1999	n/a	n/a	70
1996	n/a	n/a	70	1954 3R5 1/2-ton Pickup, 1999	n/a	n/a	60
1940 President Business Coupe, 1996	n/a	n/a	70	1954 Commander Starlight Coupe,			
1940 President Club Sedan, 1996	n/a	n/a	70	2001	n/a	n/a	70
1940 President Stock Car, 2003	n/a	n/a	70	1954 Commander Starliner HT, 2001......	n/a	n/a	70
1940 President World's Fair Car, 1996	n/a	n/a	70	1955 Commander De Luxe Starlight			
1941 Champion 2-door Sedan, 1997........	n/a	n/a	70	Coupe, 2002	n/a	n/a	70
1941 Champion 4-door Sedan, 1997........	n/a	n/a	70	1955 Commander Regal Starlight Coupe,			
1941 Champion Business Coupe, 1997 ...	n/a	n/a	70	2002	n/a	n/a	70
1941 Champion Coupe Delivery, 1997.....	n/a	n/a	70	1955 Commander Starliner HT, 2002......	n/a	n/a	70
1941 Cruising Sedan DeLux-tone trim	n/a	n/a	NPF	1955 E38 Dump, 2002	n/a	n/a	70
1941 M 16 Tractor & Dump, 1997	n/a	n/a	70	1955 E38 Tractor, 2002	n/a	n/a	70
1941 M 5 Pickup, 1997..........................	n/a	n/a	60	1955 E7 1/2-ton Pickup, 1999	n/a	n/a	60
1941 President DeLuxe-tone, 1997..........	n/a	n/a	70	1955 President Speedster, 2002	n/a	n/a	70
1941 President Landcruiser Skyway,				1955 President Starlight Coupe, 2002	n/a	n/a	70
1997	n/a	n/a	70	1955 President Starliner HT, 2002..........	n/a	n/a	70
1941 Sedan Coupe in Skyway trim	n/a	n/a	NPF	1956 2E38 Dump, 2002	n/a	n/a	70
1946-48 M 5 Pickup, 1997.....................	n/a	n/a	60	1956 2E38 Tractor, 2002	n/a	n/a	70
1947-49 Champion Business Coupe,				1956 2E38 Tractor and Fruehauf Van			
1998	n/a	n/a	70	Trailer, 2003	n/a	n/a	150
1947-49 Commander (all body styles),				1956 2E7 1/2-ton Pickup, 1999	n/a	n/a	60
1998	n/a	n/a	70	1956 Golden Hawk, 2002	n/a	n/a	70
1949-53 2 R 16 Dump, 1999...................	n/a	n/a	70	1956 Power Hawk, 2002	n/a	n/a	70
1949-53 2 R 16 Tractor, 1999	n/a	n/a	70	1956 Sky Hawk, 2002	n/a	n/a	70
1949-53 2 R 5 Pickup, 1999...................	n/a	n/a	60	1957 3E7 1/2-ton Pickup, 1999	n/a	n/a	60
1950 Business Coupe, 1998	n/a	n/a	70	1957 Golden Hawk, 2003	n/a	n/a	70
1950 Champion 2-door Sedan, 1998........	n/a	n/a	70	1957 Golden Hawk 400, 2003	n/a	n/a	70
1950 Champion 4-door Sedan, 1998........	n/a	n/a	70	1957 Silver Hawk, 2003	n/a	n/a	70
1950 Champion Convertible, 1998	n/a	n/a	70	1958 3E7 1/2-ton Pickup, 1999	n/a	n/a	60
1950 Champion Starlight Coupe, 1998....	n/a	n/a	70	1958 Golden Hawk, 2003	n/a	n/a	70
1951 Auto Cannon, 2002	n/a	n/a	300	1958 Packard Hawk, 2003	n/a	n/a	70
1951 Comander Starlight Coupe, 1998....	n/a	n/a	70	1958 Silver Hawk, 2003	n/a	n/a	70
1951 Commander 2-door Sedan, 1998	n/a	n/a	70	1959 4E2 1/2-ton Pickup, 1999	n/a	n/a	60
1951 Commander 4-door Sedan, 1998	n/a	n/a	70	1959 4E7 1/2-ton Pickup, 1999	n/a	n/a	60
1951 Commander Business Coupe,				1959 4E7D 1/2-ton 4x4 Pickup, 1999......	n/a	n/a	60
1998	n/a	n/a	70	1960 5E7 Champ 1/2-ton Pickup, 2000 ...	n/a	n/a	60
1951 Commander Convertible, 1998	n/a	n/a	70	1961 6E7 Champ 1/2-ton Pickup			
1952 50th Anniversary Loewy Spider,				(fleetside), 1999.................................	n/a	n/a	60
1999	n/a	n/a	70	1961 6E7 Champ 1/2-ton Pickup			
1952 Commander 2-door Sedan, 1998	n/a	n/a	70	(stepside), 2000.................................	n/a	n/a	60
1952 Commander 4-door Sedan, 1998	n/a	n/a	70	1962 7E45E 96 BBC Diesel Dump, 1999	n/a	n/a	70
1952 Commander Convertible, 1998	n/a	n/a	70	1962 7E45E 96 BBC Diesel Tractor,			
1952 Commander Starlight Coupe, 1998.	n/a	n/a	70	1999	n/a	n/a	70
1952 Commander Starliner HT, 1998......	n/a	n/a	70	1962 7E7 Champ 1/2-ton Pickup			
1953 Commander Convertible (top				(fleetside), 1999.................................			60
down), 1999	n/a	n/a	70	1962 7E7 Champ 1/2-ton Pickup			
1953 Commander Convertible (top up),				(stepside), 2000.................................	n/a	n/a	60
1999	n/a	n/a	70	1963-64 8E7 Champ 1/2-ton Pickup			
1953 Commander Loewy Landau Coupe,				(fleetside), 1999.................................	n/a	n/a	60
1999	n/a	n/a	70	Tractor and Car Carrier, All years	n/a	n/a	160
1953 Commander Starlight Coupe, 1999.	n/a	n/a	70				

Shrock Bros. 1961 6E7 Champ 1/2-ton Pickup, 1:72-scale, 2000. Photo courtesy Jim Geary

Shrock Bros. 1962 7E45E 96 BBC Diesel Dump, 1:72-scale, 1999. Photo courtesy Jim Geary

Shrock Bros. 1958 Packard 3E12D 4x4 Pickup, 1:43-scale, 1999. Photo courtesy Jim Geary

SKIPPY

	C6	C8	C10
Pedal Car, (American National ?), Chrysler Airflow, 1936, 54" long	9000	15,000	25,000

SKOGLUND & OLSON

Little is known about Swedish cast-iron toymaker, Skoglund & Olson

	C6	C8	C10
Bugatti Racer, cast-iron, 1929-30, 7-1/2" long	2000	3500	5500
Bus, cast-iron, 10-1/2" long	850	1400	2200
Central Garaget Wrecker, cast-iron, white w/raised letters along sides, 11-1/4" long	800	1350	2000
Chevrolet Coupe, cast-iron, spare tire in rear, rubber tires, 8"	NPF	NPF	NPF
Dump Truck, cast-iron, rubber tires, long bed, 10-1/2" long	NPF	NPF	NPF
Ladder Truck, cast-iron, rubber tires, 16" long..	NPF	NPF	NPF
Lincoln Zephyr, aluminum, rubber tires, skirted rear fenders, 9-1/2" long	NPF	NPF	NPF
Lincoln Zephyr, cast-iron, rubber tires, nickel plated, skirted rear fenders, 9-1/2" long	NPF	NPF	NPF

Skoglund & Olson Bus. Photo courtesy James S. Maxwell and Virginia Caputo

	C6	C8	C10
Log Truck, cast-iron, rubber tires, 17" long..	NPF	NPF	NPF
Oil Tank Truck, cast-iron, 10-1/2" long ..	1000	1900	2600
Rapair Ramp, cast-iron, scaled to fit S&O cars/trucks, 14-1/2" long.....................	125	225	350
Sedan, cast-iron, four doors, spare tire in rear, rubber tires, 8" long	NPF	NPF	NPF

Skoglund & Olson Tank Truck. Photo courtesy Bertoia Auctions

Skoglund & Olson "Central Garage" Wrecker. Courtesy Bertoia Auctions

SMITH-MILLER

Smith-Miller trucks entered an already competitive market in 1945. These cast-metal and aluminum trucks, produced in Santa Monica, California, should have failedówho wouldíve thought that a new toy vehicle company could compete with such toy giants as Buddy "L," Structo, Marx, and Hubley. Despite the stiff competition, Smith-Miller Toys stayed on the market for a full ten years outclassing virtually all toy trucks.

Their first trucks had two different classes, expensive replicas or smaller, no-name trucks that resembled Fords. During their last year they changed their profile from Mack Trucks to Auto-Car diesels with opening doors and working steering wheels.

Smith-Miller is once again in operation using original and new parts. For more information contact the company online at: www.smith-miller.com, or through the mail at: Smith-Miller, Inc., 68 Mulberry Ave., Lake Havasu City, AZ 86403, (818) 703-8588.

Contributors: John Taylor, P.O. Box 63, Nolensville, TN 37135-0063.

	C6	C8	C10
B Mack Associated Truck Lines, fourteen wheels	NPF	NPF	NPF
B Mack Jr Fire Truck, warning light, battery-operated, four wheels, rare	1400	2650	3950
B Mack Orange Dump, ten wheels, rare ..	950	1850	2800
B Mack P.I.E., eighteen wheels	400	625	850

Smith-Miller B Mack Orange Dump, ten wheels. Photo courtesy Tim Oei

Smith-Miller GMC Drive-O Steerable Dump, six wheels, 1949. Photo courtesy Bob Smith

Smith-Miller GMC Searchlight Truck with trailer. Photo courtesy Bob Smith

Smith-Miller L Mack Aerial Ladder Truck, eight wheels. Photo courtesy Bob Smith

Smith-Miller L Mack Bekins Van, ten wheels.

Smith-Miller L Mack Army Materials Truck seven-piece cargo load, ten wheels. Photo courtesy Bob Smith

Smith-Miller L Mack Material Truck, minus two barrels and four timbers. Photo courtesy R.F. Sapita

Smith-Miller L Mack Personnel Carrier, ten wheels. Photo courtesy Bob Smith

Smith-Miller L Mack Merchandise Van, six wheels. Photo courtesy Ray Funk

Smith-Miller GMC Material Truck, No. 402-M, four barrels, two timbers. Photo courtesy Calvin L. Chaussee

Smith-Miller GMC Bank of America, No. 404-B, four wheels. Photo courtesy Calvin L. Chaussee

	C6	C8	C10
Chevy Bekins Van, fourteen wheels, plain tires, hubcaps	300	400	600
Chevy Coca-Cola, four wheels, plain tires, early	425	638	850
Chevy Flatbed Tractor-Trailer, fourteen wheels, unpainted wood trailer, plain tires, hubcaps, early	200	300	450
Chevy Ice Truck, c.1945	350	575	800
Chevy Milk Truck, four wheels, plain tires, hubcaps, early, 1945-46	300	500	950
Ford Bekins Van, fourteen wheeler, plain tires, hubs, one of the earliest Smith-Millers (?), 1944	350	450	650
Ford Coca-Cola, four wheels, wood soda cases, 1944	600	1000	1400
GMC Be Mac T-Trailer, fourteen wheel, 1949	265	350	650
GMC Coca-Cola Truck, twenty-four plastic bottles in six cases, four wheels, 1954-55	425	875	1925
GMC Drive-O Steerable Dump, six wheels, cable w/hand control, 1949	325	550	925
GMC Dump Truck, 1950-53, six wheels	185	280	470
GMC Furniture Mart Pickup, four wheels, 1953 Truck	250	350	500
GMC Machinery Hauler, ten wheels	200	300	450
GMC Marshall Field & Company Tractor-Trailer, ten wheel T-Trailer	400	650	1000
GMC Mu Grocery	250	350	500
GMC Peoples First National Bank and Trust Company Armored Truck, lock and key, 1951	225	400	525
GMC Rexall Drug, four wheels, rare	475	815	1550
GMC Searchlight Truck, Hollywood Film Ad w/trailer, 1953	550	900	1600
GMC U.S Treasury Armored Truck, w/lock and key, 1952	250	375	500

	C6	C8	C10
L Mack Aerial Ladder, SMFD, eight wheels	440	660	880
L Mack Army Materials Truck, three barrels, two boards, one large crate, one small, ten wheels	460	690	925
L Mack Army Personnel Carrier, ten wheels	460	690	925
L Mack Bekins Van, all white, ten wheels	750	1200	1800
L Mack Blue Diamond Dump, ten wheels	800	1300	1800
L Mack International Paper Co., ten wheels, rare	700	1000	2100
L Mack Lyon Van, six wheels	550	875	1200
L Mack Material Truck, two barrels, six timbers, six wheels	350	550	750
L Mack Merchandise Van, six wheels	475	775	1200
L Mack Merchandise Van and Trailer, twelve wheels	850	1400	2500
L Mack Mobile Tandem Tanker, twelve wheels	800	1300	1800
L Mack Orange Hydraulic Dump, ten wheels, rare	750	1650	2950
L Mack Orange Material Truck, ten wheels, three barrels, two boards, one large crate, one small	650	950	1200
L Mack P.I.E., fourteen wheel	450	800	1050
L Mack Sibley's Van, six wheels (rare)	600	900	1500
L Mack Tandem Timber, six wheel, eighteen or twenty-four timbers (varies), 36" long	420	630	950
L Mack Telephone Truck, six wheels	600	1000	1400
L Mack West Coast Transport, six wheel	800	1300	1800
MIC Aerial Ladder	375	565	750
MIC Fruehauf Road Star Tractor-Trailer, fourteen wheels	400	600	950
MIC House Trailer	380	550	750
MIC Hydraulic Dump, ten wheels	500	850	1250
MIC Lift Gate Truck, six wheels, two barrels, 18" long	500	800	1100

Smith-Miller L Mack Merchandise Van and Trailer, twelve wheels. Photo courtesy Bob Smith

Smith-Miller, L Mack Army Materials Truck, 10 wheels, w/barrels and canvas top. Photo courtesy R.F. Sapita

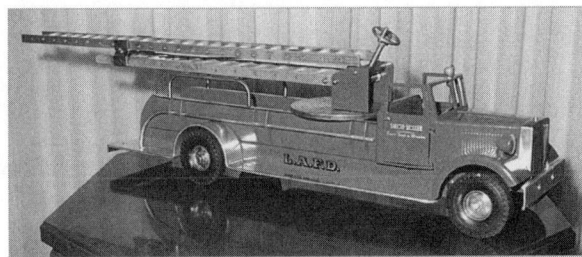

Smith-Miller MIC Aerial Ladder. Photo courtesy Ray Funk

Smith-Miller MIC Tow Truck, six wheels. Photo courtesy Tim Oei

Smith-Miller GMC Mobilgas Tanker, No. 409G, fourteen wheels, two hoses. Photo courtesy Tim Oei

Smith-Miller GMC Silver Streak Express Tractor Trailer, No. 311-E, fourteen wheels. Photo courtesy Bob Smith

Smith-Miller Tow Truck, No. 401, 15". Photo courtesy Calvin L. Chausee

Smith-Miller MIC Lift Gate Truck, six wheels, two barrels. Photo courtesy Bob Smith

Smith-Miller Coca-Cola Truck, No. 206-C, sixteen Coca-Cola cases, four wheels, 14". Photo courtesy Richard MacNary

Smith-Miller GMC Silver Streak Express Tractor Trailer, No. 311-E, fourteen wheels. Photo courtesy Bob Smith

Smith-Miller GMC Machinery Hauler. Photo courtesy Ray Funk

	C6	C8	C10
MIC Lincoln Capri (for MIC House Trailer), steerable	425	700	950
MIC P.I.E. Tractor-Trailer, fourteen wheels	600	1000	1400
MIC Teamsters Hydraulic Dump, ten wheels	650	1000	1500
MIC Teamsters Tow Truck, six wheels	800	1400	1800
MIC Teamsters Tractor-Trailer, fourteen wheels	750	1100	1700
MIC Tow Truck, Official Tow Car, six wheels	500	800	1200
MIC Tow Truck, six wheels, unpainted, polished	400	775	1025
MIC Tractor-Trailer, polished aluminum trailer, No. decals, fourteen wheels	375	600	850
NEC Lumber Truck, six wheels, nine timbers	600	1000	1450
No. 201-L Lumber Truck, sixty boards, six wheel, 14" long	300	400	550
No. 202-M Material Truck, three barrels, three cases, eighteen boards, four wheels, 14" long	450	675	900
No. 203-H Heinz Grocery Truck, six wheels, 14" long	250	400	675
No. 204-A Arden Milk Truck, twelve milk cans, four cases, four wheels, 14" long	350	550	800
No. 205-P Oil Truck, four drums, six wheels, 14" long	275	415	550
No. 206-C Coca-Cola Truck, sixteen Coca-Cola cases, four wheels, 14" long	450	675	900
No. 208-B Bekins Vanliner, fourteen wheels, 22-1/2" long	325	500	850
No. 209-T Timber Giant, three logs, fourteen wheels, 23-1/2" long	260	350	550

	C6	C8	C10
No. 210-S Stake Truck, fourteen wheels, 23-1/2" long	250	375	500
No. 211-L Sunkist Special, fourteen wheels, 23-1/2" long	250	350	500
No. 212-R Red Ball, fourteen wheels, 23-1/2" long	250	350	500
No. 301-W GMC Wrecker, four wheeler	250	350	500
No. 302-M GMC Materials Truck, four barrels, three timbers, 1948	250	350	550
No. 303-R GMC Rack Truck, six wheels	250	350	500
No. 304-K GMC Kraft Foods, four wheels, yellow cab and box, "Kraft" decals, 1948, 14" long	275	475	575
No. 305-T GMC Triton Oil, three drums	175	263	350
No. 306-C GMC Coca-Cola, four wheels, sixteen Coke cases	450	675	900
No. 307-L GMC Redwood Logger Tractor-Trailer, thtree logs	500	800	1100
No. 308-V GMC Lyon Van Lines Tractor-Trailer, fourteen wheels	375	575	800
No. 309-S GMC Super Cargo Tractor-Trailer, fourteen wheels, ten barrels	250	350	500
No. 310-H GMC Hi-Way Freighter Tractor-Trailer, fourteen wheels	250	350	500
No. 311-E GMC Silver Streak Express Tractor Trailer, fourteen wheels	212	318	425
No. 312-P GMC Pacific Intermountain Express (P.I.E.) Tractor Trailer	300	450	600

This Smith-Miller catalog page illustrates the No. 402 Dump Truck and the No. 401 Tow Truck. Photo courtesy Ray Funk

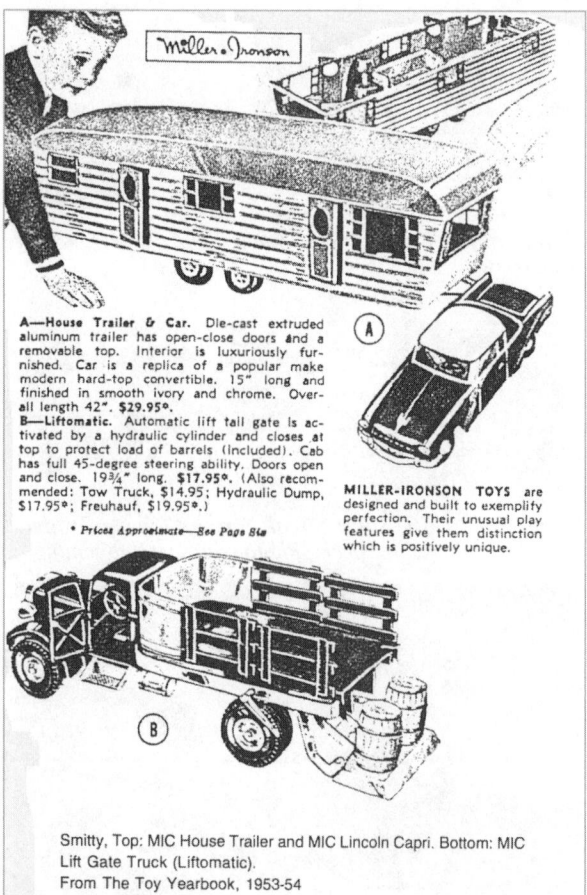

Smitty, Top: MIC House Trailer and MIC Lincoln Capri. Bottom: MIC Lift Gate Truck (Liftomatic). From Toy Yearbook 1953-54.

	C6	C8	C10
No. 401 Tow Truck, 15" long	350	550	800
No. 401-W GMC Wrecker, six-wheels....	350	525	700
No. 402 Dump Truck, 11-1/2" long	250	350	500
No. 402-M GMC Material Truck, four barrels, two timbers............................	250	350	500
No. 403 Scoop Dump, 14" long	275	325	550
No. 403-R GMC Rack Truck, six-wheels	225	380	550
No. 404 Lumber Truck, 19" long............	375	560	750
No. 404-B GMC Bank of America, lock and key, four wheels, 1949, 15" long ..	200	400	500
No. 404T Lumber Trailer, 17" long	200	300	400
No. 405 Silver Streak Six-wheel Tractor, 28" long..	170	255	440
No. 405-T GMC Triton Oil, six wheels, three drums	250	400	500
No. 406 Bekins Van, six- wheel tractor and four-wheel trailer, 29" long..........	325	495	750
No. 406-L GMC Lumber Tractor-Trailer, fourteen wheels, eight timbers	250	350	500
No. 407 Searchlight Truck, marked "Hollywood Film ad," 18-1/2" long	800	1500	2500
No. 407-V GMC Lyon Van Tractor-Trailer, ten wheels	350	500	700

Smith-Miller B Mack Lumber Truck and Trailer, No. 404-T, twelve wheels. Photo courtesy Bob and Alice Wagner

Smith-Miller GMC Lyon Van Tractor-Trailer, No. 407-V, ten wheels. Photo courtesy Bob Smith

This Smith-Miller catalog page illustrates a No. 404 Lumber Truck, No. 408 Blue Diamond, and a No. 404T lumber trailer. Photo courtesy Ray Funk

A look at the cover of a 1954 Smith-Miller catalog. Photo courtesy Ray Funk

This Smith-Miller catalog page illustrates the No. 406 Bekins Van and the No. 405 Silver Streak. Photo courtesy Ray Funk

This Smith-Miller catalog page illustrates a No. 407 Searchlight Truck, No. 403 Scoop Dump and a No. 409 P.I.E. truck. Photo courtesy Ray Funk

	C6	C8	C10
No. 408 Blue Diamond Ten-wheel Dump Truck, 18-1/2" long......................	650	1100	1600
No. 408-H GMC Machinery Hauler, thirteen wheels, marked "Fruehauf"	300	450	600
No. 409 Pacific Intermountain Express (P.I.E.) Six-wheel Tractor Semi, w/eight wheel aluminum trailer, 29" long.............................	500	750	1000
No. 409-G GMC Mobilgas Tanker, fourteen wheels, two hoses	270	400	750

	C6	C8	C10
No. 410 Aerial Ladder Semi, six-wheel tractor and four-wheel trailer, 36" long, "SMFD	450	850	1500
No. 410-F GMC Trans-Continental Tractor-Trailer, fourteen wheels, marked "Trans-Continental Freighter"	250	350	550
No. 411-E GMC Silver Streak Tractor-Trailer, fourteen wheels, yellow cab, 28" long	200	400	600
No. 412-P GMC P.I.E., fourteen wheels..	250	375	500

SOLIDO

Solido's military line seems to sell for between $50 to $100, in Mint condition. The following list is of their civilian line.

	C6	C8	C10
40th Anniversary Gift Set, includes Tiger Tank, M3 Halftrack, M20 Scout Car, M10 Halftrack, M20 Scout Car, M10 Tank Destroyer, 1984	75	155	200
M-20 U.S. Armored Car	30	45	65
Renault R35 Tank	30	45	65

10 Series (1973-80)

	C6	C8	C10
10 Renault 5 TL, hatchback, 1972-80	NPF	NPF	NPF
12 Peugeot 104, 1973-80, sedan w/hatchback	NPF	NPF	20
12B Peugeot 104, Driving school car, 1977-80	NPF	NPF	NPF
13 Matra 670, Racing car, 1973-77..........	NPF	NPF	NPF
14 Matra 670, race car, 1973-80	NPF	NPF	35
15 Lola T280, race car, yellow, 1973-76 .	NPF	NPF	30
16 Ferrari Daytona, race car, 1973-80	NPF	NPF	30
17 Gulf Mirage, race car, 1973-80	NPF	NPF	30
18 Porsche Can Am, race car, white body 1973-80, yellow body 1974-77, red body 1977-80	NPF	NPF	50
19 Volkswagen Golf, 1975-80	NPF	NPF	NPF
20 Alpine Renault A441, race car, 1975-80	NPF	NPF	20
21 Matra Simca, coupe, 1973-80	NPF	NPF	NPF
22 Renault 12 Station Wagon, hatch opens, 1975-80	NPF	NPF	20
23 Peugeot Ambulance, wagon, white body, 1974-80	NPF	NPF	NPF

	C6	C8	C10
23B Peugeot Police Car, wagon, blue body, 1974-80	NPF	NPF	NPF
23C Peugeot Break, wagon, 1977-80	NPF	NPF	NPF
23D Peugeot Fire Car, wagon, red body, 1979-80	NPF	NPF	NPF
24 Porsche Carrera RS, opening doors, 1974-80	NPF	NPF	25
25 BMW 3.0 CSL, white body, 1974-80 .	NPF	NPF	35
26 Ford Capri Rallye, 1974-80	NPF	NPF	30
27 Lancia Startos, 1974-80	NPF	NPF	30
28 BMW 2002, coupe, 1975-80	NPF	NPF	35
29 Citroen CX 2200, sedan, 1975-80	NPF	NPF	25
30 Renault 30, sedan, 1975-80.................	NPF	NPF	35
31 Delage D8 120 1939, 1939 convertible, 1975-80	NPF	NPF	20
32 Citroen 15 Six, 1939 sedan, black body, 1974-80	NPF	NPF	NPF
33 Fiat X19, coupe, 1974-80	NPF	NPF	NPF
34 Simca, sedan, 1974-76	NPF	NPF	NPF
35 Duesenberg J Type, 1931 convertible, removable hood, 1976-80	NPF	NPF	25
36 Porsche 914, rally car, white body, 1975-78	NPF	NPF	NPF
37 Renault 17TS Rally du Maros, race car, light blue body, 1976-80	NPF	NPF	25
38 Gulf Ford GR8 LeMans, race car, light blue body, orange "Gulf" decals, 1976-80	NPF	NPF	35
39 Simca 1308, sedan, 1976-80	NPF	NPF	20
40 Peugeot 604, sedan, 1976-80	NPF	NPF	NPF
40 Peugeot 604, sedan, 1976-80	NPF	NPF	25
41 Alfa Romeo 33, race car, red body, 1976-80	NPF	NPF	NPF
42 Renault 4, van, white body, various models had different colors and decals, 1976-80	NPF	NPF	NPF

Solido's 40th Anniversary Gift Set from 1984 consisted of a Tigre Tank, M3 Halftrack, M20 Scout Car and an M10 Tank Destroyer. Photo courtesy Harvey K. Rainess

Back row, left to right: No. 200 Combat Car M20; No. 202 Patton Tank; No. 203 Renault 4x4 Truck; No. 204 Antiaircraft Gun. front row, left to right: No. 205 105mm Howitzer; No. 206 250mm Howitzer; No. 207 Russian Pt-76 Tank. Starlux 30mm soldier and Britains 54mm Gunner included for scale. Photo courtesy Ed Poole

	C6	C8	C10
43 Renault 14, sedan, 1976-80	NPF	NPF	NPF
44 Ferrari BB, coupe, 1976-80	NPF	NPF	NPF
45 Ford Escort, 1976-80	NPF	NPF	NPF
46 Rolls-Royce Phantom III, 1939 convertible, top up, 1976-80	NPF	NPF	NPF
47 Mercedes-Benz 280, sedan, 1977-80	NPF	NPF	NPF
48 Delahaye 135M, 1939 convertible, top up, 1977-80	NPF	NPF	NPF
49 Porsche 928, coupe, 1977-80	NPF	NPF	NPF
51 Delage D8, 1939 Coupe de Ville, town car, 1977-80	NPF	NPF	NPF
52 Lancia Beta, coupe, 1977-80	NPF	NPF	NPF
53 Ford Fiesta, 2-door hatchback, 1977-80	NPF	NPF	NPF
54 Fiat 131, rally car, 1977-80	NPF	NPF	NPF
55 Cord L29, 1930 convertible sedan, 1977-80	NPF	NPF	NPF
56 Citroen 2CV, sedan, 1977-80	NPF	NPF	NPF
57 Alpine A442, race car, yellow body, 1977-80	NPF	NPF	NPF
58 Renault Gordini, hatchback, 1977-80	NPF	NPF	NPF
59 Renault 40 CV, 1926, phaeton, 1977-80	NPF	NPF	NPF
60 Simca 1308 Taxi, sedan, taxi decals, 1977-80	NPF	NPF	NPF
61 Ford Escort Rally, rally car, 1977-80	NPF	NPF	NPF
62 Hispano-Suiza H6B, 1926 phaeton, brown interior, 1977-80	NPF	NPF	NPF
63 Porsche 911 Turbo, coupe, 1977-80	NPF	NPF	NPF
65 Citroen CX Break, wagon, 1978-80	NPF	NPF	NPF
66 Land Rover, 1978-80	NPF	NPF	NPF
67 Mercedes-Benz 540K, 1939 convertible, 1978-80	NPF	NPF	NPF
68 Porsche 934 Turbo, 1979-80	NPF	NPF	NPF
69 Alfasud Trophee, race car, 1978-80	NPF	NPF	NPF
70 Opel Kadett GTE, rally car, #31, 1978-80	NPF	NPF	NPF
71 Rolls-Royce Phantom III, 1939 town car, 1978-80	NPF	NPF	NPF
72 Citroen, hatchback, 1978-80	NPF	NPF	NPF
73 Lancia Stratos, race car, #10 blue body or #19 white body, 1979-80	NPF	NPF	NPF
75 BMW CSL, race car, #21 orange body, 1978-80	NPF	NPF	NPF
76 Simca Chrysler Horizon, sedan, 1978-80	NPF	NPF	NPF
77 Rolls-Royce Phantom III, 1939 convertible, top down, 1978-80	NPF	NPF	NPF
78 Delahaye 135M, 1939 convertible, top down, 1978-80	NPF	NPF	NPF
80 Cord L29, 1929 coupe, 1979-80	NPF	NPF	NPF

	C6	C8	C10
81 Peugeot 104, rally car, #59, 1978-80	NPF	NPF	NPF
82 Alfa Romeo, white body, 1979-80	NPF	NPF	NPF
85 Cadillac 452A, 1931 landaulet with white roof, 1979-80	NPF	NPF	NPF
86 Porsche 936, LeMans race car, #4, 1979-80	NPF	NPF	NPF
87 Alpine Renault, race car, yellow body, 1979-80	NPF	NPF	NPF
88 Bugatti Atalante, 1939 coupe, 1979-80	NPF	NPF	NPF
89 BMW 530, 4-door sedan, race decals, 1979-80	NPF	NPF	NPF
90 Peugeot 305, sedan, 1979-80	NPF	NPF	NPF
91 Renault 18, sedan, 1978-80	NPF	NPF	NPF
96 Jaguar XJ 12, sedan, tan interior, 1980	NPF	NPF	NPF
97 Renault Reinastella, 1934 sedan, 1980	NPF	NPF	NPF

100 Series (1957-72)

	C6	C8	C10
100 Jaguar D, Le Mans race car, 1957-71	NPF	NPF	NPF
101 Porsche Spyder, race car, silver body, 1957-65	NPF	NPF	NPF
102 Maserati 250 F1, race car, red body, 1957-65	NPF	NPF	NPF
103 Ferrari 500 TRC, race car, red body, 1958-65	NPF	NPF	NPF
104 Varwall Formula 1, race car, "Vanwall" decals, 1958-68	NPF	NPF	NPF
105 Mercedes-Benz 190 SL, convertible, driver, 1958-66	NPF	NPF	NPF
106 Alfa Romeo Giulietta Spider, roadster w/top down, 1958-68	NPF	NPF	NPF
107 Aston Martin, race car, 1959-68	NPF	NPF	NPF
108 Peugeot 403 Cabriolet, convertible w/top down, 1959-63	NPF	NPF	NPF
109 Renault Floride, convertible w/top down, driver, 1959-65	NPF	NPF	NPF
110 Simca Oceane, convertible w/top down, driver, 1959-63	NPF	NPF	NPF
111 Aston Martin DB4, coupe, 1960-65	NPF	NPF	NPF
112 Panhard DB, Le Mans race car, 1960-71	NPF	NPF	NPF
113 Abarth Fiat, 1961-1970	NPF	NPF	NPF
114 Citroen Ami 6, sedan, 1961-65	NPF	NPF	NPF
115 Rolls-Royce Silver Cloud	NPF	NPF	NPF

200 Series (1961-80)

	C6	C8	C10
200 Combat Car M-20, 1961-80	30	45	65
201 UNIC Rocket truck, 10 tires, French decals, olive drab, 1961-80	NPF	NPF	NPF
202 Patton M-47 Tank, olive body w/U.S. or French decals 1962, tan body w/Israeli decals 1969	30	45	65

Back row, left to right: No. 222 Tiger Tank; 226 German Armored Car; 231 Sherman Tank; 232 M10 Tank Destroyer. Front row, left to right: Renault R35 Tank; 234 Somua S35 Tank; 237 Panzer IV Tank; 241 German Half-Track. Photo courtesy Ed Poole

Left to right: Solido No. 253 General Lee U.S. Tank; No. 245 GMC 6X6 U.S. Truck. Decals were supplied and left to the buyers' imagination to apply. Toy soldier is a French Stralux and was added for scale. Photo courtesy Ed Poole

	C6	C8	C10
203 Renault 4x4 Truck, covered truck, red fire extinguisher, 1962-80..............	30	45	65
204 Antiaircraft Gun, 1962-80.............	30	45	65
205 Cannon, olive drab, 1962-80.........	NPF	NPF	NPF
206 105mm Howitzer, 1962-80	30	45	65
207 Russian PT-76 Tank, red star, #51, 1963-77	30	45	65
208 SU 100 Tank, tan body 1963, olive body 1964	NPF	NPF	NPF
209 AMX 30T Tank, olive body French decals 1965, tan body Egyptian decals 1976	NPF	NPF	NPF
210 Patton M-47 Tank, olive body, same as 202 w/radio controls, 1965-76........	NPF	NPF	NPF
211 Berliet T12 Tank Transport truck, semi truck w/flatbed, 1967-80	NPF	NPF	NPF
212 Mercedes Jeep and Trailer, olive body 1966, tan body 1968...................	NPF	NPF	NPF
214 Berliet Aurochs, transport vehicle, "OPS" decals, olive drab, 1967-76	NPF	NPF	NPF
215 Renault 4x4 Police truck and 2 motorcycles, blue body, 1968-70.........	NPF	NPF	NPF
218 PT-76 Rocket Tank, olive body, same as 207 but launcher instead of turret, 1971-80	NPF	NPF	NPF
219 M-41 Tank Destroyer, no turret huge gun instead, olive drab body, 1969-76.	NPF	NPF	NPF
221 Alfa Romeo GTZ Police Car, blue body, 1967-71	NPF	NPF	NPF
222 Tigre I Tank, German decals, gray or tan body, 1970-80	30	45	65
223 AMX Anti-Aircraft Tank, olive body, #19, two guns, 1970-76..............	NPF	NPF	NPF
224 XM706 Commando, amphibian, olive body, U.S. decals, 1970-78	NPF	NPF	NPF
224B XM706 Police, commando vehicle, white body, police decals, 1970-78	NPF	NPF	NPF
225 BTR 40 Lance, rocket carrier, olive body, 1971-77	NPF	NPF	NPF
226 German Armored Car, dark gray, 1975-80	30	45	65
227 AMX 13 VCI, armored car, Red Cross decals, 1971-76	NPF	NPF	NPF
228 Jagdpanther Tank, German tank, camoflaged or dark gray paint, 1971-80	NPF	NPF	NPF
230 AMX 12 Tank, w/90 gun, olive body, 1972-76	NPF	NPF	NPF
231 Sherman M4 A3 Tank, olive body, 1972-80	30	45	65

	C6	C8	C10
232 M10 Tank Destroyer, armored car, U.S. or French decals, 1972-80	30	45	65
233 Renault R35 Tank, 1973-80..............	NPF	NPF	NPF
234 Somua S35 Tank, 1973-80...............	30	45	75
235 Simca 4x4 truck and 105mm Cannon, set includes covered truck that pulls cannon, 1973-79...................	NPF	NPF	NPF
236 Panther G Tank, German decals, cammo or dark gray body, 1973-80.....	NPF	NPF	NPF
237 Panzer IV Tank, German decals, 1974-80	30	45	65
238 AMX Missile Launcher, olive body, 1977-80	NPF	NPF	NPF
240 Panhard AML 90, armored car, olive or tan body, 1973-80..........................	NPF	NPF	NPF
241 Hanomag SDKFZ 251 Half-track, German decals, 1974-80	30	45	65
242 Dodge 6x6 Truck, olive body, U.S. decals, 1975-80	30	45	65
243 KPZ Leopard Tank, German decals, olive body, 1975-80	NPF	NPF	NPF
244 Half-Track M-3, U.S. decals, 1976-80	30	45	65
245 GMC 6x6 M-34 Truck, 1975-80.......	30	45	65
245 GMC 6x6 U.S. Truck, 1975-80	30	45	65
247 Berliet Alvis, 6-wheel transport vehicle, 1975-80	NPF	NPF	NPF
248 M41 Tank Destroyer, gun on tank body, no turret, 1976-80	NPF	NPF	NPF
249 AMX Tank, olive body, two guns, French decals, 1975-80	NPF	NPF	NPF
250 AMX 13T Tank, olive body, French decals, 1975-80	NPF	NPF	NPF
251 6x6 Amphibian, 1976-80	NPF	NPF	NPF
252 M7BI Priest Assault Gun, U.S. decals, 1976-80	30	45	65
253 General Lee U.S. Tank, 1978-80	30	45	65
254 AMX 10, armored vehicle, olive body, 1979-80	NPF	NPF	NPF
255 Berliet Foam Truck, tanker truck, 1979-80	NPF	NPF	NPF
256 Jeep and Trailer, jeep pulls 2-wheeled trailer, 1979-80	30	45	65
257 Tank Truck, Saviem, 1979-80	NPF	NPF	NPF
259 Citroen C 35 Ambulance, olive body, Red Cross decals, 1978-80	NPF	NPF	NPF
262 Richier Crane Truck, olive body, telescoping boom, 1979-80.................	NPF	NPF	NPF

300 Series (1960-80)

	C6	C8	C10
300 Berliet TBO 200 CV Titan, tan semi truck, 1960-72.......................	NPF	NPF	NPF
301 UNIC Sahara Titan Tank Truck, semi with 4 tanks, 1961-72	NPF	NPF	NPF
302 Willeme Titan Truck, cab w/open semi, 1961-72	NPF	NPF	NPF
303 Camion Berliet Dump Truck, 1967-78	NPF	NPF	NPF
304 Bernard T12, refrigerator truck, 1963-72	NPF	NPF	NPF
305 Berliet T12 SR, loader truck, 1967-77	NPF	NPF	NPF
306 Berliet Stradair Dump Truck, 1967-73	NPF	NPF	NPF
307 Berliet Stradair Truck, covered truck, 1968-73	NPF	NPF	NPF
308 Willeme Elf Tank Truck, 1968-72	NPF	NPF	NPF
316 Saviem SM 300 semi, open semi truck w/crane, 1972-79	NPF	NPF	NPF
317 Berliet transporter, green semi w/white cab, 1972-79..........................	NPF	NPF	NPF

Solido Vehicles (Starlux 30mm GIs included for scale). Back row left to right: 242 Dodge 6X6 Truck, 244 Half-Track M-3, 245 GMC 6X6 M-34 Truck, 252 M7BI ¡Priestî Assult Gun. Front Row: 253 General Lee Tank, 253 Jeep & Trailer, GMC Truck (?), Air Compressor and Dodge Ambulance (numbers unknown). Photo courtesy Ed Poole

	C6	C8	C10
318 Saviem SM 300 Elf Tanker, "Elf" logo decals, 1972-77	NPF	NPF	NPF
319 Saviem SM 300 Esso Tanker, "Esso" logo decals, 1972-77	NPF	NPF	NPF
320 Saviem SM 300 Shell Tanker, "Shell" logo decals, 1972-77	NPF	NPF	NPF
321 Saviem Car Carrier & Trailer, "Causse Walon" decals, 1974-80	NPF	NPF	NPF
330 Citroen C35 Circus Van, white body, red interior, 1979-80	NPF	NPF	NPF
331 Mercedes Circus Truck, red cab, white semi, 1979-80	NPF	NPF	NPF
332 Saviem Flatbed Semi, w/animal cages, lion and tiger figures, 1979-80	NPF	NPF	NPF
333 Circus Box Office Semi, semi truck, 1979-80	NPF	NPF	NPF
334 Richier Circus Crane Truck, red body crane truck w/ "Amar" decals, 1979-80	NPF	NPF	NPF
335 DAF Animal Semi, animal transport, 1979-80	NPF	NPF	NPF
336 DAF Circus Semi, stake sided open semi, red and white, 1979-80	NPF	NPF	NPF
350 Berliet Toner Gam Fire Engine, red body, 1972-80	NPF	NPF	NPF
351 Berliet Airport Foam Tender, tanker w/nozzle, red body, 1972-80	NPF	NPF	NPF
352 Berliet Ladder Truck, fire ladder truck, red body, 1973-80	NPF	NPF	NPF
353 Toner Gam Richier/Grue Telescopique Truck, yellow or red body, crane and boom, 1973-80	NPF	NPF	NPF
354 Berliet Forest Fire Truck, w/trailer, red body, 1973-80	NPF	NPF	NPF
355 Peugeot Minibus, 1976-80	NPF	NPF	NPF
356 Peugeot Bus, 1976-80	NPF	NPF	NPF
357 UNIC Dump Truck, yellow body, 1974-80	NPF	NPF	NPF

Early Solido Military Model and Box (M-20 U.S. Armored Car in French markings); Crewman is a 30mm Starlux, also made in France. Photo courtesy Ed Poole

	C6	C8	C10
358 Mercedes Service Truck, boom arm and basket extend from truck, 1974-80	NPF	NPF	NPF
359 Simca Snowplow Truck, red or yellow body, 1974-80	NPF	NPF	NPF
361 Mercedes Ladder Truck, red body, "Service Departemental" decals, 1975-80	NPF	NPF	NPF
362 Hotchkiss Fire Truck, engine, red body, 1975-80	NPF	NPF	NPF
363 Freuhauf Semi, covered yellow semi, cab different colors, 1975-80	NPF	NPF	NPF
364 Mercedes Bucket Truck, 1975-80	NPF	NPF	NPF
365 International Harvester Shovel, 1976-80	NPF	NPF	NPF
366 Saviem Wrecker, 1977-80	NPF	NPF	NPF
367 Volvo-BM LM 1240 Wheel Loader, 1977-80	NPF	NPF	NPF
368 Citroen C35 Ambulance, red body, 1977-80	NPF	NPF	NPF
369 DAF Semi Tanker, 1977-80	NPF	NPF	NPF
370 Saviem Semi Truck, 1977-80	NPF	NPF	NPF
371 Citroen Ambulance, 1977-80	NPF	NPF	NPF
372 Peugeot J7 Police Bus, 1977-80	NPF	NPF	NPF

SONICON

(Japan)

	C6	C8	C10
Sonicon Bus, battery-operated, Japanese, 13" long	288	432	575

SONNY

A trademark of the Dayton Toy & Specialty Co., "Son-ny" or Sonny as collectors know it, was a line of pressed steel trucks and other wheeled toys that was first issued in the 1920s. The line survived only into the mid-1930s.

Sonny Dump Truck, 26-1/2". Photo courtesy Joe and Sharon Freed

Sonny "Railway Express Co." Truck, 2". Photo courtesy Bob Smith

Sonny "USA 1120" Anti-Aircraft Truck. Photo courtesy Bertoia Auctions

Sonny Trucks, as shown in a 1928 Butler Bros. catalog.

	C6	C8	C10
Army Truck, open cab, 27" long.............	500	850	1250
Dump, 1920s, 26-1/2" long......................	600	900	1400
Moving Van	400	700	1000
Parcel Post Van	700	1200	1900
Police Patrol Paddy Wagon....................	600	900	1400
Railway Express Co. Truck, 26" long......	800	1200	2000

	C6	C8	C10
US 1120 Artillery Truck, 26" long	325	480	650
USA 1120 Anti-Aircraft Truck, olive drab, crank-operated cannon, 1920s, 24" long..	600	925	1450

STANLEY & COX

Little is known about the Stanley & Cox Mfg. Co., other than the World War II-era production of this wooden tank.

	C6	C8	C10
Tank, wooden, WWII	32	48	65

Stanley & Cox Tank, wooden, with original box. Photo courtesy Jack Matthews

STANLEY WORKS

Based in New Britain, Conn., the Stanley Works company issued construction sets in the 1930s using the ìStanloî brand name. Stanley also released a number of kits as accessory sets to train layouts.

	C6	C8	C10
Stanlo Coupe, build-it, 5-1/2" long, 1920s..	85	128	170

STAR BAND

	C6	C8	C10
Star Brand Shoes Are Better Racing Car, The Winner, tin lithographed, 8-1/2" long	650	1050	1500

STEELCRAFT

The Murray-Ohio Mfg. Co. of Cleveland, Ohio. released the Steelcraft line of pressed-steel trucks in the 1920s.

	C6	C8	C10
Army Truck, Mack, c.1930, 22" long	650	1000	1450
Army Truck, Mack, c.1930, 26" long	375	562	750
Bloomingdale's Delivery Truck, 25" long	NPF	2000	NPF
Buick Pedal Car, early 1930s, 46" long ...	2000	4500	8000
Cadillac Pedal Car, 1926..........................	1500	2500	5000
Cadillac Pedal Car, 38" long	2500	4500	9000
City Delivery Truck, orange and black, 19" long..	150	325	475
City Fire Dept. Ladder Truck, early........	500	800	1200
City Ice Co. Mack Truck, 24" long	375	562	750
City Ice Cream Co.	250	375	500
City Milk Co., 18" long............................	300	650	1100
City Trucking Co., 21" long....................	200	NPF	NPF
Coca-Cola Truck, twelve bottles on side .	400	600	800
Cream Crest Truck, 18" long	270	405	540
Dump Truck, 1934, 24" long	150	275	425
Dump Truck, Airflow	1500	2500	3500
Dump Truck, early 1934, 23" long	275	425	575
Dump Truck, Mack, 1930s, 20" long.......	150	225	300
Dump Truck, Mack, 26" long	450	700	1000
Dump Truck, Mack, early 1930s, 25" long..	300	450	600
Dump Truck Pedal Car, 62" long............	2000	4000	6600
Fire Hook and Ladder Airflow Pedal Truck..	1600	2700	3800
Fire Truck, 25" long	750	1100	1500
Ford Pedal Car, 1930, 30" long...............	650	1100	1650
Fro-Joy Ice Cream Truck, c.1933	250	575	1000
GMC Scissor Dump Truck, 26" long.......	550	850	1400
GMC Trailer Truck	1200	2000	2800
Hydrox Ice Cream Truck, 1933, 22"........	400	600	800
Inter City Bus, pressed steel, 1920s, 24" long..	250	500	950
Lazarus Delivery Truck, 25" long,..........	800	NPF	NPF
Lincoln Pedal Car, 46" long	1500	2500	4000
Lincoln Zephyr Pedal Car, 1941	1400	2500	4000
Little Jim Fire Truck	600	900	1200

	C6	C8	C10
Little Jim Mack Dump Truck, red/black, c.1928 (Little Jims were sold by J.C Penney's)	600	900	1400
Mack Ladder Truck, 26" long..................	450	675	900
Mack Moving Van, rare, 1920s, 25" long	NPF	2000	NPF
Mack Pedal Car Dump Truck, 44" long ..	700	1100	1500
Mack Police Patrol, 25" long	1400	2500	4000
Macon Zeppelin, pressed steel, white w/electric headlight, 24" long..............	250	500	700

Steelcraft vehicles as shown in an October 1932 Butler Bros. catalog.

Steelcraft Pontiac Pedal Car, 1935, 36".

Steelcraft Lincoln Pedal Car, 46". Photo courtesy Sotheby's

Steelcraft Cream Crest Truck, 18". Photo courtesy Bob Smith

Steelcraft Little Jim Mack Dump Truck, late 1920s. Photo courtesy Bob Smith

Steelcraft Bloomingdale's Delivery Truck, 25". Photo courtesy Bob Smith

Steelcraft New York Trucking Co., headlights work, 1930s, 23-1/4". Photo courtesy John Gibson

Steelcraft Sheffield Farms Truck, 1930s, 21". Photo courtesy Bertoia Auctions

Steelcraft City Fire Dept. Ladder Truck. Photo courtesy Tim Oei

Steelcraft Mack Moving Van, 1920s. Photo courtesy Tim Oei

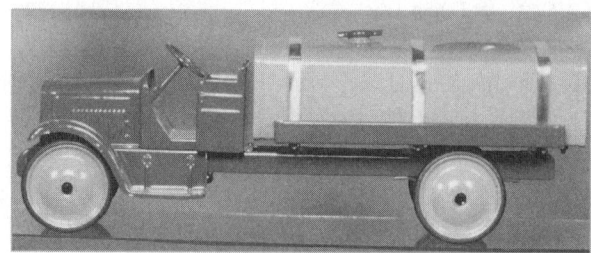

Steelcraft Tank Truck, sheet metal, 25-1/2". Photo courtesy Bertoia Auctions

Steelcraft U.S. Mail, late 1920s, 27-1/4". Photo courtesy Calvin L. Chaussee

	C6	C8	C10
Mandrel Bus Van	1100	1800	2400
Marion Steam Shovel, pressed steel, black w/red roof, "Marion" on back of cab	200	300	400
Model T Roadster Pedal Car, license No. 65-287, 50" long	450	675	900
New York Trucking Co., headlights work, 1930s, 23-1/4" long	800	1100	1400
Pedal Car, Pontiac, 1935, 36" long	NPF	NPF	NPF
Playboy Ice Cream Co., c. 1933, 23" long..	400	700	1200
Racer Pedal Car, 1941	800	1300	1800
Railway Express Truck, 26" long	1100	1600	2600
Richfield Oil Tanker	800	1300	1800

	C6	C8	C10
Road Roller, 16-1/2" long	238	357	475
Roadster Pedal Car, 38" long	1800	2900	4500
Rockwood's Chocolate Gold Coin Express Truck, c. 1934, 19" long........	475	925	1375
Sheffield Farms Truck, 1930s, 21" long ..	500	800	1300
Shell Motor Oil Truck, w/oil barrels.......	300	450	600
Southern Dairies Step Van, 1933	350	700	1150
Steam Shovel, 26" long...........................	225	338	450
Supplee Ice Cream, 21" long	NPF	NPF	8000
Tank Truck, sheet metal, 25-1/2" long	650	1100	1500
U.S Mail, c.1928, 27-1/4" long	1150	1725	2300
Van, "City Delivery," 1934, 19" long......	225	450	900
Wrecker, "Play Boy Trucking," c. 1933, 21" long..	250	500	950

STEER O TOYS

Steer O Toys was based in Chicago, Ill. and little else is known.

	C6	C8	C10
Convertible, Kaiser-Nash type, plastic, push down to operate, 12" long	300	450	600

Steer O Toys Convertible, 1950s, Kaiser-Nash type, 12". Photo courtesy Tim Oei

STRAUSS

Ferdinand Strauss, born in Bavaria in the late 1800s, immigrated to the United States where he became a toy importer in the early 1900s. By 1914, he had four New York toy shops. When war disrupted the importing of toys, he began manufacturing them. In 1918, he was located in East Rutherford, N. J., with fifty employees. Eventually Strauss was known as "The Founder of the Mechanical Toy Industry in America."

Strauss seems to have been wholly or partially out of business in the late 1920s, and then resumed, turning out wind-ups and other toys until at least 1941-1942. He is also famous for having given employment to the very young Louis Marx.

Contributor: Bob Smith

	C6	C8	C10
Big Show Circus Truck..........................	1600	2350	3200
Big-Show Circus, tin wind-up, containing lion and tamer, more in cage, no engine compartment, c.1925, 9" long...	900	1600	2300

Strauss Big Show Circus, lion and tamer, tin windup, 1920s, 9". Photo courtesy Sotheby's

Strauss Interstate Bus, tin windup, 10-1/2". Photo courtesy Sotheby's

Strauss Jitney Bus, tin windup, 1920s, 10". Photo courtesy Bob Smith

Strauss Leaping Lena, tin windup, 8". Photo courtesy Bob Smith

Strauss Yell-O-Taxi, 8-1/2". Photo courtesy Bob Smith

Strauss Racer, No. 21, tin windup, 1920s. Photo courtesy Bob Smith

Strauss Red Flash Racer, tin windup, 9-1/2". Photo courtesy Bob Smith

Strauss Green Racer, 1920s, 8-1/2". Photo courtesy Bob Smith

	C6	C8	C10
Bus Deluxe, 1920s, 12" long	1100	1900	2700
Check-A-Cab	550	775	1100
Circus Wagon, 10" long, has engine compartment	1350	1975	2700
Circus Wagon, containing lion and tamer, 8-1/2" long, no engine compartment	900	1600	2300
Green Racer, wind-up, 8-1/2" long	200	300	550
Haul Away Truck, dump body, No. 22	340	460	680
Hooligans Hack	400	550	800
Interstate Bus Double Decker, tin wind-up, green and yellow, 1920s, 10-1/2" long	475	700	1125
Jitney Bus, No. 66, tin wind-up, c.1921, 10" long	400	650	850
Kraka Jack Car, 1920s, 5-1/2" long	250	325	500

	C6	C8	C10
Leaping Lena, tin wind-up, 8" long	500	700	1000
Long Haulage Truck	450	625	900
Old Jalopy, The, w/four college kids	200	250	400
Racer, No. 2 1, tin wind-up, c.1923	300	450	750
Racer, Red Flash Racer, windshield, tin wind-up, c.1919, 9-1/2" long	350	500	800
Red Star Van	500	700	900
Reo Racer, tin wind-up	325	438	650
Standard Oil Truck 73	425	588	850
Timber King Log Truck, w/driver, wind-up, 1920s, 18" long	335	455	670
Trikauto, No. 53	288	382	575
Water Sprinkler Truck	550	775	1100
What's It? Car, No. 53, 1925, 9-1/2" long	700	1000	1400
Yell-o Taxi, No. 59, 8-1/2" long	525	850	1150

STROMBECKER

Strombecker was a trade name used by the Strombeck-Becker Mfg. Co. of Moline, Ill. Noted for its wooden toys, the company began in the 1930s and survived until taken over by the Dowst Mfg. Co. (parent company of Tootsietoy).

Strombecker Truck Hauler. Photo courtesy Perry Eichor

The Strombecker Truck Hauler´s cab was used as a wrecker. Photo courtesy Perry Eichor

STRUCTO

Structo, of Freeport, Illinois, was founded in 1908 by three men: brothers Louis and Edward Strohacker and C.C. Thompson. They initially manufactured Erector Construction Kits. About 1919, they started making toy vehicles. In 1935, J.G. Cokey bought a majority of the business. When µhe died in 1975, the toy patents and designs were taken over by the Ertl Company.

Many of Structo's cast cabs were painted and these trucks almost always had solid black rubber wheels. Most of the wheels were finished with a plated disk over the wheel's center, which gave the appearance of a bright metal hubcap; although, some of the early trucks were issued with plain rubber wheels, without the plated disk hubcaps. For the most part the trucks with painted cabs were issued from around 1951-1954. Series No. 600 and No. 700 models represented this style.

In the early 1950s, Structo offered another group of cast cab-overs that were equipped with powerful wind-up motors and front axles that could be positioned for steering. All windups were made with distinct headlights. Rather than simply being cast into the cab detail, the headlights had a clear plastic lens with a metal rim. Series No. 800 models represented this style.

In 1955, Structo improved their cast cab-over design in several ways. The cabs were given a bright ìchromeî finish and running lights were added to the roof of the cab's detail. The all rubber wheels were replaced with wheels consisting of cast metal ìmag-likeî rims with solid rubber tires. Series No. 600 and No. 700 models represented this style.

Late in the cast cab-over period, around 1958, Structo introduced a few tractor-trailer models with cast cabs and steel frames, not aluminum. These new but limited designs featured a good fifth wheel detail and saddlebag gas tanks.

Contributor: Randy Prasse, 916 Hayes Avenue, Racine, WI 53405, e-mail: prasse@racineweb.net

Prewar

	C6	C8	C10
Aerial Fire Truck, No. 902, 1950s	100	150	200
Aerial Fire Truck, red, conventional Studebaker-style front, rotating ladder base, two ladders, 1936-38, 28" long...	40	600	800
Aerial Fire Truck, No. 305, red/yellow, three yellow 18-inch ladders, raising hood, 1940, 29-1/2" long	200	400	600
Aerial Truck Rider, No. 301, red/yellow, same as 1940 model No. 403, 1941, 29-1/2" long	250	500	750
Aerial Truck Rider, No. 403, red/yellow, same as No. 305 only with seat in back on trailer, raising hood, 1940, 29-1/2" long	250	500	750
Air Mail Transport, No. 421, green, tractor/trailer, white balloon tires, "Air Mail Transport" decals, 1927-29, 24" long...	300	500	800

	C6	C8	C10
Ambulance, No. 416, green, white balloon tires, canvas side skirts on rear sides, scarce, 1927-32, 17" long	300	600	800
Army Searchlight Unit, No. 207, plastic light and generator, battery-operated, rubber tires, rotating searchlight, 1941, 16" long..	200	400	700
Army Tank, No. 103, green, 10 wooden wheels, turret with machine gun, makes sound when cranked, 1939-40, 12-3/4" long	150	300	500
Army Tank, No. 102, green, same as previous years but with black metal wheel guards and fenders, 1941, 12-1/2" long	150	300	500
Army Truck, No. 203, green, canvas cover over rear troop area, raising hood, 1940-41, 21-3/4" long................	250	500	750
Army Truck, No. 415, green, white balloon tires, canvas cover over rear troop seating area, 1927-32, 17" long..	200	400	700
Army Truck, No. 252, green, w/canvas cover over rear troop area, 1939, 22-1/4" long	250	500	750
Auto Transport Trailer, No. 706, w/cars, 1953-54	115	175	250
Barrel Truck, No. 609, early 1950s..........	115	175	225
Barrel Truck, No. 811, wind-up, early to mid-1950s	115	175	225
Bearcat Auto, No. 10, red, kit car with windshield, 1919-23, 16" long.............	500	800	1200
Bearcat Racer, clockwork, 12-1/4" long ..	400	600	800
Bed set, No. 108, faux maple finish, side by side or stackable, fits 20" dolls, 1940-41, 20" long	75	125	150
Bing-It Game, No. 102, red/yellow, like full-size carnival bell-ringing game, "Show Your Strength," rare, 1939, 18-1/2" long	200	300	400
Camper, w/cloth top, 12" long	55	82	110
Caterpillar, No. 44, green/red, pre-assembled "Ready Built" w/two-wheel trailer, "Structo" embossed, 1924-26, 11-1/2" long	200	400	600
Caterpillar, No. 44, green/red, pre-assembled "Ready Built," w/two-wheel trailer, 1922-23, 11-1/2" long	200	400	600
Caterpillar, No. 44, green/red, pre-assembled "Ready Built," w/disk harrow, 1920-21, 11-1/2" long	200	400	600
Cattle Trailer, No. 708, 1950s.................	100	125	175
Cement Mixer, 1950s, 20" long	100	150	350
Chain Tread Climbing Tank, No. 58, green, large tank with steel tracks, scarce, 1930-32, 12-1/2" long.............	500	800	1500

Structo 50th Anniversary Gold Cadillac, No. 201958, 6-3/4". Photo courtesy Randy Prasse

Structo Auto Transport, No. 706, 1954, 27". Photo courtesy Randy Prasse

Structo Auto Transport, No. 706, 1955, chrome cab, 27".
Photo courtesy Randy Prasse

Structo Cadillacs, metal, each 6-1/2". Photo courtesy Ron
Fink

Structo Caterpillar Tractor and Disk, No. 44, 1920-21, 11".
Photo courtesy Randy Prasse

Structo Dump Truck, 1930s, 20". Photo courtesy Calvin L.
Chaussee

Structo Mechanical Dumper, 1940s, 19-1/2". Photo
courtesy Harvey K. Rainess

Save with Structo
Bank included with
the No. 811 Structo
Barrel Trucks. Photo
courtesy Randy
Prasse

Structo Barrel Truck, No. 811, 1951-53, 12-3/4". Photo
courtesy Randy Prasse

Structo Deluxe Cattle Transport, No. 712, 1955-56, 24".
Photo courtesy Randy Prasse

Structo Dump Truck, 1940s, 19". Photo courtesy Calvin L.
Chaussee

	C6	C8	C10
Communications Center Truck, 21" long	175	265	350
Contractor's Sand Unit, No. 410, red/gray, three-piece set includes No. 107 Sand Loader and No. 200 Dump, small hand shovel, 1941, 15-3/4" long	300	500	700
Contractor's Truck, No. 42, orange, pre-assembled "Ready Built", 1922-26, 12" long	600	800	1000
Coupe, convertible, 1920s	350	545	760
Delivery Truck, electric lights	150	225	300
Deluxe Auto, No. 12, orange, kit car with windshield, convertible top bonnet and spare tire on rear, 1919-26, 16" long	600	1000	1500
Deluxe Auto, No. 20, orange, same as No. 12 only in assembled form, 1924-26, 16" long	600	1000	1500
Doll House Furniture, No. 104, green/yellow/blue, chairs, table and davenport, 1939	100	150	200
Dump Rider, blue, seat in rear of toy, wooden-handled steering mechanism through roof, 1936-38, 18" long	300	500	700
Dump Truck, early, Mack type	200	300	400
Dump Truck, orange/black, C-cab style, 1933-35, 23-1/2" long	250	500	750
Dump Truck, No. 200, red/yellow, box raises automatically, raising hood, 1940-41, 21" long	200	400	600
Dump Truck, No. 404, black/red, pull toy with no motor, large white balloon tires, 1924-26, 14-1/2" long	200	400	600
Dump Truck, green, C-cab style, 1933-35, 23-1/2" long	250	500	750
Dump Truck, yellow/red, four hard rubber wheels with plated caps, spring-loaded dump box, 1936-38, 24" long	300	500	700
Dump Truck, No. 250, red/yellow, two-tone truck with manual lift handle, 1939, 23" long	200	400	600
Evening Ledger Truck, yellow, aka the Popeye Truck, unknown production term, extremely rare, 1933-35, 22" long	1500	2500	4000
Excavator, No. 57, black/orange, steam shovel with steel Caterpillar-style tracks, scarce, 1927-32, 29" long	600	800	1200
Express Truck, red/white, stubby Studebaker-style front, hard rubber tires with steel caps, 1936-38, 18" long	700	1000	1500
Fire Dept. Emergency Patrol Truck, red bubble light, 1950s, 12" long	55	82	110
Fire Insurance Patrol, No. 407, red, white balloon tries, open rear with bench seats and brass bell, 1927-29, 18" long	200	400	600
Fire Insurance Patrol, No. 424, red, white balloon tires, open rear with bench seats and brass bell, 1930-32, 18" long	200	400	600
Fire Patrol, No. 321, red/yellow, two ladders, two extinguishers and fireman's axe, raising hood, 1940, 26" long	200	400	600
Fire Patrol, No. 301, red, two ladders, two extinguishers and fireman's axe, 1939, 26" long	200	400	600
Fire Patrol, No. 205, red/yellow, two ladders, raising hood, 1940, 26-1/2" long	200	400	600
Four-Wheel Dump, yellow/red, stubby Studebaker-style front, hard rubber tires with steel caps, 1936-38, 18" long	600	900	1200

Structo Dump Truck, 8-1/2". Photo courtesy Ron Fink

	C6	C8	C10
Garbage Truck, "Sanitation Dept."	110	160	225
Garbage Truck, 21" long	75	115	175
Gasoline Truck, No. 866, wind-up, steerable front axle, Structo 66 decals, red cab w/red body, early 1950s, 13-1/2" long	150	200	300
Gasoline Truck, No. 912, 1950s, 13" long	75	112	150
Giant Dump Truck, No. 21, red, same as No. 14 only in assembled form, 1924-26, 18" long	700	1200	1700
Giant Dump Truck, No. 14, red, kit truck with dumping box mechanism, 1919-26, 18" long	700	1200	1700
Giant Grab Bucket, No. 111, green/red, with clam bucket, 1924-26, 21-1/4" long	100	200	300
Giant Grab Bucket, No. 111, green/yellow/blue, with clam bucket; no yellow (1930-32), 1927-32, 21-1/4" long	150	250	400
Giant Grab Bucket, No. 66, red/green, smaller version of No. 111, 1927-32, 14" long	100	200	300
Giant Steam Shovel, No. 110, black/orange, with scoop shovel bucket, 1927-32, 22-1/2" long	150	250	400
Giant Steam Shovel, No. 110, black/orange, with scoop shovel bucket, 1924-26, 21-1/4" long	150	250	400
Grab Bucket, No. 52, black/red, with clam bucket, 1924-26, 13" long	100	200	400
Grain Trailer, No. 704, early and mid-1950s	115	175	225
Guided Missile Launcher, No. 906, w/plastic launcher, missiles made of wood and vinyl, 1950s, 13" long	70	105	140
Guided Missile Launching Truck, truck metal, plastic missiles, rubber tires	60	75	110
High Wheel Tractor, No. 11, green/red, kit tractor with one red trailer, 1919-26, 10" long (16" long overall)	500	900	1500
High Wheel Tractor, No. 19, green/red, same as No. 11 only in assembled form, 1924-26, 10" long	500	900	1500
Hi-Lift Dump, No. 844, wind-up, early 1950s	110	165	220
Hi-Way Transport, No. 404, blue/yellow, same as 1919 model No. 401 with blue and yellow paint scheme, raising hood, 1940-41, 30-1/2" long	200	400	600
Hi-Way Transport, orange, stubby Studebaker-style front, hard rubber tires with steel caps, 1936-38, 18" long	600	900	1200

	C6	C8	C10
Hi-Way Transport, yellow/green, stubby Studebaker-style front, hard rubber tires with steel caps, 1936-38, 18" long	600	900	1200
Hi-Way Transport, No. 401, red/white two-tone with diagonal paint line on side of trailer, 1939, 32-1/2" long........	200	400	600
Hook and Ladder, No. 205, red/yellow, two ladders, raising hood, 1941, 26-1/2" long	200	400	600
Hook and Ladder, red, black hard rubber tires, hose reel and four ladders on sides, brass bell, 1933-35, 25" long	250	500	700
Hook and Ladder, No. 251, red, two ladders, 1939, 26" long	200	400	600
Hook and Ladder, No. 406, red, white balloon tires, hose reel and four ladders on sides, brass bell, 1927-32, 24" long...	250	500	750
Ladder Rider, red, seat in rear of toy, wooden-handled steering mechanism through roof, 1936-38, 22" long	300	500	700
Ladder Truck, 1950s	95	150	225
Lawn Furniture set, No. 104, red, four pieces including chairs, table and davenport; green (1941), 1940-41	100	150	200
Lift Crane, No. 114, black/red, with lift hook on chain, 1924-26, 13" long........	100	200	300
Machinery Hauler, 1940s	120	180	240
Machinery Truck, No. 607, early 1950s ..	125	195	250
Motor Express Stake Truck, No. 601, also known as Freeport Motor Express Truck, early 1950s	55	83	110
Motor Transport, No. 420, blue, tractor/trailer, white balloon tires, "Motor Dispatch" decals, 1927-32, 24" long...	300	500	800
Moving Van, No. 410, orange, black balloon tires with red center hubs, enclosed rear, 1927-29, 17" long	200	400	700
Moving Van, No. 427, open cab, orange, black balloon tires with red center hubs, enclosed rear, 1930-32, 17" long	200	400	700
Overland Freight Trailer, No. 704, early 1950s...	100	150	200
Package Delivery, No. 603, early 1950s ..	100	160	200
Packard Dump Truck, No. 405, red, white balloon tires, also included w/No. 56 Sand Sifter set, 1927-32, 17-1/2" long..	200	400	600
Pickup Truck, 13" long	90	135	180
Pile Driver, No. 122, green/red, similar to No. 65 and No. 68 but w/vertical pile driver mechanism, scarce, 1927-32, 14" high...	200	400	600

	C6	C8	C10
Police Patrol, No. 409, black, white balloon tires, enclose rear paddy wagon appearance, 1927-29, 17" long.	200	400	700
Police Patrol, No. 426, blue, white balloon tires, enclosed rear, paddy wagon appearance, 1930-32, 17" long.	200	400	700
Police Patrol, No. 320, blue, automatic ringing gong, two bench seats in open back, raising hood, 1940, 23" long	250	500	750
Porch Furniture, No. 106, red/green, three pieces including chairs and glider swing, 1940	100	150	200
Pumping Fire Engine, No. 605, red, operable water tank with pump, hose and reel, two ladders on sides, 1940, 26" long...	200	400	700
Pumping Fire Engine, No. 601, red, operable water tank w/pump, hose and reel, two ladders on sides, 1939, 26" long...	200	400	700
Pumping Fire Engine, red, operable water tank, pump and hose, two ladders on sides, 1933-35, 21" long	300	600	800
Pumping Fire Engine, No. 449, red, operable water tank, pump and hose, two ladders on sides, 1927-32, 21" long...	200	400	700
Racing Auto, No. 8, green, kit car, 1919-26, 16" long	600	1000	1500
Racing Auto, No. 17, green, same as No. 8 only in assembled form, 1924-26, 16" long..	600	1000	1500
Refrigerator, No. 105, white, battery-operated light when door opened, rare, 1940-41, 14" long	100	175	250
Renault Tank, clockwork, green w/red turret...	260	400	520
Roadster, clockwork, 1920s, 16" long	600	1000	1400
Roadster, No. 40, red, pre-assembled "Ready Built", 1920-26, 10-1/2" long .	400	800	1000
Sand Elevator and Bin, No. 107, red/yellow, two pieces, nine sand buckets attached to crank-operated chain, four wheels; red/black (1941), 1940-41	150	300	400
Sand Loader, No. 51, black/red, winding elevator track w/sand buckets, 1924-32, 13" high	200	300	400
Sand Sifter set, No. 56, black/red, complete with sand sifter operation, sold with No. 405 Dump Truck, scarce, 1927-29, 72" long	400	800	1200
Sand Sifter set, No. 56, black/red, complete sand sifter operation with			

Structo Freeport Motor Express, No. 601, 1951-52, a.k.a. Motor Express Truck, 12-3/4". Photo courtesy Randy Prasse

Structo Freeport Motor Express, No. 601, 1953, a.k.a. Motor Express Truck, 12-3/4". Photo courtesy Randy Prasse

Structo Gasoline Truck, No. 866, 1951-54, 13-1/2". Photo courtesy Randy Prasse

Structo Log Truck, No. 940. Photo courtesy Thomas G. Nefos

Structo Machinery Hauling Truck with original box, No. 607, 1951, 13". Photo courtesy Randy Prasse

Structo Excavating Company, No. 605, 1951-54, a.k.a. Shovel Dump, 12-3/4". Photo courtesy Randy Prasse

Structo Pick-Up Truck, 1940s, 17". Photo courtesy Calvin L. Chaussee

Structo Grain Trailer, No. 704, 1953-55, 20-3/4". Photo courtesy Randy Prasse

Structo Machinery Hauling Truck, No. 607, 1953, 13". Photo courtesy Randy Prasse

Structo Package Delivery Truck with original box, No. 603, 1954, 13". Photo courtesy Randy Prasse

Structo Excavating Company, No. 606, 1955-56, a.k.a. Deluxe Shovel Dump, 12-3/4". Photo courtesy Randy Prasse

Structo Pick-Up Trucks, metal, each 6". Photo courtesy Ron Fink

Structo Police Patrol Truck, No. 426, 17". Photo courtesy Thomas G. Nefos

Structo Pumper, 1920s, 22". Photo courtesy Bertoia Auctions

	C6	C8	C10
No. 405 Dump truck, scarce, 1930-32, 72" long	200	300	400
Shovel Dump, No. 605, also known as Structo Excavating Company, early 1950s	100	150	200
Six-Wheel Dump, orange/black, stubby Studebaker-style front, hard rubber tires with steel caps, 1936-38, 18" long	600	900	1200
Small Steam Shovel, No. 50, green/red, vertical boiler tank and smoke stack, 1924-26, 13-3/4" long	150	250	350
Speed Wagon, No. 425, orange, black balloon tires, open truck box with drop-down tailgate, scarce, 1930-32, 17" long	300	500	700
Speed Wagon, No. 408, green, white balloon tires, open truck box w/drop-down tailgate, scarce, 1927-29, 17" long	300	500	700
Stake Delivery Truck, No. 310, red/white, removable stakes, raising hood, 1940, 25" long	300	500	800
Stake Truck, C-cab style, orange/green, working lights, 1933-35, 21-12" long	300	700	1200
Stake Truck, No. 254, red/yellow two-tone truck with removable plated stakes, 1939, 22-1/2" long	250	500	750
Stake Truck, No. 204, yellow/red, removable sakes, raising hood; blue/yellow (1941), 1940-41, 21-3/4" long	250	500	750
Stake Wagon Truck, black/red, C-cab style, 1933-35, 21-1/2" long	250	500	750

	C6	C8	C10
Standard Rider, red, seat in rear of toy, wooden-handled steering mechanism through roof, 1936-38, 18" long	300	500	700
Station Wagon, No. 206, shown in catalog but excluded from the 1941 line, 1941	NPF	NPF	NPF
Steam Shovel, No. 100, blue/yellow/black, crank controls; no blue (1940), 1939-41, 21" x 18"	100	150	250
Steam Shovel, 16"	57	87	115
Steam Shovel, 14" x 11"	75	150	200
Steam Shovel, No. 65, black/red, smaller version of No. 110, 1927-32, 18-3/4" long	100	200	300
Steam Shovel, No. 112, green/red, with scoop shovel bucket, 1924-26, 14-1/2" long	100	200	300
Steel Cargo Trailer, No. 702, early to mid-1950s	125	175	225
Straight Truck, white, black hard rubber tires with painted whitewalls, 1933-35, 22" long	250	500	700
Tank, olive drab w/orange turret, ten metal wheels, 12-1/2"	300	450	600
Tank, No. 48, 11" long	225	338	450
Telephone Bank, No. 101, black/orange/red, bell rings when coin is deposited; only black (1940), 1939-41, 10-1/2" long	75	125	200
Tractor and Grader, No. 61, large blue/orange crawler with green pull-behind grader, scarce, 1930-32, 30" long	600	1000	1800
Tractor and Sand Trailer, No. 45, black/orange, same as No. 44 but with three trailers, 1927-29, 16" long	400	600	800

Structo "Ready Mix" Cement Truck, 14". Photo courtesy Calvin L. Chaussee

Structo "Ready Mix" Cement Truck, 1960s. Photo courtesy Bob Smith

Structo "Rocker," 23-1/2". Photo courtesy Calvin L. Chaussee

Structo "Sanitation Department" Garbage Truck, 1960s. Photo courtesy Bob Smith

Structo Steel Cargo Company, No. 702, 20-3/4". Photo courtesy Randy Prasse

Structo Steel Company, No. 705, 1956, 24-1/2". Photo courtesy Randy Prasse

Structo Tank, No. 48, 11". Photo courtesy Mapes Auctioneers & Appraisers

Structo Tank, olive drab w/orange turret, 10 metal wheels, 12-1/2". Photo courtesy Joe and Sharon Freed

Structo "Telephone Co." Photo courtesy Bill Kaufman

Structo Timber Toter, No. 714, 1955-57, 21". Photo courtesy Randy Prasse

Structo "Telephone Co." Photo courtesy Bill Kaufman

Structo Toyland Construction Co., No. 844, 1953-54, 12-1/2". Photo courtesy Randy Prasse

*Structo Toyland Construction Co. Elevated Dump, 12".
Photo courtesy Calvin L. Chaussee*

*Structo Toyland Garage Wrecker, No. 822, 1951-52,
12-1/4". Photo courtesy Randy Prasse*

	C6	C8	C10
Tractor and Sand Trailer, No. 44, black/orange, similar to old version of No. 44 with high seat and cast nickel-plated driver, 1927-29, 16" long	300	500	700
Tractor and Trailer, No. 402, green/red, pull toy with no motor, 1924-26, 17-1/2" long	200	400	600
Tractor and Trailer, No. 39, green/red, one-piece tractor and cab, solid black wheels, wind-up motor, 1924-26, 13" long	200	400	700
Tractor Train, No. 45, green/red, same as No. 44 but with three trailers, 1924-26, 28-1/2" long	300	500	700
Tractor, Trailer and Scraper, No. 46, blue, crawler with red four-wheel wagon and gray two-wheel scraper, 1930-32, 23-1/2" long	200	500	700
Transport Trailer, No. 700, early 1950s	90	135	180
Transport Unit, No. 505, red/white, three piece set, same as 1939 model No. 500, raising hood; red/gray (1941), 1940-41, 35" long	300	600	800
Transport Unit, No. 500, three-piece set with tractor and same trailers as No. 300 and No. 401 sets, 1939, 32-1/2" long	300	600	800
Trench Digger Truck, black/yellow, conventional Studebaker-style front, chain-operated crane, 1936-38, 26" long	500	700	1000
Truck, "Structo Telephone Co.", 1948, 12" long	38	56	75
Truck and Steam Shovel, yellow/blue, stubby Studebaker-style front, hard rubber tires with steel caps, 1936-38, 18" long	700	1000	1500
Truck and Trailer, No. 300, blue/yellow two-tone tractor and stake trailer, automatic coupling system, 1939, 25-1/2" long	250	500	750
Truck Assortment, No. 317, blue Dump Truck, Stake Truck, Lumber Truck, heavy gauge metal, rubber wheels, original box folds to form garage, price per set, 1920s, each 9" long, 3-1/2" wide, 3-1/2" tall	175	250	400
Truck/Steam Shovel, No. 400, orange/black, flatbed truck with steam shovel on back, 1939, 28" long	300	500	700
Truck/Steam Shovel, No. 402, yellow/black, flatbed truck with Steam Shovel on back, includes ramp, raising hood, 1940, 32" long	300	500	750

	C6	C8	C10
Truck/Steam Shovel, No. 402, yellow/black, flatbed truck with Steam Shovel on back, includes ramp, raising hood, 1941, 32" long	200	400	600
U.S. Mail Truck, No. 428, green, black balloon tires w/red center hubs, enclosed rear with lattice, 1930-32, 17" long	200	400	700
U.S. Mail Truck, No. 411, green, black balloon tires with red center hubs, enclosed rear with lattice, 1927-29, 17" long	200	400	700
Van, No. 300, open top, red/gray, open grain-hauler style trailer with tailgate, 1941, 25-1/2" long	300	500	800
Whippet Tank, No. 48, heavy spring clockwork motor, may read "Patented 1920," green/red, pre-assembled "Ready Built" (1922-26); also yellow, with gun on turret (1927-29); only green/red with gun (1930-32), 1922-32, 12" long	200	400	600
Wrecker, "Toyland Garage"	50	75	125
Wrecker, No. 822, "Toyland Garage," wind-up, early to mid-1950s	100	135	200
Wrecker, No. 201, blue/white, tow arm with crank-operated tow chain and hood, raising hood; blue/yellow (1941), 1940-41, 21-1/4" long	250	500	750
Wrecker, No. 253, blue/white two-tone truck with manual crank tow arm and winch, 1939, 22" long	300	600	800
Wrecking Auto, No. 115, red/black, with tow arm and winch mechanism, 1924-26, 16-1/2" long	200	400	600
Yuba Tractor, No. 16, black/red, kit tractor with steel tracks and one red trailer, 1920-23, 13-1/2" long (20" long overall)	80	1200	1800

Postwar

	C6	C8	C10
10 Pc. Truck Assortment, 1955, 2 cabs plus one each #702, #706, #714, cattle trailer, Model No. 725	225	495	695
12 Pc. US Highway Set, 1958, Orange, dump, grader, maintenance, pick-up plus 8 road signs, Model No. 550	95	245	425
15 Pc. Farm Set, 1958, Various, caddy, dump, pick-up/horse trailer, 6 wheel transport, Model No. 93	125	175	225
17 Pc. Coast To Coast Fleet, 1956-57, Various, 2 cars plus lumber trailer, #175, #935, #950; 2 cars, Model No. 925	175	295	495

	C6	C8	C10
17 Pc. USA Combat Convoy Set, 1958, Green, transport, searchlight and missle trucks w/soldiers, Model No. 520	155	205	375
3 Pc. Truck Assortment, 1954, One each: #75, #76, #77, Model No. 91	125	175	255
3 Pc. Truck Assortment, 1955, One each: #105, #201, #300, Model No. 325	175	225	345
3 Pc. Truck Assortment, 1956-57, Various, one each: #106, #201, #300, Model No. 326	175	225	345
3 Pc. Truck Assortment W/Garage, 1956-57, One each: #75, #76, #77 with garage storage box, Model No. 92	155	195	295
3 Pc. Truck Assortment W/Garage, 1958, Various, one each; dump, log and stake truck, Model No. 94	155	195	295
32 Pc. Big Job Transcontinental Set, 1956-57, Various, 2 cabs plus one each #702, #706, #714, cattle trailer, Model No. 726	225	495	695
4 Pc. Truck Assortment, 1954, One each: #21, #30, #40, #50, Model No. 90	95	125	175
5 Pc. Highway Builder Set, 1958, Various, one each: #106, #201, #300 plus 2 metal road signs, Model No. 510	175	225	395
5 Pc. Turnpike Builder Set, 1956-57, Various, one each: #321, #340, #404 combo, Model No. 327	195	275	395
6 Pc. Fire Department, 1958, Red and white, pumper, hook & ladder, ambulance, road signs, Model No. 570	175	225	395
8-Wheel Transport Truck, 1954, Orange, 7.25Lx2.5Wx2.25H, also in 1957 as 6 wheeled, red version in farm set, Model No. 40	25	55	75
Aerial Fire Truck, 1948, Red, 24Lx6.75Wx6.25H, 1 raising/ 2 side ladders & bell on hood, Model No. 250	115	175	255
Aerial Fire Truck, 1949, Red, 24Lx6.75Wx6.25H, 1 raising, 2 side ladders & bell on hood, Model No. 250	115	175	255
Aerial Fire Truck, 1950, Red, 24Lx6.75Wx6.25H, 1 raising/ 2 side ladders & bell on hood, Model No. 250	115	175	255
Aerial Fire Truck, 1951, Red, 24Lx6.75Wx6.25H, with plastic fireball motor under the hood, Model No. 250	115	175	255
Aerial Fire Truck, 1952, Red, 24Lx6.75Wx6.25H, with plastic fireball motor under the hood, Model No. 250	115	175	255

	C6	C8	C10
Aerial Hook & Ladder, 1961, Red, 30.75Lx6.25Wx6.25H, two metal ladders, crank operated lift ladder, Model No. 902	65	115	145
Aerial Hook & Ladder, 1962, Red, 30.75Lx6.25Wx6.25H, two metal ladders, crank operated lift ladder, Model No. 902	65	115	155
Aerial Hook & Ladder, 1963, Red and red, 30.75Lx6.25Wx6.25H, two metal ladders, crank operated lift ladder, Model No. 902	65	105	145
Aerial Hook & Ladder, 1964, Red and red, 30.75Lx6.25Wx6.25H, two metal ladders, crank operated lift ladder, Model No. 902	55	95	135
Aerial Hook & Ladder, 1965, Red and red, 30.75Lx6.25Wx6.25H, two metal ladders, crank operated lift ladder, Model No. 900	55	95	135
Aerial Hook & Ladder, 1966, Red and white, 29.25Lx6.25Wx 6.25H, two metal ladders, crank operated lift ladder, Model No. 901	55	85	125
Aerial Hook & Ladder, 1967, Red and red, 29.25Lx6.25Wx6.25H, two metal ladders, crank operated lift ladder, Model No. 381	55	85	125
Aerial Hook & Ladder, 1968, Red and red, 29.25Lx6.25Wx6.25H, two metal ladders, crank lift ladder "9" decal on side, Model No. 381	55	85	115
Aerial Hook & Ladder, 1969, Red and red, 30.25Lx5.5Wx7H, typhoons design with crank operated extension ladder, Model No. 381	35	45	55
Aerial Hook & Ladder, 1972, Red and red, 17.5Lx6Wx7.25H, typhoon design with 2 ladders and extension ladder, Model No. 381	35	45	55
Air Force Anti-Aircraft Set, 1959, Red and blue, scarce, canvas covered truck, missile launcher, searchlight, Model No. 506	115	195	245
Air Force Radar Truck, 1959, Blue and red, 12Lx5.25Wx12.5H, scarce, radar dish on roof of box, 2 plastic soldiers, Model No. 102	55	95	125
Air Force Truck, 1958, Blue and red, 17.25Lx7.25Wx8H, includes soldiers and canvas top, spare tires on side, Model No. 212	115	155	195
Air Force Truck, 1968, Blue, 8.75Lx3.5Wx4H, scarce, Kom-pak			

Structo Transport, No. 700, 1951-54, 21-1/2". Photo courtesy Randy Prasse

Structo Transcontinental Express, No. 710, 1957, late 1956-57, blue trailer, 24". Photo courtesy Randy Prasse

	C6	C8	C10
design with clear cover on bed, 4 blue soldiers, Model No. 175	45	75	115
Air Terminal Service Set, 1962, Red and white, includes #195, #303, #307, Model No. 908	115	135	175
Airlines Lift Truck, 1961, Copper and white, 12.5Lx5.25Wx7H, lever lifts cargo box with scissors lift mechanism, Model No. 303	55	75	95
All Steel Dump Truck, 1966, Grey and orange, 8.75Lx3.5Wx4H, Kom-pak design, Model No. 125	15	25	45
All-In-One Wild Animal Set, 1960, Pink, blue, yellow, 5.5Lx4Wx 2H, smaller animals fit inside larger animals, Model No. 105	15	25	35
American Airlines Sky Chef, 1962, Blue and white, 12.5Lx5.25Wx 7H, lever lifts cargo box with scissors lift mechanism, Model No. 303	75	95	125
American Rev-O-Lution, 1972, White and black, 10Lx4.5Wx5H, sport model design with american flag on doors, Model No. 775	25	35	45
American Rev-O-Lution, 1973, White and black, 10Lx4.5Wx 5H, sport model design with american flag on doors, Model No. 775	25	35	45
Animal Set, 1969, Yellow and green, 2 pc. set contains #837 and #870, Model No. 961	35	55	75
Army Engineers Dump & Sand Loader, 1964, Army green, 21.5Lx5.5Wx8.25H, includes 4 plastic soldiers, Model No. 411	55	75	95
Army Engineer's Set, 1963, Army green, includes #190, #400, #409, all in army green, Model No. 915	115	135	175
Army Troop Carrier, 1966, Army green, 8.75Lx3.5Wx4H, Kom-pak design with clear plastic cover2 soldiers, Model No. 115	15	25	45
Army Troop Transport, 1959, Green, 18.75Lx6.75Wx9H, canvas top with "USA" printed. 4 plastic soldiers, Model No. 412	55	75	95
Auto Elevator, 1960, Red and yellow, 9Lx3.5Wx9H, scarce, plastic parking garage, crank release car down ramp, Model No. 111	75	95	115
Auto Haulaway, 1955, Blue and orange, 25Lx4.5Wx6.5H, with two cars, loading ramp and "S" grill cab, Model No. 175	105	175	195
Auto Haulaway, 1956-57, Blue and orange, 25Lx4.5Wx6.5H, with two cars, loading ramp and "S" grill cab, Model No. 175	105	175	195
Auto Haulaway, 1958, Yellow and red, 21.5Lx4.5Wx6.5H, smaller model with 2 cars and loading ramp, Model No. 946	75	115	155
Auto Transport, 1954, White and red, 27Lx5.5Wx6.75H, with 4 die cast cars and loading ramp, Model No. 706	95	155	205
Auto Transport, 1960, Met. green, 22Lx5.5Wx6.5H, 4 metal cars plus loading ramp, Model No. 402	55	75	95
Auto Transport, 1961, Copper, 22Lx5.5Wx7H, includes one car and one truck plus loading ramp, Model No. 502	35	65	95
Auto Transport, 1962, Yellow and green, 22Lx5.5Wx7H, two metal cars, one metal truck plus loading ramp, Model No. 502	75	115	155
Auto Transport, 1963, Met. gold, 22Lx5.5Wx7H, one metal car, one metal truck plus loading ramp, Model No. 402	35	55	75
Auto Transport, 1964, Red and yellow, 22Lx5.5Wx7H, includes 1 metal car and 1 metal truck & loading ramp, Model No. 402	55	75	95
Auto Transporter, 1967, Red and yellow, 28.25Lx5.75Wx5.5H, large, open car carrier, ramps adjust, 3 plastic cars, Model No. 492	85	125	155
Auto Transporter, 1968, Red and yellow, 28.25Lx5.75Wx5.5H, large, open car carrier, ramps adjust, 3 plastic cars, Model No. 492	85	125	155
Automatic Dump Truck, 1964, Copper, 8.75Lx3.5Wx4H, spring dump mechanism, Model No. 125	15	25	55
Automatic Dump Truck, 1965, Green and yellow, 8.75Lx3.5Wx4H, spring dump mechanism, Model No. 125	15	25	55
Automatic Under Counter Dishwasher, 1959, Pink and grey, 7Lx7.75Wx13H, works with water, battery operated, Model No. 10	15	55	75
Barrel Truck, 1951, Red and blue, 12.75Lx5.5Wx5H, wind-up motor and two oil can banks, Model No. 811	135	195	255
Barrel Truck, 1952, Red and blue, 12.75Lx5.5Wx5H, wind-up motor and two oil can banks, Model No. 811	135	195	255
Barrel Truck, 1953, Red and blue, 12.75Lx5.5Wx5H, wind-up motor and oil can bank, Model No. 811	135	195	255
Barrel Truck, 1954, White and red, 12.75Lx5.5Wx5H, rare, made only in 1954. Replaced #811, no wind-up, Model No. 609	115	175	205
Barrel Truck, 1955, Yellow and red, 12.75Lx5.5Wx5H, non-wind-up model, no oil can bank, Model No. 913	75	115	175
Barrel Truck, 1956-57, Yellow and red, 12.75Lx5.5Wx5H, non-wind-up model, no oil can bank, Model No. 913	75	115	175
Big 2-Dozen Assortment, 1972, 17.75Lx14.75Wx16.5H, all 3 weird wheels designs in a store display - 24 cars total, Model No. 265n/an/a	250		
Big 2-Dozen Assortment, 1973, 17.75Lx14.75Wx16.5H, all 3 weird wheels designs in a store display - 24 cars total, Model No. 265n/an/a	250		
Big Job Transcontinental Fleet, 1958, Various, 2 cabs plus 1 each trailers: steel, auto, freight, cattle, Model No. 540	225	495	695
Blacktop Bandit, 1972, Plum and black, 10Lx4.5Wx5H, sport model design with dragster styling, Model No. 780	25	35	45
Blacktop Bandit, 1973, Yellow and black, 10Lx4.5Wx5H, sport model design with dragster styling, Model No. 780	25	35	45
Boat With Outboard Motor, 1959, Red and white, 13.25Lx 4Wx3.25H, boat only, from #601 set, convertible boat and motor, Model No. 803	55	75	95

	C6	C8	C10
Boat With Play Motor, 1959, Red and white, 9.5Lx3Wx2.5H, boat only, from #206 set, convertible boat and motor, Model No. 802	35	55	75
Boog-A-Loo, 1969, Pink and white, 9.5Lx4.5Wx5H, sport model design with 5" blond doll, Model No. 766	25	35	45
Boog-A-Loo, 1970, Pink and white, 9.5Lx4.5Wx5H, sport model design with 5" blond doll, Model No. 766	25	35	45
Boon Dock'r, 1972, Red and green, 23Lx5.5Wx5.25H, sport model design with buggy towing boat & trailer, Model No. 758	25	35	45
Boon Dock'r, 1973, Orange and green, 23Lx5.5Wx5.25H, sport model design with buggy towing boat & trailer, Model No. 758	25	35	45
Bottom Dump, 1953, Orange, 21.5Lx6.5Wx6.5H, with plastic fireball motor under the hood, Model No. 320	75	105	155
Bottom Dump, 1953, Orange, 21.5Lx6.5Wx6.5H, with plastic fireball motor under the hood, Model No. 320	75	105	155
Brain Barrel, 1972, Brown, 2.75Lx3.5Wx3H, 2 wheeled design with brown "Wooden" barrel & bald driver, Model No. 250	10	15	20
Brain Barrel, 1973, Brown, 2.75Lx3.5Wx3H, 2 wheeled design with brown "Wooden" brrel & bald driver, Model No. 250	10	15	20
Bridge Set, 1970, Yellow and white, 22.25Lx3.5Wx5.5H, road tow'ds design with stake truck, 2 trailers & 4 pc. Bridge, Model No. 290	15	25	35
Bridge Set, 1972, Yellow and white, 22.25Lx3.5Wx5.5H, road tow'ds design with stake truck, 2 trailers & 4 pc. Bridge, Model No. 290	15	25	35
Built-In Cooking Range, 1959, Pink and grey, 7Lx7.75Wx13H, plastic burners on top, cabinets open, pots and pans, Model No. 4	15	35	55
Built-In Double Oven, 1959, Pink and grey, 7.25Lx7.75Wx13H, battery operated, rotisserie in top oven unit, Model No. 14	15	35	55
Built-In Double Sink, 1959, Pink and grey, 7Lx7.75Wx13H, works with water, battery operated, Model No. 8	15	55	75
Bulldozer, 1959, Copper and cream, 11.75Lx7Wx6.75H, cream blade, yellow wheels and motor, also on #502 set, Model No. 205	35	55	75
Bulldozer, 1960, Yellow, 11.75Lx 7Wx6.75H, black tires and motor, blade tips up, Model No. 210	35	55	75
Bulldozer, 1961, Yellow, 11Lx 6.5Wx6.5H, rubber tracks, Model No. 206	35	75	95
Bulldozer & Earth Mover, 1966, Green and yellow, 25.5Lx 7.5Wx7H, combination bulldozer towing bottom dump earth mover unit, Model No. 460	55	75	95
Bulldozer & Earth Mover, 1967, Green and yellow, 24.5Lx 6.5Wx5.75H, combination bulldozer towing bottom dump earth mover unit, Model No. 574	45	65	85

	C6	C8	C10
Bulldozer & Earth Mover, 1968, Green and yellow, 24.5Lx 6.5Wx5.75H, combination bulldozer towing bottom dump earth mover unit, Model No. 574	45	65	85
Bulldozer & Scraper, 1966, Green and yellow, 25.5Lx7.5Wx7H, combination bulldozer towing scraper unit, Model No. 461	55	75	95
Buzzin' Bugggy, 1972, Yellow, 2.75Lx3.5Wx3H, 2 wheeled design with open dune buggy style, Model No. 218	10	15	20
Buzzin' Buggy, 1971, Yellow, 2.75Lx3.5Wx3H, 2 wheeled design with open dune buggy style, Model No. 218	10	15	20
Buzzin' Buggy, 1973, Yellow, 2.75Lx3.5Wx3H, 2 wheeled design with open dune buggy style, Model No. 218	10	15	20
Cabin Cruiser, 1960, Red and white, 12Lx4Wx3H, plastic hull, wooden deck and cabin, battery op motor, Model No. 212	55	95	125
Caddy Sedan, 1954, Various, 6.25Lx2.5Wx2H, same scale as appear on auto transport set, Model No. 20	15	25	35
Camper, 1960, Teal and red, 23.25Lx4.5Wx6.5H, red and white canvas over truck bed, boat and trailer, Model No. 211	55	95	125
Camper, 1961, Met. green, 21.5Lx 4.5Wx5H, rampside truck towing boat and trailer, Model No. 202	45	65	85
Camper, 1962, Green and yellow, 10.5Lx4.5Wx6.5H, rampside truck with plastic camper in bed of truck, Model No. 203	55	75	95
Camper, 1963, Teal, 10.5Lx 4.5Wx6.5H, rampside truck with plastic camper in bed of truck, Model No. 203	55	75	95
Camper, 1964, Teal and teal, 10.5Lx4.5Wx6.5H, plastic camper in truck bed, Model No. 203	35	65	85
Camper, 1965, Teal and white, 10.5Lx4.5Wx6.5H, plastic camper in truck bed, Model No. 203	35	65	85
Camper, 1966, Lt. blue and white, 10.5Lx4.5Wx6.5H, plastic camper in truck bed, Model No. 203	25	55	75
Camper Truck, 1967, Lt. blue and dk. blue, 10.5Lx4.5Wx6.5H, dk. blue rampside truck with lt blue plastic cover, Model No. 235	25	55	75

Structo Transcontinental Express, No. 710, 1956, 24".
Photo courtesy Randy Prasse

	C6	C8	C10
Camper Truck, 1968, Lt. blue and Dk. blue, 10.5Lx4.5Wx6.5H, Dk. blue rampside truck with Lt. blue plastic camper, Model No. 235.	25	55	75
Camper Truck, 1969, Gold and white, 10.5Lx5Wx6.5H, typhoons design with white plastic camper in bed, Model No. 235.	25	35	45
Camper Truck, 1970, Lime green and white, 9.25Lx4.25Wx5H, hurricane design with white plastic camper, Model No. 835.	15	25	35
Camper Truck, 1972, Orange and white, 9.25Lx4.25Wx5H, hurricanes design, Model No. 835.	10	20	30
Camper Truck, 1973, Orange and white, 9.25Lx4.25Wx5H, hurricanes design, Model No. 835	10	20	30
Camper With Boat & Trailer, 1965, Teal and red, 20Lx4.5Wx6.5H, #203 with plastic boat on trailer, Model No. 304.	45	85	105
Car Carrier, 1965, Teal and teal, 22Lx6Wx7H, new, 2 plastic cars (T-Birds) and loading ramp, Model No. 413.	55	75	95
Car Carrier, 1966, Grey and yellow, 22.25Lx6Wx7H, 3 plastic cars (Mustangs & T-Birds) loading ramp, Model No. 418.	45	65	85
Car Carrier, 1967, Red and yellow, 22.25Lx6Wx7H, 3 plastic cars (Mustangs & T-Birds) loading ramp, Model No. 331.	45	65	85
Car Carrier, 1968, Red and yellow, 22.25Lx6Wx7H, 3 plastic cars (Mustangs & T-Birds) loading ramp, Model No. 331.	45	65	85
Car Carrier, 1969, Red and yellow, 22.5Lx5.5Wx5.5H, typhoons design with 3 plastic cars (Mustangs/T-Birds) ramp, Model No. 331.	35	45	55
Car Carrier, 1970, Red and yellow, 22.5Lx5.5Wx5.5H, typhoons design with 3 plastic cars (Mustangs/T-Birds) ramp, Model No. 331.	35	45	55
Car Carrier, 1972, Red and yellow, 22.5Lx5.5Wx6H, typhoon design with 3 plastic cars and ramp, Model No. 330.	45	55	65
Cattle Trailer, 1953, White and red, 21.5Lx5.5Wx7.5H, no loading ramp or animals, Model No. 708.	95	155	205
Cattle Trailer, 1954, White and red, 21.5Lx5.5Wx7.5H, no loading ramp or animals, Model No. 708.	95	155	205
Cattle Trailer, 1955, Green and orange, 21Lx5Wx7.75H, new pressed steel cab design, Model No. 960.	75	135	195
Cattle Transport, 1956-57, Green and orange, 21Lx5Wx7.75H, Model No. 960.	75	135	195
Cattle Transport, 1958, Green and orange, 21Lx5Wx7.5H, with plastic farm animals, Model No. 961	75	115	155
Cattle Transport, 1959, Red and white, 21.25Lx5.25Wx7.5H, farms decals on white trailer, Model No. 304	45	65	85
Cattle Transport, 1960, Red and white, 21.25Lx5.5Wx7.5H, plastic mirrors, windshield wipers and horn, Model No. 403	45	65	85
Cattle Transport, 1961, Green and white, 23.5Lx6.5Wx8H, white trailer with green doors, Model No. 503	35	65	95
Cattle Transport, 1962, Yellow and green, 23.5Lx5.5Wx8H, green trailer with yellow doors, Model No. 503	55	75	95
Cattle Transport, 1963, Red and red, 22.25Lx6.5Wx8H, new cab - over design, plus steering wheel and seat detail, Model No. 503	35	65	95
Cattle Transport, 1964, Red and red, 22.25Lx6.5Wx8H, Model No. 503	45	75	95
Cattle Truck, 1965, Green and white, 16.5Lx4Wx5H, white plastic insert panels in side of trailer, Model No. 150	25	45	75
Cattle Truck, 1966, Teal and white, 16.5Lx4Wx5.25H, Kom-pak design white insert panels in side of trailer, Model No. 150	25	45	75
Cement Mixer, 1965, Grey and orange, 14Lx6.75Wx5.25H, axle driven gear operates barrel, Model No. 450	45	65	85
Cement Mixer, 1965, Red and white, 8.75Lx3.5Wx5H, axle driven gear operates barrel, Model No. 136	15	35	65
Cement Mixer, 1966, Grey and orange, 9.75Lx4Wx4.5H, Kom-pak design with dumping barrel, Model No. 136	15	25	45
Cement Mixer, 1966, Grey and orange, 15.5Lx6.75Wx5.25H, axle driven gear operates barrel, POW-R-R sound, Model No. 450	45	65	85
Cement Mixer, 1967, Grey and orange, 9.75Lx4Wx4.5H, Kom-pak design with dumping barrel, Model No. 153	15	25	45
Cement Mixer, 1967, Grey and orange, 16.5Lx6.5Wx7.5H, axle driven gear operates barrel, POW-R-R sound, Model No. 432	45	65	85
Cement Mixer, 1968, Red and yellow, 16.5Lx6.5Wx7.5H, axle driven gear operates barrel, Model No. 270	35	55	75
Cement Mixer, 1968, Grey and orange, 9.75Lx4Wx4.5H, Kom-pak design with dumping barrel, Model No. 153	15	25	45
Cement Mixer, 1969, Red and yellow, 14.5Lx7Wx7.5H, typhoons design with axle driven barrel, Model No. 270	25	35	45
Cement Mixer, 1969, Dk. orange and white, 12.25Lx7Wx7H, thunder-bolt design with steer-o-matic front wheels, Model No. 632	25	35	45
Cement Mixer, 1969, Dk. orange and white, 9.5Lx4Wx4.25H, hurricanes design with axle driven barrel, Model No. 853	15	25	35
Cement Mixer, 1970, Dk. orange and white, 9.5Lx4Wx4.25H, hurricanes design with axle driven barrel, Model No. 853	15	25	35
Cement Mixer, 1970, Red and yellow, 14.5Lx7Wx7.5H, typhoons design with axle driven barrel, Model No. 270	25	35	45
Clam Bucket, 1956-57, Yellow and green, 16.75Lx7Wx7.25H, Model No. 101	75	105	125
Clam Bucket and Machinery Truck, 1956-57, Yellow and green, 32Lx7.25Wx13.75H, with plastic fireball motor under the hood, Model No. 404	105	175	205

	C6	C8	C10
Combination, 1958, Green and orange, 32Lx7.5Wx6.75H, #106 power shovel and machinery hauling low-boy, Model No. 405	75	135	195
Combination Refrigerator/Freezer, 1959, Pink and grey, 7.25Lx7.75Wx13H, swing out shelves, freezer drawer, plastic food, Model No. 12	15	35	55
Combination With Two Trailers, 1951, Blue cast cab with #702 and 704 trailers, Model No. 706	155	215	275
Combination With Two Trailers, 1952, Blue cast cab with #702 and 704 trailers, Model No. 706	155	215	275
Concrete Mixer, 1960, Copper and yellow, 6.25Lx5.5Wx13.25H, scarce, plastic cement mixer with clear barrel w/marbels, Model No. 114	75	95	115
Construction And Paving Set, 1961, Varies, 4 pc. set includes #309, #609, #700 plus barricade, Model No. 907	95	135	175
Contractor Set, 1965, Varies, 3 pc. set includes #125, #136, #140, Model No. 180	55	85	125
Contractor Set, 1966, Grey and orange, 3 pc. Kom-pak set includes #125, #136, #140, Model No. 180	55	85	125
Contractor Set, 1967, Grey and orange, 3 pc. set includes #141, #153, #183, Model No. 192	55	85	125
Contractor Set, 1972, Yellow, combination of #579 set and #184 set plus 10 street signs, Model No. 967	35	55	75
Contractor Set, 1973, Yellow and orange, combination of #580 set and #184 set plus 10 street signs, Model No. 967	35	55	75
Corner Counter-Top Cabinet, 1959, Pink and grey, 12Lx 9.75Wx13H, 2 lazy susan shelves, drawer opens, pots and pans, Model No. 6	15	35	55
Counter-Top Cabinet, 1959, Pink and grey, 7Lx7.75Wx13H, cabinet doors open, includes pots and pans, Model No. 2	15	35	55
Cub Pick-Up, 1963, Lt. blue, 10.75Lx5Wx5H, white plastic convertible roof, doors open, Model No. 250	35	55	75
Cub Pick-Up, 1964, Blue and white, 20.75Lx5Wx6H, white plastic convertible roof covers cab, doors open, Model No. 250	25	55	75
Cub Pick-Up, 1965, Blue and white, 20.75Lx5Wx6H, white plastic convertible roof covers cab, doors open, Model No. 250	25	55	75
Cub Station Wagon, 1963, Teal and white, 10.75Lx5Wx5H, same body as #250 but white plastic roof cover whole body, Model No. 325	55	75	95
Cub Station Wagon, 1964, Teal and white, 10.75Lx5Wx5H, white plastic convertible roof cover body, doors open, Model No. 325	25	55	75
Cub Station Wagon, 1965, Teal and white, 10.75Lx5Wx5H, white plastic convertible roof cover body, doors open, Model No. 325	25	45	65
Cub Station Wagon & Horse Trailer, 1963, Teal and white, 20.5Lx5.25Wx6H, same as #190 plus 2 wheel horse trailer and 2 horses, Model No. 403	75	95	115
Cub Station Wagon With Horse Trailer, 1964, Teal and white, 20.5Lx5.25Wx6H, #325 cub station wagon & trailer, 2 plastic horses, Model No. 403	45	75	95
Deluxe Auto Transport, 1955, Chrome and yellow, 27Lx6Wx 6.75H, with 4 die cast cars and loading ramp, Model No. 706	75	135	195
Deluxe Auto Transport, 1956-57, Chrome and yellow, 27Lx6Wx6.75H, with 4 die cast cars and loading ramp, Model No. 706	75	135	195
Deluxe Auto Transport, 1958, Chrome and yellow, 27Lx 6Wx6.75H, with 2 cars, 1 truck and loading ramp, Model No. 707	75	135	195
Deluxe Auto Transport, 1959, Green and yellow, 31.5Lx 5.5Wx6.75H, two cars, one truck with loading ramp, plastic "S" grille, Model No. 401	65	95	125
Deluxe Camper, 1960, Gold, 27.5Lx6Wx6.5H, #207 truck plus #212 boat on trailer, Model No. 602	55	95	125
Deluxe Camper, 1962, Green and yellow, 21.5Lx4.5Wx6.5H, #203 plus boat and trailer, Model No. 304	75	105	135
Deluxe Camper, 1963, Blue and white, 20Lx5Wx5H, same as #190 plus boat and trailer, Model No. 404	65	95	125
Deluxe Cattle Transport, 1955, Chrome and green, 24Lx6Wx 8.5H, with loading ramp and metal farm animals, Model No. 712	75	155	195
Deluxe Cattle Transport, 1956-57, Chrome and green, 24Lx6Wx 8.5H, with loading ramp and metal farm animals, Model No. 712	75	155	195
Deluxe Cattle Transport, 1958, Yellow and brown, 25.75Lx6.25Wx8.5H, includes plastic farm animals, Model No. 275	95	155	205
Deluxe Dump Truck, 1961, Met. green, 11.75Lx5.5Wx5.75H, lever operates dump box, Model No. 309	35	65	85
Deluxe Dump Truck, 1962, Yellow and red, 11.75Lx5.5Wx5.75H, lever operates dump box, Model No. 309	35	65	85
Deluxe Earth Mover, 1958, Orange, 22Lx6.5Wx6.5H, with plastic fireball motor under the hood, Model No. 322	65	105	125
Deluxe Hydraulic Dumper, 1959, Copper and yellow, 20.5Lx 8Wx7H, hydraulic cylinder controls dump box, Model No. 500	65	95	125

Structo Transcontinental Express, plastic and metal, 1950s. Photo courtesy Harvey K. Rainess

	C6	C8	C10
Deluxe Kitchen-Laundry Ensemble, 1960, Pink and grey, 7 pc. set, includes #8, #12, #4, #10, #14, #16, #2- 1959 models, Model No. 27	115	155	195
Deluxe Moving Van, 1955, Chrome and yellow, 24Lx 6Wx8.5H, with loading ramp, Model No. 710	105	175	205
Deluxe Moving Van, 1956-57, Chrome and blue, 24Lx 6Wx8.5H, with loading ramp and mini grocery freight, Model No. 710	105	165	205
Deluxe Moving Van, 1958, Chrome and blue, 31Lx6Wx8.5H, with loading ramp and mini grocery freight, Model No. 710	105	165	205
Deluxe Moving Van, 1959, Yellow and red, 26.25Lx6Wx8.5H, red cab with bulb horn on roof, Model No. 504	55	95	125
Deluxe Power Wrecker, 1959, Blue and white, 23Lx7Wx9.25H, battery operated winch & lights, Model No. 702	75	125	175
Deluxe Road Grader, 1958, Orange, 18.75Lx7.25Wx7.5H, with plastic fireball motor under the hood, Model No. 301	55	95	115
Deluxe Road Grader, 1959, Copper and yellow, 18.75Lx7.25Wx 7.5H, copper with yellow wheels and engine, Model No. 301	35	55	75
Deluxe Rocker Dump, 1958, Orange, 20.25Lx6.25Wx6.5H, with plastic fireball motor under the hood, Model No. 312	65	105	125
Deluxe Rocker Dump, 1959, Copper and cream, 20.25Lx 6.25Wx6.5H, bronze dump, cream tractor with yellow wheels & motor, Model No. 312	45	75	95
Deluxe Transport, 1961, Red and white, 23.5Lx6.5Wx8H, North American Vanlines decals on trailer, Model No. 504	55	95	155
Deluxe Van Truck, 1962, Blue and white, 25.5Lx6.5Wx8.5H, express with rocketship on decals, Model No. 600	75	115	135
Deluxe Van Truck, 1963, Red and white, 25.5Lx6.5Wx8.5H, white trailer with red doors, Model No. 601	55	85	105
Deluxe Van Truck, 1964, Red and white, 25.5Lx6.5Wx8.5H, white trailer with red doors, Model No. 601	55	85	105
Deluxe Van Truck, 1965, Red and white, 25.5Lx6Wx8.75H, white trailer with red doors, Model No. 601	55	85	105
Deluxe Van Truck, 1966, Red and silver, 24Lx6Wx8.75H, unpainted steel trailer with "Structo Freight Lines" decal, Model No. 609	45	65	85
Die-Cast Dump Truck, 1961, Varies, 7.25Lx2.5Wx2.25H, packaged on bubble pack for in-store display, Model No. 79	35	55	75
Dig 'N Dump Set, 1970, Orange and white, 20Lx3.25Wx4.25H, road tow'ds design with shovel & dual dump boxes in tow, Model No. 280	15	25	35
Dig'n Dump, 1972, Orange and white, 20Lx3.25Wx4.25H, road tow'ds design with shovel & dual dump boxes in tow, Model No. 280	15	25	35
Dirt Tracker, 1972, White and black, 10Lx4.5Wx5H, sport model design with dual wheels #1 logo & flags on doors, Model No. 770	25	35	45
Dirt Tracker, 1973, Yellow and black, 10Lx4.5Wx5H, sport model design with dual wheels #1 logo & flags on doors, Model No. 770	25	35	45
Dispatch Truck, 1961, Met. green, 13Lx5.25Wx5H, similar to 1950's barrel truck, plastic mirrors, wipers & horns, Model No. 208	55	75	95
Display For Farm Set, 1966, Rare, boxed set for dealer trade show & store display, Model No. 9371	155	195	245
Display For Highway Set, 1966, Rare, boxed set for dealer trade show & store display, Model No. 9101	155	195	245
Display For State Fair Set, 1966, Rare, boxed set for dealer trade show & store display, Model No. 9521	155	195	245
Double Hydraulic Load & Dump, 1958, Black and yellow, 24.5Lx7.75Wx7H, hydraulic dump lift arm on dump box & front bucket, Model No. 252	125	165	205
Double Hydraulic Load & Dump, 1959, Copper and yellow, 23.75Lx7.75Wx6.75H, yellow bucket dumps over top into dump box, Model No. 252	55	75	95
Duluxe Camper With Boat & Trailer, 1959, Red and white, 29Lx6Wx6H, red truck with white roof, battery op boat motor, Model No. 601	75	125	175
Dump Truck, 1948, Red, 20L x 6.75W x 6.25H, long bullet headlights, Model No. 200	95	155	225
Dump Truck, 1949, Red, 20Lx6.75Wx6.25H, long bullet headlights, Model No. 200	95	155	225
Dump Truck, 1950, Red, 20Lx6.75Wx6.25H, long bullet headlights, Model No. 200	95	155	225
Dump Truck, 1951, Red, 20Lx6.75Wx6.25H, with plastic fireball motor under the hood, Model No. 200	75	135	195
Dump Truck, 1952, Red, 20Lx6.75Wx6.25H, with plastic fireball motor under the hood, Model No. 200	75	135	195
Dump Truck, 1953, Red, 20Lx6.75Wx6.25H, with plastic fireball motor under the hood, Model No. 200	65	105	155
Dump Truck, 1953, Red, 20Lx6.75Wx6.25H, with plastic fireball motor under the hood, Model No. 200	65	105	155
Dump Truck, 1954, Green and orange, 8.25Lx2.5Wx2.5H, spring dump action, Model No. 50	35	65	95
Dump Truck, 1954, Green and orange, 10.25Lx3.25Wx3.5H, spring dump action, Model No. 75	35	55	75
Dump Truck, 1955, Yellow and red, 20Lx6.75Wx6.25H, spring dump action, Model No. 201	55	95	125
Dump Truck, 1956-57, Gold and blue, 10.25Lx3.25Wx3.5H, spring dump action, Model No. 75	35	55	75

	C6	C8	C10
Dump Truck, 1956-57, Green and orange, 20Lx6.75Wx6.25H, spring dump action, Model No. 201	55	95	125
Dump Truck, 1959, Blue and yellow, 9Lx3.5Wx3.5H, Model No. 75	35	55	75
Dump Truck, 1959, Black and yellow, 15.75Lx6.75Wx6.75H, red roof and plastic "S" grille, no windshield, Model No. 201	55	95	115
Dump Truck, 1959, Copper and cream, 10.75Lx4.5Wx4.5H, Model No. 70	55	75	95
Dump Truck, 1963, Green, 11.75Lx5.5Wx5.75H, new cab - over design, plus steering wheel and seat detail, Model No. 300	35	65	85
Dump Truck, 1964, Green, 11.75Lx5.5Wx5.75H, cab-over design, plus steering wheel and seat detail, Model No. 300	35	65	85
Dump Truck, 1965, Met. green, 11.75Lx5.5Wx5.75H, cab - over design, plus steering wheel and seat detail, Model No. 300	35	65	85
Dump Truck, 1966, Red, 11.75Lx5.5Wx5.75H, spring dump mechanism, Model No. 300	25	45	65
Dump Truck, 1966, Green and yellow, 13.5Lx5.5Wx5.75H, lever action dump box, Model No. 316	25	45	65
Dump Truck, 1967, Red, 13.5Lx 5.5Wx5.75H, lever controls dump action, Model No. 303	25	45	65
Dump Truck, 1968, Red, 13.5Lx 5.5Wx5.75H, lever controls dump action, Model No. 303	25	45	65
Dump Truck, 1969, Grey and orange, 13Lx5.5Wx6H, typhoons design with spring action dump box, Model No. 311	25	35	45
Dump Truck, 1969, Red, 13.5Lx6Wx5.5H, typhoons design with lever action dump box, Model No. 303	25	35	45
Dump Truck, 1969, Dk. orange and white, 10.5Lx4Wx4.25H, hurricanes design, Model No. 841	15	25	35
Dump Truck, 1970, Red, 13.5Lx6Wx5.5H, typhoons design with lever action dump box, Model No. 303	25	35	45
Dump Truck, 1970, Dk. orange and white, 10.5Lx4Wx4.25H, hurricanes design, Model No. 841	15	25	35

Structo Weekender, 1960s. KP Photo courtesy Ron O'Brien

	C6	C8	C10
Dump Truck, 1972, Yellow, 13.5Lx6Wx5.5H, typhoon design, Model No. 303	15	25	35
Dump Truck, 1973, Gold and white, 10.75Lx4Wx4.25H, "Structo 841" stencilled on side of dump box, Model No. 841	10	20	30
Dump Truck and Sandloader, 1962, Yellow and red, 21.5Lx 5.5Wx8.25H, crank operated conveyer belt takes sand up to truck, Model No. 501	55	85	115
Dump Truck and Sandloader, 1963, Green and chartreuse, 21.5Lx5.5Wx8.25H, crank operated conveyer belt takes sand up to truck, Model No. 409	55	85	115
Dump With Front-End Loader, 1958, Yellow and blue, 23Lx6.75Wx6.25H, spring loaded dump with front loader bucket, Model No. 202	105	135	175
Dumper, 1960, Copper, 11.5Lx 5.5Wx6H, whitewall tires, plastic horn on roof, Model No. 209	45	75	95
Earth Mover, 1955, Orange, 21.5Lx6.5Wx6.5H, with plastic fireball motor under the hood, Model No. 320	75	105	155
Earth Mover, 1956-57, Orange, 22Lx6.5Wx6.5H, same tractor as #311, bottom panels open to dump, Model No. 321	95	125	155
Earth Mover, 1960, Yellow, 21.5Lx6.5Wx6H, black tires and motor, Model No. 322	35	55	75
Emergency Fire Patrol Searchlight Unit, 1959, White and red, 19.5Lx5.75Wx7.5H, white trailer with red battery operated searchlight unit, Model No. 303	55	95	125
End Loader, 1953, Orange, 15.25Lx6.25Wx6.75H, with plastic fireball motor under the hood, Model No. 340	65	95	145
End Loader, 1954, Orange, 15.25Lx6.25Wx6.75H, with plastic fireball motor under the hood, Model No. 340	65	95	145
End Loader, 1955, Orange, 15.25Lx6.25Wx6.75H, with plastic fireball motor under the hood, Model No. 340	65	95	145
End Loader, 1956-57, Green, 15.25Lx6Wx6.75H, with plastic fireball motor under the hood, Model No. 340	65	95	145
Explorer Vanguard Tracking Station, 1959, Red, 7.75Lx4.5Wx10H, scarce, various buttons, globe revolves in TV screen, Model No. 801	95	155	195
Farm Pick-Up And Trailer, 1959, Yellow and blue, 27.5Lx 6.25Wx6H, 7 plastic animals included, Model No. 213	55	95	125
Farm Set, 1962, Varies, includes #507, pick-up and trailer similar to nationwide set, Model No. 914	115	135	175
Farm Set, 1963, Teal and white, includes #314 with trailer and #403, Model No. 914	115	135	175
Farm Set, 1964, Teal and white, 5 pc. set includes #314 & trailer, #250 cub pick-up & trailer, Model No. 914	95	125	155

	C6	C8	C10
Farm Set, 1965, Teal and white, 5 pc. set includes #310 & trailer, #250 cub pick-up & trailer, Model No. 914	95	125	155
Farm Set, 1966, Green and yellow, 5 pc. set includes #194 & trailer, #310 & trailer, 4 animals, Model No. 937	95	125	155
Farm Set Showcase Display, 1965, Rare, boxed set for dealer trade show & store display, Model No. 9140	155	195	245
Farm Stake Truck & Horse Trailer, 1962, Red and white, 23.25Lx 6.25Wx6H, same as #312 plus tow behind trailer and 4 animals, Model No. 507	75	95	125
Farm Trailer Truck, 1958, Blue and red, 20.5Lx5.5Wx5.5H, with plastic animals and loading ramp, Model No. 945	75	115	155
Farm Truck, 1958, Green and red, 13Lx5.75Wx4.5H, with plastic farm animals, Model No. 938	65	95	125
Farm Truck & Trailer, 1958, Blue and yellow, 28Lx6Wx6.25H, pick-up with pick-up box trailer & plastic farm animals, Model No. 213	115	155	195
Fire Department Set, 1959, Red and white, 3 piece set, includes #701, #901, #303 (minus searchlight unit), Model No. 975	125	195	275
Fire Rescue Truck, 1961, Red, 12Lx5.75Wx5.25H, plastic hose reel with braided hose, two ladders, Model No. 307	35	65	95
Fire Rescue Truck, 1962, Red, 12Lx5.75Wx5.25H, plastic hose reel with braided hose, two ladders, Model No. 307	35	65	95
Fire Rescue Truck, 1963, Red, 12Lx5.75Wx5.25H, plastic hose reel with braided hose, two ladders, Model No. 307	35	65	95
Fire Rescue Truck, 1964, Red, 12Lx5.75Wx5.25H, plastic hose reel with braided hose, two ladders, Model No. 307	35	65	95
Fire Rescue Truck, 1964, Red, 8.75Lx3.5Wx3.5H, 2 plastic ladders, Model No. 105	15	35	65
Fire Rescue Truck, 1965, Red, 8.75Lx3.5Wx3.5H, 2 plastic ladders, Model No. 105	25	45	65
Fire Rescue Truck, 1965, Red, 13.25Lx5.75Wx5.75H, red light on roof (non-operable), 2 metal ladders, Model No. 308	45	75	105
Fire Rescue Truck, 1966, Red, 12.75Lx5.75Wx5.75H, red light on roof (non-operable) 3 ladders, sim. hose reel, Model No. 313	45	65	95
Fire Rescue Truck, 1966, Red, 8.75Lx3.5Wx3.5H, Kom-pak design with 2 ladders, Model No. 105	25	45	65
Fire Rescue Truck, 1967, Red, 12.75Lx5.75Wx5.75H, turbine cab. lever operated ladder, Model No. 453 .	55	75	95
Fire Rescue Truck, 1967, Red, 8.75Lx3.5Wx3.5H, Kom-pak design with 2 ladders, Model No. 121	25	45	65
Fire Rescue Truck, 1968, Red, 12.75Lx5.75Wx5.75H, turbine cab. lever operated ladder, Model No. 453 .	55	75	95

	C6	C8	C10
Fire Rescue Truck, 1968, Red, 8.75Lx3.5Wx3.5H, Kom-pak design with 2 ladders, Model No. 121	25	45	65
Fire Rescue Truck, 1969, Red and white, 12.5Lx6Wx6.5H, thunderbolt design with steer-o-matic front wheels, Model No. 653	25	35	45
Fisherman, 1962, Blue, 21.5Lx 4.5Wx5H, rampside truck towing boat and trailer, Model No. 202	45	65	85
Fisherman, 1963, Teal, 21.5Lx 4.5Wx5H, rampside truck towing boat and trailer, Model No. 204	45	65	85
Fisherman, 1964, Teal and red, 20Lx4.5Wx6H, rampside pick-up towing plastic boat on trailer, Model No. 204	35	65	85
Fisherman, 1965, Teal and red, 20Lx4.5Wx5H, rampside pick-up towing plastic boat on trailer, Model No. 204	35	65	85
Fisherman, 1966, Lt. blue and red, 20Lx4.5Wx5H, rampside pick-up towing plastic boat on trailer, Model No. 204	35	65	85
Fisherman, 1967, White and red, 20Lx5Wx4.75H, jeep towing plastic boat & trailer, no doors on jeep, Model No. 210	45	65	85
Fleetside Pick-Up, 1959, Copper and cream, 14.5Lx6Wx6H, 6 mini grocery box play freight, Model No. 202	45	75	95
Freight Hauler, 1956-57, Blue and yellow, 20.5Lx5.25Wx5.5H, with grocery freight, Model No. 935	75	105	155
Freight Trailer, 1954, Red and red, 17.75Lx5Wx4.5H, new pressed steel cab design, Model No. 930	115	155	195
Freight Trailer, 1955, Yellow and red, 17.75Lx5Wx4.5H, Model No. 930	115	155	195
Gasoline Truck, 1951, Red and red, 13.5Lx5.5Wx5H, wind-up motor, Model No. 866	135	195	255
Gasoline Truck, 1952, Red and red, 13.5Lx5.5Wx5H, wind-up motor, Model No. 866	135	195	255
Gasoline Truck, 1953, Red and red, 13.5Lx5.5Wx5H, wind-up motor, Model No. 866	135	195	255
Gasoline Truck, 1954, Red and red, 13.5Lx5.5Wx5H, wind-up motor, Model No. 866	135	195	255
Gasoline Truck, 1955, Red and yellow, 13.5Lx5Wx4.5H, non-wind-up model, Model No. 912	75	115	175
Gasoline Truck, 1956-57, Blue and yellow, 13.5Lx5Wx4.5H, Model No. 912	75	115	175
Gasoline Truck, 1958, Blue and yellow, 13.5Lx5Wx4.5H, Model No. 912	75	115	175
Giant 24-Pack Assortment, 1972, 17.75Lx16.5Wx16.5H, all 4 weird wheels designs in a store display - 24 cars total, Model No. 219	n/a	n/a	250
Giant 24-Pack Assortment, 1973, 17.75Lx16.5Wx16.5H, all 4 weird wheels designs in a store display - 24 cars total, Model No. 219	n/a	n/a	250
Giant Bulldozer, 1962, Orange, 11.5Lx7Wx5H, levers operate blade, rubber tracks, Model No. 405	55	75	95

	C6	C8	C10
Giant Bulldozer, 1963, Chartreuse, 11.5Lx7Wx5H, scarce chartreuse color - only used in 1963 production year, Model No. 405	55	75	95
Giant Bulldozer, 1964, Orange and black, 11.5Lx7Wx5H, blade raises and lowers with lever controls, Model No. 405	45	65	85
Giant Bulldozer, 1965, Orange and black, 11.5Lx7Wx5H, blade raises and lowers with lever controls, Model No. 405	45	65	85
Giant Bulldozer, 1966, Orange and black, 11.5Lx7Wx5H, blade raises and lowers with lever controls, Model No. 405	45	65	85
Giant Bulldozer, 1967, Orange and black, 11.5Lx7Wx5H, blade raises and lowers with lever controls, Model No. 514	45	65	85
Giant Bulldozer, 1968, Orange and black, 11.5Lx7Wx5H, blade raises and lowers with lever controls, Model No. 514	45	65	85
Giant Bulldozer, 1969, Red and yellow, 12Lx6.75Wx7H, blade raises and lowers with lever controls, Model No. 514	25	35	55
Giant Bulldozer, 1970, Lime green and yellow, 12Lx6.75Wx7H, blade raises and lowers with lever controls, Model No. 514	25	35	55
Giant Bulldozer, 1972, Yellow, 12Lx6.75Wx7H, blade raises and lowers with lever controls, Model No. 514	25	35	55
Giant Bulldozer, 1973, Yellow, 12Lx6.75Wx7H, "Structo 11" stencilled in black on blade, Model No. 514	25	35	55
Giant Bulldozer Truck & Trailer, 1962, Orange, 29Lx7.25Wx 6.25H, structo construction company on decals, Model No. 850	95	135	175
Giant Gantry Crane, 1972, Yellow, 32.5Lx12.25Wx14H, hand crank pulley system with crane mechanism, Model No. 555	25	35	45
Giant Gantry Crane, 1973, Yellow, 32.5Lx12.25Wx14H, hand crank pulley system with crane mechanism, Model No. 555	25	35	45
Gold Plated Cadillac, 1958, Gold, 6.75Lx2.25Wx2H, same as used on car carriers. 50th Anniversary decal on roof	125	175	225
Grading Service Set, 1962, Yellow and red, 25Lx6Wx5.75H, same truck as in #501 set plus #207 bulldozer on trailer, Model No. 701	75	105	135
Grain Trailer, 1953, White and orange, 20.75Lx5.5Wx5.5H, replaced freight trailer, sliding rear door, Model No. 704	95	155	205
Grain Trailer, 1954, White and orange, 20.75Lx5.5Wx5.5H, sliding rear door, Model No. 704	95	155	205
Grain Trailer, 1955, White and orange, 20.75Lx5.5Wx5.5H, shown in catalog with green cab but have not seen, Model No. 704	95	155	205
Green Beret Truck, 1967, Green, 8.75Lx3.5Wx4H, Kom-pak design with clear plastic cover 2 soldiers, Model No. 126	15	25	45
Guided Missile Launcher, 1959, Red and silver, 12.25Lx5.25W x10.25H, plastic missile launcher on bed, metal "S" grille, Model No. 203	75	95	125
Hammer Tower, 1960, Yellow and red, 6.5Lx4.75Wx9H, scarce, hammer button and marbles shoot up through tower, Model No. 110	35	55	75
Heavy Construction Set, 1967, Red and yellow, 4 pc. set includes #303, #432, #514 and barricade, Model No. 941	65	95	135
Heavy Construction Set, 1968, Red and yellow, 4 pc. set includes #270, #303, #514 and barricade, Model No. 941	65	95	135
Heavy Duty Dump Truck, 1958, Blue and orange, 20Lx6.75Wx 6.25H, spring dump action plus red light on roof, Model No. 200	75	105	135
Heavy Duty Steam Shovel, 1948, Blue, 21.5L x 6.25W x 7.75H, rubber tracks, Model No. 105	75	135	195
Heavy Duty Steam Shovel, 1949, Blue, 21.5Lx6.25Wx7.75H, rubber tracks, Model No. 105	75	135	195
Heavy Duty Steam Shovel, 1950, Blue, 21.5Lx6.25Wx7.75H, rubber tracks, Model No. 105	75	135	195
Heavy Duty Steam Shovel, 1951, Blue, 21.5Lx6.25Wx7.75H, Model No. 105	65	125	175
Heavy Duty Steam Shovel, 1952, Blue, 21.5Lx6.25Wx7.75H, Model No. 105	65	125	175
Heavy Duty Steam Shovel, 1956-57, Green and orange, 26.5Lx 7Wx6.75H, 2 cranks and rubber tracks, Model No. 106	55	95	125
Highway Builder Set, 1959, Varies, 11 pc. set includes #201, #205, #302, road signs, plastic workers, Model No. 900	95	155	195
Highway Builder Set, 1960, Copper, includes #209, #210, #305 plus road barricade, Model No. 903	95	135	175
Highway Builder Set, 1961, Copper, includes #206, #305, #309 plus road barricade, Model No. 905	95	135	175
Highway Builder Set, 1962, Varies, includes #207, #501 plus sand hopper and one barricade, Model No. 913	115	135	175
Highway Builder Set, 1963, Varies, includes #190 and #409, Model No. 913	115	135	175
Highway Builder Set, 1964, Varies, includes #207, #300, sand hopper, sand loader & barricade, Model No. 913	95	125	155
Highway Builder Set, 1965, Varies, includes #207, #300, sand hopper, sand loader & barricade, Model No. 913	95	125	155
Highway Builder Set, 1966, Green and yellow, 4 pc. set, includes #207, #316, sand hopper & sand loader, Model No. 910	95	125	155
Highway Builder Set, 1967, Green and yellow, 4 pc. set includes #183, #303, #501 and sand hopper, Model No. 909	65	85	115

	C6	C8	C10
Highway Builder Set, 1968, Yellow and green, 4 pc. set includes #183, #306 set, #501, Model No. 932	65	85	115
Highway Builder Set, 1969, Green and yellow, 4 pc. set includes #183, #306 set, #501, Model No. 932	55	75	105
Highway Builder Set, 1970, Green and yellow, 4 pc. set includes #183, #306 set, #501, Model No. 932	55	75	105
Highway Builder Set Showcase Display, 1965, Rare, boxed set for dealer trade show & store display, Model No. 9130	155	195	245
Highway Department Set, 1967, Red and yellow, 4 pc. set includes emergency, dump, wrecker & pickup trucks, Model No. 197	75	105	155
Highway Maintenance Service, 1958, Orange and green, 12Lx4.5Wx7H, with lift/swivel boom arm, Model No. 939	65	95	125
Highway Truck Assortment, 1959, Varies, 13 pc. set, includes #70, #76 plus 6-wheel truck, log truck & signs, Model No. 400	115	155	195
Hi-Lift Bulldozer, 1962, Yellow, 11.25Lx5.75Wx3.75H, rubber tracks, lever controls bucket, Model No. 207	25	55	75
Hi-Lift Bulldozer, 1963, Chartreuse, 11.25Lx5.75Wx 4H, scarce chartreuse color - only used in 1963 production year, Model No. 207	55	75	95
Hi-Lift Bulldozer, 1964, Yellow and black, 11.25Lx5.75Wx4H, metal levers operate the bucket, Model No. 207	25	45	75
Hi-Lift Bulldozer, 1965, Yellow and black, 11.25Lx5.75Wx4H, metal levers operate the bucket, Model No. 207	25	45	75
Hi-Lift Bulldozer, 1966, Orange and black, 11.25Lx5.75Wx4H, metal levers operate the bucket, Model No. 207	25	45	75
Hi-Lift Bulldozer, 1967, Orange and black, 11.25Lx5.75Wx4H, metal levers operate the bucket, Model No. 501	25	45	75
Hi-Lift Bulldozer, 1968, Orange and black, 11.25Lx5.75Wx4H, metal levers operate the bucket, Model No. 501	25	45	75
Hi-Lift Bulldozer, 1969, Orange and black, 12Lx6Wx6.5H, metal levers operate the bucket, Model No. 501	25	35	55
Hi-Lift Bulldozer, 1970, Lime green and yellow, 12Lx6Wx 6.5H, metal levers operate the bucket, Model No. 501	25	35	55
Hi-Lift Bulldozer, 1972, Yellow, 12Lx6Wx6.5H, metal levers operate the bucket, Model No. 501	25	35	55
Hi-Lift Bulldozer, 1973, Yellow, 12Lx6Wx6.5H, "Structo 11" stencilled in black on blade, Model No. 501	25	35	55
Hi-Lift Dump Truck, 1951, Red and blue, 12.5Lx5.5Wx5.25H, wind-up motor with scissors lift box, Model No. 844	105	155	215
Hi-Lift Dump Truck, 1952, Red and blue, 12.5Lx5.5Wx5.25H, wind-up motor with scissors lift box, Model No. 844	105	155	215

Structo Toys as shown in a 1929 Butler Bros. Christmas catalog.

	C6	C8	C10
Hi-Lift Dump Truck, 1953, White and red, 12.5Lx5.5Wx5.25H, wind-up motor with scissors lift box, Model No. 844	105	155	215
Hi-Lift Dump Truck, 1954, White and red, 12.5Lx5.5Wx5.25H, wind-up motor with scissors lift box, Model No. 844	105	155	215
Hi-Lift Dump Truck, 1955, Chrome and green, 12.5Lx 6Wx5H, same as #844 from past years. Mag wheels, Model No. 644	115	195	225
Hi-Lift Dump Truck, 1956-57, Chrome and blue, 12.5Lx 6Wx5H, same as #644 from 1955 only blue dump box, Model No. 644	115	195	225
Hi-Lift Dump Truck, 1958, Blue and yellow, 12Lx5.25Wx 5.75H, with scissors lift mechanism, Model No. 914	65	95	125
Hook and Ladder Truck, 1955, Red, 33.25Lx6.75Wx7H, with raising & two ladders, cast metal siren on roof, Model No. 260	95	155	205
Hook and Ladder Truck, 1956-57, Red, 33.25Lx6.75Wx7H, with raising & two ladders, cast metal siren on roof, Model No. 260	95	155	205
Hook and Ladder Truck, 1958, Red, 33.5Lx6Wx7H, with raising & two ladders, cast metal siren on roof, Model No. 261	95	155	205
Hurricane Construction Set, 1970, Orange and white, 3 pc. set including #841, sand hopper & 10 pc. Road sign set, Model No. 965	65	85	105

	C6	C8	C10
Hurricane Contractor Set, 1969, Dk orange and white, 2 pc. set contains #841 and #853 plus sand hopper and signs, Model No. 965	35	55	75
Hydraulic Cement Mixer, 1968, Green and yellow, 16.5Lx 6.5Wx7.5H, same as #270 but with hydraulic dump action on barrel, Model No. 271	45	65	85
Hydraulic Dump Trailer, 1958, Yellow and green, 20.5Lx 5.5Wx5.75H, with hydraulic lift arm on trailer dump, Model No. 941	115	155	195
Hydraulic Dump Truck, 1965, Red, 14Lx5.5Wx6.25H, hydraulic cylinder controls dump box, Model No. 401	35	55	75
Hydraulic Dump Truck, 1965, Grey and orange, 14Lx 5.5Wx 6.25H, hydraulic cylinder controls dump box, Model No. 425	45	65	85
Hydraulic Dump Truck, 1966, Met. blue, 13.75Lx5.5Wx6.25H, same body style as #316 but with hydraulic dump control, Model No. 419	35	55	75
Hydraulic Dump Truck, 1966, Grey and orange, 13.75Lx 5.5Wx6.25H, hydraulic cylinder dumps box, POW-R-R-R sound, Model No. 425	45	65	85
Hydraulic Dump Truck, 1967, Yellow and green, 12Lx 6Wx 6H, turbine cab. hydraulic controlled dump, Model No. 319	35	55	75
Hydraulic Dump Truck, 1967, Red and yellow, 13.5Lx5.5Wx 6.25H, hydraulic controlled dump box, Model No. 309	35	55	75
Hydraulic Dump Truck, 1967, Grey and yellow, 12.75Lx6Wx 6H, hydraulic dump box, POW-R-R-R sound, Model No. 423	45	65	85
Hydraulic Dump Truck, 1968, Red and yellow, 13.5Lx5.5Wx 6.25H, hydraulic controlled dump box, Model No. 309	35	55	75
Hydraulic Dump Truck, 1968, Grey and orange, 12.75Lx6Wx 6H, hydraulic dump box, POW-R-R-R sound, Model No. 423	45	65	85
Hydraulic Dump Truck, 1968, Yellow and green, 12Lx6Wx 6H, turbine cab. hydraulic controlled dump, Model No. 319	35	55	75
Hydraulic Dump Truck, 1969, Yellow and green, 13Lx 6Wx6H, typhoons design with hydraulic dump box, Model No. 319	25	35	45
Hydraulic Dump Truck, 1969, Dk. orange and white, 12.25Lx 5.5Wx6.25H, thunderbolt design with steer-o-matic front wheels, Model No. 626	25	35	45
Hydraulic Dump Truck, 1970, Yellow and green, 13Lx6Wx 6H, typhoons design with hydraulic dump box, Model No. 319	25	35	45
Hydraulic Dumper, 1960, Met. green, 14.75Lx6.25Wx6.5H, plastic mirrors, windshield wipers and horn, Model No. 404	35	55	75
Hydraulic Dumper, 1961, Met. green, 13.75Lx5.5Wx6.25H, hydraulic cylinder controls dump box, Model No. 407	35	65	85
Hydraulic Dumper, 1962, Green, 13.75Lx5.5Wx6.25H, hydraulic cylinder controls dump box, Model No. 407	35	55	75
Hydraulic Dumper, 1963, Red, 13.75Lx5.5Wx6.25H, hydraulic cylinder controls dump box, Model No. 401	35	55	75
Hydraulic Dumper, 1964, Copper, 13.75Lx5.5Wx6.25H, hydraulic cylinder controls dump box, Model No. 401	35	55	75
Hydraulic Hook & Ladder, 1959, Red and red, 31Lx6.25Wx 7.25H, open cab, plastic "S" grille, metal ladders, Model No. 901	75	115	135
Hydraulic Hook & Ladder, 1960, Red and red, 31Lx6.25Wx 7.25H, open cab, two metal ladders, hydraulic lift ladder, Model No. 901	75	125	175
Hydraulic Hook & Ladder Truck, 1958, Red, 33.25Lx6.75Wx7H, with raising & two ladders, red flashing light on roof, Model No. 266	95	175	215
Hydraulic Lift Dump Truck, 1955, Green and orange, 21Lx8Wx 7H, hydraulic dump lift arm on dump box, Model No. 250	95	155	205
Hydraulic Lift Dump Truck, 1956-57, Yellow and green, 21Lx 8Wx7H, hydraulic dump lift arm on dump box, Model No. 250	95	155	205
Hydraulic Lift Dump Truck, 1958, Orange and green, 21Lx8Wx 7H, hydraulic dump lift arm on dump box, Model No. 250	125	165	205
Hydraulic Sanitation Truck, 1959, Blue and white, 18Lx6Wx7.5H, hydraulic cylinder controls dump box, Model No. 454	65	95	125
Hydraulic Sanitation Truck, 1961, White, 18Lx6Wx8H, all white design, Model No. 606	55	95	115
Hydraulic Sanitation Truck, 1962, Grey and white, 18Lx6Wx8H, with manual lift arm that dumps into body, Model No. 606	75	105	125
Hydraulic Sanitation Truck, 1963, Blue and white, 18Lx6Wx8H, with manual lift arm that dumps into body, Model No. 602	75	105	125
Hydraulic Sanitation Truck, 1964, Grey and white, 18Lx6Wx8H, with manual lift arm that dumps into body, Model No. 602	75	105	125
Hydraulic Sanitation Truck, 1965, Grey and white, 18Lx6Wx8H, with manual lift arm that dumps into body, Model No. 604	55	75	95
Hydraulic Sanitation Truck, 1966, Grey and white, 18Lx6Wx8H, manual lift bucket dumps into body, POW-R-R-R sound, Model No. 604	55	75	95
Hydraulic Sanitation Truck, 1967, Grey and white, 16.5Lx5.75Wx 7.75H, manual lift bucket dumps into body, POW-R-R-R sound, Model No. 474	55	75	95
Hydraulic Sanitation Truck, 1968, Grey and white, 16.5Lx5.75Wx 7.75H, manual lift bucket dumps into body, Model No. 268	45	65	85

	C6	C8	C10
Hydraulic Trailer Dump, 1963, Chartreuse, 20.75Lx6.25Wx 5.75H, scarce chartreuse color - only used in 1963 production year, Model No. 603 .	65	95	125
Hydraulic Trailer Dump Truck, 1964, Grey and orange, 20.75Lx6.25Wx5.75H, also available as "Scotch-O-Lass" private label-add 50, Model No. 603	55	75	95
Hydraulic Trailer Dump Truck, 1965, Grey and orange, 20.75Lx5.75Wx5.75H, also available as "Scotch-O-Lass" private label - add 50, Model No. 603	55	75	95
Hydraulic Trailer Dump Truck, 1966, Grey and orange, 21.5Lx5.75Wx5.75H, turbine cab, hydraulic controlled dump, Model No. 610	45	65	85
Ice Cream Truck, 1966, White and teal, 12Lx6Wx6.5H, scarce, bell rings as truck moves, built-in coolers & detail, Model No. 712	75	115	155
Jack And Jill Pump, 1960, Copper and yellow, 8Lx4.25Wx 11.25H, scarce, plastic marble toy, structo pre-school series, Model No. 112	75	95	115
Kennel Truck, 1966, Teal and white, 8.75Lx3.5Wx4H, Kom-pak design with clear cover and 6 dogs, Model No. 130	15	35	55
Kennel Truck, 1967, Yellow, 8.75Lx3.5Wx4H, Kom-pak design with clear cover and 6 dogs, Model No. 137	15	35	55
Kennel Truck, 1968, Yellow, 8.75Lx3.5Wx4H, Kom-pak design with clear cover and 6 dogs, Model No. 137	15	35	55

Structo, circa the early 1930s.

	C6	C8	C10
Kenya Karryall, 1967, Green and yellow, 9.25Lx4.25Wx4.25H, scarce, Kom-pak design, 4 cages with 4 hand-painted wild animals, Model No. 176	45	75	115
Kenya Karryall, 1968, Green and yellow, 9.25Lx4.25Wx4.25H, scarce, Kom-pak design, 4 cages with 4 hand-painted wild animals, Model No. 176	45	75	105
Kitchen Ensemble, 1960, Pink and grey, individual appliances still available, see 1959 for values	15	35	55
Kitchen Ensemble, 1960, Pink and grey, 3 pc. set, includes #8, #12, #4- 1959 models, Model No. 23	75	125	155
Kitchen-Laundry Ensemble, 1959, Pink and grey, 9 piece 1/4 scale set, Model No. 50	95	155	195
Kitchen-Laundry Ensemble, 1960, Pink and grey, 5 pc. set, includes #8, #12, #4, #10, #16- 1959 models, Model No. 25	95	155	175
Kom-pak Animal Set, 1968, Teal and white, 4 pc. set includes #137, #163, 6 dogs, 4 ponies & fence coral, Model No. 196	55	85	115
Kompak Assortment, 1965, Varies, 3 pc. set includes #100, #105, #110, Model No. 170	55	85	125
Kom-pak Contractor Set, 1968, Green and yellow, 4 pc. set includes #153, #183, #184, Model No. 193	55	85	115
Kom-pak Pony Van, 1968, Teal and teal, 16.5Lx3.5Wx4.5H, clear roof on trailer with coral & 3 ponies, Model No. 163	35	55	75
Kom-pak Sandy, 1968, Green and yellow, 8.75Lx3.5Wx3.5H, Kom-pak design with plastic sand hopper, Model No. 184	25	45	65
Kom-pak Sandy, 1969, Green and yellow, 9Lx5.25Wx8.5H, Kom-pak design, Model No. 184	25	35	45
Kom-pak Sandy, 1970, Green and yellow, 9Lx5.25Wx8.5H, Kom-pak design, Model No. 184	25	35	45
Kom-pak Sandy, 1972, Yellow, 9Lx5.25Wx8.5H, sand hopper and dump truck, Model No. 184	15	25	35
Kom-pak Sandy, 1973, Yellow and orange, 8.5Lx5.5Wx9.5H, sand hopper and dump truck, Model No. 184	15	25	35
Lad-A-Bout, 1970, Lime green and white, 9.5Lx4.5Wx5.25H, sport model design with 5" black male doll, Model No. 769	35	45	55
Litter Picker, 1972, Chrome and orange, 2.75Lx3.5Wx3H, 2 wheeled design with trash can style, Model No. 252	10	15	20
Litter Picker, 1973, White and orange, 2.75Lx3.5Wx3H, 2 wheeled design with trash can style with propeller, Model No. 252	10	15	20
Little Miss Structo Washer/Dryer, 1962, Teal, 7.25Lx8Wx10H, washes & spins, battery operated, Model No. 16	15	25	55
Little Miss Structo Washer/Dryer, 1963, Teal, 7.25Lx8Wx10H, washes & spins, battery operated, Model No. 16.	15	25	55

	C6	C8	C10
Livestock Set, 1965, Teal and white, 22.25Lx6.5Wx8H, white insert panels in side of trailer, 5 pc. fence & 4 animals, Model No. 505	45	65	85
Livestock Truck, 1960, Red and white, 14.75Lx6Wx7.25H, white plastic stake panels and 2 plastic animals, Model No. 306	35	55	75
Livestock Truck, 1961, Red and white, 14.5Lx6.25Wx7.5H, stake truck with 2 plastic animals, Model No. 306	35	65	85
Livestock Truck, 1962, Red and white, 14.75Lx6.25Wx5.5H, white metal stake panels, Model No. 312	55	75	95
Livestock Truck, 1964, Blue and white, 14.75Lx6.25Wx5.5H, white metal stake panels, 2 plastic cows, Model No. 314	55	75	95
Livestock Truck, 1965, Blue and white, 14.75Lx6.25Wx5.5H, white stakes, 5 pc. plastic fence, 4 animals, Model No. 310	55	75	95
Livestock Truck, 1967, Red and yellow, 14.75Lx3.25Wx5.5H, yellow metal panels, Model No. 260	25	45	65
Livestock Truck, 1968, Red and yellow, 14.75Lx3.25Wx5.5H, yellow metal panels, Model No. 260	25	45	65
Livestock Truck, 1969, Teal and white, 9.5Lx4.25Wx4H, hurricanes design with white stake panels and 5 animals, Model No. 870	15	25	35
Livestock Truck, 1970, Green and white, 9.5Lx4.25Wx4H, hurricanes design with white stake panels and 5 animals, Model No. 870	15	25	35
Livestock Truck, 1972, Blue and white, 9.5Lx4.25Wx4H, hurricanes design with white panels and 5 animals, Model No. 870	10	20	30
Livestock Truck, 1973, Blue and white, 9.5Lx4.25Wx4H, hurricanes design with white panels and 5 animals, Model No. 870	10	20	30
Livestock Truck Set, 1966, Teal and white, 14.75Lx6.25Wx 5.5H, white stakes, 5 pc. plastic fence, 2 plastic cows, Model No. 310	35	65	85
Livestock Van, 1966, Teal and white, 22.25Lx6.5Wx8H, white insert panels in side of trailer, 5 pc. fence & 4 animals, Model No. 505	45	65	85
Livestock Van, 1967, Teal and white, 21.25Lx7.75Wx5.75H, turbine cab, white panels on side of trailer, Model No. 344	55	75	95
Livestock Van, 1968, Teal and white, 21.25Lx7.75Wx5.75H, turbine cab. white panels on side of trailer, Model No. 344	55	75	95
Livestock Van, 1969, Teal and white, 21.75Lx5.5Wx7.5H, typhoons design with fifth wheel detail, Model No. 344	25	35	45
Livetstock Truck, 1963, Blue and white, 14.75Lx6.25Wx5.5H, white metal stake panels, Model No. 314	55	75	95
Log Trailer, 1954, Orange and orange, 17.75Lx5Wx4.5H, with five wooden logs, Model No. 940	115	155	195
Log Trailer, 1955, Green and orange, 17.75Lx5Wx4.5H, with five wooden logs, Model No. 940	115	155	195
Loonie Looper, 1972, Yellow and orange, 2.75Lx3.5Wx3H, 2 wheeled design with airplane styling including propeller, Model No. 251	10	15	20
Loonie Looper, 1973, Yellow and orange, 2.75Lx3.5Wx3H, 2 wheeled design with airplane styling including propeller, Model No. 251	10	15	20
Lumber Truck, 1954, Red and blue, 10.5Lx3.5Wx3.25H, with five wooden logs, Model No. 77	35	55	75
Lumber Truck, 1956-57, Red and blue, 10.5Lx3.5Wx3.25H, with five wooden logs, Model No. 77	35	55	75
Machinery Hauler, 1960, Copper, 19.5Lx7.5Wx6.5H, includes #210 dozer, Model No. 509	55	75	95
Machinery Hauling Truck, 1954, Red and yellow, 12.5Lx5.5Wx 4H, flatbed with winch and "S" grill cab, Model No. 151	75	125	155
Machinery Hauling Truck, 1956-57, Red and yellow, 12.5Lx 5.5Wx4H, flatbed with winch and "S" grill cab, Model No. 151	75	125	155
Machinery Truck, 1951, orange and blue, 12.75Lx5.5Wx5H, with loading ramp and chain winch, Model No. 607	95	155	205
Machinery Truck, 1952, Orange and blue, 12.75Lx5.5Wx5H, with loading ramp and chain winch, Model No. 607	95	155	205
Machinery Truck, 1954, White and blue, 12.75Lx5.5Wx5H, rare, made only in 1954. Hubcaps, loading ramp, Model No. 607	95	155	205
Machinery Truck & Steam Shovel, 1948, Orange and blue, 21.5Lx6.75Wx6.25H, comes 2/#105 steam shovel & loading ramp, Model No. 402	115	175	245
Machinery Truck & Steam Shovel, 1949, Orange and blue, 21.5Lx6.75Wx6.25H, comes w/#105 steam shovel & loading ramp, Model No. 402	115	175	245
Machinery Truck & Steam Shovel, 1950, Orange and blue, 21.5Lx6.75Wx6.25H, comes w/#105 steam shovel & loading ramp, Model No. 402	115	175	245
Machinery Truck & Steam Shovel, 1951, Orange and blue, 21.5Lx6.75Wx6.25H, with plastic fireball motor under the hood, Model No. 402	100	155	195
Machinery Truck & Steam Shovel, 1952, Orange and blue, 21.5Lx6.75Wx6.25H, with plastic fireball motor under the hood, Model No. 402	100	155	195
Machinery Truck & Steam Shovel, 1953, Orange and blue, 21.5Lx6.75Wx6.25H, comes w/#105 steam shovel & loading ramp, Model No. 402	95	155	195
Machinery Truck & Steam Shovel, 1954, Orange and blue, 26.5Lx6.75Wx14.25H, comes w/#105 steam shovel & loading ramp, Model No. 402	95	155	195

Structo catalog from 1939. Photo courtesy Randy Prasse

	C6	C8	C10
Mechanical Hydraulic Dump, 1959, Red and white, 12.25Lx 5.25Wx5.5H, scarce, hydraulic cylinder controls dump box, Model No. 204	75	115	135
Merry-Go-Round, 1969, Yellow and red, 9.5Lx4.25Wx5.75H, hurricanes design with carousel, Model No. 874	25	35	45
Minuteman Tow Truck, 1969, Dk. orange, 9.25Lx4Wx4H, hurricanes design with crank operated tow rope, Model No. 812	15	25	35
Minuteman Tow Truck, 1970, Dk. orange, 9.25Lx4Wx4H, hurricanes design with crank operated tow rope, Model No. 812	15	25	35
Mobile Anti-Missile Unit, 1959, Blue and yellow, 27Lx7.5Wx 11.25H, scarce, battery op spotlight & missile launcher on trailer, Model No. 620	85	115	175
Mobile Communications Center, 1958, Red and blue, 20Lx 6.25Wx6.25H, includes antenna tower & morse code buttons, Model No. 270	115	155	195
Mobile Crane, 1959, Green and yellow, 19.25Lx6.25Wx7.25H, battery operated boom and cab, Model No. 902	85	135	195
Mobile Crane, 1960, Copper and yellow, 19.25Lx6.25Wx7.25H, half-track with single-driver cab, Model No. 800	75	115	135
Mobile Crane, 1961, Yellow, 15.5Lx6.5Wx7.25H, double cranks control crane arm and clam bucket, Model No. 700	55	95	115
Mobile Crane, 1962, Yellow, 15.5Lx6.5Wx7.25H, double cranks			

	C6	C8	C10
control crane arm and clam bucket, Model No. 800	55	95	115
Mobile Crane, 1963, Chartreuse, 15.5Lx6.5Wx7.25H, scarce chartreuse color - only used in 1963 production year, Model No. 801	75	105	155
Mobile Crane, 1964, Orange, 15.5Lx 6.5Wx7.25H, cranks control the boom and clam bucket, swivels, Model No. 801	75	95	125
Mobile Crane, 1965, Orange, 16.5Lx 5.5Wx7H, cranks control the boom and clam bucket, swivels, Model No. 801	75	95	125
Mobile Crane, 1966, Orange, 16.5Lx 5.5Wx7H, cranks control the boom and clam bucket, swivels, Model No. 801	75	95	125
Mobile Merry-Go-Round Truck, 1967, Yellow and red, 9.25Lx 4.25Wx5.75H, scarce, Kom-pak design, circus carousel spins when truck moves, Model No. 174	55	85	125
Mobile Merry-Go-Round Truck, 1968, Yellow and red, 9.25Lx 4.25Wx5.75H, scarce, Kom-pak design, circus carousel spins when truck moves, Model No. 174	55	85	125
Mobile Outer Space Launcher, 1959, Red and blue, 19.5Lx6Wx12.75H, scarce, 2 plastic missiles launch. Launcher swivels, Model No. 503	95	135	195
Mobile Power Shovel Unit, 1958, Green and yellow, 32.5Lx 6.75Wx8H, half-track truck with steam shovel on back, Model No. 272	95	155	205
Mobile Steam Shovel Unit, 1956-57, Green and yellow, 32.5Lx 6.75Wx8H, half-track truck with steam shovel on back, Model No. 272	95	155	205
Monster Machine, 1971, Green, 2.75Lx3.5Wx3H, 2 wheeled design with exposed "Chrome" engine, Model No. 215	10	15	20
Monster Machine, 1972, Green, 2.75Lx3.5Wx3H, 2 wheeled design with exposed "Chrome" engine, Model No. 215	10	15	20
Monster Machine, 1973, Green, 2.75Lx3.5Wx3H, 2 wheeled design with exposed "Chrome" engine, Model No. 215	10	15	20
Motor Express Truck, 1951, Grey and orange, 12.75Lx5.5Wx5H, cast cab "Freeport Motor Express" decals, Model No. 601	75	125	195
Motor Express Truck, 1952, Grey and orange, 12.75Lx5.5Wx5H, cast cab "Freeport Motor Express" decals, Model No. 601	75	125	195
Motor Express Truck, 1953, White and red, 12.75Lx5.5Wx5H, cast cab "Freeport Motor Express" decals, Model No. 601	75	125	195
Motor Express Truck, 1954, Yellow and blue, 12.5Lx 5.25Wx4.5H, stake truck with "S" grill cab, Model No. 150	75	125	155
Motor Express Truck, 1956-57, Yellow and blue, 12.5Lx 5.25Wx4.5H, stake truck with "S" grill cab, Model No. 150	75	125	155

	C6	C8	C10
Motorized Giant Gantry Crane, 1973, Blue and yellow, 32.5Lx 12.25Wx14H, motor operates all action, battery operated, Model No. 558	35	45	55
Nationwide Rental Truck & Trailer, 1962, Green and yellow, 21Lx5.75Wx5.5H, scarce, same design as #311 plus tow behind trailer, Model No. 500	75	125	155
Nationwide Rental Truck & Trailer, 1963, Green and yellow, 21Lx5.75Wx5.5H, scarce, same design as #311 plus tow behind trailer, Model No. 500	75	125	155
Nationwide Rental Truck & Trailer Set, 1962, Green and yellow, scarce, same as #500 set plus larger open trailer, Model No. 904	115	155	195
Nationwide Rental Truck & Trailer Set, 1963, Green and yellow, scarce, same as #500 set plus larger open trailer, Model No. 904	115	155	195
Overland Freight Trailer, 1951, Blue and orange, 20.75Lx 5.5Wx5.5H, blue cast cab with orange stake trailer, Model No. 704	115	175	225
Overland Freight Trailer, 1952, Blue and orange, 20.75Lx 5.5Wx5.5H, blue cast cab with orange stake trailer, Model No. 704	115	175	225
Package Delivery Truck, 1951, Orange and green, 13Lx5.5Wx 5H, cast cab, tail gate with chain, Model No. 603	75	125	195
Package Delivery Truck, 1952, Orange and green, 13Lx5.5Wx 5H, cast cab, tail gate with chain, Model No. 603	75	125	195
Package Delivery Truck, 1953, White and orange, 13Lx5.5Wx 5H, cast cab, tail gate with chain, w/hubcaps, Model No. 603	75	125	195
Package Delivery Truck, 1954, White and orange, 13Lx5.5Wx 5H, cast cab, tail gate with chain, w/hubcaps, Model No. 603	75	125	195
Package Delivery Truck, 1955, Yellow and green, 13Lx5.5Wx 4.75H, with tailgate and chains, Model No. 911	55	95	155
Package Delivery Truck, 1956-57, Blue and yellow, 13Lx5.5Wx 4.75H, with tailgate and chains, Model No. 911	55	95	155
Panic Panel, 1971, Orange, 2.75Lx 3.5Wx3H, 2 wheeled design with panel wagon sides, Model No. 216	10	15	20
Panic Panel, 1972, Orange, 2.75Lx 3.5Wx3H, 2 wheeled design with panel wagon sides, Model No. 216	10	15	20
Panic Panel, 1973, Orange, 2.75Lx 3.5Wx3H, 2 wheeled design with panel wagon sides, Model No. 216	10	15	20
Parcel Service Truck, 1958, Yellow and green, 12.25Lx 5.25Wx7H, with mini grocery freight, Model No. 942	75	115	155
Paving Department, 1962, Varies, same as #913 but #408 replaces sand loader trailer, Model No. 916	125	155	195
Paving Department, 1963, Varies, includes #190, #305, #400, #401, #408, Model No. 916	115	135	175
Pickup, 1964, Red and yellow, 8.75Lx3.5Wx3.5H, metal with rubber tires, Model No. 100	15	25	55
Pickup, 1967, Green, 8.75Lx 3.5Wx3.5H, Kom-pak design, Model No. 101	15	25	45
Pickup, 1968, Teal, 8.75Lx3.5Wx 3.5H, Kom-pak design, Model No. 101	15	25	45
Pickup And Delivery, 1960, Met. green, 14Lx5.75Wx6.5H, whitewall tires, plastic horn on roof, Model No. 207	45	75	95
Pickup Truck, 1966, Teal, 8.75Lx 3.5Wx3.5H, Kom-pak design, Model No. 100	15	25	45
Pick-Up Truck, 1954, Various, 6.5Lx2.5Wx2.25H, same scale as appear on auto transport set, Model No. 21	15	25	35
Pick-Up Truck, 1958, Red and yellow, 19.25Lx6.5Wx6H, includes mini grocery freight, Model No. 210	95	125	155
Pick-Up Truck, 1963, Red, 13.25Lx5.25Wx5.5H, Model No. 311	35	65	85
Pick-Up Truck, 1964, Red, 13.25Lx 5.25Wx5.5H, plastic window, yellow interior, whitewall tires, Model No. 311	55	75	95
Pick-Up Truck, 1965, Teal and white, 8.75Lx3.5Wx3.5H, metal with rubber tires, Model No. 100	15	25	55
Pick-Up Truck With Horse Van, 1958, Blue and yellow, 10.5Lx 2.5Wx3H, includes 2 plastic horses, Model No. 100	55	85	105
Pipe-Layer Set, 1970, Blue and white, 20Lx3.25Wx4.25H, road tow'ds design with grab bucket & dual trailers in tow, Model No. 285	15	25	35
Pipe-Layer Set, 1972, Blue and white, 20Lx3.25Wx4.25H, road tow'ds design with grab bucket & dual trailers in tow, Model No. 285	15	25	35
Police Emergency Truck, 1966, Blue and white, 12Lx6Wx7.5H, bell rings as truck moves, 3 ladders, hose reel, Model No. 716	55	95	125
Police Emergency Truck, 1967, Blue and white, 12Lx6Wx7.5H, bell rings as truck moves, 3 ladders, hosse reel, Model No. 727	55	95	125
Police Emergency Truck, 1968, Blue and white, 12Lx6Wx7.5H, bell rings as truck moves, 3 ladders, hose reel, Model No. 727	55	95	125
Pony Van, 1969, Lime green, 16.5Lx3.25Wx5H, Kom-pak design with clear roof on trailer and 3 colts, Model No. 163	25	35	45
Pony Van, 1970, Lime green, 16.5Lx3.25Wx5H, Kom-pak design with clear roof on trailer and 3 colts, Model No. 163	25	35	45
Power Shovel, 1958, Orange, 26.5Lx7Wx6.75H, 2 cranks and rubber tracks, Model No. 106	55	95	115
Power Shovel, 1959, Copper, 26.5Lx7Wx6.75H, rubber tracks, Model No. 302	35	55	75
Power Shovel, 1960, Yellow, 26.5Lx7Wx6.75H, black rubber tracks, Model No. 305	35	55	75
Power Shovel, 1961, Yellow, 26.5Lx7.5Wx7H, rubber tracks, Model No. 305	35	55	75
Power Shovel, 1962, Yellow, 26.5Lx7.5Wx7H, rubber tracks, Model No. 305	35	55	75

	C6	C8	C10
Power Shovel, 1963, Chartreuse, 26.5Lx7.25Wx7H, scarce chartreuse color - only used in 1963 production year, Model No. 305	55	75	95
Power Shovel, 1964, Yellow, 26.5Lx7.25Wx7H, rubber tracks, 2 cranks operate boom and bucket, Model No. 305	35	65	85
Power Shovel, 1965, Orange, 26.5Lx7.25Wx7H, rubber tracks, 2 cranks operate boom and bucket, Model No. 305	35	55	75
Power Shovel, 1966, Orange, 26.5Lx7.25Wx7H, rubber tracks, 2 cranks operate boom and bucket, Model No. 305	35	55	75
Power Wrecker, 1960, Blue and white, 23Lx7Wx9.25H, battery operated winch & lights, Model No. 802	75	125	175
Propur-T, 1973, Blue and white, 10Lx4.5Wx5.75H, new design for 1973, Model No. 768	25	35	45
Pumper, 1960, White, 19.75Lx7.25Wx6H, scarce, open cab, operating water tank and hose, Model No. 603	95	125	175
Pumper, 1961, Red, 19.5Lx7.25Wx6.5H, operating water tank and hose, two ladders, Model No. 708	55	95	125
Pumper, 1962, Red, 19.5Lx7.25Wx6.5H, operating water tank and hose, two ladders, Model No. 708	55	95	125
Pumper Fire Truck, 1959, Red and red, 20Lx7.25Wx6H, open cab, plastic "S" grille, sprays water through hose, Model No. 701	55	95	155
Pumper Fire Truck W/Light, 1958, Red, 22.75Lx7.25Wx7H, pumps water through truck & hydrant, flashing light, Model No. 262	105	165	205
Race-A-Roo, 1970, Gold and white, 9.5Lx4.5Wx5H, sport model design with 5" white male doll, Model No. 760	25	35	45
Rampside Pick-Up, 1961, Copper, 10.5Lx4.5Wx5H, plastic bed liner and drop-down door in side of bed, Model No. 195	35	55	75
Rampside Pick-Up, 1962, Red, 10.5Lx4.5Wx5H, plastic bed liner and drop-down door in side of bed, Model No. 195	35	55	75
Rampside Pick-Up, 1963, Red, 10.5Lx4.5Wx5H, plastic bed liner and drop-down door in side of bed, Model No. 194	35	55	75
Rampside Pick-Up, 1964, Copper, 10.5Lx4.5Wx5H, plastic bed liner and drop-down door in side of bed, Model No. 194	25	55	75
Rampside Pick-Up, 1965, Copper, 10.5Lx4.5Wx5H, plastic bed liner and drop-down door in side of bed, Model No. 194	25	55	75
Rampside Pick-Up, 1966, Red, 10.5Lx4.5Wx5H, plastic bed liner and drop-down door in side of bed, Model No. 194	25	45	65
Rampside Pick-Up, 1967, Red, 10.5Lx4.5Wx5H, plastic bed liner and drop-down door in side of bed, Model No. 230	25	45	65

	C6	C8	C10
Rampside Pick-Up, 1968, Red, 10.5Lx4.5Wx5H, plastic bed liner and drop-down door in side of bed, Model No. 230	25	45	65
Rampside Pick-Up, 1969, Gold and white, 10.5Lx4.75W5.25H, typhoons design with white plastic bed liner, Model No. 230	25	35	45
Ready Mix Concrete Truck, 1956-57, Red and yellow, 21.5Lx7.5Wx9.25H, with gear on barrel, driven by axle, Model No. 271	75	105	155
Ready Mix Concrete Truck, 1958, Green and orange, 21.5Lx7.5Wx9.25H, with gear on barrel, driven by axle, Model No. 271	75	105	175
Ready Mix Concrete Truck, 1960, Teal and white, 16Lx7.5Wx9H, axle driven gear operates barrel, Model No. 604	55	75	95
Ready Mix Concrete Truck, 1962, Red and white, 15.5Lx6.75Wx7.25H, axle driven gear operates barrel, Model No. 408	35	55	75
Ready-Mix Concrete Truck, 1959, Copper and cream, 20.75Lx7.5Wx9.25H, gear powered barrel, runs off axle, Model No. 700	55	85	125
Ready-Mix Concrete Truck, 1961, Red and white, 15.5Lx7.75Wx9H, axle driven gear operates barrel, Model No. 609	55	95	115
Ready-Mix Concrete Truck, 1963, Green and chartreuse, 15.5Lx6.75Wx7.25H, axle driven gear operates barrel, Model No. 408	35	55	75
Ready-Mix Concrete Truck, 1964, Red and yellow, 15.5Lx6.75Wx7.25H, axle driven gear operates barrel, Model No. 408	35	55	75

Structo Toys as shown in the 1940-41 L. Gould catalog.

	C6	C8	C10
Refrigerated Express Truck, 1958, Yellow and brown, 21Lx5Wx 7.5H, transport trailer with refrigerator unit on front, Model No. 951	95	155	195
Ride 'Em Air Force Jeep, 1958, Blue and red, 25.5Lx11Wx 14.5H, with steering wheel and fold-down windshield, Model No. 995	105	175	215
Ride 'Em Dump Truck, 1958, Blue and yellow, 20.5Lx7.75Wx 10.25H, with seat and steering wheel, Model No. 990	95	155	195
Ride-er Air Force Jeep, 1959, Blue and red, 25.75Lx10.25Wx18H, missile launcher and missiles on hood, trunk opens, Model No. 950	75	115	175
Ride-er Chief's Car, 1966, Red and white, 25.5Lx10.25Wx12.75H, bell rings when string is pulled, Model No. 921	75	105	155
Ride-er Doodle Bug, 1963, Yellow, 25.5Lx10.25Wx 12.75H, same as ride-er fire truck from 1962, Model No. 925	75	105	135
Ride-er Doodle Bug, 1964, Yellow, 25.5Lx10.25Wx 12.75H, Model No. 925	75	105	135
Ride-er Doodle Bug, 1965, Teal and white, 25.5Lx10.25Wx 12.75H, Model No. 925	75	105	135
Ride-er Dump Truck, 1959, Blue and yellow, 20Lx7.75Wx10H, metal seat in dump box, bulb horn on steering wheel, Model No. 505	55	95	125
Ride-er Dump Truck, 1960, Blue and white, 20Lx7.75Wx10H, metal seat in dump box and bulb horn on steering wheel, Model No. 605	55	75	95
Ride-er Dump Truck, 1963, Red and white, 20Lx7.75Wx 10.25H, metal seat in dump box, Model No. 605	75	105	135
Ride-er Dump Truck, 1964, Red and white, 20Lx7Wx10.25H, metal seat in dump box, Model No. 605	75	105	135
Ride-er Dump Truck, 1965, Teal and white, 20Lx7Wx10.25H, metal seat in dump box, Model No. 605	75	105	135
Ride-er Dump Truck, 1966, White and green, 20Lx7Wx10.25H, metal seat in dump box, Model No. 605	55	85	115
Ride-er Fire Truck, 1959, Red and white, 25.5Lx10.5Wx12.75H, crank siren on hood, trunk opens, Model No. 925	75	115	155
Ride-er Fire Truck, 1960, Red and white, 25.5Lx10.5Wx12.75H, crank siren on hood, trunk opens, Model No. 925	75	115	155
Ride-er Fire Truck, 1961, Red and white, 25.5Lx10.5Wx12.75H, crank siren on hood, trunk opens, Model No. 925	75	105	135
Ride-er Fire Truck, 1962, Red and white, 25.5Lx10.5Wx12.75H, crank siren on hood, trunk opens, Model No. 925	75	105	135
Ride-er Wrecker Truck, 1961, Copper and white, 23.5Lx 7.75Wx10.25H, metal seat and crank operated boom in box, Model No. 607	55	95	125
Ride-er Wrecker Truck, 1962, Red and yellow, 23.5Lx7.5Wx 10.25H, metal seat and crank operated tow boom in box, Model No. 607	55	95	125
Riding Academy, 1965, Teal and teal, 20Lx4.75Wx6H, #250 cub pick-up plus horse trailer, 2 plastic horses, Model No. 252	55	75	95
Riding Academy, 1966, Teal and teal, 18Lx4.75Wx6H, #194 rampside pick-up plus horse trailer, 2 plastic horses, Model No. 254	55	75	95
Road Boss Car Carrier, 1972, Orange, 22.5Lx5.5Wx5.5H, with chrome stacks and air horn detail plus 3 cars, Model No. 335	35	45	55
Road Boss Car Carrier, 1973, Blue and yellow, 22.5Lx5.5Wx5.5H, with chrome stacks and air horn detail plus 3 cars, Model No. 335	35	45	55
Road Boss Hydraulic Dump, 1972, Orange, 13.25Lx5.25Wx6.25H, with chrome stacks and air horn detail, Model No. 327	25	35	45
Road Boss Hydraulic Dump, 1973, Blue and yellow, 13.25Lx 5.5Wx6.25H, with chrome stacks and air horn detail, Model No. 327	25	35	45
Road Boss Pipeline Transport, 1973, Blue and yellow, 21.75Lx5.5Wx6.5H, with chrome stacks and air horn detail, same as #328, Model No. 323	25	35	45
Road Boss Timber Toter, 1972, Orange, 21.75Lx5.5Wx6.5H, with chrome stacks and air horn detail, Model No. 328	35	45	55
Road Boss Timber Toter, 1973, Blue and yellow, 21.75Lx 5.5Wx6.5H, with chrome stacks and air horn detail, same as #323, Model No. 328	35	45	55
Road Boss Tractor Trailer Truck, 1972, Orange, 22Lx5.5Wx8H, with chrome stacks and air horn detail, Model No. 329	35	45	55
Road Boss Tractor Trailer Truck, 1973, Blue and yellow, 22Lx5.5Wx8H, with chrome stacks and air horn detail, Model No. 329	35	45	55
Road Boss Vista Dome Horse Van, 1972, Orange, 22Lx5.5Wx6H, with chrome stacks and air horn detail plus 4 black horses, Model No. 324	35	45	55
Road Boss Vista-Dome Horse Van, 1973, Blue and yellow, 22Lx 5.5Wx6H, with chrome stacks and air horn detail, 4 black horses, Model No. 324	25	35	45
Road Builder Set, 1962, Red and yellow, same as #913 set plus #400, Model No. 915	125	155	195
Road Grader, 1951, Orange, 18Lx7Wx7.5H, with plastic fireball motor under the hood, Model No. 300	55	85	105
Road Grader, 1952, Orange, 18Lx7Wx7.5H, with plastic fireball motor under the hood, Model No. 300	55	85	105
Road Grader, 1953, Orange, 18Lx7Wx7.5H, with plastic fireball motor under the hood, Model No. 300	55	85	105
Road Grader, 1953, Orange, 18Lx7Wx7.5H, with plastic fireball motor under the hood, Model No. 300	55	85	105
Road Grader, 1955, Orange, 18Lx7Wx7.5H, with plastic fireball motor under the hood, Model No. 300	55	85	105
Road Grader, 1956-57, Green, 18Lx7Wx7.5H, with plastic fireball motor under the hood, Model No. 300	55	85	105
Road Grader, 1960, Yellow, 18.75Lx7.25Wx7.5H, black tires and motor, scraper blade lifts with levers, Model No. 301	35	55	75

	C6	C8	C10
Road Grader, 1961, Yellow, 18.75Lx7Wx7.5H, plastic tires, Model No. 301	25	45	65
Road Grader, 1962, Yellow, 19Lx7.5Wx8H, covered cab, plated blade, black plastic tires, Model No. 400	55	75	95
Road Grader, 1963, Chartreuse, 19Lx7.5Wx8H, scarce chartreuse color - only used in 1963 production year, Model No. 400	55	75	95
Road Grader, 1964, Orange, 19Lx7.5Wx8.25H, plated scraper blade, black plastic wheels & engine, Model No. 400	45	65	85
Road Grader, 1965, Orange and black, 11.75Lx4Wx4H, new z-z-z sound when unit rolls, no batteries, Model No. 140	15	35	65
Road Grader, 1965, Orange, 19Lx7.5Wx8.25H, plated scraper blade, black plastic wheels & engine, Model No. 400	45	65	85
Road Grader, 1966, Orange, 19Lx7.5Wx8.25H, plated scraper blade, black plastic wheels & engine, Model No. 400	35	55	75
Road Grader, 1966, Orange, 11.75Lx5Wx4.75H, Kom-pak design, Model No. 140	15	25	45
Road Grader, 1967, Orange, 19Lx7.5Wx8H, plated scraper blade, black plastic wheels & engine, Model No. 527	35	55	75
Road Grader, 1967, Orange, 11.75Lx5Wx4.75H, Kom-pak design, Model No. 183	15	25	45
Road Grader, 1968, Orange, 11.75Lx5Wx4.75H, Kom-pak design, Model No. 183	15	25	45
Road Grader, 1968, Orange, 19Lx7.5Wx8H, plated scraper blade, black plastic wheels & engine, Model No. 527	35	55	75
Road Grader, 1969, Orange, 11.75Lx5Wx6H, black plastic wheels and motor, Model No. 183	15	25	45
Road Grader, 1969, Orange, 19Lx7.5Wx8H, plated scraper blade, black plastic wheels & engine, Model No. 527	25	35	55
Road Grader, 1970, Lime green and yellow, 11.75Lx5Wx6H, black plastic wheels and motor, Model No. 183	15	25	35
Road Grader, 1972, Yellow, 11.75Lx 5Wx6H, black plastic wheels and motor, Model No. 183	15	25	35
Road Grader, 1973, Yellow, 11.75Lx5Wx6H, "Structo 11" stencilled in black on blade, Model No. 183	15	25	35
Roadbuilder Set, 1968, Yellow and green, #580 set and #303 dump truck, Model No. 905	55	75	95
Roadbuilder Set, 1969, Yellow and green, #580 set and #303 dump truck, Model No. 905	45	65	85
Rocker, 1953, Red, 20Lx6.25Wx. 6.5H, with plastic fireball motor under the hood, Model No. 310	75	105	155

Structo ad from 1942. Photo courtesy Randy Prasse

	C6	C8	C10
Rocker, 1953, Red, 20Lx6.25Wx 6.5H, with plastic fireball motor under the hood, Model No. 310	75	105	155
Rocker, 1955, Green, 20Lx6.25Wx 6.5H, with plastic fireball motor under the hood, Model No. 310	75	105	155
Rocker Dump, 1956-57, Green, 20Lx6Wx6.5H, rubber tracks on tractor, dumps to the rear, Model No. 311	95	125	155
Rough Rider Pickup, 1970, Yellow, 9.25Lx4Wx4H, hurricanes design with open bed, Model No. 801	15	25	35
Rough Rider Pickup, 1972, Yellow, 9.25Lx4Wx4H, hurricanes design, Model No. 801	10	20	30
Rough Rider Pickup, 1973, Yellow, 9.25Lx4Wx4H, hurricanes design, Model No. 801	10	20	30
Rough Rider Pick-Up Truck, 1969, Yellow, 9.25Lx4Wx4H, hurricanes design with open bed, Model No. 801	15	25	35
Sand Hopper, 1963, Chartreuse, 8.25Lx6Wx12H, goes with construction sets, Model No. 190	15	25	35
Sand Loader, 1972, Yellow, 9.5Lx5Wx9.5H, small sand hopper with conveyor, Model No. 560	10	15	20
Sand Master Set, 1968, Yellow, 17.5Lx9Wx15H, plastic sand hopper with rubber conveyor belt, Model No. 580	15	25	35

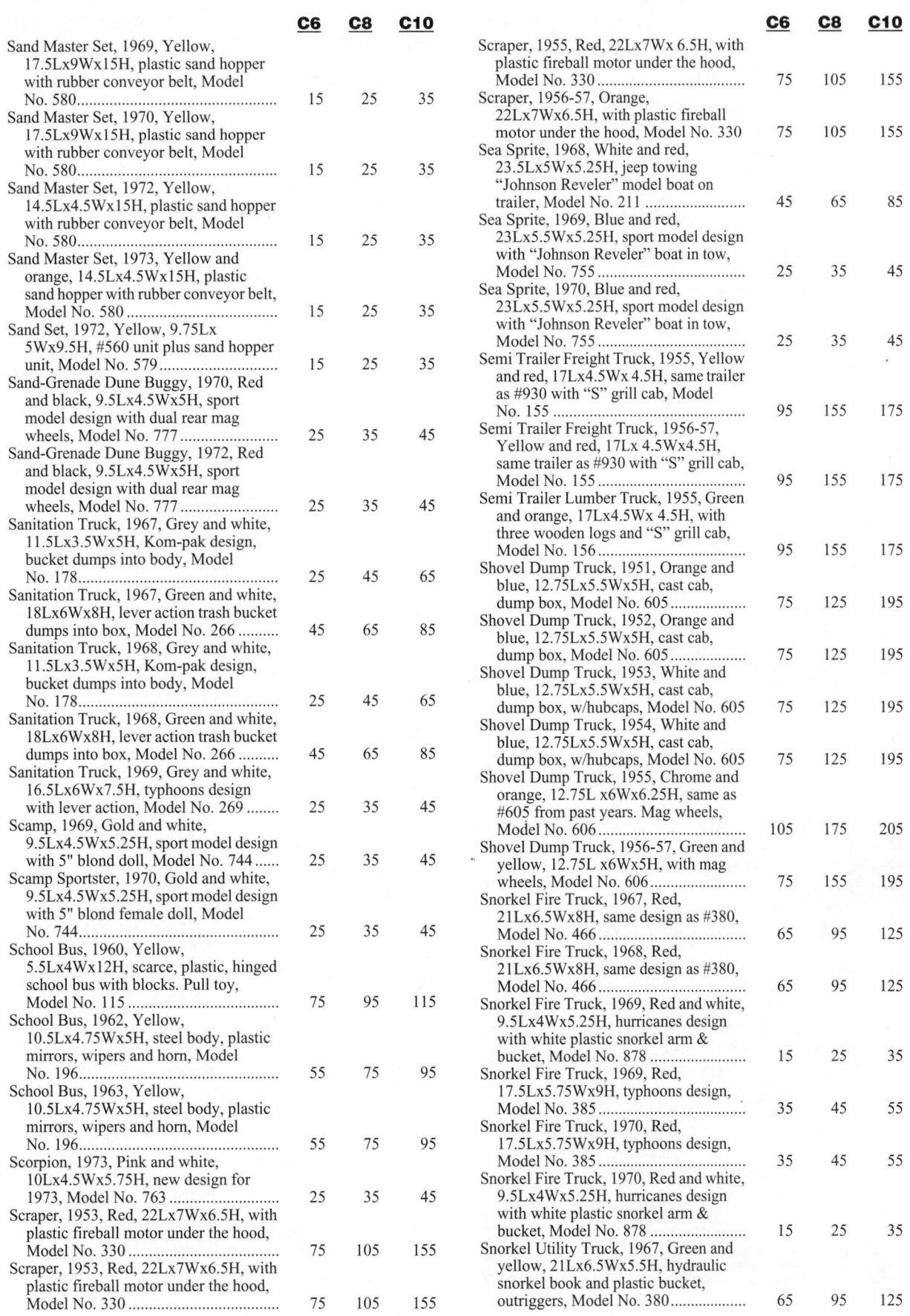

	C6	C8	C10
Sand Master Set, 1969, Yellow, 17.5Lx9Wx15H, plastic sand hopper with rubber conveyor belt, Model No. 580	15	25	35
Sand Master Set, 1970, Yellow, 17.5Lx9Wx15H, plastic sand hopper with rubber conveyor belt, Model No. 580	15	25	35
Sand Master Set, 1972, Yellow, 14.5Lx4.5Wx15H, plastic sand hopper with rubber conveyor belt, Model No. 580	15	25	35
Sand Master Set, 1973, Yellow and orange, 14.5Lx4.5Wx15H, plastic sand hopper with rubber conveyor belt, Model No. 580	15	25	35
Sand Set, 1972, Yellow, 9.75Lx 5Wx9.5H, #560 unit plus sand hopper unit, Model No. 579	15	25	35
Sand-Grenade Dune Buggy, 1970, Red and black, 9.5Lx4.5Wx5H, sport model design with dual rear mag wheels, Model No. 777	25	35	45
Sand-Grenade Dune Buggy, 1972, Red and black, 9.5Lx4.5Wx5H, sport model design with dual rear mag wheels, Model No. 777	25	35	45
Sanitation Truck, 1967, Grey and white, 11.5Lx3.5Wx5H, Kom-pak design, bucket dumps into body, Model No. 178	25	45	65
Sanitation Truck, 1967, Green and white, 18Lx6Wx8H, lever action trash bucket dumps into box, Model No. 266	45	65	85
Sanitation Truck, 1968, Grey and white, 11.5Lx3.5Wx5H, Kom-pak design, bucket dumps into body, Model No. 178	25	45	65
Sanitation Truck, 1968, Green and white, 18Lx6Wx8H, lever action trash bucket dumps into box, Model No. 266	45	65	85
Sanitation Truck, 1969, Grey and white, 16.5Lx6Wx7.5H, typhoons design with lever action, Model No. 269	25	35	45
Scamp, 1969, Gold and white, 9.5Lx4.5Wx5.25H, sport model design with 5" blond doll, Model No. 744	25	35	45
Scamp Sportster, 1970, Gold and white, 9.5Lx4.5Wx5.25H, sport model design with 5" blond female doll, Model No. 744	25	35	45
School Bus, 1960, Yellow, 5.5Lx4Wx12H, scarce, plastic, hinged school bus with blocks. Pull toy, Model No. 115	75	95	115
School Bus, 1962, Yellow, 10.5Lx4.75Wx5H, steel body, plastic mirrors, wipers and horn, Model No. 196	55	75	95
School Bus, 1963, Yellow, 10.5Lx4.75Wx5H, steel body, plastic mirrors, wipers and horn, Model No. 196	55	75	95
Scorpion, 1973, Pink and white, 10Lx4.5Wx5.75H, new design for 1973, Model No. 763	25	35	45
Scraper, 1953, Red, 22Lx7Wx6.5H, with plastic fireball motor under the hood, Model No. 330	75	105	155
Scraper, 1953, Red, 22Lx7Wx6.5H, with plastic fireball motor under the hood, Model No. 330	75	105	155

	C6	C8	C10
Scraper, 1955, Red, 22Lx7Wx 6.5H, with plastic fireball motor under the hood, Model No. 330	75	105	155
Scraper, 1956-57, Orange, 22Lx7Wx6.5H, with plastic fireball motor under the hood, Model No. 330	75	105	155
Sea Sprite, 1968, White and red, 23.5Lx5Wx5.25H, jeep towing "Johnson Reveler" model boat on trailer, Model No. 211	45	65	85
Sea Sprite, 1969, Blue and red, 23Lx5.5Wx5.25H, sport model design with "Johnson Reveler" boat in tow, Model No. 755	25	35	45
Sea Sprite, 1970, Blue and red, 23Lx5.5Wx5.25H, sport model design with "Johnson Reveler" boat in tow, Model No. 755	25	35	45
Semi Trailer Freight Truck, 1955, Yellow and red, 17Lx4.5Wx 4.5H, same trailer as #930 with "S" grill cab, Model No. 155	95	155	175
Semi Trailer Freight Truck, 1956-57, Yellow and red, 17Lx 4.5Wx4.5H, same trailer as #930 with "S" grill cab, Model No. 155	95	155	175
Semi Trailer Lumber Truck, 1955, Green and orange, 17Lx4.5Wx 4.5H, with three wooden logs and "S" grill cab, Model No. 156	95	155	175
Shovel Dump Truck, 1951, Orange and blue, 12.75Lx5.5Wx5H, cast cab, dump box, Model No. 605	75	125	195
Shovel Dump Truck, 1952, Orange and blue, 12.75Lx5.5Wx5H, cast cab, dump box, Model No. 605	75	125	195
Shovel Dump Truck, 1953, White and blue, 12.75Lx5.5Wx5H, cast cab, dump box, w/hubcaps, Model No. 605	75	125	195
Shovel Dump Truck, 1954, White and blue, 12.75Lx5.5Wx5H, cast cab, dump box, w/hubcaps, Model No. 605	75	125	195
Shovel Dump Truck, 1955, Chrome and orange, 12.75L x6Wx6.25H, same as #605 from past years. Mag wheels, Model No. 606	105	175	205
Shovel Dump Truck, 1956-57, Green and yellow, 12.75L x6Wx5H, with mag wheels, Model No. 606	75	155	195
Snorkel Fire Truck, 1967, Red, 21Lx6.5Wx8H, same design as #380, Model No. 466	65	95	125
Snorkel Fire Truck, 1968, Red, 21Lx6.5Wx8H, same design as #380, Model No. 466	65	95	125
Snorkel Fire Truck, 1969, Red and white, 9.5Lx4Wx5.25H, hurricanes design with white plastic snorkel arm & bucket, Model No. 878	15	25	35
Snorkel Fire Truck, 1969, Red, 17.5Lx5.75Wx9H, typhoons design, Model No. 385	35	45	55
Snorkel Fire Truck, 1970, Red, 17.5Lx5.75Wx9H, typhoons design, Model No. 385	35	45	55
Snorkel Fire Truck, 1970, Red and white, 9.5Lx4Wx5.25H, hurricanes design with white plastic snorkel arm & bucket, Model No. 878	15	25	35
Snorkel Utility Truck, 1967, Green and yellow, 21Lx6.5Wx5.5H, hydraulic snorkel book and plastic bucket, outriggers, Model No. 380	65	95	125

	C6	C8	C10
Snorkel Utility Truck, 1968, Green and yellow, 21Lx6.5Wx5.5H, hydraulic snorkel book and plastic bucket, outriggers, Model No. 380	65	95	125
Snorkel Utility Truck, 1969, Green and yellow, 17.5Lx6Wx9H, typhoons design with white boom and plastic bucket, Model No. 380	35	45	55
Snorkel Utility Truck, 1970, Green and yellow, 17.5Lx6Wx9H, typhoons design with white boom and plastic bucket, Model No. 380	35	45	55
Speedway Ambulance, 1973, White, 9.25Lx4Wx4H, similar to hurricane design with first aid decals, Model No. 855	25	35	45
Speedway Midget Race Hauler, 1973, Red and black, 10.5Lx 4Wx4H, flatbed with race car, Model No. 842	25	35	45
Speedway Pacer, 1973, Green, 9.25Lx4Wx4H, same as hurricane design #801 with speedway decals, Model No. 865	25	35	45
Speedway Series Ambulance, 1972, White, 9.25Lx4Wx4H, similar to hurricane design with first aid decals, Model No. 855	25	35	45
Speedway Series Pacer, 1972, Green, 9.25Lx4Wx4H, same as hurricane design #801 with speedway decals, Model No. 865	25	35	45
Speedway Series Wrecker, 1972, Purple, 9.25Lx4Wx4H, same as hurricane design #428 with speedway decals, Model No. 845	25	35	45
Speedway Water Tanker, 1973, Blue and white, 9.25Lx4Wx 4.5H, white plastic water tank on back, Model No. 868	25	35	45

Structo catalog from 1959. Photo courtesy Randy Prasse

	C6	C8	C10
Speedway Wrecker, 1973, Purple, 9.25Lx4Wx4H, same as hurricane design #428 with speedway decals, Model No. 845	25	35	45
Sportsman, 1962, Red and white, 13.25Lx5.25Wx5.5H, scarce, white plastic "Sportsman" camper top, Model No. 311	75	115	155
Stake Truck, 1954, Green and orange, 9.25Lx3.25Wx3.25H, removable stake panels, Model No. 76	35	55	75
Stake Truck, 1956-57, Gold and green, 9.25Lx3.25Wx3.25H, removable stake panels, Model No. 76	35	55	75
Stake Truck, 1959, Copper and cream, 9.25Lx3.25Wx3H, Model No. 76	35	55	75
Standard Steam Shovel, 1948, Orange, 20.5Lx6.25Wx7.75H, wooden wheels without tracks, Model No. 100	55	115	175
Standard Steam Shovel, 1949, Orange, 20.5Lx6.25Wx7.75H, wooden wheels w/o tracks, Model No. 100	55	115	175
Standard Steam Shovel, 1950, Orange, 20.5Lx6.25Wx7.75H, wooden wheels w/o tracks, Model No. 100	55	115	175
State Fair Set, 1966, Met. blue, 4 pc. set includes #203, #310, #417, 6 animals, Model No. 952	95	125	155
Station Wagon, 1966, Teal and white, 10.75Lx5Wx5H, white plastic convertible roof cover body, doors open, Model No. 325	25	45	65
Station Wagon With Boat & Trailer, 1964, Blue and red, 20Lx5Wx 5H, cub station wagon (#325) towing plastic boat on trailer, Model No. 404	35	65	85
Station Wagon With Boat & Trailer, 1965, Blue and red, 20Lx5Wx5H, cub station wagon (#325) towing plastic boat on trailer, Model No. 404	35	65	85
Steam Shovel, 1953, Blue, 26.5Lx 6.5Wx8H, 2 cranks and rubber tracks, Model No. 105	55	95	125
Steam Shovel, 1955, Orange, 26.5Lx6.5Wx8H, 2 cranks and rubber tracks, Model No. 105	55	75	115
Steam Shovel & Machinery Truck, 1955, Green and orange, 26.5Lx6.5Wx14.25H, with plastic fireball motor under the hood, Model No. 403	95	155	195
Steam Shovel (New Design), 1953, Blue, 26.5Lx6.5Wx8H, new design, 2 cranks, Model No. 105	55	95	125
Steel Cargo Trailer, 1951, Blue and red, 20.75Lx5.5Wx5.5H, blue cast cab with red trailer, no hubcaps, Model No. 702	95	135	195
Steel Cargo Trailer, 1952, Blue and red, 20.75Lx5.5Wx5.5H, blue cast cab with red trailer, no hubcaps, Model No. 702	95	135	195
Steel Cargo Trailer, 1953, White and red, 20.75Lx5.5Wx5.5H, w/hubcaps & loading ramp, Model No. 702	75	125	175
Steel Cargo Trailer, 1954, White and red, 20.75Lx5.5Wx5.5H, w/hubcaps & loading ramp, Model No. 702	75	125	175
Steel Cargo Trailer, 1955, White and red, 25.5Lx5.5Wx5.5H, shown in catalog with yellow cab but have not seen, Model No. 702	75	125	175

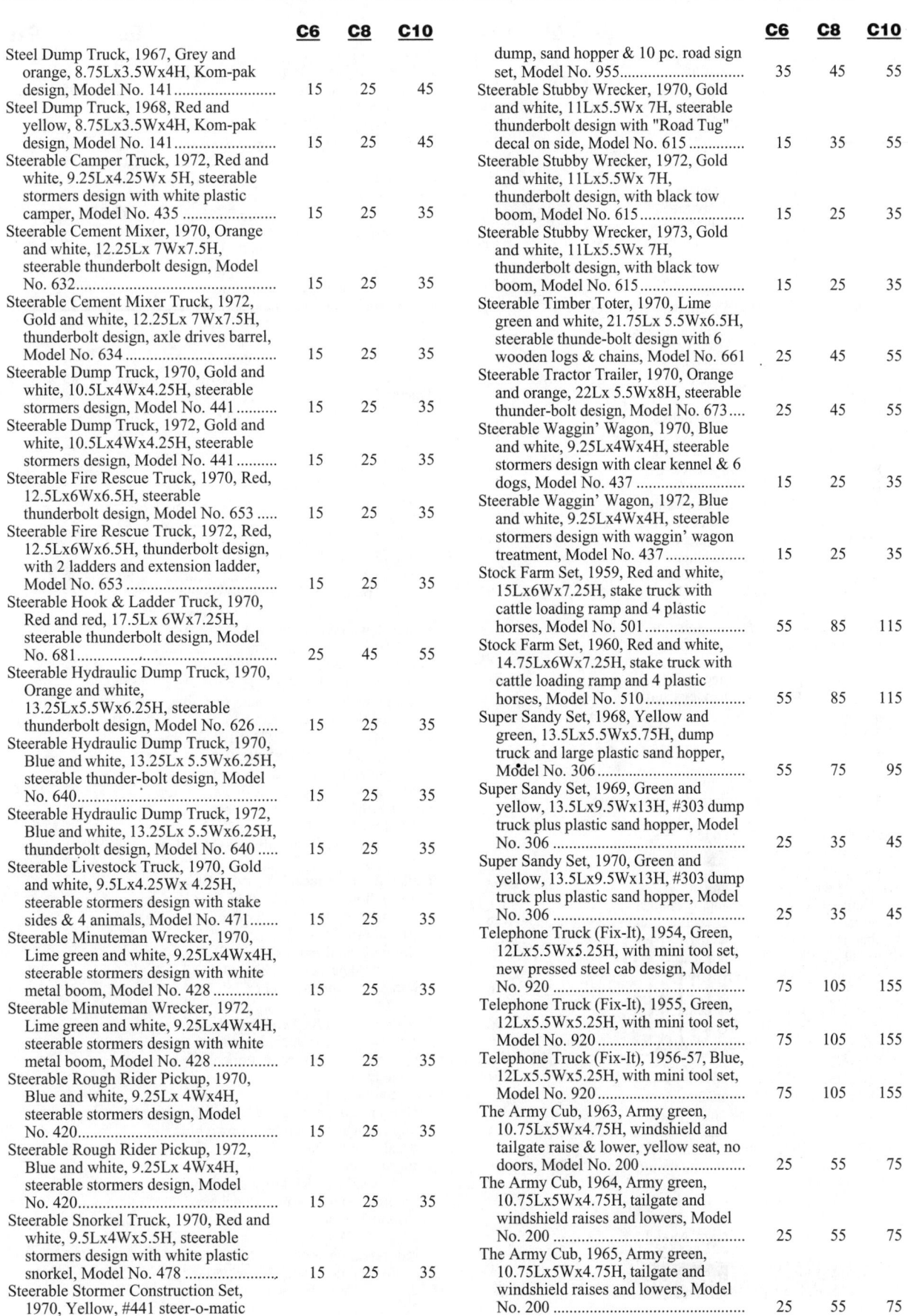

	C6	C8	C10
Steel Dump Truck, 1967, Grey and orange, 8.75Lx3.5Wx4H, Kom-pak design, Model No. 141	15	25	45
Steel Dump Truck, 1968, Red and yellow, 8.75Lx3.5Wx4H, Kom-pak design, Model No. 141	15	25	45
Steerable Camper Truck, 1972, Red and white, 9.25Lx4.25Wx 5H, steerable stormers design with white plastic camper, Model No. 435	15	25	35
Steerable Cement Mixer, 1970, Orange and white, 12.25Lx 7Wx7.5H, steerable thunderbolt design, Model No. 632	15	25	35
Steerable Cement Mixer Truck, 1972, Gold and white, 12.25Lx 7Wx7.5H, thunderbolt design, axle drives barrel, Model No. 634	15	25	35
Steerable Dump Truck, 1970, Gold and white, 10.5Lx4Wx4.25H, steerable stormers design, Model No. 441	15	25	35
Steerable Dump Truck, 1972, Gold and white, 10.5Lx4Wx4.25H, steerable stormers design, Model No. 441	15	25	35
Steerable Fire Rescue Truck, 1970, Red, 12.5Lx6Wx6.5H, steerable thunderbolt design, Model No. 653	15	25	35
Steerable Fire Rescue Truck, 1972, Red, 12.5Lx6Wx6.5H, thunderbolt design, with 2 ladders and extension ladder, Model No. 653	15	25	35
Steerable Hook & Ladder Truck, 1970, Red and red, 17.5Lx 6Wx7.25H, steerable thunderbolt design, Model No. 681	25	45	55
Steerable Hydraulic Dump Truck, 1970, Orange and white, 13.25Lx5.5Wx6.25H, steerable thunderbolt design, Model No. 626	15	25	35
Steerable Hydraulic Dump Truck, 1970, Blue and white, 13.25Lx 5.5Wx6.25H, steerable thunder-bolt design, Model No. 640	15	25	35
Steerable Hydraulic Dump Truck, 1972, Blue and white, 13.25Lx 5.5Wx6.25H, thunderbolt design, Model No. 640	15	25	35
Steerable Livestock Truck, 1970, Gold and white, 9.5Lx4.25Wx 4.25H, steerable stormers design with stake sides & 4 animals, Model No. 471	15	25	35
Steerable Minuteman Wrecker, 1970, Lime green and white, 9.25Lx4Wx4H, steerable stormers design with white metal boom, Model No. 428	15	25	35
Steerable Minuteman Wrecker, 1972, Lime green and white, 9.25Lx4Wx4H, steerable stormers design with white metal boom, Model No. 428	15	25	35
Steerable Rough Rider Pickup, 1970, Blue and white, 9.25Lx 4Wx4H, steerable stormers design, Model No. 420	15	25	35
Steerable Rough Rider Pickup, 1972, Blue and white, 9.25Lx 4Wx4H, steerable stormers design, Model No. 420	15	25	35
Steerable Snorkel Truck, 1970, Red and white, 9.5Lx4Wx5.5H, steerable stormers design with white plastic snorkel, Model No. 478	15	25	35
Steerable Stormer Construction Set, 1970, Yellow, #441 steer-o-matic			

	C6	C8	C10
dump, sand hopper & 10 pc. road sign set, Model No. 955	35	45	55
Steerable Stubby Wrecker, 1970, Gold and white, 11Lx5.5Wx 7H, steerable thunderbolt design with "Road Tug" decal on side, Model No. 615	15	35	55
Steerable Stubby Wrecker, 1972, Gold and white, 11Lx5.5Wx 7H, thunderbolt design, with black tow boom, Model No. 615	15	25	35
Steerable Stubby Wrecker, 1973, Gold and white, 11Lx5.5Wx 7H, thunderbolt design, with black tow boom, Model No. 615	15	25	35
Steerable Timber Toter, 1970, Lime green and white, 21.75Lx 5.5Wx6.5H, steerable thunde-bolt design with 6 wooden logs & chains, Model No. 661	25	45	55
Steerable Tractor Trailer, 1970, Orange and orange, 22Lx 5.5Wx8H, steerable thunder-bolt design, Model No. 673	25	45	55
Steerable Waggin' Wagon, 1970, Blue and white, 9.25Lx4Wx4H, steerable stormers design with clear kennel & 6 dogs, Model No. 437	15	25	35
Steerable Waggin' Wagon, 1972, Blue and white, 9.25Lx4Wx4H, steerable stormers design with waggin' wagon treatment, Model No. 437	15	25	35
Stock Farm Set, 1959, Red and white, 15Lx6Wx7.25H, stake truck with cattle loading ramp and 4 plastic horses, Model No. 501	55	85	115
Stock Farm Set, 1960, Red and white, 14.75Lx6Wx7.25H, stake truck with cattle loading ramp and 4 plastic horses, Model No. 510	55	85	115
Super Sandy Set, 1968, Yellow and green, 13.5Lx5.5Wx5.75H, dump truck and large plastic sand hopper, Model No. 306	55	75	95
Super Sandy Set, 1969, Green and yellow, 13.5Lx9.5Wx13H, #303 dump truck plus plastic sand hopper, Model No. 306	25	35	45
Super Sandy Set, 1970, Green and yellow, 13.5Lx9.5Wx13H, #303 dump truck plus plastic sand hopper, Model No. 306	25	35	45
Telephone Truck (Fix-It), 1954, Green, 12Lx5.5Wx5.25H, with mini tool set, new pressed steel cab design, Model No. 920	75	105	155
Telephone Truck (Fix-It), 1955, Green, 12Lx5.5Wx5.25H, with mini tool set, Model No. 920	75	105	155
Telephone Truck (Fix-It), 1956-57, Blue, 12Lx5.5Wx5.25H, with mini tool set, Model No. 920	75	105	155
The Army Cub, 1963, Army green, 10.75Lx5Wx4.75H, windshield and tailgate raise & lower, yellow seat, no doors, Model No. 200	25	55	75
The Army Cub, 1964, Army green, 10.75Lx5Wx4.75H, tailgate and windshield raises and lowers, Model No. 200	25	55	75
The Army Cub, 1965, Army green, 10.75Lx5Wx4.75H, tailgate and windshield raises and lowers, Model No. 200	25	55	75

	C6	C8	C10
The Army Cub, 1966, Army green, 10.75Lx5Wx4.75H, tailgate and windshield raises and lowers, Model No. 200	25	45	65
The Camper, 1959, Red and white, 21.75Lx4.5Wx6.75H, canvas cover on truck, convertible boat & trailer, Model No. 206	55	95	125
The Cub Set, 1963, Teal and white, 10.75Lx5Wx5H, converts to three variations with #250 and #325 roofs, Model No. 350	55	75	95
The Cub Set, 1964, Teal and white, 10.75Lx5Wx5H, converts to three variations with #250 and #325 roofs, Model No. 350	55	75	95
Tilt-Top Trailer Truck With Dozer, 1959, Yellow and green, 20.25Lx7.5Wx6H, dozer is copper with yellow plastic wheels and engine, Model No. 502	55	75	95
Timber Toter, 1955, Chrome and green, 21Lx6Wx6H, with six wooden logs and chains, Model No. 714	65	135	175
Timber Toter, 1956-57, Chrome and green, 21Lx6Wx6H, with six wooden logs and chains, Model No. 714	65	135	175
Timber Toter, 1958, Chrome and blue, 21Lx6Wx6.25H, with six wooden logs and chains, Model No. 714	65	135	175
Timber Toter, 1959, Red and blue, 21.5Lx4.75Wx5.25H, 5 wooden logs and load chains, Model No. 714	55	75	95
Timber Toter, 1960, Copper, 20.75Lx5.5Wx5.5H, plastic mirrors and horn, 5 wooden logs and chains, Model No. 323	45	65	85
Timber Toter, 1961, Met. green, 23Lx5.5Wx6H, six wooden logs and chains, Model No. 406	55	75	95
Timber Toter, 1962, Red, 23Lx 5.5Wx6H, six wooden logs and chains, Model No. 406	55	75	95
Timber Toter, 1963, Red, 23Lx 5.5Wx6H, six wooden logs and chains, Model No. 406	55	75	95
Timber Toter, 1965, Red and red, 23Lx6Wx5H, 5 wooden logs plus chains, Model No. 406	55	75	95
Timber Toter, 1966, Red and red, 23Lx6Wx5H, 6 wooden logs & chains, Model No. 406	55	75	95
Timber Toter, 1967, Red and red, 20.75Lx6.5Wx5.5H, turbine cab., 5 wooden logs and chains, Model No. 360	55	75	95
Timber Toter, 1968, Blue and blue, 20.75Lx6.5Wx5.5H, turbine cab, 5 wooden logs and chains, Model No. 360	45	65	85
Timber Toter, 1969, Red and red, 21.75Lx5.5Wx6.5H, typhoons design with 6 wooden logs and chain, Model No. 361	25	35	45
Top Chopper, 1973, Lime green and orange, 10Lx4.5Wx5.75H, new design for 1973, Model No. 765	25	35	45
Tow Truck (Fix-It), 1954, Red and red, 11.75Lx5.5Wx6H, with mini tool set. New pressed steel cab design, Model No. 910	75	105	155
Tow Truck (Fix-It), 1955, Red and red, 11.75Lx5.5Wx6H, with mini tool set, Model No. 910	75	105	155
Tow Truck (Fix-It), 1956-57, Blue and blue, 11.75Lx5.5Wx6H, with mini tool set, Model No. 910	75	105	155
Towing & Service Truck, 1958, Green and orange, 17.5Lx 6Wx7.5H, same as #210 but with tow set-up and red light on roof, Model No. 214	105	135	175
Tractor Trailer Truck, 1967, Red and silver, 16.5Lx4Wx5.25H, Kom-pak design, no decals on trailer, Model No. 160	25	45	65
Tractor Trailer Truck, 1967, Red and red, 21.25Lx7.75Wx5.75H, turbine cab. red, white & blue decal on trailer, Model No. 483	55	75	95
Tractor Trailer Truck, 1968, Red and silver, 16.5Lx4Wx5.25H, Kom-pak design, with "National Freight Lines" decal on trailer, Model No. 160	25	45	65
Tractor Trailer Truck, 1968, Red and red, 21.25Lx7.75Wx5.75H, turbine cab. red, white & blue "Structo" decal on trailer, Model No. 483	55	75	95
Tractor Trailer Truck, 1969, White and red, 16.5Lx4.25Wx5.5H, Kom-pak design with red trailer & white doors, Model No. 160	25	35	45
Tractor Trailer Truck, 1969, Red and red, 22Lx5.5Wx8H, typhoons design, Model No. 373	25	35	45
Tractor Trailer Truck, 1970, White and red, 16.5Lx4.25Wx5.5H, Kom-pak design with red trailer & white doors, Model No. 160	25	35	45
Tractor-Trailer Truck, 1972, Blue and silver, 16.5Lx4.25Wx5.5H, hurricanes design with structo van lines on trailer, Model No. 861	15	25	35
Tractor-Trailer Truck, 1973, Blue and silver, 16.5Lx4.25Wx5.5H, hurricanes design with structo van lines on trailer, Model No. 861	15	25	35
Trailer Truck, 1956-57, Chrome and red, 24.5Lx6Wx5.5H, same as #702 but with chrome cab and lift gate, Model No. 705	95	155	205
Trailer W/Mechanical Lift, 1958, Blue and yellow, 50.75Lx 5.5Wx5.75H, mechanical lift gate with mini grocery freight, Model No. 936	95	155	195
Transcontinental Express Fleet, 1960, Varies, 20 pc. set includes auto transport, express, steel trailer, Model No. 904	115	155	195
Transcontinental Express Fleet, 1961, Varies, 25 pc. set includes auto transport, express, cattle trailers, Model No. 906	125	155	195
Transcontinental Express Semi, 1960, Blue and silver, 26Lx 6Wx8.5H, unpainted aluminum trailer with blue decals, Model No. 905	55	95	125
Transport Trailer, 1951, Blue and red, 21.5Lx5.5Wx7.5H, blue cast cab with red trailer, no hubcaps, Model No. 700	95	135	205
Transport Trailer, 1952, Blue and red, 21.5Lx5.5Wx7.5H, blue cast cab with red trailer, no hubcaps, Model No. 700	95	135	205
Transport Trailer, 1953, White and red, 21.5Lx5.5Wx7.5H, w/hubcaps, Model No. 700	75	125	195

	C6	C8	C10
Transport Trailer, 1954, White and red, 21.5Lx5.5Wx7.5H, w/hubcaps, Model No. 700	75	125	195
Transport Trailer, 1955, Yellow and red, 21Lx5Wx7.75H, new pressed steel cab design, Model No. 950	75	135	195
Transport Truck, 1956-57, Red and yellow, 21Lx5Wx7.5H, Model No. 950	75	105	135
Tree Trimming Truck, 1959, Copper and green, 12Lx 4.25Wx12.5H, green boom arm and basket, Model No. 939	35	55	75
Triple Terrific 3 Pack, 1972, 14Lx5Wx5H, one each #215, #216, #217 in a 3 pack store display box, Model No. 220	n/a	n/a	150
Triple Terrific 3 Pack, 1972, 14Lx 5Wx5H, one each #250, #251, #252 in a 3 pack store display box, Model No. 262	n/a	n/a	150
Triple Terrific 3 Pack, 1973, 14Lx5Wx5H, one each #250, #251, #252 in a 3 pack store display box, Model No. 262	n/a	n/a	150
Triple Terrific 3 Pack, 1973, 14Lx5Wx5H, one each #215, #216, #217 in a 3 pack store display box, Model No. 220	n/a	n/a	150
Typhoon Car Carrier, 1973, Red and yellow, 22.5Lx5.5Wx6H, typhoon design with 3 plastic cars and ramp, Model No. 330	45	55	65
Typhoon Cement Mixer, 1973, Blue and white, 13.5Lx6.75Wx 7.5H, typhoon design with turbine cab, Model No. 325	15	25	35
Typhoon Construction Set, 1969, Grey and orange, 3 pc. set including #270, #311, #501, Model No. 966	65	85	105
Typhoon Dump Truck, 1973, Yellow, 13.5Lx6Wx5.5H, typhoon design, Model No. 303	15	25	35
Typhoon Emergency Truck, 1973, White, 12.5Lx6Wx6.5H, typhoon design with 1 red ladder on top, Model No. 358	25	35	45
Typhoon Fire Rescue Truck, 1973, Red, 12.5Lx6Wx6.5H, typhoon design with 3 ladders, Model No. 353	25	35	45
Typhoon Hydraulic Dump, 1973, Blue and white, 13Lx6Wx6H, typhoon design with turbine cab, Model No. 311	15	25	35
U.S. Army Combat Set, 1964, Army green, includes #315 & searchlight, #410, 8 plastic soldiers, Model No. 920	105	155	195
U.S. Army Combat Set, 1965, Army green, includes #315 & searchlight, #410, 8 plastic soldiers, Model No. 920	105	155	195
U.S. Army Combat Set Showcase Display, 1965, Rare, boxed set for dealer trade show & store display, Model No. 9201	175	215	275
U.S. Army Missile Launcher, 1964, Army green, 17.25Lx 6.5Wx7H, missile launcher on back, 3 missiles, 2 outriggers, Model No. 410	45	65	95
U.S. Army Missile Launcher, 1965, Army green, 17.25Lx 6.5Wx7H, missile launcher on back, 3 missiles, 2 outriggers, Model No. 410	45	65	95
U.S. Mail Van, 1965, White and blue, 12Lx5.75Wx6.5H, includes 2 plastic mail bags, Model No. 710	65	85	105
U.S. Mail Van, 1966, Blue and white, 12Lx5.75Wx6.5H, includes 2 cloth mail bags, Model No. 710	65	85	105
US Main Truck, 1958, Blue and red, 12.25Lx5.25Wx6.5H, Model No. 943	95	125	175
USA Guided Missile Launcher, 1958, Green, 12.75Lx5.25Wx 6H, with 2 plastic missiles, Model No. 906	65	105	155
USA Searchlight Truck, 1958, Green, 12.75Lx5.25Wx7.25H, with battery operated searchlight, Model No. 907	75	115	175
USA Transport Truck, 1958, Green, 12.5Lx5.25Wx7.5H, with canvas top, Model No. 905	55	95	135
Utility (Garbage) Truck, 1951, Red and blue, 21.5Lx6.5Wx7.5H, with plastic fireball motor under the hood, Model No. 500	95	155	205
Utility (Garbage) Truck, 1952, Red and blue, 21.5Lx6.5Wx7.5H, with plastic fireball motor under the hood, Model No. 500	95	155	205
Utility (Garbage) Truck, 1953, Red and white, 21.5Lx6.5Wx7.5H, with plastic fireball motor under the hood, Model No. 500	95	155	205
Utility (Garbage) Truck, 1954, Red and white, 21.5Lx6.5Wx7.5H, with plastic fireball motor under the hood, Model No. 500	95	155	205
Utility (Garbage) Truck, 1955, Blue and grey, 21.5Lx6.5Wx 7.5H, with plastic fireball motor under the hood, Model No. 500	95	155	205
Utility (Garbage) Truck, 1956-57, Blue and grey, 21.5Lx6.5Wx 7.5H, with plastic fireball motor under the hood, Model No. 500	95	155	205
Vacation Set, 1973, Orange and green, 22Lx5.75Wx10H, includes #758 and #835, Model No. 962	25	35	45
Van Truck, 1965, Red and white, 22Lx6.5Wx8H, red structo van line decals on side, Model No. 506	45	65	85
Van Truck, 1965, Red and white, 16.5Lx4Wx5H, red structo van line decals on side, Model No. 145	25	45	65
Van Truck, 1966, Red and white, 16.5Lx4Wx5.25H, Kom-pak design, Model No. 145	25	45	65
Van Truck, 1966, Dk. blue and lt. blue, 22Lx6.5Wx8H, scarce 2 tone blue color combination, Model No. 506	55	75	95
Vista Dome Army Truck, 1964, Army green, 8.75Lx3.5Wx4H, clear plastic cover over bed, 2 plastic soldiers, Model No. 115	15	25	55
Vista Dome Army Truck, 1965, Army green, 8.75Lx3.5Wx4H, clear plastic cover over bed, 2 plastic soldiers, Model No. 115	15	25	55
Vista Dome Horse Van, 1964, Met. gold, 21.75Lx5.5Wx6H, ramp on side and back of trailer, 4 plastic horses, Model No. 412	45	65	85

	C6	C8	C10
Vista Dome Horse Van, 1965, Teal and teal, 21.75Lx5.5Wx6H, ramp on side and back of trailer, 4 pc. fence, 4 plastic horses, Model No. 412	45	65	85
Vista Dome Horse Van, 1966, Met. blue and met. blue, 21.75Lx 6Wx6H, 2 ramp doors and 2 horses, 2 colts, Model No. 417	45	65	85
Vista Dome Horse Van, 1967, Met. gold, 21.75Lx6Wx6H, 2 ramp doors and 2 horses, 2 colts, Model No. 322	45	65	85
Vista Dome Horse Van, 1968, Met. gold, 21.75Lx6Wx6H, 2 ramp doors and 2 horses, 2 colts, Model No. 322	45	65	85
Vista Dome Horse Van, 1969, Met. gold, 22Lx5.5Wx6.5H, typhoons design with 4 horses, Model No. 322	35	45	55
Vista Dome Horse Van, 1970, Met. gold, 22Lx5.5Wx6.5H, typhoons design with 4 horses, Model No. 322	35	45	55
Vista Dome Horse Van, 1972, Met. gold, 22Lx5.5Wx6H, typhoon design with 4 plastic horses, Model No. 320	35	45	55
Vista Dome Horse Van, 1973, Met. gold, 22Lx5.5Wx6H, typhoon design with 4 plastic horses, Model No. 320	35	45	55
Vista Dome Kennel Truck, 1964, Teal and yellow, 8.75Lx3.5Wx 4H, clear plastic cover over bed, 6 plastic dogs, Model No. 130	15	35	65
Vista Dome Kennel Truck, 1965, Blue and white, 8.75Lx3.5Wx 4H, clear plastic cover over bed, 6 plastic dogs, Model No. 130	15	35	65
Vista Dome Livestock Truck, 1964, Blue and yellow, 8.75Lx 3.5Wx4H, clear plastic cover over bed, 2 plastic animals, Model No. 120	15	35	65
Vista Dome Troop Carrier, 1964, Army green, 13.25Lx5.25Wx 5.5H, clear plastic cover over bed, 8 plastic soldiers, Model No. 315	55	75	95
Vista Dome Troop Carrier, 1965, Army green, 13.25Lx5.25Wx 5.75H, clear plastic cover over bed, 8 plastic soldiers, Model No. 315	55	75	95
Vista Dome Troop Carrier, 1966, Army green, 13.25Lx5.25Wx 5.75H, clear plastic cover over bed, 6 plastic soldiers, Model No. 315	55	75	95
Waggin' Wagon, 1972, Lime green and white, 9.25Lx4Wx4H, hurricanes design with clear cover & 6 dogs, Model No. 837	10	20	30
Waggin' Wagon, 1973, Lime green and white, 9.25Lx4Wx4H, hurricanes design with clear cover & 6 dogs, Model No. 837	10	20	30
Waggin' Wagon Kennel Truck, 1969, Yellow, 9.25Lx4Wx4H, hurricanes design with clear kennel and 6 dogs, Model No. 837	15	25	35
Waggin' Wagon Kennel Truck, 1970, Yellow, 9.25Lx4Wx4H, hurricanes design with clear kennel and 6 dogs, Model No. 837	15	25	35
Washer-Dryer Combination, 1959, Pink and grey, 7.25Lx8Wx10H, washes & spins, battery operated, Model No. 16	15	55	75

	C6	C8	C10
Weekender, 1965, Teal and white, 12Lx5.75Wx7H, canvas awning, white plastic interior, Model No. 700	55	75	95
Weekender, 1966, Teal and white, 12Lx5.75Wx7H, canvas awning, white plastic interior, Model No. 700	55	75	95
Weekender, 1967, Teal, 12Lx 5.75Wx6.5H, molded built-in refrigerator & sink detail, Model No. 708	55	75	95
Weird Wagon, 1971, Red, 2.75Lx 3.5Wx3H, 2 wheeled design with WV bug style, Model No. 217	10	15	20
Weird Wagon, 1972, Red, 2.75Lx 3.5Wx3H, 2 wheeled design with WV bug style, Model No. 217	10	15	20
Weird Wagon, 1973, Red, 2.75Lx 3.5Wx3H, 2 wheeled design with WV bug style, Model No. 217	10	15	20
Western Auto Moving Van, 1956-57, Chrome and white, 24Lx 6Wx8.5H, private label. Same body as #710 deluxe moving van. Red doors, Model No. 711	125	185	225
Wrecker, 1961, White, 12Lx 5.75Wx6.5H, crank operated winch, plastic mirrors, wipers & horns, Model No. 302	55	75	95
Wrecker, 1962, White, 12Lx 5.75Wx6.5H, crank operated winch, plastic mirrors, wipers & horns, Model No. 302	55	75	95
Wrecker, 1963, White, 13Lx 5.25Wx5.5H, door windows and interior detail, black metal boom arm, Model No. 301	55	75	95

Structo ad from 1961. Photo courtesy Randy Prasse

	C6	C8	C10
Wrecker, 1964, White and black, 13.25Lx5.25Wx5.5H, door windows and interior detail, black metal boom arm, Model No. 301	55	75	95
Wrecker, 1966, White and red, 12.5Lx5.25Wx6.25H, red light on roof (non-operable), red interior & boom, Model No. 312	45	65	95
Wrecker Truck, 1951, Red and grey, 12.25Lx5.5Wx5.25H, wind-up motor and chain winch, Model No. 822	95	125	175
Wrecker Truck, 1952, Red and grey, 12.25Lx5.5Wx5.25H, wind-up motor and chain winch, Model No. 822	95	125	175
Wrecker Truck, 1953, White and orange, 12.25Lx5.5Wx5.25H, wind-up motor and chain winch, Model No. 822	115	155	195
Wrecker Truck, 1954, Various, 7.5Lx2.5Wx2.25H, same scale #21 pick-up but with cast tow boom arm, Model No. 30	25	55	75
Wrecker Truck, 1954, White and orange, 12.25Lx5.5Wx5.25H, wind-up motor and chain winch, Model No. 822	115	155	195
Wrecker Truck, 1955, White and orange, 12Lx5.5Wx5.25H, shown in catalog with green cab but have not seen, Model No. 822	115	155	195
Wrecker Truck, 1956-57, White and orange, 12Lx5.5Wx5.25H, wind-up, Model No. 822	115	155	195
Wrecker Truck, 1964, White and grey, 9.25Lx3.5Wx3.5H, with metal tow boom and hook, Model No. 110	15	25	55
Wrecker Truck, 1965, White and red, 12.5Lx5.25Wx6.25H, red light on roof (non-operable), red metal boom arm, Model No. 302	55	75	95
Wrecker Truck, 1965, Red and white, 9.25Lx3.5Wx3.5H, with metal tow boom and hook, Model No. 110	15	25	55

	C6	C8	C10
Wrecker Truck, 1965, White and red, 10.75Lx4.75Wx5.75H, red convertible roof, seats and metal boom arm, Model No. 251	55	75	95
Wrecker Truck, 1966, Yellow and red, 9.25Lx3.5Wx3.5H, Kom-pak design with red boom arm, Model No. 110	15	25	45
Wrecker Truck, 1966, White and black, 10.75Lx4.75Wx5.75H, black convertible roof and boom, red seat, Model No. 251	35	55	75
Wrecker Truck, 1967, White and black, 10.75Lx4.75Wx5.75H, black convertible roof and boom, Model No. 205	45	65	85
Wrecker Truck, 1967, White and grey, 9.25Lx3.5Wx3.5H, Kom-pak design with red boom arm, Model No. 112	15	25	45
Wrecker Truck, 1967, White, 12.5Lx5.25Wx6.25H, red light (non-operable) on roof, POW-R-R-R sound, Model No. 415	45	65	95
Wrecker Truck, 1968, Red, 15Lx 5.5Wx6.25H, white boom arm, red light (non-operable) on roof, Model No. 264	45	65	85
Wrecker Truck, 1968, White and black, 10.75Lx4.75Wx5.75H, black convertible roof and boom, red seat, Model No. 205	45	65	85
Wrecker Truck, 1968, White, 12.5Lx5.25Wx6.25H, red light (non-operable) on roof, POW-R-R-R sound, Model No. 415	45	65	95
Wrecker Truck, 1968, White and red, 9.25Lx3.5Wx3.5H, Kom-pak design with red boom arm, Model No. 112	15	25	45
Wrecker Truck, 1969, Yellow and red, 12.5Lx6Wx6.25H, typhoons design with red tow boom & crank winch, Model No. 277	25	35	45

STURDIBILT

Although best-known for its model airplane kits, the Sturdibilt Co. of Portland, Ore., did release at least one truck.

	C6	C8	C10
Logging Truck, (Oregon)	325	510	650

STURDITOY

The Sturdy Corporation of Providence and Pawtucket, R.I., manufactured its steel toy trucks from about 1929 to 1933.

	C6	C8	C10
Ambulance, open cab, white, red cross on sides, c.1926, 26" long	2000	3500	5000
American LaFrance Water Tower Fire Truck, 34" long	1000	1800	2750
American Railway Express Truck, green screenside body, black cab, "American Railway Express" decals, 26" long	1000	1500	2200
Armored Truck, red, solid box w/3 small sets of louvers on sides, 24" long	2200	3700	5500
Coal Dump Truck, 1920s, side shute, 25" long	1200	2000	2900
Coal Truck, 26" long	1400	2300	3200

Sturditoy Coal Dump Truck, 1920s, 25". Photo courtesy Tim Oei

	C6	C8	C10
Coal Truck, high-sided, 27" long	1400	2350	3300
Dairy Truck, 25" long	600	1000	1400
Dairy Truck, white, tank has two filler			
caps on top, 34" long	1700	3000	4300
Delivery Truck, 1920s, 26" long	1200	2000	3500
Dump Truck, 1920s, 25" long	800	1300	1800
Dump Truck, 1920s, 26-1/2" long	500	800	1200
Huckster Truck, 27" long	450	700	1000
Oil Company Tanker, 27" long	1100	1800	2500
Oil Tanker, "Gulf," 27" long....................	NPF	NPF	NPF
Police Patrol, 26" long	1100	1800	2500
Pumper, c.1930, 26" long........................	1100	1800	2500
Sand and Gravel Truck	900	1600	2000
Side Dump, 26-1/2" long	1100	1800	2530
Steam Shovel, 26" long..........................	162	243	325
Tanker, 15" long.....................................	2000	3500	7500
Traveling Store, orange w/black fenders,			
26" long..	1800	2900	4200
Trucking Co., 24" long............................	1150	1800	2600
U.S Army Truck, 26" long	550	850	1300
U.S Mail Screenside Truck, blue w/black			
fenders, "U.S. Mail" decals	1200	2000	2725
Water Tower	1500	2500	3500
Wells Fargo Armored Truck, 24" long,			
c.1927...	900	1700	2500
Wrecker, 30" long	1000	1650	2750

Sturditoy Coal Truck, 1920s, 25". Photo courtesy Bertoia Auctions

Sturditoy Dairy Truck, 34". Photo courtesy Bertoia Auctions

Sturditoy Oil Company Tanker, 27". Photo courtesy Tim Oei

Sturditoy Oil Tanker, 27". Photo courtesy Bertoia Auctions

Sturditoy Pumper, 1930s, 26". Photo courtesy Bertoia Auctions

Sturditoy U.S. Army Truck, 26". Photo courtesy Tim Oei

Sturditoy Traveling Store, 26". Photo courtesy Bertoia Auctions

Sturditoy Wrecker, 30". Photo courtesy Bertoia Auctions

SUN RUBBER

Sun Rubber of Barberton, Ohio, was founded in 1923. Toy making started in 1924 and vehicles were introduced in April 1935. The owner was Tom W. Smith Jr.

Contributor: Dave Leopard, 2507 Feather Run Trail, West Columbia, SC 29169-4915.

	C6	C8	C10
'34 DeSoto Airflow Four-door Sedan, No. 500, 4" long (SA002)	25	35	50
'40 Dodge Four-door Sedan, c.1936, No. 12001, 4-1/2" long (SA003)	25	35	50
Ambulance, late 1930s, No. 12006, 3-3/4" long (ST007)	25	35	50
Art Deco Housetrailer, fits Teardrop Sedan, No. 1025, 4-3/8" long (SA005)	NPF	NPF	NPF
Coupe, external exhaust pipes, from 1936, No. 515, 4" long (SA001)	25	35	50
Donald Duck Roadster w/Pluto (SD004)	80	100	150

	C6	C8	C10
Donald Duck Tractor (SD008)	75	90	120
Mickey Mouse and Donald Duck Fire Truck, No. 12017 (SD002)	75	90	120
Mickey Mouse Tractor, No. 12020 (SD001)	75	90	120
Open Master Truck, futuristic, No. 12111, 5-5/8" long (ST005)	25	35	55
Open Racer, boat tail, "Super" racer, No. 12012, 6-3/4" long (SR003)	30	45	60
Open Racer, full fenders on rear, No. 1000, 1936, 6-1/2" long (SR002)	35	50	70
Open Racer, two drivers, No. 505, 1936, 4-3/8" long (SR001)	25	35	50

Left to right: Sun Rubber Ambulance; Ambulance with military paint. Photo courtesy Dave Leopard's book Rubber Toy Vehicles

Sun Rubber 1934 DeSoto Airflow, four-door sedan, 4". Photo courtesy Dave Leopard's book Rubber Toy Vehicles

Sun Rubber Art Deco Housetrailer, 4-3/8". Photo courtesy Dave Leopard's book Rubber Toy Vehicles

Sun Rubber Coupe, external exhaust pipes, 1936, 4". Photo courtesy Dave Leopard

Left to right: Sun Rubber Coupe in two-toned color scheme; solid-colored Coupe. Photo courtesy Dave Leopard's book Rubber Toy Vehicles

Sun Rubber 1940 Dodge 4-door Sedan, 4-1/2". Photo courtesy Dave Leopard's book Rubber Toy Vehicles

Sun Rubber Donald Duck Roadster. Photo courtesy Dave Leopard

Sun Rubber Mickey Mouse and Donald Duck Fire Truck.

Sun Rubber Mickey Mouse Tractor.

Two different Sun Rubber Open Racers with two drivers. Photo courtesy Dave Leopard's book Rubber Toy Vehicles

Sun Rubber Open Racer, 1936, 6-1/2". Photo courtesy Dave Leopard's book Rubber Toy Vehicles

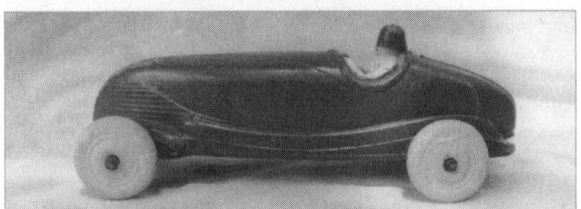

Sun Rubber Open Racer, boat tail, 6-3/4". Photo courtesy Dave Leopard

Sun Rubber Open Truck, stake sides, streamlined, 5-1/4". Photo courtesy Dave Leopard's book Rubber Toy Vehicles

Sun Rubber, (ST04) and (ST05). Photo courtesy Dave Leopard

Sun Rubber, (ST08A) and (ST04A). Photo courtesy Ed Poole

Sun Rubber Pickup Truck, stake sides, streamlined, 4-1/2". Photo courtesy Dave Leopard's book Rubber Toy Vehicles

Another view of the Sun Rubber Pickup Truck, stake sides, streamlined, 4-1/2". Photo courtesy Dave Leopard

	C6	C8	C10
Open Truck, futuristic, No. 12003, 4-1/2" long (ST004)	25	35	50
Open Truck, stake sides, streamlined, No. 1005, 5-1/4" long (ST002)	35	45	55
Pickup Truck, stake sides, streamlined, No. 510, 4-1/2" long (ST001)	25	35	50
Scout Car, four gunners, No. 12014, 1946, w/or without front winch, 6-3/4" long (SM002)	50	75	100
Station Wagon, woody, mid-1930s, No. 12007, 3-3/4" long (SA007)	25	35	50
Tank, revolving turret and gunner, No. 12015, 1946, 6" long (SM001)	50	75	100
Teardrop Sedan, 1936, No. 1010 , 5-1/2" long (SA004)	30	40	60
Town Car, brewster-type limo, exposed driver, No. 1015, 5-3/8" long (SA006)	35	50	80
Tractor/trailer, one-piece, three axles, futuristic, No. 12013, 5-1/8" long (ST003)	25	35	50
White Bus, streamlined, No. 520, 1936, 4-1/4" long (ST006)	25	35	50

Sun Rubber Scout Car, four gunners, 1946, with or without winch, 6-3/4". Photo courtesy Ed Poole

Left to right: Sun Rubber Station Wagon, woody, 1930s, 3-3/4"; military version of same vehicle. Photo courtesy Dave Leopard's book Rubber Toy Vehicles

Sun Rubber Tank with revolving turret and gunner, 6". Photo courtesy Ed Poole

Sun Rubber 1936 Teardrop Sedan, 1936, 5-1/2". Photo courtesy Dave Leopard's book Rubber Toy Vehicles

Sun Rubber Town Car, Brewster-type limo, exposed driver, 5-3/8". Photo courtesy K. Warren Mitchell

Sun Rubber Tractor/trailer, one piece, futuristic, 5-1/8". Photo courtesy Dave Leopard's book Rubber Toy Vehicles

Sun Rubber White Bus, streamlined, 1936, 4-1/4". Photo courtesy Dave Leopard's book Rubber Toy Vehicles

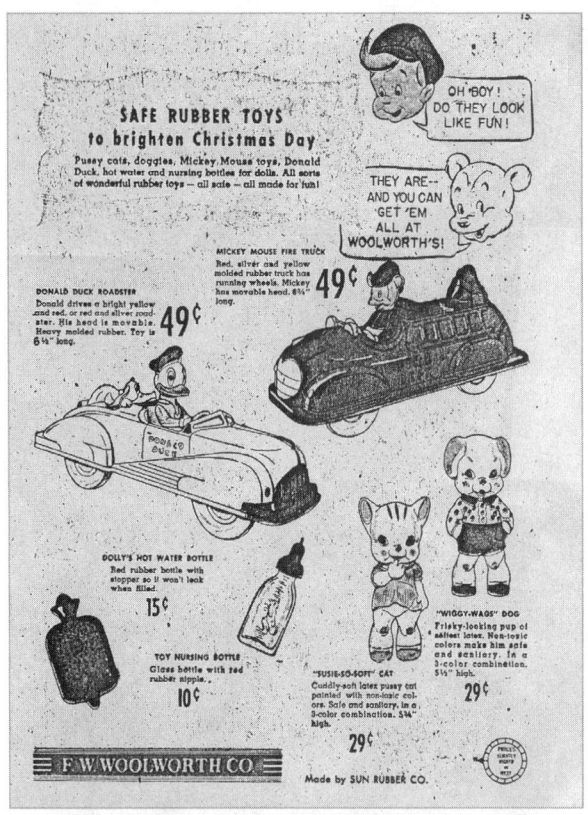

Pictured is an F.W. Woolworth catalog page of Sun Rubber toys from 1952—note the original retail prices!

A catalog page of Sun Rubber vehicles.

SUPERIOR

Superior Service Station; value in Good condition $85. Photo courtesy Ron Fink

Superior Products was a trade name used by the T. Cohn Co. of Brooklyn, N.Y., on its postwar tin litho playsets.

	C6	C8	C10
Airport Bus, plastic, assorted colors, 1950s, 4-1/2" long	15	30	45
Circus Truck	88	132	175
Dump Truck	40	60	80
Fire Chief Car, w/driver	32	48	65
Service Station, metal, 1950s	188	282	375

Superior "Garage Entrance" Service Station; value in Good condition $120. Photo courtesy Ron Fink

Superior "Sales Service" Station; value in Good condition $170. Photo courtesy Ron Fink

T.C.O.

T.C.O. was a brand name used by Tipp & Co., a German tin-toy maker.

	C6	C8	C10
Policeman on Motorcycle, tin lithographed wind-up, 11" long	185	278	370

TECHNOFIX

Technofix, a German firm, was known for its tin-litho mechanical toys.

	C6	C8	C10
Grand Prix, No. 302, tin wind-up, three cars, built-in key	125	200	275
Racer Motorcycle, tin wind-up, "No. 2, G.E. 255" w/attached key	125	200	300

	C6	C8	C10
Racer Motorcycle, tin wind-up, No. "G.E. 258" w/attached key, 1950s.......	125	225	375
Racer Motorcycle, tin wind-up, No. 15, 1950s, 7" long	125	200	350
Racer Motorcycle, tin wind-up, No. 4, 7" long	125	200	350
Racetrack, tin, mutli-color, w/two tin wind-up cars...................................	150	225	310
Ralleye 65, No. 311, racing hill, tin wind-up, three attached cars, built-in key..	150	225	310
Traffic Control Set, tin, No. 295, three wind-up cars and tin track, 3 keys, 1950s..	75	150	220

Technofix Racer Motorcycles, tin windups, 7" each. Photo courtesy Kent M. Comstock

TED TOYS

Based in Bedford, Mass., Ted-Toylers began production of its wooded toys in 1925. Edwin V. Babbit was its founder and chief designer. The short-lived firm closed its doors in 1930.

	C6	C8	C10
Racer Pull Toy, wood, two riders	125	188	250

Ted Toys Racer, wood, two riders, pull toy. Photo courtesy Perry Eichor

THIMBLE DROME (ROY COX)

Thimble Drome gas-powered race cars were the kings of the post-WWII toy racing scene. The Roy Cox Co. even manufactured its own fuel.

	C6	C8	C10
Champion Racer.....................................	288	432	575
No. 81	225	338	450
Prop Rod	68	102	135

	C6	C8	C10
Racer, No. 25	188	282	375
Racer, pusher..	170	255	340
Racer, w/engine......................................	275	363	550
Special, No. 2 Pusher, 8" long	138	205	275
Special, No. 28, w/motor	275	413	550
Special, wind-up	400	600	800

THOMAS TOYS

Thomas Toys was owned by Islyn Thomas, who founded the company in 1944 after leaving his position as general manager of the Ideal Toy Company. According to Thomas, its first toys—jeeps, planes, and vinyl dolls—were produced that year. The firm was located at 80 Clinton St., Newark, N.J. It made only toys, and at its peak had 350 employees. Thomas Toys was tied to Acme Plastics, since Acme's Ben Shapiro was a partner. Toys made by Acme from 1945 to 1950 were clearly marked "Acme." Some order sheets submitted by Thomas were printed in Acmeís name. Thomas indicated that these toys were also Thomas Toys. Sometimes, but not always, Acme and Thomas Toys used the same order numbers.

The company's molds, and perhaps some of its sculpting, were provided by Richard Koegi (perhaps Koegel), whose Koegi stampworks were in Newark. Sculpting of some of Thomas' finer-detailed toys, such as its lines of small babies, dolls, and civilians, were done by a Mr. Kaiser. In 1960, Thomas, aware of the impending impact of new, low-priced Japanese imports, sold out to Banner Plastics. Thomas then became an international plastics consultant.

Thomas was made a member of the Plastics Hall of Fame in 1977. Originally from South Wales, he was made an Officer of the British Empire by Queen Elizabeth. He had served as chief engineer for the plastic parts in the Spitfire's Merline engine (which was made in the United States). In the immediate postwar period, heading Thomas Engineering Company, he had helped restore the ravaged European community by setting up a number of companies in England and continental Europe. One of these companies was the toy company Popular Playthings in Wales, of which he was half-owner for a while. Founded in 1945, it continues in business today. Thomas is also the author of several books, including *Our Welsh Heritage* and *Injection Molding of Plastics* (Reinhold Publishing Corp.) and many technical articles.

Thomas Toys had at least three different numbering systems over the years, with the same items having their numbers changed as time went on. The items with an alphabetical code preceding the number appear to be the earliest, those with a "T" next, and those without a code the latest.

	C6	C8	C10
No. 018 Same as TMC-9, listed in 1955 as No. 18	NPF	NPF	NPF
No. 019 Jeep and Trailer, w/yellow driver in GI helmet, 1954, 8-3/8" long	14	16	18
No. 019 Jeep and Trailer, yellow civilian driver, 8-3/8" long	14	16	18
No. 024 Sport Convertible & Sedan, set consists of numbers 77 and 77S, 1955, each 4-1/4" long	20	24	28
No. 026 Wrecker, plastic, winch works, tow hook and chain, 1947-51, 5" long	35	40	45
No. 027 Sedan, plastic, assorted colors, rubber wheels, 1947-51, 4-5/8" long	NPF	NPF	NPF
No. 029 Airline Limousine, plastic, assorted colors, rubber wheels, 1947-51, 4-1/2" long	10	22	40
No. 030 Coupe and House Trailer, plastic, assorted colors, trailer detaches, 8-1/4" long	20	22	24
No. 040 Texaco Gas Truck, plastic, assorted colors, rubber wheels, 1947-50, 4" long	15	20	25
No. 041 Delivery Truck, plastic, 1947, 4" long	15	18	20
No. 048 Utility Trailer, plastic, assorted colors, plastic wheels, 1948, 2-1/2" long	10	15	20
No. 055 Airline Limo and Utility Trailer, plastic, assorted colors, 1948-51, 7" long	20	40	60
No. 067 Police-Fire Chief Radio Car, plastic, w/spotlight and radio antenna, 1949-51, each 4-1/2" long, price per each	15	20	27

	C6	C8	C10
No. 072 Plastic Motorcycle and Rider, vinyl rider detaches, handlebars steer front wheel, 1949-51, 4" long	35	45	55
No. 074 Merry-Go-Round Truck, plastic, 4-3/4" long	20	25	30
No. 077 Convertible Coupe and Driver, 1953, 1954, 4-1/2" long	9	11	13
No. 077C Convertible Coupe and Driver, 1953, 1954, 4-1/2" long	9	11	13
No. 077S Streamlined Sedan, plastic, assorted colors, rubber wheels, 1949-56, 4-1/2" long	10	15	20
No. 090 Service Motorcycle and Rider, plastic, vinyl rider, opening rear compartment, handlebars steer front wheel, 1950, 4-7/8" long	NPF	NPF	NPF
No. 098 Sedan (metalized), plastic, assorted colors, plastic wheels, add water to gas tank comes out of oil pan, 1947-48, 4-5/8" long	NPF	NPF	NPF

Thomas Toy Jeep with trailer, with driver, No. 019, 1954, 8-3/8".

Thomas Toys Motorcycle & Sidecar, No. 237, 1955, no passenger, 4".

	C6	C8	C10
No. 107 Military Policeman and Motorcycle, w/detachable policeman, 1952, 4" long	20	25	30
No. 125 Motorcycle, plated, 1950, 4" long	NPF	NPF	NPF
No. 126 Same as T-114, plastic, rubber band motor, 1951, 4-1/2" long	20	40	65
No. 128 Taxi, plastic, decals on sides and roof, taxi sign on roof, 1950, 4-1/2" long	18	33	45
No. 131 Car and House Trailer, overall length 9-1/2"	25	30	35
No. 132 Truck and Racer, 1950-52, 4" long	NPF	NPF	NPF
No. 134 Same as No. 257, 1950, 4" long	NPF	NPF	NPF
No. 135 Repair Truck with detachable ladder, 1950, 4" long	15	20	27
No. 139 Same as T-148, 1950, 4" long	NPF	NPF	NPF
No. 141 Racer, plastic, two-tone colors, plastic wheels don't turn, 1950-52, 1-5/8" long	10	20	32
No. 148 Truck and Air Compressor, 8-1/2" long	14	16	18
No. 160 International Race, plastic, two-tone colors, "5" on hood, sold w/ and w/o driver-same number, 1955, 5" long	20	35	50
No. 162 Servi-Car (driver not included), 4-1/2" long	25	30	35
No. 168 Motorcycle, 4" long	20	25	30
No. 170 Motorcycle and Sidecar w/passenger, yellow girl passenger, no driver, 4" long	NPF	NPF	NPF

Thomas Toys Jeep & Driver, No. 580, khaki soldier, jeep in red, blue or green.

	C6	C8	C10
No. 175-6 Police & Fire Chief Radio Cars, each 4-1/2" long, price per each	11	13	15
No. 177 Large Tow Truck, 5-1/2" long	12	14	16
No. 183 Army Jeep and Trailer w/Driver, 8-3/4" long	14	16	18
No. 184-5 Army Radar and Tow Trucks, each 4" long (may be the same as T-192/3) price per each	16	20	24
No. 188 Military Police Jeep w/three MPs, 1955, 1956, 4-1/4" long	10	15	20
No. 189 Maintenance Truck, w/detachable ladders, 5-1/2" long	NPF	NPF	NPF
No. 196 Army Road Roller, self-winding, 4-1/2" long	NPF	NPF	NPF
No. 212 Plated Two-Tone Racer w/Driver, 5" long (same No. 160 except top half is Special Silver Metal Plated)	NPF	NPF	NPF
No. 222 Mobile Searchlight Unit, uses batteries, 15-1/2" overall length	100	120	140
No. 222 Mobile Searchlight Unit, w/friction motor, uses batteries, 1954 overall length 15-1/2"	55	65	75
No. 234 Gas and Delivery Trucks w/Traders, overall length 6-1/4", per each	14	16	22
No. 237 Motorcycle and Sidecar, plastic, w/o passenger, 1953-55, 4" long	NPF	NPF	NPF
No. 245 Limousine and Trailer, w/luggage and rack, assembly kit (1955)	NPF	NPF	NPF
No. 25 Sedan w/Canoe and Polyethylene House Trailer, 1955, overall length 9-1/2"	30	35	40
No. 254 Polyethylene TV Truck, w/ladder, 1955, 4" long	NPF	NPF	NPF
No. 257 Polyethylene Sound Truck, 1955, 4" long	30	35	40
No. 261 Vespa Motor Scooter, 1955, 4" long	NPF	NPF	NPF
No. 267 Truck and Polyethylene Trailer, 1955, 6-1/4" long overall	NPF	NPF	NPF
No. 289 Jet Hot Rod, 1955, 5-1/2" long	NPF	NPF	NPF
No. 299 Searchlight Truck w/Friction Motor Assembly Kit, 1955	NPF	NPF	NPF
No. 303 Ferguson Tractor Assembly Kit, 1955	NPF	NPF	NPF
No. 334 Electronic Airport Traffic Control Set, contains plane, "flash" truck w/signal light, "radar" truck w/signal buzzer, remote control Morse Code Unit, 1956	NPF	NPF	NPF
No. 360 Indianapolis Speed Race, two racers w/drivers, spring-action mechanism, 1956	NPF	NPF	NPF
No. 369 Radar Signal Set, four radar vehicles, 1956	NPF	NPF	NPF
No. 449 Lumberyard Express, trailer has retractable wheels	NPF	NPF	NPF
No. 457 Jet Car	NPF	NPF	NPF
No. 519 Sport Car Transport, four sports cars included from Thomas Toys: Jaguar, Mercedes-Benz, Thunderbird, Alfa Romeo, Talbot, Corvette; 23-1/2" long when boxed	NPF	NPF	NPF
No. 520 Overland Express Van, 21-5/8" when boxed	NPF	NPF	NPF

	C6	C8	C10
No. 521 Cabin Cruiser and Trailer, fifty-six put-together parts, 22-7/8" long when boxed	NPF	NPF	NPF
No. 522 Jeep and Horse Trailer Set, includes doll family, pet, table, and bench, 18-7/8" long when boxed	NPF	NPF	NPF
No. 524 Animal Transport, No animals included, 21-1/8" long when boxed	NPF	NPF	NPF
No. 545 Speed Boat, Jeep and Trailer, w/boat driver outboard motor is rubber-band propelled	NPF	NPF	NPF
No. 558 Auto and Horse Trailer, 7-1/2" long bagged	NPF	NPF	NPF
No. 566 Military Set Jeep, Howitzer, four soldiers	NPF	NPF	NPF
No. 572 Assorted Six Sport Cars Pkg, 5-1/8" x 9"	NPF	NPF	NPF
No. 576 International Sport Cars, same as No. 581, except packed three dozen in plain box	NPF	NPF	NPF
No. 579 Authentic 8 Jeep Spare Tire, moveable windshield, w/o driver	NPF	NPF	NPF
No. 580 8 Jeep and Driver, moveable windshield, spare tire	NPF	NPF	NPF
No. 581 Chest of Sport Cars, contains six Dozen "All-Poly Cars" in six different styles: Jaguar, Mercedes-Benz, Thunderbird, Talbot, Corvette, Alfa Romeo	NPF	NPF	NPF
No. 592 Stake Trailer Truck, 24-1/2" long when bagged (probably the same as No. 524)	NPF	NPF	NPF

	C6	C8	C10
No. 597 Van Trailer Truck, 24-1/2" long when bagged	NPF	NPF	NPF
No. 604 Same as T- 114	NPF	NPF	NPF
No. 607 Auto Transport, Trailer loaded w/any four of these Sports Cars; Jaguar, Mercedes-Benz, Thunderbird, Alfa Romeo, Talbot, Corvette; 24-1/2" long when bagged	NPF	NPF	NPF
No. 614 Assortment of 8 Authentic All-Poly Ack-Ack and Search-light Jeeps, price per each	8	10	12
No. 635 Sight-Seeing Bus	NPF	NPF	NPF
No. 638 Same as No. 25, but in blister pack	NPF	NPF	NPF
T-110 No. 168 Motorcycle, plated, 4" long	NPF	NPF	NPF
T-114 Road Roller, w/ivory driver, self winding, 1953, 4-1/2' long	NPF	NPF	NPF
T-140 Same as 131	NPF	NPF	NPF
T-141 Same as No. 132	NPF	NPF	NPF
T-144 Same as No. 257	NPF	NPF	NPF
T-145 Same as No. 135 (both 1953)	NPF	NPF	NPF
T-148 Tow Truck, 4" long, 1953	8	10	12
T-152 (1953) Same as No. 148	NPF	NPF	NPF
T-171 Same as No. 162	NPF	NPF	NPF
T-174 Large Tow Truck, 5-1/2" long	12	14	16
T-179 Motorcycle, 4" long	20	25	30
T-18 Wrecker, 5" long	25	35	45
T-192/3 Army Radar & Tow Trucks, each 4" long, olive drab (may be the same as No. 184-5)	NPF	NPF	NPF
T-205 Army Jeep and Driver, khaki	NPF	NPF	NPF
T-209 Army Maintenance Truck w/detachable ladders, olive drab, 5-1/2" long	NPF	NPF	NPF
T-209 Same as No. 189 (1953)	NPF	NPF	NPF
T-215 Army Road Roller (same as No. 196)	NPF	NPF	NPF
T-223 Same as No. 77 (both in 1953)	NPF	NPF	NPF
T-242 Same as non-friction-motor No. 222	NPF	NPF	NPF
T-66 Same as No. 67	NPF	NPF	NPF
T-79 Convertible Coupe (or Sedan), 4-1/2" long (Same as No. 77 and No. 77S)	NPF	NPF	NPF
T-89 Same as No. 74	NPF	NPF	NPF
TMC-10 Jeep, 1949, 4-1/4" long	15	20	27
TMC-10 Jeep and Driver, driver is khaki soldier, jeep red, blue or green	12	14	16
TMC-13 Trailer, for jeep, 1949, 4" long	4	6	8

Thomas Toys Jet Car, No. 457.

Thomas Toys Streamlined Sedan, No. 77S. KP Photo courtesy Karen O'Brien

	C6	C8	C10		C6	C8	C10
TMC-17 Streamlined Buick Sedan, 4-5/16" long	16	19	22	TMC-40 Utility Trailer, 1949, 2-1/2" long	6	8	10
TMC-19 Airline Limousine, 1949, 4-1/2" long	15	20	27	TMC-51 Jeep and Trailer, 1949, 8-1/2" long	14	16	18
TMC-25 Limousine and Trailer, 1949, 6-3/4" long	25	30	36	TMC-53 Truck and Trailer, 1949, 9" long overall	14	16	18
TMC-32 Dump Truck, 5" long (also in 1947 Acme order sheet)	12	14	16	TMC-9 Streamlined Truck, plastic, Acme name not on hood, 1947-52, 5" long	10	12	18

TIM-MEE

Originally based in Aurora, Ill., Tim-Mee Toys specialized in dime-store plastic figures and vehicles during the 1950s and 1960s. The firm was acquired by Processed Plastics of Montgomery, Ill., and toys were issued as "Tim-Mee Toy by Processed Plastics Co."

	C6	C8	C10
Army Jeep, hard plastic, olive drab, 4-1/2" long	4	8	12
Army Tow Truck, hard plastic, 9" long	12	18	25

TIMPO

Timpo Toys was a British toy soldier manufacturer. Incorporated in the 1940s, Timpo released composition and wood figures during the materials shortages of the time. When metal was again available, the figures were cast in metal. The company switched to plastics in the early 1960s.

	C6	C8	C10
Coronation Coach, cast metal, ornate, 8 horses, 4 riders	50	100	150
Delivery Van, friction, 4" long	100	150	200
Dispatch Rider, No. 9007, cast metal, motorcycle driver	10	20	35

TIPP

Tipp's history is interesting. Founded in 1912 and named after an early director/employee (?), Miss Tipp, its ultimate owner, Phillip Ullman, was forced to flee from Germany in 1933. He went to England, where he founded Mettoy, eventually returning to Germany and recovering his company following the war.

Tipp's military vehicles and overall production are clearly not up to the quality standards of Lineol and Elastolin and current prices reflect that fact. However, some of its pieces are particularly well-crafted, such as the Hitler Mercedes car.

In the United States, Tipp tinplate pieces turn up at shows far more often, with its small Prime Mover being the most popular. Tipp military pieces sell for about a third that of Lineol and Hausser. Prices for Tipp military vehicles can be found as part of their photo captions.

Contributor: Jack Matthews

Tipp Club Sedan, 1933, electric headlights, 17". Photo courtesy Bertoia Auctions

Tipp No. 934 Fuhrer Wagon, very rare, value as shown $3,500. Photo courtesy Jack Matthews

	C6	C8	C10
Aerial Ladder Fire Truck, early	350	525	700
Bus, marked "Provincial Omnibus Co."	1500	2900	4500
Club Sedan, tin lithographed, electric head lights, clockwork motor, rear trunk opens, 1933, 17" long	500	800	11
Motorcycle and Rider, 6-1/2" high	285	418	570
Police Motorcycle, battery headlight and friction, 11" long	550	950	1300
Santa Driving Roadster, tin wind-up, tree lights up, approx. 13" long	3500	5500	9500
Sedan, eight Cylinder, c.1930, 12" long	550	900	1300
Silver Racer motorcycle, wind-up, 7-1/2" long	500	750	1000
Stake Truck, wind-up, c.1930, 10" long	135	198	270

Tipp Santa Driving Roadster, tin windup, tree lights up, 13". Photo courtesy Bertoia Auctions

Tipp Electric Tank, camouflaged, value as shown $2,000. Photo courtesy Jack Matthews

A large scenic Tipp box that held various toys.

Tipp Military Sedan, value as shown $600. Photo courtesy Jack Matthews

Tipp No. 162 with baggage cart, value as show $450. Photo courtesy Jack Matthews

Tipp Silver Racer windup motorcycle, 7-1/2". Photo courtesy Kent M. Comstock

Tipp Armored Car, early and very rare, value as shown $1,500. Photo courtesy Jack Matthews

Tipp Command Car, value as shown $1,200. Photo courtesy Jack Matthews

Tipp No. 217 Tracked Prime Mover, value as shown $990. Photo courtesy Jack Matthews

Tipp No. 217 Tracked Prime Mover, camouflaged, British crew, value as shown $1,050. Photo courtesy Jack Matthews

Tipp No. 934 Fuhrer Wagon, same as other version but in tan, value as shown $4,000. Photo courtesy Jack Matthews

Tipp No. 162/167 Field Kitchen, value as shown $450. Photo courtesy Jack Matthews

Tipp No. 162/174, value as shown $450. Photo courtesy Jack Matthews

Tipp No. 164, rare, value as shown $550. Photo courtesy Jack Matthews

Tipp No. 169/71, value as shown $600. Photo courtesy Jack Matthews

Tipp No. 169/274, value as shown $700. Photo courtesy Jack Matthews

Tipp No. 162/175, value as shown $500. Photo courtesy Jack Matthews

Tipp No. 164 early large Sedan with British crew, rare, value as shown & 1,750. Photo courtesy Jack Matthews

Tipp No. 169/240 Towing 88mm, value as shown $650. Photo courtesy Jack Matthews

Tipp No. 169/72/171 with cleated cannon wheels, value a shown $600. Photo courtesy Jack Matthews

Tipp No. 170/175 Wheeled Mortar, value as shown $600. Photo courtesy Jack Matthews

Tipp No. 176 Anti-Aircraft Truck, value as shown $950. Photo courtesy Jack Matthews

Tipp No. 184 Military Lastwagon, early camouflage and top, rare, value as shown $1,800. Photo courtesy Jack Matthews

Tipp No. 181/4 Pioneer Auto, rare, value as shown $950. Photo courtesy Jack Matthews

Tipp No. 181/4 Military Pioneer Auto, value as shown $600. Photo courtesy Jack Matthews

Tipp No. 194 Panzer Spahwagen, rare, value as shown $175. Photo courtesy Jack Matthews.

Tipp No. 197, early, An accurate shot at the shield stops the clockwork mechanism, value as shown $175. Photo courtesy Jack Matthews

Tipp No. 204 early tank, rare, value as shown $650. Photo courtesy Jack Matthews

Tipp No. 209 Tank, value as shown $750.

TIPPER

	C6	C8	C10
Fire Ladder Truck	400	600	800

TIP-TOP TOYS

Tip-Top Toys were realistic, crisply detailed, and often unique. Wheels were either metal disks or Tootsietoy-loke with lugbolts, metal hubs with rubber tires and rubber wheels. This progression helps to date the issues. Windshields and windows were open. Except where noted, cars and trucks were without bumpers.

Contributors: Perry R. Eichor, 703 North Almond Drive, Simpsonville, SC, 29681 and the late Fred Maxwell.

	C6	C8	C10
Airflow Sedan, six windows, w/bumpers (TTTV014)	NPF	NPF	NPF
Coupe, die-cast, cast rearmount; looks like Tootsietoy copy, 3-1/4" long (TTTV018)	NPF	NPF	NPF
Coupe, die-cast, rearmount tire, 3-3/16" long (TTTV006)	25	50	75
Coupe, die-cast, streamlined, 1935 Huppmobile (?) w/realistic front end (forward fenders, setback grille, large louvers, bumpers, rearmount, tow loop), 3-1/4" long (TTTV007A)	50	75	100

	C6	C8	C10
Coupe, Dodge (?) sidemounts, four windows, 1923, 3-1/8" long (TTTV001)	40	60	80
Midget racer, die-cast, easily confused w/slush Barclay No. 53, 1-7/8' long (TTTV020)	NPF	NPF	NPF
Overland Bus, die-cast, thirteen windows, 3-3/8" long (TTTV005)	25	40	60

Left to right: Tip-Top (TTTV2) and (TTTV19). Photo courtesy Ferd Zegel

Tip-Top TTTV3a w/2ea TTTV3c. Photo courtesy Ferd Zegel

The Outstanding Sellers In

(Cut actual size)
NO. 155 CANNON

(Cut actual size)
NO. 165 AIR EXPRESS

5c PEWTER TOYS

G.H. Curry Mfg. Co.
1266 So. Eastman St.
Los Angeles, Calif.

(Cut actual size)
NO. 145 SPORT COUPE

(Cut actual size)
NO. 140 RACER

Please mention TOY WORLD when writing to advertisers

Left to right: Tip-Top (TTTV8), (TTTV19), (TTTV2). Photo courtesy Ferd Zegel

NO. 25 TIP-TOP TOY ASSORTMENT

Cash in on this

The Biggest Two Bit Value This Year
Five Wheel Toys in a Four Color Box
To Retail at

25c

Manufactured by

G.H. CURRY MFG. CO.

1266 So. Eastman St.
Los Angeles, Calif.

Ad for Tip-Top Toys in the November, 1930 Toy World magazine—note that G.H. Curry advertises itself as the manufacturer. Photo courtesy Fred Maxwell

Tip-Top Coupe, 1923, four windows, 3-1/8". Photo courtesy Ferd Zegel

Left to right: Tip-Top Racer, rounded grille, strapped hood, short tail, 3-1/2"; Racer, slanted vee grille, driver, 3". Photo courtesy Ferd Zegel

Tip-Top Overland Bus, thirteen windows, 3-3/8".

Left to right: Tip-Top Sport Coupe, No. 145, 2-1/8"; Coupe, die-cast, 3-1/4" (similar to Tootsietoy). Photo courtesy Ferd Zegel

Left to right: Tip-Top Coupe, streamlined, 1935, 3-1/4"; Travel Trailer, Airstream-type, eight windows, 3-5/8". Photo courtesy Ferd Zegel

Tip-Top Stake Truck, six wheel version, 4-5/8". Photo courtesy Ferd Zegel

Left to right: Tip-Top Tanker Truck, "Gasoline", 3-1/2"; Pickup Truck, "Tow Car", 3-1/4". Photo courtesy Dave Leopard

Left to right: Tip-Top Racer, Miller-like, driver, 3"; Midget Racer, 1-7/8". Photo courtesy Ferd Zegel

Left to right: Tip-Top Pickup Truck, hinged tailgate, 3-1/4"; Panel Truck, "Parcel Delivery," 2-1/8".

Left to right: Tip-Top Racer, slanted vee grille, strapped hood, 4"; Racer, squarish grille, strapped hood, 3-1/4"; Record Racer, Bluebird, 4". Photo courtesy Ferd Zegel

Left to right: Tip-Top (TTTV8), (TTTV19), (TTTV2). Photo courtesy Ferd Zegel

	C6	C8	C10
Panel Truck, "Parcel Delivery," 2-1/8" long (TTTV010)	NPF	NPF	NPF
Pickup Truck, die-cast, "Tow Car," openwork handrails, 3-1/4" long (TTTV003A)	50	75	100
Pickup Truck, die-cast, "Tow Car," w/solid-cast handrails, 3-1/4" long (TTTV3b)	NPF	NPF	NPF
Pickup Truck, hinged tailgate, 3-1/4" long (TTTV004)	30	45	60
Racer, die-cast, Miller-like, driver, torpedo tail, six cylinder right exhaust, 3" long (TTTV024)	NPF	NPF	NPF
Racer, die-cast, rounded grille, strapped hood, short tail, 3-1/2" long (TTTV022)	NPF	NPF	NPF
Racer, die-cast, slanted vee grille, round V8 ports, driver, 3" long (TTTV021)	NPF	NPF	NPF
Racer, die-cast, slanted vee grille, strapped hood, left exhaust, boattail, 4" long (TTV025)	NPF	NPF	NPF
Racer, die-cast, squarish grille, left exhaust, driver, boattail, 3-1/4" long (TTTV026)	NPF	NPF	NPF
Racer, die-cast, strapped "16" hood, right exhaust, 4" long (TTTV023)	NPF	NPF	NPF

	C6	C8	C10
Record Racer, die-cast, Bluebird, rear fin, 4" long (TTTV027)	NPF	NPF	NPF
Small Sedan, 1933 Studebaker (?), 2-1/4" long (TTTV012)	NPF	NPF	NPF
Sport coupe, No. 145, die-cast, marked "TipTop Toy," under dash ventilator door, landau irons; shows parting-line and lower edge flash, 2-1/8" long (TTTV011)	60	80	100
Stake Truck, four- or six-wheel versions, body separately cast and fastened to chassis, 4-5/8" long (TTTV013)	75	100	125
Stake Truck, six-wheel versions, body separately cast and fastened to chassis, 5-1/4" long (TTTV013B)	NPF	NPF	NPF
Tanker Truck, die-cast, reads "Gasoline," two filler caps, 3-1/2" long (TTTV002)	40	60	80
Tanker Truck, die-cast, three filler caps, 3-1/4" long (TTTV019)	50	75	100
Tanker Truck, die-cast, three fillers, 2-11/16" long (TTTV008)	NPF	NPF	NPF
Trailer for above, two wheel dolly w/shaft, 2" long (TTTV3C)	30	45	60
Travel Trailer for Coupe, die-cast, "Airstream" type, eight windows, right-side door, 3-5/8" long (TTTV007B)	75	100	125

TOLEDO METAL WHEEL COMPANY

The Toledo Metal Wheel Company was located in Toledo, Ohio, during the early and late 1920s. It manufactured a large range of pedal cars, as well as toy trucks. Its trade name for its products was "Blue Streak."

An advertisement showing Toledo's Bull Dog Truck and its Bull Dog Dump Truck.

Another Toledo advertisement showing the Bull Dog Sprinkler Truck, Moving Van, and Coal Truck.

	C6	C8	C10
Coal Truck, No. 50, "Bull Dog," 25" long	800	1350	1875
Dump Truck, "Bull Dog," No. 46, 26-1/2" long	600	1000	1475
Fire Chief Pedal Car	3000	6000	10,000
Fire Pumper Car, red, 59" long	1250	1875	2500
Mack Express Truck, "Bull Dog," black cab and chassis, screen-sided tan express body, c.1926, 26" long	1150	2250	3200

	C6	C8	C10
Moving Van, "Bull Dog," No. 48, 26" long	550	1050	1550
Pedal Car, "De Luxe," 54" long	2500	5000	7500
Pedal Car, 46" long	1200	2200	3300
Sprinkler Truck, "Bull Dog," No. 47, 27-1/2" long	600	1100	1510
Truck, "Bull Dog," open cab, No. 45, 26" long	500	1000	1500
White Dump Truck Pedal Car, 68" long	5000	9000	14,750

TOMMY TOY

Tommy Toy, 131 Palisade Ave., Union City, N.J., had its first sale on Nov. 13, 1935. Its principal owners were Dr. Albert Greene and Charles E. Weldon. It seems to have gone out of business between August 1938 and May 1939.

The following vehicles have been identified by Charles E. Weldon Jr., son of one of the owners of Tommy Toy. The Cannon Truck, aside from the hubs, looks just like Barclay's, which was produced in the same years. Some others resemble Metal Cast, Savoye, and other makers' vehicles. However, since slush molds did tend to change hands, production of a vehicle by one company would not preclude later manufacture of the same toy by another company. American Alloy is known to have produced copies of Tommy Toy's soldiers, using new molds. The only vehicle known to bear the Tommy Toy trademark is the No. 810 Cord.

	C6	C8	C10
Aerial Ladder Truck, late 1920s-type (TTV001)	20	30	40
Airflow-type Auto, like Savoye, c.1935 (TTV002)	32	48	65
Ambulance, like Kansas Toy, late 1920s-early 1930s (TTV003)	16	24	32
Beer Truck, w/wooden barrels, late 1930s (TTV004)	14	21	28
Cannon Truck, like Barclay, mid-1930s (TTV005)	17	25	34
Convertible, no driver, mid-late 1930s (TTV006)	8	12	16
Convertible w/driver, 1935 Oldsmobile, mid-late 1930s (TTV007)	10	15	20
Cord, 810, 1935 (TTV008)	40	60	80
Delivery Truck, "Delivery Deluxe," like Savoye, late 1930s (TTV009)	18	27	36
Double-Decker Bus, closed top, early 1930s (TTV010)	16	24	32
Double-Decker Bus, open top, extended hood, like Savoye, late 1920s (TTV011)	35	52	70
Double-Decker Bus, open top, no hood, like Barclay, late 1930s (TTV012)	16	24	32
Dump Truck, late 1930s, resembles Kansas Toy, Best Toy, Manhattan Toys (TTV013)	16	24	32
General Trucking, late 1930s (TTV014)	12	18	25
Ladder Truck, mid 1930s (TTV015)	20	30	40
Milk Truck, grilled window, late 1930s (TTV017)	20	30	40

	C6	C8	C10
Milk Truck, late 1930s (TTV016)	20	30	40
Milk Truck, smooth window, late 30s (TTV018)	20	30	40
Motorcoach, mid-1930s, like Savoye (TTV19)	NPF	NPF	NPF
Oil Tanker, marked "Cap 80,000," like Metal Cast, which has different capacity number, 1930s, attaches to Tommy Toy Towing Car Coupe (TTV020)	8	12	16
Packard Coupe, mid-1930s (TTV021)	17	26	35
Police Patrol, open windows, late 1920s-early 1930s type (TTV022)	70	105	140
Police Patrol, solid windows, late 1920s-early 1930s type (TTV023)	35	52	70
Pumper, large, red hubs, late 1930s (TTV025)	11	16	22
Pumper, mid 1930s (TTV024)	12	18	25
Pumper, small, late 1930s (TTV026)	8	12	16
Racing Car, large, mid 1930s (TTV027)	16	24	32
Racing Car, small, mid 1930s (TTV028)	12	18	25
Sedan, four door, c.1935 (TTV029)	17	26	35
Sedan Towing Touring Trailer, 1936-1937 (TTV030)	20	30	40
Towing Car Coupe, early 1930s-type, like Savoye (TTV031)	16	24	32
Tractor (TTV032)	12	18	25
Wrecker, late 1930s (TTV033)	10	15	20

TONKA

In 1946, Lynn E. Baker, Avery Crounse, and Alvin Tesch founded Mound Metalcraft Co. in the basement of a small schoolhouse in Mound, Minn. The company was incorporated September 18, 1946. The primary production was a major output of hoes, rakes, and shovels, along with tie, hat, and shoe racks—toy production was merely a sideline. During the first year, the company purchased tooling from the L.E. Streeter Co. for a toy steam shovel. The tooling was refined, and Mound produced their first two toys—a steam shovel and crane. After a successful debut at the International Toy Fair in

1946, Mount Metalcraft manufactured a total of 37,000 pieces of the two metal toys—the No. 100 Steam Shovel and the No. 150 Crane and Clam.

Tonka Toys, named after Lake Minnetonka, enjoyed the first of what would be many years of successful sales in the toy truck business. A resident of Mound, Minn., Ering W. Eklof, was asked to design the first Tonka logo. In three days, the logo was designed to represent the lake area in which the plant was located. The waves reflected the waters of Lake Minnetonka and three birds were added along with a distinctive swash-type font. The logo remained unchanged from 1947 until 1955. The first Tonka catalog was printed in 1949.

The founding premise of Tonka was to provide consumers with a toy that was durable, reasonably priced, and, of course, fun. Tonka devoted great time and resources to the design and testing of each truck. Three decades after its founding, the company grew from the original small schoolhouse with a half-dozen employees, to an expansive plant covering nearly one-third of a mile along the shores of Lake Minnetonka and employing over 1,300 people that produced approximately 400,000 toys per week.

The production of Tonka Toys followed many of the same techniques used in the mass production of trucks and cars in Detroit, Mich. A new toy began as a sketch. If the sketch received favorable reviews from consumers, it was then transformed into a three-dimensional clay model. A positive reaction to a clay model meant it would be produced in Fiberglas or metal to be reviewed by those involved with child supervision and early childhood development. If the toy passed this round of inspections, detailed drawings and blueprints were prepared and manufacturing specifications were developed. When trial production samples were completed, they were sent out for the toughest test of all—the children.

Tonka's production and management staff observed the reactions of children as they played with the toys. This test judged the play value, safety, and durability of the toy. If the toy passed this final test, it was sent into production.

Since the initial production in 1947, Tonka has become a world-wide operation. Late in 1955, Mound Metalcraft changed its name to Tonka Toys, Inc. In 1991, Tonka became part of Hasbro, Inc., and Tonka trucks continue to be the No. 1 brand in the non-powered toy truck category. Each year Hasbro introduces a dynamic line of fun, innovative state-of-the-art trucks for children of all ages.

Contributors: This chapter was prepared by John Taylor and Don DeSalle for the 3rd edition. For this edition, Mark Rich assisted the editor.

	C6	C8	C10
1947			
No. 100 Steam Shovel, 20-3/4" long	135	200	350
No. 150 Crane and Clam, 24" long	135	200	350
1948			
No. 200 Lift Truck and Trailer.................	200	350	600

	C6	C8	C10
1949			
No. 100 Stearn Shovel Deluxe, 22" long...	100	250	400
No. 120 Tractor and Carry-All Trailer, w/No. 50 Steam Shovel.	155	280	475
No. 125 Tractor & Carry-All Trailer, w/No. 100 Steam Shovel	150	250	550
No. 130 Tractor-Carry-All Trailer, 30-1/2" long	100	150	350
No. 140 Tonka Toy Transport Van, 22-1/4" long	150	300	500
No. 170 Tractor & Carry-All Trailer, w/No. 150 Crane and Clam	200	300	525
No. 180 Dump Truck, 12" long	100	175	375
No. 190 Loading Tractor, 10-1/2" long ...	NPF	NPF	NPF
No. 250 Wrecker Truck, 12-1/2" long	125	250	375
1950			
No. 145 Steel Carrier Semi, 22" long	125	200	350
No. 175 Utility Hauler, 12" long..............	100	150	300
No. 185 Express Truck, 13-1/2" long	200	450	900
No. 400 Allied Van Lines Semi, 23-1/2" long	175	260	400
1952			
No. 500 Livestock Hauler Semi, 22-1/4" long	100	150	350
No. 550 Grain Hauler Semi, 22-1/4" long	125	180	350
1953			
No. 250 Wrecker, blue cab-over, red boom, 12-1/2" long	125	200	450
No. 575 Logger Semi, 22-1/4" long........	125	180	350
No. 575 Logger Semi, wood flat bed.......	125	180	350
No. 600 Road Grader, 17" long	50	75	100
No. 650 Green Giant Transport Semi, 22-1/4" long	150	300	500
No. 675 Trailer Fleet Set, two tractors (five interchangeable trailers), per set .	450	680	975

Tonka 1948 Power Lift Truck and Trailer. Photo courtesy the DeSalle Collection

	C6	C8	C10
1954			
No. 145 Steel Carrier Truck	100	185	380
No. 175 Utility Truck, orange cab, green bed	110	275	425
No. 700 Aerial Ladder Semi Fire Truck, "MFD" decals, 2 ladders, 32-1/2" long	175	260	450
No. 725 Star Kist Van, 14-1/2" long	250	575	950
No. 750 Carnation Milk Step Van, 11-3/4" long	200	400	600
No. 750 Parcel Delivery Van, 11-3/4" long	200	300	500
No. 775 Road Builder Set, Road Grader, Semi T&T Crane and Dump Truck, five pieces	350	525	900
Wrecker	100	300	500
1955			
No. 050 Steam Shovel, red, 15" long, 5-3/4" high, 5-3/4" wide	50	100	150
No. 065 Trailer, stake side	30	45	60
No. 120 Shovel and Carry-All (Loboy), red cab, blue loboy, red No. 50 steam shovel	150	300	450
No. 145 Steel Carrier, red cab, green open trailer, white "Steel" decal on side, 23-1/2" long, 5-3/4" high, 6" wide	NPF	NPF	NPF
No. 180 Dump, red cab and frame, green dump bed, 13" long, 6" high, 6" wide	100	150	350
No. 250 Wrecker, 12-3/4" long, 6" high, 6-3/4" wide, red and white, chain and hook, dual wheels on rear	100	300	500
No. 400 Allied Van Lines, 23-3/4" long, 9" high, 6" wide, orange, "Allied Van Lines" decals	150	275	500
No. 500 Livestock Truck, red cab and trailer w/slits, 24" long, 9-1/4" high, 6-1/4" wide	110	200	350
No. 550 Grain Hauler (Freighter), 23-1/2" long, 6" high, 6" wide, red cab, open silver steel box	85	150	300
No. 575 Logger, red cab, silver frame w/chains and round logs, 23-3/4" long, 6" high, 6" wide	125	275	450
No. 600 Grader, orange, 17" long, 6-3/4" high, 7-1/4" wide	75	125	200
No. 650 Green Giant Transport, refrigerator tractor trailer, 23-3/4" long, 9" high, 6-1/4" wide, white w/"Green Giant" decals	150	300	500
No. 675 Tonka Trailer Fleet, red and orange tractor cabs, livestock box trailer, steel box trailer, grain hauler box trailer, lumber box trailer	NPF	NPF	NPF

	C6	C8	C10
No. 700 Aerial Ladder Truck, 23-1/2" long, 7-1/4" high, 6" wide, "MFD" decals, aluminum ladders	100	300	450
No. 725 Minute Maid Orange Juice Van, 14-1/2" long, 7-3/4" high, 5-3/4" wide, two rear doors	275	650	950
No. 750 Carnation Milk Delivery Van, white van, 11-3/4" long, 7" high, 5" wide, side door	200	400	600
No. 775 Road Builder Set, Shovel and Carry-All, Dump truck, Road Grader	NPF	NPF	NPF
No. 800 Aerial Sand Loader, loader w/out dump truck	NPF	NPF	NPF
No. 825 Aerial Sand Loader Set, Loader and Dump Truck, 25-1/2" long, 19-1/2" high, 8" wide	275	425	875
No. 850 Lumber Truck, six-wheel, red cab, silver bed, 18-3/4" long, 5-3/4" high, 6-1/4" wide	175	260	400
No. 860 Stake Truck, six-wheel, 16-1/2" long, 6-5/4" high, 6" wide, red cab and flat bed, green stakes	175	360	500
No. 875 Builder's Supply Fleet, Pick-up, red semi cab, stake box trailer, lumber box trailer	NPF	NPF	NPF
No. 880 Pick-up Truck, red, 12-3/4" long	125	280	450
Rescue Van	200	450	800
1956			
No. 050 Steam Shovel, red, 15" long, 5-3/4" high, 5-3/4" wide	50	100	150
No. 120 Shovel and Carry-All (Loboy), 33" long total, red cab, blue loboy, red No. 50 steam shovel	188	280	475
No. 180 Dump Truck, red cab and frame, green dump bed, 13" long	100	150	300
No. 400 Allied Van Lines, 23-3/4" long, 9" high, 6" wide, orange, "Allied Van Lines" decals	150	275	500
No. 500 Livestock Truck, red cab and trailer w/slits, 24" long, 9-1/4" high, 6-1/4" wide	110	200	350
No. 550 Grain Hauler (Cargo King), red cab, green dump bed, 23-1/2" long, 6" high, 6" wide	85	150	300
No. 575 Logger, red cab, silver frame w/chains and round logs, 23-3/4" long, 6" high, 6" wide	125	275	450
No. 600 Road Grader, orange, 17" long	75	125	200
No. 650 Green Giant Transport, refrigerated tractor trailer, 23-3/4" long, 9" high, 6-1/4" wide, white w/"Green Giant" decals	155	350	600
No. 675 Tonka Trailer Fleet, red and orange tractor cabs, livestock box trailer, steel box trailer, grain hauler box trailer, lumber box trailer	NPF	NPF	NPF

Tonka 1949 "Tonka Toy Transport" Van, No. 140. Photo courtesy Calvin L. Chaussee

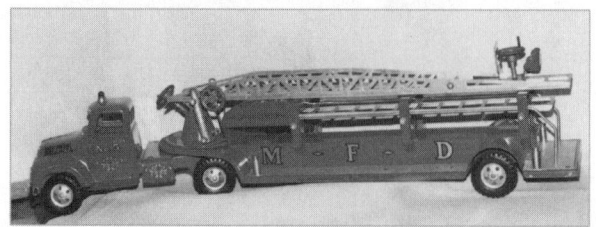

Tonka 1954 Aerial Ladder, No. 700. Photo courtesy Harvey K. Rainess

	C6	C8	C10
No. 700 Aerial Ladder Truck, red, 32-1/2" long, 7-1/4" high, 6" wide, "TFD" decals on sides, aluminum ladders	150	300	450
No. 725 Minute Maid Orange Juice Van, 14-1/2" long, 7-3/4" high, 5-3/4" wide, two rear doors	275	650	950
No. 750 Carnation Milk Delivery Van, white van, 11-3/4" long, 7" high, 5" wide, side door	200	400	600
No. 775 Road Builder Set, Shovel and Carry-All, Dump truck, Road Grader	NPF	NPF	NPF
No. 825 Aerial Sand Loader Set, Loader and Dump Truck, 25-1/2" long, 19-1/2" high, 8" wide	275	475	825
No. 850 Lumber Truck, six-wheel, red cab, silver bed, 18-3/4" long, 5-3/4" high, 6-1/4" wide	130	225	360
No. 860 Stake Truck, six-wheel, 16-1/2" long, 6-5/4" high, 6" wide, red cab and flat bed, green stakes	175	350	500
No. 875 Builder's Supply Fleet, Pick-up, red semi cab, stake box trailer, lumber box trailer	NPF	NPF	NPF
No. 880 Pickup Truck, 13-3/4" long	150	350	650
No. 900 Tonka Fire Department, Aerial Ladder, Suburban Pumper, Emergency Rescue Squad Truck, metal fire chief badge, box measures 33" long, 6" high, 13-1/2" wide	NPF	NPF	NPF
No. 925 Farm Stake Truck, white w/blue stakes, 13-1/2" long, 5-3/4" high, 6" wide	150	250	460
No. 950 Suburban Pumper, red, 17" long, 6-1/2" high, 6" wide, black fire hoses, red hydrant (rare)	150	275	450
No. 960 Wrecker, 12-1/2" long, 6-1/2" high, white truck, black boom	100	300	450
No. 975 State Highway Dept. Set, "highway yellow" (orange) color, Road Grader, Dump Truck, Pickup Truck, Hi-Way hydraulic dump truck, 6 road signs	NPF	NPF	NPF
No. 980 Hi-Way Hydraulic Dump Truck, 13" long	130	280	395
No. 990 Wrecker, white, black boom, 12" long, rare	390	525	800
Rescue Squad Van, 11-3/4" long, 7-1/2" high, packaged with the Tonka Fire Department set	225	400	850

1957

	C6	C8	C10
No. 02 Pickup Truck, blue, 12-1/2" long, 5-1/2" high, 5-1/2" wide, w/trailer hitch, tailgate has plated chains	75	150	250
No. 04 Farm Stake Truck, light blue cab and bed, dark blue stakes, 13-1/2" long, 5-3/4" high, 6" wide	190	375	480

	C6	C8	C10
No. 06 Dump Truck, red cab and frame, green dump bed, 13" long	75	150	300
No. 08 Shovel, orange steam shovel sold alone, 15" long, 12-1/4" high, 6" wide, originally retailed for $3.98	NPF	NPF	NPF
No. 10 Parcel Delivery Van, 12" long, 7" high, 5-1/2" wide, sliding door, 2 opening rear doors, "Parcel Delivery" decals	200	350	500
No. 12 Road Grader, orange, 13" long, 6" high, 6" wide	50	100	150
No. 14 Tonka Logger, red cab, silver frame w/chains and round logs, 23-3/4" long, 6" high, 6" wide	175	250	450
No. 16 Gasoline Truck, red tanker truck, 15" long, 5-3/4" high, 6" wide	350	525	1000
No. 18 Wrecker, white w/black boom, dual tires at rear, 12-1/2" long, 6-1/2" high, 6-1/4" wide	100	250	450
No. 20 Hydraulic Dump Truck, 13" long, 6" high, 6" wide	80	165	290
No. 22 Lumber Truck, bronze cab, aluminum bed, w/lumber, 18" long, 5-3/4" high, 6" wide	150	275	400
No. 24 Rescue Squad Truck, white van w/sliding side door, 2 opening rear doors, 12" long, 7-1/2" high, 5-1/2" wide	120	260	400
No. 26 Pickup with Box Trailer, blue pickup w/blue box trailer, trailer has same tailgate w/chains as pickup, 20-1/2" long, 5-1/2" high, 5-3/4" wide	125	250	400
No. 28 Pickup with Stake Trailer, blue pickup w/red stake trailer and animal, 20-1/2" long, 5-1/2" high, 5-3/4" wide	150	250	400
No. 30 Cargo King (Grain Hauler), red tractor, open aluminum trailer, 23-1/2" long, 6" high, 6" wide	100	200	325
No. 32 Stock Rack Truck with Animals, blue cab and frame, red stock rack w/sliding rear door, comes w/horse, bull, sheep, 16-1/4" long	175	365	650
No. 34 Thunderbird Express Semi, white tractor and semi, "Thunderbird" decals, 24" long, 8-1/4" high, 6" wide	150	400	600
No. 36 Livestock Van, red cab and trailer w/slits, 24" long, 9-1/4" high, 6-1/4" wide	110	200	350
No. 38 Allied Moving Van, 24" long, 9" high, 6" wide, orange, "Allied Van Lines" decals	NPF	NPF	NPF

Tonka 1954 Steel Carrier Truck. Photo courtesy Continental Hobby House

Tonka 1954 Utility Truck. Photo courtesy the DeSalle Collection

	C6	C8	C10
No. 40 Shovel and Carry-All Trailer, orange tractor, loboy and steam shovel; 32" long, 14-1/4" high, 6" wide	NPF	NPF	NPF
No. 42 Big Mike Dual Hydraulic Dump Truck, 14" long, 7" high, 8-1/4" wide, two hydraulic pumps, 2-position tail gate, twin tandem rear wheels	325	595	1000
No. 44 3-in-1 Hi-Way Service Truck, w/two snowblades, 13" long	275	400	700
No. 46 Suburban Pumper, red fire pumper, 2- 6" black rubber hoses on one side, aluminum ladder on other, black hose coiled, fire hydrant that could be hooked up to a standard garden hose, 17" long, 6-1/2" high, 6" wide	125	250	400
No. 48 Hydraulic Aerial Ladder Truck, red w/aluminum trim and ladders, 32" long, 7-1/2" high, 6" wide	200	300	500
No. 900 Tonka Fire Department Set, Aerial Ladder, Suburban Pumper, Emergency Rescue Squad Truck, metal fire chief badge, box measures 33" long, 6" high, 13-1/2" wide	NPF	NPF	NPF
No. AC-300 Hi-Way Sign Set, 6 road signs, 2 road barriers	NPF	NPF	NPF
No. AC-302 Tonka Stock Corral, wooden pieces, 6 fence sections, ramp	NPF	NPF	NPF
No. AC-304 Tonka Farm Animals, set of 6 assorted polystyrenne plastic animals	NPF	NPF	NPF
No. AC-306 Scraper Blade w/mounting Bracket, orange, attaches to any Tonka Dump truck, 7" wide	NPF	NPF	NPF
No. AC-308 "V" Blade Snow Plow w/mounting bracket, orange, attaches to any Tonka Dump truck, 9" wide, originally retailed for $1.98	NPF	NPF	NPF
No. AC-312 Stake Trailer, red, 5-1/2" long, 4-3/4" high, 5" wide	30	45	75
No. B-200 Tonka Trailer Rental Set, blue Pickup truck w/trailer hitch, 2 box trailers, 1 stake-side trailer, originally retailed for $7.95	NPF	NPF	NPF

	C6	C8	C10
No. B-202 Tonka Stock Farm, Stock Rack Truck has blue cab and frame w/red stock trailer, 6 farm animals, wooden corral pieces and ramp	NPF	NPF	NPF
No. B-204 Tonka Truck-Trailer Rental, Farm Stake truck, blue Pickup truck, stake trailer, box trailer	NPF	NPF	NPF
No. B-206 Tonka Trailer Fleet, 2 red tractors, Logger trailer, Cargo King (Grain Hauler) trailer, Livestock trailer, 4 farm animals	NPF	NPF	NPF
No. B-208 State Hi-Way Dept. Set, "highway yellow" color, Dump Truck, Road Grader, Hi-Way Hydraulic Dump Truck, Pickup Truck, road signs, originally retailed for $19.95	NPF	NPF	NPF
No. B-210 Road Builder Set, Hydraulic Dump Truck, Dump Truck, Road Grader, Steam Shovel, Carry-All Trailer (Loboy), Scraper blade and mounting bracket, originally retailed for $24.95	NPF	NPF	NPF

1958

	C6	C8	C10
No. 02 Pickup Truck, blue, tailgate opens, two chains hold it	100	150	300
No. 03 Utility Truck, red tractor and frame, open aluminum bed	100	150	300
No. 04 Farm Stake Truck, green truck, white stakes	100	150	300
No. 05 Sportsman Pickup w/Topper, blue, "Sportsman" decals, 12-3/4" long	150	225	450
No. 06 Dump Truck, red cab, green dump bed	100	150	300
No. 12 Road Grader, orange	75	112	150
No. 18 Wrecker Truck, white body, black boom, tow chain and hook	100	250	450
No. 20 Hydraulic Dump Truck, bronze, originally retailed for $3.98	125	175	275
No. 28 Pickup with Stake Trailer and Animal, blue truck, red stake trailer, plastic animal	125	175	350
No. 29 Sportsman Truck w/Box Trailer, blue Sportsman truck, blue box trailer	150	225	400
No. 32 Stock Rack Truck, white truck and frame, open red side racks	175	300	500
No. 33 Gasoline Truck, red tanker truck, "Gasoline" decals, hinged back door, hose and nozzle	350	500	900
No. 34 Deluxe Sportsman with Boat Trailer, red truck w/white roof, red trailer, gray boat w/detachable motor, 22-3/4" long	150	325	750

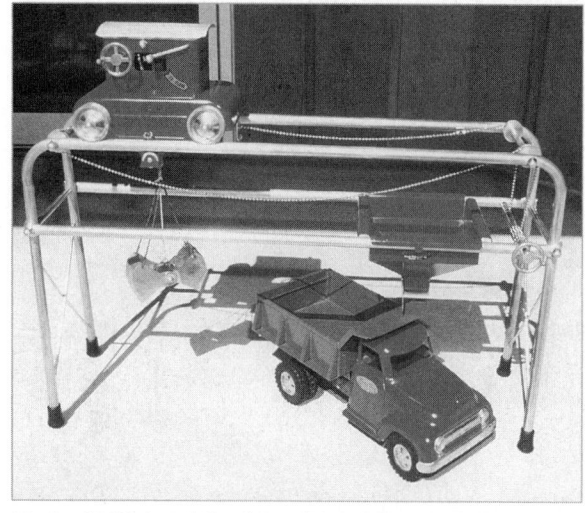

Tonka 1955 Aerial Sand Loader Set, No. 992. Photo courtesy Thomas G. Nefos

Tonka 1955 Dump Truck. Photo courtesy Thomas G. Nefos

Tonka 1955 Minute Maid Orange Juice Van. Photo courtesy the DeSalle Collection

Tonka 1955 Pickup Truck. Photo courtesy the DeSalle Collection

Tonka 1956 Dump Truck, 13". Photo courtesy the DeSalle Collection

Tonka 1955 Stake Truck, six wheel. Photo courtesy the DeSalle Collection

Tonka 1956 Allied Semi. Photo courtesy DeSalle Collection

Tonka 1956 Pumper, 17". Photo courtesy the DeSalle Collection

Tonka 1957 Suburban Pumper. Photo courtesy Mark McManus

Tonka 1957 Lumber Truck. Photo courtesy DeSalle Collection

Tonka 1957 Thunderbird Express Semi, 24". Photo courtesy the DeSalle Collection

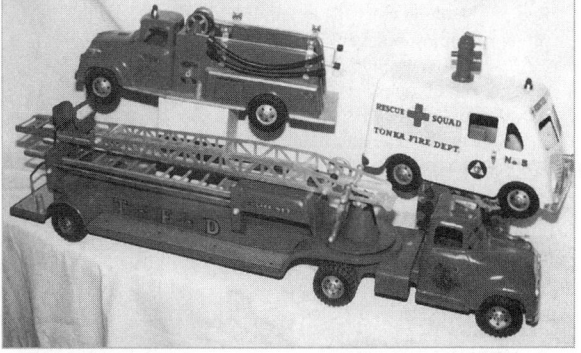

Tonka Fire Set, 1957: Rescue Squad Ladder Truck, Pumper, Hydrant. Photo courtesy Bob Smith

Tonka 1957 Hydraulic Dump Truck, bronze. Photo courtesy DeSalle Collection

Left to right: Tonka 1957 Gasoline Truck, 1958 TDF Tanker, 1958 Gasoline Truck. Photo courtesy DeSalle Collection

	C6	C8	C10
No. 35 Farm Stake w/Two-Horse Trailer, green truck w/white stakes, white horse trailer, 2 black horses, 21-3/4" long	125	250	450
No. 36 Livestock Van, red tractor and trailer, rear door becomes ramp	175	250	450
No. 37 Thunderbird Express, white tractor and trailer, "Thunderbird" decals, rear semi doors open	150	300	600
No. 39 Nationwide Moving Van, white tractor and trailer, "Nation Wide Moving" decals, rear doors open, 24-1/4" long	250	475	800
No. 41 Hi-Way Service Truck, orange hydraulic dump, scraper blade and mounting bracket, road signs	100	200	400
No. 43 Shovel & Carry-All Trailer, orange steam shovel, tractor and trailer (loboy)	200	300	500
No. 45 Big Mike Dual Hydraulic Dump Truck, orange w/large "V" snow plow	375	675	1000
No. 46 Suburban Pumper, red pumper, 2 black rubber hoses, 1 aluminum ladder, 1 rolled black rubber hose, fire hydrant connects to garden hose	125	225	400
No. 48 Hydraulic Aerial Ladder, red w/aluminum ladder that extends 36"	100	250	450
No. AC310 Box Trailer, blue, tailgate lowers	NPF	NPF	NPF
No. AC311 Boat Trailer, red trailer, gray boat, outboard motor	NPF	NPF	NPF
No. AC312 Stake Trailer, red, originally retailed for $1.98	NPF	NPF	NPF
No. AC314 Horse Trailer, white trailer w/2 horses, "Tonka Farms" decals	NPF	NPF	NPF
No. AC316 Corral and Four Animals, corral has 6 fence sections, 4 plastic animals	NPF	NPF	NPF
No. AC318 Scraper and Snow Plow w/mounting bracket, orange, 7" wide Scraper, 9" wide "V" shaped snow plow, mounting bracket	NPF	NPF	NPF
No. AC320 Hi-Way Sign Set, 6 road signs, 2 road blocks	NPF	NPF	NPF
No. B202 Tonka Stock Farm, Stock Rack Truck has white cab and frame w/red stock trailer, 6 farm animals, wooden corral pieces and ramp	NPF	NPF	NPF
No. B204 Tonka Trailer Rental Set, blue pickup w/trailer hitch, green Farm Stake truck, white stake trailer, blue box trailer	NPF	NPF	NPF
No. B205 Farm Set, white Stock Rack truck, green Farm Stake truck, red stake trailer w/animal, white horse trailer w/2 horses	NPF	NPF	NPF
No. B207 Hi-Way Construction Set, all pieces lime green, Dump Truck, Scraper blade w/mounting bracket, Road Grader, Steam Shovel, Carry-All tractor and loboy, originally retailed for $19.95	NPF	NPF	NPF
No. B209 Deluxe Farm Set, red Livestock Van, white Stock Rack truck w/red stock, green Farm Stake Truck, white horse trailer w/2 horses, corral, farm animals	NPF	NPF	NPF
No. B211 State Hi-Way Department, all pieces "highway yellow," Dump Truck w/Scraper blade and mounting bracket, Hi-Way Hydraulic Dump Truck w/"V" shaped snow plow and mounting bracket, Road Grader, Pickup truck, 6 road signs, 2 road barriers	NPF	NPF	NPF
No. B213 Tonka Fire Department, red Suburban Pumper, white tanker truck, red Aerial Ladder truck, fire chief's badge	NPF	NPF	NPF

1959

	C6	C8	C10
No. 01 Service Truck, blue, aluminum ladder, 12-3/4" long	100	150	350
No. 02 Pickup Truck, copper, tailgate snaps open/closed	75	150	250
No. 03 Platform Stake, yellow tractor and flatbed	100	200	325
No. 04 Farm Stake Truck, green tractor and flatbed, white stakes	100	200	325
No. 05 Sportsman, w/white boat strapped to roof	100	175	350
No. 06 Dump Truck, red cab and frame, green dump bed	75	150	250
No. 07 Logger, red tractor, aluminum frame, wooden logs held in place by chains	125	225	310
No. 12 Road Grader, orange	50	100	150
No. 14 Dragline, yellow, new design, 20" long	100	175	375
No. 16 Air Express, blue, box truck, opening rear doors	350	425	700
No. 18 Wrecker, white wrecker w/black boom, chain and hook	100	250	450
No. 20 Hydraulic Dump Truck, bronze w/hydraulic dump bed	100	175	275
No. 22 Deluxe Sportsman, blue pickup w/white roof, boat trailer, boat, outboard motor	150	325	500
No. 28 Pickup and Trailer, bronze pickup truck, bronze stake trailer, animal	75	150	250
No. 30 Tandem Platform Stake, bronze open-bed truck and tandem trailer, 28-1/4" long	240	450	800
No. 32 Stock Rack Truck, white cab and frame, tall red removable racks	100	200	300
No. 33 Hydraulic Hi-Way Dump, orange dump, 2 road signs,	100	225	325
No. 35 Farm Stake and Horse Trailer, Farm Stake truck w/white stakes, white horse trailer w/2 horses	125	250	450
No. 36 Tandem Air Express, blue, w/large box trailer, 24" long	325	650	1000

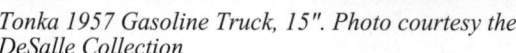

Tonka 1957 Gasoline Truck, 15". Photo courtesy the DeSalle Collection

	C6	C8	C10
No. 37 Thunderbird Express, white tractor and trailer, "Thunderbird" decals, rear semi doors open	NPF	NPF	NPF
No. 39 Allied Moving Van, orange tractor and trailer, "Allied Van Lines" decals, trailer rear doors open	125	275	400
No. 40 Car Carrier, yellow tractor and car hauler, 3 plastic cars	100	300	500
No. 41 Boat Transport, blue tractor and boat hauler, 4 white boats, 2 outboard motors, 38" long	250	350	700
No. 42 Hydraulic Land Rover, heavy-duty orange dump truck, 15" long	550	825	1700
No. 44 Dragline & Trailer, lime green, tractor, flatbed (loboy), dragline shovel, 26-1/4" long	150	275	400
No. 46 Suburban Pumper, white pumper, 2 black rubber hoses, aluminum ladder, black rubber coiled hose, hydrant hooks to garden hose	125	275	400
No. 48 Hydraulic Aerial Ladder Truck, red fire truck w/extending ladder	125	275	400
No. AC308 Scale Model Cars, Hardtop, Sedan, Wagon, retailed for $1.00 each	NPF	NPF	NPF
No. AC310 Box Trailer, bronze, tailgate lowers, 8-1/2" long	NPF	NPF	NPF
No. AC311 Boat Trailer, red trailer, gray boat, outboard motor, 12-1/2" long	NPF	NPF	NPF
No. AC312 Stake Trailer, bronze, originally retailed for $2.00, 8-1/2" long	NPF	NPF	NPF
No. AC314 Horse Trailer, white trailer w/2 horses, "Tonka Farms" decals, 8-1/2" long	NPF	NPF	NPF
No. AC316 Corral and Four Animals, corral has 6 fence sections, 4 plastic animals	NPF	NPF	NPF
No. AC318 Scraper and Snow Plow w/mounting bracket, orange, 7" wide Scraper, 9" wide "V" shaped snow plow, mounting bracket	NPF	NPF	NPF
No. AC320 Hi-Way Sign Set, 6 road signs, 2 road blocks, 4-1/2" high	NPF	NPF	NPF
No. B202 Stock Farm set, white Stock Rack Truck w/tall red stakes, coral, 4 animals	NPF	NPF	NPF
No. B203 Sanitary Service set, square back, white Sanitary truck, 2 refuse containers	450	700	1000
No. B204 Farm set, No. 35 Farm Stake and Horse Trailer, No. 28 Pickup and Stake Trailer	NPF	NPF	NPF

Tonka 1958 Suburban Pumper, No. 46 with hydrant. Photo courtesy Harvey K. Rainess

	C6	C8	C10
No. B205 Dragline and Crane set, No. 04 Dragline, No. 06 Dump Truck, No. 07 Logger	NPF	NPF	NPF
No. B206 Trailer Sales Set, tan No. 05 Sportsman, bronze No. 02 Pickup truck and 4 trailers, No. AC310 Box trailer, No. AC312 Stake trailer, No. AC314 Horse trailer w/2 horses, No. AC311 Boat trailer w/boat and motor	NPF	NPF	NPF
No. B207 Hi-Way Construction Set, lime green, No. 06 Dump truck, No. 12 Road Grader, No. 44 Dragline, tractor and flatbed trailer (loboy)	NPF	NPF	NPF
No. B210 State Hi-Way Department Set, orange, No. 06 Dump truck, No. 12 Road Grader, No. 33 Hi-Way Hydraulic Dump truck, No. 02 Pickup truck, No. AC320 6 Road signs 2 road barriers	NPF	NPF	NPF
No. B212 Tonka Fire Department Set, white, No. 46 Suburban Pumper w/hydrant, No. 48 Hydraulic Aerial Ladder, fire chief's badge	NPF	NPF	NPF

1960

	C6	C8	C10
Jolly Green Giant Special, white, green stake racks	375	450	850
No. 001 Service Truck, blue w/aluminum ladder	100	150	350
No. 002 Pickup, bronze, tailgate opens	100	200	375
No. 004 Farm Stake Truck, teal w/white stakes	100	200	325
No. 005 Sportsman, tan w/boat strapped to top	100	275	400
No. 006 Dump Truck, red and metallic green, retailed for $3.98	75	125	290
No. 008 Timber (Logger), red cab, aluminum frame, logs	150	225	300
No. 012 Road Grader, orange, tilting scraper blade	50	100	150
No. 014 Dragline, lime green shovel w/black bucket, no trailer	65	125	200
No. 018 Wrecker, white sidewalls, black boom, retailed for $4.98	100	150	325
No. 020 Hydraulic Dump, bronze, "hydraulic" decals	75	150	300
No. 022 Deluxe Sportsman, blue pickup w/white roof, blue boat trailer, white/red boat, outboard motor	100	250	400
No. 028 Pickup & Trailer, bronze pickup, bronze stake trailer, plastic animal	100	150	300
No. 035 Farm Stake and Horse Trailer, tan truck, white stakes, white trailer, 2 black horses	125	180	350
No. 037 Thunderbird Express, red tractor w/white roof, red trailer w/horiz. white stripe, black "Thunderbird" decals, 14 tires, rear doors open	150	350	550
No. 039 Allied Moving Van, orange w/"Allied" decals	125	250	450
No. 040 Car Carrier, yellow w/3 scale cars	100	225	450
No. 041 Boat Transport, blue transport, 4 white boats, 2 outboard motors, 38" long	250	450	850
No. 046 Suburban Pumper, red, black hoses, hydrant attaches to garden hose, ladder	100	250	350

	C6	C8	C10
No. 048 Aerial Ladder, red, aluminum ladder extends to 36"	125	250	350
No. 100 Bulldozer, orange, 8-7/8" long, plated roller wheels only in 1960	75	125	200
No. 105 Rescue Squad, white, used same body as Sportsman, boat strapped to top, 13-3/4" long	100	250	450
No. 110 Fisherman Pick-up, w/sportsman, cover, "Fisherman" decals, 14" long	100	175	375
No. 115 Power Boom Loader, 1960 only, blue truck and flatbed trailer, aluminum loader, 18-1/2" long	300	650	1000
No. 120 Cement Mixer, red truck w/white hopper, 15-1/2" long	100	150	300
No. 125 Lowboy and Bulldozer, lime green tractor, flatbed (lowboy) and bulldozer, 26-1/4" long	190	375	675
No. 130 Deluxe Fisherman, blue truck and trailer, new boat w/windshield and white canopy, outboard motor	150	350	625
No. 135 Mobile Dragline, rare, orange cab and flatbed w/dragline mounted on	100	250	500
No. 140 Sanitary Truck, white, hydraulic	350	550	900
No. 145 Tanker, first Tonka w/major use of plastic, adapter attaches to garden hose, 4 qt. capacity, 28" long	100	250	450
No. B200 Stock Farm, red Farm Stake truck w/white stakes, red Stake trailer, corral, 4 animals	NPF	NPF	NPF
No. B201 Timber Company, No. 115 Power Boom Loader, No. 08 Timber truck	NPF	NPF	NPF
No. B204 Farm Set, No. 35 Farm Stake and Trailer, 2 horses, No. 28 Pickup and Stake Trailer, 0	NPF	NPF	NPF
No. B206 Trailer Sales, tan No. 05 Sportsman w/boat, teal No. 02 Pickup truck, tan box trailer, teal stake trailer, white horse trailer, teal boat trailer w/white boat, outboard motor	NPF	NPF	NPF
No. B207 Hi-Way Construction Set, lime green, dump truck, road grader, dragline, tractor and lowboy	NPF	NPF	NPF
No. B215 Bulk Storage, rare, No. 145 Tanker, two 2-qt. holding tanks	NPF	NPF	NPF
No. B218 Paving Department, No. 06 Dump truck, No. 12 Road Grader, No. 100 Bulldozer, No. 120 Cement Mixer	NPF	NPF	NPF
No. B220 State Turnpike, orange, Pickup, Hydraulic Dump truck, Mobile Dragline, Bulldozer, road signs, barriers	NPF	NPF	NPF
No. B225 Fire Department, No. 105 Rescue Squad, No. 46 Suburban Pumper, No. 48 Aerial Ladder, originally retailed for $25.95	NPF	NPF	NPF
Standard Oil Company Wrecker Special	400	600	1200

1961

	C6	C8	C10
No. 002 Pickup, bronze, 12-3/4" long	100	190	320
No. 004 Farm Stake, blue w/white stakes, 14" long	85	175	370
No. 005 Sportsman, tan w/white boat strapped to top, 12-3/4" long	100	150	375

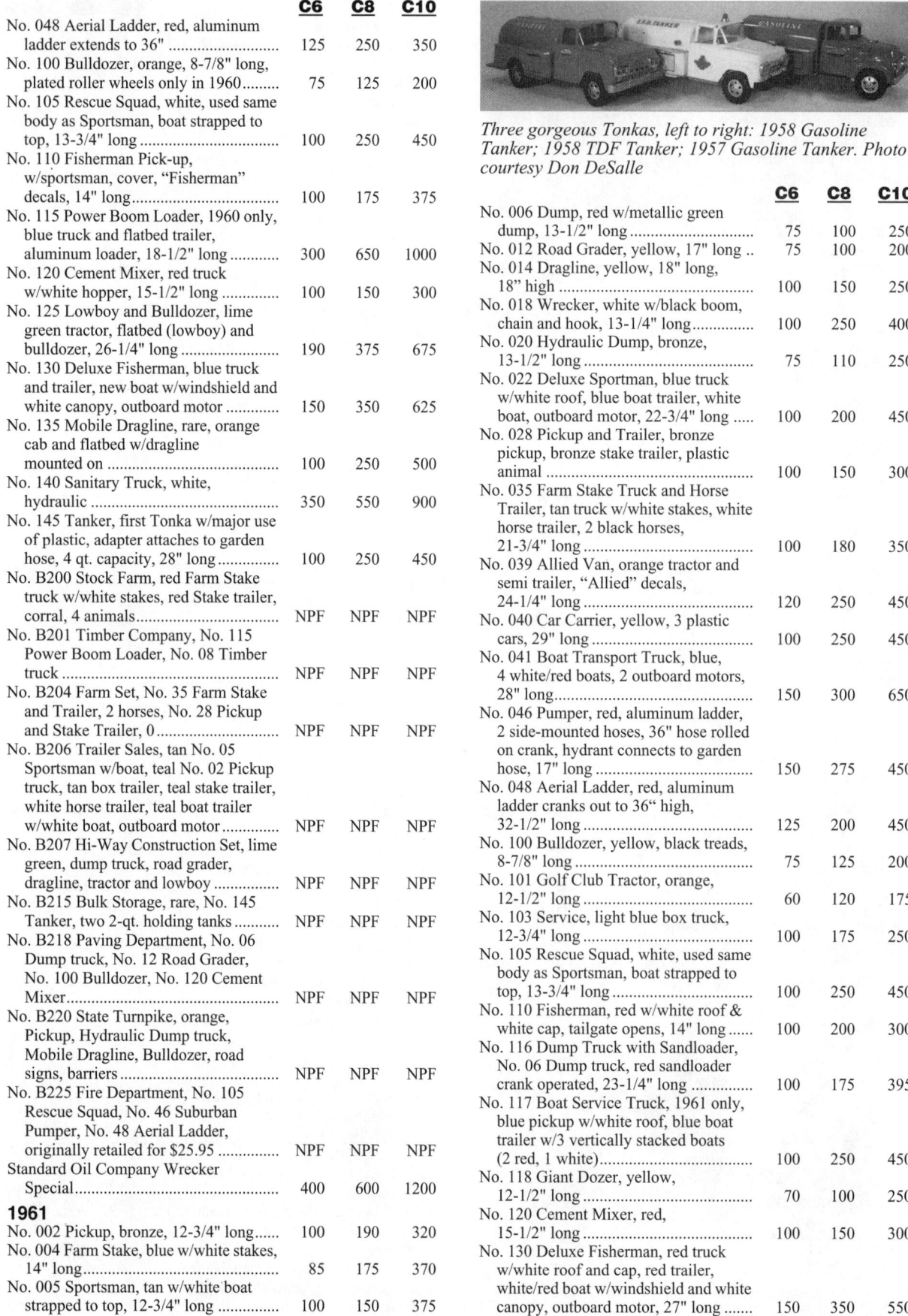

Three gorgeous Tonkas, left to right: 1958 Gasoline Tanker; 1958 TDF Tanker; 1957 Gasoline Tanker. Photo courtesy Don DeSalle

	C6	C8	C10
No. 006 Dump, red w/metallic green dump, 13-1/2" long	75	100	250
No. 012 Road Grader, yellow, 17" long	75	100	200
No. 014 Dragline, yellow, 18" long, 18" high	100	150	250
No. 018 Wrecker, white w/black boom, chain and hook, 13-1/4" long	100	250	400
No. 020 Hydraulic Dump, bronze, 13-1/2" long	75	110	250
No. 022 Deluxe Sportman, blue truck w/white roof, blue boat trailer, white boat, outboard motor, 22-3/4" long	100	200	450
No. 028 Pickup and Trailer, bronze pickup, bronze stake trailer, plastic animal	100	150	300
No. 035 Farm Stake Truck and Horse Trailer, tan truck w/white stakes, white horse trailer, 2 black horses, 21-3/4" long	100	180	350
No. 039 Allied Van, orange tractor and semi trailer, "Allied" decals, 24-1/4" long	120	250	450
No. 040 Car Carrier, yellow, 3 plastic cars, 29" long	100	250	450
No. 041 Boat Transport Truck, blue, 4 white/red boats, 2 outboard motors, 28" long	150	300	650
No. 046 Pumper, red, aluminum ladder, 2 side-mounted hoses, 36" hose rolled on crank, hydrant connects to garden hose, 17" long	150	275	450
No. 048 Aerial Ladder, red, aluminum ladder cranks out to 36" high, 32-1/2" long	125	200	450
No. 100 Bulldozer, yellow, black treads, 8-7/8" long	75	125	200
No. 101 Golf Club Tractor, orange, 12-1/2" long	60	120	175
No. 103 Service, light blue box truck, 12-3/4" long	100	175	250
No. 105 Rescue Squad, white, used same body as Sportsman, boat strapped to top, 13-3/4" long	100	250	450
No. 110 Fisherman, red w/white roof & white cap, tailgate opens, 14" long	100	200	300
No. 116 Dump Truck with Sandloader, No. 06 Dump truck, red sandloader crank operated, 23-1/4" long	100	175	395
No. 117 Boat Service Truck, 1961 only, blue pickup w/white roof, blue boat trailer w/3 vertically stacked boats (2 red, 1 white)	100	250	450
No. 118 Giant Dozer, yellow, 12-1/2" long	70	100	250
No. 120 Cement Mixer, red, 15-1/2" long	100	150	300
No. 130 Deluxe Fisherman, red truck w/white roof and cap, red trailer, white/red boat w/windshield and white canopy, outboard motor, 27" long	150	350	550

Tonka 1960 Service Truck. Photo courtesy Calvin L. Chaussee

	C6	C8	C10
No. 134 Grading Service Truck, Trailer and Bulldozer, yellow and red dump truck, yellow trailer, yellow buldozer, 25-1/2" long total	100	150	350
No. 135 Mobile Dragline	100	250	450
No. 136 Houseboat Set, red w/white roof & white cap Fisherman, red loboy trailer w/tilt, red/white houseboat, outboard motor, 29" long	200	400	800
No. 140 Sanitary Truck, white, hydraulic, 19-1/2" long	400	700	1500
No. 142 Mobile Clam, orange, cab swivels 360 degrees, 27-1/4" long	100	250	450
No. 145 Tanker, holds 4 qts., connects to garden hose, 28" long	100	250	350
No. 146 Giant Dozer and Trailer, orange, Giant Dozer, tractor and loboy, 26-3/4" long	NPF	NPF	NPF
No. 324 Houseboat, plastic, red/white, outboard motor, 13" long	75	150	225
No. 325 Animals, five assorted farm animals	NPF	NPF	NPF
No. B202 Country Club Service Set, No. 100 Bulldozer, No. 101 Golf Club Tractor, blue Pickup truck	NPF	NPF	NPF
No. B204 Farm Set, No. 28 Pickup and Stake trailer w/animal, No. 35 Farm Stake and Horse trailer w/2 horses	NPF	NPF	NPF
No. B206 Trailer Sales Set, No. 05 Sportsman; No. 22 Deluxe Sportsman Pickup, trailer, boat, and outboard motor; blue stake trailer, tan box trailer, white horse trailer	NPF	NPF	NPF
No. B215 Bulk Storage, No. 145 Tanker, 2 storage tanks that fill from garden hose	NPF	NPF	NPF
No. B216 Road Builder, yellow/red dump truck, yellow No. 12 Road Grader, No. 100 Bulldozer, yellow loboy trailer, red Sandloader	NPF	NPF	NPF
No. B218 Paving Department, No. 12 Road Grader, No. 06 Dump, No. 100 Bulldozer, No. 120 Cement Mixer	NPF	NPF	NPF

	C6	C8	C10
No. B219 Construction, orange, Hydraulic Dump, No. 118 Giant Dozer, No. 142 Mobile Clam	NPF	NPF	NPF

1962

	C6	C8	C10
No. 125 Animals, five animals, 2 horses, 2 cows, 1 steer, originally retailed for $1.00	NPF	NPF	NPF
No. 1348 Aerial Ladder, red, aluminum ladder extends to 36" high	100	150	350
No. 200 Jeep Dispatcher, blue, white interior, black steering wheel, 9-3/4" long	50	75	100
No. 201 Serv-I-Car, white, 3 wheels, dump box, 9-1/8" long	75	125	200
No. 2100 Airport Service, No. 249 Universal Jeep, No. 201 Serv-I-car, No. 420 Luggage Service Tractor and luggage trailer, extra luggage trailer	NPF	NPF	NPF
No. 2110 Marina, No. 302 Pickup, red/white 13" Houseboat on red loboy trailer, red/white Motorboat w/windshield on red trailer, red/white Speedboat w/windshield and white canopy, each boat has outboard motor	NPF	NPF	NPF
No. 2120 Farm Set, No. 735 Farm Stake and Horse trailer w/2 horses, yellow pickup w/yellow stake trailer and animal	NPF	NPF	NPF
No. 2130 Super Service, No. 518 Wrecker, No. 200 Dispatcher Jeep, No. 201 Serv-I-car, Stake trailer, Box trailer	NPF	NPF	NPF
No. 2150 Road Builder, No. 512 Road Grader, No. 406 Dump Truck, red Sand Loader, yellow Bulldozer on green loboy trailer	NPF	NPF	NPF
No. 2190 Construction, No. 406 Dump Truck, No. 620 Cement Mixer, No. 524 Dozer Packer, No. 402 Loader	NPF	NPF	NPF
No. 249 Jeep Universal, dark blue, white interior, black steering wheel, side-mounted spare tire	75	125	175
No. 250 Tractor, orange, 8-5/8" long	50	75	100
No. 300 Bulldozer, yellow	50	75	100
No. 301 Utility Dump, 12-1/2" long, revised Golf Club Tractor, 1962 only	100	150	300
No. 302 Pickup, red w/white roof, tailgate opens	95	150	250
No. 308 Stake Pickup, yellow, 12-5/8" long	50	100	200
No. 350 Jeep Surrey, fringe top, pink, striped interior and roof, spare tire, 10-1/2" long	75	125	200
No. 402 Loader, yellow and green	40	60	80

Tonka 1961 Hi-Way Goose Neck Lowboy w/Giant Dozer. Photo courtesy DeSalle Collection

Tonka 1961 Dump Truck. Photo courtesy the DeSalle Collection

	C6	C8	C10
No. 404 Farm Stake Truck, red w/white stakes.....................	50	95	150
No. 405 Sportsman, blue pickup w/white roof and cap, red boat strapped to top..	75	100	200
No. 406 Dump Truck, red cab w/metallic green dump	75	150	275
No. 410 Jet Delivery Truck, blue w/white side panels, 14" long, 1962 only	200	350	850
No. 420 Airlines Luggage Service, blue cart, trailer, 5 suitcases, 16-5/8" long...	100	250	400
No. 512 Road Grader, yellow	45	68	90
No. 514 Dragline, yellow	150	225	300
No. 516 Jeep Runabout, blue jeep w/white interior, blue trailer, red/white boat w/windshield and white canopy, outboard motor, 25-5/8" long	75	175	350
No. 518 Wrecker, new body style, white wrecker w/black boom	75	175	300
No. 520 Hydraulic Dump, orange	75	100	220
No. 524 Dozer Packer, orange, 18-1/4" long, Packer has eleven tires, sold only in 1962..................................	100	250	400
No. 528 Pickup & Trailer, green truck w/white roof, white Stake trailer, plastic animal	50	75	150
No. 530 Camper, blue style-side truck w/white camper attachment, 14" long..	75	150	250
No. 616 Dump Truck and Sand Loader, red/yellow Dump, red Sand Loader	75	125	240
No. 618 Giant Dozer, orange, black treads	100	150	200
No. 620 Cement Mixer, red w/white mixer	85	150	300
No. 735 Farm Stake and Horse Trailer, blue truck w/white stakes, white horse trailer, 2 black horses	75	125	225
No. 739 Allied Van, orange tractor and van, "Allied" decals	125	250	350
No. 834 Grading Service Truck, green/yellow dump, yellow trailer, green bulldozer	70	100	150
No. 840 Car Carrier, yellow w/3 plastic scale cars	100	150	300
No. 926 Pumper, red, aluminum ladder, black hoses, rolled black hose, fire hydrant attaches to garden hose	100	150	300
No. 942 Mobile Clam, orange, originally retailed for $9.00	100	150	320

1963

	C6	C8	C10
No. 050 Mini-Tonka Jeep pickup, red, 9-1/4" long	35	52	70
No. 056 Mini-Tonka Stake Truck, blue, 9-1/4" long	35	52	70
No. 060 Mini-Tonka Dump, red, 9-3/4" long	30	50	75
No. 068 Mini-Tonka Wrecker, white w/red boom, 9-1/2" long	30	50	75
No. 070 Mini-Tonka Camper, pink truck w/white cap, 9-5/8" long.....................	75	112	150
No. 1001 Trencher & Loboy, yellow tractor and loboy, No. 534 Trencher, 28-1/2" long	75	112	150
No. 125 Animals, six animals, 2 horses, 2 cows, 2 bulls, originally retailed for $1.00	NPF	NPF	NPF
No. 1348 Aerial Ladder Truck, red, aluminum ladder extends to 36" high ..	100	150	200
No. 200 Jeep Dispatcher, blue, white interior, black steering wheel, 9-3/4" long	30	50	75

	C6	C8	C10
No. 201 Serv-I-Car, white, 3 wheels, dump box, 9-1/8" long	55	82	110
No. 2100 Airport Service Set, No. 249 Universal Jeep, No. 201 Serv-I-car, No. 420 Luggage Service Tractor and luggage trailer, extra luggage trailer, 10 suitcases	150	225	300
No. 2120 Farm Set, No. 404 Stake, white Horse trailer, red Stake Pickup, red Box trailer, 2 horses, animal	NPF	NPF	NPF
No. 2140 Outdoor Living, all vehicles light green, Surrey Jeep, Camper, Jeep Runabout, boat trailer, boat w/windshield and white canopy..........	NPF	NPF	NPF
No. 2160 Contractor Set, No. 534 Trencher, No. 512 Road Grader, No. 406 Dump, green sand loader	NPF	NPF	NPF
No. 250 Tractor, yellow w/red seat..........	75	112	150
No. 251 Military Jeep Universal, olive drab, white decals, 10-1/2" long	25	38	50
No. 300 Bulldozer, yellow w/black treads	55	82	110
No. 302 Pickup, red w/white roof, trailer hitch	35	52	70
No. 308 Stake Pickup, green w/green stakes..	50	95	150
No. 350 Jeep Surrey, pink, black steering wheel..	50	75	100
No. 352 Loader, yellow	40	60	80
No. 354 Style-Side Pickup, 14" long	40	60	125
No. 404 Farm Stake Truck, white w/red stakes..	60	90	150
No. 406 Dump Truck, red w/green dump bed...	45	68	90
No. 422 Back Hoe, yellow, rear facing seat, 17-1/8" long.................................	100	175	350
No. 425 Jeep Pumper, red, connects to garden hose, ladder, 10-3/4" long	100	175	400
No. 512 Road Grader, yellow, red clearance lights	80	120	160
No. 514 Dragline, yellow w/black bucket	60	90	120
No. 516 Jeep Runabout, blue jeep w/white interior, blue trailer, red/white boat w/windshield and white canopy, outboard motor, 25-5/8" long	75	150	300
No. 518 Wrecker, white w/red boom, red roof light still has metal base	45	75	150
No. 520 Hydraulic Dump Truck, red	45	70	100
No. 522 Style-Side Pickup & Stake Trailer, light green truck w/white roof, white stake trailer, 22-3/4" long	75	125	250
No. 524 Dozer Packer, yellow	200	300	400
No. 530 Camper, blue style-side truck w/white camper attachment, 14" long .	25	50	75
No. 534 Trencher, yellow/black, front bucket, rear hoe, 18-1/4" long	40	75	150
No. 536 Giant Dozer, orange, black treads...	110	160	225
No. 616 Dump Truck & Sand Loader, red/yellow dump, yellow sand loader ..	100	150	235
No. 620 Cement Mixer, red truck w/white mixer	75	125	250
No. 625 Stake Pickup & Horse Trailer, green stake pickup, white horse trailer w/2 black horses, 21-3/4" long overall	75	125	175
No. 640 Ramp Hoist, red truck and flatbed, white roof, 19-1/4" long	175	350	550
No. 720 Terminal Train, fifteen suitcases, red tractor, 3 white trailers, 33-5/8" long	105	175	300

Tonka 1961 Sanitary Truck, No. 140.

Tonka 1961 Tanker, No. 145. Photo courtesy Harvey K. Rainess

Tonka 1962 Cement Mixer. Photo courtesy the DeSalle Collection

Tonka 1963 Camper with original box. Photo courtesy the DeSalle Collection

Tonka 1963 Dump Truck & Sand Loader. Photo courtesy the DeSalle Collection

	C6	C8	C10
No. 739 Allied Van, orange tractor and van, "Allied" decals	118	175	235
No. 840 Car Carrier, yellow w/3 plastic scale cars	42	63	85
No. 926 Pumper, red, aluminum ladder, black hoses, rolled black hose, fire hydrant attaches to garden hose	60	90	120
No. 942 Mobile Clam, orange	75	112	150

1964

	C6	C8	C10
No. 050 Mini-Tonka Pickup, red, white plastic wheels	NPF	NPF	NPF

Tonka 1964 Ramp Hoist, green, very rare. Photo courtesy the DeSalle Collection

Tonka 1968 Air Force Jeep, No. 2252. Photo courtesy Calvin L. Chaussee

Tonka 1964 Jeep Pumper. Photo courtesy the DeSalle Collection

Tonka 1968 Jeep Wrecker and Plow, No. 2435. Photo courtesy Calvin L. Chaussee

	C6	C8	C10
No. 056 Mini-Tonka Stake, blue body, white stake bed	NPF	NPF	NPF
No. 060 Mini-Tonka Dump, light green/yellow	NPF	NPF	NPF
No. 068 Mini-Tonka Wrecker, white w/red boom	NPF	NPF	NPF
No. 070 Mini-Tonka Camper, purple w/white camper cap	NPF	NPF	NPF
No. 076 Mini-Tonka Grader, yellow	NPF	NPF	NPF
No. 077 Mini-Tonka Mixer, red w/white mixer, 9" long	30	50	75
No. 086 Mini-Tonka Van, blue cab, white semi, 16" long	36	54	72
No. 090 Mini-Tonka Livestock Van, red, 16" long	50	75	100
No. 096 Mini-Tonka Carrier, light green, "modern" cab, 18-1/2" long, two scale Corvettes	50	75	150
No. 103 Mini-Tonka Mini 3-Pack, No. 50 Pickup, No. 56 Stake, No. 68 Wrecker	NPF	NPF	NPF
No. 110 Mini-Tonka Mini Contractor Set, yellow, Pickup, Dump, Mixer, Road Grader	NPF	NPF	NPF
No. 125 Animals, six animals, 2 horses, 2 cows, 2 bulls	NPF	NPF	NPF
No. 200 Jeep Dispatcher, blue, white interior, black steering wheel, 9-3/4" long	NPF	NPF	NPF
No. 201 Serv-I-Car, white, 3 wheels, dump box, 9-1/8" long	NPF	NPF	NPF
No. 2120 Farm Set, blue Farm Stake truck w/white stakes, blue Stake Pickup, white Horse trailer w/2 horses, white Stake trailer w/animal	NPF	NPF	NPF
No. 2140 Outdoor Living, light green, Camper, Jeep Surrey, Jeep Runabout w/trailer and boat	NPF	NPF	NPF
No. 2170 Military Set, olive drab, No. 536 Military Giant Dozer, No. 304 Jeep Commander, No. 380 Troop Carrier, Road Grade	NPF	NPF	NPF
No. 250 Military Tractor, olive green tractor, black seat	55	70	100
No. 251 Military Jeep Universal, olive green, steering wheel, spare tire	35	55	75
No. 300 Bulldozer, yellow	NPF	NPF	NPF
No. 302 Pickup, red w/white roof	NPF	NPF	NPF
No. 304 Jeep Commander, olive green, steering wheel, spare tire, plastic "canvas" top, 10-1/2" long	30	50	75
No. 308 Stake Pickup, blue w/white roof	NPF	NPF	NPF
No. 315 Dump Truck, orange, 13-1/2" long	40	60	90
No. 350 Jeep "Surrey", pink jeep, pink striped roof and seats	NPF	NPF	NPF
No. 352 Loader, yellow/black	NPF	NPF	NPF
No. 375 Jeep Wrecker, white Jeep w/black boom, 11" long	75	130	200
No. 380 Troop Carrier, olive drab styleside pickup w/plastic "canvas" cover, 14" long	70	100	150
No. 384 Military Jeep & Box Trailer, olive drab, side-mounted spare tire, 19-3/8" overall	50	75	150
No. 404 Stake Truck, red	70	120	170
No. 406 Dump Truck, green cab, yellow dump bed	35	55	85
No. 422 Backhoe, yellow, truck w/rotating backhoe on rear	NPF	NPF	NPF
No. 425 Jeep Pumper, red, black steering wheel, attaches to garden hose	100	150	275
No. 504 Stake Pickup & Trailer, light green w/white roof, light green trailer, 2 animals, 21-5/8" long	50	75	185
No. 512 Road Grader, yellow	75	120	160
No. 514 Dragline, yellow w/black bucket	60	90	120
No. 516 Jeep Runabout, blue jeep w/white interior, blue trailer, red/white boat w/windshield and white canopy, outboard motor, 25-5/8" long	75	150	300
No. 518 Wrecker, white w/red boom	45	75	150
No. 520 Hydraulic Dump, blue w/white roof, hydraulic action	45	70	100
No. 525 Jeep & Horse Trailer, light green jeep, white horse trailer, 2 horses, 19-1/4" long	45	68	135
No. 526 Shovel, yellow w/black shovel, handle operates shovel	20	40	60
No. 530 Camper, light green styleside pickup, white camper cap	25	50	75
No. 534 Trencher, yellow, black front bucket, yellow back hoe	40	75	150
No. 536 Military Giant Dozer, olive drab, black treads	100	160	220
No. 616 Dump Truck & Sand Loader, red and yellow dump, red sand loader	75	125	175
No. 620 Cement Mixer, red, white	75	125	225
No. 640 Ramp Hoist, park green and white, very rare	300	650	900
No. 739 Allied Van Lines, orange tractor and van, "Allied" decals, black knob on door	75	125	175
No. 840 Car Carrier, yellow, 3 plastic scale cars	45	65	95
No. 900 Mighty Tonka Dump Truck, one of the most popular Tonka vehicles ever made; there were 9,655,000 sold between 1964 and 1983	65	100	230
No. 926 Pumper, red, aluminum ladder, black hoses, rolled black hose, fire hydrant attaches to garden hose	60	90	120
No. 942 Mobile Clam, yellow	50	100	150
No. 998 Aerial Ladder, two auxiliary ladders	50	75	100

TOOTSIETOY

Tootsietoy is one of the best-known names in the world of the toy collecting, and for good reason.

The toys, products of a Chicago concern that now has a century of manufacturing behind it, have long appealed to parents because of their cheap price, and to kids because of their high play value. The Tootsietoy line through the years has included toy cars, trucks, trains, dollhouse furniture, airplanes, and toy soldiers. During the company's heyday, roughly from the 1930s through 1960s, a person would have had to search long and hard to find a child with no knowledge of the trademark.

Dowst and Company started in 1876 in the publishing trade, and moved into manufacturing after the 1893 Columbian World Exposition in Chicago, where the new die-casting technology was introduced to the public. By then named Dowst Brothers, the company released its first die-cast body, free-axle toy car in 1911, the generic Limousine. The first specific-model car, the Model T Ford touring car, followed in 1914. The name Tootsietoy was adopted in the early 1920s and was registered in 1924 as the company's trademark. Theodore Dowst, who joined the firm in 1906, is generally seen as the guiding force behind the grownth of toy production at Dowst Brothers. He remained with the company even after its purchase by Nathan Shure in 1926, until 1945. For most collectors, the toys of the Ted Dowst period are the most noteworthy.

High points in the world of Tootsietoy collecting include the 1933 Graham series, notable for its use of three-piece construction, with separately die-cast bodies, chassis, and radiator grilles, and the 1935 LaSalles, which used four-piece construction, adding a casting for the rear bumpers. Collectors also avidly seek the 1932-33 Funnies series cars, which featured such comic figures as Andy Gump, Uncle Walt, and Moon Mullins.

Interest seems to be growing in the various advertising toys Tootsietoy produced through the years, ranging from the 1932 Wrigley's Railroad Epress truck to more recent U-Haul and Coast to Coast vehicles. Collector demand for post-war toys remains stable at a fairly low level; and it may not grow stronger any time soon, given the heavy contemporary interest in detailed scale models as opposed to made-for-play toys. On the other hand, interest in the post-Vietnam toys is inching upward, reflecting the maturing of the later Baby Boomers.

Contributors: John Gibson, 9713 Pleasant Gate Lane Potomac, Maryland 20854. Mark Rich, P.O. Box 971, Stevens Point, WI, 54481-0971 provided the 4th edition pricing updates.

Miniature Vehicles	C6	C8	C10
0510 Midget Assortment Boxed Set, eight-piece	105	140	175
0510 Midget Assortment Boxed Set, ten-piece	150	200	250
0610 Midget Assortment Boxed Set, twelve-piece	160	210	265
1628 Bus	6	9	12
1629 Wrecker	7	10	14
1630 Racer	5	7	10
1631 DeSoto Airflow Sedan	5	7	10
1632 Zephyr Railcar	7	10	14
1634 Fire Truck	7	10	14
1635 Delivery Van	6	9	12
1635 Delivery Van (Ambulance)	7	10	14
1666 Army Tank	4	6	8
1667 Armored Car	5	7	10

Prewar Tootsietoys	C6	C8	C10
--- 1935 Ford V8 Roadster Fire Chief's Car	105	140	175
--- Box Trailer and Roadscraper Raker, sold only in boxed set farm tractor No. 7003	81	108	595
--- Ford Model A Van, marked "U.S Mail," sold only in sets	50	75	95
--- Graham Commercial Tire & Supply	165	220	275
--- Graham Coupe, four-wheel, Bild-A-Car	65	100	150
--- Graham Roadster, four-wheel, Bild-A-Car	100	150	195

	C6	C8	C10
--- Graham Sedan, four-wheel, Bild-A-Car	65	100	150
--- TransAmerica Bus, sold only in sets	165	220	275
0023 Racer, w/driver intact	45	68	90
0101 Buick Coupe	20	35	50
0102 Buick Roadster	25	45	65
0103 Buick Sedan	20	25	50
0104 Mack Insurance Patrol	25	40	60
0105 Mack Tank Truck	36	48	60
0108 Caterpillar Tractor, original treads only	15	25	35
0109 Ford Pickup Truck	20	30	45
0110 Bluebird Daytona Record Car	25	35	75
0111 1934 Ford V8 Sedan	35	50	70
0111 1935 Ford V8 Sedan	25	35	50
0112 1934 Ford V8 Coupe	30	50	75
0112 1935 Ford V8 Coupe	25	35	45
0113 1934 Ford V8 Wrecker	72	96	120
0113 1935 Ford V8 Wrecker	30	50	65
0114 1934 Ford V8 Convertible Coupe	30	50	70
0114 1935 Ford V8 Convertible Coupe	39	52	65
0115 1934 Ford V8 Convertible Sedan	45	72	90
0115 1935 Ford V8 Convertible Sedan	35	52	65
0116 Ford V8 Roadster	25	40	60
0117 Zephyr Railcar	35	60	n/a
0118 DeSoto Airflow Sedan	20	35	60
0120 Oil Tank Truck	15	25	35
0121 Ford Pickup Truck	25	40	55
0123 Ford Lewis's Camelback Van	195	260	325
0123 Ford McLeans Camelback Van	280	380	475

Tootsietoy made various prewar Graham Sedans.

Tootsietoy Graham Commercial Tire & Supply Co. Van, 1935. Photo courtesy John Gibson

Tootsietoy Wrigley Box Van, No. 1010. Photo courtesy John Gibson

Tootsietoy Massey-Ferguson Farm Tractors, No. 1011, in red-and-silver and green-and-silver color schemes. Photo courtesy John Gibson

	C6	C8	C10
0123 Ford Miller & Rhoads Camelback Van	300	400	500
0123 Ford Shepards Camelback Van	285	380	475
0123 Ford Special Delivery Camelback Van	25	38	50
0123 Ford Wieboldt's Camelback Van	285	380	475
0180 Lincoln Zephyr & Roamer House Trailer, w/o wind-up motor	435	655	875
0180 Lincoln Zephyr & Roamer House Trailer, w/wind-up motor	660	880	1100
0187 Mack Auto Transport, w/up-tilted trailer and three vehicles	360	480	600
0190 Mack Auto Transport, w/four Buicks	165	220	275
0190 Mack Auto Transport, w/three Buicks	135	180	225
0191 Contractors Tipper Set	100	150	200
0192 Mack Tootsie Toy Dairy, two-piece cab, three trailers	75	100	225
0192 Mack Tootsietoy Dairy, one-piece cab, three trailers	100	168	210
0198 Mack Auto Transport, one-piece cab, three 1935 Fords	195	260	325
0198 Mack Auto Transport, yellow, two-piece cab, three '34 Fords	360	480	600
0230 LaSalle Sedan	15	20	30
0231 Coupe	15	20	30
0232 Open Touring Coupe	25	35	45
0233 Boattail Roadster	20	35	55
0234 Box Van	15	20	30
0235 Oil Tank Truck	20	25	40
0236 Fire Engine, Hook and Ladder	20	25	40
0237 Fire Engine, Insurance Patrol	15	25	40
0238 Fire Engine, Hose Wagon	20	30	40
0239 Station Wagon	15	35	55
0511 Graham Roadster, five-wheel	50	115	150
0512 Graham Coupe, five-wheel	50	115	150
0513 Graham Sedan, five-wheel	50	115	150
0514 Graham Convertible Coupe, five-wheel	50	125	175
0515 Graham Convertible Sedan, five-wheel	50	125	175
0516 Graham Town Car, five-wheel	50	115	150

	C6	C8	C10
0611 Graham Roadster, six-wheel	50	115	150
0612 Graham Coupe, six-wheel	50	115	150
0613 Graham Sedan, six-wheel	50	115	150
0614 Graham Convertible Coupe, six-wheel	50	125	175
0615 Graham Convertible Sedan, six-wheel	50	125	175
0616 Graham Towncar, six-wheel	50	115	140
0712 LaSalle Coupe	100	200	300
0713 LaSalle Sedan	140	200	275
0714 LaSalle Convertible Coupe	150	225	325
0715 LaSalle Convertible Sedan	140	200	300
0716 Briggs Lincoln prototype, "Doodlebug"	50	75	100
801 Mack Express Stake Semi-trailer, one-piece cab	78	104	130
0801 Mack Express Stake Semi-trailer, two-piece cab	96	128	160
0802 Mack Domaco Tank Semi-trailer, one-piece cab	87	116	145
0802 Mack Domaco Tank Semi-trailer, two-piece cab	111	148	185
0803 Mack Long Distance Hauling Semi-trailer	150	200	250
0804 Mack City Fuel Coal Truck, four-wheel	90	180	250
0804 Mack City Fuel Coal Truck, ten-wheel	60	120	175
0805 Mack Tootsietoy Dairy Semi-trailer Truck	105	140	175
0806 Graham Wrecker	50	110	150
0807 Delivery Motorcycle, adapted from 5103	175	260	350
0808 Graham Tootsietoy Dairy	85	132	175
0809 Graham Ambulance	85	132	175
0810 Mack Railway Express Co. Truck, w/"Wrigley's Gum" ad, one-piece cab	70	150	225

Mack Tootsietoy Dairy Semi-trailer Truck.

Tootsietoy Doodlebug, Briggs Lincoln prototype, 1935, No. 716. Photo courtesy John Gibson

Tootsietoy Mack Stake Truck, No. 4638. Photo courtesy Phillips NY

Tootsietoy Shell Oil Truck, No. 1009. Photo courtesy John Gibson

	C6	C8	C10
0810 Mack Railway Express Co. Truck, w/"Wrigley's Gum" ad, two-piece cab	70	150	225
1006 Standard Oil Truck	25	50	75
1007 Sinclair Oil Truck	25	50	75
1008 Texaco Oil Truck	25	50	75
1009 Shell Oil Truck	25	50	75
1010 Wrigley Box Van	45	60	85
1011 Massey-Ferguson Farm Tractor	150	300	400
1016 Auburn Roadster, jumbo torpedo-single color	15	30	45
1016 Auburn Roadster, jumbo torpedo-two tone	36	48	60
1017 Coupe, jumbo torpedo-single color	20	30	40
1017 Coupe, jumbo torpedo-two tone	30	40	50
1018 Sedan, jumbo torpedo-single color	23	34	45
1019 Pickup Truck, jumbo torpedo-single color	23	34	45
1019 Pickup Truck, jumbo torpedo-two tone	23	34	45
1026 Cross Country Bus, jumbo torpedo, fully skirted	45	60	75
1027 Wrecker, jumbo torpedo, single color	23	34	45
1027 Wrecker, jumbo torpedo, two tone	36	48	60
1033 Buck Rogers Attack Ship	75	150	225
1040 Fire Engine, hook and ladder	40	60	75
1041 Fire Engine, hose Car	35	50	80
1042 Fire Engine, insurance patrol w/single ladder and rear fireman	38	56	75
1042 Fire Engine, insurance patrol, open end	25	40	60
1043 No. 111 Ford Sedan and Small House Trailer	51	68	85
1044 Roamer House Trailer, w/door and tin bottom	297	396	495
1045 Greyhound Deluxe Bus, open front fenders and tin bottom	55	83	110
1045 Greyhound Deluxe Bus, Streamliner, open front fenders, 1937, 5-3/4" long	35	50	75

	C6	C8	C10
1046 Station Wagon	43	64	85
4528 Limousine	20	40	65
4570 Ford, Model T, Open Tourer	33	50	65
4610 Ford Model T Pickup Truck	30	50	70
4629 (Yellow Cab) Sedan	10	20	30
4630 (Federal) Grocery Delivery Van	45	70	100
4631 (Federal) Bakery Delivery Van	50	85	110
4632 (Federal) Market Delivery Van	55	85	110
4633 (Federal) Laundry Delivery Van	50	85	110
4634 (Federal) Milk Delivery Van	55	85	110
4634 Army Supply Truck	25	40	55
4635 (Federal) Florist Delivery Van	75	175	220
4635 Armored Car, 1938-41	25	35	65
4636 Buick Coupe	30	42	65
4638 Mack Stake Truck	25	40	60
4639 Mack Coal Truck	60	120	160
4640 Mack Tank Truck	25	40	55
4641 Buick Touring Car	25	45	70
4642 Long Range Cannon	7	15	30
4643 Mack Anti-Aircraft Gun	25	40	55
4644 Mack Searchlight Truck	25	40	55
4645 Mack US Mail - Airmail Service	40	70	100
4646 Caterpillar Tractor, original treads only	20	30	50
4647 Renault Tank, original treads only	23	34	45
4648 Steamroller	75	150	200
4651 Fageol Safety Coach, 1927	28	40	60
4652 Fire Engine, hook and ladder	45	60	75
4653 Fire Engine, water tower	51	68	85
4654 Farm Tractor for Army Field Battery Set, No. 5071	60	100	145
4654 Huber Star Farm Tractor, 1927, assorted colors, black chassis	60	100	145
4655 Ford, Model A Coupe, 1928	25	35	50
4656 Buick Coupe in tinplate garage	60	90	150
4657 Buick Sedan in tinplate garage	60	90	150
4658 Mack Insurance Patrol, in tinplate garage	135	208	260
4665 Ford Model A Sedan	20	30	40
4666 Bluebird I Daytona Record Car	36	48	60
4670 Mack Tractor and two Semi-trailers, "A&P," "American Express"	180	240	300

Tootsietoy Mack Express Stake Semi-trailer, No. 801, two-piece cab. Photo courtesy John Gibson

Tootsietoy Mack Domaco Tank Semi-trailer, No. 802, two-piece cab. Photo courtesy John Gibson

Left to right: Tootsietoy Station Wagon, No. 1046, 1940; reissued postwar Station Wagon. Photo courtesy John Gibson

Tootsietoy Ford Model T, Open Tourer. Photo courtesy David Richter

Tootsietoy Federal Milk Delivery Vans.

Tootsietoy Florist Delivery Van, No. 4635, 1924. Photo courtesy John Gibson

Left to right: Tootsietoy 1935 Ford Coupe; 1934 Ford Coupe.

Tootsietoy Overland Bus Lines, No. 4680.

Tootsietoy Mack A&P Trailer Truck, No. 4670, 1929. Photo courtesy John Gibson

Tootsietoy Kayo Ice Wagon, No. 5105, articulated version, from 1932 Tootsietoy Funnies Series. Photo courtesy John Gibson

Tootsietoy Moon Mullins Police Wagon, No. 5104, non-articulated, from the 1932 Funnies series. Photo courtesy John Gibson

Tootsietoy Mack Long Distance Hauling Semi-trailer, No. 803. Photo courtesy John Gibson

Tootsietoy Mack City Fuel Coal Truck, No. 804. Photo courtesy The Graham Works.

	C6	C8	C10
4680 Overland Bus Lines	54	72	90
5101 Andy Gump Roadster, articulated...	225	340	500
5101 Andy Gump Roadster, standard	175	265	350
5102 Uncle Walt Roadster, articulated	225	340	500
5102 Uncle Walt Roadster, standard	175	265	350
5103 Smitty Motorcycle, articulated	225	340	500
5103 Smitty Motorcycle, standard	175	265	350
5104 Moon Mullins Police Wagon, articulated	225	340	450
5104 Moon Mullins Police Wagon, standard	175	265	350
5105 Kayo Ice Wagon, articulated	240	320	400
5105 Kayo Ice Wagon, standard	150	225	300
5106 Uncle Willie Rowboat, articulated..	240	320	400
5106 Uncle Willie Rowboat, standard	135	210	275
6001 Buick Roadster, GM series	45	60	75
6002 Buick Coupe, GM series	45	60	75
6003 Buick Brougham, GM series	20	35	70
6004 Buick Sedan, GM series	25	35	55
6005 Buick Touring Car, GM series	50	75	110
6006 Buick Screenside Delivery Truck, GM series	25	35	50
6-01 No Name Roadster, GM series	50	100	140
6015 Lincoln Zephyr, plain version	270	360	450
6015 Lincoln Zephyr, wind-up	450	600	750
6016 Lincoln Wrecker, plain version	200	425	600
6016 Lincoln Wrecker, wind-up	570	760	950
6-02 No Name Coupe, GM series	72	96	120
6-03 No Name Brougham, GM series	72	96	120
6-04 No Name Sedan, GM series	50	100	135
6-05 No Name Touring Car, GM series...	93	124	155
6-06 No Name Screenside Delivery Truck, GM series	90	120	150
6101 Cadillac Roadster, GM series	57	76	95
6102 Cadillac Coupe, GM series	57	76	95
6103 Cadillac Brougham, GM series	40	60	85
6104 Cadillac Sedan, GM series	57	76	95
6105 Cadillac Touring Car, GM series	50	90	120
6106 Cadillac Screenside Delivery Truck, GM series	66	88	110
6201 Chevrolet Roadster, GM series	20	45	90

	C6	C8	C10
6202 Chevrolet Coupe, GM series	20	45	90
6203 Chevrolet Brougham, GM series	40	60	85
6204 Chevrolet Sedan, GM series	20	35	75
6205 Chevrolet Touring Car, GM series..	60	150	200
6206 Chevrolet Screenside Delivery Truck, GM series	66	88	110
6301 Oldsmobile Roadster, GM series	25	45	75
6302 Oldsmobile Coupe, GM series	25	35	50
6303 Oldsmobile Brougham, GM series .	25	35	50
6304 Oldsmobile Sedan, GM series	25	35	50
6305 Oldsmobile Touring Car, GM series	25	35	50
6306 Oldsmobile Screenside Delivery Truck, GM series	66	88	110
6665 Ford Model A Sedan	25	35	50

Postwar

	C6	C8	C10
1040 Hook and Ladder, 4" long	20	25	40
1041 Hose Car, 4" long	35	50	80
1931 Ford B Hot Rod, 3"	5	10	20
1940 Ford Special Deluxe Convertible, 6" long	25	41	55
1940 Ford V8 Hot Rod, 6" long	15	25	35
1941 Chrysler Windsor Convertible, 4" long	20	30	45
1941 International K1 Panel Truck, 4" long	20	30	55
1941 White Army Half Track, 4" long	18	26	35
1942 Chrysler Thunderbolt Experimental Roadster, 6" long	13	26	40
1946 International K11 Oil Tanker, 6" long	12	23	35
1947 Chevrolet Coupe, 4" long	13	19	25
1947 Futuristic-Looking Pickup Truck, commonly called Hudson	37	56	75
1947 Jeepster, 3" long	2	5	15
1947 Kaiser Sedan, 6" long	25	45	55
1947 Mack L Line Closed Side Stake, 6" long	25	35	55
1947 Mack L Line Dump Truck, 6" long	20	35	55

Tootsietoy Fire Engine, Hook & Ladder, No. 1040. Photo courtesy John Gibson

Tootsietoy Roamer House Trailer, No. 1044, with door and tin bottom. Photo courtesy John Gibson

Tootsietoy Graham Wrecker, No. 0806. Photo courtesy Phillips NY

Tootsietoy No. 0804 "City Fuel Co." rarer 4-wheel version, issued 1936, in catalog from 1936-38. Photo courtesy The Graham Werkes

Tootsietoy No. 4630 "Store Name" Federal Delivery Van; Emil Kraus, State at 18th, an Erie, PA store, 1924. Photo courtesy John Gibson

Mack Tootsietoy Dairy, No. 192, one-piece cab, three trailers. Photo courtesy Phillips NY

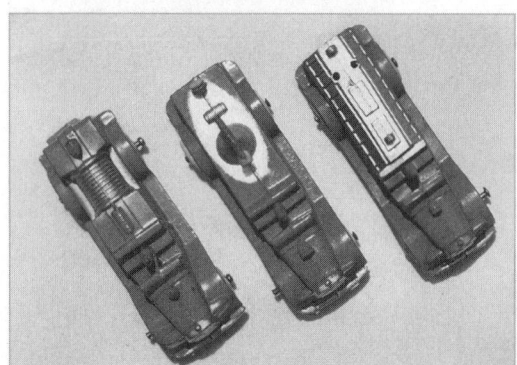

Left to right: Tootsietoy Insurance Patrol, No. 238; Hose Wagon, 236; Hook & Ladder, No. 236. Photo courtesy John Gibson

Tootsietoy Buick No. 103 Sedan in No. 4657 tinplate garage. Photo courtesy John Gibson

Tootsietoy, Left to right: Mack "A&P" Tractor, No. 4670; Overland Bus Lines, No. 4680; Fegeol Safety Coach, No. 4651; and Federal "Milk" Delivery Van, No. 4634. Photo courtesy Phillips NY

Tootsietoy 1935 Ford Wrecker, No. 113. Photo courtesy John Gibson

Tootsietoy, Left to right: Ford Model A Sedan, No. 4665; Ford Model A Coupe, No. 4655; Unnumbered "U.S. Mail" sold only in sets; Doodlebug, No. 0716. Photo courtesy Phillips NY

Tootsietoy Graham Town Car, No. 0516, 1930s.

	C6	C8	C10
1947 Mack L Line Fire (ladder) Trailer, 6" long................................	35	64	85
1947 Mack L Line Fire Pumper, 6" long .	35	64	85
1947 Mack L Line Log Truck, 6" long	35	64	85
1947 Mack L Line Moving Van, 6" long .	25	38	55
1947 Mack L Line Stake Trailer, 6" long	55	85	125
1947 Mack L Line Tootsietoys Coast to Coast, 6" long................................	35	64	85
1947 Mack L Line Tow Truck, 6" long ...	25	35	55
1947 Offenhauser Hill Climber Racer, 3" long................................	10	20	35
1947 Studebaker Champion, five-window coupe, 3" long.................	39	52	65
1948 Buick Estate Wagon, yellow and maroon w/black wheels, 6" long..........	20	30	50
1948 GMC 3751Greyhound Bus, 6" long	23	34	45
1949 Buick Roadmaster, four-door sedan, 6" long.....................................	25	40	65
1949 Ford Custom, four-door sedan, 3" long.....................................	15	20	35
1949 Ford Custom Convertible, 3" long ..	10	20	35
1949 Ford F1 Pickup, 3" long	15	20	35
1949 Ford F6 Oil Tanker, 4" long...........	10	15	25
1949 Ford F6 Oil Tanker, 6" long...........	25	50	100
1949 Ford F6 Stake Truck (pickup), 4" long.....................................	13	19	25
1949 Mercury Fire Chief Car, 4" long	15	20	40
1949 Mercury Sedan,, four-door, 4" long	13	20	30
1949 Oldsmobile 88 Convertible, 4" long	15	25	35
1950 Chevrolet Ambulance, 4" long........	15	20	35
1950 Chevrolet Deluxe Panel Truck, 3" long.....................................	8	17	25
1950 Chevrolet Deluxe Panel Truck, 4" long.....................................	25	30	40
1950 Chevrolet Fleetline, two-door fastback; sedan, 3" long	10	15	20
1950 Chrysler Windsor Convertible, 6" long.....................................	50	90	120
1950 Dodge Pickup Truck, 4" long..........	20	30	40
1950 Jeep CJ3, Army version, 3" long.....	10	15	30
1950 Jeep CJ3, Army version, 4" long.....	10	15	30
1950 Jeep CJ3, Civilian version, 3" long .	10	15	30
1950 Jeep CJ3, Civilian version, 4" long .	10	15	30
1950 Plymouth Special Deluxe, four-door sedan, 3" long	15	20	30
1950 Pontiac Chieftan Deluxe Coupe Sedan, 4" long........................	15	25	45
1950 Pontiac Chieftan Fire Chief Coupe Sedan, 4" long........................	20	35	50
1950 Twin Coach Bus, (Transit Coach), 3" long.....................................	18	27	40

Tankers were among the vehicles featured in this reproduction of a Tootsietoy catalog page that originally ran in 1933.

Tootsietoy Pontiac Safari Station Wagon, mid-1950s, 9".

Tootsietoy Jeep CJ3, 1950, 3". Photo courtesy Ed Poole

Tootsietoy No Name Touring Car, GM Series, No. 6-05, 1933.

Tootsietoy Cadillac Touring Car, GM series, No. 6105. Photo courtesy John Gibson

Tootsietoy 1947 Futuristic-looking Pickup Truck, commonly called the Hudson, sold only in boxed sets. Photo courtesy John Gibson

Tootsietoys as shown in the 1933 Butler Bros. catalog.

Tootsietoy No Name Screenside Delivery Truck, GM series, No. 6-06. Photo courtesy John Gibson

Tootsietoy Chrysler Thunderbolt experimental roadsters. Photo courtesy Gerald F. Slack

Tootsietoy 1948 Buick Super Estate Wagon, open grille, postwar. Photo courtesy John Gibson

Tootsietoy 1948 Buick Super Estate Wagon, open grille, postwar. Photo courtesy John Gibson

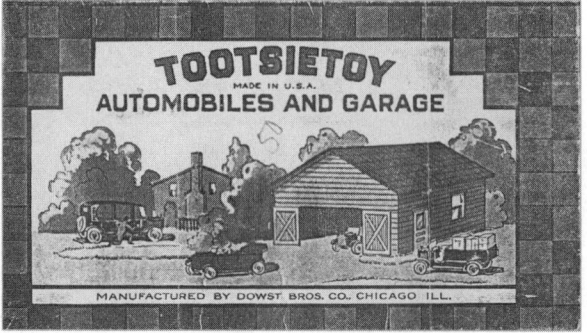

An early Tootsietoy boxtop.

	C6	C8	C10
1951 Buick LeSabre Experimental Roadster, 6" long	25	50	75
1952 Ford Mainline, four-door sedan, 3" long..................................	10	20	30
1952 Lincoln Capri, two-door hardtop, 6" long..................................	20	35	50
1952 Mercury Custom Sedan, four-door, 4" long..................................	15	30	40
1953 Chrysler New Yorker, four-door sedan, 6" long..........................	25	35	55
1954 American LaFrance Pumper, 3" long..................................	15	20	35
1954 Buick Century Estate Wagon, 6" long..................................	20	30	50
1954 Ford Ranch Wagon, 3" long............	15	20	35
1954 Ford Ranch Wagon, 4" long............	15	25	35
1954 Jaguar XK120 Roadster, 3" long.....	10	15	25
1954 MG TF Roadster, 3" long................	15	20	35
1954 MG TF Roadster, 6" long................	15	25	45
1954 Nash Metropolitan Convertible, 3" long..................................	25	35	60
1954-55 Corvette Roadster, 4" long........	15	20	35
1955 Austin Healy 100-6, unassembled kit, 6" long................................	150	225	300
1955 Chevrolet BelAir, four-door sedan, 3" long..................................	15	30	50
1955 Ford Customline V8, two-door sedan, 3" long..........................	15	20	30
1955 Ford F600 Stake Truck w/tin cover, 6" long..................................	15	25	35
1955 International RC180, 6" long w/rocket launcher, Army version........	120	180	200
1955 International RC180, w/boat transport	30	45	60
1955 International RC180, w/car transport	35	50	70
1955 International RC180, w/gooseneck trailer	30	40	55
1955 International RC180, w/grain trailer	30	50	70
1955 International RC180, w/moving van	30	50	65
1955 International RC180, w/oil tanker, no decals	30	50	65
1955 Mack B Line Cement Mixer, 6" long..................................	20	35	55
1955 Mack B Line Hook & Ladder, 6" long..................................	38	56	75
1955 Mack B Line Log Trailer, 6" long...	43	64	85
1955 Mack B Line Moving Van, w/doors, 6" long..........................	90	120	150
1955 Mack B Line Moving Van, w/o doors, 6" long..........................	60	80	100
1955 Mack B Line Oil Tanker, 6" long ...	23	34	45
1955 Mack B Line Open Stake Truck, 6" long..................................	63	94	125
1955 Mercedes 300SL Gullwing (doors intact), 9" long..........................	150	225	300
1955 Oldsmobile 98 Holiday, four-door hardtop, Army version, 4" long	20	27	40
1955 Oldsmobile 98 Holiday, two-door hardtop, 4" long..........................	13	20	35
1955 Pontiac Safari Station Wagon, No. 895, 9" long..............................	180	240	300
1955 Thunderbird Coupe, 3" long............	15	20	30
1955 Thunderbird Coupe, 4" long............	15	30	40
1956 Austin Healy 100-6, four-passenger roadster, 6" long..............................	20	30	60
1956 Caterpillar Roadscraper, 6" long.....	15	25	40
1956 Chevrolet Cameo Pickup, 4" long...	15	25	40

A catalog ad depicting various Tootsietoy vehicles.

	C6	C8	C10
1956 Dodge D100 Panel Truck, 6" long..	18	36	55
1956 Ferrari Racer, 6" long......................	30	40	65
1956 Ford F600 Army Gun Truck, 6" long..................................	20	30	45
1956 Ford Farm Tractor, 6" long	30	40	65
1956 Jaguar XK140 Coupe, 6" long	8	17	25
1956 Lancia Racer, 6" long......................	30	50	75
1956 Mercedes 190SL, 6" long................	15	25	40
1956 Packard Patrician, four-door sedan, 6" long..................................	12	23	35
1956 Porsche Spyder Roadster, 6" long...	20	25	40
1956 Triumph TR3 Roadster, 3" long	4	8	12
1957 Ford F100 Styleside Pick-up w/o rear window, 3" long	4	8	12
1957 Ford F100 Styleside Pickup w/rear window, 3" long..........................	8	11	15
1957 Ford Fairlane 500 Convertible, 3" long..................................	6	12	18
1957 Greyhound Sceni-Cruiser Bus, 6" long..................................	23	34	45
1957 Jaguar type D, 3" long....................	10	15	25
1957 Plymouth Belvedere, two-door hardtop, 3" long..........................	6	12	18
1959 Chevrolet Semi Cab, w/Army flatbed	180	240	300
1959 Chevrolet Semi Cab, w/dean van lines	180	240	300
1959 Chevrolet Semi Cab, w/hook and ladder	180	240	300

	C6	C8	C10
1959 Chevrolet Semi Cab, w/log trailer...	180	240	300
1959 Chevrolet Semi Cab, w/mobile trailer......................	180	240	300
1959 Chevrolet Semi Cab, w/three boat trailer......................	180	240	300
1959 Chevrolet Semi Cab, w/three car transport......................	180	240	300
1959 Chevrolet Semi Cab only	105	140	175
1959 Oldsmobile Dynamic 88 Convertible, 6" long..........................	20	25	40
1959 Pontiac Star Chief, four-door sedan, 4" long......................	15	25	40
1960 Chevrolet El Camino, 6" long.........	20	25	40
1960 Chevrolet El Camino w/camper/boat, 6" long.......................	25	35	85
1960 Chrysler Windsor Convertible, 4" long......................	15	25	35
1960 Ford Falcon, two-door sedan, 3" long......................	4	8	12

	C6	C8	C10
1960 Ford LTD, two-door hardtop, 4" long......................	10	19	25
1960 International Metro Step Van, 6" long......................	126	168	210
1960 Jeep CJ5, Army version, 6" long	18	26	35
1960 Jeep CJ5, Civilian version, 6" long......................	15	20	30
1960 Jeep CJ5, Snowplow version, 6" long......................	38	56	75
1960 Rambler Super Cross Country Station Wagon, 4" long......................	15	25	35
1960 Studebaker Lark Convertible, 3" long......................	4	10	25
1960 Volkswagen Beetle, 3" long...........	10	20	35
1960 Volkswagen Beetle, 6" long...........	20	33	45
1962 Ford Econoline Pickup, 6" long	15	25	35
Atomic Cannon/155mm Howitzer, 5-1/4" long......................	100	150	200
Metro Van, HO Series.............................	21	28	35
School Bus, HO series	10	15	20

TOY FOUNDERS

Another firm specializing in postwar plastic toy production, Toy Founders Inc. was based in Detroit, Mich.

	C6	C8	C10
Kaiser Convertible, wind-up, 1947, 11" long	150	265	360
Kar Kit, clockwork, car, makes 3 types, 11" long	150	265	360

TRAILER CO.

Trailer Co. was based in Los Angeles, Calif. during the 1920s.

	C6	C8	C10
Traveleer Land Coach Traveler, 1927	180	270	360

TRU-SCALE INTERNATIONAL TRUCKS

Early in the 1940s, Joseph Carter founded the Carter Machine Company. Following World War II, Carter began to manufacture a line of toys. At first, Carter's toy line mainly consisted of International and John Deere farm tractors and implements. In the 1950s, Carter began his new line of 1:16-scale trucks under the Tru-Scale trademark. He felt that the International truck model would be the best choice,

because International had been building trucks since 1907. The first Tru-Scale model was in the "S" series. This was the model then in production by the International Truck Company. The models marked with the "I.H." logo on the doors were sold by International Harvester outlets only. Any models marked "Tru-Scale" on the doors would have been sold through other retail outlets.

As the International Truck Co. redesigned its body style, Carter followed the design with its comparable

Tru-Scale International Service Truck, No. 1, green and white, circa 1953. Photo courtesy Bob Smith

Tru-Scale International Service Truck, No. 3, red and white, circa 1959. Photo courtesy Bob Smith

Tru-Scale International Service Truck, No. 4, orange and white with white tires, 1960s. Photo courtesy Bob Smith

Top to bottom: Tru-Scale International Pickup Truck, No. 6, red and white, TS decal, circa 1961; International Pickup Truck, No. 6A, blue and white, circa 1961. Photo courtesy Bob Smith

Tru-Scale International Grain Truck, No. 7A, green, I/H decal, circa 1959. Photo courtesy Bob Smith

Tru-Scale No. 10. Photo courtesy Bob Smith

Tru-Scale International Pickup Truck, No. 5, red and cream, circa 1957. Photo courtesy Bob Smith

Tru-Scale International Grain Truck, No. 7, blue, I/H decal, circa 1957. Photo courtesy Bob Smith

Tru-Scale No. 8. Photo courtesy Bob Smith

Tru-Scale International Ten-wheel Hydraulic Dump Truck, No. 9, circa 1957. Photo courtesy Bob Smith

model. While thought of as a toy, one must consider the fine detail and workmanship that went into the Tru-Scale models. Paint colors were correct, the grille styling and fender lines followed the real truck body lines, and they were very well detailed for a pressed-steel toy.

After the "S" series, the "A" series, "B" series, and "C" series trucks followed, in respective order. The models were made as pick-up trucks, service trucks with tool boxes, dump trucks with single or dual axle, semi-tractor trailer trucks with open or enclosed trailers, and also as grain trucks. The dump trucks came with either a hydraulic cylinder or manual control, depending on which model or year it was produced. The later "C" series came with plastic windows and whitewall tires with full hubcaps. Another feature was the finger-tip steering that worked by applying pressure on the front of the cab to steer the front wheels. Tru-Scale also produced some Private Label trucks, such as Ryerson Steel and Yale Trucking.

In 1971, Carter Tru-Scale sold the business to Ertl, which used parts of the Tru-Scale line for the new Ertl die-cast International "Loadster" series. Ertl discontinued the Tru-Scale line of International trucks.

Contributor: Bob Smith, RATS Toy Shows, 255 Tryon Park, Rochester, NY 14609. (585) 288-7153, bird@oldtoysonline.com.

	C6	C8	C10
No. 01 Tru-Scale S series International Service Truck, green/white, c.1953	225	400	650
No. 2 Tru-Scale A series International Service Truck, red/white, c.1957	225	400	650
No. 2a Tru-Scale S series International Pickup Truck, light blue/white, c.1953	175	325	550

Top to bottom: Tru-Scale International Service Truck, No. 2, red and white, circa 1957; International Pickup Truck, No. 2A, light blue and white, circa 1953. Photo courtesy Bob Smith

	C6	C8	C10
No. 3 Tru-Scale B series International Service Truck, red/white, c.1959	175	350	575
No. 4 Tru-Scale C series International Service Truck, orange/white, whitewall tires, windshield, c.1961	200	350	575
No. 5 Tru-Scale A series International Pickup Truck, red/cream, c.1957	200	350	575
No. 6 Tru-Scale C series International Pickup Truck, red/white, T/S decal, c.961	200	350	575

Tru-Scale No. 11. Photo courtesy Bob Smith

Tru-Scale No. 14. Photo courtesy Bob Smith

Tru-Scale No. 13 (restored). Photo courtesy Bob Smith

Tru-Scale Top to bottom: No. 15 and No. 15a. Photo courtesy Bob Smith

	C6	C8	C10
No. 6a Tru-Scale C series International Pickup Truck, blue/white, I/H decal, c.1961	150	275	475
No. 7 Tru-Scale A series Internati6nal Grain Truck, blue, I/H decal, c.1957	200	350	575
No. 7a Tru-Scale B series International Grain Truck, green, I/H decal, c.1959	150	275	475
No. 8 Tru-Scale S series International Ten-wheel Hydraulic Dump Truck, orange/white, c.1953	225	375	600
No. 9 Tru-Scale A series International Ten-wheel Hydraulic Dump Truck, orange, c.1957	225	375	600
No. 10 Tru-Scale B series Six-wheel Manual Dump Truck, orange, c.1959	200	350	575
No. 11 Tru-Scale B series Ten-wheel Hydraulic Dump Truck, orange, c.1959	175	300	500

	C6	C8	C10
No. 12 Tru-Scale C series Six-wheel International Dump Truck, red/white, c.1961	175	300	500
No. 13 Tru-Scale B series Semi-Tractor and Van Trailer, red/white, c.1959	300	450	700
No. 14 Tru-Scale C series Semi-Tractor and Van Trailer, green/ white, "Yale Trucking," c.1961	325	500	750
No. 15 Tru-Scale B series Semi-Tractor Hydraulic Dump Truck, dark red, c.1959	175	325	550
No. 15a Tru-Scale C series Semi-Tractor Stake Truck, red/ yellow, "Ryerson Steel," c.1961	200	350	575
No. 16 Tru-Scale/Ertl, Ertl Int'l. Fleetstar Cab w/Tru-Scale Dump Trailer, white/green, c.1971, "Anderson Payload"	200	375	600
No. 16a Tru-Scale International C series Semi-Tractor Hydraulic Dump Truck, orange/yellow, c.1961	175	325	550

TRU-TOY

Tru-Toy was a brand name used by the Carter Tru-Scale Machine Co. of Rockford, Ill.

	C6	C8	C10
Tru-Toy Steer-O-Car, 13" long	112	168	225

TURNER, JOHN C.

John Turner began in the trade working first with D.P. Clark and later with the Schieble Toy Co. He went off on his own in 1915. Within two years, he was producing a line of friction cars. In 1925, he was issued a patent for a new flywheel design made of metal disks, giving the appearance of large flat washers fitted together. The Turner flywheel is noticeably different from other manufacturers' mechanisms. Turner was located in Dayton and Wapkoneta, Ohio from about 1915 into the 1940s.

Contributor: Bob Smith, RATS Toy Shows, 255 Tryon Park, Rochester, NY 14609. (585) 288-7153, bird@oldtoysonline.com.

	C6	C8	C10
Ahrens Fox Ladder Truck, 1920, 15" long	550	820	1250
Ahrens Fox Pumper, 16" long	700	1175	1750
Army Truck, 1940s, 15" long	100	200	425

Turner trucks as shown in the August 1937 issue of Toys and Bicycles.

Turner Ahrens Fox Ladder Truck, 15". Photo courtesy Rodney A. Heesacker

	C6	C8	C10
Army Truck, 1940s, 15" long..................	100	200	425
Auto Transport, No. 85; Tractor and auto trailer; red, cream and green; two cars; 1938; 27" long..	250	450	675
Bulldog Mack Closed Cab Dump Truck, 23" long..	300	475	700
Chemical Truck, 1930s, rubber wheels, two ladders, bell, hose and reel, 29" long..	250	450	700
Contractor Equipment, No. 62, Steam shovel on flatbed truck, box trailer, red and green, 31" long	NPF	NPF	NPF
Crane Truck, 22" long............................	350	525	750
Delivery Van, 1920s, 12-1/2" long	950	1575	2350
Dump Truck, 1935-37, 17" long	200	375	600
Dump Truck, 1940s, 15-1/2"..................	250	400	625
Dump Truck, 1940s, 21"..........................	150	275	500
Dump Truck, 28" long, Dodge.................	150	250	475
Dump Truck, C-Cab, 22" long.................	200	525	850
Dump Truck, C-Cab, 28" long	325	575	975
Dump Truck, friction, early 1930s, 15-1/2" long	225	400	625
Dump Truck, No. 90, 1930s, 7" long	175	350	575
Fire Engine Pumper, 15" long.................	800	1475	1950
Fire Engine Pumper, early, 26" long........	600	875	1350
Garage, No. 97, 21-1/2" long, 19-3/8" wide, 11-3/4" high	NPF	NPF	NPF
Garage, pressed steel, 21" long, 15" wide	200	300	450
Garage Set, No. 98, Garage, Ladder Truck, Dump Truck	NPF	NPF	NPF

	C6	C8	C10
Hook and Ladder, No. 81, ringing bell, 2 ladders, hose and reel, 1930s, 31-1/2" long	275	475	725
Hook and Ladder, red and gold, 3 ladders, No. 38 steel wheels, No. 36 rubber wheels, 27-1/2" long..................	275	450	650
Intercity Bus...	550	825	1150

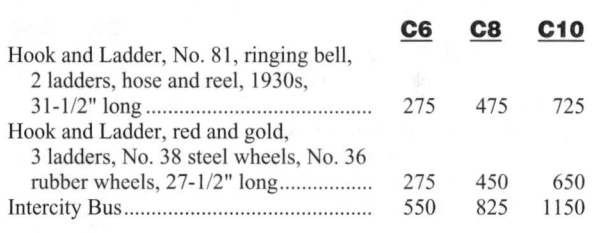

Turner trucks, as shown in a catalog advertisement.

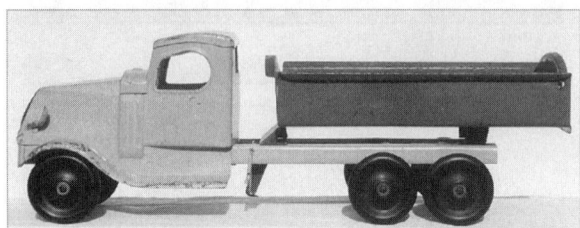

Turner Bulldog Mack, closed cab, 1930s, 23". Photo courtesy John Taylor

Turner Crane Truck, 22". Photo courtesy Calvin L. Chausee

Turner Dump, friction, early 1930s, 15-1/2". Photo courtesy Calvin L. Chaussee

Turner Dump, friction, early 1930s, 15-1/2". Photo courtesy John Taylor

Turner Dump, Dodge, 28". Photo courtesy John Taylor

Turner Overland Bus, pressed steel. Photo courtesy James Apthorpe

	C6	C8	C10
Ladder Truck, 1940s, 22".........................	300	450	5650
Limousine..	2050	3575	5150
Lincoln Sedan, 26" long...........................	2050	3575	5150
Mack Ladder Truck..............................	175	350	575
Overland Bus, pressed steel	NPF	NPF	NPF
Packard (?) Roadster, 26" long, friction...	950	1575	2350
Packard Racer, 1924, 26" long.................	850	1475	2150
Packard Roadster, 1920s, 16-1/2" long	650	1025	1450
Panel Truck, early, 13" long....................	300	450	650
Pick-Up (Stake) Truck, No. 97, 1930s, 7" long...	175	350	575
Shovel Truck, 1930s, 17" long.................	300	475	700
Speed Truck, C-cab, No. 40, c.1930, 22".	200	450	850
Speedster, 1920s, 17" long......................	550	825	1150
Stake Truck, 1940s, 10-1/2" long.............	150	275	500
Stake Truck, c.1938, 22" long..................	150	275	500
Steam Shovel, 14" long...........................	125	175	300
Tow Truck, electric lights, 20" long	175	275	400

Turner Speed Truck, 1930s, 22". Photo courtesy John Taylor

	C6	C8	C10
Tow Truck, rare, 1940s, 15" long	250	400	625
Water Truck, copper tank	200	300	450
Yellow Taxicab, flywheel drive, orange/black, four riders, c.1927, 9-3/4" long	350	550	775

UNIQUE ART MFG. CO.

Unique Art Mfg. Co. was in business from 1916, when it introduced its Merry Juggler and Charlie Chaplin. In 1931 it was located at Waverly and Peshine Avenues in Newark, New Jersey. Its president was Wm. Marbe, and there were 28 employees. By 1934, there were 275 employees.

	C6	C8	C10
Artie the Clown in his Crazy Car, tin.......	300	450	600
Capitol Hill Racer, w/2" tin racing car, 1930s, 17-1/2" long.............................	100	150	200
Daredevil Motor Cop, tin, 1940s, 8-1/2" long	500	750	1000
G.I Joe and His Jouncing Jeep, tin, post WWII, 7" long	165	247	330

	C6	C8	C10
Krazy Kar, tin, new in 1921	300	450	600
Lincoln Tunnel, tin, moving vehicles, cop, 1935, 24" long..............................	225	310	500
Motorcycle Cop, tin, 1930s, 9" long........	220	330	440
Rodeo Joe Crazy Car, tin	158	235	315
Rollover Motorcycle Cop, tin, 1935	200	300	400

Unique Art G.I. Joe and his Jouncing Jeep, 7". Photo courtesy Mapes Auctioneers and Appraisers

Unique Art Rodeo Joe Crazy Car.

VARNEY SCALE MODELS

Toy train manufacturer Varney Scale Models was founded by Gordon Varney in 1936, just six months after he picked up his first issue of *Model Railroader* magazine. In addition to its HO-gauge trains, the firm produced some vehicle accessories for train layouts.

	C6	C8	C10
No. 2473 Ford Sedan, HO scale, assorted colors	NPF	NPF	NPF
No. 2474 Ford Pickup, HO scale	NPF	NPF	NPF
No. 2475 Ford Panel Truck, HO Scale	NPF	NPF	NPF

VICEROY

Viceroy was a Canadian toy manufacturer. It had several locations and specialized in rubber and vinyl toys and dolls. Some were authorized versions of Sun Rubber toys.

	C6	C8	C10
Donald Duck Roadster, 6/2/03 (VD002)	62	93	125
Donald Duck Tractor, 4/3/04 (VD006) ...	62	93	125
Open Racer, 4/1/02 (VR002)	22	33	45
Open Racer, Sun Rubber type, 6-1/2" long (VR001)	30	45	60

*Viceroy Donald Duck Tractor, 4-3/4".
Photo courtesy Dave Leopard's book* Rubber Toy Vehicles

*Viceroy Open Racer, Sun Rubber type, 6-1/2". Photo
courtesy Dave Leopard's book* Rubber Toy Vehicles

*A pair of Viceroy 4-1/2", Open Racers. Photo
courtesy Dave Leopard's book* Rubber Toy Vehicles

*Viceroy Donald Duck Roadster, 6-2/3". Photo courtesy
Dave Leopard's book* Rubber Toy Vehicles

VIKING

Little is known about Viking other than that it was based in Ohio.

	C6	C8	C10
Dump Truck, 27" long	550	850	1300

VINDEX

Vindex was a division of National Sewing Machine Co. of Belvidere, Ill., from 1928 to 1932. The sturdy, high-quality toys were more expensive than the competition which probably led to the company's demise during the Depression. Vindex is best known for its farm toys, and *Farm Mechanics* magazine often offered Vindex toys as premiums. The motorcycles, which feature the Henderson logo, ceased production after 1931.

Contributor: Kent M. Comstock, 532 Pleasant St., Ashland Ohio 44805, 419-289-3308, 800-443-TOYS.

*Vindex Coast to Coast Bus, 1930s, 12". Photo
courtesy Bertoia Auctions*

Vindex Case 3-Bottom Tractor Plow, 10-1/4". Photo courtesy Bertoia Auctions

Vindex John Deere Van Brunt Drill, 9-3/4". Photo courtesy Bertoia Auctions

Vindex Motorcycle with removable cop, red or green, 9". Photo courtesy Kent M. Comstock

Vindex Motorcycle VM2, rider missing. Photo courtesy Bertoia Auctions

Vindex Motorcycle VM3. Photo courtesy Bertoia Auctions

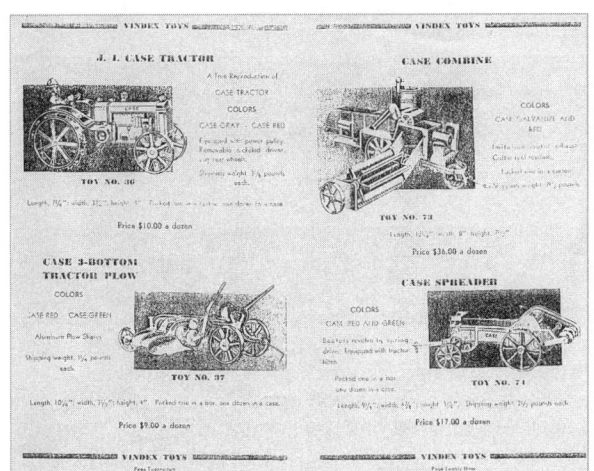

Another catalog page of Vindex farm toys.

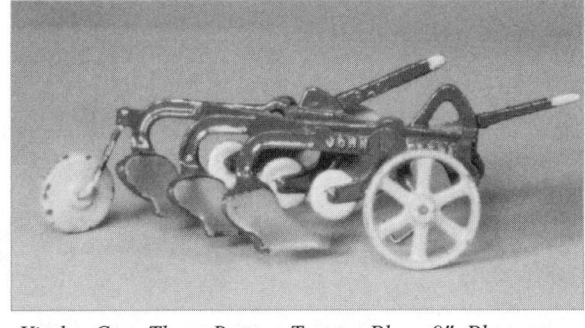

Vindex Case Three-Bottom Tractor Plow, 9". Photo courtesy Bertoia Auctions

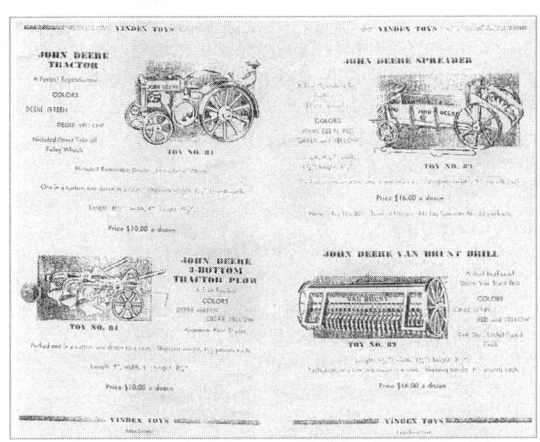

A look at some of the farm toys offered by Vindex.

Vindex P&H Power Shovel, 12" and 17" when extended. Photo courtesy Bertoia Auctions

Vindex Hay Loader, Case, 9". Photo courtesy Bertoia Auctions

	C6	C8	C10
Case Hay Loader, 9" long	3000	4500	5200
Case Manure Spreader, 12" long..............	500	1250	2000
Case Model L Tractor, 6-1/2" long	500	750	1030
Case Three Bottom Tractor Plow, 10-1/4" long	1000	2500	3700
Coast to Coast Bus, cast iron, c.1930, 12" long	1250	1875	2500
Combine	850	1500	2300

	C6	C8	C10
John Deere 3-bottom Tractor Plow, 9" long,..	900	1400	2400
John Deere Manure Spreader, horse drawn	500	1100	1800
John Deere Thresher, 15" long	1500	2800	3900
John Deere Tractor, Model D, 6-1/2" long	950	1700	2600
John Deere Van Brunt Drill, 9-3/4" long	1000	1800	2900
Model L Tractor, 7" long	500	1000	1500
Oldsmobile Sedan	3000	5500	10,000
P&H power shovel, cast-iron, wheels in Caterpillar base, handle revolves rig, 12" (17" extended)	2500	5500	8000
Packard Club Sedan, 1929	10000	15000	26000
Pickup Truck, cast-iron, 7-1/2" long........	300	450	600
Pontiac Coupe, 7-3/4"	800	1400	1900
Racer, cast-iron, "2," 11-1/2" long	900	1400	2100

Motorcycles

	C6	C8	C10
Motorcycle w/removable policeman, marked "Henderson," red or green, 9" long (VM001)	1000	1500	2500
Motorcycle w/Package Truck, "Henderson PDQ Delivery" w/removable blue rider, red or green, 9" long (VM003)	1800	2500	3500
Motorcycle w/sidecar, w/two removable policemen, red or green, marked "Henderson," 9" long (VM002)	1200	1800	3000

WALKER & STEWART

	C6	C8	C10
Mack Box Van, cast-iron, 5-1/2" long	95	153	190
Mack Open Bed Truck, cast-iron, 5-1/2" long	95	153	190

WANNATOY

Wannatoy was among the first toy makers off the starting block at the end of World War II. Of the millions of children born during the war, and the millions more who arrived soon afterward, a good percentage played with Wannatoys.

What seems to have been the company's first offering, the twenty-five-cent futuristic Coupe, was a hit toy for Christmas of 1945, selling a million units that season. With streamlined, Deco-influenced body and bubble top, the Coupe continued to sell well into the 1950s.

By 1950, the company had a modest but diverse line, sold through dimestores, that included toy semi-trailers, construction trucks, cars, airplanes, and ships. For at least one season the company offered toy assortments in see-through mesh Christmas stockings, ready to hang from the mantle.

Wannatoy was the trademark of Dillon Beck Manufacturing Co., based in New Jersey. Dillon Beck made toys of acetate, a hard plastic with a tendency to warp through time. Toward the end of its life as a toy maker, probably in the mid to late 1950s, the company produced soft plastic toys.

Contributor: Mark Rich, P.O. Box 971, Stevens Point, WI 54481-0971.

Wannatoy Woodie Jeep. Photo courtesy Dave Leopard

	C6	C8	C10
Miscellaneous			
Transit Bus, plastic, two-tone in assorted colors, 1950s, 5-1/2" long...................	15	25	
Miscellaneous Vehicles			
Cadillac, 9" long	8	12	
Cement Mixer, 1948 to mid 1950s, 3-1/4" long	9	14	
Convertible, 6" long.................................	7	11	
Coupe, futuristic, bubble top, 3-1/2"........	11	16	
Jaguar, mid-1950s, 6" long	10	15	

	C6	C8	C10
Jet Auto, bubble top, 1948 to mid-1950s, 3-1/2" long	18	26	
MG, clear windshield, mid-1950s, 4-12" long	11	16	
Race Car, tail fin, late 1940s through early 1950s, 2-1/2" long	6	8	
Sedan, early 1950s, 9-1/2" long	18	26	
Woodie Jeep, 3-1/2" long	14	21	

Trucks

	C6	C8	C10
Dump Truck, 1946 to mid 1950s, 3-1/2" long	6	9	
Earth Hauler, 1949 to mid-1950s, 4-1/4" long	10	15	
Hauling Truck, tractor-trailer, 1950s, 5" long	7	11	

	C6	C8	C10
Ladder Truck, closed cab, white ladder, 1947 to mid-1950s, 6" long	11	16	
Ladder Truck, open cab, white ladder, 1946 to mid-1950s, 4-1/2" long	9	14	
Oil Tanker, tractor-trailer, 1950s, 5" long	7	11	
Service Truck, mid-1950s, 5" long	11	16	
Stake Truck, tractor-trailer, 1950s, 5" long	7	11	
Steam Shovel, 1949 to mid 1950s, 4" long	12	17	
Tank, revolving turret, 1950s, 3-3/4" long	10	15	
Tractor, w/front scoop, 1948 to mid-1950s, 4" long	11	16	
Van Truck, soft plastic, 5" long	4	6	
Van Truck, tractor-trailer, 1950s, 5" long	7	11	

WARREN

Warren, of New York City, was a toy soldier company owned by John Warren Jr., from about 1936 to 1939. Its two vehicles were converstions of toys made by Kenton and are of particular interest to toy soldier collectors.

	C6	C8	C10
Scout Car (W173)	300	450	600
Staff Car (W174)	300	450	600

WEEDEN

Weeden was founded in 1882 by William N. Weeden, in New Bedford, Massachusetts. In 1884, he made his first toy steam engine. His toys included engines, vehicles, and boats. Weeden toys were produced into at least the 1940s.

	C6	C8	C10
Steam Auto, steam, early, 8-3/4" long	1500	3000	4500
Steam Fire Pumper	1200	2000	3000
Steam Road Roller, brass, tin, cast iron, steam toy fired by alcohol, 1920s, 7" long	250	375	500

	C6	C8	C10
Steam Tractor, 9" long	250	375	500

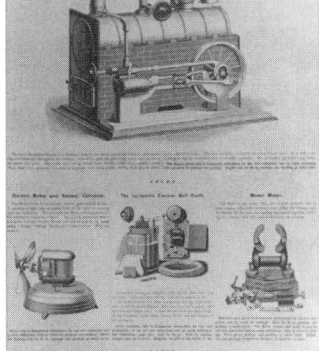

Weeden's steam-operated toys were big sellers for years. Toys pictured here are from the October 31, 1895 issue of The Youth's Companion magazine.

*Weeden Auto, live steam, 8-3/4".
Photo courtesy Sotheby's New York*

WELLMADE DOLL & TOY CO.

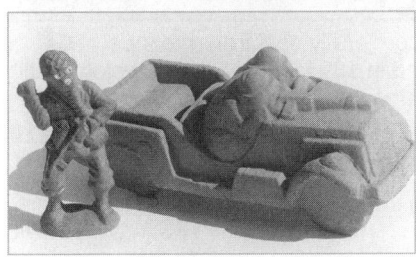

A variation of the 7-1/2" composition Jeep made either by Wellmade or M.A. Henry. Photo courtesy Ed Poole

Left to right: Wellmade composition jeep, 7-1/2"; 3-1/2" jeep that appears to be by M.A. Henry—which also made an 8" composition jeep. Photo courtesy Ed Poole

Based in New York City, the Wellmade Doll & Toy Co. specialized in composition and stuffed dolls and toys, and released only a few vehicles.

	C6	C8	C10
Jeep, composition, 3-1/2" long	NPF	NPF	NPF
Jeep, composition, 7-1/2" long	37	56	75

WELLS (ENGLAND)

	C6	C8	C10
Automite Racer, plastic, 9" long	60	90	120
Dump Truck, 1930s, tin wind-up, 12" long	275	415	550
Go Cart, gas operated	90	135	180
Mustang, 13" long	75	112	150

	C6	C8	C10
Racer, tin wind-up, No. 77, 11-1/4"	300	400	500
Rolls Royce limo, 9" long	130	195	260
Texaco, Fire Pumper	60	90	120
Texaco, Tanker	42	64	85
Touring Sedan, tin wind-up, 11" long	312	468	625

WEN-MAC

Known as AMF Wen-Mac, from Los Angeles, Calif.

	C6	C8	C10
Automite Racer, plastic, 9" long	NPF	NPF	NPF
Go Cart, gas powered	NPF	NPF	NPF

	C6	C8	C10
Mustang, 13" long	NPF	NPF	NPF
Texaco Fire Pumper	NPF	NPF	NPF
Texaco Tanker	NPF	NPF	NPF

WESTERN TOY CO.

	C6	C8	C10
Jeep Pedal Car, aluminum	375	562	750

WILCO PROMOTIONAL TOYS

A division of Hess, Wilco trucks were re-issued Hess promotional trucks with the blue, white, and red color scheme of the Wilco company. Last year's Hess truck would become this year's Wilco truck. They were released through 2000.

	C6	C8	C10
1967 Tanker, split window w/blue body and white trim	n/a	n/a	550
1968 Oil Tanker Ship, green body	n/a	n/a	1200
1985 Semi Tanker Truck, bank, blue body, white trim and red letters	n/a	n/a	95
1986, 1933 Chevy tanker, bank, blue body, white trim and red letters	n/a	n/a	485
1988 Semi Box Truck, no barrels, white body, blue trim w/red and blue letters	n/a	n/a	25
1989 Race Car Transporter, white body, blue trim, red and blue letters	n/a	n/a	35
1990 Aerial Ladder Fire Truck, white body, blue trim w/red letters	n/a	n/a	30
1991 Semi-Tanker Truck, white body, blue trim, red letters	n/a	n/a	25

	C6	C8	C10
1992 Race Car Transporter, white body, blue trim, red letters	n/a	n/a	25
1993 Eighteen Wheeler Box Truck, w/race car, white body, blue trim, red letters	n/a	n/a	25
1994 Patrol Car, white body, blue trim, red letters	n/a	n/a	25
1995 Rescue Truck, white body, blue trim, red ladder	n/a	n/a	25
1996 Flatbed Semi w/Helicopter, white body, blue trim, red letters	n/a	n/a	25
1997 Emergency Truck, white body, blue trim, red letters	n/a	n/a	25
1998 Toy Truck and Racers, white body, blue trim, red letters	n/a	n/a	25
1999 Recreational Van w/Dune Buggy, white body, blue trim, red letters	n/a	n/a	25
2000 Toy Truck w/Space Shuttle, final model	n/a	n/a	25

WILKINS TOY COMPANY

Wilkins, of Keene, New Hampshire, was begun by James S. Wilkins as the Triumph Wringer Company. But the tiny model Wilkins produced to promote his product proved so intriguing to prospective customers and their children, that requests for them poured in. The real thing was quickly forgotten as Wilkins turned to toy making.

Its toys were generally cast iron and steel. The firm was acquired in 1894 by Kingsbury, which is still in business, though now as a tool and die maker.

	C6	C8	C10
Aerial Ladder Truck, wind-up, 1910, 18" long	300	450	600
Auto Surrey, wind-up, pressed steel, 1911, 7-1/2"	NPF	NPF	NPF

Wilkins Aerial Ladder Truck, windup, 1910, 18". Photo courtesy Phillips NY

Wilkins Auto Surrey, 1911, light pressed steel withy cast-iron wheels, windup, 7-1/2". Photo courtesy Phillips NY

Wilkins Automobile Racer, silver, light stamped steel, 10". Photo courtesy Bob Smith

Wilkins Hook and Ladder Open Truck, steel, 9-1/4". Photo courtesy Phillips NY

Wilkins Truck Wagon.

	C6	C8	C10
Automobile Racer, silver, clock-work motor, light stamped steel, 10" long, c.1905	750	1100	1700
Dray, driver, barrels, tiller	400	600	800
Fire Pumper, driver, c.1924, 11" long	550	850	1200
Fire Pumper, driver, clock-work, c.1924, 9-1/2" long	225	338	450
Fire Station, c.1911, 13" long	NPF	NPF	NPF
Hook & Ladder, early, 14-1/2" long	600	900	1250
Hook & Ladder, early, 26" long	NPF	NPF	NPF
Hook & Ladder Open Truck, steel, wind-up motor, 9-1/4" long	175	250	325
Ladder Truck, wind-up, early, 15" long	450	695	925
Motor Truck Wagon, eighteen barrels, driver, 13" long	300	450	600
Panama Dump Truck, gray, light stamped steel, clock-work motor, c.1919, 14" long (also made as Kingsbury in 1923, different wheels, same value)	400	600	800
Runabout, w/driver, 1911	650	1000	1500
Tractor, 8-1/2" long	165	248	330

Wilkins Fire Station, 1911, opening doors, ringing bell, which released engine from house.

	C6	C8	C10
Tractor & Trailer, 17" long	225	338	450
Truck, open cab, very early, clockwork, 11" long	450	675	900
Truck Wagon, w/cast-iron driver, clockwork, 190ss, 7"	NPF	NPF	NPF

WOLVERINE

Wolverine, of Pittsburgh, Pa., was founded in 1903 by B.F. Bain. The company got its name from Bain's Michigan hometown. In later years, Wolverine became a subsidiary of Spang Industries. In 1970, it moved to Boonville, Arkansas.

The "Sandy Andy," in all its variations, was probably Wolverine's most successful and famous toy.

	C6	C8	C10
Autolift, includes 2-1/2" tin car and four sections of track, 1930s, 10-1/4" high	150	225	300
Caterpillar Tractor w/Trailer, c.1930, wind-up, 20" long	305	458	610
Coke Coal Truck	88	132	175
Dump Truck, white, 12" long	55	82	110
Fire Dept. Truck	90	135	180
Jackie Gleason Bus, "Away We Go, Honeymooner's Special" on tin litho, 1955, 14" long	125	275	400
Loop-A-Loop, includes small car No. 30, 1930s, 19" long	125	188	250
Magic Auto Race, two cars, 1940s	50	150	200
Motor Race, one spinner, four cars	50	100	150
Motor Race, two spinner, six cars	150	200	250
Motorcycle Rabbit, 9-1/2" long, 1930s	90	135	180

Wolverine Mystery Car and Trailer, 1950s. Photo courtesy Calvin L. Chaussee

Wolverine "U.S.A. Transport" Army Truck. Photo courtesy Ken Butler

	C6	C8	C10
Mystery Car, 13" long	138	205	275
Mystery Car and Trailer, press down to make car move, c.1953	218	327	435
Mystery Taxi, No. 33	200	300	400
Ring-A-Long Bus, No. 161, tin, wood wheels, 13-1/2" long	45	90	145
Sky View Taxi	115	172	230
Speeding Bus, tin lithographed, driver and occupants, press down on rear to move, marked "5 Via Main St." and "19302," 14" long	105	158	210

	C6	C8	C10
Sunny Andy Tank, 14" long	130	195	260
Taxi, tin, 13" long	180	270	360
U.S Army Staff Car, 12" long................	130	195	260
U.S.A Transport Army Truck	150	225	300
U.S.A. Transport Bus, tin, 14" long........	75	150	225
White Mustang Dump Truck, 14" long ...	75	112	150
White Stake Truck	102	153	205
Wolverine Express Bus, "Mystery Motor," 14" long.................................	100	150	200

Wolverine Dump Truck, 12".

Wolverine Mystery Taxi.

WOOD COMMODITIES CORP. (NEW YORK)

	C6	C8	C10
Jeep, steel, 10-1/2" long	60	80	100
Jeep, wooden, WWII, 2 versions	40	60	80
Tank, wooden, WWII..............................	25	38	50

Wood Commodities Jeep, wooden. Photo courtesy Jack Matthews

Another version of Wood Commodities' Jeep. Photo courtesy Perry Eichor

Wood Commodities Tank. Photo courtesy Jack Matthews

Wood Commodities Jeep, steel, 10-1/2". Photo courtesy Richard Jansen

WOODHAVEN

Research by John Monteleone has established that in the 1930s, Herman Joerger bought Animate Toy and, about the same time, Ranger Toys. He sold the business to his son, Herman Joerger Jr., who, in turn, sold it to his son, Kurt, the present owner. The firm made toys until at least 1939. It was located in Woodhaven, New York. Now called Woodhaven Telesis Corporation, it makes sheet metal parts to order.

	C6	C8	C10
Animate Climbing Tractor, tin windup....	125	188	250
Robot Bus, tin litho, 1930s, 14" long.......	58	110	165

Woodhaven Animate Climbing Tractor, tin windup. Photo courtesy John Monteleone

WYANDOTTE

Wyandotte Toys began in the fall of 1921, when William Schmidt and George Stallings decided that instead of making steel parts for the automobile industry, they would make toys. All Metal Products initially became well known for its large line of toy guns, rifles, and water pistols, but also would be increasingly known for pressed-steel vehicles and airplanes, mechanical toys and games, target sets, musical tops, doll carriages, and other sturdy toys for boys and girls.

Arthur Edwards bought into the growing company and became its president and general manager, running the company until his death in 1932. He was succeeded by his son C. Lee Edwards. By the mid 1930s, Wyandotte Toys was a major mid-price contender in the toy business. It was not unusual for Wyandotte to issue different sizes of the same toy. One might find the same stake truck in four sizes, ranging from 4-1/2 inches to fifteen inches. Additionally, the backed enamel toys came in many colors and color combinations, with special color runs for the Easter holiday. Lithographed toys also figured

EQUIPMENT VARIATIONS

brt	black rubber tire
bwmw	blask & white metal wheels
bww	black wood wheels
e/l	electric lights
eww	embossed wood wheel
lmw	litho metal wheels
pmw	pressed steel wheels
rpw	red plastic wheels
trk	truck
wmw	white metal wheels
wpw	white plastic wheels
wrt	white rubber tires
www	white wood wheels
ymw	yellow metal wheels
yww	yellow wood wheels

BODY ABBREVIATIONS

AS/CG	Air Speed/convex grille	**FN**	Flat Nose	**RW**	Rounded Windshield
AS/FG	Air Speed/flat grille	**LN**	Long Nose	**SB**	Soap Box Racer
AW	All Wood	**LN/T**	Long Nose & Trailer	**SC**	Square Cab
BT	Boat Tail Racer	**LS**	LaSalle	**SE**	Sleepy Eye
CB	Checker Board	**LS/T**	LaSalle & Trailer	**SN**	Shark Nose
CD	Cord	**OC**	Open Cab	**SP**	Speedster
CD/T	Cord & Trailer	**OE**	Open Eye	**SPC**	Sportsman's Convertible
CE	Construction Equipment	**PL**	Plastic	**SW**	Shaded Windshield
CO	Cab Over	**PV**	Panel Van	**TT**	Toy Town
CV	Convertible	**RC**	Rooster Comb	**WF**	Wide Face
FM	Farm Equipment	**RR**	Rocket Racer		

prominently, and with the Wyandotte Circus No. 503 truck and trailer of 1936, it reached the pinnacle of lithography.

During World War II, Wyandotte made clips for the M-1 rifle and was able to offer a reduced toy line of all-wood toys, but it would not be until after the war that it would get back to major toy production.

In April 1947 long-time employee William Wenner was elected president. In 1950, Wyandotte bought Hafner Manufacturing Company, with the thought of increasing market penetration by marketing its toy train line. In 1951, C. Lee Edwards, Mary Reberdy, and the estate of his late father, sold their interests to a new set of owners. The new directors hoped to reorganize the company successfully. It was during this time that one plant was moved to Martin's Ferry, Ohio, another to Pequa, Ohio, and one to the McCord Corporation for its gasket division.

The year 1955 saw both C. Lee Edwards and William Wenner retiring and selling their stock that was acquired as part of the 1951 reorganization. The company was also undergoing financial problems at the time. It has been reported that Louis Marx, of Marx Toys, to assume a larger market share for his own company, purchased some of the Wyandotte and Haffner toy lines and sent them to his Mexican operations. All Metal Products (Wyandotte Toys) filed for bankruptcy Nov. 6, 1956, thereby closing this chapter in toy history.

Values listed are estimates only and should be used ONLY as a guide. Prices vary due to availability and condition of toys. As to pricing, the West Coast is usually higher than the East Coast, while the Midwest is usually lower than the East Coast. What you, the collector, offer to pay and eventually pay, is the true value. Offer or pay only what you feel a piece is worth.

Contributor: John Taylor, P.O. Box 63, Nolensville, TN 37135-0063. Brian Seligman, 11004 S. W. 37th Manor, Davie, FL 33325.

Cars

	C6	C8	C10
Advertising Car, LN, www; red car w/display board on roof reads "Take a ride w/Sophie," "Sophie Tucker and her ROI; TAN show on the radio / C.B.S. Mon. Wed. Fri." on one side and "Roi-Tan Cigars / An auto a day is given away / a brand new 1939 Chevrolet" on the other side, 1936/40, 4-3/8" long	90	165	325

	C6	C8	C10
Air Speed Coupe, AS / CG, wrt; No. 309, 1934/37, 6" long	70	95	120
Air Speed Coupe, AS / FG, wrt; No. 309, 1934/37, 6" long	70	95	120
Air Speed Coupe and Trailer, AS / FG (and CG); wrt/brt, No. 341, 1934, 11-1/4" long	135	190	295
Ambulance, FN, bww; side ports, inset front grille, No. 224, 1939, 6-3/8" long	40	65	125

Wyandotte Advertising Car, 1936/40, 4-3/8" long. Photo courtesy Brian Seligman

Wyandotte Air Speed Coupes, 6" long. Photo courtesy Brian Seligman

Another view of the Wyandotte Air Speed Coupe, 6" long. Photo courtesy Brian Seligman

Two examples of Wyandotte's No. 341 Air Speed Coupe and Trailer. Photo courtesy Brian Seligman

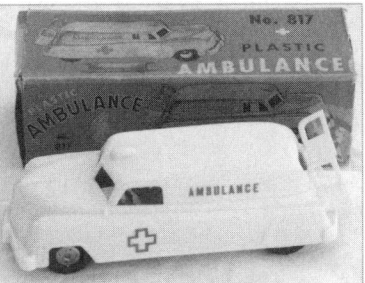

Wyandotte Ambulance with original box, No. 817, 1952/53, 9-1/2" long. Photo courtesy Brian Seligman

Wyandotte Ambulance, No. 224, 1939, 6-3/8" long. Photo courtesy Brian Seligman

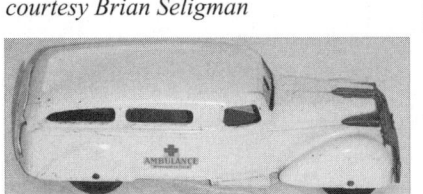

Wyandotte Ambulance, No. 340, 1936/38, 11-1/4" long. Photo courtesy Brian Seligman

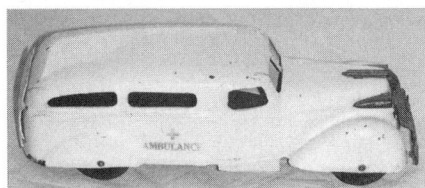

Wyandotte Ambulance, 1939, 11-1/4" long. Photo courtesy Brian Seligman

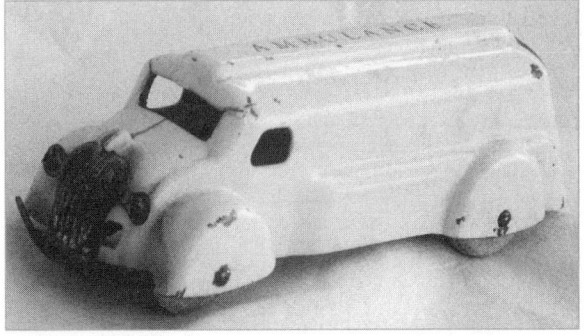

Wyandotte Ambulance, No. 379, 1938, 6-3/8" long. Photo courtesy Brian Seligman

Cardboard Wyandottes from the WWII era; Jeep, Armored Car, and Ambulance. Photo courtesy Jack Matthews

Wyandotte Cadillac, No. 3100, 1955, 8-3/4" long. Photo courtesy Brian Seligman

Wyandotte Cadillac, 1952/54, 5-5/8" long. Photo courtesy Brian Seligman

Cardboard Wyandottes from the WWII era; Jeep, Armored Car, and Ambulance. Photo courtesy Jack Matthews

Wyandotte Convertible, No. 652, 1947/48, 12" long. Photo courtesy Brian Seligman

Wyandotte Cadillac, 1952/54, 5-5/8" long. Photo courtesy Brian Seligman

Two examples of Wyandotte's No. 102 Convertible, 1936/40, 4-3/8" long. Photo courtesy Brian Seligman

Wyandotte Cord, 1936-37, 13-3/8" long. Photo courtesy Brian Seligman

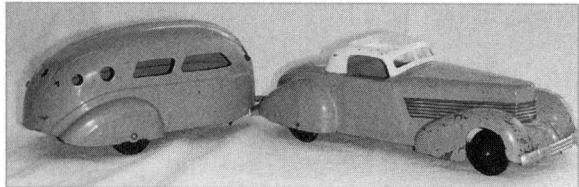

Wyandotte Cord and Trailer Set, No. 363, 1938/39, 23-1/2" long. Photo courtesy Brian Seligman

	C6	C8	C10
Ambulance, LN, brt; friction, "Ambulance and Red Cross," stretcher, 1952, 6-1/2" long..................	70	90	120
Ambulance, LN, brt; white plastic body / metal chassis, friction motor and siren, marked "Ambulance" and "Red Cross," stretcher, opening rear doors; No. 817, 1952/53, 9-1/2" long	40	65	145
Ambulance, LN, bww; marked "Ambulance" stamped on side, opening rear hatch, 1939, 11-1/4" long	65	90	165
Ambulance, LN, bww; w/"Ambulance" and "Wyandotte Toys" decals, opening rear hatch, No. 340, 1936/38, 11-1/4" long	65	95	175
Ambulance, RC, wrt; four side ports, "Ambulance" stamped on top, surface mounted grille, No. 379, 1938, 6-3/8" long	45	70	130
Army Jeep, AW, bww; marked "Jeep," No. 368, 1942, 9" long	45	80	175
Cadillac, "true scale," brt/white hubs; plastic, friction motor, many colors; No. 3100; 1955, 8-3/4" long	60	95	155
Cadillac, PL, pw; plastic, many colors, 1954, 3" long...	40	60	120
Cadillac, PL, pw; plastic, many colors, used on auto transports, 1952/54, 5-5/8" long	35	55	110
Convertible, CD, brt on wood hubs; marked "Zephyr," pull back wind-up motor; No. 600, 1936/37, 13-3/8" long	125	350	550
Convertible, CD, brt; "Fire Dept.," brass bell, wind-up motor w/attached key, No. 384, 1939; 17-3/8" long	145	325	575
Convertible, CD, brt; "Fire Dept.," brass bell, Zephyr motor, No. 601, 1938/39, 17-1/4" long	120	300	525
Convertible, CD, brt; marked "Fire Dept.," Zephyr motor, hood mounted brass bell, 1938, 13-3/8" long	120	300	525

Two examples of Wyandotte's Two-door Roadster. Both are from 1934 and measure 6-3/8" long. Notice the circus wheels on the car on the right. Photo courtesy Brian Seligman

	C6	C8	C10
Convertible, CD, bww; "Fire Dept.," wind-up motor w/attached key, hood mounted brass bell, 1937, 13-3/8" long	145	325	575
Convertible, CD, bww; 1938/39, 13-3/8" long	75	275	425
Convertible, CV, wrt/www; also part of the garage set (1938/40), No. 102, 1936/40; 4-3/8" long.........................	20	50	90
Convertible, SPC, brt; non-woody, plastic driver and windshield, attached key wind-up, license plate "WY 652," No. 652, 1947/48, 12" long.................	150	200	275
Convertible, SPC, brt; sportsman convertible, retractable top, woody look sides, license plate "WY650," No. 650 (No. 651 w/wind-up motor) 1947/48, 12" long	145	190	245
Cord and Trailer Set, CD/T, bww; rear door opens in trailer, No. 363, 1938/39, 23-1/2" long	100	300	575
Coupe, two-door, LN; wrt or www; car also came w/two car garage set, No. 103, 1936/40; 4-3/8" long....................	20	50	90
Coupe, two-door, RW, eww; circus type, 1934, 6-3/8" long	35	60	95
Coupe, two-door, RW, wrt; 1934, 6-3/8" long	35	60	85

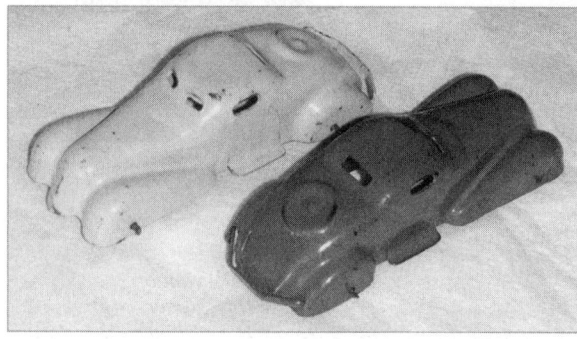

Two views of Wyandotte's No. 103 Two-door Coupe with wood wheels from 1936/40. Photo courtesy Brian Seligman

Wyandotte Coupe, two-door, w/box, electric lights, 1933, 8-1/4" long. Photo courtesy Brian Seligman

Left to right: Wyandotte Coupe, two door with grille, No. 312, 1934/36, 4-1/2" long; Wyandotte Coupe, two door without grille, No. 312, 1934/36, 4-1/2" long. Photo courtesy Brian Seligman

Wyandotte Coupe, two-door, rumble seat, 1932, 8-1/4" long. Photo courtesy Brian Seligman

Wyandoote Coupe, two-door, 1932, 4-7/8" long. Photo courtesy Brian Seligman

Wyandotte Coupe, two-door, rumble seat, 1933, 8-1/4" long. Photo courtesy Brian Seligman

The back of Wyandotte's No. 501 Two-car Garage Set. Photo courtesy Brian Seligman

The front of Wyandotte's No. 501 Two-Car Garage Set. Photo courtesy Brian Seligman

The front of Wyandotte's No. 754 Super Service Garage Set. Photo courtesy Brian Seligman

The back of Wyandotte's No. 754 Super Service Garage Set. Photo courtesy Brian Seligman

Wyandotte Garage Set with plastic door and two 2-3/4" cars, No. 4000, 1952.

The front of Wyandotte's No. 4003 Toytown Fire Dept Garage Set. Photo courtesy Brian Seligman

The back of Wyandotte's No. 4003 Toytown Fire Dept Garage Set. Photo courtesy Brian Seligman

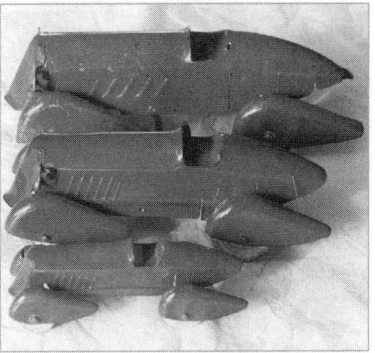

Top to bottom: Wyandotte Racer, boattail, 10-1/4"; Racer, boattail, No. 333, 8-5/8"; Racer, boattail, No. 310, 5-7/8". Photo courtesy Brian Seligman

Wyandotte La Salle (land cruiser), No. 357, 1936/39, 15" long. Photo courtesy Brian Seligman

Wyandotte La Salle with Travel Trailer, No. 358, 1936/38, 26-1/2" long. Photo courtesy Brian Seligman

Wyandotte La Salle (land cruiser), 1939, 15" long. Photo courtesy Brian Seligman

Top to bottom: Wyandotte Racer, boattail, white rubber tires, 8-5/8"; Racer, boattail, yellow wood wheels, 8-5/8". Photo courtesy Brian Seligman

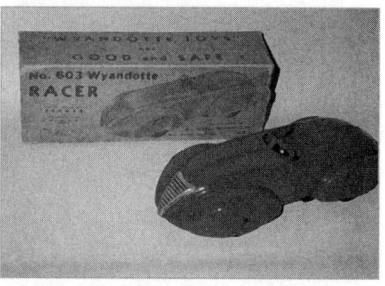

Wyandotte Racer, No. 603, 1937, 10" long. Photo courtesy Brian Seligman

	C6	C8	C10
Coupe, two-door, RW, wrt; w/grille, trunk mounted spare tire, No. 312, 1934/36, 4-1/2" long	35	60	95
Coupe, two-door, RW, wrt; w/out grille, trunk mounted spare tire; No. 312, 4-1/2" long, 1934/36	35	60	95
Coupe, two-door, SW, wrt/red hubs; no light; 1933, 8-1/4" long	45	90	155
Coupe, two-door, SW, wrt; electric lights, 1933, 8-1/4" long	55	100	155
Coupe, two-door, SW, yww; 1932; 4-7/8" long	60	80	105
Coupe, two-door, SW, yww; rumble seat, 1932, 8-1/4" long	55	95	155
Garage Set, metal lithographed double door garage w/a 4-3/8" coupe and convertible, marked "Two Car Garage," No. 501, 1938/39; 3-3/4" x 4-3/4"	65	110	250
Garage Set, metal lithographed single door fire station garage w/one or two 6" fire trucks, "Toytown Fire Dept," No. 4003, 1952, 8" x 6"	50	75	135
Garage Set, metal lithographed single door garage, "Super Service," vehicles included varied, No. 754, 1952, 8-1/2" x 8-1/2"	50	80	150

	C6	C8	C10
Garage Set, plastic single door garage w/two 2-3/16" plastic cars, on back of each is imprinted; No. 4000, 1952, 2-3/4" x 2-1/2"	50	80	140
La Salle (land cruiser), LS, brt or wd hubs; hood opens, no electric lights, 1939, 15" long	75	130	290
La Salle (land cruiser), LS, brt; key attached spring motor, No. 383, 1938, 15-3/4" long	75	150	225
La Salle (land cruiser), LS, wrt; hood opens, electric lights, No. 385, 1939, 15" long	95	150	350
La Salle (land cruiser), LS, wrt; No. 357, 1936/39, 15" long	65	150	225
La Salle w/Travel Trailer, LS/T, wrt; opening rear trailer door, No. 358, 1936/38, 26-1/2" long	145	275	525
Racer, boattail, BT, bww; red w/electric lights, 1934, 10-1/4" long	95	150	300
Racer, boattail, BT, wrt; green/red, electric lights, No. 333, 1934, 8-5/8" long	60	105	155
Racer, boattail, BT, wrt; green/red, No. 310, 1933/34, 5-7/8" long	50	70	125
Racer, boattail, BT, yww; red w/electric lights, 1933; 8-5/8" long	75	105	195

Two views of Wyandotte's No. 319 Rocket Racer. Photo courtesy Brian Seligman

Wyandotte Racer, bottail, 1933/34, 5-7/8". Photo courtesy Brian Seligman

Left to right: Wyandotte Sedan, four door, without grille, No. 311, 4-1/2"; Sedan, four door, with grille, No. 311, 4-1/2". Photo courtesy Brian Seligman

Wyandotte Racer, Indy style, 7" long. Photo courtesy Brian Seligman

Wyandotte Sedan, four door, plastic, No. 311, 1950s, 2-1/4" long. Photo courtesy Brian Seligman

Wyandotte Sedan with Travel Trailer, No. 7625, 1938, 11-3/4" long. Photo courtesy Brian Seligman

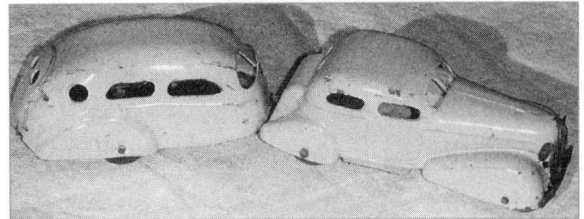

Wyandotte Sedan with Travel Trailer, No. 346, 1938, 11-3/4" long. Photo courtesy Brian Seligman

Two versions of Wyandotte's No. 220 Sedan. Photo courtesy Brian Seligman

Wyandotte Sedan, four door, No. 425, 1939, 11" long. Photo courtesy Brian Seligman

Two versions of Wyandotte's No. 316 Sedan. Photo courtesy Brian Seligman

Wyandotte Sedan, four door, No. 316, 1938, 6" long. Photo courtesy Brian Seligman

Left to right: Wyandotte Sedan, four door, embossed wooden wheels, 1934, 6-1/4"; Wyandotte Sedan, four door, white rubber tires, 1934, 6-1/4". Photo courtesy Brian Seligman

Wyandotte Sedan, four door, No. 344, 1938, 9" long. Photo courtesy Brian Seligman

Two versions of Wyandotte's No. 334 Four-door Sedan. Photo courtesy Brian Seligman

Two versions of Wyandotte's No. 266 Soap Box Derby Racer. The car on the left has red tires, while the model on the right has black. Photo courtesy Brian Seligman

Wyandotte Sedan, four door, No. 311, 1934/37, 4-1/2" long. Photo courtesy Brian Seligman

Left to right: Speedster, No. 378, 6-3/4" long; Wyandotte Speedster, No. 603, 10"; Wyandotte Speedster, with top, 10". Photo courtesy Brian Seligman

Wyandotte Toy Town, large scale, No. 1009, 1941, 21" long. Photo courtesy Brian Seligman

Wyandotte Speedster, 1938, 10" long. Photo courtesy Brian Seligman

Wyandotte Earth Mover, No. 1602, 1952/55, 20-1/2" long. Photo courtesy Brian Seligman

Wyandotte Road Grader, No. 1603, 1952/55, 19" long. Photo courtesy Brian Seligman

Wyandotte Sand Loader and Dump Truck, No. 401, 1954/56, 10-3/4" truck, 10-5/8" tall sand loader. Photo courtesy Brian Seligman

	C6	C8	C10
Racer, Indy style, brt; lithographed body w/attached head of driver, marked "Wyandotte" and "7," also "Jet Streak" version; 7" long	50	70	145
Rocket Racer, rr, wrt or bww; wood rear wheel, No. 319, 1935/36, 6-1/4" long	60	80	145
Sedan w/Travel Trailer, LN/T, wrt or bww; opening rear trailer door, No. 346, 1938, 11-3/4" long	60	150	245
Sedan, four door, CO, bpw; touring sedan (Nash style), No. 220, 1939/41, 6" long	40	65	110
Sedan, four door, CO, pmw; touring sedan (Nash style), No. 425, 1939, 11" long	80	150	325
Sedan, four door, LN, lmw/brt; enclosed chassis; No. 344, 1938, 9" long	70	95	190
Sedan, four door, LN, wrt; No. 316, 1938, 6" long	40	70	115
Sedan, four door, LN; wood wheels, 1938, 9-1/8" long	70	110	225
Sedan, four door, PL; no tires, embossed at license plate is "yand," used on small car carriers, No. 311, 1950s, 2-1/4" long	15	25	35

	C6	C8	C10
Sedan, four door, RC, wrt; electric lights; No. 334 (No. 339 w/o lights), 1934/35, 9" long	70	110	225
Sedan, four door, RC, wrt; No. 316, 1934/35; 6" long	40	70	115
Sedan, four door, RW, eww; 1934, 6-1/4" long	35	60	90
Sedan, four door, RW, wrt; 1934, 6-1/4" long	40	55	95
Sedan, four door, RW, wrt; w/grille, trunk mounted rear spare, No. 311, 1934/37, 4-1/2" long	40	70	110
Sedan, four door, RW, wrt; w/out grille, trunk mounted rear spare, No. 311, 1934/37, 4-1/2" long	35	65	100
Sedan, four door, SW, bww; sometimes included w/auto transport; 1934, 5" long	45	60	80
Soap Box Derby Racer, SB; early red version w/red wd wheels and attached driver helmet, "Soap Box Derby" and "Thunderbird 226," 1941, 6" long	90	195	260
Soap Box Derby Racer, SB; red version w/red wd wheels and blue version w/black wd wheels, marked "Soap Box Derby" and "Thunderbird 226," No. 226, 1941, 6" long	75	150	195

Wyandotte Sand Loader and Hopper, No. 402, 5-1/2" high, 3-3/4" base, 20" reach. Photo courtesy Brian Seligman

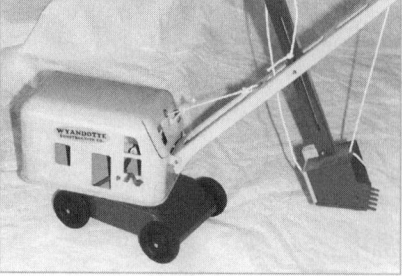

Wyandotte Steam Shovel, early 1950s, 7" x 4" body, 12" boom, 6-1/2" x 3-7/8" chassis. Photo courtesy Brian Seligman

Wyandotte Truck Mounted Digging Combination, No. 236, 1952; 5" long, 8-1/4" with boom. Photo courtesy Brian Seligman

Wyandotte Truck Mounted Digging Combination, 1952, 16-1/4" long. Photo courtesy Brian Seligman

Wyandotte Winch Truck, 1949/53, 23" long. Photo courtesy Brian Seligman

Wyandotte Winch Truck with Removable Steam Shovel, No. 1201, 1952, 22" long. Photo courtesy Brian Seligman

Wyandotte Winch Truck with Removable Steam Shovel, 1953, 19-1/2" long. Photo courtesy Brian Seligman

Wyandotte Winch Truck, 1953, 22" long. Photo courtesy Brian Seligman

Wyandotte Army Truck, 1941, 17-1/2" long. Photo courtesy Brian Seligman

Wyandotte Auto Transport, No. 130, 1953, 12-5/8" long. Photo courtesy Brian Seligman

Wyandotte Tractor, No. 603/602, 1954, 5" long. Photo courtesy Brian Seligman

Wyandotte Auto Transport, 1956/57, 22-1/2" long. Photo courtesy Brian Seligman

Wyandotte Auto Transport, 1932, 21-5/8" long. Photo courtesy Brian Seligman

Wyandotte Auto Transport, No. 130, 1953, 12-5/8" long. Photo courtesy Brian Seligman

Wyandotte Auto Transport, 1940s/50s, 9-1/2" long. Photo courtesy Brian Seligman

Wyandotte Bank Truck (also called Bus Bank), No. 375, 1936-40, 6-3/8" long (front and back view). Photo courtesy Brian Seligman

Wyandotte Army Truck, 1941, 17-1/2" long. Photo courtesy Brian Seligman

Wyandotte Bus, No. 1002, 1941, 21" long. Photo courtesy Brian Seligman

	C6	C8	C10
Speedster, SP, bww; pull back spring motor, cord-like roof over cockpit, 1938, 10" long	65	110	190
Speedster, SP, bww; pull back spring motor, No. 603, 1937, 10" long	60	100	165
Speedster, SP, bww; w/lithographed driver and passenger, No. 378, 1937/38, 6-3/4" long	50	100	225
Speedster, SP, bww; w/out lithographed driver and passenger, No. 378, 1937/38, 6-3/4" long	50	80	190
Toy Town, large scale, TT, brt on wood hubs; delivery wagon, "Toytown Delivery," license plate "WY____," lithograph of driver in window, rear doors open, No. 1008, 1941, 21" long	70	150	375
Toy Town, large scale, TT, brt on wood hubs; grocer wagon marked "Meats and Groceries," license plate "WY1008"; lithograph of driver in window, rear doors open, No. 1008, 1941, 21" long	70	150	375
Toy Town, large scale, TT, brt on wood hubs; w/roof rack, estate station wagon, marked "Toytown Estate," w/woodie-like sides, license plate "WY1009," lithograph of family in widows, rear doors open, No. 1009, 1941, 21" long	70	175	350
Toy Town, large scale, TT; brt on wood hubs; w/out roof rack, estate station wagon, marked "Toytown Estate," w/woodie-like sides, license plate "WY1007," lithograph of family in widows, rear doors open, No. 1007, 1941, 21" long	70	150	325

Construction

	C6	C8	C10
Caterpilar Grader, CE; all plastic construction except for metal blade, black and yellow, 1952, 12" long	50	70	110
Caterpilar Scraper, CE; all plastic construction except for metal blade, black and yellow, 1952, 12" long	50	70	110
Caterpilar Wagon, CE; all plastic construction, black and yellow, 1952; 12" long	50	70	110
Earth Mover, CE, brt; orange, "Heavy Duty," operable rear dump, front scoop, plastic engine and smoke stack, "Highway Engineers," 1952/55, 20-1/2" long	60	85	130
Earth Mover, CE, brt; orange, "Heavy Duty," operable rear dump, plastic engine and smoke stack, "Highway Engineers," No. 1602, 1952/55, 20-1/2" long	60	85	130
Electric Conveyor, CE, brt; color?; No. 402, 1955, 14-1/2" long	40	65	190
Road Grader, CE; brt; orange, steerable front wheels and adjustable grading blade, "Power Grader"; No. 1603, 1952/55, 19" long	60	85	130
Road Roller, CE; plastic and tin, multi color, friction motor, "Construction," No. 905, 1952, 6-1/2" long	20	50	105
Sand Loader and Dump Truck, CO/CB, brt; sand loader w/string operated dump hoist, "Wyandotte" on side of truck and "Wyandotte Construction Company" on side of sand loader, No. 401, 1954/56, 10-3/4" truck, 10-5/8" tall sand loader	90	150	250
Sand Loader and Hopper, CE bww; red and green super scoop shovel; No. 401, 7" high, 5-1/2" square; sand hopper No. 347; 1938; N/A; when 11-1/4" dump truck was added it was known as the "Highway Construction Set," No. 402, 5-1/2" high, 3-3/4" base, 20" reach	75	125	275
Steam Shovel, CE, brt; "Wyandotte Construction Company," also came w/lithographed body and "Sturdy Construction" on side, early 1950s, 7" x 4" body, 12" boom, 6 1/2" x 3-7/8" chassis	35	60	105
Truck Mounted Digging Combination, CE/PL, brt/dual rear; plastic, "Scooper," No. 236, 1952; 5" long, 8-1/4" w/boom	10	30	75
Truck Mounted Digging Combination, CO, brt (four rear tires); lithographed cab w/"Wyandotte" on side, lithographed crane body "Sturdy Construction Co," "Diesel," w/clamshell bucket, steel chassis "Wyandotte, Construction, Engineering" decal, 1952, 16-1/4" long	185	225	295
Truck Mounted Digging Combination, CO, brt; plastic cab w/lithographed grille and dash, steel chassis, clam shell bucket, "Sturdy Construction," No. 1012, 1952; 14-1/2" long	185	225	305
Winch Truck w/Removable Steam Shovel, CO, brt; all plastic; No. 238, 1952, 10" long	60	75	100
Winch Truck w/Removable Steam Shovel, CO, brt; late 1940s/50, 7" long	65	80	100
Winch Truck w/Removable Steam Shovel, CO, brt; No. 236, 1952, 8-3/4" long	65	80	100
Winch Truck w/Removable Steam Shovel, CO, brt; plastic motor, rubber exhaust pipe, sliding rear ramp, removable crane, 1953, 22" long	80	100	145
Winch Truck w/Removable Steam Shovel, CO, brt; steam shovel on wood wheels w/"Wyandotte Construction Co" decal; 1953; 19-1/2" long	80	100	145
Winch Truck w/Removable Steam Shovel, CO/OE, brt; steam shovel on tracks, No. 1201, 1952, 22" long	80	100	140
Winch Truck w/Removable Steam Shovel, OE, brt; on red plastic hubs, tractor and flatbed w/treaded steam shovel, tool box w/tools behind cab, 1954, 22-1/2" long	50	75	145
Winch Truck w/Removable Steam Shovel, WF, brt; "Wyandotte Construction Co." on side of removable crane, 1949/53, 23" long	85	105	145

Farm Equipment

	C6	C8	C10
Farm Set, tractor w/stake trailer "Valley Farms Produce," harrow, spreader and coupler, 1955	NPF	NPF	NPF
Tractor, FM; plastic; brt; No. 603/602, 1954, 5" long	40	65	95

Wyandotte Bus, No. 377, 1936-40, 6-3/8" long (front and back view). Photo courtesy Brian Seligman

Wyandotte Bus, No. 233, 1939, 6-3/8" long. Photo courtesy Brian Seligman

Wyandotte Circus Truck, No. 503, 1936, 19-1/4" long. Photo courtesy Brian Seligman

Wyandotte Circus Truck, 1941, 19-1/4" long. Photo courtesy Brian Seligman

Wyandotte Dairy/Milk Truck, 1949, 12" long. Photo courtesy Brian Seligman

Wyandotte Dairy/Milk Truck, No. 4002, 1952, 7-1/2" long. Photo courtesy Brian Seligman

Wyandotte Dairy/Milk Truck, No. 805, 1952, 4-7/8" long. Photo courtesy Brian Seligman

Wyandotte Delivery Truck, No. 345, 1938-39, 11-3/8" long. Photo courtesy Brian Seligman

Wyandotte Delivery Truck, No. 353, 1952, 11-1/2" long. Photo courtesy Brian Seligman

Wyandotte Delivery Van, 1954, 6" long. Photo courtesy Brian Seligman

Wyandotte Delivery Van, No. 120, 1954, 9-7/8" long. Photo courtesy Brian Seligman

Wyandotte Diaper Delivery Truck, No. 805, 1952, 4-7/8" long. Photo courtesy Brian Seligman

Wyandotte Delivery Van, 11" long. Photo courtesy Bob Smith

Wyandotte Dump Truck, 1934, 7" long. Photo courtesy Brian Seligman

Trucks

	C6	C8	C10
Army Truck, bww; marked "Army Supply," all wood construction; No. 214; 1941/42; 9-1/2" long	45	80	175
Army Truck, LN, brt; "Army Engineer Corp. No. 42," canvas cloth top; 1941; 17-1/2" long	60	90	150
Army Truck, LN, brt; "Army Engineers Corps," canvas cloth top; No. 1006; 1940-41, 21" long	65	95	155
Army Truck, LN; brt; marked "Army Supply Corp.," canvas cloth top; No. 433, 1941, 11-3/4" long	45	75	145
Auto Transport, CO, brt; lithographed cab and trailer, marked "Car a van Lines" and "Automotive Transport"; three 5-1/2" Cadillacs, loading ramp, 1956/57, 22-1/2" long	45	70	135
Auto Transport, CO, brt; plastic cab and lithographed trailer; marked "#455" "Auto Transport," "Wt.714," "Cap.4," and "Tires.90-20"; No. 455, 1952; 10" long	35	50	120
Auto Transport, CO, brt; plastic cab, marked "Wyandotte" or "Auto Transport" on the side, 1952, 10-1/4" long	50	70	150
Auto Transport, CO, pmw; red/yellow lithographed cab w/red and yellow trailer and four "Cadillac" cars, ramp for upper cars and tailgate lowers for lower cars, "AUTO TRANSPORT," No. 1104, 1952/53, 22" long	55	75	155
Auto Transport, CO, red cab, w/four plastic cars; 1940s/50s, 9-1/2" long	30	40	110
Auto Transport, CO, SC, brt; w/four "Cadillacs; No. 611; 1955; 42" long	45	70	145
Auto Transport, CO; brt; plastic cab w/metal trailer, "Haul A Car," four plastic cars; No. 482; 1950s, 8-3/4" long	20	45	110
Auto Transport, OE, CB, brt; lithographed cab and trailer, four cars, marked "Transmobile Jr.," "Transcontinental Auto Freight Lines," and "I.C.C. 2034 / LT.WT. 6800 / CAPY 9000," No. 130, 1953; 12-5/8" long	50	70	145
Auto Transport, OE; brt w/red plastic hubs; lithographed cab w/rear toolbox and five tools, four cars w/ramp, marked "Car o van," 1954, 23" long	50	65	145
Auto Transport, SW, yww; green cab and black trailer w/four vehicles, electric lights, 1932, 21-5/8" long	105	190	325
Auto Transport, SW, yww; orange cab and trailer w/four vehicles, 1932, 21-5/8" long	95	175	350
Auto Transport, SW, yww; orange cab and trailer w/three vehicles, 1932, 19" long.	65	165	340
Baggage Truck, LN, brt; marked "Baggage," w/freight cart, 1941, 11-3/4" long	45	75	125
Baggage Truck, SN, bmw; marked "Baggage," 1953; 11-1/2" long	40	70	145
Bank Truck (also called Bus Bank), RC, bww; green/red/orange, four portholes on each side, rear hatch w/coin slot and key, sealed chassis, No. 375, 1936-40, 6-3/8" long	40	65	125

	C6	C8	C10
Bread Truck, PV, wpw; red plastic body and metal red frame, marked "Silvercup Bread," friction, 1952, 4-7/8" long	45	75	105
Bus, CO, brt; no roof rack or decal, rear door, No. 1002 1941, 21" long	90	150	290
Bus, CO, bww; blue; same window and rear panel design as No. 377, but different nose w/inset grille design, open chassis, No. 233, 1939, 6-3/8" long	40	70	130
Bus, CO, bww; no roof rack, rear door, "Coast to Coast Bus Line," No. 1002 (Heavy Duty Motor Bus), 1939-40, 21" long	90	150	300
Bus, CO, bww; roof rack and rear door, No. 1002, 1938, 21" long	90	155	325
Bus, CO; brt; no roof rack, rear door, "Coast to Coast Bus Line," No. 1002, 1941, 21" long	90	150	300
Bus, RC, bww or wrt; green/red/orange/yellow, eight windows on each side and rear panel w/two windows and embossed spare tire, sealed chassis; No 377, 1936-40; 6-3/8" long	40	70	135
Cement Truck, CO, brt; "Cement Mixer / Sell / Rent," may have had attached mixer; 1940/50, 5" long	20	50	75
Cement Truck, CO, brt; plastic cab, attached mixer No. 239, 1952, 8-1/2" long	20	45	65
Circus Truck, LN, 1941; two-piece, red cab and lithographed double trailers w/swing down rear ramps, reads "Greatest Show On Earth," cardboard animals on metal stands, w/long nose-style cab, scarce, 19-1/4" long	250	475	1300
Circus Truck, RC, eww; two-piece, red cab and lithographed double trailers w/swing down rear ramps, reads "Greatest Show On Earth," cardboard animals on metal stands; No. 503, 1936, 19-1/4" long	200	425	1200
Coal Truck, SN, ymw; front scoop, lithographed dump bed w/tailgate, marked "COAL," "FUEL and SUPPLY CO.," and "444," No. 444, 1949, 13" long	50	130	225
Contractor Truck, LN, bww; "Contractor Truck," No. 434c, 1941, 11-1/4" long .	45	65	135
Dairy/Milk Truck, LN, brt/brt on hubs, No. 362; 1937/38, 17-3/8" long	55	75	145
Dairy/Milk Truck, LN, brt; w/one milk bottle "Drink More Milk," No. 431, 1941, 11-3/4" long	60	80	150
Dairy/Milk Truck, LN, bww; w/two milk bottles, No. 349, 1939, 11-1/2" long	50	75	145
Dairy/Milk Truck, PL, rpw; w/two crates of milk, marked "Sunshine Dairy," "Milk," and "Cream," box reads "Early Bird Milk Wagon and Horse," No. 4002, 1952, 7-1/2" long	50	75	145
Dairy/Milk Truck, PV, brt; plastic yellow body and metal red frame, "Sunshine Dairy," friction, No. 805, 1952, 4-7/8" long	20	35	110
Dairy/Milk Truck, SN, ymw; "Sunshine Dairy Farms," "Milk," and "Cream," w/one milk bottle, 1949, 12" long	50	85	140

Wyandotte Dump Truck, No. 326 1931-32, 9-5/8" long. Photo courtesy Brian Seligman

Wyandotte Dump Truck, 1931/32, 15-1/4" long. Photo courtesy Brian Seligman

Wyandotte Dump Truck, 1933-34, 15" long. Photo courtesy Brian Seligman

Wyandotte Dump Truck, No. 328, 1934, 12-3/4" long. Photo courtesy Brian Seligman

Wyandotte Dump Truck, No. 222, 1939/41, 6" long. Photo courtesy Brian Seligman

Wyandotte Dump Truck, No. 326 (later version), 1931/32, 9-5/8" long. Photo courtesy Brian Seligman

Two versions of Wyandotte's, No. 318, Dump Truck. Photo courtesy Brian Seligman

Two versions of Wyandotte's No. 315 Dump Truck. The truck on the right is slightly longer because it has a grille. Photo courtesy Brian Seligman

Wyandotte Dump Truck, 1934/37, 15-1/2" long. Photo courtesy Brian Seligman

Wyandotte Dump Truck, 1932, 5-5/8" long. Photo courtesy Brian Seligman

Wyandotte Dump Truck, No. 318, 1934-37, 6" long. Photo courtesy Brian Seligman

Wyandotte Dump Truck, 1941, 12-1/4" long. Photo courtesy Brian Seligman

Wyandotte Dump Truck, 1933, 7" long. Photo courtesy Brian Seligman

Wyandotte Dump Truck, 1934, 7" long. Photo courtesy Brian Seligman

	C6	C8	C10
Delivery Truck, LN, bww; opening rear door; green/red/grey/yellow, "City Delivery" stamped on side, same body as No. 340 ambulance, No. 345, 1938-39, 11-3/8" long	60	75	145
Delivery Truck, PV, brt; red plastic body/metal chassis, "Toy Town Delivery" and "Super Service," lithographed grille and dashboard, opening side and rear doors, No. 353, 1952, 11-1/2" long	50	65	115
Delivery Van, CO, wmw; lithographed cab and body, "Minitown Parcel Service," and "Courtesy Pays," w/white "w" in black circle, 1952, 12" long	55	100	190
Delivery Van, LN, 1938; brt/ws hub, spring motor w/attached key, No. 382, No. 362 w/out motor, 16" long	80	95	175
Delivery Van, LN; wood wheels, 1938-39, 16-3/8" long	50	65	115
Delivery Van, OE, brt; lithographed cab and body, cab w/rear van body, "Express Delivery Service," "Local," "National," and "I.C.C. 120/Cap. 4500/WT. 3250," No. 120, 1954, 9-7/8" long	35	70	140
Delivery Van, OE, brt; lithographed cab and body, cab w/rear van body, "Wyandotte Trucking," "Speedy Delivery," "New York Chicago San Francisco," 1954, 6" long	25	50	85
Delivery Van, SE, brt; 1949, 12" long	30	55	95
Diaper Delivery Truck, PV, brt; white plastic body and red metal frame, mark "Dy-Dee Wash," and "Stork," friction, No. 805, 1952, 4-7/8" long	20	45	110
Dump Truck, AW, bww; marked "Highway Dept. Dump," all wood construction, No. 1009, 1942, 13-1/4" long	45	80	175
Dump Truck, CO, bpw; No. 222, 1939/41, 6" long	20	35	95
Dump Truck, CO, brt/wd hubs; 1941, 21" long	45	70	120
Dump Truck, CO, brt; all plastic; No. 159, 1952, 5-1/2" long	20	35	70
Dump Truck, CO, brt; late 1940s/50s, 5" long	25	45	70
Dump Truck, CO, brt; lithographed cab, marked "Giant" on side of dump bed, w/11-3/4" shove, No. 1023, 1954/55, 20-1/2" long	55	95	250
Dump Truck, CO, brt; marked "Automatic Loading," No. 331, 1955-56, 13" long	65	85	150
Dump Truck, CO, brt; marked "Giant," No. 1023, 1950s, 11-1/4" long	60	90	190
Dump Truck, CO, brt; red plastic cab, w/12" shovel, "Giant Construction Co." on side of dump body, No. 1014, 1953/54, 21" long	60	105	250
Dump Truck, CO, brt; side dump, No. 301, 1953-54, 21-1/2" long	60	75	125
Dump Truck, CO, bww/mw; No. 426, 1940/45, 12-1/4" long	40	55	105
Dump Truck, CO, bww; side dump No. 391, 1939/47, 17-3/8" long	45	70	130
Dump Truck, CO, bww; w/shovel; Heavy Duty Dump Truck, No. 1001, 1938/41, 21" long	65	105	145

	C6	C8	C10
Dump Truck, CO, mw; front end loader, lever action rear dump, plastic cab and chassis, lithographed body, marked "Sand," No. 443, 1952, 12" long	30	50	125
Dump Truck, CO, mw; plastic cab and metal dump body, 1952, 20" long	35	95	155
Dump Truck, CO, ymw; plastic cab, tailgate, No. 352, 1952; 11" long	50	65	125
Dump Truck, CO/SC, brt; hydraulic lift, opening tailgate, No. 300, 1955, 21-3/4" long	60	75	120
Dump Truck, LN, bww; mechanical, attached key, shovel, No. 381, 1938-39, 16" long	65	95	135
Dump Truck, LN, bww; No. 318, 1938, 6" long	35	55	110
Dump Truck, LN, bww; side lever/rear dumping action, w/wheelbarrow, 1941, 12-1/4" long	45	70	135
Dump Truck, LN, bww; w/5-1/4" wheelbarrow, No. 343c, 1938/41, 11-1/4" long	60	80	145
Dump Truck, LN, bww; w/shovel, No. 361, 1938-39, 16" long	50	75	120
Dump Truck, OE/CB, brt/mw; No. 124, 1955, 12" long	60	80	110
Dump Truck, RC, brt/red hubs; w/lights working lights: No. 354, w/non-working headlights: No. 351, 1934-37, 15-1/4" long	65	95	135
Dump Truck, RC, brt; electric lights; No. 326, 1934, 10" long	40	60	115
Dump Truck, RC, brt; imitation lights, No. 324, 1934, 10" long	40	60	110
Dump Truck, RC, bww; Easter Style, pink cab and purple dump body w/chicken stamped on sides, No. E318, 1937/38, 6" long	40	75	205
Dump Truck, RC, wrt; red/green/ orange; No. 318, 1934-37, 6" long	40	65	95
Dump Truck, SE/CB, brt; marked "Wyandotte," front scoop; No. 122, 1953, 10" long	50	65	120
Dump Truck, SN, bww; marked "Sand Gravel Excavation," No. 1023, 1949, 12" long	60	80	135
Dump Truck, SN, ymw/bww; 1949, 12" long	40	55	110
Dump Truck, SW, eww; 1933, 7" long	50	70	100
Dump Truck, SW, wrt/red hubs; electric lights, 1933-34; 15" long	55	95	165
Dump Truck, SW, wrt/red hubs; No. 328, 1934, 12-3/4" long	65	85	125
Dump Truck, SW, wrt; larger version of 5-1/4" truck, 1934, 7" long	40	60	110
Dump Truck, SW, wrt; w/grille, green or red; No. 315, 1934/36, 5-1/4" long	40	65	105
Dump Truck, SW, wrt; w/o grille, green or red, No. 315, 1934/36, 4-7/8" long	40	65	105
Dump Truck, SW, yww; 1932, 5-5/8" long	20	45	110
Dump Truck, SW, yww; side lever w/slide track mechanism, dual rear wood wheels, No. 326, 1931-32, 9-5/8" long	60	80	145
Dump Truck, SW, yww; side spring release mechanism, dual rear wood wheels, 1931/32, 15-1/4" long	75	150	225
Dump Truck, SW, yww; side spring release mechanism, dual rear wood			

Wyandotte Dump Truck, 1949, 12" long. Photo courtesy Brian Seligman

Wyandotte Dump Truck, side dumper, "Wyandotte Construction Co." Photo courtesy Bob Smith

Wyandotte Dump Truck, No. 324, 1934, 10" long. Photo courtesy Brian Seligman

Wyandotte Dump Truck, No. 122, 1953, 10" long. Photo courtesy Brian Seligman

Wyandotte Fire Truck, No. 329, 1932/34, 10" long. Photo courtesy Brian Seligman

Wyandotte Fire Truck, No. 428, 1949, 12" long. Photo courtesy Brian Seligman

Wyandotte Fire Truck, No. 428, 1949, 12" long. Photo courtesy Brian Seligman

Top to bottom: Wyandotte Fire Truck, No. 329, 1932/34, 10"; Wyandotte Fire Truck, No. 308R, 1932, 6". Photo courtesy Brian Seligman

Wyandotte Dump Truck, No. 343c, 1938/41, 11-1/4" long. Photo courtesy Brian Seligman

Wyandotte Fire Truck, No. 1004, 1940/41, 27-1/4" long. Photo courtesy Brian Seligman

Wyandotte Lumber Truck/Log Hauler, 1952, 10-1/4" long. Photo courtesy Brian Seligman

Wyandotte Ice Truck, one ice cube and one pair of ice tongs, No. 123, 1954, 10-1/4" long. Photo courtesy Brian Seligman

Wyandotte Medical Truck, No. 430, 1940/41, 11-3/4" long. Photo courtesy Brian Seligman

Wyandotte Ice Truck, No. 432, 1949, 12" long. Photo courtesy Brian Seligman

	C6	C8	C10
wheels, No. 326 (later version), 1931/32; 9-5/8" long	60	80	145
EXPRESS (see tractor-trailer)			
Fire Truck, CO, 1952; ymw, plastic cab and metal lithographed trailer, No. 382 20-1/2" long	65	95	135
Fire Truck, CO, brt; all plastic, No. 157, 1952, 5-1/2" long	65	80	110
Fire Truck, CO, brt; attached green ladder, reads "Wyandotte Fire Department" and "Fire Chief Hook and Ladder Truck," late 1940s/50, 11" long	30	50	115
Fire Truck, CO, brt; hook and aerial ladder truck, plastic cab and metal lithographed trailer, marked either "Hook and Ladder CO. NO. 3" or "Wyandotte Fire Department," plastic rear driver; No. 457, 1952, 11" long	50	75	125
Fire Truck, CO, brt; lithographed trailer, toolbox w/tools, "Hook and Ladder" and "1," No. 1021, 1955/56, 24" long	60	110	225
Fire Truck, CO, brt; plastic cab and metal lithographed trailer, mechanical, crank to raise ladder, 1952, 20" long	65	95	155
Fire Truck, CO, brt; w/bright metal hubs; plastic and steel, friction, siren and red flashing light, lever release ladder, 1952, 11" long	35	60	135
Fire Truck, CO, six bww; "Hook and Ladder No. 10," 29" expanding ladder, hood bell, No. 1004, 1940/41, 27-1/2" long	65	125	250
Fire Truck, LN, brt; friction, siren and ladder, No. 156, 1952, 7-1/2" long	30	50	75
Fire Truck, LN, brt; red plastic body w/metal chassis, friction motor and siren, marked "Fire Dept. Rescue Squad," stretcher, opening rear doors; No. 818, 1952/53, 9-1/2" long	35	50	125
Fire Truck, LN, bww; bell, two ladders, No. 366, 1941, 17-1/2" long	50	70	145
Fire Truck, LN, bww; lithographed grille and rear bed, bell, two 7-1/2" ladders, "Engine Co. No. 4," No. 428, 1941, 11-3/4" long	50	70	135
Fire Truck, OC, wrt; red body w/three green ladders, No. 308R, 1932, 6" long	65	80	120
Fire Truck, OC, wrt; red body w/three ladders, axle activated bell, No. 329, 1932/34, 10" long	65	90	125
Fire Truck, SC, wpw; red w/white ladders, all plastic, "W" on wheels, No. 150, 1952; 6-1/4" long	20	35	70
Fire Truck, SE, brt; lithographed cab and body, lithographed "control panel" inside body, 1952, 10-1/2" long	65	90	145
Fire Truck, SN, brt; bell, two or three ladders, "Engine Co. No. 4," No. 428, 1949, 12" long	45	70	125
Fire Truck, WF, 1949; brt, lithographed trailer, "Hook and Ladder" and "10," 24" long	65	125	225
Garbage Truck, CO/SC, brt; dump action and rear loading sliding gate, marked "Metropolitan Department of Public Service" and "Help Keep our City Clean," No. 332, 1956/57, 17" long	70	150	325
Gardener's Truck, CO/CB, mw/brt; marked "Gardening," "Ferry's Seeds,"			

	C6	C8	C10
"Fill," "Dirt," "Trees," "Shrubs" decal, wheelbarrow and round nose shovel, No. 121; 1953; 10-1/4" long	50	60	125
Ice Cream Cart, PL; all plastic, sliding lid and bell, 1953, 4-1/2" long	30	50	100
Ice Truck, LN, brt; one ice cube and one pair ice tongs, ink stamped "Toy Town Ice Co.," No. 432, 1941, 11-3/4" long	45	60	135
Ice Truck, LN, bww; two ice cubes and one pair of ice tongs; No. 348; 1938/39, 11-1/2" long	45	60	125
Ice Truck, LN, wmt; lithographed body, marked "Toy Town Ice Co." and "Crystal Clear," No. 432, 1941, 11-3/4" long	45	60	135
Ice Truck, SE/CB, lmw; lithographed body, marked "Igloo Ice Company," one ice cube and one pair of ice tongs; No. 123 1954, 10-1/4" long	50	60	135
Ice Truck, SN, ymw; lithographed body, "Toy Town Ice Co.," "Crystal Clear" and "23"; No. 432, 1949; 12" long	45	60	135
Lumber Truck/Log Hauler, CO, bmw; lithographed cab, "Timberland Lumber Supply," No. 426, 1950, 12" long	50	65	145
Lumber Truck/Log Hauler, CO, brt; all plastic, six logs included, No. 176, 1952, 9-1/4" long	45	50	110
Lumber Truck/Log Hauler, CO, brt; lithographed tractor, open log trailer, three logs included, 1956/57, 24" long	50	75	165
Lumber Truck/Log Hauler, CO, brt; metal cab and trailer, three logs included, 1956/57, 11-1/2" long	50	75	135
Lumber Truck/Log Hauler, SE, b/wmw; lithographed cab, flat bed has four plastic posts, marked "Lumber Supply," four logs included, 1952, 10-1/4" long	45	50	130
Medical Truck, LN, bww; reads "Medical Corps" w/a Red Cross on side of canvas cloth top, No. 430, 1940/41, 11-3/4" long	65	90	140
Oil/Gas Tanker, CO, brt; rear fold down hatch; No. 1003 (Heavy Duty Gas Truck), 1939/40; 21" long	60	90	165
Oil/Gas Tanker, RC, bww; four embossed top hatches and fold down rear hatch; sealed chassis, No. 225, 1939, 6-3/8" long	30	55	120
Oil/Gas Tanker, RC, wrt ('35-36), brt ('37); four imitation top hatches and fold down rear hatch, sealed chassis, No. 330, 1936/37, 10-1/2" long	65	90	145
Oil/Gas Tanker, RC, wrt; four embossed portholes on each side, rear panel w/two windows and embossed tire (like bus), open chassis, 1939; 6-3/8" long	30	55	120
Oil/Gas Tanker, RC, wrt; four embossed top hatches and fold down rear hatch, sealed chassis, No. 376, 1936/38, 6-3/8" long	30	55	120
Painting Truck, SE, brt; "Jiffy Painting," "Decorating" and "Quick Service," w/two ladders, 1953, 10-1/4" long	50	65	130
Pickup Truck, PL, 1952; plastic, brt, No. 155, 5-1/2" long	10	40	65
Pickup Truck, PL, brt; plastic, 1950s, 7-7/8" long	10	40	65

Wyandotte Fire Truck, 1949, 24" long. Photo courtesy Brian Seligman

Wyandotte Ice Truck, No. 432, 1941, 11-3/4" long. Photo courtesy Brian Seligman

Wyandotte Oil/Gas Tanker, No. 376, 1936/38, 6-3/8" long. Photo courtesy Brian Seligman

Wyandotte Oil/Gas Tanker, Two versions of Wyandotte's No. 330, Oil/Gas Tanker, 10-1/2" long. Photo courtesy Brian Seligman

Wyandotte Oil/Gas Tanker, No. 225, 1939, 6-3/8" long. Photo courtesy Brian Seligman

Two views of Wyandotte Oil/Gas Tanker, 1939, 6-3/8" long. Photo courtesy Brian Seligman

Wyandotte Painting Truck, "Jiffy Painting-Decorating," 10-1/2" long. Photo courtesy Brian Seligman

Wyandotte Pickup Truck, plastic, 1950s, 7-7/8" long. Photo courtesy Brian Seligman

Front and back view of Wyandotte's Railway Express from the late 1940s, 6-1/2" long. Photo courtesy Brian Seligman

Wyandotte Railway Express Truck, late 1940s/52, 12-1/2" long. Photo courtesy Brian Seligman

Wyandotte Riding Truck, No. 356, 1935/36, 16-1/4" long. Photo courtesy Brian Seligman

Wyandotte Stake Truck, 1931/32, 15" long. Photo courtesy Brian Seligman

Wyandotte Stake Truck, Easter, 1939/41, 11" long. Photo courtesy Brian Seligman

Wyandotte Stake Truck, No. 314, 1933, 4-5/8" long. Photo courtesy Brian Seligman

	C6	C8	C10
Railway Express Truck, CO, brt; "Wyandotte Toys" and REA lithographed on each side, late 1940s, 6-1/2" long	25	40	100
Railway Express Truck, CO, brt; REA lithographed, "Nation Wide," "Air; Rail Service" and "Railway Express Agency," late1940s/52, 12-1/2" long	50	70	165
Railway Express Truck, CO, ymw; plastic cab and lithographed body, "Nation-Wide" "Air-Rail Service," late1940s/52, 11" long	50	70	115
Riding Truck, RC, brt; No. 356, 1935/36; 16-1/4" long	65	95	275
Riding Truck, SC, brt on metal wheels; "Towing Service Car," wrecker boom w/chain operated winch, No. 1705, 1956/57, 32-1/2" long	75	105	200
Riding Truck, SC, brt; fire truck w/electric spot light and siren, No. 1704, 1952/56, 32-1/2" long	75	105	230
Stake Truck, CO, brt and bpw; "Wyandotte Toys" embossed on driver's side of cab; No. 221 1939/46, 6" long	20	50	100
Stake Truck, CO, brt; late 1940s/50s, 5" long	35	60	75
Stake Truck, CO, brt; lithographed cab, fourteen tires, rear opening door, steerable, 1955, 22-1/2" long	65	105	160
Stake Truck, CO, brt; mini hand truck, "Express," No. 1000, 1939/41, 21" long	65	105	155
Stake Truck, CO, mw; No. 426, 1940/45, 12-1/4" long	40	65	125
Stake Truck, CO, six brt; plastic cab w/lithographed grille and metal trailer marked "Wyandotte Truck Lines, " rear spare tire, 1952; 23" long	90	135	180
Stake Truck, LN, bww; 1940/41, 12-1/4" long	50	75	125
Stake Truck, LN, bww; w/5-3/4" hand truck, No. 342c, 1938/39, 12" long	65	75	145
Stake Truck, LN, mw; Easter Style, pink cab w/light green bed, rabbit stamped on side, "Funny Bunny Wants To Stay," 1939/41, 11" long	45	85	210
Stake Truck, LN, mw; w/5-3/4" hand truck; No. 342c, 1938; 11-1/4" long	65	80	145
Stake Truck, LN, wrt mounted on wood hubs; mechanical w/attached key, No. 380, 1938/39, 16" long	65	90	165
Stake Truck, LN, wrt or brt mounted on red hubs; hand truck, No. 360, 1938/39, 16" long	60	95	155
Stake Truck, LN, wrt/bww; No. 317, 1932 / 37, 6" long	40	65	110
Stake Truck, RC, bww; Easter Style, pink cab w/light green bed, rabbit stamped on side, No. E317, 1937/38, 6" long	35	75	165
Stake Truck, RC, imw; Easter Style, pink cab w/light green bed, rabbit stamped on side, "Funny Bunny Wants to Stay," No. E325, 1937/38, 10" long	45	85	210
Stake Truck, RC, wrt brt mounted on red hubs; electric lights, No. 360, 1934/37, 15-1/4" long	75	105	170
Stake Truck, RC, wrt or brt; dual rear wood wheels, 1935/36, 10" long	55	80	150
Stake Truck, RC, wrt, bww; No. 317, 1934/37; 5-5/8" long	40	55	85
Stake Truck, SE/CB, brt/bmw; "Pickwick Pastures," "Livestock," "Dairy Cows" and "Wyandotte," No. 129, 1954, 11-3/4" long	35	60	115
Stake Truck, SN; bmw, 1949, 12" long	40	60	100
Stake Truck, SW, brt; electric lights, No. 323, 1932, 9-5/8" long	60	85	175
Stake Truck, SW, eww; 1934/35, 6-7/8" long	50	75	95
Stake Truck, SW, wd wheels; w/ and w/o electric lights, No. 352, 1933/34, 15" long	60	95	170
Stake Truck, SW, wrt on red hubs, No. 327, 1934/35, 12-1/8" long	75	150	220
Stake Truck, SW, wrt or brt on metal spoke wheels, No. 325, No. 323 has non-spoke wheels, 1931, 9-5/8" long	60	85	175
Stake Truck, SW, wrt; No. 317, 1934/35, 6-3/8" long	50	75	95
Stake Truck, SW, wrt; No. 327, 1934/35, 12-1/8" long	75	150	220
Stake Truck, SW, wrt; w/grille, green or red, No. 314, 1934, 5-1/4" long	40	70	115
Stake Truck, SW, wrt; w/out grille, green or red, No. 314, 1933, 4-5/8" long	40	70	115
Stake Truck, SW, yww or wrt on red hubs; No. 323, 1931, 9-5/8" long	60	85	175
Stake Truck, SW, yww; dual rear wood wheels, 1931/32; 15" long	60	85	145
Stake Truck, SW, yww; dual rear wood wheels, No. 325, 1931/32, 9-3/8" long	50	75	145
Television Truck, PL, brt; red plastic body w/yellow metal frame, "Television Repair Service," friction, No. 803, 1954, 4-7/8" long	20	35	110
Tow Truck, CO, brt on yellow plastic hubs; "Moto; Fix," "Toolkit," "Towcar," "Towing-Repairs," "Tire Change" and "Parts," w/tools and two spare tires, all metal construction, 1954, 15" long	75	90	150
Tow Truck, CO, brt/red hubs; lithographed cab and body, "Towing Service," tools and two spare tires on boom, w/a "W" in red circle, roof mounted light; 1954/56, 15" long	65	90	145
Tow Truck, CO, brt; "Towing; Day and Nite," 1956/57, 13-7/8" long	45	65	115
Tow Truck, CO, brt; late 1940s/50, 4-3/4" long	45	60	75
Tow Truck, CO, brt; plastic cab, lithographed body, "24 hr," "Tire Change," "Towing Repairs," "Official Service Car," "We Have The Tools To Do The Job" and "Wyandotte," two spare tires on boom, tools, plastic cab No. 1015, 1953/54, 15" long	65	90	145
Tow Truck, CO, brt; plastic No. 237, late 1952, 6" long	45	60	75
Tow Truck, CO, brt; plastic, "Wrecker Service," late 1952, 5-1/4" long	45	60	75
Tow Truck, CO, bww; rear hoist, 1940s, 12-1/4" long	40	70	105
Tow Truck, LN, brt on wood hubs; "AAA Service," No. 1005, 1940, 22-1/2" long	50	90	150
Tow Truck, LN, brt on wood hubs; marked w/a "W," No. 1005, 1941, 22-1/2" long	50	90	140

Wyandotte Stake Truck, No. 352, 1933/34, 15" long. Photo courtesy Brian Seligman

Wyandotte Stake Truck, No. 317, 1934/35, 6-3/8" long. Photo courtesy Brian Seligman

Wyandotte Stake Truck, No. 360, 1934/37, 15-1/4" long. Photo courtesy Brian Seligman

Wyandotte Stake Truck, No. 360, 1938/39, 16" long. Photo courtesy Brian Seligman

Wyandotte Stake Truck, 1940/41, 12-1/4" long. Photo courtesy Brian Seligman

Wyandotte Stake Truck, Easter, No. E325, 10" version (top) and No. E317, 6" version (bottom). Photo courtesy Brian Seligman

Wyandotte Stake Truck, No. 317, 1932/37, 6" long (two versions). Photo courtesy Brian Seligman

Wyandotte Stake Truck, No. 327, 1934/35, 12-1/8" long. Photo courtesy Brian Seligman

Wyandotte Stake Truck, No. 221, 1939/46, 6" long. Photo courtesy Brian Seligman

Wyandotte Stake Truck, No. 325, 1931/32, 9-3/8" long. Photo courtesy Brian Seligman

Wyandotte Stake Truck, No. 327, 1934/35, 12-1/8" long. Photo courtesy Brian Seligman

Wyandotte Stake Truck, No. 129, 1954, 11-3/4" long. Photo courtesy Brian Seligman

Wyandotte Stake Truck, brt on red hubs, electric lights, 1934/37, 15-1/4" long. Photo courtesy Brian Seligman

Wyandotte Stake Truck, 1949, 12" long. Photo courtesy Brian Seligman

	C6	C8	C10
Tow Truck, LN, brt; lithographed grille, "Service + Wrecker," "Toy Town Only 24 hr Service," No. 365, 1941, 17-1/2" long	50	90	150
Tow Truck, LN, bwt; lithographed grille, "Service + Wrecker," No. 365 1938, 17-1/4" long	50	90	225
Tow Truck, LN, bww; "Official Service Car," rear hoist, No. 429, 1940/41, 11-3/4" long	50	85	130
Tow Truck, SE, lmw; "Wyandotte Automobile Society," "Towing and Repairs" and "Towing Service Nite and Day," rear crank operated hoist, 1953, 9" long	45	70	145
Tow Truck, SN, bmw/ymw; marked "Official Service Car" and w/a "W" in a circle, rear hoist, No. 429, 1949; 12" long	50	75	120
Tractor Trailer (semi), CO, brt /two sets rear dual wheels; plastic cab and metal open trailer, removable chains and side pieces, 1952, 23" long	85	110	225
Tractor Trailer (semi), CO, brt on die-cast hubs; removable wooden stake panels, "Motor Freight Lines," No. 6001, 1953; 24-1/2" long	75	100	130
Tractor Trailer (semi), CO, brt; "Green Valley Stock Ranch," lithographed cab marked w/"Wyandotte" and "W" in a dot on cab; No. 390, 1950s, 17-1/2" long	80	95	165
Tractor Trailer (semi), CO, brt; "Highway Freight"; No. 392, 1939/41, 17-3/8" long	55	80	135
Tractor Trailer (semi), CO, brt; "Produce Van," "Refrigerated Cargo" and "Coast to Coast", 1953, 7-3/4" long	40	60	105
Tractor Trailer (semi), CO, brt; "Valley Farms Livestock Produce," 1953, 8-1/2" long	40	60	105
Tractor Trailer (semi), CO, brt; "Wyandotte Express Co," No. 390, 1939/41, 17-3/8" long	50	75	125
Tractor Trailer (semi), CO, brt; "Wyandotte Van Lines," "Coast to Coast" and "Moving Packing Storage," 1953, 7-3/4" long	40	60	105
Tractor Trailer (semi), CO, brt; gray or red plastic cab, lithographed trailer, "Produce Van," "Refrigerated Cargo" and "Coast to Coast," 1952, 9" long	35	50	100
Tractor Trailer (semi), CO, brt; gray or red plastic cab, lithographed trailer, "Wyandotte Van Lines," "Coast to Coast" and "Moving-Packing-Storage," No. 456, 1952, 9" long	35	50	100
Tractor Trailer (semi), CO, brt; grey or red plastic cab, lithographed trailer, "Freeway Van," 1952, 9" long	35	50	100
Tractor Trailer (semi), CO, brt; lithographed cab, cattle truck, loading ramp, 1956/57, 24" long	70	90	120
Tractor Trailer (semi), CO, brt; plastic cab, "Coast to Coast Truck Lines," 1952, 23" long	85	110	145
Tractor Trailer (semi), CO, brt; plastic cab, "Deluxe Highway Express," 1952, 23" long	65	80	125
Tractor Trailer (semi), CO, brt; side dump, "Wyandotte Construction Co.," No. 391, 1939/41, 17-3/8" long	65	95	145
Tractor Trailer (semi), CO, bww / brt; lithographed cab w/marked "Wyandotte" and "W Trucking," orange trailer w/"Shady Glen Stock Ranch" decal, 1952/53; 17" long	40	60	175
Tractor Trailer (semi), CO, fourteen brt on die-cast hubs; die-cast cab and aluminum trailer, "Grey Van Lines," "De Luxe Long Distance Moving," "Affiliated w/Greyhound Lines," also comes in "Chun King Orient Express" and Allied Van Lines versions; side and rear doors open, 1954, 24" long	90	150	275
Tractor Trailer (semi), CO, fourteen brt on red plastic hubs; "Wyandotte Van Lines" (also "Gambles"), retractable landing gear, double rear doors, No. 1850, 1952/54, 23" long	95	130	250
Tractor Trailer (semi), CO, fourteen brt, lithographed cab, marked "Wyandotte Van Lines" on trailer, No. 1605, 1955, 22-1/2" long	95	130	175
Tractor Trailer (semi), CO, pmw; side dump w/shovel, 1952/53, 17" long	45	70	145
Tractor Trailer (semi), CO, six brt w/wood hubs and metal inserts; rear door w/mounted spare tire, three front/two rear reflectors, marked "Van Truck," No. 1500, 1941; 25" long	60	105	150
Tractor Trailer (semi), CO, six brt; baggage truck w/hand truck and baggage, No. 380, 1952, 17" long	70	90	125
Tractor Trailer (semi), CO, ymw; red plastic cab, lithographed trailer, "Wyandotte Van Lines," "National," "Local," 1952, 14-3/4" long	50	70	155
Tractor Trailer (semi), CO; all plastic parts, removable side stake panels, No. 175, 1952, 9-1/4" long	35	50	100
Tractor Trailer (semi), CO; six brt w/wood hub and metal inserts; rear door w/mounted spare tire, mini tarpaulin, marked "Highway Freight," No. 1501, 1941, 25" long	60	100	195
Tractor Trailer (semi), OE, brt; lithographed cab marked w/"Wyandotte Trucking" and "ICC W-1260" "TARE 7000" and "GROSS 18000" on side, orange trailer w/"Shady Glen Stock Ranch" decal, 1953, 17" long	45	70	165
Tractor Trailer (semi), OE, brt; lithographed cab marked w/"Wyandotte" in bubble on side, red side dump body w/"Motor Fleet Hauling Service" and "W" decal, 1953, 17" long	45	70	165
Tractor Trailer (semi), OE, brt; lithographed cab w/"Wyandotte" in bubble on side, orange trailer w/"Shady Glen Stock Ranch" decal, 1954, 17" long	45	70	165
Tractor Trailer (semi), SN, brt; "Wyandotte Van Lines," "National" and "Local"; No. 356,1949, 15" long	65	80	125

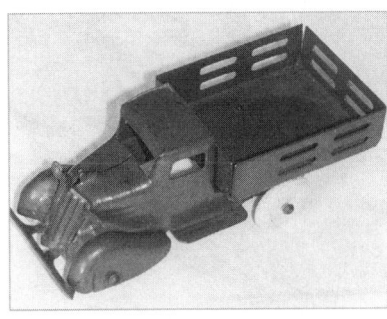

Wyandotte Stake Truck, No. 317, 1943/37, 5-5/8" long. Photo courtesy Brian Seligman

Wyandotte Stake Truck, No. 323, 1932, 9-5/8" long. Photo courtesy Brian Seligman

Two versions of Wyandotte's 1931 Stake Truck, 9-5/8" long. Photo courtesy Brian Seligman

Wyandotte Stake Truck, 1949, 12" long. Photo courtesy Brian Seligman

Wyandotte Television Truck, No. 803, 1954, 4-7/8" long. Photo courtesy Brian Seligman

Wyandotte Tow Truck, No. 365, 1938, 17-1/4" long. Photo courtesy Brian Seligman

Wyandotte Stake Truck, dual rear wheels, 1931/32, 9-3/8" long. Photo courtesy Brian Seligman

Wyandotte Tow Truck, No. 429, 1949, 12" long. Photo courtesy Brian Seligman

Wyandotte Tow Truck, 1953, 9" long. Photo courtesy Brian Seligman

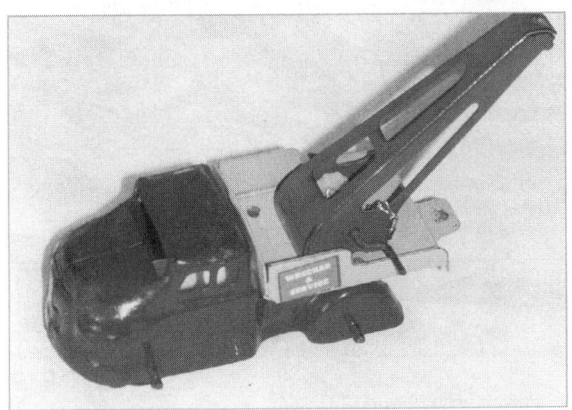

Wyandotte Tow Truck, late 1940s/50, 4-3/4" long. Photo courtesy Brian Seligman

Wyandotte Tractor Trailer (semi), No. 391, 1939/41, 17-3/8" long. Photo courtesy Brian Seligman

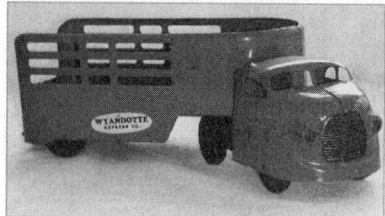

Wyandotte Tractor Trailer (semi), No. 390, 1939/41, 17-3/8" long. Photo courtesy Brian Seligman

Wyandotte Tractor Trailer (semi), 1956/57, 24" long. Photo courtesy Brian Seligman

Wyandotte Tractor Trailer (semi), 1953, 17" long. Photo courtesy Brian Seligman

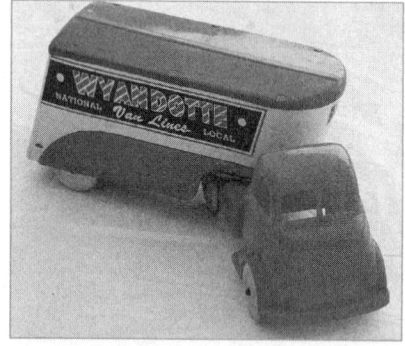

Wyandotte Tractor Trailer (semi), 1952, 14-3/4" long. Photo courtesy Brian Seligman

Wyandotte Tractor Trailer (semi), 1952/53, 17" long. Photo courtesy Brian Seligman

Wyandotte Tractor Trailer (semi), 1953, 17" long. Photo courtesy Brian Seligman

Wyandotte Tractor Trailer (semi), 1952, 9" long. Photo courtesy Brian Seligman

Wyandotte Tractor Trailer (semi), similar to the "Produce Van" of 1952, but with different cab, 9" long. Photo courtesy Brian Seligman

Wyandotte Tractor Trailer (semi), No. 456, 1952, 9" long. Photo courtesy Brian Seligman

Wyandotte Tractor Trailer (semi), 1953, 7-3/4" long. Photo courtesy Brian Seligman

YONE

Yone of Japan was best known for its battery-operated toys in the baby boomer era. It did release a number of vehicle toys.

	C6	C8	C10
Ford Falcon, wipers work	45	68	90
Monster Car, tin wind-up, monsters at windows, 1960s	48	72	95